Encyclopedia
of Security
Management

Encyclopedia of Security Management

Techniques & Technology

Edited by

John J. Fay, CPP

Manager of Security
British Petroleum Exploration Inc.

Butterworth-Heinemann
Boston   London   Oxford   Singapore   Sydney   Toronto   Wellington

Library of Congress Cataloging-in-Publication Data
Fay, John J.
    Encyclopedia of security management: techniques & technology / edited by John
J. Fay
        p.   cm.
    Includes bibliographical references and index.
    ISBN 0-7506-9327-4 (casebound)
    ISBN 0-7506-9660-5 (paperback)
    1. Private security services-Management—Encyclopedias.
2. Industry--Security measures--Management--Encyclopedias. I. Fay,
John, 1934- .
HV8290.S365 1993
658.4'7—dc20   93-13264
                                                          CIP

British Library Cataloguing-in-Publication Data
A catalogue record for this book is available from the British Library.

Butterworth-Heinemann
313 Washington Street
Newton, MA 02158

10 9 8 7 6 5 4

Printed in the United States of America

Dedicated with great affection to my wife and best friend
Calvina, whose good sense and patience
helped bring this book into print.

Preface

The security field continues to evolve rapidly, becoming broader and more complex with each passing year. The single common thread tying the field together is the discipline of management. This book is for and about security managers, the practitioners whose innovativeness and energy are fueling the great changes of our age.

Security management must be applied wherever protective effort is to be organized on a significant scale -- in government, the military, or the business sector. The security manager in one arena can take advantage of technical advances in other arenas when the advances have been described in a useful format. This book is dedicated to that purpose.

The product of rapid evolution is specialization, which can be both positive and negative. The manager who specializes in computer security, for example, may possess great knowledge about electronic data bases but not know very much about the behavioral sciences or the traditional management functions. While this can be accepted as the price tag of progress, it presents a real problem in a discipline committed to control, direction, and elimination of complexity.

As specialization increases, the generalists decline -- not because they are unneeded, but because the broadening opportunities are not present in the workplace. The usual experience of a security practitioner is to spend formative years in a relatively specialized area, such as supervising contract guard services, conducting investigations, or installing alarm systems. When promoted to a managerial level, the individual brings to the new job a limited, one-dimensional viewpoint. Saddled with enlarged responsibilities that call for proficiency in many aspects of managing, the individual is suddenly in a sink or swim situation. Some survive, in a sense overcoming the weight of specialization, to become generalists. The few that reach the very top often owe their success to personal efforts on a grand scale. We observe that these are individuals who have acquired a broad understanding of the profession and have developed strong skills in planning, organizing, directing, and controlling.

Continuous learning is required of a security manager who is determined to stay current. The area of electronic technology, with myriad security applications, has practically exploded in recent years. At the same time, steady advances have been made in the time-honored ways that human and financial resources are harnessed to the work of security organizations. The professional security practitioner needs an authoritative reference source to keep abreast.

This encyclopedia offers to the aspirant, student, or practitioner, whether at the entry or senior executive level, a collection of authoritative information that impinges directly upon the security management function as it is performed in many different industries. It proposes, for example, to make the novice aware of the opportunities that are presented in the diverse nature of security jobs; to make the retail store investigator aware of cash register auditing techniques used by his or her counterpart in the lodging industry; to make the electronic access control designer aware of group dynamics; to make the consultant knowledgeable about finance; and to give the top security executive improved insights into the work of the front-line technicians. In addition, this book endeavors to make all security practitioners aware of the truly remarkable strides that have been made in electronic technology, the forensic sciences, human motivation, and the like.

Authoritativeness has been assured by the professional standing of the individual contributing authors. The editor's contacts with professionals engaged in the subjects presented have made possible original contributions by leading authorities. In many cases, a contributing author is also the author of a recognized text or is a frequent contributor of articles to the security trade magazines and professional journals.

viii   **Preface**

To the extent feasible, the authors have followed a prescribed editorial formula designed to tell the reader what the topic is all about, how it works, what it does, how it is used and the problems it solves or creates. A reader who has no substantive knowledge of a topic will, after referring to the article, obtain the basics, i.e., purpose, objectives, modes of operation, and scope. A reader whose education and experience provide at least a peripheral understanding of a topic will gain an appreciation of the potentials for applying the information to the reader's own job, business, or industry.

Contributing Authors

Rachel A. Ankeny, M.A. Research Assistant, Reid Psychological Systems, Chicago, IL; Student Affiliate, American Psychological Association. Bachelor of Arts, University of Minnesota; Masters of Arts, Loyola University of Chicago.

David W. Arnold, Ph.D., Esq. General Counsel/Vice President Research, Reid Psychological Systems, Chicago, IL; General Counsel, Association of Personnel Test Publishers, Washington, DC; Senior Human Resource Planning Specialist, United Airlines, Chicago, IL; Manager of Assessment Centers, Supermarkets General Corporation, Woodbridge, NJ. Member, American Bar Association; member, American Psychological Association; member, American Psychological Society; member, Chicago Bar Association; member, Illinois Bar Association; member, Society for Industrial and Organizational Psychology; member, Personnel Testing Council of Metropolitan Washington; Secretary, Association of Personnel Test Publishers; committee member, State Affairs Committee of Society for Industrial and Organizational Psychology; Research Committee Chairman, Personnel Testing Council of Metropolitan Washington. *Who's Who Among Rising Young Americans*. Bachelor of Arts, University of Minnesota; Master of Arts, University of Nebraska; Doctor of Philosophy, University of Nebraska; Juris Doctor, Loyola University. Author of "Clearing the Air About Honesty Tests," *Corporate Security Digest*; "A Response to 'New Polygraph Law: No Dangerous Weaponry Involved'," *TIP*; "Legal, Ethical, and Business Reasons for Preemployment Integrity Testing," *Employment Testing*; "Evaluating the Integrity Test," *Security Management*; "Introduction to the Model Guidelines for Preemployment Integrity Testing," *Journal of Business and Psychology*; "Invasion of Privacy: A Rising Concern for Personnel Psychologist," *TIP*; "Are Integrity Tests Valid? The Controversial OTA Study: Background to the Debate -- Publishers' View," *Employment Testing*; "To Test or Not to Test: Legal Issues in Integrity Testing," *Forensic Reports*; "Integrity Testing: The Debate Continues," *Security Management*; "Recent Legislative Initiatives and Reactions by the Psychological Community," *TIP*; "Potential Legislative Inroads into Personnel Psychology: Appropriate Reaction Measures," *Journal of Business and Psychology*; "To Test or Not to Test: The Status of Psychological Testing Under the ADA," *Journal of Business and Psychology*.

Randall I. Atlas, Ph.D., AIA, CPP. Vice President of Atlas Safety & Security Design, Inc., Miami, FL; Adjunct Associate Professor of Criminal Justice, Florida International University and University of Miami; Technical Assistance Consultant for the National Institute of Corrections, Longmont, CO. Member, American Institute of Architects -- Architecture for Justice Committee; member, American Society of Industrial Security -- Architecture Engineering Committee; member, American Correctional Association -- Design & Technology Committee; member, American Society of Safety Engineers; member, National Safety Council; member, National Association of Criminal Justice Planners; member, Environmental Design Research Association; member, National Fire Protection Association; member, American Society of Testing Materials; member, Human Factors Society; member, American Jail Association; member, National Youth Crime Watch -- Advisory Board; member, Florida Jail Association; member, Greater Miami Chamber of Commerce -- Crime Prevention Committee; member, National Institute of Justice -- Leadership Position; member, Security by Design -- Leadership Position; member, Advisory Task Group -- Leadership Position. Doctorate of Criminology, Florida State University; Master of Architecture, University of Illinois; Bachelor of Criminal Justice, University of South Florida; Bachelor of Architecture, University of Florida. Author of "Crime Prevention Through Building Codes," *Building Security*, 1981; "Crime Site Selections for Assaults in Four Florida Prisons," *Prison Journal*, 1986; "Stairs, Steps, and Slipping,"

Florida Architect Journal, 1987; "Crime Prevention Through Building Codes," *Journal of Security Administration*, 1986; "Secure Homes: The Future of Anti-Crime Technology," *Futurist*, 1988; "Designing Security for People, Information, and Property," *Florida Real Estate Journal*, 1988; "How to Protect Your Home," 1988; "Just When You Thought It Was Safe," *Professional Safety*, 1989; "Building Design Can Provide Defensible Space," *Access Control*, 1989; "Design for Safety: Building Code Update," *Florida Architect Journal*, 1989; "Security Design" -- a monthly featured article in *Protection of Assets Bulletin*; "Pay It Now or Pay It Later," *Security Management*, 1990; "Architect Input Among First Steps in Design," *Access Control*, 1991; "Offensible Space: Obstruction of Law Enforcement Through Environmental Design,"*Security Management*, 1991; "Handicap Accessibility Affects Security," *Access Control*, 1992; "Will ADA Affect Security?" *Security Management*, 1992; "Need for Involving Security in Building Planning," *Campus Security Report*, 1992; "Security for Buildings," *Architectural Graphic Standards*, Wiley Publishers, 1992; "Post-Occupancy Evaluation of Building Security," *Post-Occupancy Evaluations*, 1993; "Impact of ADA on Corrections," *Construction Bulletin*, National Institute of Corrections, 1993.

Terry J. Ball. Owner, Gillespie *Polygraph*, Lynnwood, WA; former Corporate Director of Loss Prevention, Schuck's Auto Supply; former Regional Manager of Loss Prevention, Pay n' Save Corporation; expert witness in retail security. Member, American Polygraph Association; past member of the Board of Directors, Northwest Polygraph Association; member, American Association of Police Polygraphists; member, Who's Who in Security; member, American Society for Industrial Security. Bachelor of Science, Criminal Justice Administration, Central Missouri State University; graduate, Missouri Highway Patrol Basic Training Academy; graduate, Utah Academy of Forensic Polygraph; graduate, Reid College of Interviewing and Interrogation; graduate, Missouri Rural Major Case Squad Training Academy. Author of "The Computer Sleuth Attacks Register Theft," *Security Management*, 1987.

J. Kirk Barefoot, CPP. Security Consultant (self-employed), Savannah, GA; Director of Risk Managment (Retired), Cluett, Peabody & Company, New York, NY; former Director of Security, McKesson Corporation, San Francisco, CA; former lecturer in security management courses at the University of Delaware, John Jay College, and the University of New Haven. Member, American Society for Industrial Security; life member, American Polygraph Association; Board member (former) ASIS; first president of A.P.A. Recipient of the John E. Reid Memorial Award, American Polygraph Association. Bachelor of Science, Washington State University. Editor and principal author of "The Polygraph Story," American Polygraph Assocation; author of *Undercover Investigation*, 1st and 2nd Editions; *Employee Theft Investigation*, 1st and 2nd Editions; co-author of *Corporate Security Administration and Management*, Butterworth-Heinemann; and various articles in *Security Management*.

Robert L. Barnard. Independent Technical Security Consultant, Annandale, VA; Related Position, Chief, Intrusion Detection Branch, Fort Belvoir, VA; seminar presenter, University of Delaware. Member, American Society of Industrial Security (ASIS); member, American Society of Test and Materials (ASTM); Chairman, Committee F12.40 (1976-1984). Bachelor of Science, Physics, American University. Author of *Intrusion Detection Systems*, Butterworth-Heinemann; "When Security Covers the Expanded Picture," *Security World*; "Performance Standards for Ultrasonic and Microwave Motion Detectors," *Signal*; "Designing Your Intrusion Detection System, Part I & II," *Security World*.

Joseph A. Barry, CFE, CPP. Security Consultant, Barry's Consultants, Inc., Naples, FL; former General Manager, ML Aviation Ltd., North America; former Director of Government Security Programs, Senstar Incorporated; former Manager of Government Services, Aritech Corporation;

former Vice President for Marketing and Training, Management Safeguards, Inc.; former Director of Security, Systems Division, Analytical Systems Engineering Corporation (ASEC); former Director of Security and Law Enforcement, U.S. Army Material Command. Member, American Society for Industrial Security (ASIS); member, Criminal Investigation Division Agent Association; member, National Association of Fraud Examiners; member, American Correctional Association; Peer, Quintillian Institute; former Chairman, Boston Chapter, ASIS; former Chairman, Standing Committee on Physical Security, ASIS; former member, Professional Certification Board. 1972 Military Citizen of the Year, Junior Chamber of Commerce, Hampton Road, VA. Master of Science in Police Administration, Michigan State University; Bachelor of Science, University of New Hampshire; graduate, U.S. Naval War College; graduate, Armed Forces Staff College. Author of numerous professional articles in *Security, Security Management, Bureau of Business Practice* and *Fortune*.

Norman D. Bates, J.D. President, Liability Consultants, Inc., Framingham, MA; Adjunct Faculty, College of Criminal Justice, Northeastern University, Boston, MA. Member, American Bar Association; member, American Society for Industrial Security; member, Association of Trial Lawyers of America; member, Board of Trustees, Civil Libility Institute of Massachusetts; member, Massachusetts Bar Association; member, Board of Directors, Children's Law Center of Massachusetts; Boston Chapter Vice Chairman, American Society for Industrial Security. Professor of the Year Award (1989), College of Criminal Justice. Bachelor of Science, College of Criminal Justice, Northeastern University; Juris Doctor, Suffolk University School of Law. Author and co-author of numerous articles and chapters of books including "Contemporary Issues in Healthcare Security," *Security Supervisor's Training Manual,* International Association for Hospital Security, 1988, and "Hotel Security," *Handbook on Crime Prevention*, 2nd Edition, 1988, Butterworth-Heinemann.

Curt P. Betts, PE. Structural/Security Engineer, U.S. Army Corps of Engineers, Protective Design Center, Omaha, NE. Member, American Society for Industrial Security (ASIS); member, Society of American Military Engineers (SAME); member, American Society of Civil Engineers (ASCE); Chairperson, Standing Committee on Security Architecture and Engineering, ASIS. Bachelor of Science in Civil Engineering, Colorado State University; graduate work in structural engineering at University of Nebraska. Author of "The Intrusion Detection Misconception" and "Requirements Definition, What You Say Is What You Get," *Security Management*; "Security Engineering" (co-author), *The Military Engineer*, "The Security Engineering Design Process, An Evaluation Procedure for Physical Security Requirements," *Structure for Enhanced Safety and Physical Security*, ASCE; "A Procedure to Integrate Protective Measures Over a Range of Terrorist and Criminal Threats," *Proceedings of the 1990 Carnahan Conference on Security Technology*; "Integrating Delay and Detection: A Challenge to Industry and Government," *Proceedings, 7th Joint Government -- Industry Symposium on Security Technology*, American Defense Preparedness Association (ADPA); "The Army Security Engineering Design Process," *Proceedings, 5th Joint Government -- Industry Symposium on Security Technology*, ADPA; "Anti-Terrorism Physical Security System Design Process for U.S. Army Facilities," *Proceedings, 3rd Joint Government -- Industry Symposium on Security Technology*, ADPA; *The Security Engineering Manual*, U.S. Army Corps of Engineers Protective Design Center; *Technical Manual 5-853-1/Air Force Manual 88-56*, Vol. 1, *Security Engineering Project Development and Technical Manual 5-853-2/Air Force Manual 88-56*, Vol. 2, Security Engineering Concept Design, U.S. Department of Defense.

B. Steve Bias, CPP, CFE, CPO. Director of Public Safety, Nova University, Fort Lauderdale, FL; Adjunct Instructor, School of Justice and Safety Administration, Miami, FL; former Director of Loss

Prevention, Bi-Lo Supermarkets, Inc., Greenville, SC; former Commander of Internal Affairs, Hollywood Police Department, Hollywood, FL. Member, American Society for Industrial Security; member, International Association of Campus Law Enforcement Administrators; member, National Association of Fraud Examiners; life member, Florida Association of Campus Safety and Security Administrators; life member, Florida Police Benevolent Association and the Fraternal Order of Police; Chairperson, Educational Institutions Standing Committee, ASIS; former Chairperson, Miami Chapter, ASIS; past President, Florida Chapter IACLEA (FACSSA); past President, Broward County Police Benevolent Association; past President, Hollywood Fraternal Order of Police; recipient of the ASIS Region XIII Award of Merit, 1991. Bachelor of Science, Nova University. Author of cover article, *Security*, April, 1991, "Behavioral Analysis," *Security New Canada*, "Recruiting Campus Public Safety Management," Campus Law Enforcement Journal, "Police Benevolent Centurion," *Campus Security Report*, December, 1991, and *School Security Report*, September, 1991.

G. J. (Jack) Bologna, JD, CFE. Associate Professor of Management, Siena Heights College; Adrian, Michigan; President, Computer Protection Systems, Inc., Plymouth, Michigan. Member, National Association of Certified Fraud Examiners; the Academy of Management, Academy of Criminal Justice Sciences; American Academy of Forensic Sciences; Institute for the Prevention of Financial Crime; member, Editorial Board of the *Journal of Assets Protection and Data Processing* and *Communications Security*. Outstanding Teacher of the Year in 1987, Siena Heights College. Bachelor of Arts in Accounting, Detroit Institute of Technology; law (Juris Doctorate), University of Detroit. Author of two newsletters: *Forensic Accounting Review* and *Computer Security Digest*; author of *Computer Crime: Wave of the Future*, Assets Protection Press; *Strategic Planning for Corporate Directors of Security and Risk Management*, Assets Protection Press; *Corporate Fraud: The Basics of Detection and Prevention*, Butterworth-Heinemann; *Fraud Auditing and Forensic Accounting*, John Wiley & Sons, Inc.; *Computer Security Handbook*, Macmillan; co-author of *The Accountant's Handbook of Fraud and Commercial Crime*, John Wiley & Sons, Inc.; *Handbook of Corporate Fraud Prevention and Investigation*, Butterworth-Heinemann.

Norman R. Bottom, Ph.D., CPP, CST, CFE, CPO. Professional security consultant and expert witness; Editor-In-Chief, *Journal of Security Administration*; Vice President, BLSS, Inc.; Teaching Associate, Bryant Systems; former Director of Security, Miami-Dade Community College District; former Associate Professor and Director of Graduate Studies, Indiana University of Pennsylvania; former Associate Professor, Northern Michigan University; former Assistant Professor, East Tennessee State University; former Deputy Sheriff, Washington and Sullivan Counties, Tennessee; former Vice President/Manager for Arundel Investigative Agency and Fidelifacts of Maryland; former Operations Manager, Metalimport, Ltd., London, England; former Intelligence Analyst, Defense Intelligence Agency; Honorable Discharge, USAR. Member, Fraternal Order of Police; Fellowship of Christian Police Officers; Presbyterian Church of America; Academy of Criminal Justice Educators -- Security/Crime Prevention Section; Academy of Security Educators and Trainers (ASET); Association of Former Intelligence Officers; Illuminating Engineering Society of North America; National Association of Legal Investigators; American Society for Industrial Security (ASIS). Former President and Chairman of the Board, ASET; former Chairman of the Board, International Foundation for Protection Officers; former Chapter Chairman, National Liaison Officer, Standing Committee Vice Chairman, ASIS. Co-author of *Introduction to Security & Loss Control*, Prentice-Hall; *Industrial Espioniage*, Butterworth-Heinemann; *Security & Loss Control*, Macmillan Press. Author of *Security & Loss Control Negligence*, Hanrow Press; *The Parking Lot and Garage Security Handbook*, Hanrow Press.

Dan M. Bowers. Consulting Engineer, Randallstown, MD; former Vice President for Electronic Security Systems, Burns International Security Services; former Research Staff member, Thomas J. Watson Research Laboratory, IBM; former Project Manager, National Security Agency; former Editor-in-Chief, *Minimicro Systems*; former Project Manager, Potter Instrument Company; former Department Manager, Computer Control Company. Senior member, Institute of Electrical and Electronic Engineers; member, American Society for Industrial Security; member, Association for Computing Machinery; senior member, Instrument Society of America. Bachelor of Science in Physics with Honors, The Pennsylvania State University; Master of Electrical Engineering, The Catholic University of America; doctoral studies at New York University and the Polytechnic Institute of Brooklyn. Author of *Access Control and Personal Identification Systems*, Butterworth-Heinemann; *Access Control and Personal Identification Systems: Buyers' Guide and State-of-the-Art Report*, 5th Edition; *Physical Security Equipment: Buyers' Guide and State-of-the-Art Report*; numerous professional papers and articles in the areas of security, computers, and management.

James F. Broder, CPP. Consultant, Confidential Management Services, Inc., San Dimas, CA; former Security Consultant, Marsh and McLennan, Inc.; former Special Agent, U.S. State Department; former Assistant and the Chairman, Investigations Sub-Committee, U.S. House of Representatives. Member, American Society for Industrial Security; member, Society of Former Special Agents of the FBI; member, Association of Former Intelligence Officers; past member, Congressional Staff Association, U.S. House of Representatives; past member, International Association of Professional Security Consultants. Legion of Merit, Vietnam. Bachelor of Arts, Criminology, University of California. Author of *Risk Analysis and the Security Survey*, Butterworth-Heinemann; *Investigation of Substance Abuse in the Workplace*, Butterworth-Heinemann; *Resources Control in Counter-Insurgency*, Agency for International Development, U.S. State Department; "Case Management and Control of Undercover Operations for Business and Industry," *Professional Protection*; contributing author, *Effective Security Management*, Butterworth-Heinemann.

Lonnie R. Buckels, CPP. Head, Information Security, Telecommunications and Space Sector, Hughes Aircraft Company, El Segundo, CA; former Branch Manager, Industrial Security, McDonnell Douglas Corporation, Huntington Beach, and Long Beach, CA; former part-time Instructor, Golden West College, Huntington Beach, CA; former substitute Instructor, California State University at Long Beach. Member, American Society for Industrial Security; Chapter Chairman, Greater Los Angeles Chapter, ASIS; National General Chairman, 20th Annual Seminar and Exhibits, ASIS; member, National Classification Management Society; member, Research Security Administrators; member, California Association of Administration of Justice Educators; recipient of the James S. Cogswell Award, Douglas Aircraft Company, Long Beach, CA, and Hughes Aircraft Company, Torrance, CA; Silver Beaver and District Award of Merit, Boy Scouts of America. Associate in History, El Camino College, Torrance, CA; Bachelor of Arts in History, California State College at Long Beach; Bachelor of Science in Criminal Justice (Security Adminstration Option), California State University at Long Beach; Douglas Management Institute Certificate. Co-author of "Is an Ex the Best Candidate?" and "The Security Manager's Apprentice," *Security Management*; author of "A Murphy's Law Corollary in Personnel Selection," "The Perils of 'P'," "The Plague of Security Misconceptions," and "Professionalism -- An Impossible Task?," *Security Management*; "While Waiting for the Call That Never Came," *Greater Los Angeles Chapter Newsletter*.

Joseph P. Buckley, III. President, John E. Reid and Associates, Inc., Chicago, IL; past and present Lecturer, Northwestern School of Law, Federal Law Enforcement Training Center, Institute of Internal Auditors, and the American Society for Industrial Security; licensed Detection of Deception

Examiner. Governor of Illinois appointee as Chairman of the Detection of Deception Committee, 1978-1982; Vice President in 1981, President in 1982 and 1983, and Chairman of the Board in 1984 of the Illinois Polygraph Society; Chairman, Public Relations Committee, 1979-1980 and 1984 to present, and Vice President, 1979-1980, of the American Polygraph Association; member, Investigations Committee of the American Society for Industrial Security; and member of various professional associations including the American Society for Industrial Security, International Association of Chiefs of Police, American Management Association, Chicago Crime Commission, Special Agents Association, and Academy of Security Educators and Trainers. Bachelor of Arts, Loyola University; Master of Science in the detection of deception, Reid College of Detection of Deception. Co-author of *Criminal Interrogation and Confessions*, 3rd Edition, 1986; co-author of "Abdominal and Thoracic Respiration Recordings in the Detection of Deception," *Polygraph*, March 1972; "Relative Accuracy of Polygraph Examiner Diagnosis of Respiration, Blood Pressure and GSR Recordings," *Journal of Political Science and Administration*, 1975; "The Use of Behavior Symptoms in the Search for the Truth: A Tool for the Prosecutor," *Prosecutor*, 1985; "The Influence of Race and Gender on Specific Issue Polygraph Examinations," *Polygraph*, 1991; "The Influence of Race and Gender on Preemployment Polygraph Examination Results," *Polygraph*, 1991; "The Influence of Race and Gender on Blind Polygraph Chart Analyses," *Polygraph*, 1991; "Criminal Interrogation Techniques on Trial," *Prosecutor*, 1991; author of "Polygraph Technology," a chapter in the text *Modern Legal Medicine, Psychiatry and Forensic Science*, 1980; "The Nine Steps of Interrogation," *Security Management*, May, 1983; "The Use of Polygraphs by the Business Community," *Management Review*, January, 1986; "How Do I Know If They Told Me the Truth?," *Internal Audit Advisor*, March and April, 1986; "Nobody's Perfect," *Security Management*, May, 1987; "Read Between the Lines," *Security Management*, June, 1987; "Interrogation," a chapter in the text *The Encyclopedia of Police Science*, 1989; "The Behavioral Profile of a Liar," International Association of Credit Card Investigators Newsletter, first quarter, 1991; "The Behavioral Analysis Interview," *International Association of Credit Card Investigators Newsletter*, second quarter, 1991.

Loren L. Bush, Jr., CPP. Chief, Program Development and Review Section, Nuclear Regulatory Commission, Washington, DC; former Chief, Nuclear Security Division, Defense Nuclear Agency, Washington, DC; former Operations Officer, 8th Military Police Group (Criminal Investigation), Long Binh, Vietnam. Member, American Society for Industrial Security; Chairman of the Host Chapter Seminar Committee of the 29th Annual Seminar and Exhibits, ASIS; Regional Vice President of ASIS; Chairman of the Washington, DC Chapter of ASIS; member of the Utilities Security Committee, ASIS. Recipient of the ASIS Regional Vice President of the Year Award; the American Legion Award for Leadership and Integrity; Legion of Merit, Bronze Star and three Commendation Medals (U.S. Army); and recipient of seven outstanding performance awards from the Nuclear Regulatory Commission. Bachelor of Science, University of Florida. Author of "A Joint Responsibility," *Security Management*, 1991; "Fitness for Duty Programs," *The Federal Register*; NUREG-1354, "Fitness for Duty in the Nuclear Power Industry: Responses to Public Comments," *The Federal Register*; NUREG-1385, "Fitness for Duty in the Nuclear Power Industry: Responses to Implementation Questions," *The Federal Register*; and NUREG-0903, "Survey of Industry and Government Programs to Combat Drug and Alcohol Abuse," *The Federal Register*.

John M. Carroll, Ph.D. Professor Emeritus, Department of the University of Western Ontario, London, Canada; past holder of academic appointments in seven universities in the United States, Sweden, Australia, and South Africa; past consultant to the Royal Canadian Mounted Police, the U.S. Naval Research Laboratory, police forces in six countries, and business firms; former Managing Editor of *Electronics*; Registered Professional Engineer. Member, American Society for Industrial Security. Bachelor of Science, Lehigh University; Master of Science (Physics), Hofstra University;

Doctor of Science (Industrial Engineering), New York University. Author of *Computer Security, Confidential Information Sources, Controlling White Collar Crime*, and *Managing Risk*, all published by Butterworth-Heinemann; author of more than 100 professional papers.

Joseph A. Cascio. Staffing Manager, Romac & Associates, Houston, TX; former Security Services Manager, Kaiser Permanente Medical Care Program, Oakland, CA; former Detective, Violent Crimes Unit, Chicago Police Department, Chicago, IL. Member, American Society for Industrial Security; former Chapter Officer, International Association for Healthcare Security and Safety. Bachelor of Arts in Management, St. Mary's College of California.

Nancy H. Cole, MA. Forensic Document Examiner, Palo Alto, CA. Member, Association of Forensic Document Examiners (AFDE); member, British Academy of Forensic Sciences (BAFS); member, California Trial Lawyers' Association (CTLA); member, Technical Support Division; member, International Association of Credit Card Investigators (IACCI); member, California Check Investigators Association (CCIA). Bachelor of Fine Arts, Carnegie-Mellon University; Master of Arts, Stanford University. Served on Board of Directors of Association of Forensic Document Examiners; founding editor of the *Journal of Forensic Document Examination*; Co-Chair of Criminalistics Section, 1988 International Congress of Forensic Sciences (ICFS), Beijing, China; presented keynote paper for experts' section of Kriminal Expo '92, International Conference and Exhibition on Criminal Investigation and Justice, Budapest, Hungary, 1992. Author of "J'Accuse: A Study of the Handwriting Concerned in the Dreyfus Case," *Journal of Forensic Document Examination*, Vol. 1, 1987; "Medico-Legal Problems of Last Will and Testament," presented before the International Congress of Forensic Sciences (ICFS) under the aegis of the Forensic Medical Association of China, Beijing, September, 1988; published in the *Journal of Forensic Document Examination*, Vol. II, 1988; "A Study in Guided Hand Writings," presented before the American Academy of Forensic Document Examination, Vol. IV, 1991; pending publication, "From the Attic to the Computer Showroom: A Survey of the Methods and Tools of Document Examination and the Challenges of Document Crime Detection in the '90s."

Russell L. Colling, CPP, CHPA. Executive Vice President, Hospital Shared Services of Colorado, Denver, CO; Adjunct Professor, Security Management, Webster University, Denver, CO; former Assistant Vice President, Chicago Wesley Memorial Hospital, Chicago, IL; former Security Compliance Officer, Martin Marrieta, Denver, CO; former Police Officer and Chief of Police, Saugatuck, MI. Member, American Society for Industrial Security; founding president, charter member and life member, International Association for Healthcare Security and Safety; past Chairman/member, Metropolitian Law Enforcement Association, Denver, CO; past Chairman/member, Colorado Law Enforcement Memorial Committee; member, American Hospital Association , Ad Hoc Security Committee; member, Board of Directors, School of Criminal Justice Alumni Association, Michigan State University; member, Editorial Advisory Board, *Security Journal*; Editorial Advisory Board, *Hospital Security and Safety Management*; recipient of first Russell L. Colling Literary Award, International Association for Healthcare Security and Safety; Bachelor of Science, Michigan State University; Master of Science, Michigan State University; Editor, *Security Officer Basic Training Manual*, International Association for Healthcare Security and Safety; Editor, *Supervisor Training Manual*, International Association for Healthcare Security and Safety; author, "Hospital Security: Is the Patient at Risk," *Journal of Healthcare Protection Management*; author of *Hospital Security*, 3rd Edition, Butterworth-Heinemann.

Pamela A. Collins, Ed.D. Coordinator and Associate Professor, Security and Loss Prevention Program, Eastern Kentucky University, Richmond, KY; Independent Security Consultant, Toyota

Motor Manufacturing, Lexington, KY, King Faisal Specialist Hospital in Riyadh, Saudi Arabia, The Council for 21 Independent Colleges in Kentucky, and several contract security corporations and legal firms; Dimension Faculty, The Union for Experimenting Colleges and Universities; former Specialist-Industrial Security, General Electric of Ohio; former Plant Protection Department, General Electric of Ohio; former Fire Protection Engineer, Industrial Risk Insurers of Texas. Member, American Society for Industrial Security; member, Southern Criminal Justice Association; member, Somerset Community College Advisory Board; member, Classification Management Society; member, National Association of Chiefs of Police; Chair, Standing Committee on Academic Programs in Colleges and Universities, American Society for Industrial Security; former Chair, Standing Committee on Academic Programs in Colleges and Universities, American Society for Industrial Security; former Co-Chair, Standing Committee on Academic Programs in Colleges and Universities, American Society for Industrial Security; former Vice-Chairman, Lexington Chapter of American Society for Industrial Security; former Secretary/Treasurer, Lexington Chapter of American Society for Industrial Security. Educational Doctorate, University of Kentucky; Master of Loss Prevention Administration, Eastern Kentucky University; Bachelor of Security and Loss Prevention Administration, Eastern Kentucky University. Author of "Evaluation of False Alarm Rates -- With Emphasis on Reduction and Improved Efficiency for Police Departments," *1989 Carnahan Conference Journal*, University of Kentucky, Lexington, KY; "Big Plan on Campus," *Security Management*.

Charles P. Connolly, MPA, CPP. Vice President, Wells Fargo Guard Services, Parsippany, NJ; former Vice President, New York City Health and Hospitals Corporation; former Police Commissioner, Yonkers, NY; former Captain, New York City Police Department; Adjunct Professor, John Jay College of Criminal Justice, Rockland Community College, Mercy College, St. Thomas Acquinas; former Editorial Consultant for Stoeger Publications; Training Consultant for Northwestern University and University of Delaware. Member, American Society for Industrial Security, International Association of Chiefs of Police, International Association of Healthcare Security and Safety, Police Executive Research Forum, American Academy of Professional Law Enforcement, FBI, National Academy Association, FBI National Executive Institute; Chairman, ASIS Law Enforcement Liaison Council; member, Board of Directors, FBI NEI; former Chairman, New York State Peace Officers Advisory Council, IACP's Public Safety Directors Committee; former member, NYS Police Standards and Goals Task Force, IACP's Organized Crime and Private Security Committees' former president, New York State and Eastern Canada Chapter of the FBI National Academy; Visiting Instructor, FBI Academy (LEED's Program) and NYC Police Department Executive Development Program. Recipient of the FBI Bart Hose Memorial Award (1986); Distinguished Alumni, John Jay College of Criminal Justice (1992). Bachelor of Science and Master of Public Administration, John Jay College of Criminal Justice; graduate of FBI National Academy (93rd Session) and National Executive Institute (6th Session). Author of *Feasibility Study on Development of a Standard Hospital Security Staffing Formula*, a 168 page research publication funded by the National Institute of Justice, Department of Justice, Washington, DC; and author of numerous law enforcement and private security articles.

Francis J. D'Addario, CPP, CFE. Director of Loss Prevention, Hardee's Food Systems, Inc., Rocky Mount, NC; founder, Crime Prevention Associates Inc., Chapel Hill, NC; former Director of Corporate Security, Jerrico Inc., Lexington, KY; former Regions Security Manager, Southland Corporation, Dallas, TX. Member, American Society for Industrial Security; member, International Association of Crime Prevention Practitioners; member, National Food Service Security Council; Vice President, Board of Directors, National McGruff House Network; Security Advisory Board member, North Carolina State University; Chairperson, American Society for Industrial Security's

Food Service Security Committee. Recipient of the National Food Service Security Council's Life Achievement Award and Jerrico Inc.'s Key Man Award. Associate of Arts, Baltimore Community College. Author of *Loss Prevention Through Crime Analysis*, Butterworth-Heinemann; "Security Self-Sufficiency, Survival of the Urban Retailer," "The Siege of Washington," "Cops, Convicts and Computers," "Con Men Don't Wear Plaid" and "The Anatomy of a Statistic," *Security Management*. Designer of Loss Vision loss analysis software, copyrighted 1990.

Kurt H. Decker, Esq. Partner, Stevens & Lee, Reading, PA; Adjunct Professor of Industrial Relations, Graduate School of Industrial Relations, Saint Francis College, Loretto, PA; Adjunct Professor of Law, School of Law, Widener University, Harrisburg, PA; former Assistant Attorney General, Governor's Office, Bureau of Labor Relations, Commonwealth of Pennsylvania, Harrisburg, PA. Member, American Bar Association, American Bar Association's Labor and Employment Law Section, American Society for Industrial Security Ad Hoc member Privacy Committee, American Society for Public Administration, Industrial Relations Research Association, International Industrial Relations Research Association, Pennsylvania Bar Association, Pennsylvania Bar Association's Labor and Employment Law Section, Society for Human Resource Administration; Editor, *Journal of Individual Employment Rights*; Board of Editors, *Journal of Collective Negotiations in the Public Sector*. Recipient of the Philadelphia Bar Association's Media Achievement Award. Bachelor of Arts, Thiel College; Master of Public Adminstration, the Pennsylvania State University; Juris Doctorate, Vanderbilt University School of Law; Master of Laws (Labor), Temple University School of Law. Author of *An Introduction to Workplace Privacy Rights, Procedures, and Policies*, Labor Relations Press; *A Manager's Guide to Employee Privacy Law, Policies, and Procedure*, John Wiley & Sons, Inc.; *Covenants Not to Compete*, John Wiley & Sons, Inc.; *Drafting and Revising Employment Contracts*, John Wiley & Sons, Inc.; Drafting and Revising Employment Handbooks, John Wiley & Sons, Inc.; *Employee Privacy Law and Practice*, John Wiley & Sons, Inc.; *Employee Privacy Forms and Procedures*, John Wiley & Sons, Inc.; *The Individual Employment Rights Primer*, Baywood Publishing Co., Inc.

Sal DePasquale, CPP. Senior Consultant, Lockwood Greene Engineers, Spartanburg, SC. Member of American Society of Criminology, Risk and Insurance Management Society, American Society for Industrial Security, and World Future Society; member of U.S. Delegation on Criminal Justice to U.S.S.R., Czechoslovakia and Italy, 1991. Master of Criminal Justice, University of South Carolina; Bachelor of Arts, University of Delaware. Publications include: "Pharmaceutical Plant Security Design: A Strategic Approach," *Pharmaceutical Engineering*, May, 1990; "Security Master Plan Provides Positive Impact," *Access Control*, March, 1990; "Use This Security Master Plan to Better Minimize Risks," *Security*, May, 1989.

Robert D. Dey. Supervisory Special Agent, Drug Enforcement Administration, Houston, TX; former D.E.A. Special Agent in Galveston, TX, and Detroit, MI. Member, Texas Summit Committee, Ad Hoc Advisory Committee to the Texas Commission on Alcohol and Drug Abuse; member, Drug Prevention Curriculum Committee, Education for Self-Responsiblity, Texas Education Agency; past member, Statewide Advisory Council to the Texas Commission on Alcohol and Drug Abuse; past member, Statewide Advisory Council to the Southwest Regional Center for Drug-Free Schools and Communities; past member of the Board of Directors of the Bay Area Council on Drugs and Alcohol; charter member and past member of the Board of Directors of Houston's Drug-Free Business Initiative; present member of the Board of Directors of Gloria Dei Lutheran Church, Houston, TX. Bachelor of Business Administration, Western Michigan University. Editor/compiler of *Guidelines for a Drug-Free Workforce*, Drug Enforcement Administration.

Calvina L. Fay. Executive Director, Houston's Drug-Free Business Initiative, Houston, TX; Guest Lecturer at the University of Houston, Houston, TX, Texas Southern University, Houston, TX, Brazosport College, Brazosport, TX, Texas A&M University, College Station, TX, and Texas State Technical Institute, Houston, TX; expert witness in the area of workplace drug testing; former Owner and Chief Executive Officer, Forward Edge, Inc., Houston, TX. Member, International Narcotic Enforcement Officers Association; Advisory Council member of the Drug Education Cooperative, State of Texas Region IV Education Service Center; Steering Committee member, Red Ribbon Campaigns, Texans' War on Drugs; Chairperson of Business Committee, Drug Abuse Prevention Month; Chairperson of the Public Relations Committee, Houston Crackdown Community Partnership; and member, Texas Task Force of the President's Drug Advisory Council. Bachelor of Science, Century University, Albuquerque, NM; Certified Trainer of Technicians in the enzyme multiplied immunoassay technique for the detection of drugs in urine; Certified Trainer of Technicians in the use of Alco Sensor equipment for the detection of alcohol in the blood. Author of *The Supervisor's Handbook for Preventing Drug Abuse in the Workplace*, Forward Edge, Inc.; *Drug Abuse Education in the Workplace*, Forward Edge, Inc.; and author/editor of two regional newsletters.

John J. Fay, CPP. Security Manager, British Petroleum Exploration, Houston, TX; Adjunct Professor, Criminal Justice Department, University of Houston; former Director of Security, The Charter Company, Jacksonville, FL; former Director, National Crime Prevention Institute, University of Louisville; former Chief of Plans and Training, Georgia Bureau of Investigation, Atlanta, GA; former Chief of Training Standards, Georgia Peace Officer Standards and Training Council, Atlanta, GA; former Special Agent, U.S. Army Criminal Investigation Division; former Lecturer, Police Science Division, University of Georgia; former Adjunct Professor, University of North Florida. Member, American Society for Industrial Security, Texas Police Association, Houston Metropolitan Criminal Investigators Association; former Chapter Chairman, Jacksonville, Florida Chapter of ASIS; former Regional Vice President, ASIS; former member of the Professional Certification Board. Honor Society, University of Nebraska at Omaha; Bronze Star Medal with Oak Leaf Cluster (Vietnam); Meritorious Service Medal (Vietnam); U.S. Army Commendation Medal. Bachelor of General Education, University of Nebraska at Omaha; Master of Business Administration, University of Hawaii. Author of *Drug Testing*, Butterworth-Heinemann; *Butterworths Security Dictionary*, Butterworth-Heinemann; *The Alcohol/Drug Abuse Dictionary and Encyclopedia*, Charles R. Thomas Publishers; *The Police Dictionary and Encyclopedia*, Charles R. Thomas Publishers; *Approaches to Criminal Justice Training*, University of Georgia Press; and *Managing Drug Abuse in the Workplace*, Forward Edge, Inc.

Harold A. Feder, BA, LLB, JD. Attorney, President, Feder, Morris, Tamblyn & Goldstein, P.C. Denver, CO; Adjunct Law School Professor, University of Denver College of Law; former Special Assistant Attorney General, State of Colorado, 1960-1971; former Trial and Defense Counsel, General Courts Martials, 1961. Fellow, International Society of Barristers; Fellow, American Academy of Forensic Sciences; Fellow, Colorado Bar Foundation; member, Colorado Trial Lawyers Association; member, Denver, Continental Divide, Colorado and American Bar Associations; member, Association of Trial Lawyers of America; member, Federal Bar Association; member, National Association of Certified Fraud Examiners; past President, Colorado Trial Lawyers Assocation, 1971-72; Governing Council, Law Practice Management Section, American Bar Association, 1980-86. Volunteer of the Year Award, Alzheimer's Association, Metro Denver Chapter, December, 1991; Founder, Public Justice Foundation, 1986; Martindale-Hubbell "a-v" Rating; listed in *Who's Who in America*, *Who's Who in the West*, and *Who's Who in American Law*; Colorado Supreme Court Committee, Drafting Rules for Mandatory Arbitration, 1989; Honorary Board member, Special Olympics for the Mentally Retarded, 1978 -- 1983; Civil Justice Reform Act Commission member, 1991 to present; President's Council, Crow Canyon Archeological Center, 1991 to present. Bachelor of Arts, University of Colorado, 1954; Bachelor of Laws, University of Colorado, 1959; Juris Doctorate,

University of Colorado, 1968. Author of *Succeeding As An Expert Witness -- Increasing Your Impact and Income*, Van Nostrand Reinhold, 1991; "Toxic Torts for the General Practitioner," *The Colorado Lawyer*, Feb., 1992; "Effective Trial Preparation, Post Discovery Checklist," *Trial*, July, 1992; "Physical Social, Psychological, and Property Damages from Toxic Contamination," *Trial Diplomacy Journal*, Spring, 1989; "Successfully Marketing a Small Law Firm," *Legal Economics*, 1989; chapter author of *Law Firm Agreements and Disagreements*, Practicing Law Institute, 1988; "Inverse Condemnation: A Viable Alternative," *Denver University Law Journal*, Vol. 51, No. 4, 1974.

Hans Mayer Gidion, FSSDip. Private consultant, Forensic Examiner of Questioned Documents, Augusta, GA; former Special Agent, U.S. Army Criminal Investigation Division; former Commanding Officer, Executive Officer, Chief Document Examiner, and Questioned Documents Analyst, U.S. Army Criminal Investigation Laboratories at facilities in the Continental United States and Far East. Diplomate (Certified), American Board of Forensic Document Examiners (ABFDE); Diplomate (Certified), Forensic Science Society of England (FSS); member, American Society of Questioned Document Examiners (ASQDE); member, International Association for Identification (IAI); member, Forensic Science Society (FSS), England; charter member and member, Southeastern Association of Forensic Document Examiners (SAFDE); member, National Association of Criminal Defense Lawyers (NACDL). Legion of Merit and Meritorious Service Medal, U.S. Army; Police Medallion and Certificate of Appreciation from the Superintendent, Tokyo Metropolitan Police Department; former editor and contributing author to the *U.S. Army Criminal Investigation Laboratory (Pacific) Quarterly Newsletter*, and author of numerous professional articles relating to the forensic examination of questioned documents.

Richard J. Gigliotti. Manager, Security, Chem-Nuclear Geotech, Inc., Grand Junction, CO; former Security Director, UNC Naval Products, Montville, CT; former Manager, Loss Prevention, Colt Firearms, Hartford, CT; former Adjunct Faculty member, Mohegan Community College, Norwich, CT, and Eastern Connecticut State University, Willimantic, CT; Guest Lecturer, Indiana University, University of New Haven and Northeastern University. Member, American Society for Industrial Security, International Association of Chiefs of Police (former member, Committee on Private Security), Connecticut Police Chiefs Association (former member, Private Security, Public Affairs, Legislative and Firearms Committees); member, Governor's and General Assembly's Task Force on Private Security in the State of Connecticut; expert witness on security matters, U.S. District Court, New Haven, CT. Recipient of Chief Samuel Luciano Award as outstanding scholastic graduate, Connecticut Police Academy; U.S. Army Commendation Medal. Bachelor of Arts, Norwich University. Author and presenter of "The Crucial First Hour -- Hostage Incident Management for Industrial Security Departments," and author of *Emergency Planning for Maximum Protection and Security Design for Maximum Protection*, Butterworth-Heinemann; "Understanding Private Security," *Connecticut Police Chief*, "How to Stretch Your Security Dollar," *National Safety News and Journal of Healthcare Protection Management*, "Should Security Personnel Be Armed?," *Assets Protection*, "The Fine Art of Justification," *Security Management*, "What's Your Level of Physical Security?," *Security Management*, "Words Instead of Weapons," *Security and Protection (U.K.)*, "The Crucial First Hour," *Assets Protection, Journal of the Institute of Nuclear Materials Management, Journal of Healthcare Protection Management*, "Security Officer Evaluation Guide," *OSI Nuclear Security Safeguards*, "Filling the Void in Police Education," *Law and Order*, "Disparity Between the Ranks," *The Police Chief*, and "Guidelines for the Use of Deadly Force," *Law and Order* and *The Peace Officer*.

Richard P. Grassie, CPP. President, TECHMARK Security Integration Services, Hanover, MA; former Director, Security Programs Development, Analytical Systems Engineering Corp., Boston,

MA; former Program Manager, Law Enforcement Technical Assistance Program, Westinghouse National Issues Center, Washington, DC; former Lecturer, Criminal Justice Programs, University College, Northeastern University, Boston, MA; former Officer, Department of Defense Special Weapons Security Program. Member, American Society for Industrial Security; Standing Committee member, ASIS Security Architecture & Engineering and Substance Abuse Committees; member, American Defense Preparedness Association; member, Executive Committee, ADPA Facility Security Technical Working Group. Recipient of the American Spirit of Honor Medal, Association of the Army, Navy and Air Force. Bachelor of Science, University of Massachusetts; candidate, Master of Science, Northeastern University, Boston, MA. Author of numerous articles on security design and integration and countermeasures development for *Security Management* and other magazines; co-author of U.S. Department of Justice publications addressing crime analysis, criminal warrant service, and the Integrated Criminal Apprehension Program (ICAP).

John Dale Hartman. Licensed Private Investigator, Commonwealth of Pennsylvania; Criminal and Civil Trial Litigation Investigator and Consultant to government and the insurance, commercial and legal communities; Instructor, Pennsylvania State Police; court-recognized expert witness on private law enforcement in the Commonwealth of Pennsylvania; Guest Lecturer and Curriculum Developer at the university, college, and proprietary school level. Member, American Society for Industrial Security. Recipient of various commendations for investigative services and instruction. Bachelor of Arts in the Administration of Justice, University of Pittsburgh; candidate, Master of Arts, Graduate School of Public and International Affairs-Law and Justice Program, University of Pittsburgh. Author of *Legal Guidelines for Covert Surveillance Operations in the Private Sector*, Butterworth-Heinemann.

Richard J. Heffernan, CPP. President of R.J. Heffernan and Associates, Inc., Branford, CT. Member, American Society for Industrial Security; Chairman of the ASIS Standing Committee on Safeguarding Proprietary Information; former committee member, ASIS Standing Committee on Educational Institutions; faculty member, ASIS Assets Protection Course I and II; member, High Technology Crime Investigation Association; member, Society for Competitive Intelligence Professionals; member, National Forensic Center. Recipient of the 1991 ASIS Standing Committee Chairman of the Year Award. Author and originator of the *ASIS Technology Theft Surveys* technique. Author of "ASIS Technology Theft and Proprietary Information Protection Assessment Survey," *Security Management*, 1993.

Robert D. Hulshouser, CPP. Internal Affairs Manager, Metropolitan Edison Company, Reading, PA; Adjunct Instructor, Security Administration, Reading Area Community College; Lieutenant Colonel, U.S. Army Reserve, Willow Grove, PA; former Security Agent, Pennsylvania Power and Light Company, Allentown, PA; former Assistant Professor of Criminal Justice, West Chester University; former Assistant Professor of Criminal Justice, Lehigh County Community College, Schnecksville, PA; former commissioned officer, U.S. Army Military Police Corps with assignments in Europe, South Vietnam, and the United States. Member, American Society for Industrial Security; member, Security Committee, Edison Electric Institute; member, Pennsylvania Crime Prevention Officers' Association; member, Berks County Chiefs of Police Association; member, Law Enforcement and Security Administration Advisory Committee, Reading Area Community College; Chairperson, Standing Committee on Privacy and Personnel Information Management, ASIS; Chapter Chairman, Schuylkill Valley Chapter, ASIS. Recipient of Company Volunteer Recognition Award, Metropolitan Edison Company; Official Commendation from the City of Allentown, PA, for service as a Police Academy Instructor; member, People to People, Private Investigation and Security Delegation to Russia; invited presenter on the topic of "Hiring and Retention of Quality Employees" to the ASIS Norden Chapter and Skandia Insurance, Stockholm, Sweden; listed in the 1st Edition, *Who's Who in*

Security, National Security Institute, Inc., 1989; Bronze Star, U.S. Army. Bachelor of Arts, Ripon College; Master of Arts, Pacific Lutheran University; interviewed and featured in professional magazines and journals that include: *Security, Personnel Advisory Bulletin, Security Management,* and the *Utility Supervisor*.

Robert B. Iannone, CPP. President, Iannone Security Management, Inc., Fountain Valley, CA; Adjunct Professor, Department of Criminal Justice, California State University, Long Beach, CA; former Manager of Security, Hughes Aircraft Company, Torrance, CA; former Manager of Security and Investigations, Rockwell International Corporation, El Segundo, CA; former Security Inspector, Douglas Aircraft Company, Long Beach, CA; former Adjunct Professor, Administration of Justice, Golden West College, Huntington Beach, CA. Member, American Society for Industrial Security; former Chapter Chairman, Greater Los Angeles Chapter, American Society for Industrial Security; member, National Classification Management Society; former member, Board of Directors, Research Security Administrators. Recipient of the James S. Cogswell Award, Department of Defense. Bachelor of Science, California State University, Long Beach, CA; Master of Science, LaVerne University, LaVerne, CA. Co-author of "Security, Higher Training, and Internship," *Security Management* and "Is an Ex the Best Candidate?," *Security Management*.

Ronald C. Jason. Retired Officer, U.S. Coast Guard; former Security Training Officer, UNC Naval Products, Uncasville, CT; former Nuclear Accounts Manager, Globe Security Services, Inc.; former Chief, Security Branch, U.S. Coast Guard Academy, New London, CT; former Assistant Chief, Reserve Administration Branch, 3rd CG District, Governors Island, NY. Twice recipient of the Coast Guard Achievement Medal. Author of *Security Design for Maximum Protection*, Butterworth-Heinemann, *Emergency Planning for Maximum Protection*, Butterworth-Heinemann, and various professional articles that have appeared in *Security Management* and *Assets Protection*.

Brian C. Jayne, M.S.D.D. Research and Development, John E. Reid and Associates, Chicago, IL; Dean of Reid College of Detection of Deception, Chicago, IL. Member, American Polygraph Assocation, Wisconsin Polygraph Assocation; past President, Wisconsin Polygraph Assocation. Bachelor of Science University of Wisconsin -- Platteville; Master of Science, Reid College of Detection of Deception. Author of "Purposeful Non-Cooperation: A Diagnostic Opinion of Deception," *Polygraph*; "The Polygraph Technique I and II," *Wisconsin Public Defender Newsletter*; "The Psychological Principles of Criminal Interrogation," *Criminal Interrogation and Confessions*, 3rd Edition, Williams and Wilkins; "Control Question Theory in the Polygraph Technique," *Polygraph*; "Interrogating Suspects Regarding the Sale of Drugs," *The Narc Officer*; "The Reid Control Questions Technique," *The Complete Polygraphy Handbook*, Lexington Publishers; "The Employee Polygraph Protection Act of 1988," *The State Patrol Journal*; "A Comparison Between the Predictive Value of Two Common Preemployment Screening Procedures," *Polygraph*; "Detect Unscrupulous Applicants," *Recruitment Today*; "Contributions of Physiological Recordings in the Polygraph Technique," *Polygraph*; "The Ways and Means of Screening -- The Interview," *Security Management*; "The Use of the Polygraph Technique by Municipal Attorneys," *The Municipal Attorney*; "Polygraph Comes of Age," *The Docket*; "A Prosecutor's Guide to the Polygraph Technique," *Prosecutor*; "Interrogation Techniques on Trial," *Prosecutor*.

Brian M. Jenkins. Senior Managing Director, Kroll Associates, Los Angeles, CA; consultant on terrorism to government and business; former Chairman, Political Science Department, the Rand Corporation; former Captain, Special Forces (Green Berets), U.S. Army. Recipient of awards for valor in combat in the Dominican Republic and the Republic of Vietnam, and recipient of the U.S. Army's highest award for work as a member of the U.S. Army in Vietnam Long-Range Planning Task Group.

Author of *International Terrorism: A New Mode of Conflict*; editor of and contributing author to *Terrorism and Personal Protection* (Butterworth-Heinemann); co-author of *The Fall of South Vietnam*; Author of more than 100 professional works dealing with political violence; Associate Editor of two scholarly journals, *Terrorism* and *Conflict*; and Editor-in-Chief of *TVI Report*, a quarterly journal in the area of terrorism, violence, and insurgency.

Steven Kaufer, CPP. Security Management Consultant; Founder and President, Inter/Action Associates, Inc., Palm Springs, CA; founded and later sold Checkmate Security; developed the method for security surveys that has been adopted by numerous security companies. Member, International Association of Professional Security Consultants; American Society for Industrial Security; National Fire Protection Assocation; Professional and Technical Consultants Association; National Bureau of Professional Management Consultants; and the Defense Research Institute; Designee as a Certified Professional Consultant to Management by the National Bureau of Professional Management Consultants, and as a Certified Protection Professional (CPP) by the American Society for Industrial Security; former Southern Vice President and Chairman of Legislative Affairs for the California Alarm Association. Attended Arizona State University. Publisher of *Security Topics Newsletter*.

Steven R. Keller, CPP. Principal Consultant, Steven R. Keller and Associates, Inc.; Deltona, FL; Executive Producer, Horizon Institute, Inc. and Horizon Productions, Deltona, FL; former Executive Director of the International Association of Professional Security Consultants; former Executive Director of Protection Services, the Art Institute of Chicago; former Director of Corporate Security, Mother Earth News Publishing Company, Hendersonville, NC; former Assistant Director of Security and Special Agent, Federal Reserve Board, Washington, DC; former Police Officer, Sergeant, Detective, Metropolitan Police Department, Washington, DC. Member, American Society for Industrial Security (ASIS); member, International Association of Professional Security Consultants (IAPSC); member, Board of Directors, IAPSC; member, American Association of Museums (AAM); former Chairman, ASIS Museum, Library and Archive Committee; former Chairman, ASIS Professional Practices Sub-Committee during writing of the *Suggested Guidelines in Museum Security*; member, ASIS Museum, Library and Cultural Property Committee; member, AAM Security Committee; Certified Hypnotist (Forensic). Recipient, Security Executive Achievement Award; recipient, ASIS President's Award of Merit; recipient, ASIS Distinguished Achievement Award; recipient, Smithsonian Institution's Leadership Award; recipient, IAPSC Outstanding Achievement Award; listed in *Who's Who in the Southeast*; listed in *Who's Who Among Emerging Leaders in America*. Bachelor of Arts, Public Administration, American University, Washington, DC; Seminar Faculty, New York University and the Smithsonian Institution's National Conference on Museum Security; former faculty ASIS Seminars, International Security Conferences; former member of Editorial Board, Security; author or contributing author of six books; author and executive producer for 24 video training tapes in management and security; author of over 20 articles in professional publications and journals including *Security, Security World, Security Management, Security Industry Product News, Leaders, Curator, International Security Review, Building Design and Construction, Construction Specifier, Specifying Engineer,* and *The Protection Officer*.

Daniel B. Kennedy, Ph.D., CPP. Professor and Chair, Department of Criminal Justice and Security Administration, University of Detroit Mercy, Detroit, MI; Consulting and testifying expert in premises liability and negligent security litigation; former Probation Officer and Police Academy Director. Member of American Society for Industrial Security, International Association of Chiefs of Police, and International Society of Crime Prevention Practitioners; former Chairman, Academic Programs Committee of American Society of Industrial Security; recipient of Chairman of the Year,

American Society for Industrial Security; Faculty Award for Excellence, University of Detroit. Bachelor of Arts, Master of Arts, and Doctor of Philosophy, Wayne State University, Detroit, MI; graduate of the National Crime Prevention Institute. Author of seven books and over 60 professional articles appearing in such periodicals as *Security Journal, Journal of Security Administration, Security Management, Journal of Police Science and Administration, Justice Quarterly,* and *Journal of Criminal Justice.*

Howard R. Keough, BS, CPP. Risk Management Officer/Contingency Planner, Safir and Associates, Fairfax, VA; Associate Instructor, Computer Security, Northern Virginia Community College, Annandale, VA; Instructor, ADP Environments, Computer Education, McLean, VA; Independent ADP Security Consultant, Rockville, MD; Project Manager, McAuto Systems, Gaithersburg, MD; Branch Chief, Information Systems Security Group, Central Intelligence Agency, McLean, VA; Special Agent, U.S. Office of Naval Intelligence, Guam; Special Agent, U.S. Secret Service; Chairman, Chesapeake Chapter, American Society for Industrial Security (ASIS); Vice Chairman, Washington, DC, Chapter, ASIS; member, Standing Committee on Computer Security, ASIS; Chairman, Computer Security Subcommittee, Washington, DC, Chapter, ASIS; member, Subcommittee on Terrorist Countermeasures, Washington, DC, Chapter, ASIS; member, Association of Former Special Agents, U.S. Secret Service, Washington, DC; member, American Society for Industrial Security; member, Association of former Special Agents, U.S. Secret Service; member and Chairman, Chesapeake Chapter, ASIS; member and Vice Chairman, Washington, DC, Chapter, ASIS; member and Chairman, Computer Security Subcommittee, Washington, DC, Chapter, ASIS. Bronze Star Medal, U.S. Army; three Certificates of Appreciation as Program Chairman, Standing Committee on Computer Security, ASIS. Bachelor of Science, New York University; School of Law, New York University (2 years). Author of 13 articles and book reviews published by *Security Management*.

Carl E. King. Chief Executive Officer, Team Building Systems, Inc., Houston, TX; Chief Executive Officer, Insights Corporate Selection Systems, Houston, TX; Chief Executive Officer WNCK, Inc., Houston, TX; Major, U.S. Marine Corps, Retired. Member of International Association of Chiefs of Police; American Society for Industrial Security; Private Security Services Council of American Society of Industrial Security; FBI National Academy; National Order of Battle Field Commissions. Listed in *Who's Who in Finance and Industry, 1989-1992*; listed in *Who's Who in Security, 1989-1992*; named to *Inc.* magazine's 1990 list of 500 Fastest Growing Companies; finalist for Houston's Entrepreneur of the Year; recipient of two Purple Hearts, the Bronze Star, Presidential Unit Citation, and other Vietnam awards. Bachelor of Science in Criminal Justice, University of Nebraska at Omaha; Bachelor of Laws, Lasalle Extension University, Chicago, IL; Master of Arts in Business Management, Central Michigan University; graduate of the Federal Bureau of Investigation National Academy, Quantico, VA; graduate of the Military Police Officers Advanced Course. Author of "Why Test for Alcohol?," "When Is a Drug Not a Drug?," and "Alcohol Abuse on the Job," *Security Management*.

Robert L. Kohr, CSP, CPP. Senior Consultant, Arthur D. Little, Inc., Cambridge, MA; Principal, Kohr & Associates, Mt. Airy, MD; Director of Design and Director of Technical Services for Loss Prevention, Marriott Corporation, Washington, DC. Member, American Society of Safety Engineers; member, American Society for Industrial Security; member, American Society for Testing and Materials; member, National Safety Council; member, National Fire Protection Association; member, Building Officials and Code Adminstration International; member, American Hotel and Motel Association; Secretary, ASTM F13 and C21.06. Bachelor of Science, Geology, Virgina Polytechnic Institute and State University. Author of *Accident Prevention for Hotels, Motels, and*

Restaurants, Van Nostrand Reinhold; "Washroom Safety, Things to Consider," and "Slip, Slidin' Away," *Safety & Health*; "Safety Factor in Bathroom Design," "Recognizing and Preventing Slip and Fall Accidents," "How Safe Are Marble Floors," and "It Could Be A Crime," *Lodging*; "Security By Design" and "Mastering the Challenge of Securing a Budget Motel," *Security Management*; "A Study of the Comparative Slipperiness of Floor Cleaning Chemicals," "Worker Safety in the Kitchen: A Comparative Study of Footwear versus Walking and Working Surfaces," and "Bucknell University F-13 Workshop to Evaluate Various Slip Resistance Measuring Devices," *Standardization News*; "Slip Resistance and the Designer," *Progressive Architecture*.

Herman A. Kruegle. Vice President, Visual Methods, Inc.; former Section Head, Electro-Optics Division, ITT Avionics, Clifton, NJ; former Manager, Laser and Electro-Optical Systems Division, Holobeam, Inc., Paramus, NJ; former Assistant Chief Engineer, Spectroscopic and Electro-Optical Laboratory, Warner and Swasey Co. Member, Institute of Electrical and Electronic Engineers (IEEE); member, American Society for Industrial Security (ASIS); Chairman, 1992, 1993, Closed Circuit Television Manufacturers Association (CCTMA). Awarded six patents in security, electro-optical, and laser fields. Bachelor of Science in Electrical Engineering, Brooklyn Polytechnic Institute; Master of Science in Electrical Engineering, New York University; Licensed New York State Professional Engineer. Author of numerous publications in professional security and electro-optics journals; contributing author, *Handbook of Loss Prevention and Crime Prevention, Controlling Cargo Theft, Museum, Archive and Library Security*, Butterworth-Heinemann; author of *Lens Primer Series*, CCTV Source Book; author of *CCTV Surveillance*, Butterworth-Heinemann.

Richard LaBoda. U. S. Postal Inspector, U. S. Postal Inspection Service, Houston, TX; member, American Society for Industrial Security; member, Texas Crime Prevention Association; member, Sheriffs Association of Texas; member, Houston Metropolitan Criminal Investigators Association; member, Federal Investigators Association. Recipient of the Wichita Kansas Police Department Bronze Wreath for Meritorious Service. Bachelor of Science and Master of Arts, Western Connecticut State University, Danbury, CT.

Robert F. Littlejohn, CPP. Director of Security, Avon Products, Inc.; former Vice President of Investigations, Pinkerton's, Inc.; former Commander of Operations, New York City Police Department; former Deputy Director of Emergency Management, City of New York; former Adjunct Professor of Management, Graduate School of Business and Public Administration, Long Island University; Colonel, U.S. Army Reserve, U.S. Military Academy at West Point. Member, American Society for Industrial Security and member of various security and law enforcement professional associations. Recipient in 1984 of the Congressional Medal of Merit for outstanding public service. Baccalaureate (magna cum laude), City University of New York; Master's, C.W. Post College; graduate of the Industrial College of the Armed Forces and of the U.S. Army Command and General Staff College. Author of numerous professional articles including "Crisis Management: A Team Approach," *American Management Association*, 1984.

Lynn Wilson Marks, BCFDE. Forensic document and handwriting examiner; owner, Lynn Wilson Marks & Associates, San Antonio, TX. Member, Association of Forensic Document Examiners; member, Forgery Investigators Association of Texas; member, International Association of Credit Card Investigators; member, International Graphonomics Society; past President, Association of Forensic Document Examiners (AFDE); Board Certification Chairman, AFDE, 1992-1993; Abstract Review Committee (Questioned Document Section) for the 1993 International Graphonomics Society's Paris Conference. Author of "Forensic Document Examination in Medical

Malpractice Cases," *Lawyer's Cooperative Publishing*, "Opinions and Their Meaning," *The Subpoena, San Antonio Bar Association Journal*.

Harry L. Marsh, Ph.D.   Associate Professor, Indiana State University, Terre Haute, IN; former Special Agent, Defense Investigative Service; former Special Agent and Detachment Commander, Air Force Office of Special Investigations.   Member, American Society for Industrial Security; member, Academy of Criminal Justice Sciences.   Bachelor of Arts, Rutgers University; Master of Science, Central Missouri State University; Doctor of Philosophy, Sam Houston State University. Author of "Corporation/University Cooperation in Security Education Programs: A Model for Professionalization of Security Personnel," *Security Journal*; "A Profile of Partnership," and "An Ironclad Case for Professionalism," *Security Management*.

Leon C. Mathieu.   Senior Investigator, Corporate Security, Legal Department, Conoco, Inc., Houston, TX; former Chief of Investigations, The Charter Company, Jacksonville, FL; former Detective, Metropolitan Dade County Police, Miami, FL; former Insurance Adjuster, Employer's Service Corporation, Coral Gables, FL; former Instructor, Miami-Dade Community College, Miami, FL; member, American Society for Industrial Security; former Chapter Chairman, Jacksonville, Florida, Chapter of ASIS; member, International Society of Crime Prevention Practitioners; member, Houston Metropolitan Criminal Investigators Association.   Bachelor of Science, Florida International University; Master of Science, Nova University.

Chris E. McGoey, CPP, CSP.   President, McGoey Security Consulting, Phoenix, AZ; Publisher of security books, Aegis Books, Oakland, CA; former Security Manager, Neiman-Marcus, San Francisco, CA; former Corporate Loss Prevention and Region Security Manager, Southland Corporation, Dallas, TX; former Security Consultant, Big Bear Markets, San Diego, CA; former Security Manager, S.S. Kresge Corporation, San Diego, CA; former Criminal Investigator, Santa Clara County Public Defender's Office, San Jose, CA.   Member, International Association of Professional Security Consultants; member, American Society for Industrial Security; member, Retail Security Association of Northern California; member, California Crime Prevention Officers Association; member, California Association of Licensed Investigators; member, National Association of Legal Investigators; Board of Directors, International Association of Professional Security Consultants; District Governor, California Association of Licensed Investigators.   Recipient of the President's Award for District Governor of the Year, California Association of Licensed Investigators; recipient of the Governor's Crime Prevention Award, State of Nevada.   Associate of the Arts, Police Science, Chabot College, Hayward, CA; Bachelor of Science, Criminal Justice Administration, San Jose State University; Master of Science, Criminal Justice Administration (12 units completed), San Jose State University.   Author of "Security; Adequate...or Not?," "The Complete Guide to Premises Liability Litigation," and "Premises Liability Investigation," *CALI,*; "A Model of Management," and "Effective Security Design Must be Flexible," *Access Control*.

Bonnie S. Michelman, CPP, CHPA.   Director of Police and Security, Massachusetts General Hospital, Boston, MA; Lecturer in Security, Northeastern University, Boston, MA; affiliated with Liability Consultants, Inc., Framingham, MA; Manager of the Metro-medical District for First Security Services Corporation, Boston, MA; Assistant Vice President for Support Services, Newton Wellesley Hospital.   Chairperson of the Boston Chapter of the American Society for Industrial Security; Vice President/Secretary, International Association for Healthcare Security and Safety. Master of Business Administration, Bentley College; Master of Criminal Justice, Northeastern University; Bachelor of Science in Government, Clark University.   Author of several articles on security management.

Richard L. Moe, CPP. Director of Assets Preservation for S&A Restaurant Corp., Dallas, TX; former Director of Assets Protection for Metromedia Steakhouses, Inc., Dayton, OH; former Security Manager for Argonne National Laboratories-West, Idaho Falls, ID; former Director of Security for Sambo's Restaurants, Inc.; Lieutenant Colonel, U.S. Army (Retired). Member, American Society for Industrial Security; member, International Security Management Association; member, National Food Service Security Council (NFSSC); member, International Association of Chiefs of Police; Chairman, National Food Service Security Council; Chairman, Food Service Security Standing Committee, ASIS; Chairman, Santa Barbara Chapter, ASIS. Recipient of ASIS Standing Committee Chairman of the Year Award, recipient of NFSSC Award for Life Time Achievement in Food Service Security. Bachelor of Science, University of Arizona; Master of Science, George Washington University.

Kenneth C. Moore, CPP. Aviation Security Consultant, Kenneth Moore Associates, Dublin, CA; former Manager of Security, Apple Computer, Inc., Cupertino, CA; former Manager of Security, United Airlines, Chicago, IL; former Manager of Security, J.C. Penney Co., New York, NY; former Special Agent, Federal Bureau of Investigation; former Special Agent, Office of Special Investigations, U.S. Air Force. Member, American Society for Industrial Security; member, former Special Agents of the Federal Bureau of Investigation; member, Worldwide Aviation Safety and Security Association; member, International Association of Airline Security Officers; member, National Business Aircraft Association; member, Aviation Crime Prevention Institute; member, Aircraft Owners and Pilots Association; member, California Association of Licensed Investigators; member, High Technology Crime Investigation Association; Certified Protection Professional. Bachelor of Science, University of Oregon; Master of Science, Criminal Justice Administration, San Jose State University. Author of *Airport, Aircraft, and Airline Security*, 2nd Edition, Butterworth-Heinemann; "Airline Security in the Year 2000," an article in *Security in the Year 2000 and Beyond, An Anthology*, ETC Publications.

John R. Morris. President, VIDEOTRONIX, Inc., Burnsville, MN and Denver, CO; former Vice President of North American Video Corporation. Member, American Society for Industrial Security; member, Minnesota Association of Parking Professionals. Author of "Plugging into the Systems," *Security Management*.

Dale A. Moul, CPP. Vice President, Safeguards, Security and Training Systems, Battelle Memorial Institute, Columbus, OH; former Manager, Safeguards and Security Program Office, Battelle; former Division Manager/Director of Special Projects, Wackenhut Advanced Technologies Corporation, McLean, VA; former Military Police Officer and Counterintelligence Officer, U.S. Army. Member, American Society for Industrial Security (ASIS); member, ASIS Standing Committe on Disaster Management; member, Institute of Nuclear Materials Management; Certified Security Lead Auditor under ANSI/ASME N45.2.23; former member of the Virginia State Bar. Bachelor of Science, Michigan State University; Juris Doctor (Law), University of Maryland. Co-author of U.S. Nuclear Regulatory Commission reports NUREG/CR-3251, *The Role of Security During Safety-Related Emergencies at Nuclear Power Plants*; NUREG/CR-4093, *Safety/Safeguards Interactions During Safety-Related Emergencies at Nuclear Power Reactor Facilites*; NUREG/CR-5081, *Tactical Exercise Planning Handbook*; and NUREG/CR-5172, *Tactical Training Reference Manual*.

Edmund J. Pankau, CFE, CLI, CPP. Chief Executive Officer, Intertect, Inc., Houston, TX; Director of Security, Space Commerce Corporation, Houston, TX; former Special Agent, Intelligence Unit, U.S. Treasury Department. Member, American Society for Industrial Security; member, National

Association of Certified Fraud Examiners; member, National Association of Legal Investigators; Regent, National Association of Certified Fraud Examiners, 1990-91; Instructor, Federal Financial Investigators Examination Council. Bachelor of Science in Criminology, Florida State University, 1971. Author of *Check It Out*, Contemporary Press; *How to Investigate by Courthouse and Computer*, Thomas Publications; and *How to Make $100,000*, Paladin Press.

E. Floyd Phelps, CPP. Assistant Director, Department of Public Safety, Southern Methodist University, Dallas, TX; Adjunct Professor, School for Continuing Education, University of Texas at Dallas; former Security Investigator, Safeway Stores, Inc., Dallas, TX; former Regional Asset Protection Manager, Handyman/Homers Home Centers, Inc., Dallas, TX. Member, American Society for Industrial Security, Forgery Investigators Association, Texas Narcotic Officers Association, Texas Crime Prevention Association, Texas Parking Association; member of the National Standing Committee for Educational Institutions Security; former member of the Mayor's Council for Dallas Against Drugs. Recipient of the Dallas County Sheriff's Office Citizen Certificate of Merit in 1986. Contributor to *Computer Security -- Readings from Security Management*, ASIS Reprint Series; author of "Bug Bites," "Campus Security 101," "Day of Reckoning," "Physical Education in Campus Security," "Methods of Theft from a Register," all published in *Security Management*. Licensed by the State of Texas as a Security Consultant.

Philip P. Purpura, CPP. Coordinator, Criminal Justice and Paralegal Departments, Florence-Darlington Technical College, Florence, SC; Security Consultant; former Security Manager and Investigator. Member, American Society for Industrial Security; member, Academy of Criminal Justice Sciences. Master of Science, Criminal Justice, Eastern Kentucky University; Bachelor of Science, Criminal Justice, University of Dayton. Author of *Retail Security & Shrinkage Protection*, (1993), *Security & Loss Prevention: An Introduction*, 2nd Edition, 1991, *Modern Security & Loss Prevention Management*, 1989, Butterworth-Heinemann; and *Security Handbook*, 1991, Delmar Publishers.

David D. Schein. Attorney and business consultant; Managing Partner, Law Offices of David D. Schein; Executive Vice President and General Counsel, Claremont Management Group, Inc.; frequent Lecturer at Rice University Graduate School of Business; Director of Health Access Texas; Director of the Houston Council. Member, American Bar Association; member, Texas Bar Association; member, Houston Bar Association. Named to *Who's Who in American Law*; 1992 Republican candidate for the Texas House of Representatives, District 148. Juris Doctorate, University of Houston; Master of Business Administration, University of Virginia; Bachelor of Arts, University of Pennsylvania. Author of "How to Prepare a Company Policy on Substance Abuse Control," *Personnel Journal*; "Should Employers Restrict Smoking in the Workplace," *Labor-Law Journal*; "Facing the Drug-Test Challenge," *Sam's Buy-Line*; "Americans with Disability Act," *Leaps Newsletter*; quoted in *Occupational Health and Safety, Convenience Store Management, Communication World, Houston Chronicle, The Houston Post, Lawrence (KS) Journal-World*, and *American Society of Association Executives Newsletter*.

William J. Schneider. Senior Associate, TECHMARK Security Integration Services, Portland, ME; Certified Engineer in Training (Mechanical), Commonwealth of Virginia; former Manager, Security Sytems Engineering, Analytical Systems Engineering Corporation, Boston, MA; former Chief Executive Officer, Anti-Terrorism Consulting, Inc., Ayer, MA; former Officer, U.S. Army Special Forces Group, Fort Devens, MA. Member, American Society for Industrial Security; member, American Defense Preparedness Association. Recipient of numerous military decorations. Bachelor of Science, U.S. Military Academy, West Point, New York; candidate, Juris Doctorate,

University of Maine. Co-author of "Counting on Design," *Security Management*, and "Anti-Terrorism Countermeasures Development," *Carnahan Conference on Security Technology*.

James A. Schweitzer. Information security consultant; former Corporate Manager, Information Security for Digital Equipment Corporation, and Manager, Systems Security Technology at Xerox Corporation; former Chair and Editor for ACM Special Interest Group, Security, Audit, and Control. Member of the American Society for Industrial Security Standing Committee on Computer Security; member of International Board of Editors for the Computers & Security journal; member of the National Security Agency team which reviewed information security in industry (1988). Certificate in Data Processing; Bachelor of Science from Duquesne University; and Master of Business Administration from Indiana University. Author of three current books on security management and information security, including *Managing Information Security*, 2nd Edition, Butterworth-Heinemann.

Bonnie L. Schwid, BS. Board Certified Forensic Document Examiner, Anagraphics, Milwaukee, WI; Document Integrity Services, San Antonio, TX; Board Certified member, Assocation of Forensic Document Examiners, International Graphonomics Society. Member, American Society for Industrial Security; public member of the Board of Governors of the State Bar of Wisconsin (appointment by State Supreme Court); former public member of the Professional Responsibility Committee of State Bar of Wisconsin; former Treasurer, Vice President, President, Certification Chair and present Second Vice President of the Association of Forensic Document Examiners. Recipient of the Excellence in Training award in competition sponsored by the Wisconsin Chapter of the American Society of Training and Development; electee to *Who's Who in America's Colleges and Universities*. Bachelor of Science, Cardinal Stritch College, Milwaukee, WI; board certification in Forensic Document Examination by the Assocation of Forensic Document Examiners. Author of "Forgeries and Altered Documents," *Milwaukee Lawyer*; "Examining Forensic Documents," *Wisconsin Lawyer*; "Forgery Workshop Aids Tellers," *Wisconsin Banker*; presenter of "Language and Handwriting," to the post graduate program, University of Trier, Germany, the Puerto Rico Association of Forensic Sciences, the Document Section of the Pan American Association of Forensic Sciences, the regional meeting of the National Association of Legal Investigators, the University of Wisconsin Linguistics Department, the American Safe Deposit Association, and various law enforcement organizations and banking associations.

Charles A. Sennewald, CMC, CPP, CPO. Independent Security Management Consultant in Escondido, CA; former Security Director for the Broadway Department Stores; former Chief of Campus Police, Claremont, CA; former Deputy Sheriff, Los Angeles County; former assistant Professor at California State University at Los Angeles. Founder and first President, International Association of Professional Security Consultants; former President and current board member of the International Association of Protection Officers; former Standing Committee Chairman and member of the American Society for Industrial Security. Recipient of *Security World* magazine's Merit Award; twice designated by the U.S. Department of Commerce as the Security Industry Representative on missions to Sweden, Denmark, Japan, China, and Hong Kong. Bachelor of Science, California State University at Los Angeles. Author of four Butterworth-Heinemann books: *Effective Security Management, The Process of Investigation, Security Consulting*, and *Shoplifting*.

Clifford E. Simonsen, Ph.D., CPP. President, Criminology Consultants International, Camano Island, WA; Adjunct Professor, Graduate School of Criminal Justice, Chaminade University of Honolulu; former Chairman of the Corrections and Security Program, Edmond Community College, Lynnwood, WA; former Associate Superintendent, Washington State Reformatory, Monroe, WA;

former Manager of King County Jail, Seattle, WA; former Chairman of Criminal Justice Department, City University, Seattle, WA; retired Military Police Officer (Colonel), United States Army. Member, American Society for Industrial Security; member American Correctional Association; member, Academy of Criminal Justice Sciences; member, International Academy of Criminology; former Chairman, Puget Sound Chapter of ASIS; Chairman of CPP Committee of the Puget Sound Chapter; Editorial Board member, *Security Journal*; member of Educational Committee, American Correctional Association; Representative to National Conference on Correctional Policy, ACA. Korean National Police Medal of Merit, 1969; Distinguished Citizen Award, State of Washington, 1976; Meritorious Service Award, International Association of Halfway Houses, 1979; Legion of Merit, U.S. Army, 1984; Outstanding Achievement as a Scholar Award, Washington Council on Crime and Delinquency, 1989; Certified Protection Professional (CPP), American Society for Industrial Security; Certified Vocational/Technical Instructor (Security), State of Washington; certified Community College Instructor (Criminal Justice), State of Florida; certified in Operational Research and Systems Analysis, Department of Defense; Certified Professional Trainer, New Mexico Department of Public Safety. Bachelor of Science, University of Nebraska at Omaha in Law Enforcement and Corrections; Master of Science, Florida State University in Criminology and Corrections; Master of Public Administration, Ohio State University in Correctional Administration; Doctor of Philosophy, Ohio State University in Administration of Justice/Deviance; graduate of Military Police Officer Basic Course, Military Police Officer Advanced Course, U.S. Army Command and Staff College, OR/SA Executive Course, Army Management School, Industrial College of the Armed Forces, and the U.S. Army War College. Co-author of *Corrections in America: An Introduction*, 6th Edition, Macmillan Publishing Company; author of *Building A More Successful Security Program Using Guidelines and Modes for Policies and Procedures*, STA Publications; author of *Juvenile Justice in America*, 3rd Edition, Macmillan Publishing Company; co-author of *Criminal Justice in America; the System, the Process, the People*, Saunders Press; author of *Psychopathic Offender Legislation in the United States*, Sophia and Oratio Publishers. Author of many articles, including "The Man/Machine Interface as Interacted by the Ecology of the Security Person," *Proceedings of the 7th Annual Symposium on the Role of Behavioral Science in Physical Security*, Defense Nuclear Agency, 1981; "The Indispensable Person Syndrome," *Security Management*, April 1987; "Why Not Plug Into the 'Invisible Empire'?," *Security Management*, February, 1988; "The Window of Indifference," *Security Management*, May, 1988; "Stitching Up a Suit-Proof Policy," *Security Management*, July, 1989; "Policies and Procedures: Better Protection Than a Bullet-Proof Vest?," *Corrections Today*, July, 1989; "Breaking Bureaucratic Bonds," *Security Management*, September, 1991; "How to Take a CPP Test," *Dynamics*, May-June, 1992; and "What Value Do Ethics Have in the Corporate World?," *Security Management*, September, 1992.

Vicki Simpson-Looney. Sales Manager, ABM Security Services, Houston, TX. Member, American Society for Industrial Security; leadership positions in the Houston Chapter of ASIS include 1991 Chapter Secretary, 1992 Vice Chairperson, and 1993 Chairperson. Associate Degree, Howard Payne University. Co-author of "Have I Got a Deal for You!: A Guide to the Selection of a Security Guard Contractor," *Security Management*; "Guide to Selecting a Guard Contractor," Butterworth-Heinemann; "Do's and Don'ts of Security Management," *FACETS*, Community Association Institute.

Philip C. Sunstrom, CPP, CHS. Director of Security and Loss Prevention, Saddlebrook Resorts, Inc., Wesley Chapel, FL; former Manager of Hospitality Security and Safety, The American Club, Kohler, WI. Member of the American Society for Industrial Security; member of the National Association of Chiefs of Police; Chairman of the Standing Committee on Lodging Security, American Society for Industrial Security. Bachelor of Arts, Concordia University.

John D. Sutton. Senior Project Engineer, Raytheon Services, Nevada, Las Vegas, NV; former Project Manager, EG&G Special Projects, Albuquerque, NM; former Program Manager, Wackenhut Advanced Technologies Corporation, Fairfax, VA; Electronic Maintenance Officer, U.S. Marine Corps (Retired). Member, American Society for Industrial Security (ASIS); former Chairman, ASIS Standing Committee on Security Architect and Engineers; former Program Chairman, ASIS Security A&E Workshop. Recipient of 19 military decorations and numerous Letters of Commendation. Bachelor of Arts with honors and with distinction in Public Administration, San Diego State University; Master of Science candidate, Safety and Systems Management, University of Southern California. Author of "Know Your QC's," *Security Management*.

Ronald L. Thomas, CPP. Researcher, Children's Hospital of Michigan, Detroit, MI; Director of Investigative Operations, Corporate Business Intelligence, Inc., Dearborn, MI; Adjunct Professor, Department of Criminal Justice/Security and Safety Administration, University of Detroit, Detroit, MI; former Police Officer, City of Dearborn, MI; former member of the Drug Enforcement Administration's Great Lakes Narcotic Task Force, U.S. Department of Justice; former Deputy U.S. Marshal; Licensed Private Investigator, State of Michigan. Member, American Society for Industrial Security. Associate Degree, Henry Ford Community College; Bachelor of Science, University of Detroit; Master of Science, University of Detroit; Doctor of Philosophy candidate, Research and Evaluation, Wayne State University. Author of "How to Choose a Private Investigator," *Security Management*; "Crime Prevention Through Environmental Design: The Site Plan Review Process in Ann Arbor, Michigan," *ASLET Journal*; and "Crime Prevention Through Environmental Design," *Michigan Municipal Review*.

G. Randolph Uzzell, Jr., CPP. Director, Corporate Security, Burlington Industries, Inc., Greensboro, NC. Member, American Society for Industrial Security, Academic Advisory Council (ASIS), Standing Committee on White Collar Crime (ASIS), Standing Committee on Substance Abuse (ASIS); former member, Standing Committee on Disaster Management (ASIS) and Standing Committee on Physical Security (ASIS); former Chairman, Standing Committee on Physical Security (ASIS) and North Carolina Chapter (ASIS); member, North Carolina State University Industrial Security Advisory Board and the Textile Security Roundtable. Recipient on two occasions of the Joe Hinnerman Outstanding Volunteer Leader award, North Carolina Chapter of ASIS, and, while Chairman, the I.B. Hale Award as Outstanding Chapter in ASIS; recipient of Outstanding Committee Chairman of the Year for ASIS. Associate Degree, Wingate College, Wingate, NC; Bachelor of Arts, University of North Carolina at Chapel Hill; Bachelor of Administrative Sciences, Guilford College, Greensboro, NC.

Martin L. Vitch, CPP. Senior Security Specialist, C.H. Guernsey and Co., Oklahoma City, OK, and Atlanta, GA; former Security Specialist in the application of interior and exterior intrusion detection technology, U.S. Army Material Command, Atlanta, GA; Guest Instructor in a variety of educational and training venues; former Investigator with the Internal Revenue Service; former Municipal Law Enforcement Officer; former Independent Security Consultant. Member, American Society for Industrial Security and member of the ASIS Standing Committee on Physical Security. Associate of Arts from Miami Dade Community College and the Bachelor of Business Administration from Florida Atlantic University. Author of U.S. Army Special Text 190-30-1, *Employing/Evaluating the Operation of Intrusion Detection Systems (IDS)*, and numerous articles published in the security literature.

J. Branch Walton. Director, Corporate Security, Cummins Engine Company, Inc., Columbus, IN; Adjunct Assistant Professor, Indiana University, Bloomington, IN; U.S. Secret Service-Retired;

former Special Agent in Charge, Springfield, Illinois Office; Assistant Special Agent in Charge, Office of Training; member of the Presidential Detail (Nixon and Carter presidencies); Instructor, Office of Training, Kansas City and Omaha Field Offices. Member, ASIS; member, ASIS Academic Programs Committee; past Secretary, Indianapolis Chapter of ASIS; member, American Society of Law Enforcement Trainers; member, International Security Management Association (ISMA); member, Board of Directors and Treasurer, Academic Scholarship Chairperson, ISMA; member, State Department Overseas Security Advisory Council; member, Academic Advisory Committee, Eastern Kentucky University; member, Academic Adivsory Committee, National Crime Prevention Institute (NCPI), University of Louisville; member, Red Cross Advisory Board, Bartholomew County, IN; past member, Illinois Local Governmental Law Enforcement Officers Training Board; past member, Illinois Attorney General's Law Enforcement Adivsory Board; past member, Federal Law Enforcement Training Center and Public Police/Private Security Feasibilty Study Group; Consultant, Palumbo Partners, Inc., Miami Beach, FL; Consultant, Security Services International, Philadelphia, PA. Bachelor of Science, University of Nebraska; Master of Science, Wichita State University; post graduate studies at Indiana University. Author of "Terrorism and VIP Protection," *CJ the Americas*; "Out of Harms Way," *Security Management*; "An Ironclad Case for Professionalism," *Security Management*; "Phone Fraud," *Security Management, Careers in Investigations*, and *Preparing for Careers in Law Enforcement and Private Security*, W.C. Brown Publications; and "VIP Protection and Terrorism," a paper presented to the American Society of Criminology.

Terry F. Whitley, CFE, CPP. Senior Security Coordinator, Star Enterprise, Houston, TX; former Director of Corporate Security, Enron Corporation, Houston, TX; former Senior Security Representative, Phillips Petroleum Company, Houston, TX; former Security Representative, Shell Oil Company, Houston, TX; former Criminal Investigation Supervisor, U.S. Army Criminal Investigation Command. Member, American Society for Industrial Security; member, National Association of Certified Fraud Examiners; member, Institute of Internal Audit; member, Assocation of Former Intelligence Officers; member, CID Agents Assocation. Bachelor of Science in Police Adminstration/Psychology, Hardin-Simmons University; Master of Science in Criminal Justice, Troy State University; Master of Education, Boston University.

Jerry L. Wright, CPP. Director, Crime Prevention Unit, Ann Arbor Police Department, Ann Arbor, MI; President, Wright & Associates, Inc., Ann Arbor, MI; Instructor, National Crime Prevention Institute, Louisville, KY; Instructor, Eastern Kentucky University, School of Loss Prevention, Richmond, KY; volunteer consultant, Criminal Justice Services, American Assocation of Retired Persons, Washington, DC. Member, American Society for Industrial Security; member, Crime Prevention Association of Michigan; member, International Society of Crime Prevention Practitioners; member, Washtenaw Law Enforcement & Industrial Security Association; member, National Crime Prevention Institute Alumni Association; member, International Association of Crime Analysts; member, American Society of Law Enforcement Trainers; Chairperson, Crime Prevention/Loss Prevention Committee, American Society for Industrial Security; Chapter Chairperson, Greater Ann Arbor Area Chapter, American Society for Industrial Security; past Vice President, Crime Prevention Association of Michigan; past Chairperson, Washtenaw Chapter, American Red Cross. Recipient of the Professional Excellence Award, Ann Arbor Police Department; recipient of the Chapter Award for Chartering the Greater Ann Arbor Area Chapter, American Society for Industrial Security. Bachelor of Business Administration, Cleary College. Author of "Crime in the Lodging Industry," *Michigan Lodging Association*; "Loss Prevention Program Equals Reduced Employee Theft," *Michigan Lodging Association*; "Tele-Communication Security," *Practitioner*; "Crime Prevention Through Environmental Design," *Michigan Municipal Review*; and

"Crime Prevention Through Environmental Design: The Site Plan Review Process in Ann Arbor, Michigan," *The ASLET Journal*.

G. H. Zimmer, Jr., CPP. Principal, Checkmate Strategies Group, Phoenix, AZ; Lieutenant Colonel, U.S. Army, Retired. Member, American Society for Industrial Security; member, International Association of Professional Security Consultants; member, Association of Former Intelligence Officers; member, Operations Security (OPSEC) Professional Society; former member Chulalonkhorn University Political Science Seminar, Thailand; former Deputy Chief, U.S. Mission, South East Asia Treaty Organization Intelligence Conference, Thailand. Bronze Star Medal, U.S. Army; Defense Meritorious Service Medal with Oak Leaf Cluster, Department of Defense; Meritorious Service Medal with Oak Leaf Cluster, U.S. Army; Medal of Brightness, Republic of China; Memorial Medal, Republic of China; Cross of Gallantry with Gold and Bronze Stars, Republic of South Viet Nam. Bachelor of Science, U.S. Military Academy; Master of Arts, Claremont Graduate School; Master of Business Administration, Nova University. Author of "The Key to OPSEC," *Security Management*, and "The Insider Threat," presented to the ASIS Forum at Phoenix, AZ.

A

ACCESS CONTROL: KEYPAD SYSTEMS

Keypads are the embodiment of the combination lock technique of access control. While it is certainly possible to contrive devices that utilize other forms of the combination lock or stored code principle, keypads are universally used because they are easy to operate and therefore cause minimum delay and confusion to the prospective entrant.

Also, keypads are both mechanically and electronically simple to create from the manufacturer's point of view. Keypad access controls are available in four basic forms, as follows.

Keypad Access Controls

Mechanical Keypad. These devices usually have four or five keys (but can have as many as 10) which operate a mechanism that is similar in concept to the tumblers in a rotary combination lock. When the mechanical interposers have been properly aligned by depression of the correct sequence of pushbuttons, the door bolt may be manually opened.

Electrical-Mechanical Keypad. These devices may have the mechanical mechanism described previously for ensuring that the correct code has been entered. This mechanism then closes a switch that electrically causes the door bolt to be opened. There are also versions in which the pushbuttons operate a set of electrical relays that, when activated in the correct sequence, electrically open the door bolt.

Electronic Keypad. These devices are the most popular form of keypad access control. The keys themselves are simple pushbutton switches, and the sequence in which the keys are depressed is decoded by digital logic circuits. If the sequence is correct, an electrical solenoid is energized, thus unlocking the door. As in all digital logic operations today, the intelligence is frequently conferred by a microprocessor rather than discrete logic chips.

Computer-Controlled Keypad. These devices come in two forms, a local intelligent unit, and a central computer-controlled device. The local intelligent unit contains its own microcomputer (which is little more than the microprocessor used for decoding purposes), to which additional functions have been added such as increased memory and perhaps some input-output capability.

In addition, this microcomputer can perform some more extensive functions -- such as personal identification, zoning, and digit scrambling -- than merely opening the door. The centrally controlled device is connected to a conventional computer, which can range from the PC-size up to the largest of real-time computers used for building automation control.

When so connected, the simple keypad can become part of a sophisticated security and facility management system that provides all of the features of which access control technology is capable.

Keypad Access Codes

All keypad access control devices require that the correct sequence of numbers be depressed on a set of pushbuttons to open a door or other mechanism. As in all combination lock devices, the level of security which is provided is considerably dependent upon the number of combinations that are available.

If there are 10 keys and the prospective entrant is required to depress only one to gain entrance, there is 1 chance in 10 of getting in, even if the correct number is not known; if 2 keys are required chances are reduced to one in a hundred, and if 3 keys are required it is down to a one in a thousand shot.

The simplest method of attacking a keypad access control is to try all of the possible numerical combinations. This can be done all at once if the keypad is located in an unattended area where no one is likely to take note of a person standing at the keypad for a long period of time; or it can be done piecemeal, trying a hundred or so combinations at a time over the span of a few days or even weeks.

As a measure of the effort and time required, if the attempted penetrator can enter a code every 3 seconds, less than an hour will be required to enter all of the possible codes in a 1,000-

combination system, and the probability is that the correct code will be found in about one-half hour. A number of defenses have been developed to deal with this weakness.

Number of Combinations. Obviously, the more possible combinations provided, the less attractive and feasible is the approach of trying all of the combinations. While 10,000 combinations will require 8-1/2 hours at 3 seconds per combination, 100,000 combinations would need 3-1/2 days of round-the-clock effort.

Frequent Code Changes. Frequent code changes are another defense means, and are particularly effective against those who attempt to find the correct code by trying a few hundred combinations at a time over a long period. By the time a significant portion of the possible codes has been tried, the code will have been changed and the prospective penetrator must start over.

Of course, there is a non-zero probability that the correct code will be hit on the first day, just as there is a probability of winning the lottery without playing every number. One of the difficulties with frequent code changes is that all of the authorized entrants must be informed each time the code is changed.

Time Penalty. A feature available with many keypad access control systems is time penalty. It deactivates the system for an amount of time, which is usually adjustable, after an unsuccessful attempt has been made to enter a code. This can greatly increase the amount of time required to enter a large number of codes, while penalizing the authorized entrant who has simply made a mistake with only a few-seconds wait. If the time penalty were set, for example, at 7 seconds, this would raise the time required to try 1,000 combinations from less than 1 hour to nearly 3 hours, and for 100,000 combinations from 3-1/2 continuous days to a week and a half.

Combination Time. Another feature of many keypad systems is combination time. It allows a fixed amount of time, usually adjustable, for the code to be entered. The theory behind this is that authorized persons have the number memorized and can readily enter it, whereas anyone taking excessive time is probably up to no good, and may be, for example, reading numbers from a list of those not yet tried, and checking them off.

Error Alarms. Error alarms are a more forceful form of dissuasion of the interloper. In its simplest form, an alarm is sounded whenever there is an incorrect entry of the code sequence. The alarm can be a local bell, siren, or light to call attention to the portal, or it can annunciate within the protected premises or at a guard station. Because even authorized entrants can sometimes make a mistake and enter the code incorrectly, single alarms are not usually annunciated, although they may unobtrusively light a bulb or appear on a log or as a line on a cathode ray tube (CRT), simply as cautionary indicators.

Sounding of an alarm is usually made to follow two or more successive wrong entries, and eliminates the try-all-the-codes attack, provided, of course, that a means of responding to the alarm has been incorporated into the total security system.

Methods of Code Storage

The code or codes that are to be recognized as correct by the keypad access control system must be stored within the system. This is accomplished in a number of different ways, depending upon the kind of keypad system and the proclivities of its designers. The more common methods are as follows.

Mechanical Units. Mechanical units store the code in portions of their internal mechanism, such as detents, rotating cylinders, and interposers. Some mechanical units utilize replaceable sheets of metal or composition board with holes or notches in the appropriate positions for each code, i.e., a mechanical read-only memory.

Changing of the code requires access to the interior of the mechanism, usually from the side of the unit that is inside the secured area, but sometimes from the front with special tools and knowledge of the current code. None requires more than a few minutes to change the code.

Electrical Units. Electrical units usually store the code in the position of a set of switches or jumper wires. When the code punched into the buttons matches the positions of the switches or jumpers, current flows to the relay, which allows the bolt to be removed and the door to be opened. To change the code, one merely changes the position of the switches, or moves the jumper wires, having first obtained access to the interior of the unit, usually from inside the protected premises. The operation should take less than a minute.

Electronic and Computerized Units. Electronic and computerized units sometimes use the switch simply because they are easy to perform and provide visible indication of the code to the serviceperson. Most often, however, these more sophisticated systems feature sophisticated methods of code storage appropriate to their high station in the hierarchy of keypad devices, solid-state memory being the most common.

There is read-only memory (ROM), the solid-state equivalent to a template, which must be physically replaced every time there is to be a code change. There is EAROM (electrically alterable read-only memory) and its kinfolk, which act like ROM for code storage but can be reprogrammed (re-coded) electrically without having to be removed from the unit.

There is conventional computer memory storage for the local microcomputer that is contained in the portal unit. There is also the ability, in centrally controlled systems, to store the code only in the central computer itself.

Changing of the code in most of these setups is done from the keypad itself; a master code allows access to the memory, and the new code is entered through the keypad. The unit need not be physically opened, and the operation can be accomplished in seconds.

The ROM version requires that the unit be opened and the ROM replaced. For this reason, ROM coded units are not usually used in situations where frequent code changes are anticipated. In the centrally controlled systems, the new code is entered once into the computer console – using, one hopes, the strictest of security procedures and precautions, and is immediately in force for all keypads in the system, either because it is sent downline for storage in each unit, or because the individual keypads must refer to central each time they are comparing an entered code. There are also, of course, systems in which the individual keypads may have different codes and all may be entered at the central computer console.

Dan M. Bowers

Source Bowers, D.M., Access Control and Personal Identification Systems. (Butterworth-Heinemann, Boston, 1988).

ACCESS CONTROL: PAST, PRESENT, AND FUTURE

Past and Present

The development of electronic locks in the 1950s was hailed as a major scientific achievement in access control. A significant technology advantage was the reduced role of the human assessor of authorization procedures. Even though the early electronic locks required the presentation of some type of credential that was recognized for itself and not to the individual presenting the credential, the technology was light years ahead of systems in use up to that point.

Introduction of personal identification number (PIN) codes in the 1960s began to remedy this weakness. The card codes were made up of part facility code and part individual identity code, and they could be read by a machine capable of recording events. They could handle some 500 people and could terminate an access authorization without retrieving the credential. The codes were assigned and stored in plastic cards allocated to specific persons.

Coded badges or credentials came in various shapes and sizes, the majority approximating today's credit card; and they operated on principles that are familiar to most security practitioners -- optical coding, magnetic code, magnetic stripe, passive electronic (proximity), metallic stripe, or watermark. Generally, the more secure the card, the higher its cost, with Weigand and proximity at the top in both security and cost.

Watermark, developed in England and used primarily there and on the Continent, did not extend to this side of the Atlantic until the late 1980s. This technology, used alone or in conjunction with other card technologies, offers a high level of security at modest cost.

Card-based systems offered such features as multiple level access, occupant listings, anti-passback, and automated access logging. Card readers, enrollment consoles, central controllers, and printers made their appearance in the industry. The initial stand-alone units could handle one to four doors, and on-line systems offered multiple readers, computers or PCs, mass storage, multiple doors, and transaction storage and recall. Distributed processing gave these systems enough intelligence to enable card readers to make local decisions at the reader. This feature provided protection against the adverse effects of central controller or PC failure. Options such as fail-safe or fail-secure, time zones, alarm monitoring, and multiple access levels became available.

The old, non-coded picture badges were, of course, a source of anxiety because they could be altered, duplicated, or just ignored by the security force. The story is told of a consultant working for 3 days inside a major Michigan prison with the face of a Boston terrier on his altered badge before a new guard challenged him. Coded badges were at first assumed to be more secure than photo identification badges, but by the mid 1970s it became clear that the coded badges were vulnerable to counterfeit and picture exchange techniques.

In the mid-1970s, names and descriptions such as Vikonics Model VS 1021 and Viscan loop configuration, multiplexer, 16 channel, CPU A and CPU B, magnetic tape recorders, and Harco's Nova 3 (16k) made their appearance, marking further advances in access control technology. It was during this period that an article entitled *Caveat* was published, describing a new, semi-automated identity verification system utilizing identification of a person through measurement of speech, fingerprint, or handwriting characteristics. Major Wayne F. Messner of the U.S. Air Force presented a paper on the same subject to the 1974 Carnahan Conference and the road to today's biometric access control technology was clearly indicated. By measuring and comparing unique individual characteristics, it was possible to identify people with a higher degree of reliability than had ever before been known. A breakthrough in access control had occurred.

Initial efforts to develop this technology were undertaken by several private sector companies, with U.S. Department of Defense support. These early efforts led to today's offerings in signature dynamics, voice print, fingerprint, hand geometry, palm print, retinal scan, iris scan, facial comparison, and keyboard recognition.

The question of error rate was raised, resulting in a close examination of the number of times an authorized credential or person was denied access (Type I error), and conversely the number of times that unauthorized persons or credentials would be accepted (Type II error). We began talking about "the crossover point" -- where denial of unauthorized admissions was maximized without severely affecting first- or second-time-try access by authorized personnel. This clearly showed that even with today's biometric systems, we could not expect to have our cake and eat it too. The more we attempted to deny access to the unauthorized, the more we caused additional delay to those who were authorized, and vice versa.

When coded card and PIN numbers were reviewed in terms of error rate, they fared poorly. In Type I, there was no relationship to the person -- only to the card -- and considering swipe error, you or anyone else with my card would be granted access 95 to 98% of the time. The same was true for the PIN, except that the entry error rate resulting from acceptance of my PIN entered by someone else was at the 84 to 87% range. The difference between these rates and 100% was due to human and reader errors, such as no card read on first swipe or wrong pin key pushed by accident. Today's error rates for biometric access equipment, measured in times per 100,000 or per million, guarantee far better security than cards or PINs alone. The combination of card reader and PIN pad, plus the excellence of items such as the Hirsch Electronics scrambler key concept, helped to raise the security efficiency of the older technology. The industry, however, had accepted the superiority of biometrics.

The next advance was to integrate the biometric technology with existing nonbiometric systems. A first approach was integration through software by removing a coded card reader and replacing it with a biometric reader that understood and communicated with the old system by the 0's and 1's, or by electronic pulse codes. This made it possible to upgrade interior security needs without altering the complete system. The next stage involved insertion of biometric data into the older generation of cards, providing for the use of dual readers at critical points in the system. This meant that a transaction could not be initiated unless the reader had determined that the biometric sample was the same as the owner's enrollment sample. After that, the balance of the coded card information would be released to accomplish the access mission.

The follow-on step was to integrate biometric technology with the new technology of smart cards. These cards brought to access control the full processing capability that had heretofore been found only in computers or PCs. It became possible to combine the data processing and storage capability of the smart card with the security of biometric verification.

The Future

What will the access control market look like at the end of this century? According to the Hallcrest Report II, security equipment revenue should, by then, have grown to some $15 billion, with access control increasing its share by more than 14%. Electronic tracking and tagging devices are expected to enjoy a similar growth, while the sensor market share growth rate will slow down but still exceed the U.S. national average for manufactured goods. An educated guess is that the sensors of tomorrow's security systems could be sold almost exclusively by access control system dealers. A new generation of long range article tracking items, identification tracking devices, and people tracking sensors will play more logically to access control systems.

During the 1990s, we can expect that most of the coded cards we know (the not-so-smart cards) will be used in conjunction with biometric technology. Lost, borrowed, or stolen cards will therefore cease to be a concern. At check cashing facilities, point-of-sale dual readers will accept biometric samples, make verification comparison, and authorize or deny the transaction. These biometrically re-educated cards may well be used in tool rooms, for visitor control and identification in correctional facilities, in welfare control programs, and in countless other applications. Stand-alone card/biometric units in homes and in business locations will offer low-cost protection against illegal entry. Between the stand-alone processing capability and the information in the card, decisions can be made on the spot, saving time and money, and virtually guaranteeing security.

We can look ahead to the time when the card itself will evolve into the reader of tomorrow. The authorized card holder wishing to make a purchase or other transaction will need only sign the back of the card with an inkless pen; the pressure, direction, and speed of the signing will be compared with enrollment data stored in the card for verification.

Fingerprint smart cards can be made to work in a similar manner by applying the card holder's finger to a point on the card that serves as a reader for comparing against data in the card. We can

look forward to having the sound of our voice unlock our car door, turn on the ignition, and operate the vehicle. The phone company can employ this same technology in connecting calls and billing customers; it can be set up to detect impairment by alcohol or other drugs so that dangerous items will be rendered useless to a person under the influence.

Current research by a North American camera company in the field of optics will allow a moving person to hold up a hand some 15 to 20 feet from a pinpoint reader and have both fingerprint and palm print read long before the person reaches the locked portal. Future access control systems will alarm only on the unauthorized person while recognizing, logging, and allowing those who are authorized to pass without bringing the transaction to the attention of the assessment device. A commonplace capability will be to identify, not by card but by biometric characteristics, everyone present in a facility and the location of each at any given moment.

Access control as a sophisticated technology arrived on the scene in the 1950s, picked up the pace from the 1960s through the 1980s, and in the 1990s went into high gear. New frontiers now being charted hold even greater promise for the first decade of the next century.

Joseph A. Barry III

ACCESS CONTROL: PEOPLE, VEHICLES, AND MATERIALS

Access controls regulate the flow of people, vehicles, and materials into, out of, and within a protected facility. They apply to many categories of people: employees, visitors, contractors, vendors, service representatives, etc. Access controls apply to vehicles, such as employee automobiles entering and leaving parking lots, and trucks moving to and from shipping and delivery platforms.

Access controls can be applied to materials, such as raw goods moving to the production line and finished goods moving to the shipping department or warehouse. Although access controls are most often in place as a means for protecting assets (which include the people being regulated), they play an important part in facilitating movement in a manner that meets the operating needs of the protected facility.

People Control

Employees. The basic tool for controlling the movement of employees is an identification card. The use of an employee identification card as part of a system for controlling access will depend on the number of employees and the sensitivity of the protected facility. A workplace with a few employees in a low security situation will not require an access control system or one that is elaborate in any meaningful respect. A location containing many employees will have difficulty operating without some form of access control. This will be especially true when there is a need to also control access to restricted areas within the protected facility. Large or small, simple or sophisticated, for the system to operate efficiently, it must be clearly understood by those affected by it and be supported by management.

Visitors. A variety of techniques are applicable to visitor access control; for example, a visitors lounge, appointments made in advance and registered with a receptionist, personal vouching by employees, positive identification of the visitor, search of items carried into the premises by the visitor, screening by metal detector, escort while on the premises, and temporary badges that self-destruct.

Relevant information collected at the time of issuing the badge would be the name of the visitor, date of visit, time entering and leaving, purpose, specific location visited, name of sponsoring/escorting employee, and temporary badge number. In a safety-sensitive environment, visitors may be required to be briefed and to wear special protective equipment, such as a helmet, safety glasses, robe or steel-reinforced footwear. A record or log of visits is wise. In some situations, contact between employees and visitors should be discouraged; for example, on the loading dock where larcenous conspiracies may evolve between truck drivers and employees of the shipping and receiving departments.

Electronic Access. Systems for controlling access by use of electronic technology are appropriate in highly populated working environments and where asset protection is essential. The typical approach is to issue to each authorized person a plastic key card that contains coded information capable of being read by electronic devices placed at the entry/exit points of the protected facility.

Three types of key cards on the market are the magnetically encoded card, the magnetic pulsing card, and the proximity card. The first has small magnets within the card. When the card is brought into contact with a reader device at the entry point door, the card's magnetically encoded data is transmitted to a computer processor. If the card's data corresponds to the access requirements, entry is granted; if not, entry is denied. Magnetic pulsing works in a fashion similar to the magnetically encoded card. Magnets and wires encased in the card emit positive and negative pulses that are sensed by the reader device at the entry point.

The proximity card contains circuits tuned to a radio frequency emitted by the reader at the point of entry. When the card is brought within the detecting range of the radio frequency, the reader will sense the unique characteristics of the card and transmit these data to the computer. If the data meet the entry criteria, the lock mechanism at the entry point disengages. This type of key card is called a proximity card because it does not have to be brought into physical contact with a reader, such as by inserting or swiping, but merely by placing it in the proximity of the reader. Other card systems offer a variety of personal identification principles based on fingerprints, signature recognition, voice characteristics, retinal patterns, and hand geometry.

Traffic Control

In comparison to electronic access control, traffic control can be relatively simple yet extremely frustrating. This is because automobiles, and the operation of them, can, for some individuals, be an emotional issue. Where employees park and how they park, although uncomplicated, can be difficult to manage.

Traffic control at a protected facility can begin at points outside of the property line. Whether the control is administered by local police officers or security officers who have been deputized for the limited purposes of traffic control, the essential point is that some degree of influence can be brought to bear on vehicles before they cross the property line. Once inside the premises, but not necessarily inside the facility's outer line of protection, control of vehicles can be enhanced through the designed characteristics of the roadway(s), such as median dividers and one-way directions of travel, signage, traffic signals, and the use of uniformed security officers at intersections and at entry points.

More entry points translate into more security officers, assuming that every vehicle entry point requires a human presence for security purposes. Management may decide that during times of high vehicle traffic, typically the morning and evening rush hours, the number of entry/exit points can be increased without having an officer present at every one. Electrically operated gate arms can be set to automatically open during rush hours without presenting access cards, and to operate in the normal mode during other hours.

From the standpoint of theft prevention, traffic control around the facility's loading dock is important. To ensure that the vehicles and drivers in the loading dock are there on legitimate business, the access control system may feature closed-circuit television (CCTV) cameras to monitor activity; a loading dock door that can be operated remotely from an interior location, such as the security center; an intercom for drivers to obtain notice of arrival and opening of the loading dock door; and the presence of a security officer to monitor and/or inspect departing cargo.

Traffic control may also involve control of vehicles moving within the protected facility. An out-of-doors holding area for cargo received at a seaport may, for example, have trucks and heavy loading and stacking machinery moving simultaneously throughout a relatively large and congested area. Control in this situation can be directed at both theft prevention and accident prevention.

Materials Control

An access control system can be engineered to accommodate the free movement and tracking of materials ranging from supplies and raw goods that feed the business, to unfinished products being created within the facility, to finished goods leaving the facility. Included in this capability are the tools used by the business, whether office equipment, such as desktop computers, or plant equipment, such as mechanical and engineering devices. The access control system can be put to good use in regulating the movement of these materials into, within, and from the protected facility.

Three methods have been found to be successful in deterring loss producing incidents: inspection of entering packages, accounting for property removed, and inspection of departing vehicles.

Inspection of Entering Packages. This method of access control is intended to prevent introduction to the premises of dangerous or undesirable items, such as bombs and drugs. The arrangement usually involves a location outside or on the fringe of the premises where package deliveries are made. Package deliveries include bags picked up at the local post office by a company employee, packages delivered by UPS and the other alternatives to the postal service, items delivered by couriers, and small shipments not sent through the company's routine support and supply channels.

Inspection is made by persons trained in how to recognize the visual indicators of mail bombs; how to use bomb detection equipment, such as an X-ray viewer, metal detector, or so-called explosives sniffing equipment; and how to use specially trained dogs for detecting explosives. The place of inspection is likely to be isolated from people and may contain a bomb barrel, bomb blanket, or a specially reinforced vault or room for storing questionable items. While inspection may be focused on the detection of bombs, it will include attention to other forms of contraband, such as firearms, drugs, alcohol, and pornographic materials.

Accounting for Property Removed. In this method, the employer is attempting to exercise control of company-owned property leaving the protected facility. The arrangement usually involves cooperation between management and the security officer force. Management, usually persons in supervisory and management positions, are given the authority to authorize subordinates to remove company property from the premises for a business-related purpose, such as taking a personal computer home to work on a word processing project. A property removal pass, signed by the supervisor, describes the property to be removed; the supervisor keeps a copy of the pass; the employee presents the original and a copy of the pass to the security officer at the exit point; the security officer compares the pass against the property, retains the copy of the pass, and allows the employee to proceed; and the security department holds its copy of the pass as a record of property having left the premises. When the employee returns the property, the supervisor signs his or her copy of the pass plus the original copy held by the employee. The transaction is complete at this point and a record has been made of the removal and the return of the property.

Inspection of Departing Vehicles. This method is also intended to control removal of company property. In some industries, removal of property is based on safety considerations, such as in the nuclear power industry where the taking of fissionable material would constitute a major hazard to public safety. Whatever the industry and whatever the reason for making inspections, management will have observed certain necessary prerequisites; for example, ensuring that the inspection program will not violate laws, contracts, or agreements with a bargaining unit or the employees; ensuring that the employees, visitors, or others who will be affected by the inspection program have been informed; and training the security officers to conduct the inspections in a manner that will not violate constitutional protections and reasonable standards of fairness and privacy.

Management may decide that inspection need not be made of all departing vehicles but of a percentage high enough to discourage attempts to pass through the system undetected. When this option is taken, the method for selecting the vehicles to be inspected must be based on a random technique. If the decision is to inspect 20% of departing vehicles, a counting device at the exit point would count the departing vehicles and annunciate by horn and/or light every fifth vehicle so that both the driver and the security officer can go about the business of conducting the inspection.

John J. Fay, CPP

ACCESS CONTROL: PROXIMITY SYS-TEMS

There are two basic classes of proximity access control systems: those in which the user initiates the transmission of the code to the system, such as in the garage-door opener, and those in which the system automatically senses the presence of a coded device without the user having to perform any action other than moving the coded device within the prescribed range of the sensor. We call these two classes the user-activated and the system-sensing proximity access control systems.

User-Activated Systems

In a user-activated system, the system itself sits in a quiescent, listening mode until it is activated by a signal that is transmitted (usually by radio or sometimes by a light beam) from the access token carried by the user. Upon receiving such a signal, the system compares the received code with its stored access code (set, in the usual way, into jumpers, switches, or electronic memory). If the received code is correct, the system unlocks the portal; if the code is not correct, the system goes back to its listening mode. In order to transmit the signal, the token in a user-activated system must contain a power source, along with the electronics to generate the code and superimpose it upon a radio transmission. The power source is a battery in all currently offered tokens, but devices having other power sources are being developed. Since it must contain the battery plus the required electronics, the token in a user-activated system is usually rather bulky; observe your garage-door opener.

Within the class of user-activated systems there are two basic types, as follows.

Wireless Keypads. In a wireless keypad system, the user depresses a sequence of keys on an ordinary keypad, similar to that in the conventional keypad access control system. As the keys are depressed, the coded representation of the keys is transmitted on a radio frequency. The system detects the transmission and decodes it.

Preset Code. The code, in this system, is preset into the device (for example, the garage-door opener), and a single depression of a pushbutton causes the code to be sent all at once. This is the equivalent in concept to coded-card and other portable-key systems.

System-Sensing Systems

The system-sensing proximity systems utilize a variety of different concepts, operate at a wide variety of distances, and are dispersed over a wide range of costs. Some require that the token contain its own battery power and some derive their power from the system that interrogates them. Some of the battery-powered units will run for months between battery changes, and some must be recharged daily. The several types of system-sensing systems are as follows.

Passive Devices. Passive devices contain no battery or other power, and communicate the code to the interrogator (the reader of the system) by reradiating the interrogating radio frequency (RF) signal back to the system at a frequency different from the original. This is the same principle upon which electronic article surveillance (EAS) systems operate, except that EAS tokens (tags) need have only one frequency at which they can reradiate (scream), and they all scream at the same frequency. They therefore contain only one code bit and can communicate only two items of information, screaming or not screaming. In order to provide the degree of encoding capability that is required in an access control system, passive proximity cards are capable of reradiating at several different frequencies simultaneously, and have dozens of frequencies from which the reradiation can be selected. For example, the proximity access control system with which Schlage brought proximity into its current popularity uses a passive card that contains four printed tuned-circuits that enable it to reradiate at any four frequencies selected from the 80 frequencies which the system can detect (except that adjacent frequencies may not be used in order to improve the accuracy with which the system can detect the codes). This provides a total system code capacity of over one million combinations.

A second technique for passive proximity is known as surface acoustic wave technology, which provides the coding in the form of crystalline material on the surface of the card; the crystalline material is excited by the interrogating RF field, modulating the reradiated signal with the code.

Field-Powered Devices. These devices contain a relatively sophisticated complement of electronic circuitry, usually including solid-state storage for the code bits, microprocessor-level intelligence, a radio transmitter circuit with antenna, and a power supply circuit capable of extracting sufficient power from the interrogating field to operate the internal circuitry and to accomplish a brief, weak transmission of the code. Since the interrogating field that supplies the power for the device is maintained by the access control system, the code transmission will occur when and only when the device is brought within the appropriate distance of the interrogator. Despite the quantity of electronics that the device contains (about the same contained in a smart card), this proximity device, which is offered by several different vendors, can be obtained in credit-card form, in a disk the size of a dime, or in the form of a medicine capsule-size cylinder that can be (and is) implanted in a salmon.

Transponders. A transponder is an automatically operated two-way radio set. It contains a radio receiver, a radio transmitter, a receive-send antenna, and microprocessor logic with solid-state code storage, all powered by an internal battery. The access control system transmits an interrogation signal that is received and recognized by the device, which then transmits a return signal containing the access code. This operation is similar to the ordinary poll response through which a computer communicates with its network of terminals, and to the IFF (identification, friend, or foe) systems used on military radar systems (and, similarly, on air traffic control radar) to identify aircraft by interrogating an on-board transponder (enemy aircraft presumably do not have properly coded transponders on board). Transponder systems are more popular in the manufacturing segment of the article identification market, where the transponders are attached to automated vehicles, for example, that carry goods in warehouses and through production lines. Some vendors are beginning to approach the access control market using this technology.

Continuous Transmission. Continuous transmission tokens are coming into use. The "Father of Proximity Systems" is the Modular Automated System to Identify Friend from Foe (MASTIFF). This system features a device that is battery powered and contains electronic logic and a radio transmitter which continuously transmits the entry code. When the device is sufficiently proximate to the system and its receiver, the transmission is detected and the code is received and recognized. The token is about the size of a cigarette pack that must be left on-premises every night so the battery can be recharged.

Codes and Coding

Since there is a wide variety of proximity access control systems that operate on diverse principles and use markedly different technologies, there is a consequent wide variation in the methods that they use to store the access code, in the number of code bits that they can store, and the resulting number of possible code combinations that they can provide. Clearly, coding in these devices must be discussed separately with respect to each type.

Wireless keypads have the same coding capabilities as their wired brethren since they are functionally the same devices. A three-digit code on a 10-key pad gives 1,000 combinations, four digits give 10,000 combinations, and so forth.

Preset code devices are limited in coding capacity only by the number of code switches that the manufacturer decides to incorporate into the equipment, and the electronic logic that is provided to organize and transmit all of the code bits. Most of the devices that operate at the garage-door-opener level have 10 code bits, which provide 1,024 different combinations. To date, these devices have not been aimed at the high-security market with millions of combinations, personal identification, time and space zoning, and other sophisticated features.

Passive devices, using the current technologies, have theoretical coding capabilities in the millions of combinations. Commercially available systems offer personal identification capabilities in the range of 4,000 persons, along with time and space zoning and facility coding. This provides an adequate access control and personal identification system for most commercial and industrial situations.

Microprocessor-controlled devices comprise the remaining bases of proximity access control systems: the field-powered devices, the transponders, and the continuous-transmission system. Here also, as in the smart card, the amount of code storage that is made available is the designer's choice. Since solid-state memory requires very little space, tens of thousands of bits will fit onto an area the size of a fingernail. Consequently, the designers have not been stingy with code capacity, which ranges from millions to billions (even the English billions) of combinations.

There are, as in other forms of access systems, widely varying performance characteristics, features, functions, and options among the different kinds of proximity systems, and as always, there is no single choice as to which is best for every kind of application. The user's security system design must take into consideration the attributes of the various kinds of systems, and determine which, if any, of the proximity systems correspond to actual needs. Following are some of the parameters that should be evaluated during the design process.

Activation Distance. The distance at which a proximity system can be activated by its token or card, or the distance within which the card or token can be sensed by the system, varies from 2 inches to nearly 50 feet with the various forms of proximity systems. The passive devices, which depend upon a low-level reradiation of the interrogating signal, have the least range, from 4 to 6 inches for the tuned circuit (which requires that the prospective entrant hold the purse or wallet containing the access card up to the reader) up to a few feet for the surface wave. The field-powered devices are not much more powerful, since they must be relatively close to the source of the interrogating field to obtain enough power to operate: 6 inches to 12 inches distance is typical, with one vendor claiming operation up to 6 feet.

Devices powered by a self-contained battery are limited in range only by the power of the battery and the space provided to configure an efficient antenna within the device; some are intentionally held to a distance of a few feet (as a practical matter, effective security is not well served if portals can be opened while the authorized entrant is a considerable distance away), but others -- such as the garage-door opener -- can operate at about 50 feet or so.

Hands-Off Versus Triggered. User-activated systems, that is, the wireless keypads and preset-code devices, require the user to push buttons or depress keys to transmit the code to the system. All of the others require no user action, and thus need not be removed from pocket, wallet, or purse in order to perform their intended function.

Concealment of the System. Since there is no need for readily accessible and therefore very visible wall-mounted keypads, card readers, or reader slots, most proximity access control systems can be installed in an unobtrusive manner. Readers and interrogators consist of simple antennae, and these can be readily hidden or camouflaged to look like something else. This, in itself, can add to the security of an installation.

Physical Protection. Since electromagnetic and optical waves pass rather readily through sturdy materials (such as cement, wood, and brick for RF; and bulletproof and even tinted glass for optical), all parts of a proximity system, including the antenna, can be physically protected from assault and tampering, unlike conventional card and keypad systems that must have a card reader or keypad accessible in an unprotected area.

Form and Size of Device. Proximity tokens come in a range of sizes, from one that could fit into an empty medicine capsule, to another the size of a dime, to the conventional credit card configuration, to cuboid packages ranging from the size of a matchbox, to nearly the size of a pocket novel.

Currently, the only credit card versions are passive systems, but the activity in smart cards is certain to lead to field-powered and transponder proximity systems having tokens in the credit-card configuration. The capsule- and dime-sized tokens currently used for implanting into fish and attaching to small manufactured parts, are already beginning to be made into credit card versions. The larger of the current versions is comprised of two groups. One consists of portable keypads, which need to be relatively large or else the keypad will be impossible to manually operate; and garage-door kinds of user-activated systems, in which size is of relatively little concern.

The second group is comprised of devices that are currently marketed for manufacturing and inventory control applications, for which their size is not inconvenient. If and when the latter group begins to be adapted for access control use, one of the engineering tasks required will be repackaging. With today's proximity access control systems, the choice of token is between the credit card and a module that fits into the shirt pocket.

Cost of Token. The system portion of a proximity access control installation differs little in cost from a conventional card access system. The tokens,

however, which must be issued to each authorized person, vary over a wide range of cost. The passive cards are on the high end of standard access cards, that is, $4 to $7 before imprinting, photographs, clips, and other accouterments. Preset-code and other active tokens range from $15 to $75, with the wireless keypads on the high end of the range. Field-powered devices tend to run in the $10 vicinity.

The devices that are currently used in the manufacturing area generally contain more sophisticated electronics than are required in devices for access control, and a $100 price tag is not uncommon. This identifies another area that must be re-engineered before these systems can compete effectively in the access control marketplace.

Code Changes. As in the other methods of access control, an important concern when selecting a proximity system is the ease with which code changes can be effected so as to provide additional security. With the passive cards, the code is constructed into the card when it is manufactured -- the tuned circuits are contained in an internal sandwich, and the surface acoustic wave coding is contained in the surface coating -- and changing the code would require issuing new cards, similar to the case with Wiegand or Hollerith cards.

Most field-powered tokens have the code stored in solid-state memory, but this memory is not accessible and alterable like the memory in a personal computer (PC); rather it is fixed when the circuitry is constructed and molded into the device. These are also unchangeable coded tokens. All the other tokens provide a convenient means for changing the code (and these are, not surprisingly, all of the more expensive tokens).

The preset-code, garage-door types have internal code switches. The devices that contain microprocessors and solid-state memory, which include all of the manufacturing-oriented and transponder systems, and at least one field-powered device, can all be re-coded at the user's whim, usually using a separate programming unit supplied by the manufacturer with the system.

Dan M. Bowers

Source Bowers, D.M., Access Control and Personal Identification Systems. (Butterworth-Heinemann, Boston, 1988).

AGE DISCRIMINATION

Persons 40 years of age or older are protected by the Age Discrimination in Employment Act (ADEA). The law prohibits arbitrary age discrimination in hiring, discharge, pay, promotions, fringe benefits, and other aspects of employment. Retaliation against a person who files a charge of age discrimination, participates in an investigation, or opposes an unlawful practice is also illegal.

The law applies to private employers of 20 or more workers; federal, state, and local governments; employment agencies; and labor organizations with 25 or more members. Labor organizations that operate a hiring hall or office that recruits potential employees or obtains job opportunities also must abide by the law.

Provisions of the Act

Health Insurance Benefits. Employers must offer all employees and their spouses 65 years of age and older the same group health coverage under the same conditions as is offered to employees and their spouses under age 65.

Pension Accruals. For pension plan years beginning on or after January 1, 1988, for employees who have at least one hour of service in such plan years, it is unlawful to cease or reduce the rate of pension benefit accruals or allocations because of age. Limitations on the amount of benefits, years of service, or years of participation may be permissible. However, the limitations must be imposed without regard to age.

Remedies for Violations of the Law. A lawsuit may be brought by the Equal Employment Opportunity Commission (EEOC) or individuals may file suit on their own behalf 60 days after filing a charge with EEOC and the appropriate state agency. Should EEOC take legal action first, a private suit may not be filed.

Remedies for violations of the ADEA include payment of lost wages and benefits, interest, liquidated damages, attorney's fees, and court costs. Damages may be recovered for a period up to 2 years prior to the filing of the suit, except in cases of willful violations, where damages up to 3 years prior to the filing of suit may be recovered.

The Commission's policy is to seek full and effective relief for each and every victim of employment discrimination, whether it is sought in court or in conciliation agreements reached before litigation. In pursuing its mission of eradicating discrimination in the workplace, the Commission intends that its enforcement be predictable, provide effective relief for those affected by discrimination, allow remedies designed to correct the source of discrimination, and prevent its recurrence.

Exemptions. The law does not bar age discrimination where age is a bona fide occupational qualification. It also does not bar employers from differentiating among employees based on reasonable factors other than age. Employers may observe the terms of a bona fide seniority system or any bona fide employee benefit plan, such as retirement, pension, or insurance plans, which is not a subterfuge to evade the purposes of the Act, except that no such seniority system, benefit, or benefit plan shall excuse mandatory retirement on account of age or a refusal to hire because of age.

State and local governments may make age-based hiring and retirement decisions for firefighters and law enforcement officers if the particular age limitation was in effect on March 3, 1983, and the action taken is pursuant to a bona fide hiring or retirement plan that is not a subterfuge to evade the purposes of the Act. Institutions of higher education may involuntarily retire at age 70 an employee who is serving under a contract of unlimited tenure or a similar arrangement. The ADEA does not prohibit the compulsory retirement of certain bona fide executives or high policymaking personnel.

U.S. Equal Employment Opportunity Commission

Source Laws Enforced by EEOC. (U.S. Equal Employment Opportunity Commission, Washington, DC, 1988).

AIDS

Acquired immune deficiency syndrome (AIDS) is a syndrome caused by a virus known as the human immunodeficiency virus (HIV), which infects and destroys certain white blood cells, thereby undermining the body's ability to combat infection. HIV belongs to a group of viruses known collectively as retroviruses because they reverse, in part, the order in which genetic information is usually processed. HIV has the ability to insert a copy of itself into the genetic material (DNA) in different types of cells throughout the body. Each time the host cell divides, the virus is blindly copied. Viruses are very difficult to attack because of their similarity to healthy material. Interfering with the reproduction of the virus may kill the healthy cell. Scientists are not yet sure of the trigger, but for some reason there is a rapid reproduction of the virus, killing the good cell, and the virus spills out into the bloodstream.

Although HIV occupies many types of cells, it favors the T4 cell, the backbone of the immune system. Once the army of T cells has been sufficiently reduced, the body is all but defenseless.

A victim can be infected with the HIV for years without ever developing symptoms of AIDS, and can transmit the virus even in the absence of symptoms. AIDS victims do not die from AIDS itself, but from "opportunistic infections" such as pneumonia, malignancies, and a type of skin cancer.

Transmission

Despite reports to the contrary, the AIDS virus is not transmitted through casual contact. Studies have confirmed that the virus is not spread by sneezing, coughing, breathing, hugging, handshaking, sharing eating and drinking utensils, using the same toilet facilities, and other forms of non-sexual contact.

There is no evidence of AIDS virus transmission in schools, offices, churches, or other social settings, and there are no known cases of police or security officers becoming infected through performance of their duties. Except for a very small number of cases of infection in health care workers attributed to accidental needle sticks or other exposure to infected blood, there are no reports of infection as a result of occupational contact.

AIDS is transmitted through exposure to contaminated blood, semen, and vaginal secretions. This occurs primarily through sexual intercourse and needle sharing by intravenous drug users. Transmission from infected mother to fetus or infant has also occurred.

Effects on the Body

HIV may lay dormant within the body of a carrier indefinitely. There may be no symptoms. The only sign of infection may be a positive blood test for antibodies to the virus. Months or years after infection, symptoms develop. They can be mild or severe, prolonged, and persistent. Symptoms include swollen lymph glands in the neck, underarm, or groin; recurrent fever and night sweats; rapid, unexplained weight loss; constant fatigue; diarrhea; diminished appetite; and unusual spots in the mouth. Symptoms can be crippling, sometimes fatal. Symptoms worsen and the body becomes overwhelmed by fatal infections and cancer. The two most common are pneumocystis carinii pneumonia (lung infection) and Kaposi's sarcoma (cancer).

Detection

The initial blood test, called the ELISA (enzyme-linked immunoassay), detects antibodies that the immune system produces to fight off the invading HIV virus. It has an accuracy rate of 99% when licensed test kits are used under optimal laboratory conditions. In actual practice, false-negative and false-positive results can be common. Therefore, this test is usually validated by the Western blot test, especially in the United States.

A positive result means infection with HIV and an infected person is capable of transmitting the disease. The positive result does not mean the person has AIDS, or even that the person will get AIDS, although this is likely. Some carriers have remained asymptomatic longer than 10 years.

A negative result means no antibodies have been detected. However, false negative results can be common within the first 6 to 12 weeks after infection. Hence, the tested person may be advised to repeat the test later.

Testing is recommended for anyone seeking treatment for sexually transmitted disease; homosexual and bisexual men; past or present IV drug users; persons with history of prostitution or multiple sex partners; women whose past or present sexual partners were HIV-infected, bisexual, or IV drug users; persons with long-term residence or birth in an area with high prevalence of HIV infection; and anyone who received a transfusion between 1978 and 1985.

Prevention

The safest avoidance method is a mutually exclusive sexual relationship between two uninfected people who do not use drugs. If there is a chance one partner is infected, they should abstain from sex.

If abstention is not possible, sexual activity should be restricted and accompanied by the use of a latex condom (which is not foolproof) in tandem with the spermicidal agent nonoxynol-9. Petroleum-based products (like Vaseline) should never be used with latex condoms.

Drugs, including alcohol, can reduce inhibitions leaving a person open to high-risk behavior.

International Travel

The risk to international travelers is determined less by geography than by individual behavior. Travelers should avoid intimate encounters with any person whose HIV status is unknown, especially prostitutes and IV drug users.

Illegal drugs should not be taken intravenously or needles shared for any reason. Diabetic travelers should carry enough syringes for the entire trip.

The United States, Australia, New Zealand, Canada, Japan, and the western European countries have greatly reduced risk of infection from transfusion. All donated blood in these countries is tested for antibodies to HIV. Less developed nations may not have a formal HIV testing program for blood or biological products. When in a less developed country, the traveler should:

• Avoid locally produced blood clotting factor concentrates if at all possible. If transfusion is necessary, ideally blood should be tested for HIV antibodies by trained laboratory technicians using a reliable test.

• Make sure needles used to draw blood or give injections are the single-use disposable type, prepackaged in a sterile container.

Some countries screen incoming travelers intending to stay more than 3 months. Any person with AIDS or whose test indicates infection with HIV may be barred. For most countries, diagnosis of seropositivity requires documentation of at least two reactive ELISAs and a follow-up Western blot test.

Protecting against Exposure

The AIDS virus is difficult to transmit and is quite fragile when outside the body. It can be destroyed by heat, many common household disinfectants and bleaches, and by washing with soap and hot water.

Transmission has also been traced to blood transfusions and to blood products given to hemophiliacs. This source of infection, however, has been eliminated through changes in screening and treating donated blood products.

No case of infection from giving mouth-to-mouth resuscitation has ever been reported from any part of the world. In the event of a "high-risk casualty," it would be advisable to employ a disposable mouthpiece. Blood-to-blood contact can be avoided by keeping open wounds covered and wearing gloves when in contact with bleeding wounds. In an emergency, direct mouth-to-mouth should not be withheld if a mask or airway device is not available.

Concerns of security personnel include:

• Human bite: Transmission through saliva is highly unlikely, but if bitten the first aid procedure is to milk the wound to make it bleed, wash it thoroughly, and seek medical attention.

• Spitting: Contrary to popular belief, transmission through saliva is highly unlikely.

• Urine/feces: The virus is in very low concentrations in urine, and not at all in feces. Transmission is highly unlikely.

• Cut/wound: Needle stick studies show low risk of infection. Caution in handling sharp objects and searching in areas hidden from view is advised.

• Body removal and contact with blood or body fluids: Those who must come into contact with blood or other body fluids in connection with a dead victim should wear gloves. Afterwards, wash thoroughly with soap and hot water. Clean up blood spills with one part water to nine parts household bleach.

• Dried blood: Despite low risk of infection, caution dictates wearing gloves, a mask, and protective shoe coverings if exposure to dried blood is likely, for example, at the scene of a death or injury.

John J. Fay, CPP

Source Fay, J.J., The Alcohol/Drug Abuse Dictionary and Encyclopedia. (Charles C. Thomas, Springfield, IL, 1988).

AIDS AND HEPATITIS B: WORKER EXPOSURE

The acquired immune deficiency syndrome (AIDS) and hepatitis B diseases merit serious concern for workers, especially those in the health care industry and persons who provide first responder assistance, such as CPR and first aid.

Workers at risk of blood, body fluid, or needle stick exposures are at the highest risk of infection. They include physicians, dentists and other dental workers, podiatrists, laboratory and blood bank technologists and technicians, phlebotomists, dialysis personnel, medical technicians, medical examiners, morticians, housekeepers, laundry workers, and others whose work involves contact with blood or other body fluids, or with corpses.

Other personnel, such as paramedics, emergency medical technicians, law enforcement personnel, security officers, firefighters, lifeguards, and others whose jobs might require first response medical care and potential contact with blood or body fluids are also at risk.

Work-related AIDS and hepatitis B infections have been reported from every state. The seriousness and immediacy of the problem have prompted the Occupational Safety and Health Administration (OSHA), in cooperation with the U.S. Public Health Service, to provide workers with information on the Centers for Disease Control recommended practices to protect against occupational exposure to these diseases. The recommended practices include precautions for the appropriate handling of blood and other body fluids. Following these precautions should help prevent the spread of these diseases in the workplace.

AIDS

AIDS is a bloodborne and sexually transmitted disease in which a virus invades the body, damages the immune system, and allows other infectious agents to invade the body and cause disease. ARC (AIDS-related complex) refers to a variety of conditions caused by infection with the AIDS virus. These conditions range from mild symptoms to life-threatening ones.

AIDS/ARC is caused by the human immunodeficiency virus (HIV). It is spread through body fluids, primarily blood and semen.

Although other fluids have not been shown to transmit infection, all body fluids and tissues should be regarded as potentially infectious. HIV is transmitted by sexual contact, by needle sharing, and through contaminated blood products. An infected woman can pass the virus to her fetus.

Despite reports to the contrary, HIV is not transmitted by casual contact, such as touching or shaking hands; eating food prepared by an infected person; or from drinking fountains, telephones, toilets, or other surfaces.

Hepatitis B

The usual symptoms of acute Hepatitis B infections are flu-like and include fatigue, mild fever, muscle and joint aches, nausea, vomiting, abdominal pain, diarrhea, and jaundice. Severe hepatitis B virus (HBV) infections may be fatal. Chronic carriers of HBV may develop a chronic hepatitis that may progress to cirrhosis, liver cancer, or death.

A hepatitis B vaccine is available that is safe and effective in the prevention of HBV infection. This vaccine is recommended for persons at risk of HBV infection, including health care workers and emergency personnel.

Protection against Exposure.

The Centers for Disease Control (CDC), with advice from health care professionals, has made recommendations to protect workers from HIV and HBV infections. These precautions are prudent practices that apply to preventing the transmission of these viruses and other similar bloodborne-type infections and that should be used routinely.

Personal Protective Equipment.
•Use gloves where blood, blood products, or body fluids will be handled.
•Use gowns, masks, and eye protectors for procedures that could involve more extensive splashing of blood or body fluids.
•Use pocket masks, resuscitation bags, or other ventilation devices to resuscitate a patient to minimize exposure that may occur during emergency mouth-to-mouth resuscitation. Employers should place these devices where the need for resuscitation is likely.

Workplace Practices.

•Wash hands thoroughly after removing gloves, and immediately after contact with blood or body fluids.

•Use disposable needles and syringes whenever possible. Do not recap, bend, or cut needles. Place sharp instruments in a specially designated puncture-resistant container located as close as practical to the area where they are used. Handle and dispose of them with extraordinary care to prevent accidental injury.

•Follow general guidelines for sterilization, disinfection, housekeeping, and waste disposal. Use appropriate protective equipment. Place potentially infective waste in impervious bags and dispose of them as local regulations require.

•Clean up blood spills immediately with detergent and water. Use a solution of 5.25% sodium hypochlorite (household bleach) diluted at 1 to 10 parts water for disinfection, or other suitable disinfectant.

Education.

•Know the modes of transmission and prevention of these infections.

Other Recommendations for Prevention.

•Treat all blood and body fluids as potentially infectious.

•Get an HBV vaccination if at substantial risk of acquiring HBV infection.

Potential Exposures

Exposure to bloodborne pathogens may occur in many ways, including needle stick and cut injuries or spray of body fluid from the victim to the rescuer's eyes, mouth, or other mucous membranes. Employees working as medical rescuer responders or those tasked with providing first aid and/or cardiopulmonary resuscitation as a job function are assumed to be at high risk for bloodborne infections due to possible exposure to body fluids from potentially infected individuals. Other employees who may be directly exposed to such body fluids, depending on their job assignments, include house keeping and laundry personnel, and fire fighters. Any employee directly exposed to body fluids is considered to be at risk of occupational exposure to HIV and/or HBV. Other employees are not at greater risk of contracting bloodborne diseases than members of the general population. Neither HBV nor HIV is transmitted by casual contact in the workplace.

Post-Exposure Evaluation

Following an exposure incident, a confidential medical evaluation and follow-up should be made immediately available to the exposed employee. There should be documentation of the route(s) of exposure, and details of how the exposure incident occurred. These should include identification and documentation of the source individual, unless identification is infeasible or prohibited by state or local law.

An exposure incident means a specific eye, mouth, or other mucous membrane, non-intact skin, or parenteral (piercing mucous membranes or skin barrier) contact with blood or other potentially infectious materials that results from the performance of one's job duties.

The source individual's blood should be tested as soon as possible and after consent is obtained. If consent is not obtained, it should be documented that legally required consent cannot be obtained. When the source individual's consent is not required by law, the source individual's blood, if available, should be tested and the results documented.

When the source individual is already known to be infected with HBV or HIV, testing for the source individual's known HBV or HIV status need not be repeated. Results of the source individual's testing should be made available to the exposed employee, and the employee informed of applicable laws and regulations concerning disclosure of the identity and infectious status of the source individual.

Enforcement

Various OSHA standards apply to exposure to the hazards of potential infection of both the HIV and the HBV viruses. These standards cover personal protective equipment, sanitation, and waste disposal.

In addition, the General Duty Clause of the OSHA Act requires employers to provide "employment and a place of employment which are free from recognized hazards...." Employers must comply with either OSHA standards and the General Duty Clause or with state standards.

States with approved plans to operate their own occupational safety and health program enforce standards comparable to the federal standards and are encouraged to enforce state counterparts to the General Duty Clause. State plan standards, unlike federal standards, apply to state, county, and municipal workers as well as to private employers.

Occupational Safety and Health Administration

Source   OSHA Public Affairs Pamphlet. (Occupational Safety and Health Administration, Washington, DC, 1992).

AIR CARGO SECURITY

The first commercial business of U.S. airlines was the carriage of mail, which began in 1918, 8 years before the introduction of commercial passenger traffic. At first, cargo carriage increased much more slowly than the carriage of air mail. For example, it was not until 1956 that air freight passed air mail as a source of revenue for United Airlines. Today, air cargo carriage increases at a rate that can only be called dramatic.

A number of security problems are peculiar to air cargo operations. For one thing, air cargo has a greater proportion of high-value shipments than any other method of freight carriage; as a result, the potential for loss is much greater.

Identifying the point at which a loss occurred is always a problem and is even more difficult for air cargo, due to its greater exposure. In all other forms of freight carriage, shipments are picked up, transshipped, and delivered at loading docks. In addition to this, air cargo must be moved (usually in "trains" of carts) from the carrier freight terminal to the flight line, where it is loaded onto the aircraft. This results in increased exposure and additional handling.

When the freight is to go in the belly of a passenger airplane, the exposure is further increased because the freight must then go to the passenger terminal ramp, where it is exposed to other persons. At many airports, the tractors (tugs) towing the carts travel to and from the flight line along a route that passes unlighted (and sometimes unfenced) parking lots or dark adjacent streets. This creates opportunities for goods to be quickly passed to a waiting accomplice or stashed for later pickup by the driver.

Air cargo shipping is basically a nighttime operation. In the United States, 90% of all air mail and 90 percent of all air cargo -- domestic and international -- arrives or departs between 10:00 p.m. and 7:00 a.m. Darkness has always been attractive as a cover for criminal acts, and air cargo theft is no exception to this general rule.

Physical Security of the Freight Terminal

Air freight terminals should be fenced on as many sides as possible. Quite obviously, they cannot be fenced on a side facing an adjacent airport ramp, but fencing should separate air freight terminals from public access roads and all parking lots. If a fence is to be an effective barrier, a well-lighted clear space of 20 to 30 feet must be maintained on each side. Where freighters are loaded next to public access roads, adequate fencing and lighting are particularly essential.

The opportunities for an off-duty air freight employee or other accomplice to drive along-side the fence and receive goods passed over the fence must be reduced. If this means of theft is a frequent and continuing problem, the only solution may be to cover the suspect area by low light-level closed-circuit television capable of clearly distinguishing activities that might otherwise go unseen.

Gates into the freight facility should be limited in number to no more than are absolutely essential to the efficient operation of the terminal. These gates should be staffed by guard personnel, and employees leaving or entering the premises should have to pass a guard post on their way in or out of the facility. Patrols by local and airport police departments and by company guards can provide added perimeter security.

Parking

The parking lot should be separated from the air freight facility by a fence, and employees should not be allowed to park on the terminal side of this fence. Employees should have no occasion to go to their cars during a shift; indeed, some carriers enclose the employee parking lot and secure it during the shift.

The fact that many employees have access to the entire airport as part of their work assignment presents special problems requiring a variety of solutions. Employees may park their cars in a lot some distance from the terminal but convenient to the route they will be taking later in their shift, perhaps with a piece of attractive freight that can be off-loaded near the car.

A primary step toward control seems to be a company rule that requires employees to park in specified company lots and threatens them with dismissal if they park elsewhere.

Dock Security

Areas where cargo is stored should be well lighted, whether they are inside the terminal building or outside. Properly placed dock lights maintain good visibility inside trucks parked at the dock and make it difficult for persons in the truck to tell if they are being observed.

Loading dock doors should be kept closed, except when a truck is backed up to the dock for loading or unloading. Where hot weather is a problem and it is necessary to keep the doors open for ventilation, gates of chain link or wire mesh can be used.

The Airport Security Council recommends an exceptionally good dock practice. The council suggests that a barrier or at least a 4-inch wide yellow painted line be located about 10 feet back from the edge of the dock and that signs be suspended over the line advising that no one other than employees is allowed beyond that point. Cargo should not be left within that area of the dock; where efficient operation requires that the rule be breached, cargo left in this accessible area should never be unattended. The lines may require frequent repainting, but they serve a useful purpose and should be maintained.

Terminal Access

Rest room facilities should be provided where truckers can reach them without walking through the freight terminal. Where no such facilities are available within the 10-foot limit, truckers should be escorted while within the terminal. Coffee machines can be provided in an anteroom located so that truckers need not walk through the terminal to reach them. There is no logical reason why employees from other airlines or freight carriers should be allowed beyond the designated transfer area. Unless they are specifically

assigned to air freight duties, not even employees of the carrier operating the terminal should have any more access to the terminal than an outsider. Air carrier employees working in supply or storage functions should not be allowed to meet freight shipments at planeside or to walk through the freight terminal looking for incoming shipments; they should be required to come to the same pickup areas as other consignees.

Closed-Circuit Television (CCTV)

Closed-circuit television (CCTV) is used in a number of air freight terminals, sometimes effectively and sometimes ineffectively. If thefts are primarily caused by collusion between an air freight employee and a driver, CCTV at the loading platform can be of little assistance; a shipment being stolen through collusion will look no different to the television camera than a shipment being legitimately loaded. On the other hand, if the problem is pilferage at the dock, a camera at that location can be of some assistance.

The breakdown area where carts and containers are unloaded is an excellent point for camera coverage. It is at this location that particular items are spotted for theft and perhaps set aside or placed back in the cart to be towed to the cart storage area, where the item can be picked up at the employee's leisure. If limitations of space require that carts be held outside the terminal awaiting break-down of shipments, a television camera should cover this area. For areas in which little or no activity is scheduled, various kinds of video alarms can be employed. These alarms can activate a tape recorder, a light, or an audible signal. The scene is scanned constantly, and any movement in the area covered by the video alarm sensor will trigger an alarm condition. One such device stores the path of intrusion visually on the monitor.

One method of protecting high-value items or freight that is particularly theft prone is to place the material in a designated area of the terminal or the ramp where it can be monitored by CCTV connected to a lapse-time video recorder.

Guard Force Operations

A uniformed guard force, properly used, can assist in reducing cargo theft at an air freight terminal. It is essential that guards be permanently assigned to air freight duties and trained in air freight methods and procedures. They must be able to look at the airbill or other documentation and know whether it is being properly handled. They should be able to look at receiving and shipping documents and know whether the shipment is in its proper location and whether the count is accurate.

Guards should be cautioned against fraternization with air freight employees. If possible, locker space for guards should be entirely separate from that of the other employees at the location. The guards are working in a crime-preventing capacity and must accept the fact that personal friendships with employees could hinder their authority and theft-deterring function.

The use of armed company guards to follow high-value shipments as escorts to and from aircraft should not be overlooked. If the volume of freight precludes their use on every high-value shipment, escort guards should follow all shipments over an established dollar amount appropriate to that location. At some stations, airport police will provide an escort for shipments valued at or above a particular dollar amount.

Accountability

What loss-prevention measure is simpler and what procedure is more basic to good freight management than the elementary practice of counting and weighing freight when it is received and when it is delivered? If shipments are not counted there is no certainty whether the missing items actually were received by the carrier, were received but disappeared in transit, or were loaded for delivery and removed after that point.

Counts are also essential in order to stop pilferage of loads by truck drivers. At its simplest, pilferage may be attempted in several forms. Drivers may accept delivery of an entire load but claim the shipment is short one or more boxes by their count. If the supervisor signs off one short on the shipment to avoid the labor and time of unloading the truck and making a recount, the box belongs to the driver. If the shipment is recounted, the driver cannot be accused of theft, only of miscounting. A way to counter this scam is to ensure that it will not be attempted; supervisors must insist, as a matter of policy, that

whenever the count of the driver and the count of the air freight employee do not agree, the shipment must be recounted, without exception.

Caution must be exercised in counting palletized freight; where there are supposed to be 12 cases on each layer, the trucker may have stacked the bottom layers so that they contain as few as 9 cases to the layer. Unless a count is made while the boxes are being stacked, rather than waiting until the stacking is completed, the deception may not be caught.

Truck Seals

If seals are used on departing trucks, the guard should verify that the seal on the truck is the one indicated by the number on the airbill. Otherwise, the trucker can use a seal obtained from another source, and replace it with the correct seal after rifling the cargo. (Obtaining the necessary extra seal, as well as the designated seal before it is used to seal the cargo, usually requires the cooperation of an air freight agent, and collusion is to be suspected when such seal errors are found.)

Collusion

Theft becomes easier and its detection much more difficult when collusion is involved, whether it is collusion between employees or between an air freight employee and a trucker. Occasionally, even contract guards are a part of the theft. Successful minor pilferage -- if not checked -- leads to collusion, the source of the largest thefts and the greatest theft losses.

When an employee has a collaborating truck driver, the ease of theft is remarkable; the freight is simply loaded aboard the cooperating driver's truck and driven off the premises. Onlookers who see large boxes of wearing apparel or console television sets being stolen assume they are watching a normal pickup or delivery.

A rotation system should be established as a routine to preclude the same trucker and air freight agent working together on a daily basis. Spot checks conducted by supervisors are another measure useful in countering collusion. Another procedure useful in combating collusion is to divide responsibility; that is, to have one agent pull (and count) the freight and another release the freight to the trucker.

Fraudulent Pickups

A fraudulent pickup occurs when freight is delivered to an individual not authorized to receive it. Shipments released to an unauthorized individual can force the carrier to pay the claim. In its more flagrant application, fraudulent pickup may involve an entire truckload of cargo. At those stations where fraudulent pickups have become a problem, dual-lens cameras (which simultaneously photograph the driver and the papers -- driver's license, pickup order, and airbill) have been of great assistance, principally in deterring such attempts. Both the identity of the individual and the individual's authority to receive the shipment must be established in every case of delivering a shipment. If both cannot be established, the shipment should not be released.

Protection of Documentation

Some fraudulent pickups involve valid but stolen documentation, which demonstrates the need to protect shipping and receiving documents. Air freight pickup counters should never be left unattended, particularly where documentation is kept behind the counter. Blank airbills, too, must be protected; an airbill in the hands of an individual who knows how they should be filled out can be costly.

Containerization and Security

A significant percentage of air freight moves in containers packed by shippers at their own facilities. Containerization offers the advantages of unitizing shipments and delivering them to the carrier in containers, rate reductions because of the reduced carrier handling costs, reduced packaging costs, and reduced risk of theft.

All cargo received, whether from a shipper or from another carrier, should be promptly inspected for damage. When damage is found or when it appears entry may have been gained to a piece of freight being received, specific exception to the shipment must be made on the proper forms. Exceptions must be specific as to the extent, type, and location of the evident damage, and an inventory of the contents must be made at that time. A camera should be used to make a photographic record of damaged or improperly

packaged merchandise. A Polaroid camera is best for this, as it instantly provides pictures that can be affixed to the documentation. In addition to the Pickup and Delivery Manifest, an Over, Short, and Damage (OS&D) report should be made on every damaged shipment passing through the terminal.

Container Seals

A number of freight forwarders and shippers seal their containers before delivery to the air carrier. This practice considerably benefits the air carrier because an unbroken seal at the destination eliminates any possibility of carrier liability for shortages discovered after arrival. When a sealable container is delivered to the air carrier without a seal, air carrier freight personnel should affix a seal. The seal number should be entered on the airbill, and the shipper's representative should be asked to sign or initial the airbill to signify that he or she was present when the seal was affixed.

High-value items should be loaded into sealable containers whenever possible, sealed with one or more seals as necessary (the LD-3 container, for example, requires four seals), and the seal numbers transmitted as part of the advance advice message sent to the destination station. For the practice to be effective, the seal numbers must also be verified at the destination station.

High-Value Shipments

The Department of Transportation broadly defines high-value cargo as "cargo that because of its monetary value, utility, desirability, or history of frequent theft, requires greater protection than other commodities normally handled at that facility." This definition correctly covers a wide range of cargo, from diamonds to garments, and from gold to guns.

Articles of Extraordinary Value. A narrower definition of high-value cargo was used by the now-defunct Civil Aeronautics Board in requiring specific procedures for the handling of certain high-value items generally referred to as articles of extraordinary value (AEV). Carriers refer to this general list in defining what should be treated as high-value items.

The AEV list includes artworks; bills of exchange; bonds; bullion or precious metals; clocks, watches, and parts; currency; deeds; evidences of debt; furs, fur clothing, and fur-trimmed clothing; gems, cut or uncut (including diamonds for industrial use); gold and silver bullion, coined and uncoined; cyanides, dust, or sulfides; jewelry (other than costume jewelry); money; pearls; platinum; promissory notes; negotiable securities; postage or revenue stamps; and stock certificates.

Special procedures applicable to high-value cargo generally include advance arrangements of not less than 24 hours before shipment, delivery or shipment to the carrier not more than 3 hours prior to the departure of the flight, and written assurance that the consignee will accept delivery within 3 hours and/or not later than 24 hours after the scheduled arrival time at the destination.

Upon receipt, high-value shipments should be carefully and thoroughly inspected for damage, piece count, and proper packaging. Unless the flight is leaving almost immediately, the item should be locked in the high-value security cage and entered in a log maintained for the security cage.

Signature accountability should be maintained all the way to the aircraft; if accountability cannot be traced, investigating a theft after the fact is of little value. If the runner is required to obtain the signature of the individual at planeside to whom the package was delivered, the possibility of theft immediately lessens; individuals are less likely to steal -- or be careless with – a package if they know that their signature is the last one on a receipt. Where such a hand receipt system is used, the time should be part of the receipt.

On shipments of particularly high value, generally over $25,000, special escorts should be arranged, either through airport police, carrier company guards, or armed contract service.

Delivery of the AEV item to the aircraft should be as late as possible; lengthening the time the shipment remains in the security cage reduces the time the shipment is vulnerable to theft. Once the item is placed aboard the aircraft, the aircraft should be kept under surveillance until it taxis away from the ramp.

The procedures followed at the station of origin must be followed at the destination station. High-value shipments must be met, and there must be signature accountability for the shipment from the aircraft to the high-value security cage. The destination station should have been notified that an AEV shipment was enroute by means of an advice message, usually through the company's internal telex system.

Air carriers, particularly international carriers, may wish to adopt a signature service, wherein a form such as a Special Handling Notice is used to indicate a high-value shipment. The Special Handling Notice is to be signed by an authorized person at each point of interface from origin to destination.

Circuitous routings should be avoided; high-value freight, particularly, should be sent on direct, nonstop, daylight flights whenever possible. Split shipments of AEV items should be prohibited. A split shipment occurs when part of a shipment goes out on one flight and part on another.

One effective preventive measure in use by many carriers is to refuse to accept any item for shipment packaged so that it is smaller than 1 cubic foot in size. This eliminates the small, easily pocketed, high-value theft, and makes the article much more difficult to conceal.

Attractive Merchandise

The Department of Transportation's definition of high-value cargo rightfully includes classes of items that, because of their desirability or history of frequent theft, need greater protection; yet, the procedures of most carriers call for extra precautions only for tariff-defined AEV items. Wearing apparel, the largest volume item moved by air freight, is perhaps the most glaring example of this. This single commodity accounts for some of the heaviest claim losses sustained by air carriers and forwarders -- in some cases, as much as over half of all the company's theft-related losses.

Attractive merchandise can be any commodity in which the carrier is experiencing heavy losses; generally, these items are desirable, readily resold products such as stereo equipment, video cameras, electric power tools, and appliances.

The controls placed upon attractive merchandise should be generally the same as those used for AEV items. This includes special advice messages to downline stations, storage in secure areas, and signature account.

High Value Security Cage

A specific room or cage designed for the secure storage of high-value cargo should be available at each air freight terminal. The secure area should be large enough to handle all the terminal's high-value freight at any one time. If all attractive merchandise is included in this category, the room may need to be quite large. The physical security and the construction of the cage or room should be commensurate with the value of the goods stored there. Some excellent guidelines are given in the Department of Transportation's Cargo Security Advisory entitled *High Value Commodity Storage*.. The cage or crib should be located so as to be constantly visible to supervision; it should never occupy an isolated location. When CCTV is available, cameras can be used to observe the cage. Damaged cartons awaiting repair should not be placed in this cage unless the merchandise they contain is truly valuable; another lockable room should be provided for the storage of all over, short, and damaged material. A control log should be maintained for every high-value cage. The contents of the high-value cage should be periodically inventoried by a supervisor, ideally at least once a shift.

Cargo Theft Investigation

An early Department of Transportation study found that 85% or more of thefts were committed during working hours by employees, by authorized drivers, or by both. Therefore, investigators should not be looking for burglars and unauthorized visitors. An analysis of claim reports can help in determining what is being stolen and where it is being stolen. At one airline, cargo shipments originate at any one of 100 or more stations. An analysis of loss statistics revealed that more than 80% of the losses were occurring at 13 stations, while the remaining 90 or so stations accounted for less than 20% of the losses. Sound management requires that primary attention be directed toward those stations where the major portion of their losses are occurring.

U. S. Customs Service

U. S. Customs Service has a responsibility for cargo coming in from outside the United States.

The Customs Service can levy heavy penalties on companies that import items "contrary to law." Under that definition, shippers that are robbed at U. S. airports or ports can be fined if the cargo is stolen before it clears Customs. The fine can be a penalty equal to 100% of the cargo's value, in addition to the obligation to reimburse the owner of the cargo.

Kenneth C. Moore

Source   Moore, K.C., Airport, Aircraft and Airline Security. (Butterworth-Heinemann, Boston, 1991).

AIR FORCE OFFICE OF SPECIAL INVESTIGATIONS

The Office of Special Investigations (OSI) is a separate operating agency reporting to the Secretary of the Air Force through the Air Force Inspector General. The organization has active duty, civilian, and reserve special agents located worldwide. These agents investigate violations of the military and civilian laws of the United States and help protect the people, property, and the security of the United States Air Force.

Most of OSI's people are active duty military, both officers and non-commissioned officers. Civilian special agents also comprise a significant portion of OSI's criminal investigative and counterintelligence force. Along with agents, OSI members include specialists in areas such as information management, supply, computers, finance, personnel, and other specialized support fields.

OSI was founded in 1948 to provide a centralized organization to investigate allegations of procurement fraud. Agents are assigned to major Air Force acquisition and logistics centers which spend the bulk of the Air Force budget. Major emphasis is put on cases involving product substitution, bribery, cost mischarging, and criminal defective pricing.

OSI has joined with other Department of Defense (DOD) and federal investigative agencies in joint federal task forces. Task forces investigate bid rigging, kickback schemes involving prime and subcontractors, and major accounting violations involving "top 100" contractors. Combining the specialized talents of various agencies into one cohesive unit makes complex fraud matters easier to investigate and prosecute.

A priority for OSI is the investigation of use, possession, sale, and distribution of illegal drugs. OSI's efforts to interdict the flow of illegal drugs includes an antismuggling program. This program uses time-sensitive drug and contraband smuggling intelligence information to protect Air Force personnel, facilities, programs, and missions.

OSI also conducts independent research to identify criminal behavior patterns that often leads to the development of new investigative approaches and techniques, and are shared with other law enforcement agencies.

As the Air Force's lead agency for antiterrorism and protective services, OSI undertakes various activities designed to counter the terrorist threat. In addition to investigating terrorist incidents involving Air Force personnel and property, carefully selected OSI agents are called upon to conduct protective service operations to ensure the safety of Air Force and other U.S. and visiting foreign government officials.

Protective operations take place throughout the world wherever and whenever the safety of the dignitary is in question. OSI also provides specialized antiterrorism training to persons likely to be terrorist targets.

Within the Air Force, OSI is solely responsible for the counterintelligence mission: to counter the threat to Air Force interests posed by foreign intelligence services and terrorist groups. To effectively do this, OSI performs a variety of broad counterintelligence and security services.

The OSI counterintelligence collections program is designed to identify and assess threats to the Air Force and other DOD interests worldwide. It is OSI's first step in neutralizing or minimizing threats from foreign intelligence services and terrorist groups. Acquired information is analyzed, assessed, and disseminated to appropriate Air Force commanders and U.S. agencies for security planning, and use in antiterrorist and counterintelligence operations. Another counterintelligence service is the defensive awareness briefing program, which informs Air Force personnel of espionage and terrorism threats.

Foreign intelligence targeting and penetration attempts directed against the Air Force continue to be a serious threat to the Air Force's mission. OSI works to detect, neutralize, and destroy the effectiveness of the targeting of Air Force resources by foreign intelligence services.

The Countermeasures Program and Technical Support Operations constitute the primary mission areas of OSI Technical Services. The first seeks to ensure the technical security of sensitive Air Force facilities. The second is a traditional law enforcement function. Since its creation, Technical Services has continually expanded its inventory to include sophisticated state-of-the-art equipment.

Forensic consultants are assigned at regional locations throughout OSI and provide on-scene investigative assistance in cases involving notorious, complex, or serial crimes. They are an Air Force asset for all child abuse investigations worldwide. In this capacity, they also serve as members of the DOD Family Advocacy Command Assistance Team.

Computer crime investigators are invaluable whenever a computer is used to commit a crime, a computer is the target of the crime, or if evidence of criminal activity may reside on a computer. The computer crime investigators design and develop data bases so complex information can be organized, retrieved, and analyzed during complicated investigations. They also assess computer security.

OSI is in the forefront of psychological applications in criminal investigations and counterintelligence. These psychological advances focus on supporting investigations, providing human reliability, and directing research. Psychological profiling, psychological autopsy, and forensic hypnosis are frequently used behavioral science techniques. Specialists are available for consultation or on-scene assistance at all OSI locations.

OSI is solely responsible for all polygraph matters within the Air Force, and is a leader in the federal polygraph community. One mission of this program is to provide an invaluable investigative tool for use in criminal, fraud, and counterintelligence investigations. A second mission is the counterintelligence polygraph program to detect and deter espionage against the United States. It applies to individuals involved in many special security programs.

OSI agents work closely with such agencies as the FBI, the Drug Enforcement Administration, U.S. Secret Service, U.S. Customs Service, Interpol, state police agencies, and local county sheriffs' offices to ensure rapid exchange of criminal intelligence and mutual assistance. Continuous cooperation occurs between OSI and a large number of allied agencies in countries where the Air Force is located.

U.S. Air Force Office of Special Investigation

Source AFOSI Public Affairs Pamphlet. (Headquarters, U.S. Air Force Office of Special Investigation, Bolling Air Force Base, Washington, DC, 1992).

AIR FORCE SECURITY POLICE

Originally established as the Air Force Office of Security Police in September 1979, a redesignation to a field operating agency status in February 1991 brought about a change in the name to Headquarters Air Force Security Police Agency. The Agency reports directly to the Air Force Chief of Security Police, Headquarters U.S. Air Force.

The Air Force Security Police Agency implements security and law enforcement policies and programs for the Air Force worldwide. Its staff also manages programs for the Security Police and Combat Arms Training and Maintenance career fields for over 40,000 active duty, Air Reserve, Air National Guard, and Department of Defense civilian and contract personnel.

Programs managed by the Air Force Security Police Agency are: air base ground defense; aerospace systems security; maintenance of law and order; prisoner rehabilitation and correction; vehicle traffic management; safeguarding classified information; security police personnel management; security police training; and firearms. The Agency also manages the Department of Defense Military Working Dog program which includes providing explosives and drug detector dog team support for civilian law enforcement agencies. The term "security police" identifies both security and law enforcement personnel. Together they form the ground combat arm of the Air Force responsible for protecting vital resources.

History

The position of Air Provost Marshal came into being in March 1943 at the direction of General H. H. "Hap" Arnold, Commander of the Army-Air Forces. When the Air Force became a separate entity in January 1948, its military police became "air police." The Air Provost Marshal came under the Air Force Inspector General. This title was redesignated as the Director of Security and Law Enforcement in 1960, and in 1967 air police became security police.

In 1975 the security police function left the inspector general's umbrella and became a separate agency reporting to the Air Force Chief of Staff. The Chief of Security Police title replaced the Director title. The Air Force Office of Security Police moved from Washington, DC, and established itself at Kirtland Air Force Base, New Mexico, in 1978. In 1979, it became a separate operating agency, again under the Inspector General. In 1991 another reorganization placed the Chief of Security Police back under the Air Force Chief of Staff at the Pentagon. The Kirtland center is now Headquarters, Air Force Security Police Agency, a field operating agency under Headquarters, U.S. Air Force Security Police.

Mission

The primary security police mission is to maintain operational readiness through the deterrence of enemy forces and protection of war-fighting resources on a 24-hour, 365 day-a-year basis. This is accomplished through an interwoven system of strategically located base area and entry control points, armed vehicle and foot patrols, and sensor/detection equipment.

When employed as air base ground defenders to repel attacks by enemy forces, Security Specialists are also armed with light and heavy machine guns, automatic grenade launchers, recoilless rifles, light anti-armor weapons, mortars, and defensive munitions and pyrotechnics.

Their safeguarding of nuclear weapons systems includes use of sophisticated electronics systems for intruder detection. Response forces are equipped with M60s, M203s, and specially designed armored vehicles.

Law Enforcement Specialists

Armed with 9 millimeter pistols, Law Enforcement Specialists perform various functions: protection of resources, installation entry control, traffic services, and maintenance of law and order through crime prevention and criminal investigations. Military Working Dogs, trained at Lackland Air Force Base in San Antonio, Texas, assist them on patrols and with detection of drugs and explosives. Additionally, Law Enforcement Specialists are responsible for confinement and corrections programs.

Administration of the U.S. Air Force Corrections Program is a function of law enforcement. Personnel are charged with prisoner care at the base level where short-term sentences are served, at regional corrections facilities, and at the long-term facility at Fort Leavenworth, Kansas.

Trained in standard police functions, Law Enforcement Specialists also serve as desk sergeants, becoming proficient with interagency computer information terminals, traffic radar devices, and chemical breathalyzers.

U.S. Air Force Security Police

Source   United States Air Force Public Affairs Pamphlet. (Headquarters, U.S. Air Force Security Police, U.S. Department of Defense, Washington, DC, 1992).

ALARMS: EVALUATION OF FALSE ALARM RATES

The use of alarms can be traced back to biblical times when guards were hired to keep the watch and raise the "alarm." Alarm systems as we know them developed concurrently with the telephone, beginning in the early 1850s. Alexander Bell and his partner Edwin T. Holmes thought the telephone was just a novelty. Bell's interests turned to other areas, but Holmes used the same technology to design an alarm that would protect against fire and threat.

The alarm industry in the United States has evolved considerably in technology and sophistication. Alarm monitoring services provide remote supervision of conditions at users' premises. Commercial and residential subscribers seek protection against fire, vandalism, burglary, and other emergencies. The central station alarm office responds to an alarm by notifying an appropriate authority or by taking other action. Although not as common, some alarm systems are connected directly to the police department. Commercial users, particularly those with high security needs, such as financial institutions and

furriers, require more secure transport. The capability for a dedicated circuit that provides transport of alarm signals and line integrity is available with some phone companies.

Each year Americans spend several hundred million dollars for electronic security equipment. The interesting outcome of this increased consumer demand for alarm systems is that the subscriber accounts for a very large percentage of false alarms due to misuse and abuse of the system.

Police and insurance company records show that burglaries, robberies, and vandalism are costing the American public well over a billion dollars a year. In response to that growing demand by the American consumer is an estimated 14,000 firms that provide alarm component systems. Approximately 6,600 central monitoring stations serve the market and 580 meet more stringent Underwriters Laboratory requirements often demanded by commercial customers.

Most police administrators realize that an increase in the demand for service must be met by a corresponding increase in efficiency in order to offset fiscal constraints plaguing most public agencies today. As citizen demand for police services increases, many police departments across the country are experiencing budget reductions.

Accompanying these factors is the continual pressure to maintain or improve police departments' quality of service, innovative approaches to crime prevention, reduction of community fear of crime, and improved response time to emergency calls. All of this is to be accomplished without increasing staffing levels.

Dimensions of the Problem

False alarms greatly impact a police department's ability to function effectively and efficiently. Not only do false alarms seriously compromise alarm effectiveness, they also create many problems:

• Unproductive workloads.
• Potential for injury to citizens and responding police officers.
• Unnecessary out-of-service time for officers investigating false alarm calls.
• Removal of officers from their primary duties of preventive patrol and law enforcement.
• Unnecessary police radio traffic.

•Unnecessary workload by complaint operators answering repeated automatic dealer alarms and calls from companies.

•Complacency caused by repeated responses to alarm locations that continually report false alarms.

The Nassau County Police Department in Long Island, New York, received 72,000 alarm calls in 1982. Of these, 99% were considered to be false. The department estimates that personnel and operating costs for false alarm calls is well over $1.5 million. The growing problem, in addition to the cost, is the amount of personnel hours being wasted by the officers responding to such alarms.

According to a survey conducted by Security Distributing and Marketing (SDM) in 1984, over 2,000 police departments surveyed considered false alarms a serious problem in need of corrective action. However, 93% of these police departments endorsed the concept of electronic security systems to prevent burglary and/or to signal a burglary attempt.

Normally, local law enforcement personnel are questioned by the community as to the effectiveness of burglar alarms. Ninety-eight percent of the officers surveyed indicated they would recommend an alarm to business owners and 89% to homeowners. Obviously, this stresses the importance of police attitudes relative to marketing of alarm systems. Although police departments continue to maintain a positive response to alarm recommendations, approximately 48% agree that there are serious problems with false alarms. Many of the police departments surveyed have taken action to deal with the problem of false alarms.

Dealing with the Problem

In addition to the survey conducted by Security Distributing and Marketing, numerous surveys and articles have been written on the subject of false alarms; police departments are generally addressing the problem through one of the following approaches.

The first of these is ordinances, which are fines levied when an alarm owner generates excessive false alarms. Fines or fees levied against alarm owners are common not just because the revenue generated helps cover the cost of administering the ordinance, but also because

police believe penalties help deter future inadvertent alarms. The specifics of an ordinance differ from city to city and state to state. For example, in Pasadena, California (which was probably the nation's first city to pass an alarm ordinance), fines were not imposed 15 years ago. However, during this same time period a similar ordinance was passed in Lower Merion Township, Pennsylvania, where the police department imposed monetary penalties at the outset. Consequently, the diversity in false alarm ordinances continues to emerge in police departments across the country.

Fines are not the only measure cities have taken in their ongoing battle with false alarms. A more powerful deterrent than a monetary penalty is the decision by police to simply not respond. Legally, police departments do not have to answer alarms calls. According to some of the departments who use it, the no-response policy is successful. Of the 19 states surveyed by SDM, 7 have a no-response policy.

Generally, alarm users are allowed a predetermined number of false alarms. After the first false alarm signal, police send a letter saying the equipment may be faulty and should be tested. After the second false activation, another letter warns that police will not respond if the problem is not corrected. On the third false call, police terminate response. To reinstate service, either the installing company must send the police a letter indicating the system has been repaired, or the system owner must send a letter indicating that the employees who operate the alarm have been trained in its proper use. Currently there is mixed opinion on refusing alarm responses, according to SDM.

Many security professionals believe that private security will eventually assume responsibility for response to alarms. Also, the "Hallcrest Report: Private Security and Police in America" predicted that private security firms would be filling the gap left by underfunded and understaffed police departments. This is already taking place in San Diego, California, where Pacific Security will, before contacting the police, dispatch armed security officers to the premises of subscribers who have a history of false alarms. According to the survey conducted by Hallcrest Systems in 1982, 57% of law enforcement administrators favored transfer of alarm response. About 40% of central station managers either favored or opposed this concept.

In New York City, special police officers (SPO) who have police power for certain crucial incidents occurring on property being protected by them are utilized for initial alarm response to determine the need for police action. This concept of private security response has received strong market support in some areas of the country and some residential alarm firms are offering the service as a key sales feature.

However, those police departments surveyed by SDM strongly oppose alarm companies responding to their own alarms. The third method police departments are utilizing to deal with false alarms has been the development of what is called priority response. The level of response is lowered by downgrading the classification of an alarm call, depending on the number of false activations the system has had. This differs from no-response because regardless of the number of false alarms, a police officer always responds, but more and more slowly. Some police departments, such as Southfield, Michigan, have altered this method slightly by not responding to the lowest priority status alarms. The difficulty with these approaches is that most police departments have not carefully and systematically planned for a comprehensive system, which includes:

•Reduction of false alarms due to subscriber error.

•Reduction of sub-standard equipment and improper installation.

•Control over the use and application of alarm systems which affect the police communication center.

•Elimination of questionable alarm dealers.

•Providing feedback on alarm effectiveness to alarm system dealers, users, and crime prevention practitioners and the alarm industry.

To use an old phrase, the actions thus far have been to "treat the symptom, not the disease." Consequently, many departments have been unsuccessful in obtaining their projected goals for false alarm reduction. One reason is the lack of analysis and development of empirical data from which conclusions can be drawn as to the effectiveness of specific models that could be used by a police department plagued with high rates of false alarms.

The responsibility for dealing with false alarms rests equally with private security alarm companies, users, and police departments. In order to improve the efficient use and management of police patrol forces and reduce community fear of crime and victimization, these groups need to work together to form combinations of strategies that will:

•Decrease the amount of patrol time spent answering false alarms and the unnecessary out-of-service time for officers investigating false alarm calls (notifying businesses or homeowners and securing the building or residence).

•Decrease complaint operator's time spent answering automatic dealer alarms and calls from alarm companies.

•Decrease the excessive cost for handling false alarm calls.

•Address the issue of complacency and apathy caused by repeated response to alarm locations that continually report false signals; it has the potential of leading to an unjustified and heightened community fear of crime and victimization.

•Develop educational programs for alarm customers on the proper use and operation of alarms.

•Develop an effective method of screening alarms prior to police notification.

•Develop training programs for police personnel in the identification and use of various alarm systems.

•Utilize private alarm response units or patrol services that augment police response by verifying that a burglary is in progress.

The alarm industry has made considerable strides in recent years toward the reduction of false alarms. At the same time, alarm control ordinances have proliferated. Law enforcement and private security seem to agree on the need for state licensing and regulation of the industry; however, how best to do so is quite debatable. Many departments are enforcing ordinances that result in fines and possibly arrests. Others simply do not respond to those alarms that have a history of "crying wolf." A third alternative, labeled "priority response," classifies alarms by the number of false activities the system has experienced. Whatever the approach, much of the interest is in controlling false alarms. Yet the question is, which method is more effective?

Pam Collins, Ed.D.

Sources
Alarm Industry in Transition: Competition & Technology. (Security Letter, New York, September, 1987).

Armel, A.L., Framing False Alarm Laws: Part 2. (Security Distributing and Marketing, June, 1987).

Barnard, R.L., Intrusion Detection Systems: Principles of Operation and Applications. (Butterworth-Heinemann, Boston, 1981).

Cavallini, N.M., and R.E. Bartlett, Fire Alarm Data and False Alarm Analysis. (The University of Rochester, Rochester, NY, 1971).

Cole, R.B., Protect Your Property: The Application of Burglary Alarm Hardware. (Charles C. Thomas, Springfield, IL, 1972).

Cunningham, J.E., Security Electronics. (Howard W. Sams & Co., Inc., Indianapolis, IN, 1970).

Cunningham, W.C., Law Enforcement and Alarm Company Relationships in the 80s. (Alarm Signal, 1982).

Depasquale, S., Alarm Awareness. (Security Management, Arlington, VA, April, 1986).

Fitch, R.D. and E.A. Porter, Accident or Incendiary. (Charles C. Thomas, Springfield, IL, 1968).

A Hands-on Checklist for Evaluating Complex Alarm Systems, Such as for Aircraft. (Security Letter, New York, March, 1987).

Harris, K., A Case Study: False Alarm Prevention. (Alarm Signal, September, 1982).

How Has it Affected the Alarm Industry? (Security Management, Arlington, VA, January, 1986).

How to Select a Security Servicing Company. (Interstate Alarm Systems, Inc., Pontiac, MI, 1979).

Improving Residential Security. (U.S. Department of Housing and Urban Development, Washington, DC, 1973).

In Pursuit of Alarm Industry Facts. (Alarm Signal, March, 1986).

Installation, Test and Evaluation of a Large-scale Burglar Alarm System for a Municipal Police Department. (National Institute of Law Enforcement and Criminal Justice, Law Enforcement Assistance Administration, U.S. Department of Justice, Washington, DC, 1971).

Lewin, T., Security: Everything You Need to Know about Household Alarm Systems. (Park Lane Enterprise, Minneapolis, MN, 1982).

Mangan, D.L., DOE-Sponsored Evaluations of Interior Intrusion Detection Systems. (ORES Publications, Lexington, KY, 1978).

Market Study Finds Continued Opportunities for Intrusion Detection Equipment. (Security Business, New York, October, 1987).

Mechanically Actuated Switches for Burglar Alarm Systems. (United States Department of Justice, Washington, DC, 1974).

Nassau County Police Upset Over False Burglar Alarm Calls. (Crime Control Digest, June, 1983).

National Institute of Justice Standard for Control Units for Intrusion Alarm Systems. (U.S. Department of Justice, Washington, DC, 1984).

Ohlhausen, P., What's New in Wireless. (Security Management, Arlington, VA, July, 1986).

Orey, W.J., Keep the Heat Off. (Security Management, Arlington, VA, September, 1987).

Pinpointing the Culprits Behind False Alarms. (National Burglar and Fire Alarm Association, New York, 1979).

The Prevalence of Crime. (Alarm Signal, March, 1982).

Revised House Bill Bars AT&T and Divested BOCs from Providing "Any Alarm Service." (Alarm Signal, May, 1982).

Sanger, J., More Kinks & Hints. (Butterworth-Heinemann, Boston, 1986).

Solomon, E., Does Your Fire Alarm System Ring True? Part 1. (Security Management, Arlington, VA, October, 1986).

Solomon, E., Does Your Fire Alarm System Ring True? Part 2. (Security Management, Arlington, VA, November, 1986).

Sound Sensing Units for Intrusion Alarm Systems. (U.S. Department of Justice, Washington, DC, 1977).

Understanding Crime Prevention. (National Crime Prevention Institute, University of Louisville, Louisville, KY, 1986).

White, T.W., K.J. Regan, J.D. Waller, and J.S. Wholey, Police Burglary Prevention Programs. (U.S. Government Printing Office, Washington, DC, 1975).

Whitehurst, S.A., Protecting Residential America. (Security Distributing and Marketing, February, 1983).

ALARMS: PRINCIPLES OF OPERATION

Most alarm system sensors operate on the following principles, either singly or in conjunction with another:
- Breaking an electrical circuit
- Interrupting a light beam
- Detecting sound
- Detecting vibration

• Detecting motion
• Detecting a change in capacitance
• Detecting heat

Breaking an electrical circuit can be accomplished in a variety of ways: metallic foil and/or wire, grid wire sensors, pressure mats, and door contact switches, to name a few. There is no application for these types of sensors in a maximum-security environment if they are used alone. Each can be used to the advantage and to the limits of a practitioner's imagination when they are supplemented with other types of sensors.

Interrupting a light beam is the basic principle behind photoelectric sensors. They may be susceptible to occlusion by snow, rain, smoke, or dust, and can be bypassed if an adversary has knowledge of sensor locations and applications. Photoelectric sensors should never be used exclusively but may be incorporated into the overall protection system.

Detecting sound can be quite effective in a maximum-security setting when used in conjunction with other types of sensors. Sound detectors are limited in their application, however, to areas where natural background noise is minimal and where sensitive or classified information is not discussed.

Vibration-sensitive sensors are used on barriers, including ceilings and floors. They are designed to sense vibrations associated with a penetration attempt. They too have their drawbacks in that use is restricted to areas where excessive vibrations are not usually found.

Detecting motion can be accomplished in a variety of ways. Two of the most common security applications of this capability are ultrasonic and microwave sensors. Ultrasonic sensors detect a change in a transmitted pattern of acoustical energy. While very effective indoors, their use outside is questionable.

Microwave sensors operate in essentially the same manner; however, radio waves are transmitted rather than acoustical energy. Any change in the frequency of the radio waves reflected back to the receiver initiates an alarm. Their use in a maximum-security environment can be quite effective also.

Their principal disadvantage is that radio waves are not easily confined and may penetrate beyond the confines of the area to be protected, thus resulting in inadvertent activation, that is, false alarms.

Detecting capacitance change in an electrostatic field can be quite effective in addition to other principles of detection. A capacitance or electrostatic intrusion detection system can be installed to establish an electrostatic field around the object to be protected. This field is tuned by a balance between the electrical capacitance and the electrical inductance. The body capacitance of an intruder who enters the field unbalances the electrostatic energy of the field, setting off an alarm.

Detecting heat is the principle employed by passive infrared intrusion devices. These detectors are used quite effectively in the maximum-security setting due primarily to their resistance to false alarms when properly installed.

A passive infrared detector is a line-of-sight device and should not be installed so that it is "looking" at open flames, neon signs, or anything that emits heat while in motion. This type of device detects changes in the radiation of heat from the area being protected. Body heat, emitted by an intruder while in motion, will be detected.

Richard J. Gigliotti
and Ronald C. Jason

Source Gigliotti, R., and R. Jason, Security Design for Maximum Protection. (Butterworth-Heinemann, Boston, 1984).

ALCOHOL TESTING

Alcohol's cost to society is staggering. The Research Triangle Institute of North Carolina reports alcohol abuse was responsible for $50.6 billion in reduced productivity in 1988, compared with $25.7 billion in losses from drug usage. Our nation spent $9.5 billion in health care costs for alcohol-related problems, compared with $1.2 billion for drug-related problems.

The Employee Assistance Society of North America reports that absenteeism among alcoholics and problem drinkers is as much as 8.3 times higher than for other employees. Alcohol abusers also have a two to three times greater risk of being involved in industrial accidents.

The Society's studies show that up to 40% of industrial fatalities and 47% of industrial injuries are due to alcohol abuse. Even nonalcoholic members of an alcoholic's family will use as much as 10 times more sick leave than will other employees.

Alcohol problems are not limited to the workplace. The U.S. Department of Health and Human Services reports that alcohol was involved in half of all highway deaths last year, resulting in 25,000 fatalities. It is also a factor in 50-70% of all murders, fatal accidents, and fire death; and in over half of all arrests. Considering alcohol's impact on our nation and our businesses, alcohol testing should be considered a part of a responsible drug screening program.

Blood Alcohol Content

Law enforcement agencies have long used breath tests to measure the level of alcohol in the blood of persons suspected of committing crimes. Most states have set 0.10% blood alcohol content (BAC) as the maximum level of alcohol a person may have in the body system while operating a motor vehicle. Some states use a 0.08% BAC standard. The Department of Transportation recently set limits of 0.04% BAC for pilots, bus and truck drivers, train crews, and marine crews.

Loss of driver attention and control is generally understood to occur at BAC levels of 0.03% and 0.04%. Studies show that some impairment may be measured with any detectable level of alcohol, and for this reason there is a growing consensus that the acceptable level should be lowered or that zero tolerance be applied. The relatively high BAC level of 0.10% comes from an earlier period in which the professional community was in general agreement that any person exhibiting a BAC at that level was unquestionably intoxicated to operate any dangerous machinery.

In the industrial setting, where impairment is known to increase the risk of accidents, the rule of thumb is that 0.04% should be the highest acceptable BAC level for employees operating equipment.

The several methods of analyzing blood for alcohol content can be divided into two basic categories: pre-evidentiary and evidentiary testing. Pre-evidentiary tests produce preliminary or presumptive test results. They are like field tests or screening tests designed to indicate the need for more definitive testing conducted in a laboratory environment. Evidentiary tests are the definitive, highly analytical tests whose findings are widely recognized in the scientific community and accepted as evidence in a court of law.

Pre-Evidentiary Testing

Three types of pre-evidentiary tests stand out. Two are based on the application of scientific principles to the examination of body substances (i.e., breath and saliva) and the third is based on the empirical observations of a person trained in the identification and interpretation of physiological symptoms associated with alcohol-induced impairment.

Breath Tests. Hand-held, disposable breath testers are inexpensive, accurate and easy to administer. Where it is necessary to test for alcohol abuse -- such as at the scene of an accident or when an employee appears to be intoxicated -- a disposable breath tester can provide nearly instant visual proof that the subject should be further tested.

A positive breath test provides a "reasonable cause" justification for conducting a more definitive test, such as a blood test. Since disposable breath testers are priced at only a few dollars each, they are cost-effective.

A variety of disposable breath testers are on the market. One brand works as follows. The test administrator squeezes a tube containing silica gel granules. The squeezing action breaks a small glass ampule of potassium dichromate inside the tube. The subject then blows through the tube for a period of 12 seconds. If alcohol is present in the breath, the granules in the tube change color.

Testers can be purchased that are factory-calibrated for BAC levels at the 0.02%, 0.04%, 0.05%, 0.08%, and 0.10% ranges. When using the 0.10% tester, the color change becomes distinct in most of the granules when the BAC is higher than 0.05% and the color change becomes complete when the BAC exceeds 0.10%.

Saliva Tests. In these tests a sterile swab is used to collect a sample of saliva from the subject's mouth. The swab is then directly rubbed against a sensitized plate. A color change on the plate indicates the presence of alcohol. Unfortunately, the test materials have a limited shelf life and must be kept cool. On the positive side, the saliva test costs less than the breath test.

Observational Tests. Observational tests are almost exclusively limited to motor vehicle traffic enforcement. A driver suspected of driving while under the influence of alcohol is examined by a law enforcement officer specially trained (and sometimes certified) in the administration of such tests. The tests usually involve a combination of psychomotor exercises, such as touching the nose and walking a line, and a systematic search for physiological indicators, such as dilated pupils and irregular eye movements, e.g., strabismus and nystagmus. Although these techniques can be applied to making fitness-for-work determinations, they are not generally accepted in the workplace.

Evidentiary Testing

The methods of evidentiary testing for alcohol are different from drug testing due to the rapid breakdown of alcohol, both in the body and in any sample collected.

Because alcohol moves through the kidneys and is held in the bladder until expelled, a urine test can report an alcohol level in the danger zone even though the subject is no longer affected by the intoxicant.

Conversely, it's possible for the urine to show very little alcohol while the blood contains a great deal. Another potential problem with urinalysis is the evaporation rate of alcohol during transportation, leading to a discrepancy between the alcohol content at the time of collection and at the time of testing.

Blood testing is the most accurate method of proving excess alcohol content, but it is intrusive and costly. It is also inconvenient because the person to be tested must be transported to a medical facility and the collected blood sample must then be transported to a forensic drug testing laboratory. In the case of a highly intoxicated subject, the BAC is likely to drop significantly during the time spent getting to a blood collecting facility.

Blood and urine tests should be conducted by a forensic laboratory that specializes in such tests, such as a laboratory certified by the National Institute on Drug Abuse. An NIDA-certified laboratory will use testing methodologies and chain-of-custody procedures capable of withstanding intense court scrutiny.

Breath analysis machines, such as the Breathalyzer and Intoximeter, are evidentiary testing devices that work with high accuracy and are usually recognized in judicial proceedings. These devices are extensively used by law enforcement officers but are only rarely used in the private sector. They are costly, require certified operators, and must be calibrated continuously, making them difficult for use by the average company.

Carl E. King

AMERICAN SOCIETY FOR INDUSTRIAL SECURITY

The American Society for Industrial Security (ASIS) is the world's largest organization of security professionals. Its members provide protection to the people, property, and information assets of a diverse group of private and public organizations.

ASIS members are management specialists who formulate security policy and direct security programs for banks, classified aerospace facilities, communications networks, hotels, museums, educational institutions, hospitals, shopping malls, domestic and foreign governments, and countless other businesses and institutions. Security administrators from the nation's leading firms are included in the membership.

Since its founding as a professional membership society in 1955, ASIS has continued to grow in size and to play a leading role in advancing professionalism in the field of security. The Society's global network is organized on local, regional and international levels.

ASIS members initiate and supervise loss prevention programs to thwart internal and external offenses. These offenses range from acts of terrorism, the pirating of classified documents, industrial espionage, and counterfeiting, to insurance fraud, arson, white collar crime, computer crime, and organized crime. Members are also responsible for preventing or minimizing losses from natural and manmade disasters such as fires, riots, strikes, and civil disorders.

Representatives of companies or organizations supplying security equipment, materials, and services used by security practitioners can be affiliate members of ASIS as well. ASIS acts as a conduit for the security professions; providing programs and resources that enable members to update and exchange information and expertise. ASIS accomplishes this through a certification system, a variety of educational programs, regularly scheduled meetings and conferences, a series of professional publications, legislative monitoring activities, and the specialized functions of numerous standing committees and councils.

The Society sponsors the Certified Protection Professional (CPP) program for the advancement of the security profession. Candidates for CPP accreditation must meet educational and experience requirements, and pass a written examination. Membership in ASIS is not a prerequisite. CPPs must qualify for recertification every 3 years through educational and other professional development activities.

To keep members informed of the latest developments in security practice and technology, and to further integrate specialized knowledge and skill, ASIS has established more than 25 standing committees. One group of committees concentrates on the specialized functions of security practitioners in specific types of organizations, such as government installations, retail outlets, financial institutions, hospitals, transportation facilities, hotels and motels, restaurants, museums, libraries, schools, and public utilities.

A second group of committees focuses on security functions germane to most fields. These include physical security, disaster planning, crime prevention, and fire protection, as well as safety, drug abuse, terrorism, computer security, coupon fraud, and white collar crime.

ASIS does not lobby. Since ASIS is a professional membership society and not a trade association, it does not represent the special interests of any one group. Instead, ASIS seeks to advance the interests of the security profession as a whole. The Society plays an educational role in the legislative process by keeping lawmakers informed of the profession's position on security-related issues.

It also monitors local, state, and federal legislation, and the activities of regulatory agencies to keep members up-to-date. When called upon, the Society also gives written and oral testimony on federal legislation regulating the private security sector.

American Society for Industrial Security

Source ASIS Membership Pamphlet. (American Society for Industrial Security, Arlington, VA, 1992).

AMERICANS WITH DISABILITIES ACT: KEY FACTS

Title I of the Americans with Disabilities Act of 1990 prohibits private employers, state and local governments, employment agencies, and labor unions from discriminating against qualified individuals with disabilities in job application procedures, hiring, firing, advancement, compensation, job training, and other terms, conditions, and privileges of employment. An individual with a disability is a person who:

• Has a physical or mental impairment that substantially limits one or more major life activities;

• Has a record of such an impairment; or

• Is regarded as having such an impairment.

A qualified individual with a disability is an individual who, with or without reasonable accommodation, can perform the essential functions of the job in question. Reasonable accommodation may include, but is not limited to:

• Making existing facilities used by employees readily accessible to and usable by persons with disabilities;

• Job restructuring, modifying work schedules, reassignment to a vacant position; and

• Acquiring or modifying equipment or devices; adjusting or modifying examinations, training materials, or policies; and providing qualified readers or interpreters.

An employer is required to make an accommodation to the known disability of a qualified applicant or employee if it would not impose an "undue hardship" on the operation of the employer's business. Undue hardship is defined as an action requiring significant difficulty or expense when considered in light of factors such as an employer's size, financial resources, and the nature and structure of its operation. An employer is not required to lower quality or production standards to make an accommodation, nor is an employer obligated to provide personal use items such as glasses or hearing aids.

Medical Examinations and Inquiries

Employers may not ask job applicants about the existence, nature, or severity of a disability. Applicants may be asked about their ability to perform specific job functions. A job offer may be conditioned on the results of a medical examination or inquiry, but only if the examination or inquiry is required for all entering employees in the job. Medical examinations or inquiries of employees must be job related and consistent with the employer's business needs.

Drug and Alcohol Abuse

Employees and applicants currently engaging in the illegal use of drugs are not covered by the Americans with Disabilities Act, when an employer acts on the basis of such use. Tests for illegal drugs are not subject to ADA restrictions on medical examinations. Employers may hold illegal drug users and alcoholics to the same performance standards as other employees.
U.S. Equal Employment Opportunity Commission

Source Facts About the Americans with Disabilities Act. (U.S. Equal Opportunity Commission, Washington, DC, 1992).

AMERICANS WITH DISABILITIES ACT, TITLE I: A SUMMARY FOR THE SECURITY PROFESSIONAL

On July 26, 1990, President Bush signed the first major piece of civil rights legislation since the Age Discrimination in Employment Act. The Americans with Disabilities Act (ADA) does not repeal or replace the Rehabilitation Act of 1973 because that Act only applied to government grant recipients and federal contracts.

The new law substitutes the terms "disabled" and "disability" for the old terminology relating to "handicap." Laws in many states already protected disabled individuals from employment discrimination. However, enforcement has been irregular, at best. The enforcement provisions of the new law will be through the Equal Employment Opportunity Commission (EEOC.)

The new law is divided into five sections. Title I covers employment. Title II applies to public service. This section deals primarily with public transportation, but does not apply to airlines, which are covered under a separate act. Title III will have a major effect on public and private entities providing "public accommodation." This is so broad that it ranges from hotels to doctor's offices to golf courses.

Title IV requires telecommunications companies to provide access via relay services for disabled persons. Title V contains numerous provisions that relate to some or all of the other sections.

Administrative Details

The effective date of the Act is July 26, 1992, for employers of 25 or more employees; July 26, 1994, for employers of 15 or more. Employers of less than 15 employees are not covered.

Employers engaged in industries involved in commerce are covered. This is basically every business that serves the public. Also covered are state and local governments, employment agencies, labor organizations, and joint labor management committees.

Individuals with a disability who are qualified for the position they are seeking or in which they are presently employed are protected. This includes persons who have a physical or mental impairment that substantially limits one or more major life activities, have a record of such impairment, or are regarded as having such an impairment. The employee or applicant must be able to perform "essential functions" of a position with or without reasonable accommodation. The employer decides these functions, and, if a written position description is prepared before advertising for or interviewing applicants, this description shall be considered evidence of the essential functions. Notices must be posted, as with other civil rights acts. Not protected are drug abusers and alcoholics, persons who have sexual deviate disorders, gambling and other compulsive disorders, and mental illnesses induced by drug abuse.

Substance Abuse

The issue of substance abuse under the ADA promises to be an irritation to security professionals. Three specific aspects of the ADA are worth noting.

•There is an emphasis on "illegal use of drugs." This classic poor wording focuses on only part of the substance abuse problem. The law protects employees who have completed rehabilitation; are in rehabilitation; or are incorrectly suspected of drug use. This provision could lead to challenges against drug tests.

DOCUMENTATION OF A REQUEST
FOR REASONABLE ACCOMMODATION

Federal law requires the employer to document each request for reasonable accommodation under The Americans with Disabilities Act. This form is designed for that purpose.

Requester:_____   Job Title:_____

Person to Whom Request Was Made:_____   Date of Request:_____

Step 1: Analyze the Job

What is the purpose of the job?_____

_____

List the Essential Functions of the Job

1_____   4_____

2_____   5_____

3_____   6_____

Step 2: Consult with the Requester

Circle the essential functions the requester is unable to perform: 1   2   3   4   5   6

Why? What are the job-related physical or mental limitations claimed by the requester?

_____

_____

_____

Can the requester suggest an appropriate, acceptable accommodation? Describe it.

_____

_____

_____

_____

Note: If the requestor suggests an appropriate, acceptable accommodation, go to Step 5. Otherwise, continue on to Step 3.

Step 3: Identify Possible Accommodations

Document the guidance obtained from local, state, and federal agencies that represent the interests of disabled workers.

Source   Recommendations

_____   _____

                                                          _____

_____   _____

                                                          _____

_____   _____

                                                          _____

Assess the feasibility of each accommodation identified. Would the accommodation be effective? Practical? Reasonable? Appropriate? Acceptable to the parties concerned? Describe below.

_____

_____

_____

_____

Step 4: Select the Accommodation

Consider the requester's preference. While the requester's preference is important and should be considered, the employer has discretion to choose among all effective and reasonable accommodations. On the below lines, name the accommodation selected and explain the reason(s) for the selection.

_____

_____

Step 5: Implement and Make a Record of the Accommodation

Name of company official who approved the accommodation: _____

Date of implementation:_____

Details of implementation:_____

•The ADA contains specific approval of drug policies and procedures, not limited to drug testing. Also approved are Department of Defense, Department of Transportation, and Nuclear Regulatory Commission substance abuse programs.

•The ADA is very specific to workplace alcohol abuse, as opposed to alcohol abuse generally. This could create problems for disciplining an employee for a DWI off duty.

Reasonable Accommodation

Reasonable accommodation includes:

•Making existing facilities readily accessible; and

•Job restructuring, modification of work schedules, or reassignments; modification of examinations and policies; providing readers or interpreters, etc.

This leads to the question, How much accommodation? The limitation relating to reasonable accommodation requires employers to show that corrective actions will cause undue hardship. Factors to be considered include:

•Nature and cost of accommodations;

•Finances of company and number of employees;

•Impact of accommodations upon a specific facility, number of employees, and finances of the facility involved;

•Type of operation of facility impacted and the relationship between that facility and the company as a whole.

Discrimination

Discrimination under the ADA includes:

•Classification due to disability that adversely affects opportunities;

•Contracts that cause discrimination, including union contracts, and possible trap-benefit plans;

•Standards or methods that lead to discrimination;

•Classification based on a relationship to a disabled individual;

•Failure to accommodate (see previous discussion).

•Failure to properly validate employment tests regarding impact on disabled;

•Using tests where administration of testing tends to screen out the disabled -- unless the skill sought is the one being tested.

Defenses

The defenses under the ADA for employers include:

•Establishing that hiring standards are job related;

•Proving business necessity;

•Showing that reasonable accommodation is not possible;

•Showing that the individual is a direct threat to the safety of others;

•That the employer is a religious organization or Indian tribe;

•The employer can reject or reassign a food handler with an infectious disease.

Medical Examinations

Pre-Employment Medical Examinations. These are somewhat limited. Drug tests are not considered to be medical examinations and therefore are not limited under the ADA. If the pre-employment examination is used to exclude an applicant, the examination must be shown to be job related.

Post-Employment Medical Examinations. These are very limited unless they are health and safety related, or if they are voluntary.

Records. Medical records must be kept separate from other personnel records.

David D. Schein

Source   The Americans with Disabilities Act. (Federal Register, Washington, DC, July, 1991).

ANONYMOUS LETTERS

Perhaps the most perplexing cases for the security manager involve anonymous letters. These may be handwritten, handprinted, typewritten, painted on walls, or consist of letters or words pasted together. In the corporate world, people send anonymous letters to recommend an employee for promotion, to warn the employer about an employee, or to inform the company about the activities of a particular person. Most often, however, disgruntled employees send anonymous letters as a way to vent frustration. In a series of letters, the nature of the notes may progress from minor complaints to harassing or even threatening statements. Elements of disguise surround anonymous letters as the author attempts to mislead, often with false information.

Categories of Anonymous Letters

Anonymous letters fall into the following categories: graffiti, altruistic letters, benevolent or "friendly" letters, harassing or disturbing letters, and letters that are criminal in nature.

Graffiti. We see graffiti in a variety of places: public rest rooms, on the outside of buildings or automobiles; or even on stockroom merchandise. People create graffiti with spray paint, lipstick, chalk, markers, or, in criminal cases, with blood. Messages may be scratched onto a surface with a sharp instrument. The purpose behind graffiti is to draw attention to a specific cause, person, or organization.

Altruistic, Benevolent, or "Friendly" Letters. Altruistic letters are most likely found in non-profit corporations, written by persons who wish their contributions to be anonymous. Benevolent or "friendly" letters, on the other hand, may comfort the reader, involve recommendations for promotion, or may warn or inform the reader about someone. Anonymous letters of recommendation often praise one individual while discrediting another. In these cases, the author is often the person recommended, or a relative, spouse, or lover of the person recommended. Unless written by the "recommendee," the letters are most often naturally written, absent of disguise.

A recent case involved a friendly letter and the theft of jewels valued at $15,000. Due to the circumstances surrounding the disappearance of the valuables, security suspected an inside job. Shortly thereafter, someone mailed the jewels to the store. Inside the package was a brief, anonymous note from "a relative" of the thief. The security manager submitted the original questioned note and envelope for examination. Handwriting samples from all employees who

were working at the time of the theft were also included for analysis. The available writings (from employee files) were insufficient for comparative analysis, so the document examiner aided the security manager in obtaining dictated writings from the employees [1]. Examination of the additional samples clearly pointed to the primary suspect. The document examiner made a near certain identification, despite the author's attempt to disguise the writing.

Harassing or Disturbing Letters. These, the most common of anonymous letters, while seldom preceding physical harm, do cause mental anguish to the recipient. Many are spitefully written, often containing foul or explicit sexual language. Others result from a disgruntled employee seeking revenge.

One harassing letter case involved a former business partner who, upon dismissal, subscribed his adversary to every professional publication imaginable. He further irritated his former partner by arranging for sales demonstrations and equipment deliveries to the company. In short, he made life miserable for his associate. The chief executive officer retained a document examiner who determined that while some documents were in the suspect's natural writing, others were disguised. The examiner identified the suspect as having prepared all of the harassing documents.

Letters That are Criminal in Nature. Extortion letters and letters threatening character, reputation, health, or life fall into this category. It is wise to take seriously all correspondence of this type. The criminal may have written them or had them written by direction. In one case, a CEO received a typewritten letter threatening to expose a marital indiscretion if he did not meet certain conditions. Security traced the type style to a specific office, narrowing the list of suspects. Word usage further shortened the list. Unfortunately, there was only circumstantial evidence to connect the suspect to the letters. Fortunately, however, he did not follow through on his threats.

Handling an Anonymous Letter Case

It is imperative to learn as much as possible about the time, method, and place of the letter's delivery. Examine and note with careful attention

> Manager,
>   A relative of ours works at your store and brought these home either by accident or on purpose. We want nothing to do with this. We are hoping that she will talk to you about this. Thank you.

Anonymous letter mailed to the store.

There is good agreement throughout the note, despite evidence of disguised writing. For example, compare the questioned and the suspect's writing of "a-g-e-r" in the word "manager." Also, notice the proportion of the second "p" in the word "purpose." An idiosyncratic feature is the initial hook of the "h" in words "hoping" in Figure 1 and in "Thank You" in Figure 2. Other characteristics can be seen as well.

Dictated writing sample from a suspect.

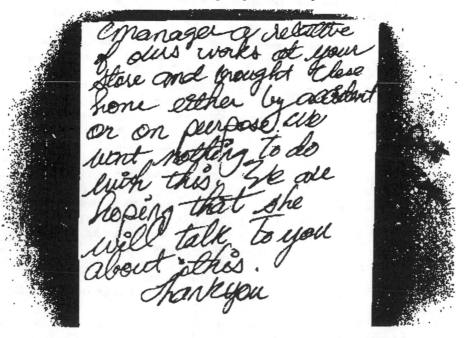

the postmark on the envelope. Note the type of paper and envelope used. Does the note contain handwriting, handprinting, block lettering (all capitals)? What type of writing instrument is used? Is it typewritten, or letters and words pasted together? Consider no detail insignificant.

Immediately place the document in a protective evidence envelope. Be certain to retain the envelope and any extraneous material(s). Handle the evidence as little as possible. Do not overlook possible fingerprint testing and blood typing from saliva analysis of the stamp or envelope flap.

Ask yourself, who will this letter affect? Who will benefit from it? Who knows the details discussed? Read the letter aloud several times. Who does the letter sound like? What education level does the writer portray? It is not uncommon for an anonymous writer to feign an uneducated person. This tactic is seldom effective once an expert evaluates the letter.

What is the motive behind the letter(s)? Remember, possible motives include revenge, jealousy, "sour grapes," spite, and blackmail; others are obscene, give information on stolen property, or make a recommendation.

Contact the document examiner as soon as possible. The examiner can assist you in narrowing a list of suspects and can make recommendations for proceeding with the case. The examiner can also provide or help you prepare customized request writing forms, as needed.

The document expert will ask to examine the originals of the letter(s) and the standards for comparison from all suspects. If the note is in handprinting, the exemplars also must be handprinting; if handwriting, the exemplars must be handwriting; if written in block letters then the examiner will need block-lettered samples. Few people write in block lettering, so these are often only available by taking dictated standards.

In a typewriting case, obtain typewritten samples from the machine(s) that the suspect might have access to. Take the ribbon out of these machines immediately. The document examiner can read the text on a used ribbon.

If the anonymous letter is written from a pad of paper, get the tablet(s) from the desk of the suspect(s). The document examiner can run an ESDA (Electrostatic Detection Apparatus) on these sheets. This technique brings out indented writings from underlying sheets of paper. In one case, the document examiner ran an ESDA on a sheet of tablet paper. The paper contained the indentation of the anonymous letter, in its entirety. Case solved.

When faced with an anonymous letter case, act quickly. The sooner the document examiner is contacted, the greater the chance for a successful outcome. Anonymous letters can be a real dilemma for the security manager. Working with a forensic document examiner helps him to meet this challenge.

Lynn Wilson Marks

Note

1. It is always wise to obtain handwriting samples from everyone who could have committed the act, even when a primary suspect has been identified. This serves two purposes: first, it may put the suspect off guard and second, it may lessen the possibility or success of a wrongful dismissal action against the employer following termination of the suspect.

ARCHITECTURAL SECURITY: INTEGRATING SECURITY WITH DESIGN

The "form follows function" tenet of 20th century architecture holds that the specific functional requirements of a building should determine design criteria. A structure must permit efficient job performance, meet the needs of the user, and protect the user from safety hazards and criminal acts. In practice, however, the tenet is often reversed when design is focused on form rather than on function. Aesthetics, preferences for construction materials, and harmony with surroundings has predominated at the expense of the activities planned to occur within the structure.

Throughout history people have sought to control their physical environment. In this century, the creation of large cities, the further industrialization of labor, and a growth in lawlessness have led to an interest in crime prevention controls that operate at the fundamental levels of societal life. Among these is the concept of crime prevention through environmental design.

Architects worry about the fortress mentality of security professionals while security professionals are concerned about the failure of architects to include security elements in the design of buildings from the ground up. The conflict is not over whether to include security equipment in the building design; rather, the conflict lies between a building's openness on the one hand and the reasonable control of access to it on the other.

Making a building secure when it was not originally designed to be secure is an expensive proposition. Architects have to sacrifice much more of a building's openness in retrofitting for security than would be the case had the building been designed for security from the outset. Protection and operating expenses are greater than they need to be because of a lack of forethought during the design of a facility. This condition is particularly evident in many of today's buildings, where modern design and materials can result in facilities that are especially vulnerable.

Theoretical Background

Oscar Newman's concept of "defensible space" focused on the vulnerability of urban housing environments to crime because of poor design. Research has shown that criminals do not move about randomly through their environment looking for a target but use a spatial search process to try to find victims or targets that match their perceptual generalizations. When a match occurs, crime is likely to occur.

Deciding to commit a crime can be seen as a process of selecting a crime target and determining a crime method by taking cues from the environment.

P. and B. Brantingham's model of crime site selection is based on the following four propositions.

•Individuals who are motivated to commit specific crimes vary in character, strengths, and resources.

•The commission of an offense is the result of a multistage decision process that seeks out and identifies, within the general environment, a target or victim positioned in space and time.

•The environment emits many signals or cues about its physical, spatial, cultural, legal, and psychological characteristics.

•An individual motivated to commit a crime uses cues learned from experience and observed in the environment to locate and identify victims and targets.

Practical Realities

Theory holds, then, that crime can be curbed by altering the conditions that provide the opportunities for criminal behavior. While this may be eminently sensible, great financial resources are required to alter the conditions. After a building has been constructed and put into use, the anticipated cost of physically changing it tends to overwhelm the anticipated benefits of crime reduction. Even in new construction projects, owners and investors are reluctant to commit the extra funds required to incorporate the physical features called for in the crime prevention through environmental design theory.

Reluctance to design for security is related to more than dollars. Modern buildings strive to attain openness and free-flowing movement. Design ideas that constrain and restrict are not on the agendas of the owners and not in the minds of the architects. Security features are often seen as obtrusive and lacking in aesthetical value. It seems to not matter that the world is an increasingly less safe place to work and live.

For a building to be made truly crime-resistant, security considerations must be in the architectural drawings from the very beginning. The drawings should reflect a comprehensive security perspective -- one that takes into account the interrelationships between electronic security equipment, security officer services, and, most importantly, the routine and exceptional activities of the users of the building.

A common mistake, for example, is to establish an intrusion detection system without at the same time ensuring that intrusion alarms will be evaluated by a trained individual and that responses to alarms will be prompt, appropriate, and consistent with the needs of the building occupants.

We often see in facilities not designed for security a menu of problems associated with the control of human movement. These problems include vehicles backed up in and around garages and exterior entrances, employees bottle-necked at electronically controlled doors, criminal opportunists roving the stairwells in search of victims, and robberies at public service counters that were not installed with security in mind.

We also discover that electronic sensing devices do not function properly because someone failed to notice that a hanging ceiling or a wall extension would interrupt the sensing function.

The use of glass and foliage, which enhance the feeling of openness, can cause false alarms because sunlight will affect infrared detectors and motion detectors will activate when plants and trees are moved by air currents of the cooling system. Microwave detectors will react to cables moving in elevator shafts, vibration detectors will go off when the mail cart passes, and the fire department will be on the way when a cigar is lit under a smoke alarm.

False alarms cannot be taken lightly because they undermine confidence in the entire security program and they place an unnecessary burden on the response units. Also, when the false alarm rate is high, the building occupants tend to develop symptoms of the "cry wolf" syndrome and, as a result, may not react quickly and properly when an alarm is warning them of a true life-threatening condition.

In addition to the loss of life and property consequences that can flow from an improperly designed electronic system, there is the prospect of being held liable, both criminally and civilly. The governmental agencies that hold regulatory authority in matters affecting public safety are increasingly under pressure from society, generally to seek criminal prosecution when violations result in death or injury. Next, the extremely litigious nature of the security industry poses great potential loss in terms of compensatory and punitive awards and loss of reputation. A property owner or manager who makes security-sensitive design decisions without the input of a competent security professional is taking on a very large risk.

Security as a Design Requirement

Architects and designers can make the greatest contribution to meeting a project's security objectives. Architects generally make the basic design decisions about circulation, access, building materials, fenestration, and many other features that can support or thwart overall security aims.

Building clients and design professionals are not the only ones concerned about security during the design process. Many jurisdictions require a security review by the police as part of the building permit approval process, much the same as with fire safety requirements. Inspectors evaluate the plans for obvious spots where assaults, mugging, break-ins, and other crimes of opportunity may exist. Many jurisdictions have security ordinances that require certain lighting levels, and secure door and window designs and hardware.

If security is treated as one of the many design requirements, then the implementation and costs for such measures will be no more a burden to the project owners than fire safety features or landscaping requirements. The basic premise of security design is that proper design and effective use of the built environment can lead to a reduction in the incidence and fear of crime, and to an increase in the quality of life. The environmental design approach to security recognizes the space's designated or redesignated use -- which defines the crime problem -- and develops a solution compatible with that use. Good security design enhances the effective use of the space at the same time it prevents crime.

The emphasis in security design falls on the design and use of space, a practice that deviates from the traditional. The traditional approach focuses on denying access to a crime target through physical or artificial barriers, such as locks, alarms, fences, and gates. This approach tends to overlook opportunities for natural access control and surveillance. Sometimes the natural and normal uses of the environment can replace or work in harmony with mechanical hardening and surveillance techniques. An intelligent use of the environment will present three basic strategies: access control, surveillance, and territorial reinforcement.

Access Control. This strategy embraces the tried and true custom of utilizing security guard forces, and the less understood and infrequently applied strategy of making use of terrain and spatial characteristics and natural circulation patterns. Access control can be augmented by mechanical safeguards such as locks and card key systems. The central objectives of an access control strategy are to deny access to a crime target and to create in the mind of the criminal a belief that an attack on the target will present personal risk.

Surveillance. A strategy based on surveillance is directed at detecting intrusion attempts, keeping an intruder under observation, and launching a response to an intrusion or an attempt at intrusion. A surveillance strategy can take advantage of terrain features, such as landscaping;

building features, such as raised entrances; organized methods, such as patroling; and electronic supplements, such as closed-circuit television.

Territorial Reinforcement. The thrust of this strategy is that physical design can create or extend the sphere of influence naturally exercised by the users of the territory. The idea is that an individual's sense of proprietorship concerning a place of work or domicile can be enhanced and extended by conscious individual action and by cooperating with others in a variety of crime-suppressing activities.

In a residential setting, individual actions can include installing lights, fences, locks, and alarms; cooperative actions can include neighborhood watch and patrol programs; and confronting suspect criminals who enter the neighborhood can combine individual and cooperative action. Territorial reinforcement communicates to criminals a message that they don't belong, that they are at risk of being identified, and that criminal behavior will not be tolerated by the residents.

The Architect Is the Key

The architect is the key to opening the opportunities inherent in the crime prevention through environmental design approach. The architect is the essential element in creating a structure that will work in tandem with the various crime prevention through environmental design (CPTED) strategies. However, to be effective in this regard, the architect must be skilled in three areas.

Determining Requirements. Security needs must be determined early in the project's programming and problem-defining stage. The design team should analyze the designated purpose of how the space or building will be used. The designated purpose will be clear when designers examine the cultural, legal, and physical definitions of what the prescribed, desired, and acceptable behaviors are for that space. The space can then be designed to support desired behaviors and the intended function of the space. The design team should inquire about existing policies and practices, so that this information will be integrated in the programming process.

Knowing the Technology. Rapid and substantial advances in the technology of security systems make keeping up-to-date a challenge. Many construction projects, even those that may be seen as routine, will require the services of an architect knowledgeable in security principles and applications. An important competency is to understand and bring into existence the expressed needs of the security professionals representing a building's owner or manager. Within this competency is the ability to know when an expressed security need cannot be filled by a particular design idea and how to lead the security professional to an alternate idea.

Construction management, usually for reasons of economy, will sometimes invite an electronic security system vendor to act as an unpaid security consultant in matters involving major design decisions. The problem in such an arrangement is that the vendor's expertise will be in manufacturing and selling a product, not in providing an unbiased consulting service. The vendor's design recommendations are likely to reflect what will be best for the vendor in the short term without regard for the building occupants in the long term. Experience has shown this to be a primary reason underlying the poor performance of electronic security systems.

This is not to say that vendors should be excluded from contributing to the design, only that their contributed ideas should be critically examined by the design team. Good sense dictates that all ideas, irrespective of source, be looked at from every perspective. The architect's best contribution to a project may be in providing a constructively critical analysis of security design concepts.

Understanding the Implications. Designs must integrate the complicated and sometimes conflicting goals of security and safety. The tendency to want to lock out the undesirables can create serious safety drawbacks in situations that require quick and unhampered egress. Space and function are variables that must also be brought into balance with security objectives.

Security and safety needs can be integrated in a five-stage approach. First is the problem statement, which explores the users' needs and leads to the development of functional requirements. Second is developing the scope of work from the problem statement, client expectations, and staff available. This stage should lead to a signed contract. Third is the design and documentation of the building and systems. It is at this stage that most architects go through schematic design, design development, and construction documents. Stage four is the administration and supervision of construction, and stage five involves acceptance testing, training, and setting up the building for occupancy.

Design Planning

Whenever possible, security planning should begin during the site selection process. The greatest opportunity for achieving a secure operation begins with locating a site that meets architectural requirements and also provides security advantages. The security analysis in site planning should begin with an assessment of conditions on-site and off-site, taking into account topography, vegetation, adjacent land uses, circulation patterns, sight lines, areas for concealment, location of utilities, and existing lighting. Other key factors for site security planning are off-site pedestrian circulation, vehicular circulation, access points for service vehicles and personnel, employee access and circulation, and visitor access and circulation. Site analysis is a starting point in security defense planning. It considers the perimeter and grounds of the facility, including walls, plantings, fences, berms, ditches, lighting, and natural topographic separations.

The next security level is the perimeter or exterior of the building. The building shell and its openings represent a crucial line of defense against intrusion and forced entry. The area being protected should be thought of as having four sides as well as a top and bottom. The principal points of entry to be considered are the windows, doors, skylights, storm sewers, roof, floor, and fire escapes. Doors are by nature among the weakest security links of a building because they inherently provide poor resistance to penetration. Attention must be paid to the door frame, latches, locks, hinges, panic hardware, the surrounding wall, and the door leaf. Window considerations for secure design include the type of glazing material, the window frame, the window hardware, and the size of the opening. The building shell itself is a security consideration for the simple reason that the type of construction

will determine the level of security. Most stud walls and metal deck roof assemblies can be easily and rapidly compromised with common hand tools. Unreinforced concrete block walls can be broken quickly with a sledge hammer or by impact of a motor vehicle. The architect's challenge is to provide security that is attractive and unobtrusive, while providing balanced and effective deterrence to unauthorized access.

Finally, the architect should design for internal space protection and specific internal point security. These security features may be necessary for the areas within a facility that warrant special protection. The level of protection may be based on zones, with access to the zones limited to persons with the required level of security clearance.

Zoning

Application of the zoning concept means control of human movement. The idea is to allow employees, visitors, vendors, and others to reach their destinations without hindrance, and at the same time prevent them from entering areas where they have no business. Controlling access to each department of a building screens out undesirable visitors, reduces congestion, and helps employees spot unauthorized persons.

Zoning design goals are accomplished through the use of unrestricted zones, controlled zones, and restricted zones. Some areas of a facility should be completely unrestricted to persons entering the area during the hours of designated use. The design of unrestricted zones should encourage persons to conduct their business and leave the facility without entering controlled or restricted zones. Unrestricted zones might include lobbies, reception areas, snack bars, and public meeting rooms. Controlled zone movement requires a valid purpose for entry. Once admitted to a controlled area, persons may travel from one department to another without severe restriction. Controlled zones might include administrative offices, staff dining rooms, security offices, office working areas, and loading docks.

Restricted zones are essentially limited to designated staff. Particularly sensitive areas within restricted zones frequently require additional access control. These might contain classified records, chemicals, drugs, cash, and the like. Security zoning is a standard design feature of hospitals, jails, courthouses, laboratories, and industrial plants.

Electronic Systems

Devices intended to detect building intrusions is a major element of security design. The performance of a security device should be measured in terms of its probability of detecting an intruder, its vulnerability to intentional defeat, and its nuisance alarm rate. With this understanding, an architect can design and specify site intrusion detection devices, building penetration sensors, motion and volume sensors for key interior areas, access control systems, personnel identification systems, and security central control stations.

The architect should take steps to assure generous wiring in tamperproof conduit and to provide a backup, uninterruptible power supply system.

Much has changed in security technology. Today's alarm systems work differently than systems of only a few years ago. Devices, like CCTV cameras, are much smaller and less costly, making them useable and affordable in many more situations. An interesting advance is the verified or dual technology technique used with interior motion-detection systems. Infrared detectors feel the change in temperature as a target crosses a zone, while microwave or ultrasonic detectors sense motion. Both technologies must be triggered to cause an alarm.

Security planning is aimed at preventing crime in the built environment. The architect plays a key role in the shaping of the environment and of the cues and signals that the building sends to the user and visitors. Whether the building turns out to be safe, secure, and comfortable is a factor of how well the architect understands the intended uses. However, good architecture cannot prevent all misdeeds. The crimes that a building environment can deter by natural, mechanical, and organized means are overwhelmingly external -- that is, crimes from outsiders breaking in, robbery, or assault. These stranger-to-stranger crimes produce the greatest fear but not the greatest economic losses.

Internal crime represents the greatest potential loss. Terrorism of the future may not be bomb attacks on buildings but theft and destruction of assets within buildings. Can architecture make a difference in preventing internal crime? Possibly, for if a living or working environment is perceived as defensible, the occupants are likely to take greater responsibility in protecting their individual and common territories. Establishing defensible space is not the panacea that proponents have hoped, nor is it irrelevant to crime as some detractors have contended.

Randall Atlas, Ph.D, AIA, CPP

Sources

Anderson, D., and M.T. McGowan, Untitled. (Progressive Architecture, March, 1987).

Behrends, J., Designing for Security. (Progressive Architecture, March, 1987)

Brantingham, P and B., A Theoretical Model of Crime Site Selection. (American Society of Criminology, Dallas, November, 1977).

Keller, S., Designing for Security. (Building Design and Construction, March, 1988).

Krupat, E., and P. Kubzansky, Designing to Deter Crime. (Psychology Today, October, 1987).

Newman, O., Defensible Space: Crime Prevention Through Urban Design. (MacMillan, New York, 1973).

Repetto, T., Residential Crime. (Ballinger, Cambridge, 1974).

Vonier, T., General Building Design Guides. (Progressive Architecture, March, 1987).

Walters, J., Design and Deterrence. (Security Management, December, 1984).

ARCHITECTURAL SECURITY: INTERFACING WITH THE ARCHITECT

The renovation, addition, or new construction of a place of business will often bring an architect into a working relationship with a security professional. The security professional may be an employee of the business or an outside consultant. In either case, the security professional will be representing owner/management interests with respect to the security features of the facility to be built or modified. The architect will similarly represent owner/management interests but may have a diverging view on security features.

The architect may regard the security professional as simply a conduit for obtaining basic information about the facility or as a valuable source for obtaining security concepts that can be incorporated into the design of the facility. The architect's perception of the security professional's interfacing role may range from low-value functionary to high-value contributor. The architect might also mentally ask, "Will the security professional be a hindrance or a help? A doubter to be won over? An adversary to be beaten or neutralized? Or an ally and partner?"

The security professional may see the architect in similar terms. On the negative side, the security professional may be worried that the architect will sacrifice security in favor of aesthetics; on the positive side, the security professional may hope that the architect will know of design features to establish or enhance particular protective concepts. The relationship, especially at the outset, is fraught with possible conflict, but at the same time holds a great potential for success.

User Information

The architect will have a great number of questions concerning use of the facility. For example:

•Who are the users? How many are staff, visitors, service people, sales representatives, guests, and uninvited persons? Is it a multi-tenant facility?

•What do the users do in the facility? What are the major occupational tasks? What equipment is required and how much space is needed? Does the facility have accommodations for dining, exercising, sightseeing, or caring for children?

•When do the users arrive and leave? What are the opening and closing hours? Do employees work shifts or on flex time?

•What are the patterns of people movement in the facility? Do people move laterally, as in a campus-style facility; or vertically, as in a high-rise building?

•What are the patterns of vehicle and property movement? What are the ingress and egress routes to the facility? Parking provisions? Shipping and receiving? Internal transfer of goods and materials?

The answers to these questions have security implications for the security professional and design implications for the architect. While the security professional may know or have ready access to the answers, the architect will not. This will be an early interface opportunity.

Security and Design Implications

What are the implications of user activity? They vary widely, of course, but let's take as an example the operation of a contract janitor service. The implications of a security nature might be:

•Conduct background checks of the contract company and/or the janitorial staff.

•Verify employment and issue identification cards to janitorial staff.

•Establish security control of after-hours access by janitorial staff.

•Establish procedures for determining entry and exit times of janitorial staff.

•Control and account for mechanical keys and key cards issued to janitorial staff.

•Establish procedures for monitoring removal of property by janitorial staff, for example, in trash bags.

These security concerns could then translate into design implications for the architect:

•Establish an electronic access control system that will control and record movement of janitorial staff.

•Place garbage dumpsters in areas convenient to janitorial staff.

•Install a closed-circuit television (CCTV) system for monitoring unsupervised janitorial work in sensitive areas.

•Conveniently locate service doors and service elevators.

•Establish an alarm system that can be deactivated by security personnel while protected areas are being cleaned.

This is a simple illustration of the relationship between the security professional and the architect. The former articulates the problem or need, and the latter finds design solutions. The value of the architect, then, at least from the security perspective, is dependent upon the ability of the security professional to accurately determine the facility's security needs and to present those needs in a format that is meaningful and useful to the architect.

Security Vulnerability Assessment

Very often the process for determining and presenting security needs is called the security vulnerability assessment process. The assessment will identify the assets in need of being protected, identify the kinds of risks that may affect the protected assets, determine the probability of risk occurrence, and determine the impact in dollars if the risk does occur.

The process is a rational approach to anticipating adverse events of a security nature and taking proactive steps to prevent or mitigate the effect of the events. The architect, and the owner/management, need to be provided with information upon which to base decisions concerning design features that prevent or mitigate loss.

For example, if information theft is a risk posing severe loss potential, should expensive high security vaults be installed to protect sensitive data? Instead, should the information be stored in less secure containers at a considerable saving? Each decision has a trade-off, and the security professional's function is to define the risks and estimate the costs.

A well-conducted assessment will show the current and required security profiles of the facility; it will highlight areas where greater or lesser security is needed; it will serve as an organizing and collecting mechanism for facts that justify security expenditures; and will serve as a record for defending negligent security claims, especially claims that relate to the foreseeability and reasonable security doctrines. Finally, as much as anything else, the assessment can be the basis for developing a comprehensive security plan for the facility.

Randall Atlas, Ph.d, AIA, CPP

ARCHITECTURAL SECURITY: QUALITY CONTROL

A security manager has direct responsibility for quality control (QC) in many areas, but perhaps none so important as in the area of security design. When an architect and engineering firm have been selected to design a security system, one of the security manager's earliest concerns will be the operation of a QC program that insures conformance to specifications.

The heart of any QC program is documentation. In a good QC plan, all information is documented and filed for future reference. In addition, correspondence is tracked, using some type of transmittal and logging technique, and daily logs are kept, delineating those events that have even the smallest impact on the completion of the project.

A sound QC plan addresses the required deliverables, from shop drawings to manufacturers' technical data. A thorough review of submittal data becomes important when equipment arrives at the installation site, for it is at this point that the security manager finds out if what was promised was actually delivered.

Very careful attention to detail is a given in a QC effort, not for the sake of ensuring that the documentation is correct, but for ensuring that the work product represented by the documentation has been delivered and that responsibility can be fixed when it is not delivered. Besides being clear and complete, important documents must be both traceable and retrievable -- a condition that can be important when the system is presented for acceptance.

The inspector staff is the backbone of any QC organization; it provides assistance, advice, and direction. QC inspectors are highly specialized individuals who are usually jacks-of-all-trades and masters of some. The on-site inspectors are walking sources of specifications, with reference documents in their hands and thousands of details in their heads. A well organized inspector staff ensures that the installation is done right and within schedule. Organizing an effective QC team is not easy. It takes dedication on the part of all concerned and the selection of the right people for the right job. The on-site presence of principals is highly motivating to the QC staff.

The QC manager must hold veto power and have a direct link to upper management. The QC manager cannot be expected to report to a construction manager and properly execute his or her duties. Construction documentation will usually spell out the duties and authority of the QC manager, including reporting relationships.

Common sense is an essential element when developing a QC plan. For example, everything should be inspected and people cannot be allowed to inspect their own work. The plan must provide a system of checks and balances with which everyone can live. Using the divisions of contract specification (such as concrete, welding, earthwork, electrical, plumbing, and structural), the QC planner can take the full project into account and develop individual checklists for the field installation inspections, including checks that are witnessed.

The planner will focus attention on tests made of procured materials, the off-site integration of subsystems prior to their shipment to the site, field installation testing, and acceptance testing. Because testing procedures are critical, they should be approved before testing begins. Test instruments are always an issue: they should be called for in the specifications, along with guarantees that they will work properly.

An accurate record of calibration of test instruments is a good example of the kinds of files the security manager can request from the QC manager. Certificates of calibration, which are easily attainable from a calibration laboratory, should accompany all test instruments used for the installation. An amazing array of test instruments is available; even more amazing is that calibration laboratory personnel will usually understand the instruments and articulate their calibrations precisely.

A properly organized QC plan will lead the installation of a security system, not follow it. QC procedures benefit everyone during the installation phase of a project because they bring discrepancies to the surface early enough to prevent expensive retrofitting later.

John D. Sutton

ARMY CRIMINAL INVESTIGATION DIVISION

The U.S. Army Criminal Investigation Division Command (USACIDC) is the Army's sole agent for worldwide investigation of serious crimes committed by members of the Army or committed against the Army. Serious crimes are felonies punishable under the Uniform Code of Military Justice by more than one year of confinement. As a major Army command, USACIDC uses the latest equipment, systems, and investigative techniques to accomplish its mission.

Before World War I, the Army relied on private agencies, such as the Pinkerton Detective Agency, to investigate serious crime. In 1917, the Military Police Corps was established to function as uniformed policemen servicing the American Expeditionary Forces in France.

The crime rate mounted, however, and the need for a detective element became apparent. Therefore, in November 1918, General John J. Pershing, commanding the Army Expeditionary Forces, directed his provost marshal to organize a criminal investigation division to investigate crimes committed against the Army in France.

The CID, as the division was called, was headed by a division chief, who was the Criminal Investigation Division's advisor to the provost marshal general on all matters pertaining to criminal investigations. Today, USACIDC still retains the "D" in its acronym as a historical reminder of the first Criminal Investigation Division.

When the division was first formed, there was no central control of investigative efforts within the CID and investigators consisted of selected personnel from military police units within each command. Between World War I and World War II, the Army returned to its former policy of relying on local civil law enforcement officials for investigating crime in the Army. But the growth of the Army, after the onset of World War II, was paralleled by an expanding crime rate.

Therefore, in January 1944, a Criminal Investigation Division of the Provost Marshal General's Office was established to provide staff supervision over criminal investigations, as well as to coordinate investigations between commands and set standards for investigations.

USACIDC has worldwide responsibility with clearly defined missions and functions. The organization is tailored to the geographic needs of the Army, providing centralized control over serious investigations, and reports directly to the Army chief of staff and the secretary of the Army.

U.S. Army Criminal Investigation Division

Source USACIDC Public Affairs Pamphlet. (U.S. Army Criminal Investigation Division Command, Falls Church, VA, 1992).

ARSON

In most types of crime, an investigation will follow the known fact that a crime was committed. Arson is an exception. An investigation must take place before it is even known that arson occurred.

Unfortunately, arson investigations are often inadequate or not performed at all. This is often due to a shortage of investigators who have been trained in the techniques of arson investigation. In addition, evidence of the crime is likely to have been destroyed by the fire or by the suppression of the fire. The result is that many fires are declared to have innocent origins when in fact they were deliberately set.

Arson Motives

Willful and malicious intent is an essential element in proving the offense of arson. The establishment of a motive adds weight to evidence tending to prove intent. Common motives are fraud, crime concealment, revenge, jealousy, spite, sabotage, intimidation, suicide, excitement, and pyromania.

Proving the element of intent in a building fire can be advanced when the following questions are answered through the inquiries of the investigator:

•Were alarms or communications systems tampered with?

•Was property removed prior to the fire?

•Were interior and exterior doors and windows open or closed?

•Was the ventilating system tampered with?

•Was the fire department called immediately?

•Were flammable materials in the building?

•Was internal fire fighting equipment in working condition?

•Was there any evidence of tampering?

In respect to proving intent regarding an automobile fire, the investigator needs to address these questions:

•Were payments being made regularly?

•Was the lien holder or finance company about to repossess the vehicle?

•Was the vehicle the subject of a domestic problem, such as divorce?

•Was the owner dissatisfied with the vehicle?

•Were accessories removed from the vehicle prior to the fire?

•Did the owner or prior owner have an insurable interest?

Accelerant Indicators

The detection, recovery, and analysis of fire accelerants are of major concern to the arson investigator. The areas most likely to contain residue of liquid fire accelerants are floors, carpets, and soil, since, like all liquids, they run to the lowest level. In addition, these areas are likely to have the lowest temperatures during the fire and may have had insufficient oxygen to support the complete combustion of the accelerant. Porous or cracked floors may allow accelerants to seep through to the underlying earth. Other places where accelerants may be discovered are on the clothes and shoes of the suspect.

Because scientific laboratory equipment cannot always be brought to the scene of a suspected arson, the investigator must rely upon a personal ability to detect the possible presence of accelerants through smell and sight. The sensitivity of the human nose to gasoline vapor appears to be on the order of 1 part per 10 million. As such, the nose is as sensitive as any of the currently available vapor detection equipment. Experienced arson investigators will agree that their noses are as sensitive to gasoline as the equipment available to them. However, not all flammable liquids are gasoline. A factor called olfactory fatigue and the possibility of an arsonist using a strong smelling substance to mask the presence of an accelerant are further reasons why a determination of arson should not rest solely upon detection by smell.

In addition to the sensitivity of the human nose, there are certain visual indicators of arson. These indicators reflect the effects on materials of heating or partial burning, which are used to indicate various aspects of a fire such as rate of development, temperature, duration, time of occurrence, presence of flammable liquids, and points of origin. The interpretation of burn indicators is a principal means of determining the causes of fires. Interpretation of burn patterns is a most common method of establishing arson. Some of the burn indicators are as follows.

Alligator Effect. This is the checkering of charred wood, giving it the appearance of alligator skin. Large, rolling blisters indicate rapid, intense heat, while small, flat alligator marks indicate long, low heat.

Crazing of Glass. This indicator is seen in the formation of irregular cracks in glass due to rapid, intense heat. Crazing suggests a possible fire accelerant.

Depth of Char. The depth of burning wood is used to determine length of burn and thereby locate the point of origin of the fire.

Line of Demarcation. This is the boundary between charred and uncharred material. On floors or rugs, a puddle-shaped line of demarcation is believed to indicate a liquid fire accelerant. In the cross section of wood, a sharp, distinct line of demarcation indicates a rapid, intense fire.

Sagged Furniture Springs. Because of the heat required for furniture springs to collapse from their own weight and because of the insulating effect of the upholstery, sagged springs are believed possible only in either a fire originating inside the cushions or an external fire intensified by a fire accelerant.

Spalling. This is the breaking off of pieces of the surface of concrete, cement, or brick due to intense heat. Brown stains around the spall indicate the use of a fire accelerant.

Arson Checklist

It is difficult, if not impossible, to list all evidence and factual material that may be available to the investigator. The following list highlights the basic areas that should not be overlooked.

Establish That a Fire Occurred.
- The date and time of the burning.
- The address or location where burning occurred (official designation).
- A brief, accurate description of the building structure or premises, including the kind of construction material; the age or approximate age; the dimensions or approximate dimensions.
- The fire station that received the alarm.
- The time that the fire station received the alarm.
- The fire apparatus, if any, that attended the fire, and the time that the fire apparatus was officially in operation.
- The time that the fire apparatus was withdrawn from the burning, or the time that the fire department declared the burning extinguished.
- The official designation of the incident by fire department records.

Establish Value and Ownership.
- The approximate value of the property.
- The insurance coverage on the property, or of items and articles of particular value; data as to mortgages, liens, loans, and the financial status of the suspect; and any action, pending or past, against the suspect or against any member of the suspect's family.

- The inventory of stock, fixtures, equipment, and other items of value within the premises, and the damage as a result of the fire.
- The name of the occupant at the time of the fire; and if the dwelling was vacant, the length of time that the premises had remained unoccupied.
- Alterations or changes made in the building while it was occupied by the last tenant, such as the addition of partitions, electric wiring, or stoves.
- Evidence that any articles were removed from the premises or were recently repaired, altered, or adjusted in any way.
- Evidence indicating who was responsible for the security of the building: who possessed the keys to the building, and who could have had additional keys made.
- Information as to whether windows or doors were normally closed and locked; whether some windows were, of necessity, left unlocked although they were closed; or whether some, or all, of the windows were normally left open.
- The name of the owner of the property, including all aliases.
- The name of the insured.

Collect Information and Evidence.
- The name of the person who discovered the fire, and the person's observations concerning the location(s) in the building where burning or smoke were observed.
- The time that the fire was discovered.
- The circumstances under which the fire was first discovered.
- The name of the person who turned in the alarm.
- The means by which the fire was reported.
- The time interval between the discovery of the fire and the report to the fire department.
- Weather data, such as the atmospheric temperature and the direction of the wind at the time of the burning, and information concerning any electrical storms that may have occurred at that time.
- How the burning occurred, if known.
- The type of burning, e.g., flash fire, explosion, smoldering fire, or rapidly spreading fire; the approximate intensity of the burning; and whether there were separate fires.
- The presence, color, and odor of smoke during the fire.
- The color, height, and intensity of the flames.

•The direction of the air currents within the building during the burning, as deduced from partially burned wallpaper, depth of charring, or soot deposits.

•The quantity of air within the building during the fire, as revealed by the heaviest concentrations of smoke and soot.

•The direction in which the burning spread.

•Significant noises that were noticed before or during the burning.

•The name of the person who was in the building at the time of the burning or who was in the building last.

•The area that suffered the greatest damage.

•The physical evidence discovered.

•Evidence of possible devices or means by which the burning was started, e.g., candle, match, timing device, or flammable material (mechanical, electrical, chemical, or combination of the three).

•Blistered paint, charred wood, melted metal, glass, or other material that may be found at the suspected or known point of origin.

•The presence among the debris of peculiarly colored ashes and clinkers, or traces of paraffin, saturated rags, waste, excelsior, or other fire spreaders.

•The identification of the material burned, e.g., oils or chemicals. (Laboratory examination of samples of soot may supply this information.).

•If a death occurred, all the pertinent data and facts revealed by the autopsy.

•Photographs or sketches of the scene, interior and exterior, during the burning and after the burning was extinguished, supplemented with notes and evidence.

•Photographs and impressions of evidence of forced entry at any of the doors, windows, hatches, skylights, or other points of entry.

•The condition and location of fire-fighting equipment, such as hoses, extinguishers (full or empty), damaged alarm mechanisms, and sprinkler systems.

•Information from inspections of the premises that may have been made prior to the fire. (Such data may be obtained from city or local fire departments, insurance carriers, city or local construction permits and accompanying inspections, and from insurance underwriting groups.).

•Evidence of the careless storing or placing of flammable materials such as gasoline, paint, oils, chemicals, lighter fluid, and cleaning fluid.

•The location and condition of all electric lights, drops, extensions, appliances, and fuses.

•The condition of electric wiring, including exposed wiring; evidence of recent repairs, inside and outside; evidence of splices, connections or alterations, and when, if known, such alterations were made and by whom; load carried by the wires; prescribed load of the fuses through which the lines were fed; and testimony as to whether or not heat was ever noticed in the wires or terminals before the fire.

•The number and type of machines, if any, in the room or building; when they were last used; the amount of power they consumed; and when they were last tested and serviced.

•The number of electric motors in the room or building; how they were safeguarded against dust, debris, and tampering; their horsepower, voltage, and purpose; whether they were of the "open" or "sealed" type; the length of time they were generally in operation, and their defects, if any.

•The condition of gas pipes, bottled gas pipes, steam pipes, air pipes, and water pipes.

•The number and type of stoves within the room or building; whether fires were in the stoves; the kinds of fuel used; the locations of the sources of fuel in relation to the stoves; whether the stoves were self-insulated; when the ashes were last removed; where removed ashes were placed; when the stoves were last cleaned or serviced; and whether they had pilot lights or similar continually burning flame.

•Glass objects that may have accidentally caused the fire by concentrating the rays of the sun.

•The facts pertaining to any suspicious items or devices that may have been found among the debris.

•The methods used to extinguish the burning, e.g., water, foam, and carbon dioxide.

John J. Fay, CPP

Source   Special Agent Manual. (Georgia Bureau of Investigation, State of Georgia, Atlanta, 1979).

AUDIO DETECTORS

Audio detectors are not motion detectors in the same sense as are active or infrared detectors. They do not generate an energy pattern to detect motion, nor do they detect thermal energy emanating from someone in the protected area, as do infrared detectors. Audio detectors listen for audible noises generated by an intruder's forced entry into the protected area or for noises from destructive activities within the area. Since they are often used to detect forced entry, audio detectors can be classified as penetration detectors. However, they are classified here as motion detectors because any noise that satisfies the detector alarm criteria, whether it is associated with penetration or movement, will initiate an alarm.

Audio detectors consist of a number of microphones strategically located within the protected area to listen for sounds in the audio frequency range. These sounds are sent to the signal processor in the control unit. The signal processor includes a manual sound level adjustment for setting the sound level alarm threshold above the normal audible background sounds in the protected area.

In certain applications it is difficult to satisfactorily adjust the sound level threshold for the prevailing background sound levels. If the threshold is set too high above the normal sounds in the protected area, actual intrusion sounds may not be detected. If the threshold is set just above the normal background sounds, exterior noises might exceed the alarm threshold and cause false alarms.

Two signal processing techniques are used to minimize such false alarms from exterior noises. One technique is to use an adjustable pulse counting circuit; the second technique is to use cancellation microphones. Pulse count circuits can be set to initiate an alarm only after counting a selected number of noise bursts or pulses within a specific time period. If there are not a sufficient number of noise pulses within the designated time period to satisfy the alarm criteria, the accumulated pulses will be cancelled after about 10 minutes. The count circuit will then be ready to start counting the next series of noise pulses. This feature reduces false alarms from noises that exist for only a short time such as thunder or back-firing vehicles.

The second technique to reduce false alarms from exterior noises or common interior noises is to use cancellation microphones. Cancellation microphones are installed outside the protected facility or near any interior noise sources to listen for sounds that could be received by the microphones. Signals received by the cancellation microphones are used to cancel the corresponding signals received by the detection microphones. This signal cancellation is accomplished in the signal processor. Typical outside noises that could be cancelled are those from trucks, airplanes, trains, etc., while inside noises might be from compressors, generators, and fans.

Although the pulse count circuits and cancellation microphones do not appreciably affect the detection effectiveness against a low-skill-level intruder, they do reduce the probability of detecting the intruder with a higher skill level. An unskilled intruder, such as someone entering a facility for vandalism, will usually generate sufficient noises while breaking and entering to satisfy the signal processing alarm criteria. However, the more serious threat will be made by an intruder who moves very quietly by exercising patience and caution. In such a case, the intruder may escape detection. This is especially true if cancellation microphones are used and the intruder strikes during the occurrence of loud outside noises such as thunder and high wind.

Audio detectors are available that detect only high frequency sounds generated during forced penetration through masonry construction materials such as cinderblock, brick, and concrete. They can also detect torch cutting or hacksawing through expanded steel grills and steel bars. These materials generate energies over a broad frequency range when they are subjected to forced penetrations or cutting. The frequencies generated during these attacks extend well into the ultrasonic frequency range.

One of the limitations in the application of audio detectors is that audible energies or noises are likely to cause them to go into alarm when they should not. To reduce this vulnerability, these audio detectors use bandpass filters that pass only high frequency signals above 20KHz to the signal processor. Because these detectors will not detect low frequency energies, they should not be used to detect penetrations through soft materials such as sheet rock and wood. Forced penetrations through soft materials may not generate a sufficient quantity of high frequency energy to be detected.

Robert L. Barnard

Source   Barnard, R. L., Intrusion Detection Systems. (Butterworth-Heinemann, Boston, 1982).

AUDITING: GO/NO-GO TESTING BY COMPUTER

For a long time, auditors have wanted a simple go/no-go test. They would like to have a program that could be run against a questioned program, one that would say, okay, or, here is trouble. There are three possible programs to implement. None of the programs do all that is desired, but each can be helpful in special circumstances.

The first is the code-comparison program. It compares production programs, line for line, with other copies that have been stored under secure conditions. It is the actual load modules that are compared. These are also known as object programs and exist in the form of numerical sequences of machine-readable code. In order to instruct the computer, a program must follow this form. The program is written by the programmer; the so-called source program is automatically converted to an object in a process called compilation. This process uses a systems program called a compiler. Compilers exist for computer languages such as COBOL and FORTRAN. By making comparisons with the load modules, we are able to exclude the possibility of someone subverting an applications program by tampering with the compiler.

The disadvantages of using a code-comparison program are twofold. First, to be effective, it should be run each time the object program is loaded into the computer. Code-comparison programs are slow to run and, consequently, their use may incur an unacceptable amount of overtime. More significant is the fact that every time a change is made to the object program, a corresponding change must be made to the program used for comparison. The making of the change, which must be made to the source program, and the recompilation of the exemplar, must be accomplished under secure conditions. This also takes a lot of time and may constitute an unacceptable interruption of the routine work of the data-processing department.

A second kind of go/no-go test may be accomplished by using an integrated test facility (ITF). An ITF consists, in the first instance, of a computer controlled directly by the audit department or by the security department. This computer must be capable of emulating any computer used in the company to process sensitive jobs. Emulation is a software-based procedure that causes one computer to look, operationally, exactly like another. Traditionally, emulators were used when a company bought a newer, larger, and faster computer but did not want to go to the trouble and expense of rewriting all of the company's application programs.

It is then established that a copy of every sensitive applications program used by the company must be deposited with the ITF. Moreover, every time a new program is written or an old one revised, a copy must be sent to the ITF. In a sense, the ITF is a shadow data-processing department even though it need not be capable of large-scale production operations.

With the ITF infrastructure in place, the audit or security department embarks on a continuing program of taking and processing random samples of sensitive production jobs at irregular intervals, and compares the results with the results produced by the regular data-processing departments. Moreover, the ITF may be directly connected to the data-processing department over high-speed data communications lines to enable samples of work to be taken without human intervention, indeed without regular employees even becoming aware that their work is under surveillance. The ITF procedure may expose the most sensitive information of the corporation. It is therefore essential that ITF employees and ITF communications circuits be cleared to the highest level and that the communications circuits be secured, using encryption if necessary. These requirements may substantiate an argument for putting the ITF under operational control of the security department.

The third approach to go/no-go testing is the exact opposite of the integrated test facility. In the ITF, samples of real data were processed through a computer system known to be as correct as possible, and the results were compared with those obtained in regular operations. Presumably, any discrepancy could then be attributed to unauthorized changes having taken place in the operational system.

The third approach uses test decks. A test deck is a simulated job comprised of data specifically contrived to exercise the operational system in all its allowable modes of operation. The results of having run the test deck when the system was new are stored under secure conditions. The same is also true for the test deck. Any discrepancy between a recent run against the test deck and the original run when the system was new can be taken as evidence that unauthorized changes have been made in the operational system.

Just as in the case of the code-comparison program where the standard of comparison must be continually updated to reflect authorized changes, so also must the configuration of the ITF be continually updated as well as the expected results of running the test deck.

Years ago, the most common form of input to a computer was a deck of punched cards, hence the name test deck. Today's test decks may be magnetic tapes, disk packs, floppy or mini disks, decks or prepunched card/badges, or sheaves of documents coded for optical-character-recognition (OCR), magnetic-ink-character-recognition (MICR), or universal packaging code (UPC) scanning.

Test decks are used to:
• Evaluate a system of accounting controls. Do controls exist that will properly reject spurious or erroneous data?
• Test the worst-case limits of applicability. How will the system behave when confronted with zero or negative values, or with extremely high values?
• Discover erroneous logic embedded in the programs. Every case is distinct, but totals should rise when incremented, and fall when decremented. If this not the case in every instance, it should be seen as a symptom that logical errors exist.
• Determine the effectiveness of system controls. Will controls continue to function when faced with a higher rate?
• Evaluate the viability of the user/computer interfaces. Can the integrity of the system survive user errors?
• Find weaknesses in accounting controls that could lead to fraud. The way to do this is to insert potentially fraudulent transactions and observe how the system reacts to them.
• Improve system quality and the effectiveness of controls. Find out what conditions cause unpredicted behavior, and insert program steps to counter them.

These are some of the improprieties that can be uncovered by use of test decks:
• Duplicate payments, which often requires bypassing serial checks.
• Fictitious employees and vendors.
• Ability to pay more than the allowable maximum.

• Payments to former employees and former creditors.
• Employees working under two social security numbers.
• Overtime payments to exempt employees, that is, management or office staff ineligible for overtime pay.
• Credit extended or goods shipped to customers who have exceeded credit limits.
• New employees and new vendors added without authorization.
• Credit customers added without credit check.
• Shipments authorized on insufficient, zero, or negative inventory; or from reserved stock, that is, stock earmarked for specific authorized use.
• Checks issued with a blank amount, or issued with some absurd amount like a million dollars.
• Checks issued with payee blank.
• Payroll checks issued to employees who did not work.
• Unauthorized overtime payments.
• Discounts allowed beyond maximum limit.
• Checks treated as though they were cash.

John M. Carroll

Source Carroll, J.M., Controlling White Collar Crime. (Butterworth-Heinemann, Boston, 1982).

AUTOMATIC TELLER MACHINE SECURITY

Automatic teller machines (ATMs) are one of the more innovative -- and one of the most popular -- new facilities to be offered by banks in recent times. They are also, by nature of being unattended and frequently remotely located, the most vulnerable to criminal attack. A primary concern is limiting access to the ATM (thereby limiting access to individual bank accounts) to only the depositor who owns the account. This is accomplished by using the bank card, which is a plastic card with magnetic-stripe encoding, along with a keypad or keyboard into which the customer's unique number (personal identification number or PIN) must be entered. The fact that this card-plus-keypad system has proven adequate in the ATM application, where there exist both a prime motivation (there is real money in the box) and an ideal opportunity (unattended, frequently remote, and available 24 hours a day), provides a powerful endorsement for the level of security provided by this combination of two simple security systems. In the early days of ATMs there were frequent instances of "jackpotting" through manipulation of the access cards and codes, but the card-plus-PIN technique has now been well proven.

Having thus adequately secured access to the ATM terminal, the remaining electronic exposure in this facility is the telephone wire that carries transaction information to the bank's computer and returns the authorization signal. (In their early days, ATMs were self-contained units that did not have the capability to communicate with the central computer; this eliminated the communications security problem, while raising a number of other problems.) Some institutions have incorporated rudimentary encryption of the information on these lines, but such codes are relatively easily broken or mimicked (the perpetrator listens in on the line for a long enough time to determine what code opens the cash box), and a more sophisticated rolling-key cryptographic system is expensive. There is no such thing as a free lunch.

Many of the risks associated with ATMs are not amenable to solution by electronic security systems. For example, some unauthorized use is by family and friends of the cardholder. There is no electronic system that can ascertain that a person does or does not have the permission of the cardholder to make a withdrawal.

Further, a substantial amount of fraudulent use is by the cardholder. Personal identification systems such as those using fingerprint recognition and other biometric characteristics could be used to limit ATM transactions to the cardholder, but they have thus far proven to be too expensive. Within the next decade such protection may become routine.

The second most common form of ATM fraud is committed by bank employees who are adept at creating fictitious accounts and running cash into them, learning the PINs of actual accounts and making duplicate cards to access them, and other time-tested means that have been used on bank accounts since long before the ATM appeared. These methods of fraud and embezzlement can be prevented by proper systems and procedures within the banking system, and can be detected by the use of an effective auditing software product.

The primary security need of an ATM installation, however, is the physical protection of the machine itself, since the ATM is located outside of any physically protected area, and may in fact be in a remote or even high-crime location. The ATMs must resist physical assault by those who may have a relatively long time to work on the assault unobserved: the same heavy-metal construction and alarm systems that have proven effective on vaults and night depositories are used. The customer and the cash obtained by the customer from the ATM must be protected: a secure and lockable enclosure, closed-circuit television (CCTV) monitoring, adequate lighting, and a call-for-help intercom are usually provided. Finally, the personnel who replenish the cash box and remove the deposits must also be protected: two-person deliveries, radio communications, and other means that are standard within the armored-car industry are used. The provisions for protecting the customer are also useful in protecting the servicing personnel.

Dan M. Bowers

Source Bowers, D.M., Access Control and Personal Identification Systems. (Butterworth-Heinemann, Boston, 1988).

AVIATION SECURITY: AIRLINE TICKET THEFT AND FRAUD

A great deal of confusion exists for the average consumer in purchasing airline tickets. Even for legitimate tickets purchased through reputable travel agencies, the public is aware that a multitude of fares exist to get from point A to point B. The fares may differ not only by carrier and class of service but by advance notice, which days of the week the passenger is traveling, and whether or not the traveler is staying over a Saturday night. It is quite possible for a person who paid $150 for a ticket to be sitting next to someone who paid $500 for the same flight.

Because everyone is looking for the lowest possible fare, passengers have become extremely resourceful in buying tickets. There is a "gray market" in airline tickets. Some of these tickets are great buys, and some will create problems for the purchaser.

An important contribution has certainly been made by the use of available computer memory to identify stolen tickets. If a ticket is listed on an airline's computer as stolen, the airline employee can qualify for a cash reward by retaining the ticket to prevent its use. Many carriers subscribe to TRW's Validata system, which provides its subscribers with the same service. Validata is said to average between 50 and 100 detections per day of forged or stolen tickets, voided credit cards, and bogus checks. British Airways was the first carrier to have used a system known as "TicketCheck," manufactured by Rand McNally & Co., the major manufacturer of airline tickets. TicketCheck is merely a bar-code reader wand that scans the ticket number, air fare box, and other key sections.

Ticket Thefts

Because stolen tickets are so easy to sell, travel agencies have long been plagued with burglaries and armed robberies. The Airlines Reporting Corporation (ARC) reports that the number of travel agents increased from 37,807 in 1990 to 39,424 in 1991. Burglaries of these travel agencies declined from 76 in 1990 to 49 in 1991. The number of tickets stolen in these burglaries declined from 17,131 to 11,843, respectively. In 1990 there were 10 armed robberies of travel agents compared with 13 in 1991. Not only is ticket stock stolen, but validators and validator plates are taken also, so that the tickets will be easier to pass. It has been estimated that each stolen ticket represents an average loss of $800 to the carrier.

Use of Stolen Tickets

The sale of stolen tickets remains highly profitable. The tickets are usually sold to individuals in such places as bars or beauty parlors by fellow patrons who profess to want to do the buyers a favor.

The active pursuit of stolen or fraudulent tickets is often hampered by a mistaken opinion that pervades the airline industry itself. Many believe that if a stolen ticket is used on a flight, the only cost to the airline is the meal served to the freeloading passenger; the plane was flying to the destination anyway, and the seat would probably have been empty otherwise.

This is a highly questionable thesis. Stolen tickets are most attractive at peak travel periods, and a revenue-paying passenger would often have occupied that seat. Stolen tickets can cost the

carrier their full face value in cash; many stolen tickets are resold to professional ticket refund fraud operators.

Also, when the stolen ticket of one airline is used for travel on another and there is no loss-sharing agreement, the issuing airline must reimburse the actual carrier. Where tickets from travel agencies are involved, however, the airline honoring the stolen ticket usually must absorb the loss on the premise that by failing to check the stolen ticket bulletin the airline assumed the risk. Where loss-sharing agreements are in effect, however, all parties suffer loss.

Unreported Ticket Sales

Fraud involving unreported ticket sales occurs more often with ticket agents than airline employees. Discrepancies detected by the airlines are handled as an accounting matter, and agents are invoiced for the value of the unreported tickets. It is worth noting that such unreported sales have often proved to be a prelude to a prime default on the part of the travel agency, and thus should be regarded as a warning signal by the airline.

Ticket fraud by airline employees continues to occupy a major portion of the investigative time of most airline security specialists. The most common fraud method is for a ticket agent to sell a ticket for cash, pocket the money, and destroy the auditor's coupon, usually believing the discrepancy will not be caught. Indeed, the mills of accounting operations often do grind slowly, and the thief may enjoy a run of 2 to 3 months before accounting establishes that there is no auditor's coupon that matches the used ticket. Once a theft has been detected by the accounting process, investigation focuses on identifying the ticket agent.

Counterfeit Tickets

The first counterfeit airline tickets appeared in 1970, mostly in the Pacific and Southeast Asia regions. The first counterfeits were of poor quality and consequently easy to detect. In 1973, prompt action by carriers led to the arrest of four counterfeiting suspects in London. Thus far, the emergence and availability of color copiers has not created counterfeiting problems for the industry, in part because of the alertness of airline carrier personnel in spotting and picking up counterfeit tickets as they are presented for travel or refund.

Altered Tickets

Normally, alteration involves the purchase of a legitimate ticket for a destination a short distance away. Then the ticket is altered to a transcontinental or international flight. This necessarily includes altering the indicated fare to reflect an increased amount. The next step is to get rid of or "launder" the altered ticket as quickly as possible.

Miscellaneous Charges Order (MCO)

Miscellaneous charges orders (MCOs) are issued for air or surface transportation, excess baggage charges, land arrangements for tours, deposits or partial payments for tickets, and for refundable balances. They may be issued to any carrier and, as such, are negotiable documents. Although they cannot be directly used for transportation, they are exchangeable for a ticket or cash.

Ticket-by-Mail (TBM) Fraud

Tickets by mail (TBMs) is an important marketing system. It essentially operates by allowing travelers to make reservations by phone using an established credit line (such as a credit card) and receive their tickets by mail. The system is perverted when callers obtain tickets by providing false information. The fraudulently acquired tickets are then used, sold, or laundered by a process of exchange and refund through other carriers. In some cases, the tickets are presented for refund at the ticket counter of the issuing carrier.

The implementation of precautionary measures has helped airlines limit the losses associated with telephone or mail arrangements. For example, a caller's request to have a ticket mailed to an address other than the billing address of the credit line is routinely refused. Most carriers also require the credit line to be cleared or to receive some other form of payment before the ticket is placed into the mail.

The normal avenue of prosecution of TBM fraud offenders is through the federal criminal justice system. In many cases the pre-prosecution investigations are coordinated with the Postal Inspection Service when the fraud involves controlled deliveries of tickets. The decision to prosecute, however, is often declined by the U.S. Attorney's Office. Many prosecuting attorneys feel that the victim airline is a contributor to the fraud by mailing out tickets on the basis of a phone call and therefore should be prepared to absorb the loss. They are reluctant, as they put it, to be "used as a collection agency" for the airlines.

Prepaid Ticket Advice (PTA) Fraud

A prepaid ticket advice (PTA) occurs when a passenger calls to order a ticket, gives his or her name, credit card number, and other authorizing information, and asks that the ticket be held for pickup at the airport, often in the name of a person other than the card holder. The perpetrator of this kind of fraud obtains the legitimate credit card information of another individual.

The best precaution, exercised by some carriers, is to require the individual ordering the PTA to come in to a ticket office or airline ticket counter and complete the transaction, usually paying an additional fee for the PTA service. This provides an airline employee the opportunity to check identification and verify the transaction.

Refund Fraud

Not all stolen ticket blanks are used for travel. The individual who holds the ticket may fill it out for substantial travel and attempt to obtain a refund. For this reason, it is essential that all tickets presented for refund be checked through the computer or against blacklists to make certain that they are not stolen tickets. If a ticket was purchased with a credit card, the card number should also be checked.

In the case of refunds, floor limits should be established to ensure that refunds over a specific dollar amount will be processed through the airline accounting office and paid by check. If a check or draft issued in payment of a refund provides space for the signature and address of the payee, the agent—without fail—should witness the filling-in of this information by the payee. This requirement is in addition to the agent's responsibility for positively identifying the individual presenting the ticket for refund and for determining that a refund is legally due.

If refund drafts or checks are mailed, they should at least be sent by certified mail. The best method is to send all refund requests to the home office refund department, where receipt of payment for the ticket can be confirmed prior to issuing the refund.

On occasion, the auditing department will become aware that an employee is falsely claiming to have refunded a ticket for a passenger. In some cases, employees have taken tickets from passengers as they boarded or from the ticket lift, and made refunds to themselves on tickets that belonged to passengers who actually flew. This version of pocketing is best controlled by mailing sampling letters to passengers shown to have received a refund. If the passenger denies having received a refund and claims to have flown as planned, investigation should begin. The use of these sampling letters on a continuing basis will usually isolate dishonest employees before they can do a great amount of damage.

Applicable Laws

Under Title 18, Section 2314, Interstate Transportation of Stolen Property (ITSP), the FBI is authorized to investigate the interstate transportation of "stolen goods, securities, moneys, fraudulent State tax stamps, or articles used in counterfeiting."

The definition of the word "securities" is given in Section 2311 as including "any note stock certificate, bond debenture, check, draft, warrant, traveler's check, letter of credit, warehouse receipt, negotiable bill of lading, evidence of indebtedness" and numerous other "securities," but airline tickets are not specifically named. Although legislation has been proposed from time to time to correct this, none has yet been passed. Under the ITSP statute, the aggregate amount of loss must be more than $5000.

Prosecutions relating to airline tickets can be supported under a number of federal statutes. Among them are: Fraud by Wire, 18 U.S.C. 1343; Mail Fraud, 18 U.S.C. 1341; Consumer Protection, 15 U.S.C. 1644; Theft from Interstate Shipment, 18 U.S.C. 659; Interstate Transportation of Stolen

Property, 18 U.S.C. 2314, 2315; Crime on a Government Reservation, 18 U.S.C. 7 and applicable enclave statutes; and the Electronic Funds Transfer Act, 18 U.S.C. 1951(a), (b)(1).

Kenneth C. Moore

Source Moore, K.C., Airport, Aircraft and Airline Security. (Butterworth-Heinemann, Boston, 1991).

AVIATION SECURITY: GUIDELINES FOR CORPORATE AND GENERAL AVIATION

Background

This document is intended for use primarily by the professional security staff of a business enterprise that owns and operates aircraft in support of its corporate goals. However, it may also be useful to owners of general aviation aircraft desiring guidelines for improving the security of their investment.

Corporate aircraft operators are not exempt from criminal activities and, although extremely unlikely, from attempts by terrorists to promote a particular cause through exploitation of the company's aviation assets. The military-defense-industrial complex, international corporations with operations in countries with civil unrest, corporations whose products and operations are of a controversial nature, and corporations experiencing labor unrest are all potential targets for acts of air piracy, sabotage, extortion, bombings, and other criminal acts. The safe operation of corporate aircraft must equate security planning with flight planning. Responsibility for the security of aircraft rests with the aircraft owner or operator. This responsibility is not affected by the type of aircraft or its use.

Airport operators are required, in most cases, to provide for the physical security of the air operations area as an integral part of their overall responsibility for the operation of that airport. These guidelines are intended to complement these efforts, where possible, and direct the user at all times to coordinate their efforts with the responsible airport operator.

The first line of defense against threats to the safety of corporate aircraft operations is the protection against unauthorized access to the aircraft and ground support facilities or areas.

Aircraft owners and operators who are involved in establishing or maintaining protective measures for corporate aircraft should also consider the presence or absence of an airport security program, as required by regulations of the Federal Aviation Administration (FAA).

General Considerations

A corporate security plan should be a written document detailing positive measures to protect the aircraft at its home base, inflight, and at airports where the aircraft is parked during a transit status. Access to the plan should be limited to those who have an operational need to know, in order to preserve its integrity.

A security awareness program in a corporate aviation department should be established to promote initial and recurrent security training of all personnel — clerical, maintenance personnel, and flight crews — not just the employees who are directly responsible for security. System testing should also be an integral part of the program and should include all elements of the plan.

The security plan must have the full support of the chief executive officer of the organization, and those responsible for it should be held accountable for its success to the same degree as in other corporate efforts.

Basic Aircraft Protection Measures

I.   Where possible, the aircraft should be parked in a locked or guarded hangar.

A.   Dependence upon a locked hangar for protection should include strict access control.

B.   Placement of an aircraft within a hangar does not eliminate the necessity for securing the aircraft.

II.   Security of an unattended aircraft may be improved through the use of devices such as special anti-tampering tape on doors, windows, ports, and inspection plates that -- once applied -- cannot be removed under normal conditions. Tape that is weatherproof, heat resistant, and available with self-destroying slits will enhance the tamper-detection capability.

III.   Due to the widespread unauthorized possession of master keys to manufacturer-installed locks, and the possibility of loss of key

control with the passage of time, the security of manufacturer-installed locks may not always be assured. If in doubt, consideration should be given to the replacement of the locks on corporate aircraft with high-quality, professionally installed locks.

Reminder: Positive key control is used to protect many valuable corporate assets; the flight department contains or transports many of them and should, therefore, be subject to the highest control standards in the corporation.

IV.   All avionics and removable items in the aircraft should be marked for positive identification.

A.   Positive identification of each item is an absolute necessity to facilitate investigative and recovery efforts.

B.   A color marking, in addition to engraved aircraft registration numbers, or any other unique identifying numbers or symbols, is recommended. The engraved marking provides a means of positive identification and the color marking provides a significant theft-deterrent value.

V.   Non-installed items of value or of unusual interest should not be stored in the aircraft if it is to be unattended for any extended period of time. If storage in the aircraft is absolutely necessary, these items should be secured.

VI.   A thorough inventory of the contents of the aircraft should be maintained on file at its home base. The inventory should include serial numbers and other identifying data. Color photographs of the aircraft exterior and interior spaces should also be maintained.

VII.   Consideration should be given to the use of anti-theft devices such as alarms or removable wheel locks. While such devices are not foolproof, they provide a deterrent and could result in a diversion of an attack on an unprotected aircraft. Such devices may also bring about an early detection and apprehension by authorities. This is an especially important consideration at airports where the corporate aircraft will remain unattended overnight when the aircraft is not hangared.

VIII.   The display of corporate logos and product or organizational identification media is not recommended.

IX.   Aircraft parked on the ramp should always be parked in a well-illuminated area and away from perimeter gates and fencing.

X.   Positive identification of all passengers is a must. If a passenger is not a known corporate official or guest, identification and trip authorization should be verified before the individual is allowed access to the aircraft.

XI. Safeguards should be established assuring that all baggage to be loaded on board the aircraft matches those passengers on board, and that the baggage was not left unattended and accessible prior to its loading.

XII. Safeguards should be established for cargo to be transported on board the aircraft to assure that each package is received from a known source and has been authorized by the flight department.

XIII. Procedures should be established for the search of passengers, baggage, and packages or cargo in the event that credible threats are received, or in the event of other questionable circumstances.

XIV. All persons working on the aircraft should be positively identified, especially at airports where other than corporate employees are called upon to perform maintenance or repair work.

XV. The pre-flight inspection should include efforts to detect foreign objects and evidence of tampering with the aircraft.

XVI. Crew vigilance should be heightened while the aircraft is being refueled by persons representing a company that does not normally do business with the flight department.

XVII. Once engines are started, be suspicious of any attempts to delay, stop, or otherwise impede the departure from other than air traffic control (ATC) authorities.

Home Base Security Considerations

I.   Hangar the aircraft whenever possible.

II. Designate the hangar as a closed or restricted area and control access into it from the public side of the airport.

A.   Depending upon the size of the flight department, use corporate identification badges unless precluded by an airport authority operating under an approved FAA security program.

B.   Unless under escort, visitors should not be permitted into the hangar area where aircraft are stored, or in the immediate ramp area where the aircraft are readied for flight.

C.   Pedestrian doors to the hangar should deny access to unauthorized persons. Doors that open into an office area should be designated for passengers, visitors, or delivery access to the flight department.

1.   Consider establishment of a waiting lounge for passengers to wait until boarding is announced, or pending identification and approval for boarding.

2.   If large, air-side hangar doors are left open for ventilation, expansion-type barriers should be deployed to delay unauthorized access into the hangar area.

3.   Where possible, visual observation of the hangar and ramp parking areas should be maintained.

D.   All unauthorized personnel should be challenged. Suspicious individuals should be immediately reported to the supporting law enforcement agency.

E.   An alarm system is recommended to protect the hangar during unoccupied periods. Guards with adequate communications equipment offer added protection of extremely valuable or threatened assets.

F.   Employee and non-employee parking should be separated.

III. The air side should be physically separated from the public side in the vicinity of the hangar. A 7-foot chain link fence with a three-stranded barbed wire overhang is the minimum recommended.

A.   Vehicle parking, or the storage of items on the ground, within 20 feet of the perimeter fence should be prohibited, as such objects provide an easy means to go over the fence.

B.   Outside illumination of the hangar and immediate fencing is highly recommended.

C.   Consideration should be given to lease provisions allowing control of the ramp areas where corporate aircraft are parked or are readied for flight. The controlled area should be sufficient to provide a buffer zone between the aircraft and non-controlled access areas. The marking of a controlled area as a restricted area is sometimes accomplished by lines and symbols painted on the ramp surface.

Note: Markings applied to a ramp area are very often subject to requirements set by the FAA and the airport operator. The latter should be consulted prior to applying any permanent ramp markings.

IV. A policy should be established and enforced requiring passengers to board through the operations office or passenger lounge, and, except for maintenance and service support, prohibiting vehicles on the ramp side.

When cargo must be transported to the aircraft, flight department personnel should admit the vehicle to the ramp only after verification of authenticity of the shipment and the driver, and, following that, accompany the delivery van to the aircraft.

V. Positive access controls should be enforced, including the positive identification and recording of all visitors.

VI. Assure that a comprehensive emergency or bomb threat plan is in effect and that the telephone numbers of the airport's supporting law enforcement agency and explosive ordnance disposal resources are readily available.

VII. Ensure that the facility is periodically visited by the airport's supporting law enforcement patrols.

Remain-Over-Night (RON) Airport Considerations

I. Prior to any departure from the home base, the servicing fixed-base operator (FBO) at any remain-over-night (RON) airport should be contacted in advance and advised of any unusual security requirements needed to protect the aircraft while at that airport

II. Consideration should be given to providing the flight crew with the telephone number of the law enforcement agency having jurisdiction at the RON airport and the telephone number of the nearest FAA security office.

III. Aircraft should be hangared whenever possible. If it is not, the aircraft should be parked in a well-illuminated area away from perimeter gates and fencing.

A. In threat conditions, especially outside the United States, arrangement for a guard on the aircraft should be considered a necessity.

IV. When taxiing to the parking location, a non-flying crewmember should carefully scan the area to detect any unusual conditions.

V. The flight crew should visit the aircraft at least once daily at RON airports to inspect the aircraft and assure that it is properly secured and that there are no signs of tampering.

VI. The keys to the aircraft should never be left with the FBO unless they are properly secured and controlled to the satisfaction of the pilot in command.

VII. If maintenance or repairs are required of a firm not normally providing services to the flight department, a flight crew member should be present, and the repairperson should be positively identified as an employee of the servicing firm.

VIII. A security inspection of the aircraft to detect tampering or foreign objects is vital prior to any departure from a RON airport.

In-Flight Security Considerations

I. Flight crews should frequently review plans developed by the security department to handle in-flight emergencies and threats. Plans of action should include actions to take in the event of a bomb threat, attempted hijacking, or terrorist attack. These plans should be consistent, to the greatest extent possible, with those plans developed to protect other corporate assets from similar threats.

II. If the cockpit is separated by a door from the cabin, unauthorized personnel should not be permitted into the cockpit.

III. In the event of a hijacking (air piracy):

A. A special emergency condition exists when a hostile act is threatened or committed by a person(s) aboard an aircraft that jeopardizes the safety of the aircraft or its passengers.

B. The pilot of an aircraft reporting a special emergency condition should:

1. If circumstances permit, apply distress or urgency radio telephone procedures and include the details of the special emergency.

2. If circumstances do not permit the use of prescribed distress or urgency procedures, transmit on the air/ground frequency in use at the time as many of the following elements as possible, spoken distinctly and in the following order:

a) Name of the station addressed (time and circumstances permitting).

b) The identification of the aircraft and present position.

c) The nature of the special emergency condition and pilot intentions (circumstances permitting).

d) If unable to provide this information, use code words and/or transponder codes that will alert air traffic controllers to the emergency.

Note: The transponder codes and code words are available to responsible officials of the flight department from the nearest FAA security office. Flight crews should be thoroughly familiar with their meaning and use. Mistaken use of these codes and code words will result in a great deal of inconvenience to air traffic controllers and the responsible crew member.

C. If it is possible to do so without jeopardizing the safety of the flight, the pilot of a hijacked aircraft, after departing from the cleared routing over which the aircraft was operating, will attempt to perform one or more of the following, circumstances permitting.

1. Maintain a true airspeed of no more than 400 knots, and preferably an altitude of between 10,000 and 25,000 feet.

2. Fly a course toward the destination that the hijacker has announced.

D. If these procedures result in either radio contact or air intercept, the pilot will attempt to comply with any instructions received that may direct him/her to an appropriate landing field.

E. In the event of a hijacking or any other disturbance, or upon learning an unauthorized person may be aboard the aircraft, the flight crew should:

1. Get the aircraft on the ground under any pretext.

2. Get the passengers and then the flight crew off the aircraft, if possible.

3. Allow the law enforcement authorities to deal with the hijackers or other disturbances.

IV. Flight crew briefing for bomb threat search procedures and in-flight and hijack incident management procedures are available to responsible officials of the flight department from the nearest FAA security office.

Law Enforcement Considerations

I. Theft, damage, or destruction of general aviation (including corporate) aircraft, or contents thereof, is a criminal offense over which the law enforcement agency having jurisdiction where the offense was committed has primary jurisdiction. All such offenses should be promptly reported to that agency for investigation and prosecution.

II. The interstate transportation of a stolen aircraft is a violation of Title 18 of the U.S. Code, and is a federal offense investigated by the FBI. Such offenses may be reported directly to the local FBI office or reported through the local law enforcement agency.

III. Arson, malicious damaging, destruction, disablement, or wrecking of any civil aviation aircraft used, operated, or employed in interstate, overseas, or foreign air commerce; or any aircraft engine, propeller, appliance, or spare part with intent to damage, destroy, disable, or wreck any such aircraft; or with like intent, placement of a destructive substance in, upon, or in proximity to any such aircraft or components or times used in connection with the operation of the aircraft or components or times used in connection with the operation of the aircraft or cargo carried; or with like intent wrecks, damages, destroys, disables, or places a destructive substance in or upon or in proximity to support facilities used in connection with the operation; or with like intent, willfully incapacitates any member of the crew of such aircraft, is a violation of Title 18, U.S. Code, and is a federal offense investigated by the FBI. (Note: the aircraft must be employed in interstate, foreign, or overseas air commerce).

Forgery of Certificates and False Marking of Aircraft. Any forgery, counterfeiting, alteration, or false marking of a certificate issued under the authority of the Federal Aviation Act and/or the willful display of markings that are false or misleading as to the nationality of registration of the aircraft are federal criminal offenses under Title 49, U.S. Code, and are investigated by the Civil Aviation Security Division, FAA.

Interference with air navigation through display of a light or signal in such a manner to be mistaken for a true signal in connection with an airport or other air navigation facility, or any removal, extinguishing of, or interference with the operation of any such true light or signal is a federal criminal offense under Title 49, U.S. Code, and is investigated by the FAA.

Interference with flight crew members while aboard an aircraft within the special aircraft jurisdiction of the United States by assaults, intimidation, or threats so as to interfere with the performance by such member of his/her duties or lessen the ability of the flight crew member to perform his/her duties is a federal offense under Title 49, U.S. Code, and is investigated by the FBI.

Aircraft piracy, i.e., any seizure or exercise of control, by force or violence, or threat of force or violence with wrongful intent, of an aircraft within the special aircraft jurisdiction of the United States is a federal criminal offense, punishable by death or imprisonment for not less than 20 years.

Guidelines for International Travel

I.   Prior to the start of any foreign trips, consult with the Department of State Travel Advisory Service and provide a briefing for all persons on board before the flight.

II.   When traveling to an area of economic strife, make advanced arrangements to provide for a reliable contract guard service.

III. Know the telephone numbers of the nearest U.S. Embassy or consulate and, if unsure of any political, economic, or other local factors that might affect security, contact them directly before departure.

IV.   Advise all crew members and passengers enroute to a foreign location to be cautious when accepting gifts or packages of which the contents are unknown.   Query all aboard prior to departure of their knowledge of all personal or business-related goods acquired outside of the United States.

V.   Physically inspect all goods for which any uncertainty exists.

Federal Aviation Administration

Source   Security Guidelines for Corporate and General Aviation. (Federal Aviation Administration and U.S. Department of State, Washington, DC, 1992).

AVIATION SECURITY: PROTECTION OF AIRLINES AND AIRPORTS

Historical Perspective

The era of hijackings came into its own in 1968. Prior to that time there had been only 12 U.S. hijackings since 1930, but in 1968 there were 22 hijackings or "skyjackings" as they were called. Nineteen of those were to Cuba. The skyjackings peaked in 1969 and began to taper off in 1970 and 1971.

The first major use of hijacking as an instrument of international terror occurred in 1970 when terrorists hijacked a TWA 707 on a flight from Frankfurt, a Swissair DC-8 on a flight from Zurich, and a Pan Am 747 on a flight from Amsterdam. The fourth plane to be hijacked was a BOAC VC-10. The Pan Am plane was blown up on the ground in Cairo. The other three were flown to Jordan where nearly 500 passengers and crew suffered 6 days of confinement in the plane before being allowed to exit. The three planes were then blown up.

On the day before Thanksgiving in 1971, Dan Cooper hijacked a Northwest Orient 727 out of Portland, Oregon, and parachuted from the tail stairs with a ransom of $200,000. There were other parachutist hijackers who were given money as a result of extortion threats to blow up aircraft.

Others, such as felons fleeing prosecution, committed hijackings.   During this time, passengers were screened only if they met a profile and were designated as "selectees." After two particularly brutal hijackings in October and November 1972, President Nixon ordered mandatory 100% screening for all passengers beginning January 5, 1973.   The hijackings decreased dramatically, but still occurred.

After 125,000 Marielitos came to the United States on a 5-month-long boat lift from Cuba in 1980, a number of them began hijacking aircraft to go back to Cuba.   These were known as the "homesick Cuban" hijackings and the weapon of choice was usually a bottle filled with flammable liquid. These hijackings got so numerous that the FAA broadcast radio and television commercials in English and Spanish to dissuade the Cubans from further attempts.

Other Incidents

In addition to the hijackings, there were attacks on airport terminals. The first of these occurred in May 1972 at Lod Airport, Tel Aviv.   Three Japanese passengers debarking from an Air France Flight picked up their luggage from a conveyor belt, unzipped them, and took out automatic weapons.   They began firing and lobbing grenades at the crowd in the waiting room. Twenty-five were killed and 76 wounded.

On December 27, 1985, airport attacks at Rome and Vienna occurred within 5 minutes of each other.   At Rome's Leonardo da Vinci Airport, terrorists sprayed bullets at passengers waiting to check in for an El Al flight and others at nearby Pan Am and TWA counters. The toll was 15 dead and 74 wounded. A few minutes later an attack began at Vienna's Schwechat Airport. The toll there was 3 dead and 47 wounded.

While over the years there have been numerous terrorist incidents involving airlines and airports, a few should not be forgotten, if only for the lessons learned.

June 27, 1976, Entebbe, Uganda. An Air France flight from Tel Aviv to Athens and Paris was hijacked by armed terrorists out of Athens. They demanded the release of 53 terrorists in custody in five countries. The terrorists released 150 to 250 hostages. On July 3, Israeli commandos successfully carried out a spectacular rescue operation. Three of the remaining hostages were killed during the attack. Thirty individuals were killed and 42 were injured during the entire incident.

October 13, 1977. Lufthansa Flight 181, Mogadishu, Somalia.. During this 110-hour hijacking, the West German government refused to bow to the demands of the hijackers. In a daring raid on October 18, reminiscent of Entebbe, West German commandos freed 82 passengers and four crewmembers, and killed three of the four hijackers.

June 14, 1985. TWA Flight 847, Athens to Rome. TWA Flight 847, enroute from Athens to Rome with 145 passengers, was hijacked by two terrorists and flown to Beirut. A third terrorist had been unable to get a seat and was not allowed to board. The terrorists demanded the release of over 776 Shi'ite prisoners held in Israeli jails. At the first stop in Beirut, 19 women and children were released. The plane began to shuttle from Beirut to Algiers to Beirut to Algiers and back to Beirut, all between Friday, June 14, and Sunday, June 16. At the first Algiers stop, which lasted 5 hours, 21 more passengers were released. The plane then flew back to Beirut.

It was there that U.S. Navy diver Robert Stethem, age 23, was beaten, murdered and his body thrown out onto the tarmac. About a dozen additional hijackers were brought on board and six or eight passengers with Jewish-sounding names were removed. Then the plane flew back to Algiers. The hijackers released three hostages

on arrival and after negotiations with Algerian officials, they released 58 others. Then, the plane went to Beirut for the third time. Finally, 39 of the original 153 passengers and crew remained. Those hostages were taken to locations in Beirut while the three-man crew was kept on board. Seventeen days after the hijacking began, the hostages were released.

On January 15, 1987, Mohammed Ali Hamadi, age 22, was arrested at Frankfurt airport trying to enter West Germany with liquid explosives concealed in liquor bottles. He was charged with the hijacking and has subsequently admitted his role, denying however, the killing of Stethem. On May 17, 1989, Hamadi was convicted by the Hesse State Supreme Court and sentenced to life imprisonment for hijacking, murder, and possession of explosives.

April 2, 1986. TWA Flight 840, Rome to Athens, Explosion. TWA Flight 840, enroute from Rome to Athens, experienced an in-flight explosion as it descended through 15,000 feet over Greece, preparatory to landing at Athens. The explosion tore a 9 by 4 foot hole in the side of the fuselage and killed four Americans, including an 8-month old girl. A bomb had been placed under seat 10F. Police centered their investigation on a Lebanese woman who had flown from Beirut to Cairo on March 25 and from Cairo to Athens on the same plane on the morning of April 2 and had sat in seat 10F. She had arrived late for the flight and had been driven to the plane in an airline car rather than on a bus. Airport officials said she was thoroughly searched even though she arrived late.

The Izzeddin Qassam unit of the Arab Revolutionary Cells, which in turn is linked to Palestinian renegade Abu Nidal, claimed responsibility. They said it was in retaliation for U.S. missile attacks on Libyan targets the previous month during the showdown over the right of foreign ships to use the waters of the Gulf of Sidra.

September 5, 1986. Pan Am Flight 73, Karachi, Pakistan. Four Arab males, dressed as security people and driving a vehicle similar to a security vehicle with a flashing amber light, were allowed to drive to a 747 loading passengers for Frankfurt to join those already enroute from Bombay. They stormed the aircraft with weapons, firing numerous shots in the process.

One of the controversies surrounding this incident was that the cockpit crew became aware of what was occurring and immediately escaped, leaving the hijackers with 13 flight service personnel and over 300 passengers as hostages. Some felt the crew should have stayed. However, most authorities strongly supported their action.

Early into the hijacking, a businessman from California was shot and his body was dropped onto the tarmac. The climax of the 16-hour hijacking occurred when the plane's auxiliary power unit, which powers the lights and air conditioning, failed. Not realizing what had caused the lights to go out, the hijackers apparently panicked. They began spraying the aircraft with automatic weapons fire and detonating grenades into the center area of the aircraft where all the hostages had been gathered. At least 22 were killed and more than 100 were injured. Pakistani commandos did not respond until after all but the very seriously wounded had departed the aircraft. Intelligence indicated that the Abu Nidal group was responsible. As a postscript, the two security guards who allowed the terrorists onto the field were sentenced to one year in prison for their negligence.

December 7, 1987. PSA Flight 1771, Los Angeles to San Francisco. David Burke was fired from USAir on November 19, 1987, after being caught on camera stealing $69 in liquor receipts. The Friday before the incident, Burke had held his girlfriend and her 6-year-old daughter at gunpoint on a forced 6-hour drive. Burke boarded Flight 1771 after bypassing screening as a familiar airline employee, using airline identification, which had not been turned in when he was terminated. Over Paso Robles, California, he shot his target, Raymond Thomson, the USAir Customer Service Manager in Los Angeles. He then shot the cockpit crew, causing the aircraft to crash. All 43 people on board were killed. This incident was primarily responsible for the adoption of an FAA regulation requiring a computerized access control system at airports.

December 21, 1988. Pan Am Flight 103, Lockerbie, Scotland. Pan Am Flight 103, which originated at Frankfurt and was enroute to New York, exploded in the air over Lockerbie, Scotland, about one hour out of London. The explosion killed 258 passengers and crew, and another 11 people were killed on the ground. A

double detonator device was used; the first trigger was activated by barometric pressure and in turn activated a timing device. This type of device is believed to have been designed to thwart the airline practice of putting cargo through a pressure chamber to activate barometric triggers.

This incident aroused particular controversy because of an anonymous call received at the U.S. Embassy in Helsinki on December 5, 1988, advising that sometime within the next 2 weeks a bombing would be attempted against a Pan Am flight from Frankfurt to New York. The information was given to American diplomatic missions in Europe and the Middle East and to Pan Am, but not to the general public.

November 27, 1989. Avianca Flight 203, Bogota. A bomb placed under a seat exploded, killing 107. A new word, "narcoterrorism," was born.

Airline and Airport Responsibilities

The federal government has charged the air carriers with the responsibility for screening passengers and for the safety of their baggage and cargo. Air carrier regulations require each carrier to have in place a security program designed to "prevent or deter the carriage aboard airplanes of any explosive, incendiary, or a deadly or dangerous weapon on/or about each individual's person or accessible property and the carriage of any explosive or incendiary in checked baggage."

Initially the carriers wrote their own programs to carry out the FAA directives. The confusion and inequities of that system became immediately apparent and the carriers got together and wrote the Air Carrier Standard Security Program (ACSSP), which was agreed to by the FAA and adopted by all carriers. Each carrier was still free to determine how to adapt the program to company operations.

Like the carriers' ACSSP, each airport is required to submit a security plan to FAA for approval. In general, the airport operator is responsible for the security of the airport, the air operations area (except for areas exclusive to a carrier), and for providing law enforcement support.

A new section of the law requires most airports to install a computerized access control system. This requirement was the outgrowth of the downing of PSA Flight 1771 by David Burke.

The imposition of this requirement has been a highly controversial one among airport operators.

Screening of Passengers and Carry-on Luggage. It is the air carrier's responsibility to screen passengers and their carry-on luggage. In almost every case in the United States, this is accomplished by contract baggage screeners. Passengers are screened for carrying metal by walking through a metal detector. Carry-on items are generally screened by X-ray, although in some small airports, a hand search is still conducted.

Explosives Detection. In the early years of the screening program the emphasis was directed toward thwarting hijackers. Thus, screening equipment was designed to detect metal and show where guns and knives were located. Now the threat has shifted from hijacking to explosives. Some of the old screening methodologies and technology have had to be modified to meet the new threat. The FAA is doing a considerable amount of research into explosive detection systems (EDS). One of the most controversial ones has been the TNA (thermal neutron activation) device. In August 1989, the FAA issued an order requiring airlines to install EDS at about 15 U.S. and 25 foreign airports. TNA, which costs about $1 million per system, was strongly recommended. There were questions about the effectiveness of TNA and the carriers fought the recommendation. The President's Commission on Aviation Security and Terrorism agreed with the carriers and their recommendation to hold off on future proposals was enacted into the Aviation Security Improvement Act of 1990.

It appears now that future EDS methods will rely on several technologies rather than just one. X-ray is being shown to be a useful adjunct to other detection devices, particularly when used with new technology that displays organic and inorganic material in separate colors. Most manufacturers are now using two monitors, one color and one black and white, in order to provide for backscatter imaging, another technology that greatly enhances the ability to detect explosives with X-ray.

Technology that was initially rejected as being too slow to process the large numbers of bags required is now being utilized to provide further screening for bags that may have caused one type of detector to alarm or that aroused suspicion on an X-ray. By narrowing the target to just a few bags, more time can be taken for closer examination.

At the current time, only checked bags destined for international travel are routinely screened. There are no immediate plans to institute screening of checked bags on domestic flights. This could change if technology improves significantly, or if there is a serious incident resulting from an explosion in hold baggage.

Another method used to reduce the risk of a bomb being placed on a flight is passenger/baggage reconciliation. Particularly in the case of Pan Am 103, the President's Commission stated, "The undisputed facts before the Commission show that passenger/baggage reconciliation is a bedrock component of any heightened security system." The purpose of passenger/baggage reconciliation is to prevent unaccompanied bags from being placed on a flight; the theory being, that a terrorist is less likely to place a bomb on an aircraft where he or she is a passenger. The ACSSP now requires both a positive match and an X-ray or a hand search of all checked baggage in specific designated countries.

International Law

The International Civil Aviation Organization (ICAO), formed in Chicago in 1944, took no action on air piracy until June 1970, and even omitted the problem in its 1963 Convention on Offenses and Certain Other Acts Committed Onboard Aircraft. The 1970 ICAO action was a resolution condemning all acts of violence directed against personnel, airports, and facilities, and it called for strengthening existing extradition arrangements.

Efforts to achieve multilateral action through international law have met with some success, and the United States is a signatory to the three agreements developed so far. The first, the *Convention on Offenses and Certain Other Acts Committed on Board Aircraft* (the Tokyo Convention of September 1963), the so-called "Crimes Aboard Aircraft Convention," contained a commitment by the party nations to take custody of the perpetrators of criminal acts aboard aircraft and expedite the continued journey of the aircraft, its crew and its passengers. Some 123 nations are parties to this treaty, including the United States.

The second treaty, the *Convention for Suppression of Unlawful Seizure of Aircraft* (the

Hague Convention of December 1970), commonly referred to as the "Hijacking Convention," provides that party nations, some 128 in number, will apprehend and prosecute or extradite hijackers and ensure that hijacking is subject to severe penalties. The Hague Convention was implemented in the United States on August 5, 1974, as Public Law 93-366. Title I is known as the Anti-Hijacking Act of 1974, and Title II, the Air Transportation Security Act of 1974. It significantly changed the Federal Aviation Act of 1958.

The third treaty, the *Convention for the Suppression of Unlawful Acts Against the Safety of Civil Aviation* (the Montreal Convention of September 1971), usually cited as the "Sabotage Convention," calls for apprehension and prosecution or extradition of aircraft saboteurs, and severe penalties. It calls on the 128 party nations to take all practicable measures to prevent sabotage and to forewarn all affected nations of such offenses when it has reason to believe they will be committed.

The need for enforcement strength continued until July 1978 when Canada pressed for a joint declaration by the seven economic powers convened in Bonn, Switzerland. The so-called Bonn Declaration, the only affirmative agreement reached at that summit, asserted that Canada, the Federal Republic of Germany, France, Italy, Japan, the United Kingdom, and the United States were intensifying their joint efforts to combat international terrorism by agreeing to cease all flights to any country that refused to extradite or prosecute hijackers or did not return a hijacked aircraft, and to halt all incoming flights from any country by the flag airline of the offending nation. The President's Commission on Aviation Security and Terrorism has recommended that the signatories to the Bonn Declaration adopt an annex declaring that members would also halt air services in cases of unpunished attacks at airports and airline ticket offices. The Tokyo Summit Statement on International Terrorism, issued May 5, 1986, committed the heads of the seven major democracies to "make maximum efforts to fight against the scourge" of terrorism.

Kenneth C. Moore

Sources

Moore, K.C., Airport, Aircraft and Airline Security. (Butterworth-Heinemann, Boston, 1991).

Report of the President's Commission on Aviation Security and Terrorism. (U.S. Government Printing Office, Washington, DC, 1990).

B

BACKGROUND CHECKS: RECORD SEARCHES

Background checks refer to a wide variety of investigations into the history of a job applicant. A background check can be as simple as a single call to a previous employer, or it can involve weeks of exhaustive work by investigators building a full biography of an individual. In the private sector, background checks take two forms: confirmatory, in which an employer makes calls to verify information an applicant has provided about his or her educational, military, and employment history; and investigative, where an employer digs for information that an applicant might try to hide, such as previous terminations or a criminal history.

Getting Started

Types of Records. There are many sources of public information available to employers, in both public and private records. State and county regulations sometimes limit an employer's access to information in public records, or limit the use of information found. It is important to know the local laws and stay within them.

There are two types of information sources: government agencies and private industry data banks. Government sources include police and court records, military records, professional licenses, social security records, and a host of others. Private data banks are numerous and generally comprehensive. They include credit histories, association memberships, education records, telephone numbers, and utility records.

Preparing for the Background Check. The burden of the search and the risk of breaking the law can be reduced in three important ways.

First, have the applicant sign a release authorizing the employer to obtain -- and make the hiring decision based on -- information from public records. These releases protect the employer and also warn potential applicants. If an applicant is providing fraudulent information, the applicant may decide to withdraw the application.

In using the release, the employer needs to remember that the majority of applicants are honest and that care should be taken to not offend them. The fraudulent applicant will understand the reason behind the polite presentation of the release, and will react accordingly.

Second, the employer should get adequate information from the applicant. Within reason, the more complete the information, the better. It will help to go over the background information with the applicant to make sure the information is accurate and complete. Check for full names, complete social security and driver's license numbers, full addresses, and a full employment history going back 5 years with no gaps; then use that information to do the background checks.

Third, gear the search to verification of the data provided. It is possible for a particularly adept professional criminal to create a false history that will stand up to a complete check, but it is difficult. Fortunately, most employers are unlikely to encounter such an applicant. For the purposes of the average business organization, verifying background information provides reasonable security at a reasonable price. It also speeds the search process. If the employer is unable to verify the information the applicant provides, the employer may decide to not hire.

Searching Records

Here are typical records an employer can tap.

Voter Registration Records. This is the first place to start, because voter registration records provide complete information, including full names, current and former addresses, and even signatures.

Driver's License Number. Because of today's high liability insurance rates, an applicant's driving record is of obvious importance if the applicant is going to be driving on company business, whether in a personally owned vehicle or a company vehicle. An employee with a history of reckless driving can endanger the public safety, and the employer will pick up the tab when a lawsuit gets filed. Obviously, an employer has a right to know about an unusual amount of tickets, DWI citations, or suspended licenses. Furthermore, such information can give insight to the character of the applicant. A person with DWI citations might have more than a problem driving a car — there may be a substance abuse problem as well.

Social Security Verification. Growing responsibility is being placed on the employer to verify that an applicant has a social security number and, if not a citizen, that the applicant can legally work in the United States. Since many databases use social security numbers as identifiers, an applicant can hide a wide range of past problems just by changing the spelling of the name and a digit or two in the social security number.

There is a simple check that can be made. The first three numbers of a social security number refer to the state in which it was issued (or, in some cases, to a special class of number). A chart that shows and explains this numbering system can be obtained from the local social security office. If the number presented by the applicant does not match the state in which the applicant grew up, the employer should start asking questions.

Criminal Arrests/Convictions. Arrest and conviction records are kept in county courthouses all across the country. In many cases, they are also kept in state files. In most states, these are public records that anyone can get just by walking up to the counter and asking for them.

A conviction record can be important, particularly if it is related to the job being offered, such as a check fraud conviction of an applicant applying for a job with financial responsibilities. While such a fact should not necessarily be the only criterion in making a decision not to hire, it may be used if the employer can show job-relatedness.

With respect to arrest records, care must be exercised because in some jurisdictions and in some circumstances it is illegal to disadvantage a job applicant on the basis of arrest information.

Civil Suit Records. Records of civil suits can sometimes provide important information about an applicant. If an applicant has an unusually litigious nature (demonstrated by being listed as a plaintiff in a number of suits), he or she might not make a productive member of the employer's team. The same may be true if the applicant is a defendant in a number suits. This is not to say an applicant should not be involved in a suit — that's

a constitutional right — but it may provide insight into a past unusually punctuated with lawsuits.

Workers' Compensation Claims. Some people make a living out of worker's compensation claims. Fraudulent claims are a major factor in the high cost of insurance premiums at some companies. Other applicants have no intention of making a false claim, but have a history of injury that may make them unsuitable for the job in question. Each state keeps a record of worker's compensation claims, and the employer can search those records to see if applicants under consideration have a history of injuries or claims, especially claims they have not disclosed in their applications.

Educational Degree Verification. Many employers take an applicant's word for educational attainments, and rarely check with the academic institutions. Yale University claims to get only five inquiries a month from employers checking references. Often, applicants list the college they attended and either list a degree different from the one they actually received, or claim a degree when they didn't actually graduate. Others simply falsify their entire educational history, or lack of it. An employer can query the institution and get a written statement of the actual degree received. This can be invaluable in jobs where a degree really counts, particularly with younger employees, whose lack of on-the-job experience may make a degree their only asset. The federal Family Educational Act may limit access, and it is vital to have a release.

Military Records. The Freedom of Information Act allows the employer to access military records easily. Through the Defense Locator Service in Washington, DC (or locator services for the individual services), an employer can receive a verification of military service and the place and time of discharge.

Professional Associations and Licensing Boards. Almost every profession has associations and licensing boards. If an applicant claims to have worked in an occupation that has such an organization, the employer may find valuable information from the applicant's local association. If an applicant claims to have been a realtor, for instance, but didn't belong to the local Board of Realtors, the employer may want to ask why.

Associations may also know of complaints filed against the applicant.

Credit Reports. It may be important to have an idea of an applicant's fiscal responsibility. A credit report can show debt load, payment history, and information on civil actions, such as judgments, liens, and bankruptcies. If there is a job-related concern, this may be very valuable information. Additionally, credit reports can verify information such as previous addresses and previous employers. In double-checking the information the applicant has given, the employer may attain a clearer picture of the applicant's sense of responsibility and reliability.

Vehicle Registration. Before making a hiring decision for a job that requires use of a personally owned vehicle, the employer may want to make sure the applicant really owns the vehicle identified in the application. Vehicle registration files make this possible.

Database Services. These services access databases across the country and can provide the employer with extensive records searches for inexpensive fees. In today's mobile environment, a local search is likely to miss important data. A search of counties where an applicant is thought to have lived may uncover more information, although an applicant with an out-of-state criminal record may not disclose having lived in that state or in the county where the applicant's criminal record is on file. This by itself is sufficient reason to conduct a separate inquiry along other lines to identify former home addresses. One such line of inquiry is a credit check, which will almost always reflect the individual's home address.

Database services are popular because most employers do not know their way around county records and find it inconvenient to go through the process to check on every applicant. The database services are usually operated by professionals with investigative backgrounds who may be able to offer the benefit of their expertise in enhancing and expediting a search.

Success with a database service will depend on the quality and quantity of the identifying data provided by the requester. For each name subjected to a check, there will be hundreds (if not thousands) of persons with the same name. Good information presented to the database at the front end will produce good information at the back end.

Response Times. The time required to get the requested information back from the various agencies depends on the type of information and the agency reporting it. Social security number verifications normally come back within 24 hours. Arrest and conviction records, as well as workers compensation records, can take anywhere from 2 days to 2 weeks, depending on the state. A database service can process a request within minutes, but has no control over the agencies from whom it is requesting the information. When agencies require requests to be made in writing, as some still do, the database service can handle that for the employer.

It is easy to understand why companies often overlook background checks: it is difficult to get information, and hard to handle the rejection from people who are intent on not giving information. Most employers limit themselves to a couple of calls to previous employers, just to check dates of employment.

Some will hire a private investigator or a specialized background checking service to make a report on an applicant, but usually this is reserved for key positions, because of the costs involved. The irony is that most of the information the private investigator brings in is publicly available. The problem is that most employers have no idea how to go about getting it.

Carl E. King

BACKGROUND INVESTIGATIONS

The purpose for conducting a background investigation is an attempt to verify the applicant's statements (verbal or in writing) that he or she is qualified for the position and a person of high integrity. These procedures can be divided between record checks and background interviews. The efficacy of a background investigation is somewhat limited in that it can only develop information to disqualify job applicants; the absence of adverse information does not necessarily offer reassurance of the applicant's integrity. The reason for this is self-evident: when an individual engages in acts of dishonesty he or she does so secretly to avoid discovery. Consequently, the applicant prevents others from knowing about most past acts of dishonesty. The following list cites a few limitations of background investigations:

- The applicant was never caught for the crimes committed.
- The applicant was guilty of a crime but was acquitted in court or charges were dropped.
- The applicant plead guilty to a lesser charge.
- References provided by the applicant are not likely to be aware of the applicant's acts of dishonesty.
- Past employers are reluctant to provide honest evaluations for fear of subsequent law suits.
- Past employers are frequently unaware of an applicant's dishonesty.
- Financial records that indicate, for example, a poor credit rating, bankruptcy, or wage garnishments do not represent a bona fide occupational qualification (BFOQ) for many positions.

Records Check

With the applicant's permission, an employer can access many public records relevant to a hiring decision. One category of these verifies the applicant's qualification, such as possession of a required license, certification, or permit, and the applicant's educational background. Because of the frequency with which applicants falsify their qualifications, a "verification" records check is highly recommended.

A second category of records check attempts to confirm the absence of negative information, e.g., motor vehicle reports and criminal convictions. Before making this type of records search, an agency or company must first decide which records will provide information that satisfies a BFOQ. For example, it would be relevant to check a driving record for an individual applying as a truck driver. On the other hand, if the position does not require driving, the applicant's driving record is not a BFOQ.

Some employers use the threat of a background investigation in an attempt to elicit truthful responses on a written application. The application may read, "The information indicated on this application will be verified through a background investigation." Statistics indicate that such a caveat is ineffective in eliciting truthful responses from most dishonest applicants. The dishonest applicant, after all, is a risk taker and realizes that if the application is completed truthfully he or she will not be offered the position. Therefore, the dishonest applicant has nothing to lose by lying on the application in hope that no background investigation is conducted.

Some employers incorrectly believe that conducting a records check is a waste of time and money because most records are legally unavailable and require much effort to obtain. To the contrary, more than 91% of the nation's 3,100 counties release criminal conviction records, all 50 states make motor vehicle reports available, and more than 97% of post-secondary institutions will confirm an applicant's credentials.

The recommendation, therefore, is that an employer follow through with a records check if the information sought is relevant to the position under consideration -- keeping in mind, of course, that the absence of negative information in a record does not necessarily indicate that the applicant has not engaged in dishonest or irresponsible behavior. It is becoming a much more accepted practice for employers to require that the applicant provide his or her own records, including proof of licensure or certification, college transcripts, criminal record check and a motor vehicle report when appropriate. The benefits of this practice are (1) cost savings to the employer, (2) a deterrent for dishonest applicants to not apply for the position, and (3) a legal safeguard against incorrect information contained within a record, i.e., because the applicant reviews his or her own records incorrect information will be identified.

Background Interviews

Interviews with an applicant's past employers, co-workers, neighbors, or other individuals who may have information about the applicant is time-consuming and too often does not result in developing adverse information about an applicant. Alternatively, most employers will simply verify dates of employment and the position the applicant held with previous employers. This conservative attitude is in response to a concern that a negative reference may result in a defamation of character lawsuit. To complicate matters, it is common for retail businesses and financial institutions to offer an employee who has been caught stealing or using drugs during work hours a "favorable reference" in exchange for the employee's voluntary resignation. This practice, of course, is to avoid claims of wrongful discharge as well as to avoid paying unemployment compensation.

The least likely sources of negative information about an applicant are the references listed on an application form. These individuals were selected by the applicant precisely because they will provide favorable information.

Following are guidelines for conducting background interviews:

• Conduct interviews in person rather than by telephone. It is important that the interview be conducted in a private environment to alleviate the source's concern that others may overhear negative information offered.

• Select sources who are likely to be aware of the applicant's integrity and yet willing to offer candid information. Examples of these sources are past co-workers who worked at or below the level of the applicant; past neighbors who no longer socialize with the applicant; and law enforcement officers who may be aware of the applicant's reputation, even though the applicant does not have a criminal record.

• If negative information is developed through a background interview, it should be corroborated if used as the grounds for denying the applicant employment. The best source of corroboration, of course, is through the applicant's own admissions.

When conducting a background interview, the investigator should introduce the purpose for the interview as "verifying" information already learned about the applicant. Because this approach implies that other sources have previously offered information, the source will feel more comfortable in divulging adverse information.

The investigator should avoid promising confidentiality to the source since the applicant ultimately will be offered an opportunity to explain any negative information developed through a background interview. The investigator should also avoid asking opinion questions that begin with phrases such as, "Do you think..." or "Do you consider..." Questions that prompt a source to render a judgment often produce misleading answers.

Finally, the investigator should not ask negative questions. Examples of negative questions are, "He didn't have any drug problems that you're aware of?" or "She wasn't in any trouble with the law that you know about?" Invariably, a source will agree with the negative assumption within the question. Rather, the investigator should phrase questions in a direct and objective manner with an implied expectancy of a positive response. By doing so it is much easier to identify sensitive areas through the source's verbal and nonverbal behavior. Under this circumstance, of course, the investigator would pursue related topics within that area to develop specific information.

Examples of a few of these questions are:

• How many different employers has (APPLICANT) worked for during the time you've known him?

• How many times have you seen (APPLICANT) drink alcohol at lunch or on a break at work?

• Has (APPLICANT) used marijuana, speed, or cocaine in your presence?

• Has (APPLICANT) ever told you that he or she used drugs?

• Has (APPLICANT) ever offered to sell you merchandise that you think may have been stolen?

• Has (APPLICANT) ever told you that he stole merchandise or money?

• Does (APPLICANT) belong to any gangs?

• What contact has (APPLICANT) had with the police?

Conducting a thorough background interview is a time-consuming process that requires an investigator with expertise in interviewing and investigation techniques. Because of this, conducting such background interviews is typically reserved for positions requiring high trust and authority. The investigator conducting such interviews should approach each source with a mental set believing that the source possesses adverse information about the applicant and will divulge it if the right questions are asked. Operating from this mental set, the investigator will be more successful in eliciting information and also more confident in the source's truthfulness when only positive information is developed.

Bryan C. Jayne

BARRIER DETECTORS

Barrier detectors are used in intrusion detection systems across entrances leading into protected areas and across probable routes an intruder would take inside the protected areas. Photoelectric detectors are the most popular inside-barrier detector. The newer, active infrared detectors form an invisible beam of light in the infrared frequency range between a transmitter located on one side of the area requiring protection and a receiver located on the opposite side. When anyone interrupts or breaks the beam, the infrared energy is blocked from the receiver, thus initiating an alarm.

Trip-wire devices are also in use as barrier detectors, but they are becoming unpopular because they must be set up and taken down at closings and openings. This task quickly becomes a nuisance, especially if the protected area has more than one or two trip-wire devices.

Barrier detectors can be easily avoided, especially if they are visible or the intruder is aware of their existence, because the barrier usually consists only of a single beam or trip-wire. The beam or trip-wire is installed about 30 inches from the floor. At this level, if the intruder can see it, the intruder can simply crawl under the beam undetected. If the beam is lower than 30 inches, the intruder can probably step over it.

Therefore, any barrier detector should be concealed or disguised to minimize its vulnerability to defeat; at least two beams should be used to reduce the vulnerability to an intruder crawling under the barrier.

Photoelectric Detectors

Photoelectric beam detectors consist basically of a light transmitter and a separate receiver. The light transmitter is located on one side of the entrance or area requiring protection, and the receiver is positioned on the opposite side of the entrance to receive the radiant energy from the transmitter.

In earlier photoelectric detectors, an incandescent lamp was the light source in the transmitter. The light, radiating from the lamp, passed through a lens that columnated the light source. The light then passed through a red filter to reduce its visibility. The columnated beam was projected onto a photoelectric cell in the receiver. The photoelectric cell converted radiant energy into an electrical signal that was amplified for the detector processor.

In actual application, the photoelectric detector initiated an alarm when interruption of the radiant energy incident on the photocell satisfied the alarm criteria. The red beam of light, formed by the incandescent lamp, was visible and therefore easy to bypass.

Photoelectric detectors are used for many applications other than as intrusion detection devices. Some of these applications include automatic door openers, automatic feed packaging systems, safety barriers, and many other similar automatic systems. In these types of applications, the visible light beam does not affect the function of the device.

But for the photoelectric device to be an effective intrusion detection barrier, the light beam should be virtually invisible to the naked eye. The gallium arsenide light-emitting diode (LED) is now being used because it generates a beam of light in the infrared frequency range that is virtually invisible to the naked eye. Thick fog and smoke in the area of the beam will scatter the light particles, making the beam visible, especially near the transmitter. Gallium LEDs are solid-state devices that are highly shock- and vibration-resistant and they have about a ten-year life expectancy.

Photoelectric detector light beams should be modulated to minimize the possibility of an intruder defeating the detector with another light source. Modulating the light beam requires only that the light beam be pulsed at a specific frequency. The results of the modulation is that the intensity of the light source is recognized by the detector processor. This feature makes it very difficult for an intruder to substitute another light source, even a pulsed light source, to compromise the detector.

An added benefit of modulation is that detectors, using modulated light beams, are less susceptible to false alarms from sunlight or other light sources. Both the constant beam and the modulated beam photoelectric detectors should initiate an alarm when 90% or more of the beam is interrupted for a period of no greater than 75 milliseconds.

The detector's obscuration time is the time the light beam is obscured from the receiver. The momentary interruption caused by an intruder moving at a rapid speed through the light beam would be detectable.

Trip Wire Devices

A trip-wire device consists of a spring-loaded switch and spring-loaded wire that can be stretched across the entrance to a protected area or across any path an intruder might take after entering the area. The trip-wire is connected to the switch that initiates an alarm if the wire is bumped, stretched, or retracted. When anyone comes in contact with the wire, the wire stretches, disconnecting the switch that initiates an alarm. The wire is also part of a supervised circuit to detect cutting. Some trip-wire devices have the wire attached to a retractable spool for storing the wire when the area is open. An advantage of a trip-wire is that it will not initiate an alarm unless someone or something comes in contact with the wire. Therefore, false alarms from trip-wire devices are minimal.

Robert L. Barnard

Source Barnard, R.L., Intrusion Detection Systems. (Butterworth Heinemann, Boston, 1982).

BARRIERS: PERIMETER AND VEHICLE

Perimeter Barriers

A perimeter barrier is any element that impedes or prevents an aggressor from crossing a perimeter boundary. Common perimeter barriers include fences, walls, ditches, and hedges. Perimeter barriers are commonly required to serve as barriers to people or vehicles. The form of barrier to accomplish each is quite different.

The effectiveness of perimeter barriers in resisting personnel entry is frequently highly overestimated. Tests have shown that a 7-foot chain-link fence provides only a few seconds of delay to an aggressor attempting to climb over it. This delay approaches 10 seconds for attempts to cut through it. Even installing such fence enhancements as barbed tape does not significantly increase the delay time of the fence. Walls can easily be climbed, ditches can easily be crossed, and hedges can easily be penetrated. These lead to the conclusion that perimeter barriers should not be assumed to be effective barriers against people. There are fence enhancements that may increase delay up to 1 minute, but they are very expensive.

Perimeter barriers such as those previously mentioned can serve other purposes, however. Perimeter barriers can serve as a deterrent to a "casual intruder." They also effectively delineate boundaries. Another significant purpose for perimeter barriers is to enhance detection. A person climbing a fence or wall is easier to see than a person crossing a boundary without such a barrier.

In addition, perimeter barriers can be used as a platform for mounting intrusion detection sensors. People may be easily detected as they climb or cut through a sensored fence. In general, fences should be used to firmly establish a perimeter. This is especially true where a perimeter intrusion detection system is installed.

Vehicle Barriers

Vehicle barriers are used to prevent vehicles from penetrating a perimeter. They may be active or passive. Active barriers require an action to deploy them. Passive barriers are in place at all times.

The application of vehicle barriers also depends on the anticipated tactics of the driver of the vehicle. If the driver is likely only to try to park the vehicle as close to a building as possible without being noticed, the threat may be considered a stationary or parked vehicle tactic. If the aggressor is likely to attempt to ram through the perimeter, the threat is a moving vehicle tactic.

Barriers for the parked vehicle tactic need only define the perimeter. They do not need to prevent the vehicle from crossing it, but should provide enough resistance that an aggressor attempting to cross the boundary would be easily noticed. Passive perimeter barriers for this tactic may include high curbs, low hedges, or fences. Active vehicle barriers for this tactic may include common fence gates and traffic arms.

Barriers for the moving vehicle tactic must arrest the motion of the vehicle. To design such a barrier, the designer must know the weight of the vehicle and the speed it may attain on an approach to the barrier. The barrier is designed to resist the kinetic energy of the vehicle, which is a function of the vehicle weight and its velocity squared. Because the velocity is squared, providing means to slow the vehicle will limit the barrier resistance requirements, which will lower its cost. In general, the maximum vehicle speed can be obtained based on the distance to the barrier, the acceleration capabilities of the vehicle, and any obstacles that might slow the vehicle.

Perimeter barriers for the moving vehicle tactic include fences reinforced with cable, walls, planters, and concrete-filled steel bollards (posts). Any barrier, such as a highway median barrier, must be carefully anchored to the ground to stop a vehicle.

Ditches and berms may also stop vehicles, but they must be steep and high enough to high center the vehicle. Active vehicle barriers for this tactic are specially manufactured for this purpose. They are commonly used at entries through the perimeter. Most of them retract into the ground, slide out of the way, or are lifted out of the way. Retractable barriers include wedge-shaped steel barriers of various configurations, pipe bollards, and other complex configurations.

Sliding barriers take the form of steel gates, and lifting barriers take the form of reinforced traffic arms using cables or steel beams. Any of these may be obtained from manufacturers by specifying the vehicle weight and speed. The speed with which the barriers are required to deploy or retract is also an important consideration.

Vehicle barriers are frequently employed to keep vehicle bombs away from buildings. Where they are provided for this purpose they must be at the appropriate distance from the building to resist the blast effects. The barriers must also extend around the entire perimeter so that any possible vehicle approach is equally likely to be stopped at the speed that the vehicle is capable of attaining at that location.

Curtis P. Betts, P.E.

BEHAVIORAL MONITORING: A COUNTERMEASURE TO INDUSTRIAL ESPIONAGE

Industrial espionage, the illegal aspect of competitive intelligence, is frequently focused on information gathering activities that depend for their success on the aid of an employee who is well-placed in the targeted company. We often call this conspirator the Insider. In other contexts, he or she would be called a mole.

The information being sought is typically within the control of the Insider who has a legal and/or ethical duty to protect it.

The Insider

Traditional security systems are designed for the most part to defend against the outside enemy, and as a result are often ineffective against the inside enemy. The Insider has placement, has a legal right to move through access control points, and has certain defined rights to possess sensitive information. The Insider's activities are not questioned so long as he or she operates within the bounds of normal work behavior, and is practically invulnerable to exposure until an unauthorized act has been detected.

Detection of an unauthorized act usually occurs with a discovery that sensitive information has been compromised, i.e., that the damage has been done. The implication here is that prevention may be the best strategy for countering the Insider. Three tactics can be included in a preventive strategy:

•Strictly enforce the rules relating to need to know and accountability of documents.

•Enlist the support of employees and heighten their security consciousness.

•Conduct behavioral monitoring of employees who have access to sensitive information.

The first two tactics are well known to security professionals and are integral to any security program in place to protect information. The third tactic, however, is not widely practiced. This article will look at the dimensions of an organized program for monitoring the behavior of employees whose unique positions make them stand out as prospective industrial spies.

The Psychology of the Insider

The Insider is likely to rationalize that unresolved personal needs can be met through espionage. These cognitive factors (needs and rationalization) may produce visible behaviors that point to possible spying activities.

Dr. Howard Timm of the Defense Personnel Security Research and Education Center provided valuable insight to the cognitive factors of Insider espionage [1]. He described five cognitive factors that an Insider will attempt to rationalize:

1. The Insider must perceive an opportunity to act and to gain some benefits from the act. The benefits can be financial reward, revenge, or attainment of an ideological objective.

2.   The Insider must contemplate a criminal act. The idea of the act will usually come from an external source.   The idea can be passively planted, such as by a story in the public media, or actively as a deliberate contact by a recruiter to enlist the Insider.   Whatever the source, the planted seed will germinate in the Insider's thought processes.

3.   The Insider must have a strong desire to bring about the outcome projected to result from the act. Value will be attached to the outcome.

4.   The Insider must have insufficient internal control mechanisms to prevent the act. The act will seem acceptable and not morally wrong. The Insider may view the circumstances as being special and that he or she has a special, redeeming role to play.

5.   The Insider must believe there are insufficient protective measures to prevent the act or that, if caught, the likely value of the act will outweigh any punishment for it.

Observable Behaviors

Many of the Insider's unresolved needs are likely to be in the area of socialization. The Insider may be experiencing problems with a spouse or lover, family, friends, or co-workers. The Insider may feel lacking, unfulfilled, or disappointed in the social setting, in sexual affairs, and in workplace relationships.   Low self-esteem may be rationalized by placing blame on others, such as supervisors and employer, and a desire for revenge may begin with fantasies of vindication and triumph over antagonists.

The Insider may attempt to fill unresolved needs by making alliances with persons or programs that appear to be worthy adversaries to the Insider's antagonists. The employer's major competitor, for example, may be seen as an ally or as a weapon for avenging imagined grievances.

Following are a number of observable behaviors that may indicate a potential or actual Insider:

1.   Resisting supervision; violating rules; criticizing management or ownership; and criticizing the organization or its activities.

2.   Engaging in excessive political activism characterized by a need to convert others; expressing a narrow fanatical viewpoint; and refusing to accept opposing viewpoints.

3.   Borrowing money and not paying debts.

4.   Attempting to buy friendship; unexplained affluence; and a sudden, unusual change in work attitude and habits.

5.   Showing curiosity about sensitive information without having the right and need to know; keeping sensitive documents long after the need for possession has ended; and asking to be involved in classified work.

6.   Working when other employees are absent, such as late at night or on weekends; spending an inordinate amount of unsupervised time at a copying machine; and taking documents home.

7.   Forming new relationships with non-work related associates; meeting with new associates at odd hours and locations; and appearing nervous and being suspicious of others.

8.   Abusing alcohol or drugs; being absent without excuse from the job; arriving late and leaving early; being sick and being involved in accidents at a higher-than-normal rate; and showing poor judgment in making decisions.

Items 1 through 3 are likely to occur prior to the Insider making the commitment to engage in spying; items 4 through 7 are likely to be associated with having made the commitment or with actively spying; and item 8 behaviors can be present before, during, and after spying.

A most telling and apparent indicator is an unexpected and highly positive change in work behavior. The newly committed Insider will want to shun conduct that might lead to discharge (thereby closing off the opportunity to spy) and to drop any activities that call attention to the Insider's disenchantment with the organization. The Insider will want to spy in a manner that minimizes being caught in the act or being identified as the spy after the act has been discovered.   Where once a problem in supervision, a poor performer and a fomenter of unrest, the Insider may make a remarkable turnaround in the other direction. The Insider may intuitively understand that maintaining a low profile is a key to success in spying; if not, the Insider's controller or task master will make that clear.   The Insider may also receive special training in espionage techniques.

Behavioral Patterns

Unusual behaviors, by themselves, may not indicate potential or actual espionage. In some individuals, unusual behaviors happen to be normal behaviors. Two questions can help the security manager differentiate between innocent and suspicious conduct: Are the behaviors new? Are there any reasons to explain the new behaviors?

We are creatures of habit. We follow a variety of daily routines without conscious thought. Each of us has a unique pattern of activities from the moment we get up in the morning until we retire for the evening. Although what we do may be strongly influenced by forces outside of our control, we still manage to act with regularity and individuality. We find a particular pattern that suits us and we stick to it.

The indicators of Insider activity may be observed in the deviations from the pattern; and because a person's pattern is visible, it is therefore evaluable. The deviations can be examined for the meanings they hold.

A lack of a discernible pattern may also be significant. The Insider may be consciously avoiding any pattern at all or of avoiding certain activities within a pattern that might lead to discovery.

A Program for Behavioral Monitoring

The first thing that needs to be said about behavioral monitoring is that it is not for every organization. The process is intrusive, labor intensive and costly, and is justified only when the protection of sensitive information is crucial to the organization's viability.

Behavioral monitoring is a proactive and subtle process that relies on an environment of understanding, mutual trust, and concern for the protection of sensitive information. Management and employees at all levels have to understand the program and be committed to its success.

Define the Protected Information and Identify the Knowledge Workers.

A first step in establishing a monitoring program is to identify the specific types or categories of information to be protected and the employees who will have access to it (knowledge workers.) An option is to compartmentalize protected information so that no single employee will have knowledge of the full spectrum of information or of its major segments. Restricted areas, access controls, accountability, special storage, and a long list of security safeguards would be complementary provisions.

Profiles.

A unique feature of behavioral monitoring is the creation of a profile for each employee. A profile describes the employee's particular pattern. The pattern might reflect details concerning work routines, social acquaintances, and personal traits. Deviation from the pattern would be a signal, although not necessarily a red flag signal.

Peer Appraisals and Psychological Testing.

A part of the process is to conduct peer appraisals and psychological testing. Peer appraisals are typically conducted through the use of a questionnaire distributed to work peers of the person being appraised. Behavioral characteristics are included in the appraisal. Psychological tests conducted at various points in time may show a change that merits investigation. Periodic record checks can also shed light on changes that may be of interest.

The profile, peer appraisal and psychological test results of an employee can serve as benchmarks of what would be the normal, expected conduct of the individual. Monitoring reports can be compared against the benchmarks. Slight fluctuations from the norm can be expected.

Policy and Procedures.

Prior to program start-up, a written policy should be formulated by management and thoroughly communicated to the employees. Written procedures should also be developed for carrying out the policy.

It may help to underscore the gravity of the program by requiring each employee to acknowledge by signature that the policy has been read, understood and accepted. This signed acknowledgment would be in addition to the nondisclosure and confidentiality agreements signed by knowledge employees having access to particularly sensitive data.

Training and Education.

A follow-on activity is to train supervisors and educate employees. Line supervisors, security personnel, human resources specialists, and others responsible for program execution need to be given skills in how to recognize the indicators of Insider behavior and knowledge of what to do when the indicators are present. The training should include presentation of an approved methodology for making a "reasonable belief" determination prior to conducting an Insider inquiry.

In the area of employee education, the monitoring program should be a major agenda item in the security department's ongoing efforts to promote security acceptance and awareness by all employees. A key element should be the provision of constructive notice to the employees that the organization reserves the right to conduct inquiries that may involve examination of the employees' financial records, credit reports, police and medical records, and interviews of coworkers, friends, and neighbors. At the same time, of course, the organization must take extraordinary steps to ensure that inquiry information is protected against unauthorized disclosure, except as may be required by law.

G.H. Zimmer, Jr., Cpp

Note

1. For greater detail, see "Who Will Spy" by Howard Timm. (Security Management Magazine, 1991).

BOMBINGS: CRIME SCENE SEARCH

Bombing crime scenes, in spite of their massive destruction, must be searched on the theory that everything at the scene prior to the explosion is still in existence unless it has been vaporized by the explosion. Locating and identifying items is the problem. The often-used statement that so much is destroyed by the explosion that the cause must remain unknown is rarely true. Due to various factors the exact amount of explosives used cannot be determined based on an evaluation of the damage at the scene. The purpose of a bomb scene search is to determine what happened, how it happened, and gather evidence. The actual searching is conducted by specialists employed or acquired by the governmental agency having investigative jurisdiction.

Search Procedures

The following steps assist in the preparation, supervision, and evaluation of activity connected with the scene of a bombing.

Plan of Action. Formulate a plan adapted to the particulars of the bomb crime scene. This plan will include consideration of the creation of an on-scene command post; establishment of lines of supervision; assignment of various tasks such as photographing, fingerprint processing, crowd control, and collecting evidence; protecting the crime scene; obtaining necessary equipment; periodically evaluating progress; providing pertinent information to the public; safety; etc.

Command Post: Consider establishing an on-scene command post, particularly at a large bombing that may require days or weeks to complete the crime scene search. The command post should coordinate efforts among investigative personnel and between representatives of other agencies and utilities, as well as handle inquiries from sightseers, persons associated with the scene, relatives of victims, and the press.

One person should be in overall charge of the bombing investigation, another over the actual crime scene search, and another over the collection of the evidence. These three individuals must maintain close coordination and expeditiously exchange information on a continual basis. The evidence coordinator will report directly to the individual responsible for the overall bombing investigation.

Safety. Evaluate safety conditions at the outset of the crime scene search and on a continual basis throughout the search. Consider the possibility of a second bomb, a "jammed" bomb, or live explosives in the debris, as well as the safety of crowds, nearby residents and personnel at the crime scene. Utilities, weakened walls, and the like that may create dangerous situations should also be considered.

Protection of the Crime Scene. Take adequate safeguards to protect the crime scene from fire, law enforcement, utility, and rescue personnel, as well as others such as sightseers, victims, and individuals with a personal interest in the property. Also, since most residues remaining after an initiation of an explosion are water soluble, the crime scene should, as much as possible, be protected against exposure to excessive moisture, be it from rain, snow, broken water pipes, or other sources.

Photographs. Take appropriate photographs to give a photographic presentation of the crime scene. These photographs should be made immediately before, periodically during, and at the completion of the crime scene activity. Properly identify each photograph, coordinate the photographs with diagrams and/or blueprints or maps, and consider the advisability of aerial photographs.

Bomb Scene Specialist. If without a specialist trained in handling and processing bomb scenes, make arrangements for obtaining such an individual. Although the basic principles of conducting a crime scene search apply in a bomb scene search, individuals with specialized knowledge of explosives, improvised explosive devices, damage produced by explosive charges, and other facets associated with bomb scene searches are extremely valuable to the effective and efficient processing of the scene. These specialists need not be qualified bomb disposal specialists. They should be the first persons, if possible, to be selected for the evidence and crime scene search coordinator positions.

Equipment. Promptly make arrangements to obtain the necessary equipment to move the debris and material at the scene. Although the equipment needed at the scene varies, the following have been used:

• Shovels, rakes, brooms, boltcutters, wire cutters, sledgehammers, hammers, screwdrivers, wrenches, chisels, hacksaws, magnets, flashlights, knives, measuring tapes, and traffic wheel-measuring devices.

• Screens for sifting debris, wheelbarrows, metal trash cans, power saws, cutting torch equipment, ladders, portable lighting equipment, metal detectors, large plastic sheets, photographic equipment, and a parachute harness with related rope and pulleys.

• Truck, front-end loader, bulldozer, crane, and shoring materials.

• Hard hats, safety goggles, gloves (work and rubber types), foul weather clothing, coveralls, and work shoes.

• Crime scene processing kit containing equipment and supplies used for the collection, preservation, and identification of physical evidence.

If the bombed target was a vehicle, bring an identical vehicle, if possible, to the scene for use as a model in identifying fragmented and mutilated items.

Search for Evidence. Bear in mind the search for evidence at a bombing crime scene is important because the crime scene may contain principal evidence that will lead to the identification of the bomber(s) and/or assist in the successful prosecution of the matter. The following guidelines are general in nature since the exact method of searching will depend on various uncontrollable factors:

• It is extremely important that the area be photographed before a search begins, and when evidence is located.

• Place one person in overall charge of the collection of the evidence from the various collectors as valuable evidence may not be admissible in court if a proper "chain of custody" cannot be established. Include the location where the items were found. A diagram of the crime scene is always useful.

• Do not stop the search after a few items of evidence have been found.

• Look for signs of safety fuse, detonating cord, blasting caps, electrical wire, dynamite wrappers, batteries, clock and timing devices, electronic and electrical components, metal end cap from a TNT block, plastic end cap from a C4 block, explosive residues, and unconsumed explosives.

• While searching for the previous items, avoid overlooking other valuable evidence, such as fingerprints, hair, fibers, soil, blood, paint, plastic, tape, tools, tool marks, metals, writing paper, printing, cardboard, wood, leather, and tire tread-shoe print impressions.

• Conduct a well-organized, thorough, and careful search to prevent the necessity of a second search. However, have a secure "dump" area for debris in the event a second search becomes necessary.

• Normally, initiation of the search should start at the site of the explosion and work outward. If the bomb crater is in earth, obtain soil samples from the perimeter of the crater as well as from the sides and bottom, making sure to dig into the substrata. If the crater is in another material, obtain similar samples.

• Sift small debris through a 1/4-inch wire screen onto an insect-type wire screen. Usually these screens are placed on 2-foot square wooden frames constructed from 2-inch by 4-inch lumber.

• X-ray the bodies of living and deceased victims who were in close proximity of the explosion site for possible physical evidence and, if possible, have the evidence removed. (Their clothing should be retained as it may contain explosive residues.)

•Search a greater-than-sufficient distance from the site of the explosion in order to have a chance at finding evidence that may have been widely scattered.

•Determine the possible flight paths of bomb components to prevent needless searching.

•Search trees, shrubbery, telephone poles, and the roofs, ledges, and gutters of buildings. Instances have occurred where physical evidence has been "carried away" on the tires of fire and rescue vehicles.

•Establish a search pattern for large areas. A line of searchers moving forward has been found to be a satisfactory method. A bomb scene specialist should follow the line of searchers to evaluate the items found, control the searchers, and furnish guidance. If a second search is desired, the positions of the searchers on the line should be rotated. Charting the area to be searched will ensure a thorough search pattern.

•Retain all items foreign to the scene and items that the searchers cannot identify after seeking the assistance of those familiar with the bombed target.

Federal Bureau of Investigation

Source The Handbook of Forensic Sciences. (Federal Bureau of Investigation, U.S. Department of Justice, Washington, DC, 1984).

BOMB THREATS: INCIDENT MANAGEMENT

The proposition is well accepted that the organization's security manager is invested with the main responsibility for managing bomb threats. Even when there has been no history of threats and no reason to believe the organization has become a target, the security manager must anticipate the possibility and have a program in place.

Prevention Activities

Being ready to respond to a bomb threat is one thing; taking preventive action is another. A balanced program for the management of bomb threats will include proactive steps, for example:

•Coordinate with intelligence collection units of law enforcement agencies to learn the operating locales of criminal and terrorist groups known to use bombs; stay current with new developments in bomb construction and the methods of operation of groups that use them; and determine if the organization is a potential target.

•Confer with security counterparts to learn the bomb incident experiences of other organizations. Set up information sharing agreements.

•Liaise with bomb disposal experts who can be helpful to the organization in conducting training programs for plan respondents, for employees generally, and for certain employees whose duties would bring them into contact with mail bombs. This last group would comprise mail room employees and executive secretaries.

•Control suspect packages entering the workplace. Considerations can include examining packages at an offsite location that poses minimum danger in the event of an explosion; using bomb detection equipment; and training the package examiners in the visual techniques for spotting the indicators of package bombs.

•Maintain a positive means of identifying and channeling people who enter and move within the workplace.

•Educate employees to look for and report strangers in the workplace, and educate employees and visitors alike to not leave personal items, such as briefcases and gym bags, unattended in public areas of the facility.

•Conduct periodic inspections of the workplace to identify areas where a bomb could be planted with minimum chance of detection and at the same time cause major property damage or personal injuries. The areas to think about are the facility's power plant, flammable storage rooms, telephone switching center, computer room, and executive offices.

•Educate employees, generally, and security and maintenance personnel, specifically, to be alert for suspicious persons and activities in areas that are accessible to the public, offer bomb concealment opportunities, and are sensitive in terms of damage and/or injury.

•Require security officers during each tour of duty to make random checks of public areas to look for unauthorized persons who may be hiding in or reconnoitering the facility.

•Ensure physical protection of key assets. Fire resistant safes and vaults can protect sensitive documents, cash, small valuables, magnetic media, and similar materials against bomb damage.

•Educate fire wardens and other emergency respondents to look for and report unusual activities that might signal the early stage of a bombing attempt.

An intelligent and determined adversary is likely to find a chink in even the best defensive armor. Without considering the elaborate schemes, some of the readily available means for introducing a bomb into a workplace are: on the person of an employee, by postal or commercial delivery service, and by motor vehicle into the facility's garage. Once inside, placement of a bomb is mainly a matter of the attacker's nerve and knowledge of the premises. The attacker might choose to place the bomb in a rest room, janitor's closet, stairwell, receiving platform, lobby, or elevator.

Security management must regard, as a top priority, the degree of control exerted by the security force at access points. Control at the perimeter is the first and most important line of defense in a proactive strategy. Although most bomb threats prove to be hoaxes or are resolved by disarming the bomb before detonation, we cannot rule out the skilled attacker intent upon inflicting maximum harm without warning. The best preventive course in such a case is to deny access.

The Bomb Threat

A bomb threat is rarely made in person and sometimes is transmitted in writing. A bomb threat in writing should be handled carefully, touched by as few persons as possible, and the envelope or any other accompanying materials preserved as evidence. Observing these simple precautions can be extremely helpful to a post-incident investigation.

Nearly all bomb threats are made by telephone. Two reasons can be attributed to a bomb threat call:

•The caller has certain knowledge that a bomb has been or will be placed. The caller wants to minimize personal injury or property damage by alerting persons at the target area. The caller is likely to be the bomber or an accomplice.

•The caller wants to disrupt the normal activity and cause inconvenience. In most cases this type of call will not involve placement of

anything, although in some few cases a simulated bomb will have been placed.

When prior preparation and practice have not been made, panic can result from a bomb threat call. Panic is an infectious fear capable of spreading quickly, and when present, the potential for injury is substantially increased. One of the ways that the potential for panic can be minimized is to train persons in how to receive a bomb threat call. Training would teach the recipient of a bomb threat call to:

•Keep the caller talking for as long as possible. Ask the caller to repeat the message. Take notes. Try to take down the exact words used by the caller.

•Ask the caller to specifically state where the bomb is located and when it is set to detonate. Ask what part of the facility should be evacuated first.

•Ask for a description of the bomb. What does it look like? How is it packaged? What is it made of and how does it work?

•Ask why the bomb was placed and what group is responsible. Ask the caller if he or she was the person who placed the bomb. Ask where the caller is now.

•Tell the caller that the facility is occupied and that a detonation could result in death and serious injury to many innocent people.

•Listen closely to the caller's voice. Is the caller male or female? Calm or excited? Accent? Speech impediment?

•Pay attention to background noises that may give a clue as to the caller's location. Traffic sounds, music, and voices heard in the background may be important.

•Keep the line open after the call has ended. It may be possible to trace the call.

•Notify the Security Department immediately after the caller hangs up. Be ready to be interviewed by a security representative and to pass over the notes made during the call.

A checklist form for receiving a bomb threat call can be very helpful. The form can be made a part of the training and distributed to employees for posting close to the telephone.

Formal training in how to receive a bomb threat call should be supplemented by informal refreshment through an ongoing program of security awareness and education. The objective is to condition the employees (most particularly telephone operators, receptionists, executive secretaries, and security officers) to properly handle a bomb threat call and then immediately notify the Security Department.

Evaluating a Bomb Threat Call

The very first task of the security manager who has been informed of a bomb threat is to evaluate it. Interviewing the person who received the call and examining the notes taken during the call are preliminary to making any judgment. The evaluation takes into account the details and characteristics of the call itself, prior calls, and similar threats that have been made in the community or against counterpart organizations.

Evaluation is essentially a process of judging the credibility of the threat. Is the call a hoax or is it real? In this process, absolutes are not possible. The security manager is weighing probabilities and if an error is to be made, it has to be made on the side of caution.

For example, in looking at the details of a call, the security manager may learn that the caller was a young female, probably a teenager; giggling sounds and music were heard in the background; and the caller's answer to the question as to motive was that "it seems like a good idea." In this case, the security manager may conclude that the call is probably a hoax.

In another case, the security manager may be looking at entirely different indicators, such as nervousness in the caller's voice, an expressed grievance against the organization, knowledge of the workplace or of persons who work there, and a knowledge of bomb construction. The conclusion here is that the threat is probably or most probably real. When the indicators are not clear cut, the security manager has to act as if the threat were real.

The senior managements of many organizations will insist, as a matter of policy, that bomb threat evaluation be a shared process in which the security manager presents his findings to one or more senior executives before decisions are made to search or evacuate.

Search and Evacuation Options

Some organizations will require, even when searching and evacuating are deemed unnecessary, that all employees be informed of the receipt of a bomb threat and those that wish to leave may do so without penalty. The concern appears to be with the liability that may arise if a bomb explodes after the management received a warning that it chose not to disclose.

Three possible options proceed from a judgment of the threat: (1) to search without evacuating; (2) to evacuate partially or fully, and then search; and (3) to fully evacuate and not search.

Searching without Evacuating. This option is appropriate when the bomb threat call is judged to be a hoax or probable hoax.

Immediate and total evacuation would at first glance seem to be the only possible response to a bomb threat. Upon close analysis, however, we can note at least two factors that operate against automatic evacuation. First, there is the matter of safety. Even the most orderly evacuation can produce injuries from tripping and falling. There is also the risk of moving large numbers of people along designated exit routes where a bomb might be planted or assembling them in an area where even a small explosive device would cause many casualties.

Evacuation is also disruptive to work. While the protection of life certainly outweighs any economic loss, repeated threats and evacuations would soon escalate productivity losses to an unacceptable level.

Evacuating Partially or Fully and Then Searching. This option is appropriate when the call is assigned a greater degree of credibility. For example, if the caller indicates that the bomb is in a particular area, employees from that area and surrounding confines would be evacuated. Similarly, full evacuation would be appropriate if the caller is credible and indicates multiple bomb locations or refuses to name any specific location.

Fully Evacuating and Not Searching. This option is rarely taken because it is only appropriate when the call is given a high degree of credibility and when not enough time is available to conduct a search. In selecting this option, management is essentially saying it is better to get out and wait until the bomb goes off, if it goes off at all, or wait until more than sufficient time elapses to permit a conclusion that the threat was false.

These three options represent preliminary courses of action that can be changed as circumstances change. The option to search

BOMB THREAT GUIDANCE AND CHECKLIST

If you receive a bomb threat telephone call, use the checklist and follow this guidance:

Be calm. Be courteous. Listen carefully. Do not interrupt the caller.

Get as much information as possible from the caller, but avoid the impression you are working from a checklist.

If possible, alert your supervisor while the caller is on the line.

Take notes, try to get the caller's remarks "word for word."

It is very important to obtain answers to these questions:

1. When is the bomb going to explode?

2. Where is the bomb right now?

3. What does the bomb look like?

4. What is the bomb made of? (Obtain details about its parts.)

5. What will cause the bomb to explode?

6. Who placed the bomb? Why?

7. What is your name? Where are you now?

Try to keep the caller talking. If necessary, pretend difficulty with your hearing. Try to weave these general questions into the conversation:

8. What did you say? I'm sorry, I didn't understand what you said.

9. How do I know this is not a joke?

10. What group do you represent?

11. Why are you doing this?

Notify your supervisor and Security immediately. Discuss the incident only as needed.

Call received by:

Time call began: Time call ended: Date:

(Go to second page.)

Record the caller's remarks "word for word" as much as possible.

_____

_____

_____

_____

The caller was most probably:
❑ Male   ❑ Female   ❑ Child   ❑ Teenager
❑ Young Adult   ❑ Middle-aged   ❑ Older person   ❑ White
❑ Black   ❑ Hispanic   ❑ Other:

The caller seemed to be:
❑ Sober   ❑ Drunk   ❑ Mentally Disturbed   ❑ Joking
❑ Nervous   ❑ Calm   ❑ Excited   ❑ Angry
❑ Emotional   ❑ Rational   ❑ Irrational   ❑ Coherent
❑ Incoherent   ❑ Sincere   ❑ Laughing   ❑ Determined

The caller talked:
❑ Loud   ❑ Soft   ❑ With a high pitch
❑ Fast   ❑ Slow   ❑ With a deep voice
❑ Raspy   ❑ Slurred   ❑ With a nasal sound
❑ Fast   ❑ Slow   ❑ With a stutter or lisp
❑ With good pronunciation   ❑ With a disguised voice

The caller's language was:
❑ Educated   ❑ Good   ❑ Poor   ❑ Profane
❑ Full of slang words or expressions. (Include these in comments.)

The caller had an accent that I would say was:
❑ Local   ❑ Not local   ❑ Foreign (where?)

The caller seemed to be familiar with the Company's:
❑ Location   ❑ Equipment   ❑ Personnel   ❑ Operations

In the background I could hear:
❑ Party Noises ❑ Bar sounds   ❑ Another person or persons
❑ Music   ❑ House Sounds   ❑ Office Sounds
❑ Street Sounds ❑ Trains   ❑ Airport Sounds
❑ Voices   ❑ No sounds   ❑ Factory Machines

The origin of the call seemed to be:
❑ Local   ❑ Long Distance   ❑ From within the Company

Comments:

_____

_____

_____

without evacuation might be upgraded if a second bomb call increased the credibility of the threat, or if during the search a suspect bomb was discovered. The size and location of a suspect bomb will influence the extent of evacuation. For example, a suspect bomb about the size of a cigarette pack that is found in a non-safety sensitive area might not require a total evacuation.

As a general rule, at least 300 feet of lateral area around a suspect bomb should be cleared of all non-essential response personnel. The vertical areas above and below a suspect bomb should also be cleared. If a suspect bomb is found on a floor of a multi-story building, the floor involved plus the floors immediately above and below should be cleared.

Does total evacuation mean that every person must leave? The answer is always yes when there is reason to believe a discovered bomb is capable of inflicting damage or injury. In the absence of that belief the answer could be no. Some persons, such as security officers and maintenance employees, may remain to perform essential life-protecting and shutdown duties when the risk to them appears to be low.

Searching Considerations

Bomb searching is in most cases conducted by persons familiar with the workplace and almost never by police officers. Public safety policy often discourages the participation of police department personnel in bomb searches on private property, unless probable cause exists to believe that a bomb is in fact present. Probable cause can be established by the details of the bomb threat call or by the discovery of a suspect bomb. With a belief established, the police are more likely to want to be actively involved in making or directing the search. Although employees at the workplace will have a greater familiarity with the possible places of bomb concealment, officers trained in bomb disposal will know how to avoid booby traps and mistakes that can lead to detonation.

Three key points need to be emphasized: first, that the search be thorough; second, that the search be careful; and third, that when a suspect bomb is found, it be approached only with great caution.

Putting the key points into practice means that: (1) for a search to be thorough it is best to do it with people familiar with the physical environment, i.e., security officers, maintenance workers, and other employees who know the nooks and crannies; (2) that for a search to be careful it should be done by people who are trained, i.e., that the organization give training to its bomb searching personnel; and (3) that the dangerous nature of bomb disposal requires people with highly specialized qualifications, i.e., that a suspect bomb be approached and handled only by duly authorized and certified bomb disposal technicians.

A search team's thoroughness will be affected by the size and configuration of the workplace to be searched. It might be fair to say that making a thorough search is not easy in any working environment. Even small environments uncomplicated by multiple workstations, equipment, and labor-intensive activities will present problems. Large and complex environments, such as manufacturing plants and high-rise office buildings, are searchable on a genuinely thorough basis only with substantial expenditure of effort and time. A 20-story office building, for example, might require 48 hours of uninterrupted looking with a 20-person team before it can be said that every conceivable hiding place has been examined.

It will seldom be possible in a large and complex environment to conduct a comprehensive search because time will not allow looking into false ceilings, examining every file cabinet, and removing panels from equipment. Neither will it be acceptable to disrupt or shut down work operations for two full working days while a search is in progress. A practical solution might be to prioritize, as part of the planning process, those places that should be thoroughly searched within the time available for searching. Note that the principle of searching with thoroughness remains uncompromised but that selectivity is introduced with respect to what should be searched.

In prioritizing the search effort, two variables standout: probability and criticality. How probable is it that a bomber would be able to penetrate the organization's security defenses, and if the probability is high, how probable is it that a bomb or bombs would be placed in some areas as opposed to others? An evaluation of probability might lead to a search priority that concentrates on areas that are outside the umbrella of high security control, such as lobbies,

BOMB THREAT NOTIFICATION CHART

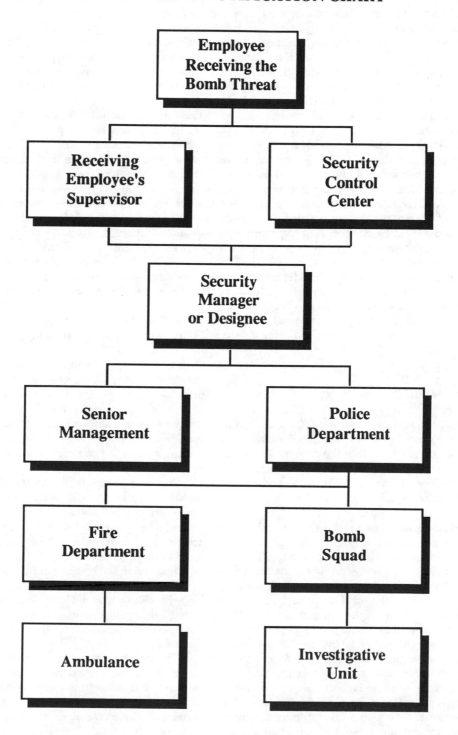

garages and other areas easily accessible to the public.

An evaluation of criticality might establish a priority for searching in areas where greatest damage can be done to the organization's most valuable assets. Criticality, however, needs to be balanced by probability. For example, it may not be sensible to set a high priority on searching the computer center when the probability is low that a bomb could be brought into the computer center without detection.

A technique associated with the prioritization of searching is the use of a card system. Each area or object to be searched is represented by a card that describes its location and other details, such as a particular telephone number to be called when the search has been completed. The cards are coded or numbered according to priority and are kept by the security manager or other person responsible for directing search team activities. At the search team briefing that precedes the starting of a search, the cards are handed out to team members. At the end of the search, checkmarks or signatures on the cards can provide a quick reference for ensuring that no areas were overlooked.

Search Methods

As mentioned earlier, the time requirements and the disruption of a comprehensive search make that method impractical in most cases. Two other general search methods present themselves for consideration: the non-evacuation method and the post-evacuation method.

The Non-Evacuation Method. The decision to not evacuate would be based on a judgment that the bomb threat call is a hoax and that persons in the workplace are not in danger. But because a bomb threat call is never judged to be absolutely false, a search should be made even when evacuation is not deemed appropriate.

The non-evacuation method is performed in a "walk-through" manner, but not in a cursory manner. A searcher is typically working alone, and is making searches of one or more specific areas that are likely to be occupied by employees who may or may not have been informed of the bomb threat. The searcher is typically a security officer, maintenance worker, or other person known to the employees.

The searcher moves in a steady, unhurried pace looking for objects that seem to not belong. Employees can be a source of information in determining if an object is really suspicious or simply not in its proper place. In areas where there are few or no employees present, the searcher can give closer attention to containers, closets, and areas that are out of direct sight.

The Post-Evacuation Method. When employees are absent, such as following an evacuation or during non-working hours, the searcher can move into workstations, offices, and conference rooms to examine shelves, waste baskets, storage bins, and the like. Even though each searcher can move faster when employees are not in the way, the time gained is expended in looking with more intensity. Also, if the post-evacuation search is conducted after hours, the search team will not be at full force because maintenance employees and other day workers who would normally assist in the search are likely to be off duty.

Discovery of a Suspicious Object

One of the fundamentals is to not touch a suspicious object. A searcher, however, will need to do a certain amount of touching in the routine course of looking into, behind, and under the many items that can conceal a bomb. But at the instant a suspicious object is seen, all touching should stop. The searcher then needs to alert persons nearby to leave the area.

The next step is to notify the security manager or other person coordinating the search. The responsive actions that can follow include:

• Questioning employees who may be able to account for the presence of the suspicious object.

• Ordering a partial or full evacuation.

• Notifying the bomb disposal team.

• Notifying the fire department.

• Readying first aid supplies and calling for standby medical personnel and equipment.

• Asking the police to assume command of the situation.

The bomb disposal team leader or the fire officer in charge may ask for further information, such as the location of the suspect device relative to stored fuels, chemicals, flammables, power plant, and fire exits. Requests may be made to identify other possible hiding places, to open doors or windows for the purpose of dissipating

BOMB THREAT PROCEDURES

These procedures apply to bomb threats at the Company's home office.

1.   Bomb Threats Made by Telephone. Guidance for receiving telephonic bomb threats is provided in the Bomb Threat Guidance and Checklist form.

2.   Bomb Threats Received in Writing. A bomb threat is rarely made in person and sometimes transmitted in writing. A bomb threat made in writing should be handled carefully, touched by as few persons as possible, and the envelope or any other accompanying materials retained and preserved. Observing these simple precautions can be extremely helpful to a post-incident investigation.

3.   Bomb Threats Made Through a Second Party. A probability exists that a bomb threat will be made through a second party, such as the police department or fire department. If this should occur, the initial notice would come from the police department by telephone or in person. This initial notification might be supplemented by a police patrol being sent to stand by to render possible assistance.

4.   The Initial Response to a Bomb Threat. Receptionists and secretaries have been oriented to call the Security Control Center upon receipt of a bomb threat call. The objective is to channel into the Security Control Center any initial notice of a bomb incident.

When the Security Control Center receives or is informed of a bomb threat, the initial action will be to notify the Security Manager and the Supervisor of Safety and Security.

5.   Bomb Threat Evaluation. Evaluation of a bomb threat will be made by the Manager of Security or the Supervisor of Safety and Security in conjunction with senior management. Evaluation will be made on the basis of all facts available at the time. Many of the available facts will be obtained from the person who received the bomb threat. Evaluation is essentially a process of judging the credibility of the threat. When a threat is judged to be false, the evaluator may elect to take no action. An example might be a bomb threat made by a child over the telephone. When a threat is judged to have possible credibility, one of three decisions will initially result from the evaluation:

      a.   To search without evacuation.
      b.   To evacuate, partially or fully, and then search.
      c.   To evacuate and not search.

6.   The Decision to Evacuate. The decision to evacuate will be made by the CEO, and in his absence, the Director of Administration. If either of these persons is unavailable, the senior member available from the Security Department will make the evacuation decision.

7.   Communications. The primary means of communication will be the telephone. Employees who use wireless communications will be instructed to turn off such devices. This is done because a bomb can be engineered to detonate by radio frequency.

8.   The Announcement to Evacuate. The announcement to evacuate will be made on the public address system by the security officer in the lobby. The announcement will include brief instructions to employees to take with them any personal belongings (particularly purses, briefcases and lunch boxes); to make quick visual surveillances of their immediate work areas for the purpose of detecting suspicious objects; and to report their suspicions to the security officer in the lobby as they exit the building.

The announcement message may vary from case to case because:

a.   The decision to evacuate will take into consideration the location of a suspect bomb relative to the fire stairwells. If a suspect bomb is believed to be in or near a stairwell, the evacuation announcement will include instructions that direct evacuees away from the danger zone while exiting the building.

b.   Total evacuation will not be an automatic response. Partial evacuation would be an appropriate response in those instances where the bomb threat caller mentions a specific location.

c.   The size and location of a suspect bomb will influence the extent of evacuation required to achieve safety. The bomb disposal unit will provide guidance regarding the probable damage effects of the suspect bomb. This information will determine the extent of evacuation required.

9.   Search Responsibilities. Security officers are responsible for searching the office areas. Maintenance employees are responsible for searching the common and public areas, for example, the lobbies, stairwells, restrooms, elevators, and mechanical rooms. Searches by security officers will begin and conclude upon instruction of the Security Manager or the Supervisor of Safety and Security.

10.   Discovery of a Suspicious Object. If a suspicious object is found, the finder will call the Security Control Center without delay, insuring first that the suspect device is not touched or moved by another searcher or an uninformed bystander. These actions will follow the discovery of a suspicious object:

a.   The console operator will notify the Security Manager and the Supervisor of Safety and Security.

b.   The Security Manager or the Supervisor of Safety and Security will ask the police to take command of the situation with respect to handling of the suspect bomb.

c.   A partial or full evacuation, depending on the circumstances, will be immediately implemented.

d.   The console operator will ensure that:

(1)   the fire department has been notified.
(2)   first aid supplies have been readied for possible use.
(3)   the ambulance service has been notified.
(4)   the CEO's office has been informed.
(5)   the fireman's key for elevator operation is readily available for use by fire department personnel, if needed.

The police may ask for help when a device is found. This help might be to:

a.   Place calls to the bomb disposal unit or other elements within the police department.

b.   Open doors to dissipate a possible blast effect.

c.   Confer with knowledgeable employees to learn of other possible hiding places where a secondary device could be concealed.

d.   Question employees who may be able to account for the device being in fact an innocent object.

11.   Fire Wardens. Fire Wardens will perform their established functions with respect to evacuation, but will not be used to search or perform other actions directly related to the bomb threat.

12.   The Assembly Area. The assembly area will be the ground floor level of the parking garage. Fire wardens will be used to ascertain who is missing from each floor and to issue instructions to assembled employees.

13.   Coordination. The Security Control Center will serve as the focal point of telephone communications during a bomb incident. At the earliest possible moment following the initiation of a bomb incident, the Security Manager and the Supervisor of Safety and Security will proceed to the Security Control Center to coordinate management of the incident.

14.   Evacuation of the Security Control Center. If the Security Control Center is within the danger zone posed by a suspect bomb, all personnel in that area will evacuate to the assembly area. Before leaving the Security Control Center, the telephones will be placed on call forwarding to the office of the Director of Administration. The Security Manager and the Supervisor of Safety and Security will proceed to the Director of Administration's office to coordinate management of the incident from that location.

15.   Police Involvement. The initial notice to the police department of a bomb incident will result in a patrol unit being sent to the building. Depending on the nature of the threat, the police will decide what other notifications are appropriate with respect to the fire department, paramedics, and bomb disposal unit. The principal functions of the police will be to:

a.   Provide guidance to security management.

b.   Conduct certain limited searches of areas surrounding a suspect device.

c.   Dispose of suspect devices.

blast effects, and to establish traffic control around the facility to permit free movement of emergency vehicles.

Command and Control

The security manager will find it advisable to pre-designate a location where the response coordinators can assemble at the outset of a bomb threat. The pre-designated location should be easily accessible to bomb incident response personnel, contain the applicable bomb threat response procedures, and have adequate communications, such as a radio network and telephones that can quickly connect to key persons inside and outside of the organization.

John J. Fay, CPP

BOMB THREATS: PLANNING

Three key steps are involved in establishing a program to manage bomb threats: (1) develop a plan, (2) prepare implementing procedures, and (3) train the persons responsible for responding to bomb threats.

The bomb incident plan describes the goals or objectives of the program; the major preventive, anticipatory and responsive functions of units within the organization; the responsibilities assigned to particular positions; the interfaces with outside response agencies, such as police and fire departments; the equipment required; and the strategy for bringing the various elements of the program together into a synchronous whole.

The plan provides an overall framework that allows management to exercise a variety of response options at the outset and during the course of the incident. Because the plan commits to action a number of units and persons that operate outside the security department, development of the plan will require the security manager to work through and coordinate with all of the interested parties.

The interested parties inside the organization are likely to be the security officer force, building maintenance workers, fire brigade team, and fire wardens. If the organization is a tenant, the landlord or building management office will be involved. Outside parties could include an explosives detection team, a bomb disposal team, fire control units, ambulance services, and post-incident investigative units.

A Bomb Threat Planning Model

Preparing a plan is more than just putting pen to paper. The plan itself will be the product of a logical planning process. A model that works well in effectuating a security planning process has six sequential steps or phases that occur in a cycle. The model has applicability to a wide range of security management activities. The six steps are: (1) assess the risk, (2) decide policy, (3) prepare a plan, (4) implement the plan, (5) test the plan, and (6) evaluate results. The sixth step loops back to step 1 by providing input to risk assessment.

Assess the Risk. In assessing risk, the security manager judges the organization's exposure and vulnerability to a bomb attack. The assessment attempts to answer a number of questions:

- Is the organization a target?
- What is the probability of an attack?
- Who are the likely attackers?
- What are the motives and capabilities of the attackers?
- What will be the form and delivery method of the attack?
- Is the organization vulnerable to an attack?
- What are the organization's specific areas of vulnerability?

Some answers may be found in the intelligence findings of government intelligence and law enforcement agencies, commercial firms that provide intelligence on a subscription or fee basis, professional associations that serve industries, and from inquiries made by the organization. Other answers may be found by the security manager in conducting security surveys and audits of the organization, special studies commissioned to outside consultants, and in many cases by the application of reasoned judgment.

Decide Policy. The security manager's portfolio may not include deciding policy, at least not without senior management review, but will normally place the security manager in a position of providing input to the setting of security policy. This will be particularly true when the policy relates to bomb incidents -- an area in which the security manager is the organization's best possible resource.

A given in the setting of policy is the recognition that a 100% level of security cannot be attained, no matter how much money and effort the organization may be willing to expend. Something less than absolute protection will be the objective, usually at a level reflecting a balance between cost and effect.

The security manager plays a central role in determining the level and striking the balance. When the homework has been done, the security manager is able to delineate to management the increases and decreases of risk associated with proposed increases and decreases in security. For example, the operation of a fire warden program in support of a bomb incident plan has dollar costs that can be readily determined and placed into contrast with the reasonably estimated dollar costs of injury, death, property destruction, and loss of business opportunity.

BOMB THREAT PLANNING MODEL

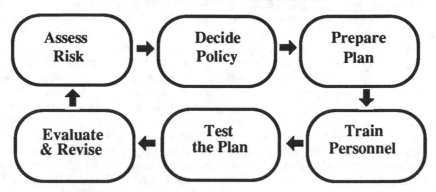

Prepare a Plan. Although bomb threat plans can vary widely, a well-devised plan will usually contain these elements:

• A statement of the policy that authorizes the plan. The statement will generally cite the plan's goal. The goal is likely to be threefold: (1) provide for the safety of people, (2) protect property against damage or destruction, and (3) restore the organization to normal operations.

• A description of the threat and an assessment of risk.

• Definitions of terms that are important to understanding the plan and assigning accountability.

• A delineation of job positions and units, including external agencies, which have plan responsibilities. The delineation will reflect lines of communication and formal authority.

• A description of the facility in terms of its geographical and demographical location, access routes, physical construction, entry points, utility interfaces, hours of operation, types of work activities, and numbers and types of persons within the facility.

• A description of the resources, such as a command center and public address system, available to the bomb threat response effort. This description could also mention evacuation routes and assembly areas.

• An identification of various procedures that carry out the plan, for example, procedures used by (1) maintenance personnel in shutting down the facility's basic utility systems, (2) fire wardens in evacuating the facility, (3) security officers in conducting bomb searches, and (4) ordnance personnel in removing suspect bombs.

While it may not be possible to predict and plan specifically for all possible bomb threat scenarios, the security manager should set up general arrangements that, in the course of execution, can be adjusted to meet the needs of the situation.

Implement the Plan. The implementing procedures flow from the plan, and provide detailed guidance to the responders. The security manager may assume or be assigned the responsibility for writing several sets of procedures; for example, the procedures that variously guide the security officers, the fire brigade team, and the fire wardens.

Where the bomb incident plan may be general, the procedures are specific, and where response actions may be set out in the plan as major functions, the procedures will show them as action steps. Bomb threat procedures are in the nature of directives and leave little room for interpretation. This is so because the potential for severe consequences affords no allowance for mistakes in judgment.

Test the Plan. A plan can be tested partially or fully. A partial test might consist of a practice response on or at certain floors and locations. The exercise may be to simulate a bomb threat call, initiate a search, and evacuate employees. The responding personnel would use the response equipment, such as the alarm system, public address system, radio communications equipment, and so on.

For the human element involved in mounting a response, testing of the plan is synonymous with training. Testing through the use of practice is highly effective in providing plan respondents with the critical knowledge and skills. Hands-on activities are a natural extension of the briefings and orientations that precede evaluation, and training administrators agree that the learning acquired through doing is powerful and lasting. In the absence of testing on a regular basis, plan execution will unquestionably suffer.

Evaluate Results. The exercise should be assessed objectively and an after-action report prepared of the lessons learned. The response procedures, as well as the plan itself, can be modified in light of experience gained through testing.

Every test should be evaluated, but evaluation does not end there. The organization's readiness and ability to respond is measurable on an ongoing basis, not just when tests are conducted. Weaknesses that are discovered in the routine operation of equipment, in the carrying out of written procedures, or in the performance of people are observable, and therefore potentially correctable, when evaluation is continuous.

Evaluation keeps the planning cycle in motion by involving the security manager in a never-ending assessment of risk. As the dimensions of risk change, the security manager engineers offsetting changes in the plan, procedures, and testing.

John J. Fay, CPP

BUDGETING: AN OVERVIEW

In any operation of size and complexity, budgeting will be an essential element of management planning and control.

Three purposes of budgeting stand out:
- Estimate the costs and expected revenues of planned activities.
- Provide a warning mechanism when variances occur in actual costs and revenues.
- Exercise uniformity in the matter of fiscal control.

Over all is the comprehensive or master budget. It is the forecast of all transactions within a given period, set up in a manner that will deliver timely reports of financial results to responsible managers. The comprehensive budget enables the preparation of financial statements, such as the profit and loss statement and balance sheet.

Within the comprehensive budget can be found a variety of smaller budgets that address the activities of departments and functions within the business. A budget director may be assigned to coordinate preparation of the individual budgets, and the process of preparation may follow a particular approach or technique.

A security manager's budget may include a major purchase. A preparatory step in considering a large expenditure is to determine the cost-benefit ratio. The ratio is attained by dividing costs by benefits. For example, if the installation of an access control system is estimated to cost $500,000 with an anticipated service life of 10 years, and annual guard costs will be reduced $100,000 per year as a result, the cost benefit ratio is 0.5:1 (meaning that the costs are half of the benefits, or the benefits are twice as great as the costs). The ratio in this example was arrived at by multiplying the annual guard cost savings by the number of years of useful service that can be expected from the access control system. This figure ($1,000,000) represents the benefit, and is divided into the cost of the system ($500,000). When the ratio is less than 1, it is favorable; and unfavorable when it is higher than 1.

Zero-Based Budgeting

A technique growing in popularity is zero-based budgeting. In this approach, a manager's budget for the upcoming budget period starts with zero dollars. Funds are placed into the manager's budget only to the extent that planned expenditures have been justified in detail.

A manager is often required to analyze planned activities in terms of purpose, cost, and value added. The benefits to be derived are weighed against the benefits that will be lost if the planned activity is carried out at a lesser level or not done at all. Implied is the requirement to explore different alternatives for achieving the same results. For example, the manager may analyze the pros and cons of using an in-house computer service or contracting with an outside agency.

Zero-based budgeting also forces managers to look at different levels of effect for performing an activity. The levels may range from zero activity to maximum or optimum activity. At each spending level, the manager would show the costs and the corresponding effect. A security manager, for example, might be required to analyze a guard operation arranged to function at the 50%, 75%, and 100% levels of spending. The security manager would describe the probable outcomes of operating at different cost levels. This approach forces each manager to examine other alternatives for getting the job done, and at the same time gives to management the alternative of reducing or eliminating an activity.

The budgeting process can be extensive, perhaps requiring a budget committee, typically consisting of the chief executive officer, the chief financial officer, and the budget director. The committee would develop spending policy and manage overall costs.

John J. Fay, CPP

Source Heyel, C., The Encyclopedia of Management. (Van Nostrand Reinhold, New York, 1982).

BUDGETING: JUSTIFICATION OF NEEDS

At the core of budget justification is the consideration that, when the budget is presented, upper management will ask: "Why do you need the money that you are requesting?" It is to the loss prevention manager's advantage to be prepared with well-researched answers supported by adequate documentation. For instance, if the manager is requesting additional funds for more loss prevention strategies to curb crime, then a summation of crime incidents for the previous year can support the justification. But this is only one way of justifying a loss prevention budget.

Justification can follow a cost-benefit approach. For example, the loss prevention manager may be able to show that the company's loss statistics related to crime, fire, and accidents are low in comparison to the same sets of statistics reported by comparable companies in the same industry and/or geographical area. These are the benefits that can be converted to dollars and they can logically incorporate related savings, such as lower insurance premiums and the value of property recovered. Benefit dollars are then compared against the cost dollars. Costs in this case might represent an enhanced pre-employment process for screening out applicants with crime histories, a fire prevention and suppression program, and a safety hazard

reduction program. Savings data like these make it so much easier for the loss prevention manager to justify his or her budget.

Other factors that actually or potentially create costs should be described. These can vary widely. The factors might relate to an increase in cash flow, the installation of dangerous machinery in a manufacturing process, or a union contract that is about to expire. Each of these factors will necessitate a cost-producing loss prevention effort of some type, e.g., increased cash flow may require new methods for collecting and storing funds, dangerous machinery may require operator training, and labor unrest may require activation of the company's strike plan. These are the details, complemented by dollar figures, which go into the justification of a budget.

The loss prevention manager should not fall into the trap of over-emphasizing results that are reactive in nature, such as the number of employees who were caught stealing. While results like these are certainly reportable they tend to suggest the failure of proactive or preventive controls. Profit enhancement through the medium of loss reduction is made possible by preventive controls. Because upper managers understand this proposition well, they are attuned to results that indicate problems of control.

A loss prevention budget is usually constructed through a process of give and take between the loss prevention manager and the supervisor to whom the manager reports. The process is adversarial but constructive. The loss prevention manager presents, the supervisor questions and challenges, and the process moves on until an agreement is reached. The budget reflects an understanding that certain essential services will be provided within certain described cost parameters.

The negotiating nature of the process, although tempered by good intentions on both sides, suggests that the loss prevention manager would be advised to come to the table with some well-developed insights to the supervisor's style, personality, interests, and idiosyncrasies. More importantly, the loss prevention manager will want to know the supervisor's cost containment objectives and the objectives passed down to the supervisor from an even higher level. The present financial condition of the company and its prospects for the future will shape budget requests generally. The loss prevention manager needs to put all of these considerations together in constructing a budget, defending it, and getting it approved.

Philip P. Purpura, CPP

Source Purpura, P.P., Security and Loss Prevention, 2nd Edition. (Butterworth Heinemann, Boston, 1991).

BUDGET PLANNING

Management is the coordinated application of resources to accomplish objectives. In this definition, managers carry out the functions of planning, organizing, directing, and controlling. The work activities of these functions consume resources that are purchased and are therefore measurable in dollars. The dollars planned to be expended are shown in budgets. There are many types of budgets. They can be used to show expenditures for projects that start and end, processes that never end, capital equipment purchases, a department's monthly activities, or the total organization's yearly activities. Budgets come in all sizes and shapes, serve a variety of purposes, and involve many different techniques.

All budgets have one thing in common, however; they have a close relationship with the planning function. This is so because the work activities planned to occur must be funded by dollars set aside in the budget. A budget can be viewed as:

• A plan stated in financial terms.
• An allocation of funds required to achieve planned objectives.
• A record of work activities in terms of monies appropriated.
• A tool for measuring the success of planned activities.

Let's use a simple situation to illustrate the relationship between planning and budgeting. Assume the security manager, in planning for the next fiscal year, concludes that a valuable work activity of the department will be to operate a rape avoidance program. The objective of the program is to minimize loss to the company resulting from lower productivity of employees who miss work or are distracted at work due to actual or perceived rape incidents. The security manager's plan is to conduct one rape avoidance presentation each quarter of the next year; the presentations will be made by a rape avoidance expert; a video tape on the topic will be

purchased; and the presentations will be held in the company's learning center, using in-house audiovisual equipment. The presentations will be announced by posters placed in the coffee bars and each attendee will receive a booklet that is available for sale from the community rape crisis center. The security manager estimates that 100 employees will attend each presentation. The budget might look like this:

Speaker fees	
Four @ $200 each	$ 800
Film purchase	$ 250
Posters	
Artwork	$ 150
Printing	$ 100
Booklets	
400 @ .50 each	$ 200
Total	$1500

This simple illustration does not take into account other costs, such as the security manager's time in managing the program, and the cost of the learning center and audiovisual equipment. Those costs might be rolled into other categories in the security manager's overall budget, and within that overall budget the rape avoidance project would be a very small item.

Forecasting

Work activities of today are based on yesterday's plans and tomorrow's expectations. Plans cannot be made without forecasting the future and what the future will bring. For example, a security manager's projection of growth in the company's employee population is a forecast of increased pre-employment screening activity; increased vehicle and pedestrian movement into, within, and from the premises; and increased pressure on the pass section to issue new access control badges.

It is well recognized that while forecasting is important in making rational decisions, the activity itself is more art than science. The value of a forecast is not in its relative accuracy, but in the fact that the activity requires the manager to give balanced consideration to factors that might influence the future. Because the past has never been a perfect predictor of the future, the manager is on mushy footing when making plans based solely on historical data.

Success at forecasting usually rests on a competency to judge under what conditions past occurrences can be relied upon. The manager must also be able to differentiate between new facts that are important and those that are irrelevant. The security manager cannot plan for the unknown or the unpredictable, but must instead concentrate on making an intelligent assessment of probabilities.

While the average line employee is thinking of work in terms of today, the manager is thinking about work stretched across substantially larger blocks of time. Thinking ahead is not necessarily a measure of intelligence, but of the conditioning effects of experience in meeting life's responsibilities.

Charles A. Sennewald, CPP

Source Sennewald, C.A., Effective Security Management, 2nd Edition. (Butterworth Heinemann, Boston, 1985).

BUREAU OF ALCOHOL, TOBACCO AND FIREARMS

The Bureau of Alcohol, Tobacco and Firearms (ATF) is an agency of the United States Department of the Treasury. ATF responsibilities are law enforcement; regulation of the alcohol, tobacco, firearms, and explosives industries; and ensuring the collection of the federal taxes imposed on distilled spirits and tobacco products. ATF has federal jurisdiction under the following laws: 1935 Federal Alcohol Administration Act; The Internal Revenue Code of 1954 as it relates to distilled spirits, tobacco products, and firearms; 1968 Gun Control Act (as amended); 1970 Title XI of the Organized Crime Control Act (Explosives Control Act); 1976 Portions of the Arms Export Control Act; 1968 Trafficking in Contraband Cigarettes Act; 1982 Anti-Arson Act (amended Title XI); and 1984 Armed Career Criminal Act.

The mission of ATF is to:

• Curb the illegal traffic in and criminal use of firearms. Special emphasis is placed on the apprehension of armed narcotics traffickers and repeat offenders who possess firearms by effectively enforcing federal firearms laws.

• Investigate bombings and other violations of federal explosives laws. Investigate arson-for-profit schemes. Remove safety hazards caused by improper storage of explosive materials.

• Regulate the alcohol, tobacco, firearms, and explosives industries.

• Trace the origin and movement of firearms recovered by law enforcement agencies worldwide.

• Assure the collection of all alcohol, and tobacco tax revenues, and obtain a high level of voluntary compliance with alcohol and tobacco tax laws.

• Suppress commercial bribery, consumer deception, and other prohibited trade practices in the alcoholic beverage industry.

• Assist the states in their efforts to eliminate the interstate trafficking in, and the sale and distribution of, cigarettes in avoidance of state taxes.

Bureau of Alcohol, Tobacco and Firearms

Source Public Affairs Pamphlet. (Bureau of Alcohol, Tobacco and Firearms, Washington, 1992).

BURGLARY: ATTACKS ON LOCKS

A door lock is usually all that prevents movement into a protected area, whether commercial or residential. Occasionally, a door lock will be supplemented with a padlock. Most door locks are key-operated. They consist of a cylinder or other opening for inserting a key that mechanically moves a bolt or latch. The bolt (or deadbolt) extends from the door lock into a bolt receptacle in the door frame.

The cylinder part of a lock contains the keyway, pins, and other mechanisms. Some locks, called double-cylinder locks, have a cylinder on each side of the door and require a key for both sides. With a single-cylinder lock, a thief may be able to break glass in or nearby the door and reach inside to turn the knob to release the lock. The disadvantage is that a key to the lock on the inside of the door must be readily available for emergency escape, such as during a fire.

The key-in-knob lock works on the same principles as the cylinder lock except, as the name implies, the keyway is in the knob. In the single key-in-knob lock the keyway is almost always on the outside door knob and a push or turn button for locking/unlocking is on the inside knob. The double key-in-knob lock has a keyway on the outside and inside knobs, which increases security but also decreases safety.

From the standpoint of forced entry, the cylinder lock is somewhat resistive in that it cannot be ripped easily from the door because it is seated flush or close to the surface. One model of the cylinder lock features a smooth, narrow ring around the neck of the cylinder. The ring moves freely so that even if it can be grasped by a tool, it cannot be twisted. The cylinder lock is vulnerable to a burglary tool called the slam hammer or slam puller. The device usually consists of a slender rod with a heavy sliding sleeve. One end of the rod has a screw or claw for insertion into the keyway. The other end has a retaining knob. When the sleeve is jerked away from the lock, striking the retaining knob, the lock cylinder or keyway is forcibly pulled out.

By contrast, the key-in-knob lock is somewhat more vulnerable because the knob itself can be hammered off; pried off with a crowbar; or pulled out by a grasping tool, such as channel lock pliers. Once the inner workings of the lock are exposed, the burglar can retract the bolt to open the door.

Probably one of the simplest attack techniques is slip-knifing. A thin, flat and flexible object, such as a credit card, is inserted between the strike and the latch bolt to depress the latch bolt and release it from the strike. Slip-knifing of sliding windows is accomplished by inserting a thin and stiff blade between the meeting rail (stile) to move the latch to the open position; slip-knifing of pivoting windows is done by inserting a thin and stiff wire through openings between the rail and the frame and manipulating the sash operator.

Springing the door is a technique in which a large screwdriver or crowbar is placed between the door and the door frame so that the bolt extending from the lock into the bolt receptacle is pried out, enabling the door to swing open. A 1-inch bolt will hinder this attack.

Jamb peeling is the prying off or peeling back the door frame at a point near the bolt receptacle. When enough of the jamb is removed from the receptacle, the receptacle can be broken apart or removed, allowing the door to swing open. A metal or reinforced door frame is the antidote.

Sawing the bolt is inserting a hacksaw blade between the door and the door frame and cutting through the bolt. The countermeasure is to use a bolt made of a saw-resistant alloy or a bolt that is seated in such a way that it will freely spin on its side, thereby taking away the resistance needed for the saw blade to gain purchase.

Spreading the frame involves the use of a jack, such as an automobile jack, in such a way that the door jambs on each side of the door are pressured apart to a point where the door will swing free from the bolt receptacle. A reinforced door frame and a long deadbolt are countermeasures.

Kicking in the door is a primitive, but effective technique. In this case, the attack is against the door so that even the best locking hardware will have little deterrent effect. The countermeasure is a metal door or a solid wood door, at least 1-3/4-inches thick, installed in a wooden door frame at least 2-inches thick, or a steel door frame. An escutcheon plate can be used to shield the bolt receptacle.

A more sophisticated attack technique is lock picking. It is seen infrequently because of the expertise required. Lock picking is accomplished by using metal picks to align the pins in the cylinder as a key would to release the lock. The greater the number of pins, the more difficult it is to align them. A cylinder should have at least six pins to be resistive to lock picking.

The high-security form of the combination lock requires manipulation of one or several numbered dials to gain access. Combination locks usually have three or four dials that must be aligned in the correct order for entrance. Because only a limited number of people will be informed of the combination, the problems associated with compromised mechanical keys and lock picking are removed. Combination locks are used at doors and on safes, bank vaults, and high-security filing cabinets; in most cases, the combination can be changed by the owner on an as-needed basis.

With older combination locks, skillful burglars may be able, often with the aid of a stethoscope, to discern the combination by listening to the locking mechanism while the dial is being turned. Another attack method is for the burglar to take a concealed position at a distance from the lock and with binoculars or a telescope observe the combination sequence when the lock is opened.

The combination padlock has mostly low-security applications. It has a numbered dial and may be supplemented with a keyway. On some models, a serial number impressed on the lock by the manufacturer will allow the combination to be determined by cross-checking against a reference manual provided by the manufacturer to dealers. Although a convenience, it is a risk to security.

In a technique called padlock substitution, the thief will remove the property owner's unlocked padlock and replace it with a similar padlock. After the property owner locks up and leaves, the thief will return, open the padlock and gain entry. The preventive measure is to keep padlocks locked even when not in use.

John J. Fay, CPP

Sources

Fennelly, L.J., Handbook of Loss Prevention and Crime Prevention. (Butterworth Heinemann, Boston, 1982).

Purpura, P.P., Security and Loss Prevention. (Butterworth Heinemann, Boston, 1984).

BUSINESS ETHICS

Ethics in business are the standards of conduct and judgment in respect to what is perceived as right and wrong. An intrinsic element of ethics is the specification of responsibility for human actions. Ethical standards go beyond merely describing conduct that we habitually accept; they seek to define higher goals and the means for attaining them.

The security manager encounters ethics in two dimensions: first, as the employer's instrument for developing business conduct policy and investigating improper conduct by others; and second, as an employee who is personally obligated to conduct business in accordance with the established policy.

The security manager knows well such unethical practices as misuse of proprietary information, kickbacks, and conflicts of interest. The controls for preventing and detecting offenses are clear cut and easily understood administrative mechanisms. It may be less clear to the security manager the expectations of senior management regarding the manager's decisions and conduct that impact the company's bottom line. For example, a security manager whose principal duties involve selling a security product may be caught between the choices of using persuasive, but deceptive, selling techniques and being scrupulously honest. How does senior management view the situation? Does the promise of profit take precedence over truth?

The continued deterioration of ethics in business should lead us to a closer examination of personal and corporate morality. Mainstream ethicists believe that an act is either intrinsically correct or incorrect, and that we have a duty to always act correctly. Others argue, however, that the reality of the human condition is that we all seek to engage in acts that derive pleasure, and acts that produce the greatest amount of pleasure for the greatest number of people are morally correct.

Code of Ethics

A traditional approach for promoting ethical conduct is the adoption of a code of ethics. Problems arise, however, due to concerns about who will create the code, who will be affected by it, what it will cover, and the sanctions that may be applied to violators.

In attempting to reconcile the various concerns about a code under development, the drafters may produce an ineffectual document. On the one hand it may be so watered down as to have no real impact on behavior, or on the other hand, include unattainable principles. In many cases it is impossible to select between competing and sometimes incompatible interests when moral questions are being examined.

A great difficulty lies in reconciling morality and profit. Realistically, a moral principle is not acceptable if it condemns business activity; as a result there is a natural tendency within business to see profit-making as a legitimate, if not moral, end in itself.

Principles of Business Conduct

A business is driven by the forces of economic reality, is constrained by the limits of custom and law, and is shaped by the human values of its workforce. A business, then, is an institution of people and ethics as well as an enterprise of profit and loss.

The ethical performance of a business is a matter of spirit and intent, as well as a matter of law. A company's business practices are the expression of management's philosophy and will often contain these basic principles:

• Businesses that succeed are those that conduct their affairs with honesty and integrity. These qualities are characterized by truthfulness and freedom from deception.

SAMPLE BUSINESS ETHICS POLICY

General. The Company has a policy of strict compliance with laws which are applicable to its businesses, wherever conducted. In some instances, law and regulations may be ambiguous and difficult to interpret. In such cases we would seek legal advice to which we have access in each business and at the corporate level in order to assure that we are in compliance with this policy and are observing all applicable laws and regulations. Compliance with the law means not only observing the law, but conducting our business affairs so that the Company will deserve and receive recognition as a law-abiding organization.

Entertainment, Gifts, Favors and Gratuities. The Company's guidelines governing levels of entertainment, gifts, favors, and gratuities, whether offered by employees or extended to them, are summarized below. They are acceptable if:

•They cannot be construed as intended to affect the judgement of the recipient so as to secure preferential treatment and
•They are of such limited nature and value that they could not be perceived by anyone to affect the judgement of the recipient and
•Public disclosure would not be embarrassing to the Company or the recipient. All relations with government or public officials should be conducted in a manner that will not adversely reflect on our reputation or the official's integrity and with the expectation that all such actions will become a matter of public knowledge.

Political Contributions. Corporate contributions, direct or indirect, and of whatever amount or type, to any political candidate or party, or to any other organization that might use the contributions for a political candidate or party, are illegal at the federal level and in some states. In those states where such contributions are legal, they should be made only upon the approval of the Director, State Government Affairs. In addition, political contributions at the federal or state level by any employee who is a "foreign national" (i.e., an employee who is not a citizen of the United States or has not been admitted for permanent residence) are illegal.

We may from time to time take stands on issues of public policy, particularly those that affect the Company's interests or those of its several constituencies. In such cases, we may elect to express our views publicly and spend company funds to ensure that our position is broadly disseminated. We may also provide financial support to groups that advocate positions essentially consistent with our own. The Company encourages individual employees to participate in the political process, including voluntary contributions to the Company's political action committee and to candidates and parties of their choice. However, no influence shall be exerted by any employee on another employee to make any personal political contribution or to engage in any political activity inconsistent with that employee's own personal inclination.

Accountability. The law requires that the Company and the businesses for which it is responsible keep accurate books, records, and accounts to fairly reflect the Company's transactions and that we maintain an adequate system of internal accounting controls. Therefore, it cannot be over-emphasized that our books and records should have the highest degree of integrity. Employees should fulfill their responsibilities to assure that books, records, and accounts are complete, accurate, and supported by appropriate documents in auditable form.

All vouchers, bills, invoices, expense accounts, and other business records should be prepared with care and complete candor. No false or misleading entries and no undisclosed or unrecorded funds or assets should be permitted for any reason. No payment is to be made for purposes other than those described in the documents supporting the payment.

Antitrust Laws. The Company endorses the view that a viable free-enterprise system rests upon the fundamental proposition that free and open competition is the best way to assure an adequate supply of goods and services at reasonable prices. Therefore, in carrying out his or her duties, every employee shall strictly adhere to the letter and spirit of the antitrust laws of the United States and with competition laws of any other country or any group of countries which are applicable to our business.

It is recognized that the antitrust laws are complex and difficult to interpret. They also have application to a very broad range of activities. In these circumstances, employees should take the initiative to consult the Law Department whenever the proper course of action is in doubt. We consider compliance with the applicable antitrust laws so vitally important that neither claims of ignorance and good intentions, nor failure to seek timely advice will be accepted as an excuse for noncompliance.

Conflict of Interest. The term "conflict of interest" describes any circumstance that could cast doubt on our ability to act with total objectivity with regard to interests of our business. We not only want to be loyal to the Company, we want that loyalty to come easily, free from any conflicting interests.

While we fully respect the privacy of employees in the conduct of their personal affairs, we insist that each employee fully discharges his or her obligations of faithful service to the business. Activities which involve the unauthorized use of time, equipment, or information, which significantly interfere with business interests will be avoided. Of particular concern are situations in which our personal interests may conflict with the interests of our business in relations with present or prospective suppliers, customers, or competitors.

The use of an employee's position or the assets or influence of the organization for personal advantage or for the advantage of others is prohibited. In order to avoid potential conflicts with regard to accepting outside employment regarding consultancies, directorships, part-time or free lance activities, the employee should discuss the particulars with his or her immediate supervisor prior to accepting employment.

Generally, it is our policy that employees may not, except at the direction of the Company, undertake any discussions or activities with potential participants, lenders, advisors or attorneys relative to the possible purchase of any business for which the Company is responsible. This applies whether or not that business has been applied for divestiture.

If an employee desires to undertake any such activity on his or her own behalf or on behalf of others, before doing so he or she should advise the Chief Financial Officer of the Company who will determine in each case whether such activity can be conducted in such a way so as to protect the best interests of the Company.

Prohibited Investments. The Company prohibits employees from purchasing or dealing, either directly or indirectly, in any:

•Interest (or option to purchase or sell interest) in any organization or concern that the employee knows is a candidate for acquisition by the corporation or is under consideration for some other business arrangement with the corporation. This provision, however, does not apply to ownership of stock or securities amounting to less than one-half of one percent of the outstanding stock of any publicly held corporation. For purposes of this policy, a "publicly held corporation" is one whose shares are listed on a recognized stock exchange or are included in the daily over-the-counter list of quotations of the National Association of Securities Dealers and published in the Wall Street Journal.

•Interest in any supplier, competitor or customer with whom we do business.
•Contracts, options, or any other form of participation in the commodities' futures or trading markets and in any commodity which we sell.

These prohibitions apply to purchasing and dealings by members of the employee's household or by a third party if intended to benefit the employee. They apply only to "purchasing and dealing" and do not apply to acquisitions by inheritance or gift nor do they apply to employees who are members of collective bargaining units.

Managers are requested to take necessary actions to ensure their employees are aware of these prohibitions.

Employees should also be urged to discuss any questions they may have pertaining to prohibited investments with their immediate supervisor or designated ethics coordinator within their operating company or staff department.

Other prohibitions, in addition to those above, may be prescribed by individual business who will make these prohibitions known to affected employees.

Use of Classified Information. Company classified information is found in many types, forms and locations. Security measures applicable to the protection of information are to be followed.

It is our policy that all classified business information is used solely for our own purposes and is not to be provided to unauthorized persons or used for the purpose for furthering a private interest or making a personal profit.

We would ensure that all material non-public information concerning the securities, financial condition, earnings, or activities of the Company remain protected until fully and properly disseminated to the public. Examples of areas of particular sensitivity are current interim earnings figures or trends, possible acquisitions or divestitures, exploration and production plans, and new plants, products, or processes.

Procurement. We require that our employees maintain the highest ethical principles in the acquisition of goods and services. Procurement practices and procedures should:

•Provide equal opportunity to all qualified firms wanting to do business with us.
•Treat all suppliers and contractors fairly and consistently.
•Be meticulously applied.

During the bidding process, difficulties may arise when bidders offer unsolicited price reductions or other concessions after bid submission, or attempt to enter into other post-bid negotiations which go beyond the normal bid clarification process. Acceptance of such unsolicited offers during bidding is contrary to our procurement policy.

Bids are considered confidential and are never to be provided to anyone outside the Company, and, within the Company, only to authorized personnel. Further, pains must be taken to treat all bidders equally during the bid period, especially with respect to bid document interpretations and clarifications.

The Company procurement policy, reflecting ethical business practice, is issued by the Corporate Materials and Contracts Department. Businesses and staffs are expected to establish their own procedures consistent with such policies.

Non-Compliance. Compliance with this Business Conduct Policy carries the highest priority throughout the Company. Failure to comply with the principles of business conduct may unnecessarily expose us and our employees to risks in the form of administrative sanctions, civil proceedings and/or criminal prosecution.

Management is responsible for instituting preventative measures, ensuring that violations of Business Conduct Policy are thoroughly investigated by competent professionals experienced in ensuring equal respect is given to the rights of employees and objectives of the Company and the business for which it is responsible, and taking the appropriate administrative and/or disciplinary actions consistent with the infraction.

Legal Violations. Diversion of Company assets, fraud embezzlement, theft, and intentional damage to equipment and similar events all represent criminal actions against the Company. It is our policy to seek and assist the prosecution of persons who are believed to have committed criminal acts against the Company. Particulars of the case will be presented to the appropriate law enforcement agency for a determination in pursuing prosecution. In addition, any criminal loss exceeding $75,000 requires an investigative audit with assistance from Internal Audit and Corporate Security.

Policy Violations. Violations of this policy on business conduct more often will not result in violations of law; however, they result in violating the spirit and intent of ethical behavior. These may include: unauthorized use or disclosure of classified information; accepting gifts or entertainment of material value that affects our ability to be impartial; records manipulation; and conflict of interest. Management's response to such cases usually will be handled internally and disciplinary procedures will be applied where deemed appropriate.

Follow-Through. There are two broad actions we can take to ensure that our written commitment to ethical business conduct pays off in practice.

The first is to provide a mechanism that will help us handle difficult judgement decisions in those "gray areas" where it is often hard to pinpoint right from wrong. None of us should be uncomfortable in handling a question of ethics.

When such situations arise, we must seek counsel. The system is very simple. Ask the person to whom you report.

All managers are to maintain an open-door policy with regard to questions of ethics. They are to make themselves easily available to any of us who have such questions. We are reminded that the time to bring up a question of moral standard or ethical behavior is before the fact, rather than after the fact. We must never hesitate to talk to our supervisors about a question of business conduct, no matter how small or insignificant it may seem to be.

The second action consists of several steps that will make attention to this policy an integral part of managing our business. These steps are as follows:

•The Director, Corporate Security is assigned oversight of a follow-through program.
•Each business and staff group will establish a procedure to ensure that at least once a year these principles of business conduct are reviewed with their managerial employees. Additionally, each business and staff group will designate at least one person to whom any employee may communicate freely on matters concerning the interpretation, application, or suspected violation of these principles. Such designees will, routinely, keep the Director, Corporate Security apprised of activities/inquiries with respect to these principles which arise in the ordinary course of business.

> •Urgent issues of this nature will be immediately communicated to the Director, Corporate Security, who will consult, as appropriate, with the Audit and Law Departments as to the appropriate course of action.
> •Any allegation or suspicion that unethical or illegal activities are taking place will be reported to Corporate Security and, where appropriate, will be thoroughly investigated in a competent, fair, and confidential manner, with equal respect being given to the rights of the employee and the objectives of the Company.
> •The General Auditor will establish procedures to monitor management's compliance with our principles of business conduct and will annually report the results of this effort to the Chief Executive Officer of the Company and to others as he or she may direct.

•There is no conflict between pursuit of profit and attention to ethics. Business generally will prosper in an environment that is fair, open, and morally secure.

•Employees are the key to ethical business conduct, and their behavior is strongly influenced by the way they are treated and how they view management. Ethics flourish in an environment that fosters individual self-respect, loyalty, and dedication.

A business ethics policy will usually express these overriding principles in a more specific format, setting out personal standards, responsibilities and sanctions. The policy provides a framework against which individual employees can measure their own personal conduct and management can establish a supportive climate by communicating the principles and setting the example.

John J. Fay, CPP

Sources

Principles of Business Conduct. (BP America, Cleveland, 1990).

Heyel, C., The Encyclopedia of Management. (Van Nostrand Reinhold, New York, 1982).

BUSINESS INTELLIGENCE: AN OVERVIEW

Business intelligence is both a product and a process. As a product, it is information with use and value that can be applied by decision makers to the organization's particular purposes or goals. As a process, it is a combination of ethical and legitimate activities that involve the collection, evaluation, analysis, integration, and interpretation of data obtained from open and covert sources. Industrial espionage is a loose, generic term that describes the harnessing of the business intelligence process in a manner that may or may not be entirely legitimate or which involves the use of a legitimately developed intelligence product to achieve an illegal end.

Open sources of business information are publicly available. They include information presented by the news media, public records, government reports and reports issued by business competitors, such as annual reports and stock offerings. On the gray fringe are the competitors' internal newsletters, proposals to prospective clients, and similar documents that are usually not confidential and which would be impossible for the authoring organizations to control in any meaningful way.

For the user of open information, the caveat is extreme caution because the data is often a potpourri of fact, fiction, half-truths, and deliberate distortions. The challenge to the collector of publicly available information is to ferret out the factual portions and combine them with pieces of data obtained from other sources.

Covert sources of information include informants, paid and unpaid, witting and unwitting. They may be the targeted organization's regular, temporary, and contractor employees, as well as suppliers, vendors, clients, and other competitors. They may also be the wives, children, or friends of these individuals.

Also included are the collector's operatives who may be in-house employees or outside contractors, and may range in skill from amateur to veteran professional. Operative activities can consist of recruiting and directing informants, going undercover into the targeted organization, intercepting written communications to and from the target, maintaining visual and photographic surveillance of the target's activities, conducting audio surveillance with the use of covert listening devices, and posing as headhunters to possibly acquire from the target's key employees sensitive information that may be inadvertently leaked during a bogus job interview. The more odious tasks involve searching the competitor's trash, breaking and entering, and blackmailing the vulnerable.

The information sought by industrial spying is usually proprietary in nature, i.e., it is information owned by a company or entrusted to it that has not been disclosed publicly and has value. Trade secrets, patents, business plans, research and development discoveries, and the like are examples. Proprietary information is generally under the owner's protective shield, except when it is also classified government data entitled to protections afforded by the government.

The dark side of business intelligence has only recently come to be acknowledged as a serious threat to the viability of a business and, in a larger sense, to entire industries and national economies. As companies, industries, and nations move to dependence on technologically intense products and services, as is the case in the United States, business spying will expand and intensify. Adding fuel to this fire is the availability of national spying infrastructures that can be converted from military to business objectives.

John J. Fay, CPP

C

CAMPUS SECURITY: A HISTORICAL PERSPECTIVE

The future of campus security is guided by its past. Only by understanding where it has been and where it is now, can campus security determine where it needs to go. The history of security on college campuses provides the basis for charting the "big plan" for campus security.

Although the histography of American universities has been limited, with regard to the examination of campus security as an infrastructure, much of the historical discourse suggests that security provided an element of control in response to increased violence and student demonstrations. This article, however, provides a different explanation for the development of campus security and is based upon the recent completion of an institution-specific comparative case study [1].

In fact, the research indicated that the evolving infrastructure of campus security was largely a response to the need for control over the outsider. The outsider represents the universities' fear of individuals or groups who pose a threat to the campus inhabitants and property.

The history of campus security represents a unique infrastructure that has a long and rich history dating back to the 15th century. This 15th-century informal campus security system was at Oxford University. Individuals performing what could be described as security-related activities were referred to as bedels. As servants appointed to execute the orders of the chancellor and the proctor, they would serve writs, collect fines, and escort "evil-doers" to prison. The bedels were charged with keeping order, making lists of offenders, and seeing to the punishment and fines. Money that was collected from the fines was used to pay the bedels for maintaining security on the campus at night.

Yale University is noted for adopting the first formal campus security department in 1894. The college had previously responded to crime and student violence informally with the assistance of the Blue Skin Club started by Julian Sturtevants, a Yale undergraduate. Sturtevants, along with three close friends, formed the club to report all violations of college rules.

As a result of the increased strain of "town-gown" relations and the recommendation of a special task force, local police were used at night to patrol the campus. Ultimately, these officers were hired away from the city to form the Yale campus police.

The history of student control has been described as a struggle or series of negotiations between students and administrators for control. This struggle provides an explanation for the student unrest, violence on campus, and the subsequent initial impetus for campus security.

The Revolutionary War brought about many contributory factors that led to student revolt. The purpose and role of higher education in this country became less defined. Students entering colleges during these post-war years pursued a path different from their earlier predecessors, who were usually preparing for the ministry. These new college students were not as willing to passively accept administrative and faculty demands.

Post-revolutionary presidents and professors had been trained as ministers in 18th century colleges. Their philosophies and ideologies contrasted violently with the new student culture. They were unyielding to student complaints and consistently traditional in disciplinary actions. The colleges' ability to persist in student control was fostered by support from the local community who were fearful of civil disorder. This continual war between faculty and students etched out a student culture very different from that of the 18th century. Unquestionably, student control both on campus and off was a major concern for college administrators and faculty who normally handled all disciplinary action. Not surprisingly, faculty-student relations were embittered and extremely confrontational. Students during this period battled not only with interclass rivalries, but outsiders as well.

Although the literature suggests a correlation between the emergence and growth of campus security and student revolt, there is very little discussion on campus security prior to the 1950s. There are references, however, to the night watchman, who emerged from the physical plant or buildings and ground departments. The night watchman has been described as the early predecessor to our modern day campus security officer. During the early 20th century the watchman's responsibilities were varied, but normally consisted of performing maintenance-oriented tasks; checking building locks and lights; and most importantly, watching for fires. With the advent of prohibition in the early 1930s the watchman acquired the additional responsibilities of observing for and reporting those violating rules such as curfew, drinking on campus, and entertaining members of the opposite sex in dormitories.

Although the concept of security in the university setting began as a fire watch system, commonly staffed by building nightwatchmen, in the years following World War II more and more colleges began to develop formal security departments.

The student demonstrations of the 1960s were very instrumental in increasing the numbers of these departments across the country. The 1960s also represented a change in the role of administration. The practice of *in loco parentis*, in the place or position of a parent, was replaced by legal concepts that recognized the civil rights and responsibilities of students. Consequently, the campus assumed a more open atmosphere that recognized the citizen rights of students. Changes from restricted and sexually segregated dormitories to a more open environment with co-educational residences resulted in a significant social transformation of college campuses.

During the mid to late 1970s, campus security departments experienced even greater growth. Often, the growth resulted from violent crimes that occurred on campus. These periods in the history of campus security, each acting on the other, gave way to changes in the role of campus security and describe what has typically happened across the country.

Campus security, therefore, can best be described as an infrastructure that serves as a necessary support service that has evolved in response to a perceived obligation by administration to provide a safe and secure environment for the campus community.

This service orientation refers to the handling of a wide variety of situations in which the law may have been violated, but the campus security officer chooses to deal with the situation by employing some alternative to invoking the criminal process. For example, an officer may intervene to arbitrate quarrels, to pacify the unruly, and to aid people in trouble. With a service orientation the officer may be continuously looking for violations, however minor, for the purpose of intervening, and

perhaps preventing an arrest situation from developing.

In contrast, campus security officers, with a law enforcement orientation, often approach situations by invoking criminal statutes in which a violation or offense has occurred. Their ultimate goal is to make an arrest or to report the actions of the individual in order to obtain some form of punitive action against the person. This type of orientation is consistent with that of student control and emphasizes a need to maintain law and order within the campus community.

The student demonstrations of the 1960s acted as a catalyst for the reorganization and enhanced responsibilities of a number of campus security departments. Many universities, in an effort to diminish the "watchman" images of their campus security officers, promoted a law enforcement orientation for their security departments. As a matter of fact, many departments have changed their name to public safety rather than that of campus security.

Furthermore, the inherited explanation that campus security developed because administrators needed another means of controlling students does not adequately describe what took place historically at the private colleges examined for this article. The years prior to and following the Civil War were not accompanied by any notable problems of student unrest at either college. Rules governing student control were relatively unchanged and consistently enforced until the end of the 19th century. Contrary to the historical discourse, student control was not an element of great concern to the leaders of the private colleges in these two cases.

The issue of service, however, continues to play a far more significant role in the development of campus security and is much more complex than just an attempt by administrators and faculty to control student life. The historical analysis, albeit of only two institutions, pointed to the importance of service and the providing of a safe and secure environment on those campuses. Interestingly, campus security at both private colleges had very little, if any, problems with student control. The locus of control for campus security was not over the student, but over the would-be outside villain or criminal waiting to prey upon the unsuspecting campus community. Emphasis upon enforcement was not based upon the need to control students, but from fear of the outsider.

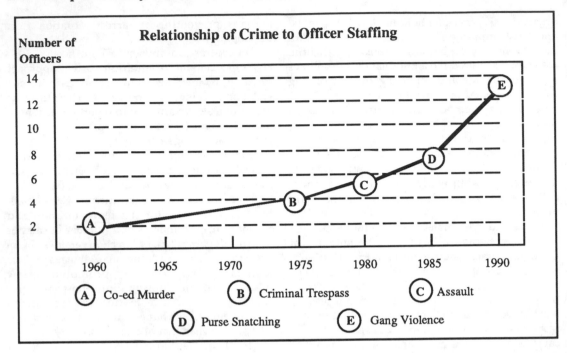

Number of Officers

Relationship of Crime to Officer Staffing

14
12
10
8
6
4
2

1960   1965   1970   1975   1980   1985   1990

(A) Co-ed Murder   (B) Criminal Trespass   (C) Assault

(D) Purse Snatching   (E) Gang Violence

What this suggests is that colleges have not completely relinquished the concept of in loco parentis. As a matter of fact, contrary to the widespread agreement that the relationship is no longer one of in loco parentis, the doctrine is very much alive at these private colleges. True to its definition, that of surrogate parent, in loco parentis is one of the guiding forces behind campus security.

Vestiges of this concept still exist, but greater emphasis is placed upon a parental role of protection rather than discipline. Student control, for these two colleges, has never completely been out of administration's hands. The growth and development of security can be attributed to the concern for providing a safe and secure environment. This is evidenced by the provided chart which illustrates that every increase in staffing was preceded by an act of violence or crime directed toward the college or campus community.

This perceived need for student control has been linked closely with the history of campus security. Therefore, the importance of understanding student control is critical to a historical explanation for campus security in this country. What the historical argument has not taken into consideration, however, are issues relating to service/enforcement orientations and

the significance of corresponding policies and procedures.

There is very little discussion in the literature on policies and procedures, and their relative importance in defining role orientation. There is clearly a lack of direction for both public and private universities regarding their support service roles. Guidance toward providing policy makers with information that could help clarify policy matters regarding campus security appears to be a very scarce commodity.

In order to develop a more comprehensive understanding of the importance of policies and procedures to role orientation, the following questions were asked of administrators, faculty, students, and officers at the private colleges:

• Who establishes policies and procedures for the campus security department on issues relating to student discipline, rules of conduct, crimes, and offenses?

• Is the perceived versus actual role of campus security by faculty, students and administration compatible with the orientation of the security department?

• If perceptions are incompatible, what impact does this have on policy formation and program effectiveness?

Predictably, the mission statements for both private colleges were relatively the same, emphasizing the importance of providing an atmosphere free from fear for personal safety, property loss, or accident. The purpose of the security department could best be described as creating and maintaining a feeling of confidence by the campus community.

Interestingly, beyond a generic policy statement the security departments at both colleges operate without specific and current procedural guidelines. Both departments rely primarily on a system of "management by memo." The difficulty of this type of management, for the officer, is that it provides minimal guidance or direction on events or decisions they may have to make where specific policy has not been established. This is very similar to "management by crisis" where reaction occurs after the fact. This style fosters a reactionary approach to dealing with those situations facing campus security on a daily basis.

The significance of this is that both departments have a service-oriented policy statement and the officers' responsibilities clearly suggest an emphasis on adopting a service orientation. Therefore, the current method of administrative management is in direct conflict with the proactive approach suggested in the departments' mission statement. The interviews that were conducted at the two private colleges showed that perceptions vary dramatically between students, faculty, administration, and even among the officers themselves. This perceptual confusion of role orientation is linked to policy and procedural deficiencies at both colleges.

Although each institution had developed a list of duties and responsibilities the officers were to perform, they had not given formal guidance as to how to adequately complete the identified tasks. Therefore, officers commonly responded differently to similar situations. These procedural inconsistencies reduced the ability of the security departments to distinguish between public police and private institutional needs. This also inhibited the clarity of role orientation for those in the campus community.

The listing of job responsibilities, service activities, and management by memo cannot serve as a department's formal policies and procedures, because it provides minimal guidance or direction on events or decisions officers may have to make. These types of documents, in and of themselves, provide merely a listing of activities or

responsibilities the officer may be required to perform, but offer no guidance on how they are to be accomplished. They may not even be realistic given the resources and staffing levels. Therefore, the lack of policies and procedures often results in frustration and subsequent decline in morale.

The significance of this upon the "big plan" is that policies and procedures provide the necessary foundation on which role orientation is developed, and that greater emphasis should be placed upon their comprehensive development and implementation. In order to learn from the past, the future of campus security should not continue to be driven by external forces, whether it be student control or control from the outsider. The focus should be upon internal issues, and how campus security as an infrastructure of the university can become more effective as a support service to the campus community. The future for campus security depends upon the development of sound policies and procedures that complement as well as demonstrate a commitment to providing quality of service and results in a safe and secure college environment.

The big plan holds that campus security should be viewed as a requisite component of American higher education and as an integral part of the campus infrastructure, providing a unique and necessary support agency.

Pam Collins, Ed.D.

Notes

1. The campus security departments of two private colleges served as the basis for a dissertation research entitled *Campus Security: An Historical Analysis of the Campus Infrastructure with Emphasis on Service/Orientation and Its Relation to Policies and Procedures*, 1991, Pamela A. Collins.

CASH REGISTER AUDITING: A COMPUTER-AIDED APPROACH

Because the investigation of cash register overages and shortages is the primary responsibility of many retail security or loss prevention managers, they often get the first call when a store's cash register totals do not balance.

The security manager may decide to proceed with an investigation based on the store manager's assessment that the loss was caused by theft. If such suspicions have not been aroused, the security manager may choose to keep an eye on the situation, waiting for the problem to disappear or reoccur.

But what if the store manager ignores the problem, fearing it's disclosure would reflect negatively on his or her management abilities? Or what if the manager is part of the overage or shortage problem?

As security professionals, we must be able to identify, analyze, and investigate cash register problems without waiting for referrals from store managers. While we should not ignore their calls for assistance, we should temper our views of the information provided by store managers with facts from our own ongoing analysis and investigation. By regularly looking at store overages and shortages, we can not only anticipate problems, but also get an unbiased view of the source of the problem.

One way to accomplish this review is through a highly structured, systematic approach to the analysis and investigation of cash register overages and shortages. The system, which is applicable to both large and small retail environments, is divided into two phases: analysis and investigation. While each phase works independently, together they offer the security professional a powerful tool. By using this investigative technique in conjunction with a personal computer, the security manager can:

1. Quickly focus on problem stores in the company or within a certain locale.

2. Eliminate needless and costly investigations.

3. Be assured all problems are being investigated.

4. Rank stores from those with the biggest problems to those with the smallest and work as deeply into this list as time and staff will allow.

5. Limit time in the office so more time can be spent in the field identifying solutions.

6. Match employee's schedules to the occurrence of repeated overages and shortages.

7. Sort and rank all employees according to their "percentage of responsibility," a statistical ranking formula indicating a relative factor of responsibility for the occurrence of overages and shortages.

As stated earlier, the discovery of cash register overages and shortages in retail stores requires a two-phase response. During the analysis phase, all the overage and shortage problems at the store in question are compared against each other. This study produces a sorted list that ranks the store's problems in order of seriousness. Then, during the investigation phase, specific steps can be taken to identify personnel responsible for the overages and shortages, gathering sufficient evidence to substantiate disciplinary action or criminal prosecution.

Unfortunately, too many security managers seem to jump directly into the investigative phase without properly analyzing the data or the problem. This mistake will not cause much trouble if only one store is involved, it only wastes time. But, if the security manager is responsible for more than 50 stores, wasting time and resources on unnecessary investigations is a disaster. Placing emphasis on analysis can prevent such waste.

The analysis phase has three categories: monthly analysis, store historical analysis, and employee analysis.

The Monthly Analysis

The monthly analysis is the first step in ranking the stores and analyzing the security staff's ability to handle overage or shortage problems. This analysis lists, sorts, and ranks stores by the seriousness of their problems. Once this information is known, the security manager can allocate staff time accordingly. The monthly analysis is divided into six steps.

List Monthly Totals by Store. To begin the monthly analysis, overages and shortage figures for the month, and overage and shortage figures for the year to date are needed for each store. Be sure to take the time to ensure the accuracy of figures. No matter where the figures originate, make sure they are correct and complete.

Add Monthly Totals to Year-to-Date Totals. The monthly figures should be added to a year-to-date list of overages and shortages for each store. A glance through this second list will highlight stores with a cumulative total high enough to warrant investigation, even though other stores may show higher monthly totals for the current month.

Sort and Rank Both Lists. Once the new monthly figures are added to the year-to-date figures, both lists are sorted and ranked from the greatest shortage to the greatest overage.

Prepare Monthly Summary Sheets. Most security managers sort and rank these monthly overage and shortage figures. Circulate this monthly summary sheet to operations executives to show them the monthly status of overages and shortages. The number of entries on this sheet will depend, of course, on the number of stores in the chain and the security department's investigative capabilities. The summary sheet gives information to use when making the decision as to whether an investigation is necessary.

Complete Investigative Sheets. Investigative sheets are a detailed study of the overage and shortage activity at a particular store. These investigative sheets list the monthly overage and shortage history for the present year and the previous year. This data will give a clear picture of a pattern at any particular store. The investigative sheet also provides the opportunity to list comments about trends, past investigative efforts, and future plans.

Investigative sheets can be the backbone of a system for scheduling investigations. They are completed on the top 10 stores identified through the monthly and year-to-date figures on the summary sheets.

Once an investigative summary sheet is completed on the stores with the greatest problems in each category for each month, the investigative staff is quickly able to select the 10 stores that require their immediate attention. This selection can be made in a group session with all members of the loss prevention staff in attendance.

Decide and Select. At this point, enough information has been gathered to decide which stores the investigators will concentrate on in the coming month. This decision is affected by four factors:

1.   The size of the security staff.
2.   The distance between stores.
3.   The company's policy regarding requirements for terminating an employee.
4.   The availability of investigative and shopping services.

Once it has been decided which stores will be investigated in the coming months, a master schedule is completed, showing the exact completion dates and times for investigative services.

The Store Historical Analysis

The next step is to take a different view of the month's statistics through a store historical analysis. This analysis takes a closer look at the activity in each store through daily, rather than monthly or annual, overage and shortage figures. Through this examination, patterns may come to light. Problems occurring on a regular basis might indicate a planned incident or might help identify employees who need more training.

The store historical analysis sets up key data for examination. It consists of four phases:

Collect Data. The collection of data is the most important part of any overage or shortage analysis and accuracy must be assured. A daily report should be prepared for each register in the store.

Correct for Errors. Once this data is compiled, the majority of common errors can be identified quickly and corrected. Whenever people handle money, errors occur. The two most frequent are change errors, where incorrect amounts are exchanged between registers, and wash errors, where money put into the register at setup is counted incorrectly.

To get an accurate picture of a store's unexplained overages and shortages, these counting errors and paperwork errors must be factored out. Look for corresponding overages and shortages at the same register on subsequent days, or corresponding overages and shortages at different registers on the same day.

As a general rule, if the difference between the two figures is 10% or less of the smallest of the two figures, it is an error that should be corrected. Amounts less than $5 can be ignored since their cause is frequently hard to determine and they only water down the figures of the more significant problems.

Analyze the Data. Next, enter these daily figures on a blank monthly calendar. Identify key days or special events that took place within the month, such as paydays, days the store manager was off, holidays, or days when popular events such as rock concerts or football games took place. Identifying these special days is important because overages and shortages occurring on or close to these days might indicate a pattern that reveals the dishonest actions of one or more employees.

Decide and Select. Examination of the pattern leads to a decision to focus on particular employees at one or more particular stores and to select all or certain of the suspected employees for further investigation.

Steps in Analyzing Overages and Shortages

Monthly Analysis

1. List monthly totals by store.
2. Add monthly totals to YTD totals.
3. Sort and rank YTD and monthly totals.
4. Complete summary sheets.
5. Decide and select.

Store Historical Analysis

1. Collect data.
2. Correct for errors.
3. Analyze data.
4. Decide and select.

Employee Analysis

1. Separate overages and shortages.
2. Divide each group into subgroups of $5-10; $10-20; and over $20.
3. List monthly shorts and overs.
4. List employee schedules.
5. Calculate percent of responsibility.
6. Sort and rank each list.
7. Produce total page.
8. Decide and select.

Employee Analysis

An employee analysis is the last stage of the preliminary investigation. During this phase, individual employees who might be responsible for the overages and shortages under investigation can be uncovered. This conclusion can be reached by comparing each employee's work schedule with the occurrence of the overages and shortages. Obviously, an employee could not have been responsible for an overage or shortage unless he or she was working the day it occurred. The employee analysis consists of the following six steps.

Separate Overages and Shortages. In the retail loss prevention environment, it is easy to focus attention on shortages only. However, any thorough investigation should contain an analysis and investigation of repeated overages as well. To begin an employee analysis, these two figures are collected and compiled on separate sheets.

Divide Each Category into Subgroups. Each category can then be divided into the following groups for analysis: $5 to $10, $10 to $20, and more than $20. Once again, shortages and overages of less than $5 can be ignored. Using separate sheets for each category of overages and shortages will make the analysis easy to understand.

List Information. To get a picture of employee involvement, a grid is prepared. The dollar amounts of the overages and shortages are listed across the top of the grid, and the employee names are listed down the left column. The schedules for all employees should be examined and the sheet marked to indicate whether an employee worked on the day a particular overage or shortage occurred.

Calculate the Percent of Responsibility. Calculating the percent of responsibility involves mathematically analyzing an individual's overall probability of being responsible for each overage or shortage. The mathematical formula that determines this weighted factor compares the number of days an employee worked of the total work days per month and the number of times an employee was present when a shortage or overage occurred.

The scale identifies employees whose total work days approach the total number of days they are present when problems occur. These are indeed the employees an investigation should target.

Employees who work less frequently during the month but more often when events occur will receive a higher factor. For example, consider a store manager who works 6 days a week and a cashier who works 3 days a week. On the surface, it might appear the manager would score higher on the scale because he is at the store more often. But the formula corrects for this situation. The manager will actually score lower than the cashier, since the cashier worked almost the same number of days as the number of days a shortage occurred. Conversely, if both the cashier and the manager had been present on the days a shortage occurred, the cashier would have scored higher on the scale because she worked fewer days in the month.

Analyze the Data. Once a detailed examination of the shortages is completed using this formula, the same method of examination is used to analyze the overages. Placing these two summary charts side by side shows many employees who can be removed from suspicion.

Decide and Select. Again, a point is reached to make a decision about who is most likely involved and to decide to continue the investigation further.

Computer-Aided Analysis

The survey method outlined in this article can be of substantial use to any investigator looking into a series of problems with cash register overages and shortages. Done manually, however, it can be very time consuming. Repeated multiple numerical analysis can be done quickly and efficiently using a personal computer (PC) and a specially designed software program [1].

Once data has been entered into the computer, it can be stored, copied, archived, and manipulated in a variety of ways. Data on overages and shortages and employee schedules that are contained in a mainframe computer can be retrieved and loaded into the PC, eliminating the need for the investigative staff to perform the data entry functions. In short, a computer-aided program can save countless hours of paperwork and free valuable time for investigative work in the field.

Terry J. Ball

Note

1. The author has developed a software program for conducting the numerical analysis. It is called "Computer Sleuth." More information can be obtained by contacting the author in care of Gillespie Polygraph, Post Office Box 56, Lynnwood, WA 98046.

CCTV: APPLICATIONS IN SECURITY

Installation of closed-circuit television cameras (CCTV) around a site perimeter would require adequate light or use of cameras designed for operation in low light. The cameras would require protection from the elements; depending on the prevailing climate, housings and enclosures, mounting brackets, scanners, pan/tilt units, and the like should not necessarily be chosen on a dollars-and-cents basis. Keeping the costs down by accepting a lower-quality item, or overextending equipment by attempting to use an item designed for indoor or light duty in an outdoor or heavy-duty application, will probably result in unsatisfactory service because of breakdowns and necessary replacement of prematurely worn or broken parts.

Cameras should be installed high enough to provide an unobstructed view and prevent surreptitious tampering or redirection. They should, whenever possible, be placed below sources of area light to prevent their inadvertent pan through a bright light and the resultant "bloom" that will temporarily blind them. All such perimeter cameras should be equipped with pan/tilt capabilities and zoom lenses. At facilities where the perimeter is an isolation zone wherein no authorized movement will be taking place, the use of a video motion-detector system may offer excellent backup to a perimeter microwave intrusion-detection system.

At facilities that require visitors to sign in and be searched prior to authorized entry, CCTV monitoring of the officer on duty at the entry control post and the individual being processed assures a measure of protection for the officer. Aggressive actions by the person or persons attempting to gain entry would result in the immediate closure of that access point and the dispatch of assistance forces.

Where the facility has security-controlled remotely operated doors, CCTV cameras positioned at that point allow the identification of individuals to determine their access authorization.

Where the door is an entry or exit point to a controlled area that prohibits the introduction or removal of certain items, a CCTV installation enables the security officer to observe the individual to ensure this prohibition is being observed prior to activating the door-release mechanism. Used in this manner, CCTV is part of the site access control system.

The use of CCTV would be of great benefit in facilities where precious metals or minerals are mined, refined, or processed; used in the manufacture of a product; stored as raw stock or as a completed product awaiting shipment; or displayed for sale or as art objects.

Because of the high dollar value of a relatively small amount of precious metal and certain rare or strategic minerals, the unauthorized diversion of any quantity would result in a monetary or other unacceptable loss to the owner. Where the potential for such diversion exists or where losses are already being experienced, the installation of a quality CCTV surveillance system that offers total coverage of all areas is highly recommended, prevailing laws notwithstanding. (This would preferably be in conjunction with the institution of a system of access controls, personnel and package searches, and other procedures to curtail such diversion.) The cameras should be equipped with pan/tilt features as well as zoom lenses.

Where the spaces being monitored contain machinery or material that obstructs the camera view, consideration should be given to:

•Removing the obstructions to allow a clear field of vision.

•Rearranging the items in the space to allow a clear field of vision.

•Using more cameras so that no area within the monitored space(s) can hide a human or provide cover for an unauthorized act.

•Using a tracked system that allows more flexibility in camera position (but has certain disadvantages).

In reality, a combination of these features would be the best solution. The use of translucent domes for all cameras is recommended so that personnel in the monitored spaces cannot see in which direction the camera may be pointing and therefore do not know if they are under observation.

All cameras should be monitored in an on-site central alarm station that is continuously manned. Depending on the amount of station activity, it may be necessary to assign one or more security officers exclusively to monitor the CCTV surveillance system. The console should be equipped with a bank of dedicated monitors, one for each of the cameras; at facilities with a great many cameras, two or three may share the same dedicated monitor through the use of a sequential switcher. Immediately in front of the operator should be a single larger monitor by which all cameras are monitored through another sequential switcher. The system must allow the operator instantly to switch the scene from any camera onto the main screen and begin video recording of the scene displayed. (The video recorder should be equipped with a built-in or in-line time/date generator.)

Some facilities use fake CCTV cameras to give the illusion of surveillance; however, this seldom fools in-house personnel for long. Other facilities opt for a mix of real and fake cameras, but this system also only buys a little time before site personnel learn which are real and which are not.

Where a facility has two or more alarm stations capable of independent operation, each should have a CCTV camera viewing all activities within the space but monitored at the other station. This dual monitoring enables either station to observe any unauthorized activity in the other, so that corrective or compensatory action may be initiated.

In addition, both of these scenes could be monitored in the security supervisor's office or in some other protected on-site location that has the capability to freeze doors and summon on- or off-site assistance.

For a facility with a number of remote or isolated guard posts on access roads, CCTV surveillance of the approaches would be a psychological boost to the officers assigned there, plus afford an extra measure of protection for the site by early warning of an unauthorized or forced entry. At facilities where highly volatile or explosive materials are stored in outdoor or remote areas, CCTV surveillance within the storage perimeter and even among the materials would eliminate the necessity for an officer patrol to conduct periodic checks. This has the added safety feature in that the officer could accidentally be the cause of a major catastrophic loss, whereas the camera system could not.

Medical research facilities or pharmaceutical laboratories are often engaged in the development of new drugs or in disease research involving the use of live viruses, some of which are extremely virulent. They frequently use CCTV to observe experiments and, at certain facilities, test animals to monitor the development of a disease and the results of experimental immunizations. Because the bacteria and viruses are sometimes deadly, CCTV surveillance and positive control of all personnel entering, working in, and leaving is a necessity.

In the area of training, CCTV has enormous potential and should prove itself extremely versatile. For example, a facility that trains its security officers in the use of firearms can use video tape to record the progress of students through each phase of range firing. Students can then view their performance and most will be able instantly to recognize their mistakes. The instructor can go over the video record, showing students point by point where they could make corrections or adjustments. Another use of CCTV for training is in recorded indoctrination or welcoming addresses, taping of site drills or training exercises for later critique, and even play-acting scenarios where aggressors are detected on-site committing any of a variety of unauthorized deeds. Each officer to be tested is suddenly confronted with the evidence and required to act quickly and decisively. The officer's actions are then evaluated by the instructor and other officers present to decide if they were proper and timely.

At sites or facilities that may be the scenes of a riot, strike violence, or protest demonstration, CCTV video recording is highly recommended. The recorder should have a time/date generator to validate the recorded information. The camera operator should be positioned behind potential violent action and high enough to have an unobstructed field of view.

The operator should attempt to get clear shots of all such acts, as well as of all rear area agitators and vehicles (including license plates) involved in violent acts or that appear to be adversary command centers. The operator must avoid becoming enveloped by violent action, and if not already in a position of safety, should have an avenue of safe escape.

When alarm console operators monitor only fixed cameras, they must be alert for attempts to defeat the system by placement of a photo of the area being viewed, taken from the same angle at which the camera is mounted, before the camera. To the security officer monitoring the CCTV console, this photo could make it appear that all was well within this space when, in fact, it was effectively blocking his view of the area. Other ways in which the system may be circumvented include repositioning cameras so that they do not provide total area surveillance or breaking the signal transmission line between camera and monitor.

At facilities with no response force, or where the officer on duty at the monitoring station is not familiar with the areas being monitored, such simple ploys have a chance for success. Where response force personnel are available, however, they should be immediately dispatched to the scene of any alarm or assessment system component failure or malfunction to check on the cause. In cases where camera repositioning only is required and the response force is able, they should be directed to do this. When a space being monitored is not protected by an alarm system, a security patrol should check it frequently or a security officer can be posted there as a compensatory measure in the event of camera or monitor failure.

Where monitoring of personnel is necessary, such as in a penal or mental institution, CCTV can provide comprehensive coverage with a minimum number of personnel. Again, some method is required of ensuring that problems or situations observed are promptly responded to by qualified persons.

Richard J. Gigliotti
and Ronald C. Jason

Source Gigliotti, R. and R. Jason, Security Design for Maximum Protection. (Butterworth-Heinemann, Boston, 1984).

CCTV: BASIC COMPONENTS

The closed-circuit television (CCTV) field offers a bewildering assortment of cameras, monitors, lenses, housings, brackets, transmission systems, and recorders, ad infinitum. The features offered by the various manufacturers are innovative in many cases and can even be custom-packaged to suit a particular need or specification. Every system, however, is composed of certain basic elements.

Cameras

The latest state-of-the-art cameras are solid-state electronic fabrication. They are very compact, highly reliable, and capable of offering dependable service in a range of environmental conditions. The ever decreasing sizes available have led to innovations in their security application wherever undetected monitoring is desired. They have been built into such innocuous items as a standard exit sign, a department store mannequin, an index card file, and a popular brand AM/FM table radio. The list of objects that may be used to hide a surveillance camera is governed only by the space available.

For most security applications, the use of monochrome (black-and-white) cameras is recommended. These give satisfactory picture resolution and are far less expensive than color cameras.

Lenses

No matter how good or expensive a camera may be, it is useless (or nearly so) without the proper lens. For most applications, a fixed-focus lens is adequate. It should be matched to the camera and designed for the purpose, such as ability to function in ambient light conditions, clarity of images at the focal distance specified, field of view at the desired viewing distance, and so on. In applications where the camera's position can be changed through remote control, the most versatile lens has zoom capabilities. Again, it should be matched to provide image clarity through the entire zoom range and desired field of view, under ambient light conditions.

Because the CCTV industry, like any other highly competitive technological field, has developed a set of manufacturing standards, the lenses offered by most manufacturers are often usable with a competitor's product. This allows greater flexibility in designing a specialized system and ensures that several makes of camera may be intermixed in the same system without the necessity for stocking separate lenses for each brand.

Signal Transmission

Video signal transmission systems include coaxial cables, fiber-optics, and microwave. In most installations the system will be coaxial cable or fiber-optics, since they permit the highest picture resolution receivable at the monitor. To assure minimum interference and signal loss, it should be designed and installed by a qualified professional with experience in this field, rather than assigned to a maintenance department in hopes of saving on installation costs. Microwave optical systems offer the flexibility of a video signal transmission across line-of-sight spaces where it would be impossible or impractical to string coaxial cable.

Optical fiber systems transmit the signal from camera to monitor. Because such a system contains no metal in the transmission lines, it offers several distinct advantages over conventional coaxial cable. Coaxial cables use copper wire with a metallic sheath to prevent signal loss or interference. Absence of these metals makes an optical fiber system less vulnerable to tampering or attack because metal-detecting devices are useless in locating signal-carrying lines.

Because the signal passes through the optical fiber as light, the transmission of an electrical impulse is eliminated. This makes such a system impervious to normal interference-producing pieces of equipment and allows the transmission line to be routed through spaces or areas where this was not previously possible. This versatility in installation, coupled with its abilities to transmit a great many signals over a very few glass strands, its light weight, and low cost (relative to multistranded metal cable) offer the individual or company contemplating a complex and widespread CCTV system a very attractive alternative to conventional means of signal transmission.

Another transmission system offers interesting possibilities by converting the video signal into an audio signal, then sending it anywhere in the world by telephone. The manufacturer claims that visual data can be transmitted almost instantaneously to any place that can be reached by telephone, and with few exceptions, anything that can be televised with CCTV can be televised with this system.

Special training of the user is not required to utilize the system, which has been designed for simplicity of operation for use with cellular telephone systems.

Housings

Cameras installed outdoors, even in protected areas, must provide dependable service regardless of the prevailing weather and environmental conditions. For this reason they must have housings that not only protect the camera against dust and moisture, but ensure that service continues with no interruption. Housings therefore incorporate a variety of accessories, including heaters, lens-cover wipers, hoods, and the like.

Monitors

After ensuring that site CCTV cameras and lenses are matched and protected from the elements by an adequate housing, and that the video signal is being transmitted by the most efficient method, the next consideration should be the monitor on which the signal will become a comprehensible picture. There are numerous monitors available that have been designed and built to provide dependable 24-hour continuous service. The clarity and quality of the picture are the result of the resolution capabilities inherent in the camera, lens, and transmission mode over which the video signal is sent.

The monitor, however, must be capable of reassembling these electronic signals onto a display screen made up of a number of very fine, closely spaced lines. These, in turn, must be capable of reproducing all 10 shades of gray on the Electronic Industries Association (EIA) resolution test chart. The more lines available on the viewing screen, the better the picture. The industry standard viewing screen had provided about 525-line resolution, but as technology and manufacturing methods improve, this figure has increased to 600, 700, and even over 800 lines of resolution.

Monitors are available with screens of varying sizes. In general, the smallest screen that should be considered is the 9-inch, unless the scene being monitored is a small space where positive identification of an individual is not necessary, or the camera has been placed close to the object being viewed, such as gauges on a piece of equipment that requires remote monitoring. In specialized cases such as this, the smaller monitors may be acceptable.

In a multimonitor alarm station, the 9-inch monitors are adequate for fixed monitoring. One or more 17-inch units are recommended where sequential switchers pass the scenes being displayed on the banked individual monitors before the guards at that post. The larger monitor allows for easier and quicker identification of personnel and activities.

Video Recorders

While video tape records have been in existence for a number of years in the television broadcast industry, it was only with the introduction of down-sized and more affordable recorders aimed at the home or small consumer market that this equipment began to receive serious consideration by security practitioners.

Like the sound tape recorder after which it appears to be modeled, the video version uses a magnetic tape on which the images to be recorded are placed. This tape requires no special processing and is ready for viewing merely by rewinding for playback. Recorders generally found in security use are of two types, one that is designed for permanent or semi-permanent installation in the alarm station where it is instantly available to record any unusual event; and a compact portable, which when coupled with a suitable camera and power pack, enables the security department to go to the scene of a contingency and provide a complete visual record of the event. This package is also a valuable training tool. At the scene of a riot, demonstration, or strike, the portable system can be an especially valuable security tool.

Additional advantages of a video recorder over a conventional photographic film camera include the fact that, like a sound recorder, it is used to play back the recorded tape. Depending on the existing requirements, sound may be recorded on the video tape at the time it is recorded, or it may be added later to an already recorded tape. The similarities between sound and video tape recorders continues, as both can be edited, erased, and reused.

The video tape recorders most commonly used in a security environment use either a 1/2-, 3/4-, or 1-inch recording tape. While all are capable of providing adequate service, the 1-inch models have best reproduction capabilities.

Features offered by commercially available video recorders include multiple playback modes (slow motion, quick motion, freeze frame); full remote-control capability; timer switch (for time-controlled unit start and stop); tape counter with memory; auto rewind at end of tape; a meter to show accumulated hours of operation; internal power backup; external battery connections; direct-drive capstan motor; automatic alarm search (locates all recorded alarms); built-in-time/date generator; electronic security lockout (secures recorder from unauthorized tampering); time-lapse recording; ability to be coupled to alarm sensors to start video recording at a normal speed from a time-lapse mode; audio dub feature; and tape reels or cassettes.

Accessories

Included in this category are such items as pan/tilt units, scanners, video switchers, mounting brackets, controls, video signal equipment, consoles, and miscellaneous other items.

Sequential switchers are control units that, among other things, provide a visible signal to the alarm station operator for whichever camera is being viewed on the monitor screen. Depending on the manner in which it is programmed, automatic switching from one camera to the next in a routine sequence may be altered by the operator either to speed up or slow down the sequencing. This allows a longer period for detailed viewing of each area under CCTV surveillance or rapid assessment of each area to detect major changes in the scene. The sequential switcher also provides the capability for locking one camera out of rotation and placing the view onto a separate monitor screen for unbroken surveillance.

When a video record of a security contingency will be needed as evidence in civil or criminal court proceedings, the use of a time/date generator appears warranted. If the recorder being used does not have this as a built-in capability, an accessory generator is available. It is connected in-line between the camera output and the monitor, and superimposes a continuous display consisting of the month, day, and year, plus time of day in hour, minutes, and seconds. This information is placed on the scene being recorded on video tape, and becomes a visual record to show a judge and jury or site management officials the second-by-second course of events that constituted an unusual event or emergency.

There are large numbers of mounting brackets available, which, through an evolutionary process, have become basically similar in design. The products of various manufacturers differ somewhat, however, in methods of surface mounting, product finish, construction material, and so on. Because of the varied positions selected for camera mounting and the different weights the bracket must support, units are available that allow an indoor ceiling mount; an indoor wall mount (both basically light-duty units where the weight of the camera is not excessive and no camera motion is necessary); a universal wall/ceiling mount, which

would be considered suitable for medium duty; heavy-duty indoor wall mount and outdoor mount; pedestal mounts; heavy-duty scanner mounts for building corners; combination mounting bracket and automatic scanning device; and pole mounts.

Some CCTV camera enclosures differ from housings in that they protect equipment that is subjected to stresses on the pan/tilt or scanner drive mechanism caused by heavy winds and snow or ice buildup in addition to the weight of the camera and housing. These extra stresses can lead to early mechanism failure. A camera inside an enclosure is free to move with no external influence by wind, or snow or ice load.

The enclosure is basically a sphere that is available with a clear lower half where there is no desire to hide the fact that an area is under CCTV surveillance. In areas where discreet surveillance is necessary, such as furriers, gem merchants, and museums, the lower enclosure may have tinted or reflective mirror finish to hide the camera inside. The tint or coating does not affect the camera's ability to provide clear and distortion-free surveillance. Another spherical enclosure has a number of projections that appear to be camera lenses; however, only one actually is a lens. Its deterrent value is in an adversary not knowing that only one is real or knowing which lens is real. Another system uses compressed air for noiseless movement of the camera along a track up to 150 feet long. It is suitable for covering large areas such as building exteriors, bonded warehouses, and correctional facilities.

A scanner is a motor-driven device on which a CCTV camera is mounted. Once it has been adjusted, it allows the camera to traverse or pan through an arc of up to 355 degrees. A pan/tilt unit is also a powered device on which a camera is mounted; however, unlike the scanner, it can be remotely operated through its arc with stops at any point. The camera can also traverse in a vertical direction up to 90 degrees for a better look at a subject. These units are usually available in indoor and outdoor models. One manufacturer even has models suitable for service in an explosive atmosphere.

Specialized Equipment

For specialized operations, CCTV equipment is available that is built into an attaché case and contains an independent power supply. Where undetected monitoring of a space is desired but the physical layout or contents preclude the use of conventional CCTV cameras, the approach may be to place a miniaturized camera behind a wall or in the ceiling connected to a pinhole lens inserted into the room.

The lens, equipped with a fiber-optic transmission line, can be hidden by placing it inside an innocent device such as a fire sprinkler head, smoke or heat detector, or an air conditioning vent. Lenses are also available that allow a two- or three-way split image on the same monitor of the same scene at different magnifications.

Richard J. Gigliotti
and Ronald C. Jason

Source   Gigliotti, R. and R. Jason, Security Design for Maximum Protection.   (Butterworth-Heinemann, Boston, 1984).

CCTV: CAMERAS FOR SECURITY

The closed-circuit television (CCTV) camera's function is to convert the focused visual (or infrared) light image from the camera lens into a time-varying electrical video signal that contains the intelligence in the scene image. The lens collects the reflected light from the scene and focuses it onto the camera image sensor. The camera processes the information from the sensor and sends it to a viewing monitor via coaxial cable or other transmission means.

There are two generic types of CCTV sensors: (1) tube and (2) solid-state. Tube types represent the majority of existing security installations, but the solid-state types are expected to eventually replace all of them. The tube cameras use electron beam scanning techniques and the solid-state cameras use charge coupling techniques.

Camera Scanning Function

The monochrome or color television camera in the security CCTV system analyzes the scene by scanning it in a series of closely spaced lines in the case of a tube camera, or picture elements (pixels) in the case of a solid-state camera. This technique generates the codes and electrical signal as a

function of time so that the scene can later be reconstructed on the monitor.

Unlike film cameras or the human eye, or low-light-level (LLL) television image intensifiers that see a complete picture one frame at a time, a television camera sees an image point by point until it scans the entire scene. In this respect the television scan is similar to the action of a typewriter where the type element starts at the upper left-hand corner of the page, moves across the page to the right-hand corner, and in this way a single line of type is completed. The typewriter carriage then returns to the left-hand side of the paper, moves down to the third line (skips a line), and starts over again. At the left-hand side the typewriter carriage again moves from the left to the right, typing out another line, then returns and moves down again, with this action continuing until the typewriter has reached the bottom of the page. This completes one field or half the television picture. If the page is then moved back so that the typewriter begins typing on the second line at the left just below the first line and the same action continues again, moving down two lines at a time, each line in-between the originally typed lines is filled in, and by the time the typewriter gets to the bottom of the page, the full page is completely typed. This completes two fields and is equivalent to one full video frame.

Scanning is accomplished in the tube camera, through the use of magnetic or electrostatic deflection of an electron beam whereas in the solid-state camera electrical clocking circuits are used to scan the sensor pixel array.

The television camera consists of: (1) an image sensor, (2) some form of electrical scanning system with synchronization, (3) timing electronics, (4) video amplifying and processing electronics, and (5) video signal synchronizing and combining electronics to produce a composite video output signal. The camera has synchronizing signals so that a monitor, a recorder, a printer, or other CCTV routing or processing equipment can be synchronized to produce a stable display or recording.

In operation, the lens forms a focused image on the camera sensor. In the tube camera the television picture is formed by extracting the light information on the target area as the electron beam moves across the light-sensitive area of the tube in a process called linear (or raster) scanning. The entire picture is called a frame and is composed of two fields. Each frame contains 525

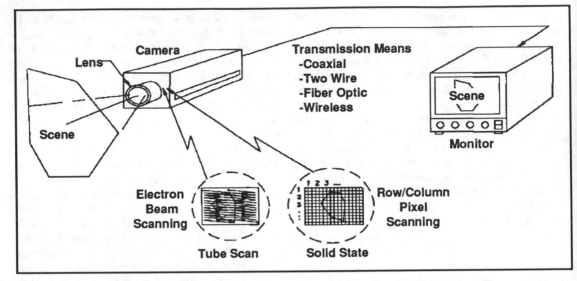

CCTV System with Lens, Camera, Transmission Means and Monitor

horizontal lines in the U.S. National Television System Committee (NTSC) system based on the 60-Hz power line frequency and a duration of 1/30 second per frame (30 frames/second). The European system, based on a 50-Hz power line frequency, has 625 horizontal lines and 1/25 second per frame. In the NTSC system the electron beam scans the picture area twice, with each scan producing a field. Each field contains 262-1/2 television lines with the two fields producing a complete frame having 525 television lines total. A 2:1 interlaced scanning technique is used to reduce the amount of flicker in the picture and improve motion display. This scanning mode is called two-field, odd-line scanning.

For the solid-state camera, in place of the moving electron beam in the tube, the light-induced charge in the individual sites -- picture elements (pixels) -- in the sensor are clocked out of the sensor into the camera electronics. The time-varying video signal from the individual pixels clocked out in the horizontal rows and vertical columns generate the two interlaced fields.

Sensor Types

Several different sensor types are available for CCTV security applications. These include: (1) vidicon, silicon diode, Newvicon, and Saticon tube types; and (2) silicon charge transfer devices (CTD), metal-oxide semiconductor (MOS), and

charge injection device (CID) solid-state types. The most widely used are the charge-coupled device (CCD) and the MOS.

In LLL applications these tube and solid-state sensors are combined with image intensifiers to produce the silicon intensified target (SIT), intensified SIT (ISIT), and intensified CCD (ICCD) cameras.

Solid State Cameras

The solid-state camera uses a silicon array of photosensor sites (pixels) to convert the input light image into an electronic video signal, which is then amplified and passed on to a monitor for display.

Most solid-state sensors fall into the category of devices called charge transfer devices (CTD), which can be subdivided into three groups depending on the manufacturing technology used: (1) charge coupled device (CCD), (2) charge priming device (CPD), and (3) charge injection device (CID). A fourth type is the metal-oxide semiconductor (MOS).

By far the most popular devices used in security camera applications are the CCD, MOS, and CPD, with the CID reserved primarily for military and industrial applications. The solid-state imaging devices used in security CCTV applications are small, light weight, rugged, and consume low power.

Solid-State Sensor

The solid-state sensor CCTV camera performs a function similar to that of the tube camera, but the sensor and scanning system is significantly different. It has no electron beam scanning of the visual image on the sensor area, and an area array of pixels replaces the camera tube. The typical sensor has hundreds of pixels in the horizontal and vertical directions equivalent to several hundred thousand pixels over the sensor area. A pixel is the smallest sensing element located on the sensor that converts the light energy into an electrical charge and signal.

Scanning and Timing. The CCD imager works by a process called charge coupling. It is the collective transfer of the electrical charges produced by the image stored in the CCD storage element (pixel) and moved to an adjacent storage element by the use of external synchronizing or clocking voltages that, in effect, push out the signal, line by line, at a precisely determined clocked time and produce the video signal. The signal represents the light intensity at each pixel location, which is the intelligence in the picture.

Typical device parameters for a CCD available in the market today are 488 by 380 pixels (horizontal x vertical) in formats of 1/3-, 1/2-, and 2/3-inch, in a 4 x 3 (H x V) aspect-ratio television presentation.

The MOS-type sensor exhibits high picture quality but has a lower sensitivity than the CCD. In the MOS device the electric signals are read out directly through an array of MOS transistor switches, rather than line by line as in the CCD sensor.

The CID device differs from all other solid-state devices in that any of the pixels can be addressed or scanned in a random scan sequence rather than in the row/column sequence used in the other sensors. The advantage of this capability has not been realized in the security field but is used in industrial and military applications where non-raster scan sequences or patterns offer advantages.

Most CCD image sensors have wide spectral ranges and are usually useful over the entire visible range and into the near infrared (IR) spectral region above 800 to 900 nanometers.

One of the significant advantages of charge coupled image sensors over vacuum tube sensors is the precise geometric location of the pixels with respect to one another. In a camera tube the video is "read" from a photosensitive material by a scanning electron beam.

The position of the beam is never precisely known because of some uncertainty in the sweep circuits resulting from random electrical noise, variations in power supply voltage, or other variations.

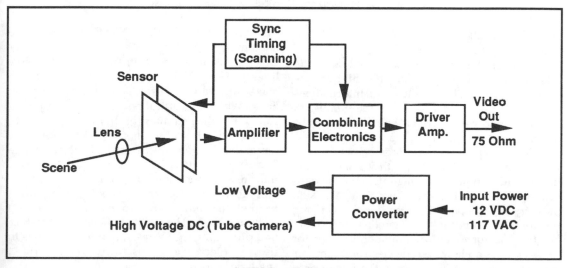

CCTV Camera Block

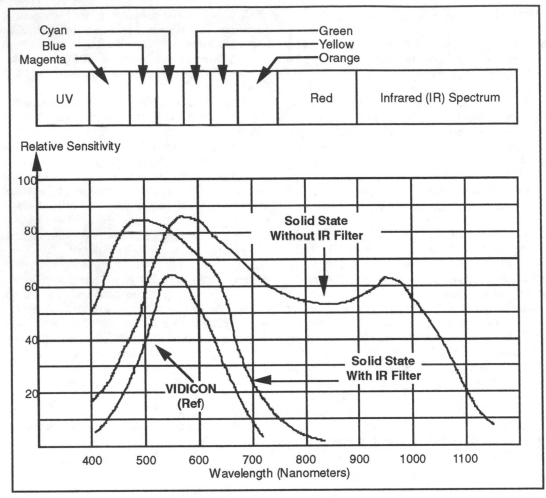

CCD Spectral Response and IR Blocking Filter Transmission

CCTV Resolution

CCTV resolution is a critical measure of the television picture quality; the higher the resolution, the higher the level of information. CCTV resolution is measured by the number of horizontal and vertical television lines that can be discerned in the monitor picture.

The U.S. NTSC standard provides a full video frame composed of 525 lines, with 504 lines for the image, and a vertical blanking interval composed of the remaining 21 retrace lines. The television industry has adopted the practice of specifying horizontal resolution in television lines per picture height. The horizontal resolution on the monitor tube depends on how fast the electron beam can change its intensity as it traces the image on a horizontal line.

With the 525-line NTSC system, the maximum vertical resolution achievable in any CCTV system is approximately 353 television lines. The 625-line system can produce a maximum vertical resolution of 438 television lines. While the vertical resolution is determined solely by the number of lines chosen (U.S. standard 525 lines), the horizontal resolution is dependent upon the electrical performance bandwidth of the individual camera, transmission, and monitor system.

Most standard cameras with a 4.5-MHz bandwidth produce a horizontal resolution of 550 television lines. The traditional method of testing and presenting CCTV resolution test results is to use the Electronic Industry Association (EIA) resolution target.

One comparison made between the solid-state and tube camera is resolution, i.e., how much detail is seen in the picture. The resolution for a good tube security camera is 500 to 600 television lines. Solid-state data sheets often quote the number of picture elements (pixels) instead of television lines of resolution. However, unless the number of horizontal pixels is converted into equivalent television lines, the horizontal resolution is not known.

To approximate the horizontal resolution from the horizontal pixel count, multiply the number of horizontal pixels by 0.75. Only recently have solid-state sensors been available that can match the resolution of average tube cameras.

Low-Light-Level Sensors

LLL cameras such as the SIT, ISIT, and ICCD share many of the characteristics of the tube and solid-state types described previously but include means to respond to much smaller light levels found in scenes illuminated by natural moonlight, starlight or some other very LLL artificial illumination. These cameras use image intensifiers coupled to imaging tubes or solid-state sensors, and can amplify the available light up to 50,000 times and view scenes hundreds to thousands of feet from the camera under nighttime conditions. Complete SIT tube and ICCD camera systems have sufficient sensitivity and automatic light compensation to be used in surveillance applications from full sunlight to overcast moonlight conditions.

The ICCD camera is a new LLL camera class whose sensitivity approaches that of the best SIT cameras and eliminates the blurring characteristics of the SIT under very LLL conditions. The ICCD camera combines a tube or microchannel plate (MCP) intensifier with a CCD image sensor to provide a sensitivity similar to that of an SIT camera.

For dawn and dusk outdoor illumination, the best CCD cameras can barely produce a usable video signal. SIT and ICCD cameras can operate under the light of one-fourth moon with one 0.001 foot candle (FtCd) of illumination. The ISIT camera can produce an image from only 0.0001 FtCd, which is the light available from stars on a moonless night. SIT, ISIT, and ICCD offer a 100 to 1,000 times improvement in sensitivity over the best CCD cameras because these cameras intensify

light whereas the tube and CCD cameras only detect it. By contrast, the best CCD camera has a minimum sensitivity of 0.00093 FtCd.

Format Sizes

There are four existing image format sizes for solid-state and tube sensors. These are 1/3-, 1/2-, 2/3-, and 1-inch (tube only). All sensor formats have a horizontal x vertical geometry of 4 x 3 (H x V) aspect ratio as defined in the EIA and NTSC standards. For a given lens, the 1/3-inch format sensor sees the smallest scene image (smallest angular field of view) and the 1-inch sees the largest. The 1/2- and 1/3-inch solid-state formats are presently the most popular, with the direction going toward the smaller sensors. The 2/3- and 1-inch vidicons and other tube cameras, while popular years ago and still in extensive use in existing installations, are primarily being sold for replacement use and when high resolution requirements exist. The SIT tube cameras using the 1-inch tube to provide LLL capabilities are likewise being replaced by their solid-state counterpart, the ICCD.

Color Cameras

Solid-state color cameras developed for the consumer video cassette recorder (VCR) and camcorder use a single solid-state sensor with an integral three-color filter and automatic white balancing circuits. These sensors incorporated into a CCTV camera provide a stable, long-life color camera with good sensitivity suitable for indoor and outdoor security application.

There are presently two techniques to produce the color video signal from the image sensor produced by the color visual image from the lens: (1) single sensor and (2) three sensor with prism. Most color cameras used in the security industry are of the single sensor type. The single sensor camera has a complex color imaging sensor with three integral optical filters on the image sensor to produce the three primary colors -- red, green, and blue (R, G, B). These colors are sufficient to reproduce all the colors in the visible spectrum.

Solid-state CCD and MOS color cameras are available in 1/3-, 1/2-, and 2/3-inch formats. Most of those used in security applications have single-chip sensors with three-color stripe filters integral with the image sensor. Typical color sensitivities for these cameras range from 0.7 to 1.4 FtCd (7 to 15 lux) for full video, which is less sensitive than their monochrome counterpart. The resolution of most color cameras ranges from 250 to 380 television lines, corresponding to standard VHS and 8-millimeter formats, with VCR recorder capabilities.

Cameras with higher resolutions of 420 to 470 television lines are available for use with the higher resolution S-VHS and Hi-8 (8-millimeter) recorders. Color cameras with a 2/3-inch format producing 250 to 350 television line resolution require an array with 780 (H) x 490 (V) (380,000 pixels).

Most color cameras incorporate automatic white balance compensation as an integral part of the camera so that when the camera is initially turned on, it properly balances its color circuits to a white background as determined by the type of light illuminating the scene. The camera constantly checks the white balance circuitry and makes any minor compensation for variations in the illumination color temperature (spectrum of colors in the scene it is viewing).

The availability of solid-state color cameras has made a significant impact on the security CCTV industry. Color cameras provide enhanced television surveillance because of the increased ability to identify objects and persons when using color rather than monochrome.

Lens Mounts

All security cameras have a lens mount in front of the sensor to mechanically couple whatever objective lens or optical system is used to image the scene onto the camera.

The two widely used lens mounts in the CCTV industry are the C and CS mounts. Until recently, all 1-, 2/3-, and 1/2-inch cameras used an industry standard mount to couple the lens to the camera called the C mount. This camera mount has a 1-inch diameter hole with 32 threads per inch (TPI). The lens has a matching thread (1-32 TPI) that screws into the camera thread. The distance between the lens rear mounting surface and the image sensor for the C mount is 0.69 inches (17.526 millimeters).

A second new mount adopted by the CCTV industry for 1/3- and 1/2-inch sensor format

cameras is the CS mount, in which the camera has a 1-inch diameter hole with a 32 TPI thread (same as the C mount) and the lens has a matching thread. The distance between the lens rear-mounting surface and the image sensor for the CS mount is, however, 0.492 inches (12.5 millimeters), which is 5 millimeters (0.2 inches) shorter than for the C mount. This shorter distance means that the lens collecting light for the sensor is closer to the sensor by 5 millimeters and can be made smaller in diameter for an equivalent FOV.

A C mount lens can be used on a CS mount camera if a 5-millimeter spacer is interposed between the lens and the camera, and the lens format covers the camera format size. The advantage of the CS mount system is that the lens is smaller, lighter, and less expensive than its C mount counterpart.

Herman A. Kruegle

CCTV: COVERT TECHNIQUES

Overt closed-circuit television (CCTV) security equipment is installed in full view of the public, and is used to observe action in an area while simultaneously letting the public know that CCTV surveillance is occurring. This technique often has the effect of deterring crime. Covert CCTV is used so that the offender is not aware he or she is under surveillance and to produce a permanent recording on a video cassette recorder (VCR) for later use in confronting, dismissing, or prosecuting the person committing the offense. The covert camera and lens are out of view of anyone in the area under surveillance, and therefore unsuspecting violators are viewed on CCTV, their actions recorded, and often are apprehended while committing the illegal act. Although the camera uses small optics and is hidden, the result can be a high-quality CCTV picture of the area and activity.

An independent reason for using covert CCTV is to avoid changing the architectural aesthetics of a building or surrounding area. Covert CCTV cameras are concealed in common room objects or are located behind a small hole in an opaque barrier (wall, ceiling). Cameras are camouflaged in common objects such as lamps and lamp fixtures, table and wall clocks, radios, books, etc. A very effective covert system uses a camera and lens camouflaged in a ceiling-mounted sprinkler head.

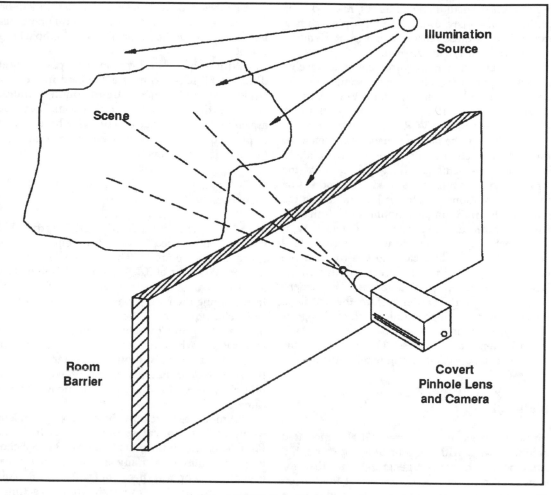

Covert CCTV Surveillance

There are lenses with a small front lens diameter so that the lens and camera can view the scene through a 1/16-inch diameter hole. These lenses have a medium to wide field of view (FOV) from 12 to 78 degrees to cover a large scene area, but still permit identification of persons, and monitoring activities and actions. Other special pinhole lens variations include right angle, automatic iris, sprinkler head, and fiber optic, and small pinhole cameras combining a mini-lens and sensor into a small camera head and other complete miniature cameras.

In low-light-level (LLL) applications, a charge coupled device (CCD) camera with a very sensitive sensor and infrared (IR) light source or an image intensifier are used. Since many covert installations are temporary, wireless transmission systems are used to send the CCTV camera signal to the monitor, VCR, or video printer.

CCTV lens and camera concealment is accomplished by having the lens view through a small hole, a series of small holes, or from behind a semi-transparent window.

A number of suitable lens and camera locations include: (1) ceiling, (2) wall, (3) lamp fixture, (4) furniture, and (5) other articles normally found in a room. CCTV cameras are installed in one or more locations in the room, depending on the activity expected.

Since the diameter of the front lens viewing the scene must, by necessity, be small to hide it, these lenses are optically fast, and collect and transmit as much light as possible from the reflected scene to the television sensor. As a consequence, small-diameter lenses, referred to as pinhole lenses, are used. The term pinhole is a misnomer, as these lenses have a front diameter anywhere from 1/8 to 1/2 inch.

The lens/camera requirement is to receive reflected light from an illuminated scene, have the lens collect and transmit the light to the camera sensor, and then transmit the video signal to a video monitor and/or VCR and video printer.

The hole in the barrier is usually chosen to be the same diameter (d) or smaller than the pinhole lens-front lens element. When space permits, the straight-type installation is used. In confined or restricted locations with limited depth behind the barrier, the right-angle pinhole lens/camera is used. In both cases to obtain the full lens FOV, it is imperative that the pinhole lens-front lens element be located as close to the front of the barrier as possible to avoid "tunneling" (vignetting). When the pinhole lens-front element is set back from the barrier surface, the lens is, in effect, viewing through a tunnel, and the image as viewed on the camera sensor has a narrower FOV than the lens can produce. This is seen on the monitor as a porthole-like (vignetted) picture.

Pinhole Lenses

Pinhole lenses and cameras can be mounted behind a wall, with the lens viewing through a small hole in the wall. A generic characteristic for almost all pinhole-type lenses is that they invert the video picture and therefore the camera must be inverted to get a normal right-side-up picture. Some right-angle pinhole lenses reverse the image right to left and therefore require an electronic scan reversal unit to regain the correct left-to-right orientation.

Pinhole lenses have been manufactured for many years in a variety of focal lengths (FL) (3.8, 4, 5.5, 6, 8, 9, 11 millimeters), in straight, right angle, manual-, and automatic-iris configurations. The focal length (FL) of most of these lenses can be doubled to obtain one-half the FOV by using a 2x extender. The 16- and 22-millimeter FL are achieved by using a 2x magnifier on the 8- and 11-millimeter lenses, between the lens and the camera. This automatically doubles the optical speed or f/number (F/#) of each lens (halves the optical speed). In many applications, the required FL and configuration are not known in advance, and the user must have a large assortment of

pinhole lenses, or take the risk that the job will be done using an incorrect lens. This dilemma has been solved with the availability of a Pinhole Lens Kit.

With this kit of pinhole lens parts, eight different FL lenses can be assembled in either a straight or right-angle configuration in minutes. An additional four combinations can be assembled for a disguised sprinkler head covert application. All lenses have a manual iris (automatic-iris optional).

Mini-Lenses

Mini-lenses are small fixed focal length (FFL) objective lenses used for covert surveillance when space is at a premium. The lenses will typically have focal lengths of 3.8, 5.5, 8, and 11 millimeters and front barrel diameters between 3/8 and 1/2 inch, making them easy to mount behind a barrier or in close quarters. These small lenses do not have an iris, and therefore, should be used in applications where the scene light level does not vary widely or with shuttered cameras. Mini-lenses, like other FFL lenses and unlike standard pinhole lenses, do not invert the image on the camera.

Mini-lenses have only three to six optical lens elements, fast optical speeds of f/1.4 to f/1.8. Pinhole lenses, on the other hand, are 3 to 5 inches long, and have as many as 10 to 20 optical elements and optical speeds of f/2.0 to f/4.0. This makes the mini-lens approximately five times faster (five times more light) than the pinhole lens.

Small Covert Camera

The most compact covert CCTV installation uses a flat board CCD camera and integral mini-lens. The complete camera is only 1.38 times 1.38 times 2.2 inches long. The 11-millimeter FL lens extends 0.3 inches in front of the camera. The camera operates directly from 12-volt DC, requires only 2.5 watts of power, and produces a standard composite video output.

Sprinkler Head Pinhole Lens

A very effective covert system uses a camera and lens camouflaged in a ceiling-mounted sprinkler

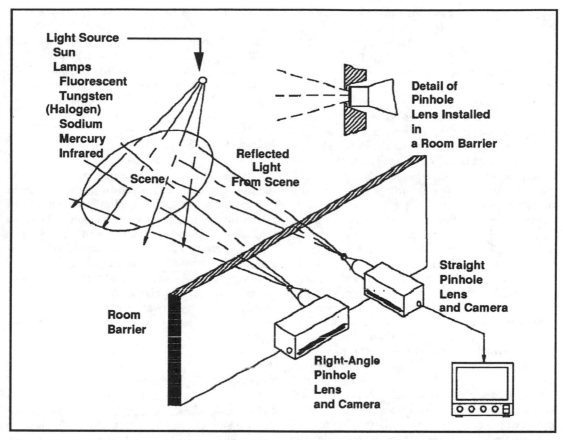

Straight and Right-Angle Pinhole Lens Installations

head. Of the large variety of covert lenses available for the security television industry (pinhole, mini, fiber optic), this unique lens hides the pinhole lens in a ceiling sprinkler fixture, making it extremely difficult for an observer standing at floor level to detect or identify the lens and camera, and the surveillance sprinkler unit goes unnoticed. This unique combination of pinhole lens and overhead ceiling-mounted sprinkler head provides an extremely useful covert surveillance television system.

The covert surveillance sprinkler installed in the ceiling in no way affects the operation of the active fire suppression sprinkler system; however, it should not be installed in locations that have no sprinkler system so as not to give the false impression to fire and safety personnel that there is a real and active sprinkler system.

The only portion of the system visible from below is the standard sprinkler head and the small (3/8 x 5/8 inch) mirror assembly. In operation, light from the scene reflects off the small mirror which directs it to the front of the pinhole lens. The 11 or 22-millimeter pinhole lens in turn transmits and focuses the light onto the camera sensor. The small mirror can be adjusted in elevation to point at different scene heights. To point in a particular azimuth direction, the entire camera-sprinkler lens assembly is rotated with the mirror pointing in the direction of the scene of interest.

If the sprinkler head assembly is removed from the right-angle lens, all that protrudes below the ceiling is a small mirror approximately 3/8 times 5/8 inch. This technique provides a very low profile and is difficult to detect by an observer at ground level.

The pinhole/mirror system provides an alternative to some dome applications. The system can be fixed or have a 360-degree panning range, or a limited pan, tilt, and zoom capability, depending on the design.

Fiber-Optic Lenses

In applications where it is required to view a scene where the camera is located 6, 8, or 12 inches behind a thick concrete wall, a rigid coherent fiber-optic conduit or a borescope lens is used to extend the objective lens several inches to several feet in front of the camera sensor.

Difficult television security applications are sometimes solved by using coherent fiber-optic bundle lenses. They are used in surveillance applications when it is necessary to view a scene on the other side of a thick barrier or inside a confined area.

The lens is installed behind a thick barrier (wall) with the objective lens on the scene side, the fiber-optic bundle within the wall, and the camera located on the protected side of the barrier. The lens viewing the scene can be a few inches or a few feet away from the camera. The rigid fiber version is a fused array of fibers and cannot be bent.

The fiber-optic lens should not to be confused with the single or multiple strands of fiber commonly used to transmit the time-modulated television signal from a camera over a long distance (hundreds of feet or miles), to a remote monitor site. The fiber-optic lens typically has 200,000 to 300,000 individual fibers forming an image-transferring array.

A minor disadvantage of all fiber-optic systems is that the picture obtained is not as "clean" as that obtained with an "all lens" pinhole lens. There are some cosmetic imperfections that look like dust spots, as well as a slight geometrical pattern caused by fiber stacking. For most surveillance applications the imperfections do not result in any loss of intelligence in the picture.

Configuration

In the case of the rigid fiber-optic bundle, the individual fibers are fused together to form a rigid glass rod or conduit. The diameter of the rigid fiber-optic bundle is approximately 0.4 inch for a 2/3-inch format sensor, 0.3-inch diameter for a 1/2-inch format, and 0.2-inch diameter for a 1/3-inch format. The rod is usually protected from the environment and mechanical damage by a rigid metal tube (0.5 inches in diameter for 2/3-inch format). It should be noted that the image exiting the fiber-optic lens is inverted with respect to the image produced by a standard objective lens. This inversion is corrected by inverting the camera.

Infrared (IR) Sources

There are numerous commercially available thermal lamp and light-emitting diode (LED) IR sources for covert CCTV applications. They vary from short range, low power, wide-angle beam to long range, high power, narrow-angle beam types.

A single IR LED emits enough IR energy to produce a useful picture at ranges up to 5 or 10 feet with a CCD camera. By stacking many (several hundred) LEDs in an array, higher IR power is directed toward the scene and a larger area at distances up to 50 to 100 feet may be viewed.

Special Configurations

CCTV cameras and lenses are concealed in many different objects and locations. Examples of some objects include an overhead track lighting fixture, emergency lighting fixture, exit sign, table top radio, table lamp, wall or desk clock, shoulder bag, attaché case, etc.

The emergency lighting fixture operates normally and can be tested for operation periodically. The fixture's operation is in no way affected by the installation of the CCTV camera.

The exit light fixture is another convenient form for camouflaging a covert CCTV camera system. The right-angle pinhole lens and CCD camera are located inside the unit and view out of either arrow on the exit sign, providing an excellent covert CCTV camera system.

A large wall-mounted clock is an ideal location for camouflaging covert CCTV camera/lens combination. The lens views out through one of the black numerals. In this case, the flat camera (approximately 7/8-inch deep) and right-angle mini-lens is mounted directly behind the numeral 11 on the clock. The camera uses offset optics so that the camera views downward at approximately a 15-degree angle even though the clock is mounted vertically on the wall.

Wireless Transmission

Covert CCTV applications often require that the camera/lens system be installed and removed quickly from a site, or that it remain installed on location for only short periods of time. This may mean that a wired transmission means cannot be installed and that a wireless transmission means from camera to monitor (or VCR) is necessary. This takes the form of a VHF or UHF radio frequency (RF), microwave, or lightwave (IR) video transmitter of low power mounted near the television camera. The RF transmitters are of low power -- from 100 milliwatts to several watts -- and transmit the video picture over ranges from 100 feet to several miles.

Microwave transmission systems operate in the 2- to 22-gigahertz range and require FCC licensing and approval, but can be used by government agencies and commercial customers as well. One condition in obtaining approval is to have a frequency search performed to ensure the system causes no interference to existing equipment in the area. Most microwave systems have a more directional transmitting pattern than for the RF transmitters. Most microwave installations are line of sight, but the microwave energy can be reflected off objects in the path between the transmitter and the receiver to direct the energy to the receiver. The higher frequency of operation and directionality makes microwave installation and alignment more critical than the RF transmitters.

Pinhole lenses are used for surveillance problems that cannot be adequately solved using standard FFL or zoom lenses. The fast f/#s of some of these pinhole lenses make it possible to provide covert surveillance under normal or dimly lighted conditions. The small size of the front lens and barrel permit them to be covertly installed for surveillance applications.

A large variety of mini-, pinhole, fiber-optic, and borescope lenses are available for use in covert security applications. These lenses have FL ranges from 3.8 to 22 millimeters, covering FOVs from 12 to 78 degrees. Variations that include manual and auto iris, standard pinhole, mini and off-axis-mini, fiber optic, and borescope provide the user with a large selection from which to choose.

Herman A. Kruegle

CCTV: LIGHTING CONSIDERATIONS

An important parameter affecting the performance of any monochrome or color closed-circuit television (CCTV) security system is the scene lighting. Whether the application is indoor or outdoor, daytime or nighttime, the amount of available light, its color (wavelength) energy spectrum must be considered and evaluated, and compared to the sensitivity of the cameras used. In daytime applications some cameras must have protection from high light levels in the form of an automatic iris lens or shutter. In nighttime applications the light level and characteristics of available and artificial light sources must be analyzed and matched to the camera spectral and illumination sensitivities to ensure a good video picture. If additional lighting is installed, the appropriate lamp type -- tungsten, tungsten-halogen, metal arc, sodium, mercury, etc. -- must be chosen. Where no additional lighting is permissible, the existing illumination level, color spectrum, and beam angle must be evaluated and matched to a CCTV lens/camera combination, which will provide an adequate picture to gather the necessary scene intelligence. An axiom in CCTV security applications is: the more light the better the picture. The quality of the monitor picture is affected by how much light is available and how well the sensor responds to the colors in the light source. This is critical when color cameras are used since they require more light than monochrome cameras.

Scene Illumination

The energy from light radiation is composed of a spectrum of colors including "invisible light" produced by long wavelength infrared (IR) and short wavelength ultraviolet (UV) energy. Most CCTV cameras respond to visible and some IR light. The illumination can be either from natural sources such as the sun, moon, or starlight, or from artificial sources such as tungsten, mercury, fluorescent, sodium, or other lamps.

Light Output

Factors to consider in scene illumination include source: (1) spectral characteristics, (2) beam angle, (3) intensity, and (4) variations in intensity.

The factors to be considered in the scene include: (1) reflectance, (2) complexity, and (3) motion.

The CCTV camera image sensor responds to the reflected light from the scene. In planning a television system it is necessary to know the type of illumination and intensity of light falling on a surface, and how the illumination varies as a function of distance from the light source. The radiation from the illuminating source reaches the television camera by first reflecting off the objects in the scene.

Because the different CCTV camera types respond to different colors, it is important to know which type light source is illuminating the surveillance area, and what type to add to achieve the required television picture quality. Since each source produces light at different wavelengths or colors, maximum utility from any camera is obtained when the camera is sensitive to the light produced by the natural or artificial source of illumination.

Beam Angle

Another characteristic important in determining the amount of light reaching a scene is the beam angle over which the source radiates. Light sources are classified by their light beam pattern,

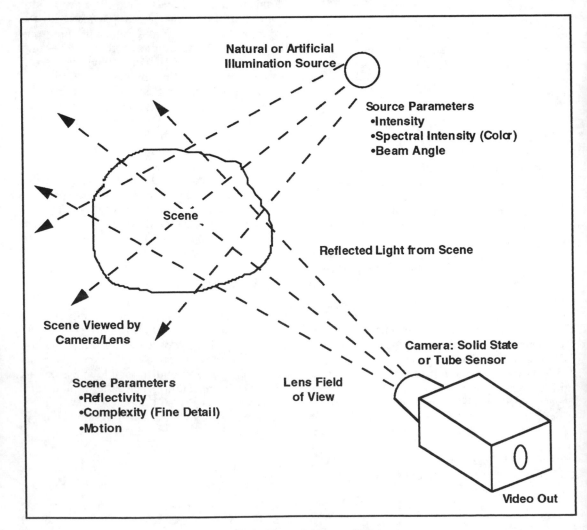

CCTV Camera, Scene and Source Illumination

i.e., they emit a wide, medium, or narrow beam of light. The requirement for this parameter is determined by the field of view (FOV) of the camera lens used and the total scene to be viewed. The natural sources are inherently wide while artificial sources are available in narrow beam (a few degrees) to wide beam (30 to 90 degrees).

A wide-beam flood lamp illuminates a large area and has a fairly uniform intensity of light reaching each part of the scene to produce a uniform picture. A narrow beam or spot light illuminates a small area and consequently areas outside of it will appear darker, the scene will be non-uniformly illuminated, and a non-uniform picture will result. If a lamp illuminates only a part of the scene area, the camera-lens combination FOV should only view the area illuminated by the lamp. This source beam angle problem does not exist for areas lighted by natural illumination such as the sun, which usually uniformly illuminates the entire scene.

Natural Light Sources

Natural light sources include the sun, moon (reflected sunlight), and stars. The sun contains a continuous spectrum producing energy at all wavelengths and colors that the monochrome and color cameras are sensitive to. This radiation includes blue, green, yellow, orange, red, and near IR parts of the spectrum. In the case of the sun, during the first few hours of sunrise and during the last few hours at sunset, the spectrum is shifted toward the orange-red region, and hence things look predominantly orange and red. During the midday hours the sun is the brightest and most intense, and hence the blues and greens are brightest and produce the most balanced white light. Sun and moonlight contain IR radiation in addition to visible light spectra and are broadband light sources (containing all colors and wavelengths). Artificial sources can be broadband or narrow-band (containing only a limited number of colors).

Monochrome vs. Color

All monochrome cameras are sensitive to the visible spectrum with some, particularly silicon tube and charge-coupled device (CCD) solid-state cameras, sensitive to the visible and near IR

spectrum. Monochrome cameras can operate with either narrow or broadband sources since they respond to any or all of the full spectrum of energy, and color rendition is not a problem.

The situation is more complex and critical for color CCTV systems. Color cameras are sensitive to all the color wavelengths in the visible spectrum as is the human eye, and are designed to be insensitive to near IR wavelengths. For the camera to be able to see all the colors in the visible spectrum, the light source must contain all the colors of the spectrum. To get a good color balance in the picture the illumination source should match that of the sensor sensitivity. Most color cameras have what is called an automatic white balance control, which automatically adjusts the camera electronics to obtain the correct color balance; however, the light source must still contain the colors in order for them to be seen on the monitor. Broadband light sources such as the sun and tungsten or tungsten-halogen light sources produce the best color pictures because they contain all the colors in the spectrum. Narrow-band light sources such as a mercury arc or sodium vapor lamp do not produce a continuous spectrum of colors and therefore poor color rendition results. A mercury lamp has little red light output and therefore red objects appear nearly black when illuminated by them. A high-pressure sodium lamp contains large quantities of yellow, orange, and some red light. An object that is blue or green illuminated under it will look dark, gray, or brown on the color monitor because the lamp does not emit these colors. A color camera viewing a scene illuminated with a low-pressure sodium lamp produces only yellow light and the scene will be all dark except for yellow objects, which will appear normal.

Artificial Light

Artificial light sources consist of two general types: (1) tungsten or tungsten-halogen having solid filaments, and (2) gaseous or arc lamps having a low- or high-pressure gas in an enclosed envelope. The arc lamps can be further classified into: (1) high-intensity discharge (HID), (2) low-pressure, and (3) high-pressure short-arc types. The HID lamps are represented by the mercury, metal-arc, and high pressure sodium. The low-pressure arc lamps are represented by the fluorescent and low-pressure sodium and xenon.

Long-arc xenon lamps are used in large outdoor sports areas, etc.

Tungsten Lamp

The incandescent filament (tungsten) lamp is the oldest lamp type used for artificial illumination, and the least efficient, having a maximum efficacy of 35 lumens/watt, and a life expectancy of about 1,000 hours. The incandescent lamp radiates all the colors in the visible spectrum as well as energy in the near IR. It provides an excellent illumination source for both monochrome and color cameras. Its two disadvantages when compared with arc lamps are low efficiency (costs more to operate) and short operating lifetime.

Tungsten-Halogen Lamp

A significant advancement made to the tungsten lamp was the use of a halogen element (iodine or bromine) in the quartz envelope of the tungsten lamp, with the lamp operating in what is called the tungsten-halogen cycle. This mode of operation increases its rated life to 2,000 hours even though the lamp operates at a high temperature and light output. The halogen chemical cycle permits the use of more compact bulbs than those of tungsten filament lamps of comparable ratings and permits either increasing the lamp life, or increasing lumen output and color temperature to values significantly above those of conventional tungsten filament lamps.

High-Intensity Discharge (HID) Lamp

The high-intensity discharge (HID) lamp has an enclosed arc and is in widespread use for general lighting and security applications. The three most popular HID lamps are: (1) mercury enclosed in a quartz tube, (2) metal halide with a quartz tube, and (3) high-pressure sodium with a translucent tube.

Each of these three different types differs in electrical input and light output characteristics, life, color, shape, and size. HID lamps require an electrical ballast and a high-voltage starting device. Unlike incandescent or fluorescent lamps, they require several minutes of warm-up to achieve full brightness after ignition. If turned off

momentarily, they require several minutes before they can be turned on (re-ignited) again. Dual-HID bulbs are now available that include two identical HID lamp units in one envelope, of which only one is operating at a time. If the first lamp is extinguished momentarily, the cold lamp may be ignited immediately, allowing the first lamp to cool down for a subsequent operation.

The primary advantages of the HID lamp over other lamps are long life and high efficiency. Lamp lifetime is typically 16,000 to 24,000 hours, with light efficacy ranging from 60 to 140 lumens/watt. These lamps cannot be electrically dimmed without drastically affecting the starting warm-up luminous efficiency, efficacy, color, and life. HID lamps are the most widely used lamps for general illumination for industrial and commercial buildings, flood lighting, street lighting, sports fields, etc.

One class of HID lamps is the high-pressure sodium lamp. This lamp contains a special ceramic arc tube material that produces a high luminous efficiency yielding a yellow-orange color spectrum as compared with single color (yellow) low-pressure sodium arcs. However, because the gas is only sodium, the sodium HID lamp has only a small amount of blue, green, and red in the spectrum. For this reason the lamp is not suitable for color CCTV security applications. The primary and significant advantage of the high-pressure sodium lamp over virtually all other lamps is its high luminous efficiency, which is approximately 140 lumens/watt. It also enjoys a long life of approximately 24,000 hours. The sodium lamp is an extremely good choice for monochrome surveillance applications.

The mercury arc lamp has an efficiency between tungsten and high-pressure sodium. Its use as a light source with monochrome CCTV cameras provides only fair results since the light output is primarily in the blue region of the visible spectrum where silicon tube and solid-state cameras are insensitive. It is for this reason that while the mercury lighting might appear good to the human eye, it is not the lamp of choice for CCTV security.

The short-arc xenon has a color temperature of approximately 6,000 degrees K, which is almost identical to that of sunlight. However, since the xenon lamp output is composed of specific colors, as well as a continuum (and some IR radiation), it does not produce as well-balanced a color picture as results from a sun-illuminated scene.

Low-Pressure (LP) Arc Lamp

Fluorescent and low-pressure (LP) sodium lamps are examples of LP illumination sources. These lamps have tubular bulb shapes and long-arc lengths (several inches to several feet) and require a ballast for operation. The most common type is the fluorescent lamp having a relatively high efficacy of approximately 60 lumens/watt. LP lamps are used for large area illumination and produce a fairly uniform illumination pattern. Fluorescent lamps are available in various "colors" such as cool white (most popular) and blue white.

LP sodium lamps are another second class of LP lamps and produce a near single color (monochromatic) yellow light output. The LP sodium lamp has the highest efficacy of any lamp type built to date, approximately 180 lumens/watt. While the efficacy is high, its limitation is its monochromatic yellow color, which limits it to security and roadway lighting applications in which only monochrome CCTV cameras can be used. If used with color, only objects that are yellow will be seen as yellow and all other colors will be seen as brown or black.

A unique feature of the LP sodium amber light and one of its advantages is that it provides better "modeling" (shows up texture and shape) of any illuminated surface, both for the human eye and for CCTV camera, providing a clearer scene with more contrast.

Infrared (IR) Lighting

A covert IR lighting system is used when it is required to avoid calling attention to a secured site or the presence of a security system, to avoid alerting intruders, or to avoid disturbing neighbors or the public.

The IR source produces a monitor image from an illumination source that is invisible to the eye. This technology is commonly referred to as seeing in the dark, i.e., there is no visible radiation and yet a CCTV image is discernible.

There are two generic techniques for producing IR lighting. One method uses the IR energy from a thermal (incandescent or xenon) lamp. The lamp uses an optical filter to block the visible radiation so that only the IR radiation is transmitted to illuminate the scene. The second uses a non-thermal IR light emitting diode (LED) or LED array to generate IR radiation. Both

techniques are used and can produce narrow or wide light beams resulting in excellent images when the scene is viewed with a tube or solid-state silicon camera.

Thermal Infrared (IR) Source

The incandescent lamp is a good illumination source for IR CCTV applications when the light output is filtered with a covert filter. The filter blocks or absorbs the transmission of visible radiation and transmits only the near IR radiation. When an IR transmitting/visible blocking filter is placed in front of these lamps, only the IR energy reaches the scene to illuminate it and reflect back to the CCTV camera lens. A significant portion of the emitted spectrum of the lamp radiation falling in the near IR region that is invisible to the human eye is sensitive to tube and solid-state silicon cameras (monochrome).

Infrared-Emitting Diodes (LED)

The solid-state LED IR source using an array of gallium arsenide (GaAs) semiconductor diodes emits a narrow band of IR radiation and essentially no visible light. These devices are highly efficient -- typically 50% conversion of electrical to optical (IR) radiation -- do not dissipate much heat, and usually do not require special cooling.

Electrical power produces IR energy in the LED and directs it towards the magnifying dome lens and is emitted out in the direction of the scene. To produce sufficient light to illuminate the entire CCTV scene, an array of 100 to several hundred diodes are used. The IR output power from each diode adds linearly to the other diodes, the sum total illuminating the scene with sufficient IR energy to produce a good CCTV picture.

Lighting Costs

A factor of prime consideration in any CCTV security system is that of energy efficiency. Translated into dollars and cents this relates to the number of lumens (light output) per kilowatt of energy input that additional lighting might cost or

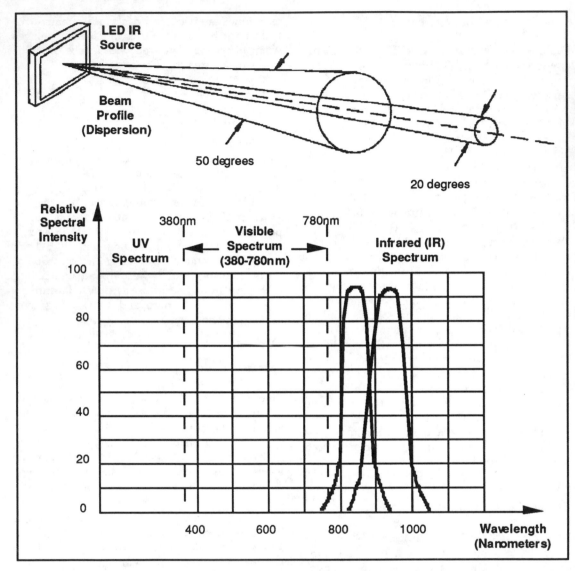

Light-Emitting Diode (LED) Source Output

that could be saved if a low-light-level (LLL) television camera system was used.

Since the light level affects the quality and quantity of intelligence contained in the picture scene on the monitor, it is important to know what type of lighting should be used and how much lighting is necessary to produce a good picture.

A site survey will determine whether lighting is adequate or if more must be added. There are computer design programs available to calculate the location and size of the lamps necessary to illuminate an area with a specified light level. Color cameras require higher levels of lighting (5 to 10 times).

The costs for lighting an indoor or outdoor area are dependent on several factors including initial installation, maintenance, and operating costs (energy usage). The initial installation costs for incandescent lighting are the lowest, followed by fluorescent lighting and then by HID lamps. All incandescent lamps can be connected directly to the electrical AC supply voltage without requirements for any electrical ballasting or high-voltage starting circuits. Some incandescent lamps are prefocused with built-in luminaries to produce spot or flood beam coverage. Fluorescent lamps are installed in diffuse light reflectors and require only a simple ballast and igniter for starting and running. The HID lamps are used most extensively because of their high efficacy and long life. They require more expensive ballasts, which add to the installation, but their overall efficiency is highest.

Lighting operating costs are a function of the electrical power input to the lamp vs. the light output (efficacy). Significant differences in operating costs exist for different lamp types. Comparing the lamp life and efficiency for the incandescent, mercury vapor, high-pressure sodium, and fluorescent lamps, it is noted that there is a significant saving in operational costs (energy costs) between the high-pressure sodium and fluorescent lamps as compared with the mercury vapor and standard incandescent lamps. Factors of a 2 or 3 to 1 savings in operational costs when choosing the more efficient lamp over the less efficient are achieved.

Lamp Life

Lamp life plays a significant role in determining the real cost efficiency between different light sources. This takes the form of actual lamp replacement costs each time a lamp must be replaced, in addition to the labor costs involved in replacing the lamp. A further factor is the additional risk involved because the lighting is not available so that security is not maintained.

The lamps having the longest lamp life are the high- and low-pressure sodium, and the HID mercury lamp, each providing approximately 24,000 hours of average lamp life. The next most efficient are most fluorescent lamps having a life of 10,000 hours. At the bottom of the list is the incandescent and quartz-halogen lamps, with average lamp life of approximately 1,000 to 2,000 hours, respectively. If the maintenance of changing lamps is of prime consideration, high-pressure sodium lamps should be used. There will be a difference of 12 trips to the site to replace a defective incandescent lamp compared with a sodium lamp. This is a significant cost difference in addition to the reduced security resulting during the replacement time of the burned out lamp.

The quality of the final CCTV picture and the intelligence it conveys is a strong function of the natural and/or artificial light sources illuminating the scene. For optimum results, an analysis of the light source(s) parameters (spectrum, illumination level, beam pattern) must be made and matched to the spectral and sensitivity characteristics of the camera. Color systems require careful analysis and should only be used with natural illumination during daylight hours or with broad spectrum, color-balanced artificial illumination indoors or at night. If the illumination level is marginal, measure it with a light meter to obtain the actual light reaching the camera from the scene. If there is insufficient light for the standard CCTV camera, augment the lighting with additional fill-in sources or choose a more sensitive camera. As with the human eye, lighting is a key factor to clear sight.

Herman A. Kruegle

CCTV: OPTICAL SYSTEMS

The function of the closed-circuit television (CCTV) lens is to collect the reflected light from a scene and form a sharp image of the scene on the camera sensor. The proper choice of lens constitutes an important decision in a CCTV system since it determines the amount of light received by the camera sensor, the field of view (FOV) that the camera will see, and, to a large extent, the quality of the picture obtained on the monitor. In describing the function of a CCTV lens a good analogy can be made to the human eye. The lens in both the human eye and the CCTV camera collect the reflected light from the scene or the light coming directly from a luminous light source, and focuses the scene onto the person's retina or the CCTV camera sensor. The eye is analogous to a fixed focal length (FFL) automatic iris CCTV lens and a camera sensor.

There are many different types of lenses used in CCTV security applications. The most common is the FFL lens, which is available in wide, medium, and narrow FOVs. When a wide scene area and close-up views are required, the variable FOV zoom lens mounted on a pan/tilt is often used. Covert applications use a pinhole lens that has a small front diameter and can easily be hidden out of view of the observer. There are many other specialty lenses including split-image, fiber-optic, right-angle, and auto-focus.

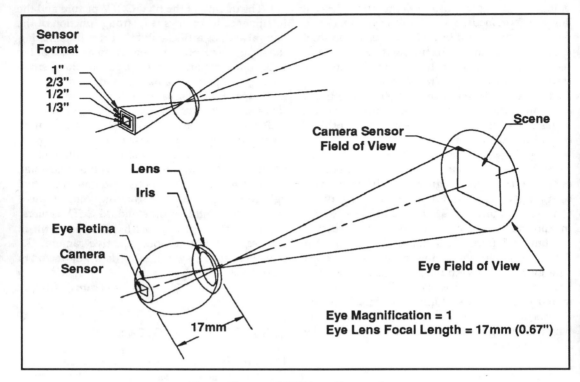

Human Eye and CCTV Lens/Camera Sensors

Lens Functions/Properties

Lenses are used to image the scene that the camera "sees" onto the solid-state or tube sensor. The CCTV lens and camera sensor system differs from the human eye in that the lens has one FFL and the retina is one size, whereas in the CCTV system the lens may have many different focal lengths and the sensor may have different sizes. The unaided human eye is limited to seeing a fixed and constant FOV, whereas the CCTV system can be modified to obtain a range of FOVs. To accommodate the wide changes in light level, the eye has an automatic iris diaphragm that opens and closes to optimize the light level reaching the retina to provide the best image. The camera lens has a manual or automatic iris to regulate the light level reaching the sensor.

In CCTV practice a lens with a FL and FOV similar to that of the human eye is referred to as a normal lens with a magnification M=1. The CCTV lens and camera format corresponding to the M=1 condition is a 25-millimeter FL lens on a 1-inch camera sensor format, a 16-millimeter FL lens on a 2/3-inch, a 12.5-millimeter FL on a 1/2-inch, and an 8-millimeter FL on a 1/3-inch.

There are many tables, graphs, nomographs, linear and circular slide rules, and a handy aid called a Lens Finder Kit for determining the angles and sizes of the scene viewed at varying distances by a CCTV camera with a given sensor format and FL lens.

A lens with a FL shorter than normal is referred to as a wide-angle lens; a lens with a FL longer than normal is referred to as telephoto or narrow-angle lens. A telephoto lens used with a CCTV camera provides the same function as a telescope used with the human eye: they magnify the image viewed, narrow the FOV being observed, and effectively bring the object of interest closer to the eye or sensor.

The lens FL is the distance behind the lens at which the image of a distant object (scene) would focus. On the scene at some distance (D) from the lens is shown the projected area that the sensor sees. Using the eye analogy, the sensor and lens

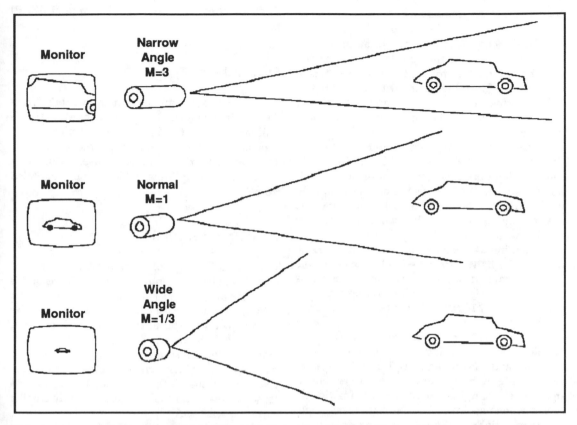

Lens Field of View (FOV) for Magnification of 1, 3 and 1/3

project a scene W (wide) times H (high) (the eye sees a circle). As with the human eye, the CCTV lens inverts the image, but the human brain and the electronics in the camera re-invert it to provide an upright image.

To obtain the angular FOV for 1-inch sensors, multiply the angles for the 1/2-inch sensor by 2. To obtain the angular FOV for 1/3-inch sensors, divide the angles for the 2/3-inch sensors by 2.

Optical Speed (f/#)

The optical speed or f/number (f/#) of a lens defines the light-gathering ability of the lens. In general, the more light the lens collects and transmits to the camera image sensor, the better the picture quality eventually seen on the monitor. This light-gathering ability is dependent on the size of the CCTV optics: the larger the optics the more light that can be collected. With the human eye there is no choice since most people have

about the same size eyes (approximately 7-millimeter lens diameter). The CCTV front lens diameters vary over a wide range and therefore their optical speed varies significantly. An important factor to consider is that the f/# varies as the square of the diameter of the lens. In practical terms this means that a lens having a diameter twice that of another can transmit four times as much light.

Fast lenses have a low f/#, such as f/1.3 or f/1.6. The lens optical speed is related to its FL and diameter (d) by the equation:

$$f/number = f/\# = focal\ length/diameter = FL/d.$$

The larger the FL, given the same lens diameter, the "slower the lens" (i.e., less light reaches the sensor). A "slow" lens might have an f/# of f/4 or f/8. In general, faster lenses collect more light energy from the scene, are larger in physical size, and are more expensive.

Manual and Automatic Iris

The CCTV lens iris is manually or automatically adjusted to optimize the light level reaching the sensor. The manual iris CCTV lens has movable metal "leaves" forming the iris with the amount of light entering the camera determined by rotating an external iris ring that opens and closes these leaves.

This ring is usually marked in numbers such as 1.0, 1.4, 2.0, 2.8, 4.0, 5.6, 8.0, 11, 16, 22, C, representing optical speed, f/# or f stops. The C indicates when the lens iris is closed and no light is transmitted. The difference between each of the iris settings represents a difference of a factor of two in the light transmitted by the lens.

Opening the lens from say f/2.0 to f/1.4 doubles the light transmitted. Only one-half the light is transmitted when the iris opening is reduced from say f/5.6 to f/8. Covering the range from f/1.4 to f/16 spans a light attenuation range of 256 to 1.

Solid-state sensor charge-coupled device (CCD) and metal-oxide semiconductor (MOS) cameras, and silicon and Newvicon tube cameras can operate with manual iris lenses over limited light level changes, but require automatic iris lenses when used over their full light level range, i.e., from bright sunlight to low-level nighttime lighting. Vidicon tube cameras compensate fairly well over their useful light range without any automatic iris lens.

Automatic Iris Operation

Automatic iris lenses have an electro-optical mechanism responding to the camera video signal whereby the amount of light passing through the lens can be varied or adjusted depending on the amount of light available from the scene and the sensitivity of the camera used. The system works something like this: if a bright scene is being viewed, i.e., too much light for the camera, the video signal will be large in amplitude. This signal information is used to activate a motor or galvanometer, which causes the lens iris to close down, thereby reducing the amount of light reaching the camera to a level the camera can accommodate.

At a predetermined signal level the motor or galvanometer stops and maintains this level of light through the lens. Conversely, when too little light reaches the camera, the opposite will happen.

Standard Lens Types

CCTV lenses are available in many varieties from the simple, small, and inexpensive "bottle cap," 16-millimeter FL , f/1.6 lens; to complex, large, expensive, motorized, automatic iris zoom types. There are covert pinhole lenses used to uncover theft, such as shoplifting, which can be concealed from sight.

Fixed Focal Length (FFL)

The FFL lens is the most common CCTV lens and is available with a manual or automatic iris and is optically fast -- from f/1.3 to f/1.8 -- providing sufficient light for most cameras to provide a good quality picture. These lenses have a C or CS (1 inch times 32 threads per inch) mounting. The C mount has been a standard in the CCTV industry for many years, with the CS introduced a few years ago to match the trend to smaller camera sensor formats and their correspondingly smaller lens requirements.

The difference between the C and CS mount is in the distance between the mounting surface and the sensor: 0.69 inches for the C mount and 0.492 inches for the CS lens.

Wide-Angle Viewing

While the human eye has peripheral vision and can detect the presence and movement of objects over a wide-angle (160 degrees), the eye only sees a focused scene in about the central 10 degrees of the eye's FOV. No television camera has this unique eye characteristic. The CCTV FOV can be increased (or decreased), however, by replacing the lens with one having a shorter (or longer) FL. The eye cannot change its FOV, which is approximately 45 degrees. To increase the FOV of a CCTV camera, a short FL lens is used.

A 4.8-millimeter FL lens on a 2/3-inch sensor is an example of a wide-angle lens and has a 96 degree horizontal by 72 degree vertical FOV. A super-wide FOV lens for a 1/2-inch sensor is the 2.6-millimeter FL lens, which has approximately a 117 horizontal by 88 degree vertical FOV.

Using a wide-angle lens reduces the resolution or ability to discern objects in a scene.

Wide-Angle (Telephoto) Viewing

Outdoor security applications often require viewing scenes hundreds or thousands of feet away from the CCTV lens and camera. Long FL lenses magnify these scenes and are necessary to detect and/or identify objects, persons, or activity at these ranges. When the lens FL increases above the standard (normal) lens (M=1 condition), the FOV decreases, the magnification increases, and the lens is called a telephoto or narrow-angle lens. Lenses with a FL from 2.6 millimeters up to several hundred millimeters are refractive or glass type. Above approximately 300 millimeters FL, refractive glass lenses become large and expensive, and reflective mirror optics or mirror/glass optics are used. These long FL telephoto lenses are called Cassegrain or catadioptric lenses, and have focal lengths between a few hundred and a few thousand millimeters.

Zoom-Variable Focal Length

The zoom lens is a cleverly designed assembly of lens elements that can be moved to change the FL from a wide- to normal to a narrow-angle (telephoto) while the image on the sensor remains in focus. Adjusting its zoom ring setting has the effect of varying the FL and angle of view through a specified range of magnifications. This permits viewing narrow-, medium-, and wide-angle scenes. As a result, a scene can be made to appear close-up or far away, giving the impression of camera movement, even though the camera remains in a fixed position.

Since the FL of a zoom lens is variable and its entrance aperture is fixed, its f/# is not fixed. Therefore, an 11- to 110-millimeter zoom lens may be f/1.8 when set at 11-millimeters FL, and f/4 when set at 110-millimeters FL with the f/# for any other FL in between the two settings being in between these two values.

A large variety of manual and motorized zoom lenses are available from inexpensive 8- to 48-millimeters FL to a large and expensive (13.5-600 millimeters) used in high-risk security areas for industry, military, and government agencies.

Zoom lenses are usually mounted on a pan/tilt mechanism so that the lens can be pointed in almost any direction. The pan/tilt and lens controller remotely controls pan, tilt, zoom, and focus. By varying the lens zoom control and moving the pan/tilt platform, a wide dynamic FOV is achieved.

A zoom lens designed into a computer-controlled surveillance system uses an electronic preset function, whereby the zoom ring and focus ring positions are monitored electrically and are memorized by the computer during system setup. These positions can then be automatically repeated on command by the computer at a later time. In a pan/tilt surveillance application this allows the computer to point the camera/lens combination to a predetermined preset set of conditions: (1) azimuth and elevation angle, (2) focused at a specific distance, and (3) iris set to a specific f/# opening. In response to an alarm sensor, if a camera must point in another direction, the preset feature significantly reduces the time required to acquire the new target and eliminates the human factor.

Pinhole Lenses

A pinhole lens is a special security lens with small front diameter so that it can be hidden behind a wall, ceiling, or in some other object and be inconspicuous to the observer. Some objects in which covert camera/pinhole lenses have been installed include emergency lighting fixtures, exit signs, ceiling mounted lights, sprinkler heads, table lamps, and mannequins. Any object that can house the camera and pinhole lens and can disguise or hide the front lens element is a candidate for a covert installation. Pinhole lens variations include straight and right-angle, manual and automatic iris, narrow-taper or stubby front shape, and mini-pinhole.

The narrow (slow) tapering design permits easier installation than the stubby (fast) taper and also has a faster optical speed since the larger front lens collects more light. The optical speed (f/#) of the pinhole lens is important for the successful implementation of a covert camera system. The lower the f/#, the more light reaching the television camera and the better the television picture.

The sprinkler head pinhole lens is hidden in a ceiling sprinkler fixture, making it extremely

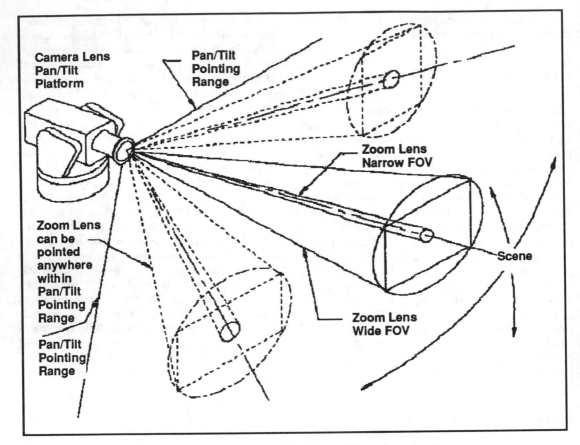

Dynamic FOV of Pan/Tilt Mounted Zoom Lens

difficult for an observer standing at floor level to detect or identify the lens/camera.

The pinhole lens and camera combination is concealed in and above a ceiling with only a modified sprinkler head in view below the ceiling. For looking in different directions, a panning sprinkler head and moving mirror configuration is used.

Mini-Pinhole Lens

Another generic family of covert lenses is called the mini-lens. These lenses are very small and optically fast. Mini-lenses can be used in places unsuitable for larger pinhole lenses because of their small size, typically 3/8-inch diameter by 1/2-inch long. The mini-pinhole lenses have optical speeds from f/1.4 to f/1.8. An f/1.4 mini-pinhole lens transmits five times more light than an f/3.5 pinhole lens. A useful variation of the

standard mini-lens is the off-axis mini-lens, which is mounted offset from the camera axis and causes the camera to "look" off to one side, up, or down, depending on the direction it is offset.

Special Lenses

Some special CCTV security lenses deserving mention include fiber optic and borescope, split image, and right angle.

Fiber-Optic Lens. Fiber-optic lenses should not to be confused with the single or multiple strands of fiber commonly used to transmit the television signal from the camera site to a remote monitor site. The coherent fiber-optic lens consists of a bundle of several hundred thousand glass fibers positioned adjacent to each other. It transmits a coherent image from an objective lens, over a distance of several inches to several feet,

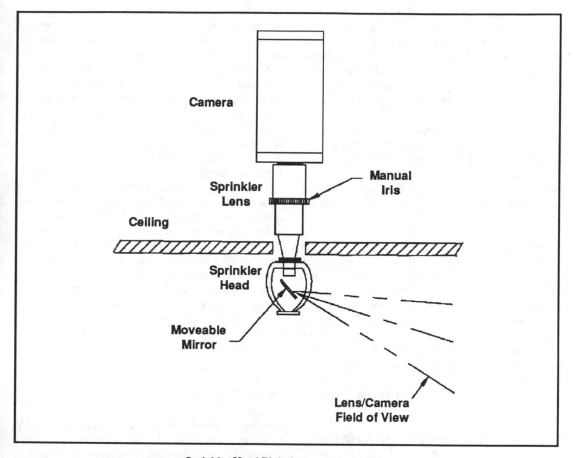

Sprinkler Head Pinhole Assembly Installation

where the image is then transferred again by means of a relay lens to the camera sensor. The meaning of the term coherent is that each point in the image on the front end of the fiber bundle corresponds to a point at the rear end of the fiber bundle.

Since the picture quality obtained with fiber-optic lenses is not as good as the quality obtained with all glass lenses, they should only be used when no other lens/camera system will solve the problem. Fiber-optic lenses are available in 1/2-inch diameter rigid up to 1 1/8-inch diameter flexible configurations with optical f/#s from f/4 to f/8.

Borescope Lens. The borescope lens consists of a long rigid tube measuring 6 to 30 inches in length and having a 0.125- to 0.5-inch diameter. The tube has multiple, small internal lenses to transmit the image from a front lens to the rear lens and onto a camera sensor.

Because of the small diameter of the lenses, only a small amount of light is transmitted, resulting in slow f/#s, typically f/11 to f/30. This slow speed limits their application to well-illuminated environments and sensitive cameras. The image quality of the borescope lens is better than that of the fiber-optic lens since it uses all glass lenses.

Split-Image Lens. The split-image lens places the images of two independent scenes onto a single television camera. This is done using two separate objective lenses, with the same or different FL and combining them onto one camera sensor.

The split-image lens has two C or CS lens ports (mounts) so that the two objective lenses view two scenes with the same camera. Depending on the orientation of the bifocal lens system on the camera, either a vertical or horizontal split is obtained. Any FFL, pinhole, zoom, or other lens that mechanically fits onto the C or CS mount image splitter can be used. The adjustable mirror on the side lens permits looking in many directions.

The scene FOV covered by each lens is one-half of the total lens horizontal FOV. By rotating the split-image lens 90 degrees about the camera optical axis, a horizontal split is obtained. A three-way optical image splitting lens can view three scenes, with each scene occupying one-third of the monitor screen.

Right-Angle Lens. The right-angle optical system permits use of normal or wide-angle lenses (2.6 millimeters, 110 degree FOV) to look at right angles to the camera axis. The right-angle lens permits mounting cameras parallel to a wall or ceiling while the lens views the scene. This cannot be accomplished by using a mirror and a wide-angle lens directly on the camera since the entire scene will not be reflected by the mirror to the lens on the camera.

Herman A. Kruegle

CCTV: THE INTEGRATION OF SYSTEMS

In the past, it was common to see security control rooms overloaded with closed-circuit television (CCTV) monitors. As a business grew, its security needs also increased, so more cameras were added to the original system. There were often more monitors than security personnel could possibly watch. To reduce the number of viewing screens, many security departments added video switches and made multiple cameras sequence automatically on fewer monitors. As more cameras were added, more positions on a video switcher were used.

Unfortunately, this cure created a different problem. Realistically, security personnel cannot watch more than four cameras on one monitor, and if multiple monitors are used, even four can be too many.

Despite this reality, many security departments added sequencing cameras because it was a quick solution. The typical management attitude was, "We have extra camera positions, let's use them."

When a CCTV system is properly designed, it will monitor large areas that cannot be covered by personnel accurately; work with other systems to alert security personnel for potential problems; and provide evidence after problems have occurred (through time-lapse videotaping) to assist in prosecutions or recovery of lost goods. CCTV and videotape recording systems are tremendous tools for helping security personnel do many tasks, such as access control, perimeter protection, quality control, traffic control, and inventory control.

Generally, as the variety of uses of CCTV grows, there is a need to re-evaluate how these systems are to be controlled. Depending on a company's size, it is not always possible to reduce the number of video monitors needed to accomplish multiple tasks, so CCTV monitors should call attention to emergency situations or activities that are different from the norm. This is accomplished by using a variety of systems that automatically call up cameras to show that an unusual condition exists. The following are examples.

CCTV Systems

Access Control. Some companies use CCTV systems with visual badge readers on a split screen. This system enables security personnel to see a badge and, at the same time, view the person using the badge. Cameras can be called up automatically when a badge is placed in the badge reader.

New systems also use various card access control systems that connect directly with CCTV switching systems. When a card is used, cameras are automatically called up and displayed on the viewing screen (the scene may also be recorded for future reference).

Some systems also tie into personnel files that store color photographs of all authorized personnel. Thus, security officers can see not only people entering the building, but can compare people with photographs from the personnel file. Because this system calls up information for an officer automatically, several entrances and exits can be monitored at one time.

Video Motion Detection. A video motion detector analyzes the signal sent from a video camera. If changes are made in the scene, the signal changes and the motion detector will alarm the CCTV system. These devices have become so sophisticated in the last few years that some systems can detect a change in the video pattern that even the human eye cannot detect. Such sophisticated motion detectors are used at nuclear plants for perimeter protection.

Sound Systems. There are many ways to incorporate sound systems into a CCTV system. The simplest is an intercom installed at the entrance of a building that transmits the audio to a master station and calls up a camera on an automatic switcher. When someone makes an inquiry at the entry point, a security officer can respond without having to touch a single controller.

There are also sophisticated vox switches that monitor sound activities in areas such as stairwells, lobbies, and elevators. These switches are programmed to allow for normal traffic movement but will automatically alarm if sound levels go beyond a predetermined threshold. These devices can connect with a CCTV system.

Many of these systems are used in parking garages for patron protection. Sound systems can be designed so the camera, speakers, and microphones are all built into the same package. Again, when these areas are triggered by the vox switch, cameras will automatically come up on the screen, the voice path will open automatically, and a security officer can respond with a minimal amount of action.

Black-and-White Solid-State Cameras. CCTV systems have come a long way since the use of large 1-inch black-and-white vidicon tube cameras. Today, most cameras are solid-state and use either a metal-oxide semiconductor (MOS) or charge-coupled device (CCD) type of sold-state chip. These new camera formats have minimized service costs, reduced the number of service calls, and improved the overall picture quality and performance of CCTV systems.

Color Solid-State Cameras. In the past, to obtain a color CCTV system, security departments had to use a three-stage color tube camera. These cameras were expensive, were effective only when lighting was adequate, and required constant service. With today's new chip technology, a color system is much more attractive in cost and quality. Today's color CCD cameras do not cost

much more than black-and-white CCD cameras. There are several advantages of color systems. They are more realistic for monitoring personnel (it's a color world), are less tiring on the eyes, and provide more information.

Video Multiplex Systems. Another means of minimizing the number of monitors security personnel have to watch is to use a new concept called video multiplexing. This system allows up to 16 cameras to be viewed simultaneously on one video screen. In most systems, the pictures are compressed in their entirety so a full view of each camera is seen on the corresponding quadrant. These systems also include automatic full screen call-up on alarm and some include built-in activity detection that brings active camera scenes to full screen. By using a combination of video multiplexers and video switching, security managers can design various configurations. Cameras can sequence individually on each section of the multiplexer, or multiple screens can sequence on one single monitor.

To give an example, in a parking garage each level uses four cameras to monitor traffic. These cameras can be displayed through a quad multiplex system and multiple floors can then sequence through a microprocessor-based controller system, enabling a security officer to watch the entire parking ramp as the system sequences from the ground floor to the top floor.

Reproduction of Pictures. In the past, the only way to generate a hard-copy picture from a video system or a time-lapse videotape recorder was through a Polaroid oscilloscope camera with a special cathode-ray tube hood. New devices on the market today -- video thermal printers, thermal film process printers, and ink-jet printers -- provide for both black-and-white and color copies with excellent quality.

Whether a business has an existing system that has become unmanageable or is designing a new system for the future, consideration should be given to using several technologies to accomplish immediate and future needs. No one system alone can accurately provide the protection needed by today's security departments.

Unfortunately, no single manufacturer provides a system that will do access control, multitask alarm monitoring, microprocessor-based video and audio switching, sound threshold detection, motion detection, and video and audio multiplexing. As a result, there has been an emergence of qualified integrators doing systems design, complete installation, and service. Because this field is ever changing, these types of contractors are in tune to future products that will meet future needs. Many consultants and engineers rely heavily on systems contractors (integrators) as information sources for their specifications.

The key to finding the right systems contractor is to look for one who provides performance specifications rather than equipment specifications. Contractors who have the client's best interest in mind are the ones who will find equipment to fit client needs and will not try to change those needs to fit their equipment.

Jack Morris

CCTV: THE MANY ROLES OF CCTV IN SECURITY

Closed-circuit television (CCTV) is a reliable, cost-effective deterrent to crime and a means for the apprehension and prosecution of offenders. In view of high labor costs, CCTV more than ever before has earned its place as a cost-effective means for expanding security and safety, reducing asset losses and reducing the cost of security. Most safety and security applications require several different types of equipment including CCTV surveillance, fire and intrusion alarm, and access control.

Theft Reduction

Thievery causes loss of assets and time, and is a growing cancer in our society. It reduces the profits of all organizations, be they government, retail, service, manufacturing, etc.. CCTV is effective in counteracting these losses in small and large companies alike, thereby increasing corporate profits. The public at large has accepted the use of CCTV systems in public and industrial facilities while the reaction by workers to its use is mixed.

The integration of CCTV with a properly designed security system can be an extremely profitable investment to any organization. One objective of the CCTV system should be to deter crime so as to prevent thievery. It has been shown that CCTV is an effective psychological deterrent to crime. If an organization or company can prevent an incident from occurring in the first place, the problem has been solved.

A second objective is the apprehension of offenders and successful dismissal or prosecution of them. A successful thief needs privacy in which to operate and it is the function of the CCTV system to prevent this. The number of thefts cannot be counted exactly, but the reduction in shrinkage can be measured.

Theft takes the form of removing valuable property and/or information from a facility. Lost information takes the form of computer software, magnetic tape and disks, optical disks, microfilm, data on paper, etc. Real property losses include vandalizing and defacing buildings; graffiti on facilities and art objects; and destroying furniture, business machines, or other valuable equipment. CCTV surveillance systems provide a means for successfully deterring such thievery and/or detecting or apprehending the offenders.

Management Function – Master Plan

The protection of assets is a management function. Three key factors that govern the planning of an assets protection program are: (1) preventing losses from occurring, (2) providing adequate countermeasures to limit actual losses and to limit unpreventable losses, and (3) top management support of the protection plan.

The Role of CCTV in Assets Protection

CCTV plays an important role in the protection of assets by permitting detection of unwanted entry into a facility beginning at the perimeter location and by monitoring internal activity.

The CCTV security system consists of an illumination source, lens, camera, transmission, switching, recording, and printing means. To make best use of all aspects of CCTV technology, the practitioner and end user must understand the lighting sources needed to illuminate the scene, the CCTV equipment and its capabilities, and the surveillance limitations during daytime and nighttime operation.

Videocassette recorders (VCRs) and hard-copy video printers provide CCTV security with a new dimension, i.e., going beyond real-time

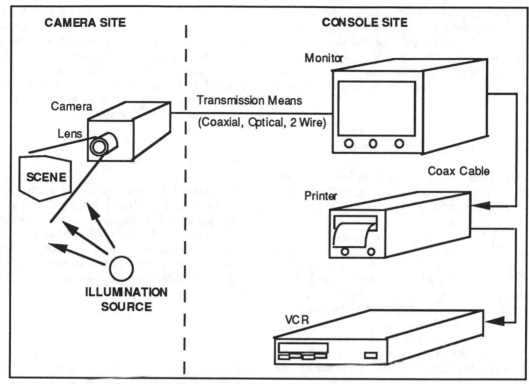

Single Camera System

camera surveillance. This archiving ability is of prime importance since it permits permanent identification of activities and personnel necessary for dismissal or prosecution of an offender in a court of law at a future time.

Color vs. Monochrome

Most CCTV surveillance applications use monochrome equipment, but the solid-state camera has made color systems practical. The driving functions responsible for the accelerated development and implementation of the excellent CCTV equipment available today has been the widespread use of CCTV by consumers, made possible through technological advances and the resulting availability of low-cost VCRs and associated camera equipment. Solid-state color cameras for the consumer VCR market accelerated the availability of reliable, stable, long-life color cameras and time-lapse VCRs for the security industry. Color is important in surveillance applications because objects that are easily identified in a color scene are difficult to identify

in a monochrome scene. For this reason, color cameras will replace most monochrome types as the sensitivity and resolution increases, and the cost decreases.

CCTV as Part of the Emergency and Disaster Plan

An organization should have a method to alert employees in the event of a dangerous condition, and a plan to provide for quick law enforcement, fire and/or emergency response. Every organization regardless of size should have an emergency and disaster control plan that includes CCTV as a critical component. CCTV can:

1. Protect human life by enabling security or safety officials to see remote locations, to view what is happening, where it is happening, what action is most critical, and what areas to attend to and in what priority.

2. Warn of an oncoming disaster.

3. Prevent or at least assess document or assets removal by intruders or unauthorized personnel.

4. Document via VCRs the equipment and assets in place prior to the disaster for comparison to the remaining assets after the disaster.

5. Help in restoring the organization to normal operation and procedures.

6. Reduce exposure of physical assets and optimize loss control.

Documentation of the Emergency

CCTV can aid in determining whether machinery, utilities, boilers, furnaces, etc., have been shut down properly, whether personnel must enter the area to do so, or whether other means must be taken to take it off-line. It can be used to verify that all personnel have left a potentially dangerous area.

The use of CCTV is an important tool that can be used to monitor assets during and after a disaster to ensure that material is not removed and that it is monitored. After the emergency situation has been brought under control, CCTV and security personnel provide the functions of monitoring the situation and maintaining the security of assets.

For insurance purposes, and for critique by management and security, documentation provided by CCTV recordings of assets lost or stolen and personnel injuries or deaths can support that the company was not negligent, and that a prudent emergency and disaster plan was in effect prior to the event.

CCTV can play a critical role in evaluation of a disaster plan to identify shortcomings and to illustrate correct and incorrect procedures to personnel.

Stand-By Power and Communications

It is likely that during any emergency or disaster, primary power and/or communications from one location to another will be disrupted. Stand-by power will keep emergency lighting, communications, and strategic CCTV equipment on line as needed during the emergency. When power is lost, the CCTV equipment is automatically switched over to the emergency power backup equipment (gas-powered generator or uninterruptible power supply (UPS)). A prudent security plan anticipating an emergency will include a means to power vital safety and security equipment to ensure its operation during a crisis event. Since critical CCTV and audio communications must be maintained over remote distances during such an occurrence, an alternate means of communication (signal transmission) from one location to another should be supplied either in the form of protected auxiliary hard-wired cable or a wireless system.

Security Investigations

CCTV is used for covert security investigations where the camera and lens are hidden from view by any personnel in the area so that positive identification and documentation of an event or person's actions can be made. Lenses and cameras can be discreetly hidden in rooms, hallways, and specific objects in indoor or outdoor locations to provide such surveillance.

Safety

CCTV equipment is used for safety purposes whereby security personnel can identify unsafe practices to prevent accidents or respond to those needing immediate attention. CCTV cameras should be distributed throughout a facility, in stairwells, loading docks, and other potentially dangerous locations to permit security and safety personnel to respond to safety violations and accidents.

CCTV is used when an area is evacuated to determine if all personnel have left the area and are safe. Security personnel can use CCTV for pedestrian and vehicular traffic monitoring and control, to locate high traffic areas, and how to best control them.

CCTV plays a critical role in public safety to monitor vehicular traffic on highways, city streets, truck and bus depots, public rail and subway facilities, and airports.

Guard Role

A guard using CCTV can significantly increase security effectiveness. CCTV represents a low capital investment and low operating cost as compared with the overall cost for a guard. A guard can often be replaced with CCTV equipment when monitoring remote sites.

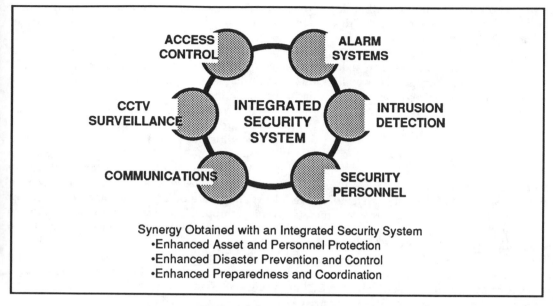

ACCESS CONTROL

ALARM SYSTEMS

CCTV SURVEILLANCE

INTEGRATED SECURITY SYSTEM

INTRUSION DETECTION

COMMUNICATIONS

SECURITY PERSONNEL

Synergy Obtained with an Integrated Security System
•Enhanced Asset and Personnel Protection
•Enhanced Disaster Prevention and Control
•Enhanced Preparedness and Coordination

Integrated Security System

Training of Employees and Security Personnel

CCTV is an effective training tool for management, security personnel, and employees that improves employee efficiency and increases productivity. It is in widespread use because it so vividly and conveniently demonstrates security procedures for the trainee to implement. Actual, real-life situations demonstrate to the trainee what can happen when procedures are not followed, and the improved results obtained when plans are properly executed by trained personnel.

Scenes from actual exercises can demonstrate good and poor practices, breaches of security, unacceptable employee behavior, and proper guard reaction. Training videos are used for rehearsals or tests of an emergency or disaster plan. At a later time all members of the team observe their response and are critiqued by management or other professionals to improve their performance.

Synergy through Integration

CCTV equipment is most effective when integrated with other security hardware to form a coherent security system. The hardware used in synergy with CCTV is electronic access control,

fire and safety alarms, intrusion detection alarms, and communication channels.

Functionally, the integrated security system can be regarded as a design-coordinated combination of equipment, personnel, and procedures that utilizes each component to enhance every other component to assure optimum achievement of the stated objective.

Each element chosen is analyzed to determine how it will contribute to prevent loss or protect assets and personnel. As an example, if an intrusion occurs, at what point should it be detected, what should the response be, and by what means should it be reported and recorded? In a perimeter-protection role, CCTV can be used with other intrusion detection devices to alert the guard at the security console that an intrusion has occurred.

When an intrusion occurs, multiple CCTV cameras located throughout the facility follow the intruder to permit implementation of the planned response by guard personnel or designated employees. Management determines the specific guard reaction and response. If the intruder has violated some form of barrier or fence, the intrusion-detection system should be able to determine that a person passed through the barrier and not an animal, bird, insect, leaves, debris, etc. (false alarms). CCTV provides the most positive means for making this determination and communicating it to the security personnel reaction force, with enough information to permit them to initiate a response.

The synergistic integration of CCTV, access control, alarms, intrusion detection and security guards into a system increases the overall security of the facility and maximizes assets protection and employee safety.

Fire and Safety

The greatest potential for CCTV is its integration with other safety-related sensing systems (smoke detectors, alarms), and its use to view remote areas having potential safety problems or fire hazards. In the case of a fire, CCTV cameras act as real-time eyes at the emergency location, permitting security and safety personnel to send the appropriate reaction force. Having CCTV cameras on location before personnel arrive shortens the reaction time to a fire or other disaster. A CCTV camera can quickly ascertain whether an event is a false alarm, a minor alarm, or a major event. In a fire alert, the automatic sprinkler and fire alarm system alerts the guard to the event, but the CCTV "eye" views the scene and permits more effective use of personnel and ensures that they are not diverted to false alarms unnecessarily. The synergistic combination of audio and CCTV from a remote site enhances the intelligence received from the remote site.

Security Surveillance Applications

CCTV applications are broadly classified into indoor or outdoor: those suitable for a controlled indoor environment, and those suitable for harsher outdoor environments. The indoor location requires the use of artificial lighting, which may or may not be augmented by daylight entering the viewing area, and is only subjected to mild indoor temperature and humidity variations, dirt, dust, and smoke. The outdoor location uses sunlight during daytime and artificial lighting during nighttime, and can encounter environmental precipitation (fog, rain, snow), wind loading, dirt, dust, sand, and smoke. Some typical safety and security applications for which CCTV provides an effective solution include:

1.   Overt observation of hazardous areas with the potential for life threatening or injurious situations, including toxic, radioactive, high fire or explosion potential, X-ray radiation, or other nuclear radiation.

2.   Visual observation of a scene that must be covert (hidden) is accomplished by means of a small camera and lens rather than locating a person in the area.

3.   Where significant events must be viewed or recorded when activity occurs, at a normally low-activity area such as at a perimeter or other location.

4.   Simultaneous surveillance of many locations by one person from a central security location to trace the entry and path of a person or vehicle through a facility from the entry point to the final destination in the facility or interdiction by the security force.

5.   Provide a high-quality hard-copy printout of unauthorized entry, activity, or event using a VCR and/or printer system.

CCTV Access Control

CCTV access control uses television to remotely identify a person requesting access, whether as a pedestrian or in a vehicle. Identification is accomplished by comparing the person's face with a photo on an identification card carried by the person. The live and replicated facial image is displayed side-by-side on a split-screen monitor. If the two images match, the security guard unlocks the door and allows entry. The CCTV access control system can be combined with an electronic access control system to increase security and provide a means to track all attempted entries.

For medium- to low-level access control security requirements, electronic card reading systems are adequate after a person has first been identified at some exterior perimeter location. To provide higher security than a simple identification card and electronic card reading system can provide, it is necessary to combine the electronic card reader with either biometric descriptors of a person, and/or CCTV identification. For the highest level of access control security, the video image of the person and other pertinent information is stored in a video image file and then retrieved and used as part of the identification process.

The synergy of a CCTV security system implies the following functional scenario:

1. An unauthorized intrusion or entry or attempted removal of equipment is detected at the time of the event by some alarm sensor.

2. A CCTV camera located somewhere in the alarm area is pointed manually or automatically (from the guard site) to view the alarm area.

3. The alarm sensor and CCTV camera information is transmitted immediately to the security console and monitored by personnel and/or recorded for permanent documentation.

4. The security operator receiving the alarm information acts according to a security plan to dispatch personnel to the location or to take some other appropriate action.

5. After appropriate action the guard resumes normal security duties to view any future event.

The use of CCTV plays a crucial role in the overall security plan. During an intrusion or theft, the CCTV system provides information to the guard to make an assessment of the security problem and provide an appropriate response. Suitable alarm sensors and CCTV cameras permit the guard to follow the progress of the event and assist the response team by providing tactical information.

With an intrusion alarm and visual CCTV information, all the elements are in place for a reliable transfer of information to the security officers in a timely fashion. For proper effectiveness, all parts of the security system must work properly: the alarm, CCTV, and guard response.

The motivation for an organization to justify expenditures on security and safety equipment is that there must be a positive return on investment, i.e., the value of assets not lost must be greater than the amount spent on security. Experience has shown that CCTV does play a crucial role in the success of a security and safety plan. A well-planned security and safety system has the potential to reduce thefts, protect assets, and save lives. When disaster strikes, an organization should have an emergency and recovery plan in place.

Herman A. Kruegle

CENTRAL INTELLIGENCE AGENCY (CIA)

The United States has carried on foreign intelligence activities since the days of George Washington, but only since World War II have they been coordinated on a government-wide basis.

Even before Pearl Harbor, President Franklin D. Roosevelt was concerned about American intelligence deficiencies. He asked New York lawyer William J. Donovan to draft a plan for an intelligence service. The Office of Strategic Services was established in June 1942 with a mandate to collect and analyze strategic information required by the Joint Chiefs of Staff and to conduct special operations.

During the war, the OSS supplied policy makers with essential facts and intelligence estimates, and often played an important role in directly aiding military campaigns. The OSS never received complete jurisdiction over all foreign intelligence activities. Since the early 1930s the Federal Bureau of Investigation (FBI) had been responsible for intelligence work in Latin America, and the military services protected their areas of responsibility.

In October 1945, the OSS was abolished and its functions transferred to the State and War Departments, but the need for a postwar centralized intelligence system was clearly recognized. Eleven months earlier, Donovan, by then a major general, had submitted to President Roosevelt a proposal calling for the separation of OSS from the Joint Chiefs of Staff with the new organization having direct presidential supervision.

Donovan proposed an "organization which will procure intelligence both by overt and covert methods and will at the same time provide intelligence guidance, determine national intelligence objectives, and correlate the intelligence material collected by all government agencies."

Under his plan, a powerful, centralized civilian agency would have coordinated all the intelligence services. He also proposed that this agency have authority to conduct "subversive operations abroad," but "no police or law enforcement functions, either at home or abroad." Donovan's plan drew heavy fire. The military services generally opposed a complete merger. The State Department thought it should supervise all peacetime operations affecting foreign relations. The FBI supported a system whereby military intelligence worldwide would be handled by the armed services, and all civilian activities would be under the FBI's own jurisdiction.

In response to this policy debate, President Harry S. Truman established the Central Intelligence Group in January 1946, directing it to coordinate existing departmental intelligence, supplementing but not supplanting their services. This was all to be done under the direction of a National Intelligence Authority composed of a presidential representative and the Secretaries of State and War, and Navy Rear Admiral Sidney W. Souers, who was the Deputy Chief of Naval Intelligence, was appointed the first Director of Central Intelligence.

Twenty months later, the National Intelligence Authority and its operating component, the Central Intelligence Group, were dis-established. Under the provisions of the National Security Act of 1947 (which became effective on September 18, 1947) the National Security Council and the Central Intelligence Agency (CIA) were established.

Most of the National Security Act's specific assignments given the CIA, as well as the prohibitions on police and internal security functions, closely follow both the original 1944 Donovan plan and the presidential directive creating the Central Intelligence Group.

The 1947 Act charged the CIA with coordinating the nation's intelligence activities and correlating, evaluating, and disseminating intelligence that affects national security. In addition, the Agency was to perform such other duties and functions related to intelligence as the NSC might direct. The Act also made the Director of Central Intelligence (DCI) responsible for protecting intelligence sources and methods.

The office of Deputy Director of Central Intelligence (DDCI) evolved gradually. Until 1953, Deputy Directors were appointed by the Director, and it was General Walter Bedell Smith, the fourth DCI, who established the Deputy Director of Central Intelligence in the role he has since played in CIA.

Congress recognized the importance of the position in April 1953 by amending the National Security Act of 1947 to provide for the appointment of the Deputy Director of Central Intelligence by the President with the advice and consent of the Senate. This amendment also provided that commissioned officers of the armed forces, whether active or retired, could not occupy both DCI and DDCI positions at the same time. The DDCI assists the Director by performing such functions as the DCI assigns or delegates. He acts for and exercises the powers of the Director during his absence or disability, or in the event of a vacancy in the position of the Director.

In 1949, the Central Intelligence Agency Act was passed, supplementing the 1947 Act by permitting the Agency to use confidential fiscal and administrative procedures and exempting CIA from many of the usual limitations on the expenditure of federal funds. It provided that CIA funds could be included in the budgets of other departments and then transferred to the Agency without regard to the restrictions placed on the initial appropriation. This Act is the statutory authority for the secrecy of the Agency's budget.

In order to protect intelligence sources and its methods of operation from disclosure, the 1949 Act further exempted the CIA from having to disclose its "organization, functions, names, officials, titles, salaries, or numbers of personnel employed."

Under these Statutes, the Director serves as the principal adviser to the President and the National Security Council on all matters of foreign intelligence related to national security. The CIA's responsibilities are carried out subject to various directives and controls by the President and the NSC.

Today, the CIA reports regularly to the Senate Select Committee on Intelligence and the House Permanent Select Committee on Intelligence, as required by the Intelligence Oversight Act of 1980. The Agency also reports regularly to the Defense Subcommittees of the Appropriations Committee in both houses of Congress. Moreover, the Agency provides substantive briefings to the Senate Foreign Relations Committee, House Committee on Foreign Affairs, and the Armed Services Committees in both bodies, as well as other Committees and individual members

Central Intelligence Agency

Source Factbook on Intelligence. (Central Intelligence Agency, Washington, DC, 1992).

CIVIL RIGHTS ACT OF 1991: A SUMMARY FOR THE SECURITY PROFESSIONAL

President Bush signed the new Civil Rights Act on November 21, 1991. This Act amends and extends existing civil rights laws significantly. It is intended to cause, and will cause, fundamental changes in the way business relates to applicants and employees.

Because of the integral role security professionals play in the employment process, especially the evaluation of applicants, a working understanding of the Act is necessary. The summary of the Act is divided by major subtopics, as noted.

Civil Rights Act of 1866

The Civil Rights Act of 1866 was enacted following the Civil War and was intended to correct some of the more serious problems of integrating Black Americans into society following the abolition of slavery. Very little happened with this law until the 1950s and 1960s. It was viewed as impacting business and housing relationships, not primarily employment. In 1964, the "new" Civil Rights Act was passed. This law specifically addressed the employment function. It also established the Equal Employment Opportunity Commission (EEOC).

By the mid 1970s, the 1964 Act began to have an impact on employers. However, this Act did not provide for jury trials or punitive damages, and had strict procedural limits. It was then that plaintiff employment attorneys resurrected the "old" Civil Rights Act of 1866.

There were limits to using the old Act. The burden of proof was greater, and it only applied to race discrimination. A frequent use was when a race discrimination claimant had missed the EEOC filing deadline. However, in 1989, the U.S. Supreme Court limited the application of this law to the formation of the employment relationship, and disallowed a case where a black female claimed harassment.

The 1991 Act amends the 1866 Act to cover the entire employment relationship. This is despite the fact that the entire employment relationship is already covered by the 1964 Act. The significance for the small employer is that there is no 15-employee requirement for coverage under the 1866 Act. This expands the rights of applicants and employees to make claims against all employers for any employment-related problem where race may be a factor.

A subtle change over the last 10 years also makes this amendment more significant. Hispanics, Arabs, and Jews have now been recognized by the courts as "racial" groups. This brings them under the protection of the 1866 Act.

Punitive Damages

Historically, other than the 1866 Act, punitive damages have not been available in Civil Rights lawsuits. Despite the fact that many state legislatures are moving to reduce punitive damages due to their adverse economic impact, Congress has now expanded the availability of punitive damages. The following questions and answers explain the new punitive damage provision of the 1991 Act.

Q: When are punitive damages available?
A: When intentional discrimination is proven under the Civil Rights Act of 1964, where the claimant cannot recover under the 1866 Act; or when intentional discrimination is proven by a disabled claimant under the Rehabilitation Act of 1973 or the Americans with Disabilities Act of 1990. No punitive damages awards are available where the employer can show a good faith attempt at reasonable accommodation. The key here is that the claimant is unlikely to win at all if it cannot be shown that the employer failed to attempt reasonable accommodation.

Q: What is "intentional discrimination?"
A: The claimant must show that the discriminatory practice was done with "malice or with reckless indifference to the federally protected rights of an aggrieved individual." (Section 102 of the 1991 Act). Traditionally, ignorance of the law is not an excuse. However, for small businesses, there is usually some limited leeway. For a larger organization, it will be presumed that its managers know the law. In the case of the larger business, discrimination will therefore most likely be found to have been done with "reckless indifference."

Q: What are the punitive damage limits?
A: Limits are based on the number of employees:

15 to 100 employees	$50,000
101 to 200 employees	$100,000
210 to 500	$200,000
501 plus	$300,000

There are no limits on punitive damages under the 1866 Act. Businesses rarely have insurance coverage for employment matters. Punitive damages are also generally not covered by insurance.

Jury Trials

Jury trials have not been available in employment discrimination cases except for age discrimination and 1866 Act cases. Now, jury trials are available where intentional discrimination is claimed, which will be most cases.

The downside for businesses is that juries rule in favor of the employment claimant two-thirds of the time. The availability of juries also means a high likelihood that the new punitive damages will be awarded. Jury trials are also more time consuming and more expensive than non-jury trials.

Burden of Proof in Disparate Impact Cases

There are hiring and promotion standards and pre- and post-employment tests that appear to be neutral, but actually disadvantage certain protected classes. An example is a requirement of a high school diploma for a groundskeeper position. Many minorities who would be able to perform the duties of the position would be eliminated by the diploma requirement.

The discrimination claimant need only show that there is "disparate impact." That is, that it is not intentional discrimination, but that one protected class is impacted by an employer's rule or test. The next step for the employer is to either prove that there is no disparate impact or prove that the employment rule or test is required due to "business necessity" *and* that the rule or test is "job related."

In addition, the claimant can also win by showing that a targeted employment practice could be replaced by one with less discriminatory impact. Employers must be very careful in setting employment and promotion standards, and in the administration of pre-employment and promotional tests.

One piece of good news for companies that operate drug-free workplace programs is that drug testing, in most cases, even if it has a disparate impact on some protected classes, will continue to be a permitted activity by employers under the 1991 Act.

Test Cutoff Scores

A new provision forbids employers from setting different cutoff scores for different employment groups. Interestingly, attempts like this have been done in the past, not always successfully, as a means for boosting employment of protected groups.

Discrimination Need Only Be a Factor

In order for claimants to recover in the past, they normally had to show that the reason for the adverse employment decision was due to the discriminatory act. Employers could win by showing that the main reason for the employment action was non-discriminatory. Now, claimants need only show that some bias was involved in the employment decision in order to recover damages. However, reinstatement or promotion may not be ordered, but attorney's fees and costs, and other undefined damages may be recovered as long as they are related to the biased actions.

Finality of Consent Judgments

This new rule may be of some help to very large employers. In the past, some employers, generally large ones like AT&T, have entered into involved "consent decrees" to avoid continued litigation costs. These consent decrees are agreements that generally have provided for special hiring preferences or training for certain protected groups.

Once a consent decree is entered into, groups of employees, frequently white males, may find their employment opportunities reduced. This amendment requires impacted employees to intervene at the time the decree is developed, rather than waiting years until the impact is felt. This will now give a business the freedom to enter into a consent decree, without running the risk that it will be sued years later by a group of employees.

Overseas Employees

This provision will have an impact on multi-national business. Only the Age Discrimination in Employment Act (ADEA) has been applied overseas to date. This was a result of an amendment to the ADEA several years ago. The courts have generally refused to apply the Civil Rights Act of 1964 to overseas employees. The 1991 Act amends both the 1964 Act and the Americans with Disabilities Act to specifically cover U.S. citizens working for a covered employer outside of the United States.

The amendment also specifically states that if a foreign corporation is controlled by a covered U.S. employer, then the foreign corporation will be covered. A claim cannot be brought where compliance with the U.S. discrimination laws would cause a violation of the laws of the foreign country where the workplace was located. This caveat may be helpful in parts of Africa and the Middle East. The exception will be narrowly interpreted, however.

This Amendment was effective November 21, 1991, for actions occurring after that date. The 1991 Act is silent on the effective date of the other changes discussed in this article. This is presently a hot area of debate between employers and the EEOC. The latest court decisions have tended to consider the law not retroactive.

Challenge to Seniority Systems

In a move that is opposite to the finality of consent decrees, discussed previously, an employee claiming to have been injured by a "seniority system that has been adopted for an intentionally discriminatory purpose..." will be able to challenge that system:

1. When the system is adopted;
2. When the employee becomes subject to the system; or
3. When the employee is injured by the application of the system.

While unionized workforces are only about 15% of the total workforce, this provision is still a concern. Employers and unions ought not to have to deal with attacks on a seniority system years after the fact. Virtually all claimants will allege that the system they are unhappy with was "intentionally discriminatory."

Expert Fees Now Recoverable

The Civil Rights Act of 1964 has been interpreted by the courts to not provide for reimbursement of expert witness fees when a winning party is awarded attorney's fees. This amendment states that expert witness fees can now be recovered as part of attorney's fees. This will make an adverse judgment that includes attorney's fees even more expensive for employers.

Ninety Day Limit for Age Discrimination Suits

Previously, an ADEA claimant was told that the EEOC had stopped processing his or her charge. The claimant then had until the end of the two year period after the covered act to file suit. Now, the ADEA will be parallel to other discrimination actions, in that the EEOC will issue a "90 Day Right to Sue Letter." This should provide some help to employers.

David D. Schein

Source Americans With Disabilities Act, The Federal Register. (U.S. Government Printing Office, Washington, DC, 1992).

CLASSIFICATION OF INFORMATION

Classification of information is a process of assigning protection categories to sensitive materials, usually documentary materials. The process also logically includes marking the sensitive materials according to the appropriate protection category, establishing distribution limitations, defining storage and disposal requirements, and assigning specific responsibilities for protection and accountability. Classification of information is a widely used process in the government and business sectors.

Government Sector Programs

Government classification programs assign documents to the following categories:

•Restricted Data. This category relates to the research, design, and production of nuclear weapons. It was established by the Atomic Energy Act of 1954, as amended.

•Formerly Restricted Data. This category is peculiar to Armed Forces operational personnel in respect to downgraded nuclear weapons data.

•National Security Information. The NSI category contains information about the diplomatic and military security of the United States. It was established by Executive Order 12356.

•Code Word. Various special categories pertaining to intelligence activities are given code words that govern the classification of information.

Each category of information, has three levels of importance. These are:

•Top Secret. Information that would cause serious damage to the national security.

•Secret. Information that would damage the national security.

•Confidential. Information that might damage the national security.

The military services issue regulations which control individual classification programs. Classification guides assign information to categories and levels of protection. The Defense Industrial Security Regulations (DISR) control the classification program for Department of Defense (DOD) contractors. Department of Energy (DOE) guidance is contained in DOE Order 5650.2A, *The Classification Program*, and various topical classification guides. All other governmental agencies that handle classified information have similar regulations, orders, or procedures.

Business Sector Programs

For reasons not unlike those held by government, the business sector regularly engages in the practice of classifying information. Businesses in competition with one another are naturally adversarial. They are concerned with the dilution of competitive advantage that results from compromise of sensitive information. In some businesses, information is the stock in trade and loss or damage to it is a direct bottom line issue.

Steps for Establishing a Classification Program

Because it is neither cost effective nor physically possible to protect the totality of a business organization's information, the management must identify the really sensitive information of a private or proprietary nature and endeavor to keep it safe. Non-sensitive, non-valuable private information and information already available to the public does not merit protection. A classification program will set the criteria for making distinctions between information that should be protected and that which should not.

Step 1. Establish the Categories of Information. The first task is to identify those categories of information that should be protected. For example: strategic planning (financing, marketing plans and new acquisitions); research and development (new technologies and processes); operations (product information, production and delivery schedules and trade secrets); litigation (patent protections, mergers, takeovers, liability defenses, and offenses); and privacy act information (employee salaries and medical data).

Step 2. Establish Levels of Information. The next step is to develop a manageable range of classification levels and to label each level with an appropriate descriptor, such as secret, restricted, confidential, and private.

Each level would be defined on the basis of a commonly understood factor, such as loss or damage. The highest level, which might be labeled "Secret," could be defined as information, which if disclosed, would cause serious damage to the interests of the organization. Serious damage could be a dollar value set by the organization, and logically very few information topics would fall within the "Secret" classification.

Information that requires protection but has minimum loss or damage potential would be at the lower end of the range of classification levels.

Information assigned a "Private" designation might relate to data important to the private or personal interests of individual employees, such as salary information.

Because classification adds cost and inconvenience, the number of levels should be held to a minimum and controls should be in place to prevent "over-classification" of documents.

Step 3. Establish Policies, Procedures, and Guidance. Every program needs direction, and policies and procedures can provide it. Policies dedicate management support, set goals and assign responsibilities. Procedures explain the duties of authors and reviewing officials. Classification guides, usually classified themselves, provide detailed instructions for assigning categories and levels. These guides are essential to classification consistency.

Step 4. Select the Reviewing Officials. The selection of qualified reviewing officials is essential to the success of the classification program. In general, they should be mature and knowledgeable in their areas of expertise. They should also have broad industry knowledge. Frequently, a company may need two levels of reviewing officials: an original reviewing official to make classification decisions based upon a unique knowledge of the company and industry, and a derivative reviewing official to make classification decisions based upon classification guidance. When a derivative reviewer cannot make a classification decision, the matter is referred to an original reviewer for final determination.

In making a classification decision, a reviewing official is prepared by training and experience to subject a document to three inquiries:

•Are there words or phrases in the document that are specifically classifiable under guidance?

•Are there portions of the document that , when taken together, reveal classifiable information?

•Does the document, when compared with other information known to the public, reveal classifiable information? This is known as a "missing link" and is the most difficult classification decision.

Step 5. Downgrade and Declassify. Unlike a diamond, a document's value does not last forever. The declining value of information must be taken into consideration and a mechanism put into the program to downgrade or declassify. Documents of low value and sensitivity that no longer conform to the original classification decisions need to be purged from the program. By reducing the inventory of documents, the security manager can better concentrate attention on the remaining bulk of information that continues to require safeguarding.

Protection of a business organization's valuable information may be essential to its growth, profitability, or even survival in a highly competitive environment. A classification of information program is a key aid in providing the needed protection.

G.H. Zimmer

COAST GUARD

The Coast Guard is responsible for enforcing or assisting in the enforcement of all applicable Federal laws on the navigable waters of the United States and high seas. In its capacity as the primary maritime law enforcement agency for the United States, the Coast Guard cooperates with other agencies in the execution of their law enforcement responsibilities. The Coast Guard is specifically tasked to regulate and enforce federal laws governing navigation, vessel inspection, port safety and security, marine environmental protection, and resource conservation, including federally controlled fisheries. Traditionally, the Coast Guard has also been significantly involved in the enforcement of general criminal laws and customs and immigration laws pertaining to the maritime environment.

U.S. Coast Guard

Source Public Affairs Pamphlet. (United States Coast Guard, Washington, DC, 1992).

COMPUTER CRIME: INVESTIGATIVE CONSIDERATIONS

Computer-related crime is one of today's more challenging forms of investigations. Unfortunately, some security professionals are intimidated when they learn that a computer has been used in the commission of a crime. Often they believe solving such a crime is beyond their capability. This is simply not true.

Solving computer crimes often requires complex investigations, but these investigations are similar to other difficult investigations most security personnel have faced. With a little confidence, the average investigator can play a major role in computer-related crime investigations.

To touch briefly on the nature and scale of computer crime, the average computer-assisted embezzlement nets $450,000, according to the FBI, while stealing by hand nets only $19,000. A business executive might look at computer crime this way: If a company is operating with a 5% profit margin, it would take a million dollars in sales to make up the loss incurred in one average computer embezzlement. An IBM study of 339 computer-related crimes found the average loss to be $500,000. The study also found manufacturing companies to be as vulnerable as banks. The damage from such crimes is actually greater than any study shows, however, as less than 15% of all computer crimes are reported to authorities, some experts say.

The lack of a universal definition of computer-related crime adds to the difficulty of prosecuting it.   From the investigator's perspective, computer-related crime is a criminal act, as defined by statute, in which a computer is used or an act is committed against a computer. Computer-related crime has generally been characterized by the use of a computer to steal money, services, property, or information for invasion of privacy, extortion, and even committing a terrorist act. The exact definition depends on which state the act is committed in, provided the state has a statute. It also depends on whether the act meets the federal guidelines of Title 18, passed in 1984 and amended in 1986. The 1986 amendment has greatly expanded federal involvement in computer-related crime.

The Who and What of Computer Crime

In investigating computer-related crimes, it helps to know who the criminals are. The average computer criminal is a well-educated, skilled professional. Generally, the person is respected in the workplace and the community and has no records of criminal behavior. In addition to the monetary incentive, he or she is often motivated by the excitement and the challenge of carrying out the crime.

What types of crimes do these model citizens commit? Computer-related crime comes in two basic categories. In the first, a computer is the target of the crime. A computer may be stolen or the information in it may be erased, modified, destroyed, or disclosed.   In fact, cases have occurred in which computers and computer disks have been stolen and held for ransom.

In the second category, computers are used as the instrument of the criminal act. The computer may be used to steal money, bonds, or other negotiable instruments. In some cases, false data have been put into a computer to mislead individuals examining the financial condition of a company.

Obviously, computer-related crime includes a broad spectrum of criminal activity.   The following are some of the more common crimes.

•Embezzlement. Probably the most common is input fraud. An individual, possibly in the accounting department, creates a corporation, gives it an account number, fabricates invoices, and generates a check to pay those invoices or modifies payment records to generate or redirect payment.

•Theft of Information. Individuals steal data such as trade secrets, sensitive research material, client lists, and marketing plans, often to sell to competitors.

•Theft of Equipment. The thief generates a shipping order and has the equipment delivered to a drop site. The thief then erases the shipping order in the computer, thus leaving no documentation. When the company discovers it is short in inventory, it will have trouble determining where the loss occurred.

•Theft of Services. Sometimes an employee uses the employer's mainframe or minicomputer to run a business on the side. In one case, an Air Force employee was running an entire real estate business with an Air Force computer. In other situations, computer personnel have rented corporate computer time to private individuals.

•Theft of Services via Access Code. Large corporations assign individuals access codes that permit them to call anywhere in the world through a computerized telephone switching system. These access codes can be compromised either by a computer hacker or through negligence on the part of an employee. In one instance, stolen access codes cost a company over a million dollars in one year.

•Electronic Funds Transfers.   Many multinational companies have terminals linked directly to banks so they can initiate funds transfers on their own, without having to work through a bank official. An individual could call up the bank computer from a terminal and move funds from an account in Zurich to one in Houston. Although most major corporations have protected their systems by designating where funds can be transferred, sometimes the procedures for authorizing new locations are not guarded, thus leaving the entire system vulnerable.

The Investigative Team

Who should investigate computer-related crime? Trained investigators, but not necessarily computer-crime specialists. A veteran FBI agent recently put the role of investigators in perspective this way: "The traditional investigator is the backbone of the prosecution in a computer crime case. He or she gathers the evidence, interviews witnesses, and presents the case in such a way that the judge, the jury, and even the prosecutor are able to understand every aspect. The investigator basically boils down the technical issues so everybody can understand them."

The central figures in a computer-related crime investigation should be the director of security and the investigative staff. This is not to imply the director of security does not need outside assistance in the investigation; rather, the director should be the team coordinator.

After carefully analyzing the case, the security director might decide assistance is needed from the data processing and legal departments; perhaps even a prosecutor should be brought on early in the case. It is not a one-person show; the director of security is simply the team coordinator.

Here are some suggested roles for the key team players:

• Director of Security. The director of security coordinates all investigative activities. He or she ensures that the experts perform their tasks and sees that those tasks are coordinated with other team members. He or she also ensures that the entire investigation is carefully documented; the team should keep a chronological file of all information it develops, and all records and evidence must be properly marked and catalogued.

• Investigator. The investigator follows up on all information developed by team members. He or she interviews suspects and witnesses, and develops and debriefs informants. The investigator plans and conducts surveillances, background checks, and asset searches on suspects; if appropriate, he or she can place an undercover operative in the workplace. The investigator must work very closely with the director of security to develop a prosecutable case.

• Information Systems Specialist. This individual provides team members with the technical knowledge needed for the investigation. He or she imparts the hardware, software, and procedural know-how to the rest of the team. The information systems specialist also assists in translating the case into language a judge and jury can easily understand. Ideally, this person is a certified data processing auditor capable of withstanding a vigorous attack from the defense.

• Lawyer. The lawyer is a litigation expert. He or she reviews the evidence with the investigator as it develops and guides members of the team to explore additional avenues as needed. The lawyer also files the civil and criminal complaints.

• Accountant or Auditor. This team member searches paper and computer files for symptoms of fraud and deviations from standard corporate procedure. He or she also ensures the meticulous recording of all pertinent facts.

The Challenge

Like other complex investigations, computer-related investigations present certain problems that demand meticulous attention. Following are a few of those problems:

• Lack of Uniform Reporting. As mentioned earlier, many companies do not report computer crimes. Some companies, for example, fear such a disclosure would affect the price of their stock. In addition to concealing the true extent of such crimes, cover-ups also tell employees computer crime is not likely to be prosecuted.

• Lack of Interest by Prosecutors. Just as some companies are reluctant to prosecute computer crime, some prosecutors hesitate to take on the task of prosecuting these complex criminal acts. In many large U.S. cities, prosecutors have more cases than they can possibly handle. When it comes to prosecuting white-collar crime cases, they are extremely choosy. Some district attorney offices have informally put a dollar threshold on cases, such as not taking on a fraud case involving less than a million dollars. This practice further frustrates security professionals who have vigorously pursued computer fraud investigations.

• Charging the Suspect. This aspect is confusing, particularly for a corporation covering a number of states. The charge depends on the specifics of the computer-crime statute in the state in which the crime was committed. The federal statute adopted in 1984 and amended in 1986 may apply when two computers are used in different states.

• Evidence. Evidence is critical in the prosecution of all crimes. Unfortunately, evidence in computer-related crimes can be easily and quickly altered, leaving nothing for the prosecution. The information systems specialist can teach investigators how to preserve evidence. Armed with this information, investigators can seize and search equipment without damaging vital data.

• Documentation.   Computer tapes and magnetic disks – common forms of evidence – are often indistinguishable from each other. Extreme care must be taken to establish a chain of custody. Accurate marking and documentation are very important when such evidence is to be presented to a jury.

• Technical Jargon.   Computer-related crime cases are often presented to a judge, jury, and prosecutor in a very complex manner. Investigators must eliminate technical jargon to simplify the presentation of these cases so they can be easily understood.

• Informants. Informants in computer-related crime prosecutions tend to be individuals from the computer community. Although they may have voluntarily come forward and supplied information about a crime, when it comes time to prepare the case for prosecution, they often refuse to cooperate and may even change their stories completely. Because of the mixed allegiance of some computer informants, an investigator must not base a case solely on information an informant has provided.

• Audit Trail.   Often an audit trail does not exist in a computer-related crime. As one security expert has stated, "There's nothing inherent in a computer that requires it to leave fingerprints or footprints. You're dealing with records that can be erased without a trace. You're not looking at handwriting forgery, you're not looking at entries in books that have been obviously altered, you're looking at something that can be erased, altered without a trace. In one of the most clever cases I have ever been involved in, an individual entered the operating system of the computer – the brain -- and manipulated the computer to control reports that would have suggested something was wrong."

The Investigative Process

The investigative process for computer-related crime does not differ dramatically from other complex white-collar criminal investigations. The investigative process involves three phases.

Discovery. Unfortunately, not all data processing personnel or users view computer problems as criminal acts; they ordinarily think of a problem as a malfunction.   Personnel must be indoctrinated with the idea that a computer problem could be a criminal act. With this mind-set, they are more likely to discover a crime early.

During the discovery phase, key personnel should be notified without delay. The director of security should be brought into the process immediately to begin coordinating the work of other team members.   Information should be handled on a need-to-know basis and the case should be discussed only with the team members. Information leaks provide suspects with time to destroy evidence, fabricate stories, and otherwise jeopardize the success of the ongoing investigative process.

Planning. In the next step the security director begins planning the investigation. Short-term and long-term objectives are identified along with a corresponding investigative strategy. The security director needs also to determine if management wishes to take the case to a prosecutive stage. There may be a compelling reason, such as evidence of mismanagement, for the organization to not want to publicize the matter.

If the choice is to aim for prosecution, a management-approved action plan needs to be put in place for the allocation of resources, the assignment and coordination of specific investigative tasks, and the provision of authority. In addition, a case management system should be set up to help the security director stay in control of the operation.

Case Preparation. At this stage the team is ready to begin preparing a case. An early step will be to confer with the team's legal counsel to identify the statutes violated and the pertinent elements of proof. It is also advisable at this point to invite the prosecutor into the investigation. Even if the prosecutor declines to enter the investigation at this fairly early stage, valuable insights might be obtained with respect to the prosecutor's personal views and operating policies with respect to computer-related crime.

In most states, the company will have to prove that the criminal act happened, that it was not supposed to happen, and that controls were circumvented. For example, to charge a person under New York computer-crime law, the person who perpetrated the act must be shown to have broken through a password system or have been notified by the system that the information was confidential. If the circumstances do not fit the computer-crime statute in the state in which the crime was committed, some other law may apply. Many cases that do not fall under computer-crime statutes fall under either larceny or theft-of-service statutes.

After determining the appropriate statute, the legal counsel should meet with team members to outline the proof needed for a conviction. An infinite number of investigative tasks may be required, depending on the complexity of the case at hand. The two most critical items, however, are the expert testimony of the electronic data processing (EDP) auditor and the security director's meticulous documentation.

In a murder case, a gun may surface as evidence. The gun is marked, sent to a laboratory for a ballistics check, and safeguarded by the property clerk. The weapon is then taken from the property clerk and shown to the jury as the means by which the crime was committed. In a computer-related crime, however, the equivalent of the gun may be a computer's program. The difficulty comes in convincing a jury that the defendant used the computer in an unlawful manner at a particular point in time. This is a task for the EDP auditor. He or she must determine what should have been in the computer at the time of the crime, what was in the computer at that time, who put it there, and who benefited from the change.

The EDP auditor's efforts can be supported by information developed through a variety of investigative functions, such as interviewing witnesses, exploiting confidential informants, using undercover agents, and surveilling suspected activities with concealed video cameras. A hidden camera can be very valuable in clearly establishing the identity of the person who used a particular machine at a particular time.

The investigative team must meticulously document each sequence of evidence: who was involved; what machines and programs were used; where and when they were used; and how they were used and how their unauthorized use constituted a violation. Even when the organization declines to prosecute, the investigation should be conducted thoroughly and fully. The final report of investigation should be a foundation for taking action against the violators and for taking proactive steps to prevent recurrence.

The investigation of computer-related crime is clearly a responsibility that falls within the security manager's portfolio. Although a computer is by its very nature a highly technical device, the violator involved with the computer is human and therefore limited to activities that can be detected by the application of good old fashioned investigative techniques. A security investigator or manager confronted with a computer-related crime would do well to approach the matter with the same level of confidence that would apply in other types of crime.

Robert F. Littlejohn, CPP

COMPUTER SECURITY: ANALYZING RISK

The term computer security means more than a protective focus on a piece of computer hardware. It embraces a much wider range of protection that considers environmental influences and other threats; the security of the building housing the computer; the power (type and demand load); the cabling, disks, and tapes holding the information; the information's value to the data owners; and the communications system. Each requires different forms of protection. Broadly speaking, protection must address the three distinct aspects of computer security: the information's confidentiality, its accuracy and integrity, and the availability of the data to its users when needed.

All these considerations are based on a thorough risk analysis. The risk analysis must address factors that are physical in nature, such as the building that houses the computer system, and factors that are technical, such as the connectivity of the system's components. Administrative factors that regulate human involvement must also be examined.

No one person should attempt to conduct a risk analysis alone, but rather, the effort should follow a team approach. The team will ideally include specialists representing hardware, software, communications, security, automated information, senior management, and the end user or data owner. The security representative should bring to the effort an understanding of risk management principles.

The team should have regularly scheduled meetings, preferably chaired by the senior management representative whose authority will maximize attendance. The team can call upon other persons in the company for assistance or guidance; for example, problems or questions related to conduits can be presented to an invited participant from the facilities maintenance group, or safety issues can be addressed with input from the organization's safety manager.

A matter of special interest to the analysis team will be electrical power. There are several forms of electrical power; some power companies recommend what is called laboratory power. This type of power is that usually supplied to hospitals and, more recently, to computer centers. Laboratory power refers to a system with a minimum of power surges and/or sags and is usually accomplished by use of power surge equipment that absorbs the intensity of a sudden increase in power. The sags are minimized by equipment that rejuvenates the level of power.

As to types of power sources, some computer installations have a dual power feeder system. This means two power lines to service the installation, each one coming from two separate power sub-station sources but not two lines from the same sub-station.

The other type of power source is an uninterruptible power source (UPS). There are three types of UPS systems. The first is an industrial battery array that can automatically supply the demand load in nanoseconds. The battery array provides sufficient power to permit the computer installation to power down gracefully with no loss of data. The drawback to this system is that it only furnishes power for periods lasting 15 to 30 minutes.

The second type is a diesel-powered generator that, when automatically brought on line, requires two or three whole seconds to activate. The advantage to this form is that it can supply power continually for as long as the diesel fuel can be replenished. The third form of UPS is a turbo-powered generator that can provide the demand load indefinitely. The last two UPS types are similarly priced.

When we think of demand load for an automatic data processing (ADP) facility -- not necessarily the entire installation or building in which the facility is housed -- we must provide minimally for computing power, lights, air-conditioning needs, and whatever is required for the fire and intrusion alarm systems. This last item is necessary in the event the outage was induced by deliberate human intent.

Generally, all automated data processing installations are similar; however, each one has characteristics that make it unique. For that reason, no master analysis can be developed that will be directly applicable to each and every data processing facility. There are several risk analysis software packages that are very good, but the need for a team to answer the several questions asked and the need to apply those answers directly to a given facility remains. By way of illustration, not all facilities have problems with the threat of earth tremors; quakes or floods; or being located in basements where all water, steam pipes, and building entry power paths are usually located.

An explanation of the difference between a threat and a vulnerability may be helpful. In a broad sense, a threat is something that, if it occurs, could cause damage or loss to a physical or personal entity. A vulnerability is the susceptibility of the entity to a given threat. For example, a computer facility in Kansas faces the threat posed by tornadoes and is vulnerable to the extent that it is not designed to withstand tornadoes.

Further, it is in the nature of threats that the severity of the consequences is inversely related to the frequency or probability of occurrence, i.e., that as the disastrous nature of an event increases, the chances of it happening decrease. This is at the heart of risk analysis and is the basic reason for developing programs to prevent or mitigate loss and damage.

The security representative must not only consider the potential of a threat occurring, but the estimated extent of damage to be sustained. When estimating the potential impact of a threat's occurrence, it is wise to use a worst-case scenario. By assuming the worst, the recovery can at least be completed no later than planned, or sooner and at less cost if the damage turns out to be less than what was projected.

Any vendors to be used in a disaster recovery program will need to be alerted to equipment that may need to be replaced or repaired in the event of disaster. In this way the vendors can better assure rapid satisfaction of hardware and software needs.

The determination of threats and vulnerabilities is only half the job; the team must also develop safeguards and in that process must consider the cost of safeguards relative to the value of the assets. A cost-benefit analysis might reveal that the initial high cost of a safeguard can be recovered when spread over time. To illustrate, the cost to install a closed-circuit television (CCTV) system could be $250,000 plus a small yearly maintenance fee, but the system could result in reducing the need for a large guard force after the first year of use. Generally, each shift could be reduced to three: one supervisor, one screen monitor, and one alarm respondent. If each shift had 8 members, the total reduction would be 5 per shift or 15 total. Assuming each guard costs the organization $25,000 plus benefits each year, the first year's savings would be $150,00 followed by $400,000 per annum thereafter (less a small CCTV maintenance cost). The preceding is merely an illustration of a high-cost/high-savings safeguard and should not be considered as a recommended solution or a denigration of guard forces.

Howard Keough

COMPUTER SECURITY: DISASTER RECOVERY

The focus of the disaster recovery business has been in a state of change since the mid-1980s. In past years, the industry had concentrated almost exclusively on backup capabilities that could be called into service, should a disaster occur. Now, the focus is on mitigating points of vulnerability that could result in a system loss. Finding the single point of failure, or the weakest link in the chain, is the central objective.

The disaster recovery industry has had a relatively short history that has evolved with the advent of computerization. As businesses have become dependent on systems and could not revert quickly to manual practices, it has become evident that system downtime could prove catastrophic. In the early days of disaster recovery, the emphasis was placed on establishing backup facilities; today, that is not enough.

During the past decade, computer operations have shifted from batch processing operations to real-time environments. This shift has coincided with the concepts of "just-in-time" manufacturing and with the trend toward drastic reductions in inventory. In batch processing environments, business operations simply required a backup

operating system for disaster recovery. In real-time, however, downtime is intolerable.

In contrast to the focus on backup data procedures, today's planners must analyze the total infrastructure of computer operations, identify single points of failure, and develop strategies to mitigate exposures. This requires an extensive analysis.

Computer operations require power, environmentally controlled operating facilities, telecommunications services, and skilled operating personnel, among a litany of other supporting functions. Failure of one component may mean compromise of the entire system. For business in the 1990s, that could mean catastrophe.

Disaster Recovery Analysis

An analysis begins by defining operating components. If the focus is computer operations, which it is in most cases, this would include each component of hardware, software, database, operating personnel, telecommunications, and the supporting infrastructure of power and environmental controls. Each component must be listed and categorized based on criticality.

Possible threats are defined next and placed in categories based on the probability of occurrence. Threats include natural disasters, accidents, criminal events, and even operational threats such as mismanagement of the system or of the people operating it. Threats are correlated with each element of the system and an order of priority established, so the most vital elements are considered first. This correlation notes which threats are applicable to specific system components and which are not.

The vulnerability of each element is defined by outlining the process by which a specific element may be subject to a specific threat. Through this process, the Achilles heel of the overall operation is identified.

In the final phase of analysis, countermeasures are selected to mitigate the exposures noted in the vulnerability analysis. This involves eliminating single points of failure and providing substantial backups for critical system components that may compromise the entire operation. Exposure mitigation may be considered the single most important aspect of disaster recovery planning.

Emergency Plans

Of course, exposures can never be completely eliminated. Consequently, emergency plans are needed that define procedures for actions to take in the event of a system loss, despite the effort to mitigate exposures. These procedures can be subdivided into the following phases as outlined below.

Phase 1: Prewarning.
a. Evacuation procedures
b. System shutdown procedures
c. Identification of shelter facilities

Phase 2: During the Event.
a. Endurance techniques
b. Survival techniques

Phase 3: Immediately after the Event.
a. First aid accommodations
b. System shutdown procedures
c. Notification of response authorities
   1. Police
   2. Fire
   3. Rescue
   4. Utility crews
d. Security of the scene
   1. Control of access
   2. Preservation of evidence
e. Traffic control
f. Removal of injured
g. Notification of regulatory agencies
h. Summon emergency management team
i. Implement containment strategy

Phase 4: Post-event.
a. Clean-up
b. Repair
c. Alternate site operation
d. Notification to next of kin
e. Legal services
f. Mental health services

Phase 5: Resumption of Normal Operations.
a. Plan for return to facilities and operation restart

Data Gathering

Following is an outline of tasks essential for developing the content of the plan:

I. Conduct interviews within the organization in order to:
   A. Identify key systems.
   B. Define shutdown and evacuation requirements.
   C. Examine feasibility of alternate site operation.
   D. Identify chain of command and succession of authority.
   E. Identify likely issues that management will need to address during the event.
   F. Define regulatory agency reporting requirements.

II. Meet with response agencies (such as police, fire, rescue services, the emergency management agency, and public utilities companies) in order to:
   A. Determine the methods of interagency communication.
   B. Note who is to be called.
   C. Identify the needs of emergency response forces.
   D. Identify routes to, from, and within the site.
   E. Define utility needs.
   F. Define action steps and responsibilities for preserving the scene.
   G. Identify key safety considerations.

Formal Document

The collected data should be presented in a formal document that addresses the following issues.

Plan Coordinator. One person should be identified as responsible for preparing the plan document, communicating it to interested parties, revising and updating the plan, and organizing training to facilitate proper execution.

Management Authority. The plan should delineate the chain of command that will apply in the carrying out of plan functions, provisions should be made for succession of authority, and the duties of key figures will be described so as to leave no doubt concerning personal accountability. This portion of the plan might also take note of legal and corporate restrictions.

Security Response. This plan element defines the tasks to be performed by security, such as facilitating access by public authorities, directing traffic, controlling spectators, preserving the scene, rendering first aid, coordinating evacuation, and making notifications to emergency response personnel.

Communications. The plan should spell out the methods for establishing and maintaining communications among the various agencies involved in responding to a disaster. A number of separate networks are likely to be utilized in moving critical messages simultaneously.

Agency Notifications. The plan should include a detailed listing of agencies that are required to be notified in a disaster. The nature of the disaster will determine the agencies to be contacted and the order of contact. The agencies likely to be identified in the plan include the Federal Emergency Management Agency (FEMA), Federal Aviation Administration (FAA), Environmental Protection Agency (EPA), and Occupational Safety and Health Administration (OSHA).

Support Services. These include hazardous waste cleanup, fire salvage, office repair, cleaning, and other specialized services that may be required to remove materials left in the wake of a major disaster. This part of a plan also addresses the use of specialized professionals such as psychologists and lawyers.

Public Relations. A strategy for dealing with news media and making next of kin notifications should be included. It will assign responsibilities for prompt collection of information of interest to the media and identify the authorized spokespersons. Families of persons injured or killed in the disaster will be informed quickly, according to procedures that respect privacy needs.

Disaster Response Equipment and Facilities. The plan should identify the equipment and facilities that will be fully or partially dedicated to disaster-response activities. These include an emergency management center, first aid-triage center, salvage and storage areas, media center, and alternate operating site. The technicians who provide the related services, such as communications coordinators and paramedics, might also be mentioned in this section of the plan.

Alternate Site. The plan might include provisions for moving employees and equipment to an alternate location in order to maintain continuity of essential business operations. In this event, the company will need to include as response agencies (although not as emergency responders) the vendors who will provide the alternate site, transport to and set up equipment at the alternate site, provide temporary backup equipment, prepare the alternate site for operation, and so forth.

Resumption of Normal Operations. The plan should give guidance for resuming normal operations. Points to be considered include cleaning up, restoring utilities, ensuring that safety risks have been removed and obtaining public authority approval for a return to business as usual.

Sal Depasquale, CPP

COMPUTER SECURITY: FIVE STRATEGIES

Five basic strategies are possible in recovering from severe damage to a major computer system.

Strategy 1: Recover in Company-Owned Facilities

One variant is to maintain a standby facility to replace any central facility rendered unusable. This is one of the most expensive backup policies and is probably not cost-effective except for very large enterprises in which continuity of data-processing service is highly critical and where there is a high degree of intracompany compatibility in hardware, software, and procedures. An example might be a large commercial bank or telephone company.

A second variant is to recover using other company-owned central facilities. This can be expensive unless the recovery processing is intended to be done on the second or third shift. Otherwise, this strategy implies that at least one central facility must continually operate below its optimal loading.

Strategy 2: Recover by Hiring Service Bureau Facilities

This method used to be popular when computer manufacturers operated demonstration sites and arranged to back up their customers in case of emergency. Some manufacturers still provide this service, but it will usually be adequate backup only for small users whose regular processing is done on minicomputers.

Using a commercial service bureau is costly and can give rise to several problems. First, procedures must be sufficiently well documented that service bureau employees can perform the work with minimal direction from operations supervisors. There is also the question of what to do with temporarily redundant data-processing staff. On the one hand, it is wasteful to pay them simply for standing by, and, on the other hand, dangerous to lay them off because you may not be able to hire satisfactory personnel after the emergency.

Some applications are best handled by service bureaus when the hiatus is to be of short duration, such as while airing out and mopping up the aftermath of a minor computer room fire. Critical programs such as customer order processing, payroll, accounts payable, accounts receivable, inventory control, pricing and billing, and general ledger are prime candidates for this treatment. Some companies contract out all payroll and order processing.

If you adopt the service bureau strategy, you should form a continuing relationship with your service bureau, occasionally contracting out temporary overloads on these critical systems so that bureau personnel learn how to handle your work.

Strategy 3: Share Backup Facilities with Another Company

This can be very good or very bad, depending on the other company and what facilities are to be shared. If the cooperative arrangement involves second or third shift sharing of another company's primary central facility, there are at least three problems: (1) you will eventually become an unwelcome burden on the other company; (2) there will probably be some software and hardware incompatibilities, which your systems programmers will have to resolve with minimum interference with the host company; and (3) your host may get to know more about your business than is good for you.

In a variant on sharing, two non-competitive companies share the cost of a standby site. In one such case, a major branch banking institution is sharing the cost of a standby with a large regional telephone company.

Strategy 4: Rent a Hot Site

A hot site is a standby alternate site whose hardware and operating software duplicate your own. It is operated by a third party who rents backup service to many companies -- often 100 to 200 of them. Comparing the hot site with other backup site strategies is like comparing a vacation cottage, even one shared with your brother-in-law, with a room at the Holiday Inn.

If you have to use the hot site, you will have to move in with your data files and application programs plus your whole operating crew. For this reason, accessibility to transportation and communications facilities is essential. If two hot-site clients suffer a disaster in the same time period, you might find no room in the inn.

Hot-site backup is not cheap. If you choose it, you should arrange for at least one recovery exercise to make sure designated employees know what to do in a real emergency.

Strategy 5: Acquire a Shell Site

The shell-site concept presupposes that the critical part of a backup facility is its support systems and that computing hardware can readily be replaced by the manufacturer. This may be true if you regularly replace your equipment with state-of-the-art hardware and stick to products of manufacturers not likely to go bankrupt.

Some site operators have syndicated memberships in shell sites. What you get is an empty building with heating, ventilation, air-conditioning, water, conditioned electric power, data communications lines, shielding, and cabling installed. You have only to bring your personnel, software, and data, and have a hardware supplier provide a new computer and all necessary peripheral equipment components.

There are many variants of the shell site. Suppliers of temporary buildings will erect one on your own site, sometimes with hardware included, especially if you use one of the more popular minicomputers. Other structures have been used as well: modular homes, house trailers, and even semitrailers.

John M. Carroll

Source Carroll, J.M., Computer Security, 2nd Edition. (Butterworth-Heinemann, Boston, 1987).

COMPUTER SECURITY: THE VIRUS THREAT

A virus is a small program that has an "appending" capability; that is, the virus program can attach itself to any other program that meets certain specifications set by the writer of the virus. For example, almost all virus software checks to see if a program is already infected. Also, virus software will check to see that the virus can be appended only to an executable program (e.g., in MS-DOS, an .EXE or .COM program), since execution of the infected program generates reproduction and further distribution of the virus. Virus software often is delivered to an unsuspecting personal computer (PC) user in some misleading and attractive cover. (In this guise, the virus is a Trojan horse, but the terms are not synonymous.) It may be imbedded in a commercial software package normally costing hundreds of dollars but offered "free" on a hackers' network, or it may be implanted in an attractive display or computer game. A clever virus is very difficult to identify; experts estimate 4 to 6 weeks of concentrated effort are required to find virus code in the average complex applications package.

Once attached to another program, the virus can reproduce itself when the host program is run, attaching itself to any other programs with which the infected program comes in contact. Thus the virus can spread through a system or network much like a physical virus can spread through a population of human carriers. The virus program may carry within itself certain instructions. These may be harmful, but they can also be beneficial or merely neutral. Consider the now-famous IBM Christmas virus. Its ostensible purpose was only to send a greeting to many people, but in doing so it overloaded the network by replicating itself on everyone's mail lists, thereby sending each user scores of similar greeting messages, until the network could no longer cope.

Other viruses have delivered Trojan horses, programs that look like friendly helpers, such as data compressors; but when run, the program may delete the disk directory, thereby making the disk and its contents useless to the computer user. Technical experts can see potential in using virus software to correct problems in networks. An early version of such software was the "worm" program developed and used at the Xerox Palo Alto Research Center in the early 1970s to fix a network problem. The virus did its job, but then it could not be shut off without extensive effort.

Experience with virus software attacks shows that the virus software threat is real and has serious implications but that the actual risk has not substantially materialized. Consider that few virus attacks on commercial systems have been noted (the most famous, the IBM Christmas virus, is believed to have been a mistaken attempt to send a greeting, not sabotage). And, with few exceptions, no viruses have been found in public domain software. Rather, they have been distributed through commercial software packages (many of these were "pirated" or counterfeit copies passed around among university students). Finally, almost all attacks have occurred in the research and university environments (the Internet Attack of 1988, for example), where the use of "free" software is common or where access is easy for many people. In such situations, people pass around floppy disks and exchange software freely, an ideal environment for spreading a "software plaque."

Risks and Antidotes

With our current knowledge concerning potential virus software and methods of attack, very little can be done to prevent initiation of a virus software attack. (Positive protection against the virus threat would require major changes in the way computers are built and used, e.g., limited resources for users, no programming or compiling for anyone not defined as a programmer, limited transitivity, and limited sharing. Obviously, with the computers being developed and delivered today providing increasing user power, this will not happen soon.) If the virus attacker is clever, the attack will probably succeed to some degree. Internally initiated attacks, where the virus is introduced intentionally or unwittingly by an authorized user, appear to be the greatest risk at this time. A lesser risk is penetration through a network, perhaps from a secondary network.

However, companies can take prudent steps to lessen risk and damage.

Risks from virus software attacks vary among types of systems and machines. Computer mainframes are considered to be relatively secure from virus attacks. One should not rule out an attack on a mainframe by a trusted insider, but consider that event unlikely because of the rigorous technical reviews, input and program library controls, as well as management overviews on software activity. Large networks are a moderate risk, not only from insiders or authorized outsiders, but also from ubiquitous hackers.

Significant numbers of PCs may be used; some may be connected to networks. Certain workstations have a dual personality; that is, they can run PC emulation on a network. These workstations and PCs use MS-DOS, the environment posing the most severe risk. This is so because there is much software available, and it tends to be distributed through unauthorized copies and modified versions that are not attributable to identified authors.

Prudent information managers should consider the following six measures to help guard against catastrophic losses of information or compromises of information integrity due to virus attacks.

1. Provide an awareness and training program, so that users of computers will know what a virus program is and will be alert to symptoms of virus attacks.

2. Perform an analysis of exposure, so that managers will know what risks they may be accepting in choosing a course of action. Note that current risk analysis systems do not provide for handling the infectious characteristics of a virus attack, which may gradually extend over an entire company or network.

3. Take reasonable precautions, including careful selection and testing of all new software and backup of files and operating systems. Current software "inoculation" packages may provide limited protection, but only against viruses already seen. Since there are an unlimited number of potential forms, the use of such packages is questionable in most situations.

4. Ensure that computer users can reasonably recognize danger signs. Recognition allows the user to report suspicions and allows the company or agency to take action appropriate to the

situation. Among signs of a virus attack are multiple, concurrent machine failures, unexplained increases in the amount of disk space occupied, and changes in the length of programs.

5. Plan for a reaction to suspected "infection." The organization must be prepared to take action to isolate the suspected infected system(s) and to begin recovery through the use of stored backup copies of operating systems and data.

6. Plan for recovery. By using backup tapes and disks, the system must be restarted in a "clean" state. The backup tapes and disks will be useless if they are not produced with reasonable frequency and kept for some significant time. A time-delay Trojan horse program could already be present on backup files when the virus attack becomes known.

Practical Suggestions

Security against virus software attacks may be viewed as having two stages: (1) strengthening the systems infrastructure to make it more robust, or healthy, so that it can recover from an attack, and (2) putting measures in place to minimize damages

Systems Robustness. All new programs must be thoroughly tested for quality and acceptability. This should be a function performed by some central agency, such as the data center quality control function or the information center. In most cases involving PCs, however, practical wisdom says that we will have to rely on individual users to test new software. Preferably, testing should extend over several weeks and should be done on an isolated system.

Public domain software (also known as shareware or freeware) should not be used unless obtained directly from the author, usually on payment of a small fee. Commercial software packages should be used only if obtained from reputable suppliers in sealed, tamper-revealing packages.

Preinstallation software quality checks should be performed at mainframe sites at installation of an application or operating system software. The data center should obtain from the software supplier (the computer manufacturer in most cases) some method to ensure "certification" that the software delivered is clean and free from improper changes.

Minimizing Damage. All critical files should be backed up with a minimum of two versions. Operating systems software must be backed up on disk and stored securely, with release only when authorized.

Where the user deems it appropriate to the business situation, inoculation software should be installed. This may provide more psychological than actual protection, however, since the virus has so many potential forms.

James A. Schweitzer

Source   Schweitzer, J.A., Managing Information Security. (Butterworth-Heinemann, Boston, 1990).

COMPUTER SECURITY: THREE BASIC PRINCIPLES

There are three principles basic to computer security: the never-alone, limited-tenure, and separation-of-duties principles.

Never-Alone Principle

The first is the never-alone principle. Insofar as the personnel resources of the center permit and consistent with the director's threat evaluation studies, two or more persons designated by the electronic data processing (EDP) center director and known to be professionally competent and reliable should witness every security-relevant action and attest to it by signing a suitable memorandum or log.

The following items represent what is meant by security-relevant actions:

1. Issue and return of access control items or credentials.
2. Issue and return of EDP media.
3. Systems initialization and shutdown.
4. Processing sensitive information.
5. Hardware and software maintenance.
6. Test and acceptance of hardware.
7. Modification of hardware.
8. Permanent systems reconfiguration.
9. Design and implementation of database.
10. Design, implementation, and modification of applications programs.
11. Design, implementation, and modification of operating systems.
12. Design, implementation, and modification of security software.

13. Changes to documentation.
14. Changes to emergency or contingency plans.
15. Declaration of a state of emergency.
16. Destruction or erasure of important programs or data.
17. Reproduction of sensitive information.
18. Changes to EDP operating procedures.
19. Receipt, issue, or shipment of valuable material.

Limited-Tenure Principle

The second security management principle is that of limited tenure. No person should ever be left in any security-related position so long that he or she begins to believe that the position is exclusive or permanent or the duties wholly predictable. How often people are switched around will have to depend on the availability of personnel and the extent to which employee dishonesty is perceived as a threat.

To implement limitation of tenure, crews should be randomly rotated among shifts, individuals should be randomly rotated among crews, mandatory vacation periods should be enforced, and provision should be made for cross-training so that the practice of limited tenure can become a feasible policy.

Separation-of-Duties Principle

The third and most important management principle is separation of duties. Insofar as the personnel resources of the center permit and consistent with management's appraisal of the threat of employee dishonesty, no person should have knowledge of, be exposed to, or participate in any security-related function outside of his or her own area of responsibility.

There are 10 pairs of EDP functions that, for the sake of security, must be performed by different individuals or groups. They are:

1. Computer operations and computer programming.
2. Data preparation and data processing.
3. Data processing and EDP quality control.
4. Computer operations and custody of EDP media.
5. Receipt of sensitive or valuable material and transmittal of same.

6. Reproduction, issue, or destruction of sensitive information and the granting of authorization for these acts.

7. Applications programming and systems programming.

8. Applications programming and database administration.

9. Design, implementation, and modification of security software.

10. Control of access credentials and any other function.

John M. Carroll

Source Carroll, J.M., Computer Security, 2nd Edition. (Butterworth-Heinemann, Boston, 1987).

COMPUTER TECHNOLOGY: MANAGING SECURITY IN THE INFORMATION AGE

In the mid 1950s, the world entered the information age and began to leave the industrial age. Evidences of this change are found in the automation of so many aspects of our daily lives, the unprecedented flow of information, the rapid development of all kinds of technology, and the painful transition from production-line factory industries to information-based businesses. The computer has become the heart of the business enterprise; business managers have come to rely on it for the data necessary to make all kinds of business decisions. Information is now the essential ingredient required for profit and success.

Challenge and Opportunity

Astute security managers will see change as both a challenge and an opportunity. The challenge is to provide an effective security system for business while taking into account rapidly evolving technology, intense competition, and tight profit margins; the opportunity is in making security a contributor to profits.

Why should business executives or security managers care about change? They must care, first, because in almost every business, security represents an important expense, probably in the tens of millions of dollars for a big company; and second, because in the information age the viability of a business and its ability to continue to perform profitably may well depend on protecting

its core assets. The security function is at the center of change, both as a protector of assets and a participant in the pursuit of profit.

A security department in the information age must be equipped and prepared to meet today's and tomorrow's threats with well-trained staff and modern equipment. To perform these tasks successfully, the security function must have a competence for understanding and managing technological aspects of total security program. Author John Naisbitt (1982) and management consultant John Diebold (1979) described this new age as the "age of technology and information value."

Computers allow the generation of timely and accurate information to a degree that was unknown 30 years ago. The information explosion has allowed for the management and control of worldwide businesses; at the same time, computing technology has created serious vulnerabilities. In the meantime, more and more applications of information technology are being installed, often creating more vulnerabilities. Security managers must be prepared to deal with the fact that time-sensitive information provided by computing is now the most valuable of business resources. There is impressive evidence of this value.

The Characteristics of Change

Migration of Profits. Profits, and hence business investments, are migrating from industrial age businesses to information-based businesses. In the major industrial sectors, information business revenues already exceed all but automotive and oil revenues.

To continue to operate profitably, businesses must adopt the high technology appropriate to their industries. In the automobile industry, for example, we have seen mass adoption of computer-aided design and robotics. Many businesses are seizing opportunities for new markets and profits based on information about their traditional customers. Developing and keeping technological information is a major strategic management goal that requires security.

Rapidly Evolving Technology. The product development cycle and product life cycle are shortening as technology development and applications rapidly deliver new and more

A Glossary of Computer Security Terms

A **breach** is a break in a system's security that results in admittance of a person or program. A breach will generally fall into one of three categories: user irresponsibility, user probing, and user penetration. A breach usually occurs through the log in process, and is often the result of informed guesses and other trial-and-error attempts by the intruder.

A **user violation** is the misuse of authorized access. For example, a user may utilize his access privilege to copy a sensitive file and sell it to a competitor.

User probing is a deliberate attempt by an insider or a knowledgeable outsider to exploit weaknesses in system controls in order to gain access. The prober may steal or damage information. A form of probing is hacking. The hacker's only motivation may be the intellectual challenge of defeating a system's controls against unauthorized intrusion, but the intrusion is nonetheless an invasion of confidential information even in the absence of malice.

User penetration is an attempt to break through security controls for the purpose of gaining control of the system. Once controlled, the system can be subverted to the penetrator's purpose; for example, transfer funds or ship goods. Penetration implies malicious intent, and often involves sophisticated penetration methods.

A **captive account** is a type of account that limits the activities of the user. Typically, the user is restricted to using certain command procedures and commands. A captive account is also called a **turnkey account** or a **tied account**.

An **electronic serial number (ESN)** is a number assigned to an electronic device that is connected to a computer. For example, a cellular phone may have an ESN that is automatically reported to the base station every time a call is made from the phone. A computer at the base station verifies that the number is valid before allowing the call to go through. The ESN also makes it possible for the telephone company to identify subscribers to whom calls are being placed on a stolen cellular phone.

Erase-on-allocate is a technique that applies an erasure pattern when a new area is allocated for placing data in a file. The new area is covered with the erasure pattern so that when the file is later erased anyone attempting to recover remaining data will obtain only the erasure pattern.

The erase-on-allocate strategy can also include **high-water marking**, a technique that tracks the furthest extent that a file has been written into an allocated area. The technique then prohibits reading data that lies beyond the written area of the current file, on the premise that any information outside the existing boundary was intended to be discarded at the time the previous file was erased.

The companion technique for preventing data scavenging is **erase-on-delete**, a method that applies the erasure pattern when a file is deleted or purged.

Evasive action is an automatic response of a system to prevent a break-in when the system identifies pre-designated criteria characteristic of a break-in attempt. For example, when an unauthorized user attempts to log in on a trial-and-error basis, the evasive action locks out all log-in attempts by the user for a set period of time.

A **gateway** is a device for providing isolation and controlling the flow of information between a computer system and authenticated users on networks connected to the system. Gateways are commonly placed at the host computer site between the host computer applications and the links to networks. The key function of a gateway is to permit (or deny) passage of authenticated users to network destinations.

Login is the series of actions involved in authenticating a user to a system and creating a process that runs on the user's behalf. A **proxy login** permits an authorized user at a remote site to log in as if the user were at a local site.

A user gains access by meeting the requirements of an initial screening process that usually requires both a user name and a password so the system can check authorization and impose restrictions. Different types of logins can be used for accommodating different modes of access, such as access through a terminal or through a telephone.

Logins fall into two broad categories: interactive and noninteractive. An **interactive login** prompts the user to input certain information, and the system responds to the input. The procedure is analogous to opening a combination lock by rotating the dial and stopping at the required digits in the proper order.

A **noninteractive login** is performed by the system without user involvement. An example is the startup of a batch process or a subprocess initiated in a sequence of events set in motion following a previous login.

Security enhancements that can be built into a log-in procedure include forced hang-ups on multiple log-in failures; disabling an account for a period of time following a break-in attempt; automatic account expiration; and account restrictions based on time, day and location.

A **password** is a character string that a user provides at log-in time to validate identity and prove access authorization. There are user passwords and system passwords.

In many environments, a **user password** is sufficient to gain access. A user password is associated with one user only and must be correctly supplied when the user attempts to log in. A primary and a secondary user password can be required. A **primary password** is normally associated with the user name that is supplied with it.

A **secondary password** is provided immediately after the primary password has been correctly submitted. In addition to minimizing unauthorized access through guessing, the primary/secondary approach enhances security by requiring the physical presence of more than one authorized user at login.

A **system password** may be required before login can be initiated at a particular terminal. System passwords can be used to tighten security generally by controlling access to all or most terminals, or they may focus specifically on terminals which may be targets for unauthorized entry.

Passwords may be either selected by the user or automatically generated. They may consist of letters, numerals or a combination of both. Password vulnerability can be minimized by establishing a minimum password length and specifying a password expiration period. A user may also be required to select a password from a list of nonsense words created by a random password generator. In some situations, only the system manager is allowed to select and change passwords. These are called **locked passwords**.

Password aging is the practice of tracking the length of time a password has been in effect and informing the user to change the password at minimum intervals. Many systems limit the number of password entry attempts as a deterrent to intrusion by guessing. After five unsuccessful attempts, for example, the system may disconnect the terminal, go into a **lock-up** condition, or activate an alarm.

The user's obligation with respect to password security is to: (1) select a password that cannot be easily guessed, (2) not put the password into writing where it can be seen by someone else, (3) not tell anyone the password, (4) not include the password on any file, (5) change the password frequently, (6) change the password if there is any chance it has been compromised, and (7) use a different password for each different system.

Another protection is to store passwords in a one-way encrypted form. **One-way encryption** ensures that noone, including the system manager, can determine a user's password. If the user forgets his password, the system manager can assign a temporary and automatically expiring password to allow the user to log in. After logging in, the user is able to select a new password.

A **hash table** is a place within a system where passwords are stored in a hashed or compacted form. The system will put the passwords into a fixed length, usually 16 or 32 bits. More bits provide better security against hacking attempts.

Privileges is a means of protecting the use of certain functions that can affect a system's integrity and resources. Generally, a system manager grants and denies privileges according to a user's needs.

Scavenging is reading information from a deleted file. In many systems, the contents of a previously deleted file remain intact on a disk until overwritten with the contents of a new file. Even when overwritten, residual magnetic impressions may remain. These impressions can be read by special equipment designed for this purpose. The first line of defense against scavenging is to control access to disks. A second line of defense is to overwrite deleted disk space with an erasure pattern.

A **secure access control device** is a hardware or software device that adds an additional level of access control by requiring the person attempting to access a computer system to provide a unique one-use password. Examples of access control devices are smart tokens and dial back units.

Shareware is software that is available from the owner on a "try before you buy" basis. **Freeware** is a term commonly used to refer to any no-cost or specifically free software. **Shareware** refers to copyrighted software which can be copied and used for evaluation, but for which payment is expected for permanent use.

Public domain software is software in general distribution where the origin is undetermined or where the author has explicitly granted permission for it to be freely copied and distributed. **Shrink wrap** refers to software that is packed in tamper-resistant plastic and sold in retail outlets.

A **Tempest attack** is an attack on a system's information by capturing and interpreting emissions radiated from the system. All electronic information processing devices emit unintentional signals which if analyzed can reveal information content. For example, a system attacker may isolate and interpret the characteristic emissions caused by keys being pressed on a keyboard, thus revealing passwords and the content of messages.

A **tiger team** is a team of experts who assess the security measures of a computer system by conducting unannounced penetration attempts, such as trying to circumvent access controls of a data center. A chief purpose of the team is to uncover weaknesses in the system's physical and procedural safeguards. The team members are typically employees or consultants, and the attempted penetrations are performed in a non-destructive fashion.

A **virus** is a segment of self-replicating code that iteratively attaches itself to application programs or to other executable system components in such manner as to gain control of the host module's execution. A virus will replicate itself from user to user and system to system. It can be designed to remain dormant for a specified period or be triggered by a specific event, such as removal of the virus author's name from the employer's payroll. A virus may be programmed to cause data damage or to compromise information.

A virus may be benign or malignant. A **benign virus** replicates but does not damage; for example, it might display messages on the screen but not act maliciously. Although a benign virus may be free of intent to damage, it is still a problem because it occupies memory and disk space and can interfere in unexpected ways.

A virus-infected program can infect another executable (object) program in the computer's disk storage system by secretly requesting the computer's operating system to append a copy of the virus code to the object program. When the newly infected program is itself loaded into memory and invoked, the virus in it takes control and performs hidden functions, such as infecting yet other programs. The virus code may include a marker so that the virus won't infect an already infected program because multiple infections would cause the object file to grow ever larger, leading to early detection.

The **host program** is the program to which the virus attaches. The host may be a part of the operating system, a hardware device driver, a utility, a part of the system boot process, or an application, such as word processing.

The **infection** is the invasion of the virus into the host. **Isolation** is the process a virus uses to identify and distinguish itself from the host program. **Activation** is the final phase of the virus life cycle. It may involve partial or total destruction of its environment, the issuance of a message, or some other system disturbance. The **activation period** is the time delay between initial system infection and virus activation.

A **virus remnant** is the remains of a virus after activation. **Viral strain** is the original virus design that makes it distinct from other viruses. **Viral variety** is a modification of a viral strain, appearing in a slightly different functionality.

A **Trojan horse** is a hostile software program that performs a useful function but also has a hidden, destructive purpose. The destructive functions may include deleting or creating files and displaying false information. A Trojan horse is a virus when it is additionally designed to replicate, and is called a **logic bomb** when it is designed to destroy or erase files. A bomb can initiate a "trigger event" but does not replicate.

A **warning banner** is a notice on the screen display of a computer terminal which warns the user concerning access. Examples of warning banners are "Warning: Log-on attempts are audited" and "Unauthorized access beyond this point is not permitted." The display of a warning banner before log-on is debatable. Some believe it will discourage unauthorized log-on attempts, while others will argue that a banner should appear only after an intruder has demonstrated intent by attempting to key in information.

A **worm** is a command procedure or executable image placed on a system for the purpose of seeking unauthorized access. It seeks to enter through any flaws in file protection and, if successful, will modify the file so that it carries a copy of the worm. Each time an unsuspecting user executes the code containing the worm, the worm propagates itself into poorly protected procedures or images. It replicates and spreads but does not attach to other programs, and unlike a virus, does not require a host to survive and replicate. A worm usually spreads within a single computer or over a network of computers. A **worm hole** is the path followed by the worm, usually a path of least resistance.

A **substrate** is the entity or combination of entities upon which a virus or worm acts. It is analogous to the nutrients which a bacterium needs for growth. For an executable virus, the substrate is the computer and its executable software. For a memory worm, the substrate is the computers, the memory, and communications links.

Progeny are the copies or subsequent generations of a replicated virus or worm.

A **disinfectant** is a program that locates and repairs software that has been infected by a virus or prevents infected applications from being loaded and executed.

A **vaccine** is a program that watches for suspicious attempts to modify files.

Source: Fay, John J., *Butterworths Security Dictionary*, Butterworth Publishing, Stoneham, MA, 1987.

efficient products and services. The developer of a new product will look for a "window" of opportunity to launch a sales program. If the developer fails to bring the product to market within the time frame of the window, competitors will leapfrog the technology, rendering the product obsolete and non-marketable. New product strategies and developments require increased vigilance to ensure their privacy and, hence, value to marketing plans and accomplishments.

Intensified Competition. Obtaining and holding a competitive position in the marketplace depends on continuous research and repeated successful product development and delivery. A company's reputation may rest on its ability to deliver new and exciting products at a high standard of quality. A failure in innovation, utility, or quality may result in business failure. Ideas are asset values, perhaps greater and more important than such traditional resources as plants and materials. Information protection is mandatory for providing continued market position.

Technocracy. Skilled, technologically knowledgeable employees are essential to business success; as a group, however, these people tend to have loyalties to their field rather than to their employer. The computer brought with it a special class of employees who worship at the altar of technology. For them, the disciplines for processing information have higher value than the information being processed. A serious security implication is presented with respect to the protections that must be afforded to information in the custody and care of computer technocrats.

Changing Ethics. The system of moral values that served to make society and business work properly is disintegrating. The general employee population appears to have adopted situational ethics as a norm, so that an individual's reaction to a moral challenge depends on the circumstances rather than on a commitment to established principles of conduct. Information value and security awareness are essentials for any company in a competitive, technology-oriented business.

Changing Organizational Structures. The introduction of technology to traditionally manual workplaces causes organizational changes. One such change is a restructuring of the organization that often results in a shorter hierarchical chain or a flattening of the organization. A large chunk of middle management is removed, leaving employees with less or different supervision. Employees are suddenly empowered with new freedoms, greater access to assets, and less direct monitoring of their activities. The traditional roles of line, staff, and management are changing, and new high-tech jobs are beginning to appear in which skilled specialists deal mostly with machines. A part of any program to establish employee loyalty must be an awareness of safeguards and employer rights.

These trends have important effects on how we manage and secure our businesses. The security manager's understanding of information age trends will be at the foundation of the organization's security program.

James A. Schweitzer

Source Schweitzer, J.A., Computers, Business and Security. (Butterworth-Heinemann, Boston, 1987).

CONSTRUCTION SECURITY

Construction sites present unique protection challenges for the security manager. Dynamic site conditions and unattended construction assets, especially after hours, offer attractive targets for both vandals and thieves. Loss of valuable construction materials plus crippling damage to construction equipment or even the facility under construction results in direct losses for all concerned.

Those directly affected include the constructor who owns the equipment, the insurer that underwrites the project, and the prospective tenant who must endure schedule delays and associated escalating costs. The following protection guidelines for construction sites are offered to guide constructors and their security managers in planning for safe, secure sites.

Perimeter

Perimeter barriers such as fences or walls should be utilized for site protection. A chain

Sample
CONTRACTORS EQUIPMENT CRIME PREVENTION QUESTIONNAIRE

DOCUMENTATION

Do you have an up-to-date list of all equipment and other property (hereafter called equipment) that is insured? Yes [] No []
Does the list include:
  •Original date of purchase? Yes [] No []
  •Original cost including accessories? Yes [] No []
  •Serial or other ID #? Yes [] No []
  •Description including size, weight & model? Yes [] No []
  •Location of serial or ID # on equipment? Yes [] No []
Do you have current photographs to help in identification by police and insurance company authorities? Yes [] No []
Do you keep a daily record of where equipment is located while on job sites? Yes [] No []
Do you keep a daily list of equipment in the yard? Yes [] No []
Are these lists compared to account for equipment? Yes [] No []
Is this comparison done by someone not authorized to assign equipment to job sites or transfer equipment from job site to the yard or another job site? Yes [] No []

  •What is the title of this person?   _____
_____

  •To whom does this person report?_____
_____

Does your auditor personally see all equipment? Yes [] No []
Does the scope of his audit include
  •Verification of equipment values? Yes [] No []
  •A comparison of serial or ID number shown on your equipment list with a representative proportion of your equipment? Yes [] No []
  •A comparison of insurance values to replacement or current market value for each piece of equipment? Yes [] No []

EQUIPMENT SAFEGUARDS

Do you paint your equipment in a unique way? Yes [] No []
Do you punch or engrave your equipment with your own ID numbers? Yes [] No []
How are they applied?_____
_____
_____

Does your equipment include anti-theft devices or double locking systems? Yes [] No []
Is heavy equipment that is not corralled overnight disabled in an effective way? Yes [] No []
Describe and include the serial or ID number and description of each piece of equipment. (Use a separate piece of paper and attach it to this report.)

KEY CONTROL & SECURITY

How many sets of keys do you have for each piece of equipment? _____

Who has charge of those keys?_____
Are the keys to equipment stored in your yard accounted for by someone not authorized to assign or transfer equipment to job sites or to the yard or another job site? Yes [] No []

•What is the title of this person?_____

•To whom does this person report?_____
Are keys for equipment assigned to job sites collected at the end of each day's work and accounted for? Yes [] No []

•By whom?_____
Does your job Daily Report include a statement as to the disposition of all equipment and keys? Yes [] No []
Are your Daily Reports reviewed to verify the location of equipment and disposition of keys each succeeding day? Yes [] No []

•By Whom?_____

YARD SECURITY

When on the job site, is your equipment corralled at day's end? Yes [] No []
Do you maintain adequate fire break or separation between equipment and other property stored overnight in the corral? Yes [] No []

•Approximate distance of separation on all sides:_____
Is your job site corral lighted and fenced in on all sides and locked? Yes [] No []
Do you employ a watchman at night and on weekends and holidays? Yes [] No []
Have the local police and/or fire department been notified of your job sites and requested to increase their surveillance? Yes [] No []

GENERAL

Are you a member of any trade group (such as Associated General Contractors of America, National Equipment Dealers Association, or similar organizations)? Yes [] No []
•Name of group:_____
•Does the group have a Crime Prevention Program? Yes [] No []
•Do you subscribe to it? Yes [] No []
Do you have a written Crime Prevention Plan currently in effect for your firm? Yes [] No []
•Is it administered by a key person? Yes [] No []
•State the title of the person:_____
•Is a copy of your Crime Prevention Program available upon request for review? Yes [] No []

link fence at least 7 feet in height with triple strands of barbed wire can serve as a significant barrier to the professional thief. Where possible, the fencing at the construction site should be located to satisfy security fencing after construction. If possible, a clear zone 20 feet wide should be maintained adjacent to the fence. This clear zone will render the area useless as a hiding place for criminals and for equipment marked for theft at a later time.

A continuing evaluation of relative risk, both with respect to diversion of assets and to vulnerability to adversary action, should be carried out by the site security supervisor and monitored by construction management. High-risk areas should be provided with above-average lighting, more frequent patrols, and the earliest application of supplemental electronic surveillance and detection devices.

Access Points

The fewer access points that a site has, the easier it is to control the flow of personnel and materials. As a minimum, a check point at the main gate should be established. If the project is of sufficient size, a security guard house can be set up to process personnel and serve as a command center for the guard force.

Job trailers should be placed at the entrance whenever possible. They should be placed a minimum of 20 feet away perpendicular to the fence. By placing trailers at the entrance, the site construction superintendent has better control, both psychologically and physically during the day. Strangers should be made to check in prior to going to the job site.

To reduce the amount of traffic through the access control point, it may be possible to construct a warehouse or storage area on the site perimeter. This would allow for off-loading away from construction activities. All access points should be posted with a warning of a search program and vehicle and package search should be carried out on a random basis for both ingoing and outgoing traffic.

Parking

Employee parking should be separated from visitor parking, with both isolated from the

warehouse or staging area to prevent workers from putting stolen items into their vehicles during the day.

Lighting

Since most construction site theft and/or vandalism occurs at night, an adequate lighting system is a must. Sufficient illumination discourages and deters entry to the site and provides a means of surveillance for the security force. Whenever possible, construction security lighting should be the same type of fixtures as specified for final site lighting. Individual lights should be installed to avoid throwing any glare in the eyes of security personnel or casting annoying lights into adjacent streets or neighboring facilities. If glare can be directed at the intruder, it is most effective in reducing the intruder's ability to see the patrolling security guard/police. To provide maximum security, all poles and other equipment should be located at least 10 feet inside the perimeter barrier so that they are not readily accessible to damage or destruction.

Job Trailer Security

A cardboard box is just about as much protection against theft as a job trailer. Professionals and amateurs alike in the crime community are fully aware that job trailers are easy targets to get expensive office equipment, including FAX machines, copiers, computers, and telephones. To help deter this kind of theft, job trailers should be hardened. Place wrought iron cages over the windows and any glass doors. Install shades over the doors and windows, and keep them closed at night. Weld all hinges and ensure that the door locks are adequate. Do not store keys in job trailers. Install lock-down pads for computers, typewriters, copiers, etc. Install an alarm system with an automatic call up feature. Ensure that electronic sensors are installed to monitor unconventional points of entry, such as vents, ceilings, and side walls.

Property Identification

All portable property should be marked by etching or die-stamping with an appropriate identification mark upon entry onto the site. An excellent method of marking equipment is a permanent acid etch indelible ink with a continuous roller stamp that marks the metals quickly. Marking materials aids greatly in recoveries. Employees and visitors should be advised that the property is marked and their cooperation in reducing theft solicited. Details of the types of marking should be given to law enforcement.

Key Control

Keys and keycards should be issued only to persons authorized access. Those in use should be checked in at the end of each shift or workday, and a log should be maintained showing in and out times, and other pertinent information. Keys and cards should be recovered from reassigned or terminated personnel. Locks or cores should be changed upon reported loss of keys, or codes changed and cards made unusable. A record of all keys, locks, and cards should be maintained and kept in a location secured by a combination lock.

Direct losses to contractor equipment are estimated to be in excess of $1 billion annually. Major causes of loss include fire, theft, vandalism, collision, upset, and overturn. An unusually large number of losses are the result of lack of training, inattention, oversight, and carelessness. Substance abuse, both drugs and alcohol, are increasingly contributing to losses and accidents. In order for these losses to be mitigated, management must recognize the importance of establishing loss control programs within their companies. The sample crime prevention questionnaire accompanying this article can be used by management to focus attention upon loss prevention and to establish security practices for the construction site [1] [2].

Richard P. Grassie, Cpp

Notes

1. This paper was adapted from a presentation made by John Thomas at the ASIS Facility Design Workshop, Minneapolis, MN., June 1990.

2. The Contractors Equipment Crime Prevention Questionnaire was provided through the courtesy of Inland Marine Underwriters Association, 14 Wall Street, New York, NY 10005.

CONSULTING: A NEW ROLE FOR THE SECURITY MANAGER

Downsizing, dismantling, and debt are key elements in corporate America's unfolding strategy. What does this mean? It means that a corporation may be worth more dead than alive. A company is in danger when the total value of its shares drops below that of its assets. A business becomes undervalued when speculators can sell its offices, plants, equipment, and real estate for more than they pay to buy the company. To counter the threat of takeovers, many corporations switch to a three-dimensional (3-D) strategy of downsizing, dismantling, and debt.

The 3-D strategy has consequences not only for individual employees and companies, but also for corporate America as a whole. The 3-D mentality has led to large numbers of personnel layoffs as companies attempt to reduce overhead, increase responsiveness, and gain a competitive edge. Estimates indicate that millions of managers have lost their jobs due to downsizing and dismantling and the trend has only begun. Although the recent wave of streamlining has greatly improved profit margins, it has so decimated executive ranks that the business world may never recover. It has destroyed the careers of loyal, long-term workers who knew their companies best and were committed to continued success.

The resulting lack of commitment and loyalty from employees who survive massive cuts presents increased challenges for the remaining managers. More essential than ever is a manager's ability to work within the organization's reconfigured structure to have impact, to get recommendations approved, and, on a personal level, to be seen as a flexible, innovative contributor. Security managers specifically need to find ways to exert influence, particularly when they do not have direct control over the many aspects of security. Unfortunately, there are no easy solutions.

The Security Manager as a Consultant

So, in this era of disillusionment and uncertainty, how can security professionals get their ideas accepted, adopted, and financed? One way to solve this problem is for the security department to function as consultants to other corporate divisions. Experience shows the way people feel about the security department will determine whether they follow security recommendations. Thus, managing client relationships is very important in a consulting environment.

Every phase in the consulting process is a stepping stone to successful project completion. Often, both the security consultant and the client try to hurry through the preliminary steps and get on with implementation. The consultant is eager to go ahead with a solution that requires his or her expertise. The client wants the comfort of knowing that something is being done. However, in rushing toward solutions and neglecting preliminary phases, both parties overlook skills and steps that are crucial to success. Hurried contracting, shotgun diagnosis, and impersonal feedback are the breeding ground for problems in implementation.

A Consulting Model

A four-phase model -- contracting, diagnosis, feedback, and implementation -- can ensure that security staff recommendations are acted on. This process was originally introduced by Peter Block in his landmark book *Flawless Consulting* . Block's concepts and procedures can be applied specifically to the field of security.

Initially, the consultant must build the foundation for a 50-50 relationship with the client. A cooperative relationship offers the best chance for achieving the ultimate goal of the consulting project, namely, to solve the client's problems so they stay solved and to enable the client to solve future problems.

Contracting. The goal of the first phase is to gain the client's personal commitment by negotiating responsibilities and establishing an equitable relationship. During contracting, the following elements should be covered:

•Scope. This is a statement of the study's focus. For example, the scope might state, "The study will be a physical security survey of the corporate headquarters building. It will include security lighting, CCTV, intrusion devices, and access control. The study will not include the factory or distribution area."

•Objectives. The consultant should outline his or her best estimate of the benefits the client can expect, that is, what will be accomplished if the study is successful. For example, "The objective of the study is to identify the effectiveness of the present security system and to recommend upgraded technology and other improvements."

•Informational Leads. Access to people and information is the key to effective consulting and should be discussed during the contracting phase. For example, "To complete our security study, I must have access to the plant engineer and department directors. I also need a list of policies and procedures. I will interview at least 10 additional employees to identify their attitudes toward security at the corporate headquarters."

•Consultant's Role. Only through client involvement can the consultant gain the support needed for successful implementation. A clear statement of intent that expresses a desire for equal responsibility in identifying problems, integrating findings, and developing recommendations and action plans indicates the consultant's desire for a cooperative effort. For example, "My primary role is to give you a clear picture of your current level of security and what I believe your future needs to be. I would like to present you my analysis of the situation and then together we will develop recommendations on what changes should be made. A major part of my role is to help you solve this problem for yourself the next time."

•Administration. The client should know what product he or she will receive -- whether it is a written or oral report, what the time schedule is for that report, and whether to expect any interim reports. The individual receiving the report also should be aware of any additional copies that will be supplied to other people. Reporting procedures vary depending upon whether the consultant position is internal or external. Normally, an external consultant reports only to the client, while an internal consultant may often be required by policy to report to other individuals in a chain of command.

•Obligation. A binding relationship between consultant and client should develop during contracting. Very candidly, the consultant should determine what the client really wants by asking directly what his or her expectations are. This information is the heart of the contracting process and the key to a successful project. The client may be allowing only 2 weeks for a 4-week project, or a project that should have a budget of $30,000 may only have been allotted $2,000.

After carefully eliciting the client's wants, the consultant must clearly express what he or she needs to make the project successful. Some essentials include sufficient time and budget to do the job properly; access to the right people, records, and documentation; and the commitment of key company personnel to the completion of the project.

After clarifying these needs, the consultant should ask for feedback on control and vulnerability. Unfortunately, many a project fails because the client enters it based on some type of coercion, either direct or indirect, or the client agrees to the project but feels he or she does not have adequate control over procedures.

The consultant must ask, "Is this project something you really want? Are you satisfied with the way we have set up this project?" If the client is not totally committed to the project, this does not mean the consultant should withdraw. He or she will, however, better understand potential difficulties from the beginning.

Finally, two finer points should be included in contracting. First, the consultant should offer support in terms of a statement emphasizing the client's expertise and involvement, such as "You are aware of the type of security problems that exist. That is going to be a great help to us in conducting our study."

Second, all points of agreement should be restated. For example, "I will begin the study on Monday at 10:00 a.m. The study will take 3 days. At the conclusion of the study, I will give you an oral briefing followed by a written report within 2 weeks. On Friday, I will provide you with a list of the key personnel I wish to interview."

Diagnosis. The second phase in the consulting model is diagnosis. The purpose is not to develop voluminous amounts of research material, but to mobilize energies and resources to solve the problem. During the diagnostic phase, the consultant discovers the underlying dimensions of the real problem and helps the client through professional and compassionate behavior. Diagnosis usually begins when the client presents a perceived problem, or what Block calls the presenting problem.

Importantly, however, the consultant cannot accept what is presented as the true problem without data collection and analysis. The problem presented by the client may be quite different from the real, underlying problem. As a result,

diagnosis also requires a redefinition of the problem.

The client's presented problem often includes hidden technical and business components. Organizational problems include how these business and technical aspects are managed. For an internal consultant, addressing organizational involvement is a risky, but necessary, chore.

The diagnostic phase is as important as the contracting phase. In addition to the points already covered, the client should be involved in data collection and interpretation. The collected data should also be trimmed down to a manageable size and should use language understandable to people outside the security field. These steps lead to the feedback phase of the model.

Feedback. The feedback phase is the consultant's showtime — the moment to present findings and recommendations, and to reach a mutual decision with the client on an appropriate action. Normally, voluminous research information will have accumulated during the previous phases. The consultant's challenge is to decide what information should be presented to the client.

One good way to determine information priorities is to list those four or five key items most important to the client. This list can then guide the decision on what to report and how to organize the information. Questions helpful in organizing a feedback presentation include the following:

•Does the client have control over changing current practices?

•Are the discovered problems important to both the client and the organization?

•Is the client organization committed to solving the problems?

The feedback phase is often tricky. The client must answer tough questions and accept the reality of the problems. During the presentation, the consultant should strive to be neutral, direct, nonjudgmental, and compassionate. Only after the information and recommendations have been imparted can implementation begin.

Implementation. The most powerful tool for leverage during implementation is the consultant's behavior -- the rapport he or she has developed with the client during the consulting process. Ideally, this relationship is built on honesty and trust, which reduce the client's feelings of vulnerability and loss of control as implementation moves forward.

Finally, as one project ends, it sets up a new beginning that may turn into a future business opportunity. At this point, the consultant should provide the client with feedback on project management. The consultant should also request an evaluation of his or her performance during the project and outline how the two parties might effectively work together in the future.

Organizations today are fighting for survival. They are downsizing, dismantling, and taking on debt. Many are fighting hostile takeovers. Within this climate, top management wants to know how staff managers can be more cost-effective and enhance the bottom line. Security professionals do not need special glasses to see that now is the time to ponder this question. A timely application of sound consulting techniques may be the answer.

Robert F. Littlejohn, CPP

Source Block, P., Flawless Consulting. (Learning Concepts, Austin, TX, 1981).

CONSUMER PRODUCT SAFETY COMMISSION

Every year consumer products are associated with the deaths of many thousands of Americans and injuries to several million others. Many of these deaths and injuries involve products commonly found around the home such as bicycles, toys, lawn mowers, household chemicals, furniture, appliances, and power tools. Although the cause of these accidents is more often user behavior rather than product failure, the cost to the American public is staggering -- the cost of injuries treated in hospital emergency rooms alone exceeds $10 billion per year.

Believing that something could and must be done to reduce the number and severity of these deaths and injuries, Congress passed the Consumer Product Safety Act. The President signed the law on October 27, 1972; and the U.S. Consumer Product Safety Commission (CPSC) was activated on May 14, 1973. Congress directed the Commission to "protect the public against unreasonable risks of injuries and deaths associated with consumer products." The more serious risks include amputation, electrocution, burns, asphyxiation, and cancer.

This independent regulatory agency of the federal government has worked to prevent injuries and deaths by:

• Working with industry to develop voluntary safety standards;

• Issuing and enforcing mandatory standards, where appropriate;

• Banning products for which no feasible standard would adequately protect the public;

• Obtaining the recall or repair of products that fail to comply with mandatory standards or that present substantial hazards or imminent hazards to consumers;

• Conducting research on potential hazards; and

• Conducting information and education programs.

Under the Consumer Product Safety Act, Congress granted the Commission broad authority to issue and enforce safety standards prescribing performance requirements, warnings, or instructions for use of consumer products.

The Commission also regulates products covered by four acts previously administered by other federal agencies: The Flammable Fabrics Act; The Federal Hazardous Substances Act; The Poison Prevention Packaging Act of 1970; and The Refrigerator Safety Act.

Consumer Product Safety Commission

Source Public Affairs Pamphlet. (U.S. Consumer Product Safety Commission, Washington, DC, 1992).

CONTRACT SECURITY: CONTRACTING FOR GUARD SERVICES

Choosing the right contract security service can be one of the most difficult and perplexing decisions put before a security manager. When virtually all security service contractors claim to offer the best screened, trained, and supervised guards at the best price, the security manager will not find it easy to make a choice or feel very comfortable that the choice is right.

Not surprisingly, general criticism of security service contractors consistently centers on the selection, training, and supervision of guards. Security managers often complain about contract officers and their supervisors who fail to meet expectations. The underlying causes usually relate to inadequate recruitment and screening, poor training, and supervision that is not given at all or is given infrequently or badly.

How can the security manager choose a competent contractor so as to avoid these problems? How does he or she find and invite qualified contractors to bid on a job; evaluate bid proposals; award the job; and ensure that the selected contractor is delivering the services cost-effectively and in the manner specified? This section addresses the critical questions, yet at the same time encourages the security manager to consult with legal, financial, and insurance resources.

Assess Needs

An accurate determination of the organization's security needs must be made before identifying the services that meet the needs. Such a determination can be effected through a comprehensive security survey -- one that will look at both the physical nature of the premises to be guarded and the work processes within. The survey should include these objectives:

- Identify the assets that require protection.
- Identify the probable threats to the assets.
- Identify the vulnerabilities of the assets.
- Evaluate the likelihood of threat occurrence.
- Evaluate the probable magnitude of loss from threat occurrence.

A comprehensive survey will address the standard issues, e.g., perimeter protection, locks and locking devices, intrusion detection, access control of people and vehicles, property movement control, safeguarding sensitive information, employee protection, executive protection, and contingency planning. An examination of these security concerns should produce an understanding of the security techniques and methods suitable for establishing protection. The term "level of protection" can be understood in this context to mean the extent to which the identified techniques and methods are put into operation.

The techniques and methods pertinent here represent the functions performed by contract guards such as checking passes, patrolling, responding to alarms, escorting people and property, investigating minor incidents, and providing first-responder medical assistance. Once the needs and corresponding service functions have been identified, the security

manager is able to determine the number of guards required, when they will be required, the tools and equipment they will need, and the abilities they will need to bring to the job to be effective.

The security manager may want to hire an outside consultant to conduct the survey. A different perspective may yield valuable insights. A word of caution, however: select a consultant on the basis of expertise -- not on the basis of an offer, free or otherwise, from a prospective bidder for guard services.

Identify and Evaluate Possible Bidders

The security manager should be looking for a contractor who will be strong in three broad areas: (1) quality performance of guard services, (2) positive and prompt responses to concerns expressed by the security manager, and (3) competitive pricing.

Finding a contractor who can deliver in all of these areas is not easy, especially if the security manager has had little prior experience in using contract guard services. A security manager who is charged with starting up a contract guard operation or switching to contract guards from in-house guards is likely to encounter problems outside of his or her personal experience. Even security managers who have used contract guards throughout their entire careers will admit to the headaches connected to acquiring contract guard services.

The security manager's sources of information concerning prospective contractors include industry contacts, such as those found within the memberships of the American Society for Industrial Security (ASIS), the Building Owners and Managers Association (BOMA), the American Commercial Real Estate (ACRE), and the International Real Estate Management (IREM); local Chamber of Commerce and Better Business Bureau; state licensing and regulatory agencies; law enforcement agencies; and various other industry-related groups.

The main idea at this stage is to gain as much knowledge as possible concerning potential contractors prior to inviting the bids. Items of interest include:

- Operating philosophies and attitudes.
- Compliance with state licensing and/or regulatory agencies.

• Types and amounts of insurance coverage in effect or available.

• Depth, availability, and experience of management.

• Size, experience, and turnover rate of the workforce.

• Types and costs of employee benefit packages available.

• Wage scales and merit increase programs.

• Types and costs of uniforms, equipment, and supplies.

• Personnel screening and types of tests administered.

• Training programs conducted for officers, supervisors, and other staff.

• Operational capabilities.

• Supervision methods.

• Financial condition and length of time in business.

• Auxiliary services available.

• Billing and payroll procedures.

• Clients and references.

If after examining these items, the security manager believes that the contractor will be a viable bidder, a tour of the contractor's office is in order. It will also be in order to visit at least two of the contractor's clients who have similar operations. Visits like these will allow the security manager to view the contractor in action, both on the contractor's home ground and at the premises of clients.

While touring the contractor's office, the security manager should look at uniforms and equipment in stock, obtain a briefing on hiring and assigning practices, review payroll and billing procedures, and sit in on a training session. At a customer's site, the appearance and demeanor of the assigned officers will be of interest, as will be the comments of the client they serve.

The security manager should choose carefully those companies who will be invited to bid. Soliciting bids from firms who are either underqualified or overqualified is a waste of everyone's time. The security manager should take the time to get to know the prospective vendor's operating philosophies; review carefully the vendor's experience level, reputation for service, references, and financial condition; and evaluate the hiring procedures, training programs, supervision scheme, and operating capabilities. Finally, the security manager should determine if the vendor has a caliber of management staff equal to the organization's security needs.

Prepare the Solicitation for Bids

A great deal can be said in favor of defining, up-front and in detail, what the contractor will be expected to provide. The security manager should be candid about the nature of the work; the environment in which the work will be performed; the skills, knowledge, and abilities required for minimally acceptable performance; and the repercussions of unacceptable performance. Most contractors will be sincere in wanting to provide the desired degree of service. It will be up to the security manager to articulate the characteristics of service from the beginning.

Wages and Benefits. An important element in the solicitation will be an expression of the organization's intent with respect to wages and benefits for the contract guards. The figure allocated for pay and fringe benefits to the guards will be the significant driver among all costs. Pay at the low end of the scale will invariably translate to less than adequate security; at the high end of the scale the probabilities will be significantly better for obtaining quality performance. Wages should differentiate between rank (e.g., security officer versus sergeant) and function (e.g., patrol officer versus console operator), and it should specify increases with respect to promotions, longevity, and merit.

As a general rule, 62 to 66% of the contractor's billing rate will be paid out in wages. If the organization is only willing, for example, to pay $10.00 per hour for officers working in the rank of sergeant, those officers will receive between $6.25 and $6.75 per hour. The security manager has to ask himself if that level of pay will attract and keep an employee capable of performing the duties of a sergeant.

The benefits portion of the officers' compensation package will be a major factor in holding turnover at a tolerable level. A contractor simply cannot attract and retain qualified officers without providing competitive benefits, such as health coverage, hospitalization, vacation, holiday pay, and sick leave.

Clearly, there is a relationship between pay and services. The security manager cannot expect a contractor to provide highly skilled and motivated guards in exchange for poor wages and benefits. The willingness of the organization to set a fair rate for work will be an indicator to the contractor as to the organization's overall concern for security. Also, and very importantly, the specification of wages and benefits in the bid will make it possible for the organization to compare bids on a dollar-to-dollar basis.

Written Standards. Like the wages and benefits package, the solicitation should set out the organization's minimum standards. Personnel standards might require candidates to have a high school education or equivalent, a personal history free of felony convictions, the ability to pass a reading and comprehension test, and so forth. The security manager may want to use the organization's standards as a guide. For example, if the organization requires its own applicants to pass a drug test, then it may be appropriate for the guards to also be drug tested.

Training specifications might include receiving a general orientation about security officer work, such as the laws that apply to security officer duties, followed by site-specific training that focuses on the unique nature of security at the organization's place of business. Training specifications often include CPR and first aid. The security manager might additionally specify that written and performance tests be used to ensure that officers possess the knowledge and skills critical to the job, and that test results and training records be available for the security manager's inspection.

Supervision specifications might require the contractor's account supervisor to meet once per week with the security manager to discuss operational aspects, or for the contractor's regional manager or higher-level executive to confer periodically on broad issues related to contract administration. A challenging specification would be to require the account supervisor to be a graduate of a recognized course in asset protection or hold status as a Certified Protection Professional (CPP).

Uniforms and equipment can be the subject of standards. The solicitation can specify the type of uniform, that uniform items be new, that they consist of various pieces of wear, and, that when worn, they will reflect custom tailoring and updating. Equipment, such as radios, flashlights, and foul weather gear, can be described in detail, such as by manufacturer and model.

Operational standards will specify the number of officers to be employed; job titles and ranks; the hours and days of employment; the place or places of employment; the functions to be performed; the environmental conditions in which the functions will be performed; the tools and equipment to be used, including deadly weapons and items supplied by the organization; and any special considerations that might involve mental or physical stress, discomfort, or unusual working conditions.

Insurance standards could include requirements for comprehensive general liability, automobile liability, umbrella coverage, workers' compensation, and evidence of coverage, naming the organization as an additional insured party.

Specifications might be appropriate with respect to the accuracy of billings. For example, the contractor might be compelled to "pay a fine" for every fifth invoice that is found to be inaccurate. A requirement along this line would be intended to prevent, or at least minimize, billing errors.

A cost disclosure requirement would give to the security manager a breakout of how the billing rate is determined. A disclosure would show all costs related to payroll administration, overtime, training, uniforms, equipment, insurance, benefit costs, general and administrative costs, and net profit. A right-to-audit clause might also be appropriate.

Incentives can be built into the specifications. Rewards can be set for the contractor when absenteeism and tardiness are kept below a set level; rewards can accrue to the organization when the number of billable hours rises above a set level.

The security manager should leave no doubt as to his or her intent to be involved in the delivery of services. Involvement begins with the bid and bid selection process and continues through the life of the contract.

The method of monitoring and the method for communicating the results of monitoring can be described. The bid solicitation can ask the prospective bidder to identify the person to whom monitoring reports should be submitted and to describe the contractor's manner of response to adverse reports.

Experience has shown that managers who carefully screen contractors and set workable, measurable standards will be successful in selecting a competent contractor. Conversely, security managers who do not get actively involved in the selection process, do not monitor contract performance, and do not provide feedback to the contractor will have limited success in selecting a quality contractor and administering the contract.

Evaluate the Bids

A starting point in this process is to begin by looking closely at each bid package. Was the proposal submitted on time and in the prescribed fashion? Did the bidder follow directions, provide the information requested, and arrange the information in the order and format specified? Is the proposal complete, clear, and concise?

While these may seem like minor points, the care with which a vendor responds to specifications is often reflective of capabilities and attitude. Careful attention to detail reflects a strong interest in getting the work and a resolve to meet the specifications. A poorly constructed offer is a red flag that the bidder has low interest or may not be capable of delivering the services as specified.

In evaluating bid content, the security manager may want to construct a chart or some similar administrative tool that will allow point-by-point comparisons. A method of weighting may help the security manager give greater values to some issues over others based on relative importance.

The key issues need to be looked at very carefully. Typically, the key issues are personnel screening and selection, training, supervision, wages and benefits, insurance, operational capabilities, and cost. While cost may be a primary consideration in all cases, selecting the low bidder may not be in the organization's best interest.

A contractor will need to earn a respectable profit in order to conduct business properly. If a profit is not reflected in the bid, the contractor will not have the capacity or incentive to handle the account properly. A bid that reflects no profit or a profit in the range of 1 to 2% may be an attempt by the bidder to get a "foot in the door." Once selected, the contractor may attempt to dilute the standards or renegotiate the contract.

Award the Contract

After a contractor has been selected and notified, the security manager should notify each of the bidders who were not selected. The unsuccessful bidders devoted considerable time and energy in responding to the solicitation, earning them at least an explanation as to why they were not chosen.

The contract will typically specify length of contract; cancellation and renewal options; start date, terms of payment, and billing procedures; equipment costs to be billed; insurance for the protection of the client; right of the client to remove or replace any contract employee assigned; right of the client to interview and approve contractor employees assigned to the account; the nature of supervision and management administered by the contractor to the account; health insurance, paid holidays, sick leave, and vacation benefits; the client's right to audit; and the minimum starting wage for each job classification and longevity and merit increases.

Some loose ends will probably need to be tied up before the contractor can start to work, and one or more meetings will be necessary to get things rolling on an even keel. A quality contractor will be flexible in resolving issues important to both sides, and the contract awardal stage is the best time to obtain agreement on unresolved issues. The client's needs should be projected as primary, but not to the extent that the contractor will feel bullied into accepting unreasonable conditions. If agreement cannot be reached, legal counsel for both sides may need to be brought into the picture.

Monitor Performance

Up to this point, the security manager has been a leading participant, conferring and coordinating with a variety of persons on both sides of the contract. These have included purchasing agents, attorneys, and representatives of the bidding companies. Now, however, the security manager must move from being a facilitator to a compliance monitor. Some believe this is where the really hard work begins.

By now the security manager and one or more counterpart representatives of the contractor have a general understanding of the services that are required and how they are to be provided. While a formal plan may not exist on paper, each side pretty much knows what to expect. Some important blank spots may remain to be filled in. For example, written instructions will need to be developed for each of the security officer positions and for dealing with special incidents, such as fire emergencies, bomb threats, and severe weather. The contractor will usually prepare these instructions with input from and approval by the security manager.

In the early days of contract performance, the security manager should be looking for minor problems, not for the purpose of being critical, but to keep minor problems from growing into major problems. A common friction point has to do with conflicts in style. The security manager has to feel comfortable working with the contractor's supervisors and be confident in their ability to get the job done. If the comfort and confidence are not there, the security manager will do both sides a favor by asking for a change in assignments.

On the other hand, the security manager should allow the contractor to give the service. Too much involvement by the security manager may turn out to be confusing to the contractor, resulting in a further downturn in service. The trick is to find a balance between watching and intervening.

The standards that were developed in the solicitation and incorporated into the contract are the criteria for measuring performance. The security manager's interest is to learn if the assigned officers met the hiring qualifications, completed the required training, passed the required tests, are wearing the prescribed uniforms, and are using the prescribed equipment. The security manager wants to know if the account supervisors are conducting inspections and making liaison calls at the prescribed frequency, and if the contractor's invoices are accurate to the prescribed percentage.

When the contractor has a quality control (QC) program that regularly evaluates its own services, the security manager may suggest that the standards set by the security manager be rolled into the evaluation criteria of the QC program.

Acquiring good contract guard services is investing in security. The investment can be rewarding when the services work out well over the long-term. The security manager plays a key role in selecting a competent contractor and working with the contractor to develop a combination of services that correspond to the organization's needs.

Vicki S. Looney
and Terry F. Whitley

CORPORATE SECURITY: PROTECTING ASSETS IN AN EVOLVING ORGANIZATION

At least since the end of World War II, the security industry has been radically and rapidly evolving. The main driving forces of change have been the steady escalation of crime and the increasing inability of law enforcement to be effective in dealing with crimes against businesses. A whole new industry has risen up to meet market demands fueled by business fears, and with it we have seen the maturation of an entity that has come to be called the proprietary security organization or simply corporate security.

Corporate security's raison d'etre has been the protection of the employer's assets against threats of crime, and the methods of protection have relied to a great extent on concepts borrowed from other fields. Intelligence gathering, crime analysis, investigating, and target hardening are examples of methods acquired from law enforcement; and from sister organizations in the business environment corporate security has learned how to conduct audits and inventories, how to secure confidentiality agreements, and how to track and control the physical movement of people and property. Corporate security has also necessarily developed an expertise in the application of electronic technology to the tasks of assets protection.

In short, corporate security is the child of change and the product of its environment. It was born out of a need and grew up learning how to cope and survive. It is what it is and does what it does because of the dictates of external and internal forces. Carried with this condition is the inherent danger that change can become so demanding that corporate security may be unable to cope, and therefore not survive, at least not in the way it presently operates.

A New Form of Change

A change with profound and sweeping proportions is in fact brewing now. The change has to do with human values, but first a little background.

Business organizations are turning up the pressure to improve results. It is not just that results matter more today, because results have always mattered, but what we are seeing is a shift in the way results are delivered. To be sure, change is essential if organizations are to succeed in a tough, competitive world, and organizations are being judged more harshly than ever before, both by their managements and shareholders.

Change is turning organizations into clusters of clever people doing clever things, and clever people have to be handled rather more sensitively than was the case in the good old days. The tried and true concepts of control and supervision are giving way to persuasion and to leadership. Business managers now speak of visions and empowerment. An entirely new rationale is taking shape in which traditional controls are increasingly unwelcome.

For the corporate security manager, the mandate is to achieve the same or a higher level of results, except go about it differently. This is neither simple nor easy. On the one hand, the organization's top leadership wants the corporate security manager to embrace bold new concepts, yet on the other hand wants no dilution in the protection of assets. Whether the corporate security manager likes it or not, he or she is caught up in a process of learning, adapting, and, above all, accepting the proposition that the change which has begun will continue well into the foreseeable future, and that corporate security must be a constructive part of the process.

Being a part of the process is another way of saying that the corporate security manager will continue to adapt. Successful adaptation is to continue to be effective in protecting the organization's assets, but to apply techniques that fit the ways of the new organization. But what does the new or evolving organization look like, and what are its ways?

The Shamrock Organization

Some insights can be found in Charles Handy's excellent book, *The Age of Unreason*. Handy describes what he calls the shamrock organization. The first leaf of the shamrock is the core of professional workers. These are the managers, the high fliers, the skilled technicians, and key professionals who are absolutely critical to the organization. Without them, the business cannot possibly succeed. They work hard and long, and are paid well.

Life in the professional core is collegial, resembling that in a consultancy or a professional partnership. The core structure is relatively flat, with few layers of rank. The concept of superiors and subordinates has been replaced by that of colleagues and associates.

The size of the professional core in many corporations has gotten smaller and is continuing to shrink. Two cost-driven reasons stand out: a preference for a flat organizational structure is making many positions redundant, and more and more professional core functions are being assigned to outside contractors.

The second leaf of the shamrock organization are contractors; generally, people who do specialized work. While the work may have value, it is not necessarily critical or central to the business. Contractors are able to perform these jobs better and at lower cost than regular employees, requiring less management time and attention in the bargain.

The third leaf is the flexible labor force, the part-time and temporary workers. They move in and out of the company as the needs of the business expand and contract. The services are not always done conveniently and to great satisfaction, but they are economical. In many U.S. corporations, flexible labor is the fastest growing segment of their workforces.

Shamrock types of organizations have been emerging at least since the early 1980s when downturns in profits forced many major corporations to make significant reductions in human-power. Hit hardest were the professional cores. When times improved, businesses were determined not to be caught the same way twice. Work that in earlier times would have been returned to the professional core was farmed out to contractors, and some of the lower-level jobs were converted to part-time and temporary status.

Instead of one workforce, many corporations now have three. Each workforce has a different contribution to make, a different commitment to the organization, a different scheme of remuneration, and a different set of expectations. Clearly, there are a number of interesting problems associated with delivering security services in such an arrangement.

Security Problems in the Shamrock Organization

Let's take a look at some of the security problems. In the professional core we see more people conferring and sharing information across large expanses of geography, and the information they work with has been pulled from many centers of expertise. A greater amount of sensitive information is being generated and opened to a larger number of key players in many parts of the globe.

Business information, including the most sensitive possessed by an organization, is valuable to the extent it is put to work. Although the corporate security manager's instinct is to keep sensitive information under lock and key, the reality is that sensitive information is widely scattered and in flux at any given time for the simple reason it is in use or in movement. Information in the process of being used or moved about is at the same time most vulnerable to compromise. The utilitarian value of the information at the moment of use may only be fractional by comparison to the cost of its loss.

In the professional core we are also seeing more people making spending decisions. This is called trust and empowerment, but the corporate security manager knows that more hands on the purse strings can lead to spending that is dishonest.

In the second of the three-leaved workforce, corporate security has to be concerned when the organization makes sensitive materials available to contractors, especially when contractors work for competitors. Sensitive materials include things like business plans, trade secrets, proprietary processes, customer lists, and executive salaries.

There is the possibility of contractors learning how to pass through protected computer gateways that lead to valuable data or to third parties connected to the system. When the know-how of access is in the hands of a disgruntled contractor, the organization can be damaged severely. Hacking, viruses, worms, and Trojan horses are possibilities, as well as disablement of a critical system by the support contractor as the result of a contractual dispute.

With regard to the third part of the workforce, there are few reasons to believe that the part-timers and temporaries who replaced regular employees are of the same caliber. One should anticipate in this group a higher level of drug-related accidents and incidents, pilferage, vandalism, confrontational behavior, and occasional acts of violence. The vendors of flexible labor are focused on providing human-power, not on conducting pre-employment background checks. Without screening, the professional core will likely be working next to people with pasts checkered by crime.

Controls Based on Motivation

The motivations that supported ethical business conduct in the old organization are changing in the shamrock organization. A concern for assets, for example, is not a motivator to people who get their paychecks elsewhere. The sense of mutual interest found in the employee/employer relationship may not be present in service arrangements, and it would be foolish to believe that vendors will place the client's economic good ahead of theirs. While persons in the professional core may have careers, love the challenge of their work, and take pleasure when the organization succeeds, the people who work on an out-sourced basis look at things much differently.

The traditional techniques of organizational control, such as locking things away, compartmentalizing information, and limiting spending authority, lose their effectiveness in organizations with cultures that stress individual trust. This is not to say, however, that all of the traditional controls will disappear: it is more likely they will be modified and new controls invented as the organization continues to evolve. A good guess is that the successful controls will be founded on principles of motivation, such as the influence of peers and informal groups. Motivation may be the only means of bridging the gap between rules and the desired human behavior.

The rapidly expanding work practices that rely on desktop computing are a case in point. The provision of personal computers (PCs) to employees is the giving of trust and empowerment to a large portion of the workforce. The autonomy inherent in desktop computing, combined with the power and flexibility of the technology, present new problems in control. Mainframe computers with large databases have physical, procedural, and technical safeguards, but this is not always the case with desktop systems. The desktop risks include data loss and theft, use of time and equipment for unauthorized purposes, and pilferage of hardware and software.

Although the employer may have rules and provide training concerning desktop computing, the problem is one of compliance. The highly personalized nature of a desktop work station makes it very difficult to monitor computing activity in a non-intrusive way. While it is technically possible to monitor by connecting desktop equipment to networks, observing employees with closed-circuit television (CCTV) cameras, and providing closer overall personal supervision, these are not the accepted practices in a corporation that operates on trust.

Controls based on motivation would rely on the orientation, education, and training given to employees; the personal examples set for them; and, above all, an organizational culture which holds that when given a choice, people can be trusted to act in the best interests of the organization. The designers and implementers of the controls will come from the professional core. The corporate security manager will be a key player in designing the asset-protecting controls -- controls that, on the one hand, will be workable and effective, and, on the other hand, consistent with principles of trust and empowerment. The corporate security manager will help gain acceptance of the controls by exercising the skills of teaching and leading.

A Best Practices Approach

Corporate security in the evolving organization can take the initiative in a best practices approach that enables others in the organization to learn about what works well. Best practices are those things that are done with excellence, both in and out of the corporation. Following are three hypothetical examples.

Corporation A switched from in-house security officer services to services provided by an outside contractor. The corporate security manager played a central role in negotiating the contract and monitoring contractor performance. Over a period of time, the corporate security department acquired considerable knowledge about contract administration. Many lessons were learned about how to hire honest, emotionally stable, and drug-free security officers; how to organize security officer operations so that services did not get in the way of the corporation's business processes; and how to train, develop, and generally treat security officers so that in return the corporation obtained quality performance accompanied by low turnover. These best practices had value to other units in the

corporation that were making the switch to contractor services.

Corporation B did pioneer work in establishing a drug- and alcohol-free workplace for its employees in the safety-sensitive environment of petroleum exploration and production. Through trial and error, corporate security learned how to educate employees against alcohol and drugs; trained supervisors to spot the indicators of impairment; and used chemical testing as a tool for steering employees away from abuse and for bringing afflicted employees into contact with treatment professionals. Corporate security shared this competency with the corporation's most important partners -- the drilling contractors. A best practices approach transferred the positive elements of the antidrug program to the contractors; and it was in the corporation's best interests to do so because, after all, the contractors performed jobs having high criticality in terms of physical loss, personal safety, and damage to the ecology.

Corporation C observed that the corporate security department of a competitor regularly worked with the internal audit department to conduct investigative audits of vendors. The audit methodology of the competitor contained some innovative ideas for discerning patterns of collusion. Corporation C adopted and modified the methodology as a best practice.

These examples are in the nature of finding positives and putting them to work to the corporation's advantage. A best practices approach adds value and blends very well with control functions performed by a corporate security department.

Being a Contributor to Assets

It is important to remind ourselves that questions always arise about the value of providing protective services to assets that are static or in a state of decline. When the cost of protection increases or remains steady and at the same time the value of the asset falls off or remains unchanged, there is a natural tendency to want to reduce or eliminate the protection. This is an obvious fact, but it deserves mention because in the evolving organization corporate security needs to shift its focus to the enhancement of assets. The objective should be to move from simply being the watchdog of assets to being a contributor to assets. A best practices approach could be one facet of a larger effort to find and add value to the company's bottom line.

Finally, it seems appropriate to observe that the winds of change in the last half of the 20th century have produced problems for nations, companies, and people. Inevitably, the enterprise we call corporate security has been affected and has risen to meet the challenges. Even greater challenges lie ahead as business organizations continue to restructure, innovate, and take on new cultures. There is no reason to suppose that the first half of the next century will bring any lessening of change, and if corporate security is to evolve in harmony with the organization, it must change the ways of protecting assets.

John J. Fay, CPP

Sources

Frank, J., B. Shamir, and W. Briggs, Security-Related Behavior of PC Users in Organizations, Information and Management 21. (Elsevier Science Publishers, Amsterdam, 1991).

Green, G., Introduction to Security. (Butterworth-Heinemann, Boston, 1981).

Handy, C., The Age of Unreason. (Harvard Business School Press, Boston, 1989).

CORPORATE SECURITY: RELATIONSHIPS AND FUNCTIONS

Certain organizational principles are essential to effective security operations. First, along with the company audit staff, the security function constitutes top management's principal line of protection and assurance against fraud, theft, malfeasance, destruction of property, and exposure or destruction of information. The audit and security functions must report to a neutral position at a level that ensures independence of action.

Second, the security function must have clear lines of direct communication to the top levels of management. If a case arises that potentially involves middle or senior managers, reporting of the evidence and planning for action must be carried out at a management level that is safe from chance exposure.

A security function that reports below the executive vice-president level always faces a possible challenge to a course of action because of personal interests on the part of senior people in the chain of authority.

In a large company, organizational relationships must be consistent throughout all parts of the business. If a preferred organizational structure has been defined, that structure should be repeated in the various units. Variations in the way security is carried out are unacceptable, unless there is valid reason based on business requirements. Personal preferences or status considerations are not good reasons, and they can interfere with effectiveness.

The security function, then, must be so organized and placed as to allow effective implementation of policy, responsiveness to business requirements, and efficient reactions to local emergency and routine security needs.

Leadership

The security manager must set the tone for the entire security operation across the company. In a small- to medium-sized business, this may be self-evident. For the large, multinational corporation, a strong leadership role is absolutely essential and requires a significant effort on the part of the security manager.

Leadership in security assumes two elements: (1) to establish effective working relationships with key business management people, and (2) to ensure proper performance of essential security functions.

The security manager must set the pattern for security activities throughout the company. The established pattern is based primarily on the working relationship established with company executive management. In the end, the effectiveness of the security function is a product of the security manager's interpersonal skills, the reporting channels provided, and clear directives reflecting top-level business management goals. These are interrelated elements in which the security manager is clearly the key player.

Working Relationships

The security manager must understand the workings of the business and must continually re-evaluate security functions in light of changing business requirements. The business situation is never static, requiring the security manager to be constantly tuned in to changing competitive, financial, and strategic factors. For the technology-driven businesses of the information age, the entire security program should be subject to a complete review at least every 3 years.

This means that the policies and standards -- the framework for the security activity -- must be taken apart and reconsidered, line by line, in light of current business situations and requirements. If the policy statements were well written in the first place, all that may be required will be an updating with very few or no substantive changes.

An effective security function will be supported by good directives. The basic directive is, of course, policy. The policy must reflect business operating philosophies and current practices that can only be ascertained through interaction with upper-level decision makers. Involving senior management in developing and approving security policy is an important test of a security manager in creating support for the security program.

Core Functions

Although separate parts of the corporation may have unique requirements, the corporation as a whole will have a number of core needs.

Providing Guidance. The security manager provides guidance to the organization through the dissemination of policies, procedures, and standards. Policies set goals and provide broad direction; procedures provide specific instructions for carrying out policies, and standards set minimum expectations or the level of expected excellence. Standards address a wide area: for people, they can set minimums for education, training, skills, knowledge, and job-related physical attributes; for equipment, they can set minimums for size, speed, resistance, response, delay, and so forth; and for processes, they can set controls, checks, balances, and verifications. Standards can also incorporate rules set by safety dictates and regulatory and licensing rules.

Protecting Employees. This core function can be met by the use of security officers controlling entrance points, patrolling the premises, and providing escort services; personal protection services for senior executives at work, at home,

and during travel; advisory services for employees who travel in high-risk areas; and first-responder emergency services that provide CPR and first aid for employees who become ill or injured at work.

Managing Contingencies. The security manager plays a central role in the organization's methods for responding to serious incidents. A serious incident is typically an event that results or can result in death, very serious injuries, or widespread public condemnation of the organization. Incidents that fall into this category include major accidents, ecological damage, kidnapping, civil disorder, and violence in the workplace. Preparation for crises include developing plans, marshaling resources for plan execution, setting up a crisis management team, and conducting rehearsals.

Conducting Investigations. Criminal offenses committed against the corporation are investigated by the security department. Because the products of investigations, e.g., reports, witness statements, and physical evidence, are the foundation for prosecution and for obtaining restitution, they must be high quality in all respects. The implication here is that the security department must have the use of competent investigators, either from within or from contract sources.

James A. Schweitzer

Source Schweitzer, J.A., Computers, Business and Security. (Butterworth-Heinemann, 1987).

COUNSELING

An inherent function of supervision is to assist employees in solving personal problems that detract from their effectiveness in the workplace. Counseling can occur in almost any situation that brings the individual employee and the supervisor together for the purpose of helping the employee overcome problems.

Guidance should serve all employees and not be seen as a negative activity related only to employees with problems. Counseling given to good employees can make them even better employees. But when guidance is focused exclusively on workers who perform below the established standards, other employees may be reluctant to willingly participate in counseling for fear of being stigmatized.

A principal purpose of counseling is to help individuals learn to deal with personal problems. To be an effective counselor, the supervisor must be able to communicate on an interpersonal basis and possess patience, confidence, and good judgment. A facet of good judgment is to recognize that for an individual to deal with a personal problem there must first be a willingness to act decisively, and that one of the cardinal sins of counseling is to make decisions for the individual. An overly directive approach is apt to encourage dependence rather than self-reliance.

The opportunities for a supervisor to counsel are frequent and varied. Certainly one of the earliest opportunities is when an employee first arrives on the job. The new employee needs to become oriented geographically, meet co-workers, and learn the formal and unwritten rules of the organization. The supervisor is a main source of information, particularly with regard to showing the employee where and how he or she fits into the pattern of work activities, explaining job standards, and answering questions. A good orientation will often prevent small initial problems of adjustment from escalating to larger problems at a later time.

The direct supervisor, more than any other individual in the organization, is positioned to evaluate the subordinate's productivity, attitude, and potential. Knowing something about the subordinate both as a worker and a person is necessary if the supervisor is to assist the subordinate in meeting the organization's expectations and at the same time satisfy personal goals.

Counseling Methods

Two general methods of counseling are widely recognized: the directive and non-directive methods. A third method uses the two methods together and is called the co-analysis method.

Directive Counseling. This approach is supervisor-centered. The supervisor takes the initiative in the dialogue, with the supervisor choosing the subject. The directive approach is appropriate when the employee needs to understand requirements and to identify employee deficiencies that stand in the way of

meeting them. This approach can succeed only when the employee sincerely wants to face and solve personal problems. Although the supervisor may be very skilled in this approach, the critical element for success lies entirely within the employee.

Non-Directive Counseling. The employee is the central actor in non-directive counseling. The employee is encouraged to talk, to clarify personal thinking, and to discover a solution to problems through objective examination and honest articulation. The supervisor's role is to encourage the employee to take the initiative in discovering solutions, and moving positively and constructively to implement them. This approach can be helpful in removing emotional blocks and releasing the employee's motives for improvement.

Co-Analysis. This approach falls somewhere between the extremes of the directive and non-directive methods. It is intended to join the supervisor and the employee in a mutual effort intended to work out a program for removing the employee's problems. Co-analysis can only succeed when the employee accepts the supervisor as a partner and sincerely wants to change. Success will also be a function of how well the supervisor can bring the employee to a clearer understanding of the problems and to obtain agreement of the solution-oriented actions required of the employee.

Conducting a Counseling Session

A counseling session cannot be effective without preparation. All pertinent information concerning the employee should be gathered and studied by the supervisor. Details that may be significant to the counseling process should be committed to memory so that the flow of the session will not be interrupted by referring to written materials. The presence of files or records and the taking of notes during the session can detract from a productive outcome.

The place of counseling should be relatively free from distractions and out of general view. An employee being counseled does not want to feel conspicuous, and the absence of privacy will inhibit the employee's willingness to open up. Seating, lighting, room temperature, and the physical setting should be comfortable for both the employee and the supervisor. Because the supervisor will need the employee's undivided attention, the employee's chair should face toward the supervisor and away from background distractions such as a window or open door.

The starting point will be critical. In the first few minutes the supervisor will set the tone of the discussions and attempt to open a two-way dialogue. This is often called establishing rapport, a subtle and important activity that can be difficult. The idea is to help the employee open up by getting a conversation going, usually about a topic of personal interest such as hobbies, achievements, or current events.

Encouraging the employee to talk and participate actively may cause the employee to feel constructively involved by describing the problem and playing a part in solving it. In the early part of the meeting, the supervisor should look for information that will define the dimensions of the problem. By asking questions that require more than yes or no answers, the supervisor can gain insights to the employee's motivations, attitudes, and dislikes. The responses may clarify the problem for the supervisor and provide clues to obtaining the employee's cooperation in taking corrective actions.

A counseling session should end on a positive note. The employee should walk away with a sense that something constructive has occurred. Even more importantly, the employee should leave with a commitment to take actions that were agreed upon in the meeting and the understanding that the supervisor will be expecting to see the evidence of them. Even if the employee is only helped to perceive the actual nature of the problem, this in itself is progress.

The supervisor will not always play a part in the problem-solving process. A supervisor's competency in recommending solutions will not usually extend to problems rooted in drug and alcohol abuse, marital and family stress, financial difficulties, and mental disorders. The role of the supervisor in these situations is to refer the employee to a specialized resource, such as an employee assistance program.

When an employee is referred to another resource, the supervisor should follow up to be sure the problem is being addressed. Specialized assistance should be regarded as a helping hand, not as a substitute for supervision. Responsibility to correct the employee's unacceptable performance remains in the venue of the supervisor even when third-party specialists provide the diagnosis and treatment.

A record should be made of every counseling session. The record should document the major discussion points, actions and deadlines agreed upon, and commitments of both the employee and supervisor. In some cases, the supervisor may want to give the employee a copy of the record for use as a reference in meeting the commitments.

John J. Fay, CPP

Sources

Fay, J.J., Approaches to Criminal Justice Training, 2nd Edition. (University of Georgia Press, Athens, GA, 1988).

Jucius, M.J., Personnel Management. (Richard D. Irwin, Inc., Homewood, IL, 1955).

COUNTERFEITING

Counterfeiting of currency is one of the oldest crimes in history. It was considered treasonous and punishable by death in some countries in the past. During the Civil War of the United States, approximately one-third of the existing currency was counterfeit. The U.S. Secret Service was formed in 1865 to combat this crime. Although not on the scale of the Civil War period, counterfeiting is still a major concern to the Secret Service and to other law enforcement agencies in this country and throughout the world. U.S. currency is widely circulated and accepted around the world and is therefore favored by counterfeiters.

The Security Features of U.S. Currency

Along with the paper used for making currency, the design incorporates several security features: the border, portrait, red and blue embedded fibers, placement of seals and serial numbers, and intaglio printing from meticulously engraved plates. The Treasury Department is now incorporating two new security features. First is a polyester strip or security thread embedded in the paper to the left of the federal reserve seal. The strip is printed with the letters USA and the note's value, e.g., USA 50 or USA 100. This printing is repeated along the strip in an up-and-down vertical pattern. Visible when held to a light, the strip cannot be reproduced in the reflected light of copy machines.

The second feature is repeated microprinting of the words "The United States of America" along the sides of the portrait. The letters are too small to be read without a magnifier or for distinct copier reproduction. To the naked eye, the printing appears like another line.

These two new features should deter opportunistic criminals from using state-of-the-art copying machines to generate spending money on an as-needed basis. More dedicated and experienced counterfeiters will be frustrated by the difficult, costly, and time-consuming task of producing notes that incorporate representations of the strip and the microprinting. These features are first appearing in $50 and $100 federal reserve notes, series 1990. Other denominations are gradually being phased in, with the possible exception of the $1 denomination.

Detecting Counterfeit Currency

Counterfeiters do not have the same sophisticated equipment and paper stock that are available to the Bureau of Engraving and Printing. Counterfeiters normally use offset or photomechanical printing equipment and high quality bond paper, and invariably the final product is an inferior bill. They will often attempt to create red and blue fibers by printing colored lines on the paper.

The most effective method of detecting a counterfeit bill is to compare it with a genuine bill of the same denomination and series. The idea is to look for differences, not similarities, and pay attention to the quality of printing and to the paper's characteristics. A genuine bill will have blue and red hair-like fibers embedded in the paper and a pattern of squares in the portrait background. On counterfeits, the blue and red fibers will be missing and some of the portrait squares may be filled in. The delicate lines in the portrait itself may be broken or missing. The portrait usually appears flat or lifeless, the background is usually too dark, and both tend to merge with each other. For example, the hairlines will not stand out and appear life-like as is the case with a genuine bill. Similarly, the portrait in a genuine bill appears life-like and stands out distinctly from the fine screen-like background.

On the federal reserve and treasury seals of the counterfeit notes, the saw-tooth points on the circumference are usually uneven, blunt, and broken off. On the genuine note, the saw-tooth points are even, clear, and sharp. Serial numbers of the counterfeit may be in the wrong color or shade and may not be properly aligned or spaced. In the genuine bill, they are evenly spaced, aligned and have a distinct style. The border of the counterfeit may have fine crisscross lines that are not clear or distinct. The genuine has clear, distinct, and unbroken fine lines. The paper of the counterfeit may contain a watermark, and red and blue lines may be printed on the paper to simulate the distinctive fibers of a genuine bill.

Other Currency Violations

Three other types of violations deserve discussion. These involve the use of (1) copy machines, (2) raised notes, and (3) flash notes. Advanced technology in the copy machine business has made it easy to photocopy currency. High quality color copiers are producing a better counterfeit product. The security strip and microprinting features described earlier are designed to counter this new counterfeiting method.

A raised note is a low-denomination bill that has been altered by attaching to it the corners of a high-denomination genuine bill. The raised note will have all of the distinguishing features of a genuine bill except that the numbers in the corners do not match the other features on the bill. Thus, what appears at first glance to be a $20 bill may have a portrait of George Washington and say "one dollar" on both front and back. These bills can be deceiving at first glance but are easily identified when given just a little extra examination.

Flash notes are novelty or advertising items that are confusingly similar to genuine currency and are thus capable of being passed as genuine currency. Although federal law addresses this subject, the law is often violated unintentionally. Guidance is available from the local Secret Service office.

Countermeasures

A security manager of a retail organization or any organization that regularly receives currency from the public in its normal business processes can set up procedures for employees to follow when a suspect bill has been passed. The procedures can include:

•Do not return the bill to the passer.

•Note the passer's description, the description of any companion, and the license number of any vehicles used.

•Delay the passer while the police or the Secret Service are being called. Keep in mind that the passer can be someone knowingly passing a counterfeit bill or may be an innocent "holder in due course" of the note. If the passer notices the close examination of the questioned bill, the passer's resultant demeanor may very well reflect intent.

•If unsure as to the genuineness of the bill, call the local Secret Service office and obtain guidance over the phone as to checks that can be made.

•Place initials and the date on the edge of a bill retained as suspect counterfeit currency. This is for chain of evidence purposes in case of judicial action.

•Handle the bill as little as possible to preserve fingerprints. Place it in an envelope or other protective cover and surrender it only to the police or the Secret Service.

Additional Information

Genuine currency may sometimes be questioned because of unusual appearance. Federal reserve notes with green Treasury Seal and serial numbers are the only bills printed today. United States notes ($2, $5, and $100 denominations; red Treasury Seal and serial numbers) and Silver Certificates ($1, $5, and $10 denominations; blue Treasury Seal and serial numbers) are no longer printed but may occasionally appear in circulation. Older bills such as the 1934 series have some features obviously different from current currency. The green color of bills can change to an orange color under some circumstances, such as when exposed to bleach.

J. Branch Walton

Sources

Your Money Matters. (U.S. Secret Service, Washington, DC, 1992).

Counterfeiting and Forgery. (U.S. Secret Service, Washington, DC, 1992).

COURTS: PROSECUTION IN STATE COURTS

A chief prosecutor is the attorney who advocates for the public in felony cases, as well as in a variety of other cases. A prosecutor's responsibilities are limited geographically. A prosecutorial district follows county lines and typically consists of a single county but may include two or more.

In 1990 approximately half of these officials had the title of either district attorney or county attorney. A chief prosecutor may have a staff of "assistant prosecutors," attorneys who do much of the actual case work.

The prosecutor usually does not know of a felony matter until a law enforcement agency makes an arrest. Because 95% of prosecutors receive felony cases from three or more arresting agencies, an opportunity exists for considerable variation in the time between arrest and notification of the prosecutor's office. About 73% of law enforcement agencies in the United States are state or local police departments and 18% are county sheriff's departments; the remainder are special agencies such as transit police or campus police.

Some prosecutors are notified only after the arresting agency has filed papers in a special or "lower" court. This court conducts necessary pre-trial events, such as informing the accused person of the charges, setting bail, and assigning defense counsel.

When a staff attorney handles all phases of a criminal case, the processing is known as "vertical" case assignment. A career-criminal unit is an example of a vertical case assignment in which certain assistant prosecutors handle repeat offenders from the targeting stage onward. "Horizontal" assignment means that different assistants specialize in different phases -- drafting complaints, conducting trials, or doing appellate work.

Indigent Defendants

The U.S. Constitution guarantees rights to citizens as they relate to the federal government and federal criminal prosecutions. Such rights are not automatically applicable to state governments and state criminal prosecutions. In lawsuits concerning specific rights, the U.S. Supreme Court decides the applicability of such rights to the states.

The Sixth Amendment to the U.S. Constitution establishes the right of a criminal defendant to have assistance of counsel for his or her defense. The Supreme Court has ruled that counsel must be available to any defendant who is at risk of a federal or state sentence of incarceration. This right extends to indigent defendants unable to pay a lawyer. If an indigent defendant who faces a penalty of incarceration wants a lawyer, the state must either provide a lawyer or seek a lesser penalty.

Filing

After a document charging a person with a crime is submitted to the felony court, an event known as a case "filing," the court takes control of the case. Most felony cases begin with the filing of an indictment issued by a grand jury. In most other felony cases, the charging document is an "information" filed by the prosecutor. Either type of document states who the accused person is and what illegal acts were committed. To proceed on the basis of an information rather than an indictment, the prosecutor normally must present the case in a preliminary hearing, which in some places occurs in a lower court. In a preliminary hearing, the judge reviews the facts and circumstances of the case to determine whether there are reasonable grounds ("probable cause") to believe the accused person committed the crime for which he or she is being charged. The accused person may waive any right to have the matter reviewed by grand jury. Such waivers often occur, particularly when the accused decides to plead guilty early in the case.

The Fifth Amendment to the Constitution establishes that a citizen accused of a felony has the right to have a grand jury, rather than the prosecutor, decide whether he or she shall be prosecuted. Except in cases that could involve a death sentence, the accused may waive this right. The grand jury right does not apply to prosecutions in state courts. About half of the states, however, have laws allowing or requiring the use of grand juries in felony cases.

Where grand juries are used, an indictment takes precedence over the prosecutor's view of whether probable cause exists in a case. The court rather than the prosecutor convenes grand juries. In districts with grand juries, however, judges of a

lower court or a felony court often screen cases for probable cause, providing for greater grand jury efficiency.

Criminal History Data

When a person is arrested or brought before a court on a criminal charge, usually a government agency keeps a permanent official record of the event. These records enable prosecutors to find out about a person's "criminal history." That knowledge can help prosecutors make proper decisions.

Plea Negotiation

In a vast majority of felony convictions, the defendant pleads guilty rather than requests a trial. The high percentage of guilty pleas is a key factor in minimizing case backlogs. Guilty pleas often result from negotiations: the defendant agrees to plead guilty to a lesser charge or to a charge for which the prosecutor recommends a reduced sentence. The court may impose deadlines on negotiations when responding to requests for extensions of time or continuances. Requests for more time to negotiate a plea agreement are sometimes made on the day of trial, even when witnesses, juries, and court personnel have already assembled.

Speedy Trial

The Sixth Amendment of the U.S. Constitution guarantees to the accused in a criminal trial, whether federal or state, the right to a speedy trial. In recent years legislatures and courts have established limits on the time following an arrest that a prosecutor has to bring the case to trial. Such speedy trial requirements often apply when a defendant is held in custody, but do not apply when the defendant has been granted pre-trial release.

Jury Trial

The Sixth Amendment to the U.S. Constitution gives state and federal felony defendants the right to trial by jury. This right may be waived in favor of trial by judge. An estimated 4% of all felony convictions are the result of a judge trial.

In some jurisdictions the prosecutor also has the right to have a case tried by a jury. In such jurisdictions, the jury may be used even if the defendant prefers a judge trial, although how the proceedings are carried out is decided by the trial judge. The prosecutor may exercise this right to a jury trial for many reasons, including belief that

• A jury is more likely than a particular judge to convict.

• A jury is likely to impose or recommend a desired sentence.

• A jury trial will attract more public attention to a defendant's heinous conduct.

Policies and Practices after Trial

A convicted defendant remains under the court's jurisdiction until sentencing. Between conviction and sentencing, information is often gathered to enable the judge to impose an appropriate sentence. In most districts the judge requests a pre-sentence report containing information about the defendant, family and employment circumstances, mental or physical health problems, and history of drug or alcohol abuse. This information may have an important bearing on the choice between a sentence of confinement and a sentence of probation.

A convicted defendant may appeal to a higher court, asking it to review any defect in the proceedings of the original trial. Only certain major issues, such as the sentence or what trial evidence was admitted or excluded, will serve as a basis for the appeals court accepting the appeal. Under some circumstances the prosecutor may also appeal. The special conditions for a prosecutorial appeal usually do not include the prosecutor's view of the determination of guilt in a particular case.

An appeal involves two main activities: preparing the written document (brief) that explains both the case and the defects complained of, and presenting this material verbally to the appeals judges (oral argument).

Department of Justice

Source Special Report. (Bureau of Justice Statistics, Washington, DC, 1992).

CRIME: KEY CONCEPTS

Corpus Delicti

The term corpus delicti means "body of the crime." It is often used erroneously to describe the corpse of the victim in a homicide case. Actually, the term relates to the essence of an offense and thus implies that every offense must have a corpus delicti.

In proving an accused's guilt of a specific crime, the prosecution establishes three general facts:

• That an injury or loss particular to the crime involved has taken place.

• That the injury or loss was brought about by somebody's criminality, meaning that the injury or loss resulted from a criminal act as opposed to an accident or other cause.

• That the accused, possessing the requisite state of mind (i.e., intent), was the person who caused the injury or loss.

The first two facts described previously constitute the corpus delicti. The third fact simply establishes the identity of the offender.   For example, the corpus delicti in a larceny would be (l) the loss of property (2) by an unlawful taking. In an arson offense, it would be (1) a burned house (2) that was deliberately set on fire.

Criminal Intent

Criminal intent is a clearly formulated state of mind to do an act that the law specifically prohibits, without regard to the motive that prompts the act, and whether or not the offender knows that what he or she is doing is in violation of the law.

It is generally regarded as falling into two categories: general criminal intent and specific criminal intent.   General criminal intent is an essential element in all crimes. It means that when the offender acted, or failed to act, contrary to the law, he or she did so voluntarily with determination or foresight of the consequences. For example, general criminal intent is shown in the offense of assault and battery when the offender voluntarily applies unlawful force to another with an awareness of its result.   In larceny, general criminal intent (often called larcenous intent) is shown by an intent to knowingly take and carry away the goods of another without any claim or pretense of right, with intent wholly to deprive the owner of them or to convert them to personal use.

Specific criminal intent requires a particular mental state in addition to that of general criminal intent. The laws relating to certain crimes may describe an additional, specific mental purpose. For example, the crime of murder has a general criminal intent in that the offender voluntarily applies unlawful force with an awareness of its result. In addition, the crime of murder in a particular jurisdiction may require a showing that the offender acted with premeditation to commit murder.

The terms *overt act* and *malice* are often associated with criminal intent. An overt act is an outward or manifest act from which criminality may be inferred; for example, an act done to carry out a criminal intention. In the crime of conspiracy, the overt act is an essential element of proof.

Malice is a mental state accompanying a criminal act that is performed willfully, intentionally, and without legal justification. The term malice aforethought is the state of mind or attitude with which an act is carried out, i.e., the design, resolve, or determination with which a person acts to achieve a certain result. In the death of another, it means a knowledge of circumstances that according to common experience would indicate a clear and strong likelihood that death will follow the contemplated act. Malice aforethought is usually coupled with an absence of justification for the act.

Motive and intent are separate concepts in criminal law. Motive is the desire or inducement that tempts or prompts a person to do a criminal act. Intent is a person's resolve or purpose to commit the act. Motive is the reason that leads the mind to desire a certain result. Intent is the determination to achieve the result.

Motive is an important investigative consideration, but is not an essential element of a crime. Intent must be established for a crime to exist. A good motive (as might be represented in a mercy killing) does not keep an act from being a crime, and an evil motive will not necessarily make an act a crime. Furthermore, an accused would not be acquitted simply because a motive could not be discovered.

The basic urge that led the offender's mind to want the result of the forbidden act is immaterial as to guilt. Proof of motive, however, may be relevant and admissible on behalf of either side at trial. Motive can be especially pertinent where the evidence in a case is largely circumstantial. In some statutes, proof of motive may be required.

Federal Offenses

There can be no federal crime unless Congress first makes an act a criminal offense by the passage of a statute, affixes punishment to it, and declares what court will have jurisdiction. This means that all federal crimes are statutory. Although many of the statutes are based on common law, every federal statute is an express enactment of Congress. Nearly all crimes are defined in Title 18 of the U.S.Code.

Generally speaking, federal crimes fall into three large areas: crimes affecting interstate commerce, crimes committed in places beyond the jurisdiction of any state, and crimes that interfere with the activities of the federal government.

Crimes affecting interstate commerce are described in a variety of acts, e.g., the Mann Act, the Dyer Act, the Lindbergh Act, the Fugitive Felon Act, etc. They cover a wide variety of offenses over which Congress has plenary control.

Crimes committed in places beyond the jurisdiction of any state might include, for example, murder on an American ship on the high seas or on a federal enclave such as a military reservation ceded to the United States by a state. It should be noted that when an offense, not covered by a federal statute, is committed on a federal enclave, the case can be tried in a federal court under the laws of the state where the enclave is located. The offense of murder, for example, is not defined in a federal statute. If murder occurs on a military reservation in Texas, the federal government can prosecute the case using the Texas statute covering murder. This procedure is authorized by the Assimilative Crimes Act.

Crimes that interfere with the activities of the federal government include fraudulent use of the mails, robbery of a federal bank, violation of income tax laws, espionage, and many similar offenses. Federal courts have no jurisdiction over crimes against the states, and vice versa. It can happen, however, that an offense will violate both a state law and a federal law, e.g., robbery of a federally insured state bank. In such a case, both the federal and state court will have jurisdiction.

Federal death penalty laws include these violations: (1) espionage by a member of the Armed Forces in which information relating to nuclear weaponry, military spacecraft or satellites, early warning systems, war plans, communications intelligence or cryptographic information, or any other major weapons or defense strategy is communicated to a foreign government; (2) death resulting from aircraft hijacking; (3) murder while a member of the Armed Forces; (4) destruction of aircraft, motor vehicles, or related facilities resulting in death; (5) retaliatory murder of a member of the immediate family of a law enforcement official; (6) murder of a member of Congress, an important executive official, or a Supreme Court justice; (7) espionage; (8) destruction of government property resulting in death; (9) first degree murder; (10) mailing of injurious articles with the intent to kill or resulting in death; (11) assassination or kidnapping resulting in the death of the President or Vice President; (12) willful wrecking of a train resulting in death; (13) murder or kidnapping related to robbery of a bank; and (14) treason.

Parties to Crime

Persons culpably concerned in the commission of a crime, whether they directly commit the act constituting the offense, or facilitate, solicit, encourage, aid or attempt to aid, or abet its commission are called the parties to the crime. In some jurisdictions, the concept is extended to include persons who assist one who has committed a crime to avoid arrest, trial, conviction, or punishment.

The parties to a felony crime fall into four categories: (1) principals in the first degree, (2) principals in the second degree, (3) accessories before the fact, and (4) accessories after the fact.

Generally, a principal in the first degree is the actual offender who commits the act. If the offender uses an agent to commit the act, the offender is still a principal in the first degree. There may be more than one principal in the first degree for the same offense.

A principal in the second degree is one who, with knowledge of what is afoot, aids and abets the principal in the first degree at the very time the felony is being committed by rendering aid, assistance, or encouragement. A principal in the second degree is typically at the crime scene, nearby, or situated in such a way as to render assistance. Under the concept of "constructive presence," a principal in the second degree could be a considerable distance removed from the crime while it is being committed. An example might be a lookout who monitors police radio communications at a remote location and calls burglar accomplices at the crime scene to alert them of police patrol movements.

An accessory before the fact is a person who, before the time a crime is committed, knows of the particular offense contemplated, assents to or approves of it, and expresses a view of it in a form that operates to encourage the principal to perform the deed. There is a close resemblance between an accessory before the fact and a principal in the second degree. The difference relates to where the accessory was and the nature of the assistance rendered at the time the crime was committed. If a person advises, encourages, and gives aid prior to the act, but is not present at the act and not giving aid at the time of the act, the person would be regarded as an accessory before the fact.

An accessory after the fact is a person who, knowing that another has committed a felony, subsequently aids the felon to escape in any way or prevents arrest and prosecution. The person may help the felon elude justice by concealing, sheltering, or comforting the felon while a fugitive, or by supplying the means of escape or by destroying evidence. An accessory after the fact must have an intention to assist the felon and must actually do so. Mere knowledge of the felon's offense and a failure to report it does not make a person an accessory after the fact.

Preliminary Offenses

There are three crimes that are preparatory in nature and serve as part of a larger purpose. Each of them is a means of reaching a criminal end. These so-called preliminary crimes are: solicitation, attempt, and conspiracy.

Solicitation consists of the offender's oral or written efforts to activate another person to commit a criminal offense. The essence of the crime is to incite by counsel, enticement, or inducement. The offense of solicitation is complete if the offender merely urges another to violate the law and otherwise does nothing himself.

Attempt has two elements. First, there must be a specific intent to commit a particular offense, and second, there must be a direct ineffectual overt act toward its commission. There must be some act moving directly toward the act. Mere preparation, such as obtaining tools or weapons, may be insufficient to establish the crime, especially when made at a distance in time or place.

Conspiracy is the combination of two or more persons working in some concerted action to accomplish some criminal or unlawful purpose, or to accomplish some purpose in a criminal or unlawful manner. If there is a common understanding among the participants to achieve a certain purpose or to act in a certain way, a conspiracy exists without regard to whether there is any formal or written statement of purpose, or even though there is no actual speaking of words. There may be merely a tacit understanding without any express agreement.

John J. Fay, CPP

Source

Fay, J.J., Butterworths Security Dictionary. (Butterworth-Heinemann, Boston 1987).

CRIME PREVENTION: A COMMUNITY APPROACH

A community approach to crime prevention starts with the notion that law enforcement agencies have a central, but not necessarily dominant, role in protecting citizens from crime. Traditional law enforcement methods, although response-oriented, do in fact cause criminals to perceive personal risk and thus play an important role in preventing crime; but the larger role belongs to the citizens themselves.

Citizens typically are limited in the actions they are able to take to thwart crime because of their inability to effectively exercise full control over their environments. (The environments referred to here are those of the victim, not of the criminal.) This does not mean that a citizen is powerless because, even in the most limited sense, a potential victim can reduce criminal motivation by minimizing the opportunity of the criminal to succeed. Empirically, we observe that the absence of opportunity results in less crime, and theoretically we hope that the absence of opportunity will lessen the chances that an

otherwise honest person will develop criminal habits.

We observe also that crime prevention activities in some communities have been both a cause and an effect of efforts to overcome severe crime problems, and that a successful outcome seems to hinge on the harmonious involvement of many skills and interest groups. Successful outcomes that were comprehensive and lasting appeared in many cases to result from a willingness to innovate and experiment. The doctrine of crime prevention, if such can be said of this emerging quasi-science, is interdisciplinary in nature, amenable to an ongoing process of discovery and change, and useful to the extent that it is applied and successes shared. Strategies and tactics in successful programs often were not carved in stone. What worked in one situation at one point in time did not always work later in other situations.

Community Strategies

A fundamental strategy of community-centered crime prevention is to simultaneously promote public awareness of crime problems and to inform citizens of their options and the resources available to them. The strategy naturally embraces a two-pronged approach. First, to broadly mobilize the public against crime in general, and second, to develop specific courses of action for dealing with crime that has been directed at specific neighborhoods, businesses, and organizations.

The principal actions often include the provision of teaching and counseling services, especially those that give particular attention to key groups that hold leadership positions in the community. This approach naturally leads to group projects that harness collective efforts. One of the more unique and promising projects of a group nature has occurred in some municipalities where city officials, such as planners and code administrators, have joined with architects and builders to design into new construction projects physical security features that encourage active citizen involvement in their neighborhoods and which at the same time discourage deviant behavior.

Crime Prevention Through Environmental Design, or CPTED, is a name often assigned to group projects like these. A central tenet of

CPTED is the concept of informal social control, which holds that crime in a small community or neighborhood can be reduced through:

•Intensified use by residents of streets, parks, and land around the structures in which they live.

•Increased watchfulness of residents for intruders who manifest unacceptable behavior.

•An increased tendency of people to look out for the property and well-being of their neighbors, and to interact with law enforcement.

•An enhanced ability to discriminate between outsiders and residents, and an ability to communicate by actions that deviant behavior will not be allowed.

•A strong sense of shared interests in improving and maintaining the quality of life in the physical environment and social climate of the area.

An example of a strategy founded on informal social control is the Neighborhood Watch program. This program and others like it encourage citizens to watch for crime and report observations to the police. The usual tactics include:

•Making open areas easily observable and increasing human activity in them.

•Establishing workable relationships between residents, businesses, and police for the common purpose of eradicating crime.

•Promoting a neighborhood identity, developing social cohesion, and attracting new financial investments.

•Conducting no-cost security surveys to residents and businesses; and providing guidance for implementing survey recommendations.

•Holding public meetings, creating special interest groups concerned with reducing particular crimes, and setting up community-operated response units such as crisis hot line, rape crisis center, rumor control, rap line, child abuse center, and block parent groups.

•Seeking to improve the quality of police patrol operations by creating a dialogue between the police and community leaders.

•Encouraging residents to report crimes and criminals.

A Model Community-Centered Program

Every program created from a model will have unique characteristics that require it to be different in some respects from the model it emulates. The reader will find in the following model a range of flexibility sufficient to meet the particular needs of programs operating within a neighborhood, a cluster of neighborhoods, or a community.

Obtain and Analyze Data Relating to the Neighborhood. Types of data worthy of analysis include crime and loss patterns, police patrol deployments, census tracts, terrain and topography descriptions, socioeconomic and demographic patterns, and political infrastructures. The purpose of the analysis is to identify major crime locations, trends, sources of crime, cultural strengths, and weaknesses of residents vis-a-vis the presence of crime; evaluate police effectiveness and efficiency; define perceptions by the police and of the police; identify leaders and leadership groups in the community; identify resources that exist and that need to be acquired; and assess the divisiveness and/or cohesiveness of the neighborhood.

Analysis of the obtained data is directed at determining what crimes are likely to impact particular targets, the criminals likely to commit the crimes, how the crimes are likely to occur, and when they are likely to occur. The process of analysis typically includes the collection and processing of data related to crime rate by opportunity; the varieties and preferences of attack methods; the preferred times of attacks by day, week, month, and other time variables; the characteristics of suspects; the targets preferred by criminals; and losses by type and value.

A consideration at this point is to look forward in time to when an accounting will be made of the program's effectiveness. The administrators of the program could identify a comparable neighborhood not planned to be covered under the program and use the comparable neighborhood as a control area or baseline against which success or failure can be measured.

Establish Goals and Objectives. A program's goals and objectives will vary according to the interests it serves. A community-centered program can operate at one or a combination of three levels. At the client or individual level, the overall goal is to design crime risk management systems that meet the needs of homes, businesses, institutions, and other entities that are owned or managed by one or a few individuals.

At the multiple-client level, the goal is to design crime risk management projects through which many citizens in neighborhoods, shopping centers, industrial areas, and similar localities can collectively work together to improve security. At the public-policy level, the goal is to design crime risk management activities that units of government can carry out to improve security within a large jurisdiction and across jurisdictional lines. The program's objectives will reflect tangible, measurable, and realizable outcomes that fall within the overall goal. The objectives are the milestones for progress and the indicators for efficiency and effectiveness.

Establish Criteria for Participation in the Program. What percentage of the neighborhood's population should be involved? What residents should be invited to perform organizing roles? What should those roles be? What kinds of projects are appropriate and likely to succeed, especially as first ventures? What kind of resistance can be expected? How can resistance be turned to advantage? These are questions to be answered at this stage in the development of the program.

Approach Neighborhood Leaders. Those who have been identified as having significant influence should be approached first. The local leaders should be invited to participate in the development of strategy and to act as a sounding board for program effectiveness. The program must be perceived as a neighborhood effort, with neighborhood involvement and direction.

Educate Residents through a Wide Variety of Programs. Work through the neighborhood leaders and the groups they lead. Generate interest, support, and an awareness of the program. The basic goal is to build a foundation for citizens and police to work together. This implies that police officials, from top on down, also need to be educated concerning program objectives.

Provide Feedback to Residents and Police. The residents need to know how the program is working (e.g., arrests made, convictions obtained, property recovered, and victims assisted) and the police need to know how the residents regard the work they are performing (e.g., timeliness of responses, courtesy, and visibility).

Formulate Crime-Specific Tactics Based on Accumulating Experiences. Ongoing analyses of crime data in the neighborhood will reveal times, places, and methods of criminal attack. Preventive and response tactics can be inferred from the analyses.

Implement Crime-Specific Tactics as They Are Developed. Existing tactics will call for modification, new tactics will emerge, and combinations of tactics can be attempted. Whatever tactics are selected, they should be applied comprehensively so that criminals will simply not move to another location and carry on as before.

Assess Performance and Evaluate the Program. Periodically look objectively at the successes and failings of the program's organizers, the residents, and the police. The purpose is not to pass final judgment but to determine what modifications are necessary to improve operation of the program. This means identifying weak and strong points of program operations and deriving suggestions for changes. Periodic assessments will focus on efficiency indicators as opposed to effectiveness indicators, which are measured in an overall program evaluation.

At a pre-established point in time (e.g., 2 years after start-up), an overall evaluation will examine the impact of the program on reducing crime. The data obtained in the first and second stages of the model, such as crime rates and objectives, can serve as baselines for measurement.

The impact of a crime prevention program can be evaluated by measuring the degree of progress made in meeting specific objectives set for the program and progress toward the general goal of crime reduction. This involves comparing initial program assumptions against assumptions derived from the realities of program operations. An overall evaluation can suggest new approaches, techniques, and human and physical resources.

John J. Fay, CPP

Sources

Jeffrey, C.R., Crime Prevention Through Environmental Design. (Sage Publications, Beverly Hills, CA, 1977).

Understanding Crime Prevention. (Butterworth-Heinemann, Boston, 1986).

CRIME PREVENTION THROUGH ENVIRONMENTAL DESIGN (CPTED): DEFENSIBLE AND OFFENSIBLE SPACE

Defensible Space

Oscar Newman coined the expression "defensible space" as a surrogate term for a range of mechanisms that combine to bring the environment under the control of its residents. Among these mechanisms were real and symbolic barriers, strongly defined areas of influence, and improved opportunities for surveillance.

Newman suggested that defensible design features could return to residents the productive use of public areas in housing environments. Hallways, lobbies, grounds, and surrounding streets have usually been considered beyond the control of building inhabitants.

Defensible space design concepts for urban dwellers led law enforcement to include crime prevention in its arsenal of crime fighting strategies. The theory of defensible space came from a major research effort known as Crime Prevention Through Environmental Design, or CPTED. The emphasis of the effort was to return control of the built environment to law-abiding users.

Early on in the CPTED movement, crime prevention practitioners learned that implementation of the concepts could not be easily realized. Although persons familiar with CPTED were in general agreement that CPTED could be a workable enterprise, the persons most directly affected by its implementation were seldom in agreement. Consensus was difficult, if not impossible, to achieve among the residents, property owners and managers, neighborhood and community leaders, and businesspeople in areas selected for application of CPTED concepts.

Money was a major impediment to bringing the concepts into operation. The funds needed to change the physical features of the environment proved to be enormous and elusive. Disruption of the accepted and normal routines of human activity was also an obstacle. Although people might agree that the proposed changes would be positive, they were not willing to tolerate the disruption necessary to effect the change. As a result, CPTED-based design strategies have not been successfully implemented in most low-income urban public housing areas and crime in these environments continues to escalate with no hope of positive change.

CPTED Concepts

The relative lack of success at implementing CPTED strategies does not, however, denigrate the underlying concepts and the importance of the purposes they serve. In neighborhoods where the strategies have been attempted (usually through private funding), they have been found to be effective in:

•Spotting criminals; identifying persons or strangers who do not belong in the specific setting.

•Spotting unusual or unacceptable behavior.

•Providing protective monitoring of children, the elderly, and the defenseless.

•Making timely reports of problems to the police.

•Improving the neighborhood's ability to resist crime by the use of standard target-hardening techniques.

Success, however, depends in large part on the residents themselves. They must have a sense of responsibility and control over the residential environment; they must have reliable access to effective methods of intervention; they must have a strong commitment to and personal involvement in protecting the environment from crime; and they must be able to overcome their natural fears of predatory criminals and the reprisals that sometimes follow police intervention.

The fundamental CPTED hypothesis is that four elements of physical design, operating either individually or in concert, can contribute to the creation of a secure environment.

Territorial Definition. The first element is the territorial definition of the physical areas in a residential environment that fall under the influence of the inhabitants. This definition is made by subdividing the environment into zones within which residents can easily adopt proprietary attitudes. Research has shown that residents tend to take charge of, and assume security and safety responsibilities for, public space to the extent that they feel empowered to do so.

Territorial behavior is evidenced when a person or group personalizes or marks a particular place and communicates to outsiders a sense of ownership that will not be surrendered or easily breached. A defensive response by the person or group is likely to occur when the territorial boundary is violated.

A range of territories makes up a person's territorial network. These include public, secondary, and private territories. The longer a person resides in a territory, the more psychologically comfortable and familiar he or she becomes with it. For example, public territories, such as bus seats or city sidewalks, are the least personalized. Secondary territories, such as neighborhoods, which are also characterized by shared ownership among members of a group or culture, are more familiar and personalized. Primary territories, such as homes and apartments, are the most personalized.

Newman envisioned that defensible space would evolve in a social and spatial hierarchy from private to semiprivate to semipublic to public space. The latent sense of territoriality naturally present in the human psyche would impel residents to survey and clearly articulate the boundaries of their private territories, and to gradually spread their control and influence over those public territories they perceived to be defensible and worth defending. Territorial behavior would be supported and enhanced by architectural schemes developed by enlightened planners and designers.

Surveillance. The second element is the positioning of windows in a manner that allows residents to survey the public space adjacent to and surrounding their individual residences. An adjunct to this element is the elimination of blind spots that would impede observation of criminal activity.

The rationale is to capitalize on the natural fear that criminals have about being caught in the act or arrested later on the basis of a positive identification. Since most criminals look for the easy opportunities, they will be dissuaded from committing crimes in neighborhoods where they are likely to be observed and possibly arrested. An atmosphere of mutual concern in a neighborhood is presumed to have a discouraging effect on criminal operations.

The key here is not the windows, but the willingness of the residents to use the windows for watching and to report suspicious activities. Even the best positioned windows will do no good if not used or if there is nothing to see, but most importantly for its success, this element of design depends on the courage and determination of residents to report what they observe in order to effect the arrests of criminals and to serve as witnesses to effect legal sanctions. There is no value in surveillance if the watchers are apathetic or afraid to act.

Building Forms. The third element is adaptation of structural forms to establish an image of security. The idea is to eliminate any appearances that would suggest vulnerability of the inhabitants, and to promote deterrence by presenting appearances of unity and commitment against criminal activities.

Poor building definition can create spaces that are not conducive to effective monitoring or intervention. Such spaces may be ideal for the burglar to effect a breaking and entering, the rapist to lie in wait for a victim, or for drug dealers to ply their trade. Except for criminals, these spaces may be dangerous to enter. The configuration of the residential structures and their accessories (e.g., parking lots, driveways, fences, walkways, and shrubbery) can be designed to remove spaces amenable to crime.

Building forms inspired by CPTED are not criminal-proof. A good defensible space design will not guarantee good security or safety. Known criminals and strangers are likely to be found in architecturally defined safe places, such as lobbies or playgrounds. Again, the key to making building forms work in furtherance of crime prevention is the people who live there. The people who live in the territory must assert their dominion over it.

When residents project an aura of vulnerability, they detract from the image of security. People who feel threatened often project their fears and criminals are known for their abilities to sense victim fears. Fear can be diminished when residents support each other, act in unity, and generally commit to freeing their territories from the influence of crime. Neighborhood watch programs and the like promote individual and group resistance to crime. These are the lubricants for making CPTED strategies function smoothly.

Compatible Building Placement. The fourth element is enhancing security and safety by locating residential developments in functionally sympathetic urban areas adjacent to non-threatening activities. Placing compatible-use building types together is a key concept in zoning and building codes and land use plans.

Offensible Space

CPTED strategies are being applied widely and very effectively in a manner that can be viewed as offensible rather than defensible. This is in the context of criminals practicing the principles of defensible space in pursuit of illegal activities. For example, to:
  •Spot and assess intrusion to their territories.
  •Report problems to those in command,
  •Operate a communications network to warn of danger.
  •Delay or impede intrusion attempts.
  •Minimize internal threats, such as theft by co-criminals.

Criminals have access to the two key requirements for successfully defending their territories: financial resources and consensus. Criminals, most especially those in the drug trade, have the funds needed to create a defensible physical environment. They also enjoy a unity of common purpose in their endeavors, and where consensus cannot be achieved in that channel there is always the power of intimidation.

At the criminals' places of business — places like clandestine drug labs, crack houses, auto theft chop shops, and warehouses for stolen goods -- it is not unusual to find sophisticated access control and intrusion detection systems that variously delay, detect, assess, and neutralize attempts at unauthorized entry. These premises feature high-security walls, fences, lighting, doors, and locks; they have communication systems; and the structures often take on fortress-like appearances. The territory is well-marked and the signs of defense are both real and symbolic. The natural feelings of ownership and protectiveness lead the criminals to upgrade and embellish the safeguards. They also develop a stronger commitment to defend the territory rather than abandon it in the face of attack.

Where the enterprise is located within or in close proximity to a law-abiding population, the criminal element seeks to extend its sphere of control into the immediately adjacent areas. Resistance to the encroachment is typically low, due mainly to the socially disparate and heterogeneous nature of the non-criminal population.

The solution to offensible space may lie in a comprehensive, multilevel approach to crime prevention. Jeffery (1971) proposes primary, secondary, and tertiary prevention strategies. Whatever the approach, the focus needs to be on causes as opposed to symptoms.

Coordinated efforts have been launched in a few communities to extirpate offensible space sites. Citizens and law enforcement officers have identified the locations; various regulatory officials of local government have authorized destruction or confiscation of criminal premises; and criminal justice officials have applied the Racketeer Influenced and Corrupt Organization (RICO) Act and similar laws to administer fines and forfeitures.

Offensible space is a reflection of society's inability to deal with crime in the community. That inability springs from a wide range of negatives: lack of money, agreement, and purpose; fear of change, disruption, and reprisal; and a general malaise within the victimized population. On the positive side, we have the know-how for eradicating the offensible space problem through the application of defensible space concepts. Since each is the mirror of the other, our strategy should be to beat the criminals at their own game by being more skillful than they in applying the concepts.

Randall Atlas, Ph.d., AIA, CPP

Sources

Altman, I., Environment and Social Behavior: Privacy, Personal Space, Territory, and Crowding. (Brooks/Cole Publishing Co., Pacific Grove, CA, 1975).

Altman, I. and M.M. Chemers, Culture and Environment. (Brooks/Cole Publishing Co., Pacific Grove, CA, 1980).

Brower, S., Streetfront and Backyard: Two Ways of Looking at Neighborhood Open Spaces. (Department of Planning, City of Baltimore, 1979).

Elements of CPTED. (Westinghouse Electric Corporation, Arlington, VA, 1975).

Jeffery, C.R., Crime Prevention Through Environmental Design. (Sage Publications, Beverly Hills, CA, 1971).

Merry, S., Defensible Space Undefended: Social Factors in Crime Control Through Environmental Design. (Urban Affairs Quarterly, Vol. 16, No. 4, June 1981), pp. 397-422.

Molumby, T., Patterns of Crime in a University Project. (American Behavioral Scientist, Vol. 20, No. 2, November/December 1976), pp. 247-259.

Newman, O., Defensible Space: Crime Prevention Through Urban Design (Collier, New York, 1973), p. 8.

Taylor, R., and S. Gottfredson, The Defensibility of Defensible Space: A Critical Review and Synthetic Framework for Future Research, Understanding Crime, Vol. 18 (Sage Publications, Beverly Hills, CA, 1980), pp. 53-71.

CRIME PREVENTION THROUGH ENVIRONMENTAL DESIGN (CPTED): THE SITE PLAN REVIEW PROCESS

Background

It is a well-established fact that the environment in many communities is an inherent contributor to crime and the fear of crime. Poorly lighted and deserted street layouts, easily entered doors and windows, routine pedestrian and vehicle patterns, and landscaping designs offering places of concealment for the criminal are just a few examples.

Sociologists, criminologists, and practitioners in crime prevention have long studied the question of crime and one conclusion stands out: law enforcement alone is not the answer. In recent years, there has been extensive interest in applied research focusing on the direct influence of the physical environment on crime and the fear of crime in urban community settings.

The conceptual thrust of the Crime Prevention Through Environmental Design (CPTED) program is that proper design and effective use of the physical environment can produce behavioral effects that will reduce the incidence and fear of crime, thereby improving the quality of life. These behavioral effects can be accomplished by reducing the propensity of the physical environment to support criminal behavior.

Environmental design, as understood in CPTED principles, is rooted in the patterns of the human/environment relationship. It incorporates several concepts. The term environment means the people and their physical and social surroundings. For our purposes, the environment may be defined as that which has recognizable territorial and/or system limits. The term includes physical, social, managerial, and law enforcement influences that seek to positively affect human behavior in the give and take of people interacting among themselves and with their environment. The CPTED approach seeks to prevent certain specified crimes (and the fear attendant on them) within a specifically defined environment by manipulating variables that are closely related to the environment itself. The approach does not purport to develop crime prevention solutions in the broad realm of human behavior, but rather to offer solutions in the narrow context of the relationships between people and their surroundings.

Environmental and psychological approaches to crime prevention and security were initially popularized by architect Oscar Newman in his book *Defensible Space*. These concepts have been successfully incorporated in various commercial, residential, and transportation designs. Buildings that incorporate CPTED have been found to be resistive to criminal activity.

Further support of CPTED was presented by criminologist C. Ray Jeffery in his book *Crime Prevention Through Environmental Design*. Jeffery's thesis was that urban environments can influence behavior in two ways. First, the physical surroundings in which people live have an effect on each individual. Noise, pollution, overcrowding, uncollected refuse, and unsightly buildings contribute to a deterioration in human resolve to confront crime. Second, social characteristics to which people must respond, such as alienation, loneliness, anxiety, and dehumanization, may be keys to changing criminal behavior.

Jeffery's argument parallels that of Newman. For example, Jeffery says that with regard to the physical characteristics of the environment, buildings are all too often constructed so as to be dangerous, with corridors and passageways hidden from public view. Elevators, basements, storage, and washroom areas are fraught with danger due to poor design. Large-scale housing developments are not secure in that they are often isolated from the main flow of traffic, both human and automobile, and as such are closed to public use and view. Jeffery argues for the upgrading and re-designing of abandoned buildings and better planning in the construction of homes, apartments, parks, and streets. These recommendations serve as the backbone of the defensible space argument.

Historically, the needs of people to protect their lives sparked the emergence of public and private police measures. As those needs began to be met, attention turned to the protection of private property. Today's protections for home and business premises routinely include a wide variety of physical safeguards, alarm systems, and controlled access. Tomorrow's protections are aimed at entire communities and are developed from CPTED principles.

Working relationships are becoming commonplace among crime prevention practitioners, architects, and planners. Very often, the objective is to incorporate CPTED principles into municipal housing and building codes, and to set up review and approval mechanisms for judging the crime prevention features of planned construction.

The trend is relatively new, which may account for the absence of a generally understood and accepted methodology that can be followed by design professionals, planners, law enforcement crime prevention specialists, and security managers.

Professional and trade articles have picked up on the theme by pointing to instances where the lack of a standard methodology has prevented agreement among the various parties involved in major community construction projects. What are the steps for resolving conflicts that surface when the budget director imposes spending limits, when the architect insists on aesthetic integrity, when the fire marshal wants all doors unlocked, when the security consultant wants things locked up, when business leaders demand that construction not interfere with commerce, when residents want to protect property values, and when neighborhood leaders want to keep cultural values intact?

The two key barriers to agreement are ineffective communication and a lack of understanding concerning competing needs. To be positive contributors to the process, crime prevention specialists must be excellent communicators, both in writing and speaking, and be skilled in interpersonal dynamics. They must know the process through which design decisions are reached, know the objectives of others involved in the process, and be skilled in finding areas where agreement and compromise are possible. Finally, the crime prevention representatives need to be well grounded in CPTED principles.

The Site Plan Review Process

The remainder of this article will examine site plan review as practiced in Ann Arbor, Michigan.

When architects and developers are contemplating the development of property within the city of Ann Arbor, they are responsible for researching all city ordinances and regulations that might pertain to the proposed development. These ordinances and regulations fall under eight different city departments: Building, Engineering, Housing, Police, Historic Commission, Parks and Recreation, Fire, and Planning. The Planning Department staff plays a coordinative role by guiding the research of the ordinances that may apply to the proposed development.

As of the writing of this article, the Ann Arbor Police Department's crime prevention unit has been involved in several hundred site petition reviews. A petition submitted for approval of a planned development requires police comments. One or more experienced, trained police officers will be tasked to study the probable impact of the development upon crime in the geographical area surrounding the development or in the community broadly. The officers making the study are competent in spotting problems such as poor lighting, places of concealment, inadequate barriers, and unprotected entry points. They are also skilled in making cost-effective recommendations to correct the problems identified in the petition. A source of assistance to the officers in making the analyses and formulating suggestions are the writings of Newman and Jeffery.

A great gap lies between the drawing board and the final reality of the completed development. Even when crime prevention safeguards have been built into the development, the safeguards sometimes do not work for a number of reasons. The beneficiaries ignore or fail to use the safeguards because they have not been properly educated about them; departments and agencies responsible for operation and maintenance become lax; and people generally tend to shift protective responsibilities to the police. Instead of looking at crime prevention as a personal responsibility and taking advantage of safeguards that have been built into the physical environment, such as alarms, locks, and barriers, some citizens expect the police to prevent crime by doing everything and being everywhere at once.

Contributing to the problem are the perceptions of municipal staff who work in non-law enforcement disciplines, such as engineering, health, and welfare. Since crime fighting is not on their agendas, they lack an understanding of and an empathy for law enforcement. They expect the police to be the exclusive agency for dealing with crime, and they are disappointed when they discover that the police do not have all the answers and are not right all of the time. The police are not blameless, either. They are sometimes clannish and are often put off by technical experts, such as architects and planners, who tend to speak in arcane technical languages.

Aiding the Process through Training

Much more has to be done to communicate among the players in municipal government, and with leaders in the private and business sectors. More than anything else, the Ann Arbor experiences show the need for an interdisciplinary understanding both of the dimensions and nature of crime, and the site planning review process.

A positive step in that direction proved to be a two-pronged training effort. The first prong was a training seminar designed to educate the non-law enforcement planners in the fundamentals of CPTED. The seminar presented the strategies of natural access control, natural surveillance, and territorial reinforcement. The planners learned to differentiate between various crime prevention techniques and in practice sessions identified environmental designs that were good or bad in CPTED terms.

The second prong was training that taught the crime prevention officers the functions and operations of the city planning department and the particulars of the site plan review process. Much of the training was hands-on in that it required the officers to attend review meetings and public hearings, and to learn how to read blueprints.

The officers discovered that zoning and subdivision regulations are the "police powers" of a municipal planning agency. Authorized in most cases by state legislation, these powers are used as tools to regulate the use of private land and are

the basic points of reference to the crime prevention unit in preparing input to the site plan review.

Zoning is essentially an exercise of the basic power of the state and its political subdivisions to protect the public health, safety, morals, and general welfare of the community. Zoning ordinances therefore open the door to consideration of protective measures recommended by crime prevention staff. In short, crime prevention personnel have a legitimate say in planned land uses that might breed criminal activity.

Subdivision regulations are a companion to zoning ordinances. They regulate things like building set-backs; street locations and design; residential clustering; and locating schools, parks, and public facilities. Consequently, subdivision regulations are important to the crime prevention officer. Many of the standard crime deterrents, such as protective lighting, fences, and controlled entry points, can be introduced through promulgation of subdivision regulations. Conditions that attract crime can also be regulated; for example, placing automatic teller machines in unobservable locations and leaving keys in unattended vehicles.

Building codes, which are usually administered through a city's inspection department, represent yet another tool for introducing crime prevention concepts. Building codes set specific requirements and minimum standards for such items as structural soundness, door and window sizes, locking hardware, and alarm and access control systems, as well as plumbing, electrical, and other utility installations.

Putting the Process to Work

Ann Arbor's crime prevention staff holds responsibility for studying a petitioner's plan with respect to lighting, public safety, and applicable security ordinances. Using information gathered from crime analysis data, demographic data, land use patterns, general observations, and the solicited comments of residents or users, the crime prevention staff drafts its findings. The findings are often in the form of a list of security concerns, and the usual protocol is to disclose and discuss the concerns, openly and frankly, at a meeting attended by city planners and the developer's representatives.

From cost and liability standpoints, the site plan review process is invaluable. It can prevent poor design that may have to be retrofitted at a later time, at considerable added cost and inconvenience, and it can introduce positive design features that will effectively rule out litigation based on the foreseeability doctrine and other allegations of negligent security.

The process has particular application in projects involving:
- Large residential and/or industrial developments.
  - Business and commercial developments.
  - Government and health care facilities.
  - Parks and recreational areas.
  - Redevelopment and retrofitting.
  - Target hardening of existing facilities.

Site plan review presents the ideal opportunity for reducing crime through the application of CPTED principles. Although in this article site plan review is described through the experiences of a municipality, the process has validity in non-governmental sectors.

Jerry L. Wright, CPP
and Ronald L. Thomas, CPP

CRIME SCENE SEARCH

A crime scene search is a planned, coordinated, legal search by competent law enforcement officials to locate physical evidence or witnesses to the crime under investigation.

Only persons who have a legitimate investigative interest should be allowed into the crime scene. This number should be kept to a minimum. Too many people in a crime scene can lead to evidence being moved or destroyed before its value as evidence is recognized.

The person in charge of the investigation will make a preliminary survey of the crime scene. The purposes of the survey are to:
- Form objectives of the search -- what is to be found.
- Take special note of evidence that may be easily destroyed, such as blood, shoe prints in dust, footprints, etc.
- Organize the search:
  1. Make assignments for photographs, fingerprints, plaster casts, and the handling of evidence.
  2. Decide on a search pattern, i.e., lane, grid, spiral, or zone searches.
  3. Issue instructions to assisting personnel.

The investigator's original notes prepared at the crime scene will be used to refresh memory at the trial. They should be an accurate description of the crime scene including:
- Date, time, and location of the search.
- Weather and lighting conditions.
- Identity of others participating in the search.
- Assignments given to personnel.
- Condition and position of evidence found.

A crime scene sketch is a handmade pictorial representation of conditions at a crime scene. It is useful in clarifying investigative data and making the situation easier to understand by eliminating unnecessary detail. A sketch does not replace photographs at the crime scene and should be used to show:
- Dimensions of furniture, doors, windows, etc.
- Distances from objects to entrances and exits.
- Distances between objects.
- Measurements showing the exact location of items of evidence. Each object should be located by two measurements from nonmovable items, such as doors, walls, etc.

Crime scenes will not remain undisturbed for very long, and therefore should be photographed as soon as possible, preferably before anyone is allowed into the scene.

At the exterior crime scene:
- Establish the location of the scene by photographs from a distance to include a landmark.
- Take medium distance photographs to record the relative positions of closely related items of evidence.
- Take close-up photographs of individual items of evidence.

At the interior crime scene:
- Establish the location of the building through photographs.
- Photograph rooms and other interior areas from typical observation points using a wide-angle lens when necessary to show relative positions of all items within the area.
- Take medium-distance photographs to show the relative positions of closely related items of evidence.
- Take close-up photographs of individual items of evidence.

Evidence photographs are needed to:

•Record the condition of individual items of evidence before recovery. (Photographs must show the evidence in detail and should include a scale, investigator's initials, and the date).

•Reproduce tire and similar impressions that can be recorded in no other way, or prior to attempts to lift or cast.

•Photographs should show identifying data as indicated previously.

The next steps are usually to process the scene for fingerprints, shoe print/tire tread casts and/or lifts, blood and body fluids, fibers and trace evidence, tools and tool marks, weapons, residues, and documents.

All evidence must be collected legally in order to be admissible in court at a later date. Evidence found during a search is displayed to another investigator so that both investigators can testify to its source, and all evidence should be fully described in the searcher's notes and photographed in place prior to being picked up.

Articles of an evidentiary nature should be carefully marked for identification, preferably on the article itself, in a manner not to injure the evidence itself and not to be obliterated. These markings, to include initials, date, and case number, enable the person finding the evidence to testify, at a later date, to the finding of it.

Each item of evidence is placed in a suitable container, such as pillboxes, plastic vials, or strong cardboard boxes. The container is identified and sealed, and chain of custody documentation initiated.

Federal Bureau of Investigation

Source The Handbook of Forensic Evidence. (Federal Bureau of Investigation, U.S. Department of Justice, Washington, DC, 1984).

CRISIS MANAGEMENT: FOUR LESSONS LEARNED

On February 7, 1990, the American Trader, an oil tanker under charter to British Petroleum, was holed by its own anchor, spilling 40,000 gallons of crude oil into waters off the coast of Southern California. James Ross, President of BP America, delivered these comments to the American Petroleum Institute at Dallas, Texas, in September 1990.

It was with mixed feelings that I accepted the opportunity to speak at this conference. On the one hand, anyone who sets himself up as an expert in crisis management for the oil industry deserves what he gets. On the other, we have so much to do and so far to go as an industry that we all should contribute what we can, when we can.

I do not suggest that BP has all the answers. We clearly don't. Nonetheless, as a major partner in Alyeska, which has undertaken immense spill prevention and response improvements, and as the owner of the crude oil spilled off Huntington Beach, California, earlier this year, our company considers crisis management a very salient topic. We've done some hard thinking, planning, and development for crisis response. I'm happy to share that experience with you, and we at BP look forward to benefiting from your insights and experience through this forum and others like it. Oil spills aren't the only crisis we might have to face, and there's always a danger in re-fighting only yesterday's wars, but today I will focus on oil spills.

In the past, our experience with actual spill costs taught us that the operational costs of response and cleanup were of primary concern, because historically they constituted most of the costs incurred. Secondarily, we were concerned with the costs of damages exacted through liability legislation and lawsuits. Finally, we were only marginally concerned with the indirect costs of political and regulatory outcomes from spills. That has all changed.

In today's world those cost priorities are reversed. The costs of political and regulatory responses to spills are where the real money is. Awards for damages resulting from greatly increased liability and from the increased assessments for environmental and other damages are now larger than in the past -- and they continue to grow. Operational response costs, from initial response to demobilization, while larger than in the past, are no longer at the top of the list. They pale by comparison -- particularly when we realize that the cleanup costs are borne by a few companies while the follow-on legislated costs affect virtually everybody in the business.

Why have these changes occurred? Clearly, broad societal forces have raised public awareness of environmental issues generally. But, I believe our industry is particularly vulnerable -- an easy target. We are large, pretty clearly defined in most people's minds (however inaccurately) -- and we've managed to let our industry image remain low for decades. So we have no built-up store of good will and credibility to draw on. In this public climate, the politics of punishment are very powerful. I don't think I need to elaborate much on this point. Ask Alyeska. Ask Exxon.

Public expectations have changed. Our traditional view of risk and appropriate response no longer corresponds with public attitudes and expectations. This was brought home to us at BP by the research of Dr. Peter Sandman, a professor of risk communications at Rutgers University. In his analysis, he has postulated that risk consists of two components: the hazard itself, and the "outrage" associated with it. His argument, with which I wholeheartedly concur, is that as an industry we have tended to concentrate on the hazard, which we deal with objectively, operationally, and professionally. But we tend to relegate the public "outrage component" to a decidedly secondary status.

In a spill there are the hazards of environmental damage, health exposure, and economic loss, for instance -- which we tend to prepare for. Then there is the outrage, in which public perceptions declare the risk in far different terms.

I would argue that this significant change in the priority accorded the outrage component of a crisis calls for an equally significant change in our industry's approach to crisis response. This is especially important if the industry intends to hold down the costs of a spill. I'd like to outline some thoughts on this shift, and relate it to BP's experience at Huntington Beach.

We did well at Huntington Beach, and are proud of that. We had a crisis response plan in place, and had just recently completed an exercise that provided us with a leg up for the response. We received much praise from people and governmental agencies in California. Our media coverage was remarkably favorable. But in truth, we also had a lot of luck.

The head of BP Oil in America happened to be in California when the spill occurred, and he had been the senior incident manager in our recent exercise, so we had an experienced senior executive on the scene remarkably promptly. I happened to be in Washington, DC, where I could communicate promptly with legislators and the appropriate agencies.

Currents, winds, and tides afforded us some breathing space to defend the beaches and get a relatively high percentage of the oil out of the water by skimming.

From more recent experience with much less significant incidents, we know that we have more to do to be ready -- much more. I assure you that we are not complacent. We are not counting on good luck.

In my judgment, the increase in public concerns, and the heightened significance of outrage, suggest four key lessons that I believe should guide us for the future.

Lesson 1: Get it Done, Rather Than Argue about Whose Problem It Is

In any crisis, not least of all a major oil spill, time is a key factor. We at BP estimate that a spiller has about 36 hours to establish the perception that it is on top of the situation -- doing effective, logical things and communicating well about what is happening. In this context, the spiller is the company most associated with the spill, liability exclusion clauses notwithstanding.

Responsibility is not the same as liability. In the case of the Huntington Beach spill, BP was prepared from the outset to assume responsibility for a swift and well-supported response. We were publicly on record on day 1 in assuring that BP's resources were available to the actual spiller, a marine transportation company.

We took the view that the early hours of the crisis were too precious to waste on bickering or waiting for someone else to be the "responsible" party.

In the past, our industry could take some comfort from liability legislation, which was designed as much to limit liability as to assign it. Today, liability is becoming increasingly complex as expanding and conflicting liability laws are proposed, passed, and amended. The concept of limited liability is giving way to unlimited liability. Moreover, it is increasingly the case that the company with the deepest pockets is the target of public outrage, no matter what the law of the moment specifies.

You will not be surprised to hear that a company's public acceptance of responsibility where liability is unclear gives its legal counsel some concern. But in these circumstances, lawyers can be quick to focus on the immediate damages, and too slow to perceive the larger political and regulatory costs.

I would also suggest as both a practical and philosophical point that in a rapidly changing, and increasingly populist, regulatory environment, seeking precedent is looking in the wrong direction -- backward instead of forward.

Our industry also has some inherent areas of conflict that have impeded our effectiveness in the past, and these deserve attention if we are to become as effective as we need to be in the future.

Joint ventures are one such potential source of conflict. For example, we are one of seven owners of Alyeska, the initial spill response organization acting as agents for the ship and cargo owners in Prince William Sound. Where there are complex organizational arrangements, there will be concern over policies, resources, and responsibilities. The penalties for the likely delays if crisis arrangements are not spelled out and exercised in advance are inadequate early response, and no credible public story as to why. All of us in joint ventures should look to our crisis behavior before the crisis occurs.

There is an inherent conflict between the spiller and the insurance industry, which wants to save on cleanup costs. As I have argued, operational costs are often the least of the costs we are likely to face in the event of a major spill. Cleanup cost avoidance might have been the best strategy in another era, but it is a recipe for public disaster today. We need to be better prepared in this area. There is also a natural conflict between the international shipping legal regime and local legislation and public demands. This is a highly intractable area, but one we must do with what we can.

Entrepreneurial lawyers are themselves a source of conflict. While there may be no way for us as individual companies or an industry to eliminate this source of friction, our actions, especially in handling claims, can directly affect the level of their success for clients who want to take us to the cleaners -- out of frustration or a sense of powerlessness, or perhaps just greed. With time at a premium, there is clearly a need -- an imperative -- to do the common-sense, "right thing" promptly. Decide who owns the problem in some legal or technical sense after the fact.

Lesson 2: The Operational Response Must Be Effective, and Preparation Is the Key

Acceptance of responsibility is a necessary early response, but it is no substitute for effective operations. It is undeniable that public perception is more of a driver today than in the past, but thinking of new ways to manage perceptions while doing business the same old way won't wash.

The operational response -- people, equipment, communications, and facilities -- must be prompt and excellent. Heightened public awareness and concerns have raised public expectations. People know more about what should be done in event of a spill -- and they expect more. Effective response is more than paper plans and paid-up insurance. Our Huntington Beach response benefited from our having more than just a plan.

The first skimming vessel was on scene in just over 2 hours from the time of the spill. Within 2 hours of notification, our crisis team was in the air. Within less than 24 hours, we had 36 BP specialists on site. The call out was prompt because the names and phone numbers were current. We had put names and faces with specific tasks in advance, so that our crisis response team members knew who they were and with whom they would be working.

We at BP believe that the best initial response is overkill. Our management approach is to assume the worst, and send the top team and more resources than are likely to be required. Our plans call for getting senior people and a large number of functional specialists on-site quickly. Once there, and the situation becomes clearer, the effort can be scaled back. The management requirement can then be determined based on a more dispassionate assessment of need. I probably do not need to tell you how counter-intuitive this is, and how much institutional resistance it can provoke, but first assessments are notorious for being unrealistically low and there is little opportunity to re-gain the initiative once a situation develops faster than the response.

Despite the admitted reliance on overkill in initial response, there is a strong case to be made for avoiding a bureaucratic response. We do try to push the operational decisions -- the actual incident response -- downward while keeping a public focus at the senior management level. As an illustration of this approach, we like to refer to two unsung heroes of Huntington Beach: our Long Beach office administrator and her American Express Card. She fired that card like a machine gun -- and certainly for amounts above her normal purchase authority.

It isn't possible to list all the ways that a common-sense approach rather than a bureaucratic or legalistic response can keep public frustration in check. Such an approach pays dividends, especially in handling claims quickly, paying local bills promptly, and acting decisively on local matters.

Lesson 3: Share the Solution with Those Who Share the Problem

A spill is no longer just an oil company problem. It is a public problem and an industry problem as well. Therefore, it is necessary to share the solution to the problem with those affected by it -- government agencies at all levels, especially environmental agencies; affected communities (even if they are not directly impacted by the spill); environmental groups who will respond on behalf of their perceived constituencies; and others in our industry who will be affected.

Openness directly affects public outrage and was a high-payoff approach for us. At Huntington beach, we depended less on elaborate plans and more on cooperation in the execution. We worked closely on a continuing basis with government agencies. We were particularly careful to give local government an open door, and to pay attention to the rather long parade of political figures who felt it necessary to be seen and heard, and photographed on the beach. We are convinced that by working with them, we avoided jurisdictional disputes and a ton of controversy.

Sharing the solution means more than giving others a say. It also means sharing decision making with them, responding to their priorities and concerns, and demonstrating a commitment to their interests in the response effort. For instance, when our operational team was asked by the community to clean oil off a particular public pier, that project was promptly completed, even though it would not have otherwise had a high priority. The positive feedback from that minor incident meant that we had bought a lot of good will for a small gesture.

Similarly, when some spilled oil clearly not from our spill, was shown to our operating team, they dealt promptly with it. It was not the time to say, "It's not ours; we don't care." Again, that small attention made a disproportionate contribution to good will.

Sharing the solution also means seeking (and more importantly, accepting) help -- from government agencies, from other industry sources, and from volunteers in environmental groups and the community. As with any other response activity, this had to be planned. It doesn't just happen.

At Huntington Beach, the police offered to respond to people who called the department for information about the spill. We were delighted to provide them updates -- and it took a burden off us.

We also relied on other industry participants. Over 100 people from Chevron, Arco, Unocal, Exxon, and Shell took part in the spill response. The press was not slow to recognize that the industry was responding to the spill, and willingly.

There were also many bird rescue volunteers from environmental groups and the public, and large numbers of volunteers for a variety of other tasks. To be perfectly candid, many of them were a major potential nuisance at first -- enthusiastic, but untrained and unequipped. It really did seem easier to leave the work to contractors, but we decided to accept their help. We provided them with training and equipment, and ensured that they worked safely. In the end, we were paid off handsomely. These volunteers became effective workers and among our strongest supporters in the community.

Sharing the solution also means sharing preparation with those same interested parties. They should be part of planning, training, rehearsal of follow-up, and critique. After the spill had become a recent memory, we went back to the scene to contact the people and agencies we had worked with. In the end, we couldn't tell who was thanking whom and who was praising whom. It just seemed that we had been working together on our problem.

Lesson 4: Win the Communications Battle by Reaching Out with Facts and Concern

The "crisis" in crisis management is not primarily the event itself, but rather the public outrage. Were it not for the outrage, we would need prompt response management, but not crisis management.

In a crisis, we must communicate where the news was being made, which was virtually everywhere. We had spokespersons at the headquarters, on several beaches, at the bird rescue facility, and everywhere others were holding press conferences. We did not feel that we could wait for the newsmakers and the news media to come to us. The outreach proved fruitful for getting our point of view into print and on the air. By attending other people's press conferences, we reduced the opportunities for conflict -- the most natural of news stories. Instead, the new stories tended to revert to factual information, which was what we were striving for.

We also decided at the outset to become the best available source of factual information -- good and bad. By doing so, we found that we were frequently sought out as the first recourse, and not as the last resort. We had more opportunity to be heard and to set the framework for the news as it was reported. But a word of caution: When the event occurs, there is a real temptation to present only the favorable facts, or to put a positive interpretive "spin" on facts. Our experience confirms the greater advantages of building a reputation as a highly credible source.

The combination of reaching out to other constituencies and being the best source of facts built the kind of credibility it takes to overcome bad news or bad information. By way of example, we were surprised one morning by a particularly hostile article based on the views expressed by one government agency. We did not have to respond to that article. Numerous other government agencies and community groups did so on our behalf -- resulting in a major positive story the next day.

So those are the four lessons we took away from our Huntington Beach experience:

•Get it done, rather than argue about whose problem it is.

•The operational response must be effective; and preparation is the key.

•Share the solution with those who share the problem.

•Win the communications battle by reaching out with facts and concern.

From these lessons, we at BP have drawn one conclusion that is pertinent to this group today: We are all in this together. One loses, all lose.

BP's recent advertising research demonstrated that the Exxon Valdez spill continues to overshadow opinion of our industry. The positive results of BP's Huntington Beach experience were not remembered.

We at BP are striving to be the best in some competitive sense. Everybody in the oil industry must be "best," or we will all fall short and have to pay a price. We need to support each other not only in the event of a spill, but in the training and preparation for any crisis. We need to share more experience, more planning, and more resources. We need to share ideas.

This would represent something of a culture change for our industry, but it is timely, and it is needed. I would hope that one result of this seminar would be a commitment on the part of all of us to be part of the solution to our shared problem.

Source Public Affairs Pamphlet. (BP America, Cleveland, 1991).

CRISIS MANAGEMENT: TERRORISM

Terrorism is a serious and complex problem that defies easy solutions. Some organizations vacillate in their approach to terrorism, viewing terrorist attacks as a cost of doing business. Yet there are ways in which organizations can and should address the problem. Corporate executives along with security professionals must acknowledge terrorism and deal with it. One way to accomplish this strategy is through crisis management.

Crisis management is a dynamic concept that dramatically increases a company's efficiency and effectiveness in handling the many incidents that affect organizations. It applies sound managerial techniques designed to cope with a crisis situation while simultaneously accomplishing organizational goals. This approach also emphasizes handling the crisis in the most cost-effective way.

Over the past few years, many businesses and government agencies have set up mechanisms to identify and respond to crisis situations. Today many situations in both government and industry need a mechanism for identifying and responding to crises. As a first step in clarifying the management process that can be used to handle these crises, let's define what crisis management is not.

What Crisis Management Is Not

Crisis management is not mismanagement. Because of inappropriate planning or the lack of planning, some organizations seem to be reacting constantly to crisis situations. Without ordered priorities, an organization will never know which situations call for immediate attention and which do not. Therefore, they will not be able to continue functioning in a crisis.

Crisis management is also not a quick fix. It involves identifying, studying, and forecasting crisis situations, and deciding on specific methods an organization can use to prevent or cope with crises.

This process requires a commitment on the part of a company's executives that ensures crisis management will become an integral part of the organizational structure for the long term.

Crisis management is not solely the responsibility of a separate organizational division. Rather, it is accomplished by a team comprising a nucleus of three or four key personnel augmented by representatives from those divisions with a role in managing a particular crisis. This crisis management team should not be perceived as a task force, however; it is a permanent component of the organization. The number of individuals on the team is increased as needed by representatives from divisions the nuclear group identifies as essential for addressing a particular crisis.

Crisis team members are not selected arbitrarily. The selection process is carried out jointly by the crisis team manager and the functional division heads. This dual review should ensure that the best personnel are selected for this critical assignment.

Finally, crisis management does not require all personnel to stop their regular work to address each crisis -- the antithesis of cost-effectiveness. To avoid unnecessary costs, handling crises should cause minimal interference with the day-to-day routine. Designating a select team of individuals to both plan for and manage the crisis accomplishes this goal.

What Crisis Management Is

The term crisis management has been coined because it can apply to a wide variety of events that disrupt the normal activities of businesses, government agencies, and non-profit enterprises. The definition of a crisis will vary from organization to organization, however. Some will prefer to use the word *issue* when describing these situations, calling the planning process "the management of issues," or simply "issues management."

A terrorist act certainly qualifies as a crisis. Effective management principles designed to identify, prevent, and manage the situation are required. Crisis management provides a systematic, non-chaotic response. The response permits the organization to continue making its products or providing its services while the crisis is being managed. Furthermore, it creates an early detection or warning system through a fine-tuned audit mechanism. Many crises can be prevented or at least coped with effectively through early detection.

In addition, crisis management allows the organization to capitalize on the expertise of personnel from various disciplines who plan for and manage the situation. This cost-effective approach precludes the need for a large crisis management staff. Moreover, the development of a team approach permits all crises to be coordinated through an effective and stable group of employees.

A Crisis Management Model

A crisis management model can be used as a crisis management guide. It begins with the organization of a management structure and concludes with the management of the crisis. The model consists of the following six steps: organizational design, personnel selection, team development, audit, contingency planning, and ultimately the management of an actual crisis.

Designing the Organizational Structure. The purpose of crisis management is to use a cost-effective structure that causes minimal economic burden for an organization, particularly one that might already be fighting for economic survival. The crisis management matrix is composed of a lean, permanent staff augmented by experts from various functional divisions as needed. It is inherently flexible and adapts quickly to changing conditions.

The appropriateness of this matrix structure is further exemplified by the various crisis situations that could conceivably be related to distinct organizational elements. Thus, once a crisis threat has been identified, the crisis manager can select from the various functional divisions those personnel with the most appropriate skills and abilities to handle the crisis. Once the organizational structure has been designed, the team of individuals who will participate can be selected.

Selecting the Crisis Team. The policies used to select a crisis management team should be as similar as possible to those used normally in the organization for assigning people to new jobs. The members of the permanent crisis management team should decide what additional skills are needed to handle an impending threat successfully, identify the divisions where individuals with these skills are currently assigned, and decide from what level of management the representative should be selected. How long the task will take and whether it will be a full-time or part-time assignment should also be considered. Clarifying these points will help determine which key individuals will have the time to devote to managing a crisis.

Developing the Team. After selecting the crisis team members, the team manager becomes responsible for developing the group into a cohesive, effective unit. The manager must clearly understand the purpose of crisis management, which is to develop a proficient team to handle the crisis while others in the organization continue to perform their daily routines.

Team development is accomplished by analyzing goals (where the team is going), roles (who will be doing what), and processes (how members will function as a team). Once team members understand these principles, they will begin to transform into a dedicated unit.

Designing and Conducting a Crisis Audit. The crisis audit is the foundation of the crisis management cycle. For planning purposes, the audit assists managers in analyzing their environment, identifying potential threats, assessing the effects of each threat, determining each threat's probability, and setting threat priorities.

An important part of this audit is to weigh the probability of a threat occurring against the effect the act would have if it did occur. For example, a crisis audit at a multinational company might identify the kidnapping of a key executive as a possible threat. In conducting the audit, the crisis management team might determine the probability that an executive would be kidnapped was low. However, the impact on the company of such an occurrence would be quite high.

Therefore, the crisis team would conclude the threat of an executive kidnapping should receive a high priority on a list of possible threats, even though the chance is low that such an attack might occur.

Based on these assessments, specific threats can be divided into various levels that reflect the seriousness of the consequences. A level-one incident, for example, would seriously affect a company's ability to stay in business, while a level-two threat might cause disruption but would not completely shut down operations.

Formulating crisis objectives naturally follows the setting of priorities among possible crisis threats. Crisis objectives are not distinct from organizational objectives because the former address the factors that might impede the accomplishment of the latter. Crisis objectives should not exist unless they are used to facilitate organizational objectives at minimal cost. They should also eventually be approved by the chief executive officer (CEO) or another high-level executive. The final objectives, then, should reflect the thinking of those at the highest levels in the organization.

Specific crisis objectives should be set for each threat. For example, the crisis objectives developed to counter the threat of an executive kidnapping might include a plan for protecting those at risk at home as well as in the office.

Developing a Contingency Plan. A contingency plan, written by members of the crisis team, should consist of five components: the introduction, the objectives, the assumptions, the trigger mechanism, and the action steps. For example, a contingency plan designed to deal with a terrorist threat would begin with an overview of the crisis, identifying the group or groups presenting the threat, the target locations, and the individuals and issues that might be affected.

This introduction should be followed by a specific, yet succinct, outline of the plan's objectives. Continuing the terrorism scenario, one objective might be to implement security measures designed to protect key executives from kidnapping. These measures should be spelled out in the contingency plan along with ways to achieve them.

The next component of the contingency plan is the assumptions. Assumptions are those factors the crisis team planners cannot control, but could cause concern if they do occur. Assumptions should be thought of as a guideline that adds both focus and depth to the objectives.

In certain geographic areas, for example, it may be known that law enforcement officials are sympathetic to specific terrorist organizations. In other countries the payment of ransom may be illegal. The assumptions laid out in the contingency plan must take these factors into consideration and alternate plans must be established.

The trigger mechanism, the fourth part of the contingency plan, acts as an alarm that activates the crisis plan. The mechanism must be carefully constructed to prevent premature or delayed implementation. This mechanism can be designed so it escalates the response by degrees. Although this response will vary from organization to organization, such a system activates only those teams and resources needed to cope with the emergency at hand. Without controls, each incident would require a full response, causing severe disruption of the organization's day-to-day operations.

For example, intelligence may be developed that says a high-ranking executive of a corporation has been targeted for assassination. This information might not activate a response, but it would signal the need to start notifying appropriate people and setting up preventive measures while additional sources of information are being pursued that could confirm or deny the report.

The final component, the action plan, develops a step-by-step sequence of events designed to accomplish the objectives. These steps clearly delineate the activities required to accomplish each objective. The role of every person, division, department, or agency is outlined, designating primary players as well as backup or support players.

For example, in the terrorist kidnapping scenario, a security consultant might assume a primary role by providing expert guidance on the tactics that should be used for handling a kidnapping and negotiating the release of the hostage.

The security department might play a support role by recording telephone conversations or providing investigative support. The security staff might also be preparing a backup plan that could be implemented in the event that negotiations fail.

Managing the Crisis. At this point, the organization has implemented its crisis structure, selected and developed its crisis team, conducted its crisis audit, delineated and prioritized its objectives, and developed its contingency plan. In addition, the CEO must develop some guidelines that will establish how the crisis will be managed and who will manage it. Depending on personality and management style, some CEOs might want to be directly involved, while others might prefer to have the crisis team manager handle the incident.

Another management approach might tie the decision concerning who will handle the incident into various crisis levels. For example, a level-one crisis (such as an executive kidnapping) would have a significant effect on the organization as a whole.

On the other hand, a level-two crisis (such as a bombing that causes only property damage) would not affect the organization as widely nor threaten its survival. Certainly, depending on the circumstances, a level-two incident could escalate into a level-one crisis. The bombing of one building accompanied by a threat to bomb additional installations is an example.

Ordinarily, the CEO becomes involved in a level-one incident, either managing it directly or delineating policy. For the most part, a level-two situation will be managed by the crisis team leader. While the team leader may be responsible for keeping the CEO informed, he or she will have overall authority to manage the event.

We live in uncertain times. Terrorism has not only become a way of life, but also a way of doing business in the international arena. Business and government executives must recognize and address this growing problem. The most comprehensive yet cost-effective method of addressing the terrorist threat is through crisis management.

Robert F. Littlejohn, CPP

CRYPTOGRAPHIC SECURITY

Cryptographic security is concerned with carrying out privacy transformations on data communications so as to render them unintelligible to all but the intended recipient. Cryptology is the study of secret writing. Cryptography is the science of secret writing. Cryptoanalysis is the art of obtaining the meaning of secret writing without having been invested with the key.

There are two kinds of secret writing: codes and cyphers. In a code, a symbol or string of symbols may stand for a complete message. In the old domestic telegraph code, "73" meant "love and kisses." In a cypher, there is a one-to-one correspondence between the symbols of the original message (called plain text) and the symbols of its equivalent in secret writing (called the crypto text). The transformation of plain text into crypto text is called encryption. The transformation of crypto text into plain text is called decryption.

The transformations are called by a key. If the same key is used for encryption and decryption, the cypher is said to be symmetric. If different keys are used for encryption and decryption, the cypher is said to be asymmetric. Cyphers may be applied to the symbols of an entire message or group of messages continuously. These are called stream cyphers. A cypher may be applied to groups of symbols, say eight at a time. These are called block cyphers.

There are three kinds of cyphers: concealment, transposition, and substitution. When the ancient Greeks wanted to communicate between armies separated by hostile territory, they would shave the head of a slave and tattoo the message on the scalp. When the hair grew, the slave was sent through the lines. This was a concealment cypher.

The Greeks also used a transposition cypher called the skytale. One general wrapped a leather belt spirally around his baton and wrote a message lengthwise along it. The messenger was given the belt to wear. The general receiving the message wrapped the messenger's belt around his baton and read the message off. This was a transposition cypher because the symbols of plain text were transposed.

Julius Caesar used a substitution cypher. He prepared a cypher alphabet by starting with a keyword and omitting all repeated letters:

Cypher:
CAESRBDFGHILMNOPQTVXYZ
Plain:
ABCDEFGHILMNOPQRSTVXYZ

His famous battle report would have been: VRLG, VGSG, VGEG. When more than one kind of cypher is used in a system, say, transposition and substitution, the result is called a product cypher.

The U.S. Data Encryption Standard is a symmetric, block product cypher. It encyphers text in blocks of 64 bits, which can correspond to 8 bytes (that is, characters).

There is only one unbreakable cypher: the one-time tape or pad. It is a Vernam cypher in which the key: (1) is produced by a random physical process, such as the emanations of a noise tube or the decay of a radioactive isotope; (2) is longer than the longest possible sequence of messages; and (3) is used only once.

Some cryptographic devices used by governments and sold commercially, and some software packages for data encryption, are based on Vernam cyphers in which the key is obtained by a pseudorandom arithmetic process. All these cyphers can be broken.

Such cyphers afford only work-factor security. The technique of breaking them could involve: (1) identifying the pseudorandom number generator used: (2) recreating key strings under different keying conditions until a combination is found that begins to render one message intelligible; and (3) performing the same operation on subsequent messages until the procedure for changing the keying conditions can be deduced. More likely it involves an attack using either known or chosen plain text.

The work factor depends on the amount of encyphered text available and the time it takes to break the cypher. Work factor is reduced by: (1) cryptographic systems in which the underlying pseudorandom sequence is readily apparent; (2) systems that afford little flexibility in changing keys; (3) availability of cryptographic devices, programs, and keying data to opponents; (4) malfunction of cryptographic equipment; and (5) stupidity or carelessness on the part of the user.

On the commercial level, an opponent can obtain encryption devices and programs by purchase; on the international level, he or she could do it as North Korea did to the United States in 1968, for example, by capturing an intelligence-gathering ship like the Pueblo.

Resistance to Compromise

In the hands of a skilled electronics engineer, there is no device that cannot be torn apart and its operating principles deduced. In World War II, we deceived ourselves that we were preserving security by using white wiring running over circuitous paths and implanting thermite bombs in the allied ABK radar IFF transponder, but it did not work any more than multilayer circuit boards and integrated circuit packages did in the 1960s, and any more than large-scale-integration chips do today.

In the hands of a skilled software engineer, there is no computer program that cannot be analyzed and reconstructed from its source-code or even object-code format. It is the height of arrogance for any programmer to assume that he or she alone can read machine language or assembly code.

John M. Carroll

Source Carroll, J.M., Computer Security, 2nd Edition. (Butterworth-Heinemann, Boston, 1987).

CUSTOMS SERVICE

The collection of revenue and the control of trade are almost as old as humans themselves. Levies and tariffs on imports were well known in America from the earliest colonial times. After declaring its independence in 1776, the struggling young nation found itself on the brink of bankruptcy. Responding to the urgent need for revenue, the First Congress passed and President George Washington signed the Tariff Act of July 4, 1789, establishing a tariff and system for collecting duties. Four weeks later, on July 31, the original Customs districts and ports of entry were established by the Fifth Act of Congress.

For nearly 125 years, Customs was to remain virtually the only source of income for the government. Customs revenues made possible a period of unprecedented growth; the opening of the West; the purchase of the Louisiana and Oregon Territories, Florida, and Alaska; and the building of the National Road from Maryland and the Transcontinental Railroad. Customs collections built the U.S. military and naval academies, the City of Washington, and the list goes on. By 1835, Customs revenues had reduced the national debt to zero, and Customs is still a growing, major source of revenue for the federal government.

It is interesting to note that Customs was the parent or forerunner of a number of federal agencies. Customs officers were the agents for military pensions (forerunner of the Veterans Administration), obtained statistics on imports and exports (Bureau of Census), supervised the venue cutters (now the U.S. Coast Guard), collected hospital dues for the relief of sick and disabled seamen (later the Public Health Service), and established standard weights and measures (now the National Bureau of Standards).

A number of organizational and name changes have occurred since 1789. In 1875, Customs became a division within the Treasury Department, and in 1927, a bureau. In 1973 the Bureau of Customs became the U.S. Customs Service and remains a major branch of the Department of Treasury.

The present organizational structure of Customs was created by the President's Reorganization Plan Number 1 of 1965, Reorganization Plan Number 2 of 1973, and subsequent Headquarters reorganizations. Under the 1965 reorganization, appointed positions within the Service, except the Commissioner of Customs, were abolished and all personnel were placed under the civil service system.

The Commissioner of Customs, by authority delegated by the Secretary of the Treasury, establishes policy and supervises all activities from Service Headquarters in Washington, DC.

The mission of the Customs Service is to collect the revenue from imports and enforce Customs and related laws. Customs administers the Tariff Act of 1930, as amended. The following are among the responsibilities assigned to the Customs Service:

•Assess and collect Customs duties, excise taxes, fees, and penalties due on imported merchandise.

•Interdict and seize contraband, including narcotics and illegal drugs.

•Process persons, baggage, cargo, and mail, and administer certain navigation laws.

•Cooperate with, and enforce regulations of, numerous government agencies relating to international trade and travel.

•Detect and apprehend persons engaged in fraudulent practices designed to circumvent Customs and related laws.

•Protect American business and labor by enforcing statutes and regulations such as the Anti-Dumping Act, countervailing duty provisions, copyright, patent and trademark provisions, quotas, marking of imported merchandise, etc.

•Protect the general welfare and security of the United States by enforcing import and export restrictions and prohibitions.

•Collect accurate import and export data for compilation of international trade statistics.

Even though its mission has remained constant since 1789, changes in the size and complexities of the international community have resulted in a significant expansion of the actual responsibilities assigned to the Customs Service.

Today, in addition to enforcing our own laws, Customs is responsible for more than 400 other provisions of law on behalf of some 40 other agencies. Many of these statutes relate to environmental interests and the quality of life -- such things as motor vehicle safety and emission control, water pollution, pesticide control, and protection for endangered species of wildlife. Other laws safeguard American agriculture, business, and public health.

Customs now serves approximately 300 ports of entry throughout the United States, Puerto Rico, and the U.S. Virgin Islands, keeping watch over 96,000 miles of land and sea borders. Changing laws, changing patterns of trade and commerce, and changing methods of smuggling require the Service to continually modify operations to keep abreast of these changes.

A balanced and integrated enforcement effort supports the mission, and individual programs work in concert with overall Customs concepts. An enforcement program is needed not only to apprehend the smuggler, but to protect the revenue from fraud as well.

Protecting thousands of miles of border against entry of contraband and illegally entered merchandise presents a unique enforcement problem demanding unprecedented flexibility. In addition to the vast area requiring protection, today's professional smuggler uses aircraft, boats, and all-terrain vehicles in order to evade traditional approaches to intercepting narcotics and dangerous drugs, illegal weapons, prohibited merchandise, goods subject to quotas, and endangered species of animals.

Customs responds to this challenge with a tactical interdiction approach that integrates a highly trained professional force with sophisticated equipment, and special air and marine support to focus on critical smuggling areas. Tactical interdiction ensures a highly visible, viable, and effective deterrent to smuggling.

Of special significance to the accomplishments of tactical interdiction have been the activities of the Customs marine and air units, operating from permanent bases along the borders and coastlines. Customs aircraft closely support ground and sea components, enabling units to arrive at the right place and at the right time to intercept smuggling attempts.

Certainly among its unique enforcement operations are Customs' drug detector dog teams, which save people-hours in locating narcotics and dangerous drugs in vehicles, mail, unaccompanied baggage, and cargo. A dog and its handler can check 500 packages in 30 minutes; it would take a mail examiner several days to inspect as many parcels. Along the border, a dog can thoroughly inspect a vehicle in about 2 minutes; the same examination by an inspector would take at least 20 minutes and could never equal the instinctive accuracy of the dog's inspection.

The Customs Service's role in the interdiction of narcotics and dangerous drugs continues to change to meet the ever changing threat that illicit drug smuggling poses to U.S. security. The National Drug Control Strategy of the Office of National Drug Control Policy designated Customs as the lead agency for interdiction along U.S. borders, at ports of entry, and points in between. Customs and the Coast Guard jointly lead the federal effort for air interdiction of narcotic smuggling. The Customs Commissioner chairs the Border Interdiction Committee of the National Drug Control Policy Office. This committee, which pursues the above responsibilities, is staffed by personnel from the Customs Service, the Coast Guard, and the Immigration and Naturalization Service.

As the lead drug interdiction agency, Customs has been mandated to perform investigative and tactical enforcement functions, which include interdiction and seizure of the illicit drugs smuggled into the United States, the arrest of those violators responsible, and the seizure of the conveyances used in the smuggling attempt. To accomplish this mission, Customs relies heavily on its aviation and marine components, as well as its investigative, intelligence, inspectional enforcement, and enforcement support programs. The activities of international smuggling organizations have a serious impact on the world community and have a particularly detrimental effect on the developing nations.

Congressional legislation in 1870 established special agents for the Customs Service. Today, special agents are assigned to duty stations all over the world. In the course of their duties, they have recovered art and archaeological objects, made arrests for cargo thefts and arms smuggling, and uncovered major fraud conspiracies.

Protection of the revenue against fraud is one of the most critical missions of the Service. Fraud not only deprives the government of essential income, but it also harms the law-abiding producer, importer, and exporter.

Supporting integrated enforcement and investigative activities are a number of specialized enforcement systems, including an extensive radio communications network that enables Customs officers to communicate by voice during operations; a computer-based information system to provide a rapid access to information concerning previous violations of Customs and related laws; and sophisticated technical systems that enable Customs to detect and interdict land, sea, or air smuggling attempts.

Concern with world commerce does not stop at boundaries. U.S. Customs is an active member of the Customs Cooperation Council (CCC), an international body whose purpose is to simplify and harmonize customs procedures throughout the world to facilitate the flow of international travel and trade.

International crime problems, particularly narcotics trafficking and terrorism, have prompted a greater enforcement role for U.S. Customs in the international community. U.S. Customs provides training in narcotics interdiction and anti-terrorism funded by the State Department. U.S. Customs also provides surveys and training for commercial carriers whose equipment is under threat of being used to transport narcotics. U.S. Customs also provides short- and long-term advisory assistance in both commercial operations and enforcement procedures.

In carrying out its border-protecting mission, Customs must balance the dictates of enforcement with the requirement to facilitate the legitimate movement of passengers and cargo into the United States. Maintaining this somewhat delicate balance requires that customs utilize all available technology in its commercial initiatives and that it closely coordinate with all participants in this process. Working with the world trade community and the international transportation industry, Customs has implemented numerous automated systems and techniques to expedite the flow of commerce across our nation's borders.

Customs Service

Source   Public Affairs Pamphlet. (U.S. Customs Service, Washington, DC, 1992).

D

DECISION MAKING

Decision making is a primary function of a loss prevention manager. Often, a decision is made after a problem has developed. To aid decision making, problem analysis is helpful. Problem analysis is essentially an examination of a problem for the purpose of ascertaining the cause. Decision making is the process of arriving at the best possible solution based on an understanding of the problem's cause. The information presented here consists of a practical seven-step process for analyzing problems and making good decisions.

Decision Steps

Step 1. State the Problem. The problem should be articulated as completely as possible. The best possible solution or combination of solutions can be determined when a problem is clearly described in all its dimensions.

Step 2. Gather Pertinent Information. Since good decisions will be based upon information obtained from an objective inquiry, the wise manager will be deliberate and patient in the search for relevant data. Information can be obtained from many sources, such as talking to people, looking at records, and making forensic examinations. The particular situation will dictate the scope and intensity of the inquiry.

Step 3. Analyze the Information. The accuracy and relevancy of information are important and are enhanced by focusing primarily on problems and not symptoms. A pre-occupation with symptoms may lead the manager away from solutions that will address root causes.

Step 4. List Possible Solutions. Participatory management techniques can lead to useful ideas and suggestions. Each possible solution must be explored for implications and ramifications. Questions of concern can include the effects of a solution on personnel, costs, convenience, time, efficiency, and effectiveness.

Step 5. Select the Best Solution. The best solution may be a combination of options. The implications and ramifications can be re-examined by asking critical questions: Will the selected solution alleviate the problem? Will it create a different problem?

Step 6. Implement the Solution after Careful Planning. The solution can include considerations about personnel and resources needed, objectives, time limits, means of control and monitoring, evaluation, and feedback. Realistic objectives can be formulated that, if met, will be the evidence of success.

Step 7. Evaluate the Solution. After the solution has had sufficient time to impact the problem, the situation can be looked at again. Is the solution working? Are the objectives being met? Are modifications necessary?

Leadership

Leadership and decision making go hand-in-hand. Leadership in the traditional business sense is often viewed as the influence an individual has on others in the pursuit of organizational objectives.

Let us briefly look at the five generally recognized types of leadership styles: autocratic, bureaucratic, diplomatic, participative, and free rein.

• The autocratic style makes decisions based upon personal beliefs without regard for rules, regulations, and others' opinions.

• The bureaucratic leader operates by strict adherence to rules, regulations, policies, and procedures. Decisions are made "by the book." Lack of flexibility is a shortcoming of this leadership style.

• The diplomatic leader makes decisions by soliciting others' opinions and then using persuasion to gain cooperation.

• The participative style emphasizes group decision making.

• The free-rein leader uses a minimum of supervision; decisions are avoided when possible. This style presents difficulties for those who cannot work independently

Two other and less recognized leadership styles are called the compelling and impelling approaches. Defining and contrasting them here will add to an understanding of the important relationship between leadership style and the tasks of management.

A compelling leader uses threats, power, authority, and rules, somewhat like the autocratic leader. Minimum consideration is given to the opinions and goals of others. In contrast, an impelling leader uses forces and characteristics within the followers to reach objectives, the approach being a participatory management style.

In an emergency situation where quick decisions are necessary, the compelling leader is best. When emergency action is required, there is limited time to sit down and discuss what actions to take. On the other hand, the impelling leadership style is effective in the day-to-day, routine organization of work.

In this style, employees follow their own ideas best and are more likely to accept changes when they have had a part in planning the change. Example: Instead of ordering employees to perform a particular job a particular way, a manager can ask employees if they have any ideas. During the discussion, both the employees and the manager present ideas. In the process, the employees might suggest what the manager had in mind to begin with.

Philip P. Purpura, CPP

Sources

Jennings, E.E., The Anatomy of Leadership. (Management of Personnel Quarterly, Autumn, 1961).

Laird, D.A., and E. Laird, Psychology, Human Relations and Motivation. (McGraw-Hill Book Co., New York, 1967).

McGregor, D., Leadership and Motivation. (MIT Press, Cambridge, MA, 1966).

Owens J., The Art of Leadership. (Personnel Journal, 52 , May 1973).

DEFENSE INDUSTRIAL SECURITY PROGRAM

The Defense Industrial Security Program (DISP) operates to safeguard classified information entrusted to U.S. industry. Essentially, the program is a government/industry team relationship in which the government establishes requirements for the protection of classified information that has been entrusted to industry, and industry implements these protection requirements with government advice, assistance,

and monitorship. A User Agency is one of the federal departments or agencies participating in the DISP. The User Agencies include the Office of the Secretary of Defense (including all boards, councils, staffs, and commands); Department of Defense (DoD) agencies (National Security Agency, Defense Intelligence Agency, Defense Communications Agency, Defense Logistics Agency, Defense Nuclear Agency, etc.); Departments of the Army, Navy and Air Force (including all of their activities); Departments of the Interior, State, Treasury, Commerce, Transportation, Agriculture, Labor, and Justice; the General Services Administration; the National Aeronautics and Space Administration; the National Aeronautics and Space Administration; the Small Business Administration; the National Science Foundation; the Environmental Protection Agency; the U.S. Arms Control and Disarmament Agency; the Federal Emergency Management Agency; the Federal Reserve Board; the General Accounting Office; the U.S. Information Agency; the U.S. Trade Representative; and the U.S. International Trade Commission.

The DISP is charged with providing and administering a program for properly identifying and safeguarding U.S. and foreign classified information entrusted to U.S. industry. Industrial espionage is a management problem unless, of course, classified defense information is involved.

Classified Information Categories

Classified information is official government information that has been determined to require protection against unauthorized disclosure in the interests of national security and that has been so identified by being marked as TOP SECRET, SECRET, or CONFIDENTIAL. These classification categories are defined as:

TOP SECRET. Classified information that requires the highest degree of protection and the unauthorized disclosure of which could reasonably be expected to cause exceptionally grave damage to the national security, such as armed hostilities against the United States or its allies, disruption of foreign relations vitally affecting the national security, the compromise of vital national defense plans or complex cryptologic and communications intelligence systems, the revelation of sensitive intelligence operations, and the disclosure of scientific or technological developments vital to national security.

SECRET. Classified information or material that requires a substantial degree of protection and the unauthorized disclosure of which could reasonably be expected to cause serious damage to the national security, such as disruption of foreign relations, significant impairment of a program or policy directly related to the national security, revelation of significant military plans or intelligence operations, and compromise of significant scientific or technological developments relating to national security.

CONFIDENTIAL. Classified information or material that requires protection and the unauthorized disclosure of which could reasonably be expected to cause damage to the national security of ground, air, and naval forces in the U.S. and overseas areas; disclosure of technical information used for training, maintenance, and inspection of classified munitions of war; and revelation of performance characteristics, test data, design, and production data on munitions of war.

Intentional unauthorized disclosure of classified information constitutes a violation of federal statutes.

Only certain officials of the government have the authority to classify information as requiring protection in the interests of national security. Based upon guidance furnished by the government, contractors are required to apply classification markings to information they generate.

An integral part of safeguarding is the determination that information is classified. For this reason, the DoD and other government agencies have established a Classification Management Program for the particular purpose of ensuring correct classification, timely downgrading and declassification, and the issuance of comprehensive classification guidance to all in government and industry who need it. Responsibility for issuing this guidance rests with the User Agency, which awards contracts to industry involving classified information. Once information is classified, it must be protected by a system of personnel and physical safeguards.

Access means the ability and opportunity of a person to obtain knowledge of classified information, either directly or by entry into areas where classified information is handled. However, entry into a controlled area, per se, will not constitute access to classified information if the security measures that are in force prevent the gaining of knowledge of the classified information. It is important to remember that responsibility for determining whether a person requires access to any classified information rests upon the individual who has possession, knowledge, or control of the information.

A classified contract is a contract that requires or will require access to classified information by the contractor or the contractor's employees in the performance of the contract. The requirements for a classified contract apply to all pre-contract and post-contract activity (retention of classified material). A contract may be "classified" even though the contract document itself is unclassified.

Facility Security Clearances

The term "facility' is used within the DISP as a common designation for an operating entity consisting of a plant, laboratory, office, college, university, or commercial structure with associated warehouse, storage areas, utilities, and components, which are related by function and location.

A facility security clearance is an administrative determination by the DoD that, from a security viewpoint, a facility is eligible for access to classified information of the same or lower classification category as the clearance being granted. A facility security clearance includes the execution of the Department of Defense Security Agreement (DD Form 441).

Under the terms of this agreement, the government agrees to issue the facility clearance and inform the contractor as to the security classification of information to which the contractor will have access. The contractor, in turn, agrees to abide by the security requirements set forth in the Industrial Security Manual (ISM), which is incorporated by reference in the Security Agreement. A facility security clearance is required in order to permit a contractor to have access to classified information.

A firm becomes eligible to be considered for a classified bid or quotation by the same process used in the case of an unclassified procurement.

The firm would have to qualify as a bidder to a government procurement activity or to a prime contractor or subcontractor performing on a government contract. If the bid or potential subcontract involves access to classified information, the procuring activity or cleared prime contractor submits a request to the appropriate DIS Region to clear the prospective bidder.

A firm cannot apply for its own facility security clearance. A procuring activity of the government, or a cleared contractor in the case of subcontracting, may request the clearance when a definite, classified procurement need has been established.

The requesting facility will be contacted by an Industrial Security Representative (IS Rep) from the Cognizant Security Office in the area. At that time, the IS Rep will obtain information concerning the facility, provide the facility with instructions on completion of forms, and make an appointment to visit the facility. During the on-site visit, the IS Rep will complete the clearance processing and assist the facility in establishing a security program.

A SECRET clearance is most commonly requested and can be issued in about 100 days. For those facilities that are eligible, an interim SECRET facility clearance can be issued in approximately 30 days or less.

Normally, owners, officers, directors, partners, regents, trustees, certain executive personnel, and certain contract negotiators must be processed for a personnel security clearance in connection with a facility security clearance. This may vary, however, depending on the type of organization or business structure involved, as explained below:

1. Generally, in the case of a corporation, association, or a non-profit organization, the chairman of the board and all principal officers, (such as president, senior vice-president, secretary, treasurer); the management official in charge of the facility; and the facility security officer must be cleared.

2. In the case of a sole proprietorship, the owner must be cleared. The ISM prescribes those other executive personnel who must be cleared in connection with the facility security clearance.

3. In the case of a partnership, all general partners must be cleared. Where the number of partners is large, the partnership may see fit to delegate its responsibilities (including security) to a legally constituted executive committee. In this case, all members of the committee must be cleared.

4. In the case of colleges or universities, the chief executive officer and certain other officials shall be cleared. Specific requirements are prescribed in the ISM.

There is no direct charge to the contractor for processing a facility security clearance. Speaking of cost, however, the government is not responsible for security costs, e.g., guards, storage containers, etc., unless approved by an authorized contracting officer. Accordingly, contractors should determine their security requirements and related costs, and consider such costs when submitting a bid. Industrial Security Representatives from the Cognizant Security Office are readily available to assist contractors in determining the necessary security requirements.

As a general policy, facilities that are determined to be under foreign ownership, control, or influence are ineligible for a facility security clearance. A facility will be considered to be under foreign ownership, control, or influence when the degree of ownership, control, or influence from a foreign source is such that a reasonable basis exists for concluding that compromise of classified information may result.

As a part of the Security Agreement, a contractor agrees to prepare a Standard Practice Procedures (SPP) to place into effect the security controls and requirements prescribed in the ISM, which apply to the contractor's specific operations.

The SPP must be approved by the Cognizant Security Office prior to the issuance of the facility security clearance. An SPP is a written set of procedures or instructions to employees that spell out exactly how classified material will be protected within a contractor's facility. It is the contractor's implementation of the ISM.

The ISM prescribes the minimum security requirements that must be fulfilled by cleared contractors. The Industrial Security Representative can assist the contractor in implementing these requirements. Generally, prior to granting a facility possession of classified information, the Cognizant Security Office must ensure that the facility can adequately safeguard the type of classified information involved. This assurance is based on a determination that the facility has adequate procedures, safeguards, control, and storage capable of preventing disclosure of the classified information to unauthorized persons.

Some of the more essential considerations to the previous determinations are the presence of appropriately cleared personnel in key functions, such as receiving points, document control stations, etc.; adequate procedures for document control and accountability; area controls when required; reproduction control; an adequate security indoctrination program; etc. When these and other applicable requirements are met, the Cognizant Security Office can approve the release of classified information to the facility.

There are other requirements, such as classification markings, visitor control, subcontracting procedures, destruction, transmission, automated information systems, etc. All security requirements are set forth in the ISM.

In the DISP, a RESTRICTED AREA is a controlled area that has been established to safeguard classified material which, because of its size or nature, cannot be adequately protected during working hours by any other means. During non-working hours, this classified material can be effectively protected in approved storage containers, vaults, or strong rooms. When the material is of such a nature that it cannot be sorted properly during non-working hours, a CLOSED AREA is established. Both of these areas must have special security control measures in place.

The fact that a contractor has qualified for or has been granted a facility security clearance cannot be used for advertising or promotional purposes. However, in the recruitment of an employee for a specific position that will require a personnel security clearance, the firm may include the following statement in its employment advertisements: "Applicants selected will be subject to a security investigation and must meet eligibility requirements for access to classified information."

The facility clearance remains in effect as long as the DD Form 441 is effective. This agreement may be terminated by either party by giving 30 days notice. Generally, most facility clearances remain in effect as long as there is a reasonable need for the contractor to have access to classified information.

The government reserves the right to conduct security inspections of the facility. The authority by which these inspections are conducted is outlined in the provisions of the Department of Defense Security Agreement and the Industrial Security Manual.

The inspection is normally conducted with the assistance and in the presence of a company representative. These inspections serve a dual purpose by assuring the company, as well as the government, that no classified information is being retained outside of the company's security controls and that the information is being properly safeguarded.

A cleared facility is required to implement visit procedures to preclude all visitors from unauthorized access to classified information. It is essential that even cleared visitors requiring access to classified information are kept to a minimum, that the visit has been determined to be absolutely necessary, and that the visitor's security clearance has been verified.

There are basically two ways of disposing of classified material. The first method consists of destroying the material following those procedures outlined in the ISM. The second is returning it to the activity that provided it. However, in some circumstances, contracting officer approval must be obtained before disposing of any classified material.

There are a number of reports that must be submitted as required by the ISM. These reports are necessary whenever events or incidents occur that affect the security of classified material entrusted to a contractor. In addition, reports are sometimes required for cleared employees. The ISM specifies the circumstances when these reports shall be submitted.

In some cases, government agencies have requirements for additional safeguards. For example, if a contract requires a special access program, additional controls beyond those normally required will be necessary. Such controls can include special clearances or investigative requirements, special lists of persons determined to have a need-to-know, etc.

Industrial Security Cognizance

The Cognizant Security Office is that government office responsible for the security administration of the cleared contractor facilities within a specific geographical area. There are eight Cognizant Security Offices throughout the country, managed by the Directors of Industrial Security and supported by regional field offices.

224   Defense Industrial Security Program

The Cognizant Security Office is responsible for:

• Acting as the representative of government user agencies in matters dealing with safeguarding of classified information.

• Executing the Security Agreement for the government.

• Granting facility security clearances and interim facility security clearances as may be required.

• Conducting security inspections of cleared facilities.

• Conducting special inquiries concerning security violations and compromises.

• Implementing the industrial security education program.

• Resolving problems involving industrial security procedures.

• Advising and assisting contractors relative to the implementation of the DISP.

• Approving contractor automated information systems to process classified information.

Industrial Personnel Security Clearances

An industrial personnel security clearance is an administration determination by an authorized official that an industrial employee is eligible for access to classified information. This determination is based on investigation and review of available personal data, and a finding that access is clearly consistent with national interests.

The DoD issues security clearances for U.S. citizen employees of a contractor who require access to classified information. Clearances may be at the TOP SECRET, SECRET, or CONFIDENTIAL level. Only those persons who have a bonafide need-to-know and who possess a personnel security clearance at the same or higher level as the classified information to be disclosed may have access to classified information.

An individual may be processed for a security clearance when he has been employed by the contractor in a job requiring access to classified information and has been placed on the payroll. As an exception, a candidate for employment may be processed for a personnel security clearance provided a written commitment for employment has been made that prescribes a fixed date for employment within the ensuing 30 days, and the candidate has accepted the employment offer in writing.

An interim SECRET clearance is issued to those individuals who are eligible in less than 10 days. A final SECRET clearance will take approximately 60 days. In some cases, additional time is required. A TOP SECRET clearance takes considerably longer because of the additional investigation conducted for this higher level of clearance.

A firm is clearly entitled to employ persons with a past criminal record. When a clearance is requested for such an individual, the DoD evaluates the individual's complete record on its own merits. A clearance is denied only when all of the circumstances in the particular case, in the judgment of the DoD, warrant a determination that the requested clearance cannot be granted.

Many consultants are employed by User Agencies and cleared contractors. Consultants to User Agencies who are employed under Civil Service procedures are governed by separate regulations of the User agencies concerned. All other consultants, whether utilized by User Agencies or cleared contractors, come under the DISP if their duties will require them to have access to classified information.

Types of Consultants

Three types of consultants are described in the DISP:

• A Type A consultant is a self-employed consultant who does not possess classified material except at the using contractor's facility or on the premises of a User Agency activity. No requirement exists for a separate facility security clearance for consultants of this type, provided the using contractor or User Agency activity and the consultant jointly execute a certificate prescribing the conditions under which classified material will be handled.

• A Type B consultant for all intents and purposes is a subcontractor, and as such, requires a facility security clearance.

• A Type C consultant is one who possesses classified material at his regular employer's cleared facility with agreement between himself and his employer on their respective responsibilities for the security of the classified information. The use of Type C consultants is limited to User Agencies.

Generally speaking, a personnel clearance remains in effect as long as the individual remains continuously employed by the cleared contractor and can reasonably be expected to require access to classified information. To preclude excessive clearances, the facility should be continually reviewing the number of employees with security clearances and reduce the number of clearances whenever possible.

Defense Investigative Service

Source Questions and Answers on the Defense Industrial Security Program. (Defense Investigative Service, U.S. Department of Defense, Washington, DC, 1991).

DEFENSE INTELLIGENCE AGENCY (DIA)

The Defense Intelligence Agency (DIA) was established as an agency of the Department of Defense by DOD Directive 5105.21 on August 1, 1961, under the provisions of the National Security Act of 1947, as amended. It operates under the direction, authority, and control of the Secretary of Defense.

The chain of command for DIA extends from the Secretary of Defense, through the Joint Chiefs of Staff (JCS), to the Director. The Director of DIA acts for the JCS in intelligence matters because the intelligence directorate of the JCS was disestablished after DIA was formed. The flow of intelligence from DIA to the unified commands normally follows command channels, but direct communications are authorized between DIA and military intelligence resources at any level of DOD.

The purpose of the agency is to coordinate the intelligence efforts of the Navy, Army, Air Force, and Marine Corps. Important information gathered by the service agencies, such as assessments of the military strength of friendly and unfriendly countries, is processed through the DIA to the Central Intelligence Agency (CIA) where the information is evaluated.

Although relatively unknown to the public, the DIA plays a key role in the collection of intelligence information worldwide.

Defense Intelligence Agency

Source Public Affairs Pamphlet. (Defense Intelligence Agency, U.S. Department of Defense, Washington, DC, 1992).

DEFENSES TO CRIME

The law allows many defenses to charges of crime and it is the right of the accused to use any and all of them. The concept of defenses against prosecution may be viewed from two aspects: the basic capacity of the accused to commit the crime charged, and the applicability of certain specifically accepted defenses.

Capacity Defenses

The concept called "capacity to commit crime" demands that a person should not be held criminally punishable for his conduct unless he is actually responsible for it. Young persons and mentally afflicted persons, for example, may be recognized as not having the capacity to commit crimes, because they lack a sufficient degree of responsibility.

The infancy defense holds that children are incapable of committing any crime below a certain age, that at a higher age there is a presumption of an incapacity to commit crime, and at an even higher age certain crimes are conclusively presumed to be beyond the capability of a child. For example, it may be presumed that a toddler is incapable of stealing and a 10 year old is incapable of committing the crime of rape.

The corporation defense holds that because a corporation is an artificial creation, it is considered incapable of forming the requisite criminal intent. This defense has been largely overcome in recent years. Some crimes, such as rape, bigamy, and murder, cannot logically be imputed to a corporation.

The insanity defense holds that a person cannot be held liable for his criminal act if he was insane at the time of the act. The defense goes to the heart of the fundamental principle of intent, or guilty mind. If the accused did not understand what he was doing or understand that his actions were wrong, he cannot have criminal intent and, without intent, there is no crime.

The intoxication defense is similar to that of the insanity defense. It argues that the accused could not have a guilty mind due to intoxication. The fact of voluntary intoxication is generally not accepted as a defense. Involuntary intoxication produced by fraud or coercion of another may be a defense, and insanity produced by intoxicants may be acceptable.

Intoxication can also be offered as evidence that an accused was incapable of forming the intent to commit a crime, e.g., the accused was too drunk to entertain the idea of breaking and entering into a house at night for the purpose of committing an offense.

Specific Defenses

The alibi defense seeks to prove that because the defendant was elsewhere at the time the offense occurred, the defendant cannot be accused.

The compulsion or necessity defense argues that a person should not be charged with a crime when the act was committed in response to an imminent, impending, and overwhelmingly coercive influence. For example, a person who is ordered to drive a getaway car under the threat of immediate death would not be punishable as a principal to the crime.

The condonation defense is used in some rare cases where the law allows an accused not to be prosecuted if certain conditions are met. For example, a charge of seduction might be dropped if the parties involved subsequently marry.

The immunity defense grants protection from prosecution in exchange for cooperation by the accused. The required cooperation might be a full disclosure of all facts and testimony at trial.

The consent defense may be used when consent of the victim is involved. Where consent is offered as a defense, the consent must have been given by a person legally capable of giving it and it must be voluntary.

The entrapment defense argues that an accused should not be charged if he was induced to commit a crime for the mere purpose of instituting criminal prosecution against him. Generally, where the criminal intent originates in the mind of the accused and the criminal offense is completed by him, the fact that a law enforcement officer furnished the accused an opportunity for commission does not constitute entrapment. A key point is that where the criminal intent originates in the mind of the officer and the accused is lured into the commission, no conviction may be had.

The withdrawal defense may sometimes be used in a prosecution for conspiracy. A conspirator who withdraws from the conspiracy prior to commission of the requisite overt act may attempt a defense based on withdrawal.

The good character defense may seek to offer evidence that the accused is of such good character that it was unlikely he/she committed the act. This is not a defense as a matter of law, but an attempt to convince a jury it was improbable for the accused to have committed the crime.

The defense of ignorance or mistake of fact argues that the accused had no criminal intent. This defense seeks to excuse the accused because he was misled or was not in possession of all facts at the time of the crime. For example, this defense might be used in a case where a homeowner injured someone who he thought was a burglar in his home, but who in fact was the invited guest of another member of the family. This defense is based on the grounds that a defendant did not know certain essential facts, that he could not have been expected to know them, and that there could be no crime without such knowledge. Mistake of law is a rarely allowed defense offered by an accused that he did not know his act was criminal or did not comprehend the consequences of the act.

The statute of limitations defense seeks to prevent prosecution on the grounds that the government failed to bring charges within the period of time fixed by a particular enactment. Not all crimes have time limitations for seeking prosecution, and some crimes, such as murder and other major crimes, have no limits whatsoever.

Irresistible impulse is a legal defense by which an accused seeks to be fully or partially excused from responsibility on the grounds that although he knew the act was wrong, he was compelled to its execution by an impulse he was powerless to control.

Necessity is the defense of justification of an otherwise criminal act on the ground that the perpetrator was compelled to commit it because a greater evil would have ensued had he failed to do so. Thus, one could plead necessity if he committed arson to destroy official documents that would otherwise have fallen into the hands of a wartime enemy.

The self-defense or defense of life rule is derived from English common law, which authorizes the use of deadly force in self-defense and in order to apprehend persons committing or fleeing from felonies. In many jurisdictions, the rule has been narrowed by statute so that the use of weaponry is limited only to defense of life situations and to some specific violent felonies, for example, murder, rape, aggravated assault, arson, or burglary. This protection against prosecution relies on the premise that every person has a right to defend himself from harm. A person may use, in self-defense, that force which, under all the circumstances of the case, reasonably appears necessary to prevent impending injury.

Diminished capacity is the decreased or less-than-normal ability, temporary or permanent, to distinguish right from wrong or to fully appreciate the consequences of one's act. It is a plea used by the defendant for conviction of a lesser degree of a crime, for a lenient sentence, or for mercy or clemency.

Former jeopardy is a plea founded on the common law principle that a person cannot be brought into danger of his life or limb for the same offense more than once. The former jeopardy defense is founded on the principle that a case once terminated upon its merits should not be tried again.

Double jeopardy can only be claimed when the second prosecution is brought by the same government as the first. When the act is a violation of the law as to two or more governments, the accused is regarded as having committed separate offenses.

The "but for" rule or the sine qua non rule holds that a defendant's conduct is not the cause of an event if the event would have occurred without it.

Related to legal defenses is the bill of particulars. It is a statement by the prosecution filed by order of the court, at the court's own request or that of the defendant, of such particulars as may be necessary to give the defendant and the court reasonable knowledge of the nature and grounds of the crime charged, such as the time and place, means by which it was alleged to have been committed, or more specific information.

The concept can also apply to the defendant; for example, a defendant who intends to rely on an alibi defense may be required to furnish the prosecuting officer with a bill of particulars as to the alibi. This bill sets forth in detail the place or places the defendant claims to have been, together with the names and addresses of witnesses upon whom he intends to rely to establish his alibi. The purpose of this procedure is to prevent the sudden and unexpected appearance of alibi witnesses whose testimony in the latter stage of a trial could cast reasonable doubt on the state's case.

By compelling advance notice, the prosecutor is afforded time to investigate the alibi, as well as the credibility of the alibi witnesses, and, in so doing, establish a position for refuting the alibi defense.

John J. Fay, CPP

Source Fay, J.J., Butterworths Security Dictionary. (Butterworth-Heinemann, Boston, 1987).

DESIGN: PHYSICAL SECURITY CONSIDERATIONS

A threat analysis is a prerequisite to the security system design of a planned facility. A comprehensive survey will take into consideration the range of possible threats, including both natural and man-made, and the vulnerabilities of the facility's site. The professional conducting the survey will be concerned with such elements as likely adversaries and their capabilities, probability and frequency of threat occurrence, and the criticality of the assets to be protected within the facility. Also of concern will be the physical and psychological factors that can contribute to or detract from the protective scheme.

Physical factors, such as fences, locks, walls, and doors, should be regarded as opportunities for enhancing protection. They are fairly easy to evaluate because their effectiveness can be measured in discrete terms, such as in the minutes of delay afforded against intrusion. By contrast, the effectiveness of psychological factors is relative and arguable. They include uniformed guards, television surveillance cameras, lights, and signage that discourage unwanted entry.

Asset Value

The protection given a particular asset should be in keeping with its value. Value in this context is both extrinsic and intrinsic. Extrinsic value represents monetary worth as well as replacement cost. It can also incorporate the cost of lost business opportunity when an asset cannot be sold because it has been stolen or destroyed.

Intrinsic value corresponds to assets (which may also have extrinsic value) that are irreplaceable, unique, or of such great psychological worth that protection of them is absolutely essential. Nuclear weapons, highly toxic substances, rare paintings, and the like fall into this category because they cannot be measured in dollars alone.

Asset Protection

The selection of locations and safeguards for the protected assets will be influenced by the needs of the business to have use of them and the convertibility of the assets to personal use. Cash in a retail facility, for example, is somewhat dispersed among cashiers and is highly convertible. Sensitive information in a research facility, on the other hand, tends to be compartmented, closely held, and not very convertible to personal use. The locations of retail cashiers and the physical and procedural safeguards for protecting cash will be markedly different than those used for protecting information in the research setting.

Location also refers to a number of proximities, i.e., nearby structures and access roads, human activity in and around the facility, and the nearness of the response force to the installation. Nearness of other buildings or neighboring businesses could be an advantage if there is a mutual sense of concern. Conversely, nearby premises or business activities could serve as a magnet in attracting crime that could spill onto the protected site.

Roads around the site also carry advantages and disadvantages. For a fenced compound containing stored materials, highly traveled roads with close-up visibility will be an advantage because the protection scheme will rely upon the deterring effect of passing motorists and law enforcement patrols; for a rare metals laboratory, nearby roads may be a disadvantage because they create easy in and out access for robbers and burglars.

Nearness of human activity is pertinent because if there is activity near the assets, the security system might be effective with a combination of locks, barriers, and locally annunciated audible alarms.

The proximity of the security or law enforcement force to the location of assets will determine the timeliness of response. Physical barriers to intrusion provide delay and intrusion sensors provide notice. These are essentially useless safeguards unless reinforced by the neutralizing effect of a human response.

Physical Barriers

Delay of the intruder can be provided by structural barriers such as fences, gates, walls, roofs, floors, doors, windows, or vaults, and natural barriers such as rivers, lakes, cliffs, or any natural obstruction that is difficult to cross. Unsophisticated intruders, whose mode of operation is limited to forcible entry through doors and windows, will probably be discouraged by structurally sound barriers secured with high-security locks. These barriers are minor obstacles to the sophisticated intruder.

The length of time required for an adversary to penetrate the physical barriers is a function of its penetration resistance and the breaching method used. The time required to penetrate a physical barrier should be considered in tandem with the response time. If the barrier can be penetrated before an effective response can be mounted, the system should be modified to either increase barrier resistance time or give earlier detection of a penetration attempt.

Fences. Fences are used to channel personnel and vehicles through designated entrances during normal operations and to discourage or deter entrance into the fenced area during non-working hours. Fences may be considered a barrier to an unskilled intruder, but they are only minor obstacles to a more skilled or agile intruder. Fences are, however, usually considered the first level of protection in a security system. For this reason, fences are quite often protected with fence disturbance sensors.

The most common type of fences are chain-link fences like those installed on the perimeter of most industrial sites, utilities, and government installations. These fences are typically 7-foot high, woven metal fabric supported by steel posts, usually topped with either three or six strands of barbed wire. A single arm outrigger supports three strands of barbed wire and a V-shaped outrigger supports six strands with three strands on each arm. The barbed-wire topping increases the effective height to 8 feet.

A structurally sturdy, well-maintained fence provides a better barrier for fence disturbance sensors and will psychologically discourage intruders and resist penetration more effectively than a loose, poorly maintained fence. Some maintenance measures that should be taken are: keep the fence-line free of brush and bushes; eliminate washouts under the fence that allow easy access by crawling; remove any objects from along the fence that could be used for gaining entrance by climbing; and secure all gate-hinges hardware so that the gate cannot be easily removed even though locked.

Sometimes the major advantage of a fence is that after the intruder crosses it to get in, he must retreat through or over the fence with the assets he is trying to steal. For some assets this may not be difficult, but if the intruder is trying to steal bulky materials or large objects, the fence may impede retreat, limiting the thief as to how much he can take without opening the gate or cutting through the fence. Therefore, chain-link fences have some value in protecting bulky assets, assuming that the area is patrolled; otherwise, the intruders would be undisturbed to execute their objective.

Overall, fences serve a useful purpose by defining legal boundaries, deterring the general public, and eliminating interference from wanderers and lowly motivated intruders. Defining the legal boundary around an installation is important. If, for instance, a guard or responding police officer finds someone inside the fenced compound, there can be little doubt that the person knowingly trespassed. The effectiveness of the boundary is enhanced when it is properly posted.

Walls. Exterior walls are usually considered the first level of protection for buildings not enclosed by a fence. Depending on the type of building, the exterior walls may vary from wood siding to thick granite walls. However, the most common types of exterior walls are constructed from cinder block, brick, concrete, pre-cast concrete, or combinations of these materials. Concrete and pre-cast concrete walls offer the greatest penetration resistance, but even these are vulnerable to penetration.

Operable Openings. Operable openings are doors, windows, transoms, and similar devices that can be opened or closed to allow or prevent passage of people, air, or light. They are the usual points of entry for intruders, especially at ground level and in concealed and semi-concealed locations. Operable openings are also the hardest points to protect, simply because they are designed for passage.

The first consideration in protecting an operable opening is to determine if the opening is really needed. Many buildings, especially older ones, have windows and doors that are no longer used. The problem of protecting obsolete windows or doors can be eliminated by simply sealing them permanently in a manner that maintains the penetration resistance of the wall containing the opening. For instance, if the door to be eliminated is mounted in a brick wall, the door assembly should be removed and the opening bricked up, taking care to properly anchor the new construction. When an operable opening is less than 18 feet from the ground or less than 14 feet from another structure, it should be either physically covered with bars or grilles equipped with intrusion detection devices, or both.

Ground-level doors, especially the accessible ones, are used for gaining entrance into a facility more than any other openings. Therefore, the door locks, mounting hardware, and construction of the door assemblies should be in keeping with the integrity of the surrounding walls. Because of the high probability of an intrusion through a door, all exterior doors should have intrusion-detection devices that will detect anyone opening the door. Since ground-level windows also allow easy access, they too should be physically secured and protected with intrusion-detection devices.

Deterrents

Deterrents can be classified as either physical or psychological. Physical security deterrents are highly visible devices or barriers that are designed to delay the entry of an intruder long enough to effectuate an apprehension. A deterrent is effective only to the extent it is believed by the potential intruder to be effective. A hollow core door has less deterrent value than a steel reinforced door because the potential intruder will understand the difference in time delay and will accordingly gauge his prospects for success.

The same is true for psychological deterrents, such as uniformed security officers, watchdogs, lighting, closed-circuit television (CCTV) cameras, mirrors, etc.

The effectiveness of physical deterrents can be quantitatively measured in terms of penetration times and ranked as to the likely effect on deterring or delaying an intruder, but their effectiveness as psychological deterrents cannot be quantitatively measured. Qualitative pronouncements can be made and interpolations based on crime rates can be put forward convincingly, but assessment is subjective at best. Nonetheless, the conventional wisdom is that the tried and true security safeguards do act as important deterrents to crime.

Robert L. Barnard

Source Barnard, R.L., Intrusion Detection Systems. (Butterworth-Heinemann, Boston, 1982).

DESIGN SPECIFICATIONS

In the design of a construction project involving the installation of security equipment, whether on a large scale, such as the installation of an access control system in a new building, or on a small scale, such as the addition of new alarm equipment at an existing structure, an architect will be engaged to provide architectural direction to various parties. The involved parties might be a general contractor and subcontractors concerned with physical construction and vendors or manufacturer representatives of the security equipment to be installed. The architect is also likely to interface with a security consultant who represents the interests of the owner.

The architect will communicate critical project details in several written media, such as architectural drawings and written specifications. The written specifications are especially important because they are the checks and balances used by the architect to initially delineate the precise nature of the projected work, to monitor the work while it is in progress, and to finally compare the completed work against what was planned. The architect can write two types of specifications: proprietary and performance.

Proprietary Specifications

Proprietary specifications are appropriate when there is only one product capable of providing to the finished installation an important capability or appearance. The specifications, for example, may dictate particular equipment that is compatible with existing equipment, or may dictate particular paneling, glazing, and sealing products that will satisfy aesthetic requirements.

Proprietary specifications are fairly common to nongovernmental jobs when the private owner firmly holds preconceived preferences. Public sector jobs will often prohibit proprietary specifications unless it can be shown that the preferred product or service is critical and cannot be acquired except through proprietary channels.

A disadvantage of the proprietary approach is that it works against the benefits of competitive bidding. The sole-source nature of the proprietary approach means that a premium price will be paid due to the lack of competition. Sole-sourcing of electronic security systems is not unusual for several reasons. The owner may want equipment that will interface with equipment already in place or may be convinced that a certain brand or type of technology is superior to all others. The owner may also be motivated to obtain particular equipment capabilities that have only recently come into the marketplace as the result of a scientific breakthrough made by a single manufacturer who is protected by patent rights against competition.

Sole-sourcing, however, is almost always subjected to close scrutiny by those who control the purse strings. A security consultant, for example, who is absolutely convinced that only one particular system can meet the organization's unique needs will be challenged to present convincing evidence to that effect. Scrutiny of sole-sourcing is inevitable and may in fact be helpful by requiring the consultant to give thoughtful consideration to possible alternatives. Rapidly evolving technology and intense competition among security equipment manufacturers increase the likelihood that more than one product will be capable of doing the job.

Performance Specifications

Performance specifications will typically address functional characteristics and quality. The architect has a concern that the equipment to be acquired and installed will perform to expectations. Established industry standards, the known capabilities of the proposed equipment, and the purchaser's expressions of functional need will provide guidance to the architect in the shaping of expectations.

The performance specifications document is the medium for communicating expectations. It can be extremely helpful to the owner in identifying the contractors capable of providing equipment that will meet the established operational and performance requirements. The list of identified contractors is narrowed to a manageable number and each is invited to bid. The invitation to bid is normally accompanied by the specifications.

The stage is then set for the bidders to respond. The specifications will not usually call for equipment that operates according to a particular technology or scientific principle, but it will be left to the bidders to propose equipment that will meet the delineated standards. In some cases, the purchaser may ask the bidders to submit more than one proposal and to offer options as to major technologies or to an entirely different approach.

A primary value in formulating performance specifications is the uniformity that is introduced to the bid process. For the bidders, the specifications make clear what is needed and they are therefore guided in their production of responsive bids. Bidders are also guided when the specifications make reference to well-understood performance and quality standards.

Although performance standards will sometimes relate to a particular manufacturer's product, it is understood and expected that the bidders may propose comparable products. For the purchaser, the specifications allow the separate bids to be compared in an "apples to apples" manner. To the extent that all bids can be equalized for the purpose of making straight comparisons, the process is greatly simplified for the purchaser, with the final decision probably resting on price.

Prices may vary widely among bids on the same job for the simple reason that several technologies may be offered and each technology will have its own price tag. Pricing comparisons become more confusing when bidders offer combinations of technologies. The purchaser's goal is to attain optimum performance at minimum cost, but the route to the goal can be confusing and complex. It is in this area that a knowledgeable consultant can prove invaluable to the purchaser.

Role of the Consultant

The role of the security design consultant is significantly different with respect to the two types of specifications previously discussed. Proprietary specifications require relatively little work by the consultant because, with one or only a few options to choose from, the consultant is not tasked with making a great many comparative analyses. The operational and performance characteristics of the desired equipment are readily available from the manufacturers. The matter of selection is pretty much limited to ensuring that the purchaser's needs can in fact be met by the equipment. As stated earlier, this approach precludes any significant competitive bidding.

On the other hand, performance specifications can require much more involvement by the consultant: first, the development of the specifications; second, the selection of prospective bidders whose equipment corresponds to the specifications; third, evaluation of the bids; and lastly, testing and evaluation of the installed equipment to ensure it is performing to expectations. The value added to the project by a consultant can be considerable.

The cost of the security consultant will be more than offset by the savings gained, assuming, of course, that the services were of good quality. Judgments as to the cost-effectiveness of the consultant's services are often subjective and not easily made. They are perhaps better made after enough time has passed for an experience base to be established concerning the overall performance of the installed equipment or system.

Randall Atlas, Ph.D, AIA, CPP

DESIGN TO RESIST BALLISTICS, BLAST, AND FORCED ENTRY

Ballistics

Design to resist ballistics is heavily dependent on the ballistics to be resisted. For security applications, ballistics commonly range from 0.22 caliber handgun bullets to bullets fired from high-powered rifles (0.30 caliber or 7.62 millimeters). In extreme cases, they can include armor-piercing bullets and larger caliber bullets fired from various military weapons. For most applications, however, the high-powered rifle should represent the upper bound of the threat. Deciding on and specifying the threat weapon can be a difficult task. Ballistic standards have been developed to simplify the weapons decision and to assist manufacturers in designing bullet-resistant components. The most commonly used ballistic standards were developed by the National Institute of Justice and Underwriters Laboratories. These standards specify the weapon and the bullet associated with a particular threat, and specify a procedure for testing bullet-resistant components to resist the threat. This ensures uniformity among manufacturers.

It should be noted that design to resist ballistics does not produce bullet-"proof" components. Components are designed to be bullet "resistant." Designing components to resist ballistics can be accomplished by two basic means. The first is to design components based upon the known ballistics resistance of common building materials such as steel and concrete. This method is commonly used for such components as walls and ceilings, and may be used for doors as well. The other design method is to specify that a manufactured component must resist a particular ballistic standard and allow the manufacturer of the component to certify its ballistics resistance through testing. This method is not frequently used for common walls and ceilings, but it is the most common means of specifying doors and windows.

Doors and windows may be made of a variety of materials. Doors may include materials such as steel, armor plate, or bullet-resistant fiber glass. They may be covered with a decorative material for aesthetics. Bullet-resistant window glazing is commonly made of glass, plastics, or combinations of the two. For doors and windows, the ballistics resistance must be for the entire assembly, including the door or window frames. This is common in the ballistics-resistant component industry. If a bullet-resistant component is subjected to a threat level higher than that to which it was designed or specified, it will likely fail. The degree to which failure will endanger those on the protected side of the component depends on how much higher the threat was than that specified.

One way to limit the number of building components that must be bullet resistant is to limit lines of sight through them. This entails keeping people inside a protected area away from components such as doors and windows as much as possible, or shielding the doors and windows from vantage points with other building components. Limiting lines of sight to people or other potentially targeted assets can also be used as a lower level of protection. This entails accepting the risk that aggressors will not shoot at what they cannot see.

Blast

Design to resist explosive blasts is very complex and should be left to experienced engineers. The basic concepts are relatively straightforward, however. Before any blast-resistant design may begin, the size of the explosive must be established. For security applications, upper-bound explosive weights may range from approximately 50 or 60 pounds for hand-placed explosives to approximately 1,000 pounds for vehicle bombs. These weights are equivalent weights of trinitrotoluene (TNT). The actual explosive may be a lesser weight of another explosive such as a plastic explosive, but the weight is commonly stated as a TNT equivalent to provide a standard of measure.

Once the explosive weight is established, design to resist the explosive effects depends on the distance of the explosive from the target building. The effects of an explosion dissipate rapidly with distance. Therefore, if the explosive can be kept far enough from a building, the building may require little or no special construction. As an approximate rule of thumb, for conventionally constructed buildings (those not specifically designed to resist blast effects), the distance that a bomb must be kept away can be determined by using a simple relationship. The distance in feet that must be maintained between a potential bomb location and the building is equal to a constant, K, times the cube root of the explosive weight in pounds of TNT.

The constant, K, varies depending on the level of damage that can be accepted. If the user can accept that the building will be damaged to a level approximating 20% of its replacement cost and that the assets or people inside the building may sustain moderate damage or injury, a K of 24 may be used. If damage approximating 10% of the building replacement cost and minor damage or injury to assets or occupants is acceptable, a K of 30 may be used. If damage approximating 5%

of replacement cost and only superficial damage or injury is acceptable, a K of 40 should be used. For the latter case and a 1,000-pound bomb, the bomb must be kept at least 400 feet away from the building. The previous relationship should only be used for planning purposes. The resulting distances should be verified through analysis by a qualified engineer. Also note that in all of the mentioned cases, conventionally designed windows will most likely fail, creating an additional hazard. Retrofitting existing windows or designing new windows to resist explosive effects at the previous standoff distances is not particularly difficult or expensive, however.

If an explosive cannot be kept far enough away from the building, it will need to be designed to resist the effects of the explosive. That will commonly take heavy wall and roof construction. Retrofitting existing construction to resist close-in blast effects is very difficult and costly. Windows and doors are particularly susceptible to blast effects and designing them to resist such effects is expensive. Therefore, windows and doors should be minimized. People and assets should be located in the interior of the building away from exterior doors or windows where possible.

Forced Entry

Design to resist forced entry requires an integration of detection measures and barriers. Barriers are building elements such as walls, doors, windows, and ceilings that delay an aggressor from gaining access to an asset. Barriers are designed to provide a specified delay time to a forced-entry attempt using particular tools. These may include hand, power, or thermal tools, and even explosives. A layer of barriers is laid out to form a protective envelope around an asset. For example, for an asset within a room, all of the building elements making up the structure of that room, including doors and windows, are potential barriers.

For an effective forced-entry-resistant design, all of the building elements within such a room will have delay times as close as possible to each other. In any such layer, the element with the least delay time is the weak link in the layer and controls the delay time of the entire system of barriers. The weakest links are frequently windows and doors (especially door hardware).

Where possible, establishing multiple concentric layers of delay elements, as in rooms surrounded by other rooms, may provide the most economical design.

Detection measures are critical to providing effective protection against forced entry. Detection may be by guard or by intrusion-detection system. The purpose of detection is to notify people who can respond to an alarm that a forced-entry attempt is in progress so they can respond to and prevent the act from being successful. Where detection is by guard, the guard detects aggressors visually or audibly as they attempt to break through barriers. Where detection is by an intrusion-detection system, electronic sensors detect the aggressor attempts. Different sensor types include those that detect motion of the aggressor, the sound or vibration of forced-entry attempts, and breaching of barriers, such as the opening of doors or the breaking of windows.

The key to effective forced-entry-resistant design is to integrate delay and detection. This is done by providing detection at such a location that the aggressor will be detected before he or she begins to breach the outermost layer of barriers. The outermost layer of barriers is the layer farthest from the asset at which the delay time of that layer and all of the layers between it and the asset equals or exceeds the response time to an alarm. In this integrated system, the layers of barriers provide enough delay to the aggressors to allow the response force to arrive before the aggressors have gained access to the asset.

Curt P. Betts, P.E.

DISCIPLINE

As a rule, the word discipline evokes an emotional reaction, both to the giver and the receiver. No one enjoys being disciplined and most supervisors would rather do anything but administer it, but the fact remains that discipline is an important part of supervision.

On the brighter side, discipline need not be totally negative. A positive approach will emphasize discipline accompanied by guidance, sanctions that are balanced with fairness, and a system of rules that apply to all employees uniformly and consistently.

The word discipline is derived from the Latin word *discipulus*, which means learning. The word *disciple* is from the same root. Early Christian disciples were considered the learners or students of Christ. The word conveys an important concept in supervision, i.e., that discipline is a mechanism for correcting and molding employees in the interests of achieving organizational goals. Punishment, the negative aspect of discipline, is tangential to the larger purpose of fostering desirable behavior.

Discipline is an act of the organization, not of a supervisor personally. The process is a legitimate means to an end and condemns the employee's unacceptable behavior without condemning the employee. The process essentially says, "You're okay, but what you did is not okay."

It is also important that discipline be swift. Coming to grips with a problem immediately is better than putting it off until later. Uncorrected problem behavior tends to worsen and takes on new dimensions over time. Instead of one problem, the dilatory supervisor may discover that he has one very large problem plus a number of new ones. Discipline that is applied without undue delay has a preventive influence if only for the simple reason that the offending employee is not given time to repeat the unacceptable conduct.

A note of caution is appropriate here: the supervisor should not rush into disciplinary action. Acting swiftly is important, but is not as important as obtaining all of the facts of the situation and weighing the facts carefully to arrive at a considered and deliberate judgment.

Discipline Can Be Difficult

Discipline is a responsibility that rests squarely on the supervisor's shoulders. It cannot be passed upward to the boss or laterally to a human resources specialist. A supervisor can find lots of reasons for not giving discipline: the employee is a friend, a good person, or will get upset; the workload is too heavy right now; wait until performance appraisal time to bring it up; and, it's not a popular thing to do. These are, of course, rationalizations for avoiding a difficult responsibility.

The fact is that most employees want to work in a well-ordered environment and they recognize that discipline is an essential element of good order. While no one wants to be the object of discipline, there is an acceptance of discipline as

an expected consequence of violating a rule. Employees may wish for leniency in those situations where it is deserved but not leniency across the board. They worry that overly tolerant supervision will allow a few employees to engage in violations that adversely affect everyone.

While leniency may be somewhat negotiable between a supervisor and the supervised, there can be no compromise with respect to fairness and consistency. Even a hint of unfair or discriminatory discipline can be poisonous to the process and destructive to the supervisor's reputation.

Disciplinary Principles

Principle 1: Assume Nothing. Ensure that everyone knows the rules. Put the rules in writing; make them a regular item of discussion in formal and informal sessions; disseminate and display them prominently. An employee who does not know the rules cannot be expected to follow them, and a supervisor should not discipline an employee when there is doubt that the employee was unaware of the rule.

Principle 2: Discipline in Privacy. Receiving discipline is never a pleasant experience and can be particularly unpleasant when it is received in the presence of co-workers or others who have no legitimate role in the process. Embarrassment, anger, and resentment are the natural emotions that follow criticism given publicly. Discipline is a private matter to be handled behind closed doors or in a setting that ensures absolute privacy.

Principle 3: Be Objective. Rely on facts, not opinions and speculations. Consider all the facts and examine them with an open mind. Look for and eliminate any biases, for or against the offender. Make sure there is in fact a violation and determine the relative severity of the violation. Was the offender's act aggravated or mitigated in any way?

Principle 4: Educate the Violator. Administer discipline that is constructive. The purpose is to bring about a positive change in the violator's conduct or performance. Discipline should be a learning experience in which the violator gains new insights that contribute to personal improvement.

Principle 5: Be Consistent. Inconsistent enforcement of policy and rules should be totally unacceptable. For example, if the policy of the department is to terminate officers who sleep on the job, then all officers so caught must be terminated. To fire one and not another will breed contempt for the rules and those who set the rules.

Principle 6: Do Not Humiliate. The intended outcome is to correct, not hurt. When humiliation is made a part of the process, the offender will come away angry, resentful, and perhaps ready to fail again. Both the offender and the organization will suffer as a consequence.

Principle 7: Document Infractions. Make a record of violations. This is not to say that a negative dossier be maintained on each employee, but it does mean that instances of unacceptable performance have to be recorded. The record of an employee's failures is valuable as substantiation for severe discipline, such as termination, or as a diagnostic aid to counseling professionals.

Principle 8: Discipline Promptly. With the passage of time, an uncorrected violation fades into vagueness. The violator forgets details, discards any guilt he may have felt at the time of the violation, and rationalizes the violation as something of little importance. When opened for discussion, an uncorrected violation is likely to lead to disagreement about what "really happened" and any disciplinary action at that point can appear to be unreasonable.

Giving Clear Instructions

It is sad but true that discipline is sometimes meted out when the supervisor is partially at fault. When this occurs, it is usually not in connection with a rules violation, but with a failure of the employee to complete a task or to carry out the task in some particular way. The fault of the supervisor is in having given poor instructions.

The supervisor's instructions may not have been enunciated distinctly or presented in a logical sequence. The instructions may have been too complicated for the employee to follow, or they could have come across to the employee as

intimidating or belittling. Even when an assignment is understood, it may not be completed because emotions get in the way. Asking is always better than demanding.

Following are tips on how to assign work:
- Know the assignment yourself.
- Do not assign work above the employee's ability.
- Explain the purpose of the assignment.
- Request or suggest – do not demand.
- Give brief, exact directions.
- Demonstrate if possible.
- Do not assume the employee understands perfectly.
- Do not watch every move; let the employee feel responsible.
- Let the employee know you are available to give assistance.

Most employees want to do a good job. If care is taken in giving assignments, there will be fewer failures and fewer resulting disciplinary problems.

Self-Discipline

No manager or supervisor can ever hope to discipline others effectively if he cannot discipline himself. Self-discipline is a foundation for working with other people, helping them overcome their failures, and for setting a workplace climate where good order is the norm.

Loss of temper may make a supervisor feel better for a while, but it will not improve personal performance or the performance of the supervised. Although some subordinates may quickly respond in the face of an angry outburst, the overall effect creates confusion, resentment, and loss of confidence in the supervisor as a leader.

Arguing with subordinates is a waste of everyone's time. Explaining and discussing are very necessary to good supervision because they operate to dispel misunderstanding, but when the dialogue gets argumentative, the process of communicating breaks down rapidly.

Recognizing subordinates for good work is a tried and true technique for creating harmonious working relationships. Those who use it well find that it works best when applied sparingly. Extending a great deal of recognition generally or directing it at one or a few persons reduces the effect. But certainly the greatest error in using recognition is to give the appearance of favoritism.

Consciously or subconsciously, subordinates tend to emulate their superiors. If the supervisor displays a lack of self-discipline, so will the supervised. Self-discipline in this sense goes beyond just maintaining personal composure. It deals with all manner of traits, for example, integrity, loyalty, and demeanor.

Constructive discipline is positive. It is focused on correcting unacceptable acts rather than on the personalities of the actors, and it is a process that relies more on education than on punishment. The supervisor administers discipline promptly but not hastily, objectively but leniently when appropriate, and always with fairness and consistency. Clear communications enhance the process, privacy and confidentiality cloak it, and good records provide a history.

Charles A. Sennewald, CPP

Source Sennewald, C.A., Effective Security Management, 2nd Edition. (Butterworth-Heinemann, Boston, 1985).

DISCRIMINATION ON THE JOB: EQUAL EMPLOYMENT OPPORTUNITY

The U.S. Equal Employment Opportunity Commission (EEOC) oversees federal agency discrimination complaint processing and affirmative action planning. EEOC conducts hearings and adjudicates appeals of final agency decisions on complaints of discrimination and reprisal filed by federal employees and applicants under Title VII of the Civil Rights Act of 1964, the Age Discrimination in Employment Act, and Section 501 of the Rehabilitation Act of 1973, which prohibits discrimination in the federal sector against individuals with mental or physical handicaps.

The EEOC also investigates allegations of sex-based wage discrimination in violation of the Equal Pay Act.

If an employee or applicant for employment believes that he/she has been discriminated against by a federal agency when applying for a job, or on the job because of race, color, sex, religion, national origin, age, or handicap, he/she may file a complaint of discrimination with the federal agency where the alleged discriminatory act occurred.

Only complaints of sex-based wage discrimination in violation of the Equal Pay Act are filed directly with EEOC. In cases where the matter complained of is otherwise appealable to the Merit Systems Protection Board, the complaint of discrimination will be processed by the agency pursuant to special "mixed-case" procedures.

The complainant has the right to be represented by the person of his/her choice at any step of the process. Retaliation against a person who participates in the discrimination complaint process or opposes a discriminatory employment practice is illegal. A complaint of reprisal is filed and processed in the same manner as other complaints of discrimination.

A complainant must first consult with an equal employment opportunity (EEO) counselor at the employing agency within 30 calendar days of the alleged discriminatory act or the effective date of a personnel action before filing a complaint of discrimination or reprisal. The EEO counselor will inquire into the facts and attempt to resolve the matter informally.

The complainant has 15 calendar days from receiving a written notice of final interview with the EEO counselor to file a formal complaint in writing with the employing agency. Failure to file within the 15-day time limit may result in the rejection of the complaint.

The complainant may file a formal complaint with the employing agency without having received the written notice of final interview if the matter has not been resolved within 21 calendar days from first contacting an EEO counselor.

If the employing agency accepts the complaint, it is assigned to an investigator. If the employing agency rejects the complaint, the complainant is notified in writing of the right to appeal to EEOC's Office of Review and Appeals within specified time limits.

The investigator takes affidavits from the complainant and other witnesses, and gathers evidence about the complaint. Once the investigation is complete, the employing agency gives the complainant a copy of the investigative file.

The employing agency again tries to resolve the complaint on an informal basis after the complainant has reviewed the investigative file. A complainant and the employing agency may resolve the complaint at any step in the process.

If an informal resolution has not been reached, the employing agency notifies the complainant in writing of its proposed disposition of the complaint and of the right to a final decision with or without a hearing.

Complainants must request a hearing by notifying the employing agency within 15 calendar days of receipt of the letter of proposed disposition. Otherwise, the employing agency will issue its final decision without a hearing. A hearing is conducted by an EEOC judge. The administrative judge hears relevant testimony and considers documentary evidence of the alleged discrimination. Witnesses give testimony under oath or affirmation and can be cross-examined.

After the hearing, the administrative judge submits his/her findings and a recommended decision to the head of the employing agency. The employing agency issues its final decision, either accepting, modifying, or rejecting the administrative judge's recommended decision. The final decision is accompanied by an exact transcript of the hearing and a copy of the administrative judge's recommended decision.

The complainant may appeal the employing agency's final decision to EEOC's Office of Review and Appeals within 20 calendar days of receiving that decision and may submit supporting statements within 30 calendar days thereafter. A complainant may file a lawsuit in an appropriate U.S. District Court:

• Within 30 calendar days after receiving notice of final action taken by the employing agency; or

• After 180 calendar days from filing a complaint with the employing agency if there has been no final agency decisions; or

• Within 30 calendar days after receiving notice of final action taken by EEOC on the complainant's appeal; or

• After 180 calendar days from filing an appeal with EEOC when there has been no EEOC decision.

An age discrimination complainant can choose between two different procedures:

• He/she may file a lawsuit in a U.S. District Court instead of filing a complaint of age discrimination with the employing agency after giving EEOC at least 30 days notice of intent to file suit about an alleged discriminatory act that occurred within the previous 180 calendar days.

• He/she may file a complaint of age discrimination with the employing agency and complete all the steps of the process outlined previously before filing a lawsuit.

If the employing agency is covered by the section of the Civil Service Reform Act that allows allegations of discrimination to be raised in a negotiated grievance procedure and the applicable procedure provides for the processing of allegations of discrimination, the employee may choose to file either a complaint or a grievance, but not both.

The employee is considered to have made this choice when he/she first files either a written complaint or a written grievance. The employee cannot subsequently withdraw the earlier filed complaint or switch to the other process, once the action has started.

Equal Employment Opportunity Commission

Source Complaints of Discrimination by Federal Employees or Applicants. (The U.S. Equal Employment Opportunity Commission, Washington, DC, 1988).

DNA ANALYSIS

DNA is the basic genetic material within each living cell that determines a person's individual characteristics. Since the early 1980s, DNA testing has been used in AIDS and genetic disease research, bone marrow transplants, and in anthropological investigations. In forensics, DNA testing is typically used to identify individuals, using only small samples of body fluids or tissue -- such as blood, semen or hair -- left at a crime scene.

DNA Testing Methodologies

DNA testing includes two major components when used for forensic purposes. The first involves the molecular biological techniques that allow analysts to directly examine a DNA sample. The second component has to do with population genetics -- how to interpret DNA tests to calculate the degree to which different samples are associated. Such population studies help to determine the results of the analytical work.

DNA tests investigate and analyze the structure and inheritance patterns of DNA. Many methodologies exist, and new ones are constantly being developed. The particular test used will depend on the quantity and quality of the sample, the objective of the test, and the preferences of the laboratory conducting the procedure. All tests, however, are designed to isolate certain nucleotide sequences -- the polymorphic segments of the DNA molecule carrying marked, recurring distinctions -- and these variable segments provide the basis for discriminating among individuals' DNA.

In a forensic environment, two common analytical methods used to detect the polymorphic DNA in human samples are the Restriction Fragment Length Polymorphism (RFLP) and Polymerase Chain Reaction (PCR) techniques. The RFLP method identifies fragments of the DNA chain that contain the polymorphic segments, produces a DNA "print" of the fragments, and measures the fragment lengths. The PCR-based methods seek to determine the presence of specific alleles (alternative forms of genes that occur in different individuals), thus indicating specific genetic characteristics.

Restriction Fragment Length Polymorphism. RFLP requires the presence of as little as 50 to 100 nanograms of DNA -- an amount of DNA that may be present in a single hair follicle. The distinct stages in developing a DNA print using RFLP will be portrayed here by describing the analysis of a blood sample.

First, white cells containing the DNA are separated from the blood sample by use of a centrifuge, and the cells are ruptured to extract the DNA strands. The DNA strands are then cut, or digested, using restriction endonucleuses (REs) -- enzymes derived from bacteria that catalyze the cutting process. A particular enzyme will cut the DNA strands at the same nucleotide sequence (restriction site) each time. By cutting a person's DNA in the same place, the several alternate forms (alleles) of a gene are separated from each other. A specific allele will be of the same size and molecular weight as others of its type. The polymorphism, or individuality, of a person will be detected on the basis of differences in DNA fragment lengths.

At this point in the process, all of the DNA fragments are mixed together. Using a technique called electrophoresis, the polymorphic fragments are separated by length. The DNA is placed at one end of a plate containing agarose gel, with a positive electrode placed at the other end. DNA carries a negative electrical charge; therefore the DNA will move toward the positive electrode.

The distance that an individual fragment of DNA travels depends on the amount of its electrical charge, which is determined by its length and molecular weight. Thus, fragments of the same length and weight will travel the same distance while large DNA fragments will move more slowly than smaller fragments. This process sorts the DNA into bands based on length and weight and these length-dependent bands are the basis for DNA identification.

After electrophoresis, the next step calls for transferring the DNA fragments in the gel to a nylon membrane. In a technique called "Southern blotting," a chemical reagent (such as sodium hydroxide) acts as a transfer solution and a means to separate the double-strand fragments into single-strand fragments.

Using the zipper analogy, the strands are unzipped, exposing the building blocks. The unzipped DNA fragments are now fixed on the nylon membrane, where they are exposed to radioactive DNA probes -- laboratory-developed (thus, known sequences), DNA nucleotide fragments which carry a radioactive "marker." The probes seek out the sequence that they match and attach themselves to the complementary split DNA strands.

The probes are made radioactive so that the DNA sequences to which they become attached can be visibly tracked. The nylon membrane is placed against a sheet of X-ray film and exposed for several days. When the film is developed, black bands will appear at the point where the radioactive DNA probes have combined with the sample DNA. The result, called an "autoradiograph" or "autorad" looks much like the bar codes found on items in supermarkets and department stores.

The final step is the band pattern comparison. Genetic differences between individuals will be identified by differences in the location and distribution of the band patterns, which correspond to the length of the DNA fragments present. The actual measurement of the band patterns being compared can be done manually or by machine, but often DNA identification depends upon expert judgment.

Polymerase Chain Reaction-Based Techniques. PCR is not only an analytical tool, but also an amplification technique often used when the available amount of DNA material is insufficient for proper analysis, or when the sample is degraded by chemical impurities or damaged by environmental conditions. PCR is an in vitro process that causes a specific sequence to repeatedly duplicate itself, mimicking its natural replication process. Short pieces of purified DNA, called primers, are used to build a foundation upon which the sample DNA can build. The primers must have sequences that complement the DNA flanking the specific segment to be amplified. The sample DNA is heated to separate the double helix, producing two single strands. By then lowering the temperature, copies of the primers bind to the DNA sample's flanking sequences. A heat-stable DNA polymerase (an enzyme) is then introduced to the DNA sample causing the primers to synthesize complimentary strands of each of the single strands. This process is repeated for generally 25 cycles, amplifying the original DNA sequence approximately a million times. The amplified DNA can then be analyzed by any one of several methodologies.

Functions of DNA Testing

DNA testing provides a basis for positive identification, but it is not expected to become a suitable technology for validating identification in security settings. DNA analysis would be inappropriate in situations where a nearly immediate determination must be made as to whether a person seeking entry to a particular area, or seeking to conduct a particular transaction is, in fact, authorized to do so. The chemical analysis required to make a DNA comparison takes weeks, not minutes. DNA testing is increasingly used to determine paternity and, in forensic settings, it has been most prolifically and successfully used to identify or exonerate a suspect.

Paternity Determinations. In determining paternity, DNA has proven to be extraordinarily useful. Each chromosome contains nucleotides identical to those of each parent, as well as the nucleotides that distinguish the individuality of the person. If samples from the child and from one of the parents are available, the nucleotides of the child that are different from the known parent's DNA must have come from the unknown parent's DNA. If a sample from the suspected, but unknown, parent supplies all the "missing" nucleotides without any superfluous nucleotides,

one can conclude that the suspected individual is, in fact, the other parent.

Identification of Suspects. The forensic promise of DNA typing is substantial. Samples of human skin, hair follicles, blood, semen, or saliva containing cells or other tissues found on a crime victim or at a crime scene can be examined to identify the DNA pattern. That pattern can be compared with DNA from a suspect to make a "positive identification," or to exonerate a suspect. DNA examination techniques sometimes permit the use of extraordinarily small samples of human tissues or fluids, such as a few hairs or a single spot of blood. Moreover, DNA is durable and is relatively resistant to adverse environmental conditions such as heat or moisture. DNA degrades slowly in a decomposing body, lasting sometimes for years and allowing samples to be analyzed for some time after the death of an individual. Although some experts debate the percentage of usable tissue and fluid samples that are retrieved from all crime scenes, DNA analysis will have the greatest effect on violent crime cases, such as murder and rape, where hair, blood, semen, or tissue evidence is frequently found.

Bureau of Justice Statistics

Source Forensic DNA Analysis. (Bureau of Justice Statistics, U.S. Department of Justice, Washington, DC, 1991).

DOCUMENT EXAMINATION: AN OVERVIEW FOR THE SECURITY MANAGER

"Not invisible but unnoticed, Watson. You did not know where to look, so you missed all that was important" [1].

Scrutinizing the paper trail is vital to the successful outcome of any investigation. The forensic document examiner is an expert who can assist the security manager in making the most of documentary evidence.

Document or handwriting experts are generally associated with forgery. While the most common query is, "Who wrote or signed this document?," there may be a great deal of information lying beneath the surface that may provide critical data to the investigation. It is rare to find any case without a paper trail. Names, phone numbers, addresses, figures, bank accounts, or other documentation may provide the pivotal pieces of a puzzling case. The security manager should not overlook document examination as an important tool of the profession.

Questions to ask the document examiner may include: Who wrote the anonymous letter(s)? Was the document typed in one setting or were additional terms added at a later time? Was the document signed before or after it was typed? Were the aircraft/vehicle maintenance records "sanitized" to cover for neglect in upkeep? Were new documents created to support one party's position in a case? Were additions, deletions, or insertions made in a medical record after the fact?

The forensic document examiner conducts examinations and comparisons of questioned documents in order to determine the genuineness of a document, or to expose it as non-genuine. The document examiner must look at the whole document, as it is possible to have a genuine signature on a fraudulent instrument. There is no such thing as "half a forgery."

Services Provided

The forensic document examiner can provide:
- Consultation
- Laboratory examination and analysis
- On-site examination
- Case photography [2]
- Preparation of written reports, when necessary or desirable
- Preparation of exhibits
- Deposition or court testimony

Types of examinations include:
- Handwriting and handprinting
- Typewriting or other machine impressions
- Alterations, additions, and deletions
- Page substitutions
- Dating of documents
- Comparison and/or analysis of paper or inks

Locating a Qualified Expert

The forensic document examiner must obtain training through course work, independent study, and/or apprenticeship. Skills must be acquired through government agencies or in the private sector. Currently, no formal degree program exists for this field in the United States. Training in calligraphy (ornamental writing) or in graphology or graphoanalysis (personality assessment through handwriting) is not recognized as training in handwriting identification. Common areas of study for the document examiner include the study and evaluation processes of handwriting characteristics and patterns, techniques for examination of typewriting, photocopiers, and other machines, inks, papers, and forensic photography. A competent examiner is familiar with all aspects of the field and can handle most cases through to their completion. However, one will not claim to be an authority in every area and will confer and work closely with other specialists when required. These specialists may include ink or paper chemists and photocopier or other machine technicians, as the case dictates.

Document examiners advertise in the yellow pages, and in local and state bar journals. Little can be determined from advertisements alone. A prudent manager should retain a proven and experienced examiner.

Several document examination organizations exist. Two of these are the Association of Forensic Document Examiners (AFDE) and the American Society of Questioned Document Examiners (ASQDE), both of which maintain strict membership guidelines. It is important for the security manager to inquire as to the certification and testing requirements, as some certifying bodies have higher standards than others. The AFDE Board Certification is the only procedure that involves outside legal critics in the evaluation process.

It is wise to ask examiners for references from other investigators or clients they have worked for. These persons have observed the expert in action, and are therefore the best sources of recommendation.

Fees and Payment

The document examiner may charge by the case or by the hour. Many examiners are going to a "case fee" based upon the complexity and demands of each individual matter.

A retainer is generally required up front, as are any travel or other out-of-pocket expenses. The billing arrangement is between the document

GUIDELINES FOR WORKING WITH A DOCUMENT EXAMINER

1.   If you suspect or know you have a problem document, place the original document in a protective cover immediately. **DO NOT** fold, staple, clip, mark, or alter its condition in any way. If the document is torn, do not tape or repair it.

2.   Contact the document examiner to determine what is needed for the particular case in question. For example, if the question is one of authentic handwriting, the document examiner will furnish information on how to collect appropriate comparison materials. Use your document examiner as a resource person, consultant, and expert.

3.   For handwriting related cases, acquire contemporaneous, admissible comparison materials as soon as possible. If the questioned writing is an endorsement on a check, obtain other endorsed checks; if the question involves bookkeeping figures, then other documents containing numerals are needed; handwritten correspondence will be required to conduct an examination of anonymous letters, etc.

4.   Exemplars (also known as standards or known writings) **must be 1) legally admissible, 2) the genuine writing of the person they represent,** and **3) contemporaneous** with the disputed document. The exception would be in a case where you are looking for changes in writing. In such cases, signatures from a particular range of time would be collected.

A case can be made or lost in the taking of exemplars, as generally there is but one opportunity to obtain them. Your expert can assist you in obtaining the most valuable comparative material. There are two classes of exemplars: formal and informal.

   •*Formal Exemplars* are written at your request and usually in the investigator's presence or that of the document examiner. These exemplars may contain disguised or self-conscious writing; therefore they are of limited and/or specific value.

   •*Informal Exemplars* are written in the usual course of business. Examples include checks, real estate or other legal transactions, or correspondence.

5.   Maintain the chain of custody by using personal delivery or a courier service where each person handling the document signs for it. (Federal Express, etc.)

6.   Spell out the purpose of the examination and your understanding of the fee agreement in a letter of assignment to preserve the chain of custody and prevent communication problems.

Bonnie L. Schwid and Lynn Wilson Marks of *Document Integrity Services*, San Antonio, Texas.

examiner and the retaining party (such as a security manager or an attorney acting for the client). Additionally, the retaining party may be required to sign a fee agreement. Discussing the financial arrangements at the outset prevents misunderstandings.

Obtaining and Handling Documents

Should a search of a suspect's property be permitted, gather all items that might be helpful to the document examiner. Depending upon the case, these might include: papers, tablets, pens, stapler, staples, markers, typewriter ribbon, etc. It may be possible to determine that the wadded paper found in the suspect's trash was in fact under the original handwritten note. In such a case, the indented writing can be "brought out" by various techniques and may be used at the time of trial. If the questioned document is torn from a tablet, the edge of the paper might be matched with the remaining pad.

The possibility of fingerprints or blood typing (i.e., analysis of the saliva on an envelope flap or the reverse of a postage stamp) should not be overlooked. If a document is charred, do not attempt to touch it. Contact the document examiner immediately.

Care must be taken to ensure the document's integrity. It is preferable for the document examination to be completed prior to the application of ninhydrin for fingerprint identifications. All documents, whether they be carbon copies, photocopies, or photographs, should be treated as originals and handled as such, in the event such documents become the best evidence.

When identifying a document, discreetly initial (if that is your procedure) in a nonessential area.

• Do not initial near the portion in question.

• Do not place an identification label on the documents.

• Do not fold the document.

• Do not underline or circle what is to be examined.

• Do not staple or paper clip the documents.

• Do not attempt to mend a document. The pieces can be placed side-by-side in a transparent folder.

• Do not place photocopies in hard plastic sleeves as the toner will adhere to the plastic.

• Do place documents in a paper or plastic envelope. Mark the envelope prior to placing the documents inside. This will avoid adding indentations to the evidence.

Contact the document examiner to determine what is needed for the examination. The document examiner can furnish information on how to collect appropriate comparison material. Use the expert as a resource and consultant. Both the document examiner and the security manager can obtain these standards. However, the security manager or his investigator often are conveniently located near the place at which the query arose. Although the manager has no control over the document in question, he has a great deal of latitude in collecting a complete set of comparison materials.

For handwriting-related cases, acquire contemporaneous, admissible comparison materials as soon as possible [3]. If the questioned writing is an endorsement on a check, obtain other endorsed checks; if the question involves bookkeeping figures, then other documents containing numerals are needed; handwritten correspondence will be required to conduct an examination of anonymous letters and the like.

Exemplars

Exemplars (also known as standards or known writings) *must be* (1) legally admissible, (2) the genuine writing of the person they represent, and (3) contemporaneous with the disputed document [4]. There are two classes of exemplars: formal and informal [5].

•Formal exemplars are written at the request of the investigator and usually in the investigator's presence or that of the document examiner. These exemplars may contain disguised or self-conscious writing; therefore they are of limited and/or specific value.

•Informal exemplars are written in the usual course of business. Examples include checks, real estate or other legal transactions, or correspondence.

The forensic document examiner and the security manager, working together, can make an effective team. Documentary evidence, when properly demonstrated, is convincing testimony. As the Chinese proverb states, "The palest ink is more accurate than the most retentive memory."

Lynn Wilson Marks

Notes
1.   From A. Conan Doyle's "A Case of Identity," *The Complete Sherlock Holmes*, Doubleday, New York, 1988, p. 196.

2.   Forensic photography provides a permanent record of important documents. Records can be "created" using a photocopier, and photocopies can obscure real evidence. Therefore, photographs taken from the original documents make much stronger evidence should the originals become "lost."

3.   A list of sources for handwriting exemplars may be obtained by written request to

the author at Post Office Box 690526, San Antonio, TX 78269.

4. The exception would be when looking for changes in writing. In such cases, signatures from a particular range of time would be collected.

5. A case can be made or lost in the taking of dictated writings, as generally there is but one opportunity to obtain these exemplars. An expert can assist in obtaining the most valuable comparative material.

DRUG ABUSE: DRUGS AND CRIME

Evidence continues to grow that drug abuse and crime are linked together. Data from national studies, for example, confirm that a large percentage of inmates in state prisons were under the influence of an illegal drug or had consumed large amounts of alcohol just before they committed the crimes that led to their imprisonment. The fundamental assumptions underlying the connection between crime and drugs are:

• Individuals who use heroin, cocaine, and such drugs with severity tend to have corresponding patterns of severity in criminal behavior.

• Individuals who increase their drug abuse tend to have a corresponding increase in criminality, and vice versa.

• Individuals who regularly use heroin and cocaine tend to engage in criminal acts to support their habits, with corresponding costs to their victims, families, employers, and society in general.

Career criminals comprise a majority of the most serious offenders (i.e., the violent predators) and they have histories of heroin use, frequently in combination with alcohol and other drugs. An offender's history of drug abuse, in fact, is proving to be one of the best predictors of serious career criminality.

Research also indicates that narcotics abusers engage in violence more often than previously believed. It was once thought that the euphoria associated with narcotics abuse was inconsistent with violent acts. New data show that narcotics abusers are just as likely as other criminals to commit homicide, sexual assault, and arson, and are even more likely to commit robbery and weapons offenses. Persons who are involved with drugs from the selling and distributing side are

also at high risk for violence. Reports from several cities indicate that increases to homicide rates are related to drug trafficking.

Even more disturbing is a research finding that a very high percentage of robberies and felony assaults against young persons were committed by a small, highly criminal group of youths who were habitual criminals and were regular users of heroin, cocaine, or pills. At the same time, other data show that criminally active youths who are not also involved in illicit drug use rarely commit robberies and assaults.

Accurate figures as to the full range of economic consequences of drug abuse of all kinds are difficult to derive. It was found, however, that among heroin users, who have similarities to cocaine users, the average user regularly commits "non-drug" crimes, such as larceny, burglary, and robbery, to support his or her habit. The dollar cost to the victim is about four times that of criminals who do not use drugs or who use drugs on an irregular basis.

These costs, incidentally, are in addition to those due to other economic factors such as lost productivity of legitimate work; criminal justice system expenses for police, courts, corrections, probation, and parole; treatment and rehabilitation; and the costs experienced by private persons and businesses in protecting against crime.

Perhaps the foremost conclusion that can be drawn from research is that regular abusers of hard drugs commit an extraordinary amount of crime, and much of it is violent in nature. The major impetus for most of this criminal behavior is the users' need to support drug habits, without regard for the rights and needs of others. This may not be an entirely new finding, but one that is worth revisiting, if only for the purpose of renewing our determination to cure our society of a national disease.

Calvina L. Fay

DRUG ENFORCEMENT ADMINISTRATION

The Drug Enforcement Administration (DEA) of the Department of Justice has the responsibility, in conjunction with the Federal Bureau of Investigation (FBI), of enforcing the federal drug laws as outlined in the Controlled Substances Act of 1970, and its subsequent amendments. The DEA is also responsible for developing a national drug intelligence system and cooperating with federal, state, and local law enforcement agencies in efforts to curb drug abuse nationally.

Drug Enforcement Administration

Source Public Affairs Pamphlet. (Drug Enforcement Administration, U.S. Department of Justice, Washington, DC, 1992).

DRUG-FREE WORKFORCE: GUIDELINES

According to estimates by the U.S. Chamber of Commerce, substance abuse costs our economy $60 to $100 billion annually. Businesses today must recognize that the drug epidemic gripping our nation carries high costs. These costs are manifested in lost wages, accidents, poor workmanship, employee theft, higher insurance costs, etc. Costs to employers who do not address the issue usually exceed 2.5% of payroll. Some experts estimate that between 10% and 19% of the American workforce is drug impaired. Businesses cannot ignore or avoid the problem any longer.

Many businesses are bound by federal and state laws and regulations to develop and implement drug deterrence programs which may include testing employees. Following are some steps to be considered when developing and implementing a drug deterrence policy and program.

Steps in Policy Development

Every employer should prepare a written statement that outlines the company's position on the use of drugs. The policy should state that drug use and deteriorating performance which results from drug use will not be tolerated and will result in adverse personnel action. It should be circulated and acknowledged. The policy should outline the consequences that will result from employee drug use. Sanctions can include action up to and including termination. Employers may chose to offer one-time access to an employee assistance program for first-time violations of the company policy.

The policy should be in writing and acknowledged by all current employees and all candidates prior to their employment. Acknowledgment should be in the form of a receipt, which should be placed in permanent personnel records. The policy should be posted as well.

An appropriate waiting period should be implemented prior to enforcing the policy. This allows the firm time to educate employees about the policy and it also allows employees who need to access the employee assistance program time to do so before the policy takes effect.

In developing a drug deterrence policy, the company should determine its objective and how that objective will be achieved. In his book, *Drug Abuse in the Workplace: An Employers Guide for Prevention*, Mark A. deBernardo outlines the following steps to consider in developing a policy.

1. Commit your firm at the senior management level.

2. Review personnel records of drug-troubled employees to determine if the numbers indicate that the problem is significant.

3. Analyze personnel and productivity records for indicators of abnormal increases in absenteeism, accidents, compensation claims, turnover, theft of property, grievance proceedings, and wage garnishments. Also examine production to determine changes in productivity and meeting deadlines.

4. Determine whether drug testing will become part of the firm's program, and when, how, and who will be tested.

5. Decide what disciplinary steps will be taken for employees who are found violating the firm's drug deterrence policy.

6. Analyze the costs of employee assistance programs with regard to health insurance costs, worker's compensation, and unemployment compensation.

7. Recognize that alcohol abuse and the abuse of prescription drugs are the most prevalent problems, and must be addressed in a comprehensive company policy.

8. Coordinate the policy and program with affected company personnel to ensure that the policy complements and agrees with other policies.

9. Ensure that the firm's legal counsel reviews the policy to be sure it is consistent with existing policies, laws, and regulations.

10. Collectively bargain with unions or employee associations regarding the company's intent to implement a program, and enlist their support and cooperation.

11. Issue a statement in advance of the program that states the company's position on

drug abuse, its commitment to a drug-free workplace, and the consequences for violating the policy.

The policy should include a strongly worded statement that articulates the firm's position on drug abuse, including it's position on safety, product or service integrity, and employee performance. Further, the consequences of violating the policy should be clearly stated and fairly enforced. Employees must be made to realize that it is their responsibility to seek treatment if they wish the company's support.

In order to implement a program in a fair and orderly process, the policy must be circulated to and acknowledged by all employees. Additionally, a grace period should be scheduled to allow for employee education and supervisory training. Employee education and training are key elements that will lead to acceptance of the program. A grace period will also allow those employees who will require support to take advantage of rehabilitation benefits before the policy takes effect.

Steps in Drug Testing

Drug testing should be thoroughly researched and the protocol understood before a company enacts a program. The services of many qualified and experienced professionals are available, and they should be consulted prior to drug testing.

The following are considerations when developing a drug deterrence program.

1. Drug testing is *one phase* of a comprehensive program. It is not a "cure-all."

2. Contract with a reliable, professional drug-testing laboratory that will assure quality control and chain-of-custody for test samples. Check to determine what certifications and licenses have been awarded to the laboratory, and what credentials the professional staff has earned. The laboratory should be able to provide expert witness testimony if called upon.

3. The conduct of drug testing should be done in a *fair, consistent, and legally defensible manner*. Caution should be taken to ensure that collection, handling, and testing procedures are reliable to prevent mistakes. The policy should *apply equally to all employees* covered by the policy. All steps taken that lead up to the drug screen should be well documented in a consistent and accurate manner.

4. Require applicants and employees to sign a waiver that states it is the policy of the company to test applicants and that one of the requirements for consideration for employment is passing a drug test. Additionally, acceptance of the company's drug deterrence program is a condition of employment. For current employees, the waiver must state that the employee has read and understands the company's policy, that the company reserves the right to conduct tests, and that a positive finding may subject the employee to disciplinary action up to and including termination. All releases should include a statement that allows the testing parties to release the results of tests made to the company and other officially interested parties.

5. As a routine testing procedure, the specimen that is collected should be split into two samples, which will allow for a confirmatory test following a positive screen. The confirmatory test should be a different chemical process, such as mass spectrometry/gas chromatography. The company should not contemplate any action before the second test is conducted to confirm the results of the initial screen.

6. As a precautionary measure, the testing facility that conducts the tests should retain samples as evidence for a reasonable length of time in case of litigation.

7. The firm must ensure that it has taken every reasonable precaution to protect the confidentiality of the test results. The firm does, however, have the right to notify others, e.g., supervisors, who have a need to know.

Supervisory Training

Prior to the enactment of the drug deterrence program, the firm should train supervisors. They should learn the components of the policy, the signs and symptoms of drug abuse, and the resulting deterioration of performance. Critical to the success of the program is the supervisor's ability to *observe and document* poor performance that may be the result of drug and alcohol abuse. A supervisor should not be expected to be or act like a diagnostician. The proper role is to observe deteriorating performance and document the observations. All drug-intervention training provided to supervisors should be documented. A well-written policy combined with sound supervisory training should allow for significant progress in combating employee drug and alcohol abuse.

Robert D. Dey

Source deBernardo, M.A., Drug Abuse in the Workplace: An Employer's Guide for Prevention. (U.S. Chamber of Commerce, Washington, DC, 1988).

DRUG RECOGNITION PROCESS

The Drug Recognition Process is a systematic, standardized evaluation. It is systematic in that it is based on a variety of observable signs and symptoms, known to reliably indicate drug impairment. The conclusion is based on the complete analysis, not on any single element of the evaluation. The process is standard in that it is conducted in the same way for every person.

The recognition techniques include the evaluation of specific physical and behavioral symptoms (examination of eyes and vital signs, scrutiny of speech and coordination) that indicate if a person:

• Is currently under the influence of drugs (substances actively circulating in the blood).

• Has recently used drugs (within the last 3 days). The evaluation can also provide information about the category of drug used.

The evaluation will not identify the exact drug or drugs a person has used. The process permits the presence of drugs to be narrowed down to certain broad categories (for example, central nervous system stimulants), but not to specific drugs such as cocaine. It can be determined that a person probably used a narcotic analgesic but not whether it was morphine, codeine, heroin, or some other substance.

The evaluation does not substitute for chemical testing of persons who exhibit signs of drug influence or recent use. The process will usually supply accurate grounds for suspecting that a particular category of drugs is present in urine or blood, but sample collection and analysis must still be done if scientific or legal evidence is needed.

The evaluation process can suggest the presence of seven broad categories of drugs, distinguishable from each other by observable signs they generate in users:

1. Central nervous system (CNS) stimulants, such as cocaine and amphetamines.

2. CNS depressants, such as alcohol, barbiturates, and tranquilizers.

3. Hallucinogens, such as LSD, peyote, and psilocybin – but not phencyclidine (PCP).

4. Narcotic analgesics, such as Demerol, codeine, heroin, and methadone.

5. Phencyclidine (PCP) and its analogs.

6. Cannabis, such as marijuana, hashish, and hash oil)

7. Inhalants, such as model airplane glue and aerosols.

Recognition Techniques

Professionals who implement the drug recognition techniques should follow these 12 steps, in the given order:

1. Take a drug history. Ask a structured series of questions concerning prior drug involvement. The drug history may reveal patterns of usage that will be of assistance in the evaluation.

2. Administer a breath alcohol test. With a breath-testing device, it can be determined if alcohol is contributing to the person's observable impairment and whether the concentration is sufficient to be the sole cause of that impairment. An accurate and immediate measurement of blood alcohol determines the person's blood alcohol concentration (BAC). If the BAC is not sufficient to produce the observed level of impairment, the evaluation is continued to detect the presence of other drugs. The BAC is also useful in determining if a person is in need of immediate medical treatment or other special attention.

3. Perform the preliminary examination (pre-screen). Ask a structured series of questions, make specific observations, and have the person perform simple tests that provide the first opportunity to examine the person closely and directly. Determine if the person is suffering from an injury or some other condition not necessarily related to drugs. Begin also to systematically assess appearance and behavior for signs of possible drug influence or drug use, as well as screening out persons who do not exhibit signs of drug use. For asymptomatic persons, no further evaluation or drug testing is necessary.

4. Examine the eyes. The inability of the eyes to converge toward the bridge of the nose suggests the presence of certain drugs, such as

cannabis. Other categories of drugs can induce horizontal-gaze nystagmus, an involuntary jerking that may occur as the eyes gaze to one side or as they are elevated. CNS depressants (alcohol, barbiturates, tranquilizers) will typically cause horizontal-gaze nystagmus.

5. Administer the divided-attention psychophysical tests. These include the Rhomberg Balance, the Walk and Turn, One-Leg Stand, and Finger to Nose. Specific errors of omission or commission can point toward specific categories of drugs causing impairment. For example, a person who is under the influence of a CNS stimulant (cocaine or amphetamines) may move very rapidly on the Walk and Turn test, but may exhibit a distorted sense of time on the Rhomberg Balance test (such as estimating 15 seconds to be 30).

6. Perform the dark room examination. Make systematic checks of the size of the pupils, the reaction of the pupils to light, and evidence of drugs taken by nose or mouth. Certain categories of drugs affect the eyes, especially the pupils, in predictable ways. For example, a person under the influence of a CNS stimulant or hallucinogen will have dilated (enlarged) pupils. A person under the influence of a narcotic analgesic, such as heroin, will have extremely constricted (small) pupils, which will exhibit little or no response to the presence or absence of light.

7. Examine vital signs. Perform systematic checks of the blood pressure, pulse rate, and temperature. Certain categories of drugs (including stimulants) will elevate blood pressure and pulse rate, raise the body temperature, and cause breathing to become rapid. Other drugs, including narcotic analgesics, have the opposite effects.

8. Examine for muscle rigidity. Certain categories of drugs, such as PCP, can cause the muscles to become hypertense and very rigid.

9. Look for injection sites. Some users of certain categories of drugs routinely or occasionally inject their drugs. Evidence of hypodermic needle use (scars or "tracks") may be found in veins along the arms, legs, or neck. Injection sites are frequently found on users of narcotic analgesics.

10. Interview the person and make observations. Based on the results of the previous steps, at least a suspicion can be formed about the category or categories of drugs that may be involved.

11. Form an opinion. Based on all the evidence and the observations, it should be possible to reach an informed conclusion about whether the individual is under the influence of drugs or has recently used drugs, and if so, the category or categories of drugs that are the probable cause of the impairment.

12. Request a toxicological examination. Chemical tests provide scientific, admissible evidence to substantiate conclusions. Generally, urinalyses are performed (90% of the time); in some cases, blood tests are ordered also.

National Institute of Justice

Source National Institute of Justice Report No. 221. (U.S. Department of Justice, Washington, DC, 1990).

DRUG TESTING: A COMPARISON OF URINALYSIS TECHNOLOGIES

Employers interested in conducting drug tests often ask critical questions:

• How accurate are the technologies? Does one particular technology result in more false positive or false negative errors than others?

• Do the federal guidelines for drug testing in the workplace, especially for cutoff levels, meet the needs of the private sector?

• Is one technology consistently accurate enough to eliminate the need for routine confirmation by an alternative method?

These questions were answered in a study conducted under the auspices of the Bureau of Justice Assistance and the National Institute of Justice [1].

Accuracy of the Technologies

The study involved tests made of the five drugs examined in the federal testing program: marijuana, cocaine, phencyclidine (PCP), opiates, and amphetamines. The technologies included EMIT (the enzyme multiplied immunoassay test, manufactured by the Syva Company, Palo Alto, CA), TDx (the trade name for the fluorescent polarization immunoassay test, manufactured by Abbott Laboratories, Chicago, IL), RIA (the radioimmunoassay test, also called Abbuscreen, manufactured by Roche Diagnostic Systems, Nutley, NJ), TLC (the standard thin layer

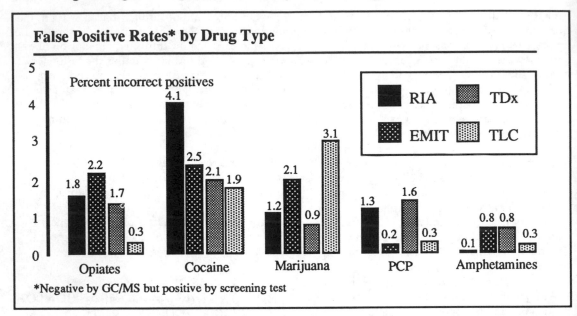

False Positive Rates* by Drug Type

Percent incorrect positives

RIA   TDx
EMIT   TLC

Opiates: RIA 1.8, TDx 2.2, EMIT 1.7, TLC 0.3
Cocaine: RIA 4.1, TDx 2.5, EMIT 2.1, TLC 1.9
Marijuana: RIA 1.2, TDx 2.1, EMIT 0.9, TLC 3.1
PCP: RIA 1.3, TDx 0.2, EMIT 1.6, TLC 0.3
Amphetamines: RIA 0.1, TDx 0.8, EMIT 0.8, TLC 0.3

*Negative by GC/MS but positive by screening test

chromatography test), and GC/MS (the gas chromatography/mass spectrometry test).

Questions have been raised within the business, scientific, and legal communities concerning the accuracy of TLC relative to other testing procedures. Test results showed a clear difference between the accuracy of the immunoassays as a group (EMIT, TDx, and RIA) and TLC. TLC performed poorly in identifying the presence of illegal drugs.

A concern frequently voiced about drug testing is the possibility that a test will label as positive a urine specimen from an individual who has not used drugs. These errors are known as false positives. The study's average false positive rate, combining results for the five drug types and using the National Institute on Drug Abuse (NIDA) cutoff levels, was about 1-2%, based on the screening test, without GC/MS confirmation.

The study also examined the extent to which the current screening technologies miss the presence of drugs in urine -- that is, the extent of false negatives. For the three immunoassays, the average false negative rate for the five drug types was about 20%, using the NIDA cutoff levels. Screening tests are designed to minimize false positive results and, as a consequence, a larger number of false negative results will occur.

The magnitude of the false negative rate was determined by the screening and confirmation cutoff levels, which followed the NIDA guidelines. The data revealed that the immunoassay cutoffs were partly the reason for the technology's failure to identify the specimens designated as positive by GC/MS. Many of the false negative specimens contained some amount of the drug, but not at concentrations high enough for the immunoassays to label the specimens positive. Accordingly, the false negative rate would be reduced by lowering the cutoff levels of the immunoassays.

Adequacy of Cutoff Levels

The study also looked at whether the current NIDA cutoff levels are appropriate, considering the strong likelihood that lower cutoff levels could lead to the detection of a greater number of drug users. To accomplish this, screening and confirmation cutoffs were selected for marijuana, cocaine, and opiates that were lower than those specified by NIDA.

The study concluded that if the cutoff levels for marijuana were lowered to 50 nanograms/milliliter, approximately one-third more users might be identified. For cocaine and opiates, lowering the cutoffs to 200 might increase detection of drug use by 10-20%. The potential impact on an employer's drug testing program could be considerable. On the up side, it would eliminate from consideration many more drug-using job applicants and identify drug-using employees who represent accident risks and

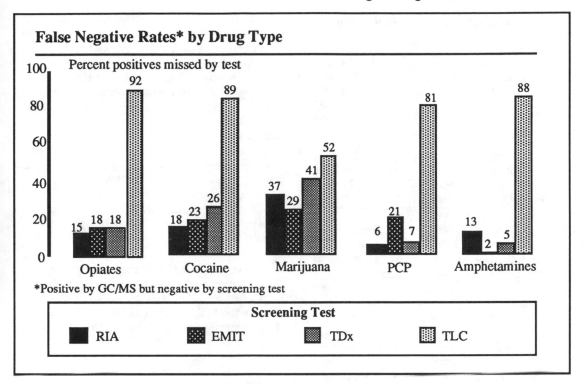

False Negative Rates* by Drug Type

Percent positives missed by test

*Positive by GC/MS but negative by screening test

Screening Test

RIA   EMIT   TDx   TLC

higher operating costs. On the down side, it would drive up the employer's costs with respect to increased use of drug treatment and an increased need for additional supervision of drug-using employees.

The Issue of Confirmation

Immunoassay technologies are not error-free. The study concluded that an average of 1 to 2 specimens may test positive in every 100 specimens, when examined by one immunoassay technology. When more than one immunoassay technology is applied to the same 100 specimens, the number of false positives may decrease, although not disappear entirely. Repeat testing by the same method or by a similar technology most probably will not eliminate all erroneous results on a long-term basis.

GC/MS confirmation of positive results, however, would eliminate virtually all false positive errors. GC/MS provides the best protection against legal challenges and gives assurance of accuracy to persons affected by drug testing.

National Institute of Justice

Source Visher, C. and K. McFadden, A Comparison of Urinalysis Technologies for Drug Testing in Criminal Justice (An Executive Summary). (National Institute of Justice, U.S. Department of Justice, Washington, DC, 1991).

Note

1. The study findings are contained in the full report of *A Comparison of Urinalysis Technologies for Drug Testing in Criminal Justice*. This article has been drawn almost entirely from a summary of that report.

DRUG TESTING: DETECTION LIMITS

Detection time in drug testing is dependent on the drug being looked for and the sensitivity of the test used. The more sensitive the test, the longer the drug can be detected. Drug concentrations are initially highest hours after drug use and decrease to undetectable levels over time. The time it takes to reach the point of non-detectability depends on the particular drug and other factors, such as an individual's metabolism.

The sensitivity of urine assay methods generally available today allows detection of

Retention Times of Drugs in Urine	
Amphetamine	48 hours
Barbiturate (short-acting)	24 hours
Barbiturate (long-acting)	2-3 weeks
Benzodiazepines	3 days
Cocaine	2-4 days
Methadone	3 days
Opiates	2 days
Cannabinoids	
Moderate use	5 days
Heavy use	10 or more days
Methaqualone	14 days
Phencyclidine	8 days

cocaine use for a period of 1 to 3 days, and heroin or phencyclidine (PCP) use for 2 to 4 days. These detection times would be somewhat lengthened in cases of previous chronic drug use, but probably to no more than double these times. Methaqualone and phenobarbital can be detected for as long as 2 to 3 weeks. On the other hand, some amphetamines and secobarbital pass through the body so quickly that a negative result is likely even with very recent use.

With regard to cannabis, several studies show that due to highly individualized excretory patterns it is possible to see positive results for as long as 4 weeks. Also, the manner in which the body stores cannabis metabolites and releases them by excretion can be erratic over a period of days or weeks. The metabolites may vary in quantity each day depending on whether fat tissue is being broken down at a high rate, as with heavy exercise, or at a low rate in a resting state. A person could give a negative result one day after last smoking marijuana and give a positive result the next day.

The metabolism of marijuana into its many metabolites is extremely complex and not fully understood. There are well over 20 compounds labeled as cannabinoids in marijuana, and since it can be taken by mouth or smoked, with variable absorption from either route, the study of its metabolism is difficult. There are literally hundreds of marijuana metabolites that are produced in variable amounts according to the user's habit and personal pattern of metabolism. For most marijuana users, absorption of the drug varies with the route of administration. Oral ingestion (eating) results in about 2-4% of the drug being absorbed, while inhalation from smoking results in 15-20% absorption, and under efficient conditions it may go as high as 50%.

Urine specimens that show positive for cannabinoids signify that a person has consumed marijuana or cannabis derivatives from within 1 hour to as much as 3 weeks or more before the specimen was collected. Generally, a single smoking session by a casual user of marijuana will result in subsequently collected urine samples being positive for 2 to 5 days, depending on the screening method employed and on physiological factors that cause the drug concentration to vary. Detection time increases significantly following a period of chronic use. Determination of a particular time of use is thus difficult. The same issues would hold for other drugs, although the time after use during which a positive analysis would be expected might be reduced to a few days rather than a week or more.

Metabolites of the active ingredients of marijuana may be detectable in urine for up to 10 days after a single smoking session. However, most individuals cease to excrete detectable drug concentrations in 2 to 5 days. Metabolites can sometimes be detected several weeks after a heavy chronic smoker (several cigarettes a day) has ceased smoking.

The concentration of drugs in urine is measured in nanograms (billionth of a gram) per milliliter of liquid of the drug or of the drug metabolite formed in the body as a result of the ingestion of a specific drug. The cutoff level is that concentration, stated in nanograms per milliliter, used to determine whether a specimen is positive or negative. Specimens with concentrations at or above the cutoff level are considered positive for the drug in question. All other specimens are considered negative. The drug testing standards most often used in laboratories are those established by the National Institute on Drug Abuse (NIDA) for testing federal employees. The NIDA cutoff level for marijuana is 100 nanograms/milliliter.

Some will argue that a lower cutoff level for marijuana might more accurately identify users, particularly those who use occasionally or in small quantities. Research has suggested that approximately one-third more marijuana users might be identified if the cutoff level were lowered to 50 nanograms/milliliter. At this level, a smaller amount of the drug is needed for a specimen to be designated positive.

Tetrahydrocannibinol (THC) can be accurately detected in blood as well as urine. Radio immunoassay (RIA) is the method commonly employed to detect THC in blood serum. The lower limit of detection is approximately 10 nanograms of THC per milliliter of serum. However, the rapid disappearance of THC from the blood limits the time of detection.

For the smoking of a single marijuana cigarette of standard street strength, the detection time is 3 to 4 hours following last use. The analysis of blood for general drug testing is therefore not feasible because of the time restriction, but it can be very valuable in situations where recent cannabis use is suspected. Although behavioral impairment and THC in the blood have not been scientifically correlated, it can be logically assumed that a person with THC in the blood in excess of 10 nanograms has very recently ingested cannabis.

Impairment, intoxication, or time of last use cannot be predicted from a single urine test. In the case of cannabis use, a true-positive urine test indicates only that the person used cannabis in the recent past, which could be hours, days, or weeks, depending on the specific use pattern. Repeated analyses over time would, however, allow a better understanding of the past and current use patterns. An infrequent user should be completely negative in a few days. Repeated positive analyses over a period of more than 2 weeks suggest either continuing use or previous heavy chronic use.

The strength and duration of cannabis effects is a direct function of how much THC the body absorbed. The amount of THC absorbed depends on the THC content of the substance ingested and the manner of ingestion.

When cannabis is ingested by smoking, the THC passes through the lungs and into the blood stream, where it is bound to blood proteins and carried throughout the body. Because THC is extremely fat-soluble (meaning it will not dissolve in water and will easily collect in the fatty tissues), it is quickly absorbed into almost all body tissues that contain fat. THC taken into the liver is converted to metabolites that are much more soluble than the original THC, and as a result they easily pass into the urine where they accumulate until the bladder is emptied.

About one-half hour after ingestion of cannabis by smoking, the THC absorbed in body tissues begins to release slowly back into the blood, which eventually carries it to the liver where it is metabolized and excreted. This process continues until all of the THC is eliminated. However, if more cannabis is ingested before the previously stored amount is voided from the body system, the new THC is added to the THC already accumulated in the fatty tissues of the body.

It can be generally stated that scientific methods exist that accurately detect and measure cannabinoids in biological specimens, particularly blood and urine. These methods can reliably determine whether or not an individual has ingested cannabis, but they cast little light on how the cannabis entered the body and the extent of impairment present at the time the specimen was collected.

John J. Fay, CPP

Sources

Fay, J.J., Drug Testing. (Butterworth-Heinemann, Boston, 1991).

Marijuana Use Measured at Alternate Detection Levels. (National Institute of Justice, Washington, DC, 1991).

Urine Testing for Drugs of Abuse, Monograph 73. (National Institute on Drug Abuse, Rockville, MD, 1986).

Visher, C.A., A Comparison of Urinalysis Technologies for Drug Testing in Criminal Justice. (National Institute of Justice, Washington, DC, 1991).

DRUG TESTING: POLICY DEVELOPMENT

The increasing utilization of drug screening technology by employers has generated a number of legal, ethical, and technical issues. An understanding of these issues is essential to the process of establishing, implementing, and enforcing an effective drug-testing policy and program.

According to estimates by the National Institute on Drug Abuse (NIDA), about one-third of all Fortune 500 companies have some type of drug-testing program. Although many of these companies are only testing job applicants and employees in hazardous positions, there is no question that routine drug testing will be common practice in the workplace.

The role of the loss prevention manager, with regard to a company's drug testing initiative, has not been clearly defined. The increased awareness of substance abuse in the workplace, however, has led industry to the point of implementing "tough" solutions to the problem.   Therefore, loss prevention must take an active role in contributing to the development of these policies and procedures. This paper has been prepared to assist the loss prevention manager in developing policies for a drug testing program.

The Developmental Process for Drug Testing Policies

The development of corporate policies for drug testing has not kept pace with the demand for drug testing programs. Thus, in their haste to implement drug testing, many corporations are churning out policies that fail to meet the objectives of the corporation or are lacking many of the fundamental components that are needed for sound policy development.

Policies are generally broad guidelines of action that relate to goal attainment.   They provide guidance to management for prioritizing major issues. The purposes of developing and implementing specific organizational policies are enhanced communication and uniformity of operational practices.

Prior to developing a formal drug testing program, an organization should identify why the program is being implemented. According to Norm Spain in his article, "Employee Drug Screening and the Law," the "why" can be determined by answering the following questions:

1. Public Safety. Do any of your employees perform duties that directly affect the life safety of the public?

2.   Employee Safety.   Do any of your employees perform duties that directly affect employee life safety?

3. Public Trust. Would your business be seriously injured if the public trust in your employees was undermined because of employee drug use?

4.   Productivity. Is a major reason for conducting employee drug screening to maintain employee productivity and to reduce absenteeism, disciplinary problems, and minor employee injuries?

5. Security. Is a major reason for conducting employee testing to reduce the motivation and need for employees to steal or embezzle company property?

6.   Corruption.   In order to reduce the opportunity for your employees to be bribed and

to abuse their positions of trust, is employee drug testing being implemented?

These criteria assist management by focusing attention on organizational objectives, and it is this objective-setting process by which policy formulation should begin. A process should start with a clear, concise statement of the central purpose of the organization.   Defining and developing these organizational controls are crucial to an effective policy. Included in the process are long-range organizational goals that help define short-range performance objectives for the company.

Long-range objectives generally extend beyond the current fiscal year.   Thus, policy formulation and implementation begins with analysis of these organizational objectives. Once they have been identified, policy development can begin and should include not only security personnel but representatives from human resources, labor relations, collective bargaining, legal, medical, and employee assistance. The use of expert advice from outside the organization may also be advisable when developing the technical aspects of the policy, program, and procedures.

Guidelines to follow when developing an organizational drug testing policy are:

Identify the Prohibited Conduct and the Consequences of Violations. Prepare a general statement that is both clear and concise; ideally, it will be no more than a paragraph or two, for example: "Reporting to work under the influence of intoxicants or narcotics and/or bringing, using, buying, or selling the same on company premises can lead to suspension or final dismissal. Persons suspected of violating this rule will be subject to the organization's Alcohol and Drug testing program."

Be Realistic. The policy should be realistic, one that "fits" the environment and situation, one that can be ratified into practice. Setting unrealistic goals will only serve to weaken the policy and undermine its credibility in the minds of the workers.

Be Consistent. An effective drug testing policy will be consistent.   This is accomplished by utilizing broad and generalized statements that are compatible with organizational objectives and controls.

Be Comprehensive. It must be comprehensive and inclusive; otherwise, there is increased susceptibility to civil action by employees. This is why it is necessary for the organization's legal department to closely review all company statements and policies.

Leave No Room for Interpretation. The policy should be in a written format and set out in plain language. This will help reduce possible misinterpretation and improve employee compliance.

State Why the Policy is a Business Necessity. The policy should contain a statement by management regarding its purpose in implementing a program. For example: "The rationale of the drug testing policy is based on the premise that use of drugs, including alcohol, by employees in the workplace is unacceptable since it can adversely affect health and safety, security, productivity, public confidence and trust."

The company's formal drug testing policy should clearly state the employer's objective and goals regarding drug use. The policy must clearly define what actions would be taken by the company in the event drug usage by the employee was confirmed. Employees should be informed of company policy and acknowledge that they understand the policy and the consequences of drug use while employed by the organization.

Pam Collins, Ed.D.

Sources

A Test Tube War on Drugs? (U.S. News & World Report, No. 100, 1986), p. 8

Belohlav, J., and P. Popp, Employee Substance Abuse: Epidemic of the Eighties. (Business Horizons, No. 26, 1983), pp. 29-34

Bensinger, P., Drugs in the Workplace. (Harvard Business Review, No. 60, 1982), pp. 48-60

Bensinger, P., and I. Glasser, Test Employees for Drug Abuse? (U.S. News & World Report, No. 100, 1986), p. 58

Drug Screening in the Workplace: Issues and Answers. (Assets Protection, No. 9, 1988), pp. 21-27

Horton, T.R., Drugs in the Workplace. (Management Review, No. 76, 1987), pp. 5-6

Wrich, J.T., Beyond Testing: Coping with Drugs at Work. (Security Management, 1988), pp. 64-73

DRUG TESTING: PREPARING TO TESTIFY

The security professional is increasingly drawn into the arena of workplace drug testing and, as a consequence, is also being called to testify at judicial and administrative proceedings that examine challenges to drug testing. Although the testing laboratory will provide most or all of the testimony in the scientific area, the security manager can expect to be called to testify concerning several related areas; for example, the company's policy, disciplinary sanctions, the measures that ensure confidentiality of testing results, and specimen collection procedures. Immediately upon receipt of the notice to appear, the security manager will need to do three things: prepare, prepare, and prepare.

The first step should be to thoroughly review the case in order to get a good grasp of the who, what, where, when, how, and why details. It will be important to know what actually happened, what should have happened, and what exactly is alleged to have happened according to the plaintiff's petition.

Next, the security manager will want to brush up on the company's rules that regulate drug testing. This will mean a study of the company's policy and procedures, with special attention to how urine specimens are collected, packaged, and transported to the laboratory. The chain of custody form, the consent to test form, and any waivers or acknowledgments that are routinely obtained from specimen donors should be examined.

The report of test results can be a troublesome matter. On the one hand, they must be handled with absolute confidentiality, but on the other hand, the company will need to have some freedom to make test reports available to the presiding officials. What can be done? Insert language in the drug test consent form that gives the company permission to release test reports at administrative and judicial proceedings.

The security manager has to regard all drug testing documents as potential evidence, either for or against the company's position. Because the other side will try to exploit any weaknesses or mistakes in documentation, the security manager should look for any and be ready to respond with accurate, confident answers.

It may be helpful to talk to the laboratory experts about the analytical techniques that were applied to the specimen in question. Full comfort may not be attainable concerning the testing science, but the security manager should at least gain a layman's knowledge of how the specimen was screened and then found to be positive. It will not be necessary to become fully versed in the technology, nor even to perfectly pronounce the tongue-twisting terms, but it will be very important to be able to explain the testing scheme and the precautions designed to rule out errors in testing.

In addition, it will be important to be able to explain why the company chose the testing scheme and how the selection of the scheme was supported by a reasonable business necessity. Documentation of the business necessity will most probably reside somewhere in the company's files. Making reference to it adds legitimacy.

Preparation should be made in how to explain the flow of communications in reporting test results and how that flow was protected against breaches of confidentiality. The security manager should expect to be questioned on the physical and procedural safeguards that were in place to protect reports and records containing test results.

Study will be in order concerning the laws or regulations that relate to the drug test in question. For example, if the test was administered in a program authorized by Department of Transportation regulations, study those regulations.

When in the witness chair, the security manager should expect attempts by the opposition to create confusion and to cast doubt on personal credibility. The plaintiff or the plaintiff's attorney will attempt through a variety of ploys and innuendoes to damage the position of the defense. The security manager may be portrayed in a less-than-favorable light, and questions will be asked in ways that are intended to advance the plaintiff's case, even at the expense of suppressing the truth. Responses to these tactics should be made calmly and confidently.

Finally, the point needs to be made that most challenges to testing are avoidable. The glitches that can occur in setting up and operating a testing program often become the foundation for challenge. The hassle of testifying and the consequences of losing a challenge are reasons enough to be constantly on the lookout for ways to minimize errors.

Calvina L. Fay

DRUG TESTING: USES IN THE PRIVATE SECTOR

Testing of job applicants and employees has long been used to ensure that workers are free of medical conditions that might interfere with safety and productivity. The rise of drug abuse in the United States has prompted many employers to establish pre-employment and in-service drug testing programs. These programs are proving to be an effective tool for managing drug abuse problems in the workplace.

The drug testing proposition essentially means that applicants will not be hired and employees will be disciplined when drug test results indicate current use of illicit substances. Possible legal challenge of a positive test result should be of special concern to management.

A principal focus of management should therefore be the selection of a qualified drug testing laboratory. The U.S. Department of Health and Human Services (DHHS) certifies laboratories that meet stringent standards relating to personnel qualifications, equipment and instrumentation, analytical methods, and quality assurance. In addition to these critical standards, the laboratory's customer will expect services that give attention to chain of custody, confidential reporting and recordkeeping, secure storage of positive specimens for later testing, and, if needed, expert witnesses to testify in court and present drug testing evidence.

The DHHS program for certifying drug testing laboratories is by far the most exacting of the various certification programs and has come to be regarded by the courts as a standard for judging workplace drug testing activities. Although many employers in the private sector fall outside regulatory purview and are therefore not required to use a DHHS-certified laboratory, many elect to do so because they recognize the advantages of high accuracy and reliability of tests and the value that courts place upon testing that meets high standards.

Definitions

The major assurance of accuracy is the series of checks built into the testing system. Two types of errors are of concern. First is the administrative error, such as incorrect transcription of test results, incorrect recording of donor identification number, and failure to maintain chain of custody. Second is the analytical error related to the precision of analysis, calibration of equipment, and interpretation of test results. In the case of administrative error, the single test result involved may or not have to be discounted, but with analytical error more than one test result may be faulty because the error may have affected other specimens tested in the same batch.

Gas chromatography/mass spectrometry (GC/MS) is a technique used mainly to confirm the positive results of screening tests. It is generally considered to be the most conclusive method of determining the presence of a drug in urine. GC/MS combines the separating power of gas chromatography with the high sensitivity and specificity of spectrometry.

An immunoassay seeks to detect in urine the presence of a drug or drug metabolite. It is based on the principle of competition between labeled and unlabeled antigens for binding sites on a specific antibody. An antibody is a protein substance to which a specific drug or drug metabolite will bind.

In the enzyme immunoassay technique, the label on the antigen is an enzyme that produces a chemical reaction that allows for the detection of a drug or its metabolite. The concentration of the drug present in the urine is determined by measuring the extent of enzymatic activity. The radioimmunoassay technique looks at the reaction produced by the injection of a radioactive-labeled substance. The presence or absence of the drug being looked for is indicated by the amount of radioactivity found. The immunoassay techniques are used mostly for screening urine samples. They are not really suitable for confirming positive test results.

Positive test results are frequently reported quantitatively in measurements called nanograms and micrograms. The concentration of the drug is expressed as a certain amount per volume of urine. Urine concentrations may be expressed as nanograms per milliliter or as micrograms per milliliter. There are 28 million micrograms in 1 ounce and 1,000 nanograms in a microgram.

A positive test that has not been confirmed by an alternate and at least equally sensitive test is called a presumed positive. For example, a specimen that has been screened by an immunoassay and found to be positive is only presumed to be positive until a second test confirms or refutes the initial finding. When the

second test is by an alternate and at least equally sensitive technique (such as GC/MS), it is called a confirmation test, and a positive result is called a confirmed positive.

When the second test is a repeat of the first test or uses a less sensitive or essentially similar technique, it is called a verification test, and a positive result is called a verified positive. A verification test falls far short of a confirmation test, especially a confirmation test by GC/MS.

The sensitivity limit of a test is the lowest concentration at which the test can detect the presence of a drug in a urine specimen. The sensitivity limit is inherently determined by scientific capabilities.

The cutoff level, on the other hand, is an administrative mechanism for distinguishing a positive result from a negative result. The absence of a drug concentration or a concentration below the cutoff level yields a negative result, whereas one above the cutoff limit yields a positive result.

The immunoassays are subject to an interference called cross-reactivity. Because immunoassays rely on immune reactions, a certain degree of interference occurs among the various drug metabolites and structurally similar compounds of a particular drug. For example, methamphetamine cross-reacts with some over-the-counter medications, such as diet pills and decongestants, and ibuprofen (the main ingredient in Advil, Motrin, Medipren, and Nuprin) has been found to interfere and cause positives for marijuana.

Cutoff Levels in Federal Workplace Drug Testing Programs	
Initial Test	
Cannabinoids	100
Cocaine	300
Opiates	300
Phencyclidine	1000
Confirmation Test	
Cannabinoids	15
Cocaine	150
Opiates	
Morphine	300
Codeine	300
Phencyclidine	25
Amphetamines	
Amphetamine	500
Methamphetamine	500
Values shown are in nanograms per milliliter.	

A few screening tests will occasionally produce positive results caused by the interference of certain foods, such as poppy seeds. Since poppy seeds come from the opium plant, a positive for opiates is possible. However, the interfering substances are well known to drug testing laboratories and are easily resolved with alternate screening techniques. The possibility of interference during screening is a very good reason for all positive screens to be confirmed.

Urinalysis

Testing for drugs is almost always done through the analysis of urine. The objective is to identify any evidence of drugs or drug metabolites in the urine. Some drug classes, such as the opiates class, can be identified directly by the presence of the drug itself. Other drug classes, such as the cannabinoids (marijuana), are identified indirectly by the presence of metabolites.

A metabolite is a compound produced from chemical changes of a drug in the body. It is a by-product resulting from the body's natural process of converting the drug to waste matter. A urine specimen that tests positive for marijuana will contain marijuana metabolites.

Urine testing is done in two steps: a screening test and a confirmatory test. When a specimen shows negative in the screen, the specimen is declared to be free of drugs and is destroyed. When a specimen shows positive in the screen, it is subjected to the confirmatory test. If the confirmatory is negative, the specimen is declared negative and destroyed. If positive, a positive finding is issued.

In some instances a second confirmatory test may be conducted, and many employers regard a positive test result as only presumptively positive until verified by a medical review officer (MRO). An MRO is a specially trained medical doctor who evaluates a positive test result in light of further evidence obtained from a physical examination of the individual, an interview of the individual, or a review of the individual's medical history. The MRO seeks to determine if the positive finding could have some other medical explanation, such as the innocent use of a legally prescribed drug.

Screening tests are most often conducted using immunoassay techniques. Immunoassays are designed to detect traces of drugs or metabolites; they lend themselves well to automation, and are accurate at the 95% level and higher. Two types stand out: enzyme immunoassay and radioimmunoassay.

Confirmatory tests are most often conducted using the GC/MS technique, which is widely considered to be the most conclusive method for confirming the presence of a drug in urine.

Certainly a most serious problem in drug testing is that of false positives. A false positive occurs when a drug or drug metabolite is reported in a urine specimen but is actually not present. False positives can be categorized into three groups:

• Chemical False Positive. This is the result of another substance in the sample being mistakenly identified as a drug. Chemical false positives sometimes occur when donors contaminate their specimens at the collection site.

• Administrative False Positive. This is the result of one person's positive test result being attributed to another person. Improper labeling and inaccurate chain of custody documentation are the usual causes.

• Operator Error. This is the result of a mistake by a laboratory technician during an analytical procedure. Inadequate operator training, poor supervision, and failure to follow testing protocols are usually at the root of operator error.

Precautions When Collecting Urine Specimens

Employers who regularly administer urine drug testing have learned that administrative or human error is more likely to occur during the urine collection process than at any other time in a drug testing program. The following precautions were born out of experience.

• The written policy that authorizes drug testing should be available at the urine specimen collection point for reading by the specimen donor prior to giving a specimen.

• At the collection point, the specimen donor should provide positive identification, such as a photo-bearing driving license.

• Written consent should be obtained from the donor at the collection point.

• Steps against contamination should include:
1. Using a specimen container of the type that is packaged at the point of manufacture in a protective plastic envelope.

2. Allowing nothing to be introduced (e.g., thermometer, litmus paper) into the specimen or its container at the collection point.

3. After the donor has voided into the container, asking the donor to place tape across the container cap, sign the label, put the container in a plastic envelope, place tape across the envelope sealing flap, and sign the tape.

Blind specimen testing is an integral part of the continuing assessment of laboratory performance. A percentage of the specimens sent to the laboratory are spiked with drugs and metabolites that the laboratory routinely looks for, and the laboratory is expected to detect the spiked drugs in concentration ranges that correspond to what can be expected in the urine of recent drug users. The idea is to imitate the type of specimens that a laboratory normally encounters both in terms of content and appearance. The laboratory, of course, has no way of differentiating between the blind specimens and the actual specimens.

Passive Inhalation

A number of defenses have been put forward to explain positive test results. Passive inhalation or inadvertent exposure to marijuana is frequently cited, but clinical studies show that it is unlikely that a non-smoking individual can passively inhale sufficient marijuana smoke to result in a high enough concentration for marijuana to be detected at the cutoff level of the standard urinalysis methods. It is extremely improbable that a person who was not smoking would be exposed to the level of smoke and for the length of time required to produce a positive test result.

John J. Fay, CPP

Sources

Fay, J.J., Drug Testing.   (Butterworth-Heinemann, Boston, 1991).

Fay, J.J., New Directions in Drug Screening. (Security Management, November, 1986).

Fay, J.J., Let's Be Honest about Drug Testing. (Security Management, December, 1988).

Fay, J.J., The Alcohol/Drug Abuse Dictionary and Encyclopedia.   (Charles C. Thomas, Springfield, IL, 1987).

Mandatory Guidelines for Federal Workplace Drug Testing Programs. (U.S. Department of Health and Human Services, Washington, DC, 1990).

E

EDUCATION: SECURITY MANAGEMENT EDUCATION IN THE TWENTY-FIRST CENTURY

Any discussion of the future necessitates that one take a broad, rather than a narrow, well-defined approach. With that caveat in place, it is suggested that security managers at the turn of the century will, of necessity, be generalists. Projected economic and demographic trends, as well as rapidly changing technology, will dictate that security managers be educated in a number of disciplines.

Traditionally, security management education has focused on security and safety courses. These areas will continue to be a major focus of security education programs; however, current trends indicate that a security manager in the 21st century will require extensive knowledge in additional areas if he or she is to be successful. The contributions of other authors in this encyclopedia suggest that the security manager of the future will require extensive knowledge in a number of disciplines that include, but are not restricted to law, computers, and management.

Law

Extensive knowledge of the law is a sine qua non for current and future security managers. With few exceptions, the states have either passed or are in the process of passing legislation governing the security industry. Additionally, many federal laws have a direct or indirect impact on security management. For example, legislation regarding employee drug testing and denying employers use of the polygraph in pre-employment screening have had a significant impact on the industry.

Future trends suggest security managers, at a minimum, must have extensive knowledge of laws relating to civil and criminal liability. The security manager must be cognizant of the legal rights of employers, employees, and clients, and the probable ramifications if those rights are violated. Employee drug testing, sexual harassment, and employee/client injury are areas in which problems of legal liability are likely to occur. Furthermore, the use of contract security forces makes it imperative that security managers understand contractual law as it applies to legal liabilities, security requirements, and job performance standards.

Knowledge of criminal law is of increasing importance due to the growing incidence of theft and workplace violence. For example, private security officers, rather than law enforcement officials, are generally the first responders to incidents of this nature and in, particular, violent incidents. Finally, increasing emphasis on environmental protection and the resultant handling, storage, and disposal of hazardous materials will demand that security mangers have extensive knowledge of environmental laws and regulations.

A thorough knowledge of the requirements of the Occupational Safety and Health Administration will be of primary importance when dealing with employee and public safety, during and after an accident involving hazardous materials. Some of the possible consequences that managers, who lack an extensive knowledge of the law, may face are: civil law suits, government fines, and criminal charges.

Computers

Computers have become one of the most pervasive elements of the constantly growing and changing electronic industry. There is every reason to believe this trend will continue into the 21st century. Thus, it is essential that security managers have knowledge of computer operations and languages, networking agreements, and telecommunications techniques. They must also have knowledge of data processing, computer programming, and computer security. They should also be capable of interpreting computer-generated data.

Currently, computer theft and fraud are two major problems that security managers must face, and there is no reason to believe these problems will be eliminated anytime in the near future. To the contrary, economic competition, both international and national, has made computer security of paramount importance. For example, the electronic theft of research and development breakthroughs can result in a large loss of income or even bankruptcy for the developing company. The latter is particularly true if the theft results in a competitor being the first to market the product or newly developed technology. Electronic theft of money and stolen computer time can also result in serious economic losses to a company during the best of times; during economic recessions they can result in the company going out of business. The proliferation of computer usage in all areas of industry and government, and the increasing economic competitiveness on a worldwide basis suggest computer security will be a problem well into the 21st century.

Business Management

Security managers of the future will have to contribute toward the economic health of their companies. Thus, they will need to be educated in managing human and financial resources.

Human Resource Management. Demographic trends indicate that by the 21st century the workforce will be older, better educated, and the percentage of women and minority employees will be higher. Increases in the number of female employees will demand the security manager be capable of developing and maintaining policies pertaining to maternity leaves and sexual harassment. An older, better educated workforce will require that managers develop the ability to motivate employees and understand the concepts of human resource development and training. Finally, successful managers will have to handle employee labor relations. They will have to understand and deal with union regulations and employees. To be successful, managers will have to develop and sharpen their skills in compromising and negotiation.

Financial Resource Management. Security mangers will be asked to do more with less in the future. Maximization of profits and minimization of costs will be of paramount importance. Thus, preparing and justifying budgets will be a major task.

Risk analysis and risk management will be essential elements in establishing budget requests. The managers must be familiar with the concepts of criticality, vulnerability, and probability if their analyses are to be effective.

Scarce resources must be expended in areas that are the most critical to the firm, that are the most vulnerable to attack, and that have the highest probability of occurring. Managers who fail to heed this tenet will not fare well in the highly competitive economic environment of the future.

The security industry becomes more complex each day. Security managers of the future are going to need broad-based educations to successfully cope with this complexity. Furthermore, it is suggested that security managers will become key personnel in company and industry management planning and operations. The security managers of the future may well become the renaissance men and women of the 21st century, because, as generalists, they will have acquired skills and knowledge in a variety of educational disciplines, including security, safety, law, computers, and business management.

Harry L. Marsh, Ph.D.

Sources

Bottom, N.R., and J. Kostanoski, Introduction to Security and Loss Control. (Prentice-Hall, Englewood Cliffs, NJ, 1990).

Hess, K., and H. Wrobleski, Introduction to Private Security, 2nd Edition. (West Publishing Company, St. Paul, MN, 1988).

Marsh, H.L., Corporate/University Cooperation in Security Education Programs: A Model for Professionalization of Security Personnel. (Security Journal, Vol. 2, No. 3, 1991).

Nemeth, C.P., Private Security and the Law. (Anderson Publishing Company, Cincinnati, 1989).

EDUCATION: UNIVERSITY INTERNSHIPS

One can fairly assume that American business will continue to achieve operational economies in the future through "downsizing" and related personnel staff reduction efforts. Departments that are particularly vulnerable to corporate re-structuring and cost containment initiatives are service and support functions, such as security.

In consideration of this dilemma, how can the security manager continue to respond to increasing job demands and responsibilities, with significantly fewer personnel assets? One possible solution to this problem may be to seek the assistance of academia in providing student interns, or "co-ops," to corporate security functions as temporary employees.

Student internships have long been accepted as required curriculum among professional academic programs, such as teaching, nursing, and engineering. In business, co-ops or interns are frequently placed in a variety of line and staff assignments to include production, information services, safety and health, communications, accounting, and procurement.

Selected students are usually assigned to employers for at least one academic term (e.g., 40 hour work week for about 10 weeks). Of course, the exact terms and conditions of internship programs may vary considerably among institutions of higher learning, as well as the professional or career disciplines that provide internship experiences for students.

Interns may be placed with or without pay and benefits. However, many enlightened businesses provide their interns with reasonable wages and, in some cases, certain benefits. If seeking intern placements, one must understand that students are usually paying full tuition to their universities for the privilege of participating in such external academic programs. Many students cannot offset the special costs associated with practicums (e.g., transportation, subsistence, and clothing) unless they receive some compensation for their efforts.

Once placed, students come under the tutelage of their business supervisors, as well as their college faculty representatives. Students are usually evaluated by their employers for job performance, and possibly for completion of special projects or assignments. The employer's evaluation is significant with respect to determining the student intern's final course grade.

The Security Practicum

To the security manager, establishment of a university internship program represents a source of highly energetic, career motivated, and gifted temporary employees. Some essential steps in developing and maintaining a viable practicum in security management include: (1) completion of a needs assessment; (2)

management approval; (3) external liaison with appropriate colleges and universities; (4) student recruitment, selection, and placement; (5) intern assignments; (6) intern supervision; and (7) intern evaluation.

Determining Need. As hard pressed as many security departments are to accomplish increasing and myriad workplace accountabilities and demands, a justifiable need often exists for additional personnel support. However, budget constraints usually preclude the hiring of full-time security staff, regardless of the actual needs of the security function. Should the security manager be experiencing "shortfalls" to the extent that additional personnel resources are needed, then use of a student intern could be justified. Interns may be very well suited to provide staff assistance in such areas as security surveys and inspections, employee training, guard force management, policies and procedures, security systems support, law enforcement liaison, and crime prevention.

Management Approval. The implementation of a security internship program is wholly contingent upon management approval. In soliciting management concurrence, the security manager must be able to justify an internship objectively, and in terms of advantages and costs. Some key factors for the security manager to consider in proposing an internship for approval could be:

• Advantages to the Employer. The employer gains an immediate low-cost and quality temporary employee. The student intern is usually very adaptable to varied job assignments and eager to learn. An internship program also gives an employer a first-hand opportunity to evaluate prospective employees in a nonthreatening and completely job-oriented environment. On another level, establishment of intern programs promotes good corporate and community relations. It is one means by which a business can effectively participate in the education and development of our youth. Furthermore, it solidifies positive interactions with the academic community. Internships equate to good corporate citizenship.

• Advantages to the Student. Internships serve to balance classroom theory with on-the-job pragmatism. The student is able to apply key

LETTER ANNOUNCING AN INTERNSHIP
(Sample)

Date

Dr. Sam Jones
Chairman, Criminal Justice Department
Smith Hall
State University
Anyplace, USA

Dear Dr. Jones:

The XYZ Company is pleased to announce a paid temporary position opening in its Corporate Security Department for a Student Trainee (Co-op) for the upcoming semester.

The Student Trainee selected for this position will serve in a supervised staff support role and will report to the Security Manager. Principal accountabilities, job requirements and applicant qualification criteria are contained in the attached position description. Preference in selection will be given to those applicants who have completed course work in appropriate security subjects and who seek eventual career placement within the private security sector. Minimum additional requirements for applicant consideration are:

1. Senior class standing or graduate degree candidacy.
2. Written recommendation of faculty advisor or department chairperson.
3. Overall GPA of at least 2.50 on a 4.00 scale, and a 3.00 average in major course subjects.
4. Availability for continuous employment throughout the period on a standard 40 hour work week basis.
5. Transportation to and from XYZ's Corporate office on scheduled work days.

Students interested in applying for this position should submit a current resumé and academic transcript to the attention of Mr. I. M. Hawkins, Supervisor-Employment.

Sincerely,

James Wilson, CPP
Security Manager

POSITION DESCRIPTION FOR AN INTERN
(Sample)

POSITION DESCRIPTION

POSITION: Student Trainee

REPORTS TO: Security Manager

ACCOUNTABILITY OBJECTIVE

This position is accountable for the provision of security services throughout the Company's service territory as directed by the Security Manager.

NATURE AND SCOPE

The incumbent shall be required to conduct security audits and surveys of operational facilities on a recurring basis, upon completion of training and satisfactory performance during supervised field practicums. Formal audit/survey reports will be prepared by the incumbent for distribution to responsible Company managers and supervisors.

This position will assist Security personnel with approved investigative activities relative to reported security incidents and/or criminal acts directed against the Company, its employees, or its customers. Initial field interviews and investigative activity reports will be prepared by the incumbent in accordance with Company Policy, and at the direction of Security Manager.

The incumbent will provide assistance to the Security section in the preparation and presentation of regularly scheduled security awareness programs for Company employees. The primary role of this position will be that of instructor aid for security training sessions given at various Company locations.

This position will provide assistance in the administration and supervision of contract guard services throughout the service territory. The incumbent will be expected to visit key protected facilities for the purpose of assisting local management in all matters relating to guard service support.

The incumbent will assist the Security Manager in other such departmental matters as may be necessary. A major project will be assigned to the incumbent as a position requirement. This project will involve a significant issue or proposal that may result in improved security services or cost benefits to the Company.

In order to successfully fulfill the requirements of this position, the incumbent shall be enrolled in a recognized undergraduate or graduate degree program with a declared major in either Security Management or Criminal Justice. Undergraduate students shall have attained senior class standing either prior to placement or at the conclusion of the work period, if the position is used in conjunction with an approved college practicum or internship program. The incumbent must possess a valid state drivers license.

PRINCIPAL ACCOUNTABILITIES

1. Performs security audits/surveys of Company facilities on both a required and an exceptional basis.
2. Assists in conducting investigations of reported incidents throughout the Company's service territory. Performs initial field interviews and investigative reports.
3. Assists in the administration and supervision of contract security guard services at protected Company facilities.
4. Assists in the preparation and presentation of security awareness and training programs for Company employees.
5. Completes a major project relative to security services for appropriate Company management.
6. Performs administrative duties as required.

concepts from his or her academic experience to "real world" problem solving. Also, the intern gains invaluable job related skills, which translate to quantifiable "resume builders" for future career placement or enhancement.

• Advantages to the College or University. Establishment of a security practicum enhances both the career curriculum and placement posture of a university or college. Such programs help to attract good students. Also, students who successfully complete approved internships usually possess a distinct advantage over non-interns, relative to eventual career placement.

College and University Liaison. Subsequent to management's approval of a security internship or co-op program, the security manager should establish ongoing communications with appropriate academic officials relative to such issues as student recruitment and selection, intern assignments and requirements, and university requirements for intern supervision and evaluation. Logically, security managers may wish to focus intern recruiting efforts in either criminal justice or security management degree programs.

However, outstanding security interns may be selected from other related academic disciplines such as computer science, accounting, and business administration.

The security manager should arrange to provide university intern placement coordinators, or department chairpersons, with formal written internship announcements that essentially describe the program and that outline minimum applicant selection criteria. Prior to mailing internship announcements, it may be prudent to first staff the letters and accompanying position descriptions with the human resources and legal departments. Also, university intern liaisons may benefit from having copies of intern position descriptions. Such descriptions serve to lend credibility to the security practicum as a valid academic program.

Student Selection and Placement. The security manager's pleasant challenge is to select the best interns from among extraordinarily talented student populations. Security practicums, particularly those offering remuneration, are highly coveted by both criminal justice and security management majors. The selection process is frequently very competitive and difficult. The task can be simplified through the development of reasonable minimum written standards that are shared with university internship coordinators and cognizant staff.

Some possible ways to enhance the student intern selection process may include: (1) treating the position exactly as an initial application for employment, and (2) conducting workplace job interviews for the most qualified candidates. Such practices add to the credibility of the internship in terms of its significance to the security function. Also, students are given valuable practical experiences in preparing cover letters, applications, and resumes, and in job interviewing.

Following selection, the new student intern must be given job responsibilities that are demanding, rewarding, challenging, and educational. A great deal of attention must be programmed for intern development by the security manager and his/her staff. It is essential to always think of the student intern as a valued staff member -- not just another "shadow" or "junior security agent."

Intern Assignments. Student interns can be effectively "coached" to perform a multitude of essential security tasks, within a relatively short period of time. The student may be well utilized in: (1) conducting security surveys and audits, (2) assisting with preliminary investigative field work, (3) assisting in the preparation and presentation of employee security training and awareness programs, (4) providing administrative support to site protection functions, (5) assisting in guard force management, (6) preparing required security reports for management, and (7) completing a major course project as mutually agreed upon by the security manager and the student's faculty internship advisor. Student assignments may be as varied and diverse as the needs of the security department dictate. The key to success in the assignment of interns rests with the security manager's commitment and personal attention to the development of each student.

Intern Supervision and Evaluation. To fully benefit from the internship experience, students should receive every possible consideration for mentorship with the security manager and

upper-level security staff representatives. Supervision in this sense is guiding and teaching, rather than controlling and directing.

Ultimately, students who are provided opportunities to relate positively with security management on a regular basis develop requisite skills and confidence for independent assignments of increasing responsibility. The security manager must be willing to invest considerably in the student's developmental process if the internship is to be successful for all parties involved.

Student practicum evaluations are typically designed to provide major input from the on-site intern supervisor. The security manager may be asked to complete weekly intern activity reports and to submit a more detailed final course evaluation.

The evaluation process may be enhanced by inviting the intern's faculty advisor to visit with his or her student at the job location on a regular basis. Through participation in the student's daily work activities, the faculty advisor gains an appreciation for the nature, scope, and demands of the security practicum. This approach provides for realistic student evaluations consistent with actual job requirements. Also, university faculty become directly involved with security concerns from a practitioner's perspective. This, in itself, assists faculty in providing a balance between theory and practice in the development of a security management curriculum.

University internships provide a viable alternative to security staff reductions and restructuring for the security manager. Moreover, internships are beneficial to employers, students, and colleges and universities alike. Student interns are often found to be incredibly capable personnel assets who can impact positively upon most corporate security departments in terms of goal accomplishments and functional capabilities.

Robert D. Hulshouser, CPP

Sources

Christian, K.E., and D. Payne, After the Sheepskin. (Security Management, April, 1987).

Fischer, R.J., and W. Durkin, A Two Way Street. (Security Management, February, 1988).

Hertig, C.A., A Solid Foundation in Academia. (Security Management, February, 1985).

Marsh, H.L., and W.A. Roth, A Profile of Partnership. (Security Management, November, 1990).

Naisbitt, J., and P. Aburdene, Reinventing the Corporation. (Warner Books, Inc., New York, 1985).

EDUCATIONAL INSTITUTIONS: PHYSICAL SAFEGUARDS

The first goal of any physical security program for an educational institution is to assess the physical and geographical characteristics within which the campus is situated. For example, an institution located in a remote rural environment would not necessarily need the same type of loss prevention measures as a school located in a downtown or urban environment. However, a number of basic principles should always be implemented because of the possibility that a criminal act can be perpetrated in any environment at any time. Many of the major universities that were once located in a relatively remote or uninhabited area have now, because of urban growth, found themselves in highly populated areas. The mass transit systems and multiple freeways have changed the exposure of the campus to outside influences.

A recordkeeping system that tracks all criminal and violent acts on the campus must be established. Federal legislation has mandated that these statistics be maintained and be made available to students, parents, faculty and staff of the university community. The utilization of these statistics can become a definite advantage in the development of a loss prevention program. The old concept of marking a geographical area with brightly colored pins is still an effective concept. Using one pin per crime and a different color for each type of crime, the map lays out a graphic display of the areas of vulnerability. This visual profile of crime is more effective to the officer on patrol than a stack of computer-generated print-outs. However, the use of computers to analyze data and generate information into a usable format is invaluable to campus security administration.

The crime statistics of the campus and also of the community surrounding the campus are invaluable in determining the direction of a physical security program. The combination of these statistics can provide valuable information on the needs of the campus and the predictable possibility of crime. A communication link with the agencies of surrounding municipalities will allow for planning and timely response to activities which could affect the campus.

The physical environment of the campus must also be surveyed. Campuses are viewed by the Administration as a free and open environment where students, guests, and employees can roam freely without fear of danger or restriction. Libraries and computer centers remain open extended hours, if not 24 hours a day. An unrealistic view of the possibility of danger permeates the thinking on most campuses. Traditionally, buildings are not designed to prevent loss. Most buildings have numerous ground-level windows that make vulnerability to break-ins a high risk. Many windows are left unlocked. Doors are usually hinged on the outside, making their removal easy.

A beginning step would be to establish a program to routinely check doors and windows to ensure they are secure after normal working hours, and to obtain information on those that were not fastened. Training personnel to use the physical security that is already available is an important process.

Campuses have become an easy target of vagrants and other homeless people who rely on the relaxed security practices to allow them access to a place to stay. With the varied dress code and economic status of a student body, it is often difficult to determine if anyone is out of place. Therefore, the securing of buildings is of paramount importance. The next step is establishing an effective key control program that ensures that all campus keys are logged, checked out, and tracked.

Key Control

The first stage to controlling access to campus facilities is to establish a database to track all doors, keys, and key holders. For quick and effective recordkeeping, a computer is recommended, although such a system can be operated manually. Important factors that must be determined are: (1) who has access to the rooms, (2) who has the authorization to grant people access to a particular area, and (3) who is responsible for issuing keys.

The most effective way to seize control of the campus key program is to change the current key system used on campus to a new key system. This action should be preceded by the establishment of a written access control policy that is authorized by campus administration. When selecting a key system one of the most important aspects is the difficulty with which the key can be duplicated off campus. The most common problem on campuses is not "break-ins" or the picking of locks but, instead, the unauthorized duplication of keys.

The market today has several lock companies with key systems which can ensure that the key blank is restricted and cannot be readily duplicated by an unauthorized source. Many keys from major lock manufacturers can be easily duplicated by local locksmiths or even conveniences stores. Even the warning "Do Not Duplicate" can be ignored by the key maker if visible. However, these warnings can be obscured from view by a piece of masking tape on which a room description is inscribed. Rarely does a locksmith remove the tape to ensure there is no such warning on the key being duplicated.

Another important factor to investigate when selecting a new key manufacturer is the size of the different key combinations possible without duplicating the same operating key in the system. Most major campuses have a large number of doors and a great many cross-jurisdictions to accommodate. It is important that the key company selected can provide the combinations required for use over an extended period of years without cross-keying or duplication of an existing combination. The system must also provide for lock changes in the future.

The third factor in the selection of the locking system is the durability, serviceability, and parts availability over a long period of time, and, of course, cost.

Recordkeeping is another important factor to maintaining the integrity of a long-range key control system. A central point of issuance should be established where campus staff and students can receive keys, at which time the appropriate documentation can be completed. The issuing office should be responsible for all records pertaining to keys and locks. All lock changes should be approved and logged to ensure that records are updated, and that lock changes meet the needs of the program and the users.

People ordering lock changes often do not know the number of options available or do not think about the overall access to the area. Questions like "Who needs access to the area?" and "Who do you want to exclude from the area?" are important. Another question that must be determined is "Who has jurisdiction of each area on campus?" Keys should be issued for real need and not for convenience. This should be the major consideration of the person who is authorized to issue keys. A list of vice presidents, deans, or department heads, and the areas over which they have jurisdiction should be established. All key requests should be in writing. Signatures should be on file for all people who can authorize keys.

Last, all lock changes and repairs should only be done by locksmiths sanctioned by the campus and under the direction of the office controlling the key program.

Access Cards

Cards that have the capability to open doors on campus should be thought of as another form of key. Many of the same principles that apply to key control should also be utilized in the issuance and control of access cards. However, there are areas where keys and cards differ in use, application, and advantages. One of the major advantages of access cards is the ease with which they can be removed from the system if a problem arises. Another plus is the paper trail that can be created by an electronic, computer-assisted system. Many access systems utilizing cards can also provide information and give an alert when doors are left ajar or left unsecured. The system can document the time a door is opened and who opened it. It can indicate when someone is tampering with the accessing hardware or an unauthorized card is being used in the system. The computer can notify the user when the system is down and when it needs repair or attention.

Campus Housing

Whether or not students are housed on campus is an important factor in the security program of the campus. The same level of protection expected of innkeepers and landlords is expected of campus administrators who operate residence halls for students. More than in any other area, loss prevention in housing is far preferable to resolving an incident after the fact. The level of security in the area of housing can be raised when the following safeguards are in place:

• The exterior doors to the residence halls should be secured at a specified time. Only persons who have been authorized to enter the residence halls should be issued a card or key to gain entry. Additional doors for emergency exit should be equipped with panic hardware on the interior and no exterior lock on the exterior.

• Each student room should have a unique key that allows access to that room only.

• The doors to student rooms should have an automatic door closer to ensure that doors are not inadvertently left ajar.

• The locks to the student rooms are changed on a timely basis every time a key is reported lost or stolen.

• One main entrance should remain available for students to enter after the doors to dorms are secured.

• Emergency telephones should be placed at the entrances to residence halls to allow timely reporting of problems or suspicious persons.

• Warning bells on entrance/exit doors should sound when doors are left open or ajar.

• Visitors and delivery persons should be supervised at all times by the persons they are visiting.

• Doors and windows should be checked during the night to ensure they are secure.

• Locks and panic devices should be maintained in good working condition at all times.

It is important that universities that maintain on-campus housing for students also maintain 24-hour security, either contract security or in-house security/police. At least one security officer should be on duty at all times.

The use of card access is highly recommended for exterior doors to residence halls. This would require an intruder to penetrate at least two barriers operating on different locking principles (i.e., the card to the front door and the key to the room). The use of card access to exterior doors provides for immediate deactivation if a card is lost or stolen,

therefore raising the level of security to the residence hall itself. Since people tend to carry keys and cards separately, there is a reduced possibility that both accessing devices will be lost or stolen at the same time. If the residence halls are not locked 24 hours a day, a specific time when the halls are locked should be established.

Lighting

Campus lighting is a highly debated security measure. Most crime prevention reports indicate that sufficient lighting inhibits criminal activity. Lighting requirements on a campus, like other institutional facilities, are often dictated by aesthetic considerations, budgetary restraints, and building codes.

In the past, a survey of exterior lighting on a campus was likely to be done by a patrol officer who would go to various places and try to read a newspaper. If the officer could read the print, the lighting was felt to be adequate. Most campuses today will assign an electrical engineer to conduct a survey using light meters.

A deceiving factor when surveying a campus visually is that bright areas seem to make the less lighted areas seem darker by comparison. Lighting levels should be set to achieve uniformity of brightness. Parking areas and highly used areas (e.g., libraries and computer centers) should be well lighted.

Parking Control

Parking control is an important factor in restricting access to the campus to those who are authorized, especially in the housing areas. This can be easily accomplished by registering vehicles and supplying the people who are authorized decals that can visibly identify them as belonging. Restricting various authorized areas of parking can be accomplished by the color of the parking permit or by restricting access to certain parking areas with gates, activated by an access card.

Emergency Call Boxes

Emergency telephones are utilized by a number of campuses. These telephone booths are dispersed throughout the campus for use by the campus community in the event of an emergency. On most campuses these telephones are activated and dial automatically to campus security when the receiver is removed. The communications center of the campus police department is instantly alerted to the location of the caller even if the person cannot speak, thereby allowing the dispatch of a patrol to the location of the call box.

Fire Alarm and Suppression Equipment

Fire alarms and fire suppression equipment are a necessity for any campus environment. An effective program will incorporate a routine maintenance and testing program.

Intrusion Alarms

Intrusion alarms should be used in areas where access is not permitted at certain times and where a quick response is imperative. Although campuses, as a general rule, tend to rely too heavily on intrusion alarms, these devices are appropriate for certain applications, such as the cashier's office, areas with expensive equipment, museums, archival vaults, and in campus clinics where controlled substances are stored.

Closed-Circuit Television

Closed circuit television (CCTV) is another type of security equipment that tends to be overused in the campus environment. Some questions that must be answered before installing CCTV devices are: Who will be monitoring the picture? Will that person know if someone is out of place? Should the image be recorded? Who will review the record?

For the most part, cameras are used with best results when the picture is viewed by someone who is familiar with the activities or people being monitored and is able to execute a timely intervention.

Making a taped record is only effective when there is a need to keep a record and when there is commitment to review the tapes to ensure that their quality meets the need. Camera equipment which is used solely as a

deterrent and is never reviewed or monitored is the least effective use of a security system.

Computer Protection

Computers represent a significant investment for any campus and lend themselves to theft because of their light weight and popularity. There are a number of methods available to protect computer and office equipment. Alarming devices can be attached directly to the computer and monitor so that any attempt to remove the equipment can be detected. A number of computers can be hooked together with a single wire, which creates a complete circuit. If the wire protecting the units is cut or removed, an alarm sounds.

Other non-electric devices include anchoring devices that secure the equipment to the desk or table. These devices require no electric supply or monitoring station.

Computers can be secured with heavy duty cable that fastens the protected item to a wall or table. Heavy bolt cutters are needed to sever the cord. It is hoped that anyone crossing the campus with this type of cutting device would be noticed. However, in any of these instances the security program is only as good as the procedural backing and operational duties of the people responding to or operating the system.

Electronic Article Surveillance Systems

Electronic Article Surveillance (EAS) systems allow items to be marked with a device or tag that sends a signal, which, in turn, activates an alarm when the protected item is removed without authorization or deactivation. These devices can also report to a central station or activate a camera to capture the incident on film.

This equipment has long been in use by retail outlets to prevent theft of high-ticket items. Campuses are utilizing this type of equipment for the protection of books, which are a significant loss expense for most campus libraries.

A program should not rely totally on electronic measures, nor should it rely totally on a police department to ensure the safety of the entire campus community. It is impossible to supply the number of officers necessary to ensure the safety of every campus member. Students, faculty, and staff should be informed of their responsibility for personal protection and protection of the campus. It is important that they be made a part of the overall security program. They should be made aware that it is necessary to pass information to the security department on suspicious persons or incidents, and make emergency situations known to the proper authorities.

E. Floyd Phelps, CPP

ELECTRIC UTILITIES SECURITY: PROTECTION OF OPERATIONS FACILITIES

For rather obvious reasons, security emphasis within the electric utility industry, has tended to focus upon protective responses to nuclear generation. However, the criticality of the overall non-nuclear electric utility infrastructure to the economic viability of the United States necessitates implementation of dynamic security countermeasures to actual and probable threats to the integrity of customer delivery systems, such as: transmission and distribution networks, non-nuclear power generation stations, energy management facilities, and telecommunications support activities.

The unique interdependency of electric companies in providing essential services to people, businesses, and government requires special security programs and systems if the continuity and reliability of these services is to be maintained at optimum levels.

Determining Criticality: A Starting Point

To the seasoned security practitioner, terms such as vulnerability, probability, and criticality form the basis of the security survey or audit process [1].

Although vulnerability/probability factors may be best identified by the security department, only cognizant management can properly articulate criticality with respect to business functions, facilities, or activities. Logically, therefore, the electric utility security manager should seek the advice of appropriate operations, generation, and customer services management in prioritizing security countermeasures relative to criticality.

Typically, facilities or functions that may receive security prioritization by management include: power generation stations, bulk power stations (230 kilovolts and above), remote combustion turbine generators, remote microwave communications sites, and energy management facilities (i.e., dispatching centers). Also, management could very well establish facility security emphasis on the basis of such other factors as public safety (e.g., inner city substations that may present greater safety exposures to the public).

In conforming to the management prioritization process, the security manager can then begin to select appropriate countermeasures through a total analysis process, involving such other factors as probabilities and vulnerabilities. From a security perspective, some very favorable results can be attained from by using such a system.

The First Result: A Policy

To be completely effective, the site and function criticality process should be codified by company policy. Beyond generic security policies, such as those relating to general physical security standards, the electric utility security manager should attempt to have promulgated a policy that clearly establishes minimum security standards for essential operations facilities. With the concurrence of management, the security manager can then specify security systems and practices that must be established at each protected facility. For example, such minimum requirements may include:

1. Power Generation Stations.
   Use of site protective services (i.e., guards) for access control; contractor processing and accountability; patrolling; emergency response; and plant safety.
   Use of security systems (e.g., alarms, CCTV, and communications).
   •Fence and gate specifications.
   •Locking systems and key/lock accountabilities.
   •Security lighting.
   •Signage.

Substation Vulnerability Analysis Worksheet
(Follow-up Inspection)

Facility _____   Prepared By _____

Date   _____   Date Of Last Survey _____

	Yes	No	N/A	Remarks
1. Fencing				
a. Are fence parts straight and serviceable?				
b. Is fence fabric taut, serviceable, and securely fastened to metal post?				
c. Is top guard taut and serviceable?				
d. Is fencing tight against the ground?				
e. Has erosion taken place along bottom of fence?				
f. Do tree branches overhang fence?				
2. Gates				
a. Are gates, including hinges and latch assemblies, in serviceable condition?				
b. Is the lower portion of any gate more than two inches from the surface?				
c. Are access gates locked?				
3. Building(s)				
a. Are doors functional and securely locked when closed?				
b. Are windows screened against intrusion?				
4. Signs				
a. Are the specified "Danger" and "No Trespassing" signs on perimeter fence?				
b. Are signs at an interval so they can be seen?				
c. Are the signs legible and in good condition?				

Page 2 of 2

	Yes	No	N/A	Remarks

5. Material storage
   a. Is material stored inside?
   b. Is material stored outside?				

6. Intrusion experience
   a. Is there any evidence of unauthorized entry into the substation?
   b. Is there any sign of vandalism?
   c. Have there been any security incident reports filed concerning this substation since last inspection?
   d. Is intrusion alarm serviceable?
   e. Have there been any criminal incidents in local area since last inspection?				

7. Other security conditions
   a. Are drainage ditches, wash out, culverts, etc., present that could threaten perimeter fence security?
   b. Are group operated switches locked?
   c. Are PF boxes locked?
   d. Are airbreak switches locked (including mechanism and coupling)?				

Additional Remarks

_____

_____

_____

_____

_____

_____

_____

_____

_____

Substation Security Project Status

Region _____   Area _____   Date _____

Items listed on this form were extracted from substation vulnerability analysis worksheets. Please forward completed project status forms to the Internal Affairs Section on a quarterly basis.

Facility	Item	Responsibility	Completed? Yes or No	Date Completed	Report Date	Remarks

2. Bulk Power Stations (230 kilovolts and above).
  • Fence and gate specifications.
  • Minimum remote alarm system capabilities for central station response.
  • Security lighting.
  • Locking system integrity.
  • Signage.

3. Remote Microwave and Combustion Turbine Generators.
  • Fence and gate specifications.
  • Remote alarms with central station monitoring.
  • Security lighting.
  • Locking system integrity.
  • Signage.

4. Energy Management Facilities.
  • Restricted access and control.
  • Selected use of computer based access control systems.
  • CCTV and other protective systems.
  • Alarm system integration and response.
  • Locking system integrity and key control.
  • Minimum construction standards.

With the implementation of a workable policy, the security manager is then positioned to sustain minimum acceptable protection programs for all essential operations facilities.

The Second Result: A Survey Program

Assuming management concurrence with a new security policy relevant to essential operations facilities, the security manager must then continually review and assess the state of security at each protected location in terms of compliance. This process can best be accomplished through the conduct of detailed security surveys or audits. Success will depend ultimately upon management's response to the security department's findings. Some very important considerations for the security manager to be attentive to, relative to the survey program, are as follows.

Survey Format and Content. The first survey at any site will be a totally detailed and exhaustive analysis of the facility from a security perspective. Subsequent surveys can be reduced to "short forms" if they are conducted at regular and timely intervals (e.g., less than 3 years).

Survey Interval. Essential operations facilities and other prioritized locations (e.g., inner-city substations) should be surveyed within relatively short intervals such as annually. Other operations functions should be surveyed at least every 3 years to ensure full compliance with company policy relative to physical security standards.

When the survey process has been institutionalized, the security manager must establish effective reporting procedures to affected management regarding survey findings. Management should also be required to respond to the security department with corrective actions or exceptions to cited deficiencies.

The Third Result: An Acceptable Compliance Program

Using a short form reporting method, the security manager can condense significant findings as "bullets" in a project status format. The project status report can list multiple locations. It also provides management with an effective method to promptly identify reported shortcomings or deficiencies by location. Management can refer to individual site security surveys for more detailed explanations regarding specific findings.

The project status report allows supported managers to respond to the security department with corrective actions. To simplify the compliance process, the security manager may wish to allow telephonic or electronic mail response to project status reports from the field. The less cumbersome the reporting process is to supervision and management, the more it will gain in credibility and acceptance.

The Fourth Result: More Complete Information

Detailed security surveys usually produce a wealth of additional information that can be used effectively by the utility company in a variety of ways. For example, during the conduct of each site survey, local or servicing police are routinely contacted on such matters as response time, crime pattern analysis, emergency contact procedures, and departmental address or organizational changes. This information can be extracted and used to update regional and corporate emergency response directories for use of security and operations personnel.

Also, directions to remote locations may need to be updated due to area construction or highway changes. The security survey is a means to revise system directories for use by company representatives, contractors, and emergency response persons.

The electric utility industry provides a necessary and vital service to myriad customers in the United States and in all developed nations. Security of the essential operations components of the electrical power system necessitates management prioritization of facilities in terms of both criticality and other significant factors.

Concurrently, the security manager is expected to develop cost-effective security countermeasures to prioritized facilities on the basis of vulnerability/probability analysis. Establishment of an ongoing survey and compliance program will ensure optimum and reasonable protection for company operations functions.

Robert D. Hulshouser, CPP

Sources

Barefoot, J.K., and D.A. Maxwell, Corporate Security Administration and Management. (Butterworth-Heinemann, Boston, 1987).

Gallery, S.M., Readings from Security Management Magazine. (Butterworth-Heinemann, 1984).

Green, G. (as revised by R.J. Fisher), Introduction to Security, 4th Edition. (Butterworth-Heinemann, Boston, 1987).

Wesley, R.L., and J.A. Wandt, A Guide to Internal Loss Prevention. (Butterworth-Heinemann, Boston, 1986).

Note

1. The authors cited provide excellent discussions regarding the security survey. Barefoot and Maxwell give a superb explanation of the differences between loss prevention inspections and surveys in the book, *Corporate Security Administration and Management.*

ELECTRONIC SURVEILLANCE AND COUNTERMEASURES

The extent of industrial espionage has yet to be fully comprehended. We do know, however, that it exists everywhere in the world, and that the United States is a particular target because of its large technological holdings. We also know that a common technique for stealing technology is electronic surveillance.

Surveillance

The basic tool of the industrial espionage operative is the microphone, placed in such a fashion as to be undetectable to the unsuspecting. Microphone wiring, when it is used, is carefully hidden or disguised and run to the recording unit along the most direct route. The recording unit is also concealed, usually in a place entirely controlled by the operative, or in a neutral area, which if discovered will not implicate the operative.

When a microphone cannot be placed within a room without detection, the operative may set up in an adjacent room and place contact microphones against the back side of the wall facing into the area to be examined. One such device is a suction cup that relies on the wall as a vibrating diaphragm for capturing sound. Another is the spike microphone, which is inserted with the point of the spike almost penetrating through the wall. Similar to the spike microphone is the pin-hole mike, a tube-like device that is inserted into a tiny, drilled hole in the wall. For direct listening into the ear (as opposed to direct recording by a recording unit), the operative may use a physician's stethoscope. The operative may also insert a non-contact type of microphone through the back side of an electrical wall plug.

If the operative does not have the advantage of being able to work in an adjacent room, he may set up in a nearby building. The microphone in this case would be the directional microphone. It is incredibly sensitive and can easily capture sounds through drapeless windows. It can also be applied in other settings, such as restaurants and parks. The directional microphone comes in three varieties: (1) the parabolic microphone that uses a small dish similar in shape to a satellite dish, (2) the shotgun microphone that is tube shaped with the microphone assembly at the muzzle end, and (3) the machine gun microphone that has a bundle of tubes shaped somewhat in the form of a Gatling gun.

Of even greater sophistication are tiny battery-powered wireless microphones that are easily concealed inside everyday items like pens, jewelry, cigarette packs and lighters, attaché cases, etc. These miniaturized and microminiaturized devices work like a handie-talkie, transmitting sound waves to a receiver/recording unit or to a booster device that sends them to an even further location where the operative is safe from apprehension.

When the advantage to be gained by spying is considerable, the cost of microphones is not a consideration. They are simply regarded as throw-away, expendable items. The life of a miniaturized microphone is relatively short because the size of the battery is necessarily small. The life span can be enhanced with an on/off switch that can be remotely operated. The on/off feature is also valuable when the operative believes that an electronic surveillance countermeasures inspection is scheduled. In many cases, an electronic sweep of a premises will be incapable of detecting nonoperating transmitters.

Telephones and telephone lines are highly vulnerable to covert listening. An inexpensive device called the "drop-in" has been sold by the millions. It is put into the mouth piece of the handset in place of the regular telephone microphone. Some activate when the handset is taken off the hook, while others are active all the time. The "drop-in" performs the function of the telephone's microphone, but in addition operates like an FM radio, sending signals to the operative's recording unit. It does not require a battery because it draws power from the telephone line. Another telephone device is an induction coil attached to or secreted near the handset.

Induction coils are often supplemented with amplifiers to ensure good reception. Drop-in microphones and coils are fairly easily detected by making either a good physical search of the instrument and its surrounding area, or by measuring the current on the telephone line. The best defense may be to educate people about discussing sensitive information on the telephone.

Almost all covert listening systems include a recording unit. The premise is that if the information is valuable enough to steal, it is valuable enough to permanently record. While the operative may be a highly trained technician, he or she cannot be relied upon to accurately report everything that was heard.

Countermeasures

Even the most determined effort to seek out surveillance devices can at best only reduce exposure. There are simply too many places where covert listening is possible. They start in the office or conference room where sensitive conversations are held, include the telephones, and extend along telephone lines to switching rooms and central telephone facilities. An electronic surveillance countermeasures inspection consists of two activities: a physical search and an electronic sweep. The search is for hidden microphones and tell-tale wiring, and involves looking and touching of the four walls, ceiling and floor, and of area contents. Electrical outlets, return air grates, and other openings on walls are examined; tiles on false ceilings are removed so that the crawl space, duct work, and conduits can be examined; rugs are lifted and carpets checked; and adjacent rooms are inspected. Furniture may be moved away from walls, turned upside down, and even disassembled; wall furnishings can be taken down and examined; lamps and electrical fixtures may be taken apart; and desk accessories and potted plants closely checked. The contents of desks, credenzas, and file cabinets are legitimate search items, as are portable items, such as coffee carts. Intense focus is always upon telephones.

The electronic sweep is much more technical. It involves use of a time domain reflectometer to detect anomalies in telephone equipment and wiring; a spectrum analyzer to detect audio signals suggestive of concealed devices; and a nonlinear junction detector that uses a low-power microwave beam to detect energy reflected from electronic components common to radio transmitters, tape recorders, nonoperating transmitters, and remotely controlled transmitters. Supplementary equipment can include audio-amplifiers and tunable receivers. A sweep is applied to the physical areas where sensitive information is discussed and to telephone terminals and frame rooms. A fundamental principle of electronic sweeping is that every detected indication of covert surveillance must be resolved as either legitimate or suspect.

Norman R. Bottom, Jr., Ph.D., CPP

ELECTRONIC SURVEILLANCE AND WIRETAPPING

Electronic surveillance is the use of electronic devices to covertly listen to conversations, while wiretapping is the covert interception of telephone communications. Eavesdropping and wiretapping can be both legal and illegal. When legal, it is carried out by authority of a warrant issued in accord with the law. The extent of such legal activity is measurable (at least theoretically) in the number of warrants issued. Illegal eavesdropping and wiretapping, on the other hand, defy measurement because they are carried out secretively.

Given the stakes in modern business dealings and the opportunities to easily steal sensitive business information, we can comfortably conclude, without fear of badly missing the mark, that the theft of business information by these illegal means is pervasive.

Surveillance Equipment and Techniques

Surveillance equipment is easy to obtain. An electronically inclined person can simply buy from an electronics wholesaler or retailer the parts and instructions for making a workable bug. Pre-built models are available by mail with no strings attached, and some retailers sell them across the counter after taking nothing more than a signed statement from the purchaser that the equipment will not be used in violation of the law.

Mall and neighborhood electronics stores sell inexpensive wireless FM microphones and transmitters that can be used for covert listening purposes. These devices can pick up conversations and send them across considerable distances to a recording unit and waiting eavesdroppers. They are sometimes advertised as innocent pieces of equipment that can be useful to mothers in monitoring the activities of their children in other parts of the house.

Miniaturization has greatly aided spying. With advances in microchip technology, transmitters can be so small as to be enmeshed in wallpaper, inserted under a stamp, or placed on the head of a nail. Transmitters are capable of being operated by solar power (i.e., daylight) or local radio broadcast. Bugging systems even enable the interception and decoding of typewriter and duplicating machine transmissions.

Bugging techniques vary. Information from a microphone can be transmitted via a wire run or a radio transmitter. Bugs can be concealed in a variety of objects or carried on a person and remotely turned on and off by radio signals. A device known as a carrier current transmitter can be placed in a wall plug, light switch, or similar electrical recess. It obtains power from the AC wire to which it is attached. Devices are difficult to detect by visual inspection when they are cleverly concealed and difficult to detect by electronic analysis when they are turned off.

Telephone lines are especially vulnerable to tapping. Telephone lines are accessible in such great numbers and in so many places that taps are easy to install and difficult to find. A tap can be direct or wireless. With a direct tap, a pair of wires is spliced to the telephone line and then connected to a tape recorder concealed someplace not too far away. The direct tap can only be detected by a check of the entire line. With the wireless tap, an FM transmitter is connected to the line, and the transmitter sends the intercepted conversation to a receiver and tape recorder. Wireless taps (and room bugs) are spotted by using special equipment. For the spy, the wireless tap is safer than the direct tap because investigators can follow the wires to the spy's hiding place.

Another technique transforms the telephone into a listening device whether it is in use or not. A technique known as the hookswitch bypass causes the hookswitch to not disconnect when the receiver is hung up. Although the telephone is disconnected, the telephone's microphone is still active. The effect is to transform the telephone into a listening bug. This technique can be detected by hanging up the telephone, tapping into the telephone line, making noise near the telephone, and listening for the noise on the telephone tap.

The spy may use a dual system in which two bugs are placed: the first to be found and the second so well concealed that it may escape detection. Discovery of the first bug is to lull management into false complacency.

Countermeasures

The physical characteristics of a building have a bearing on opportunities for audio surveillance. Some of these factors are poor access control designs, inadequate soundproofing, common or shared ducts, and space above false ceilings that enable access for the placement of devices. Physical inspections of these weak areas will hinder penetrations.

Persons untrained and inexperienced in eavesdropping and wiretapping countermeasures cannot hope to have any significant deterring or detecting impact. Only the most expertly trained and experienced specialist can effectively counter the threat, and the equipment they use is expensive. Large companies are able to afford in-house practitioners, while smaller firms rely on outside consultants.

Whether from in-house or out-of-house, the technician should be broadly familiar with security policy and strategies, espionage techniques and countermeasures, and understand the methods of information flow and storage within the business organization.

Selecting the In-House Expert. The ideal candidate for the in-house expert will have a strong educational and experiential background in electronics, especially in transmission systems; will be knowledgeable of eavesdropping and wiretapping techniques and countermeasures; and will have an active interest in the field both on and off the job. In addition to being skilled in the science of electronics, the ideal candidate will be skilled in the art of working with people; will have good verbal and writing abilities; and will be ready to work unusual hours and travel on short notice.

Selecting the Outside Consultant. The outside consultant will ideally possess the same skills as the in-house expert. Evaluating these skills can be helped by posing a number of questions to the consultant: What pertinent education and training have you had and where was it obtained? Where have you worked? What was the nature of the work? What particular countermeasures techniques do you employ? What equipment do you use? What references can you provide? Are you insured/bonded?

The security professional should also direct questions inward: Is the consultant really a vendor in disguise trying to sell detection equipment? Is the consultant all that he or she claims to be? Is there an attempt being made to scare the company into a consulting arrangement? In addition to being technically competent, is the consultant discreet? The consultant should be required to provide the evidences of education, training and licensing; a client reference list; proof of insurance; and a sampling of reports.

Equipment

The high cost of detection equipment is justified when the assets to be protected are highly valued and when a high rate of use can be made of the equipment. Following are standard items.

Non-Linear Junction Detector. This detector, which looks something like a sponge mop, contains a microwave transceiver that detects the existence of semiconductors (e.g., transistors, integrated circuits, and diodes), which are the major components of listening devices. An advantage of this portable detector is that it will detect bugs even when they are turned off or malfunctioning.

Telephone Analyzer. This device is essentially made of typical electrical test instruments. Reliability is questionable since there are so many access points to telephone lines and junction boxes. Also, certain bugs do not change electrical characteristics of telephone lines and are therefore undetectable by this piece of equipment.

High-Gain Audio Amplifier. This device is used to determine if audio information is being transmitted over a pair of wires.

Digital Volt-Ohm Meter. This device measures voltage and current. It is a good supplement to other equipment, especially for testing in a compact area, such as a false ceiling.

Tool Kit and Standard Forms. These are two additional aids for the countermeasures specialist. The tool kit consists of the common electrician's tools (e.g., screwdrivers, pliers, electrical tape). Standard forms facilitate good recordkeeping and serve as a checklist. What was checked? What tests were performed? Readings? Who performed the tests and why were they conducted? Over a period of time, records can be used to make comparisons while helping to answer questions.

When guarding against electronic surveillance and wiretapping, we must not forget about visual surveillance and other techniques for obtaining proprietary information. A spy stationed on the same floor in another building a few blocks away can use a telescope to obtain secret data, a window washer can take pictures of documents on desks or walls, a janitor is positioned to take documents discarded in the trash, and the sophisticated surveillance operative will be able to conceal miniature cameras with pinhole lenses. These techniques by no means exhaust the skills of spies.

Philip P. Purpura, CPP

Sources   Purpura, P.P., Security and Loss Prevention, 2nd Edition. (Butterworth-Heinemann, Boston, 1991).

EMBEZZLEMENT: AN INVESTIGATIVE PRIMER

Embezzlers are said to steal $4 billion to $6 billion a year from their employers. Yet their thefts are said to be rarely detected. If detected, their crimes are rarely prosecuted; and if prosecuted, their sentences are very light.

Who are these embezzlers, and what makes them behave the way they do? In the literature of criminology, the classic definition of an embezzler is someone who holds a position of trust and finds himself with an unshareable problem, usually of a financial nature, that can be resolved by "borrowing" the funds of his employer.   (Borrowing usually is a rationalization.)

The embezzler will manifest a few other characteristics as well. Embezzlers tend to have low self-esteem or compulsive personalities, i.e., they gamble, drink, or eat excessively, and might have expensive lifestyles and hobbies.

They are also said to generally commit their acts of defalcations alone, over extended periods of time, and in increasing amounts before they are apprehended. Embezzlers do not usually make "one grand hit" for $1 million and then disappear. They are not "hit and run" criminals whose disappearance stands out as a signal of loss.

Evidence of employee embezzlement initially surfaces in one or a combination of the following ways:

•From an accounting discrepancy, irregularity, questionable transaction, or asset loss detected in the course of routine, internal, external, operational, or compliance audit.

•From a complaint or allegation of misconduct made by corporate insiders, i.e., the employee's peers, subordinates, or superiors.

•From a notable change in the behavior of the culprit.

Embezzlement is legally defined as the fraudulent appropriation of property by a person to whom it has been entrusted or to whose hands it has lawfully come. It implies a breach of trust or fiduciary responsibility. The major distinction between larceny and embezzlement lies in the issue of the legality of custody of the article stolen. In larceny, the thief never had legal custody.

In embezzlement, the thief is legally authorized by the owner to take or receive the article and to possess it for a time. The formulation of intent to steal the article may occur subsequent to the time when it came into his possession or concurrently with initial possession. If initial possession and intent to steal occur simultaneously, the crime is larceny. If intent to steal occurs subsequent to initial possession, the crime is embezzlement.

The Embezzlement Environment

Embezzlement, like all crimes, is a product of motive and opportunity. Embezzlement motives include:

•Economic (need or greed).

•Egocentric (showing off).

•Ideological (revenge).

•Psychotic (obsessive-compulsive behavior).

Opportunity is created by the absence of internal controls or by weaknesses in internal controls. Motives and opportunities play off against one another. The greater the opportunity, the less the motive needed to steal. The greater the motive, the less the opportunity.

The following control environment factors enhance the probability of embezzlement:

•Inadequate rewards.

•Inadequate internal controls.

•No separation of duties or audit trails.

•Ambiguity in job roles, duties, responsibilities, and areas of accountability.

•Failure to counsel and take administrative action when performance levels or personal behaviors fall below acceptable levels.

•Inadequate operational reviews.

•Lack of timely or periodic audits, inspections, and follow-through to assure compliance with company goals, priorities, policies, procedures, and governmental regulations.

•Other motivational issues.

•Inadequate orientation and training on legal, ethical, and security issues.

•Inadequate company policies with respect to sanctions for legal, ethical, and security breaches.

•Failure to monitor and enforce policies on honesty and loyalty.

Proving Criminal Intent in Embezzlement Cases

Without a voluntary and full confession, proving "criminal intent" in embezzlement cases is the most formidable challenge to the skills and patience of investigators and auditors, mainly because evidence of such intent is usually circumstantial. Rarely will there be direct proof of a defendant "knowingly" or "willfully" violating larceny, embezzlement, or fraud laws. Such intent has to be inferred from other facts, like the defendant's education, training, experience, intelligence, sophistication in the ways of business, finance or accounting, past actions, past contradictory statements, tacit admissions, efforts to conceal records, efforts to destroy evidence, evidence of subornation of perjury or obstruction of justice, and evidence of conversion of funds to one's own use.

Common Forms of Embezzlement

Cash disbursement embezzlements are the most common fraud in books of account. They generally involve the creation of fake documents and/or false entries in some category of expense, such as purchases or payroll -- usually a phony invoice from a phantom supplier or a faked time card from a phantom employee. The fabricated purchases may be for merchandise, raw materials, repairs, maintenance, janitorial or temporary help, insurance, travel and entertainment, benefits, and so on. Fabricating the purchase of raw material and merchandise is tough to accomplish since costs of manufacture and sale are closely scrutinized by top management. If the fabricated purchases are for service or supplies rather than merchandise or raw material, the fraud is easier to execute and conceal. These expenses are not monitored as closely as costs of manufacture and sale.

Cash disbursement frauds are very common in small firms with one-person accounting departments or in situations where separation of duties and audit trails are weak or nonexistent. Computerization of small firms exacerbates the disbursement fraud problem because small business owners are too trusting of data generated by computers.

Cash receipts frauds are also common in small businesses. The classic cash receipts fraud involves the lapping of cash and/or accounts receivable; that is, borrowing from today's sales or receipts and replacing them with tomorrow's sales or receipts. In either event, the fraud requires the creation of fake data, fake reports, and/or false entries. There are several other receipts frauds of note. Skimming is holding out or intercepting some of the proceeds of cash sales before an entry is made of their receipt. This is also called fraud on the front-end.

Another form of receivables fraud can be generated by the issuance of fake credits for discounts, refunds, rebates, or returns and allowances. Here, a conspiracy may be required with a customer who shares the proceeds of the fake credit with an insider.

Investigating Embezzlement

Corporate security investigators, when not backgrounding applicants or new hires, spend much of their time investigating allegations of employee theft, fraud, and embezzlement. In a few instances, these crimes are witnessed by other employees or outsiders. The availability of such witnesses can greatly facilitate an investigation. On the other hand, it is very difficult to reconstruct a theft scenario on the basis of an asset loss alone, which is the usual case.

A loss of assets determined on the basis of a conflict between what accounting records show as cash on hand, for example, and what a physical count of cash determines its value to be, makes for a weak case for criminal prosecution. Live witnesses, videotapes, still photos, audio recordings, accounting and auditing expertise, altered documents, and falsified reports strengthen a case.

Embezzlement is a mite different from theft from the standpoint of investigative effort. There are rarely any witnesses in embezzlement cases. Accounting records may leave a trail, but the skills required to reconstruct the embezzlement are more those of an auditor than an investigator. Actually, both sets of skills are required; and for good measure, computer systems skills can prove to be an invaluable aid.

The following list of embezzlement opportunities, as rationalized by a typical embezzler, may provide some further insight.

1. What are the weakest links in this system's chain of controls?

2. What deviations from conventional good accounting practices are possible in this system?

3. How are off-line transactions handled, and who can authorize such transactions?

4. What would be the simplest way to compromise this system?

5. What control features in the system can be bypassed or overridden by higher authorities?

6. How can I introduce a fake debit into this system so that I can get a check issued or get my hands on cash?

7. What transaction authorization documents are easiest to access and forge?

Jack Bologna

EMERGENCY MANAGEMENT PLANNING

No company can consider itself immune to emergencies and no management is free of the responsibility to be prepared to meet them when they occur. An emergency management plan is a tool for meeting that responsibility. A plan is meant to anticipate what can happen and to provide for prompt and effective action should it happen. The goal of emergency planning is three-fold. It provides for the (1) protection of life, (2) protection of property and containment of loss or damage, and (3) prompt restoration of normal operations.

Anticipate the Likely Events

While it may be impossible to predict all potential emergencies and their accompanying circumstances, it is possible to anticipate most hazards and get ready to deal with them. Advanced planning enables the organization to call on the best thoughts of key personnel in every area -- security, production, safety, engineering, maintenance, finance, personnel, and others. These professionals can be tasked to think through all the eventualities and determine an appropriate response strategy. The planning approach makes possible the determination of the emergency equipment and facilities that will be required, it enables management to designate responsibility and delegate authority for emergency action, and it sets the stage for training emergency response personnel.

One of the many problems in an emergency is confusion and the panic that can easily follow. Everyone in the facility from management down to the line employee must know what to expect. Each person should know what he or she is to do, who is in charge, where to go if evacuation is ordered, etc. Key personnel need to be trained in their responsibilities for establishing a sense of order, providing reassurance to employees, minimizing panic, and giving clear directions for the protection of life and property.

Another benefit of advanced planning is the provision of mutual aid through coordination and liaison with outside agencies, such as fire and police departments, local utility companies, civil defense agencies, hospitals, local government officials, and the news media. It may also be possible for neighboring organizations -- other plants, offices, or stores -- to plan for mutual assistance through a sharing of consolidated resources.

Also of great importance in a disaster or a destructive incident of serious dimension is the preparation of reports, photographs, and damage assessment to be presented to insurance carriers following restoration of normal business activities.

Insurers should, of course, be notified as quickly as possible because in all probability they will need to conduct their own separate inquiries with respect to cause, culpability, and extent of loss.

Preparing the Plan

Whether in a manual or another form, emergency plans should be set down in writing. It is not enough to have generalized plans. Each aspect of the emergency response must be precise and specific. One of the points to be stressed is that a general "game plan" cannot be adopted for use in all emergencies. Some elements of the plan may be the same -- including even the makeup of the emergency team and the assignment of areas of responsibility -- but specific details of planning will vary according to the nature of the emergency. Different equipment requiring different human skills operating on a different schedule will be marshaled for different emergencies. These differences will be reflected in the differing challenges posed by fire, flood, earthquake, hurricane, explosion, toxic chemical leaks, and so forth.

Too many company manuals simply gather dust on a shelf or remain forgotten in a drawer. The emergency plan can escape this fate by a commitment to an ongoing program of training, practice, and revision based on experience. Key personnel representing expertise in maintenance, engineering, fire suppression, rescue and first-aid, safety, environmental quality, security, and communications should receive initial and periodic refresher training in how to respond to emergencies according to the plan.

An indispensable part of training will be practical exercises and similar "hands-on" scenarios designed to evaluate preparedness. Problems in execution that surface during practice become the focal points for revision of the plan. In this sense, a plan is a "living document."

Identifying the Threats

Most companies are well aware of the hazards of fire and few fail to take this threat into account. Fire sensors, pull stations, alarms, sprinklers, extinguishers, and the like are constant reminders of the widespread attention given to the threat of fire.

Threats posed by industrial accidents and incidents that impact the ecology are also well understood, principally through the regulatory efforts of the Occupational Safety and Health Administration (OSHA) and the Environmental Protection Agency (EPA).

Emergencies that warrant special attention in a planning document include fire and explosion, wind storm, hurricane, tornado, earthquake, flood, and major workplace accidents.

In short, a wide range of perils confront a business organization. A good starting point in emergency planning is to identify the perils that seem most likely to occur. The process here is called "risk assessment." A risk assessment can begin with a few questions:

• What emergencies are most likely to occur?

• Where and at what times?

• What is the potential for injury and/or property loss?

• How often will a given emergency arise?

The answers will come mainly from an examination of the organization's activities, particularly with respect to the vulnerability of the activities to natural phenomena, such as lightning or flash floods, and to human-induced conditions, such as toxic gas or nuclear waste releases.

The answers will also be complemented with historical and predictive data that are available from a variety of industrial and professional planning organizations and emergency response agencies in the private sector and in the government sector at federal, state, county, and local levels.

It is impossible in a general discussion to examine all of the potential emergencies that can confront a given facility, but certain factors will merit close examination. These are: (1) the hazards that may be inherent in the nature of the organization's work and the implication of those hazards to the workforce, visitors, customers, and the community at large; (2) the size and physical

A CHECK LIST FOR EMERGENCY PLANNING

Does the plan address?
  Fire and explosion
  Natural disaster
  Hazardous material release
  Bomb threat

Have standard operating procedures been developed for each of the above emergencies and do the procedures identify the:
  Responders and the leaders?
  The actions to be taken?
  The equipment and supplies to be used?
  The place and sequence of actions?
  Potential impediments to actions such as transportation obstacles?

Have authority and responsibility been clearly assigned with regard to:
  Command and control?
  Alarm equipment maintenance and testing?
  Notifications and communications?
  Response equipment maintenance, deployment, and use?
  Training, practice and evaluation?
  Public, employee, and media relations?
  First-responder and follow-up medical treatment?
  Damage assessment and containment?
  Incident investigation and analysis?
  Transportation and traffic control?
  Evacuation of personnel and critical assets?
  Utilities regulation/shutdown?
  Continuity of operations at an alternate site?
  Clean-up and restoration of activities?
  Plan review, appraisal, and revision?

Does the fire fighting response component of the plan address:
  Initial and refresher training of fire fighters?
  Fire brigade organization?
  Types and use of portable fire extinguishers?
  Care and use of stand pipe and hose systems?
  Basic fire hazards in fighting ordinary fires?
  Exit routes and escapes?
  First aid medical procedures?
  Special hazards such as toxic discharges?
  Rescue procedures?
  Personal protective equipment?
  Suppression of special hazard fires?

Does the communications arrangement provide:
  Primary and back-up modes?
  Notification lists?
  Noninterfering frequencies?
  Separate linkages with internal and external response agencies?
  A secure communications center?

  Provided by Randy Uzzell, CPP, Director of Corporate Security, Burlington Industries, Inc.,

SEVERE WEATHER PLAN
(Sample)

I. Scope

The purpose of this plan is to ensure preparedness for a severe weather emergency, such as a major tropical storm or hurricane. Identified staff departments are assigned specific responsibilities which include ensuring the safety of employees, preventing loss and damage to physical assets, and establishing communications for coordinating preparedness and response actions.

II.   Severe Weather Committee

This plan establishes a Severe Weather Committee composed of representatives from the Security Department, Administrative Services, Human Resources, Computer Services, Telecommunications, Public Affairs, the Law Department and the Safety Coordinator.

The Security Manager will chair the Committee and be responsible for calling meetings and keeping the plan current. The Committee will meet at least once each year to review this plan and determine if substantive revisions are needed. Substantive revisions will require approval of senior management. Administrative revisions, such as changes in individual committee representation and telephone numbers, will be performed by the Security Manager. The plan will be updated at least once each year and distributed to the Committee members and other concerned parties.

Committee members will be familiar with this plan and maintain the current version of the plan at ready access. In addition, each committee member will develop for use in his or her department or functional area a set of procedures for implementing the provisions of this plan. Such procedures will, for example, address these actions:
   •Identify, obtain, and keep in readiness the equipment, supplies, and materials required for responding to major storm emergencies.
   •Identify perishable supplies and arrange for their procurement in a timely manner following the detection of an approaching major storm system.
   •Establish trigger points for initiating response actions, such as shutting down computers, installing window shields, moving valuable equipment to interior space, and sending employees home.
   •Establish communications methods, both for persons who are assigned response duties and employees within the department or functional area generally.
   •Conduct training that will prepare response personnel to carry out the required procedures.
   •Provide education/awareness briefings to inform employees concerning response procedures.

III. IMPLEMENTATION

A.   Senior Executive in Charge

The Senior Executive in Charge is the CEO or a designee who is immediately available to assume direction and control of response activities. A principal responsibility of the Senior Executive in Charge is to authorize reduction or shutdown of company operations.

The Security Manager is responsible for contacting the Senior Executive in Charge upon announcement of the Phase II alert (as explained below) and to apprise the Senior Executive in Charge of the storm's status and prognosis.

B.   Alert Levels

The Security Manager will monitor the degree of severity of the storm, potential impact, and timing to determine when to move on to a higher level of alert. Four levels of alert have been identified to trigger implementation of the various procedures in the plan.

Phase I becomes effective when a major storm develops which has the potential to hit the Company's facilities. The Security Manager will at this time begin to monitor radio reports of the U.S. Weather Service.

Phase II becomes effective when a major storm develops in or enters a radius within 500 miles of the Company's facilities. The Security Manager will continue to monitor the weather reports to determine the potential impact of the storm, its magnitude, and direction. The Security Manager will keep the Senior Executive in Charge apprised of these storm developments.

Phase III becomes effective when winds ahead of a severe storm are within forty-eight (48) hours of the Company's facilities. The Security Manager will monitor all available weather information, may discuss the severity of the storm with members of the Severe Weather Committee, and may make recommendations to the Senior Executive in Charge concerning the possible shutdown of operations. The Senior Executive in Charge may elect to initiate a shutdown, partially or fully.

Phase IV becomes effective when winds ahead of the storm are within twenty-four (24) hours of the Company's facilities. If this phase is reached, the Senior Executive in Charge will be notified and asked to make a decision with respect to a shutdown.

C.   Notifications

The Security Manager is responsible for contacting members of the Severe Weather Committee and notifying the Senior Executive in Charge concerning the possibility of a major storm affecting company operations. Recommendations to the Senior Executive in Charge on whether to initiate response procedures and/or a shutdown will be based upon information obtained from broadcasts of the National Weather Service.

The Senior Executive in Charge will instruct the Security Manager to initiate response procedures and/or shutdown operations.

The Security Manager will, through personnel and equipment at the Security Control Center, implement a cascade notification so that all employees can be informed with respect to preparedness, shut down, evacuation, and related actions.

IV.   Functional Responsibilities

This section identifies the primary responsibilities of the Severe Weather Committee members. This section does not identify all the details given in the procedures maintained by each committee member.

A.   Security Manager

•Maintain this plan. Update the plan at least annually. Distribute the plan to Severe Weather Committee members.
•Chair the Severe Weather Committee. Call at least one annual meeting and call additional meetings as required.
•Maintain open communications with Senior Executives concerning major elements of this plan.
•Educate employees generally concerning this plan and how execution of the plan would affect them personally. At least once annually, in conjunction with the hurricane season, inform employees of steps they should take to protect their homes in advance of an approaching storm.
•Maintain liaison with local emergency response agencies.
•Develop and maintain a cadre of security officers who are trained/certified in the administration of CPR, first aid, and first responder medical assistance.
•Maintain a means for outside telephone and/or radio communication with local emergency response agencies.

•Monitor major weather conditions on an ongoing basis.

•Follow and evaluate major weather conditions from the time they are first reported. Prepare a storm system tracking map as needed.

•Identify and arrange for the provision of security officer manpower and security equipment or supplies that are needed to support Security Department response procedures.

•Deploy and direct security personnel during response activities.

•Provide a security officer presence at Sage Plaza and the Westport Lab during a shutdown.

B.   Administrative Services Representative

•Maintain and/or acquire at time of need those supplies, such as batteries and drinking water, that may be needed during a severe weather emergency.

•Coordinate with Property Management those response activities that are of mutual interest to the company and the landlord.

•Provide manpower for moving valuable equipment into space that affords a higher degree of physical protection and for securing materials that could pose a risk of injury or damage if left exposed to high winds.

C.   Human Resources Representative

•Provide guidance and assistance in matters relating to human resources issues arising from a severe weather incident.

D.   Computer Services Representative

•Protect and maintain main frame computers. This would include boarding up windows and erecting temporary protective barriers.

•Prepare main frame computers and computer users for a shutdown, if required.

•Provide back-up of data that might be adversely affected by storm conditions.

•Inform users of disruptions to service that may occur as the result of storm conditions and/or a shutdown.

E.   Telecommunications Representative

•Provide a back-up communications capability for use during a major storm.

•Provide a means for employees to access taped messages by telephone.

F.   Public Affairs Representative

•Provide to Telecommunications taped messages that inform callers concerning the status of work activities, opening hours, and similar details.

•Provide press releases that might be required in the event of significant property damage or personal injury.

•Monitor local broadcasts to obtain information concerning the availability of medical treatment and relief centers.

G.   Law Department Representative

•Provide advice on matters regarding liability, damage claims, regulatory compliance, documentation, or other legal issues related to a severe weather emergency.

H.   Safety Representative

•Serve as a resource to the Severe Weather Committee and as an assistant to the Security Manager during the management of a severe weather emergency.

•Serve as a contact and coordinative point for the procurement of medical emergency supplies and services that might be needed during a severe weather storm.

location of the organization, its proximity to neighboring facilities, and its relative geographical position within a surrounding community; and (3) the location of the organization relative to external hazards, such as aircraft crashes, train wrecks, chemical storage leaks, and crime.

Emergency planning involves a realistic assessment of the potential hazards, evaluating the cost of preparedness, and weighing those costs against the risk of loss, both in terms of people and property. A careful analysis along these lines can then be translated into a detailed plan of action.

The plan should name the actions that will trigger initiation of the plan, establish the authority for action, assign responsibilities for execution, and identify the physical resources that will be brought into use during emergency operations. In this regard, a plan typically will be augmented by:

- A statement of policy.
- A clearly delineated chain of command.
- An emergency command post or center.
- An alarm or warning system.
- Communications networks, internal and external.
- Notification lists.
- Procedures for evacuation and shutdown.
- Provisions for medical care and first-aid.

The importance of having an emergency plan cannot be overemphasized. Clearly, it would be impossible during an emergency to invent a plan or even to improvise as the emergency progressed. A plan requires a command and control component for coordinating the many separate, but co-dependent, activities that occur during a response to an emergency. Having no plan or a poorly conceived plan will make coordination extremely difficult, if not impossible.

Although the security manager may not be at the center of command and control decision making during an emergency, he or she will be a major player in deploying security personnel and resources. Most certainly, the security manager will be deeply involved in the important earlier activities that go into identifying the range of risks and developing a workable response capability.

Randy Uzzell, CPP

EMPLOYEE INPUT SURVEYS

Employee input surveys are instruments used to measure attitudes within a specific workforce and collect information on workplace activities that may be hard for management to obtain from other sources. These surveys usually take the form of written questionnaires. They can be as simple as a one-page sheet polling employee opinions on a specific topic, or as extensive as a full, multi-page survey of a variety of attitudes and subjects of importance to the company as a whole. The most sophisticated surveys also contain integrity tests or personality profiles, and are administered by trained consultants who facilitate a detailed process of information gathering and analysis.

Using outside consultants to administer the survey is a good idea because it can protect the integrity of sensitive information, as well as the identity of employees who share the information. The more certain employees are that their responses to sensitive questions cannot be connected back to them, the more forthcoming they are likely to be.

A typical employee input survey is an anonymous instrument in which the employee's identity is protected by use of a code. The survey may consist of several sections, the first usually being data about workforce demographics. The second section may be an integrity questionnaire or personality profile. These may provide valuable information in assessing job performance, determining the validity of information provided in the questionnaire, and in pinpointing problem areas. The third section is often a generalized questionnaire covering a wide variety of attitudes and problem areas within the general company environment. The fourth section provides 10 to 20 specialized questions dealing with specifics of the individual departments or with special companywide problems.

In years past, the practice was for an employer to conduct a survey of employee attitudes and opinions only when the employer believed that an attempt at unionization was imminent. The survey was used as a short-term tactical weapon for gaining information that might be useful in rebutting the claims of union organizers.

Employee input surveys are used with greater frequency today and for varying

---

A SAMPLING OF QUESTIONS FROM AN EMPLOYEE INPUT SURVEY

Rate the overall effectiveness of management.

1   2   3   4   5   6   7   8   9   10

Rate the effectiveness of management in preventing crime-related loss.

1   2   3   4   5   6   7   8   9   10

Have you ever seen anyone steal from the company?

[] No   []   Yes. If yes, please explain.

_____

_____

Rate the overall morale of the employees.

1   2   3   4   5   6   7   8   9   10

Is it easy to steal from the company?

[] No   [] Yes   [] Don't know

What can management do to control theft?

_____

_____

_____

---

purposes. As the differences between management and labor have blurred, and management science has become more sophisticated, employers are discovering that regularly conducted surveys can be useful tools for enhancing understanding, not just between management and labor, but among all employees and groups of employees.

Employers are also learning that healthy communications that flow up, down and laterally within the workforce are essential to productivity and hence to profits.

Surveys can be used in a number of ways. They can provide a means for assessing a perceived problem, bringing to the surface an underlying problem, predicting the probable efficacy of a solution to a problem, and identifying elements of the working environment that create or contribute to problems.

For the security manager, employee input surveys can be valuable in identifying and reducing internal theft and other types of employee crime. Most employees are honest and are offended when they see co-workers acting dishonestly. At the same time, they have learned through bitter experience that it can be unpleasant, even damaging to their careers, to blow the whistle on others. An employee input survey can be structured to provide an anonymous channel for reporting employee crime. Given a chance to get things off their chests, most employees are eager to express themselves.

A security manager who is able to collect information from employees close to criminal activity in progress will have an improved ability to better understand the true nature of the activity and to thereby engineer intelligent, effective changes. A survey is very much in order before taking expensive or radical action, and is often a precursor to undercover operations. The cost of a survey can be less than the cost of taking an ill-advised countermeasure. For example, a survey might reveal that a crime problem perceived to be widespread is, in fact, limited to only one area of the company's workplace. A companywide countermeasure would be in the nature of an expensive overkill.

When regularly used as part of a comprehensive program to improve the upward flow of communications in an organization, surveys provide an invaluable way for employees to express their concerns and for management to learn and to be guided. Surveys are used routinely to gauge employee perceptions concerning the skills of supervisors, product and service quality, advertising effectiveness, adequacy of pay and benefits, and vendor relationships. Almost anything can be surveyed and therein lies a number of questions for the security manager. What can the employees pass on concerning embezzlement, kickbacks, drug use, petty theft, and vandalism?

A survey can also have a cathartic effect, operating as a mechanism for releasing frustrations. On the one hand, it may be seen as an indicator of care and concern on the part of management and, on the other hand, as an opportunity for employees to express themselves on an issue or a small menu of issues. Just getting to be heard at the company's upper level can improve the organization's mental health.

A survey can range from a simple one-page questionnaire prepared by a supervisor for distribution to a small number of subordinates, to a lengthy and sophisticated survey prepared by a consulting firm for distribution to all employees. The common practice is to engage a consultant to ensure that the right questions are asked in the right way, that the answers are tabulated and properly interpreted, and that strict confidentiality is observed.

A sensible and cost-effective middle ground for the average company may be to engage a consultant to administer a standardized employee input survey to which company-specific questions have been added. "Off-the-shelf" surveys are available from reputable personnel consultants and typically include the services of an administrator to analyze the collected information.

Carl E. King

EQUAL EMPLOYMENT OPPORTUNITY COMMISSION

The U.S. Equal Employment Opportunity Commission (EEOC) was created by Title VII of the Civil Rights Act of 1964, which prohibits employment discrimination based on race, color, sex, religion, or national origin. Since 1979, EEOC also has been responsible for enforcing the Age Discrimination in Employment Act (ADEA) of 1967, which protects employees 40 years of age or older, the Equal Pay Act of 1963, which protects men and women who perform substantially equal work in the same establishment from sex-based wage discrimination and Section 501 of the Rehabilitation Act of 1973, which prohibits federal sector handicap discrimination. EEOC also provides oversight and coordination of all federal equal employment opportunity regulations, practices, and policies.

The EEOC has five commissioners and a general counsel appointed by the president and confirmed by the senate. Commissioners are appointed for 5-year staggered terms. The term of the general counsel is 4 years. The president designates a chairperson and a vice chairperson. The chairperson is the chief executive officer of the Commission. The five-member Commission makes equal employment opportunity policy and approves all litigation.

EEOC staff receive and investigate employment discrimination charges against private employers, and state and local governments. If the investigation shows reasonable cause to believe that discrimination occurred, the Commission will begin conciliation efforts. If EEOC is unable to conciliate the charge, it will be considered for possible litigation. The Commission's policy is to seek full and effective relief for each and every victim of employment discrimination, whether it is sought in court or in conciliation agreements before litigation, and to provide remedies designed to correct the sources of discrimination and prevent its recurrence. The Justice Department is the only federal agency that may sue a state or local government for a violation of Title VII. EEOC may sue a state or local government for violations of the ADEA and EPA. If the Commission decides not to litigate a charge, a notice of the right to file a private suit in a federal district court will be given to the charging party.

In the federal government, EEOC staff oversee agencies' affirmative action efforts and their administrative complaints process, administer the complaints hearing program, and review final agency decisions on complaints. If that review demonstrates that discrimination has occurred which has not been fully remedied, EEOC may order the agency to provide complete relief.

The mission of the Commission is to ensure equality of opportunity by vigorously enforcing federal laws prohibiting employment discrimination through investigation, conciliation, litigation, coordination, education, and technical assistance.

Sexual Harassment

A matter of interest and investigation for the EEOC is sexual harassment at work. Sexual harassment is any unwelcome sexual conduct that is either made a term or condition of employment, or has the purpose or effect of unreasonably interfering with an individual's work performance. It includes creating an intimidating, hostile, or offensive working environment.

Two forms of harassment stand out. First is the quid pro quo form in which the harasser withholds employment benefits or makes promises of rewards as a means of coercing sexual favors. The second form of harassment is to create or condone unwelcome sexual advances, requests for sexual favors, or other verbal or physical conduct of a sexual nature. In this scenario, the harasser's behavior does not

need to be linked to a tangible job benefit. Examples include slurs, jokes, gestures, innuendoes, and the display or distribution of offensive material, such as nude calendars.

The employer's policy should prohibit employee conduct of any kind that offends the dignity of co-workers. The policy should call for disciplinary action and assign to supervisors a responsibility for carrying out the policy. When violations occur, a full and prompt investigation should take place. The organization's human resources department will, in almost every case, take the lead role in making an investigation. The security department is sometimes asked to assist.

In a full investigation, three overriding questions must be answered:
- Did the conduct, as alleged, take place?
- Was the conduct unwelcome?
- Was there an abusive work environment?

The complainant should be interviewed in a neutral location and a written statement obtained. The fundamental who, what, where, when, how, and why questions need to be asked. Of particular importance, is the identification of witnesses to the conduct. The complainant should be assured that confidentiality will be observed to the greatest extent possible, but that the very nature of investigating will result in talk and speculation by co-workers.

Corroboration of the complaint should be the main focus. What persons are likely to know about the harassment? Have other complaints been made? Did the accused person commit similar acts? Documentation that may be on file of past incidents can be very valuable.

The accused person should be interviewed after all other investigative leads have been exhausted. The best approach may be to simply lay all the facts before the accused and allow a full opportunity for rebuttal. The accused's representations of innocence will, of course, deserve as much investigation as was given to the complainant's charges.

When all of the facts are in, they should be examined very objectively. It will help to adopt the perspective of a reasonable and prudent person. A thought to keep in mind is that the company's anti-harassment policy and the EEOC rules should not be used as a vehicle for vindicating petty slights suffered by hypersensitive employees. On the other hand, evidence of sexual harassment, no matter how

---

SAMPLE HARASSMENT POLICY

It is the policy of the Company to provide a workplace free of harassment of employees by other employees, including supervisors and managers. Harassment -- whether based on sex, race, color, religion, age, national origin, handicap, or veteran status -- is discriminatory, unlawful, and in violation of Company policy.

Harassment is considered an act of misconduct and may subject an individual to disciplinary action. All supervisors and managers are responsible for implementing and monitoring compliance with this policy.

Harassment is defined as unwelcome or unsolicited verbal, physical, or sexual conduct which substantially interferes with an employee's job performance or which creates an intimidating, hostile, or offensive working environment. Some types of harassment are:

•Verbal harassment, e.g., derogatory or vulgar comments regarding a person's race, sex, religion, ethnic heritage, physical appearance, and threats of physical harm.

•Visual harassment, e.g., demeaning or derogatory posters, cartoons, photographs, graffiti, drawings, gestures, leers, or distribution of written or graphic material having such effects.

•Physical harassment, e.g., hitting, pushing, or other aggressive physical contact, or threats to take such action.

•Sexual harassment, e.g., unwelcome or unsolicited sexual advances, demands for sexual favors, or other verbal or physical conduct of a sexual nature.

Any employee (temporary, permanent, or contract) or applicant for employment who feels he or she has been harassed should report such incident to his or her supervisor, to any member of management, or to the Human Resources Manager.

Any person making such a report or providing information pertaining to a report of harassment will be protected against reprisal or the appearance of reprisal in any form.

The Human Resources Department will conduct investigations of alleged harassment and in such investigations confidentiality will be maintained.

---

minor, requires corrective action. The law demands nothing less.

The options for remedial steps include developing a new policy, educating employees, training supervisors, issuing warnings, assisting victims (e.g., through administrative leave, transfer, or referral to an employee assistance program), and disciplining violators, including use of the termination sanction.

John J. Fay, CPP

Source Laws Enforced by EEOC. (The U.S. Equal Employment Opportunity Commission, Washington, DC, 1988).

EQUAL PAY

Women and men who perform substantially equal work in the same establishment are covered by the Equal Pay Act. The law prohibits employers from discriminating in pay because of sex and from reducing the wages of either sex to comply with the law. A violation may exist where a different wage is paid to a predecessor or successor employee of the opposite sex and from reducing the wages of either sex to comply with the law.

In addition, the law provides that labor organizations cannot seek collective bargaining agreements or impose procedures that cause employers to violate the law.

Retaliation against a person who files a charge of equal pay discrimination, participates in an investigation, or expresses opposition to an unlawful employment practice also is illegal. The law protects virtually all private employees, including executive, administrative, professional, and outside sales employees who are exempt from minimum wage and overtime laws. Most federal, state, and local government workers also are covered.

Many EPA charges may be violations of Title VII of the Civil Rights Act of 1964, which also prohibits sex-based wage discrimination. Such charges may be filed under both statutes. The law does not apply to pay differences based on factors other than sex, such as seniority or merit systems, that determine wages based upon the quantity or quality per item produced or processed.

A lawsuit may be filed by EEOC or by individuals on their own behalf. If the complainant is paid full back wages under EEOC's supervision or if EEOC takes legal action first, a private suit may not be filed. Remedies for violations of the EPA include payment of back wages, interest, liquidated damages, attorneys' fees, and court costs. Back wages may be recovered for a period of 2 years prior to the filing of the suit, except in the case of willful violations where back pay up to 3 years may be recovered. Remedies are tailored to the circumstances.

The Commission's policy is to seek full and effective relief for each and every victim of employment discrimination, whether it is sought in court or in conciliation agreements reached before litigation. Other relief that may be sought includes:

•Posting a notice to all employees advising them of their rights under the laws that EEOC enforces and their right to be free from retaliation;

•Corrective, curative, or preventive actions taken to cure or correct the source of the identified discrimination and minimize the change of its recurrence;

•Nondiscriminatory placement in the position the victim would have occupied if the discrimination had not occurred, or in a substantially equivalent position;

•Backpay, lost benefits, or both; or

•Stopping the specific discriminatory practices involved in the case.

Once an equal pay charge is filed, it is investigated by an EEOC investigator. If the investigation shows that there is reasonable cause to believe discrimination has occurred, the Commission will notify the charging party and the employer of this decision and will begin conciliation efforts.

If EEOC finds that there is no reasonable cause to believe discrimination occurred, the Commission will notify both parties of that decision. Charging parties have the right to request that EEOC headquarters in Washington, DC, review the district office's decision. Charging parties also will be notified of the right to file a private lawsuit.

If EEOC finds that there is reasonable cause to believe that discrimination occurred and is unable to conciliate the charge, the case will be considered for possible litigation. If the Commission decides not to litigate the case, notice of the right to file a private lawsuit in federal district court will be given.

Employers should comply with state or local laws if they set higher standards than the Environmental Protection Agency (EPA). Compliance with state and local laws does not justify noncompliance with the EPA. State and local laws regulating job conditions for employees of one sex will not make otherwise equal work unequal or justify unlawful wage rate differences.

Equal Employment Opportunity Commission

Source Laws Enforced by EEOC. (The U.S. Equal Employment Opportunity Commission, Washington, DC, 1988).

EVIDENCE IN INVESTIGATIONS

Physical Evidence

Evidence is anything that tends to prove or disprove a fact. Within that general definition, physical evidence is any material substance or object, regardless of size or shape. Generally, there are three categories of physical evidence.

•Movable Evidence. Items that can be transported or moved, such as weapons, tools, and glass fragments.

•Fixed or Immovable Evidence. Items that cannot easily be removed, such as walls of a room, trees, and utility poles.

•Fragile Evidence. Items that are easily destroyed, contaminated, or will easily deteriorate.

Evaluating Physical Evidence. In many cases the success or failure of an investigation depends on the investigator's ability to recognize physical evidence and derive understanding from it. This process of evaluation begins with the initial report of a crime and concludes when the case is adjudicated. Evaluation is usually carried out in concert with laboratory technicians, a prosecuting attorney, other investigators, experts in certain fields, and other persons whose knowledge contributes to a better understanding of physical evidence and its relationship to the many facets of the case.

Identification. Evidence must be marked for identification as soon as it is received, recovered, or discovered. Identification markings help the investigator identify the evidence at a later date. Markings are normally made by placing initials, time, and date on the items. If it is not practical to mark evidence, it is placed in an appropriate container and sealed. The container is then marked for identification.

Identification markings are supplemented by the use of an evidence tag. An evidence tag is filled out at the time the evidence is acquired. Entries on the tag are made in ink, and the tag accompanies the evidence from the moment it is acquired until it is relinquished. An evidence tag is not a substitute for marking evidence, but is an administrative convenience for locating evidence while it is in custody.

Chain of Custody. Chain of custody begins when an item of evidence is received. The number of persons who handle an item of evidence should be kept to a minimum. All persons who handle an item are considered links in the custody chain and such persons must receipt for each item whenever a transfer is made. An investigator in possession of evidence is personally liable for its care and safekeeping.

Three factors influence the introduction of evidence at trial:

•The object must be identified.
•Relevancy must exist.

•Continuity or chain of custody must be shown.

Rules of Evidence

The rules for presenting evidence in a criminal investigation are as varied as the types of evidence. Let us look at them.

Opinion testimony is a conclusion drawn by a witness, hence the term opinion testimony. Another form of testimonial information is hearsay evidence. Hearsay is a statement that is made other than by a witness. Hearsay cannot be entered into evidence unless the maker of the statement can be cross-examined.

Privileged communication is confidential information between two persons recognized by law as coming within the so-called privileged relationship rule. The following relationships are generally recognized: a husband and wife, an attorney and client, a physician and patient, and a law enforcement officer and informant.

Character evidence is evidence introduced by either defense or prosecution witnesses to prove the accused's good or bad character. Character evidence is usually introduced only when the defense raises the issue of the accused's character.

Direct evidence is evidence presented by a person who actually witnessed something. Contrast this with circumstantial evidence, which is evidence that proves other facts from which a court may reasonably infer the truth.

Admissibility is a characteristic or condition of evidence. To be admissible, evidence must be material, relevant, and competent. Evidence is material when it plays a significant part in proving a case. Examples of material evidence might be fingerprints of the accused that were found on the murder weapon, an eyewitness account of how the accused committed the crime, or stolen property found in the possession of the accused. Evidence is relevant when it goes directly to the proof or disproof of the crime or of any facts at issue. Examples of relevant evidence might be a death certificate or a medical examiner's report. Evidence is competent when it is shown to be reliable. Examples of competent evidence might be accurate business records or the testimony of an expert fingerprint examiner.

Burden of proof is a rule which holds that no person accused of a crime is required to prove his or her innocence. The prosecution must prove the guilt of a defendant beyond a reasonable doubt. Reasonable doubt means the jury must believe the charges to be true to a "moral certainty." On the other hand, the accused must prove his or her contentions. Such defenses as self-defense, insanity, and alibi are affirmative defenses that must be proved by the accused.

A presumption is a conclusion that the law says must be reached from certain facts. Presumptions are recognized because experience has shown that some facts should be accepted or presumed true until otherwise rebutted. For example, defendants are presumed to be sane at the time the crime was committed, and at the time of trial, in the absence of proof to the contrary. Presumptions are of two classes: conclusive and rebuttable. A conclusive presumption is one that the law demands be made from a set of facts, e.g., a child under 7 years of age cannot be charged with a crime. A rebuttable presumption can be overcome by evidence to the contrary, e.g., presumption of death after being unaccounted for and missing for 7 years.

Rules of Exclusion

In general, rules of exclusion deal with conditions in which evidence will not be received. They limit the evidence a witness may present to those things of which he had direct knowledge, i.e., what he saw, smelled, tasted, felt, or heard.

All evidence, direct and circumstantial, if relevant, material, and competent is admissible provided it is not opinion testimony, hearsay evidence, or privileged communication. There are exceptions regarding the admissibility of opinion testimony and hearsay evidence. An exception to the rule against opinion testimony can be made when no other description could be more accurate. For instance, a witness is allowed to testify on such matters as size, distance, time, weight, speed, direction, drunkenness, and similar matters, all of which require the witness to state an opinion. There is no requirement for the witness to be an "expert" when testifying to facts such as these.

Exceptions to the rule against hearsay can be made for the dying declaration and the spontaneous declaration. The admissibility of a dying declaration is limited to homicide cases. Because of the seriousness of homicide, a dying declaration is an exception. A dying declaration is admissible either for or against the accused. The statement must have been made when the victim believed he was about to die and was without hope of recovery. The admissibility of the declaration will not be affected as long as the victim dies; otherwise, the issue would not arise since there would be no charge of homicide.

The spontaneous declaration, a statement made under conditions of shock or excitement, may be admitted as another exception to the hearsay rule. Normally, such a statement is made simultaneously with an event or act and there is not time or opportunity to fabricate a story. It is generally accepted that the statement will be admitted if it precedes, follows, or is concurrent with the act. The statement cannot have been made in response to a question and must pertain to the act that produced it. The spontaneity of the statement is sufficient guarantee of truthfulness to compensate for the denial of cross-examination.

In prosecutions for sexual offenses, evidence that the victim made a complaint within a short time after the offense occurred (i.e., a fresh complaint) is admissible in certain cases. The fact that the complaint was made is relevant for corroborating the testimony of the victim. The statement may relate only to who and what caused the conditions, and merely indicate the credibility of the victim as a witness.

An official statement in writing made as a record of fact or event by an individual acting in an official capacity (called a "business record") is admissible to prove the truth of a matter. Records are of two types: private and public. To introduce private records, someone associated with the business must introduce them. He must show that the company kept records, that the record produced was one of these records, and that the record was the original or certified copy of the original. Public records are usually introduced by presenting certified copies.

A confession is a statement or complete acknowledgment of guilt. An admission is a statement which does not amount to a complete acknowledgment of guilt, but links the maker with a crime. Admissions are forms of hearsay. A court is inclined to apply the same rules of admissibility to admissions as for confessions.

John J. Fay, CPP

Source Fay, J.J., Butterworths Security Dictionary. (Butterworth-Heinemann, Boston, 1987).

EVIDENCE OF A FORENSIC NATURE

Evidence is that which is legally submitted to a competent tribunal as a means of ascertaining the truth of an alleged matter of fact under investigation before it. Anything that a suspect leaves at a crime scene or takes from the scene or that may be otherwise connected with the crime is evidence of a forensic nature.

Physical Evidence

"Physical," "real," "tangible," "laboratory," and "latent" are adjectives to describe the types of physical evidence capable of examination by a crime laboratory. Physical evidence can aid in the solution of a case because it can: (1) establish the criminal's modus operandi, (2) develop or identify suspects, (3) prove or disprove an alibi, (4) connect or eliminate suspects, (5) identify loot or contraband, and (6) provide leads. Physical evidence can prove an element of the offense; for example, safe insulation, glass, or building materials on a suspect's clothing may prove entry. Stomach contents, bullets, residue at the scene of fire, semen, blood, tool marks may all prove elements of certain offenses. Physical evidence can prove the theory of a case; for example, footprints may show many were at the scene, and auto paint on clothing may show that a person was hit by a particular car. For the most part, physical evidence falls into two classifications:

Evidence with Individual Identifying Characteristics. This evidence can be positively identified as having come from a specific source or person if sufficient identifying characteristics, or sufficient microscopic or accidental markings, are present. (Examples: fingerprints, handwriting, bullets, tool marks, shoe prints, pieces of glass where the broken edges can be matched, and wood where broken/cut surfaces can be matched.)

Evidence with Class Characteristics Only. This evidence, no matter how thoroughly examined, can only be placed into a class. A definite identification as to its source can never be made since there is the possibility of more than one source of the evidence found. (Examples: soil, blood, hairs, fibers, single-layered paint from a safe or car, glass fragments too small to match broken edges, and tool marks, shoe prints, or bullets, in those instances where the microscopic or accidental markings are insufficient for positive identification.)

It is desirable to have evidence that can be positively identified but the value of evidence with class characteristics only should not be minimized. In cases involving evidence with class characteristics, the following are desirable:

• A preponderance of such evidence.

• A preponderance of class characteristics within a single item of evidence, such as paint with many layers all matching or soil with foreign matter such as paint chips, odd seeds, and safe insulation.

• Elimination specimens, such as soil, vegetation, paint, carpet fibers, and other materials collected on the basis of information given in an alibi. These are analyzed to verify or disprove a suspect's statement.

Federal Bureau of Investigation

Source Handbook of Forensic Science. (Federal Bureau of Investigation, U.S. Department of Justice, Washington, DC, 1990).

EXECUTIVE PROTECTION

This section presents general guidelines that may be of value to a security manager tasked with providing executive protection services. It discusses the need for protection and provides a philosophical aspect for the security manager to consider when developing a security plan. Planning and the advance work that goes with it is the single most important function of a security manager in the matter of executive protection, whether in connection with an overall protective program or a single event.

First and foremost, it must be understood that no personal security activity, regardless of available finances and humanpower, can guarantee the safety of the individual being protected. The closest thing to a guarantee would be to place the person being protected in an isolated fortification where his/her access to potential harm (whether intentional or unintentional) would be minimal.

An example would be a maximum security prison where every person and item entering the individual's cell is thoroughly examined. Obviously, this is not an acceptable option. The security manager must work within the parameters of what is acceptable to the person being protected and what is affordable in cost to the organization.

An organization that loses a high-ranking official through assassination, kidnapping, or accident may not necessarily be permanently damaged by the loss, but it is very likely that the organization will at least temporarily suffer from the stress and confusion that immediately follows such an event. It helps to think of personal protection as a percentage game. Everything that is done to improve the safety of an individual is an increase toward attainment of a 100% secure environment. The 100% goal from a practical standpoint is unreachable, but must be strived for. The security team must recognize and accept the fact that they and the person being protected are constantly vulnerable to hazards, even when security protections are in place to the highest degree possible. A properly administered security plan reduces, but does not eliminate, the threat potential.

The security manager has to realize that the greatest threat to the protected executive is not from an intentional attack but from an unintentional occurrence. The protected executive can just as easily be killed or injured as the result of a car accident, heart attack, tripping and falling, or drowning. Security planning must not be so overly concerned with the prevention of kidnapping or assassination that the security plan overlooks common everyday hazards. The importance of advance planning in this regard cannot be overemphasized.

Many security managers do not have budgets adequate to provide continually operated protective measures for senior executives, but from time to time they are expected to set up ad hoc security arrangements for special events, such as annual stockholder meetings. Should an incident occur during a protected event, it will happen in seconds or fractions of a second. If security personnel are not alert and constantly thinking preventive actions, they may respond too late to be effective. Studies of past assassinations show

that shootings and other attacks occur in an amazingly short period of time. Alertness and anticipation on the part of security personnel should be emphasized. Accidents can occur in similar short time frames.

Management must be convinced of the need for personal protection before a security plan will go anywhere. Developing and implementing a plan can be difficult when the protected executives feel embarrassed by being the center of security attention or do not want to project an image of needing someone else to look after them. This is understandable and must be kept in mind. Collecting news clippings of violence aimed at persons in similar positions may be helpful in convincing the protected executive of the need for the protection. This form of education should be extended to the protectee's staff and family as well. Care must be taken, however, to not create a case of crying wolf.

Emphasis should also be placed on post-incident activity. In addition to the concern about preventing potentially injurious activity, the security manager needs to be prepared to respond after an incident occurs. Questions that come into play include: Does the organization have a crisis management team/plan? Are security personnel trained in CPR and first aid? What are the quickest routes to hospitals? Have kidnapping plans been reviewed with the protected person or other potential targets? Is backup transportation available in the event of vehicle breakdowns? Are procedures current and workable for contacting the protectee's doctor, family members, and close associates in an emergency?

Another point of consideration has to do with rapport. Putting the security blanket snugly in place can be affected by the personal relationships that develop between the protectors and the protected. The attitude of the protectee will be shaped by his/her perception of the individuals providing the protection. Although the security manager may hold center stage in terms of selling, explaining, and directing the protective program, and is therefore the principal image maker, the protectee will also form an opinion based on observations of the rank and file security persons assigned to the team. The main message here is that the security manager must be extremely selective in forming the protective team. Not only must the team members be competent practitioners in the art and science of personal security, they must fit neatly with the styles and personalities of the people being protected. The gorilla or gestapo type of person, for example, is rarely acceptable.

The number of kidnappings and bombings directed against businesses declined somewhat in the early 1990s but this should not be seen as the end or the beginning of the end of these forms of terroristic activity. Extremist groups in many parts of the world continue to strike out at business organizations that, to them, appear to oppose their ends or be at fault in some way.

The Irish Republican Army (IRA) in England and the Red Brigade in Europe are examples. In the United States we see businesses confronted by extremist groups with agendas that include pro-life, animal rights, conservation, protection of the environment, and military intervention overseas. We also observe an elevated security consciousness developing in the air transportation, pharmaceutical, and defense industries. The total scene is a constant shifting of threats and countermeasures as a wide range of extremist groups rise up, become active, fade out, and emerge again.

The international terrorist threat in the United States has been held in check by geographical isolation, close relationships with the bordering countries of Mexico and Canada, and to law enforcement professionalism. Terrorist attacks directed against prominent business personalities are not, however, out of the question. Security professionals must keep current with the goals, strategies, and tactics of extremist groups, and modify their protective measures accordingly.

Many publications and services on personal protection are available at little or no cost. Business and community organizations publish and distribute booklets on security and safety in the office, at home, and while traveling; police departments stock a wide variety of handouts on crime prevention and provide crime prevention surveys of homes and businesses; the American Red Cross, the American Heart Association, and other community agencies offer low-cost CPR and first aid courses; fire departments offer training in how to evacuate business buildings incident to fire or explosion; the U.S. Postal Service offers training in how to respond to suspected mail bombs; municipal, county, and state police departments, along with the Bureau of Alcohol, Tobacco and Firearms, frequently offer training in how to manage bomb incidents; the American Society for Industrial Security provides, through an electronic bulletin board, a daily summary of security incidents reported by the news media; companies that sell commercial intelligence offer advisories that can help security managers anticipate threats in volatile areas around the world; and the U.S. State Department's Bureau of Diplomatic Security and the Overseas Security Advisory Council publish protective guidelines for American businesspeople working overseas.

Past history, today's experience, and tomorrow's expectations demonstrate the need for personal protection, and in a business organization no one is more aware of that need than the security manager. The difficulty for the security manager is to communicate the need and gain acceptance of a protective program. The obstacles to listening and accepting can range from personal and corporate mindsets against executive protection to plain old considerations of cost. In this latter regard, the security manager may find himself in a position of having to compete with other managers for a shrinking number of operating dollars.

It bears repeating that protection of the business executive relies heavily on advance arrangements based on careful planning. This translates into work involving liaison with local law enforcement; hiring security-oriented professional drivers; thorough security surveys of sites to be visited, as well as residences and offices; emergency preparedness; security awareness training for the protectee, family, and staff; and thorough familiarity of team members with the geography and conditions of the areas to be visited. These are the down-to-earth activities that form the foundation of an effective protective program.

J. Branch Walton

EXECUTIVE PROTECTION: THE KIDNAPPING THREAT

U.S. business, both at home and overseas, is a target for kidnapping and other acts of violence. Terrorists use violent methods to force changes to business practices, to shape public opinion, and to bargain with governments for relief from prosecution and incarceration of their brothers-in-arms. Terrorists, as well as ordinary criminals, also use kidnapping as a means for acquiring money.

A first step in an organization's defense against executive kidnapping is to obtain approval of the protection program. Approval in most cases will be made at the Board of Directors level and will involve consideration of kidnap insurance, ransom payments, and a crisis management team (CMT). The Board's decisions will set the framework for an overall policy. The policy promulgated by senior management, with input from the security manager, is written into a kidnap plan that is cascaded down through the organization in the form of directives, procedures, and the like.

If kidnap insurance is purchased, the carrier will require absolute secrecy with respect to that fact and to any premeditation concerning intent to pay ransom demands. The carrier may also dictate who is to do the negotiating of ransom payments, require that the organization's response be conducted in accordance with applicable laws of the United States and other nations, and that prompt and full notification be given to law enforcement. A failure by the organization to meet the carrier's requirements can render the coverage null and void or reduce the carrier's obligations to pay.

Planning

Although the organization's plan for dealing with kidnapping is a highly sensitive matter, it cannot be developed with such great secrecy that it will reflect the thinking of one or a few individuals who may not have all the right answers. An initial planning group consisting of in-house and outside experts can be helpful in hitting all the bases. In addition to the security manager, who should play a key role within the group, the members might include a representative of the Federal Bureau of Investigation (FBI), an attorney, a counter-terrorism expert, a political analyst familiar with the nation or region where kidnapping is anticipated, a kidnap insurance specialist, a professional hostage negotiator, a public affairs specialist, an electronics communication expert, and a human resources specialist. Members of the initial planning group are also likely to be members of the CMT.

The early planning effort should clearly evaluate the capabilities of persons or groups who may direct kidnapping at the organization, the vulnerabilities of the organization with respect to the kidnapping threat, the current capacity of the organization to resist the threat, and the range of additional countermeasures that are necessary to lower the threat to an acceptable threshold of risk. The output of the initial planning group would become the working materials for the security manager in preparing a kidnap plan and its implementing procedures.

Plan Execution

Carrying out the plan is more than just responding to an incident. Plan execution is getting ready, paying attention to details day in and day out, rehearsing, learning from the rehearsals, and improving on procedures.

The kidnap plan will be an integral part of the organization's overall security program. The plan will be reflected in the overall program in many ways: controls on access to the executive suite and the executive's vehicle, panic alarms and closed-circuit television (CCTV) cameras in the executive reception area, bullet- and bomb-resistant materials inside the walls surrounding the executive suite, and an alarm center for monitoring sensors installed in the office (and home) environment.

The same considerations apply where the executive resides. A survey of the executive's home should be conducted and, in all probability, it will uncover weaknesses that may be corrected through investing in simple, inexpensive safeguards, such as trimming the shrubs and adding some outside lights, to more expensive and intrusive safeguards, such as watch dogs and security officers. Thought in the survey should be given to the time needed to effect an appropriate response. When a rapid response is not always certain, protection of the occupants can be enhanced by creating in the home a concealed room that features a highly resistive door, a panic button, and a telephone. A weapon inside the room is an option.

Following are brief discussions of actions that support plan execution.

Being Prepared. An important administrative step is to set up a file on the protected executive.

The file will contain details about close friends, relatives, servants and other persons who live with, work for, and frequently visit the executive; physicians, dentists, and required medications; the places where the executive and his family frequently visit, e.g., country club, church, vacation spot, weekend retreat, and the executive's favorite haunts when on the road; and proof-of-life information, e.g., a name known only to the executive and his significant other (such as the name of the family's first dog). The file can also be supplemented with photographs, handwriting samples, fingerprint cards, and voice tapes. This file can be of enormous value in launching a search for the protected executive and when communicating with kidnappers.

Being prepared also means being properly staffed and equipped. Protective staff can include a bodyguard, a chauffeur, and house and garden help. Screening and training of these persons is essential. Equipment appropriate for close-in executive protection includes defensive firearms, bulletproof wear, handie-talkies, and armor-plated vehicles.

Training. The protected executive, his or her family members, and protective staff are in the top priority for training. The next priority includes house servants and office workers. The training topics would focus on the tactics of kidnappers, the early warning signals of an attempted kidnapping, how to respond, and, if abducted, how to survive.

Maintaining a Low Profile. The protected executive should be informed of the advantages of maintaining a low profile by not unnecessarily revealing personal identity, company affiliation and position, travel plans, and planned social activities. Care should be taken when communicating with others on the telephone, in restaurants, and in public areas where conversations can be monitored. Written information of a sensitive nature should be given confidential protection and shredded when no longer needed.

Avoiding Predictable Patterns. Routes to and from work and the automobiles used should be frequently and randomly changed; the times, dates, and places of out-of-office business meetings should not follow a discernible pattern; and family and social routines should be varied.

Being Alert. A group intending to kidnap or harm the protected executive may attempt to gain entry to the residence or office through pretext. The target may be the executive's child and the method may be trickery in effecting a release of the child from the custody of a babysitter, child care center, or school. The best guidance is to anticipate possible scenarios, take pre-emptive steps, and look for and react to the early warning signals.

Abduction

The value of planning is immediately evident in the aftermath of an abduction. Preparations will be made to receive contact from the kidnappers. Contact will most likely be made directly by telephone, although it could be made indirectly through another party, such as a newspaper or radio station, or in writing. If contact is by telephone, certain protocols are in order: express a willingness to cooperate, ask to speak to the victim, and ask for the proof-of-life code. The call should be recorded.

If contact is in writing, the document and its envelope or outside container should be carefully protected so that forensic analyses (e.g., examinations for fingerprints, handwriting, and saliva on the flap or stamps) will not be adversely affected.

Contact by the kidnappers should be immediately reported to the FBI. Notifications to law enforcement agencies of other countries that have jurisdiction should also be made without delay. Attempts to handle the situation without recourse to government authorities are likely to fail. Success depends too heavily on having extensive capabilities in intelligence gathering and negotiating for the release of hostages.

By the time the kidnappers have made contact, the CMT will have been activated. The CMT leader, to whom considerable decision-making authority has been delegated, will be the key persona in coordinating major issues with law enforcement and a variety of other parties of interest. The CMT members will be variously going about the pre-planned tasks assigned to them in the plan. These tasks may include notifying next of kin, dealing with the news media, setting up a command center, establishing a rumor control function, coordinating with the kidnap insurance carrier, and conferring with the head negotiator.

John J. Fay, CPP

Sources

Fuqua, P., and J.V. Wilson, Terrorism: The Executive's Guide to Survival. (Gulf Publishing Company, Houston, 1978).

Littlejohn, R.F., Crisis Management: A Team Approach. (American Management Association, New York, 1983).

Purpura, P.P., Security and Loss Prevention. (Butterworth-Heinemann, Boston, 1984).

Reber, J., and P. Shaw, Executive Protection Manual. (MTI Teleprograms, Inc., Schiller Park, IL, 1980).

EXPERT WITNESS: AN OVERVIEW

Succeeding as an expert witness requires a basic understanding of who and what experts are. Our dispute-resolution process permits certain witnesses to render opinions based on data rather than merely reciting information. These opinions are sought to explain past, present, and future events. I will suggest ways in which you may better accomplish your tasks as an expert. Yours is a special, often controversial, position in our court and in dispute resolution procedures.

A recent article defines an expert in the following way:

A person who, by virtue of training and experience, is able to do things the rest of us cannot. Experts are not only proficient in what they do, but are also smooth and have tricks for applying these things to problems or tasks. Experts are good at plowing through irrelevant information in order to get at basic issues or actual problems. Experts are also good at recognizing problems as instances of ones with which they are familiar, generalizing alternative solutions, and making good choices among the alternatives [1].

Those authors indicate that experts can be found from a number of sources:
- Recommendations from others
- Published works
- Technical products
- Academic degrees
- Formal credentials such as licenses, awards, or honors
- Teaching experience
- Supervisory work with others
- Membership in specific organizations [2]

Federal court jury instructions advise juries as follows concerning expert witnesses:

The rules of evidence ordinarily do not permit witnesses to testify as to opinions or conclusions. An exception to this rule exists as to those whom we call "expert witnesses." Witnesses who, by education and experience, have become expert in some art, science, profession, or calling, may state an opinion as to relevant and material matter, in which they profess to be expert and may also state their reasons for the opinion.

You should consider each expert opinion received in evidence in this case, and give it such weight as you may think it deserves. If you should decide that the opinion of an expert witness is not based upon sufficient education and experience, or if you should conclude that the reasons given in support of the opinion are not sound, or that the opinion is outweighed by other evidence, you may disregard the opinion entirely [3].

How the Process Works

Preliminary Stages. Before you are selected as an expert, the conscientious attorney interviews you, sometimes at the scene of the technical challenge or at your working environment. You may also be selected without interview based on criteria previously listed.

You should have adequate time and sufficient basic information to prepare for that first interview. Approach it with appropriate questions and sufficient technical preparation to assess the degree of professional excellence required by the assignment. If your qualifications meet the needs of the case, you should confirm the relationship in writing. Critical terms are to be discussed and established in express detail.

The client -- a person, company, or government agency -- should be involved in selecting and confirming you in your role as expert witness. The client ultimately bears financial responsibility for your services and should sign or guarantee the engagement letter. If you can choose whether to take the assignment (and many times you cannot, because of your employment), you should feel comfortable with both client and attorney.

A popular misconception should be dispelled at the outset. Dramatic courtroom testimony is not the only use made of experts. Often you will be engaged for other purposes, such as arbitration, consultation, administrative hearing, office negotiation, long-range planning, or internal investigation. The process is the same regardless.

You should be made aware of all available facts, the client's understanding of the case, technical reports, research papers, official investigative records, and witnesses' statements. If the case involves places or objects, you should inspect both as soon as possible.

In cases that involve a specific protocol, locate the best, most current version. That guide will be the format for further investigation. Compare events of the case with the standard for flaws, negligence, omission, oversight, and compliance. Do not assume that only one protocol exists. Many an expert has been blindsided by that misconception.

Throughout all stages of the case, you should keep a running list of additional information required for follow-up investigation. Use it as a guide for preparing your tracking devices, either manually or as part of a computer program.

You and the client's attorney should discuss the legal principles involved in the case before you render an initial opinion about factors such as liability, culpability, fault, defect, negligent practice, or propriety. At this point, you may have developed a series of alternative hypotheses to be tested against known data, reserving final conclusions until all data are available. Your initial evaluation should be flexible and questioning. At this point, it is inappropriate for you to reach anything but tentative conclusions, and those should be kept verbal and probably private.

A cautionary word is in order. Attorneys in our system are advocates, relics of the champions of jousting fields of the past. As such, their duty is to put forward a set of facts and proofs that support the client's position.

Occasionally, zeal for the cause may shade professional and intellectual independence. It is not improper for the advocate to give you a wish list stating the most desirable conclusions from the attorney's and client's viewpoint. This does not mean, however, that you must support that view. Your integrity, reputation, and personal and professional self-esteem require that the conclusions you reach and opinions you espouse be supportable based on the available body of facts and operative knowledge. Follow the scientific methods regardless of the path it forces you to take.

In a case involving more than one expert, all expert witnesses on your side should be called together for a meeting. Each should bring results of preliminary studies and fact-gathering efforts for an exchange of data, ideas, and theories. The attorney should open the meeting by explaining that subjects about to be discussed will be part of the attorney's work product and thought process. As such, the materials should not be discoverable by opposing counsel if discovery ensues. This precaution is mandatory, particularly at early stages when various hypotheses are proposed, some of which will be discarded for lack of evidence. If the attorney does not call such a meeting, you might initiate it, just as you would do in an ordinary investigation.

A collateral benefit of the first meeting is that all experts begin to appreciate reciprocal strengths, weaknesses, and information. This is particularly necessary in multidisciplinary cases that demand a blend of sciences, skills, and expertise.

The client should be intimately involved in preparing the case and should attend the conference. At these meetings, the client will understand the amount of effort each expert must expend, and the client may then find your financial and other requests more reasonable.

Minutes of the meeting should be kept in a separate file marked "confidential" and retained by the attorney. In addition, headings on the minutes should indicate that the meeting is part of the attorney's work product and thought process. Confidentiality may be enhanced by having the client present, making the communication subject in part to attorney-client privilege and possibly not discoverable. Some existing law protects conferences such as this from discovery.

Discovery and Deposition. If the assignment is court-oriented, you may play an important role in pleadings and discovery preparation. You may be called on to word technical parts of a pleading. You can also review discovery requests and responses for completeness and technical consistency. In some cases, you can help uncover a body of technical data, forms, procedures, protocol, notes, and research materials. It is often essential that you participate at this stage to ensure that requisite technical materials are available before deposition, and to assist in reducing the costs of discovery.

Preparing for deposition, as well as interrelating previously obtained materials, should be a joint effort between you and the attorneys. If no attorney is available, proceed as indicated nevertheless. Essential items to consider in planning for your depositions include a basic understanding of what a deposition is and what its purposes are. A deposition is sworn testimony before trial, usually made in an office or at your place of work. It is designed to accomplish certain specific objectives.
- Gather information
- Uncover weaknesses in testimony
- Lock you into a position
- Assess your ability as a witness

The examination is usually done by opposing counsel, with few, if any, questions by your sponsoring attorney. The setting is generally informal, scheduled in advance, and conducted in the presence of a certified court reporter. Recording by video, as well as stenographic notes, is common. You may also assist the examining attorney at deposition of opposing experts by assessing their qualifications, capabilities, and demeanor, and framing questions for them.

The guidelines for courtroom testimony will help guide your performance as a witness. Before your deposition, you should review the following:
- Technical and fact data from the client
- Your investigative and technical materials
- Pleadings on file in the case
- Products of discovery, such as interrogatories, document production, and deposition
- Standard scientific works relevant to the subject
- Appropriate legal authorities

Agreement of counsel or court approval is usually necessary before you may be deposed. The pleadings must show that the information sought by deposition cannot be obtained by other traditional and less-expensive means of discovery. This is particularly true under the Federal Rules of Civil Procedure and in states that have adopted similar rules [4]. Depositions may be taken either for discovery or in lieu of testimony in court because you are beyond the jurisdictional limits of the court's subpoena power.

Obtaining prior court approval for your presence at deposition is an effective precaution. In some jurisdictions, such matters would be referred to local counsel, who would then determine whether you should attend the deposition. Hearing such matters in foreign territory is risky. The attorney should, at your suggestion, obtain either stipulation or a trial court order in advance of the deposition that you are expected to attend.

Preparation for Trial. Before trial, you will assist in preparing exhibits and demonstrative charts, tests, and documents. Any demonstration must be tested before the trial or hearing. Trial exhibits should be shown to opposing counsel in advance of trial, and either stipulation or court order for approval should be obtained. These are easy ways to guarantee the admissibility of a key chart, exhibit, document, or demonstration. It is proper for you to ask the attorney calling you if these details have been satisfied. Nothing can be as disappointing as preparing costly demonstrations or exhibits that are rejected at trial because of inaccuracy or lack of foundation. Exhibits and demonstrations must be accurate and technically correct. Demonstrations must be substantially similar to the subject under litigation to be admissible.

You, the attorney, and the client should be present at the final pre-trial conference of experts. The client's presence allows testimony to be sharpened and blended. Often clients forget essential facts. You can ask probing questions to remind the client of events of technical significance or inquire as to facts that will be presented at trial and may be necessary foundations for your opinions.

At this conference, all weaknesses in the case should be exposed and all strengths of the opposition examined. You and the other experts coordinate testimony among yourselves. A recalcitrant expert can be identified at this time. Inconsistencies in expert testimony should be disclosed. This conference is a dress rehearsal. All staging and timing should be practiced. Experts, attorney, and client should be brought to a peak of performance, using video or audio monitoring if necessary to identify flaws, weaknesses, and idiosyncratic behavior.

Unnecessary exhibits and testimony should be eliminated before trial. Your calculations should be re-checked. Data should be summarized whenever possible: have the raw data available in the courtroom but refer to summaries of voluminous documents or material. Rules of evidence allow this use of summary data [5].

The large amount of raw material you have evaluated before trial can enhance the weight of testimony. The data from which summaries are made must in all cases be available for examination by opposing counsel. Good practice dictates that such information be made available well before trial and be in court for opposition examination.

Preparation for trial is somewhat different from preparation for deposition. The attorney should explain to you the objectives of testimony and describe the physical setting of the hearing room in detail, including positioning of the parties, the attorneys, and the dispute resolution forum. The attorney should outline the functions of the witnesses, attorneys, jury, or other fact finder.

At Trial. During the trial, you should be aware of the importance of careful testimony, particularly the hazard of inconsistent testimony between deposition and trial. You are admonished to tell the truth and to prepare for deposition or trial testimony by reviewing the fact of the case and your work effort. You should not lose your temper. Speak slowly, clearly, and naturally. If you are familiar with the process, you will not fear the examining attorney or the setting. You must answer only the questions asked, never volunteering information beyond the scope of the question presented. You need not have an answer for every question.

Remember that most questions asked by the opposition can be answered "Yes," "No," "I don't know," "I don't remember," "I don't understand the question," or by a simple factual answer. You should not memorize your story or testimony. Avoid such phrases as "I think," "I guess," "I believe," or "I assume." These are weak and insufficient to meet scientific and technical burdens of proof of reasonable probability.

Taking a breath before answering a question is always a good idea. This allows you to appear deliberate and gives you time to digest the question and frame an answer. Be careful of trap words such as "absolutely" or "positively"; be cautious about estimating time, space, and distance. If technical information is involved, give specifics -- not estimates -- in the answer. Refer to files or notes to refresh your recollection.

Avoid fencing, arguing with, or second-guessing examining counsel. You should not deny having had prior discussions about testimony in the case if such is the fact. If you make a mistake, correct it as soon as possible. If a negative or apparently damaging fact or omission has been elicited, admit it and move on quickly. To fence, hedge, argue, equivocate, or become angry only exposes you to further cross-examination and a resultant loss of credibility. It also draws attention to the weakness. One way to handle the situation is to answer the question and then add: "But please let me explain." The examining attorney will probably not let you do that, but the attorney for whom you are working will certainly ask you to explain on re-direct examination.

You should never answer too quickly or look to counsel for assistance. Testimony in court, deposition, or hearing should never be turned into a joke. Exaggeration, underestimation, or overestimation are all indications of unwary and ill-prepared witnesses. You must translate technical terms into common, understandable language at every opportunity. Your demeanor and behavior before, during, and after testimony should be the subject of care. You should review your clothing, stance, and posture with the attorney before trial. You should know the hazards of discussing testimony in hallways, restrooms, or public areas around the hearing room. Conversations with opposing parties, attorneys, and jurors must be avoided.

A court order may be necessary to allow you to remain in a court or hearing room during trial, if either side has sought to exclude witnesses. Your assistance during trial may mean the difference between success and failure. If you continually pass notes and confer with the attorney, the client's case will appear weak to the fact finder. It is better for you to take notes and confer with the attorney during recess. At all costs, you must be viewed as a professional interested in a factual presentation, not as an advocate for either side. This is not to say your testimony is to be given without conviction. The contrary is true. Courtroom tools and gadgets that make your testimony more effective should be used. Lapel microphones, overhead projectors, and telescoping pointers allow comfort of movement and clarity of presentation.

At trial your testimony will be divided into five main parts:
•Your qualifications as an expert to render opinion testimony
•Your assignment and how it was performed
•Findings of fact based on your research
•Your expert opinions
•The reasons that support your conclusions

Your opinions may be based on facts found, research conducted, or a series of hypothetical questions developed with you by the sponsoring attorney based on facts, evidence, and proof developed at trial.

You as an expert, because of your knowledge, training, and experience, are allowed to render opinions about controversial matters during the dispute resolution processes. You may be called on to assist in all phases of investigation, preparation, discovery, and trial of contested matters. Your role is to transmit specialized information and knowledge to the fact finder. In many cases, your effectiveness will determine the outcome of the controversy. As in any stimulating setting, the expert is likely to be questioned. Anticipation of cross-examination will facilitate your persuasive response. Of particular concern are those areas which you isolate as weak. You should prepare for cross-examination and frame a strategy for answering vulnerable areas.

Harold A. Feder

Source Feder, H.A., Succeeding as an Expert Witness -- Increasing Your Impact and Income. (Van Nostrand Reinhold, New York, 1991). Reprinted with permission.

Notes
1. See "Expertise in Trial Advocacy: Some Considerations for Inquiry into its Nature and

Development," Campbell Law Review, Volume 7, Number 2, Fall 1984, p. 125.
2. See "Expertise in Trial Advocacy: Some Considerations for Inquiry into Its Nature and Development," Campbell Law Review, Volume 7, Number 2, Fall 1984, p. 125.
3. See Federal Jury Practice and Instructions, 3rd Edition, Vol. 1, (West Publishing Company, St. Paul, MN, 1977), Section 15.22, p. 482.
4. See, for example, Rule 26(b)(4), Federal Rules of Procedure.
5. See, for example, Rule 1006, Federal Rules of Evidence.

EXPERT WITNESS: THE DEPOSITION

A deposition is a legal proceeding conducted for the purpose of preserving the testimony of a witness for use in court. In this case, we are talking about a witness who is an expert witness. The deposition is usually held in a reasonably comfortable and private setting, very often the conference room of an attorney's office. The persons present are the witness, a notary public to administer an oath, a court reporter (usually a notary), and lawyers for all parties. The parties themselves or their representatives have a right to attend but seldom choose to do so.

The deposition begins by administering an oath to the witness. The lawyers take turns in asking the witness questions. A lawyer may skip a turn or take more than one turn. The proceeding is relatively informal, although serious to the outcome of the lawsuit. The reporter takes down everything said and the reporter's record will later be typed and bound in a document called a deposition or a transcript. The deposition is essentially a tool for opposing lawyers to discover what a witness' testimony will be at trial. For example, the plaintiff's lawyer in deposing an expert witness for the defense:
•Will want to discover what the expert knows concerning the facts involved in the matter being litigated. The search here is for evidence that the expert will present in support of the defendant.
•Will want to discover if the expert knows of any facts that may be damaging to the defense, e.g., that the defendant may have been careless or failed to do something.

•Will want to commit the expert to the statements made under oath so that at trial the expert's testimony cannot be changed (at least not without difficulty and damage to the defense).

•Will look for ways to discredit the expert's testimony or to use the expert's testimony to discredit the testimony of other defense witnesses. Minor contradictions among witnesses are inevitable, while major contradictions or the appearance of them can be damaging.

•Will attempt to learn the basic theory and strategy that the defense will rely on at trial. The plaintiff's attorney may decide that the defense will be formidable against the claim as stated and that the claim needs to be changed.

Although a deposition can embarrass or even damage the reputation of an expert witness, this is not a legitimate purpose of the proceeding. When it happens, it is often the result of inadequate preparation by both the expert witness and the attorney that engaged the witness.

The expert witness has three fundamental obligations. First, is to tell the truth, even if the truth will hurt. This is an obligation that sits above the outcome of the lawsuit. Second, is to be fair. This does not mean that the witness has to give equal favor to both sides, only that the witness not overstate or color the facts. Third, is to be accurate, and this is where the expert witness plays a critical part in helping the judge and jurors fulfill their responsibilities in seeing that justice is carried out.

John J. Fay, CPP

Source Baker, T.O., Operator's Manual for a Witness Chair. (Baker and Sterchi, Kansas City, MO, 1992).

EXPERT WITNESS: THE DISPUTE RESOLUTION PROCESS

The tribal councils of ancient societies frequently sought guidance from designated magicians, sorcerers, and tribal wisemen. These persons did not possess divine gifts or supernatural powers. Rather, they had the ability for keen observation of nature; physical facts; animal behavior; contents of roots, plants, and herbs; and the uniformity of times, tides, and seasons. By focusing attention on this body of data, they were able to correctly predict a number of future events. This gave them a position of superiority in primitive society. On analysis, we have not really come that far. Today you are, for similar reasons, considered to hold a special place in the dispute resolution process.

The Expert in Today's Society

Contemporary application of the expert's skills can be found in the highest halls of government and industry. Presidential and legislative panels regularly provide the executive and legislative branches of government with technical guidance. National disasters such as the Space Shuttle catastrophe of 1986 led to the convening of a blue-ribbon panel of space scientists searching for causes of the tragic flight of Challenger. Congressional panels seek scientific, technical, and fiscal experts to testify before investigating committees that attempt to unravel mysteries or develop legislation.

Administrative boards and tribunals call on forensic experts for technical guidance. Examples are the Interstate Commerce Commission, Public Utilities Commission, Federal Trade Commission, Federal Aviation Administration, Federal Reserve Board, Department of the Interior, Department of Defense, and Department of Energy. Administrative boards and agencies are composed of technical experts who call on other experts for study, opinion, and reasoned predictions as to present, past, and future events.

Local governing bodies make frequent use of experts. Among the many areas are land use; air and water pollution; zoning; building code; industrial and mining operations; wet lands; aviation; forestry; budget; economic growth; tourist and visitors' bureaus; school boards; departments of public safety, public health, and welfare; liquor control; and drug and alcohol abuse units. The list could go on. Last but not least are judicial and dispute-resolution bodies. In traffic courts, the arresting or investigating officer is the lead forensic expert, and engineers, toxicologists, and accident reconstructionists are all frequent witnesses.

Municipal courts likewise use forensic experts such as zoning code interpreters, construction experts, electric code enforcement officers, plumbing and sanitary experts, and welfare officials. Specialists of every department of the municipality are frequently called upon for expert opinion, testimony, and guidance.

Our juvenile and children's courts frequently see the child psychologist, social worker, probation officer, and guidance counselor, whose expert opinions often determine the course of a young person's life. In our probate, family, and domestic relations courts, we seek advice of economic experts, accountants, marriage counselors, therapists, physicians, and clergymen.

As an expert witness you are sought either to explain what happened in the past or predict what is likely to happen in the future. How do you do that? Because you are experienced and trained in a specialized field and a keen observer, you can teach conclusions and opinions from skillful observation of events and phenomena. These events may seem routine and commonplace to you but mysterious to the rest of the world.

In state and federal courts of general jurisdiction, not counting the areas previously enumerated, it is anticipated that at least one-third of all matters going to trial entail the use of some forensic expertise. Influence of the forensic expert in our lives today, helping shape not only future decisions but resolving present controversies over past events, assumes unusually vital proportions. There are some philosophic impediments the forensic witness must overcome before becoming truly effective.

•If forensic investigation suggests a result scientifically, technically, or factually irrefutable, why all the hassle? Why can't the experts gather around a table and resolve the dispute in a spirit of collegiality and fraternity?

•Why must I as an expert be subjected to grueling and rigorous cross-examination when the facts are so clear? After all, I am an expert, I have studied the facts, I am educated and trained in this area. I know the answer to the problem!

•I am appalled there is an expert witness who studies the same facts and reaches a conclusion contrary to mine. How can that be? The other expert must have been imposed upon by opposing counsel.

•How can the attorney know in advance the result of my study without the benefit of the weeks or months necessary for me to arrive at

those conclusions?   I refuse to have my profession insulted or my integrity challenged by an attorney who makes such a quantum leap.

These four misconceptions lie at the root of most fundamental misunderstandings between forensic witnesses and attorneys. As this text explores every aspect of the expert witness and testimony process, these misconceptions should evaporate, eliminating the major basis for combat between the professions.

It has been observed that jurors generally take to ordinary people but they do not always like or trust experts. In other words, experts tend to depersonalize themselves through their methodology, vocabulary, or general demeanor. The end result is trial presentation by a robot-like creature who has become devoid of human attributes. That situation can be reversed.

Qualities of the Effective Expert

Eight qualities identify the effective, credible expert witness:
•The expert must perform a thorough investigation.
•The expert must be personable, genuine, and natural.
•The expert must have an ability to teach.
•The expert must be generally competent.
•The expert must be believable.
•The expert must persuade without advocacy.
•The expert must be prepared.
•The expert must demonstrate enthusiasm.

Thorough Investigation

The expert must go the extra mile. Study all reports. Survey the general body of relevant data. View all relevant objects and places. Interview all relevant witnesses. Maintain field notes. Investigative tracks should be kept. Make sure your time records reflect this. Conduct tests for both inclusion and exclusion of your hypothesis. Draw and follow an investigation plan. Use the most current professional thinking, writing, and practice to develop appropriate investigative checklists.

As an expert, you should be aware of the well-recognized Frye rule, which comes from a case dealing with evidence based on scientific, professional, or technical theories [1]. Frye requires expert opinion testimony to be based on an established body of scientific, technical, or particularized knowledge, information, or study "...sufficiently established to have gained general acceptance in the particular field." You must be prepared to show that the professional, scientific, or technical premise on which you rely has been sufficiently well established to have gained general acceptance in the specific field to which it belongs [2]. However, the Federal Rules of Evidence probably represent the mainstream of current legal thinking about admissibility of expert testimony.

Personable

What qualities make you want to socialize with other people? How do you decide whom you will bowl with or take on a fishing trip? What determines whom you invite to your home?

Human beings tend to associate with those we like, those who exude feelings of warmth, friendliness, and concern. We gravitate toward people who let us talk, think, and grow for ourselves. We tend away from lecturers, know-it-alls, and people who lack humility.

What causes you to say, "I like that person"? Think about the factors that make you want to spend time with some people and not others. Be natural; be yourself. Your job as an effective forensic witness is to leave the witness stand and have the commission, court, or jurors think: "That seems like a nice person."

Ability to Teach

Think back to high school or college days. Recall a favorite instructor or coach. Recollect the qualities that made you want to learn more from that person. Visualize those attributes, and try to act like that person. This partial listing of a few of those qualities might assist your recollection:
- Well-informed
- Uses demonstrative aids
- Non-intimidating
- User of example and analogy
- Questioning
- Humble
- Non-directive
- Provides opportunities to test knowledge

- Honestly admits information gaps
- Friendly
- Sense of humor

Competence

Demonstrated ability and competence in the subject field is a mandatory element of effective expert testimony. Competence is demonstrated by thorough knowledge in the field, appropriate experience or credentials, currency of information, ability to perform as well as teach, proven results, and an ability to recognize problems, elect alternatives, and make good choices among them. Competence is the demonstrated ability to do something very well.

Believability

You have to believe to be believable. You are not merely a mirror of the position established for you by an attorney or client. You are presented with a problem, afforded opportunity to investigate and evaluate the facts, and asked to reach a supportable conclusion. As a witness dedicated to a particular conclusion, reached independently and based upon available data, you will be believable because you believe in what you are saying. On the other hand, if the conclusion you espouse is that of counsel or client, or is not supportable or supported by available data, you will not demonstrate belief. You will not be believable.

Ability to Persuade

Do you remember the last time you changed your mind on any subject? What caused you to do that? Did you read a book, attend a lecture, watch a television program, or exchange ideas with persons who had more information than you? As human beings we change our minds for various reasons. One of your objectives as an expert witness may be to cause the fact finder to change an opinion about a scientific, technical, or factual proposition. Your task frequently is to analyze what beliefs are likely to be held by the trier of fact, decide why those beliefs are held, ask yourself what it would take to convince someone that the previously held beliefs were incorrect, and then set out to convince. Your task is to persuade without becoming an advocate, to convince without argument, and to encourage a conclusion based upon irrefutable data presented in an interesting way. Effective persuasion is subtle. A person is most strongly convinced if he or she can mentally develop the ultimate conclusion rather than it being spoon-fed by the persuader.

Preparation

Thorough preparation is a relative task. It may involve detailed and extensive notes, findings, and calculations, or a general knowledge of relevant literature. It is like this story of snow peas and shrimp. Once a witness was asked her opinion about whether a man and a woman who had frequented her restaurant were married. The witness was emphatic in her recollection. She knew the people. They had appeared at her restaurant every Tuesday night for years. She had regularly served them. Her foundation testimony to that point was totally convincing. Not satisfied with the overwhelming presence of preparation and knowledge evidenced by the witness, the examining attorney pressed forward.

Q: And are you absolutely certain you served these people every Tuesday night?
A: Yes.
Q: Then I suppose you even remember what they ordered?
A: Yes
Q: What did they order?
A: Snow peas and shrimp.
Q: Every Tuesday night?
A: Every Tuesday night.

The witness concluded her testimony with her opinion that the couple was married. Her thorough preparation and familiarity with the facts, even on a collateral subject, carried her testimony on the primary issue, marital status, to a point of complete believability.

Enthusiasm

Enthusiasm for the task at hand, the subject matter, and the conclusion, can be demonstrated in many subtle ways. Facial expression and body language tell a great deal about the witness's enthusiasm for the subject. Tone of voice and inflection can suggest boredom or conviction. Imagine the difference in perception between a witness who answers simply "Yes" and the witness who at the right moment says, "You better believe it."

The Forensic Expert Questionnaire

There is an opportunity to learn from experiences of other experts. A Forensic Expert Questionnaire was prepared and sent to over 160 experts throughout the United States. One-third of the experts responded. They were questioned about how the quality of forensic testimony could be improved. Their responses rendered some thoughtful suggestions:

- Upgrading of qualifications, standards, and training
- Better review of qualifications of experts
- More accountability for performance
- Developing a list of incompetent or unethical experts
- Instituting educational programs for judges
- Instituting educational programs for attorneys
- Using more demonstrative visual aids
- Letting experts question experts
- Working more closely with attorneys
- Changing questions-and-answers process to allow more explanation

A Brief Introduction to Cross-Examination

We have seen the qualities of good expert witnesses. Another part of the process involves cross-examination. What is it all about? How does it work? Cross-examination is the most misunderstood aspect of the adversary system. It need not be a fearful experience for you. It is designed to guarantee a fair trial. Cross-examination has six general purposes. These are to establish your:

- Lack of perceptive capacity or application (stated another way, failure to do your homework).
- Inadequate recollection of the applicable facts.
- Bias, prejudice, or interest in the outcome or motivation for particular testimony.

• Questionable character, reputation, or qualifications.

• Prior inconsistent statements or conduct (stated another way, if you testified to different conclusions in another case in which the facts and evidence were approximately the same, that can be used to impeach your testimony).

• Inconsistency with recognized published authorities, so-called "learned treatises" [3].

Do not be afraid of cross-examination. It will allow you to solidify the impression you left through prior testimony. Be a good witness. Be honest. Follow the skilled, technical, professional, or scientific method. Meet the eight criteria of credible and effective expert testimony. You should be able to use cross-examination in a positive way.

Rules Are Rules

Almost every forum in which you testify, will have rules to guide you as an expert witness. Most reflective of current thinking on the subject are typically the Federal Rules of Evidence, Rules 701 through 706. The Federal Rules of Evidence characterize the rules in the federal courts, and they are similar to rules enacted by many state courts. The Federal Rules also generally reflect case and common law decisions in many jurisdictions that have grappled with aspects of expert testimony.

In synoptic form, the Rules include these provisions:

• Rule 701. General reference for the use of scientific, technical, or specialized knowledge.

• Rule 702. A liberal approach to the admission of expert testimony if that testimony will "assist the trier of act" to understand the evidence or determine an issue. This rule also sets forth a liberal standard to the question of who is an expert, leaving the determination to the discretion of the trial court.

• Rule 703. Experts may base their opinion or inference on facts or data which are not necessarily admissible or admitted into evidence at the trial.

• Rule 704. You may give testimony on any ultimate issue to be decided by the trier of fact.

• Rule 705. You may state your opinions and conclusions without disclosing the underlying facts or data of your opinion unless the court requires you to do so [4].

• Rule 706. A court may appoint its own expert witnesses to assist the dispute resolution process.

A general understanding may help alleviate some of your fear of the adversary system and our dispute-resolution process. If the evidence in a particular case is subject to only one conclusion and is cast in terms of absolute proof, the matter will probably not proceed to trial or hearing. It is the case involving questionable evidence, doubtful outcome, or conflicting exhibits and testimony that request adversarial presentation. That presentation and its ultimate objective, the dispute-resolution process, will be aided immeasurably by your service as a forensic witness.

As a reminder, justice is for the philosopher, truth is for the sage. However, it is a wise and practical society that endeavors to use the adversarial system and your expert testimony to assist in the dispute-resolution process.

Harold A. Feder

Source Feder, H.A., Succeeding as an Expert Witness -- Increasing Your Impact and Income. (Van Nostrand Reinhold, New York, 1991). Reprinted with permission.

Notes

1. *Frye v. U.S.*, 293 Fed.1013 (D.C. Cir. 1923).

2. "Using the *Frye* Rule to Control Expert Testimony Abuse." (Defense Research Institute, February, 1989), p. 23.

3. "The Expert Witness in Litigation." (Defense Research Institute, 1983), p. 6.

4. "A Practical Guide to Using Expert Testimony under the Federal Rules of Evidence." (The Practical Lawyer, Vol.31, Number 5, July, 1985), p. 21.

EXTERIOR INTRUSION DETECTION

Exterior intrusion detectors can be used for both outside and inside applications. When used out-of-doors, they must be designed to withstand the rigors and unique demands of outside conditions and must, of course, also reliably detect intrusion. Among the design considerations will be climate, weather, terrain, animals, traffic and similar forces, and stimuli.

The basic concept is to detect an intruder's movement across a boundary around the area being protected. In this sense, the concept is often called perimeter intrusion detection. Detecting an intrusion at the perimeter provides time advantages by allowing the protective force to mount a response and at the same time tighten interior safeguards surrounding critical assets.

Types of Detectors

The boundary of a protected area can be defined either by physical barriers, such as walls and fences, or natural barriers, such as a lake, river, forest, or mountain. The boundary can also be defined as an imaginary, unmarked border that delineates property lines. The types of detectors used at boundaries are fence disturbance sensors, invisible barrier detectors, buried line sensors, and electric-field sensors.

Fence Disturbance Sensors. Chain-link fences typical of the type installed around the perimeter of military installations, industrial sites, and utility complexes can be augmented with fence disturbance sensors. These devices detect mechanical forces induced in the fence by an intruder either climbing over, cutting through, or crawling under. Regardless of the intruder's method, the act of penetration will impact the fence, creating vibrations that are larger in amplitude and usually higher in frequency than vibrations induced by naturally occurring phenomena such as wind and small animals.

Invisible Barrier Detectors. Exterior perimeters with level ground can be protected by using invisible barrier detectors that generate a narrow invisible beam of electromagnetic energy. The energy is formed by a transmitter that emits a beam of either microwave or infrared energy; the beam moves through space on a line-of-sight path and is captured by a receiver. An intruder who runs, walks, or crawls through the beam will interrupt or distort the energy pattern. When the disturbance of the pattern satisfies the alarm criteria, the detector initiates an alarm. Separation between transmitter and receiver is a function of the detector application, terrain, operating environment, and certainly the types of detector (infrared or microwave). Under ideal operating conditions, infrared detectors can protect zones between 300 and 1,000 feet; and microwave detectors can protect zones between 500 and 1,500 feet, depending on the individual detector model.

Buried Line Sensors. Perimeter boundaries can be protected by buried line sensors. These sensors form a narrow sensitive area along the ground above the buried sensor line and detect intruders crossing the sensitive area. Buried line sensors are available to detect seismic, pressure, and magnetic phenomena. The seismic sensor reacts to propagated energy induced in the ground by an intruder crossing the buried sensor; the pressure sensor reacts to soil deformation produced by the weight of the intruder moving across the sensitive area; and the magnetic sensor reacts to ferrous materials either worn or carried by the intruder. Each of these buried line sensors can protect a zone at least 300 feet long.

Electric-Field Sensors. These sensors generate an electrostatic field along a combination of parallel field and sense wires. The field and sense wires are either secured to separate fence posts to form a stand-alone electric-field fence, or they are secured to stand-offs mounted to existing fence posts to form a protected barrier that is part of the existing fence. As an intruder approaches the electric-field sensor, his body distorts the electrostatic field generated by the field wire. These field distortions alter the normal electrical signals on the sense wire. When the change in the signals' characteristics satisfies the detector alarm criteria, an alarm is initiated. Depending on the sensing configuration, a single detector can protect a boundary section as long as 750 to 1,000 feet.

Robert L. Barnard

Source Barnard, R.L., *Intrusion Detection Systems.* (Butterworth-Heinemann, Boston, 1982).

F

FEDERAL BUREAU OF INVESTIGATION (FBI)

In late June of 1908, during the administration of President Theodore Roosevelt, Attorney General Charles J. Bonaparte appointed a force of special agents in the Department of Justice. Prior to this, the Department of Justice had borrowed agents from other government departments, particularly the U.S. Treasury Department's Secret Service, but Congress, perhaps in reaction to the convictions of a senator and congressmen for land fraud, passed legislation prohibiting this practice.

Thus, the attorney general and the president saw that they had to create a new investigative force. On July 26, 1908, the attorney general ordered this new force of special agents to report to Chief Examiner Stanley W. Finch. Under Attorney General Bonaparte's successor, George Wickersham, the new force was given a name, Bureau of Investigation. This bureau was renamed the Federal Bureau of Investigation (FBI) on July 1, 1935.

The early investigators of the Bureau of Investigation understandably had limited impact on the crime problems of that era. This force of investigators handled bankruptcy frauds, antitrust crimes, neutrality violations, and peonage, plus crimes on Indian reservations. Thirty-five men comprised the original staff, most of whom had investigative experience or were law-trained, and their number grew slowly. Today, the FBI has statutory jurisdiction in over 260 violations of federal criminal laws and a force of over 9,000 special agents.

Passage of the White Slave Traffic Act in 1910 proved to be a forerunner of the FBI's later emergence as a national crime-fighting agency. The act, which gave the bureau investigative authority over interstate transportation of women for immoral purposes, also prompted criticism that such legislation amounted to an invasion of state police powers. Attorney General George Wickersham, aware of the difficulties that might arise, called for prudence in enforcing the law so that violations of community regulations would be left to local authorities.

The bureau's responsibilities gradually expanded, but the number of agents needed to handle them failed to keep pace. Coping with espionage and sabotage incidents of World War I was beyond the capabilities of the small, inexperienced force of agents. Lack of training in handling the violent social unrest following the war led to abuses of civil liberties by the unskilled lawmen. Charges of political corruption reaching into the Department of Justice and the bureau itself prompted angry demands for drastic changes.

The appointment in 1924 of J. Edgar Hoover as Director of the FBI set the stage for those changes. Under Mr. Hoover, a new bureau quickly began to evolve. The fledgling director was determined that the organization would become a career service in which appointments would be made strictly on personal qualifications and abilities, and promotions would be based solely on merit. Mr. Hoover's goals were to develop a career service staffed by trained professionals and shape the bureau into an efficient crime-fighting force. High standards of personal conduct for employees, uniform operating procedures, and a training school for special agents were established.

Since 1961, the FBI has had expanded jurisdiction with respect to organized crime and two of its major sources of illicit revenue -- gambling and hoodlum loan sharking. In September 1961, the president signed into law three statutes covering the interstate transmission of wagering information, interstate transportation of wagering paraphernalia, and interstate travel in aid of racketeering. These were followed in June 1964, by a bill prohibiting sports bribery; in May, 1968, by another federal law banning extortionate credit transactions; and in October 1970, by a statute aimed at large-scale intrastate gambling operations, hoodlum infiltration of legitimate businesses, and the bribery of local officials in gambling matters.

Enactment of these laws vastly expanded the FBI's jurisdiction over professional vice and racketeering activities and enhanced its ability to penetrate the walls of secrecy surrounding organized crime. As a result, deeper insight has been gained into the structure, methods, and scope of operations of professional criminal combines in this country. Leaders of these organizations have been identified, and FBI investigations have been responsible for the conviction and imprisonment of a number of them, as well as their criminal underlings.

Throughout the years, the FBI has emphasized service functions, including those in the scientific laboratory, the fingerprint identification, the training, and the information-dissemination fields. It is the objective of these cooperative services to assist other law enforcement and criminal justice agencies to better fulfill their responsibilities to the citizens they serve. They include a broad range of programs and operations, such as the National Crime Information Center (NCIC), through which millions of records relating to stolen property and to missing persons and fugitives from justice are instantaneously available to local, state, and federal authorities across the United States.

NCIC users at present include criminal justice agencies in all 50 states, the Royal Canadian Mounted Police, and the police of Puerto Rico and the Virgin Islands.

FBI Headquarters houses the best-equipped forensic laboratory in the world. Examinations of evidence submitted by local, state, and federal law enforcement agencies constitute a major part of the laboratory's work. New scientific methods and services are continually being introduced and improved. In recent years, the analysis of business records from illicit drug trafficking has become a powerful tool in the war against drugs. Also, the forensic application of DNA-typing methods will have a profound effect on the investigation and prosecution of many crimes of violence.

Computer science has also been adapted to another high-volume area of the FBI's work -- fingerprint processing. A computerized fingerprint identification system -- known as the Automated Identification System (AIS) -- is used in the processing of many of them. AIS offers the promise of speedier and more efficient identification services than ever before possible -- with resultant increased benefits to America's criminal justice system.

While the investigative priorities of the FBI have evolved over the years, the investigations in which the FBI has achieved its reputation, such as bank robberies, fugitives, aircraft hijacking, kidnappings, assassinations, and other violent and property crimes, continue to be addressed.

Federal Bureau of Investigation

Source FBI Facts and History. (Federal Bureau of Investigation, U.S. Department of Justice, Washington, DC, 1992).

FBI: IDENTIFICATION AND LABORATORY SERVICES

The FBI's Identification Division contains the largest collection of fingerprint identification data in the world available to law enforcement agencies. Services of the division include furnishing standard forms, such as fingerprint cards, for submitting identification data; searching of fingerprint cards; making name checks to locate identification records; sending fugitive notices to enforcement agencies; making latent print examinations; examining fingers of deceased persons for possible identification; and assisting in the identification of persons killed in major disasters.

The Laboratory and the Technical Services Divisions of the FBI have capabilities in a wide range of forensic sciences: (1) document analysis, (2) scientific analysis, and (3) analysis of audio/video recordings and electronic devices. Competent expert testimony and technical assistance are provided in special situations, such as kidnapping cases, airline disasters, and photographic problems.

These divisions maintain standard reference files and collections of typewriter standards, automotive paint, firearms, hairs and fibers, blood sera, safe insulation, shoe prints, tire treads, watermark standards, safety paper standards, checkwriter standards, office copier standards, and National Motor Vehicle Certificate of Title File.

Files of questioned material consist of the National Fraudulent Check File, Bank Robbery Note File, Anonymous Letter File, National Motor Vehicle Certificate of Title File, Pornographic Materials File, National Stolen Art File, and National Stolen Coin File.

In the laboratory's National Automobile Altered Numbers File (NAANF) are surface replica plastic impressions of altered vehicle identification numbers found on stolen cars, trucks, and heavy equipment. The purpose of this file is to have a central repository for specimens of altered numbers so that comparisons can readily be made to identify recovered stolen vehicles and to link such vehicles with commercialized theft rings.

A related reference file is the National Vehicle Identification Number Standard File (NVSF), which contains standards of Vehicle Identification

Number (VIN) plates from each factory of the major manufacturers of American automobiles. The purpose of the file is to enable the FBI Laboratory to determine whether or not a submitted VIN plate is authentic. Additionally, it gives the laboratory the capability, in the event that bogus VIN plates are being prepared in an automobile factory, to identify the factory and the machine used in making the bogus plates.

Engineering Section Capabilities

The Engineering Section of the Technical Services Division is responsible for the development, procurement, and deployment of many types of technical equipment used in support of the FBI's investigative activities. In addition, this section has the capability of examining evidence of an electrical or electronic nature, conducting analysis of magnetic recordings, and providing expert testimony regarding findings. Engineering Section capabilities include the following.

Authenticity Determination. This analysis is made in cases involving allegations of tape tampering and/or alteration by a defense expert, and when the legitimacy of the recording cannot be established through chain of custody and testimony.

Signal Analysis. In this test, various analyses are conducted to identify, compare, and interpret non-voice sounds on original tape recordings, including telephone dialing, gunshots, and radio transmissions.

Speaker Identification. This test uses the spectrographic (voice-print) technique to compare the recorded voice of an unknown individual to a known recorded voice sample of a suspect. Decisions regarding speaker identification by the spectrographic method are not considered conclusive, since there is limited scientific research regarding the reliability of the examination under the varying conditions of recording fidelity, interfering background sounds, sample size, voice disguise, restrictive frequency range, and other factors commonly encountered in investigative matters.

Sound Recording Comparisons. This is an aural examination to determine if a recovered "bootleg" tape recording contains the same material as a copyrighted commercial tape.

Tape Duplication. This service provides standard format copies of unusual or obsolete tapes or disc recordings.

Tape Enhancement. This is the selective suppression of interfering noise on audio recordings, or the audio track of video recordings, to improve the voice intelligibility.

Telephone toll fraud examinations are made to identify:
- "Blue Box" and "Black Box" devices, which receive toll-free long distance telephone calls.
- "Red Box" devices, which allow free pay telephone calls.

Interception of Communications Examinations include identification of:
- Wire tap devices attached to telephone lines, which monitor, record, or transmit telephone conversations as a radio signal to a remote location.
- Infinity transmitter devices, which allow a room conversation to be monitored by a remotely activated microphone on a telephone line.
- Telephones which have been modified to monitor a room conversation when the telephone is not in use.
- Miniature transmitters, concealed microphones and recorders designed to surreptitiously intercept oral communications.

Other examinations include identification of devices used to defeat "burglar alarm" systems, FM radio transceivers, scanners and tracking devices, and electronic devices of unknown use or origin believed to have been used in the commission of a crime.

The FBI's services in these areas are available to all federal agencies, U.S. attorneys, military tribunals, in both civil and criminal matters, and to all duly constituted state, county, and municipal law enforcement agencies in the United States in connection with their official criminal investigative matters only. These services, including the loan of experts if needed as expert witnesses, are rendered free of cost to the contributing agency.

As a general rule, Laboratory Division examinations are not made if the evidence is subjected elsewhere to the same examination for the prosecution. Additionally, in order to more effectively and efficiently utilize its resources, the laboratory will not accept cases from other crime laboratories that have the capability of conducting the requested examination(s).

Because of the nature of the evidence submitted for fingerprint examinations, the previously mentioned Laboratory Division restriction does not apply. Therefore, the Identification Division will examine fingerprint evidence even if it has been or will be subjected to examination by other fingerprint experts.

FBI experts will furnish testimony regarding evidence they have examined. In the interest of economy, however, their testimony should not be requested if it is to be duplicated by another prosecution expert. It is realized that exceptions to this general policy may be required in a given instance.

Federal Bureau of Investigation

Source Laboratory Services. (Federal Bureau of Investigation, U.S. Department of Justice, Washington, DC, 1992).

FEDERAL EMERGENCY MANAGEMENT AGENCY

The Federal Emergency Management Agency (FEMA) is the central point of contact within the federal government for a wide range of emergency management activities in both peace and war.

There will always be emergencies. Planning for, responding to, and recovering from them are responsibilities shared by federal, state, and local governments and the private sector. However, the capability to meet any emergency must be based essentially at the local level, where disasters strike, with state and federal governments providing guidance and support in all aspects of the emergency management process.

Through the coordination of planning and preparedness activities, and the provision of financial and technical support, FEMA provides the vital ingredients for an effective national emergency management system -- a system that spans the full spectrum of emergencies from natural disasters to nuclear war and extends through all levels of government and the private sector.

Among FEMA's activities are:
•Coordinating civil emergency preparedness for nuclear attack.

•Planning to ensure continuity of government and coordinating mobilization of resources during national security emergencies.
•Supporting state and local governments in a wide range of disaster planning, preparedness, mitigation, response, and recovery efforts.
•Coordinating civil emergency for peacetime radiological accidents, including those at nuclear power plants, and hazardous materials incidents.
•Providing training, education, and exercises to enhance the professional development of federal, state, and local emergency managers.
•Reducing the nation's losses from fire.
•Administering the insurance aspects, the flood loss reduction efforts, and the risk assessment activities of the National Flood Insurance Program.
•Acting as lead agency for the National Earthquake Hazards Reduction Program.
•Chairing the Emergency Food and Shelter National Board.
•Developing community awareness programs for weather emergencies and home safety.

Federal Emergency Management Agency

Source This is the Federal Emergency Management Agency. (The Federal Emergency Management Agency, Washington, DC).

FEDERAL GOVERNMENT SECURITY

The types of facilities owned by government agencies vary widely. The assets to be protected within the facilities and the threats to them are also disparate. As such, it is difficult to generalize about government security. Security philosophies differ among agencies based on the nature of their work and the types of assets they must protect. Government agencies exclusive of the military and military-related agencies are addressed here.

Public Access Agencies

Many government agencies must exist within an environment of nearly total accessibility to the public that they serve. Such agencies frequently have assets little different than private sector companies that are primarily administrative in nature. The information these agencies process and store may be sensitive from the standpoint of privacy, but is unlikely to be the target of such threats as espionage. Storage of information is commonly limited to the use of locked file cabinets and locking offices after normal operating hours. Information security can also extend to data processing equipment such as computers. Much of computer security is done through procedural and software measures. Security beyond that for information is commonly directed at protecting employees from personal crimes in and near the workplace and preventing theft or vandalism. This usually entails such measures as guards or reception personnel at the entries to the buildings or offices to ensure that only people with legitimate business enter. Apprehending or ejecting "problem" people is frequently left up to either federal or local police. The form and scope of security is generally established by agency policy and local necessity.

Courts

Courts have historically been forced to deal with unruly defendants from time to time. The courts have generally been able to handle that function with unarmed or lightly armed bailiffs or guards, depending on police forces to intervene when necessary. Recently, courts have had to expand their security concerns to the personal protection of judges. This has been necessitated by assassination attempts and bombings. These threats have led the U.S. Marshals Service to institute tighter entry control into buildings that house federal courts. This has historically taken the form of having people entering the building walk through a metal detector and having them place carried packages into an X-ray screening device. These precautions are to keep people from entering the building with weapons or explosives. Other than these concerns, court security has many of the same objectives as those of administrative agencies, namely preventing personal crimes against employees, and preventing theft and vandalism.

Law Enforcement and National Security-Related Agencies

Government agencies that perform law enforcement functions or are involved in national security-related activities have a common concern. That concern is the protection of sensitive information. This includes information ranging from evidence to be used in prosecuting crimes to intelligence information used to steer our nation's foreign policy decisions. Protecting such sensitive information requires both physical and procedural security measures. Both are governed by strict agency regulations.

The procedural security measures in regulations commonly include granting clearances to people who need access to the information. The key to limiting access to information is to ensure that only people who have a need to know that information are granted access to it. In highly sensitive situations, it sometimes is necessary to institute the two-person rule, in which no individual can have access to the information alone. While much of access control is done through physical measures, much also depends on further procedural measures. These include procedures for classifying information, for accountability of it, and for handling it. There are also many procedures related to protecting information on data processing equipment such as computers or communications lines.

Physical measures in information security relate to the storage of information when it is not in use and when it is not in an electronic format. The common philosophies behind information storage are to either prevent theft of the information or to ensure that it is evident when the information has been compromised.

Measures for preventing theft usually take the form of vaults or safes in which the information may be stored. Safes are generally procured on the open market based on strict government specifications. Vaults may either be specially constructed using common building materials, such as reinforced concrete and steel, or they may be modular vaults procured similarly to safes. Where the goal is only to ensure that the compromise of the information is evident, vaults are constructed such that aggressors would have to force their way in, making it obvious that they have done so.

In either case, vaults frequently have additional security measures such as intrusion detection systems and access control. Intrusion detection systems detect aggressors as they attempt to gain access to the information. The resulting alarm allows personnel to respond to the location to attempt to prevent the aggressor from compromising the information. Access control limits who has access to a vault or safe by requiring them to know a combination or have a key in the case of mechanical locks, or requiring them to have an entry credential or a combination in the case of electronic entry control equipment. More sophisticated electronic entry control equipment includes devices that validate identity based on biological features such as finger or voice prints, or retinal patterns.

Physical security of computers and communications systems may also include special shielding or attenuation measures applied to prevent aggressors from eavesdropping on the electronic emanations from the equipment and means to prevent transmissions from being intercepted. The latter may involve encrypting the data.

Medical Facilities

Security of government medical facilities primarily focuses on the prevention of theft of controlled substances and medically sensitive items. These include drugs and drug-related equipment such as hypodermic syringes. Other medical supplies that are pilferable are also a concern, but are afforded less security. Security of controlled substances and medically sensitive items is similar to security of sensitive information. It entails physical and procedural measures related to the storage of and access to the assets. Storage is commonly in vaults or locked cabinets, depending on the nature of the substance or material. Procedural measures include restricting access to storage containers, strictly accounting for substances and materials, and locating storage containers in areas that are observable by more than one person.

Other Agencies and Facilities

Agencies other than those previously mentioned operate in a myriad of facilities that house numerous types of assets. Security ranges from providing simple locks on doors for after-hours application, to storage structures similar to vaults for the storage of money and other negotiable instruments. The scope of security measures depends on the nature of the assets, the objectives of the agency, and the perceived threat. For some

agencies, notably those with an overseas presence, protection of their people from terrorist attacks is also a significant security consideration. Again, such security is based on the threat and agency policy.

Curt P. Betts, P.E.

FENCE DISTURBANCE SENSORS

Fence disturbance sensors detect the act of an intruder either climbing over or cutting through a fence, or lifting the fence fabric to crawl under. These acts of penetrating the fence generate mechanical vibrations or stresses in the fence fabric that are usually higher in frequency and have larger acceleration amplitudes than the vibrations or stresses generated by naturally occurring phenomena such as wind and rain. These fence vibrations are detected by electromechanical switches, piezoelectric and geophone transducers, and electret transducer cables. Electrical signals from the transducers are sent to the signal processor where they are analyzed.

Fence disturbance sensors can best detect cutting, climbing, and lifting when the fabric is reasonably tight and the fence posts are well anchored. If the fabric is loose, the high-frequency vibrations and mechanical noises might be attenuated in the fence fabric before they reach the sensors, reducing the probability of detection.

Another phenomenon that can cause false alarms is the wind-induced vibration from loose objects striking the fence. All loose signs, especially metal signs, should be removed from or secured to the fence so they cannot rattle. Rattling induces high-frequency vibrations in the fence similar to a cutting penetration. Since the sensors cannot differentiate between high-frequency vibrations caused by rattling signs, loose gates, vegetation, or any other objects banging or rubbing against the fence, the fence sensors can alarm to these stimuli.

Some fence disturbance sensor transducers can be installed on every third fence fabric section or fence post. The caution is that the probability of detecting an intruder penetrating the fence is a function of the sensor sensitivity and the sensor spacing along the fence. In other words, these sensors might be able to detect many types of penetrations at this spacing, but the farther apart they are spaced, the lower their probability of detecting all penetrations. This is especially true if an intruder cuts the fence fabric or lifts the fabric to crawl under midway between the sensors. Therefore, areas requiring a high degree of security should install the individual transducers on every fence fabric section or fence post. Installing the sensors closer together, however, will increase cost, a fact to be considered in relation to the anticipated threat.

The major objection to using fence disturbance sensors to detect penetrations through perimeter fences is that an intruder can either tunnel under or bridge over the fence without being detected. But the fence effectiveness can be enhanced to reduce these threats.

The threat of tunneling under the fence can be reduced by extending the bottom of the fence into the ground, by installing another barrier in the ground along the bottom of the fence, or by captivating the bottom 2 to 4 inches of the fence fabric in an asphalt or concrete sill. An asphalt sill that extends from the fence approximately 1/2 to 1 foot on each fence side reduces the tunneling threat while facilitating mowing operations along the fence. However, adequate drainage must be provided under or over the asphalt to eliminate erosion and standing water.

The threat of bridging the fence can be reduced by extending the effective height of the fence with additional fencing, or by adding barbed wire or rolls of barbed tape on top. Adding barbed tape to the fence improves the deterrent effect of the fence but it could make the fence sensors more susceptible to false alarms in the wind.

If the intruder is not likely to tunnel under or bridge over the fence, there are several advantages to protecting the perimeter fence with fence disturbance sensors. A definite advantage is that the fence sensors are mounted directly to the fence; therefore, they do not require additional space inside the protected area as do invisible barrier detectors, buried line sensors, and electric-field sensors. Another advantage is ease of installation. The sensors and interconnecting cables can be mounted directly to the fence, following the fence contour up and down hills and around corners.

It is recommended that the fence sensors be installed in sealed electrical junction boxes and that the interconnecting cables be installed in sealed conduit, provided the conduit or junction boxes will not interfere with the operation of the sensor. Although it is initially more expensive, the conduit provides additional tamper protection and electromagnetic shielding for the sensors and signal cable. Tamper protection exists because anyone trying to cut through the conduit for access to the cables will be detected by the sensors just like an intruder cutting through the fence. The conduit also protects the cable and sensors against weathering and day-to-day abuse, thereby reducing considerable long-term maintenance problems.

Electromechanical Transducers

Electromechanical fence disturbance transducers are usually normally closed switches; however, normally open switches are also available. Normally closed switches initiate an open-circuit pulse when the switch is acted upon by accelerations generated in the fence fabric during penetration. Forces with adequate accelerations cause the electromechanical switch to momentarily open and close in a series of short pulses. The pulse rate corresponds to the frequency of the induced vibration. The number of pulses and the pulse rate depends on the attack method and the time required for the intruder to penetrate the fence. For instance, if the fence is cut there will be a number of distinct pulses, one for each time the fabric is cut. If the fence is climbed over, there will be several seconds of continuous open circuit pulses. These pulses can either be recorded in a pulse count accumulator circuit or they can activate an alarm circuit directly. Pulse accumulators are recommended because they will minimize the number of false alarms from single impacts on the fence such as when debris blows against the fence.

There are two basic types of electromechanical switches. One type uses mechanical inertia switches and the second uses mercury switches. A mechanical inertia switch consists of a single- or double-metal seismic mass that rests on two multiple contact rods or two or three electrical contacts in the normal or no-alarm position, creating a normally closed switch. The switch assembly is enclosed in a plastic case that captivates the movable mass, restricting its movement so that it always returns to rest on the contacts. The plastic case also seals the switch mass and contacts from moisture. To prevent corrosion and ensure a long contact life, the contacts and seismic mass are gold plated. The movable seismic mass in the inertia switch reacts to the minute accelerations in the vibrations generated in the fence during a forced penetration. In some inertia sensors, the seismic mass is unrestricted so that it can react to forces slightly greater than its own weight. In other inertia sensors, the movable mass is restricted by some internal force, therefore requiring a larger force to move the mass off the contacts. Inertia switches with the restricted mass are not as sensitive as the unrestricted movable mass switch, and are therefore used to protect fence gates or fence sections that have excessive movement where the undamped sensor might be susceptible to false alarming.

The mercury switch is a normally closed switch that momentarily opens on impact. It consists of a glass vial containing a small amount of mercury with electrical continuity between the two conductors. Each switch assembly is enclosed in a small tamper-protected case mounted in a near-vertical direction on the fence to function satisfactorily. On impact to the fence, the mercury is displaced from the contacts, generating a momentary open circuit or pulse.

The mechanical fence disturbance switches can either activate an alarm circuit directly or they can be connected to a pulse count accumulator circuit. An accumulator circuit counts the open-circuit pulses and activates an alarm after it has accumulated the pre-set number of pulses in a specific time period. Depending on the intruder's method of penetration, the act of intrusion will generate a large impact on the fence, such as when cutting the fabric. Some accumulator circuits can respond to both the long-duration pulses generated with a hurried climb and the short-duration pulses generated when cutting. The circuit initiates an alarm momentarily after only several long duration pulses while a greater number of short-duration pulses are required to initiate an alarm. Regardless of the counting method, the circuit should automatically bleed off the pulse counts accumulated if an insufficient number of pulses are not accumulated within the present alarm time period.

Piezoelectric Transducers

The piezoelectric transducer converts the mechanical impact forces generated in the fence during a penetration attack into electrical signals. Unlike the mechanical switches that respond to the mechanical forces by generating a series of open-circuit pulses, piezoelectric transducers generate an analog signal. The analog signal varies proportionally in amplitude and frequencies to the amplitude and frequency of the mechanically induced vibrations. The analog signals from each transducer are collectively processed and analyzed in the signal processor.

The piezoelectric crystal, which converts the mechanical forces into proportionate electrical signals, is usually a thin slab of quartz. The quartz material is physically ground to a thickness that will respond to the vibrational frequencies generated in the fence during an intrusion. This thin crystal is secured to the transducer enclosure so that it can respond to the mechanically induced forces. The induced mechanical stresses distort the crystal, generating an electrical signal that is proportional to the induced stresses. The resulting signals are amplified and sent along the interconnecting cable to the signal processor.

Typically, signals from the transducers enter the signal processor through a bandpass filter. The filter passes only those signals that correspond to the energies with vibration frequencies characteristic of the vibrations generated during a fence penetration attack. The bandpass of the filter is selected by the manufacturer after conducting penetration tests and measuring the resulting frequencies. The filter is then designed to pass those corresponding signals with the best signal-to-noise ratio. Filtering reduces the susceptibility of false alarms resulting from low-frequency vibrations induced by low velocity winds, but higher-velocity winds, above about 20 to 25 mph, generate high-frequency vibrations that are within the bandpass of the input filter. Since the processor cannot always differentiate between the valid intrusion signals and the wind-induced signals, false alarms can result.

Geophone Transducers

Geophone transducers detect the mechanical vibrations generated in the fence during a forced penetration and convert these energies into analog electrical signals that are proportional to the induced forces. A geophone transducer consists of a tubularshaped seismic mass wound with a

318 Fence Disturbance Sensors

coil of fine wire and a cylindrical permanent magnet. The magnet is fixed to the geophone housing and the seismic mass is suspended in spring balance around the magnet. When the geophone is acted upon by external mechanical forces, accelerations from these forces displace the housing and permanent magnet, while the seismic mass remains at rest. As the permanent magnet moves through the coil, the windings cut the magnetic lines of force. As the windings pass through the magnetic field, an electromotive force (emf) is induced in the coil. The induced analog signal is proportional to the external accelerations. These signals are then amplified and sent to the signal processor for analysis. When the signal amplitude and duration satisfy the alarm criteria, an alarm is activated.

Electret Cable Transducer

The electret cable transducer is a specially sensitized coaxial cable. The cable center conductor is covered with a low-loss dielectric material processed to carry a permanent electrostatic charge. A braided wire shield encloses the dielectric material. This cable assembly is covered with a weather-resistant plastic jacket. When the cable is subjected to mechanical distortions or stresses resulting from the fence penetration, electrical analog signals are induced in the transducer cable proportional to the mechanical stresses.

These signals are sent along the transducer cable to the signal processor that is usually mounted to the fence at the beginning of a detection zone. Incoming signals pass through a bandpass filter that passes only those signals characteristic of fence penetration signals. The frequency band of the bandpass filter was selected by the manufacturer based on frequency measurements made while conducting forced penetration tests. Processing only those signals within the bandpass of the input filter improves the signal-to-noise ratio. Improving the signal-to-noise ratio of the processed signal improves the detector detection capability and reduces its susceptibility to false alarms.

An optional feature is available that will enhance the central station operator's ability to verify actual intrusions. It allows the operator to listen to the fence noises causing the alarm to determine if they are naturally occurring sounds from wind or rain, or if they are actual penetration sounds. Some sounds, such as an animal climbing or bumping the fence, will be difficult to differentiate from penetration sounds, but a trained operator can differentiate between most naturally occurring noises and the noises generated during an actual penetration. The listening feature is made possible because the transducer cable is microphonic, that is, it acts like a microphone.

Taut-Wire Switches

Taut-wire switches do not detect mechanical disturbances in chain-line fences like the mechanical, piezoelectric, and geophone transducers. They are used in conjunction with barbed-wire barriers to detect anyone penetrating the barrier. Taut-wire switches consist of a movable center rod that forms one contact of a normally open switch and a cylindrical conductor that forms the other contact. In the neutral or no-alarm switch position, the center rod conductor is in the center of the switch, not touching the cylindrical contact, thus forming the normally open switch.

The switches are installed in line with individually supported strands of barbed wire configured to form the barbed-wire fence barrier. Anyone cutting, pulling, or stepping on the individual strands of barbed wire pulls the switch center conductor rod in contact with the cylindrical conductor, closing the switch, which initiates an alarm.

A unique feature of the taut-wire switch is that the switch assembly is supported in the housing by a pliable plastic material. This material exhibits cold-flow properties that allow the switch assembly always to assume a neutral force-free position when the switch housing is acted upon by gradual external force. External stresses could be caused by the fence settling or moving during the freezing and thawing seasons. This feature prevents the switches from becoming pre-stressed, altering their response to intrusion by changing the relative separation between the switch movable center conductor and the fixed cone-shaped conductor.

Robert L. Barnard

Source Barnard, R.L., Intrusion Detection Systems. (Butterworth-Heinemann, Boston, 1982).

FIBER-OPTIC VIDEO TRANSMISSION

One of the most significant advances in the transmission of communication signals has been the innovation of fiber optics. The concept of transmitting video signals over fiber optics is not new. In the early 1970s, glass fibers were able to transmit the light signal -- visible and infrared (IR) -- over distances of hundreds of feet. Now typical camera-to-monitor distances of many miles can be achieved using fiber-optic cables.

The information-carrying capacity (bandwidth) of an electrical or optical transmission system increases with increase of the carrier frequency. The carrier frequency used for fiber-optic signals is light, which has frequencies several orders of magnitude (1,000 times) higher than the highest radio frequencies. Wide bandwidths also permit multiplexing several television signals, control signals, and audio onto the same fiber-optic cable.

The fiber-optic system uses an electrical-to-optical signal converter (transmitter), a glass fiber cable for sending the light signal over the distance from the camera to the monitor, and a light-to-electrical signal converter to transform the signal back to a closed-circuit television (CCTV) signal required by the monitor. Standard coaxial cable is used at the camera and monitor ends to connect the fiber-optic system to the video devices.

Today's high performance CCTV systems require greater reliability and more "throughput," i.e., getting more signals from the camera end to the monitor end over greater distances in harsher environments. A glass fiber-optic video link offers features not available with copper wire or coaxial cable transmission:

1. It will transmit information with greater fidelity and clarity over longer distances than a wire or coaxial cable.

2. It is totally immune to all types of interference -- electromagnetic interference (EMI) or lightning -- and will not conduct electricity.

3. It will eliminate ground loops that can cause deleterious hum bars, picture tearing, or distortion.

4. Because glass fiber will not corrode, it is unaffected by most chemicals, and can be exposed to most corrosive atmospheres in chemical plants or outdoors.

5. It presents no fire hazard even in the most flammable atmosphere since there is no electrical connection to the fiber.

6. It can be mounted aboveground and on telephone poles, and is stronger than standard electrical wires or coaxial cables. This type of link withstands far more stress from wind and ice loading than electrical cables.

7. Because single or multiple fiber-optic cable is much smaller and lighter than a coaxial cable of similar information-carrying capacity, it is easier to handle and install, and uses less conduit or duct space. As an example, fiber-optical cable weighs 30 pounds per 3,300 feet with an overall diameter of 0.156 inches, while an equivalent coaxial cable weighs 330 pounds and is approximately 0.25 inches in diameter.

8. It transmits the video signal more efficiently over longer distances without a repeater (amplifier): miles for fiber optic versus thousands of feet for coaxial.

9. A glass fiber-optic video link is a more secure transmission media since it does not emit electromagnetic radiation, is hard to tap, and attempts to tap it can be easily detected.

A New Technology

In the 1950s, the practical glass-coated (clad), glass fiber was invented. The term coined for it was *fiber optics*. Active investigation continued into the 1960s [1]. In 1967, fiber attenuation was 1,000 decibels per kilometer, totally impractical for transmission purposes. Three years later losses had been reduced to less than 20 decibels (100 to 1 signal loss) per kilometer in fibers hundreds of meters long. In 1972, a 4-decibels-per-kilometer cable was announced, and in 1973, the number had been dropped to 2-decibels-per-kilometer cable. This low-loss achievement meant that wide bandwidth signals could be transmitted over long distances, and it was only a matter of time in which coaxial would be replaced by fiber-optic cables for communication systems and CCTV.

Fiber-Optic System

A fiber-optic transmission system consists of three basic components. The most critical is the glass fiber-optic cable that must transmit the light signal from the camera to the monitor. The camera signal is connected to the transmitter via standard coaxial cable, and the receiver output to the monitor or recording system via standard coaxial cable.

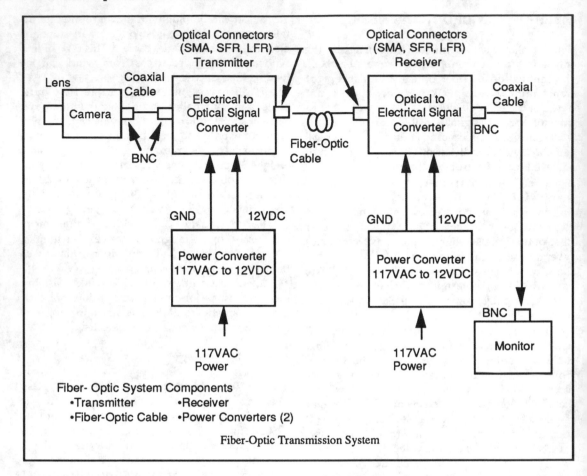

Fiber-Optic Transmission System

The optical transmitter at the camera end converts the electrical CCTV analog signal into a modulated optical signal. The IR light output from the transmitter is generated either by a light-emitting diode (LED) or an injection laser diode (ILD).

The fiber-optic cable consists of one or more glass fibers acting as a waveguide for the optical signal, and is enclosed in a protective outer jacket whose construction depends on the application. The fiber-optic receiver collects the light from the output end of the fiber-optic cable and converts (demodulates) the optical signal back into an electrical signal having the same waveform and characteristics as the original CCTV signal at the camera. This standard video signal is then sent on to the monitor, VCR, or other device. The only variation to this block diagram for a single camera is the inclusion of a connector, a splice or repeater somewhere along the cable, which may be required in very long cable runs (many miles).

Fiber-Optic Cable

The most significant part of the fiber-optic signal transmission system is the glass fiber itself. The fiber is a thin strand of very pure glass approximately the diameter of a human hair that transmits specific light frequencies with extremely high efficiency. Most fiber-optic systems operate at near IR wavelengths of 850; 1,300; or 1,550 nanometers.

The function of the fiber-optic cable is to efficiently transmit the modulated light signal from the camera, over a long distance to the monitor, and maintain its shape and amplitude. For the light from the transmitter to follow the zig-zag path of internally reflected rays, the angles of reflection must exceed the critical angle. These reflection angles are associated with what are called waveguide modes. Depending on the size (diameter) of the fiber-optic core, one or more modes are transmitted down the fiber. Like radio waves, light is electromagnetic energy. The frequencies of light used in fiber-optic video, voice, and data transmission are approximately 3.6 times 10 hertz (cycles per second), which is several orders of magnitude (100 to 1,000 times) higher than the highest radio waves. Wavelength (reciprocal of frequency) is a more common way of describing light waves. Visible light with wavelengths from about 400 nanometers for deep violet to 750 nanometers for deep red covers only a small portion of the electromagnetic spectrum. Fiber-optic video transmission uses the near IR energy extending from approximately 750 to 1,500 nanometers since the glass fibers propagate light most efficiently at these wavelengths.

Most fiber-optic security systems operate at a wavelength of 850 nanometers rather than 1300 or 1,550 nanometers. The reason for this is that 850-nanometer LED and ILD emitters are more readily available and less expensive than their 1300- or 1550-nanometer counterparts. Radiation at the 1300- and 1,550-nanometer wavelengths is transmitted more efficiently than at the 850-nanometer wavelength, and these wavelengths are used for very long cable runs (hundreds or thousands of miles).

Fiber Types and Construction

The three most common types of fiber optics are: (1) multi-mode step index, (2) graded index, and (3) single-mode (mono-mode). The three fiber types are defined by their index of refraction (n) profile (optical variation of the cross-section of the fiber core) and have different properties suitable for different applications. A fiber-optic cable consists of several components and are divided into two basic types: tight jacket and loose tube.

The optical fiber is generally surrounded by a tight jacket (strength member) or tube of plastic (loose buffer), which is substantially larger than the fiber itself. Over this material is a layer of Kevlar [3] re-inforcement material. This entire assembly is then coated with an outer jacket, typically polyvinyl chloride (PVC). This construction is generally acceptable for indoor use or dry conduit where easy cable pulls are made through a conduit.

The difference between indoor and outdoor fiber-optic cable is in the construction of the protective jacket (sheath) surrounding the fiber. Outdoor fiber-optic cable must have sufficient tensile strength and environmental properties so that it can be pulled through a conduit or overhead duct, strung on poles, or direct burial, depending on the application. Some fiber-optic plenum cables are available for indoor applications having specific smoke and flame retardant requirements. These are rated by Electronic Industries Association (EIA), Underwriters Laboratories (UL), and other codes.

If multiple signal transmission is required, multi-fiber cables (two, four, six, eight, etc.) are used. These fibers are enclosed in a single or multiple buffer tube array around a tensile strength member composed of Kevlar, and then an outer jacket of Kevlar surrounding the tubes containing the fibers. Alternatively, multiple signals are wavelength multiplexed on a single fiber using special transmitter/receivers.

Fiber-Optic Cable Sizes

The most commonly used fiber type for security applications is the multi-mode graded index fiber. This fiber is available in four primary core sizes: 50/125, 62.5/125, 85/125, and 100/140 microns. The 62.5/125 is the most commonly used.

Fiber size is expressed in microns (equivalent to one one-thousandth of a millimeter -- 1/1,000 millimeters). By comparison, the diameter of a human hair is about 0.002 inches or 50 microns. Each size has its advantages for particular applications and all four of the primary sizes are EIA standards.

The most popular and least expensive multi-mode fiber is the 62.5/125 and is used extensively in security systems. It has a low numerical aperture (NA), which allows the efficient collection of light and high bandwidth. Since it has been used for many years, most security installers are experienced and comfortable working with it. The 50/125 cable is an alternative to the 62.5/125 fiber. The 85/125 and 100/140 fibers are used in computer, industrial, and other applications.

Connectors and Fiber Termination

Coaxial cables require connectors (BNC) at their ends to interface with the camera, switcher, monitor, etc. connectors. Likewise, fiber-optic cables require connectors (SMA, SFR, LFR) to

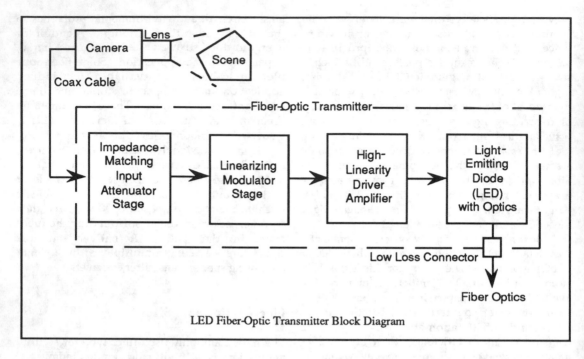

LED Fiber-Optic Transmitter Block Diagram

couple the optically transmitted signal from the transmitter into the fiber-optic cable, and at the other end to couple the light output from the fiber into the receiver. For very long cable runs, joining and fusing of the actual glass fiber core and cladding is done by a technique called splicing, which joins the two lengths of cable by fusing the two fibers (locally melting the glass), and physically joining them together so that they form a permanent connection. Most optical connectors for terminating cables, transmitters, and receivers are based on butt coupling of cut and polished fibers to allow direct transmission of optical power from one fiber core to the other. The two mating connectors precisely center the two fibers, which are then epoxied into the connector ferrules. The ferrule and fiber surfaces are then ground and polished to produce a clean surface.

Factors Affecting Coupling Efficiency

The efficiency with which the light from the end of one fiber-optic cable can be coupled into the following cable or device is a function of six different parameters: (1) fiber core lateral or axial misalignment, (2) angular core misalignment, (3) fiber end separation, (4) fiber distortion, (5) fiber end finish, and (6) Fresnel reflections. Distortion

loss and the effects of fiber end finish can be minimized by using proper termination techniques. A chipped or scratched fiber end scatters much of the light signal power, but proper grinding and polishing minimize these effects.

Lateral misalignment results when one fiber core is offset from the other. Misalignment of this nature causes the largest amount of light loss. A fiber core of 0.002-inch (50 micron) diameter displaced 0.0001 inches off the center of its connector causes a loss of 0.5 decibels (11%).

Angular misalignment losses of one fiber end with respect to another are below 1 degree (present connector design) and add only 0.1 decibels (2.3%) of loss.

Fiber end separation loss is dependent on the fiber NA. Since the optical light power emanating from a transmitting fiber is in the form of a cone, the amount of light coupled into the receiving fiber or device decreases as the fibers are separated from each other. A separation distance of 10% of the core diameter with an NA of 0.2 adds 0.1 decibels (2.3%) of loss.

Fresnel losses [4] usually add another 0.3-0.4 decibels (8%) when the connection does not use an optical index matching fluid.

The summation of all of these different losses often add up to 0.5-1.0 decibels for typical terminations and connections.

Fiber-Optic Transmitter

The fiber-optic transmitter is the electro-optic transducer between the camera television electrical signal output and the fiber-optic cable light input signal. Its function is to efficiently and accurately convert the electrical video signal into an optical signal and couple it into the fiber optic. The transmitter electronics converts the amplitude modulated CCTV signal through the LED or ILD into a frequency modulated (FM most common) light signal, which faithfully represents the CCTV signal. An LED is used for normal security applications or an ILD when a very long-range transmission is required.

The electrical video signal from the camera is modulated and converted into current variations in the LED. The LED optical output power varies directly proportional to the electrical input signal. This produces a very faithful transformation of the electrical video information into the light information, which is transmitted along the fiber-optic cable.

Fiber-Optic Receiver

The fiber-optic receiver at the output end of the fiber-optic cable is a light-to-electrical signal transducer. The receiver contains electronics for any necessary conditioning to restore the signal to its original shape at the input, and for providing signal amplification. As light exits from the receiver end of an optical fiber, it spreads out with a divergence angle (cone) approximately equal to the acceptance cone angle at the transmitter end of the fiber. The receiver detector (photodiode) has a lens to collect this output energy and focus onto the photodiode-sensitive area. After the light energy is converted into an electrical signal by the photodiode, it is linearly amplified and conditioned to be suitable for transmission over standard coaxial cable to a monitor or other device.

Multi-Signal Fiber Transmission

The fiber-optic transmission cable has a wide signal bandwidth capability and transmitting a single video signal on one single fiber easily fits within the bandwidth capability of most cables. There are special transmitters and receivers that permit multi-video channels, bi-directional video, audio, and control signals to be transmitted simultaneously over a single fiber-optic cable. These multiple, simultaneous video or control signals are sent at different wavelengths.

Fiber Optic Advantages

There are advantages in going through all the complexity and extra expense of converting the electrical video signal to a light signal and then back again to an electrical signal. Several very important properties that fiber optics offer that no electrical cabling system offers include the following: (1) complete electrical isolation, (2) complete noise immunity to radio frequency interference (RFI), electromagnetic interference (EMI) and electromagnetic pulse (EMP), (3) transmission security (hard to tap), (4) no spark or fire hazard, (5) no electrical short circuit possibility, (6) absence of crosstalk, and (7) no RFI/EMI radiation.

Electrical Isolation. The complete electrical isolation of the transmitting section (camera, lens, pan/tilt, etc.) from the receiving section (monitor, lens and pan/tilt controller, recorder, printer, switching network, etc.) is very important for inter-building and intra-building locations where different electrical power line sources are used for different parts of the system. Fiber-optic transmission totally prevents any possibility of ground loops and ground voltage differences, which could cause unacceptable performance and require the re-design of a coaxial cable-based system.

RFI/EMI/EMP Immunity. When a transmission path is run through a building or outdoors past other electrical equipment, a site survey usually cannot uncover all possible contingencies of existing RFI/EMI noise that the cable will encounter. This is also true of EMP and lightning strikes. Using fiber optics prevents any problems caused by these noise sources.

Transmission Security. Since the fiber optic has no electrical noise or light leak, there is excellent inherent transmission security. Methods to tap or compromise the fiber-optic cable are difficult and the intrusion is usually detected. To tap a fiber-optic cable, the bare fiber from the cable must be

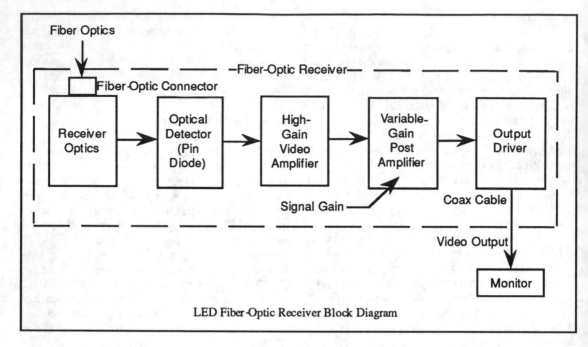

LED Fiber-Optic Receiver Block Diagram

isolated from its sheath without breaking it. This attempt will probably end the tapping attempt. In contrast, tapping a coaxial cable is easy to do and hard to detect.

No Fire Hazard. Since no electricity is involved in any part of the fiber-optic cable, there is no chance or opportunity for sparks, no possibilities of electrical short circuits, and hence no fire hazards.

Absence of Crosstalk. Because the transmission medium is light energy, there is no signal crosstalk between any of the fiber-optic cables in the same bundle as there can be when multiple coaxial cables are encased in the same electrical cable or conduit.

No RFI/EMI Radiation. Fiber-optic cables do not radiate energy, i.e., will not emit any measurable EMI/RFI radiation, and therefore other cabling in the vicinity of the fiber-optic cable will suffer no noise degradation. There are no Federal Communication Commission (FCC) requirements for fiber-optic transmission.

Video signal transmission represents a critical link that affects the ultimate quality of the video image on the monitor. Fiber-optic video, audio, and control signal transmission represents the state-of-the-art transmission means and should be considered for any CCTV security system. When comparing coaxial cable and fiber optics, total cost (material, installation, and maintenance) and performance should be considered. Fiber optic technology is presently the superior means for optimum signal transmission in security. For long distances or inter-building applications it is the clear choice.

Herman A. Kruegle

Notes

1. In 1968, the work of K.C. Kao and G.A. Hockham was reported in literature of Standard Telecommunications Laboratories, United Kingdom.

2. This work was reported in literature of Corning Glass Works in 1972.

3. Kevlar is a trademark of E. I. DuPont Corporation.

4. Fresnel losses are surface boundary reflections.

FINANCIAL AUDITING

Double-entry bookkeeping is a security measure that dates back at least 500 years. It is a specification of the principle of separation of duties. In the double-entry system, every business transaction generates two bookkeeping entries, whether buying inventory, selling merchandise, paying bills, collecting accounts, paying wages, paying taxes, or borrowing money. One of these must be a debit to one account, the other must be a credit to another account. Ideally, the accounts will be set up so that different employees handle the accounts whose entries offset each other.

Periodically, the debits and credits are added up to determine whether or not they do indeed offset each other. This is called taking a trial balance, or balancing the books. Balancing the books is a function usually assigned to a third employee who is highly trusted. Should an imbalance be discovered during the balancing procedures, another traditional safeguard, that of the audit trail, comes into play. The idea behind the audit trail is that every transaction must be evidenced by one or more source documents.

Payments can, for example, be evidenced by vouchers that authorize the issue of a check, check stubs, carbon copies of checks, and ultimately by canceled checks returned by the bank. Cash receipts can be evidenced by receipt stubs, carbon copies of receipts, cash-register tapes, memos of cash-register totals, and ultimately by the testimony of the payer backed up by the original of the receipt. Sales of goods or services must be backed up by copies of sales invoices issued to customers. Purchases of goods or services must be backed by purchase orders and purchase invoices (bills) received from vendors.

These source documents provide the information necessary to record transactions in a journal. The entries recorded in the journal (i.e., the "day" book or chronological record of transactions) in turn provide the information necessary to record the debits and credits in the proper accounts. These accounts collectively make up the ledger, or book of accounts.

The principle of separation of duties persists in respect of the audit trail. Different employees should be assigned to handle different kinds of journal entries, and ultimately to initiate different kinds of ledger entries.

John M. Carroll

Source Carroll, J.M., *Controlling White Collar Crime.* (Butterworth-Heinemann, Boston, 1982).

FINANCIAL INVESTIGATIONS: SEARCHING FOR HIDDEN INFORMATION AND ASSETS

In today's business environment, with the escalating number of failed financial institutions and the continuing spiral of litigation, many investigators find that their time is devoted to determining the financial worth of individuals and businesses. Today's investigators search a wide variety of public record sources that include courthouse records, financial documents, and on-line computer databases to help them determine if a party has sufficient assets to justify litigation or if assets are being hidden from creditors and lenders.

Fortunately for the investigator, almost every transaction conducted today is a matter of public record. Everything we do is recorded, from our daily credit card transactions to our voter registration, and from marriage records to our business registrations, lawsuit history, and real estate purchases and sales. Our major financial dealings, both in our private and public lives, become a matter of public record. This is done to protect our property rights and the rights of creditors, lenders, and others doing business with us.

The collection of the various types of data available in the public domain has become an art in itself. A growing number of private investigators and information brokers specialize in the development of information to assist their clients in making new business decisions, in locating assets in debt matters, and in determining the business background and financial ability of potential business associates.

The very same information and procedures are used in making asset searches for lenders and in locating assets in debt situations. It is just a matter of viewpoint or focus in conducting the various types of investigations or examinations that lead us to different conclusions and answers.

The key to beginning an investigation of this type is to know and understand the kinds of public records available, and how they can be used. In every area of this country, and almost every other country in the world, there are a number of public records on file that can assist the financial investigator. In the United States, the most readily available and informative place to start is the records of the county in which a person lives or does business. The county record offices (or clerks) are the chief custodians and collectors of public records. In these offices can be found the majority of documents that must be filed as a matter of law.

One of the first tasks when beginning an investigation is to learn as much as possible about the person or persons involved. Even when the target of the investigation is a corporation, the investigator's focus is on the people who manage it. Public record resources are a good place to start looking. These resources include telephone records, voter registration files, and marriage records.

Telephone Sources

Available to virtually everyone are the variety of telephone directories and criss-cross references that list the names, addresses, and telephone numbers of people according to geographical location. Experienced investigators collect telephone directories for use in identifying the new and old addresses of parties, finding their family members, or calling others with the same last names in order obtain a correct current address.

Voter Registration Records

Data can be collected from the registration of people voting in a county's jurisdiction, such as full legal name, address, date of birth, and social security number. A voter's file may also reveal a telephone number, unlisted with the telephone company, but written on the voter registration application. The file also provides a signature sample of the voter that can be compared against signatures in other documents.

Voter registration records are organized alphabetically, thereby making them useful in a manner similar to that of a telephone directory. The investigator will often find that the individual being investigated is not listed, but the spouse and children are registered as voters and reside at the same address.

Even when there is reason to believe that the subject resides apart from family members, the investigator can obtain information from the voter files about them. A search for the spouse, for example, could provide leads for locating the person under investigation.

Marriage Records

In these records the investigator can find date of birth, social security number, and proof of identity of each of the marriage partners. The proof of identity of an American citizen is usually a driver's license; a person of foreign extraction often presents a passport. In either case, the proof of identity portion of a marriage record will contain data that may be useful in opening other windows of opportunity.

A marriage record will identify the maiden name of the female. A maiden name can be very revealing because dishonest persons will often shield assets behind another name. The maiden name in a marriage record adds to the investigator's research one more name, one that may literally hit the jackpot.

After the individuals have been researched, the asset searching begins. The investigator now turns his attention to business entities. In most jurisdictions, there are two types of business entity filings: corporate filings, and assumed name or DBA (Doing Business As) records.

Corporations

The formation of corporations is recorded by the Secretary of State in each state and sometimes in each county as well. The Secretary of State requires persons who form a corporation to provide a list of the registered agent, incorporators, and the officers and directors. In many states, financial statements are also required. Financial statements provide details that may corroborate or contradict details reflected in other documents, such as applications for credit made by the subject.

Information about corporations can be obtained by calling, writing, or visiting the Secretary of State. Many states have computerized storage and retrieval systems that are accessible through modems to information brokers who sell the data to subscribers.

Assumed Name or DBA Records

These are the listings of individuals or companies who have registered a business in a county. A filing is intended to both protect the right to use the registered name and to provide a means for lenders to verify ownership of the business. Before a business can open an account at a bank, for example, it must provide a copy of the assumed name certificate or the business's corporate charter.

In many jurisdictions, assumed name records are listed alphabetically by ownership and by business name. Some jurisdictions will also have a cross-reference file to help researchers make multiple connections between owners and companies. Once the investigator has identified the individuals and the companies of interest to the investigation, the next step may be to learn something about their civil disputes with others.

Civil Records

Civil records will often provide a detailed history of financial relationships, borrowing patterns, and assets. They also identify other parties whose records can be checked or whose principals can be personally contacted.

Lawsuits are recorded at the county, state, and federal levels. This presents a bit of a problem in that the investigator will need to visit each of the separate offices where the records are kept. When searching the file indexes, the investigator should look for litigation filed for and against the subject.

The value of civil records can be seen in the following examples:

• Divorce lawsuits often identify the assets and liabilities of both the husband and wife, properties acquired prior to and during the time of the marriage, assets obtained through inheritance, the division of property at time of divorce, individual and joint bank accounts, and insurance policies. They may show the names of former spouses, friends, relatives, accountants, and business partners, and point the researcher to new investigative leads.

• Business litigation lawsuits can reflect disagreements between partners, joint owners, and shareholders, and between a company and its lenders, creditors, contractors, vendors, and employees. These records usually show financial relationships and the specific accusations that form the basis of the civil complaint.

Tax returns, financial statements, and depositions taken by attorneys seeking to discover financial information will often prove to be a treasure trove of information about bank accounts, stocks and bonds, investments, capital assets, inventory, supplies, and equipment.

When more than one lawsuit is on file, the investigator may see a pattern of dishonest business dealings. The investigator may also uncover previously used business names and their officers, and names of affiliates, subsidiaries, and associated business entities.

Business lawsuits generally identify a variety of people who have knowledge of the subject's business activities, thereby opening the door to further avenues of investigation.

• Personal injury or damage lawsuits may uncover a history of prior claims made by the subject against employers or others. Some plaintiffs will file essentially the same complaint against a succession of defendants. The investigator will want to determine the history of awards and settlements. This information may also be pertinent when the subject's assets are in question.

Bankruptcy Records

In recent years, a greater number of people have filed personal and business bankruptcy. The stigma attached to bankruptcy no longer acts as a deterrent, even for the assiduously honest and well-intentioned majority of citizens. At the same time, a minority has come to regard the filing of bankruptcy as an "in thing" to do, especially when the protections of bankruptcy can be offered up as a shield to fend off liabilities and to hide assets that rightfully belong to their creditors.

In conducting a search of bankruptcy records, the investigator should first obtain a copy of the bankruptcy petition filed by the debtor and the schedules of creditors. The schedules of creditors contain two sets of data: a list of the parties that are owed money, and a list of assets filed by the debtor with the court. The list of assets filed with the court may not be a true list if the debtor is seeking to hide assets; however, the debtor's true assets might be ascertained by contacting creditors. This is so because a usual condition imposed upon a credit seeker is to provide the creditor with a list of current assets. If the creditors are cooperative and the investigator diligent, it may be possible to locate assets still owned by the debtor that were listed in the debtor's financial statements attached to credit applications.

When the investigator compares the old and new financial statements, he might note that assets held prior to the bankruptcy filing have disappeared from financial statements filed after bankruptcy. Where have these assets gone? Some may have been liquidated quite legally, as in the case of a legitimate company caught in an economic tailspin, but others may represent transfers of assets to a trust, the spouse, children, or to third a party who has agreed to hold the assets secretly. An asset hidden in this way can be turned over to creditors if the investigator can show a relationship between the debtor and the new owner of the asset, and also show that the transfer was not an arms-length transaction.

Another interesting item to look for is the dollar value assigned to assets by the debtor. Investigators frequently find that household goods and personal items listed in a bankruptcy were set at a very low rate but later valued at a substantially higher rate (often 500% or more) in an insurance claim.

Once the information found in litigation records is added to the previously discovered personal information, the investigator is ready to search for tangible assets. These assets may include bank accounts, insurance policies, real estate, oil and gas interests, and assets acquired through inheritance. The records of each of these transactions are found in the county courthouse.

Real Property Records or Deed Records

These documents list the property transactions between individuals and business entities in a county. They provide descriptions of real estate transferred among parties, and frequently reflect purchase or sale price and mortgage details.

In the matter of hidden assets, real property records may reflect property transfers to relatives and friends or to trust entities created to place the property out of the reach of creditors. In some cases, the intent of the debtor may be to artificially diminish the true value of a property by creating sale and purchase documents that reflect a significantly lower selling and buying price. The history of property transactions is determined by researching both the records of the county tax assessor and the county recorder. The tax assessor records the name of the taxpayer making payment on a given property and provides a determination of the value of the property by its tax assessment.

The investigator should note that the tax assessor does not always value properties at 100% of their true value and should question the assessor's office about the county's valuation methodology.

The county recorder is the repository for records detailing the purchase, sale, foreclosure, and transfer of properties. Investigators may also find in these records the filing of tax and mechanics liens. Tax liens are filed by the Internal Revenue Service for non-payment of taxes, and mechanics liens are filed by repair and construction tradespeople who have not been paid for work performed in repairing or improving real estate. Since real estate is often the most valuable asset owned by an individual, the investigator should be thoroughly familiar with the methods for transferring real estate property and how those transfers are shown in public records.

Records of Oil, Gas, and Mineral Interests

The county recorder keeps documents that reflect the history of ownership of oil, gas, and mineral leases. Minerals in this sense usually mean gold, silver, copper, aluminum, and coal. The current dollar value of a lease may vary widely depending on the market worth of the commodity and the estimated volumes that exist on and nearby the property.

Probate Records

Probate records reveal the distribution of assets to heirs through a filed will. The data will identify the deceased, the heirs, and the full assets and liabilities of the estate, as well as the distribution of the estate to the heirs. Probate records are usually very detailed, listing bank accounts, certificates of deposit, insurance policies, personal effects, and real estate holdings. Probate law generally gives a right to a creditor to recover a debt before the deceased's assets are distributed to heirs. Like a bankruptcy, a probate action will list assets and liabilities, and provide for the payment of debt before assets are released.

Uniform Commercial Code Records

Also known as financing statements in some counties, these Uniform Commercial Code (UCC) records are filings made by creditors to record an obligation placed on an asset that they lend against. Typically, the assets are real estate properties, equipment, cattle, and other tangible items. A UCC filing documents the existence of a loan made by a lender and serves notice on other parties that the lender holds a secured interest in the asset pledged by the borrower.

A search of UCC records can be valuable in three respects. First, they may reveal that the borrower has obligated an asset to more than one creditor, suggesting fraud or at least a lack of credit worthiness. Second, UCC filings may lead to the discovery of assets that the subject wishes to conceal, such as might be the case when the borrower is pleading bankruptcy. Third, they might turn up the existence of otherwise unrecorded business contracts that were pledged to secure a loan or credit line. This can be useful in showing that a pleading debtor has other sources of income.

Developing Leads and Reporting the Findings

After the investigator has examined all of the public record sources in a given county, the information should be collated in a manner that reveals opportunities for acquiring information in other counties. It is not unusual for a skilled investigator to follow a single transaction through one county after another, and in the process accumulate substantial amounts of evidence.

At various points during the investigation, reports of progress are filed with the client. When the investigation has ended, a comprehensive report is prepared. The format of the report is less important than content. Conclusions made or inferences drawn need to be solidly supported by thoroughly documented facts. Report preparation has significance in respect to the client's needs, and to the possibility that the report, and the supporting file, may become evidence in a criminal or civil trial, or both.

Edmund J. Pankau

FIRE SAFETY IN THE HIGH-RISE OFFICE BUILDING

A life safety plan for a high-rise building will have three major components: people, equipment, and procedures. By far, the first component is predominant. People are the essential elements, and in fact, the other two components have no value without people. Although many parts of a life safety plan relate to equipment, such as the fire detection and alarm system, and procedures, such as evacuation, the critical key and driving force of the plan is the people component.

A safety plan provides direction to the people component in terms of their learning, preparing, and responding to major emergencies. The plan will reflect an organized and coordinated approach for responding to various contingencies, e.g., fire, severe weather and natural disasters, medical emergencies and fatalities, bomb threats, and civil disturbances. The plan is both a planning tool and a crisis control tool. On one hand, it requires preparation and readiness, and on the other hand, it assigns response obligations to specific persons or units.

High-rise structures vary widely, but nonetheless have many similarities. They are arranged vertically, are found mostly in urban and suburban areas, contain administrative offices and white collar workers, and movement internally is by elevators. Typically, the structure will be accessible by one or more transportation modes (auto, bus, rail, etc.) and have a parking garage or lot on or near the premises. The location of the structure and the traffic around it will determine the response times of various emergency responders, such as fire, ambulance, and police units.

The fairly modern high-rise building will have an electronic fire detection and alarm system. When a fire condition is detected, whether by electronic-sensing devices or human observation, well-established procedures automatically initiate a response that may include actions by security officers, building management employees, and employees of the tenant or tenants occupying the building.

Fire Detection and Alarm System

The major components of the fire detection and alarm system are likely to be a fire command center, fire alarm (manual) pull stations, ionization (smoke) detectors, thermal or heat detectors, air handling devices, alarm horns and voice communication speakers, elevators and emergency signs, firemen's telephone system, sprinkler system, and emergency generator system.

Fire Command Center. The fire command center is often located on the first floor of the building within close proximity to a security officer or other person designated to make the initial response to an alarm. The center, which is usually in a room not accessible to the public, houses panels with indicator lights showing the areas of activation equipment by floor. Fire-sensing components at places throughout the building are tied to the fire command center. These components include ionization detectors, pull stations, sprinkler heads, and other special systems appropriate for computer equipment.

When a fire-sensing component activates, a signal is registered at the fire command center. The signal may also be sent to the local fire department, the building's management office, or a security office (if it is not adjacent to the fire command center). The signal causes many responders to start their response actions simultaneously. While the fire department is on its way to the scene, building management employees are proceeding to the floor where the fire-sensing components are active, and employees on the floor are checking the floor for fire conditions. The person operating the fire command center is communicating the alarm location to the responders and making an announcement over the public address system so that building occupants can be quickly informed of the meaning of the horns, bells, and flashing lights that are annunciating (at a minimum on the affected floor, the floor above, and the floor below). Usually, the command center microphone can be activated selectively to floors, stairwells, and elevator cabs.

Sometimes the fire command center is linked to an outside monitoring station. An operator at the monitoring station reads the signal and transmits a message to the fire department dispatcher. All components of the fire alarm system are connected to the standby or emergency generator power system.

Pull Stations and Detectors. Fire alarm (manual) pull stations will be mounted on walls on each floor, often by the fire stairwell doors. Pulling a manual station will sound the alarm, as well as send a signal to the command center and other units.

Ionization detectors that react to smoke and invisible gases will be on each floor, at fire stairwell entrances, in electrical, copy, and coffee rooms. They will often be placed in passenger and freight elevator lobbies, cafeteria, and kitchen. Detectors that operate on a heat rate-of-rise principle are also common in areas where heat can be a source of ignition.

In some buildings, the alarm horn will not sound unless two or more detectors in the same zone or on the same floor go into active status at the same time. However, the alarm will automatically go into effect if within a very few minutes there is no human intervention at the alarm panel. The purpose of the few minutes delay is to allow time for the building management staff (sometimes called the fire brigade) to go to the floor covered by the activated sensor and make an on-scene evaluation. If a fire condition is confirmed, an evacuation announcement will be made on the public address system. If a fire condition is not present, the announcement will so indicate.

Certain equipment will automatically start up or shut down upon an alarm device activation. For example, stairwell pressurization fans, toilet exhaust fans, and outside air fans will start, and air-handling units and relief fans will shut down.

Alarm Horns and Voice Communication Speakers. An alarm horn and a voice communication speaker are usually located next to every stairwell door on all floors. Speakers will be situated every place that people are likely to be, including the control plant, elevator cabs, and at places where an alarm sound might be muffled (such as within a sound-treated conference room).

Voice communication originating from the fire command center usually can be made to override the alarm horn on floors selected for communication. The horn will continue to sound in areas not selected for voice communication. Upon completion of voice communication, the horn will resume. The exit lights will flash on floors where alarm horns are sounding.

Elevators and Emergency Signs. A common practice is to set up the elevator controls so that whenever two smoke detectors are activated in an elevator lobby, all cars serving that lobby will automatically go to the ground floor. An emergency sign stating "Emergency -- Use Exit Stairs" located behind the call button panel in the elevator lobby will illuminate whenever two smoke detectors in the lobby are in active status. During power outage, the emergency generator system can be set up to operate one or more elevators.

Firemen's Telephone System. Portable telephone units can be stored in the fire command center for use by responding firefighters. Telephone jacks on the elevator lobby call button panels in every elevator lobby and at both stairwell doors on every floor can provide a telephone communications network for coordinating fire fighting activities.

Sprinkler System. A modern high-rise building will be equipped with heat-activated water sprinkler heads. The panel in the fire command center will alarm and indicate the affected floor. Sprinkler pipes will have valves that remain in the open position, and if a valve is closed for any reason, the panel in the fire command center can indicate this condition.

Emergency Generator System. An emergency generator system automatically starts up in the event of a power outage. The system provides electrical service for a number of critical functions including stairwell lights, exit signs, lights in elevator lobbies, and the fire command center.

Emergency Equipment. First-aid kits, oxygen resuscitators, fire extinguishers, and bottled water can be stocked on each floor. Additionally, fire cabinets on each floor can contain extinguishers, fire hose, and nozzles. Other emergency equipment, such as portable PA systems, evacuation wheelchairs, and stretchers can be kept in the security center.

Management of a Fire Emergency

A common arrangement is for the senior building management employee present at the startup of an emergency to assume the function of fire director. This function, however, is immediately subordinated to the first arriving unit of the fire department.

In the early stages of a fire emergency, before the fire department arrives on the scene, the authority to order an evacuation of the entire building can reside with the fire director. Tenants,

such as those called floor wardens, are often empowered to order evacuation of their floors. Also, any occupant should be free to leave without waiting for an evacuation announcement.

Floor Wardens. Typically, two or more employees on each floor will be designated as floor wardens. A floor warden has these overall responsibilities:

•To educate co-workers on their respective floors concerning individual responsibilities for fire prevention, reduction of safety hazards, how to report a fire, how to evacuate, and where to assemble following evacuation.

•To prevent, report, and correct fire and safety hazards through daily inspection of the floor.

•To exercise leadership during an evacuation by directing co-workers down stairwells and ensuring that no one has been left behind.

•To provide first-responder medical assistance to persons who are in need of CPR or first aid.

In preparing to deal with a fire emergency, a floor warden should:

•Know the locations of the fire stairwells and the pull stations on the floor.

•Study the floor diagram that shows the most direct routes to the fire stairwells and ensure that the diagram is posted conspicuously.

•Obtain volunteers on the floor who will direct employees away from the elevators and down the fire stairwells.

•Inform every new person on the floor concerning what to do in case of an emergency.

•Keep a list of the persons on the floor so they can be accounted for immediately after an evacuation.

•Identify persons with medical conditions, such as asthma or pregnancy, who may need help during an evacuation. Arrange in advance with someone on the floor to provide the needed help.

•Be alert on the floor for fire hazards, e.g., overloaded electrical circuits, unattended cooking appliances, and materials blocking stairwell doors.

In responding during a fire emergency, a floor warden will immediately look throughout the entire floor for fire conditions, starting with places where fire is most likely to occur.

If a search of the floor reveals fire conditions (i.e., visible flame or smoke), the floor warden will engage a pull station, report the fire by calling the

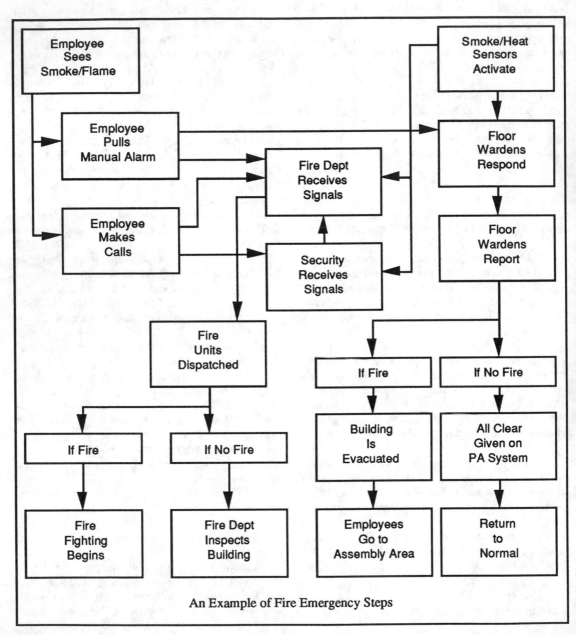

An Example of Fire Emergency Steps

fire department and the fire director, check the stairwells to ensure they are free of fire or smoke, and begin evacuation immediately. When the floor is completely evacuated, the floor warden will notify the fire director. Employees will be directed away from the elevators unless specifically directed by the fire department to do otherwise.

If a search of the floor does not reveal fire conditions, the floor warden will wait for the arrival of the fire brigade from the building management office. The fire brigade will double-check the floor to validate that the initial search was thorough. When this has been done, the building management office will make an announcement over the loudspeaker.

A floor warden does not have to wait for an evacuation announcement to be made over the loudspeaker to begin evacuation. If fire conditions are present on the floor, the floor warden will immediately begin instructing people to leave via the stairwells that have been determined to be free of fire and smoke.

During an evacuation, the floor warden will make a final search of the floor to ensure that no one has been left behind. Rest rooms, conference rooms, and closed offices will be checked. The floor wardens will assemble with their floor employees at pre-designated places outside of the building and away from arriving emergency units.

Security Officers. If the building has a security officer presence, annunciation devices can alert the officer(s) to initiate the established response actions. The most productive actions may be to operate the fire command center and/or go to the affected floor to assist the floor wardens.

If an evacuation is ordered, the security officers can assist in guiding people from the building, providing traffic control as may be needed to move fire fighting apparatus into close proximity to the building, and serving as a communications link between floor wardens at the assembly area and the fire department.

During other-than-normal working hours, the security officer(s) perform the functions of the fire brigade and the floor wardens, i.e., determine the cause for the alarm, and evacuate as needed.

Individual Employees. The floor wardens educate employees on an on-going basis to ensure that everyone will know what to do in the event of an evacuation. The employee will:

- Upon hearing the alarm, listen for and follow instructions given over the public address system or by floor wardens, building management staff, and security officers.
- Use the nearest stairwell for evacuation, unless otherwise directed.
- Not run and not smoke.
- Remain calm. Keep talking to a minimum.
- Once out of the building, proceed directly to the designated assembly area and stand by for instructions.

Training and Drills. Floor wardens should be trained in CPR, operation of oxygen resuscitators, high-rise fire safety, and should receive refresher training at quarterly meetings. Security officers should be trained in CPR, basic first aid, operation of ABC fire extinguishers, operation of oxygen resuscitators, and high-rise fire safety. Security

officers should also receive training in the post orders and special instructions that relate to fire safety at time of hire, and periodically, as part of regularly conducted refresher and advanced training. Security officers should engage in fire response drills and conduct tests of the detection and annunciation equipment on a regular on-going basis. Such drills and tests can be conducted during other-than-normal working hours.

Fire drills for the benefit of the fire director, floor wardens, security officers, the fire brigade, and all building occupants should be conducted at a frequency of at least once every 6 months. The nature of the drills are usually specified by the fire department.

John J. Fay, CPP

FLAG ETIQUETTE

In early times warring people carried identifying standards into battle. These consisted of pictures of animals or sacred symbols fastened to the tops of long rods. The ancient Greeks carried a piece of armor on a spear. Sometimes a streamer of cloth hung below the emblem. The Romans used a square of cloth hanging from a wooden crosspiece at the top of a staff. This was the forerunner of fabric flags. During the reign of the Emperor Constantine, flags were marked with Christian emblems. Some of these have survived. For example, the British national flag carries the crosses of St. George to represent England, St. Andrew for Scotland, and St. Patrick for Ireland. During the Middle Ages coats of arms, which had developed as insignia to be worn on shields, came to be used as flag emblems. Each nobleman had his own insignia or heraldic device.

Medieval flags were also used extensively in battle. In attacking, retreating, or rallying on the field, soldiers followed directions given by flags. When not used for purposes of combat, flags took on ceremonial purposes. They came to be used widely for official identification of Orders of Knighthood, cities, nations, and eventually of trade guilds and commercial companies.

Types of Flags

We generally think of a flag as a piece of fabric put on display to identify a nation, group, or person.

Sometimes a flag is used to serve as a signal. When used for identification, it is commonly marked with an emblem or device. When used for signaling, the flag may be plain. A flag is generally attached to a staff or to a halyard (rope) for raising and lowering it on a mast. Flags are generally rectangular. A triangular flag is called a pennant.

To strike a flag is to haul it down in token of surrender. To dip it is to lower it slightly and raise it again as a ceremonial greeting. To display a flag at half-mast, or half-staff, is to fly the flag part way down from the top of the staff as a sign of mourning.

Some national flags bear a design symbolizing the unity of the nation. This design is called the union. Usually the union occupies a rectangular area in the upper corner nearest the staff, as in the case of the flag of the United States. This rectangular area is called the canton. The part of the flag outside the canton is called the field, or ground.

A flag flown by ships to show nationality is called an ensign. The ensign of the United States is the same as its national flag. In many countries, however, the ensign differs from the national flag. For example, Great Britain has three ensigns with fields of different colors and a variety of emblems for special uses.

A small flag indicating nationality that flies at the bow of a ship is called a jack. It often consists of the union of the ensign and is therefore called a union jack. The United States union jack consists of 50 white stars against a blue background.

From very early times ships at sea have used flags as a means of communication. The color of a flag or the manner in which it is flown might convey the message. A flag indicating the presence on board of the fleet commander led to the term flagship. A ship in distress flies its ensign upside down, and there is an international code that uses flags to represent letters in words.

When the national flag is carried by soldiers on foot in military formation, it is referred to as a color. When carried by mounted motorized troops, the flag is called a standard. A small flag that identifies a minor military unit is known as a guidon.

The national flag of the United States is called the Stars and Stripes. The union consists of white stars against a blue background. There are as many stars as there are states of the United States, but contrary to popular belief, there is no particular star for a particular state. The field of the flag consists of seven red stripes separated by six white stripes. The thirteen stripes represent the thirteen colonies.

Respect for the Flag

It was not until this century that an official code of flag etiquette was adopted. The code has the following provisions:

•The flag is displayed outdoors from sunrise to sunset. It may be displayed 24 hours a day if illuminated during the hours of darkness.

•The flag should be raised briskly and lowered slowly.

•While it is appropriate to display the flag on any day (except outdoors during inclement weather unless an all-weather flag is used), it is especially appropriate to do so on holidays. The national flag should be displayed on certain specific holidays.

•The flag should be displayed at public institutions daily, at election polling places on election days, and at schools on school days.

•When carried with other flags in procession, the U.S. flag should be on the marcher's right. When carried in a line of flags, it should be in the front and center.

•Displayed on a wall, the union should be at top and left as the audience faces the flag.

•No other flag should be placed above the U.S. flag except a church pennant during services at sea.

•Flown with flags of other nations, all flags should be of the same size and of equal height.

•On a casket, the flag should have the union at the head and over the left shoulder of the dead person.

•Displayed over a street, the union should be to the north in an east-west street and to the east in a north-south street.

•Displayed on a speaker's platform, the U.S. flag should be at the speaker's right. Placed elsewhere in an auditorium, it should be at the audience's right. Any other flags displayed at the same time should be on the opposite side from the national flag.

•When displayed on a crossed staff, the U.S. flag should be at its right, with its staff in front of the staff of the other flag.

•Displayed with state, city, or organizational flags, the U.S. flag should be in the center and at the highest point. When flown from staffs in this manner, the U.S. flag should be raised first and lowered last.

•When flown at half-mast, the flag should first be raised to the top of the pole and then lowered to half-mast. When being lowered, the flag should be raised to the top of the pole and then lowered.

•Displayed on a projecting staff, the union should be at the peak of the staff. If the flag were attached instead to a rope stretched from a window to a tree or pole, the union should be away from the window as it would be on the staff.

•The flag should never be displayed with the union down, except as a signal of dire distress.

•The flag should never touch anything beneath it, such as the ground, floor, water, or merchandise. It should never be carried flat or with the staff horizontal. It should never be used as drapery, never festooned nor drawn back or up. It should never be used as a covering for a ceiling, nor as a receptacle for holding or carrying anything.

•No insignia or letter or picture of any kind should ever be placed upon or attached to the flag. The flag should never be used for advertising purposes in any manner whatsoever.

•When the flag is worn out, it should be destroyed in a dignified way, preferably by burning.

•The flag should not be used on a float in a parade unless it is hanging free or displayed flat. It should never be draped over any part of any kind of a vehicle. Wherever used, it should always be suspended so it will either be entirely flat or will fall free.

•When the flag is being flown with flags of states, cities, or organizations on the same halyard, the national flag should always be at the peak.

•The flag should never be used to cover a statue or monument at an unveiling ceremony.

•A salute is given the flag by all citizens when it is raised or lowered, when it passes in a parade, when the national anthem is played, and under some circumstances when the Pledge of Allegiance is given. Persons in uniform give military salute. Men and women not in uniform place the right hand over the heart. A man wearing a hat removes it with his right hand and holds it in front of his left shoulder. A person stands at attention while saluting.

John J. Fay, CPP

Source Security Officer Training Manual. (The Charter Company, Jacksonville, FL., 1983).

FORENSIC TESTING

Blood and Other Body Fluids

Forensic serology involves the identification and characterization of blood and other body fluids on items associated with a crime or crime scene. Evidence from violent crimes, such as murder, rape, robbery, assault, and hit-and-run usually bear body fluid stains.

Blood examinations aid investigations:

•In locating the possible crime scene. Identification of human blood similar in type to that of the victim can assist investigators in identifying the crime scene.

•In discovering a crime. Occasionally, the identification of human blood on a highway, sidewalk, porch, or in a car is the first indication that a crime has occurred.

•In identifying the weapon used. The grouping of human blood found on a club, knife, or hammer can be of considerable probative value.

•In proving or disproving a suspect's alibi. The identification of human blood on an item belonging to a suspect who claims that the blood is of animal origin refutes an alibi, whereas the identification of animal blood can substantiate the alibi.

•In eliminating suspects. The determination that the human blood on items from the suspect is different in type from that of the victim may exculpate the suspect. Blood similar to that of the suspect can help corroborate a suspect's claim of having a nosebleed or other injury.

Testing can determine whether visible stains do or do not contain blood. The appearance of blood can vary greatly depending on the age of the stain and the environmental conditions (such as temperature, light, and humidity) to which it was subjected. Chemical and microscopic analyses are necessary to positively identify the presence of blood in a stain and to determine whether blood is of human or non-human origin, and if non-human, the specific animal family from which it originated.

Human blood can be classified according to the four groups of the International ABO Blood Grouping System and other blood grouping systems, including red blood cell enzyme and serum protein systems, which are analyzed by electrophoresis.

The age of a bloodstain or the race of the person from whom it originated cannot be conclusively determined, and using conventional serological techniques it is not possible to identify human blood as having come from a particular person.

An investigation can also be aided by the examination of semen, saliva, and urine.

Semen. The identification of semen by chemical and microscopic means on vaginal smears, swabs, or on the victim's clothing may be of value in corroborating the victim's claims. Enzyme typing is possible on semen stains of sufficient size and quality.

DNA analysis may allow for positive personal identification of the semen source. If DNA analysis is unsuccessful and the depositor is a secretor, grouping tests may provide information concerning the depositor's ABO blood type.

Saliva. A saliva sample from a known source may be used in conjunction with the liquid blood from the same source to establish the secretor status of the individual. Saliva from a questioned source may provide information as to ABO blood type of the depositor.

Known saliva samples should be submitted from both the suspect(s) and victim(s) in sexual assault cases, and in cases where a saliva examination may provide probative information (e.g., a cigarette butt found adjacent to a homicide victim's body).

Urine. Urine may be qualitatively identified by chemical testing. Absolute identification of a stain as urine is not possible; however, no routinely reliable forensic techniques are available that provide blood group information from urine.

Secretors and Secretor Status. Secretors (which represent approximately 75% of the U.S. population) are individuals who have in their non-blood body fluids (e.g., semen, saliva and vaginal fluid) detectable amounts of substances that are chemically similar to the antigens located on red blood cells, which confer ABO blood type.

It is because of this that the ABO blood type of a secretor can often be determined from a non-blood body fluid stain from that individual.

Nonsecretors (the remainder of the population) do not exhibit these blood group substances in their non-blood body fluids.

The Lewis blood grouping system can be utilized to determine secretor status from a liquid blood sample. If, however, the secretor status cannot be determined from the known blood, then the known saliva sample can be examined.

Limitations on Seminal and Saliva Stains. Sometimes semen is mixed with urine or vaginal secretions from the victim. This can make interpretation of grouping tests more difficult inasmuch as the blood group substances from the victim's body fluids could mask the blood group substances in the semen.

To make a meaningful comparison of grouping test results on questioned semen and saliva stains, the investigator will need to obtain known liquid blood and known dried saliva samples from the victim and suspect.

Saliva on cigarette butts are often contaminated with dirt. Saliva on cigar butts is not groupable. Ash trays should not be simply emptied into a container. Rather, individual cigarette butts should be removed from the ash and debris, and packaged separately. In view of the difficulties involved in cigarette saliva grouping and the circumstantial nature of any successful result, it is often more judicious for the investigator to request latent fingerprint examinations of cigarette butts in lieu of serological examinations.

It is not necessary to submit known semen samples from the suspect in rape cases because the information necessary to make comparative analyses can be gleaned from the suspect's known blood and known saliva samples.

Rape Case Considerations

In light of recent developments in forensic DNA technology, the collection and preservation of serological evidence in a rape case warrants special consideration The forensic serologist can often provide the investigator with information beyond the fact that "semen is present" on an item if the proper samples are obtained, preserved, and submitted to the laboratory in a timely manner.

Body cavity swabs should be collected from the victim as expeditiously as possible following the assault. Once dried and packaged, these swabs should be frozen until they are submitted to the laboratory.

DNA Examinations

Deoxyribonucleic acid (DNA) is analyzed in body fluids and body fluid stains recovered from physical evidence in violent crimes. DNA analysis is conducted utilizing the restriction fragment length polymorphism (RFLP) method or other appropriate DNA methods. Evidence consists of known liquid and dried blood samples, portions of rape kit swabs and extracts, and body fluid stained cuttings from homicide, sexual assault, and serious aggravated assault cases.

The results of DNA analysis on a questioned body fluid stain are compared visually and by computer image analysis to the results of DNA analysis on known blood samples as a means of potentially identifying or excluding an individual as the source of a questioned stain. As such, this technique is capable of directly associating the victim of a violent crime with the subject or the subject with the crime scene, similar to a fingerprint. The implementation of this technique in the laboratory represents a significant advance in forensic serology.

Chemicals

Toxicological Examinations. A toxicological examination looks for the presence of drugs and/or poison in biological tissues and fluids. The toxicological findings show whether the victim of a crime died or became ill as the result of drug or poison ingestion, or whether the involved persons were under the influence of drugs at the time of the matter under investigation.

Because of the large number of potentially toxic substances, it is necessary (unless a specific toxic agent is implicated prior to examination) to screen biological samples for classes of poisons.

Examples of these classes and the drugs and chemicals that may be found within these classes are as follows:

- Volatile compounds, e.g., ethanol, carbon monoxide, and chloroform.
- Heavy metals, e.g., arsenic, mercury, thallium, and lead.
- Inorganic ions, e.g., cyanide, azide, chloride, and bromide.

- Non-volatile organic compounds, e.g., most drugs of abuse and other pharmaceuticals, as well as pesticides and herbicides.

Drug and Pharmaceutical Examinations. The forensic laboratory will determine if materials seized as suspected drugs do in fact contain controlled substances. In addition, the laboratory can examine a wide variety of items, such as boats, aircraft, automobiles, clothing, luggage, and money, for the presence of trace quantities of cocaine, heroin, phencyclidine (PCP), etc. A pharmaceutical examination will identify products for the purpose of matching recovered products with stolen products, or for proving that pharmaceuticals were switched.

Arson Examinations. The gas chromatography technique is used to determine the presence of accelerants or other substances introduced to a fire scene to facilitate destruction. Debris collected from the scene of a suspected arson can be analyzed to learn if a distillate was used to accelerate the fire and, if so, testing can classify the distillate by product, such as gasoline, fuel oil, or paint solvent. Debris most suitable for analysis will be absorbent in nature, e.g., padded furniture, carpeting, plasterboard, and flooring.

General Chemical Examinations. Qualitative and quantitative analyses can be made of miscellaneous chemical evidence. Quality analysis is helpful in cases involving theft or contamination of chemical products, malicious destruction, and assault. Analysis of writing inks can match questioned documents with known ink specimens obtained from typewriter ribbons and stamp pads. In consumer product tampering cases, analysis can determine the presence and nature of contaminants, adulterants, and alterations to containers. Chemical examinations can be useful in evaluating tear gas and dyes in bank robber packets, constituents determination in patent fraud cases, and flash and water soluble paper in gambling and spy cases.

Document Examinations

The questioned document field includes examinations of handwriting; hand painting; typewriting; mechanical impressions, such as checkwriter imprints, embossed seals, rubber stamps, and printed matter; photocopies; paper; altered documents; obliterated writing; indented writing; charred documents; and others.

Handwriting and Hand Printing. Writers can be positively and reliably identified with their writings. Other characteristics, such as age, sex, and personality, cannot be determined with certainty from handwriting. A handwriting identification is based upon the characteristics present in normal handwriting. It is not always possible, therefore, to reach a definite conclusion in the examination of handwriting. Some of the reasons for inconclusive results are:

- Limited questioned writing.
- Inadequate known samples.
- Lack of contemporaneous writing, such as when a long period of time has elapsed between preparation of the questioned writing and the known samples.
- Distortion or disguise in either the questioned writing or the known writing. In this situation, the normal handwriting characteristics are not present.
- Lack of sufficient identifying characteristics in spite of ample quantities of both questioned and known writing.

Three types of forged writings are commonly examined:

- Traced Forgery. Produced by tracing over a genuine signature, this forgery cannot be identified with the writer. A traced forgery can, however, be associated with the original or master signature from which the forgeries were traced if it is located.
- Simulated Forgery. Produced by attempting to copy a genuine signature, this forgery may or may not be identifiable with the writer, depending on the extent to which normal characteristics remain in the signature. Samples of the victim's genuine signature should also be submitted for examination.
- Freehand Forgery. Produced in the forger's normal handwriting with no attempt to copy another's writing style, this forgery can be identified with the writer.

Typewriting Examinations. Questioned typewriting can be identified with the typewriter that produced it. This identification is based upon individual characteristics that develop on the type face and on other features of the machine during the manufacturing process and through use.

Photocopier Examinations. Photocopies can be identified with the machine producing them provided samples and questioned copies are relatively contemporaneous. Two sets of questioned photocopies can be identified as having been produced on the same machine, and possible brands or manufacturers can be determined by comparison with a reference file maintained at the laboratory.

Mechanical Impression Examination. Questioned printed documents can be compared with genuine printed documents to determine if counterfeit. Two or more printed documents can be associated with the same printing, and a printed document can be identified with the source printing paraphernalia such as artwork, negatives, and plates.

A checkwriter impression can be identified with the checkwriter that produced it, and examination of a questioned impression can determine the brand of checkwriter producing it. A rubber stamp impression can be identified with the rubber stamp producing it, and an embosser or seal impression can be identified with the instrument that produced it.

Paper Examinations. Torn edges can be positively matched, the manufacturer can be determined if a watermark is present, and paper can be examined for indented writing impressions. Indentations not visible to the eye can be brought up using appropriate instruments. Some watermarks provide dating information, indicating the date of manufacture of the paper.

Writing Instruments. Chemical analysis can determine if the ink of two or more different writings is the same or different formulation. The same analysis can be conducted with an ink writing and a suspect pen. The examinations do not identify a specific pen, only that the inks are the same formulation. Ink dating examinations can also show the earliest date a particular ink was produced.

True Age of a Document. The earliest date a document could have been prepared may sometimes be determined by examination of watermarks, indented writing, printing, and typewriting. Chemical analysis of writing ink may determine the earliest date the formulation was available.

The Federal Bureau of Investigation (FBI) Laboratory maintains reference files of known standards that can be compared with questioned materials submitted for analysis.

Typewriter Standards. These consist of samples of many styles of both foreign and domestic; they permit determination of possible brands or manufacturers of typewriter from examination of questioned typewriting.

Watermark Standards. This file is an index of watermarks found in paper; it enables determination of the paper manufacturer.

Safety Paper Standards. These are samples of a variety of safety papers which enable determination of paper manufacturer when used in production of fraudulent documents, such as checks and birth certificates.

Checkwriter Standards. Sample impressions from many checkwriters allow determination of checkwriter brand or manufacturer from examination of questioned impression.

Shoe Print and Tire Tread Standards. A collection of sole and heel designs and tire tread designs helps determine the manufacturer of shoes and tires from prints or impressions left at the crime scene.

Office Copier Standards. A collection of samples from and information about many brands of photocopiers and office duplicating machines assists in determining possible brands and manufacturers of a questioned photocopy.

Explosives Examinations

Explosives examinations are visual and microscopic analyses of bomb remains, commercial explosives, blasting accessories, military explosives, and ordnance items. Tool mark examinations of bomb components are also possible.

Bomb remains are examined to identify bomb components, such as switches, batteries, blasting caps, tape, wire, and timing mechanisms. Also identified are fabrication techniques, unconsumed explosives, and overall construction of the bomb. Instrumental examination of explosives and explosive residues are carried on in conjunction with bomb component examinations All bomb components are examined for tool marks, where possible tools used in constructing the bomb are identified for investigative purposes.

Explosive Reference Files. The FBI Laboratory maintains extensive reference files on commercial explosives, blasting accessories, and bomb components. These files contain technical data plus known standards of explosive items and bomb components, including dynamite, water gels, blasting agents, blasting caps, safety fuse, detonating cord, batteries, tape, switches, and radio control systems.

Firearms

Firearms identification is the study by which a bullet, cartridge case, or shotshell casing may be identified as having been fired by a particular weapon to the exclusion of all other weapons.

The firearms examiner will provide one of three conclusions: (1) that the bullet, cartridge case, or shotshell casing was fired by the weapon; or (2) was not fired by the weapon; or (3) there are not sufficient microscopic marks to make a positive identification.

Bullets. Marks on bullets can be produced by rifling in the barrel of the weapon by a flash suppressor or possibly in loading. When a bullet and/or fragment bearing no microscopic marks of value for identification purposes is encountered, it is often useful to perform a quantitative analysis and compare the results to the similarly analyzed bullets of any recovered suspect ammunition (e.g., cartridges remaining in the suspect firearm, cartridges in suspect's pockets, partial boxes of cartridges in suspect's residence, etc.). When two or more lead samples are determined to be compositionally indistinguishable from one another, a common manufacturer's source of lead is indicated. Lead composition information, in conjunction with other circumstantial information, is often useful in linking a suspect to a shooting. Compositional analysis of shot pellets and rifled slugs can provide similar useful circumstantial information.

Cartridge Cases or Shotshell Casings. Marks on a fired cartridge case or shotshell casing can be produced by breech face, firing pin, chamber, extractor, and ejector with a fired cartridge case. The examiner may be able to determine the specific caliber, type, and possibly, the make of the weapon that was fired. A fired shotshell casing can reveal gauge and original factory loading. Wadding can indicate gauge and possibly manufacturer. From shot, the examiner can determine size.

Extractor or ejector marks on a fired cartridge or casing that match with a specific weapon means only that the cartridge or casing had been loaded into and extracted from that specific weapon. To conclude that the cartridge or case was actually fired by the specific weapon, the examiner must rely on a firing pin impression or breech face and chamber marks.

Gunshot Residues. Gunshot residues on clothing may be located, depending on the muzzle-to-garment distance, in two ways: (1) by microscopic examination of the area surrounding the hole for gunpowder particles and gunpowder residues, smudging, and singeing; and (2) by chemical processing to develop a graphic representation of powder residues and lead residues around the hole. Test patterns can be compared with those produced at various distances using the suspect weapon and ammunition like that used in the case.

When a person discharges a firearm, primer residues can be deposited on that person's hands in varying amounts. These amounts are dependent upon the type, caliber, and condition of the firearm, and the environmental conditions at the time of the shooting. Residue samples can be collected from a suspect's hands and analyzed for the presence of the chemical elements antimony, barium and lead, which are components of most primer mixtures. The analytical technique used to analyze these hand samples is dependent upon the type of hand samples collected from the suspect's hands.

Washing the hands and various other activities on the part of the shooter can remove substantial amounts of residue. Therefore, it is imperative to obtain samples as soon after the shooting as possible. Samples obtained more than 6 hours after a shooting are generally of little value and normally will not be analyzed.

Samples obtained from the hands of victims of close-range shootings (within approximately 10 feet) are generally of no value since it is not possible to differentiate between residues deposited on the hands of a shooter and victim of a close-range shooting. Therefore, samples from the hands of victims are not normally accepted for analysis.

Shot Pattern. The distance at which a shotgun was fired can be determined. It is necessary to fire the suspect weapon at various distances using the same type of ammunition involved in the case being investigated.

Hairs and Fibers

Hair and fiber examinations are valuable in person-to-person violence cases, such as rape and murder cases, because they can assist in placing the suspect at the scene of the crime by determining the interchange of hairs or fibers between the victim and suspect. Similarly, these examinations can be helpful in connecting a suspect to surreptitious crimes, such as burglary and auto theft, and in identifying the scene of the crime. Hairs or fibers found on knives, jimmy bars, and the like can identify the weapons or instruments of crime, as well as automobiles involved in hit-and-run cases. Victim and witness testimony can also be corroborated by the discovery of hairs and fibers.

Hairs. Examination of a hair can determine if it is animal or human; if animal, the species from which it originated (dog, cat, deer, etc.), and if human, the race, body area, how removed from the body, damage, and alteration (bleaching or dyeing).

The finding from a hair examination is good circumstantial evidence, but not positive evidence. An examination can conclude whether or not a hair could have originated from a particular person based on microscopic characteristics present in the hair. Age cannot be determined, but gender may be determined depending on the condition of the hair's root.

Fibers. Examination of a fiber can identify the type of fiber, such as animal (wool), vegetable (cotton), synthetic (human-made), and mineral (glass). The usual purpose of a fiber examination is to determine whether or not questioned fibers are the same type and/or color, and match the microscopic characteristics of fibers in a suspect's garment. Like hairs, fibers are not positive evidence, but are good circumstantial evidence.

Fiber examinations can include analyses of fabrics and cordage. A positive identification can be made if a questioned piece of fabric can be fitted to the known material. Composition, construction, color, and diameter of fibers are the points of comparison. Cordage or rope left at the scene of the crime may be compared with similar materials, and in some cases the manufacturer can be identified if the material contains a unique tracer.

The same principles of examination can be applied to botanical specimens, where plant material from a known source is compared with plant material from a questioned locale.

Finally, identifications can be made through comparisons of teeth with dental records and X-rays with corresponding bone structures. Examinations may be made to determine if skeletal remains are animal or human. If human, the race, sex, approximate height and stature, and approximate age at death may be determined.

The presence of a suspect at the crime scene can be established from a comparison of wood from the suspect's clothing or vehicle, or possession of wood from the crime scene. The specific wood source can be determined from side or end matching and fracture matching.

Miscellaneous Examinations. Related examinations include button matches, fabric impressions, glove prints, feathers, knots, and identifying the clothing manufacturer through a label search.

Materials Analysis

These examinations entail the use of instrumentation, such as infrared spectroscopy, X-ray diffractometry, emission spectrometry, and gas chromatography/mass spectrography (GC/MS), for identification or comparison of the chemical compositions of paints, plastics, explosives, cosmetics, tapes, and related materials.

Automobile Paints. It is possible to establish the year and make of an automobile from a paint chip by use of the National Automotive Paint File, which contains paint panels representing paints used on all makes of American cars and many popular imported cars such as Mercedes Benz, Volkswagen, Porsche, Audi, BMW, Renault, Honda, Subaru, Datsun, and Toyota. A very careful search of the accident or crime scene should be made to locate small chips because:

• Paint fragments are often found in the clothing of a hit-and-run victim. Therefore, the victim's clothing should be obtained and submitted to the laboratory whenever possible.

• Paints may be transferred from one car to another, from car to object, or from object to car during an accident or the commission of a crime. Occasionally it is better to submit an entire component, such as a fender or bumper, if the paint transfer is very minimal.

Non-Automobile Paints. Paint on safes, vaults, window sills, door frames, etc., may be transferred to the tools used to open them. Therefore, a comparison can be made between the paint on an object and the paint on a tool.

Cosmetics. Unknown or suspected cosmetics and/or makeup can be compared with a potential source in assault cases, such as rape. The investigator should be alert to the possible transfer of such materials between victim and suspect.

Plastics/Polymers. It is not possible to specifically identify the source, use, or manufacturer of plastic items from composition alone, but comparisons such as the following can be made:

• Trim from automobiles, depending upon the uniqueness of the composition, is compared with plastic remaining on property struck in a hit-and-run type case.

• Plastics comprising insulation on wire used in bombings, wiretapping, and other crimes are compared with known or suspected sources of insulated wire.

• Plastic/rubber tapes from crime scenes are compared with suspected possible sources.

• Polymers used in surgical cloth-backed tape are compared with sources.

• Miscellaneous plastic material from crime scenes is compared with possible sources.

Tape. A positive identification can be made with the end of a piece of tape left at the scene of the crime and a roll of suspect tape. If no end match is possible, composition, construction, and color can be compared as in other types of examinations.

Metallurgy

Metals or metallic objects may be metallurgically examined for comparison purposes and/or information purposes.   Determinations to ascertain if two metals or two metallic objects came from the same source or from each other usually require evaluations based on surface characteristics, microstructural characteristics, mechanical properties, and composition.

Surface Characteristics. These are macroscopic and microscopic features exhibited by a metal surface, including fractured areas, accidental marks or accidentally damaged areas, manufacturing defects, material defects, fabrication marks, and fabrication finish. The fabrication finish reveals part of the mechanical and thermal histories of how the metal was formed, e.g., if it was cast, forged, hot-rolled, cold-rolled, extruded, drawn, swaged, milled, spun, or pressed.

Microstructural Characteristics. These are the internal structural features of a metal as revealed by optical and electron microscopy. Structural features include the size and shape of grains; the size, shape, and distribution of secondary phases; non-metallic inclusions; and other heterogeneous conditions. The microstructure is related to the composition of the metal and to the thermal and mechanical treatments that the metal has undergone; it therefore contains information concerning the history of the metal.

Mechanical Properties. These characteristics describe the response of a metal to an applied force or load, e.g., strength, ductility, and hardness.

Composition. This is the chemical element makeup of the metal, including major alloying elements and trace element constituents. Because most commercial metals and alloys are non-homogeneous materials and may have substantial elemental variation, small metal samples or particles may not be compositionally representative of the bulk metal.

Broken and/or mechanically damaged (deformed) metal pieces or parts can be examined to determine the cause of the failure or damage, i.e., stress exceeding the strength or yield limit of the metal, material defect, manufacturing defect,

corrosion cracking, and excessive service usage (fatigue). The magnitude of the force or load that caused the failure can be determined, as well as the possible means by which the force or load was transmitted to the metal and the direction in which it was transmitted.

Burned, heated, or melted metal can be evaluated to determine the temperature to which the metal was exposed; the nature of the heat source that damaged the metal; and whether the metal was involved in an electrical short-circuit situation.

Rusted or corroded metal can be examined to estimate the length of time the metal has been subjected to the environment that caused the rust or corrosion, and the nature of the corrosive environment.

Cut or severed metal can be tested to identify the method by which the metal was severed -- sawing, shearing, milling, turning, arc cutting, flame cutting (oxyacetylene torch or "burning bar"), etc.; the length of time to make the cut; and the relative skill of the individual who made the cut.

Metal fragments can be analyzed to reveal the method by which the fragments were formed. If fragments had been formed by high-velocity forces, such as an explosion, it may be possible to determine the magnitude of the detonation velocity. It may also be possible to obtain an identification of the item that was the source of the fragments. In bombings, timing mechanisms can often be identified as to type, manufacturer, and model; determinations are sometimes possible as to the time displayed by the mechanism when the explosive detonated and as to the relative length of time the mechanism was functioning prior to the explosion.

Examination of nonfunctioning watches, clocks, timers, and other mechanisms can be revealing as to the condition responsible for causing the mechanism to stop or malfunction, and whether the time displayed by a timing mechanism represents a.m. or p.m.

For items unidentified as to use or source, it may be possible to identify the use for which the item was designed, formed, or manufactured, based on the construction of and the type of metal in the item. The manufacturer and the specific fabricating equipment utilized to form the item might be revealed, as well as the possible sources of the item if an unusual metal or alloy is involved.

Lamp bulbs that are subjected to an impact, such as from vehicles involved in an accident, can be examined to determine whether the lights of a vehicle were incandescent at the time of the accident.

Objects with questioned internal components can be exposed to X-ray radiography to non-destructively reveal the interior construction and the presence or absence of defects, cavities, or foreign material.

Mineralogy

Mineralogy includes materials that are mostly inorganic, crystalline, or mineral in character. Comparisons will, by inference, connect a suspect or object with a crime scene, prove or disprove an alibi, provide investigative leads, or substantiate a theorized chain of events. These materials include glass, building materials, soil, debris, industrial dusts, safe insulation, minerals, abrasives, and gems.

Glass Fractures. Glass, a non-crystalline, rigid material, can be excellent physical evidence. Fracture patterns can provide valuable information as to direction of breaking force. A physical match of two pieces of glass results in an opinion that they came from a common source to the exclusion of all other sources.

Penetration of glass panes by bullets or high-speed projectiles produces a cone pattern from which the direction and some idea of the angle of penetration can be determined. The type of projectile can also sometimes be determined. By an examination of stress lines on radial cracks near the point of impact, the direction of the force used to break the glass can be determined. This determination depends on identification of the radial cracks and the point or points of impact. By fitting glass pieces together with microscopic matching of stress lines, the laboratory examiner can positively identify the pieces as originally having been broken from a single pane, bottle, or headlight. If pertinent portions of a bottle, headlight, or taillight can be fitted together, the manufacturer and type may be determined for lead purposes.

When a window breaks, glass particles shower toward the direction of the force 10 feet or more. Particles, therefore, can be found in the hair and on the clothing of the perpetrator. Particles can also become embedded in bullets and/or objects used to break windows. Particles of broken glass from a hit-and-run vehicle are often present on the victim's clothing; many times the driver of a hit-and-run vehicle will emerge from the vehicle to determine what was hit or how seriously the victim was injured; consequently, broken glass from the accident may often be found embedded in the driver's shoes.

By microscopic optical and density comparisons, glass particles can be identified or compared with glass from a known source. The laboratory expert cannot identify the source to the exclusion of all other sources; however, it can be stated and demonstrated that it is highly improbable that the particles came from a source other than the matching known source; if two or more different known sources can be matched, the conclusion is greatly enhanced.

Soils, Dust, and Debris. Soil is any finely divided material on the surface of the earth and may contain such human-made material as cinders, shingle, stones, glass particles, paint, and rust. Soil, as a category, includes debris and industrial dusts, as well as natural soils.

Soil varies widely from point to point on the surface of the earth and even more with depth. For example, industrial dust specimens or soil near factories are often distinctive, and debris may contain particles characteristic of a specific area. Soil cannot be positively identified as coming from one source to the exclusion of all others, but the laboratory expert can associate questioned soil with a most probable source, conclude that a source cannot be eliminated, or that a point or area could not be the source of the questioned soil. Such conclusions have proven extremely valuable in the proof of criminal cases. Soil specimens will often consist of shoe prints, tire marks, burial sites, or mud taken from an area where a transfer of soil to the suspect is logical.

Safe Insulation and Building Materials. Safe insulation is found between the walls of fire-resistant safes, and in vaults and safe cabinets. It is readily transferred to tools and clothing. Samples of insulation collected at the scene can be compared to apparel, shoes, and tools confiscated from the suspect. The same principles apply where unlawful entry through a roof or wall may cause particles to adhere to the suspect or the tools used.

Photographic Examinations

Infrared, ultraviolet, and monochromatic photography can be utilized to assist in rendering visible, latent photographic evidence that is not otherwise visible to the unaided human eye. Examples of this type of evidence include alterations and obliteration to documents, invisible laundry marks, and indented writing.

Bank Robbery Film. The laboratory can examine this film to:
- Attempt enhancement of poor quality photographic exposures and/or prints.
- Compare in detail the unknown subject's clothing as depicted in the film with the clothing obtained from a suspect.
- Determine the individual's height as depicted in the film. Height is determined preferably from a height chart, but it can also be done mathematically, often to within an inch.
- Compare facial features of the unknown subject in the film with those in a known photograph of a suspect.

Miscellaneous Photographic Examinations. Various other types of photographic examinations can be conducted such as:
- Comparison of film or prints to determine if they were taken by a specific camera.
- Determine the type and date of Polaroid film, as well as preparing a print from the "throw-away" portion.
- Determine if photographs have been altered.

Considerable information can usually be obtained from photographic evidence, using hundreds of various techniques. If photographic materials are in question, they should be forwarded to the laboratory with a clear narrative as to what information or examination is desired.

Reference Files

The FBI Laboratory maintains a number of reference files that can be used for comparison purposes in the evaluation of forensic evidence.

National Motor Vehicle Certificate of Title File. Samples of genuine state motor vehicle certificates of title, manufacturer's statement of origin, and vehicle emissions stickers assist in determination of authenticity of questioned certificates. This file contains photographs of fraudulent documents to assist in association of questioned material from different cases with a common source.

National Fraudulent Check File. A computerized file contains images of fraudulent and counterfeit checks, which helps associate fraudulent checks from different cases with a common source and assists in identification of fraudulent check passers.

Anonymous Letter File. A computerized file contains images of kidnapping, extortion, threatening, and other anonymous communications. This file is matched with questioned documents from different cases with a common source.

Bank Robbery Note File. Images of holdup notes are used to link notes used in various robberies with a common source.

National Stolen Art File. This is a listing of stolen and recovered artwork, mostly paintings, reported by law enforcement agencies. Because artwork does not bear a serial number, entries in the file are based upon a description of the artwork. When available, an image of the artwork is stored, which can be recalled for reference. During a file search, both data and image will appear simultaneously. The minimum value of stolen and recovered artwork for inclusion in the file is $2,000.

National Stolen Coin File. This is a computerized listing of stolen and recovered coins reported by law enforcement agencies. Because coins do not have serial numbers, entries in the file are based upon a description of the coin along with a photograph when available. During a file search, both data and image will appear simultaneously. The minimum value of stolen and recovered coins for inclusion in the file is $2,000.

Pornographic Materials Files. A collection of evidentiary pornographic materials, printed and video, helps in determining proof of interstate travel of pornographic material, and assists in determining production and distribution channels, as well as identity of actors.

These consist of materials submitted in connection with investigations of violations of the

White Slave Traffic Act, Interstate Transportation of Obscene Materials, and sexual exploitation of children statutes. This computerized file contains over 50,000 records of commercially produced pornographic materials, and the inventory of items is in every medium including video tapes, 8-millimeter movies, books, magazines, and photographs.

These files provide reference materials for laboratory examiners, data searches for investigations (investigative lead information regarding subject, companies, or specific pornographic products), and "charge out" materials for limited courtroom use and undercover operations.

Shoe Print and Tire Tread Evidence

Shoe print and tire tread evidence found at the scene of a crime can provide important evidence for investigation and eventual prosecution of a case. For three-dimensional impressions, casts should always be made immediately following appropriate photography of the impressions. For two-dimensional impressions, the original impression is most valuable and should be retained and preserved whenever possible and practical, such as when the impression is on glass, paper, or some other retrievable surface.

Shoe and tire reference materials are maintained in the laboratory to assist in the determination of the make or manufacturer of a shoe or tire that made a particular impression. This is useful in some cases to help locate suspects or suspect vehicles.

When known shoes or tires are obtained, comparisons are made between those items and the questioned shoe prints or tire impressions. Comparisons can be made between the physical size, design, manufacturing characteristics, wear characteristics, and random accidental characteristics. If sufficient random characteristics are present, a positive identification can be made.

Tool Mark Identification

Tool mark examinations are microscopic studies to determine if a given tool mark was produced by a specific tool. In a broader sense, they also include the identification of objects that forcibly contacted each other, were joined together under pressure for a period of time and removed from contact, and were originally a single item before being broken or cut apart. The inclusion of these latter areas results from the general consideration that when two objects come in contact, the harder object (the tool) will impart a mark on the softer object. Saws, files, and grinding wheels are generally not identifiable with marks they produce.

The tool mark examiner can conclude that: (1) the tool produced the tool mark, (2) the tool did not produce the tool mark, or (3) there are not sufficient individual characteristics remaining within the tool mark to determine if the tool did or did not produce the questioned mark.

Several comparisons can be made between a tool and a tool mark. Examination can be made of the tool for foreign deposits, such as paint or metal; for comparison with a marked object; establishment of the presence or non-presence of consistent class characteristics; and microscopic comparison of a marked object with several test marks or cuts made with the tool. Examination of the tool mark can determine the type of tool used (class characteristics); the size of tool used (class characteristics); unusual features of the tool (class or individual characteristics); the action employed by the tool in its normal operation, and/or in its present condition; and most importantly, if the tool mark is of value for identification purposes.

Fracture Matches. Fracture examinations are conducted to ascertain if a piece of material from an item, such as a metal bolt, plastic automobile trim, knife, screwdriver, wood gunstock, or rubber hose, was or was not broken from a like damaged item available for comparison. This type of examination may be requested along with a metallurgy examination if questioned items are metallic in composition

Marks in Wood. This examination is conducted to ascertain whether or not the marks in a wood specimen can be associated with the tool used to cut it, such as pruning shears and auger bits. This examination may be requested along with a wood examination.

Pressure/Contact. Pressure or contact examinations are conducted to ascertain whether or not any two objects were or were not in contact with each other, either momentarily or for a more extended time.

Plastic Replica Casts of Stamped Impressions. Plastic replica casts of stamped numbers in metal, such as altered vehicle identification numbers, can be examined and compared with others, as well as with suspect dies.

Locks and Keys. Lock and key examinations can be conducted to associate locks and keys with each other.   Such associations are useful in establishing a conspiracy or link of commonality between or among individuals. It is often possible to illustrate this through their possession of keys that will operate a single, lockage instrumentality (e.g., vehicle, safe house, or padlock). Laboratory examination of a lock can determine whether an attempt has been made to open it without the operating key.

Restoration of Obliterated Markings. Obliterated identification markings are often restorable, including markings obliterated by melting of the metal as evidenced by welding marks or "puddling."

Obliterated markings can also be restored on materials other than metal, such as wood, plastics, and fiberglass. Because different metals and alloys often require specific methods for restoration of obliterated markings, the laboratory should be contacted for number restoration procedures for field processing of items too large or heavy for submission.

Federal Bureau of Investigation

Source Handbook of Forensic Science. (Federal Bureau of Investigation, U.S. Department of Justice, Washington, 1990).

FORGERIES AND ALTERED DOCUMENTS

She slowly opened the door and peered into the dimly lit closet. There was the typewriter on the top shelf, nearly buried beneath the sweaters and boxes. With sweating hands, she lifted it down and rolled a sheet of paper into it. Holding her breath, she typed a sentence and paused before typing the letter "t." It struck with the same broken mark found on the ransom note left by the murderer.

In real life, document examination cases can have the same intrigue as in the movies. This article discusses some of the basic aspects of document examination primarily from the perspective of the company and the security professional. The information, however, applies in any cases involving document problems since there is the potential for mischief whenever there are documents that convey property or send messages.

Security managers encounter documents concerning sexual harassment claims, internal fraud, forgeries, fraudulent worker's compensation claims, graffiti, threatening letters, magazine subscriptions sent by disgruntled employees, and altered records. A document examiner who is called early in the investigative stage will help design the optimal method for collecting comparison materials specific to the case.

Another benefit of this type of consultation is to get an objective opinion that could prevent a company from making a serious mistake. A personnel manager suspected an employee of writing a threatening letter. The company retained a document examiner who identified him as the author of the letter. The union retained a different expert who concluded, however, that the employee was not the writer and requested samples of writing from other workers. One was identified as the writer, and this second person confessed.

A sexual assault case shows how document examination helped the suspect. A few days after a woman filed criminal charges against a prominent businessman for molesting her daughter, a diary mysteriously came into evidence. The diary looked suspiciously clean and contrived. The pages were smooth and free of smudges or curled corners, indicating that it had not been accessed frequently. Its entries were factual and the only entries in this diary referred to the assaults.

Document examination techniques revealed that most of the diary had been created all at one time; that entries appeared only on days that cross-matched to entries on the mother's calendar; and that, while it was in the victim's handwriting, the diary was not consistent with typical teen diaries.

In the trial, the defense lawyer asked the expert whether the diary could have been dictated or made up. The prosecutor naturally objected, but the idea had been planted, and the jury acquitted the defendant. The experience took such a toll on his health, however, that he died of a heart attack within a year after his trial.

A Variety of Techniques

Although the original charge in a case may be for forgery or falsification, careful observation may reveal additional information about the document's genuineness. One page might have been substituted for another, changing the meaning of the entire document. Continuing investigation of a forgery on a check by an employee may show that the check is a counterfeit. Different inks or typewriters might have been used to add information. A carbon, facsimile, or photocopy of a document may be different from the original, or a document may have been created by transferring a signature from a different document. A non-compete agreement that was created by pasting the signature on it and then photocopying it was produced by officers of a company. In another case, a promissory note had been created by cutting out the portion of a document containing a genuine signature and typing the note above the signature. This case was easily solved by showing that the typed line and the line beneath the signature were not in alignment and that the outside edges of the paper had been cut with a scissors.

Some forgeries or alterations are obvious. When they are not, what are some general ways to recognize problems with documents and present or challenge evidence? What makes good comparison samples of handwriting? How can a security manager avoid common mistakes? How can the mistakes of an opposing attorney or investigator be detected? When an opposing attorney tries to corner an expert on cross-examination, what can be done to soften its effect?

Begin with Common Sense

Logic and common sense are important for deciding how to proceed when there is a question about a document. To preserve evidence, it can be placed in a plastic report cover and handled with gloves. Photographs will furnish a permanent record of the evidence. Samples of writing from any people who might be involved can be collected and a document examiner called as soon as possible. These samples can be from employee personnel files.

What are the most significant factors to look for in documents? Red flags include any change in normal patterns, whether the change is in the format of the documents, how natural the writing looks, or how the document looks in general. An employee's behavior can also furnish clues about possible suspects.

In a forgery by an employee, the handwriting may resemble the victim's writing. On the other hand, if written freely, it may reflect the handwriting characteristics of the suspect.

Common signs of forgery include distortion of the signature, shakiness or a drawn look, and over-writing (patching.) When a company has a forgery, it is nearly always an attempt to make the signature look like the one being forged and frequently is patterned after stolen identification, credit cards, or other known signatures. A forgery is produced by drawing the model signature or writing it in an off-hand way. Typically, the off-hand forgery reflects some of the handwriting characteristics of the forger, while the drawn forgery contains pause marks and careful, shaky lines. It is usually far more difficult to identify the writer of a tracing or carefully simulated signature than a freely written one.

Some signatures look fairly generic (common handwriting style), or exhibit limited writing skill, making them easy to forge, while others may be very artistic, illegible, and vary so much from time to time that the owner does not even recognize his own. If a signature looks distorted, disguise should be considered. People disguise their writing to cash a check without being questioned, later claiming that their signature was forged, or they try to decoy the investigator into thinking that their writing looks different from the questioned writing. It is far more likely that a forger will try to make the forged signature look like the genuine one rather than distort the writing with a shift in slant or with extra curlicues and loops as found in disguise.

Other important factors in document cases include the timing of the submission of documents when requested and the circumstances surrounding their preparation. A lengthy delay in producing comparison documents may be a signal that they are being manufactured. Is the questioned document's appearance consistent with the content and context? Are pages missing, or are all or some too clean, as in the diary case? Writing crammed into a space when it could have been written naturally and distorted or unnatural writing are suspicious if they change the meaning of the document. Variations can be found in the color of inks when they should all be the same.

Frequently it is possible to decipher the indentations made on a paper by writing on the sheet on top of it. In an investigation, anything out of the ordinary should be studied.

Comparison Materials

There are two main types of comparison materials in a handwriting case. One includes samples of "usual course of business" writing (informal exemplars) prepared about the same time as the questioned document. The other includes samples taken under direction, called "requested writing" (or formal exemplars). The informal exemplars contain normal handwriting patterns with their variations in writing characteristics. They do not contain the elements of self-consciousness found in the requested writing samples. A combination of both kinds of exemplars is the most effective when someone is accused of writing the questioned materials. If disguise is found on formal exemplars, the informal exemplars will show the type of disguise. It is highly suspicious if the suspect cannot produce informal writing samples. For example, a defendant who has recently completed college should be able to find class notes.

If both sides of an issue call document examiners, they should be provided with the same type and quantity of comparison materials. Many examinations begin with a study of photocopies because the original documents might not be available in the early stages of the investigation. This examination may be enough to reach a conclusion or provide preliminary information when there is an obvious forgery. Most often the document examiner qualifies his or her opinion pending an examination of the original document. For most situations, it is necessary to examine the original document if it exists. This is especially true for examination of medical records or documents where there is a suspicion of alterations, and where the fluency of writing, as seen in the smoothness of the ink lines, is the critical factor.

The inability to produce an original document can work in favor of the defendant. In one case, the original check in question had been microfilmed and then destroyed. Since it was not possible to be certain from the copy of the microfilm whether the defendant had written the endorsement, the prosecutor had to drop charges.

Prepare for Trial

When preparing for a hearing or trial, the discovery process helps both sides learn what evidence is to be presented. Document examiners use professionally prepared exhibits to show how a record has been altered or forged. This demonstration has a tremendous impact on a jury, especially when they have just heard the witness innocently claim its authenticity.

A document examiner can play one or more roles when a case proceeds to a hearing or trial. The company may use an expert to prove that the writing is a forgery and may try to show who did the forgery. While uncommon, there may be disagreement by experts about whose writing is on the document. One may approach the question from a different perspective than the other. For example, in one case concerning an endorsement on a check, the prosecution's expert was not certain whether the defendant wrote the endorsement of the payee. The defense expert testified that the writing was done in an "off-hand" script and did not appear contrived to make it look as though someone else had written it. Fortunately for the defense, the prosecutor did not ask the expert whether she thought that the defendant wrote the endorsement.

A company might consult with an expert merely to help with the cross-examination of an opposing witness. While an expert who only partially agrees with an opposing expert's opinion seldom testifies, the expert's help can be useful to create doubt. With the consultation of his expert, a defense attorney studied handwriting identification and comparison thoroughly in preparation of his cross-examination of the prosecution's expert. He was successful in challenging inconsistencies in the expert's testimony about the handwriting features, resulting in acquittal for his client.

Courtroom tactics for document cases require thorough preparation to understand the writing process and reasons for disagreement, if any. This preparation gives depth both to direct- and cross-examinations. Without adequate preparation, there is a risk of opening doors for an opposing expert to reinforce his or her findings and to leave the company's expert dangling instead of being able to neutralize an otherwise effective cross-examination.

Every attorney knows that it is dangerous to ask a question when there is doubt concerning the answer. As with the examination of any witness, this tactic can backfire in document cases. A prime example happened in a murder case when the defense attorney asked one dangerous question. The preliminary examination had taken place from photocopies, with a brief study of the original document directly before the trial. In an effort to discredit the examination as not being thorough enough, the defense attorney asked, "How can you make that determination from such a short study of the original document?" The reply was simply, "It was so obvious."

Some successful challenges to document examiners' testimony have attacked handwriting comparison on the grounds that it is not an "exact science." Scientific tests are used for document examination in general, ink identification, paper analysis, and many types of alterations. While there are measurable handwriting features and reasonable scientific procedures, there are aspects of document examination that are more interpretive than others. Slant, proportions of letters, spacing between letters and words, width of letters or parts of letters, and baseline stability are measurable features. Rhythm, pictorial quality, speed and fluency of writing are interpreted in their interaction as a whole within the signature.

Other successful challenges have been ego attacks. *What* an attorney asks is directly related to *how* he asks it. Some witnesses, for example, find it difficult to answer the question, "Have you ever been wrong?" They believe they should be super-human and not admit to ever having made a mistake. As a result, they may become defensive on the witness stand and their credibility suffers.

Another area of attack of experts is in regard to their credentials. Government and prosecution document examiners receive their training in crime or police laboratories, while independent examiners have diverse backgrounds. The important selection criteria is the depth of training, the reputation, and the skill of the examiner in presenting evidence. Because there is no standard curriculum for becoming a document examiner, professional organizations strive to maintain high standards for their members through testing. The Association of Forensic Document Examiners (AFDE), for example, subjects candidates for certification to strenuous testing that includes both oral and written examinations, development of a model case,

review of qualifications by a panel of judges and a mock trial presentation to a lay jury. No member of AFDE is "grandfathered" into the organization. The American Academy of Forensic Sciences, whose membership is limited to people from law enforcement, also tests candidates for certification. Neither organization recognizes graphology, the study of handwriting for personality assessment, as training in document examination.

When in trial, how is the credibility of an expert established? To minimize the expert's impact, the weak points of the opinion, if any, are brought out on direct examination. One possible explanation for a slightly qualified opinion may be that the questioned material is limited in some way. Another obstacle to a definite conclusion might be that the original documents are not available until directly before trial, comparison samples are limited in quantity or quality, or there are some unexplainable variations in the writing.

In criminal defense, it is only necessary to create reasonable doubt. To accomplish this, the expert for the defense will emphasize the points that will create that doubt.

The case examples and guidance in this article provide a basis for recognizing forgeries and alterations, for working with a document examiner, and for cross-examination of an opposing expert.

Bonnie Schwid

FRAUD: DETECTION IN THE CORPORATE ENVIRONMENT

Fraud is a generic term that encompasses all manner and forms of intentional deception. Lying, cheating, embezzlement, and theft are vernacular forms of fraud.

In the corporate context, fraud can be categorized as being internal (committed by insiders, i.e., officers, directors, employees, and agents) and external (committed by outsiders, i.e., vendors, contractors, and suppliers). Corporate fraud can also be classified as to those committed by insiders against the company (theft, corruption, and embezzlement) and those committed by insiders for the company (violation of government regulations, i.e., tax, securities, safety, and environmental laws).

In a causative context, fraud is both personal and environmental. For example, fraud perpetrators are generally motivated by economic need or greed. Environmental factors that breed internal fraud and create opportunities for embezzlement and theft include lax accounting controls and loose moral standards among the members of senior management.

Corporate frauds are often detected by accounting discrepancies noted by internal auditors and by allegations of theft, corruption, or embezzlement received by security investigators. Frauds perpetrated by senior management involve the misrepresentation of facts in financial statements.   In such cases, there may be overstatements of assets, sales, and profit, or understatements of liabilities, expenses, and losses.   Senior managers might perpetrate financial statement frauds to deceive investors and lenders, or to inflate profits and thereby gain higher salaries and bonuses.

Frauds committed by low-level employees include such techniques as falsifying expense reports and benefit claims, embezzling funds, using corporate property for personal purposes, stealing corporate property, and accepting gratuities from vendors, contractors, and suppliers. Low-level frauds are often called transaction frauds, as distinguished from fraud in financial statements mentioned previously.

Transaction frauds are most likely to occur in environments in which motives, opportunities, means, and methods abound. The following conditions indicate a high level of risk for transaction frauds.

1.   Internal controls are absent, weak, or loosely enforced.

2.   Employees are hired without due consideration for their honesty and integrity.

3.   Employees are poorly managed, exploited, abused, or placed under great stress to accomplish financial goals and objectives.

4.   Management models are themselves corrupt, inefficient, or incompetent.

5.   A trusted employee has an insoluble personal problem, usually of a financial nature, brought on by family medical needs, or alcoholism, drug abuse, excessive gambling, or expensive tastes.

6.   The industry of which the company is a part has a history or tradition of corruption.

7.   The company has fallen on bad times, i.e., is losing money or market share, or its products or services are becoming passé.

8.   Internal audit resources are inadequate.

9.   Security resources are inadequate.

How to Discern and Detect Corporate Fraud

Corporate fraud discernment and detection is as much a mindset as it is a methodology. There is no simple cookbook recipe for conducting a fraud audit, nor are there any generally accepted checklists or patterned interviews. Fraud is a human phenomenon. Humans vary a great deal as do frauds in terms of the techniques used, but accounting "red flags" do give off some inkling of fraud, for example:

- Adjusting journal entries that lack authorization and supporting details
- Expenditures that lack supporting documents
- False and improper entries in books of account
- Unauthorized payments
- Unauthorized use of corporate assets
- Misapplications of corporate funds
- Destruction, counterfeiting, and forgery of documents that support payments

In the process of committing such frauds, certain account balances may be overstated or understated. If the amount of the over- or understatement is small, detection will be difficult. The detection method is based on variance or exception notions of accounting. Expectations of normal ranges are established for each account balance; and when variances are beyond the bounds of the expected high and low range, the account balance is flagged for further review and analysis.

For example, in the accompanying chart, review the cost of sales and gross profit, and what do you find? The probability that any business's gross profit would more than double (20% to 31%) in 3 years when sales rose much more modestly is highly remote, unless the nature of its products and their markups changed dramatically or competition has changed dramatically (fewer competitors).

While the relationship between sales and cost of sales is not a fixed or constant relationship, the wide variances, as set forth previously, should cause an auditor to wonder what underlies such a gap. Some auditors call the monitoring of such gaps "red flags." They do not prove fraud, but they do indicate that something in the cost of sales is out of whack. The gap may suggest that sales are overstated, returns and allowances are understated, or the account components of cost of sales are misstated; that is, purchases and freight

	Year 1	Year 2	Year 3	Year 4
Sales	5,000	6,000	7,000	8,000
Cost of Sales	4,000	4,500	5,000	5,500
Gross Profit	1,000	1,500	2,000	2,500
Gross Profit/Sales Ratio	20.0%	25.0%	28.5%	31.0%
Sales Increase—Year-to-Year		20.0%	14.0%	12.5%
Gross Profit Increase—YTY		50.0%	33.0%	25.0%
Sales Increase over Base Year		20.0%	40.0%	60.0%
Gross Profit Increase over Base Year		50.0%	100%	150%

in are understated, ending inventory is overstated. At any rate, it is time for the auditor to probe more deeply.

Here are a few questions that can raise red flags:

1. Is profit the only corporate objective and the only criterion for performance appraisal?
2. Is the corporate culture one in which profit and economic incentives are the only motivators?
3. Is there an effective code of corporate conduct?
4. Are controls monitored for compliance?
5. Are complaints from customers, stockholders, employees, and vendors ignored?
6. Is there a reliable mechanism for examining overrides by management of internal controls?

When an allegation of employee fraud, theft, embezzlement, or corruption is received by a corporate security investigator, procedures should include:

• Assessing credibility of the complainant and the plausibility of his or her charges.

• Determining whether testimonial, documentary, and demonstrative evidence is available to support the allegation.

• Preparing a report of the facts as determined thus far and submitting same to in-house counsel for permission to open an active case.

• Determining investigative needs for other areas of expertise, i.e., auditing, computer programming, legal, handwriting and questioned document analysis, polygraph testing, and so on.

• Forming an investigative team and conducting investigations and/or audits.

Detecting Commercial Bribery

Compromising the decision or judgment of someone who has a legal, moral, or fiduciary duty to remain faithful and free of corruption is called bribery. In the typical commercial bribery situation, an outside vendor, supplier, or contractor curries favor with an inside person who has authority to make or recommend a purchase decision by offering or giving something of value to that person. Under these circumstances, both the payer and payee have a reason to conceal the transaction--the giver, because such a payment may be a crime and non-deductible; the recipient, because such receipt may be a crime and may constitute taxable income.

In each case of bribery, there is a likelihood of companion crimes, such as making false statements and false entries, and evading taxes. The concealment efforts are intended to disguise the true nature of the payment and conceal the true identities of the recipient and payer of the bribe.

Commercial bribery takes many disguised forms, e.g., the giving and accepting of cash, property, or privilege under the guise of a fee, wage, commission, charitable contribution, free sample, gift, gratuity, entertainment, loan, debt payment, free use of a vehicle, vacation home, free travel, token of remembrance, or procurement of "evening companions." The essence of commercial bribery is that a victimized firm is paying more than fair market value for the products and services it requires or getting inferior quality and untimely performance.

Proving bribery in a criminal case is no mean task, given the concealment options available to the bribe giver and bribe taker. Both are inclined to seal their lips. So how does one go about testing for and proving bribery? Several audit and investigative steps in the case of a victimized company follow:

•Analyze expense categories that are running higher than: (1) expectations, (2) cost assumptions, and (3) long-term trends; then review the documentation that supports these expenditures for evidence of contrivance.

•Check for previous allegations or complaints of payment, or receipt of bribes involving the purchasing official and vendor.

•Check for evidence of high living by the alleged bribe receiver.

•Seek out other vendors whose bids to the company have been consistently rejected even though their prices and performance appear to be competitive and comparable.

•Check for vendors whose price, quality, and performance records are consistently below standards and yet continue to get business from the firm.

Jack Bologna

FRAUD: PREVENTION AND DETECTION

There are really only two principles behind all the things we do to prevent and detect fraud. The first is that of personal accountability. It states that every sensitive transaction must be positively identified with at least one named individual. An audit trail is then the sequence of personalized transactions concerning the acquisition or disposition of some company asset.

The use of passwords, checksums, and codes are techniques that ensure the personalization of transactions. These procedures are designed so that transactions can be carried out quickly and easily by authorized, and hence named, persons;

but only with great difficulty, if at all, by unauthorized persons.

The second principle is that of forced collusion. It requires that two authorized persons participate in at least the most sensitive transactions. It rests on the premise that it is harder to subvert two people than one. This principle is reflected in the requirement for double signatures on checks, use of two keys in safety deposit boxes, never-alone-zones such as currency packaging rooms, double sign-off on security-relevant changes to computer programs, and two witnesses to the destruction of redeemed bonds.

Both these principles lead to making it more difficult, and expensive, to commit crimes (i.e., sharing the loot with more confederates, or paying more in bribes to get passwords). The rationale is that good security will make it so uneconomical for criminals to attack a company's assets that they will go elsewhere or desist altogether.

Incidentally, this is the difference between commercial crime and national security. Measures that deter thieves by making it uneconomical to steal may not deter adversaries who act from motives of patriotism or ideological conviction.

The essence of control in any large company today is control of the data-processing (DP) department. At the heart of the matter is the uncomfortable fact that DP personnel tend to identify more with their function than with the business of the company they work for. For example, in a bank, most employees regard themselves as bankers, while the DP staffers tend to regard themselves as computer people who happen to work in a bank.

For this reason, it is essential that the relationship between the DP department and the users of its services be formalized and that responsibilities be fixed for the security of data at the time it is delivered to the DP department for processing; for the security of reports at the time they are returned to the user; and for specification of the processing operations to be performed, including direct liability for loss, compromise, or error.

Today, many of the assets of the company may reside exclusively in machine-readable media: customer lists, invoices, marketing plans, and money itself. It is within the computer that changes of policy are actualized. Through the computer must flow the documents that determine the profit position of the firm. If top management loses control of the DP department, it loses control of the enterprise.

The history of computer abuse is replete with incidents where tapes containing employee names and addresses were surreptitiously supplied to union business agents for use in organizing drives, or where lists of shareholders were supplied to persons preparing a tender offer as part of an attempt to take over control of the corporation.

If some subordinate operating arm of a company is placed in a position where it can exercise undue control over the DP department, the resulting advantage it would be able to realize over other divisions could distort its relative position to the detriment of overall corporate planning.

Preventive Steps

There are at least four things that should be done routinely to help in the prevention or detection of fraud:

1.   Maintain systems and programs effectively. No item of DP equipment should be left in service with an uncorrected mechanical or electrical defect, especially when such a defect might affect a protective mechanism. Nor should a computer program having known logical errors be left in use. Such programs can give erroneous and unexpected results that may aid the depredations of an embezzler or unlawful user.

2.   Prevent and detect accidental errors. There is no way to tell whether an erroneous or unexpected result arises from accidental error or from deliberate falsification. Such falsification may be undertaken either to facilitate a defalcation, or to erase traces of one. Further, a so-called "error" can, in some cases, facilitate a defalcation by creating a distraction, or by forcing the bypassing or exposure of a protective mechanism.

3.   Prevent fraudulent manipulation of data or misuse of classified information.

4.   Prevent accidental destruction of records; ensure continuous operation. The only way to avoid accidental destruction of records is to store backup copies in a secure off-site location; otherwise operators may thoughtlessly spoil all the copies in abortive attempts to correct a systems malfunction or "bug." If backup tapes are not immediately accessible, machine-room

personnel will be forced to follow proper procedures and use simulated data while the error is being located and corrected.

Separation of Duties

A key factor in maintaining control over DP is to make sure that no one person, or clique, possesses detailed knowledge of the entire operation. There should be both spatial and functional separation of duties.

Incoming and outgoing mail rooms should be separated so clerks cannot intercept remittances and mail them home.

The functions of programming and machine operation should be separated so a programmer cannot insert codes that would cause the computer to print extra checks and then pick them up when he runs the program.

A tape librarian should keep custody of software and data so a third-shift machine operator can't make an unauthorized copy of a valuable mailing list without leaving evidence of having signed the tape out of the library.

Involving two or more persons in every sensitive action may not ensure that no unauthorized actions will occur, but it almost guarantees that someday the truth will come out.

John M. Carroll

Source Carroll, J.M., Controlling White Collar Crime. (Butterworth-Heinemann, Boston, 1982).

FREEDOM OF INFORMATION ACT (FOIA)

The Freedom of Information Act (FOIA) of 1966 [1] is a federal statute that grants access to public documents and is based on the belief that:

•An informed electorate is essential to safeguard democracy;

•Publicity is a protection against potential official misconduct;

•Privacy is a fundamental right and corresponds with a need to restrict government's intrusions into a private individual's affairs; and

•Secrecy is part of bureaucracy and may not facilitate organizational efficiency.

The FOIA evolved from three prior laws. A housekeeping statute, originally passed in 1789, gave each department head authority to "preserve regulations for the government of his department" by setting up filing and record keeping systems [2].

The Administrative Procedure Act (APA) of 1946 required that agencies publish information about their organization, powers, procedures, substantive rules, and final opinions or orders in adjudicated decisions [3]. In 1958, the APA was amended to prevent agencies from withholding information [4] and was subsequently amended by the FOIA.

The FOIA requires that all federal agency documents be publicly disclosed unless exempted. Documents described as "rules of procedure" must be published in the *Federal Register* [5]. Final opinions or orders in adjudicated agency decisions, agency policy statements and interpretations, and staff instructions affecting the public must also be available [6]. If the requested documents are exempted from disclosure, the agency need not make them available [7].

The exemptions most relevant involve those relating to confidential, commercial, or financial material [8], inter-agency or intra-agency memoranda or letters [9], personal and medical files or similar files the disclosure of which would constitute a clear unwarranted privacy invasion [10], and investigatory records compiled for law enforcement purposes [11]. Although agencies are not required to disclose information that is statutorily exempted [12], they may elect to divulge material [13].

The FOIA's interpretation in the employment privacy context poses special problems because its full disclosure policy conflicts with policies underlying other employment statutes [14]. For example, this conflict may arise under the National Labor Relations Act (NLRA) regarding the NLRA's confidentiality interest to safeguard employee rights. Problems may arise out of releasing witness testimony prior to an unfair labor practice hearing [15], or disclosing authorization cards as part of a representation election [16].

Kurt H. Decker

Sources

Decker, K., Employee Privacy Law and Procedures. (John Wiley & Sons, Inc., New York, 1987).

Decker, K., Employee Privacy Forms and Procedures. (John Wiley & Sons, Inc., New York, 1988).

Decker, K., A Manager's Guide to Employee Privacy Laws, Procedures, and Policies. (John Wiley & Sons, Inc., New York, 1989).

Decker, K., The Rights and Wrongs of Screening. (Security Management, January, 1990).

Notes

1. 5 U.S.C. § 552 (1988).
2. 5 U.S.C. § 22 (1964); recodified as 5 U.S.C. § 301 (1988).
3. 5 U.S.C. §§ 1002-1003 (1964); recodified as 5 U.S.C. § 552 (1988).
4. 5 U.S.C. § 22 (1964); recodified as 5 U.S.C. § 301 (1988).
5. 5 U.S.C. § 552(a)(1) (1988).
6. Id. § 552(a)(3).
7. Id. § 552(b) (after deletion of exempt material, the agency is required to disclose any remaining "reasonably segregatable portion").
[8] Id. § 552(b)(4) (this exemption provides that the FOIA shall not apply to "trade secret and commercial or financial information obtained from a person and privileged or confidential").
9. Id. § 552(b)(5) (this exemption provides that the FOIA shall not apply to "inter-agency or intra-agency memorandums or letters that would not be available by law to a party other than an agency in litigation with the agency").
10. Id. § 552(b)(6).
11. Id. § 552(b)(7) (this exemption shields investigatory records compiled for law enforcement purposes only to the extent that disclosure would cause one of six specified harms).
12. Id. § 552(b).
13. See *Chrysler Corp. v. Brown*, 441 U.S. 281, 293 (1979) (the "FOIA by itself protects the...[private entity's] interest in confidentiality only to the extent that this interest is endorsed by the agency collecting the information," and it held that there is no private right of action to enjoin information disclosure by a government agency).
14. See e.g., 29 U.S.C. §§ 151-169 (1988) (National Labor Relations Act).
15. See *NLRB v. Robbins Tire & Rubber*, 437 U.S. 214 (1978) (NLRB not required to release witness testimony prior to a hearing).
16. See *Committee on Masonic Homes v. NLRB*, 556 F.2d 214 (3d Cir. 1977) (NLRB not required to release authorization cards).

G

GOALS AND OBJECTIVES

Managers use goals and objectives in mission statements, business planning, project management, budgeting, and the human performance appraisal process. Goals and objectives are important in any management system (i.e., planning, organizing, controlling, directing and leading, evaluating, communicating, and reporting and feedback). Most prominently, they are the key in the planning and evaluation processes.

Definitions

The terms "goals" and "objectives" are often used interchangeably. However, they are not the same:

1. A goal, when distinguished from the term "objective," is usually a "longer-term, broader statement of intent" [1] used to describe broad ends.

2. An objective is a "specific description of an end result to be achieved. It should tell what (the end result), when (a target date or target period), and who (who is accountable for the objective)" [2].

Uses of Goals and Objectives

Managing an Organization. A systems approach to management that requires the establishment of well-defined objectives is known as management by objectives (MBO). This approach includes establishing overall objectives and priorities for a given organization in a given time period, requiring key personnel to contribute to achieving the objectives, assuring that planned results and key personnel performance are integrated to achieve organizational results, and controlling the process so that progress is monitored and feedback is provided to those accountable for the results [3]. This approach emphasizes management and the management process, but particularly planning. Strategic, long-range, or short-term plans must all have goals and objectives; i.e., broad directives, intent, vision, and narrower specific end-results to be achieved in the

planning period. For whatever reason a business plan is written (marketing, production, engineering, emergencies, etc.), the goals set the vision, and the objectives are the specific results that must be obtained to achieve success. Under MBO theory, planning is the most critical element of a management system and is the means by which the management system is implemented, because planning helps an organization determine what it must do during a given time frame, and drives the manner in which results are achieved [4]. The information sources at the end of this article provide further reading on this subject.

Budgeting is a clear-cut example of how goals and objectives are used in management systems. Budgets, by their nature, specify quantitatively what the end result is to be (e.g., $1 million net income, 5.6% return on investment), the period of expected performance, and who is responsible.

Managing a Project. After requirements for a project are determined, the objectives are defined and are used to specify the actions to be accomplished within a given period to achieve the end products of the project (i.e., the deliverables).

Measuring Employee Performance. In the performance evaluation process, objectives are established as standards of performance in individual performance plans. Objectives are the means by which required actions are documented and the standards against which performance is measured. Success or failure depends on the individual's meeting the objectives stated in the performance plan; outputs such as rewards, bonuses, pay raises, or removal are dependent on meeting, or failing to meet, the performance objectives.

To be effective, the objectives stated in an individual's performance plan should support organizational objectives (that is, the sum of the individuals should equal the whole), should use measurable standards of performance, and should be derived by agreement between the individual and his/her manager.

Writing Goals and Objectives

In the simplest terms, goals are concise statements of a vision. (For example, "We will strive to have a security program that, at all times, is state-of-the-art and provides the best available

IF THE GOAL IS TO...	AN OBJECTIVE MIGHT BE TO...
•Protect company personnel	•Reduce simple assaults that occur on company property 30 percent by December 31
•Operate a state-of-the-art security electronic security system	•Design, procure, and install an exterior intrusion detection system that has a 95 percent probability of detection at a 90 percent confidence level around Building A by January 1, 1994
•Increase the cost-effectiveness of security force operations	•Restructure the security force so there is an operating cost reduction of 5 percent during the next fiscal year
•Enhance liaison with local law enforcement agencies	•Develop a plan for local law enforcement liaison that is fully coordinated with city, county, and state officials by June; implement the plan within 30 days of approval
•Upgrade training of security force personnel	•Perform a job task analysis, develop performance objectives, revise the curriculum, and develop revised lesson plans and testing materials that reflect revised procedures by the end of the fiscal year; implement the training program six months later
•Increase educational levels of security administrative and management personnel	•In the next fiscal year, make provisions in performance plans for security administrative and supervisory personnel that assure they all have at least an associate degree within three years
•Increase communication between security personnel and company staff	•Develop and distribute a bimonthly security newsletter to company staff, beginning next fiscal year.

combination of personnel, hardware, procedures, and cost-effective use of resources to ensure that all assets are effectively protected from known threats.") They are broad statements of what an organization, program, or system will be. On a continuum, goals are between ideals (which may never be achieved) and objectives (which should be achieved, in accord with certain standards, within a given period). Goals should be challenging, yet attainable, although the time frame for achievement may or may not be specified.

On the other hand, objectives should be specific, measurable, attainable, realistic, and time-based. As such, they contain elements of quantity, quality, cost, and time. They should contain an action verb and should describe the activity to be accomplished and the results expected in the specified time frame. However, objectives do not specify how results will be achieved. Although objectives must be measurable, they may still be qualitative.

The accompanying examples of goals and objectives reveal the principles discussed earlier:

Goals and objectives are tools that have a variety of purposes for managers. They are critical to planning and are used to measure performance and the degree to which there is success or failure in any business undertaking. They can be developed for entire organizations, organizational elements, projects, and individuals or work groups. Well-thought-out goals and objectives are the foundation of a management system. Without them, any business or management venture will not have a sense of direction or purpose, and overall effectiveness will be reduced considerably.

Dale A. Moul

Sources

Guidelines for Strategic Planning, DOE/PE-0099. (U.S. Department of Energy, Office of Policy, Planning and Analysis, Washington, DC, July, 1991).

Hughes, C.L., Goal Setting: Key to Individual and Organizational Effectiveness. (American Management Association, New York, 1965).

King, W.R., and D.I. Cleland, Strategic Planning and Policy. (Van Nostrand Reinhold Co., New York, 1978).

Lynch, R.G., Management by Objectives, in Fennelly, L.J. (Editor), Handbook of Loss Prevention and Crime Prevention. (Butterworth-Heinemann, Boston, 1982).

McConkey, D.D., MBO for Nonprofit Organizations. (AMACOM, New York, 1975).

McConkey, D.D., How to Manage by Results, 4th Edition. (AMACOM, New York, 1983).

Mali, P., Management Handbook: Operating Guidelines, Techniques and Practices. (John Wiley & Sons, New York, 1981).

Mali, P., MBO Updated. (John Wiley & Sons, New York, 1986).

Odiorne, G.S., MBO II: A System of Managerial Leadership for the 80s. (Fearon Pitman Publishers, Belmont, CA, 1979).

Odiorne, G.S., MBO and Strategic Planning, in Mali, P., Management Handbook: Operating Guidelines, Techniques and Practices. (John Wiley & Sons, New York, 1981).

Pritchard, R.D., et al., Designing a Goal-Setting System to Enhance Performance: A Practical Guide. (Organizational Dynamics, Summer, 1988), pp. 69-78.

Notes

1. Dale D. McConkey, MBO for Nonprofit Organizations, AMACOM, New York, 1975, p. 213.

2. Ibid., p. 53.

3. Dale D. McConkey, How to Manage by Results, 4th Edition, AMACOM, New York, 1983, p. 18.

4. Ibid., p. 36.

GRAFFITI

Companies spend enormous amounts of money to remove graffiti. Writing can be merely a prank or may represent a more serious condition. Increasingly, companies are seeking to identify the perpetrators for discipline and as a deterrent for other employees. They are also looking for alternatives for people to find less destructive outlets for their frustrations or artistic talents. This section addresses some of the reasons people write or draw on company property, describes how to work with a document examiner to identify the author, and discusses possible actions a company might take to reduce the incidence of graffiti.

People draw or write on walls or other places when they are dissatisfied with company policy, feeling that they are being treated unfairly, angry about a co-worker or supervisor's behavior toward them, or, as when the drawings are found in rest rooms, when they just want to doodle without being identified. Many times they do not even consider or care that they are defacing property, and may draw on the walls just because others have done it. When gang members draw graffiti it is more of a territorial claim and their way of letting their presence be known to other gangs. Some graffiti is merely a prank to see if they can get away with it. For example, writing names on upper floors of buildings or other public property has been a challenge from time immemorial.

The most common location in a building for off-hand drawings and messages is in rest rooms, with men's rest rooms far outpacing the women's rest rooms for offensiveness, especially in the stall next to the toilet. Graffiti is also found extensively on lockers and walls of lounge areas. If little or no action is taken by the company, these activities seem to escalate, resulting in extensive property damage. Materials used most often include spray paint, lipstick, or magic markers. Other graffiti may be scratched into a car or wall with a sharp instrument or written on other surfaces, including propane tanks, machinery, cardboard packing boxes, and apartment walls.

Some types of graffiti include curt messages, possibly with discussions of the sexual prowess of certain men or women. Graphic designs often accompany the writing. If left in place, the messages are answered and a written dialog takes place. This type is considered "pastime graffiti." The writing or printing is not highly disguised as a rule, and the quantity of writing may be too limited to lend itself to identification. As the messages get longer and more expressive, however, it usually becomes easier to identify the writers.

One example of graffiti was found at a school. When the librarian was preparing to show a movie, she opened the projection screen and was mortified to find lewd remarks about her. Fortunately, she found the remarks before the students came into the room. The principal called in a document examiner, who studied the printing on most of the employee files and was able to identify the writer partly because of a unique formation of the letter "I." The writer confessed and was terminated immediately.

Graffiti is distinguished from anonymous or threatening letters because threatening letters are generally sent directly to the target person or written about a specific person, whereas graffiti tends to be less personal. When the graffiti is directed at a person or department, it is different from handwritten anonymous letters only by the fact that it is more public and visible.

Sexual harassment is currently a hot topic. A company that does not do everything it can to find out who writes notes or draws on walls about an employee runs the risk of being targeted and sued as contributing to the harassment. More

women than men are the target of this sort of harassment, but men are not immune.

What can the security manager do to help identify the person and work with the personnel department to prevent further graffiti? What do you look for when comparing writings, and what are some remedies that have been taken by companies? How can a forensic document examiner help you with the investigation?

The security manager will begin with his or her own investigation as to which employees are the most likely suspects. When this information is collected, the next step is to call in a reliable forensic document examiner.

A forensic document examiner is a scientist trained to compare and identify handwriting or hand printing, differentiate inks, compare typewriters, and detect and decipher alterations to documents. Additional training is focused on the presentation of evidence in hearings or trials.

To locate a qualified document examiner (commonly referred to as a handwriting expert), most security managers rely on recommendations of others who have had similar experiences. Carefully study their qualifications. Are they experienced with the study of handwriting? Are they members of a reputable professional organization? Have their expertise and skill been tested by their peers and by examining boards? Are they able to demonstrate their findings clearly and convincingly?

Training for document examiners is achieved in one of two ways. A person can apprentice in a law enforcement laboratory for several years or can study handwriting from many perspectives before learning the forensic terminology and methods. The aptitude, integrity, and skill of the individual is the key to effectiveness, whichever method of training received. Two recognized examining boards are the Association of Forensic Document Examiners, which has rigorous training and testing requirements, and the American Academy of Forensic Document Examiners, which has a testing program generally limited to law enforcement personnel.

You can photograph the graffiti if it is so offensive that your management wants it erased or painted over immediately, even before contacting a competent document examiner. That way you will preserve the evidence in case it is changed or obliterated. A black and white or color photograph that includes a measuring scale such as a ruler is appropriate. Including the scale is a required forensic technique that shows both the relative and absolute size of the letters or picture. This evidence may be needed for a hearing or disciplinary meeting, so the rules of evidence concerning proportion and scale should be met.

When you call a document examiner, he or she will most likely want to review employee files of anyone who could be connected to the graffiti. As an example, an irate customer returned a diaper to the company that had manufactured it. The diaper had a silly, but offensive, note on it about the breath of an employee of the company, naming her. The diaper was sent to a document examiner who requested writing and printing from all of the employees who could have been even remotely involved. From this sampling, the field was narrowed to one whose writing and printing were clearly the same as that on the diaper and who had worked the same shift as the person named. Just when testimony was about to be presented in an arbitration hearing, the employee who was about to be identified stipulated to the writing. It seems that she and the person she wrote about were in the habit of writing notes to each other, then destroying the diapers when the shift was over. Unfortunately for them and the company, they forgot to destroy this diaper and one other. That other one was not returned to the highly embarrassed company.

For general graffiti, document examiners begin with a study of the content and context of the writing or drawing. They look for the general style of writing and then look for how and in what ways the writing has been personalized. Unique letters or combinations of letters are the most identifiable components of the writing.

Letter formations found in the graffiti do not necessarily have to exactly match those found in the comparison writing, as a person's writing has some natural variation to it, but there is a consistency of style throughout all of the writing that is used as the basis for the identification. If the graffiti is not very expressive and has only general writing characteristics or is printed rather than written, it may become even more difficult to positively identify the person. Conditions and context are also considered. In one case, a person who was accused of murdering his wife and then writing on a wall, was given a blank paper and asked to write on it by placing it on the wall in his prison cell. Not only was the style of writing analyzed, but also the height of where he placed

the paper on the wall was considered. Therefore, if you are trying to identify a person who wrote on a building or inside wall, take the height of the writing into consideration. Who is tall enough to write at this height? People seldom bend down or use a ladder to write on a wall as this takes time and draws attention.

The list of possible suspects often can be narrowed through interviews with the personnel officer about which employees might be involved because they have disciplinary problems or have made antagonistic remarks. In addition, an investigation of the content of personnel files may reveal information about possible writers. For example, one particularly offensive drawing that was much too graphic to describe or display, was drawn with a felt tip pen and was highly detailed. The document examiner studied personnel files of the people who had most frequent access to the men's room involved and discovered an employee who filled out his application with a felt tip pen, punctuated carefully, and mentioned that he was enrolled in art classes. While it was not possible to identify him directly from the drawing, he became a strong suspect. The human resource director watched him more carefully than usual and found that he stayed out for a long time when he took breaks. Based on this and other evidence, she confronted him and obtained a confession. Because it was a union issue, the appropriate discipline was taken and the drawing stopped. The discipline also acted as a deterrent to others who might consider drawing their own pictures or enhancing his.

In addition to personnel materials, any other writing by the suspect can help the document examiner. Be sure you know your company's policy about rummaging through desk drawers and waste baskets, however, before you take that route. Some cases require personnel files of several people who possibly might be involved for a more objective analysis. This way you cannot be accused of creating bias for the document examiner. Frequently the document examiner will take samples written by the suspect in their presence to watch for elements of disguise.

What can companies do to prevent graffiti? By making it known that the act will not be tolerated and using its resources to identify the culprit, the incidence of graffiti has been reduced for many companies. Other companies have installed erasable writing boards in the stalls of the rest rooms and have initiated programs to elevate the awareness of the employees about pride in their surroundings. Open grievance options have also helped. The "handwriting may be on the wall," but with diligence, perhaps it can be eliminated.

Bonnie Schwid

H

HACKING

The large number of personal computers in the hands of the public has led to the prevalence of hacking, electronic trespass into the computer systems remotely accessible by telephone lines. Hackers are typically young, male computer enthusiasts (they range in age from 8 to 39 with the average age 14 to 15). They make a game out of defeating access-control systems. They are often loosely organized into clubs or circles. They exchange experiences and information through hacker boards -- free, privately operated electronic bulletin board services (BBS) accessible by persons with home computers capable of connecting to telephone lines.

Hackers sometimes do damage: wiping out on-line files, changing passwords so legitimate users are denied access, stealing credit card numbers and using them to obtain goods and services, and crashing systems. They constitute a vast computer underground, even conducting "tele-trials" of people who have offended them. One reporter critical of hackers was tried, convicted, and sentenced to "electronic death." The hackers were reported to have arranged to have his telephone, gas, and electricity turned off, flooded him with unordered mail-order merchandise, and fraudulently obtained his credit report and posted it on bulletin boards.

Hackers also often obtain long-distance telephone service free by using techniques such as boxing (using hardware devices or computer programs to generate the musical tones the telephone company uses to open access to long-distance trunks), stealing telephone credit card numbers, using telephone company lingo to deceive operators into thinking they are company employees making official calls, or fraudulently obtaining access codes to long-distance services.

The first thing the hacker has to know is a computer's telephone number. Most system managers wisely avoid publishing these numbers. Hackers sometimes call on public lines, however, and deceive secretaries by claiming to be legitimate users who have forgotten the number. The hacker may enter the premises with a big envelope and claim to be a private courier and then read the number off a telephone instrument.

Or, he can don olive coveralls, enter a telephone closet or vault, clip a lineman's test handset across any pair (or all pairs, if time permits) of terminals bearing red tags, dial the local ANI (automatic number identification) number, and listen while a computer-generated voice tells him the number.

If deception or penetration does not work, the hacker may obtain an autodialer and program his personal computer to record the number dialed if answered by a 1,000- or 2,000-hertz tone. Hackers do not have to dial all 10,000 numbers in the telephone exchange; computer numbers are rarely more than plus or minus 200 numbers removed from a company's published number.

Telephone Protection Devices

Devices are available that may foil the hacker who scans a telephone exchange to get computer telephone numbers. No device will help if employees are disloyal and give out the numbers, let themselves be deceived, or let unauthorized persons roam around the premises at will.

The silent answer/callback modem is a protective device. When somebody dials into a computer, it does not answer with its high-pitched tone; it does not even get the call. Instead, an intelligent modem answers with a synthetic voice and requests the user's access code (usually a four-digit number). A microprocessor checks it against a prestored list. If it is valid, the modem hangs up and calls the user back on the officially listed number (also prestored). Then the usual log-in procedure begins.

Some hackers have defeated the callback technique by call forwarding. Every telephone exchange has a test and service number. Those familiar with the procedure can deceive the operator (or computer) who answers into honoring a request to forward all calls to a given number to a different number. Provided the hacker has the user's access code, he or she will be called back on a phone under his or her control. The callback ritual can be awkward for sales representatives or executives reporting in. The best way to accommodate them is to have a schedule of time windows at which they will be allowed to log-in without callback. Employees who call in from cars may be vulnerable to interception by persons who monitor the VHF mobile radiotelephone frequencies (for example, 153 megahertz) with scanners; the same is true for executives who call in from yachts, except that the marine radiotelephone frequencies are in the 2 to 3 megahertz band. Cellular phones, operating around 890 megahertz, are also vulnerable.

Protection by Passwords

The second line of defense is the password. The hacker's usual way of breaching this defense is to steal or guess the password. Many passwords are easily guessed. One way to discourage password guessing is to impose a quota system. Each would-be user gets two or three tries, and if he or she cannot get the password right, the system logs the person off.

Quota systems, however, penalize users who are forgetful or just poor typists, but they do not bother hackers who are probably stealing long-distance service from the telephone company anyway and are not upset at being logged off. Some hackers use a telephone with an automatic redialing feature and let their personal computers try guess after guess, call after call, until they get the password right.

Some quota systems seal a user's account if the log-on quota is exceeded on the premise that such action will save files from harm. Hackers have responded to this precaution by systematically going through the whole computer system (that is, making three unsuccessful log-ins on every account, thereby bringing the system down.)

The best kind of quota system writes a warning message on the security officer's console so the officer can take action. This procedure works if the offender is on-site, but is not much good if he or she is a continent away. Provision for automatic number identification can help in tracing some hackers, but some foil that ploy by traversing complex access routes through several gateways or using a "cheesebox," an unauthorized call-forwarding device much favored by those who want to make untraceable calls.

Among the passwords that are the easiest to guess are master passwords or service passwords that often grant their users special privileges within a system. A system must, when delivered, have a master password programmed into it that enables its owner to get in for the first time, after which the owner is expected to change the password. When a large number of users must be admitted to a system at one time, a default

password is used; this too must be changed once the user gets in. Often it is not, or the user is slow in using the default password, in which case somebody else gets in first, changes the password, and has fun with the account while the owner is locked out. Default passwords are widely used in schools and colleges at the start of a semester.

Other easily guessed passwords are used by computer service persons. When allowed to choose their own passwords, users often pick words that are easy to remember. Some examples are: initials (the most common ones are JB and JM), initials backwards, personal names, street names, automobile license numbers, or the last four digits of the user's telephone number or social security number. A hacker can get some of these passwords by consulting a telephone book or city directory, or by scanning license plates in the company parking lot.

Two Bell Telephone Laboratories engineers wrote a password-breaking program that automatically tries all usual sets of initials backward and forward, 400 first names, and 100 street names. They were said to have discovered 85% of the passwords on the computer the first time they tried it. Many password-breaking programs are available on hacker boards.

It helps in guessing passwords to know about formats. The National Bureau of Standards recommends a minimum of four numbers. Many computer systems are limited to six characters; users tend to select letter sequences that are pronounceable. Some systems allow up to ten characters, and company protocols sometimes insist that they be alphabetic (upper- and lowercase) and numeric, and use at least one mark of punctuation. Passwords should be required to be changed from time to time.

There are several strategies for improving the security of passwords. One is to make them longer -- say, 10 or 12 characters instead of 6 or 8. Second is to increase the permissible number of symbols from 26 (uppercase alphabetic) to 52 (upper- and lowercase alphabetic), to 62 (upper- and lowercase alphabetic and numbers) to 90 (alphanumeric and special characteristics). Third is to use one-time passwords. Distribute a list of 500 or so, and use the top one on the list for each session. This method defeats interception of passwords by wiretaps.

Fourth is to encrypt passwords and compare the encrypted form. Password encryption can be strengthened by adding (concatenating) the password with a number that is a numeric transformation of the current date (like adding 50 to the day of the month). This procedure can be carried out automatically at each end of the line before the password is encrypted. The encrypted versions are compared for authentication.

Another improvement in password selection is a two-stage password. The user must give a project/programmer number (in a format like 9999/9999 or 9999,9999) or a user name plus a user identification and then authenticate with a password. There are even three-stage passwords: the user must give a four-digit access code to an intelligent modem before beginning the log-on procedure on the computer.

Project/programmer numbers and user names plus user identification devices (UIDs) are often used for intra-company billing, and hackers have recovered them by rummaging through company trash. Sometimes passwords are discovered in this way, although most system managers protect passwords by making them non-printing (echo suppression) or covering them with a strike-over mask.

Hackers have been known to retrieve passwords by personal reconnaissance: entering company premises ostensibly to take lunch orders and looking for passwords written on or under desk blotters, taped on or under retractable desk arms or drawers, or taped to visual display screens. Some hackers are skillful enough to discover a password by watching the user's fingers on the keyboard, a practice called *shoulder surfing*.

Deciding whether to let users choose passwords or to assign them has always been troublesome. If the user chooses them, a hacker who can learn something about the user can often guess the password; if the password is assigned, the user may write the word somewhere for fear of forgetting. One answer may be use of the pass phrase. The user selects a phrase, sometimes as long as the user likes (up to at least 128 bytes), and the log-in routine hashes and mashes it to produce a one-way encryption of it that is stored internally.

Wiretapping and Piggybacking

A truly determined hacker still has two ways to steal passwords if all else fails: wiretapping or piggybacking. To wiretap, he needs to access

either the line into the computer or out of the home or office of a legitimate user. The terminals are located in junction boxes in the basements or hallways of office or apartment buildings, or in terminal boxes on poles or in front lawns in suburban areas. An ordinary audiocassette recorder can copy the usual 300- to 2400-baud tone signals on a voice-grade telephone line. It can be played back through an acoustical modem and the result printed. Although the echo of the password is suppressed, its actual transmission from user to computer is not.

John M. Carroll

Source Carroll, J.M., Computer Security, 2d Edition. (Butterworth-Heinemann, Boston, 1987).

HANDICAP DISCRIMINATION

The Equal Employment Opportunity Commission (EEOC) enforces Section 501 of the Rehabilitation Act of 1973, which protects federal employees or applicants from discrimination because of handicap. Section 501 also requires affirmative action on the part of employers for hiring, placement, and promotion of qualified individuals with handicaps.

The EEOC Goal

The goal of the executive branch of the federal government is to be a model employer of individuals with handicaps. An individual with handicaps is one who has a physical or mental impairment that substantially limits one or more of such an individual's major life activities, has a record of such impairment, or is regarded as having such an impairment. Major life activities are such functions as caring for oneself, performing manual tasks, walking, seeing, hearing, speaking, breathing, learning, and working.

Reasonable Accommodation and Affirmative Action

EEOC regulations require federal agencies to make reasonable accommodations for the known physical and mental limitations of a qualified applicant or employee with handicaps, unless the agency can demonstrate that doing so would impose on its operations an unreasonable hardship.

A qualified individual with handicaps is one who, with or without reasonable accommodation, can perform the essential functions of the position in question without endangering the health and safety of himself/herself or others, and who meets the experience and education requirements of the position or meets the criteria for appointment under one of the special appointing authorities for individuals with handicaps.

Reasonable accommodation may include, but is not limited to, making facilities accessible to and usable by individuals with handicaps; job restructuring; part-time or modified work schedules; acquiring or modifying equipment or devices; adjusting or modifying tests; and providing readers, interpreters, and personal assistants.

EEOC regulations also prohibit the use of employment tests or other standards of selection that discriminate against qualified individuals with handicaps. Pre-employment questions about disabilities, except for job-related purposes, also are prohibited.

EEOC requires all federal agencies to develop affirmative action programs for individuals with handicaps, especially those with severe disabilities, such as deafness, blindness, missing extremities, paralysis, convulsive disorders, mental retardation, mental illness, and distortion of limbs and/or spine.

Equal Employment Opportunity Commission

Source Handicapped: Equal Employment Opportunity Guide for Handicapped Federal Employees and Applicants for Federal Jobs. (The U.S. Equal Employment Opportunity Commission, Washington, DC, 1988).

HANDWRITING ANALYSIS: SIGNATURE IDENTIFICATION

Comparison of signatures to determine authenticity is often thought by the layman to be a simple process. In fact, the opposite is often the case, the difficulty compounded because there is so little questioned writing with which to work. The following is intended only as a guideline. No two cases are exactly alike, and the investigator not trained in document examination may easily become confused. He or she should not be embarrassed to seek help from a competent document examiner.

Since there is no license required of document examiners, certification is attained through peer groups, often identified only by initials. Ask the full name of the certifying body, of whom its membership is composed, and what criteria are used in granting certification. It is strictly a caveat emptor situation, so do ask questions. Board certification is offered both by the American Academy of Forensic Science (AAFS) and the Association of Forensic Document Examiners (AFDE). The trained document examiner draws upon a large body of knowledge, both from the experience of others (learned treatise) and from his/her own experience. After completing examination and comparison of both questioned and known material, a competent document examiner will be able to give an opinion with a reliable degree of certainty, the foundation for which can be demonstrated before the trier of fact.

The rise in signature fraud may be due to economic factors, to lack of due care on the part of those accepting checks and purchase signatures, to the advent of computer technology, which has centralized much signature processing, or to a combination of these and other factors. Every signature may not be scrutinized, and in some cases all are processed electronically. In many cases a good imitation has not been necessary, since all that is needed is a good enough simulation to deceive the passing agent. At other times a non-authentic signature may be very close to its model and difficult to spot. Fortunately, those persons talented in producing nearly undetectable simulated signatures are few.

Fraudulent signatures are properly referred to as "not genuine" or "nonauthentic" signatures, not "forgeries," since the word forgery implies intent, and such knowledge is beyond the scope and practice of the document examiner.

It is not uncommon for signatures to be compared independently of any other writings. They may simply be the only writings available, or a signature may be so different from the body of writing that one portion will not serve in identifying the other.

Of all writing, a signature is that which is most often produced. Its form, therefore, is practiced and habitual. It may be highly individual, or it may be very close to copybook (the method of writing as it was taught). Often, a signature may be of higher form and written with more ease than other writings by the same person. If the signer wrote very little, then the contrast between signature and other writings may be marked. One person may have several different forms of signature, either over a period of time or under particular circumstances, especially formal and informal, and different parts of the names or initials may be combined at separate signings.

It is, therefore, imperative to request as full a representation as possible of the writer's habits in standards for comparison. Occasionally an identification can be made with one or two standards, but usually 10 or 20 are needed. Exemplars should be timely, i.e., produced close in time to the questioned signature, and they must be in the same form of writing — cursive or hand printed. In matters involving signatures by the elderly and/or infirm or the involvement of legal and/or illegal drugs, standards must be very close in time to the questioned signatures. A good source is canceled checks, since they are dated and have been produced in the "course of business." Checks should be requested in series so that the subject is prevented from choosing most-like or most-unlike samples. Request exemplars are not recommended, unless standards are insufficient; since a signature demands so little writing, a disguise is relatively easy to maintain.

The investigator should always attempt to establish how large a pool of possible signers he or she is considering. In other words, might anyone in the population of Madison, Wisconsin, have had access to the materials and model, or are the suspects limited by known factors to five or six people? In the latter case, while standards/exemplars for all six persons must be gathered, the case is considerably simplified.

Some signatures are not actually writings, but a kind of "mark," complicated or not, sometimes involving pictographs. Or they may be simply a scrawl or a collection of scratchings. If the signature is relatively simple, and/or there is a wide range of variation among the standards, the signer provides a large target, and it is not always possible in such cases to identify the non-authentic signature. Naturally, the more idiosyncratic a signature is, the more difficult it is to replicate and the easier it is to identify the non-authentic simulation.

"Range of variation" refers to the measure of difference between the exemplars. Since no one signs his or her name exactly the same way twice,

if two signatures are the same, one must be a tracing or mechanical reproduction of the other. Some signers are quite consistent and will show a narrow range of variation; others exhibit signatures that vary greatly one from the other. The process of identifying a true signature consists of comparing it with the exemplar/standard signatures in an attempt to determine whether or not it falls within the range of variation shown in the exemplar material. Thus, it is important that the exemplar material reflect as great a divergence as the examiner believes may exist between the signings of a given penman. A few "accidents" may fall outside the exemplars, but a good exemplar representation will contain all of a writer's prime variations.

Care must be taken that the differences or unique qualities cited are truly representative of one writer and not of a group or "class" of writers, such as the elderly, persons trained in a certain copybook style, or teenage girls. Occasionally group or class characteristics may be helpful in solving a questioned documents case, as for instance in a case involving Nigerian handwriting, when certain known characteristics may identify a signature as done by one of an ethnographic group, thereby narrowing down the pool of possible writers. It must be observed that there may be many similarities between two signings or similarities shared by a group of signings, yet the samples may be by different writers, all of whom share those characteristics. Only the striking idiosyncratic similarities will tie them to the same writer, and then only if there is not an unexplainable difference. However, one unexplainable difference may indicate a different writer. The mark of the expert is in knowing which similarities and which differences are significant and identifying.

Types of Simulation

Different modes of simulation produce identifiable effects.

Freehand Simulation. A signature freely drawn in an attempt to replicate a model. Such a nonauthentic signature is often markedly less fluid than the model and shows poor line quality. "Fluency" refers to the overall ease with which the signature has been produced. Highly fluent signatures are usually written quickly. "Line quality" may be defined as the type of stroke made by the writing instrument: smooth or halting, blotchy or tremulous, etc. It may be designated in all or a portion of a signature, or even in a part of one letter. Authentic signatures show a habitual pattern of pressure and release with dark and light writing strokes. This pressure pattern is habitual and very difficult to reproduce.

The slant or slope of the writing is the easiest factor to modify; nevertheless, it is difficult to modify slant by small consistent amounts, and sudden changes of slant within a name may be indicative of a given writer. Connectives between letters, relationship to a signature line, and the types of final strokes are all identifying factors. The ratio of one letter to another and the proportions of letters within themselves are often not replicated properly (as in the lower loop formation to the upper circular form of the cursive lowercase "g" or "y"). Notice here that ratio does not mean the relative size of one signature to another. Writers often adapt to the space allowed, but the ratio of one letter to another is usually constant. Often, it is of great assistance to turn the questioned and the known signatures upside down and examine the overall design and the ratio and proportion of letters.

Under 20x to 40x magnification, ticks and feather-strokes can often be observed, and sometimes there will be a dispersion of micro-dots, as well. Some writers do not lift the writing instrument entirely from the writing surface, and a drag stroke can be observed. Such strokes are seldom reproduced correctly, and when the effort to do so is made, it can be usually shown that the simulator's hand changed direction in an awkward adjustment. These tiny features of the true signature that are not observable by the naked eye are very important, since they are both habitual and may likely not be reproduced by the simulator.

When someone simulates a signature, the effort extended in the copying process usually slows the writer down. Sometimes, he/she must look up to consult the model, and that moment of hesitation may cause a blotch or an unusual pen lift. Usually, the freehand copyist will capture the rhythm (relationship of forms to the whole and fluency), but not render the individual forms accurately; or the forms will be close to the model, but the line quality and rhythm are poor. However, if the true signature is a slow, halting product, it will be much easier to replicate than one that is a rapid, fluid signing. When attempting to spot a freehand simulation, the examiner looks for labored line quality, unusual pen lifts, or places where a simulator has gone back to fix a mistake in order to make his product look more like the original. Such added marks are called "patching." Any or all of these indices may appear in true, slow, halting signings, as for example in the case of an illiterate writer, and sometimes, especially if exemplars are few, an identification may not be possible. Less likely, but possible in the true labored writing, are variations in pressure pattern.

Disclaimed Signatures. These signatures will usually bear characteristics of the natural hand of the signer, even when the idea to disclaim preceded the signing. Not infrequently, there will be a change of slant. Often, one letter will be changed from lowercase to capital or vice versa. When the writer thought to disclaim only after signing, variations will likely be found in one of the standards.

Signatures on Fraudulent Applications. These signatures often bear no relationship to the authentic signature of the person whose name has been used. Sometimes, little attempt will have been made to disguise the applicant's writing habits. Usually the slant is changed first. When a disguise is used, as is frequently done on purchase receipts, the examiner is usually successful in determining that the signature is not the true signature of the person whose name is used, but if the disguise is at all skillful, it is doubtful that the perpetrator's identity can be discovered, due to the extremely limited amount of writing. "Signatures" on anonymous writings may be consistent among themselves but as difficult to identify as the body of the writing.

Writing Surface. This will affect the look of the signature product, but it will be consistent throughout the writing and is usually readily observable. Rough surface distortion should not be confused with "tremor," that quavering of the line quality caused by a shaky hand. Tremor is often found in the writing of the aged and/or infirm. Natural tremor is very difficult, if not impossible, to replicate. Imitators will most often overdo the effect. Note: The effects of illness and infirmity on handwriting, as well as the effect of drugs, legal and illegal, may come and go.

HANDWRITING EXEMPLAR SOURCES

The following documents may be used for locating comparison writing or signatures. Microfilm can be used when originals are not available.

Public Records

Automobile title papers	Precinct Registration	Voter registration card
Notary license		

Business Records

Account books	Hotel/motel registration	Banks: safe deposit
Insurance forms or claims	Signature cards	Leases
Withdrawal receipts	Registered mail receipt	Building or gate registers
Certified mail receipt	Business licenses	Federal Express receipt, etc.
Checks (chronological)	Mortgage papers	Contracts
Payroll check endorsements	Correspondence signatures	Pharmacy register
Hospital admit/release	Employment ID badges	

Applications

College, private or special schools	Petitions	Employment
Pension	Financial aid for college	Permits
Homestead Exemption	Credit application	Insurance forms
Social Security forms	Licenses	Utilities deposits

Court/Legal Documents

Affidavits	Indigent statements	Bonds: surety, etc.
Police reports	Criminal records	Probate, receipts, waivers
Deeds	State or county ID	Depositions
Welfare records	Divorce papers	

Personal Items

Autographs (books, albums)	Charge card receipts	Auto license plate forms
Church papers	Bank withdrawal receipts	Diaries
Bible entries	Equipment rental or lease	Canceled checks
Funeral register	Checkbook register	Insurance forms
Promissory note	Leases: rent, auto	Repair authorization
Library card	Reportcard signatures	Medical card
Service contract, yard care, etc.	Military papers	Stock certificates
Notes: work memo, college	Tax returns	Passport
Traffic tickets	Pawn ticket	Travel bureau purchases

Source: Bonnie L. Schwid, Anagraphics, Inc., Forensic Examiner, Milwaukee, Wisconsin, and Vickie Willard, Forensic Examiner, Cleveland, Ohio.

Though all such factors may alter the writing and produce visible effect, it is impossible to tell from the writing what caused the effect. Some diseases, such as Parkinson's and its micrographia, produce recognizable effects, but not always. No attempt should ever be made to guess at age or to diagnose an illness from handwriting.

Vision Impairment. This may cause a writer to fail to correct mistakes that a sighted or better-sighted person would catch. The writing instrument may also not come down predictably after a pen lift, and "i " dots and "t" bars may be off. If a guide was used, the result will be a mechanically straight baseline. All of these features are difficult to replicate naturally, free of expert detection.

Guided Hand Signatures. Produced by a writer needing physical assistance, guided hand signatures will show the characteristics of the guider, unless a strict attempt was made to reproduce a model of the infirm writer's earlier signature. In such a case, especially if the model dates from some time after the onset of infirmity, identification may not be possible.

Situations Involving Prior Authorization to Sign. These situations usually involve domestic partners or employer/employee relationship. If the simulator has had ample opportunity to practice, and some of his/her simulations have passed under prior authorization, the pool of standards will likely be contaminated and the simulations may be of high quality. In some stolen credit card cases, when the signature must be produced in front of the inspecting person, much practice may have been devoted to replicating the model, making the case difficult. Caution and care will be needed to identify the perpetrator.

Writing Instrument. The writing instrument will produce an identifiable effect, but unless it is malfunctioning or the writing surface offers great resistance, the natural habits of the writer should still be evident. A felt tip pen will mask some characteristics, especially the finer ticks and feather-strokes, as might be expected, but the overall pattern of the writing will not be greatly changed, except in so far as the difficulty of handling the instrument limits the movement of the hand.

Simulations Produced by Tracing a Model.

•With Carbon or Graphite. Carbon paper or paper rubbed on the back with graphite is placed under a model, which is lightly traced onto the receiving surface. The traced guidelines are then redrawn, usually with pen. Under 20x to 40x magnification, the carbon or graphite guidelines can be seen, and the examiner is aided by the fact that it is very hard to keep the final redrawing line exactly on the guideline. Indentation may also be evident.

•With the Model against a Window or on a Light Box. A blank paper is placed over the model and the illuminated model is traced with the writing instrument. These tracings can be spotted by their absence of line quality (absence of shading in the writing strokes).

•By Indentation Utilizing a Light Box or at a Window. Here, the simulator uses a pointed instrument, sometimes a toothpick, to trace over the model signature, leaving only an indentation on the receiving surface. The indentation is then drawn over, as with carbon paper, and presents the problem of staying within the guidelines. There will be no carbon trace, but a document examiner will be able to photograph the indentations or to make an electrostatic print of them.

Photocopied Signatures. Signatures can easily be photocopied and pasted onto copy documents and then re-photocopied. If this process is skillfully done, it may get through most naked-eye processing. Only sloppy jobs will show "ghosting" shadows where divisions in the paste-up occur. Suspicion should be aroused whenever the original of a significant document is not available. The overlay of transparent typewriter grids will often show misalignment of copy portions or of the body with a signature line. Often the signature line will intersect with the signature, and it may have been partially removed or patched.

Since most copiers distort with a pull from the lower-right corner toward the right, it is sometimes possible to place copies from a given machine in the approximate order in which they were generated. Such approximations, however, are complicated by machines that enlarge and reduce, and by maintenance procedures. We look for "trash marks" or shadowline and "feed-dog" signatures that might be indicative of a certain machine at a certain point in time. Sometimes a particular copier can be identified, if one knows the characteristics of the various makes and models.

The examiner must remember that a person may have legally signed a photocopy or paste-up photocopy document, and that the document's peculiarity alone does not render it spurious. Also, though all fine detail is not rendered by photocopy processing, there may be enough information for an examiner to form an opinion as to the authenticity of a signature. The value of photocopy as evidence will depend upon how good the photocopy may be and on the degree of fineness of detail needed for identification.

Though a photocopy may be admissible as "best evidence," this does not guarantee that it will offer sufficient information for the examiner to form an opinion. Of course, the original should always be pursued, when available.

Signatures reproduced on high-resolution color photocopiers can be very, very deceptive and require the closest scrutiny. When these signatures are observed under low-power magnification using oblique light, the reflective quality of original ink will reveal itself, and there will be no indentation when a photocopied signature is involved. Alignment of underscore or typewritten name should be carefully checked.

Computer Simulation. Almost any component needed for the production of false documents by the use of computer and color copier is readily available. Very high-grade work can be produced by scanning a document into a computer, especially the MacIntosh, then manipulating and altering the document to specification and printing it out on a laser printer. If the document is then photocopied on a color laser copier, alteration to an extreme fineness of color tonality is possible.

If all other elements of a simulation appear accurate, the reflective quality of original ink will reveal itself under low magnification. Micro-encoding and paper stock should be considered, since a simulator may have neglected those elements, relying on the knowledge that the bogus document only had to be good enough to deceive the passing agent. One must not overlook the possibility that an original signature, or a signature executed by any means or the means of simulation previously discussed, may have been applied to a high-grade computer or photocopy simulation.

Thus, signature identification presents both simple and complicated problems, and the degree of complexity is often increased by the small amount of writing under question. If you have reviewed your signature question in light of these guidelines, and the answer is not now apparent to you, then it may be time to call in the help of a reputable document examiner.

Nancy H. Cole

HARD-WIRED CLOSED-CIRCUIT TELEVISION

In its broadest sense, closed-circuit television (CCTV) refers to the transmission of the video signal at baseband frequencies over coaxial cable. The transmission frequencies present in the video signal require the use of a coaxial cable unless special techniques and equipment are used. Until the introduction of fiber optics, coaxial cable was used exclusively for video transmission. The following describes the use of coaxial cable, two-wire systems using special transmitters and receivers, real-time; and slow-scan (non-real-time) using hard-wired (copper) transmission techniques.

Choosing the appropriate transmission means and hardware is important because it often constitutes the most labor-intensive portion of the CCTV installation. Specifying an incorrect cable for an application can cause a serious cost increase and/or poor performance from otherwise excellent hardware.

A CCTV signal requires approximately a 6-megahertz bandwidth; however, monochrome pictures can be transmitted for security and safety applications in a 4.5-megahertz bandwidth.

Coaxial Cable

Coaxial cable is in widespread use for short to medium distances (several hundred to several thousand feet) because its electrical characteristics best match those required to transmit the full video signal from the camera to the monitor. The CCTV signal is composed of slowly varying (low-frequency) and rapidly varying (high-frequency) components that must be transmitted. Most wires of any type can transmit the low frequencies (20 hertz to a few thousand hertz), similar to transmitting a telephone conversation or music,

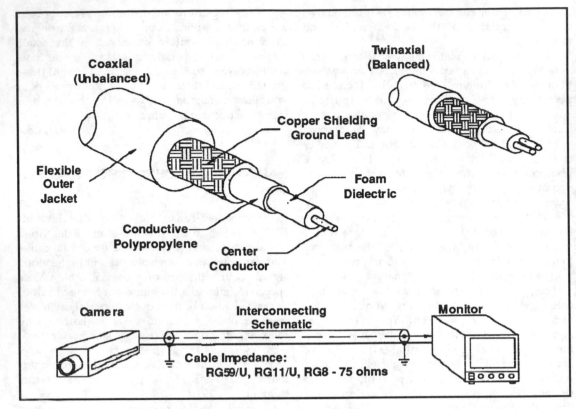

Coaxial Cable Construction

but it takes the special coaxial cable configuration to transmit the full spectrum of frequencies from 20 hertz to 6 megahertz required for a high-quality CCTV picture.

There are basically four types of coaxial cable for use in video transmission systems: 75-ohm unbalanced cable for indoor (building) installations, 75-ohm unbalanced cable for outdoor use, 124-ohm twin-axial balanced indoor cable, and 124-ohm twin-axial balanced outdoor cable.

The particular coaxial cable used for an installation depends on the environment (electrical and physical) in which the cable will be used and the distance between the camera and monitoring locations.

By far, the most commonly used coaxial cables are the unbalanced RG59/U and the RG11/U, having a 75-ohm impedance. For short camera-to-monitor distances (a few hundred feet), pre-assembled or field-terminated lengths of RG59/U coaxial cable with connectors at each end are used. For most interior CCTV installations, the RG59/U, RG6/U, or RG11/U 75-ohm unbalanced coaxial cable are used. When long cable runs (several 1,000 feet or more) are required, particularly between several buildings or if electrical interference is present, the balanced 124-ohm cable or fiber optics is used. When the camera and monitoring equipment are in two different locations, and most likely at a different electrical ground potential, an unwanted signal may be impressed on the video signal, which appears as an interference (wide bars on the video screen), making the picture unacceptable. A two-wire balanced coaxial or fiber-optic cable eliminates this condition.

Television camera manufacturers generally specify the maximum distance between camera and monitor over which their equipment will operate when interconnected with a specific cable.

In applications having cameras and monitors separated by several thousand feet, video amplifiers are required. These amplifiers are located at the camera output and/or somewhere along the coaxial cable run, and permit increasing

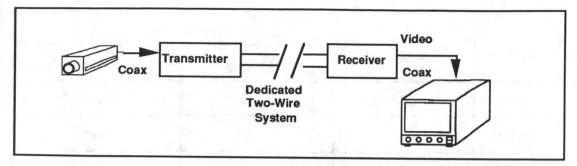

Real-Time Two-Wire Video Transmission System

the camera-to-monitor distances to 3,400 feet for RG59/U cable and to 6,500 feet for RG11/U cable.

Some special CCTV cameras transmit both the camera power and the video signal over the coaxial cable. This is referred to as videoplexing. This single cable camera reduces installation costs, eliminating power wiring, and is ideal for installing into hard-to-reach locations, temporary installations, or where power at the camera site is not available.

The RG59/U, RG6/U and RG11/U cables are available from many manufacturers in a variety of configurations. The RG-A subminiature coaxial cable with an outside diameter of .152 inches is available when a thin profile is required. The primary difference in construction is the amount and type of shielding and the insulator (dielectric) used to isolate the center conductor from the outer shield. The most common shields are standard single-copper braid, double braid, or aluminum foil. Aluminum foil type should not be used for any CCTV application. The common dielectric used is foam, solid plastic, or air, the latter having a spiral insulator to keep the center conductor from touching the outer braid.

Video coaxial cables are designed to transmit maximum signal power from the camera output impedance (75 ohms) to the receiver monitor or recorder input impedance (75 ohms) with a minimum signal loss. If the cable characteristic impedance is not 75 ohms, excessive signal loss and signal reflection from the receiving end will occur and cause a deteriorated picture.

Connectors

Coaxial cables are terminated with several types of connectors: the PL-259 connector is used with the RG11/U cable and the BNC is used with the

RG59/U cable. Older systems use the PL-259 connector on the RG59/U cables, but this practice has been discontinued in favor of the smaller BNC connector which has a fast and positive twist-on action, and has a small size. The F-type connector is used in cable television systems.

Amplifiers

When the distance between the camera and monitor exceeds the recommended length for a specific coaxial cable, it is necessary to insert a video amplifier between the camera and monitor locations to boost the video signal level, thereby permitting its use over longer distances.

Indoor and Outdoor Cable

Indoor coaxial cable is smaller in diameter than outdoor cable, and is much more flexible than twin-axial, which allows it to be formed around corners, or hidden under or adjacent to moldings.

Outdoor CCTV applications places additional physical requirements on the coaxial cable. Environmental factors such as precipitation, temperature changes, humidity, salt, or other corrosive environments are present for both aboveground and buried installations. Other aboveground considerations include wind loading, rodent damage, and storm interference.

For direct-burial-type applications, ground shifts, water damage, and rodent damage are potential problems. Most outdoor coaxial cabling is 1/2 inch in diameter or larger since the insulation qualities and outside protective sheathing must be superior to those of indoor cables. The video cable may be buried, run at

Type	Diameter (in.)	Distance (ft.)	
		Cable Only	With Amplifier
RG6/U	.280	1500	4800
RG11/U	.405	1800	6500
RG59/U	.242	750	3400
A	.15	500	N/A

Note: Impedance for all cables is 75 ohms.

Coaxial Cable Transmission Capabilities

ground level, or suspended on overhead utility poles. In severe weather locations where there are electrical storms or high winds, it is prudent to locate the coaxial cable underground, either direct-buried or enclosed in a conduit. In locations having rodent or ground shift problems, enclosing the cable in a separate conduit will protect the cable from these hostile environments.

For optimum performance the cable should have a 95% or more copper shield, and copper or copper-clad center conductor. The copper-clad center conductor is made of a center core of steel, clad with copper, and has higher tensile strength and is more suitable for pulling through conduit over long cable runs. The 95% shielding eliminates most of the outside electromagnetic interference (EMI) and there is less chance of the noise appearing as a disturbance on the monitor picture. Aluminum coaxial cable should not be used for any CCTV applications.

Potential Problems

Various potential problems should be considered when using coaxial cables for video signal transmission. Indoor problems can occur when: (1) the coaxial cable is connected to television equipment at different ground potentials in different locations in a building, and (2) the coaxial cable run passes through or nearby other electrical power distribution equipment or machinery producing high electromagnetic fields that can cause interference and noise in the

television signal. In outdoor applications, there are the two previously mentioned potential problems in addition to environmental conditions caused by lightning storms or other high-voltage noise generators, i.e., transformers on power lines, electrical substations, automobile/truck electrical noise, or other.

Ground Loops -- Hum Bars

The ground loop is by far the most troublesome and most noticeable video cabling problem. The hum bar is seen as a distortion on the monitor horizontally across the screen at two locations, one-third and two-thirds of the way down the picture. In an AC-powered camera that is synchronized or power line-locked, the bar will be stationary on the screen. In an unsynchronized camera the distortion or bar will slowly roll through the picture, recurring over and over. Sometimes the hum bars are accompanied by sharp tearing regions across the monitor or erratic horizontal pulling at the edge of the screen. When there are high voltages present in the ground loop, other symptoms, including uncontrolled vertical rolling of the scene, occur on the screen.

Electrical Interference

If there is electrically noisy power distribution equipment nearby and there is EMI, a facility site survey should be conducted. The cables should then be routed around such equipment so that there is no interference with the television signal.

When a site survey indicates that the coaxial cable must run through an area containing large electrical interfering signals caused by large machinery, high-voltage power lines, refrigeration units, microwaves, truck ignition, radio and television stations, fluorescent lamps, two-way radios, motor-generators sets, etc., a better shielded cable called a triaxial cable or fiber optics must be used. The triaxial cable has a center conductor, an insulator, a shield, a second insulator, a second shield, and the normal outer polyethylene or other covering to protect it from the environment. The double shielding affords a significantly higher reduction to the EMI radiation from the outside getting to the signal carrying center conductor.

If it is known that lightning and electrical storms will be encountered and signal loss is unacceptable, the best solution is to use fiber optics. In new installations with long cable runs (several thousand feet to several miles), or where it is known that different ground voltages exist, although balanced systems and isolation amplifiers can often solve the problem, using a fiber-optic link is the better solution.

Another category of coaxial cable is designed for use in the plenum space found in large buildings. This plenum cable has a flame-resistant outside covering and a very low smoke emission. The cable can be used in air conditioning duct returns and does not require a metal conduit. The cable designated as "plenum rated" is approved by the National Electrical Code and Underwriters Laboratory.

Two-Wire

A coaxial cable is required to optimally transmit a high-quality television picture several hundred or several thousand feet from a camera to a monitor. There are, however, some transmitters and receivers available that will transmit a video picture over a standard two-wire twisted or untwisted wire communications link.

Real-Time

A standard two-wire telephone electrical system does not have the necessary characteristics to transmit all of the high-frequency information required for a good resolution monochrome or color picture. A technique exists for transmitting the television picture over a dedicated, continuous pair of wires that can be run parallel or as a twisted pair.

This two-wire path can be a telephone system, intercom system, or any other two wires that have continuous conductive paths from the camera to the monitor location. The technique does not work if the wires run through a telephone switching station. The system uses a small transmitter and receiver -- one at each end of the pair of wires -- and transmits a low to medium resolution, real-time picture over maximum distances of 3,000 to 10,000 feet. Picture resolution of approximately 200 television lines is obtained with this non-coaxial cable system. By means of high-frequency emphasis in the transmitter or at the receiver, or both, the normal attenuation produced by the two-wire system is compensated for by excessive amplification of the high frequencies. The system will not work if there is not a conductive (resistive copper) path for the two wires.

Non-Real-Time Slow-Scan

An elegant and powerful technique for transmitting CCTV pictures anywhere on earth is called slow-scan. In this technique, the real-time video signal is electronically converted to a non-real-time signal and transmitted over any audio (3,000-hertz bandwidth) communications channel. The primary difference between slow-scan and conventional video transmission means is that single snapshots of the scene are transmitted over a period of 1 to 72 seconds, depending on the picture quality (resolution) required, rather than sending a real-time signal that changes every 1/30th of a second. The immediate effect of this sampling or snapshot technique is that real-time motion in the scene is lost and only snapshots of the motion are displayed. This is similar to a person opening his eyes once every second or once every minute (or somewhere in between) and observing the scene present. It gives the effect of slow motion but in many applications this type of information is adequate.

The coaxial cable and fiber-optic transmission techniques account for the majority of transmission means of the television camera signal from the remote camera site to the monitoring equipment. For transmitting video over very long distances -- tens, hundreds, or thousands of miles, or to span the continents -- the real-time video techniques are not a practical solution. Slow-scan offers a solution in a large city for transmitting video from one building to another that is not within sight of the first building. This non-real-time technique involves storing one television picture frame (snapshot) and sending it slowly over a telephone or other audio grade network. The received picture is reconstructed at the remote receiver to produce a continuously displayed television snapshot. Each snapshot takes anywhere from 1 to 72 seconds to transmit, with a resulting picture having from low to high resolution depending on the speed of transmission. A time-lapse effect is achieved and every scene frame is transmitted, spaced from 1 to 72 seconds apart. Since slow-scan uses ordinary voice-grade phone lines as the transmission medium, the television picture is transmitted anywhere from one location to another for the price of the phone call. The signal has an audio bandwidth from 300 to 3,000 hertz and can be stored on audio tape.

Video signal transmission is a key component in any CCTV installation and requires a good understanding if successful results are expected. Most systems use coaxial cable or fiber-optic cable, with the latter producing a better picture quality (particularly with color) and having a lower risk factor with respect to ground loops and electrical interference. In special situations where coaxial or fiber-optic cable is inappropriate, other special wired systems using real-time and non-real-time transmitter/receiver equipment are used. The choice and proper implementation of the video transmission link is as important as that of choosing the camera and lens and other monitoring equipment. Cabling equipment and installation costs often comprise a large fraction of the total system cost, and should be treated carefully to optimize system performance and picture quality.

Herman A. Kruegle

HEALTHCARE SECURITY: A MANAGER'S SURVIVAL GUIDE

Security, Loss Prevention, Assets Protection, Risk Management, and Liability Control are just a few of the labels applied to that organizational unit charged with looking after the well-being of personnel and property. While the labels may differ, the premise remains the same -- an organization cannot continue to operate with unchecked depletion of its assets.

A healthcare institution -- whether structured as for-profit or non-profit -- is basically similar to any other business. Success is, after all, predicated on adherence to sound business practices. Not the least of these practices is the protection of the organization's human and physical assets. Many healthcare administrators have come to realize that the professionalization of security staff is not merely desirable, but absolutely mandatory if the organization is to survive in an increasingly competitive industry.

Healthcare, like every other industry, has its own nuances. To successfully apply security in the healthcare environment, the security professional must understand the culture and appreciate the high value that hospital administrators place on image.

Healthcare Culture

Healthcare institutions are controlled by doctors. They may have administrative titles, such as Physician In Charge or Chief of Surgery, and perform administrative duties, such as budgeting and staffing, but they are doctors nonetheless. Although nonmedical professionals perform administrative functions and contribute business expertise to the day-to-day operations, the ultimate control of the organization is almost always in the hands of doctors.

Doctors are, as are all segments of society, individuals. Collectively, however, they are alike in many ways. The most obvious are that they are highly educated and have the scientist's propensity to be analytical and methodical. These characteristics impact the business side of healthcare. As is the case in most businesses, the culture of the organization is a mirror of the personality of those at the top. In this environment, the effective security manager is likely to be someone who shares the same characteristics or who at least recognizes the effect they have on the organization and is able to adjust.

Adjusting frequently means learning how to obtain buy-in from fellow administrators and department heads on routine security matters, and how to move major proposals through committee channels. Decisions affecting the organization as a whole are mostly made by consensus. For an action-oriented security manager, the process can be frustrating. Adjusting means, more than anything else, being patient. Once this is understood, the security manager is on the way to gaining acceptance.

Image

Personal appearance is the first impression that we make on others. In healthcare, the unwritten rule is to present a personal appearance that reflects professional competence combined with cleanliness, good grooming, and a concern for health. The model persona projects ability, confidence, and a life style consistent with the principles of health maintenance. It would be an obvious contradiction for healthcare staff to be seen by patients and visitors as lacking in personal hygiene. The stereotypical gruff, pot-bellied, coffee guzzling security manager, for example, is not tolerated. We can also observe that most healthcare institutions are smoke-free, serve nutritious food, and offer weight control and fitness programs to the employees.

It takes someone many years of education to earn the right to be called doctor. In addition, the educational process for a doctor never ends. Likewise, doctors expect their working associates to also be well educated. The security manager is no exception and must remain current on the state of the art of the profession in order to be respected and maintain credibility. The security professional should not be modest in making his or her educational and professional accomplishments known to the medical staff.

By serving on committees and stepping forward to accept challenges -- both personally and for the department -- the security manager can become a full service member of the organization. In so doing, the security manager provides added value and at the same time demonstrates a personal commitment.

In the mind of the observer, the uniformed security officer is the agent and direct reflection of the security manager. Because security officers are very visible and must deal with many people, they are vulnerable to criticism. Officers must understand that in all of their activities -- whether

preparing a report, directing traffic, or taking an authorized break -- they are projecting the department's image. It is imperative that all officers present themselves as professionals at all times. To be perceived as competent, the security manager will staff the security officer positions with the best personnel available, will train them thoroughly, and ensure they are competently supervised.

The trend in security officer titles has been away from the traditional military rank designations, e.g., lieutenant and sergeant. Less threatening designations, e.g., site supervisor and shift supervisor, are gaining in popularity.

Uniforms are also changing. Many organizations have replaced police-style uniforms with slacks and blazers. The newer uniforms work very well in healthcare. This softer look is more agreeable to healthcare administrators because it presents an image that blends well with the healthcare setting and is less intimidating to the clientele.

Another trend is to get away from the use of the term "guard," which carries images of detention and stern authority. It has also been synonymous with the term "night watchman." The preferred designator is "security officer."

The Necessary Elements

A security department's uniformed staff can consist of proprietary or contract security officers, or a combination of both. Whatever the arrangement, certain elements must be addressed for the proper delivery of security officer services.

The security manager must be directly involved in the hiring and placement process. This includes ensuring that an accurate background check has been made of the applicant; that the selected applicant has been trained in security duties generally and oriented to the healthcare organization's specific duties; that during a probationary period the officer demonstrated the required job knowledge, skills, and abilities, and adhered to the organization's prescribed standards of conduct; that follow-up and refresher training was provided to the officer at periodic intervals; and that supervision afforded the officer was regular, consistent, and competent. The security manager should also personally interview officers who are terminated, whether voluntarily or involuntarily. The information obtained may be useful in reducing unwanted turnover, making needed operational changes, and improving hiring decisions.

The training program is particularly important. At the entry level, the training has two dimensions: the basics and the specifics. The basics cover the fundamental duties and responsibilities of security officers that apply in all work environments. Examples of training topics include arrest and detention, search and seizure, use of force, and report writing. The specifics focus on duties performed at the site, i.e., the healthcare organization. Examples of topics include radiological hazards associated with magnetic resonance imaging equipment, special protections required at restricted areas such as operating rooms and storage areas for controlled substances, fire evacuation procedures, and bomb threat responses.

A matter for specific training, as well as for security equipment and procedural safeguards, is the protection of people. Patients, visitors, and staff have to be regarded as the principal focus of the security effort. Further, the staff itself presents a unique challenge because the typical healthcare organization employs a large number of females. The open nature of healthcare buildings and their surroundings presents opportunities for criminals who prey on women.

Regular staff meetings are also necessary to maintain good communications with the officers and supervisors. In addition as well, daily communication will ensure that minor issues can be dealt with before they become major ones.

The role of the security professional in healthcare has greatly expanded. The security professional must be competent in planning, budgeting, organizing, and directing. These functions require skills in communicating, team building, controlling costs, and ensuring that the security department gets its fair share of operating funds. Demands are placed on the security manager to meet protective responsibilities while being sensitive to the unique culture of the healthcare organization.

Joseph Cascio

HOSPITAL SECURITY: BASIC CONCEPTS

Although hospitals are big business, they have generally lagged behind other business, industry, education, and government institutions in developing management policies and techniques for the nonmedical functions of the organization. Included in these functions are the areas of accounting, inventory control, auditing, and security services. These deficiencies, which have been cited in the literature since the 1970s, remain valid today. This problem has resulted in part because many hospitals have treated security as a short-term situation rather than a long-range objective for protecting the organization's total assets. Another reason is that healthcare facilities pose special protection problems that are not normally encountered in other organizations. It has been said that more quick decisions and rapid reactions are required in hospitals, for more reasons, than in almost any other type of business.

Contributing to the overall lack of long-term security planning are recent changes in healthcare facilities that have escaped the attention of administrators and have failed to alter their views of protection needs. Chief among these changes is the community's perception of the healthcare facility. Society, as a whole, has come to view the healthcare facility as another big business that is exploiting them.

The healthcare facility, and in particular the hospital, the largest and most visible segment of the healthcare delivery system, is no longer as isolated as it was in the past. Hospital administrators must realize that they are no longer sheltered from the strife and anxieties of society. Nowhere is this more evident than in hospital emergency departments where violence continues to escalate each year.

Too many hospital boards and chief executive officers have failed to recognize these changes and the ways they affect the security of their organizations. This failure has resulted in substandard protection measures and subjected the organizations to valid criticism, economic losses, suffering, and undue litigation.

Crime and other negative behavior continues to increase as inner personal restraints on behavior are weakened. Our society has increasingly accepted impulsive behavior, and thus the individual has experienced a diminution of feelings of guilt and shame for inappropriate conduct. The same phenomenon coexists with an extremely high crime rate.

In addition to facing an increasing crime rate, healthcare facilities are becoming larger and have new characteristics. Hospitals are building physician office buildings adjacent to the hospital or attached to the main facilities. New and enlarged outpatient treatment facilities are commonplace, as are large parking decks and even daycare centers. The protection system must be modified to manage this new environment that not only creates unique protection situations but also brings an increasing number of people to the hospital. As the number of people in a given area increases, so does the number of probable negative interactions.

The products used in healthcare facilities are also changing. The high use of disposable products has created more items vulnerable to theft, and the problem of disposing of these products is a new area for risk management. Even equipment design provides more opportunity for loss. The lightweight, collapsible wheelchair has become a major loss item for most organizations. The downsizing of computers and electronic items such as VCRs has added to the problem. Even changes in other markets, such as telephone communications, affect hospital security. When telephones were supplied by the phone company, telephones were rarely stolen. Today, some facilities once again use the old black rotary phone in patient rooms to manage the tremendous theft problem.

Continued changes in the U.S. criminal justice system have also had a significant impact on the protection needs of all organizations, including those in the healthcare field. The emphasis on individual rights has resulted in less protection for society as a whole. Those who are inclined toward criminal acts have found these times to be particularly lucrative. Shrinking law enforcement resources place increasing emphasis on organizational security self-reliance.

Defining Hospital Security

The term *security* or *protection* for healthcare facilities might seem vague and elusive. It is in fact a relatively ill-defined concept that has taken on different connotations in different settings. In the context of protecting healthcare facilities it continues to be defined as a system of safeguards designed to protect the physical property of the facility and to achieve relative safety for all people interacting within the organization and its environment.

This definition, of course, leaves the problem of defining *relative safety*. What is safe today may

not be safe tomorrow. It is a difficult task to evaluate the environment of a particular facility to determine if relative safety has in fact been achieved. Protection, or security, is intended to reduce the probability of detrimental incidents, not to eliminate all risks. Security, then, is not static and can be viewed as a state or condition that fluctuates within a continuum. As environmental and human conditions change, so does the status of protection. It is this phenomenon that requires the constant re-evaluation of any system of protection.

Many people in the field attempt to view security too strictly or too definitively. The organization being served is the entity that provides the ultimate definition of the security system; after all, the organization provides the funding. This is not to say that the protection program and the philosophy and objectives of the principal security administrator do not have a strong influence on molding the organizational definition. In this respect, all organizations should prepare and maintain a current security mission statement.

A common error for hospital organizations is to view security as being closely aligned with the law enforcement function. Although some common ground may exist between security and law enforcement, their respective activities are different in more ways than they are similar. A balanced perspective will view security as internal protection for the organization as a single unit of society, and law enforcement as external protection that attempts to uphold the law for all of society.

Unique Aspects of Hospitals

A hospital operates 24 hours a day. Service -- or, in the language of the industrial complex, production -- cannot be shut down at 5:00 p.m. and resume again at 7:00 a.m. the next work day. The facility must remain open to admit the sick and injured at any hour, to permit the patient to see visitors, and to carry on normal business, including gift shops, cashiers, the pharmacy, physicians' offices, and the like. With people entering and exiting through numerous entrances at all hours, it is extremely difficult to determine who belongs and who does not.

Hospital patients and visitors present unique problems not found in most other social settings.

Patients are involuntary consumers, because they generally have no desire to be in the hospital or to undergo major treatment. It is often the physician who selects the facility, although the patient will likely select a physician on the basis of the facility used by the physician. With the proliferation of health maintenance organizations (HMOs), preferred provider organizations (PPOs), and the like, an increasing number of patients are being told which hospital they must use. Patients directly or indirectly pay the bills, and their wants must be considered within the organizational framework of the institution. This is no simple matter because patients are presumed to be somewhat impaired due to illness or injury. Many patients are helpless. The newborn child, for example, is certainly in a helpless state, and pediatric patients can also be classed as helpless in many situations, either because they are non-ambulatory or because they are unable to define a clear course of action in a situation that affects their welfare and safety.

Similar considerations can be applied to hospital visitors. When a member of the family or a close friend is ill, the visitor's actions and reactions to management practices may not always be completely rational. Thus, tolerance for abnormal behavior resulting from stress must be a major consideration in any hospital protection program.

Rationale for Hospital Security

The first of several basic reasons for providing a protection system is moral responsibility. Every organization, especially those serving the public, has an obligation to manage its environment in such a way that it minimizes the possibility of injury or death to all people on the premises. It is also the organization's moral responsibility to take reasonable steps to preclude the destruction, misuse, or theft of property, so that the physical facility remains intact to carry on its business without interruption.

A second justification for providing protection services is legal responsibility. The hospital corporation has a duty to exercise care and skill in the day-to-day management of corporate affairs. Specific examples of this general obligation are the duty to preserve its property by correcting fire and safety hazards, and the duty to protect people from the actions of others.

The hospital's obligation to its patients is contractual in that the hospital assumes certain responsibilities toward them. The duty of protection becomes even greater when patients are unable to take care of themselves, as in the case of the critically ill, the elderly, infants, and children.

The issue of liability in the management of patient care facilities has become more acute in recent years. A hospital may be held liable for the negligence of an individual employee under the doctrine of respondeat superior, or for corporate negligence. In terms of employee negligence, two general factors are requisite for imposing liability on the corporation. An employer-employee relationship must exist, and the employee's act or failure to act must occur within the scope of his or her employment.

Corporate negligence occurs when the hospital maintains its building and grounds in a negligent fashion, furnishes defective supplies or equipment, hires incompetent employees, or in some other manner fails to meet accepted standards, and such failure results in harm or injury to a person to whom the hospital owes a duty.

One aspect of the legal rationale is of growing concern for hospitals: punitive damages. Jury awards that punish hospitals for not taking appropriate security measures are increasing in frequency and size. An added concern is that in many jurisdictions punitive damage awards cannot be covered by insurance and must be paid from the hospital's funds.

A third important reason for maintaining a safe and secure environment is the responsibility of complying with requirements imposed by the Joint Commission on Accreditation of Healthcare Organizations (JCAHO); the Occupational Safety and Health Act; and other federal, state, and local codes.

The fourth rationale for providing a protection system is to maintain a sound economic foundation for the organization. In this regard, healthcare has faced mounting criticism, especially in regard to the rapidly escalating costs of delivering quality medical care. Critics often cite the lack of cost-containment measures, that in part relate to preventing theft and the waste of supplies and equipment. Authorities estimate that between 3% and 20% of hospital expenditures could be saved if proper security controls were implemented. Yet in most cases, the protection budget for healthcare facilities is generally less than 3% of the total operating budget.

It would seem that the economic stimulus of increased profits would be especially important to proprietary hospitals. Yet as a group they go no further than other hospitals in providing adequate loss prevention and protection systems.

Last, a safe and secure environment is required to maintain good public and employee relations. Although this reason does not appear to be as important as the others, it has probably been responsible for providing more funds for the security budget than the other four justifications combined. Hospital administrators who face bad media coverage of a security problem or restless employees threatening to walk out over a security incident somehow find the money to make necessary adjustments in the protection plan. Unfortunately, these quick solutions are generally not cost-effective and may actually be counterproductive.

Russell Colling, CPP

Source Cunningham, W.C., J.J. Strauchs, and C.W. Van Meter, Private Security Trends 1970 to 2000: The Hallcrest Report II. (Butterworth-Heinemann, Boston, 1990).

HOSPITAL SECURITY: THE ENVIRONMENT

The effective protection of any organization requires an understanding of its structure and the environment in which it functions. The term *environment* in this respect includes not only physical aspects and geographics, but also the history, mission, philosophy, processes, organizational structure, and population characteristics of the organization. According to a study by the Institute for Crisis Management, hospitals are the most crisis-prone industry in America and Canada. The study found hospitals accounted for over 12% of crises that occurred in 70 major industries. Nearly one-third of the crises found in the study were caused by accidents, while a nearly equal number resulted from violent crimes and safety problems.

Security principles are fairly universal; however, it is the manner in which these principles are applied to the specific environment that determines the security program's success. The application of security principles in the

hospital setting is unlike application in any other setting. The principles and the environment must mesh as harmoniously as possible to contribute to the delivery of quality patient care.

The Classification of Hospitals

In attempting to understand the hospital environment so that meaningful protection plans can be formulated, it is useful to classify hospitals according to type, geographical location, and ownership. The type of hospital refers to broad categories of patients or types of care. Common categories are pediatric, rehabilitative, psychiatric, general medical and surgical, and long-term care facilities. Another type, the teaching hospital, is unique in terms of research, education, and often, service to acute-care patients.

Three general classifications help define the environmental setting of the hospital. These classifications are inner-city, suburban, and rural hospital facilities. Each presents a different set of characteristics to consider in developing and implementing a facility protection program. Another way to look at the organization is in terms of ownership or control. There are four categories:

- Not-for-profit hospitals
- Investor-owned hospitals
- Federal government facilities
- State or local government facilities

Not-for-profit hospitals render the majority of the hospital care in the United States. Many of these hospitals have roots in religious organizations or were formed by citizens in a defined geographical area. The latter are often known as community hospitals.

There is a large sector of investor-owned hospitals. The growth of this type of hospital has leveled over the past several years. They are often referred to as proprietary or for-profit facilities. The majority are owned by large corporations, which in some cases own 40 or 50 hospitals.

Federal government facilities can be broadly viewed as veterans' facilities or hospitals that are operated for the military. The Defense Department's Civilian-Military Contingency Hospital System enlists civilian hospitals in the treatment of military casualties from an overseas war. Under this system, the first hospitals to be included in the new service arrangement will be hospitals located within 50 miles of the 18 major military medical centers in the United States. The majority of non-federal government hospitals are city, district, county, and state hospitals that are supported by taxes. A large number of county hospitals are in rural areas. These facilities may have as few as 12 to 20 beds and serve remote areas that are many miles from major centers.

Hospital Organization and Structure

People generally view a hospital as a place in which the sick and injured receive medical care. Throughout its evolution, this has been the hospital's primary mission. However, the hospital has important secondary functions, including the education of physicians and paramedical personnel, the prevention of disease and promotion of health standards, and the perpetuation of medical research.

A hospital is a corporate entity like any other business and should be viewed as a business within the framework of a patient care system. The hospital includes such supporting elements as income, operating expenses, politics, reporting levels, and vast interactions with the public, patients, employees, and physicians. Differences between hospitals and other businesses do exist. The chief difference is the power structure that operates in the medical facility.

Within the organization, those with certain levels of status possess the right to control the actions of those with lesser status. This right may be formal, in that it has been legitimized in the system's organization, or it may be informal, in that an individual has developed some degree of influence in the decision-making operations of the system.

Although the hospital administrator holds the institutionalized right to control the actions of others in the system, he or she is not a free agent in the decision-making process, because in the final analysis, the administrator is subordinate to the board of trustees. The final rights of power are ultimately vested in an authoritative board.

Few other organizations have as complex an organizational structure or bring together as many kinds of people, with all kinds of attitudes and dispositions, to carry out as great a variety of work as hospitals do. The fusion of these diverse talents into exactness of action, with human lives at stake, requires administrative concepts found only in the healthcare setting.

Patients and Visitors

Each year millions of patients are cared for in the U.S.'s 6,500 hospitals, 21,000 nursing homes, and thousands of outpatient clinics and physician's offices. On any given day, there are more than one million inpatients in U.S. hospitals. In addition, more than one million patients are treated daily in hospital outpatient facilities, including emergency rooms.

Although the population as a whole receives quality medical care, there is dissatisfaction with the healthcare system. A report by the Harvard School of Public Health revealed that 89% of the American public believes the healthcare system needs a major overhaul.

Visitors, including vendors and delivery people, as well as patients' friends and relatives, bring another seven million individuals to healthcare complexes every day. The number of visitors per patient varies according to the type of patient.

For example, visitors to pediatric patients greatly exceed the number of visitors to long-term, upper-respiratory-disease patients. As a rule of thumb, each patient receives approximately three and one-half visitors each day. In early 1980 the hospital industry predicted that visiting at hospitals would decrease substantially during the next 10 years -- a prediction that did not come true. Hospital public relations and marketing efforts encouraged an increasing number of people to come to the hospital to visit. A good example of increased visiting can be found in maternity patient care. Birthing rooms and the once tightly controlled newborn nurseries are often full of friends and relatives.

Friends and relatives of inpatients are not the only visitors who arrive daily at hospitals in large numbers. People who go to the hospital for clinic/outpatient services often are accompanied by others. These visitors are not only support people but also often are young children for whom no other care is available. These visitors can present unique situations for hospital security.

Hospital Employees

Hospital employees are a major component of the healthcare delivery system. The largest single cost in operating a hospital is that of labor -- the employees required directly or indirectly to render patient care. The typical hospital has approximately four employees per patient. This number, of course, varies with the mix of specialties and types of patients in each hospital. In the years ahead, continued growth and occupational diversification are expected.

In terms of occupational growth, 7 of the 10 fastest growing occupations in the United States between 1988 and 2000 will be in the healthcare field. The U.S. Bureau of Labor Statistics projects that by the year 2000, 1 in every 12 jobs will be related to healthcare. There were only 1 in 15 such jobs in 1988.

Various studies reveal that some of the most stressful occupations are in the healthcare field. It is generally well accepted that responsibility for people causes a higher level of stress than responsibility for things. The hospital employee is not only responsible for patients but also must ensure the satisfaction of other groups, including families, physicians, accrediting bodies, and licensing authorities. In a study of mental health disorders in 130 occupations, the National Institute for Occupational Safety and Health (NIOSH) found that healthcare positions were represented in 7 of the top 27 occupations.

The percentage of employees in any given position or work group varies among healthcare facilities, depending on size and primary mission. In this frame of reference, primary mission refers to whether the hospital's emphasis is on teaching, research, rehabilitation, clinical care, or medical specialty. A hospital may employ people in as many as 175 different job skills or classifications. In some job categories, as many as half of the employees are replaced each year. This places a heavy burden on management in recruiting, screening, testing, checking references, orienting, training, and supervising.

A large number of professionals work in hospitals. In general, more than 65% of the personnel in a healthcare organization have professional status. This is a handicap in terms of administrative control because a professional, highly specialized group is inherently more autonomous than a non-professional group. It is often said that the administrator of a modern healthcare facility is merely a coordinator who makes certain that all the resources come together at the right time and the right place.

Another important factor, especially from the security point of view, is that well over 75% of hospital employees are female. During the late night hours women often make up more than 95% of the work force. This concentration creates unique security problems given the higher risk of assault confronting women.

Medical Staff

Although the medical staff generally are not employees of the hospital and are not normally included in the formal organization chart, they possess legitimate formal and informal authority in their contact with other hospital personnel. Medical staff are effectively organized and usually have exceptionally good channels of communication with the board of trustees. The medical staff can be the main support of the administrator, and conversely, when the medical staff withdraws its support, the administrator almost inevitably is the loser.

The physician and the nurse are two primary caregivers, and they interact to a great degree. Physicians regard nurses as subordinates who take their orders and translate them into action for the benefit of the patient. Modern nurses view the relationship in an entirely different light. As some leaders in the nursing profession have expressed it, the nurse works with – not for -- the doctor.

Increasingly, hospitals employ physicians in certain key positions that were formerly non-paid coordinating functions. Examples include the positions of chief of staff, chief of surgery, chief of medicine, and director of medical education. A physician's authority is much more formal when he or she is directly employed by the hospital.

Attending physicians are often viewed as the hospital's customers because they are the ones who order the services that are provided by the hospital. Attending physicians decide which patients will be admitted and when, which services the patient will receive, and generally, when the patient will be discharged from the hospital. The patient, then, is the consumer of the services generated by the hospital. This is a unique case in which the customer is different from the consumer.

Physicians are not free to admit patients and provide medical care in any hospital of their choosing. The hospital must grant the physician the status of being on the hospital staff before the physician may admit patients. In larger communities most physicians are on the staff of more than one hospital. In some communities, hospitals combine their medical staff to serve multiple facilities.

Hospitals are increasingly being held responsible for the selection of staff physicians and their actions. In a sense, the hospital is caught in the middle in litigation by either the physician or the patient. If a hospital fails to approve a physician, it may be sued by that physician. On the other hand, if the physician proves to be incompetent, the hospital can be sued by the patient.

The hospital is dependent on the physician to bring the patient into the hospital system. Likewise, the physician is dependent on the hospital to provide the proper setting for patient care. The maintenance of a harmonious relationship between two such complex functions is a tremendous undertaking.

Committees

A committee is a group of people to whom some matter is committed. This group may also be called a task force, commission, or team. Committees are assembled for many reasons, one of which is the advantage of group deliberation and judgment.

Few organizations exist with more committees functioning on a routine basis than the hospital. Committees are quite beneficial in the hospital setting and serve to coordinate plans and the execution of programs. The dynamics of patient care involve so many different and varied disciplines that administrative decisions must be as fully integrated as possible.

Beyond doubt, committees are both time consuming and costly. If a committee is supposed to reach a unanimous or near-unanimous decision, the discussion is likely to be lengthy. On the other hand, if a decision is reached rather quickly, the meeting might have been unnecessary in the first place.

Committees tend to seek conclusions on which all can agree -- whether from feelings of politeness, mutual respect, or humility -- especially in small group situations. It is generally agreed that all decisions directly or indirectly affecting patient care must receive maximum input and necessary deliberations. Regardless of its demonstrable shortcomings, a primary mechanism used to reach such decisions in hospitals is the committee.

Joint Commission on Accreditation of Healthcare Organizations (JCAHO)

The Joint Commission on Accreditation of Healthcare Organizations (JCAHO) can trace its roots as far back as 1917, when the American College of Surgeons sought improvement in hospital surgery. Today's commission actually began operation in 1951 with commissioners appointed from the American College of Physicians, the American College of Surgeons, the American Hospital Association, and the American Medical Association. These four corporate members appointed a total of 20 commissioners. This model remained intact until December 1979, when the corporate membership was expanded to include the American Dental Association, which provided one more voting seat and increased board membership to 21. The commission was known as the Joint Commission on Accreditation of Hospitals (JCAHO) until 1987 when it adopted its current name.

JCAHO's purpose is to promote high-quality patient care through a process in which hospitals voluntarily seek accreditation. The word *voluntarily* is important to note. The JCAHO survey team is invited by healthcare organizations to conduct an evaluation of hospital services. JCAHO should be viewed as a self-policing program because the commission's activities are paid for by the organizations that use its program.

Standards and Inspections. The commission produces and revises its standards each year through the publication of the Accreditation Manual for Hospitals (AMH). The AMH is generally published several months before the beginning of the calendar year in which the standards will go into effect to give organizations time to review and implement standards compliance before the effective date. The AMH, which is designed for use in facility self-assessment, is the basis for the commission surveyors' report.

The JCAHO survey (inspection) team generally consists of a physician, a hospital administrator, a registered nurse, and an ambulatory care surveyor. The full team is not always used in small facilities.

Types of Accreditation. On completion of the on-site JCAHO survey, the commission staff evaluates the results of the survey, along with any other relevant data, to determine the type of accreditation status to be granted. There are three types of accreditation.

•Conditional accreditation is granted to facilities that are not in substantial compliance with JCAHO standards, but are judged to be capable of expeditious resolution of performance deficiencies. A re-survey is scheduled for 6 months after the commission's acceptance of the hospital's plan for correcting deficiencies.

•Accreditation with Type I recommendations accredits the hospital for 3 years. The commission monitors the hospital's efforts to improve in the areas of concern and to achieve significant compliance within a specified period of time.

•Full accreditation, which lasts for 3 years, also generally contains some Type II recommendations, which indicate areas that need improvement. These areas are reviewed carefully in subsequent inspections.

Once a hospital has received accreditation it is subject to re-inspection at any time during the accreditation period.

Quality Assurance and Agenda for Change. The commission continues to place a great emphasis on its quality assurance (QA) standard. In short, this standard requires hospitals to monitor and evaluate the appropriateness of patient care, to pursue opportunities to improve care, and to resolve identified problems. Ongoing measurement, analysis of measurement findings, corrective or improved actions, and documentation are all facets of the QA function.

In 1986 the commission introduced a new concept, Agenda for Change, which was in the process of being further developed in 1992. The two basic elements of this concept are the processes and the outcomes of patient care, with a goal of continuous improvement of patient care services.

JCAHO and Security. The JCAHO has been sharply criticized for failing to address the issue of security in their accreditation manuals. No JCAHO standards pertain specifically to security -- a serious shortcoming of the JCAHO accreditation process. The commission has been sharply criticized for failing to address security, which is of critical importance to quality patient care. This failure has been a significant factor in the millions of healthcare dollars spent on litigation actions that have alleged the failure of

hospitals to provide adequate security. The most tragic effects are the pain and suffering of the victim and the negative impact on the provision of quality healthcare that result from the lack of such standards.

The Plant, Technology, and Safety Management section of the JCAHO 1990 Accreditation Manual for Hospitals alludes to the provision of a safe environment. Standard PL.1 requires "a safety management program that is designed to provide a physical environment free of hazards and to manage staff activities to reduce the risk of human injury." Requirements PL.1.1 through PL.1.11 refer to traditional safety areas -- not security. Standard PL.2 deals with the area of fire safety.

In 1992 the JCAHO Board of Commissioners approved a revision of PL. 1.2 for all health facility accreditation surveys that are conducted after January 1, 1992. This revision includes the requirement (PL. 1.2.2.2) for each facility to have policies and procedures for a security management program.

Escalating Costs of Healthcare

In the United States more than $600 billion a year, or approximately 12% of the gross national product (GNP), is spent for healthcare. This expenditure, which translates to more than $2,000 per person, is higher than that of any other nation. The Chrysler Corporation calculates that employee healthcare adds $700 to every new automobile it manufactures. The cost of healthcare in the United States is expected to reach 13% of the GNP in 1995. The delivery of healthcare in the United States is in a chaotic state that will require structural, business, cultural, and philosophic changes of great magnitude.

Today, cost reduction is overshadowing the issue of access. In the past the U.S. democratic spirit fostered a belief that everyone must have equal access to the best medical care. People grew to believe that medical care was an entitlement. As a result, healthcare costs rose to unaffordable levels. Cost containment, a hospital byword of the 1980s, has been replaced in the 1990s by the term *cost reduction*. Business and industry are emerging as the major customers of health services, and they simply cannot afford the current costs. This high cost means that an increasing number of people are not insured, and the insured are being asked to assume more of the cost through higher medical plan fees, higher insurance deductibles, and increased co-payment amounts.

Baltimore-based Health Care Investment Analysts (HCIA) estimates that 1 in 10 U.S. hospitals is experiencing serious financial trouble -- that's approximately 540 facilities -- and predicts that half of these facilities are likely candidates for closure by 1993.

The Hospital's Changing Role

As the end of the 20th century draws near, healthcare delivery systems are changing at an increasingly faster pace. England is experiencing some shifting from socialized medicine to private care. In the United States, the change is toward more government control. Under Canada's changing system, everyone receives government-mandated healthcare.

Hospital care constitutes a major part of the delivery of healthcare; however, hospitals no longer occupy the role as the major hub. According to some experts, 50% of all surgery is performed on an outpatient basis, and a growing portion of hospital revenue is derived from outpatient care. It is predicted that within 10 years 70% of all healthcare services will be provided outside the hospital.

Freestanding outpatient facilities operated by for-profit entrepreneurs and by hospitals are now evident in many communities. These clinics, surgery centers, emergency services, rehabilitation units, and counseling facilities are expanding the number of medical care facilities and presenting a new way of providing medical care.

During the early 1980s hospital operations changed dramatically. One of these changes was diversification. Shrinking revenues prompted hospitals to seek opportunities outside the main facility and often resulted in a departure from direct patient care. As a whole, these diversifications did not always succeed from a financial standpoint. Not only did big profits fail to materialize but these diversifications received more than a raised eyebrow from the tax collectors, due in part to what the Internal Revenue Service (IRS) calls "unrelated business income" tax implications. Hospitals are now returning to doing what they do best, and that is takingcare of patients.

With diversification, hospitals acquired a keen sense of the need to compete for patients. The inpatient population shrank during the 1980s, and it became apparent that marketing efforts had to be directed at patients and physicians. Formal marketing to both physicians and the public has now become commonplace. Marketing to physicians includes joint ventures and recruitment programs between the physician and the hospital -- a practice that has received close scrutiny by the IRS. The first newspaper advertisements directed at the public startled many people, but now, along with other marketing media, they have become a way of life.

The hospitals of the future will provide a core of high-level inpatient services for chronic and critical-care patients, and they will resemble the critical-care units of today. The actual number of inpatient beds available will decrease, at least in the decade ahead. This reduction will be accomplished by reducing the current excess capacity through various mechanisms. Among these mechanisms will be more hospital closures and mergers, the conversion of acute-care beds to skilled-nursing beds, and the elimination of some of the beds staffed and ready for use. As a result the percentage of occupancy for staffed beds will increase somewhat, reaching perhaps 68-70 percent nationally.

The average length of hospital inpatient stays in the future is uncertain. In 1989 the average patient stay lasted 6.7 days. Industry analysts who expect the length of stay to increase cite the aging population, which raises the average acuity of the inpatient, and the transferring of the less critically ill to alternative outpatient settings.

Russell Colling, CPP

Sources

Borchert, C., Healthcare: Band-Aid Therapy Won't Help. (Colorado State Magazine, August-October, 1989).

Koska, M.T., Physician Revenues and Admissions Up 10% in 1988. (Hospitals, November, 1989).

Lutz, S., Hospitals Stretch Their Creativity to Motivate Workers. (Modern Healthcare, March, 1990).

Marketing Budgets Grow 'Respectfully" During 1989. (Hospitals, November, 1989).

McManis, G., Challenges of New Decade Demand Break with Tradition. (Modern Healthcare, January, 1990).

McLarney, V.J., JCAHO Revises Safety, Security, Power Standards. (Health Facilities Management, August, 1992).

Study: Crisis in Hospitals Rank Number One in Media Coverage. (Hospital Security and Safety Management, July, 1991).

I

IMMIGRATION AND NATURALIZATION SERVICE

For nearly a century after the American Revolution, few immigration problems arose that each state could not solve by itself. By the late 19th century, though, people began to ask questions about the effects of immigration on the nation. Did immigrants harm the United States economy by dominating certain jobs and driving down wages? Could the public be sure immigrants would not bring epidemics and disease with them from Europe? Naturalization raised questions, too. Was that process creating good, devoted citizens, or was it abused simply to gain the benefits that citizens enjoy?

These are a few of the questions of immigration policy and law. They are never permanently answered. As the nation changes over time, each generation of Americans must ask and answer them again. During the 20th century even more problems needed solutions. Should the United States impose rules on what sort of people it accepted as immigrants and citizens? The answers to these questions over time shaped United States policy and immigration law. For example, policy must balance economic conditions on one hand, and a traditional wish to welcome immigrants on the other. Events abroad, such as famine or war, also cause changes in policy; but United States immigration law and policy are generally the product of American political, social, and economic conditions.

The Immigration and Naturalization Service (INS), an agency of the Department of Justice, was established by the Immigration and Nationality Act, which charges the attorney general of the United States with administration and enforcement of its provisions and other laws relating to immigration and naturalization of aliens. Acting under the statute, the attorney general has delegated authority to the Commissioner of the Immigration and Naturalization Service to carry out a national policy that provides for selective immigration, and for controlled entry and stay of non-immigrant aliens to promote and protect the public health and safety, economic welfare, national security, and humanitarian interests of

this country. The policy provides for the reunification of families, the entry of immigrants possessing needed skills, the temporary admission of specific classes of aliens, and refugee asylum from persecution.

The mission of the INS is to:
• Facilitate entry of those legally admissible as visitors or immigrants and to grant them benefits.
• Prevent improper entry and the granting of benefits to those not legally entitled to them.
• Apprehend and remove those aliens who enter illegally and/or whose stay is not in the public interest.
• Enforce sanctions against those who act or conspire to subvert the requirements for selective and controlled entry.

The INS determines the admissibility of persons seeking entry in a timely and consistent manner, and adjusts the status of and provides other benefits to legally entitled aliens within the country with proper regard for due process. This includes assistance to those who seek permanent resident status and those who wish to become citizens through naturalization. It is the responsibility of the INS to ensure appropriate documentation of aliens at entry, to deny entry to those not legally admissible whether they attempt to enter through ports of entry or surreptitiously across the border, and to control the status of those in the country. The INS is also responsible for deterring future illegal entry and stay, including enforcement of criminal provisions against those who act or conspire to promote such entry and stay. Further, it is the responsibility of the INS to detect, apprehend, and remove those aliens whose entry was illegal and those found to have violated the conditions of their stay within the nation.

Immigration and Naturalization Service

Source Public Affairs Pamphlet. (Immigration and Naturalization Service, Washington, DC, 1992).

INCIDENT CAUSATION MODEL

The use of accident causation models is a standard approach in the safety field for identifying the causal factors of serious accidents. Generally, a model will force a consideration and careful examination of each circumstance related to the accident. The model recommended here is called the Incident Causation Model and is based on the International Loss Control Institute (ILCI) Loss Causation Model put forth by F.E. Bird, G.L. Germain, and R.G. Loftus.

The objectives of the Incident Causation Model are to determine why a security-related loss occurred, who was responsible, and what needs to be done to keep it from happening again. In the security field, we have not yet applied causation modeling in any substantive way to the analysis of causes underlying security violations.

The model can be used by security professionals to examine actual and potential loss-producing incidents. A loss-producing incident in the sense used here is an undesired event that results in harm to people or loss to property or process. It is usually the result of a violation of law, regulation, policy, procedure, or work rule. For example, in terms of harm to people, the violation may be aggravated assault; in terms of property, it may be theft; and in terms of process, the violation may be malicious disruption of work, such as sabotage, setting off a false fire alarm, or making a bomb threat.

Like other models, the Incident Causation Model can be conceptualized as a structure; in this case, the structure is a pyramid. At the top is the loss. Below it in descending order are the incident (i.e., the violation), opportunities, and management failures.

Loss

The loss is the observable and often measurable impact upon people, property, or process. It is the direct and indirect fallout of the security incident and can take many forms.

Lost Time. A security incident involving violence will, for example, create time lost by employees who are injured or affected as the result of the misconduct. Time will be lost by co-workers who assist the injured and clean up of the incident scene, and by supervisors who restore work activities, investigate the incident, prepare reports, and testify at fact-finding proceedings. Then there are the time losses associated with employees generally due to upset, shock, diverted attention, and lowered morale.

Increased Operating Costs. These are losses that result from medical claims and escalated medical insurance premiums; legal expenses associated with hearings and liability claims; penalties, fines and awards; recruiting, selecting and training people to fill in for employees displaced by the incident; and acquiring interim equipment (*Supervisors Safety Manual*, 1985:9).

Property Losses. Theft, misappropriation, and malicious damage or destruction involve property losses. In addition, they often require expenditure of supplies and equipment while dealing with the incident or compensating to overcome the immediate effects of a property loss.

Loss of Business. In this category of loss are the missed opportunities during downtime, deterioration of employee and customer goodwill, and adverse publicity.

Incident

The event that precipitates the loss is the incident. It is often rooted in a combination of violations. A theft, for example, is a violation of law, of the employer's policy, and of a work rule, and the same can be said for other violations. In many cases, an incident will consist of conduct that is prohibited in several venues.

Addressing the incident in terms of conduct helps to channel thinking to the means for controlling unacceptable conduct. Developing control measures that prevent incidents and minimize resultant losses is a fundamental responsibility of the security manager, and in this sense the Incident Causation Model has value in two respects: it can be used as a proactive tool for establishing preventive safeguards, and as a responsive tool for analyzing incidents to prevent recurrence and fix responsibility.

The incident and the loss are amenable to fairly easy examination. The opportunities and management failures, however, are not easily discerned.

Opportunities

The opportunities for an incident are the circumstances present in a situation at or immediately prior to the violative conduct. In the security practitioner's parlance, opportunities are non-secure situations. In managerial parlance, they are deviations from standards. The term "standard" implies a minimum expectation, a basis for assessing performance against the expectation, and a means for correcting and upgrading unacceptable performance.

Standards in the workplace have at least two dimensions. First are standards that we may call practices and they relate to human performance. Second are standards that we may call conditions and these relate to the work environment, such as the physical setting and the tools of the work.

When practices are substandard, they usually appear as human failures; for example, failure to control access, to lock things away, to enforce security rules, to make proper use of security resources, and to recognize and act upon the early warning signals of a violation in the making.

Substandard conditions often appear as inadequacies, such as inadequate physical safeguards, inadequate security personnel, inadequate warning systems and responses, inadequate security equipment, inadequate protections against fire and other hazards, and inadequate empowerment of security personnel to enforce security rules.

Identifying the existence of substandard practices and conditions is one thing; understanding why they exist is another. For corrective actions to be effective, the deviations must be clearly seen and fully understood. A full understanding requires asking: "Why is this the case?"

The whys or the hidden causes fall into two groups: personal factors and job factors (Bird and Loftus, 1989). Personal factors are the characteristics of the job incumbents and job factors have to do with the work itself. Substandard personal factors can include lack of knowledge, skill, or motivation and lack of physical mobility, stamina, or mental capability.

Job factors pertain to the physical nature of the workplace and of the processes through which the work takes place. Physical aspects of the job include things like building structure and layout, utilities, machinery, equipment, and supplies. Process aspects reflect the manner in which the work is carried out.

To illustrate, a failure to control access to the company's stock of blank checks (an opportunity) occurred when the stock clerk left the blank checks cabinet unattended because no one trained him to the contrary (a substandard practice resulting from a deficiency in knowledge); or the

opportunity for loss was the absence of a lock on the cabinet (a substandard condition resulting from poor physical construction), or that the accounting manager did not make access control to blank checks an element in the routine work processes of the department (a substandard condition resulting from the absence of a policy or directive). Many hidden causes are possible for each substandard practice and condition. Understanding the causes is essential to removing them.

As one might expect, the Incident Causation Model can be applied everywhere within an organization, including the Security Department. The substandard practices and conditions often found in security operations include:
- Poor and infrequent supervision.
- Poor security program and procedures.
- Poor selection of security applicants.
- Poor initial and refresher training.
- Poor assignment and utilization of personnel.
- Poor team-building and interpersonal communications.
- An absence of regularly conducted internal assessments.
- Excessive physical and psychological stresses.

The opportunities for a loss-producing incident can be tracked down without too much difficulty, but the reasons for them are not always apparent and not always fully understood. More significantly, they tend to be controversial because they point fingers at responsible managers. Patience and persistent probing are needed to get at the root causes and to expose them to rational examination When brought to light, they will suggest changes in management that are needed.

Management Failures

The connection between underlying causes and management action is analogous to the connection between diseases and preventive medicine. The causes are the diseases that produce the symptoms (the opportunities) and ill effects (loss-producing incidents). The diseases exist because the patient failed to maintain personal health (a lack of management control).

In the Incident Causation Model, the principal focal point for analysis and corrective action is at the base of the pyramid. The errors of

INCIDENT CAUSATION MODEL

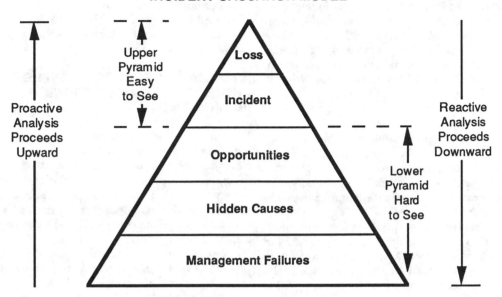

management, whether large or small and whether by line supervisors or senior executives, form the foundation for the deficiencies that lead to loss. The errors occur at the upper level in the promulgation of policy and work rules, and especially in the setting of standards. Errors at the lower levels occur in the normal course of planning, organizing, leading, and controlling (Bird and Loftus, 1989).

It does not matter if the manager's work is directed at production, quality control, cost accounting, or security, and it does not matter where the manager sits on the organizational totem pole. The simple fact is that every person in a supervisory or managerial position has an obligation to protect the employer's assets and that even the most routine tasks of management involve the use of assets.

Another simple fact is that in the rush of meeting other priorities, managers tend to push their assets-protecting obligation into the background, and even when they are not so rushed, they have no idea how to go about meeting the obligation.

Using the Model

When using the model as a tool for fact finding and preventing repetition of an incident, the security practitioner starts with an examination of the incident and works downward through the pyramid. The amount of detail increases almost geometrically as the inquiry moves from incident to opportunities and then to management failures. A single incident is likely to result from the presence of 5 to 10 substandard practices and conditions, and each practice or condition is sure to be rooted in a like number of hidden causes.

A proactive use of the model is to prevent an incident or reduce its negative effects. In this approach, sometimes called the critical incident technique (*Accident Prevention Manual for Industrial Operations*, 1988:48-49), the security practitioner starts at the bottom of the pyramid and works upward. The idea is to identify the causes of an incident and take preventive steps before the incident can happen. A logical start is to examine policies that relate to the use and care of assets. One such policy would be the security policy. Does such a policy exist? Is it in writing? Has it been communicated throughout the organization? Is it understood, followed, and enforced?

Next to be examined would be the various programs for carrying out policies. Several functional areas of interest to the security practitioner should come to mind: internal audit, safety, and some aspects of human resources, such as pre-employment screening and drug testing. Program activities will vary among organizations.

The function of security should certainly be looked at closely. Program activities may include physical safeguards, security officer operations, protection of proprietary information, investigations, security awareness, and so forth. Each program component will be operated according to well-defined standards, e.g., fences will be constructed to certain heights with certain features, and proprietary information will be marked in certain ways and stored in certain containers.

The security professional sets the standards, implements standards that fall within his or her exclusive purview, and communicates the standards to managers in order to help them carry out their security responsibilities. Finally, the security professional evaluates compliance with the established standards.

The Incident Causation Model crosses many boundaries. Although it has particular application to the security manager's domain, it reaches into all levels of the organization. In principle, the management of security is a responsibility assigned to every person performing supervisory or managerial duties. Responsibility for protecting assets entrusted to a manager is assigned to the manager, and while a security professional may assist by setting up protections, the bottom line responsibility stays with the manager.

A loss-producing incident does not happen without warning. It will be preceded by signs that are detectable. The incident will have multiple causes and will develop through a sequence of errors. The sequence moves upward from management failures to opportunities. At the opportunities level, the incident is just waiting to be triggered.

John J. Fay, CPP

Sources

Accident Prevention Manual for Industrial Operations. (National Safety Council, Chicago, 1988).

Bird, F.E., Management Guide to Loss Control. (International Loss Control Institute, Loganville, GA, 1988).

Bird, F.E., and G.L. Germain, Practical Loss Control Leadership. (International Loss Control Institute, Loganville, GA, 1988).

Bird, F. E. and R.G. Loftus, Loss Control Management. (International Loss Control Institute, Loganville, GA, 1989).

Fundamentals of Industrial Hygiene. (National Safety Council, Chicago, 1988).

Fundamentals of Modern Safety Management. (International Loss Control Institute, Loganville, GA, 1989).

Supervisors Safety Manual. (National Safety Council, Chicago, 1985).

INFORMATION SECURITY: LEVELS OF PROTECTION FOR ELECTRONIC INFORMATION

Various levels of protection may be implicit in many security systems, but for the purposes of electronic information security, the levels should be expressed explicitly. These levels are shown in the accompanying chart as a series of concentric circles. Conceptually, penetration through each succeeding level inward should be increasingly difficult.

The security elements required for the protection of security information occur at four levels. Physical, procedural, and logical protection levels are always required for information having an established value. Transformational protection is required only in special high-value cases.

Physical Protection (Level 1)

Physical security, or the separation of physical assets from potential harm, is a basic need for any kind of security program, and it is the underpinning for an information security program. Level 1 refers to all those security elements necessary to ensure that unauthorized persons are excluded from physical spaces and assets where their presence represents a potential threat.

All types of computing devices and associated communications facilities must be considered as sensitive assets and spaces, and be protected accordingly. Physical security elements include the following:

Physical Access Controls. These include guards and receptionists, door access controls (keys, magnetic cards, digital code keypads, voice recognition, hand recognition, employee badge examination), restricted areas (special authorization required), perimeter lighting and fencing, high-strength glass, closed-circuit television (CCTV) monitors, automatic door controls, and human traps.

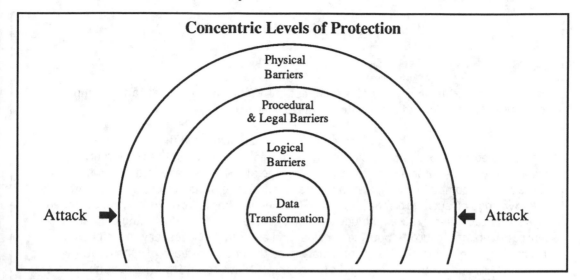

Locks and Special Protective Features. These include devices on cabinets, closets, and compartments for protecting magnetic media (tapes, disks, cartridges) and reports containing information with established value factors. Vault-type doors for media libraries, laboratories, and other sensitive areas also fall into this category of physical elements.

Procedural Protection (Level 2)

Procedural and legal security elements consist of those arrangements of employee interfaces that will ensure integrity and security of assets. Organizational and procedural elements include the following:

Authorization to Use. The information owner, the person primarily responsible for the functional area in which the information originates, is budgeted for, or which is assigned control, must decide whom to authorize to see, modify, or remove information. These authorities may be implemented through logical access control systems or by procedures. The general rationale is that a person must have a business-related "need to know."

Organizational Compartmentalization. This element is designed to provide a series of checks and balances. For example, the electronic data processing auditors should not report to the senior data processing executive, but rather to the corporate treasurer or some other disinterested senior fiscal officer. This will help objective reporting of exposures. In a data center, data control (which validates outputs) should be separate organizationally from the computer operations producing those outputs.

Procedural Assignments. This element will provide a check on integrity and security. For example, computer tapes being selected for a process by the tape librarian are also checked, before operation, by a quality assurance function. After the production run, output tapes are checked by data control and by the librarian. (The obvious analogy is the cashier and the daily cash count by a second party.)

Legal Protection. Mental information is protected by having the person knowing the information sign a confidentiality agreement.

Logical Protection (Level 3)

Logical security elements consist of those hardware and software features provided in a system that help to ensure the integrity and security of data, programs, and operating systems. Such logical elements may include the following:

Hardware Elements. These elements segregate core and thus prevent overlap, accidental or intentional, and they perform core clearing after a job to prevent the following job from seizing

A SAMPLE INFORMATION SECURITY POLICY

Summary

Protection of valuable or sensitive business information is critical to the company's continued successful and profitable business operations.

Certain business and technical information, because of its sensitivity, is classified as company registered, company private, or company personal and is to be marked accordingly. This information is to be protected at all times and in all forms (on paper, in electronic computer form, and in mental form in the minds of employees). Access to or knowledge of such information is based on need to know, following from assigned job tasks. Protection measures include avoiding careless talk, maintaining a clean desk, control over disclosure to outside parties, and avoiding unnecessary distribution internally. Public disclosure of information to the press, release of financial information, and comments on legal affairs are subject to limitations specified herein.

Policy

All units of the company will install adequate safeguards to protect the following information:

- Proprietary business and technical information
- Personal data concerning applicants, employees, and former employees
- Proprietary information of suppliers provided under contractual agreement

Classification

The company's internal classification system identifies valuable information and indicates which measures in a set of established, uniform practices are to be applied to protect sensitive business and technical information. The classifications are:

- **Company Registered** – that information, the unauthorized disclosure of which could cause serious damage to company operation. This is the highest company classification. Its use, and the access to information so classified, must be strictly limited.

- **Company Private** – information of such value or sensitivity that its unauthorized disclosure could have a substantially detrimental effect on company operation.

- **Company Personal** – that information of a descriptive, personal nature that (1) a reasonable individual determines might be limited in its disclosure or that (2) an originator determines should be limited in its disclosure.

Information owners (usually the senior function manager responsible) and, when necessary, originators of information are responsible for assigning appropriate company classification. The general counsel is the ultimate authority with regard to classification of all product-related technical material. Declassification takes place in accordance with schedules and procedures defined in the information security standards.

Handling and Marking

Company classified information in documents, electronic form, or both is to be marked, distributed, copied, mailed, hand carried off premises, stored, and destroyed only in accordance with prescribed company standards, which are specified in the information security standards.

Protection of Information

Awareness

Programs will be implemented to ensure that all employees are advised of their responsibility for protecting company classified information and the reasons therefore. All employees will read and sign the "proprietary information and conflict of interest agreement" during initial employment processing. The signed original form will be retained in the employee's personnel file.

Careless Talk

Unnecessary or careless talk about company information, plans, strategies, unannounced products, research developments relating to products, and so forth must be avoided both at and away from the job.

Under no circumstances should there be any discussion with outsiders of prospective growth, sales, earnings, research efforts, new products, contract awards, acquisitions and divestitures of business or properties, law suits, unannounced changes in management personnel, or other unpublished company information.

Clean Desk

All company employees must adhere to the "clean desk" policy. During nonbusiness hours or when a workplace is unattended for more than two hours, all business information, classified or not, must be adequately secured. Adherence to the clean desk policy and the handling of classified information must be in accordance with the information security standards.

Disclosure of Information to Outside Parties

If, in the course of business, consultants, contractors, and other outside parties must have access to company classified material, they must sign a "confidential disclosure agreement." They are to receive only such information as is necessary to comply with their contract and must conform to company information-handling procedures. A master for the form is located in the information security standards.

Publications

Company publications intended for wide distribution to employees (e.g., telephone directories and newsletters) will contain nonsensitive information. Although publication of scholarly or research material is permitted after required clearances have been obtained, company proprietary information must not be compromised.

Public Disclosure of Information

Press Relations

The company's public relations department is solely responsible for dealings with the press. The significance of information to be released must be carefully assessed by the originators beforehand. In virtually every case, clearance by the general counsel is required.

Release of Financial Information

Financial information -- other than published financial statements, SEC statements, and sundry data previously made public by authorized company officials -- is confidential information and may not be released to outside agencies, individuals, and foreign subsidiaries unless such release is approved by the CFO, comptroller, or treasurer or their designees.

Included under this definition is all data normally contained in company financial statements and notes as well as related statistical information such as products sold, supplies sold, line of business reporting, forecast of results of operations, budgets, plans, and so forth.

Legal Affairs

Any inquiries with respect to the company's legal affairs should be referred promptly to the general counsel. Legal affairs such as proposed or ongoing litigation; proceedings before governmental agencies; inquiries or investigations by federal, state, or local government; subpoenas or demands to produce company documents or other information; and contractual controversies with others can be highly sensitive and therefore must not be discussed outside the company.

Speeches and Publications

Wherever the author of any speech, article, presentation, or statement, or participant in a panel discussion, outside education program, or other activity intended for public release, is to be identified with the company, or if the content mentions the company or discusses any company matters whatsoever, the following clearance must be obtained before publication, delivery, or participation.

• For nontechnical material, clearance must normally be granted by a department manager, general counsel, and the cognizant manager of public relations.

• For technical material or material that refers to current or future products, research plans, or programs, additional approvals are required from general counsel.

Employment advertising for forward technical areas, technical training programs for customers, discussions of technical data with job applicants, organization announcements of components involved in advanced technology, new product development and other sensitive projects, and participation in trade shows and trade association meetings are all subject to prior approval requirements.

Electronic Information Security

The unique operational characteristics and inherent security risks of electronic forms of information make it essential that special security programs be implemented for these systems. The following responsibilities apply.

Information Executive

•Develop and revise policies and procedures for safeguarding information
•Prepare training programs as required
•Ensure implementation of programs
•Provide guidance and leadership in resolving information management problems
•Ensure the establishment of a security coordinator network in operating units
•Perform staff visits and reviews as necessary
•Ensure internal auditing of operating units for conformance to information policies and procedures

Operating Groups

•Develop an organization to implement information management policy
•Develop, publish, and implement information control plans to achieve adherence to policy
•Initiate policies, standards, and procedures that are necessary for local requirements and legislation
•Obtain review and concurrence of information management implementation plans by the company information executive
•Conduct operating unit compliance reviews
•Identify and correct problem situations
•Report significant information security breaches and compromises to the company information executive

Managers and Employees

•Ensure adherence to policy and related procedures
•Protect company classified material per established policies and procedures

---

●Ensure that security indoctrination is provided to employees and contract and temporary personnel assigned to the organization
●Designate security coordinators as required
●Monitor implementation of information security regulations and programs

Security Coordinators

●Be fully conversant with security policies and guidelines
●Provide counsel to their management on security matters
●Carry out tasks and programs as set forth in the security coordinator guide and perform special assignments as required

Source: Schweitzer, James A., "Managing Information Security," Butterworth Publishers, Stoneham, MA, 1990.

---

control. Hardware elements include levels of privileges that restrict access to the operating system programs, and hard-wired (firmware) programs that are not software-modifiable.

Software Elements. These elements provide access management capabilities and are the key security elements in a program to protect electronic information. A logical security system provides the means to identify, authenticate, authorize, or limit the authenticated user to certain previously stipulated actions, for each system user who may "sign on" or for each program that may be called on by the computer to process files with established value factors. Probably the most important factor in an effective authentication scheme is the will of the users to make it work.

Transformational Protection (Level 4)

Encryption. Encryption is the use of the ancient science of cryptography (literally, "secret writing") for information processing security requirements (in the sense used here, "information processing" includes computer application systems, telecommunications and data networking, computer terminals and communicating office equipment, and the use of all types of magnetic storage media).

Cryptography has been a military art throughout most of recorded history. More recently, a science of cryptography has developed as a result of demands from the community of computer users.

Encryption is accomplished through the coding-decoding of information by using mathematical formulas (algorithms) and secret or public keys. A myriad of methods exists for performing encryption, based on various mathematical principles and properties. The system chosen should: (1) protect in the environment used (e.g., against the level of threat), (2) provide protection at a cost acceptable to the user (typically, processing overhead), and (3) not interfere with business operations.

James A. Schweitzer

Source   Schweitzer, J.A., Managing Information Security. (Butterworth-Heinemann, Boston, 1990).

INTEGRITY TESTING: TECHNICAL AND LEGAL ISSUES

In recent years there has been a rising interest in the topic of written integrity tests. Much of this interest is due to the public policy and legal issues surrounding the use of these tests. This section will address some of these issues and their associated common misconceptions, while concluding that professionally developed and researched integrity tests are useful, valid, and legally supportable pre-employment screening instruments.

Recent Reviews on Validity

In response to the interest in integrity testing, two recent studies have been conducted in an attempt to determine the technical qualities of such tests. The first study ultimately produced a background paper on this topic, entitled *The Use of Integrity Tests for Pre-Employment Screening* [1], which was released by the Office of Technology Assessment (OTA) in September 1990. Considerable criticism has been expressed regarding the OTA study, both as to its methodology and the inferences drawn from the resulting data. In fact, the OTA reviewed less than 5 percent of all validity studies submitted by test publishers, users, and academic researchers. Given the flawed research methodology, it is not surprising that the OTA background paper was coincidingly flawed in concluding: "The research on integrity tests has not yet produced data that clearly supports or dismisses the assertion that these tests can predict dishonest behavior" [2]. In contrast to the study's general ambiguous conclusions, one of the OTA's own contractors, a prominent personnel psychologist, was more decisive and accurate when he wrote that "...while integrity tests are far from perfect, they are better than any available alternative for screening and selecting honest job applicants" [3].

The second study, conducted by the American Psychological Association (APA), entitled *The Prediction of Trustworthiness in Pre-Employment Selection Decisions* [4], was issued in March 1991. In contrast to the OTA study, the APA examined most available research, and its findings clearly supported the value and usefulness of integrity measures as pre-employment screening instruments. The APA report also made a number of recommendations to the publishers of integrity tests on several general improvements that should be made. For example, the APA report recommended increased openness regarding the development and scoring of the tests, better education of test users about the appropriate use of tests and test scores, and more research on the effects of language and cultural differences on test scores, to name a few. However, the APA's ultimate conclusions were that:

1. "...the preponderance of evidence is supportive of [integrity tests'] predictive validity;"
2. "...[the evidence] is consistent with the idea that these tests reflect aspects of personal integrity and dependability, or trustworthiness;"
3. "...we do not believe there is any sound basis for prohibiting [integrity test] development and use; indeed to do so would only invite

alternative forms of pre-employment screening that would be less open, scientific, and controllable" [5].

Due to the unbiased, thorough, and scientific caliber of the APA's report, many of the criticisms that had previously been aimed at the use of integrity tests have been laid to rest.

Polygraph Statutes

A common misconception regarding integrity tests is that they fall within the purview of state and federal antipolygraph statutes. To the contrary, as indicated by their operative language, many of these statutes are merely proscriptions against the evaluation of applicant or employee "deception" as measured by mechanical or electrical devices [6]. Given that integrity tests are not designed to detect lying, they are not affected by these statutes. Rather, like most personnel selection tests, they are validated and used only to predict future job behavior. Assertions that integrity tests are somehow similar or equivalent to lie detectors or truth evaluators stem from a basic misunderstanding of how these tests work.

Other polygraph statutes commonly include language similar to the Minnesota statute, which states that "no employer or agent thereof shall...require a polygraph, voice stress analysis, or any test purporting to test honesty" [7]. Since rules of legal construction require words of general description to be interpreted in a way that is consistent with specific words, statutory language such as "any test" or "other similar tests" would be interpreted to mean only instruments closely related to those previously listed.

Following this traditional approach to construction, the Minnesota Supreme Court held in *State v. Century Camera, Inc.* [8] that:

the two techniques...the polygraph and the voice stress analysis, both purport to measure physiological changes. Accordingly, we construe any test purporting to test honesty to be limited to those tests and procedures which similarly purport to measure physiological changes [9].

State administrative agencies have also determined that their lie detector statutes do not apply to written integrity tests. In a 1983 case, the

Wisconsin Equal Rights Division held that the Wisconsin lie detector act "does not apply to written psychological tests..." [10]. Since that time the division has reached the same conclusion in a number of similar cases [11]. In light of such interpretation, there is no compelling reason to believe that similar statutes would be construed differently.

Similarly, at the federal level, the Employee Polygraph Protection Act of 1988 [12] deliberately excluded the use of written integrity tests from the scope of the Act. This intent is clearly stated in the Definition section of the House Conference Report: "The conferees also do not intend to include written or oral tests (commonly referred to as 'honesty' or 'paper and pencil' tests) within the definition of lie detector" [13].

To summarize, despite the existence of the Employee Polygraph Protection Act of 1988 and various state anti-polygraph statutes, only Massachusetts and Rhode Island restrict the use of integrity testing, which they have accomplished with the passage of language specific to that purpose. The Rhode Island statute does not ban testing, but simply requires that test results not constitute the "primary basis" of an employment decision [14]. Massachusetts forbids the use of any written technique that provides a "diagnostic opinion" of honesty [15], a proscription that has so far been unchallenged in court and which may prohibit the use of application blanks, reference checks, structured interviews, and the validity scales of psychological tests as well. Such overly broad language may be vulnerable to attack on the basis of unconstitutional vagueness.

Discrimination Issues

As with any personnel selection procedure, the issue of unfair discrimination as defined by Title VII of the Civil Rights Act of 1964 [16], the Civil Rights Act of 1991 [17], and state fair employment laws is pertinent to the use of integrity tests. With integrity tests, the most common applicant challenge has been based on the disparate impact model of discrimination. In this vein, very few selection techniques can match the sheer volume of statistical evidence demonstrating freedom from disparate impact achieved by valid integrity tests. Neither the Equal Employment Opportunity Commission (EEOC) nor any state administrative agency has ever determined that

such tests create disparate impact. Although the record shows relatively few challenges for the millions of tests that have been administered, these tests have withstood at least 30 formal challenges.

Even in the unprecedented event that a complainant were to demonstrate disparate impact for an integrity test, an employer's use can be justified by demonstrating that it is "...job related for the position in question and consistent with business necessity" [18]. Since the leading publishers have extensive evidence supporting the validity of integrity tests, their use could be justified even when exhibiting disparate impact.

Proposed Legislation

Recent attempts to restrict integrity testing in particular, or pre-employment psychological testing in general, have fallen short of passing into law due to tremendous support by the business and scientific communities. For example, during Oregon's 1991 regular session, the Senate Committee on Labor considered a bill (SB 792) [19] that sought to place restrictions on the use and interpretation of psychological employment tests. Through the coordinated efforts of psychologists and business professionals to educate legislators regarding the utility of pre-employment testing, the bill's language was significantly less restrictive when it was passed by the Senate. Such educational efforts ultimately caused the bill to die in the House Committee on Labor with no further action.

Similarly, in New York, affirmative support from professional associations such as the APA and the Association of Personnel Test Publishers (APTP) was effective in opposing certain factions' attempts at creating inroads into the area of pre-employment testing. In April of 1991, a New York bill (AB 7301) [20] regarding psychological testing was introduced in response to a legislative program proposed by the attorney general. This bill sought to place prohibitions on any written or recorded test used to determine the integrity of an individual. The language of the bill was broad enough that it could be interpreted to include various personality tests, as well as clear-purpose integrity tests. In fact, the assistant attorney general handling the bill indicated that certain personality tests definitely would fall within the purview of the bill [21]. Moreover, in light of the public policy issues common to all forms of employment testing which were enumerated in the attorney general's program that fostered the bill (privacy, confidentiality, accuracy, and discriminatory impact), it is quite possible that such a bill could have been expanded to include all forms of pre-employment psychological testing.

After passing the Assembly Committee on Labor, this bill was sent to the Assembly Committee on Codes, where it remained until the legislature adjourned in July of 1991. As in Oregon, active involvement on behalf of the field of psychology and the business community ultimately forestalled the proposed legislation.

A common thread between these bills, as well as legislation that has been proposed in the past in Connecticut [22] and Iowa [23], is a desire to shield applicants and employees from being subjected to overly intrusive, non-job-related screening techniques. As legislators became more educated on pre-employment integrity testing, it became clear that their concerns were often based on a poorly defined concept of integrity testing and the notion that many of them inquired into invasive topics (e.g., religion, sexual preferences, family relations, etc.). Once pre-employment integrity tests were distinguished from clinically based tests containing items that are deemed invasive, legislation was generally re-directed towards clinical measures.

Although a few members of the U.S. Congress were initially interested in the topic of integrity tests, causing them to request the OTA to conduct the study described earlier, no legislation restricting their use has ever been introduced at the federal level. This is ostensibly due to the inconclusive findings of the OTA paper and the strongly supportive stance of the APA's subsequent paper. At present, Congress has expressed no further interest in integrity testing.

Although this article has not provided an exhaustive survey of all issues, it is hoped that it has clarified the most pertinent issues surrounding the use of these tests. That is, integrity tests are valid and legally defensible instruments that are acceptably used in all states, excepting Massachusetts. Moreover, given the ongoing process and successful track record of educating legislators, further legislative inroads are unlikely.

A further basis for considering the use of such tests is that businesses have a compelling reason for minimizing employee theft. For instance, the U.S. Chamber of Commerce has estimated that approximately 30% of all business failures are precipitated by employee dishonesty [24]. This is not surprising when you consider a *Nation's Business* report that employee theft is an estimated $40 billion annual cost to business, 10 times the toll of street crime, and increasing by 15% annually [25].

Another growing cost to business is an increase in negligent hiring suits filed against employers for dishonest acts committed by their employees. Verdicts in such suits have been known to cost employers hundreds of thousands of dollars. (See *Welsh Manufacturing Division of Textron, Inc. v. Pinkerton's, Inc.* [26].) Use of integrity tests may not only prevent hiring dishonest employees, but may also be used to show that the employer took reasonable care in selecting employees, thereby avoiding such litigation and associated liabilities.

These business needs and interests coupled with the technical and legal qualities of integrity tests make such tests a legitimate means of screening applicants. In light of security and personnel professionals' continuing recognition of these facts, the use of these instruments continues to expand.

David W. Arnold and Rachel A. Ankeny

Notes

1. U.S. Congress, Office of Technology Assessment, The Use of Integrity Tests for Pre-Employment Screening, OTA-SET-442 (U.S. Government Printing Office, Washington, DC, Sept., 1990).
2. Ibid. at 8.
3. Ibid. at 9.
4. American Psychological Association, Science Directorate, Questionnaires Used in the Prediction of Trustworthiness in Pre-Employment Selection Decisions (American Psychological Association, Washington, DC: March 1991).
5. Ibid. at 26.
6. See, e.g., Hawaii Rev. Stat. §378-29.3, Mich. Comp. Laws Ann. §338.1726a, Vt. Stat. Ann. tit. 21 §494.
7. Minn. Stat. §181.75 (1980).
8. *State v. Century Camera, Inc.*, 309 N.W.2d 735, (Minn. Sup. Ct. 1981).
9. Ibid. at 745.

10. *Blumenthal v. Kay-Bee Toy & Hobby Shops, Inc.,* ERD Case No. 8205303 (1987) .

11. See, e.g., *England v. Seifert's Pine Tree Mall*, ERD Case No. 8205634 (1983); <u>Hintz v. Fleet Farm</u>, ERD Case No. 8912545 (1991); *Nystrom v. The Holiday Companies,* ERD Case No. 8902732 (1991).

12. Employee Polygraph Protection Act of 1988 29 U.S.C. §§2001-2009 (1988).

13. H.R. Rep. No. 659, 100th Cong., 2d Sess. 11 (1988).

14. R.I. Gen. Laws §28-6.1-1 to 28-6.1-4 (1987).

15. Mass. Gen. Laws ch. 149 §19B(1), (2), (2a), (3), and (4) (West 1985).

16. Civil Rights Act of 1964 42 U.S.C. §2000e-5(g) (1988).

17. Civil Rights Act of 1991, Pub. L. No. 102-166 (1991).

18. Ibid. at §105 (k)(1)(A)(i).

19. S.B. 792, 66th Or. Leg. Ass., Reg. Sess. (1991).

20. A.B. 7301, N.Y. 1991-1992 Reg. Session (1991).

21. Halverson, NY, Legislators Push to Ban Honesty Tests, Discount Store News (June 17, 1991).

22. A.B. 5992, Conn. Feb. Sess. (1990).

23. H.F. 408, Iowa (1989).

24. A Handbook of White Collar Crime, Chamber of Commerce of the United States, Washington, DC (1974).

25. Bacas, To Stop a Thief, Nation's Business 16 (1987).

26. *Welsh Mfg. Div. of Textron, Inc. v. Pinkerton's, Inc.,* 474 A.2d 436 (R.I. 1984).

INTELLECTUAL PROPERTY RIGHTS

Most countries recognize and grant varying degrees of protection to four basic intellectual property rights: patents, trademarks, copyrights, and trade secrets.

Patents are grants issued by a national government conferring the right to exclude others from making, using, or selling the invention within that country. Patents may be given for new products or processes. Violations of patent rights are known as infringement or piracy. An example of patent protection are the Process Patent Amendments contained in the Omnibus Trade and Competitiveness Act of 1988. The Act treats unlicensed importers, distributors, retailers, and even consumers of standard products as patent infringers, if an unpatented product was produced by a U.S. patented process. The amendments apply to foreign and domestic manufacture and also to end products that are protected by U.S. process patents.

Trademarks are words, names, symbols, devices, or combinations thereof used by manufacturers or merchants to differentiate their goods and distinguish them from products that are manufactured or sold by others. Counterfeiting and infringement constitute violations of trademark rights.

Copyrights are protections given by a national government to creators of original literary, dramatic, musical, and certain other intellectual works. The owner of a copyright has the exclusive right to reproduce the copyrighted work, prepare derivative works based upon it, distribute copies, and perform or display it publicly. Copyright violations are also known as infringement and piracy.

Trade secrets are information such as formulas, patterns, compilations, programs, devices, methods, techniques, or processes that derive economic value from not being generally known and that cannot be ascertained by unauthorized persons through proper means because they are subject to reasonable efforts to maintain their secrecy. Trade secret violations are known as misappropriation and result from improper acquisition or disclosure. Distinguishing between trade secret safeguards and patent or copyright protection can be difficult. The key elements in a trade secret are the owner's maintenance of confidentiality, limited distribution, and the absence of a patent.

A non-competition or non-disclosure statement is a written agreement that grants protection to an employer from the unauthorized use of the employer's intellectual property by current or former employees. A non-competition statement will typically incorporate one or more of three basic conditions: (1) restrictions on competition by departing employees, (2) definitions of what constitutes property that the employer can legally protect from use by others, and (3) requirements that employees are obligated to cooperate with the employer in efforts to protect its intellectual property.

The Paris Convention is the primary treaty for the protection of trademarks, patents, service marks, trade names, utility models, and industrial designs. Established in 1883, the convention is the oldest of the international bodies concerned with the protection of intellectual properties. It is based on reciprocity: (1) the same protections in member states as that state grants to its own nationals, and (2) equal access for foreigners to local courts to pursue infringement remedies.

Three elements of protection must be in place for the owner to claim violation of intellectual rights: (1) the information is not readily accessible to others, (2) it was created by the owner through the expenditure of considerable resources, and (3) the owner sought to keep the information confidential.

John J. Fay, CPP

Source Fay, J.J., Butterworths Security Dictionary: Terms and Concepts. (Butterworth-Heinemann, Boston, 1989).

INTELLIGENCE: COMPETITIVE INTELLIGENCE IN BUSINESS

Competitive intelligence is essentially the collection and analysis of information. For the most part, it is the use of information readily available to the public. The fundamental purpose of competitive intelligence is to reduce the inherent risks of deciding a key business issue by providing to the decision makers an accurate understanding of the issue with respect to the competition.

Background

Competitive intelligence is not new. It reached its highest development during the Dark Ages in Europe when money lenders used their sophisticated communication systems and agent networks to conduct state intelligence. In Asia it developed along different lines but was no less important than in Europe. One of the earliest references is in Sun Tzu's *Treatise On War*. During the reign of the Prince of Wu (500 BC), Sun Tzu stressed knowing the enemy.

In modern times, intelligence is associated more closely with national intelligence agencies. However, following World War II, businesses began to go international. As corporations moved into new markets and forged alliances with

foreign enterprises, a need arose for specialized business intelligence. Japanese trading companies were probably the first to see the need for competitive intelligence.

In 1950, Eiji Toyoda, later to become the Chairperson of the Toyota Motor Corporation, went to the United States on a commercial intelligence mission. His objective was to learn all about Detroit's manufacturing methods. For over a month, Toyoda visited the Chrysler, Studebaker, General Motors, and Ford auto plants. He methodically observed the production lines, machinery, and workers. He learned what worked and what did not and kept detailed notes.

Thirty-three years later, it was America's turn. Detroit's premier manufacturer, General Motors, signed a joint-venture agreement with Toyota to produce subcompacts in California. The Americans considered this an excellent intelligence opportunity to learn about Japanese production methods.

Legal Considerations

As the world moves into the information age, there are markedly differing perceptions about the ethics and legality of information gathering. What would be called espionage, and therefore illegal, in one jurisdiction is likely in another jurisdiction to be called competitive intelligence, a legal and perfectly accepted practice. The European Economic Community (EEC), for example, has enacted very restrictive laws controlling the trans-national communication of business information. In the United States, the same activity is not a violation of law, but a routine condition of business. American companies operating within the EEC find the restrictions to be a serious impediment.

This is not to suggest that in America information of any sort is accessible or that the owners of information have no proprietary rights. The fact is that legal protections cover many types of information in the United States, but in an open society there are many types that fall outside the protection of law; for example:

•Information that can be obtained directly from public records and the media or through the Freedom of Information Act are fair game. For years, companies have sold mailing lists and demographic data about their clients. These lists are an essential marketing tool. However, credit bureaus, credit card companies, and financial institutions also provide demographic information. They provide information on real estate records, mortgage information, telephone numbers, credit records, discretionary purchasing, and company preferences.

•Direct contacts with competitor employees is all right so long as there is no attempt at subterfuge, to deceive or to conspire. A time-honored practice is to canvass a competitor's suppliers, talk to the competitor's purchasing representatives and sales people, and even hire the competitor's employees.

•Plant visits, trade shows, and scientific symposiums are still fertile hunting grounds. Reverse engineering has now become a science. Visual surveillance of a facility has been found to be acceptable.

Methods

Business needs determine the methods and techniques of competitive intelligence. For the small business, information collection may consist of nothing more than reading newspapers, trade papers, government reports, and industry periodicals. If the business participates in government contracts, it may use the Freedom of Information Act to identify competitors who have submitted bids.

A business's needs for information increases proportional to its growth. The next step up in collecting information may be to hire a clipping service to systematically search the output of the public media. The Freedom of Information Act comes into greater play in terms of discovering new patents, environmental impact statements, state filings, and Security and Exchange Commission reports.

A company's first step in establishing an in-house capability for keeping track of the competition may well consist of a database analyst, a computer, and a modem. The explosive growth of government and commercial on-line databases provides a rich source of data.

A company whose viability is strongly dependent on knowing what the competition is up to may turn the entire organization to the task of collecting data. In this arrangement, employees report every scrap of competitor information that comes their way. The information is organized, collated, analyzed, and interpreted. The product

of the process is fed back into the organization and used in routine decision making. The company becomes an intelligence organism with information as its life's blood.

Implications to Security Management

The sensible security manager will recognize two realities: first, competitive intelligence is a robust adversarial activity, and second, it is not practical to expend time and effort trying to protect information that cannot be protected.

A security manager has no control over competitor access to publicly available information or even competitor access to people who possess sensitive information, but the security manager can exercise a great deal of control over access rights into and within the workplace. The controls can range widely from background screening to sophisticated electronic detectors.

The array of protective controls need to be focused on safeguarding the genuinely sensitive information. Efforts to protect inconsequential or even marginally sensitive information can be counterproductive.

G.H. Zimmer, Jr., CPP

INTELLIGENCE: THE CENTRAL INTELLI-GENCE AGENCY (CIA) PERSPECTIVE

The Intelligence Cycle

The intelligence cycle is the process by which raw information is acquired, gathered, transmitted, evaluated, analyzed, and made available as finished intelligence for policy makers to use in decision making and action. There is scholarly debate about the nature of the intelligence process, but there are usually five steps that constitute the cycle.

Planning and Direction. This involves the management of the entire effort, from the identification of the need for data to the final delivery of an intelligence product to a consumer. It can be seen as the beginning and the end of the cycle -- the beginning because it involves drawing up specific collection requirements and the end because finished intelligence, which supports policy decisions, engenders new requirements.

The whole process is dependent on guidance from public officials. It is initiated by requests for intelligence on certain subjects by the policymakers -- the president, his aides, the National Security Council, and other major departments and agencies of government.

Collection. This involves the gathering of the raw information from which finished intelligence will be produced. There are many sources for the collection of information, including open sources such as foreign broadcasts, newspapers, periodicals, and books. Open source reporting is integral to the Central Intelligence Agency's analytical capabilities.

There are also secret sources of information. CIA's operations officers collect such information from agents abroad and from defectors who provide information obtainable in no other way.

Finally, technical collection -- electronics and satellite photography -- has come to play an indispensable part in modern intelligence, such as monitoring arms control agreements.

Processing. This step involves the conversion of the vast amount of information coming into the system to a form more suitable for producing finished intelligence, such as through decryption and language translations. The information that does not go directly to analysts is sorted and made available for rapid computer retrieval. Processing also refers to data reduction and interpretation of the information stored on film and tape through the use of highly refined photographic and electronic processes.

Analysis and Production. This refers to the conversion of basic information into finished intelligence. It includes the integration, evaluation, and analysis of all available data, and the preparation of a variety of intelligence products.

The intelligence collected is frequently fragmentary and at times contradictory. Analysts, who are subject-matter specialists, weigh the information in terms of reliability, validity, and relevance. They integrate various pieces of data into a coherent whole, put the evaluated information in context, and produce finished intelligence that includes assessments of events or developments and judgments about the implications of the information for the United States.

The CIA devotes the bulk of its resources to providing strategic intelligence to policy makers. It performs this important function by monitoring events, warning decision makers about threats to the United States, and forecasting developments. The subjects involved may concern different regions, problems, or personalities in various contexts -- political, geographic, economic, military, scientific, or biographic. Current events, capabilities, and future trends are examined.

The CIA produces numerous written reports, which may be brief -- one page or less -- or lengthy studies. They may involve current intelligence, which is of immediate importance, or long-range assessments. The agency presents some finished intelligence in oral briefings. The CIA also participates in the drafting and production of National Intelligence Estimates, which reflect the collective judgments of the intelligence community.

Dissemination. The last step, which logically feeds into the first, is the distribution of the finished intelligence to the consumers, the same policy makers whose needs initiated the intelligence requirements. Finished intelligence is hand-carried on a daily basis to the president and the key national security advisors he designates. Dissemination to policy makers is accomplished by means of various distribution lists, each designed on the "need-to-know" basis. The policy makers, the recipients of finished intelligence, then make decisions based on the information, and these decisions may lead to the levying of more requirements, thus triggering the cycle. Sound policy decisions must be based on sound knowledge, and intelligence aims to provide that knowledge.

Executive Oversight of Intelligence

Three intelligence groups serve the president.

National Security Council. The National Security Council (NSC) was established by the National Security Act of 1947 to advise the president with respect to the integration of domestic, foreign, and military policies relating to the national security. The NSC is the highest executive branch entity providing review of, guidance for, and direction to the conduct of all national foreign intelligence and counterintelligence activities. The statutory members of the NSC are the president, the vice president, the secretary of state, and the secretary of defense. The director of Central Intelligence and the chairperson of the joint chiefs of staff participate as advisers.

President's Foreign Intelligence Advisory Board. The president's Foreign Intelligence Advisory Board is maintained within the Executive Office of the president and are appointed from among trustworthy and distinguished citizens outside of government on the basis of achievement, experience, and independence. They serve without compensation. The board continually reviews the performance of all government agencies engaged in the collection, evaluation, or production of intelligence or in the execution of intelligence policy. It also assesses the adequacy of management, personnel, and organization in intelligence agencies and advises the president concerning the objectives, conduct, and coordination of the activities of these agencies. The Advisory Board is specifically charged to make appropriate recommendations for actions to improve and enhance the performance of the intelligence efforts of the United States. This advice may be passed directly to the CIA or other agencies engaged in intelligence activities.

President's Intelligence Oversight Board. The president's Intelligence Oversight Board functions within the White House. It consists of three members from outside the government who are appointed by the president. One of these, who serves as chairperson, is also a member of the president's Foreign Intelligence Advisory Board. The Oversight Board is responsible for discovering and reporting to the president any intelligence activities that raise questions of propriety or legality in terms of the Constitution, the laws of the United States, or Presidential Executive Order. The board is also charged with reviewing internal guidelines and the direction of the intelligence community. The Oversight Board is a permanent, non-partisan body.

The Intelligence Community

The person who is director of Central Intelligence is simultaneously director of the CIA and the leader of the intelligence community, of which CIA is but one component. The intelligence community refers in the aggregate to those executive branch agencies and organizations that conduct the variety of intelligence activities which comprise the total U.S. national intelligence effort. The community includes the CIA; the NSC; the Defense Intelligence Agency; offices within the Department of Defense for collection of specialized national foreign intelligence through reconnaissance programs; the Bureau of Intelligence and Research of the Department of State; Army, Navy, and Air Force intelligence; the Federal Bureau of Investigation; the Department of the Treasury; and the Department of Energy. Members of the intelligence community advise the director of Central Intelligence (DCI) through their representation on a number of specialized committees that deal with intelligence matters of common concern. Chief among these groups are the National Foreign Intelligence Board and the National Foreign Intelligence Council.

Central Intelligence Agency

Source Factbook on Intelligence. (Central Intelligence Agency, Washington, DC, 1992).

INTERIOR INTRUSION DETECTORS

Interior intrusion detectors can be classified as active and passive volumetric motion detectors, barrier penetration detectors, operable opening switches, proximity detectors, and barrier detectors. These detectors, as the title implies, are designed for interior applications, except when explicitly indicated by the manufacturer. Should consideration ever be given to utilizing interior intrusion detectors in exterior environments, extensive testing will be necessary to determine that the detectors will function properly. The primary reason for not using interior detectors outside is that they are not weatherproof or rugged enough to survive out-of-doors conditions. Another reason is that some of the detectors are very susceptible to false alarms in the outside environment, especially volumetric motion detectors. Their detection techniques are influenced by moving animals, grass, trees, etc.

Volumetric Motion Detectors

The whole volume or just a portion of the volume of a room or building can be protected using volumetric motion detectors. Whether the whole volume or just part of the volume is protected depends on the facility detection requirements. Again, depending on the requirements, motion detectors can be used to provide the primary intrusion detection for a building, or they can be used in conjunction with other interior detectors such as barrier and proximity detectors to satisfy the detection requirements. An advantage of volumetric motion detectors is that they will detect an intruder moving in the detector's zone of detection independently of his point of entry into the zone. For example, a store could use volumetric motion detectors to detect motion in the interior of the store along with magnetic door switches to detect anyone opening the entrance doors, and glass break detectors to detect breaking the showcase glass. In this type of application, an intruder coming into the store through a hole in the wall or ceiling will be detected by the volumetric motion detector just as though he had entered the store through a protected door.

The amount of volumetric coverage along with the configuration of the volume requiring protection dictates the number of detector transducers required to detect motion in the volume. A transducer, sometimes referred to as a sensor head, is the device that responds to an event or stimulus within the detection zone and produces an electrical signal for processing. The detector processor analyzes the electrical signal and activates an alarm circuit when the signal characteristics satisfy the alarm criteria.

Volumetric motion detectors consist of either a single transducer with a self-contained signal processor, or multiple transducers connected to a common signal processor. While some of the single transducer detectors have a large zone of detection, detectors with multiple transducers can be positioned to form a patterned zone of detection. This pattern can be configured to protect a specific item or to protect the most probable entrance route of an intruder. The decision to use a large-volume, single transducer detector or detectors with multiple transducers is only one of many tradeoffs that should be considered when selecting volumetric motion detectors.

There are two basic types of volumetric motion detectors -- active and passive. Active detectors fill the protected volume with an energy pattern and recognize a disturbance in that pattern when an intruder moves within the zone

of detection. Ultrasonic detectors fill the volume with inaudible acoustical energy, microwave with electromagnetic energy, and sonic with audible acoustical energy. While active detectors generate their own energy pattern to detect an intruder, passive detectors detect the energy generated by the intruder either by sensing the body heat or thermal energy in the infrared frequency range emanating from the intruder, or by sensing changes in the thermal energy background as a result of the intruder shadowing the background while moving through the protected zones. Audio detectors detect the presence of an intruder by simply listening for the noises generated by a forced entry into the protected facilities or the noises generated as the intruder carries out his objective inside the protected area.

Barrier Penetration Detectors

Forcible entry through perimeter barriers, walls, ceilings, and windows can be detected by barrier penetration detectors. There are several types of penetration detectors including vibration, heat, breakwire grids, foil tape, and security screens. Vibration detectors are available that detect low-frequency vibrations generated by a physical attack on a structural wall or ceiling, and high-frequency vibrations generated by breaking glass. The high-frequency vibration detectors are often referred to as glass breakage detectors. As the name implies, they are used to protect glass windows such as display or showcase windows.

Heat sensors are sometimes used as intrusion detectors to detect unusual thermal activity. An example of such activity would be a torch cutting through a metal barrier such as a safe and vault. Foil tape has been used for many years to protect glass windows, but it can also be installed around perimeter walls and ceilings to detect penetration. Breakwire grids are constructed with slotted wooden dowel rods lined with a fine wire that breaks if the frame is cut or broken. They are used to detect penetrations through windows or any other human-size openings, such as heating and ventilating ducts, leading into a protected area. Breakwires can also be installed in a grid pattern directly on the perimeter barrier to detect penetrations. Since the foil tape and breakwire installed directly on the perimeter barriers break easily, they should be protected against day-to-day abuse. Foil tape on windows can be protected with a clear, hard plastic coating material; however, sheet materials such as plywood or gypsum board installed directly over the breakwire patterns installed on perimeter barriers will provide lasting protection. Security screens can be used as barriers to detect penetrations through windows. Foil tape, breakwire grids, and security screens are connected directly to a control unit or signal transmitter that recognize an open circuit as an alarm. An intruder who penetrates the protected barrier breaks the foil tape or wire and thereby initiates an alarm.

Operable Opening Switches

Several types of switches are available to detect entries through operable openings such as doors and windows. These include balanced magnetic, magnetic, mechanical contact, and tilt switches. In a typical door installation, a switch detects movement between the door and the door frame. The switch is usually mounted on the door frame and the activating device, if required, is mounted on the door. When the door is opened, the activating device either opens or closes the switch contacts, thereby initiating an alarm. Operable opening switches can be connected directly to a control unit that recognizes either an open or closed circuit as an alarm condition, depending on whether the switch is normally open or normally closed.

Interior Barrier Detectors

The entrance or the most probable avenue an intruder would take when entering or moving through a protected area can be protected by interior barrier detectors. The actual barrier can be either an invisible infrared beam or a trip-wire device. The infrared beam, generated by an infrared source in the transmitter, is projected onto a photoelectric cell in the receiver. When the beam is interrupted, the incident infrared radiation projected onto the photoelectric cell is interrupted and the detector initiates an alarm. A trip-wire, as the name implies, consists of a thin wire or cord and a spring switch for terminating the trip-wire. In an actual application, the trip-wire is stretched across the entrance to the protected area and fastened to the termination switch. An intruder who comes in contact with

the wire trips the termination switch and initiates an alarm.

Proximity Detectors

Anyone coming in close proximity to, touching, or lifting a protected item can be detected by proximity detectors. They are used for protecting metal safes, art objects, jewelry on display, etc. Probably the most popular proximity device is the capacitance detector used to protect metal devices, such as safes and file cabinets. They detect changes in the electrical capacitance between the protected metal objects and the ground plane formed by the surrounding surfaces and floor. Pressure mats and tilt switches can also be used as proximity detectors. Pressure mats detect an intruder who steps on the mat installed in the vicinity of the protected item. They are also used as barrier detectors to protect entrances and the probable route through the protected facility. Although tilt switches are primarily used to protect operated openings, they can also be used as proximity detectors. In such applications, the tilt switches are fastened to valuable moveable items such as paintings and other art objects. Thereafter, if a protected item is tilted, the switch initiates an alarm. This is another example of how detection devices can be used for alternate protection applications.

Robert L. Barnard

Source Barnard, R.L., Intrusion Detection Systems. (Butterworth-Heinemann, Boston, 1982).

INTERNAL REVENUE SERVICE CRIMINAL INVESTIGATION DIVISION

History

Several important factors occurred that affected the decision of the Bureau of Internal Revenue to create the Intelligence Unit (the forefather of the Criminal Investigation Division) on July 1, 1919. To support the war effort, the first income tax law was enacted with the Revenue Act of 1913 and then significantly increased under the Revenue Act of 1916. The Revenue Act of 1917 made it necessary to quickly increase the number of revenue employees. By 1919 many serious complaints were reaching the Internal Revenue

Commissioner relative to alleged tax fraud and charges of irregularities involving revenue employees. Six Post Office inspectors were selected to become the first special agents in charge of divisions in the Intelligence Unit.

Mission

Today's mission of the Criminal Investigation Division (CID) in the Internal Revenue Service (IRS) is to enforce the criminal statutes relative to tax administration and related financial crime in order to encourage and achieve, directly or indirectly, voluntary compliance with the IRS laws. Five programs are directed to the mission.

Narcotics Crime. This program includes investigations of individuals and organizations who direct, supervise, and finance the illicit drug trade.

Abusive Compliance Crimes. These investigations focus on tax violations that involve, in a material way, commodity futures, options, government securities transactions, fuel excise tax, illegal tax protester schemes, fraudulent refund schemes, or abusive/illegal tax shelters. This category also includes investigations involving preparers of multiple/fraudulent tax returns.

Organized Crime. This program refers to those self-perpetuating, structured, and disciplined associations of individuals, or groups, combined together for the purpose of obtaining monetary or commercial gains or profits, wholly or in part by illegal means, while protecting their activities through a pattern of graft and corruption.

Public Corruption Crimes. Investigations in this area involve the violation of public trust of or by government officials/employees.

White Collar Crimes. Investigations are made of fraud against or related to a savings and loan institution, bank, or related regulatory agency, or where their employees or officials placed the solvency of the institution at risk. This category also covers cases that do not fall in any other category.

Internal Revenue Service

Source Public Affairs Pamphlet. (Criminal Investigation Division, Internal Revenue Service, U.S. Department of the Treasury, Washington, DC, 1992).

INTERNAL THEFT: PREVENTION AND CAUSES

The pundit who coined the old adage about the inevitability of death and taxes could not have foreseen a new tax that affects all of us today -- namely the "theft tax."

Many larger companies, because of size and competitive position, can easily absorb a reasonable level of loss from internal theft. At the beginning of the fiscal period, they will set aside a certain amount of money to cover anticipated theft losses. This reserve becomes part of the company's regular operating budget. The cost to produce an item will include the cost of internal theft, which in turn affects the selling price. Thus, in the end, the consumer pays the so-called theft tax in the form of a higher price.

The practice is time-honored and overall is changing only for the worse. Significant positive change will come when consumers understand they are underwriting internal theft and rise up in some way that captures the attention of management. Until then, the practice will continue and security professionals will be left to wrestle with the problems it creates.

Theft Prevention

On the brighter side, a few companies have come to realize that rising labor costs and other cost factors that fuel inflation leave very little room for theft reserves. Instead of automatically writing off theft losses, they are looking for ways to reduce them and in the process are discovering that reduction of theft can be a strong bottom-line contributor.

The past 10 years have seen the creation of more and more internal or corporate-level security departments -- departments designed not only to keep internal theft in bounds, but to reduce theft through preventive efforts coupled with a direct attack on perpetrators. Many of these corporate-level departments are now actually viewed as revenue centers because of their success in turning loss dollars into profit dollars.

A well-balanced security program will include at least two components: one to educate employees away from internal theft and the second to exercise controls that directly thwart thievery. Corporate executives, however, should recognize that the security program is designed for and intended to impact particular segments of the workforce. We know from research and experience that about 20% of all workers have great respect for the employer's property, about 60% of workers occasionally steal when given the chance, and about 20% operate on the philosophy that "whatever I can get away with is mine." Employees in the first two categories respond well to education and protective safeguards, while those in the last category are extremely resistive. They often devote considerable energy looking for and acting on ways to steal. For these employees, the practical solution is detection and termination for cause.

Internal Theft Causes

A few words of explanation are in order regarding reasons that underlie the internal theft problem and the countermeasures developed as a response.

Population Shifts. Since World War II, great shifts in population within the United States have occurred. A number of factors have contributed, such as the creation of a vast and efficient national highway system, increased worker mobility spurred by job specialization, and the choices of major employers to locate in particular parts of the country. No longer can an employer reliably determine the fitness of a job applicant based on the employer's knowledge of the applicant. Hiring decisions are often based on the uncorroborated claims of the applicant rather than on the applicant's work experience and personal character.

Limitations of Reference Checking. Employers are becoming more aware of the limitations of background investigations and the traditional reference letter, in particular. Because of a fear of lawsuits that allege invasion of privacy, the majority of today's employers are reluctant to give any information in a reference letter beyond dates of employment, job title, and salary level. More and more employers have turned to the use of paper-and-pencil honesty testing and, where permitted, polygraph testing.

Lack of Employee Loyalty. Unlike Japanese firms, which generally enjoy a high degree of employee loyalty, American companies have seen employee loyalty dwindle to the point where it can no longer be considered a viable factor in deterring internal theft.

Much of the erosion of loyalty has been brought about by labor unions that look upon members as "their people" rather than as employees of the company. Union representatives have regularly interfered with internal theft investigations by encouraging members to not cooperate and by interposing themselves as counselors and champions of "members' rights." Some union constitutions and oaths of membership contain provisions that prohibit union members from informing on other members.

Other factors associated with erosion of loyalty are the ease of cross-over of workers from one employer to another, the "bigness" of a company that detracts from the worker's sense of being a part of the family, and the continuing series of economic downturns that have forced many companies to lay off and terminate productive and loyal employees.

Restrictions on Screening. Efforts of employers to screen job applicants are also hampered by various privacy laws and Equal Employment Opportunity Commission (EEOC) restrictions. After having been sued or investigated for an alleged privacy or discrimination violation, an employer may choose to discontinue applicant screening and simply hire people at face value.

Lack of Security Expertise. The great mainstream of American business is filled with small- and medium-size companies, which lack the resources to engage full-time or contract/consultant security professionals. The result is that a very large number of businesses lack the capacity to understand the nature and depth of internal theft, much less set up defenses against it.

Organized Crime. A clear relationship exists between internal theft and organized crime. Organized crime is often involved in hijacking and fencing of stolen goods, counterfeiting and piracy of goods, embezzlement, and a variety of bankruptcy frauds that milk a company of its assets. All of these involve employee insiders. Overall, the method of operation is not so much through infiltration of the company as it is the capacity of organized crime to exert substantial leverage on employee insiders through promises of great reward or fear of violence.

Drugs. Like organized crime, there is a clear linkage between drug use and internal theft. We readily understand that theft from the employer is often used to finance the habits of drug-abusing employees. Less understood is the theft of time by drug-abusing employees who are absent from their work stations while administering or trafficking in drugs, who arrive late because of a drug hangover and leave early to get a head start on abuse, and who cheat on sick leave benefits in order to enjoy or recover from abuse.

J. Kirk Barefoot, CPP

INTERNSHIPS: THE SECURITY MANAGER'S APPRENTICE

Internship programs provide college students with opportunities to learn on the job while receiving degree credits. Internship programs have succeeded so well that many schools require students to complete one or more as a degree requirement, and on some campuses the number of prospective interns exceeds the number of available internships. Students are often caught in a Catch-22 situation created by a degree requirement (or a personal desire) that is unmatched by opportunities to gain relevant work experience with local companies. The problem seems to be rooted in a preoccupation of business leaders with the pursuit of business goals and a failure of college administrators to effectively promote internship programs.

As a result, students in Security Management degree programs are often denied the chance to develop insights and skills that can only come from working in a security management setting. This is a damaging result both for the development of the individual and the professionalization of the security field.

Employers needing to fill entry-level positions often seek candidates who have a blend of formal education, training, and related experience. A Security Management degree fills the educational requirement. The elements of

training and experience, however, are often absent in the personal portfolios of candidates. The reason is that many students were too busy pursuing their degrees to be more than superficially involved in the security profession. The internship program provides learning based on meaningful work experience.

A minimum number of hours are required from the intern for the semester. In a few cases they are paid (usually minimum wage); in most cases they are not paid. The intern is graded on participation, with the sponsor providing feedback to the school. A short-term paper describing the work is usually required and this can be reviewed by the sponsor as well.

Work and observation begins at the start of the semester and continues throughout the term. The school provides a set of expectations covering such topics as conduct, dress, and expectations of the school, supplemented by similar instructions from the sponsor. It serves a business well when internships can span two semesters. Scheduling assignments are made easier and continuity improves the quality of the work product.

A waiver can be developed addressing any inherent liability issues, if that is a matter of concern. The laws vary from state to state, and the waiver should be developed jointly with the school and the company's legal representative.

Interns should neither be used merely to supplement clerical staffing nor for mundane assignments. Obviously, there will be some duties that involve clerical effort. Interns should not be used to stand post, unless it applies specifically to their internship. They should be exposed to as many elements of the program as is permitted, including attendance at staff meetings, for example.

Interns required to comply with the Defense Industrial Security Program (DISP) can be processed for personnel security clearances. Since the clearance process can take several months, the interns can be exposed during the first semester to those elements of the DISP that do not require a clearance; during the second semester, after receiving clearances, they can be assigned more sensitive tasks.

Advantages and Disadvantages

The potential advantages to a business of an internship program include:

1.   An intern can be a valuable contributor. This presupposes that the business has interviewed the candidate and found him/her acceptable; has placed the intern under a good supervisor; and assigned to the intern a combination of tasks that when properly performed, will result in a valuable work product or service.

2.   The intern's competency and suitability for future hire as a full-time employee can be evaluated during the internship period.

3.   Projects put on hold for lack of personnel can be completed through internship contributions. Projects can include conducting studies, writing procedures, and creating security awareness materials.

4.   An intern program casts favorable light on the sponsoring company, both as a responsible corporate citizen in the surrounding community and as a supporter of security professionalization.

The potential disadvantages include:

1.   Time devoted to the internship program may draw the sponsoring company from business objectives of greater import.

2.   The sponsor may not be oriented toward training to the degree necessary to ensure good work performance by the intern and to ensure that the intern learns from the work experience.

3.   Liability issues could be presented.

Joining an Internship Program

A company that agrees to participate in an internship program will need to meet the administrative requirements of the local college or university and at the same time set up its own mechanisms for selecting interns, in-processing them, assigning supervisors, reviewing their performance and learning, and returning them to the academic setting in an improved condition. Following is an outline of action steps in setting up and operating the program within the sponsoring company.

1.   Interview candidates. Ensure that the company's criteria for employment can be met by the candidate. Fully discuss the company's expectations and requirements with respect to work hours, use of company equipment, care of company assets, dress, conduct, etc.

2.   Obtain an understanding from the school and the intern concerning the length of the internship, the beginning and ending dates, and

any days that may require the intern to be absent. Ascertain the school's requirements with respect to reports of the intern's work performance, progress, achievements, and so forth.

3.   Complete all necessary paperwork, e.g., employment application, and payroll and tax forms, if applicable.

4.   Subject the intern to the same pre-employment and post-employment screening processes that apply to regular employees.

5.   Provide an orientation to the company and to the functions of the company's security program. Caution is needed concerning disclosure of sensitive information. Issue pertinent manuals, handbooks, procedures, guides, etc.

6.   Thoroughly review safety rules, the wearing of personal protective equipment, reporting of injuries, evacuation procedures, and the like.

7.   Consider an arrangement that will permit the intern to rotate within the security department to maximize his or her exposure to many functions.

8.   Choose and brief a supervisor who can be counted on to obtain value for the company and the intern.

9.   Take the intern on a tour of the facility to establish familiarity with parking areas, rest rooms, break areas, cafeteria, etc.

10. Introduce the intern to co-workers and other employees with whom the intern will be expected to interact.

Lonnie R. Buckels, CPP,
and Robert B. Iannone, CPP

INTERPOL

The International Criminal Police Organization is an international law enforcement organization consisting of 138 member countries. The INTERPOL-U.S. National Central Bureau (INTERPOL-USNCB) facilitates international law enforcement cooperation, on behalf of the attorney general, by enabling a means of communication among domestic and foreign law enforcement organizations, and the INTERPOL headquarters or general secretariat in St. Cloud, France. Through the INTERPOL telecommunications network, and through the INTERPOL-USNCB's telecommunications linkage with state, local, and federal law enforcement agencies, the INTERPOL-

USNCB provides assistance in both domestic and foreign criminal investigative matters.

In each member country, a point of contact and coordination is established to maintain the INTERPOL function. Generally, this activity is undertaken by some component of the national police in the capital city of each country. The designated entity is known as the National Central Bureau (NCB). Although staffing patterns and size vary, each member country operates its own NCB within the parameters of its own national laws and policies, and within the framework of the INTERPOL Constitution.

The INTERPOL-USNCB, administered jointly by the U.S. Department of Justice and the U.S. Department of the Treasury, operates as a separate organization within the U.S. Department of Justice. As a law enforcement organization, it provides assistance to federal, state, and local law enforcement agencies in conducting criminal investigations in any of the INTERPOL member countries, and in the United States. Both departments provide staffing as well as professional leadership for the positions of chief and deputy chief.

The INTERPOL-USNCB functions through collaborative efforts with 13 participating federal law enforcement agencies. Currently, Department of Justice representatives from the Federal Bureau of Investigation (FBI), U.S. Marshals Service, Drug Enforcement Administration, the Immigration and Naturalization Service, and the Criminal Division are assigned at the INTERPOL-USNCB. In addition, Department of the Treasury components including the U.S. Customs Service; U.S. Secret Service; the Internal Revenue Service; the Bureau of Alcohol, Tobacco and Firearms; the Office of the Comptroller of the Currency; and the Federal Law Enforcement Training Center in Glynco, Georgia, provide detailed investigative and support personnel to the INTERPOL-USNCB. Other federal agency participants in the INTERPOL-USNCB program include the Department of Agriculture's Office of the Inspector General and the U.S. Postal Inspection Service.

Assistance may be given in investigations of the following types: criminal history checks; license plate/drivers license checks; investigations leading to arrest and extradition; locating suspects, fugitives, and witnesses; All Points Bulletins (APBs) to any and all member countries; tracing weapons abroad; locating motor vehicles abroad; and other types of criminal investigations that transcend national boundaries.

All requests for assistance must include the nature of the offense, the relationship of the subject to the investigation, and additional, supporting information to reflect that it is a valid law enforcement request for information. Other criteria, before obtaining assistance from the INTERPOL-USNCB, include the following: (1) there must be legitimate police jurisdiction to warrant initiation of an investigation; (2) any action taken cannot violate federal, state, or local laws; (3) the action cannot be in conflict with Article 3 of the INTERPOL Constitution, which stipulates that matters of a political, religious, racial, or military nature may not be handled through INTERPOL channels; and (4) the action may not violate any government regulation.

INTERPOL

Source INTERPOL. (U.S. Department of Justice, Washington, DC, 1992).

INTERROGATION: REID'S NINE STEPS OF INTERROGATION

An interview is a non-accusatory conversation where, through questions and answers, the interviewer tries to develop investigative and behavioral information that will test the veracity of statements made by a suspect, victim, or witness.

In contrast, interrogation is an accusatory procedure designed to elicit information from a person who is believed to be not telling the truth. While interrogation is most often used with an individual suspected of committing a crime, a victim who is believed to be fabricating a crime or a witness who is believed to be withholding relevant information may also be the subject of an interrogation. The process seeks to obtain an acknowledgment that the person did not tell the truth in an earlier statement to conceal guilt or to protect the guilty party.

Privacy is the principal psychological factor contributing to the successful outcome of an interview or interrogation. Typically, the questioner and the subject sit in similar chairs, directly facing each other approximately 5 feet apart and without any physical barrier (such as a desk) between them. The questioner will minimize distractions, such as phones ringing.

A second important psychological factor for successful interrogation is to conduct a non-accusatory interview prior to the accusatory interrogation. During this interview the questioner gains important insight with respect to the subject's psychological characteristics and also establishes an image of professionalism and competency. An interrogation should only be conducted when the questioner is reasonably certain that the subject has not told the truth during the interview.

The Accusatory Interrogation

The Positive Confrontation. Following the non-accusatory interview, the questioner leaves the room. After several minutes, the questioner returns carrying an investigative file, opens it, and confronts the subject with facts that clearly point to the subject's deception. This type of accusation is made only when the subject's guilt is very apparent. Otherwise, the statement should be less direct. Following the confrontation, the questioner pauses to evaluate the subject's reaction to the statement, then repeats the statement. Following this, the questioner places the investigative file aside, sits down directly opposite the subject, and makes a transition from being an accuser to a sympathetic and understanding person.

Theme Development. The next step is to present themes that are "moral justifications" for the subject's criminal behavior. One way of doing this is to place moral blame for an illegal activity on another person or an outside set of circumstances. This appeals to a basic aspect of human nature. Most people tend to minimize responsibility for their actions by placing blame on someone or something else. In a credit card fraud case, for example, the questioner might suggest that the subject was not paid enough by the employer or that someone left the card out where it was an open invitation to use. Other moral justifications include unusual family expenses, desperate financial circumstances, a friend came up with the idea, retribution for an argument, and drug or alcohol dependence.

The questioner presents the moral justification in a sympathetic and understanding way. An interest in working with the subject to resolve the problem breaks the ice. The justification is presented in an unbroken monologue that does not afford the subject an opportunity to voice denials.

Handling Denials. In fact, the more often the subject denies guilt, the more difficult it becomes for the subject to admit guilt later. Therefore, during theme development the questioner interjects a blocking statement whenever the subject enters an "I didn't do it" plea. Denials from the guilty subject are often preceded by permission phrases such as, "Can I say one thing?" or "If I could only explain" or "But sir, if you just let me talk." Each of these permission phrases will be followed by the denial, "I didn't do it." Consequently, by cutting the subject off and maintaining the flow of theme development, the questioner discourages the guilty subject's denial attempts.

Innocent subjects rarely use permission phrases before denying guilt. Instead, the innocent subject will, with any display of etiquette, promptly and unequivocally maintain innocence. An innocent subject remains steadfast in the assertion of innocence and never moves past the denial stage. On the other hand, many guilty subjects will abandon the strategy of denial, which is a defensive tactic, and move to an offensive strategy that offers objections.

Overcoming Objections. An objection is a stated reason why a subject would not or could not have committed the crime under investigation. Most guilty subjects will make objections that fall into general categories. The first of these are trait objections such as, "I wasn't brought up that way." or "I'd be too scared to do something like that." The other category of objections include factual objections that allege lack of opportunity or access to commit the crime. Examples of factual objections are, "I don't even have the combination to the safe," "I don't own a handgun," and "I was with my girl friend that night."

While both types of objections offer feeble reasons supporting a claim of innocence, most objections will have some basis in fact. For example, the subject in fact was probably not brought up to rob gas stations and in fact was probably with his girl friend at some point in time on the night of the robbery. Because of the factual basis for most objections, the questioner generally does not refute them. To do so would only encourage an argument or discussion that would break the flow of theme development. Rather, when the subject offers an objection the questioner first rewards it, perhaps with a statement such as "I'm glad you said that" or" You're absolutely right, I was aware of that before I talked with you about this." The objection is then incorporated into the theme. For example, a subject who states, "I'd be too scared to do something like this" could be told, "I'm glad you said that because it tells me that this crime was out of character for you and that you probably had never done anything like this before in your life." By handling objections in this manner the subject is made to realize that an offensive tactic will be ineffective in convincing the questioner of innocence. At this stage most subjects psychologically withdraw and focus mentally on the prospects of impending punishment.

Keeping a Subject's Attention. Following the objection stage, the guilty subject often becomes pensive, apathetic, and quiet. It is most important during this state that the questioner procure and focus the subject's attention on the theme (i.e., the psychological justification for the subject's behavior). Through this process the subject's thoughts will be diverted away from the impending punishment (which only serves to reinforce the resolve to deny guilt). To procure the subject's attention, the questioner draws nearer to the subject. A closer physical proximity helps direct the subject's thoughts to what the questioner is doing and saying. The questioner now begins to channel the theme down to the probable alternative components.

Handling a Subject's Passive Mood. At this stage, the subject may cry, which is often an expression of remorse. Many other subjects do not cry, but express their emotional state by assuming a defeatist posture -- slumped head and shoulders, relaxed legs, and a vacant stare. In order to facilitate the impending admission of guilt, the questioner intensifies the theme presentation and concentrates on the psychological justification for the unlawful act. Gestures of sympathy, such as a hand on the subject's shoulder, also aid truth-telling.

Presenting an Alternative Question. The alternative question is one in which the questioner presents two incriminatory choices concerning some aspect of the crime. Elements of the alternative are developed as logical extensions of the theme. If the theme focuses on contrasting behavior that is impulsive or spur-of-the-moment versus planned or premeditated acts, the alternative question is, "Did you plan this thing out or did it just happen on the spur of the moment?" Either choice is an admission of guilt. The alternative question should be based on an assumption of guilt, not on a yes or no proposition, such as, "Did you do this or didn't you?" A misphrased question invites denial. The first admission of guilt is established when the subject accepts either of the offered alternatives. The way now stands clear to develop the admission into a corroborated confession.

Having the Subject Relate Details. Once the alternative question is answered, the questioner responds with a statement of reinforcement such as, "Good, that's what I thought all along." Essentially, this is a statement that acknowledges the subject's admission of guilt. Following this, the objective is to obtain a brief oral review of the basic sequence of events, while obtaining sufficient detail to corroborate the subject's guilt.

Questions asked at this time should be brief, concise, and clear, calling only for limited verbal responses from the subject. It is premature to ask all-encompassing questions like, "Well, just tell me everything that happened." Furthermore, questions should be open-ended and devoid of emotionally charged terminology. Once the subject has offered a brief verbal statement about the crime sequence, the questioner should ask detailed questions to obtain information that can be corroborated by subsequent investigation. After this full verbal statement is complete, it may be necessary to return to the subject's choice of alternatives or to some other statement previously made. Discussions along these lines tend to shed light on the subject's motive, purpose, and intent at the time of the crime.

Converting an Oral Confession. In this step, the questioner tells the subject he has to leave for a few moments to check on something. The questioner leaves the interrogation room and then returns with a partner who the questioner introduces as someone who has been working on the investigation. The actual function of the partner is to be a witness to the subject's confession. The questioner then goes over the essential details in a manner that would allow the witness to testify to the correctness and voluntariness of the confession. The questioner is now ready to convert the oral confession into a written confession. One of four formats can be used:

- A statement handwritten by the subject.
- A statement written by the questioner, and read and signed by the subject.
- A statement taken down by a secretary or stenographer and transcribed into a typed document for the subject to read and sign.
- A tape-recorded or video-recorded statement.

Fundamental guidelines should be followed. In a custodial setting, even though Miranda warnings may have been given and the appropriate waiver obtained, it is advisable to repeat the warning at the beginning of the confession, referring to the fact that the subject had received them earlier.

The statement of guilt must be readable and understandable by someone who is not familiar with what the subject has done. Leading questions should be avoided, the confessor's own language should be used, and full corroboration should be established. Any errors, changes, or crossed-out words should be initialed with an "OK" written in the margin by the subject. The statement should reflect that the subject was treated properly, that no threats or promises were made, and that the statement was freely given by the subject. When the subject has completed reading the written statement, the questioner says, "Write your name here" while pointing to the place of signature. The questioner avoids saying "Sign here" because "sign" connotes a degree of legalism that may cause the subject to back out of making a written confession. The subject signs each page of the statement in front of the questioner and the witness, who also add their signatures.

Obtaining the written confession at the end of the interrogation is, of course, not the capstone. Every effort should be made to verify the statement and obtain the support evidence necessary for trial.

Joseph P. Buckley

INTERROGATION: THE KINESICS TECHNIQUE

Kinesics is the study of body language and is based on the behavioral patterns of nonverbal communication. Body language can include any nonreflexive or reflexive movement of a part or all of the body. Body language can be particularly revealing when a person communicates an emotional message to the outside world. It is said that actions speak louder than words, and it's not what you say, but how you say it that counts.

To understand this unspoken body language, kinesics experts often have to take into consideration cultural and environmental differences. The average man, unschooled in cultural nuances of body language, often misinterprets what he sees.

Some have called body language an unconscious signal, such as widening of the pupil when the eye sees something pleasant. Often the swiftest and most obvious type of body language is touch. The touch of the hand, or an arm around someone's shoulder, can spell a more vivid and direct message than dozens of words, but such a touch must come at the right moment in the right context.

We act out our state of being with nonverbal body language. We lift one eyebrow for disbelief. We rub our noses for puzzlement. We clasp our arms to isolate or protect ourselves. We shrug our shoulders for indifference, wink one eye for intimacy, tap our fingers for impatience, slap our forehead for forgetfulness. The gestures are numerous. While some are deliberate and others almost deliberate, there are some, such as rubbing under our noses for puzzlement or clasping our arms to protect ourselves, that are mostly unconscious.

No matter how crowded the area in which we humans live, each of us maintains a zone or territory around us, an inviolate area we try to keep for our own. How we defend this area and how we react to invasion of it, as well as how we encroach into other territories, can all be observed and charted, and in many cases used constructively. These are all elements of nonverbal communication. This guarding of zones is one of the first basic principles. How we guard our zones and how we intrude into other zones is an integral part of how we relate to other people.

When you are at close intimate distance you are overwhelmingly aware of your partner. For this reason, if such contact takes place between two men, it can lead to awkwardness or uneasiness. It is most natural between a man and a woman on intimate terms. When a man and a woman are not on intimate terms, the close intimate situation can be embarrassing.

We use body language to communicate approval of someone's closeness. Aside from the actual physical retreat of going somewhere else, there will be a series of preliminary signals such as rocking, leg swinging, or tapping. These are the first signs of tension, which are saying, "You are too near, your presence makes me uneasy."

The next series of body language signals are closed eyes, withdrawal of the chin into the chest, and hunching of the shoulders. They say, "Leave me alone. You are in my space." When these signals are ignored, the person will usually move to another location.

Many people who act violently have said that their victims "messed around with them," although the victims had done nothing but come close to them. The victim had intruded on the assailant's personal space.

Defending personal space involves using the proper body language signals or gestures and postures, as well as a choice of a location. Body language and spoken language are dependent on each other. Spoken language alone will not give the full meaning of what a person is saying, nor for that matter will body language alone give the full meaning. If we listen only to the words when someone is talking, we may get as much of a distortion as if we listened only to the body language.

An awareness of someone else's body language and the ability to interpret it create an awareness of one's own body language. As we begin to receive and interpret the signals others are sending, we begin to monitor our own signals and achieve greater control over ourselves, and in turn function more effectively. Research suggests there are no more than about 30 traditional American gestures. There are even fewer body postures that carry any significance in communication and each of these occurs in a limited number of situations.

Of all parts of the human body that are used to transmit information, the eyes are the most important and can transmit the most subtle nuances. While the eyeball itself shows nothing, the emotional impact of the eyes occurs because of their use and the use of the face around them. The

reason they have so confounded observers is because by length of glance, by opening of eyelids, by squinting, and by a dozen little manipulations of the skin and eyes, almost any meaning can be sent out.

The most important technique of eye management is the look, or the stare. With it we can often make or break another person. How? By giving him or her human or non-human status. Simply, eye management boils down to two facts. One, we do not stare at another human being. Two, staring is reserved for a non-person. We stare at art, at sculpture, at scenery. We go to the zoo and stare at the animals. We stare at them for as long as we please, as intimately as we please, but we do not stare at humans if we want to accord them human treatment.

With unfamiliar human beings, when we acknowledge their humanness, we must avoid staring at them, and yet we must also avoid ignoring them. To make them into people rather than objects, we use a deliberate and polite inattention. We look at them long enough to make it quite clear that we see them, and then we immediately look away. We are saying, in body language, "I acknowledge you," and a moment later we add, "But I won't violate your privacy." A look in itself does not give the entire story, even though it has a meaning. A word in a sentence has a meaning too, but only in the context of the sentence can we learn the complete meaning of the words.

If we are to attempt to interpret body language, then we must assume that all movements of the body have meaning. None are accidental. Extreme caution must be used to avoid misinterpretation of behavior. We cannot rely on any one instance to make a valid inference. All the body signals must be added up to a correct total if we are to use body language effectively.

Perhaps scratching the nose is an indication of disagreement, but it may also be an indication of an itchy nose. This is where the real trouble in kinesics lies, in separating the significant from the insignificant gestures, the meaningful from the purely random, or from the carefully learned.

We must approach kinesics with caution and study a motion or a gesture only in terms of the total pattern of movement, and we must understand the pattern of movement in terms of the spoken language too. The two, while sometimes contradictory, are also inseparable. There is a surprising lack of uniformity in body movement. Working class people will give certain interpretations to movements, and these interpretations will not apply in middle class circles.

A body movement may mean nothing at all in one context, and yet be extremely significant in another context. For example, the frown we make by creasing the skin between our eyebrows may simply mark a point in a sentence or, in another context, it may be a sign of annoyance or, in still another context, of deep concentration. Examining the face alone will not tell us the exact meaning of the frown. We must know what the frowner is doing. No single motion ever stands alone; it is always part of a pattern. We must examine other cues accompanying a particular movement to accurately assess its meaning. Body language can serve as a means of communications if we have the ability to understand it.

Kinesics and Interrogation

With respect to interrogation, the psychological assumptions underlying the kinesics technique are:

1.   The deceptive person who experiences physiological changes resulting from his fear of detection will regard the interrogation as a threat, i.e., an intensification of fear;

2.   The deceptive person's fears intensify during interrogation at moments when questioning focuses on investigative details having the greatest immediate threat to the person's self-preservation;

3.   The deceptive person is aware of physiological changes occurring in the body and may do or say things as a means to disguise the changes; and

4.   The deceptive person who does not experience fear during an interrogation will not exhibit any of the body movements that can be associated with deception.

The guilty subject has a general fear of an investigation. When the investigation calls for an interrogation of the guilty subject, the fear intensifies. During the interrogation, the guilty subject's immediate anxieties and apprehensions are directed toward those questions that present the greatest threat to exposure. In other words, a guilty person's fear of detection increases as the investigation proceeds from the general to the specific.

The deceptive person will tune in on questions that indicate trouble or danger. His mental attention and sensory organs are anticipating particular questions. There is a tendency to tune out questions that are of a lesser threat and to concentrate on questions that lead to exposure.

The interrogator cannot always know what questions will produce fear in the guilty subject. As the line of questioning moves closer to the issues having the greatest psychological threat to the subject, there is likely to be an increase in the number and intensity of deceptive behaviors.

The interrogation must be planned, and modified during execution, so as to move the line of questioning toward issues that have the greatest threat. A successful interrogation is dependent to a very large degree upon the ability of the interrogator to force the guilty subject to focus upon specific, self-threatening issues.

Not all persons who react deceptively are in fact deceptive or guilty. Some people will respond with deceptive behavior signals when subjected to accusatory questions regardless of guilt. A person of this type is sometimes referred to as a guilt complex reactor. The guilt complex reactor is extremely rare. The basic emotionality of the subject being interrogated must be taken into consideration in determining his or her potential for reaction. Generally speaking, the severity of the offense is proportional to the reaction potential of the guilty subject.

At the beginning of an interrogation the subject will undergo a temporary heightening of the emotional state. This is true whether the subject is guilty or not guilty. As the interrogation proceeds, the heightened emotional state of the innocent subject will decrease.

The reaction potential of a deceptive subject is conditioned by the number and intensity of previous interrogations; and the reaction potential of the deceptive subject may be low or beyond observation if emotional fatigue is present. The innocent apprehensive subject (not necessarily the guilt complex reactor) may give random erratic reactions.

Physiological Roots of the Kinesics Technique

The human body is composed of cells. The cells are organized into tissues, organs, and systems.

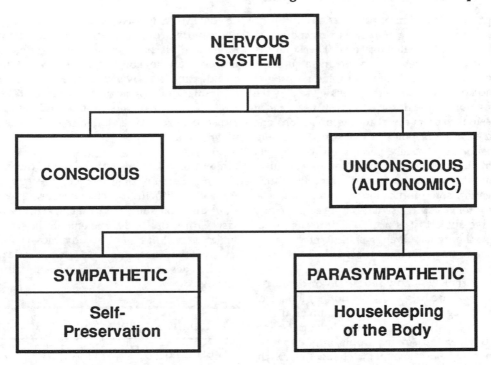

The general composition of the human body is specialized both structurally and functionally to accomplish the basic life processes. These processes are: ingestion, digestion, absorption, respiration, excretion, growth, and reproduction.

There are nine major systems of the body. You can be assisted in remembering the nine major systems by the acronym MCRENDERS. The letters of this acronym are the first letters of the major systems of the body, i.e., muscular, circulatory, respiratory, endocrine, nervous, digestive, excretory, reproductive, skeletal.

The nervous system consists of conscious functions and unconscious or autonomic functions. The autonomic functions are actions that occur without our conscious knowledge. They control the actions of the intestine and other digestive organs, the heart and blood vessels, the adrenal glands and the sweat glands. The autonomic functions are performed by motor fibers only. There are no sensory nerve fibers involved.

The autonomic functions are of two types, sympathetic and parasympathetic, which are carried out through nerve fibers in certain body organs. If an organ has sympathetic nerve fibers, it also has parasympathetic fibers. The effects of the two types of fibers operate in exact opposition. For instance, the operation of the heart is accelerated by sympathetic nerves and slowed by parasympathetic nerves. The principal purposes of the autonomic subsystem are to direct the ordinary housekeeping of the body (parasympathetic) and to prepare the body for stress (sympathetic).

The sympathetic function strengthens the defenses of the body against various dangers such as lack of water, temperature extremes, and enemy attacks. By preparing the body to fight or run, the sympathetic function produces certain physiological reactions over which the individual has little control.

The parasympathetic function causes the body to slow down, and in general manages body organs that permit the body to operate under normal, nonstressful conditions. With respect to interrogation, the significance of the parasympathetic function is that a person under stress (for example, a guilty subject) will very likely exhibit deceptive signals that are identifiable.

Deceptive Signals

What is meant by the term deceptive signal? It may be helpful to think of a deceptive signal in terms of the stimulus/response or action/reaction concept. The interrogator provides a stimulus or action that produces a response or reaction from the person being interrogated. The stimulus might be a verbal statement, a remark, a question, or the showing of a photograph or piece of evidence, or even a nonverbal message sent by the interrogator in the form of a gesture or facial expression. For every stimulus or action, one should expect a response or reaction. Sometimes the response is barely perceptible or entirely concealed. Even when the response is small or hidden, the interrogator can draw from this observation some indication of deception. The capacity for deceptive signals is present in every deceptive subject; it is up to the interrogator to provoke the signals through skillful interrogation and then to interpret the signals as he or she sees them.

Now that we know the origin of deceptive signals, what are they and what do they look like? Deceptive signals are varied and numerous. A few examples are: finger tapping; licking the lips; movement of the Adam's apple; rapid speech, stammering; eye movement; changes in pitch, tone, and volume of the voice, etc. You should note that the foregoing examples include signals that are delivered in two modes: a visual mode and an audio mode. It is not correct to think of deceptive signals as being in the visual mode only. Many strong signals are sent through speech and it is not the content of speech that is always significant, but the manner of speech. Deception may be indicated not in terms of what is said, but in the way it is said.

General Demeanor. This term has meaning with respect to the person being interrogated. A general demeanor is the outward manner, attitude, or bearing of a person in relation to other persons. For our purposes, we can regard a general demeanor as the attitudinal framework within which deceptive signals are manifested. For example, a nervous demeanor is manifested by such deceptive signals as wringing of the hands, slurred and rapid speech, knee jerking, fidgeting, and nail biting. In other words, it is the totality of behaviors (deceptive signals) that convey a general demeanor. Finally, it is possible for one or more demeanors to be exhibited simultaneously or in transition. It is possible for a person to be nervous, fearful, and angry simultaneously, or be in the process of making a transition from these attitudes to demeanors that

are defensive, evasive, and complaining. These demeanors are consistent with each other and reflect a discernible pattern. Some demeanors, however, are not consistent. Demeanors that are apologetic and overly polite are inherently contradictory to demeanors that exhibit fear and anger. A shift of this type would represent a radical change in behavior worthy of notice by the interrogator.

Major Body Movements. Many of the gestures and mannerisms of the deceptive subject are somewhat difficult to detect because they are of short duration and hard to catch. This is not the case with gross body movements in which the subject may shift his entire body, move within the interrogation room , or even attempt to leave the room. These major body movements also have messages.

When the Deceptive Subject Performs	
These major body movements...	These may be the meanings...
Shift of the torso and gross movement of head and limbs	Internal conflict or fear of the subject being discussed
Stand up	Desire to change the subject
Attempt to leave	A bluff tactic
Move chair away	Retreat from fear

Smaller gestures or mannerisms, such as facial expressions, occur at the same time a major body movement is occurring. In fact, the subject may undertake a major body movement at the moment he is aware of a revealing facial expression; the body movement is meant to mask an expression he wishes to hide. Sometimes a body movement is used to headoff or thwart a growing physiological change within the subject's body. The physiological change, of course, is the product of a threat posed by the interrogator and his line of questioning.

A deceptive subject is likely to want to place his chair as far as possible from the interrogator without giving the impression that he fears the interrogator. The deceptive subject will also want to place some substantial object between him and the interrogator; for example, position his chair so that a desk or table separates the interrogator from the suspect. The intervening object becomes something of a psychological barrier behind which the suspect finds some degree of protection.

Preparation of the interrogation room in advance will help the interrogator maintain control over major body movements of the suspect. These arrangements can include:

•The partner of the interrogator can seat himself between the suspect and the exit door.

•The suspect's chair and the interrogator's chair are placed face to face in close proximity.

•Select a chair that is not too high, too wide, nor too comfortable for the suspect to use.

The timing of a major body movement is important. What was asked or what was said immediately prior to the major body movement may have significance with respect to fears of the suspect. Keep in mind that sitting postures are preceded and followed by major body movements. The major body movements may also be revealing, especially when interpreted in conjunction with a sitting posture.

Gestures. A gesture is an activity created by the suspect to reduce tension. Most gestures are unconsciously performed. A deceptive person is likely to perform gestures without realizing it.

Some gestures are consciously initiated and deliberate. A conscious gesture may be an attempt by the deceptive subject to mislead the interrogator; it may be a gesture meant to mask an emotion the suspect wishes to conceal. Consciously controlled gestures should be viewed with suspicion. They are also indicative of a clever, willful, and self-controlled person who is determined to prevail over the interrogator.

Gestures are numerous and varied. As a group, they outnumber other forms of nonverbal communication. Gestures can be a rich source of information concerning the true feelings of a person, and can be placed into four categories: those that symbolize, those that relieve tension, those that mask inner tension, and those that protect.

Facial Expressions. A single facial expression by itself should not be interpreted to conclusively

indicate deception. More meaning can be derived by observing the variety of facial expressions displayed by a person being interrogated, especially as the expressions relate to particular questions.

When a Suspect Displays	
These facial expressions...	These may be the meanings...
Fear	Deception. May be difficult to question
Anger	Truthful person wrongly accused
Defiance	Deception. Difficult to interrogate
Acceptance	Progress is being made
Pleasure	Nervousness or flippant defiance
Blank	Deception. Suspect is careful and wary

The main value of facial expressions is the help they give in identifying the emotional state of the person being interrogated. They can be likened to road signs that guide the traveler to the desired destination. The interrogator watches for them and alters the route to the final destination.

A problem with interpreting facial expressions is the difficulty of differentiating between genuine and false expressions. Also, a person has greater conscious control over the face than any other part of body. The interrogator should ask himself if a particular facial expression is appropriate to the question posed, or if the expression is consistent with similar questions posed previously.

Of the several features constituting the face, the eyes are most important simply because of the large number and variety of eye expressions. Some researchers suggest that about 90% of all facial expressions come from the eyes.

Tips for Observing Deceptive Signals

•Determine the demeanor or combination of demeanors that represent a "normal" pattern for the individual being interrogated. Look for changes in the pattern.

•Look for consistency of behavioral signals. One quick change in behavior is not conclusive. Repeated changes from the "normal" pattern may be indicative of deception.

•Look for timing of behavioral signals. Look for deceptive signals or changes from the "normal" pattern when a fear-provoking question (stimulus) is asked. Anticipate a body language response, keeping in mind that it might be a delayed response.

•Interpret deceptive signals in clusters rather than as single observations.

•Look, listen, and follow intuition. Concentrate on watching and listening, and don't be afraid to follow your "sixth sense" in evaluating your observations.

•Compare the suspect's behavior in relation to case details and evidence. Ask yourself, "Is the outward personality of the suspect consistent with the nature of the offense, the manner in which the offense was committed, and the motive?"

•Do not challenge the suspect by telling him the specific indicators of deception you have observed. Although it may be a good practice to point out the forms of personal behavior that contradict a suspect's denial, this should be done in a general way without getting into specific detail. This tends to sidetrack the interrogation and give the suspect an opportunity to explain the symptoms as innocent phenomena.

•Prepare a checklist for recording deceptive signals. As soon as possible following or during a break in the interrogation, the checklist can be used to record the deceptive signals. The checklist can help the interrogator remember behavioral signals which otherwise would have gone unremembered and can serve as a guide in conducting further interrogation.

When two people are engaged in a normal conversation, between 30 and 60% of the time is maintained in eye contact. The implication of this fact is that abnormal or unusual eye contact occurs below or above the 30 to 60% range. For the professional investigator, interrogation is a normal, sometimes routine function. For the deceptive subject, interrogation may be a first-time or occasional experience. The deceptive subject therefore finds himself in an abnormal situation. Excessive eye shifting and looking away from the interrogator indicate deception. Prolonged eye contact may suggest that the suspect is aware of eye signals as body language and is over-compensating.

Also, a deceptive subject who is uncooperative and arrogant may stare at the interrogator to show his defiance and throw the interrogator off balance.

Eye contact is related to unwritten social rules. The character of eye contact will vary among persons of varying cultural and ethnic backgrounds. What could be regarded as deceptive eye contact by a person during questioning may in fact be perfectly normal within the person's cultural and ethnic environment.

The best way for an investigator to develop expertise in recognizing nonverbal language by cultural and social type is to study the many varieties of people engaged in routine daily activities. Although different cultures have different rules that govern eye contact, studies indicate that most cultures have these points in common:

• An extended gaze between two persons is normally a challenge and an invasion of privacy.

• Emotionally disturbed persons have abnormal eye contact.

• Strangers will look at each other longer in conversations than persons who know each other.

• The speaker in a conversation is regarded as having dominance and has greater freedom in keeping or breaking eye contact with listeners

A study of body language is a study of the mixture of all body movements from the very deliberate to the completely unconscious, from those that apply only in one culture to those that cut across all cultural barriers. We are born with the elements of a nonverbal communication. We can make hate, fear, amusement, sadness and other basic feelings known to other human beings without ever learning how to do it. Nonverbal language is partly instinctive, partly taught and partly imitative.

John J. Fay, CPP
and Leon C. Mathieu, CPP

Sources

Archer, D., and R.M. Akut, How Well Do You Read Body Language? (Psychology Today, October, 1977).

Goleman, D., People Who Read People. (Psychology Today, July, 1979).

Goleman, D., The 7,000 Faces of Dr. Ekman. (Psychology Today, February, 1981).

Inbau, F.E., and J.E. Reid, Criminal Interrogation and Confessions. (Williams and Wilkins Company, Baltimore, 1967).

O'Hara, C.E., Fundamentals of Criminal Investigation. (Charles C. Thomas, Springfield, IL, 1970).

Plutchik, R., A Language for the Emotions. (Psychology Today, February, 1980).

Schurenberg, E., Sheepish Smiles Don't Hide Embarrassment. (Psychology Today, November, 1981).

Specter, A., and M. Ketz, Police Guide to Search and Seizure, Interrogation and Confession. (Chilton Books, Philadelphia, 1967).

Swanson, C.R., N.C. Chamelin, and L. Territo, Criminal Investigation. (Goodyear Publishing Company, Santa Monica, CA, 1977).

The Special Agent Manual of the Georgia Bureau of Investigation. (Georgia Bureau of Investigation, Atlanta, 1976).

Tobias, M.W., and R.D. Peterson, Pre-trial Criminal Procedure. (Charles C. Thomas, Springfield, IL, 1972).

INTERSTATE IDENTIFICATION INDEX

The criminal arrest records of over 11 million individuals are accessible through the Federal Bureau of Investigation's (FBI's) National Crime Information Center (NCIC). In most cases, the requested records are provided in minutes. This rapid availability is invaluable to investigators, prosecutors, courts, and other users of NCIC. A cooperative federal/state effort known as the Interstate Identification Index (III) is making this record exchange possible. The III concept decentralizes the FBI's recordkeeping responsibility by making the states primarily responsible for record maintenance and dissemination. Agencies using the system have acclaimed it as one of the greatest resources since NCIC was initiated in 1967. Establishing a national system to provide automated criminal history information requires considerable effort and close coordination with many agencies. The records originate from more than 17,000 arresting agencies in the United States, as well as from some foreign countries (which submit data to the FBI when a U.S. citizen is arrested). Records are supported by information on a criminal fingerprint card completed at the time of arrest. In the participating states, the fingerprint cards are first submitted to a state identification number (SID). Two cards are forwarded for each individual so one can be retained at the state level while the other is sent to the FBI Identification Division. If no prior record is on file, the FBI assigns an FBI number and a new record is established in the Identification Division computer. A corresponding index record also is created that identifies the state of origin that will provide the record upon request. For arrests in other than the participating states, a III record is established with the FBI as the agency responsible for providing the record.

The majority of inquiries are name checks used to determine if a person has a criminal history. On the average, a positive response is provided for one out of three inquiries. The responses include identification information such as an individual's name, aliases, place of birth, physical description, scars, marks and tattoos, identifying numbers, and fingerprint classification. Based on this data, the person making the inquiry determines whether the record can be associated with the individual being inquired about. (About 5% of the positive responses will contain multiple records with similar names, birth dates, sex, and race.)

Inquiry transactions are processed quickly by the NCIC computer. The time required to search the 11 million records (more than 24 million names and aliases) is about one-fourth of a second.

In addition to inquiry capability, the III provides a means for authorized NCIC users to obtain criminal history records by using a computer terminal. Record requests must contain the unique FBI number or SID assigned to an individual. NCIC users obtain these numbers either from a III name or check, or from criminal records previously obtained in response to a fingerprint card submission.

For an NCIC user, requesting a record is simply a matter of transmitting a message from a terminal and waiting for the response to be returned (usually within a minute). The actual process of providing the record is more complex and involves as many as seven or more computers located in various parts of the country.

Federal Bureau of Investigation

Source Public Affairs Pamphlet. (Federal Bureau of Investigation, U.S. Department of Justice, Washington, DC, 1992).

INTERVIEW AND INTERROGATION

The skilled investigator is aware of the differences between interview and interrogation. The interview is the gathering of information from a person who has knowledge concerning a crime under investigation. The person being interviewed usually gives, in his own manner and words, an account of the crime or provides details concerning a suspect or other person connected to the crime.

Interrogation is the extraction of information from a person suspected of having committed a crime or from a person who is reluctant to make a full disclosure. Interrogation involves a process through which the investigator uses conversation, questioning, and observation as a means of eliciting truth. The process is adversarial in nature and depends upon the application of logic, reasoning, and understanding, without violence or coercion.

During an investigation, the investigator may need to question many types of persons, such as suspects, victims, witnesses, informers, complainants, and accusers. The choice of questioning method will be based not on the type of person to be questioned, but on the attitude and willingness of the person to provide the information being sought. For example, it might be appropriate for the investigator to interview a suspect who is entirely cooperative and to interrogate a witness who is hostile or reluctant.

Interrogation would be preferred over interviewing when the investigator determines that a person to be questioned has any of the following three reasons for not wanting to cooperate:
- Fear of self-involvement
- Inconvenience
- Resentment

Although physical evidence may play a key role in any investigation, it has been consistently true that the most prolific and valuable sources of information are the people involved.

The investigator interviews or interrogates people to achieve at least four objectives: (1) to obtain valuable facts, (2) to eliminate the innocent, (3) to identify the guilty, and (4) to obtain a confession. As the investigator moves from the preliminary task of obtaining valuable facts to a concluding task of obtaining a confession, there is an increase in the difficulty of acquiring information. That difficulty, however, is rewarded by an increase in the value of the information.

Preparation for Interrogation

Certain facts need to be obtained prior to questioning a suspect. These include facts relating to the offense, the suspect, and the victim.

Facts Relating to the Offense
- The legal description of the unlawful conduct.
- The date, time, and place of the crime in accurate detail.

DIFFERENCES BETWEEN	
INTERVIEW	**INTERROGATION**
Non-accusatory	Accusatory
Dialogue	Monologue
Variable environment	Controlled environment
Private/semi-private	Absolute privacy
Guilt unknown	Guilt indicated
No rights warning	Rights warning
Not lengthy	Usually lengthy
Cooperation	Hostility
Unstructured	Structured
Some planning	Extensive planning
Note taking okay	Note taking inhibits

•The manner in which the crime was committed and the known details of its commission; for example, the tools used, places of entry and exit, mode of travel to and from the scene, etc.

•Full description of the crime scene and the surrounding area.

•Possible motives.

Facts Relating to the Suspect

•Personal background information such as other names used, social security number, date of birth, place of birth, education, marital status, current and prior places of residence and places of employment, financial circumstances, prior arrests and convictions, etc.

•Past and present physical and mental condition, particularly with respect to drug or alcohol addiction.

•Relationship of the suspect to the victim or the crime scene.

•Possible motive and opportunity.

•Alibi.

•Personal attitude. This will help the interrogator anticipate whether the suspect will be hostile or cooperative.

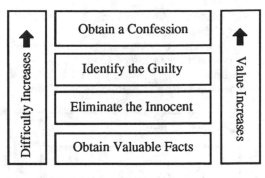

•Social attitude, including prejudices against cultural groups or social and governmental institutions.

•Home environment.

•Sexual interests, but only as they may be relevant to the crime.

•Hobbies.

•The capacity to commit the crime.

Facts Relating to the Victim

•If the victim is an organization, obtain details about organizational practices that would make the organization a criminal target, and about insurance against losses.

•If the victim is a person, obtain details about the nature of injury or loss; personal background information; attitudes toward the investigation, and social attitudes in general; and compensation of the victim through insurance claims or other victim assistance programs.

Controlling the Suspect

Privacy. Interrogation should be conducted out of sight and hearing of other persons, particularly the peers of the suspect and should be conducted on the interrogator's territory. When this is not possible, neutral territory can be used. Interrogation is never conducted on the suspect's territory.

Physical Relationships. Furniture and seating arrangements should be such as to place the interrogator in a comfortable, psychologically dominant position in relation to the suspect. Spatial relationships between interrogator and suspect influence the outcome. Four spatial zones to consider are:

•Public Zone. An area 12 feet or larger, such as a park, street, lobby of a public building, etc.

•Social Zone.   An area from 1 to 12 feet, such as a standard size room.

•Personal Zone.   An area from 1.5 to 4 feet, such as two persons facing each other.

•Intimate Zone.   An area up to 1.5 feet, such as two persons sitting knee-to-knee, face-to-face.

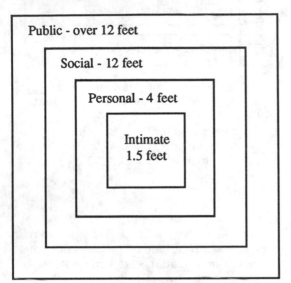

Interrogating Zones

First Contact. Control of a suspect is in great measure dependent upon the initial impression made by the interrogator.   Because first impressions are important, the appearance of the interrogator must be such that an aura of competence and self-confidence is projected.

The opening remarks of the interrogator should be appropriate in terms of how the interrogator evaluates the suspect. For example, a suspect who considers himself to be superior to the interrogator may be addressed by last name only, instructed to sit, instructed not to smoke, and manipulated in ways that quickly establish the interrogator as the person in charge.

Mental Capacity of the Suspect. Generally speaking, physiological changes that occur in a suspect's body are stronger with persons of higher intelligence.   This does not mean that the indicators of deception are always more visible; the intelligent suspect may possess a well-developed capacity to conceal inner tension. A suspect with low intelligence may not understand he is under attack or may not appreciate the full extent of the danger he confronts.   This can

happen when the interrogator fails to bring his language down to a level capable of being understood by the suspect.

A suspect may be emotionally unstable as the result of something entirely separate from the matter related to interrogation. It is difficult to interpret the behavioral signals of an emotionally unstable person. It sometimes happens that an emotionally disturbed person will exhibit non-verbal forms of communication that are exactly opposite of what they would be in a normal person.

Some behavioral signals have cultural or ethnic roots. A gesture might appear to be a deceptive signal to the investigator ,when in fact it was a typical, normal expression used by the individual during his interactions with other persons of the same culture or ethnic background. When a suspect is under the influence of drugs or alcohol, there may be a delay in the response time between stimulus (question) and reaction (deceptive signal).

Semantics

Semantics is the study of words, their meanings, and human interaction through communication. The significance of semantics to interrogation is that words are not the things for which they stand; words are only symbols; words must be interpreted; words can create emotional responses; and words can be denotative or connotative. For example, the word "home" denotes the place where one lives, but to one person it may connote comfort, intimacy, and affection, while to another person it may connote misery, estrangement, and abuse.

At some time prior to an interrogation, the investigator should seek an opportunity to evaluate the vocabulary of the person to be questioned and not assume that his interpretation of any given word is the same as the interpretation of the person being questioned. Questions must be phrased in words used and commonly understood by the person being questioned. The interrogator must be assured that the wording of each question will evoke the desired picture in the mind of the subject. Except when intended, the interrogator should avoid words that elicit an emotional response. Words like *kill, rape,* and *stab* are emotion-producing. Following are some guidelines:

Situational Analysis

If the crime facts reveal...	Then...	And then...
Strong evidence pointing to 1 or 2 suspects	Study the evidence, e.g., statements and lab results	Interrogate the suspect(s)
Weak evidence pointing to 1 or 2 suspects	Interview the suspects	Eliminate or interrogate later
Three or more possible suspects	Analyze what is known about the suspects	Select for interview 1 or 2 who might be guilty

• Questions should be simple and direct.
• Avoid legal terminology, e.g., larceny, homicide, etc.
• Questions should be short.
• The meaning of the question must be clear and unmistakable.
• Use words that the subject can easily understand.
• Unless intended, avoid accusatory questions.
• Do not lump separate crimes together in a single question.
• Where possible, a question should refer to only one element of an offense.
• As much as possible, prepare questions in writing prior to the interrogation.

Situational Analysis

Situational analysis holds that a variety of components are present in any given situation at any given particular point in time. The point in time of concern here is the early stages of an investigation in which at least three components are present: (1) the crime, (2) evidence related to it, and (3) the persons involved. Each component is analyzed individually and interrelatedly.

The Crime
• An identification of the statute violated.
• The offense elements or elements of proof.

Evidence
• Clinical facts such as crime laboratory test results and polygraph test results.

• Physical evidence.
• Testimony of witnesses.
• Documentation.

Persons
• Suspect(s).
• Other persons, such as victims, accusers, complainants, and witnesses.

Although situational analysis has application at any time during an investigation, it has critical importance during the preliminary stage. The preliminary stage can be considered that period of time from commission of the offense to the interrogation of the suspect. The preliminary stage is essentially non-accusatory in nature, whereas interrogation of a suspect is accusatory. It is during the preliminary stage that facts are analyzed through a continuing process so that the focus of investigation is narrowed to one or two suspects.

The following observations can be made with respect to the non-accusatory, preliminary stage of investigation:
• Information obtained from persons related to the crime is derived through interviewing rather than interrogation.
• The number of interviews may be extensive. There may be many possible suspects to interview, with repeat interviews of some suspects.
• A sympathetic approach is generally used when interviewing.
• "Baiting" tactics are used during interviews to provoke body language.

John J. Fay, CPP
and Leon C. Mathieu, CPP

A SHORT GLOSSARY OF INTERROGATION TERMS

active listening
  An interviewing technique in which the interviewer listens to both the facts and the feelings of the speaker.

cognitive interview
  A type of interview used in obtaining information from witnesses and victims of crime. It features four general methods for jogging memory: (1) reconstruct the circumstances, (2) report everything, (3) recall the events in different order, and (4) change perspectives. In addition, this interview technique seeks to obtain specific information relating to physical appearance, names, numbers, speech characteristics, and things said.

confession distance
  The distance between the interrogator and the person being interrogated within which the interrogator establishes feelings of friendship, acceptance, intimacy, and reassurance.

custodial interrogation
  Questioning initiated by a law enforcement officer of a person who is in custody or whose freedom of movement is restricted in any significant way. Examples would include incommunicado interrogation in a police-dominated atmosphere; interrogation of a person who is thrust into an unfamiliar atmosphere or environment; or interrogation of a person surrounded by antagonistic forces after being taken from familiar surroundings. The term has significance in respect to the rules that issued from the Miranda v. Arizona decision of the U.S. Supreme Court.

direct approach
  An interrogational approach in which the interrogator assumes an air of confidence with regard to the suspect's guilt and stresses the evidence indicative of guilt. The approach is accusatory in nature and seeks to discover why the suspect committed the act as opposed to learning if the suspect committed the act.

empathetic questioning technique
  An interview and interrogation technique in which the questioner empathizes and identifies with the subject's situation. The questioner may (1) describe the crime as being less serious than it is, (2) suggest that many people, the questioner included, have been in a similar situation, (3) suggest that the subject is the victim of circumstances that need to be fully explained in order to be understood, or (4) allow the subject an opportunity to pass moral or ethical (but not legal) blame on the victim or others. For example, in a sexual assault case the questioner might suggest that the decaying moral standards of society inevitably lead to such crimes.

end-of-line question
  A question asked by an interviewer at the end of a line of questions or at the end of an interview. For instance, "Is that all of what you saw?" or "Is there something you wish to add, change or delete?"

express questioning

Words or actions on the part of the questioner that are reasonably likely to elicit an incriminating response from a suspect. Express questioning tends to focus more on the perceptions of the suspect than the intent of the questioner. The term was used by the U.S. Supreme Court in its discussion of interrogation in the Miranda case.

implied answer question

A question phrased so as to imply its answer. In interviewing, it is a type of question to be avoided since it defeats the purpose of determining what the interviewee knows. Also called a leading question.

indirect interrogating approach

A questioning approach that is exploratory in nature, seeking to test the suspect's truthfulness in relation to facts known by the interrogator. This approach is frequently used when interrogating a suspect whose guilt is uncertain or doubtful. It is a method of obtaining information in which the witness or interviewee is asked to "tell the story" and is allowed to speak freely, prompted only as needed and with a minimum of direct questions.

interrogating zones

Distance zones between the interrogator and respondent which are regarded as being influential in the success or failure of an interrogation. Four zones are hypothesized: (1) public zone, (2) social zone, (3) personal zone, and (4) intimate zone. (See previous chart.)

interrogation distance

The distance between an interrogator and the boundary of the subject's "personal space bubble." At this distance, the interrogator is said to be confrontational and mildly aggressive.

kinesics technique

A questioning approach in which the subtle, unconscious, nonverbal behaviors of the interviewee are diagnosed and exploited by the questioner. The technique is founded on the idea that body language can be very revealing.

long pause

A technique in which the interviewer deliberately remains silent for an extended period so that the interviewee will feel compelled to offer further information if only to break the silence.

Mutt and Jeff technique

An interrogation technique in which a first interrogator presents himself to the subject as being harsh and unsympathetic. A second interrogator takes the side of the subject and seeks to gain his confidence by being kind and sympathetic.

nondirective interviewing

An interview in which the interviewer does not guide the discussion, but says only enough to encourage the interviewee to express himself freely.

---

open-end questioning

An interviewing technique in which the respondent is asked to tell what he knows in his own words and with minimum interruptions. Questions are constructed and asked so as to encourage a free, uninhibited response. The initial, prompting question is general as opposed to a question that can be answered with a yes or no response. Examples of open-end questions are: "Tell me what you saw," and "What happened then?"

wounded bird ploy

A diversionary tactic used by an interviewee to lead the interviewer away from a subject that the interviewee does not want to discuss.

Source: Fay, John, Butterworths Security Dictionary, Stoneham, MA., 1987.

INTERVIEWING: BEHAVIORAL ANALYSIS

Every investigator evaluates the behavior displayed by the person being interviewed (whether a victim, witness, or suspect) and draws some conclusion as to that person's truthfulness. This article profiles the behavioral characteristics indicative of a person who is telling the truth, as well as those characteristics that are suggestive of a person who is withholding information. Before describing the typical behaviors exhibited by truthful and deceptive subjects, some cautions must be emphasized. There is no single verbal or nonverbal behavior that automatically means that a person is lying or telling the truth. Each behavior displayed must be considered in the context of the environment and in comparison to the subject's normal behavior patterns.

The evaluation of behavior symptoms should take into consideration the subject's intelligence, emotional and psychological health, sense of social responsibility, and degree of maturity. Judgment as to a subject's truthfulness or deception should be based on the overall behavioral pattern displayed, and not upon any single observation or activity.

Nonverbal and Verbal Behavior

With these cautions in mind, the nonverbal and verbal behavior of a person during questioning may provide very valuable and accurate indications of truthfulness or deception.

Attitude. Truthful individuals usually display an attitude that can be characterized as concerned, composed, cooperative, direct, spontaneous, open, and sincere.

On the other hand, a person who is lying may appear to be overly anxious, defensive, evasive, complaining, guarded, or, in some cases, unconcerned.

Posture. In a nonsupportive environment, one where the investigator and subject are sitting in chairs facing each other about 4-1/2 to 5 feet apart, without any desk or barrier between them, the truthful subject is likely to sit upright (but not rigid or immobile) and frontally aligned with the investigator. The truthful subject will oftentimes lean forward as a sign of interest and participation, and when the subject changes posture the movement is usually casual and relaxed.

By contrast, the deceptive subject will likely maintain a very rigid and immobile posture throughout the interview. There may be a lack of frontal alignment, slouching in the chair, and a closed, barriered posture with arms folded across the chest and legs crossed. In some cases, the deceptive subject may exhibit very rapid and erratic posture changes.

Significant posture changes are likely to occur when key questions are introduced and deceptive answers given. The deceptive subject's movements are attempts to relieve or reduce internal anxiety experienced when confronted with questions that pose a personal threat and when making untruthful responses that are potentially detectable as lies. The truthful person will not usually experience this same level of high anxiety and will therefore not exhibit these same pronounced posture changes.

Gestures. In addition to significant posture changes, deceptive suspects also engage in a variety of other tension-relieving activities that include grooming gestures and supportive gestures. Examples of grooming gestures include stroking the back of the head, rearranging jewelry or clothing, dusting the pants or lint picking, and adjusting or cleaning glasses. Supportive gestures consist of placing a hand over the mouth or eyes when speaking, hiding the hands, and holding the forehead with a hand for an extended period of time. Deception is indicated when a suspect repeatedly engages in any of these nonverbal activities while making verbal responses.

Eye Contact. Deceptive persons generally do not look directly at the investigator when they answer critical questions -- they look down, over to the side, or up at the ceiling. They feel less anxiety if their eyes are focused somewhere else than on the investigator. Truthful persons, on the other hand, are not defensive and can easily maintain eye contact with the investigator.

Verbal Indicators. Generally speaking, a truthful person will answer questions in a direct, spontaneous, and sincere manner. The truthful subject will use realistic words, such as steal, embezzle, and forge, while the deceptive person will use euphemisms such as take, misuse, and write. The truthful person will exhibit a reasonable memory, not qualify the answers, and volunteer helpful information.

Conversely, the deceptive subject may delay a response or repeat the question before giving the answer. The deceptive suspect may also anticipate a question and offer an answer quickly, even before the question is completed. The deceptive person will oftentimes exhibit a remarkable memory (remembering too much or too little detail) and preface answers with such phrases as "To tell you the truth, ..." or "As far as I can recall, ..." or "To the best of my knowledge, ..."

Behavior-Provoking Questions

Since nonverbal and verbal indicators can help an investigator evaluate the truthfulness of a subject, it naturally follows that the investigator will want to engage in questioning tactics that elicit the indicators. One such tactic is to use behavior-provoking questions.

First, let's differentiate between behavior-provoking questions and questions that are routinely asked as part of the investigative process. These routine questions are designed to elicit factual information with respect to the who, what, when, where, why, and how of the matter under investigation. The behavior-provoking questions are intended to stir anxiety that will be manifested in visible and therefore detectable signals.

As the suspect responds to each routine question, the investigator will be carefully recording and evaluating the suspect's version of events. Simultaneously, the investigator will be looking for nonverbal and verbal signals connected to particular questions. Later, the investigator will want to return to those routine questions that were accompanied by the signals and probe more intently with the use of behavior-provoking questions. In other words, the routine questions are tools for identifying potentially sensitive points, and the behavior-provoking questions are tools for discovering the source of the suspect's anxiety.

This mixture of routine and behavior-provoking questions makes up the core of the behavioral analysis interview (BAI) technique developed by John E. Reid and Associates, Inc., Chicago. Theoretical models were developed, statistically tested, and validated for the predicted differences in the responses given by truthful and deceptive subjects. More than 30 behavior-provoking questions have been developed and utilized in the BAI technique.

For illustrative purposes, five of these questions are presented in a hypothetical investigation into the theft of credit cards from a bank's mail room.

1.   The purpose question: "What is your understanding of the purpose for this interview?" The truthful responder will provide an accurate description of events; may use descriptive language such as steal; and may mention numbers of cards stolen and/or victims' names, if known. The deceptive subject's response may be vague and nonspecific. The response may include non-descriptive language, such as "the incident," or "something happened," or qualifiers, such as "apparently" or "evidently" or "may have." Details are absent concerning the number of cards stolen or victims' names.

2.   The you question: "Over the past several weeks we have had a number of credit cards

disappear from the bank; specifically, the mail room. If you had anything to do with stealing these missing credit cards, you should tell me now." A truthful response is likely to be a direct, contracted, and unequivocal denial, e.g., "No, I didn't steal any credit cards." Broad, all encompassing language may be used -- "Absolutely not! I haven't stolen anything from here." The deceptive response may be a non-contracted and unemotional denial ("I do not know anything about this") or an evasive response ("I didn't even know credit cards were missing") or an objection ("Why would I risk my job by doing something like that?").

3.   The knowledge question: "Do you know for sure who did steal any of the missing credit cards?" A truthful subject will often volunteer information, "Not for sure, but I have some ideas." Concern or anger may come out, "I wish I did know, but I just don't have any idea." The deceptive subject may give an unemotional denial, "No, I do not." The subject does not offer spontaneous thoughts or feelings.

4.   The suspicion question: "Who do you suspect may have stolen these missing credit cards?" The truthful subject will give the question careful thought, and when offering a suspicion, will cite a reason for the suspicion. A deceptive response is "I don't have any idea." without giving the question any careful thought. The deceptive person may name improbable suspects, such as employees without opportunity or access.

5.   The vouch question: "Is there anyone who you work with that you feel is above suspicion and would not do anything like this?" The truthful subject will give the question thought and typically eliminate possible suspects. The deceptive subject will not vouch for others because in so doing the field of suspects is narrowed, which would have the effect of increasing the suspect's chance of exposure.

Joseph P. Buckley

INTERVIEWS: THE STRUCTURED WRITTEN INTERVIEW TECHNIQUE

Few investigators and others responsible for gathering information relating to a specific incident or problem have all the time and resources needed to accomplish this task. This is particularly true if the persons to be interviewed are not readily available because of geographical location or when it is not cost-effective to conduct an on-site investigation.

As a result, many minor incidents may either not receive a timely investigation or may not be investigated at all. A failure to conduct an inquiry can quickly send a message that no one cares, leading to additional losses.

This section presents a methodology that may have wide application in retail and other loss-sensitive environments where a loss control manager is required to conduct investigations of losses occurring at widely dispersed locations.

The Technique

The structured written interview technique (SWIT) is a method of gathering information from widely dispersed employees quickly and conveniently. This technique is an adaptation of the Reid Behavior Analysis Interview (BAI) format [1]. The approach can be of value to an investigator who needs to acquire from many people in a short period of time detailed written information but is unable personally to conduct the necessary face-to-face interviews. The process is most often the sole method of investigating an incident, although in serious incidents it can be one phase of a full and formal on-site investigation.

Questions are structured in a way that encourages and allows the respondent to provide more than a "yes" or "no "answer. The questions also go directly to the heart of the issue under investigation. A non-response or a response that seems to skirt the issue can be telling in the sense that the respondent appears to not want to provide an answer. A non-response or an evasive response is particularly significant when the investigator knows from other facts that the respondent possesses the requested information.

Even an unskilled investigator will find the SWIT to be a valuable probing tool. In the hands of an investigator who is skilled in interpreting the subtle signals that often accompany written responses the technique can be especially productive, particularly when evaluating responses given by reluctant witnesses and suspects. Written responses, for example, can be revealing in the characteristics of handwriting. A response having a physical appearance that is out of line with the appearance of other responses can be a tip-off that the individual was not at all comfortable in answering that particular question. Short, cryptic remarks written or printed with large-size letters and accompanied by punctuation marks are other common indicators. Caution needs to be the rule, however, because an anomalous response might result from nothing more than a misunderstanding of the question.

Like other investigative tools, the value of SWIT increases with experience in using it. Frequent use helps the investigator develop an awareness of written cues and the interpretive skills for making sense of them. With the SWIT, the nuances tend to take on discernible shapes and the gross cues tend to stand out. Examples of gross cues, which can be spotted by anyone, include the unnecessarily detailed and rambling response and the one-word response. Persons who give very long or very short answers may deserve follow-up face-to-face questioning. When used as a prelude to an on-site investigation, persons who provide long descriptive answers will normally tell everything they know in a face-to-face situation and should be among the first interviewed.

The SWIT can also be applied to evaluate the morale of respondents. Because morale is sometimes a contributing factor in negative incidents, such as employee theft and vandalism, the investigator may gain valuable insights.

Applying the Technique

Immediately following an incident that requires investigation, the security or loss prevention professional sends a SWIT packet to a responsible supervisor at the incident location. The packet contains a letter of instruction to the supervisor (called the Questionnaire Administrator, or QA) and a quantity of employee data sheets and questionnaires.

The data sheets are to be filled out by the QA and the questionnaires are to be filled out by the employees. Every employee, including supervisors, who are members of the work group involved in the investigation should be asked to provide information by filling out the questionnaire.

Letter of Instruction. The QA is instructed by the letter to contact and to give to each of the involved employees a questionnaire to be filled out on the spot. The employee is not allowed to take the questionnaire home or to collaborate with other employees in its completion.

The letter of instruction contains other details that help the QA carry out his or her role effectively. This role is, of course, critical to the investigation because the QA is essentially a stand-in investigator.

Employee Data Sheet. This two-part device is filled out by the QA. The first part consists of a 19-question list; the second part is a worksheet for the QA to write in the answers to the questions [2]. When finished, the worksheet will contain basic identifying data concerning the employee; the employee's relevance to the incident (e.g., whether the employee was on duty at the time or had the opportunity); and the observations of the QA in terms of the employee's work behavior (e.g., whether the employee has personal problems, is a suspected alcohol or drug abuser, etc.). The worksheet also encourages the QA to include possibly helpful information that may not be specifically addressed in the questions.

The Employee Questionnaire. This is also a two-part device. The first is a letter that identifies the incident under investigation and asks the employee to help by answering some questions. The questions comprise the second part, and they appear as a list. The list is different for each different type of offense; for example, a loss from a cash drawer or safe is different than the list pertaining to goods missing from a storage area. The employee is also encouraged to provide additional information, such as why the incident occurred and how the employee feels about being questioned.

Most of the questions go to the who, what, when, where, how, and why details. When one employee's responses are so far different from those given by the majority of employees, the investigator can conclude that the employee is confused, has poor facts to begin with, or may be lying as a means for misleading the investigator.

Not all of the questions focus directly on the incident. One such question asks the employee to name others who are above suspicion. When several respondents name the same one or two persons who are not likely to be involved, the investigator now has the names of potential witnesses whose separate accounts may serve as benchmarks for the reliability of information. Another indirect question is to ask the employee to explain why he or she did not commit the offense. This question often triggers a response that can be interpreted.

Collating and Interpreting

The returned questionnaires are collated to determine the facts of the incident, at least as they are known or perceived by most of the witnesses. Answers to the finger-pointing questions (like "Who do you believe took the money?") are carefully examined, and the investigator will look for anomalies that suggest deception or that more can be learned by privately contacting the respondent or other witness. Collation should also seek to identify employees who are known to have information but did not fill out a questionnaire.

Interpretation of responses rest on two basic premises. The first is that people will put into writing the same information that they will provide in a face-to-face interview. The second premise is that written responses, like visible body language, can be revealing.

The investigator, while evaluating a questionnaire for what it might directly or indirectly reveal, internalizes a number of central questions:

•What is motivating the writer? Is the writer candid, non-committal, guarded, evasive?

•What is the relationship between the writer and any person named as a suspect? Co-worker, friend, relative, rival, adversary, superior, subordinate?

•What, if anything, is the writer hoping to gain by completing the questionnaire? An opportunity to tell the truth, deceive, confuse?

•Is the writer providing accurate information? Has the information been corroborated?

•Is the writer deceptive, leaving out facts, exaggerating, bluffing? If so, why?

Benefits

The SWIT can be a very useful tool for gathering a large amount of data relating to a specific incident in a rapid manner with very little expenditure of funds and effort. It sends the message to everyone involved in the investigation that the employer is concerned and is asking questions.

Even when the process fails to bring the culprit to justice, the message has been delivered loud and clear that further offenses will be investigated and that eventually the guilty parties will be called to account. It is not unusual following a SWIT investigation for the suspect to quit or abandon the job.

The SWIT can also aid in identifying policy violations and inadequate management/control procedures. For example, responses to questions regarding theft of inventory often disclose deficiencies in key control procedures.

The attitudes within a work group can be revealed by the SWIT. An indicator of low morale might be consistently negative comments from employees concerning their willingness to answer questions; an indicator of apathy (or tolerance of dishonesty) might be questions answered with a single "no" or a blank spot; and an indicator of poor supervision might be sloppily completed questionnaires or a low-return rate of questionnaires.

The SWIT is both adaptable and economical. It can be applied in many different security situations. Its use in the retail environment has been well demonstrated but the process has application wherever time, distance, and money prevent investigators from getting to the scene to make face-to-face interviews.

Richard L. Moe

Source The Behavioral Analysis Interview. (John E. Reid and Associates, Inc., Chicago, 1992).

Notes

1.   The Behavioral Analysis Interview was originated and developed by John E. Reid and Associates, Inc., Chicago, from whom permission has been received for use in this article.

2.   The employee data sheet and corresponding instructions as to its use were adapted from materials generously provided by John E. Reid and Associates, Inc., Chicago.

INTRUSION ALARMS: SENSING PRINCIPLES

The fundamental components of an intrusion alarm system are the sensors, the control unit, and the annunciator. Sensors detect intrusion by feeling (e.g., pressure mats, contact switches), sound (e.g., vibration detector), or sight (e.g., light beams). The control unit receives the alarm notification from the sensor and then activates the annunciator (e.g., a bell), which usually generates a human response. The name given to an intrusion alarm system will often correspond to the sensing principle. Following are brief discussions of alarm systems in terms of sensors.

Types of Sensors

Magnetic Contact Switch. This alarm consists of a magnet mounted on a door (or window) and a magnetically operated switch on the door frame. When the door is closed, a magnetic field is generated. An alarm is activated when the magnetic field is interrupted by opening the door.

Electrical Switch. These switches are composed of electrical contacts installed in a similar fashion as magnetic switches. When the door is closed, the contacts meet and an electrical current is complete. An alarm is triggered when the circuit is broken.

Taut-Wire System. These systems are similar to magnetic contact switches and electrical switches in that a broken circuit activates an alarm. The circuit is broken when the climbing action of an intruder causes stretching of taut wire strung along a fence, wall, or similar barrier. Taut wire can also be placed across windows, doors, and other openings.

Screen Alarm. Electrically charged wires are woven into the mesh of a screen, which activates an alarm when cut. Screens can be placed on windows and doors and in walls and ceilings.

Pressure Mat. These weight-sensitive floor coverings operate on a principle similar to automatic door openers commonly in place at super markets. A pressure mat is usually placed under a rug or carpet. When stepped upon, the weight of the intruder causes an electrical contact to be closed. Another type of pressure mat operates on a release of pressure principle. For example, the alarm is activated when a protected object, such as a desktop computer, is lifted from the mat.

Vibration Alarm. This type of alarm uses microphones to detect vibrations such as vibrations caused by a forced entry. Vibration sensors are typically placed on doors, floors, ceilings, walls, file cabinets, safes, and vaults.

Capacitance Alarm. This alarm creates an invisible energy field that when interrupted signals an alarm. The energy field often envelops a high-security container such as a safe or a reinforced cabinet. The intruder's movement into the energy field sends/activates the alarm. Capacitance sensors are also called proximity sensors.

Ultrasonic. Inaudible sound waves are transmitted and sensed by a receiver. If an offender enters the area, the wave pattern changes and an alarm is sounded. These sensors are not suitable for locations where high-pitched noises take place, such as from telephones, squealing brakes, and factory whistles.

Microwave. An electromagnetic field is transmitted into a protected area. When an intruder enters the protected area, wave patterns change and an alarm is signaled. One problem is that large windows near the system may enable the microwaves to penetrate beyond the area covered and detect outside movement. Also, metal reflects microwave energy, which can distort the wave pattern and set off a false alarm.

Photoelectric. This device activates upon interruption of an invisible beam of light extending between a transmitter and a receiver. An intruder who can spot the transmitter and receiver may be able to penetrate the protected area by jumping over or crawling under the beam.

Passive Infrared. These sensors are passive in that they do not present an active beam or energy field. Rather, they react to infrared radiation caused by movement of the intruder. This detector is designed to sense the very subtle heat changes that are introduced to the protected area by the presence of the human body. Sunlight, auto headlights, heaters, and the like can set off false alarms when the sensors are poorly positioned.

Philip P. Purpura, CPP

Source Purpura, P.P., Security and Loss Prevention, 2nd Edition. (Butterworth-Heinemann, Boston, 1991).

INTRUSION DETECTION: INTRUDER TYPES

Background

It is safe to say that no two intrusion-detection systems (IDS) can ever be exactly the same. Each IDS is unique in the sense that it will be designed with careful attention to a number of variables: the nature of the threat, the assets at risk, the layout and structures of the protected area, the operating processes and culture of the organization, the characteristics of supplemental systems, such as security officer operations, and the security manager's personal philosophy and supervisory style. External forces, such as geography, law, governmental regulation, and politics, may also impact an IDS.

Although systems will vary considerably, each will at least carry out four interacting functions: delay, detect, alert, and respond. Delay is provided by the presence of physical barriers around the assets, such as safes, vaults, walls, ceilings, and fences. Detection is accomplished by sensors that pick up the presence of an intruder. The alert function is provided by alarm equipment that annunciates the place of intrusion. The respond function is executed by a trained response force.

Threat Analysis

The nature of the threat is a key variable in the design of a system. We can look at the threat variable from at least two perspectives. The first is experiential because it is concerned with past and present occurrences. We can apply labels to these two dimensions of experience: traditional and contemporary.

From the second perspective we can look at threat in terms of source. Again, two dimensions stand out: internal and external. The internal threat is sourced within the employee population, including part-timers and contractors; the external threat is sourced within elements of the population outside of the organization and they run the gamut from unskilled criminals to highly skilled ideological groups and revenge-motivated individuals.

Another way to organize our thinking about threat personalities is to apply labels. The traditional threat personalities are the insider, the opportunist, and the professional. Overlaying the traditional threat are contemporary types that we may call the ideologue and the avenger. Let's look at them.

Traditional Threats

The Insider. The inside threat is typically manifested in theft, destruction, damage, and disruption. A combination of physical and procedural safeguards is valuable in thwarting the inside threat. Access controls, at least those that regulate movement of people through perimeter and second-level defenses, will not significantly impede the insider. Barriers and sensors at the critical points of protection (i.e., the places where critical assets are kept), in conjunction with procedures followed by security personnel and the law-abiding employees, will be effective in minimizing insider-related losses.

Designing an IDS to protect against internal threat requires considerable insight and careful deliberation. The insider can be expected to have access to lock combinations and keys, to have a good working knowledge of security equipment and operating procedures, and to enjoy freedom from excessive restraint and suspicion.

The Opportunist. More often than not, an IDS is set up with the external threat in mind. The opportunistic intruder tends to follow the path of least resistance in attempting to breach security defenses and is hoping to act upon whatever opportunities may be presented. The opportunistic intruder is typically a petty, common criminal lacking in sophistication, intelligence, and skill. Once inside the protected area, he or she will move about looking for targets of opportunity, e.g., easily convertible assets such as cash, jewelry, small appliances, desktop computer equipment, and automobiles. Some intruders in this class are oriented to sexual assault crimes; they look for chances to victimize the helpless. Most IDS are designed to deter the opportunistic intruder at the outermost boundaries.

The Professional. A third type of external threat is the skilled professional who has a particular target in mind, possesses technical knowledge of security devices and how to defeat them, and has a plan of action and the resources for carrying out the plan. The skilled intruder is often patient, is willing to abort an intrusion attempt that goes awry, has a back-up plan, an escape route, a plausible story if caught, and the good sense to concentrate efforts on soft targets as opposed to those that have been hardened by countermeasures. Most security systems are not effective in keeping the skilled intruder out, although many systems will feature second- and third-level safeguards, such as proximity sensors and safes, designed to detect and delay.

Contemporary Threats

The Ideologue. The ideologue seldom operates alone; although it is not uncommon for an individual to act alone, the act is usually supported morally or materially by a group. Ideologies spring from many sources: religion, nationalism, human rights, animal rights, environmental protection, etc. Each group will have its own set of targets, an agenda and avenues for achieving goals, and a support base. Material greed and unmet psychological needs for power/sexual satisfaction are not motivators for ideological groups, although groups have a history of resorting to robbery and kidnapping to acquire operating revenue.

Group tactics can range from highly terroristic acts, such as bombings and assassination, to purely symbolic acts, such as splashing blood on walls or burning a flag on the front steps. The ideologue may or may not be skilled, is likely to be intelligent, very likely to be strongly committed and dedicated, and willing to take chances and suffer the consequences of being caught. The issue-oriented intrusion is likely to be made by several or many intruders simultaneously, causing the initial response capability at the protected area to be overwhelmed. The capacity of the security system to deal with this threat can be significantly expanded when the security manager adjusts the IDS in relation to intelligence data concerning likely adversaries, their capabilities, probable methods of attack, and determination.

The Avenger. The number of incidents involving violence by an employee (or former employee) against co-workers and supervisors has increased dramatically in recent years. The number of injuries and deaths at work has also increased.

When robbery-related shootings are factored in, workplace killings are a leading cause of on-the-job deaths.

Workplace homicides are often the result of an unstable employee being laid off or terminated; the worker returns with a gun and kills the supervisor and others who get in the way. When layoffs and terminations rise, violence also rises.

Employees who are likely to release frustration through acts of violence are also likely to have a history of violence and likely to indicate their growing frustration by changes in behavior at work. The implication here is that background checks can be helpful in identifying applicants who bring a potential for violence into the workplace, and that supervisors during periods of layoffs and terminations should be alert to radical changes in employee attitudes and performance.

The security manager should also move quickly to remove the access privileges of employees who have been let go and to set up with remaining workers and security officers an early warning system that will signal the return to the workplace of a released employee. Even more important, the security manager should have a plan and procedures for dealing with violent episodes at work.

John J. Fay, CPP

INTRUSION DETECTION: SYSTEM DESIGN COORDINATION

The designer of an intrusion detection system should thoroughly coordinate the contemplated operating and maintenance concepts with those individuals who will be affected by their implementation. These are the individuals who must operate and maintain the facility's performance within any restrictions that might be imposed by the security system.

The designer should also be concerned about those individuals who are responsible for the safety of the employees and other occupants of the premises. These are the same individuals who are usually forgotten until the security system is already installed or in the process of being installed. The designer's dread is to hear the operations manager say, "You can't install that equipment there because..." or the safety manager say, "That door can't be locked during the day because ..." This is when the designer's problems really begin.

This type of problem can be virtually eliminated if the security system design is properly coordinated before the fact. Another benefit is that the individuals who participate in the system design will have personal interest in its implementation and acceptance by both the employees and management. Management support is needed for the security system to be successful. Management must set an example by following the security procedures themselves, as well as insisting that all security procedure be followed by others and all systems maintained in operations.

Operations is defined as the group composed of people who manufacture the products, refine the minerals, generate the electricity, operate the department store, manage the office building, etc. In other words, these are the people who are directly involved with the assets that the intrusion-detection system is being designed to safeguard. Therefore, time should be taken to understand their requirements and to review the proposed system design with them. As obvious as this recommendation appears, many systems have been designed without consideration to the operator or user. The design review should start with the initial system concept and continue through the final system design and installation. Follow-up reviews after installation will alert the designer to system problems that could be detrimental to the maximum effectiveness of the system if they are not corrected. These include not only hardware and operating problems, but also problems associated with management and employee acceptance of the intrusion-detection system.

A general training session should be conducted before the system is operational to apprise employees of the need for the security system, acquaint them with the equipment, and instruct them regarding proper system operations. The training session could be highlighted by a tour of the facility to demonstrate, if possible, the operation of each piece of equipment. A well-conducted training session will eliminate many day-to-day operational problems and improve employee acceptance of the system. The acceptance might be enhanced even more if a responsible individual from management attended the training session and addressed the importance of the security system.

Additional training may be required for those employees who must comply with special operating procedures as a result of the new security equipment. For instance, if an access control system is installed to limit access to controlled areas, the employees affected by this system would require special training on its operation.

Fire and Safety Officers

Since the fire and safety officers are responsible for the safety of occupants of the facility, they should be included in the system design coordination. Both the fire and safety officers will be concerned about the types of locking and access control systems, and bars and grilles installed on windows and doors.

Maintenance Department

Probably the most overlooked department with respect to being consulted on system design is the maintenance department. Yet these are the individuals who will be given the responsibility for maintaining the equipment after it is installed. Therefore, rather than just handing them the responsibility for maintaining security equipment, they should be given the opportunity to contribute to the system's design. They should participate in selecting the equipment location within the facility, routing the equipment's interconnecting cables, and selecting the system's maintenance concept, including the confirmation of estimated maintenance costs.

Quite often the plant drawings are not kept up-to-date to depict latest equipment locations, additions, or deletions, or they do not show the new wall or the fact that new plumbing has been added -- and the list goes on and on. Sometimes these changes, especially the obvious ones, can be noted during a walk-through survey; but many of the subtle changes, such as the additional plumbing or cable trays, will probably be overlooked. The maintenance people will probably be familiar with most of these changes and additions, and therefore will be helpful in locating the security equipment and especially helpful in selecting the best cable routes.

The maintenance supervisor should certainly be consulted with regards to selecting the most appropriate maintenance concept for the intrusion-detection system. The supervisor understands his employees and knows their technical qualifications and skills. However, the supervisor will sometimes misjudge their ability to maintain the security equipment. The usual first impression is that anything containing electronic circuitry is too complicated to properly maintain. The supervisor may be right; but more often than not, the department can perform the maintenance if given sufficient training.

If the maintenance department has qualified electricians or electronics technicians who can operate a volt/ohm meter and have the manual dexterity to work with small electronics modules, then they should be able to perform most maintenance on equipment using the modular replacement concept. Sometimes it is helpful to demonstrate the equipment operation and perhaps give the supervisor a hands-on demonstration on how to trouble-shoot and repair the equipment. Another suggestion is to offer additional training for the maintenance personnel or hire an electronics technician who could perform the maintenance.

It sometimes happens that out of a sense of apprehension the maintenance supervisor will recommend that the maintenance be contracted. Quite often, however, the supervisor will experience a change of mind after witnessing the system's actual maintenance needs.

Robert L. Barnard

Source Barnard, R.L., Intrusion Detection Systems. (Butterworth-Heinemann, Boston, 1982).

INTRUSION-DETECTION TECHNOLOGY: A LOOK BACK AND AHEAD

Speaking as someone who remembers when we used pull traps for protection inside and depended upon fences, guards and dogs outside, I continue to be amazed with the progress made in protection equipment over the past 40 years. I am now looking forward to security technology that in the early 1950s would have seemed pure science fiction fantasy. Imagine sensors capable of positive identification from a person's thermal radiation, pulse rate, or heart beat. We've come a long way since trip wires!

I don't consider myself an old timer, but I do recall how elated many of us in security felt when the photoelectric beam replaced trip wires that were so primitive they worked only with clumsy

intruders. I can also remember efforts made by the Department of Defense during the Vietnam War to refine microwave technology for use in the combat situation. At the end of that war, Aerospace Research, Inc. (forerunner of today's Aritech), shifted its focus from the government to the alarm industry and ended up giving us an advanced capability called balanced signal processing.

Then in the late 1960s and early 1970s names such as Sam Bagnol, Jim Bean, and Aaron Galvin were the talk of the alarm industry [1]. Those years saw the introduction of ultrasonic balanced signal processing, and information about infrared technology began to leak out of the research and development (R&D) laboratories. Single-beam photoelectric units were augmented with multiple-beam wall or fence configurations. Ultrasonic added expanders, better ceramics, and stand-alone units. Passive infrared improvements took the industry from single element to dual element to quad element, and to various forms of interlocking.

In the early 1980s, step focus optics came on the scene to enhance stability and helped provide passive infrared curtain sensors. Anti-masking, self-test, multiple polar pulse count, uniform imaging, improved Fresnel lenses, and miniaturization all contributed to the explosion of alarm sensor offerings in the 1980s. The advent of the dual technology sensor in the middle of that decade provided for the protection of Butler buildings, pre-fabricated facilities, and other alarm-prone structures affected by environmental factors. That period also brought with it the question of sensor sensitivity vs. stability. Security practitioners had to decide between technology that was inherently more secure than stable, such as microwave and ultrasonic, or more stable and free from nuisance alarms but less likely to detect an intruder.

And then there was "gating" associated with dual technologies. An improper installation of a dual system created a potential that one technology would cancel detection by the other. One of the technologies, either ultrasonic or passive infrared, had to be placed into a lead role. This circumstance eventually led to the development of dual ultrasonic and dual passive infrared sensors.

Through the remainder of the 1980s and into the year 1990, interior sensor manufacturers focused less on developing new technology and more on making relatively modest improvements to small, inexpensive units. The late 1980s saw an industry-wide price war and margin reduction within the interior sensor community.

While all this was going on, the U.S. and Canadian governments were focusing on better ways to provide perimeter protection and exterior security. The late 1970s saw the beginnings of the base installation security system (BISS) program -- an effort to identify, develop, and field new and better ways to keep intruders out of government facilities. First came improvements on the simple shaker switch and piezoelectric fence-mounted systems, which were attempts to cancel out nuisance alarms caused by wind, thunder, and vibration. Bi-static and mono-static microwave technology was improved significantly in the 1980s. The use of active infrared beams in the outdoor environment was enhanced by "smart" processing, and efforts were made to incorporate laser where infrared had been applied.

Dr. Keith Harmon and a joint Canadian-U.S. program produced the ported coaxial cable technology -- expensive to purchase and install -- but considered by many to be more secure. Harmon was the founder of Senstar Corporation in Ottawa.

At the close of the 1980s there did not seem to be any one exterior sensing technology that, by itself, could offer the high resistance to nuisance alarms and the equally high probability of detection sought by government agencies. Multiple technology installations were still required to achieve the high-security performance demanded.

Now, in this day of highly sophisticated security systems, what new marvels may we anticipate? We already have a pulsed infrared technology representing the first move toward an intruder-tracking capability. The technology covers large areas in volumetric pattern with gaps of only 10 inches at extreme distances. With a radius of 1,500 feet, it should be able to track multiple intruders from a single sensor.

We have also acquired infrasonic technology. Both active and passive infrasonics operate on a low-frequency wave of .5 to 2 hertz. Credible as a secondary backup sensor, it would not appear to represent a major achievement in the field.

In the latter part of 1989, a product called the human body sensor (HBS) was introduced as a research effort. It detected electronic signals in the frequency between 0.004 and 0.8 hertz emanating from the human body. These signals, which are much stronger near the hands, feet, and head, form a body print of a person. With conversion of analog and digital information, the signal can identify body mass and even sex. A target can be detected up to a maximum of 12 feet from the sensor; and a pair of human feet can be read through the ceiling to a roof or floor above.

Exterior sensor research efforts include a sensor capable of picking up a parachute or hand-glider threat. From the Canadian research community comes a new cable technology similar to the existing ported coaxial product. This new cable combines features of both the transmit and receive cables currently in use, and it can be buried or used aboveground. Also at the end of the 1980s, the use of fiber optics to detect moving targets through pressure and light wave beading techniques was begun.

Although there are those who believe that the early years of the 1990s will unlikely yield major R&D advances, I am more optimistic. U.S. government focus will be on portable, deployable, reusable, and inexpensive sensors -- with names like M.L. Aviation's Guardian, Repels, IDAS, and portable microwave offerings being improved to meet these needs; and there will be breakthroughs as well.

As I look to the future, I see interior motion detection sensors coming from two directions. One is the merger of access control technologies with interior sensor development efforts (detecting individuals and determining whether or not they are authorized to access the area where the detection is made). Research in Eugene, Oregon, promises detection of an authorized individual in a room without that person moving, speaking, or touching any object. The second thrust derives from previous research work. The Detek sensor, improved and privately funded, could produce sensors capable of tracking individuals. An old non-security technology, present in almost every home in North America, may provide a new and very inexpensive means of achieving interior detection.

The more difficult world of exterior sensors will also see new successes. HBSs may be used to detect potential intruders immediately outside of buildings. Fiber optics, which today react to pressure and light wave alterations, will emerge as a carrier of both voice and sight without requiring the microphones and cameras of today. This new fiber-optic technique will provide built-in "ears and eyes" capable of both detection and assessment.

We can also expect that interior and exterior sensors will be radically changed by new accomplishments in the field of artificial intelligence. Thermal radiation of a body, pulse rate, and heart beat could provide forms of positive identification as a result of current research in both Europe and the United States. A breakthrough in laser technology will provide a new family of laser fences capable of operating at up to 1,000 feet in the densest fog and rain.

I think the next 5 years will offer some significant changes in interior sensors, and some of these will be translated into solutions for remaining exterior detection problems. On the strength of what has been achieved over the span of my own memory, I see no reason to limit the expectations of tomorrow's intrusion-detection technology.

Joseph A. Barry III, CPP

Notes

1. Sam Bagnol, when he was with Kidde, invented the ultrasonic sensor as we know it today. Jim Bean worked with Aerospace (now Aritech) and was the Johnny Appleseed of ultrasonic sensor capabilities, spreading the gospel in North America and Europe. Aaron Galvin, who worked with Aerospace and now with ADT, took balanced signal processing from the old tube technology to solid-state in 1968.

INVENTORY SHRINKAGE

Many executives in the manufacturing and retail trades hold to a time-honored belief that inventory shortages are valid barometers of how a company is doing in relation to internal theft. Seasoned security experts, however, are quick to point out that while inventory shortages (occasionally referred to as variances) may be indicators of employee theft, they are influenced by variables that can distort the true picture to such an extent that reliable conclusions cannot be drawn.

Book and Physical Inventories

Basically, there are two kinds of inventories: book and physical. The book inventory is determined as follows: at the beginning of each fiscal year, a company will have arrived at a figure of its inventory on hand by adjusting its book inventory to agree with the value of the physical inventory counted at year-end. Throughout the year, certain purchases or production of additional inventory are made by the company. When received, these amounts are added to the beginning inventory figure. Also, sales of the company's products are made throughout the year, reducing the level of the company's inventory. Therefore, these sales must be subtracted from the other figures that are normally augmented by purchases or production. At the closing of the fiscal year, the company has thus arrived at a certain figure that represents the beginning inventory, plus purchases and production, minus sales. This figure is known as the book inventory.

Once the book inventory is determined, virtually all companies are required to then make a physical count of all the inventory in their possession or under their control. This physical count may take several days and involve the efforts of many people. The figure resulting from the count gives the physical inventory. This physical inventory represents not what the company thinks it has on hand, but what it actually does have on hand. This count is compared to the book inventory.

Invariably, there will be differences between the physical inventory count and the book inventory figure. These differences can take the form of an overage or a shortage. Nominal differences usually receive absolutely no attention, as they are considered normal for any business. Significant variances, whether as overages or shortages, should be of concern to management.

Variances that are reflected as overages can be traced to a number of factors, such as price increases in commodities that went unrecorded in the books during the fiscal year and to inaccurate physical counts. Shortages can result from a variety of causes, including internal theft, undiscovered external thefts, human error, and, once again, incorrect physical counts. Other variances can be caused by incorrect compilation of the book inventory amount and improper cut-off procedures.

In most inventories, double counts are taken. It is essential that the security executive or accounting official makes sure there is no communication between the first and second counting teams. There have been occasions when the primary team, after finishing its count, has left in a pre-arranged location a number signifying the first count.

Manufacturing Inventories

In manufacturing, inventories are made of raw materials and of in-process goods.

Raw Materials. The basic accounting steps for raw materials are similar to those outlined earlier. At the beginning of the fiscal year, the company starts out with a certain amount of raw materials. Additional raw materials received by the company throughout the year are added. Raw materials withdrawn for purposes of production are subtracted from the total.

The difference between book and physical inventory balances should not be large when there is good record keeping and a sense of responsibility on the part of workers and supervisors. Because a certain amount of wastage naturally occurs in the production of goods from raw materials, the balances are not likely to be in perfect agreement, and attention to detail by the responsible workers will keep the difference within an acceptable range of tolerance. The range of tolerance for production-related waste is determined by standards that have evolved in accounting practices. When waste exceeds the standards, the effect on the inventory balance is recorded as a cost variance as opposed to an inventory variance.

In-Process Goods. An in-process inventory is a once-per-year count of unfinished goods in the production pipeline at the moment in time the inventory is conducted. To obtain an accurate count, the manufacturing process is shut down. Finished goods at the end of the production line are not counted as in-process goods, but are picked up in shipping department or warehouse inventories. The amount of in-process goods is not normally large, allowing the count to be made in a single day.

It is difficult to get a good handle on in-process inventories because accuracy is highly dependent on the competency, cooperation, and integrity of a large number of production line workers. Distortions to the count creep in through exaggerated reports of waste and

defective raw materials, sloppy physical counts, and deliberate miscounting. Oftentimes the purpose of distortion is to conceal internal theft of the manufactured product or its component parts.

Where component parts are the targets, the employer may institute a lot control program. Lot control, in its simplest form, means that at each step in the production line the unit of production must be fully intact before being passed on to the next step. In perfect practice, there can be no missing components, at least not without shutting down the line until the unit of production is made intact. In the garment industry, lot control has become a tool for controlling in-process shortages.

Distribution and Warehousing Inventories

In distribution and warehousing, the inventory approach is along the lines of the finished goods inventory that was discussed previously. Finished goods in a typical warehouse or distribution center should be influenced only by transactions that take place in the receiving and shipping departments. In other words, nothing should be added to the book inventory until it is actually received by the distribution center, and nothing should be subtracted from the book inventory until it is actually shipped out of the distribution center.

An area of concern to the security executive, and one not normally accounted for by standard inventory figures, is concealed shortages. A concealed shortage is a shortage of goods or inventory that is not obvious to the examining party. The security executive will immediately recognize that a concealed shortage may very well be the result of a breakdown in the accounting of goods shipped to the retailer or customer. For this reason, it helps to make frequent spot checks of the accounting system, including double-verification of shipments. The accounting and security departments may wish to collaborate in developing standards applicable to their workplace or industry, and to recognize deviations from the standards as signals that require closer examination.

Retailing Inventories

Inventory control is much more complex in retailing than in manufacturing, warehousing, and distributing. One of the big reasons for the increased complexity is the manner in which retail goods leave the custody of the seller. The variety and frequency of special sales and layaway programs, for example, introduce many problems for those who must do the counting.

Shrinkage and Reserves. In retailing, inventory variances or shortages are referred to as shrinkage. In virtually all retailing (and in some manufacturing companies, as well) the prevailing attitude is that a certain amount of shrinkage is inevitable. A retailer will forecast a percentage of shrinkage and account for it in the budget; if the forecast is correct, the retailer's budget is correct, and with all other things going as planned, the retailer will show profit. This is in the nature of planning for loss and not dissimilar to the concept of the self-fulfilling prophecy.

Shrinkage reserves vary from store to store and from one segment of the retail industry to another, depending on the type of business. For instance, the conventional department store management may set up reserves that provide for inventory losses of from 1-1/2 - 3% of the net sales. In the discount or mass merchandising segment of the retail industry, reserves usually range from 2 - 4%. In clothing and specialty apparel stores, reserves range from 1 - 2%.

A Contribution to Profits

The measure of a security director's performance may be the extent to which the security program has been successful in reducing internal theft as evidenced by a reduction in shrinkage. When the shrinkage turns out to be lower than what was originally projected, the security manager can be credited with having contributed to profits

J. Kirk Barefoot, CPP

INVESTIGATIONS: AUTHORITY AND LIABILITY

Generally, investigations can be separated into three categories: traditional, forensic, and covert. Traditional investigations are those inquiries utilizing common fact-gathering techniques such as interviewing, records checks, searches and seizures of evidence, and other overt efforts. Forensic investigations are those applied to the identification and collection of evidence usually related to the scene of a crime. These forms include latent fingerprint retrieval, collection of physical and other trace evidence, and incident scene photography. Covert investigations generally include surveillance and undercover operations conducted in secret unknown to the target of the investigation.

The legal guidelines that apply to each of these investigative forms and the frequency an investigator will perform these functions vary. This article centers on authority and liability aspects as they relate to the traditional investigative form.

Authority

Law enforcement as we know it today is vastly different from earlier forms. Private practitioners are assuming a far greater share of traditional public law enforcement functions than was so in the past. Present trends show this will continue.

In general, police are governmental officials appointed as peace officers who take an oath to enforce laws affecting the peace and good order of the community. The authorities granted to them are by statute. In performing their duties they are acting in the interest of the state.

Traditionally, unless specifically commissioned or working for the government, private sector officers are not sworn to an oath and do not work on behalf of the government. Rather, a private practitioner acts for the person or entity that hires him or her. In such a capacity, the private officer can do no more than can be done by the hiring entity. The actions available to the private practitioner under this traditional view is limited to the authority granted to a private citizen or to the authority held by the employer for the protection of the employer's property. As such, private practitioners have no more formal authority than does the average citizen.

However, exceptions exist. As noted previously, the legislatures of certain states have enacted statutes that provide for the commissioning of private practitioners as peace officers. These practitioners are employed by private entities such as universities, hospitals, railroads, and non-profit organizations, and possess full police powers. The courts have rules that in instances where a private agent is hired on a contractual basis by a public authority, the private agent is in fact acting with authority of the state and is subject to constitutional restrictions on the exercise of authority. We have instances where the private agent is statutorily granted certain authorities that exceed those commonly held by other citizens. An example here would be the various retail theft statutes across the country, which provide private agents with the authority to apprehend and detain suspects on probable cause. Finally, entrance requirements for persons entering the field of private security are increasing by state mandate.

The Congress is also showing an increased interest in the qualifications of private security officers, particularly with respect to basic screening and training requirements. Minimum standards and a model law for adoption by the states appear to be on the horizon. A force driving the Congress is privatization, i.e., the transfer of functions from the police to private security.

Finally, in certain instances the courts have ruled that the laws relating to the activities of government directly apply to the private sector. However, in those instances where the practitioner maintains a strictly private character, the rules may not apply.

Legal Basis of Authority. The distinctions between the public and private practitioner are rooted in the framing of basic constitutional law. The Constitution was not written to address the actions of one citizen against the other, but to delineate the manner in which the activities of government would be regulated. For example, the Fourth Amendment to the Constitution provides for the manner in which evidence can be searched for and seized, and for the manner in which persons can be arrested.

The law that relates to the civil interaction between citizens is not generally found in constitutional law, but in statutory and common law. Statutory law is that law written by the legislative branch of government in the criminal codes. The codes address which acts will be considered criminal and the penalties which will apply.

Common law is comprised of various court decisions rendered on a particular issue. In general terms this law exists where no statutory code for criminal behavior has been developed and in civil tort law addressing lawsuits. When government transgresses upon a citizen, the issue is framed in the context of constitutional rights. When one citizen transgresses against another, the issue is framed in terms of criminal activities or civil liability (lawsuit). Citizens cannot normally infringe upon the constitutional rights of another, but can commit crimes and civil torts. Private law enforcement officers are generally considered citizens and are regulated as such.

The distinctions made between public and private law enforcement rests in the authority rendered in a 1921 United States Supreme Court opinion in *Burdeau v. McDowell*, 256 U.S. 465. This case related to a private search and seizure where evidence of a crime was found and later turned over to public authorities. Charges were filed based on the evidence and the defendant was prosecuted. The case was ultimately appealed to the U.S. Supreme Court.

The court ruled that the Constitution was not enacted to redress the actions of one citizen against another, but to control the activities of government. As such, even though certain evidence may have been obtained illegally by private practitioners, when the government is not involved in the illegal search and seizure, evidence derived therefrom may be used by the government in prosecuting the party trespassed upon. The court went on to note that if a transgression in the law had occurred in the course of the private search and seizure, redress was available through both criminal codes and civil torts.

The changes in the law today center on the duality created with one law enforcement structure required to abide by constitutional restraints and the other limited by criminal and civil law alone. Certain "cut outs" in the law have been developed to address this dichotomy. In some jurisdictions (Montana and California), private agents must adhere to the same Fourth Amendment restraints applied to the public sector. In instances where private practitioners actively participate in joint efforts with the police, such private practitioners are universally considered "agents of the state" operating under the "color of law." As such, they must adhere to governmental restrictions on law enforcement. In spite of these changes and the directions they represent, the law relating to specific authorities granted to private practitioners has not kept up with the demand.

While the law is changing for the private sector, questions continue to exist on what can and cannot be done. In many instances, we must look to the only model we have available to obtain a sense of direction. That model is public law enforcement.

The laws as they relate to the public practitioners cannot be thought of as an exact blueprint for the private practitioner to follow. However, they can serve to a limited degree as an example of the methods most likely to be accepted by the courts where specific legislation or court guidance is absent. The fundamental differences between the methodology used by public practitioners vs. private practitioners are not only a function of law, but also a function of liability. As such, investigators should be keenly aware of the different exposures maintained between the public and private practitioner.

Liability

In general terms, public practitioners have significantly more insulations against liability than private practitioners. These insulations exist in the form of a limited or qualified immunity. This is a legal defense to liability that may be asserted by public practitioners, which provides that a public practitioner may not be civilly sued or criminally charged for actions when:

1. The act relates to the official duties of the public agent.
2. The public agent maintained probable cause to believe his or her actions were necessary in the enforcement of laws.
3. The actions were conducted in good faith.

In instances where these factors are not present and the actions taken were personal, malicious in nature, or lacked recognized probable cause, the limited or qualified immunity is not available to the public practitioner.

The government entity for which the officer is employed likewise maintains certain defenses to actions that are not available to their private counterparts. Federal and state employers may assert the defense of sovereign immunity. Sovereign immunity is a concept rooted in common law that is interpreted to mean, "the king can do no wrong." The theory here is that the government is acting in the best interest of the public in which it is pledged to serve. As such, any wrongdoing is either necessary or innocent; therefore, the government cannot be held liable

for the action of its employees. Local governments cannot normally assert a sovereign immunity defense. However, they can assert an additional defense to vicarious liability (liability for another), which, again, is not available to private employers. Unless the municipalities specifically permit illegal actions through the promulgation of manuals, regulations, or procedures, or through their inaction knowingly ignored the illegalities performed by their officers, the municipality cannot normally be found liable.

The significance of the protections afforded to public practitioners and their employers is this: the private sector maintains no such insulation or immunity under normal circumstances. With few exceptions, the private practitioners are held strictly liable for the consequences of their acts, regardless of whether they operated in good faith. Furthermore, under the theory of respondeat superior, private employers are held liable for all acts of their employees performed in the course of their employment, whether sanctioned or not.

The practical effect of this is that private practitioners must act cautiously because they are exposed to a higher potential for liability, while at the same time in similar situations the public practitioner can act with far greater latitude and much less risk of litigation. This adjustment in the application of procedures serves as the single greatest determinant in what private practitioners should or should not do.

As noted earlier, certain states have ruled contrary to *Burdeau* and provide that private law enforcement agents are held to the same Fourth Amendment standards as those that relate to the police. Unfortunately, these changes do not extend the same protections to the private agent as those maintained by the police.

Finally, the seemingly formidable defenses maintained by public police are under attack. The Supreme Court in Rhode Island has said that the legality of an officer's actions will be held to an industry standard in which the officer's actions are put to a theoretical reasonable human test. That is, the actions of the officer are compared to those actions that would have been taken by other officers in the same circumstance. If it is found that the officer's actions fell below accepted standards in the field, that officer may be liable.

To combat the increased risks incurred by municipalities in the lessening of defenses, a number of departments have severely limited those actions for which they will provide protection to the officers. Some entities have gone so far as to indicate that in instances of false arrests, arrests outside primary jurisdictions, and arrests off-duty, the arresting officers very likely may be acting on their own and outside the scope of insulations afforded them in their official position.

A Critical Misconception. The fact that the private practitioner is not always restrained by constitutional restrictions has often been misinterpreted to mean that they can do more than the police in a particular investigation. This is not correct. Simply because the Constitution may not be controlling their actions does not mean that prohibited police actions are legal if conducted by the private practitioner. As was set forth in *Burdeau*, if an action taken by a private party is found illegal, redress is available in either the criminal codes, civil codes, or both.

Further, where the police officer violates a constitutional guarantee such as an illegal search, for the most part, his or her primary concern is that they will lose the case. In the instance of the private practitioner, if they make a mistake, unwittingly or not, the private practitioner faces potential imprisonment and civil action. When viewed in these terms, the private agent possesses far less latitude for error in the performance of duties and faces far more serious sanctions than do police.

The significance of this last statement cannot be overemphasized. For all practical purposes even though evidence obtained by a private practitioner may prove criminality against a particular actor and may be used by the police, if the evidence is illegally obtained, the government can use the evidence to likewise criminally prosecute the private practitioner who illegally secured the evidence.

Coordination with Public Authorities. In many instances circumstances may require that the private practitioner coordinate an investigation with public authorities. This is particularly true in drug-related investigations where the private practitioner cannot possess controlled substances in any regard. This is also true in "sting" operations involving stolen merchandise. Should a private practitioner inadvertently possess stolen merchandise not owned by his or her employer, allegations of receiving stolen property may be raised. Therefore, coordinated efforts are not only invited, but in certain circumstances, legally required.

This coordination is not without its attendant liability risks. As we have seen, the public practitioner maintains certain insulations against liability not possessed by the private agent. In these coordinated efforts, the question presents itself: if the investigation should run afoul for any number of reasons, what protections would be afforded private agents? As the insulation maintained by public authorities permits far greater latitude in conducting investigations, the public practitioner is not required to operate under the same critical standard of ensured success as that of the private sector to avoid liability. With greater latitude and less risk, methods may be employed by public practitioners that maintain unacceptable risks of failure from a private perspective. If the method used does fail, the liabilities to the public agents are quite different from that of the private agent.

In all cases involving authority and liability the private practitioner should seek the advice of legal counsel. Counsel can enumerate the various risks attendant to a particular operation and can make recommendations based on these risks. In many instances practitioners may be advised to surrender the investigation to the public authorities.

John Dale Hartman

INVESTIGATIONS: FIFTH AMENDMENT PROTECTIONS

The Fifth Amendment to the Constitution generally provides that persons cannot be compelled to testify against themselves in a criminal proceeding on the grounds that they may incriminate themselves. In general terms, a person has the right to remain silent because anything said will be used against the person in a court of law. The person likewise maintains a right to counsel, as guaranteed by the Sixth Amendment, and to have counsel present during questioning. In the event a person cannot afford counsel, one will be appointed to them by the state. The subject of an interview can at anytime before or during the questioning exercise these rights by refusing to answer any further questions or make any further statement. It must likewise be ensured that the subject giving a confession fully understands these rights.

These are considered basic constitutional guarantees for anyone accused of a crime and generally comprise what has been referred to as the Miranda warning. For the most part, they only apply to interrogations by public law enforcement officials.

Public practitioners are required to provide the Miranda warning when the subject interviewed is both the "focus of the investigation" and the subject is in a "police-dominated atmosphere." In simple terms, when a suspect is interviewed in the custody or control of the police, the actor must be advised of his or her rights.

In general, the private practitioner is not required to provide the warning. Exceptions would include instances where a public practitioner is "moonlighting" in a private capacity, where the investigation conducted by the private practitioner is operated in concert with the police or there has been substantial police involvement, or where the private agent is actively working as an agent of the state. Private agents are generally not required to provide the Miranda warning because their interviews are not considered "custodial interviews" in the conventional sense under which the "reading of the rights" was instituted. A custodial interview exists where the police are controlling the movement of the suspect, whether real or perceived, and the police maintain an advantage in terms of position and training. The general concern is that the subject is at a distinct disadvantage when he or she is interviewed at a police station by trained interviewers.

This traditional thinking, while still rule of law, is now becoming more dated. The confines of a security office in many ways are no less threatening than a police station. Further, in many instances the training secured by private agents is in many ways equal to that obtained by their public counterparts. As such, many companies across the nation have instituted procedures whereby all suspects are routinely "Mirandized" prior to interview. It is the opinion of many defense lawyers that it is only a matter of time before the latitude given the private agent is replaced with a strict adherence to the basic constitutional protections provided by the Fifth Amendment.

This issue of Mirandizing carries with it a number of practical questions. The greatest one is: what should the practitioner do if the actor indicates he or she wants the benefit of counsel?

In such instances, the simple answer is to discontinue all interviewing and turn the matter over to the public authorities.

Parameters of Consent

Many investigations culminate in the private practitioner securing a statement in the form of an admission or confession. Simply because the private agent is not required to Mirandize a subject does not mean the investigator can compel a subject to confess to a crime. Such statements can only be obtained with the consent of the subject. When consent is given, often sufficient evidence to support a charge is obtained. One of the defenses available to an actor at subsequent legal proceedings is that the consent was obtained illegally and therefore is inadmissible in court.

Generally speaking, for consent to be valid and the evidence obtained to be admissible in court, a practitioner must ensure that his or her efforts meet the following standards:

1.   The actions taken must be reasonably conducted. Actions that shock the sensibilities of the court or insult the fair and honorable administration of justice are illegal.

2.   The consent must have been given voluntarily, of the subject's own free will, absent threats, promises, intimidation, or coercion.

3.   The actor must be legally competent to consent. The actor cannot be a minor, mentally incompetent, and cannot be intoxicated at the time consent is granted.

4.   A request to obtain an admission or confession must be made in private out of the presence of other persons. The interview itself must be conducted in an equally private location. Allegations of libel and slander may be raised if these requests or interviews are made in the presence of others not involved in the actions, particularly in instances where charges are not supported in court.

5.   The actor must be advised of his or her right to refuse to consent, or to withdraw the consent at anytime thereafter. Any action taken in connection with the consent must then stop.

6.   The actions consented to cannot extend beyond the parameters of the initial consent given. The scope of the actions must be outlined and agreed upon in the consent. If a party agrees to provide a statement, the party has not agreed to a search of personal effects.

7.   While a consent can be given orally, in writing, or in some circumstances by conduct or deed, it is advisable that the private agent secure a written agreement of the consent.   Most agreements come in the form of a waiver, which should be signed, dated, and witnessed.

8.   The consent given must be provided by the party against whom the action will be taken or a legal guardian for that actor.

Admissibility

Aside from consent, the primary focus on the admissibility of a confession relates to the manner in which it was immortalized. This is particularly sensitive in mechanical recordings. The laws relating to the legality of recording another's voice vary. In general terms, the laws can be segregated into two types: one-party and two-party consent. In one-party consent the law requires that at least one party to the action knows that the conversation is being recorded. The fact that the investigator knows he or she is recording the conversation and agrees to the recording satisfies the one-party consent requirement so long as the private agent is a party to the conversation. The agent cannot secretly record a conversation of others in which he or she is not involved.

In two-party consent, all parties subject to the conversation must be aware that they are being recorded, must have consented to the recording, and must be provided with the opportunity to stop the recording whenever they desire. In these instances, if a private agent secretly records the conversations he or she has with another or others, the recording is illegal and the practitioner may be subjected to illegal wiretapping sanctions. Generally, these sanctions are severe.

Please note, portable video recorders proliferate the industry and have proven their utility. Unfortunately, there is one instance where the use of the recorder may create problems. While in general what one can lawfully see may be photographically recorded, the same is not the case for what one hears.

In most VCR recorders, while visually taping an action, the recorder is likewise recording sound. In such an instance, while the visual documentation may be legal, the audio recording may not.   In instances of surveillance, practitioners must be sure to neutralize the audio capabilities of the camera.

To ensure that any consent given to a recorded statement is adequate, the following procedures should be met:

1.   In all recordings, the time, date, and place of the recording, the identity of the investigator obtaining the statement, and the party for whom the investigator works; the identity of the party providing the statement and identification information including address, telephone number, and work place; and the purpose of the interview and the identity of any co-interviewers or witnesses present should be noted at the beginning of the statement.

2.   The permissions granted to the recording should be read into the tape at both the beginning and end of the taped statement.

3.   The age of the subject, his or her date of birth, the subject's present employer, and the number of years of formal education should be read into the record. This will serve to support the competency of the subject to make the statement in question.

4.   If the tape must be turned to the second side, the permissions must appear at the beginning and end of that side.

5.   During those periods when the tape is turned over, no discussions should be had on the matter investigated and this should be confirmed at the beginning of the new side or tape.

6.   When switching sides of the tape, the time the tape recorder is turned off and the time it is turned back on should be noted.

7.   The recorder should not be turned off at any point during the interview. This will ensure the total time of the interview coincides with the total time shown on the tape. Confirmation that the tape has not been turned off should appear on the tape at the end of the statement.

8.   If for some unforeseen difficulty the tape must be turned off, the reasons why such action was necessary and the time periods involved should be noted.

9.   The subject of the interview should be granted permission to listen to the tape and to make any corrections necessary on the tape following the actual statement.

10. In instances where the subject is Mirandized prior to interview, confirmation of such protection should be shown on the tape and the "right" should be read into the record again with the subject providing affirmative responses.

11. In instances where the subject is not Mirandized, the investigator should at least

ensure the record reflects that the subject has been advised and confirms he or she understands that the employer may make use of the statement for any lawful purpose it may serve, including the institution of criminal or civil actions which may result from the investigations. Further, the subject should be advised that they may refuse to answer any question they desire, including those statements they feel may incriminate them.

12. There should be absolutely no interruptions during the interview. If there are any interruptions, they should be identified as they occur; e.g., "Officer Harris just entered the interview room."

13. The subject should confirm on tape that no threats, promises, intimidation, or coercion were used to obtain the statement. The subject should further be asked to indicate in his or her own words how he or she was treated during the interview.

14. The investigator should ensure everyone speaks loudly and distinctly during the interview so that no confusion will exist as to what was said during transcription. The subject should likewise be advised that all responses must be oral (shaking a head cannot be transcribed) and acceptable language should be used. Words such as "uh-huh" are often difficult to discern.

15. All subjects should be asked whether there is anything else they would like to add at the end of the statement.

16. Each statement should be concluded with a "thank you" and the investigator should note, "The statement is now ended."

To make certain each of these items is addressed in an interview, a script should be developed covering each point. Requirements should be made that investigators are not permitted to proceed through the litany by memory, but must refer to the script on each and every interview. This will ensure continuity in product and redundancy in the quality of the statement obtained. Further, in those instances where a subject is Mirandized, the investigator should be required to ready the warning from a card and not from memory. This will ensure a rights reading that was accurate and complete.

the desired information. While subjecting a party to verbal or physical abuse is clearly illegal and very likely may result in civil and criminal penalties against the investigator, other distressing factors may likewise be found to have created an environment that would invalidate the statement. Investigators in the private sector should likewise be certain their efforts meet the following additional guidelines:

1. The subject must be afforded the opportunity to obtain food, drink, and access to private facilities. Understanding of this should be confirmed in the statement.

2. The subject should be asked to confirm that he or she is not presently suffering from any physical or mental condition that would prohibit him or her from being interviewed.

3. Interviews should be avoided where the subject maintains physical or mental conditions that may be adversely affected to an extreme by the interview process. Should the interviewer detect indications that problems may exist, the interview should be discontinued and appropriate medical attention be summoned, if appropriate.

4. The subject must understand during the interview that he or she is not under arrest and is free to leave at any time. If the subject requests to leave, no effort to the contrary should be made.

5. A clear passageway must exist in the interview room from the point of interview to the exit door. Doors to interview rooms should not be capable of being locked from the inside.

6. The subject should be asked to confirm that every effort has been taken to ensure privacy and that there is no objection to the time and place of interview.

7. In internal investigations, the interview should be conducted during working hours.

8. The duration of an interview should be limited to a reasonable period of time. Under normal circumstances, if a confession is not obtained within 4 hours, any further effort to do so may well be viewed as unreasonable.

9. In instances where a confession is gained and the investigator has reason to believe that the subject is in an unbalanced state, assistance should be provided in transporting the subject home.

Threats, Intimidation, Duress, and Coercion

During interviews persons cannot be subjected to threats, intimidation, duress, or coercion to obtain

Promises and Guarantees

Under no circumstances should an investigator make any promises or guarantees to a subject, either explicitly or implicitly. Advising a subject that cooperation with the investigation will lead to a lesser charge or no filing of a charge will surely invalidate a confession. Investigators do not have the authority to make such promises.

Intoxication

Interviews should not be conducted while the subject is under the influence of an intoxicating substance. Intoxication clearly will only vitiate any consent provided. It should be confirmed within the statement that the subject is not under the influence of alcohol, drugs, or narcotics, which would preclude answering questions truthfully and accurately. This would include also any form of medication. If medication is involved, it should be identified and the time last taken noted. The subject should be asked to describe how he or she feels both physically and psychologically, and to acknowledge there is no reason to not conduct an interview.

In those instances where the subject is believed or professes to be a substance abuser, the investigator should identify the type of substance involved and determine if the subject is likely to undergo a drug-induced reaction during the interview, such as the withdrawal syndrome. Finally, the investigator should also attempt to establish on the record whether the subject has consumed any alcoholic beverages within the last 24 hours. If so, the investigator should determine what was consumed, the amount, and when.

Restitution

With few exceptions, unless specifically authorized by statute, investigators should not agree to restitution in lieu of prosecution. In instances where restitution is received and charges are not pressed, allegations of compounding a crime or extortion can easily be made and are difficult to defend against. Restitution should only be made under written agreement provided by corporate counsel.

Further, all arrangements relating to restitution should be coordinated with the court and any transfer of monies should occur in court. In short, then, charges must first be brought. From there, restitution can be discussed and arranged.

Acknowledgment, Release, and Indemnification

In those instances where it is agreed in court that charges will be dropped or reduced and restitution will be made, the private practitioner should ensure that the subject signs the appropriate acknowledgment admitting to the crime, and releasing and indemnifying the investigator and his or her employer from any future liabilities. Investigators should not permit a dismissal or reduction in charges under any circumstances unless such an acknowledgment, release, and indemnification is obtained from the subject.

Interviews with the Opposite Sex

In any interview, a witness must be present to serve as a safeguard in countering any number of allegations that may be made later. In those instances where the investigator is of one gender and the subject another, the witness chosen for the interview should be of the same gender as the subject. Furthermore, under no circumstances should an investigator of one gender be permitted alone with a subject of another. In those unforeseeable circumstances where the investigator is the only party present at the time, no interviewing should be conducted. The door to the interview room should be open and the investigator should assume a position in the doorway within public view, while blocking a view to the subject from the public until the witness arrives.

John Dale Hartman

INVISIBLE BARRIER DETECTORS

Invisible barrier detectors generate a narrow invisible beam of electromagnetic energy and detect a disturbance or reduction of the energy caused by an intruder running, walking, or crawling through the protected zone. The energy barrier is formed by a transmitter emitting a beam of energy to a corresponding receiver, moving along a line-of-sight path aligned with the transmitter, at the opposite end of the zone. The distance between the transmitter and receiver pair is a function of the type of detector, the application, and the operating environment. The primary application requirement for an invisible barrier detector to be effective is that the terrain between the detector transmitter and receiver be flat and free of obstructions, such as vegetation. Ground shrubbery and the like must be maintained at a height of not more than about 4 inches to prevent interruption of the beam.

There are two general types of active invisible barrier detectors: one operates at microwave frequencies and the other operates in the infrared frequency spectrum.

Microwave Detectors

Exterior microwave transmitters generate a narrow beam of microwave energy that is received by a corresponding receiver located in line-of-sight of the transmitter at the opposite end of the beam. Anyone passing through the beam will cause the receiver to react to the perturbations in the energy pattern, initiating an alarm when the resulting signals satisfy the detection alarm criteria. The maximum separation between the detector transmitter and receiver to achieve reliable detection is primarily a function of the antenna configuration.

The Federal Communications Commission (FCC) has allocated five frequency bands for operating exterior microwave detectors. These are the same frequency bands allocated for interior detectors. Of the five available frequencies, the exterior detectors presently available operate at next to the highest allocated frequency, 10,525 plus/minus 25 megahertz. This frequency is used because the higher-frequency microwave energy is more directive than the lower-frequency energies, and the energy pattern is less affected by moving or blowing grass in the area between the transmitter and receiver. Detectors operating at 10,525-megahertz frequency are restricted to a maximum field strength level of 250,000 microvolts per meter at a range of 30 meters for unlicensed use.

The narrow shape of the microwave energy beam and the maximum separation between the transmitter and the receiver is a function of the antenna size and configuration. The various detector antenna configurations being used by the microwave detector manufacturers include parabolic dish arrays, waveguide horns, stripline arrays, and slotted arrays. The maximum range of detection varies from approximately 200 feet to 1,500 feet. A 1500-foot range is difficult to cover, except perhaps for upright walkers.

Infrared Detectors

Exterior infrared detectors generate a multiple-beam fence-like pattern of infrared energy and initiate an alarm when a beam or a combination of beams is interrupted. Since the infrared energy frequency band lies just below the color red in the visible light spectrum, infrared energy is too low in frequency to be visible to the naked eye. The infrared energy is generated in the detector transmitter by a solid-state infrared source. A commonly used light source is the gallium arsenide light-emitting diode (LED). In operation, the light source should be modulated and pulsed at a specific frequency to reduce the possibility of an intruder substituting another infrared source in an attempt to compromise the detector. Modulating the beam also reduces the susceptibility of the detector alarming from sunlight or other light sources.

Energy radiating from the infrared light source passes through a co-luminating lens that forms and directs a beam of energy that is directed toward the receiver at the opposite end of the zone. Energy reaching the receiver passes through a collecting lens that focuses the radiant energy onto a photoelectric cell. The photoelectric cell is a semiconductor device that converts the radiant infrared energy into electrical signals proportional to the radiant energy. The receiver monitors the electrical signal and initiates an alarm when its magnitude drops below a pre-set alarm threshold for a specific period of time. The alarm threshold should correspond to at least a 90 % blockage for a period of about 75 milliseconds. The blockage reduces the probability of false alarms from birds flying or debris blowing through the beams. Some detectors require a loss of signal from at least two receivers to initiate an alarm. This technique reduces the susceptibility of the detectors alarming to birds and debris; however, the bottom receiver alone should initiate an alarm if it is interrupted. Otherwise, low-crawling intruders will not be detected.

The infrared fence beam patterns are formed between two separate detector columns. One column is located at one end of the protected zone and the other column is located at the opposite end. Since the exterior infrared detectors are line-of-sight devices, the area between the columns must be level and clear of any obstacles that might interfere with the transmitted energy. The separation between the two detector columns ranges from a few feet to protect entrance gates to zones as long as 1,000 feet. Weather conditions, such as heavy rain, fog, snow, or even blowing dust particles, attenuate infrared energy and can affect the operating range. In areas where these weather conditions occur, the detector range might have to be reduced to 100 or 200 feet, depending on the density of the particles.

Infrared detectors can provide perimeter penetration detection for industrial and commercial installations with level grounds that can accommodate detection zone lengths of at least 300 feet long. Infrared detectors have a high probability of detecting anyone running, walking, or attempting to jump over the infrared beams if the detector columns are at least 4 to 6 feet high. They also have a high probability of detecting anyone crawling through the energy barrier, if the ground is level between the detector columns and the lowest beam is no greater than 6 inches above the ground.

Robert L. Barnard

Source Barnard, R.L., Intrusion Detection Systems. (Butterworth-Heinemann, Boston, 1982).

J

JOB TASK ANALYSIS

Reduced to its simplest level, job task analysis is a method for describing work in terms of tasks. The method is broad and includes a variety of techniques. Technique will be influenced by the nature of the job and the purpose of the analysis. For example, the technique used to analyze investigative work for the purpose of determining job classifications is likely to be different from analyzing security officer work for the purpose of determining training needs.

The Task

The common factor in all techniques is the preparation of task statements. Preparation of good task statements requires having a clear understanding of the characteristics of a task. A task:

- Is visible and measurable.
- Has a clear beginning and end.
- Is of relatively short duration.
- Is always directed toward a specific purpose.
- Results in a meaningful product, service, or outcome.
- Is performed independently of other tasks.

A task is often confused with related terms, such as duty and job. A duty is a large cluster of closely related tasks, and a job is a group of related duties. To illustrate, the job of security console operator has several duties, which might include evaluating alarm signals, dispatching security officers, and maintaining an activity log. Within the duty of dispatching, the console operator performs certain tasks, such as operating a radio, communicating by telephone, and prioritizing responses.

We can distinguish between job, duty, and task by applying the task definition. To operate a console cannot be a task because it has no definite beginning and end, it is not relatively short in duration, and by common understanding is a broad function. Dispatching security officers cannot be a task either because the action of dispatching involves a series of steps, such as evaluating the need to respond, setting a priority

among needed responses, and deciding which officers to send, and in the process the console operator may use different pieces of equipment, such as a base station radio and telephone.

Breaking a job down into its parts has the effect of finding where and how the tasks are performed. Conceptualizing how a job is carried out, determining the equipment needed for performance, and identifying the points where the job interfaces with other jobs has value. Information of this nature can be useful input to a full range of management decisions. Finding the tasks and critically examining them can help management get a fix on the tools and equipment needed to be purchased, where they should be placed, how much space will be required, what skills and knowledge will need to be possessed by the job incumbent, and what level of compensation will be needed to attract and retain an effective performer.

The Task Inventory

Tasks are identified by persons close to the job, such as the incumbents or those who directly supervise the incumbents. The means for collecting the information can be by survey, questionnaire, personal interviews, direct observation, and by studying job descriptions, job procedures, training manuals, and the like.

Each task is expressed in a written statement that has three elements, which appear in this order:

1. An action verb that describes what is done.

2. An identification of what is being acted upon.

3. A clarifying phrase, if needed.

The task statement is declarative and understood to contain "I" or "he" or "she."

In the task statement "prepare property removal passes," the action verb is "prepare" and the thing being acted upon is "property removal passes." If property removal passes are issued only to employees, a clarifying phrase could be added so that the task statement reads "prepare property removal passes for employees."

A task statement tells what is done, not how or why it is done. Statements are short, to the point, and leave little room for interpretation. The action verb is unambiguous. It is better to state "test the fire alarm detectors" than to leave room

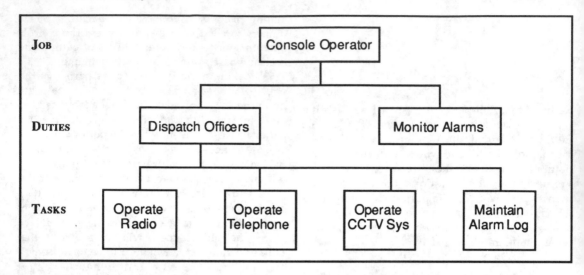

JOB		Console Operator
DUTIES	Dispatch Officers	Monitor Alarms
TASKS	Operate Radio / Operate Telephone	Operate CCTV Sys / Maintain Alarm Log

for doubt by stating "arrange to test..." or "coordinate the testing of...."

Rating the Tasks

Rating a task means to apply to it one or more questions that are important to the purpose of the analysis effort. Following are some questions and their implications:

Q: Is the task so critical that an error in performance will result in serious consequences?

A: Prospective incumbents should (1) possess a combination of skills, knowledge, and attitude commensurate to learning the task; (2) master the task in practice situations before going on the job; (3) receive intensive initial training and frequent refresher training; and (4) be compensated at a level sufficient to attract and retain.

Q: Is performance of the task hazardous to the incumbent or others?

A: The job will most probably be subject to some form of regulatory review; safety considerations must predominate; special insurance may be appropriate to reduce risk; and task mastery will be essential.

Q: Is performance of the task in this job essential to the performance of any tasks performed in other jobs?

A: The incumbent will need to be informed of the relationship of the task to the work of others, and vice versa; a back-up compensating arrangement may need to be put in place; and task competency will be a minimum.

When the question needs to be answered with more than a "yes" or a "no," the answer format can use scales, for example:

How critical is the task?
1. Not critical at all
2. Somewhat critical
3. Moderately critical
4. Critical
5. Very critical

How difficult is the task?
1. Easy
2. Easy-to-moderate
3. Moderately difficult
4. Difficult
5. Very difficult

How soon will the task be performed after the incumbent goes on the job?
1. In the first month
2. In the second month
3. In 3 to 6 months
4. In 6 to 12 months
5. After 12 months

After the persons close to the job have given their responses to the pertinent questions, the data are analyzed. A computer-assisted analytical procedure might be developed just for the study, or a software package might be purchased.

Task analysis can be done in a variety of ways, but all have one thing in common, i.e., they analyze jobs in terms of the ways in which work is actually performed. The approach is always objective, sometimes quantitative, and likely in many cases to lead to work improvement, which in the absence of analysis would not be possible.

John J. Fay, CPP

Sources

Fay, J.J., A Task Analysis of the Special Agent Job in the Georgia Bureau of Investigation. (The Georgia Bureau of Investigation, Atlanta, 1978).

Fay, J.J., Approaches to Criminal Justice Training, 2nd Edition. (University of Georgia Press, Athens, GA, 1988).

McCormick, E.J., Job Analysis: Methods and Applications. (American Management Association, New York, 1979).

Performance Content for Job Training. (The Center for Vocational Education, Ohio State University, Columbus, OH, 1977).

K

KEY CONTROL

A lock is a non-discriminating device -- it will open for anyone who possesses the correct key or combination. Ideally, in a maximum-security setting, keys to sensitive or vital areas will be stored under rigid control procedures in a locked cabinet within view of a security post that is manned around the clock. If there is no continuously manned post, the keys may be stored on-site in a container that has penetration resistance greater than that of any other sensitive area. If entry to the key repository were as easy as forcing any single door, an intelligent adversary would naturally concentrate attention there, knowing that for the expenditure of only the amount of effort necessary to gain access to the key cabinet, access can be gained everywhere.

Strong and compelling reasons exist for issuing keys to certain individuals, such as those in a supervisory or management position. Are the reasons valid? Are the keys issued because that person's duties require frequent passage through certain doors or access points, or have they been issued for the sake of convenience only? There will be employees who will argue that their duties require access to the facility during non-working hours. Some of these, such as the plant superintendent, maintenance supervisor, and security manager, will have legitimate reasons to enter the protected premises after hours, but most employees will not require after-hours access.

Issuance of keys is often a "reward" for faithful service. Perhaps the ultimate extension of this is the issuance of a master or grand master key. The loss, theft, or unauthorized duplication of a single master key negates the entire system, whereas loss of a key to a lock (or several locks) within a system has only compromised that lock or locks. Where an individual has a legitimate need for access to several different areas to carry out duties, the use of a master or grand master key would be convenient, but the convenience does not outweigh the costs that can result when the locking system has been compromised by loss, theft, or unauthorized use of a master key.

When establishing a new key control system, it is important to ensure that no key that is to reach the hands of any person outside the security management staff bears manufacturer's cut code numbers or keyway identification information. If these are the only keys available, the information should be recorded and stored in a secure space as if it were an actual key. If these numbers were obtained by an unauthorized individual, it would be a relatively simple matter to have a less-than-ethical locksmith duplicate the key. Once the information has been recorded and properly stored, the numbers may be ground off the keys or obliterated in some other manner. Unauthorized duplication would be somewhat more difficult if the keyway used a controlled key blank available only from the manufacturer and then only to the registered owner of the system. Unfortunately, more and more independent suppliers of key blanks are turning out blanks that often negate cautions taken by lock manufacturers. Because there are just so many ways to configure the guide cuts in a blank, the unprincipled locksmith may find a way to make a blank fit an altogether different keyway from that for which it was originally manufactured.

Ideally, master keys will not be used in a maximum-security environment. It is not unusual for senior executives to firmly believe they should be provided master keys because their duties require access to any part of the facility. While the premise is sound, the practice certainly is not! The possibility for loss or theft of a master key is just as good as those for any other key; the chances of unauthorized duplication is only slightly less than that for any other key.

While it is recommended that in a maximum-security setting keys not be indiscriminately issued, the realities of the situation demand that certain management or supervisory personnel have keys to aid in the execution of their duties. When this is required, a careful assessment must be made to ensure that these personnel are given only the absolute minimum number. The keys should be issued on a signature receipt form on which the individual receiving them acknowledges personal responsibilities. These include assurance that the keys will be stored in a proper penetration-resistant container when not in use or carried on the individual's person, and that the keys will never be loaned to anyone, no matter the reason (except, of course, in the event of a major emergency where failure to yield the keys could result in loss of life or major property damage). The receipt should indicate that the keys remain company property, shall not be duplicated, are subject to audit and recall at any time, and must be surrendered upon termination of employment or when the individual no longer has a need for them. An additional consideration would be the requirement that replacements for keys damaged in use will be substituted on a one-for-one basis.

Key Accounting Procedures

In the maximum-security environment, the majority of keys necessary for limited day-to-day operations will be stored in a penetration-resistant container that is located in a continuously manned security post. Proper accounting procedures require that an inventory of these keys be posted inside the container and that the keys be counted at every security shift change. The on-coming officer must assure himself that the number of keys remaining in the container and the number still signed out on the key issue/receipt record agree with the authorized container inventory. Only then can the on-coming officer sign the record indicating acceptance of the count.

For access to vital or sensitive areas, the access authorization list should specify that two authorized individuals are required to sign for the key. This ensures that no one person will have unescorted access. Ideally, the entry to the area should also be under the observation and control of yet a third person.

Some facilities have found it advantageous to use one brand or model of lock for all exterior locations that are not part of a sensitive area, and to use a different brand or model in the sensitive areas. This reduces the possibility of inadvertently using in the sensitive area a lock that may have been compromised during its use in a non-sensitive area. Ideally, whenever a lock is moved from one location to another, its core will be changed or recombinated. In this manner, the possibility that the lock may have been compromised in the past would present no problem with its use at a new location.

The last item to consider is controlling access to the supply of key blanks and key machine (if there is one on site). The possibility of unauthorized duplication of keys is great enough without making it even easier by providing the means and the method on-site. Duplication equipment and key stock should be stored in a safe or strong room when not in use, and should be under the exclusive control of the security manager. Carrying this concept to its logical conclusion, the entire lock and key system should be under security department control.

Richard J. Gigliotti
and Ronald C. Jason

Source Gigliotti, R., and R. Jason, Security Design for Maximum Protection. (Butterworth-Heinemann, Boston, 1984).

L

LAW: PRINCIPLES OF BUSINESS LAW

Business and law are inextricably linked; the law determines who may engage in business, how business is to be carried out, and the penalties that apply when the law is broken.   An understanding of the law as it relates to business is indispensable to the security manager.

An understanding of business law means knowing the origins of law, how they have changed and are continuing to change, and how they are currently applied. The particular areas of interest to the security manager are constitutional law, statutory law, case law, administrative law, and the role of ethics in influencing business conduct.

Sources of Law

Law acts as an instrument of social control and of change. Many of the laws that regulate business, for example, have evolved in response to societal demands.

In responding to the will of society, the law is in a constant state of flow, ebbing, and rising in relation to pressures from many different sources. We see this, for example, in restrictions designed to protect ecological systems. Clearly, law has a profound impact on the decisions of managers in all disciplines and at all levels in a business organization.

The security manager's view of the law will necessarily be both broad and purposeful. It will be broad in the sense that the law expresses concepts that generally ascribe to the notion that for civilization to be functional there must be a body of rules enforced by the government for the good of the people. The security manager's view will be purposeful because it will focus on functional purposes, such as prevention of crime, maintenance of order, investigation of crime, and apprehension of violators.   This view acknowledges that the law is not just a statement of rules of conduct, but also the mechanism for dealing with violations and affording remedies.

American law has four sources: (1) the U.S. and state constitutions, (2) legislation or statutory law, (3) judicial decisions or case law, and (4) the rules and regulations of governmental agencies or administrative law.   The general priority among the various sources of law is that constitutions prevail over statutes, and statutes prevail over common-law principles established in court decisions. Courts will not turn to judicial decisions for law if a statute is directly applicable.

The rules and principles that are applied by the courts fall into three groups: (1) laws that have been passed by legislative bodies; (2) case law, derived from cases decided by the courts; and (3) procedural rules, which determine how lawsuits are handled in the courts and include matters such as the rules of evidence. The first two groups are used by the courts to decide controversies. They are often called substantive law. The third group, known as procedural law, provides the machinery whereby substantive law is given effect and applied to resolve controversies.

Substantive law defines rights, whereas procedural law establishes the procedures by which rights are enforced and protected. For example, Jones claims that Smith should reimburse him for losses sustained in a burglary at the apartment that Jones rented from Smith. The rules that provide for bringing Smith into court and for the conduct of the trial constitute procedural law. Whether Smith had a duty to protect Jones against burglary and whether Jones is entitled to damages are matters of substance that would be determined on the basis of the substantive law.

Private law pertains to the relationships between individuals.   It encompasses the subjects of contracts, torts, and property. The law of torts is a chief source of litigation. A tort is a wrong committed by one person against another or against his property. The law of torts holds that people who injure others or their property should compensate them for their loss.

Constitutional Law

The Constitution of the United States and the constitutions of the various states form the foundation of our legal system. All other laws must be consistent with them. A federal law cannot violate the U.S. Constitution; all state laws must conform to the federal Constitution, as well as with the constitution of the appropriate state.

Statutory Law

Much of law is found in legislation. Legislation is the expression of society's judgment and the product of the political process. Legislative bodies exist at all levels of government. Legislation is created by Congress, state legislatures, and local government bodies. Legislation enacted by Congress or by a state legislature is usually referred to as a statute. Laws passed by local governments are frequently called ordinances. Compilations of legislation at all levels of government are called codes. For example, we have city fire codes that cover fire safety, state traffic codes that regulate the operation of motor vehicles, and, at the federal level, we have the U.S. Code consisting of statutes that regulate general conduct.

Substantial differences in the law exist among the various states simply because each state has its own constitution, statutes, and body of case law. Two methods of achieving uniformity in business law are possible: (1) having federal legislation govern business law, and (2) having uniform state laws for certain common business transactions. The latter method has produced more than 100 model uniform laws concerning such subjects as partnership, leases, arbitration, warehouse receipts, bills of lading, and stock transfers. The most important development for business in the field of uniform state legislation has been the Uniform Commercial Code (UCC).

Case Law

A very substantial part of law is found in cases decided by the courts. This concept of decided cases as a source of law is generally referred to as case law and has been a predominant influence in the evolution of the body of law in the United States. Case law is important because of the great difficulty in establishing law in advance of an issue being raised.

When a case is decided, the court writes an opinion. These written opinions, or precedents, make up the body of case law. The concept of precedent is linked to a doctrine called *stare decisis*, which means "to stand by decisions and not to disturb what is settled." *Stare decisis* holds that once a precedent has been set, it should be followed in later cases involving the same issue.

In this way, the law takes on certainty and predictability. *Stare decisis* is also flexible. If a court, especially an appeals court, finds that the prior decision was wrong or that it is no longer sound under prevailing conditions, it may overrule and change the decision. Although *stare decisis* introduces some degree of consistency, the system is far from perfect. Precedents (and statutes) vary from state to state. In some states the plaintiff in a negligent security case must be completely free of fault in order to recover damages; in most other states the doctrine of comparative negligence is used, so that a plaintiff found to be 10% at fault can recover not more than 90% of his damages.

Administrative Law

Administrative law is concerned with the many administrative agencies of the government. This type of law is in the form of rules and regulations promulgated by an administrative agency created by a state legislature or by the Congress to carry out a specific statute. For example, in a variety of statutes the Congress gives authority to the U.S. Department of Transportation (DOT) to regulate the nation's transportation systems (air, maritime, highway, railroad, pipeline, and metropolitan transit). The rules put into effect by DOT are in the nature of law to the regulated parties, e.g., the air, sea, motor, and rail carriers engaged in interstate transportation.

The powers and procedures of the administrative agencies do not always correspond exactly to the general intent of the legislature. By its very nature, most legislation is general, and interpretation is necessary to carry out the intent of the legislative body when it passed an act. The rules that implement a legislative act are often the interpretation of a government administrator. Since it is not possible to precisely express legislative intent in words that mean the same thing to everyone, the rules and regulations are often approximations that, when implemented, are quickly challenged by the affected parties.

Ethics

Ethics play a part in influencing conduct and regulating the behavior of individuals and businesses. Concern for the consequences of one's actions is clearly a powerful motivator. For example, as security professionals we are concerned about the damage to our reputations that would follow if we were found to have engaged in practices that were unethical or immoral, although not necessarily illegal. Business entities have similar fears based on economic consequences.   Personal and institutional ethical standards are having an ever-increasing impact on decisions. Almost every publicly held business has adopted a code of ethical conduct for its employees; the federal government has one for its employees; and nearly all trade and professional associations, including the American Society for Industrial Security, adhere to ethical codes. While these codes are not laws, they are usually enforced and provide penalties for non-compliance.

Ethical conduct is based on a personal commitment to do what is correct and to not do what is wrong. Ethical standards articulate values that go beyond what the law specifically demands and proscribes. The law provides a floor above which ethical conduct rises. Although ethical standards are usually considered to be extensions beyond the law, they are sometimes enacted into law when legislatures bring the law into alignment with society's views of right and wrong.

In the business environment, ethical conduct normally exists at a level well above legal minimums. It often means doing more than the law requires or less than it allows. Codes of ethics adopted by businesses can be thought of as internal work rules for all persons subject to them. Typically, they are based on fairness and honesty, and most provisions only require disclosure of facts to superiors in particular situations, while a few may dictate certain decisions and conduct. Codes of ethics state a collective sense of right and wrong, usually in the broadest of terms.

John J. Fay, CPP

Source Corley, R.N., and P.J. Shedd, Principles of Business Law, 14th Edition. (Prentice-Hall, Englewood Cliffs, NJ, 1989).

LAW ENFORCEMENT LIAISON: A CHALLENGE TO POLICE CHIEFS

Today, every major element of international and national business uses extensive personnel and financial resources to safeguard its interests. In the United States alone, private security and investigative services are provided by more than 9,000 companies that comprise a $15-billion-a-year industry. Three and possibly four times as many people are privately employed to perform security functions as are employed in policing and law enforcement at every level of government. Until recently, there has been little coordination between these sectors and minimal appreciation for each other's operational problems.

It is becoming increasingly critical for a company to identify its subtle and often sophisticated white collar crime. In the mid-1970s, annual losses to white collar criminals were estimated at approximately $40 billion. By the 1980s, estimates reached $200 billion, with analysts predicting even higher losses as we proceed toward the 21st century.

Contributing to the increases in opportunities for business fraud is the fact that society operates more on a paperless basis, as electronic impulses replace paper in the conduct of business transactions. The technological leap in communication has been extraordinary. An example is the fiber-optic cable across the Pacific that went into service in April 1989 to link the United States to Japan.   North America, Europe, part of Asia, and Australia are being strung with fiber-optic cable. A single fiber-optic cable can carry more than 8,000 conversations, compared with 48 for the traditional copper wire.

Essentially, the global economy is laying the foundations for an international information highway system that will provide the capability to communicate anything to anyone, anywhere, by any form -- voice, data, test, or image -- at the speed of light. The unanswered question is, Who will police that highway?

Within   the   business   community, recognition is being given to the notion that auditors are not investigators, and investigators are not auditors. Yet fraud detection requires open communication between these two disciplines. In order to reduce "turf mentality," the private security profession advocates cross-training, formal and informal information linkages, coordination of activities, and structured agreements on the role auditors and investigators play within the business process. In light of the emerging global economy and the potential for increased economic crime beyond a nation's borders, the issue of "turf mentality" will have to be excised between the public and private protection professionals. Innovative solutions require that both develop new perspectives and successful strategies to meet the challenge of crime, terrorism, and public disorder.

Any national strategy must include the recognition that police/private security partnerships must increase. Simply put, police would be foolish not to recognize the current momentum of such partnerships. Recognition, however, does not imply surrender of legitimate accountability on the part of law enforcement.

Protection professionals, particularly police officials, should move toward modified adaptation of the partnership, initially conceived by Sir Robert Peel in 1829 in establishing the first policing system. Peel's principle is that of a police-citizen relationship -- to wit, that the police are the public and the public are the police, the police being only members of the public who are paid to give full-time attention to duties that are incumbent on every citizen. A contemporary review of Peel's principle would allow another dimension -- that of the emerging role of private security within a democratic society.

To modernize the Peel principle, law enforcement officials, or at least a number of them, will have to change the way in which they view the role of private security. It will become imperative that they likewise change the manner in which they secure the necessary and appropriate cooperation and resources from government in order to do their job.

According to the *Hallcrest Report II, Private Security Trends (1970-2000)*, private security is America's primary protective resource in terms of spending and employment. Private security employs almost 1.5 million people, with annual expenditures of $52 billion. By comparison, roughly 600,000 people work in federal, state, and local public law enforcement, and expenditures for those services are roughly $30 billion. Among the major findings of the report are:

•The increasing growth of private security and the limited growth of public law enforcement are due to four main factors:

increasing workplace crime, increasing fear of crime, a decreasing rate of government spending for public protection, and increasing awareness and use of private security as cost-effective protective measures.

•The cost of economic crime in 1990 is estimated at $114 billion. At 2% or more of the gross national product, economic crime is out of control and on the rise.

•Private security personnel are younger and better educated than they used to be. The number of academic security programs has grown significantly, from only 33 certificate and degree programs in the mid-1970s to 164 such programs in operation currently. Furthermore, employment in private security is projected to grow at 2.3% annually to the year 2000. The U.S. Department of Labor predicts the national work force will grow by a little more than half of that projected figure.

The issue of privatization should be of great concern to future chiefs of police. We have seen much interest, even among police administrators, in transferring certain responsibilities to the private sector. More likely, as time goes on, we will see a return of non-crime and non-emergency services to the private sector. However, for many years research has suggested that 80% of what police do is non-crime related. Therefore, while police officials should recognize the growth and value of private security, they need to understand what the impact may be on their ability to generate staff and support services. Privatization has the opportunity to remove some burdens from the police to allow them to concentrate on their primary mission. It can be a double-edged sword, one edge of which may well be used to cut funding for police services.

There are a growing number of governmentally supported, private tax-incentive programs to assist business. One that is increasingly utilized is the business district tax program, which allows businesses to establish a non-profit organization to supply additional security, sanitation, and other services within a geographical area.

One of the better known organizations is New York's Grand Central Partnership, which provides additional security protection and sanitation services in a 50-square-block area of midtown Manhattan. Plans call for additional partnerships to be established in New York City, and Philadelphia is said to be considering this idea as well.

Police chiefs who have not yet given thought to developing a security partnership agenda should begin now. Police executives must learn that security should not be treated as some executives treated the growth of unions. Unions did not go away, and neither will the growth of private security programs.

If police chiefs fail to become leading players in the process, the consequent erosion of public confidence in their ability to deliver services may quicken as funding priorities shift to accommodate innovative privatization measures. The failures of joint ventures between police and security must not happen, as it will lead to corporate flight from traditional tax-base locales.

We have witnessed school systems throughout the country becoming the educational playgrounds for the "haves" and the "have-nots." The decline of neighborhoods has occurred as a result of a lack of funding and the consequent image of poor education. We have to be aware of the possibility that, as the perception of public protection tends to decrease, affluent and middle-class people will be conditioned to pay a special tax to protect themselves.

With continued growth in private protection, the notion that the best protection goes to those who can afford it will be tested, particularly in urban areas.

I am not advocating that the police attempt to stop change. I am advocating that they become a part of it. Police chiefs must begin to act politically, even though they are quick to claim that they are not politicians. They must learn the techniques of local lobbying and develop an ability to see their police service as a product that needs to be marketed.

If they fail to recognize change, they will have little control over such change and, consequently, the playing field in which police officials find themselves will continue to be uneven as we look at the growth and impact of private security.

Charles P. Connolly, CPP

Source Reprinted with permission from Law Enforcement News. (John Jay College of Criminal Justice, New York, November 15, 1991).

LAW ENFORCEMENT LIAISON: WORKING TOGETHER

In developing a mutual assistance program between private security and police, it is natural to ask a few questions: Where in the process of cooperation are we now? Where should we be if we are to enhance the protection network America deserves? How can private security and the police merge to the point of optimum success?

Let us return to the past to identify some of the obstacles that prevented an understanding of how security and police assist each other. In the past, there was an arm's length relationship between the police and the security industry, even though the security profession is no Johnny-come-lately in protection. In fact, private law enforcement has been around longer than municipally constituted public law enforcement.

Quite naturally, questions of turf have come up, and motives have been mistrusted. The police consider themselves independent. Therefore, when private security requested assistance, the police felt their responsibility to the public was somehow compromised. Other reasons the police have used to justify limited interaction with private security include the absence of standards and licensing in the security industry, skepticism over the quality of security personnel and their training, and a failure to recognize security's contribution to the public welfare.

Perceptions among law enforcement officials are changing. Recognition that public law enforcement does not and will not possess sufficient resources to respond to the needs of American businesses is probably the engine driving the interest in mutual assistance and collaboration. In fact, both professions recognize that more binds than separates them. The following are several duties both professions perform:

• Personal Safety. The private sector has a responsibility to ensure the safety of its employees, its clients, and anyone else with whom it comes into contact. That responsibility rests largely on the shoulders of employers, not local police.

• Crime Prevention Activities. Both professions have an obligation to develop crime prevention initiatives. More and more police departments have acknowledged that it is better to prevent criminal behavior than to combat it after the fact. That philosophy is a founding principle of the security profession.

•Order Maintenance. The police are responsible for maintaining public order. In areas maintained by private industry, the job of order maintenance falls to private security.

In 1975, approximately half a million police were employed in American police and sheriff departments. A similar number of persons were employed in private security. Today, the police staffing level is roughly the same as it was, while the security force level increased threefold. Why has such unequal growth occurred?

Rightly or wrongly, public officials are reluctant to raise taxes to increase public protection forces. Increasingly, we hear the plea that we must do more with less. As the police become more selective in what tasks they will perform, many new duties have fallen to private security.

Despite occasional decreases in crime rates, many people believe crime is simply out of control and there is no end in sight. Furthermore, no obvious solution is at hand. Closer cooperation in handling the increasing criminal burden is likely. Success will be measured in terms of coping with, not solving, the problems. Thus, police must target crimes that most affect the public's sense of safety. Many minor crimes must be neglected.

This inability to address certain crimes has created additional responsibilities for other parts of the protection profession. Private security must take a more assertive position in dealing with problems that cannot be addressed by public law enforcement under today's circumstances. In fact, interest is rising in privatization, in which traditional government services are contracted out to the private sector. The growth of the private law enforcement industry and the rise in crime suggest a different view of the relationship between public law enforcement and private security.

Only two relevant differences exist between the public and private protection professions: the amount of publicly constituted authority necessary to carry out a mission and the question of who pays for the services. Current protection literature notes changes in constitutional or chartered authority to perform protection activities. The public and private protection arena now contains not only police officers and peace officers, but also deputized, commissioned security personnel.

With regard to who pays for the services, policing is the result of tax levies, while private security is individually sponsored. However, the same person is paying for both services -- it is just a matter of how payment is extracted. As a taxpayer a person pays for police services, and as a consumer he or she funds private policing activities.

Private security is necessary to supplement the police if we are to get any relief from crime. Both protective services perform such basic functions as prevention, protection, enforcement, investigation, inspection, emergency services, patrol, detection and deterrence.

Private Security and Police in America: The Hallcrest Report, published in 1985 by the National Institute of Justice, Washington, DC, found that law enforcement officials, proprietary security managers, and contract security mangers agreed on the transfer of certain police-related activities to the private security side. Those activities were burglar alarm response, preliminary investigations, incident reports when victims decline prosecution, certain misdemeanor incident reports, and transporting people taken in citizens' arrests. A number of those activities are already being handled by private security in many areas of the United States.

There appears to be a growing potential for contracting private security to perform the following activities:
•Public building security
•Parking enforcement
•Parking lot patrol
•School crossing protection
•Public park control
•Accident investigations (without injuries)
•Animal control
•Traffic control
•Special event security
•Funeral escorts
•Court security
•Executive protection
•Housing project patrol

Many of these items are almost entirely a responsibility of proprietary and contract security organizations. Particularly in urban and suburban areas, traditional police responsibilities are increasingly a shared activity.

Many police administrators look favorably on such an exchange, which permits the police to focus on more serious public concerns.

Police are not the only ones who must adapt. Business people must recognize that traditional police protection may not be available. Executives must adjust to the notion that, despite the taxes paid, the demand for protection will be met primarily outside the public arena. Private security activities will need to be expanded to fill the vacuum created by police responses elsewhere. Compromise, negotiation, and partnership will be the key activities in future public/private enforcement roles.

Where should we be, and how can we get there? The need for security simply cannot be satisfied by the traditional systems of public and private protection. It is time for both protection professions to explore their opportunities -- at the local, state, and federal levels -- for cooperative options of mutual benefit. It is time for police and security administrators to develop broad cooperative strategies.

Charles P. Connolly, CPP

Source   Reprinted with permission of Security Management magazine,   American Society for Industrial Security, Arlington, VA.

LEGAL CONCERNS IN LOSS PREVENTION

Our system of justice places a high value on the rights of citizens. The loss prevention practitioner's work activities in requesting arrests, collecting evidence, interviewing and interrogating witnesses and suspects, preparing reports, seeking prosecution, and recovering company assets places the practitioner within the scrutiny of our justice system. Should the practitioner violate a citizen's rights, he or she may be held personally accountable, and where the violative act was performed as a job duty, the practitioner's employer may also be accountable. When the violative act is a crime, the issue can be decided in a criminal court and the punishment may be imprisonment and/or a fine; and when the violative act is a civil wrong, the issue may be decided in a civil court and redress made through monetary awards.

Criminal law deals with crimes against society. Each state and the federal government maintains a criminal code that classifies and defines offenses. Felonies are considered more serious crimes, such as burglary and robbery. Misdemeanors are less serious crimes, such as trespassing and disorderly conduct.

Civil law adjusts conflicts and differences between individuals. Examples of civil law cases in the security field are false arrest, unlawful detention, negligent training of security officers, and inadequate security that results in death or injury. When a plaintiff (i.e., a person who initiates a lawsuit) wins a case against another party, monetary compensation commonly results.

Law Origins

Three major sources of law are common law, case law, and legislative law. English common law is the major source of law in the United States. Common law is an ambiguous term. Generally, it refers to law founded on principles of justice determined by reasoning according to custom and universal consent. The development of civilization is reflected in common law. Specific acts were, and still are, deemed criminal. These acts, even today, are referred to as common law crimes: treason, murder, robbery, battery, larceny, arson, kidnapping, and rape, among others.

Common law is reinforced by decisions of courts of law. After this nation gained independence from England, the common law influence remained. Nineteen states have perpetuated common law through case law (i.e., judicial precedent). Eighteen states have abolished common law and written it into statutes. The remaining states have either adopted common law via ratification or are unclear about exactly how it is reflected in the state system.

Case law, sometimes referred to as "judge-made law," involves the interpretation of statutes or constitutional concepts by federal and state appellate courts. Previous case decisions or "precedent cases" have a strong influence on court decisions because they are used as a reference for decision making. Since the justice system is adversarial, opposing attorneys refer to past cases (i.e., precedents) that support their individual contentions. The court makes a decision between the opposing parties. Societal changes are often reflected in decisions. Since the meaning of legal issues evolves from case law, these court decisions are the law. Of course, later court review of previous decisions can alter legal precedent.

The U.S. Constitution provides the authority for Congress to pass laws. Likewise, individual state constitutions empower state legislatures to pass laws. Legislative laws permit both the establishment of criminal laws and a justice system to preside over criminal and civil matters. A court may later decide that a legislative law is unconstitutional; this illustrates the system of "checks and balances," which enables one governmental body to check on another.

Criminal Justice Procedure

The criminal justice system operates as a process. Following is a brief and generalized description of the process.

1. The purpose of an arrest is to bring the person into the criminal justice system so that he/she may be held to answer the criminal charges.

2. A citation is frequently used by public police instead of a formal arrest for less serious crimes (e.g., traffic violation). If the conditions set forth in the citation are not followed, a magistrate of the appropriate court will issue a misdemeanor warrant.

3. All arrests must be based on probable cause which is stated in arrest warrants. Probable cause, which is more than mere suspicion, is reasonable grounds to justify legal action. A viewing of an assault would be good probable cause.

4. Booking takes place when an arrestee is taken to a police department or jail so that a record can be made of the arrested person's name, the date, time, location of offense, charge, and the arresting officer's name. Fingerprinting and photographing are part of the booking process.

5. Because our system of justice has a high regard for civil liberties as expressed in the Bill of Rights, the accused is informed, usually right after arrest, of the Miranda rights.

6. After booking, and without unnecessary delay, the accused is taken before a magistrate for the "initial appearance." At this appearance the magistrate has the responsibility of informing the accused of constitutional rights, stating the charge, and fixing bail (if necessary).

7. Also after booking, the arresting officer will meet with the prosecutor or prosecutor's representative to review evidence. A decision is made whether to continue legal action or to drop the case. A case may be dropped by the prosecutor for insufficient evidence or when the case can be better handled by another agency, such as a mental health agency.

8. The prosecutor prepares an "information" when prosecution is initiated. It cites the defendant's name, the charge, and is signed by the complainant (e.g., the person who witnessed the crime). An arrest warrant is prepared by the proper judicial officer. The defendant may already be in custody at this point.

9. At the initial appearance, the magistrate will inform the defendant about the right to have a preliminary hearing. The defendant and the defense attorney make this decision. The hearing is used to determine if probable cause exists for a trial. The courtroom participants in a preliminary hearing are a judge, defendant, defense attorney, and prosecutor. The prosecutor has the "burden of proof." Witnesses may be called by the prosecutor to testify.

10. Federal law and the laws of more than half the states require that probable cause to hold a person for trial must result from grand jury action. The Fifth Amendment of the Bill of Rights states such a requirement. When probable cause is established, the grand jury will return an "indictment" or "true bill" against the accused. A "presentment" results from an investigation initiated by a grand jury establishing probable cause. Based on indictment or presentment, an arrest warrant is issued.

11. At an "arraignment" the accused enters a plea to the charges. Four plea options are: guilty, not guilty, *nolo contendere* (no contest), and not guilty by reason of insanity.

12. Few defendants reach the trial stage. Plea bargaining is an indispensable method to clear crowded court dockets. Essentially, it means that the prosecutor and defense attorney have worked out an agreement whereby the prosecutor reduces the charge in exchange for a guilty plea. Charges may also be dropped if the accused becomes a witness in another case.

13. Pre-trial motions can be entered by the defense attorney prior to entering a plea at arraignment. Examples: A motion to quash an indictment or information because the grand jury was improperly selected. The defense attorney may request a continuance because more time is needed to prepare the case. A change of venue is requested when pre-trial publicity is harmful to the defendant's case. The defense hopes to locate the trial in another jurisdiction so that an impartial jury is more likely to be selected.

14. The accused is tried by the court or a jury. The prosecutor and defense attorney make brief opening statements to the jury. The prosecutor presents evidence. Witnesses are called to the stand to testify; they go through direct examination by the prosecutor, followed by defense cross-examination. The prosecutor attempts to show the defendant's guilt "beyond a reasonable doubt." The defense attorney strives to discredit evidence. Redirect examination rebuilds evidence discredited by cross-examination. Recross-examination may follow. After the prosecutor presents all the evidence, the defense attorney may ask for acquittal. This motion is commonly overruled by the judge. The defense attorney then presents evidence. Defense evidence undergoes direct and redirect examination by the defense, and cross- and recross-examination by the prosecutor.

Next, the judge will "charge the jury," which means that the jury is briefed by the judge on the charge, and how a verdict is to be reached based on the evidence. In certain states, juries have responsibilities for recommending a sentence after a guilty verdict; the judge will brief the jury on this issue. Closing arguments are then presented by opposing attorneys.

The jury retires to the deliberation room, a verdict follows. A not guilty verdict signifies release for the defendant. A guilty verdict leads to sentencing. Motions and appeals may be initiated after the sentence.

Tort Law

Public police officers have greater powers than private sector officers. In conjunction with police powers, public officers are limited in their actions by the Bill of Rights. On the other hand, private officers, who possess lesser powers, are, for the most part, not heavily restricted by constitutional limitations. Authority and limitations on private officers result from tort law.

Tort law is the body of state legislative statutes or court decisions that governs citizen actions toward each other and allows lawsuits to recover damages for injury. Tort law is the foundation for civil actions in which an injured party may litigate to prevent an activity or recover damages from someone who has violated his/her person or property. Most civil actions are not based on a claim of intended harm, but a claim that the defendant was negligent. This is especially so in cases involving private security officers. Tort law requires actions that have regard for the safety and rights of others; otherwise negligence results. The essence of the tort law limitations on private officers is fear of a lawsuit and the payment of damages.

The primary torts relevant to private sector police are as follows:

1. False Imprisonment. The intentional and forceful confinement or restriction of the freedom of movement of another person. Also called "false arrest." The elements necessary to create liability are detention and its unlawfulness.

2. Malicious Prosecution. Groundless initiation of criminal proceedings against another.

3. Battery. Intentionally harmful or offensive touching of another.

4. Assault. Intentional causing of fear of harmful or offensive touching.

5. Trespass to Land. Unauthorized entering upon another person's property.

6. Trespass to Personal Property. Taking or damaging another person's possessions.

7. Infliction of Emotional Distress. Intentionally causing emotional or mental distress in another.

8. Defamation (Libel and Slander). Injury to the reputation of another by publicly making untrue statements. Libel refers to the written word; slander to the spoken word.

9. Invasion of Privacy. Intruding upon another's physical solitude, the disclosure of private information about another, or public misrepresentation of another's actions.

10. Negligence. Causing injury to persons or property by failing to use reasonable care or by taking unreasonable risk.

Civil action is not the only factor that hinders abuses by the private sector. Local and state ordinances, rules, regulations, and laws establish guidelines for the private security industry. This usually pertains to licensing and registration requirements. Improper or illegal action is likely to result in suspension or revocation of a license. Criminal law presents a further deterrent against criminal action by private sector personnel. Examples are laws prohibiting impersonation of a public official, electronic surveillance, breaking and entering, and assault.

Union contracts can also limit private police. These contracts might stipulate, for instance, that employee lockers cannot be searched, and that certain investigative guidelines must be followed.

Contract Law

A contract is basically an agreement between parties to do or to abstain from doing some act. The law may enforce the agreement by requiring that a party perform its obligation or pay money equivalent to the performance. These court requirements are known as remedies for breach of contract. Specific circumstances may create defenses for failure to perform contract stipulations. Contracts may be express or implied. In an express contract -- written or oral -- the terms are stated in words. An implied contract is presumed by law to have been made from the circumstances and relations of the parties involved.

There are several areas in the security/loss prevention field relevant to the law of contracts. The company that provides a service or device to a client company may be liable for breach of contract. Also, a contract usually states liabilities for each party. For instance, if a third party is harmed (e.g., a person illegally arrested on the premises by a private officer from a contract service hired by a client company), the contract will commonly establish who is responsible and who is to have insurance for each risk. However, in third-party suits, courts have held a specific party liable even though the contract stipulated that another party was to be responsible in the matter.

In the common law principle of *respondeat superior* (i.e., let the master respond), an employer (master) is liable for injuries caused by an employee (servant). Typically, the injured party will look beyond the employee -- to the employer -- for compensation for damages. Proper supervision and training of the employee can prevent litigation.

Another form of contract is the union contract. If a proprietary force is employed on the premises, a union contract may be in existence. As stated earlier, union contracts for regular employees may have certain guidelines for locker searches and investigations.

Arrest Law

Because our justice system places a high value on the rights of the individual citizen, private and public officers cannot simply arrest, search, question, and confine a person by whim. A consideration of individual rights is an important factor. The Bill of Rights of the U.S. Constitution affords citizens numerous protections. If we examine the Fourth and Fifth Amendments of the Bill of Rights, we can see how individual rights are safeguarded during criminal investigations.

Amendment IV. "The right of the people to be secure in their persons, houses, papers, and effects, against unreasonable searches and seizures, shall not be violated, and no warrants shall issue, but upon probable cause, supported by oath or affirmation; and particularly describing the place to be searched, and the person or things to be seized."

The Fourth Amendment stipulates guidelines for the issuance of warrants. Public and private police obtain arrest and search warrants from an impartial judicial officer. Sometimes immediate action (e.g., chasing a bank robber) does not permit time to obtain warrants before arrest and search. In such a case, an arrest warrant is obtained as soon as possible. Private police should contact public police for assistance in securing warrants and in apprehending suspects.

Amendment V. ". . . nor shall [any person] be compelled in any criminal case to be a witness against himself, nor be deprived of life, liberty, or property, without due process of law."

The Sixth, Eighth, and Fourteenth Amendments are other important amendments frequently associated with our criminal justice process. Briefly, the Sixth pertains to the right to trial by jury and assistance of counsel. The Eighth states that "excessive bail shall not be required, nor excessive fines imposed, nor cruel and unusual punishments inflicted." The Fourteenth bars states from depriving any person of due process of law or equal protection of the laws.

Probable Cause. A key factor to support a legal arrest and search is "probable cause," which means that there are reasonable grounds to justify legal action. An eyewitness viewing of a crime would support probable cause in an arrest warrant.

A knowledge of arrest powers is essential for those likely to exercise this authority. These powers differ from state to state and depend on the statutory authority of the type of individual involved. Generally, public police officers have the greatest arrest powers. They are also protected from civil liability for false arrest, as long as they had probable cause that the crime was committed. Those in the private sector have arrest powers equal to citizen arrest powers, which means that they are liable for false arrest if a crime was not, in fact, committed -- regardless of the reasonableness of their belief. An exception is apparent if state statutes point out that these personnel have arrest powers equal to public police only on the protected property. If private sector personnel are deputized or given a special constabulary commission, their arrest powers are likely to equal those of public police.

Whoever makes an arrest must have the legal authority to do so. Furthermore, the distinction between felonies and misdemeanors, for those making arrests, is of tremendous importance. Felonies are considered more serious crimes and include burglary, armed robbery, murder, and arson. Misdemeanors are less serious crimes such as trespassing, disorderly conduct, and being drunk in public. Generally, public police can arrest someone for a felony or a misdemeanor committed in view. Arrest for a felony not seen by the public police is lawful with probable cause; arrest for a misdemeanor not seen by the public police is unlawful, and a warrant is needed based upon probable cause. On the other hand, private police have less arrest powers (equal to citizen arrest powers). Basically, citizen arrest powers

permit felony arrests based upon probable cause, but prohibit misdemeanor arrests.

A serious situation evolves when, for example, a private officer mistakenly arrests a person for a misdemeanor thinking that the offense was a felony, or when the jurisdiction in which the arrest occurred does not grant such authority. Many employers in the private sector are so afraid of an illegal arrest, and subsequent legal action, that they prohibit their officers from making arrests without supervisory approval. It is imperative that private sector personnel know state arrest law.

An illegal arrest may lead to civil and/or criminal prosecution of the arrestor. False arrest may be grounds for a civil action for damages. If an illegal arrest has resulted in the death of the arrestee, an arrestor can be prosecuted for homicide.

Force

During the exercise of arrest powers, force may be necessary. The key criterion is "reasonableness." Force should be no more than what is reasonably necessary to carry out legitimate authority. If an arrestee struggles to escape and is subdued to the ground, it would be unreasonable for the arrestor to step on the arrestee's face. Although jurisdictions vary, "deadly force" is usually reserved for life-threatening situations. Unreasonable force can lead to difficulties in prosecuting a case, besides civil and criminal litigation.

Searches

A legal arrest is a prerequisite to a search. Ordinarily, a public police officer conducts a search of an arrestee right after arrest. This has been consistently upheld by courts for the protection of the officer who may be harmed by a concealed weapon. However, evidence obtained through an unreasonable search and seizure is not admissible in court; this is known as the "exclusionary rule." In reference to private sector officers, who generally have citizen arrest powers, the law is not clear and varies widely. Generally, a search is valid when consent is given and where, in a retail environment, a shoplifting statute permits the retrieval of merchandise. A search for weapons may be justified through common law, which states that citizens have the right of self-defense. The recovery of stolen goods as the basis for a search is typically forbidden, except in some state shoplifting statutes.

Though the law of searches by private police is not as well developed as for public police, court cases are evolving that are changing this situation. In the California Supreme Court decision *People v. Zelinsky*, 24 Ca. 3d.357, handed down in 1979, the court ruled, in essence, that the exclusionary rule applies to private security officers.

This decision involved a shoplifting case in which Virginia Zelinsky placed a blouse in her purse without paying for it. She was stopped outside the store and escorted to the security office. When the officers opened her purse and found the blouse, they also discovered a vial of heroin. She went to trial on a charge of possession of narcotics. Zelinsky requested the judge to suppress the heroin because it had been seized illegally. The judge denied her request stating that store detectives are not governed by the prohibition against unreasonable searches. On appeal, the California Supreme Court disagreed. What was also significant about this case was that the court had ruled that when private security officers investigate crimes, their acts are "government actions," so the full force of the Constitution governs those acts.

Questioning

An important clause of the Fifth Amendment states that a person cannot be compelled in any criminal case to be a witness against himself. What constitutional protections does a suspect have upon being approached by an investigator for questioning? Here again, the law differs with respect to public and private sector investigations.

Basic criminal law states that a person about to be questioned about a crime by public police must be advised of:

1. The right to remain silent.
2. The fact that statements can be used against the person in a court of law.
3. The right to have an attorney present, even if the suspect has no money.

4. The right to stop answering questions at any time.

These rights, known as "Miranda rights," evolved out of a 1966 Supreme Court case known as *Miranda v. Arizona*. If these rights are not read to a person (by public police) before questioning, the statements or a confession of the accused will not be admissible as evidence in court.

Are private police required to read a person the Miranda warnings prior to questioning? The courts have not yet required the reading. However, any type of coercion or trick during questioning is prohibited for private as well as public police. A voluntary confession by the suspect is in the best interests of public and private investigators. Many private sector investigators choose to read suspects the Miranda warnings as a protection against legal challenge.

Philip P. Purpura, CPP

Source Purpura, P.P., Security and Loss Prevention, 2nd Edition. (Butterworth-Heinemann, Boston, 1991).

LIABILITY: MEASURES TO PREVENT LITIGATION

Lawsuits are not necessarily inevitable. They can be avoided. When they do occur, however, steps can be taken to reduce the lawsuits' impact on an organization and its employees.

Comprehensive loss prevention programs must include components that address the liability question. For example, the process of risk assessment used by most security professionals includes identifying assets and the risks facing them, developing options that respond to the risks, weighing available solutions in light of their costs and benefits, and considering the operational feasibility of each measure. Although this process is an effective tool, security professionals often do not consider one major risk faced by their organizations: civil liability. This does not suggest that no one in the organization is concerned with the problem. However, it does suggest that security directors should have a role in its management.

The financial integrity and reputation of an organization are two assets that are severely affected by a lawsuit. Even if the suit is ultimately won by the defendant corporation, the defense absorbs considerable resources. Furthermore, irreparable harm may result to the reputation of the company or an individual from a little "bad press" when the lawsuit makes page 1 of the local tabloid. Should the defendant be exonerated by the verdict, the follow-up story will be on the bottom of page 27, if it appears at all. A more subtle asset also affected by the threat of litigation is employee morale. Managers at all levels must be concerned with protecting that particular asset too.

Options

Every business professional must recognize and address the threat of litigation and devise protective measures. That recognition must go beyond the simple response: "That's why we have insurance." Several options can be chosen and steps taken, both before and after incidents that may become the basis for a lawsuit. The best option will depend on the nature of the liability risk, type of defendant, and business structure.

The options discussed below are designed to protect the assets of the business and its owners. Primarily, these measures should be taken before an organization is faced with a lawsuit.

Insurance. Buying insurance is probably the most common response to a liability risk. The financial benefits to insurance are twofold: the policy will pay for any jury award or settlement up to its limit and, although this is not widely known, will also cover the cost of legal defense. When purchasing a policy, buyers should make sure the insurance will cover the specific risks to be avoided and should inquire whether the limits of the policy include attorney's fees generated in defending the action. The principal drawbacks to insurance as a solution are availability and cost. If the business has a history of high losses, it may not be able to purchase insurance from any carrier. If it is available, the premium cost may be so high that a business may be forced to operate without insurance, to operate with less than full coverage, or to shut down. With less than adequate coverage, the principals of a business may find themselves paying a judgment out of their own assets.

Managers should also be aware that during the discovery stage of litigation, the plaintiff will be able to find out how much coverage the defendant has. If it seems too low for an anticipated judgment, the plaintiff may seek to attach other assets. Some of the assets subject to attachment in such a case would include cash, accounts receivable, real estate, and any other tangible property. If a defendant attempts to hide or transfer such assets after a lawsuit has commenced, a court can order them returned and held so they can be liquidated later to satisfy any award.

Corporations. Security contract agencies, private investigation firms, consultants, and most any other business should consider the benefits of incorporation. The major advantage to the corporate form of ownership is that corporate assets are legally separate from those assets held individually. As a result, if the corporation is sued, the owners are usually limited in their personal liability to the extent of their actual ownership in the business. Personal assets such as the family home would not normally be exposed to seizure in a lawsuit against the company. The negative aspects of the corporate form of ownership are the extensive paperwork required to maintain the legal status of the corporation and the potential for double-taxing -- taxing of both corporate and individual income.

Those who choose to establish a corporation as a way of organizing a business must adhere to each state's requirements for the maintenance of corporate status. If the formalities are ignored, a successful plaintiff may be able to seize the personal assets of each shareholder through a process known as "piercing the corporate veil." If a court can be convinced that the corporation was established solely to isolate personal assets and that the business was not conducted in accordance with state law requirements, it will allow such assets to be seized to satisfy a judgment.

Acceptance of Risk. If insurance is too expensive or unavailable and incorporation is not appealing, a business manager may decide to accept the risk as a part of doing business. Accepting the risk of a lawsuit without doing anything to protect oneself is not generally recommended. However, if the business does not have a strong history of being sued and there are minimal assets to be seized, the manager may consider this option. A similar decision is made when security managers accept the risk of loss to certain property when the cost or feasibility of protecting it is not realistic.

An interesting turn of events occurs in some lawsuits when the plaintiff discovers there are no assets or insurance to cover the claim for damages. What can happen is that the suit is not pursued. The reason is simple economics. It does not serve anyone well for a plaintiff to win a judgment that cannot be paid. Also, since many plaintiff attorneys are hired on a contingency basis, few are willing to expend the hundreds of hours it takes to litigate a matter for which compensation is unlikely.

Preventive Measures

Preventive measures include a number of steps to reduce the risk that a harmful activity will result. These measures represent management practices that should be followed but rarely are unless the organization is threatened with legal action.

Training. In cases involving claims of police misconduct, the failure to train or the inadequacy of a training program is commonly cited as an underlying cause of the misconduct leading to a civil rights violation. Such allegations must be proven to satisfy the legal requirements of a municipality liability case.

By contrast, in cases involving private security officers, plaintiffs need not prove that the employer was at fault due to poor or no training. Employer liability is usually established by showing that the security employee was working on behalf of the employer at the time of the incident. As a result, security-related cases do not generally cite the failure to train as a cause of the wrongful acts. However, the lack of training can frequently be found to have contributed to the wrongful behavior.

Would proper training prevent or reduce the likelihood of an incident like this? From a loss prevention point of view, security managers should be asking themselves this question. A problem facing security managers is that many organizations do not appreciate the value of training programs.

Business managers frequently regard training as a budget item ripe for cutting when cash flow is poor. Reducing or eliminating training for this reason is likely to cost a company more in the end.

Business managers and owners must consider both the quality and the quantity of training programs. The quality considerations of a program should include the qualifications of the trainers, timeliness and relevance of the subject matter, and methods of instruction. Testing employees should be a way of demonstrating minimum competency. What does an organization do with an employee who is unable to pass the test? If this employee is kept on the job, the failure may become the target of a plaintiff's lawyer. He or she will argue that the security officer's inability to pass such a test is evidence of inadequacy. Also, management should know if employees are gaining any knowledge from the training sessions.

Quantity includes the number of hours allocated to training overall and to particular topics. The proportion of time should be consistent with the actual job function. Consider a retail employer who encourages his or her employees to make arrests but spends only 1 hour on the laws of arrest and court procedures in a training program for new officers. Would a jury be able to find the quantity of training adequate in view of the risk?

This discussion assumes that the organization has already developed detailed job descriptions that outline the activities which security officers are expected to perform. If job descriptions do not exist, writing them must be the first step. No training program can develop the needed skills accurately until this process is completed.

Supervision. The concept of supervision is not limited merely to the presence of a supervisor, but also includes any system, mechanism, or device that enhances control over employees and enhances the accountability of employees. The use of watch clocks, daily logs, activity reports, and spot checks by supervisors are all legitimate ways to supervise. Organizations that have security personnel or other staff performing security-related tasks must have some means of ensuring that the tasks are carried out and that they have been conducted in the manner prescribed by company policies.

Is management sure that security officers are making their rounds when no one is around to watch them? Can a jury be convinced that the security reports are accurate? These basic questions must be answerable with a degree of assurance. Management should take an objective look at the organization to see if it measures up to the adequacy test that may be applied in a future lawsuit.

Policies. The need for clear policies cannot be overemphasized. Policies are meant to provide guidelines on the proper response in a given situation. The lack of well-written and properly communicated policies will lead to excessive discretionary decision making and ultimately errors.

Policies are "two-edged swords." On one edge, if an organization does not have a policy directing employee response or if the policy is too vague, too complex, or not communicated, then inappropriate decisions are likely. Without a policy, employees will respond to situations based on their understanding of past practices or their own biases. Vague or technically difficult policies are subject to a myriad of interpretations, again increasing the chances of a wrong decision. Plain language, concise statements, and examples, where appropriate, will help employees understand the organization's position on the matter.

On the other edge of the sword is the effect of the self-imposed standard that adopted policies represent. Once the need for a policy has been recognized, the organization is expected to adhere to its parameters.

Having the properly prepared policies is never enough. They must be received and understood by each employee. Little is accomplished by having a well-written set of policies that are kept in the boss's office.

Surveys. A security survey is a valuable tool when used to prevent crime. Most surveys, however, are undertaken to locate weaknesses in a security program. They should be expanded to locate the program's weaknesses from a liability standpoint. When they are conducted, security and business managers should take into account factors establishing foreseeability of crime that have been found in earlier court decisions and have led to a finding of inadequacy.

These factors should be incorporated into the survey. For example, many cases have cited the presence of overgrown shrubbery as a contributing cause of an assault. A survey could include examination of the facility for similar hiding places and note the corrective action to be taken.

Post-Incident Measures

The Disney organization has been credited with a high rate of success in avoiding lawsuits and in winning those tried in court. Whenever a guest at its parks is injured, Disney personnel respond immediately and sincerely. Consequently, the "I'm going to get even" motive is diluted.

Although there are no published statistics this author is aware of, it is not uncommon for a plaintiff to complain about the treatment received after the incident occurred. Often this treatment comes in the form of being ignored by the defendant. Perhaps it is the fear of saying the wrong thing and having it used against the company in court that deters employers from dealing properly with a victim. Although much can safely be said to and done for a victim after an incident, certain statements can be used against a defendant in a subsequent trial. Each state varies as to what out-of-court statements are incriminating so businesses should consult with their legal counsel.

Aside from the evidentiary issues, some help should always be given after a loss has occurred. Whether the victim has been raped, fallen down in a puddle of water, or lost personal property, action should be taken to show that the organization cares. Most victims know their losses will not be fully recoverable. At the time of the loss, they do expect someone from the organization to show concern. The failure to respond serves to aggravate the person further, perhaps enough to send him or her running to a lawyer.

The last but not least step in a litigation loss reduction program is proper preparation for litigation. It is the job of the attorney to decide which legal defenses will be used, but it is the task of management to prepare the materials needed for trial. Almost every document imaginable, such as policies, training materials, memos, letters, post orders, security reports, photographs, and receipts will be demanded during the discovery stage of the suit. The better these materials are prepared, the better counsel can decide on the quality of the defense and whether to settle the matter rather than risk trial.

If a serious incident has occurred or it is apparent that a lawsuit is inevitable, the company should notify its insurance carrier to comply with policy requirements and to aid the carrier in developing a defense.

Overall, the key to a successful defense is documentation. After an incident has occurred, security reports should be written, witness statements recorded, photographs taken or sketches made, and all relevant documents put in a folder.

Lawsuits are not inevitable, but they do occur. Security-related suits will continue to rise as more victims learn of their rights. The size of awards and the cost of defense will continue to rise as well until organizations begin to develop a no-nonsense attitude about liability.

Norman D. Bates

LIGHTING: LAMP TYPES

A variety of choices is offered to a security manager when the need arises to select lamps for particular security purposes.

Incandescent

Although the incandescent lamp has a rather limited watt output and service life, it has an instant restrike/restart capability that makes it the lamp of choice for use as emergency lights for backup situations and as spotlights for augmentation lighting.

Fluorescent

Because the fluorescent lamp is sensitive to ambient air temperature, it is used primarily as an indoor lighting source in many climates. A thin coating of phosphor on the inside of the tube fluoresces and gives off visible light at an efficiency of approximately 62 lumens per watt. The fluorescent lamp offers higher wattage output and a longer life than the incandescent lamp, but produces an unwanted flickering effect that can cause disorientation among some individuals.

Also, the electromagnetic radiation given off by a fluorescent fixture can cause interference with some electronic equipment.

Metal Halide

Metal halide lamps can be very tolerant of power dips or brown-outs. They are an excellent source of light with a service life almost 20 times greater than that of incandescent lamps. Their chief disadvantage is the amount of time required to restrike/restart them after a loss of power. A loss of power of only 1/20th of a second is enough to throw a metal halide lamp off line.

Mercury Vapor

Mercury vapor lamps give good light and long service. In combination with the proper ballast, they are capable of continued operation even with significant power dips. As with metal halide lamps, a power loss of only 1/20th of a second could be enough to cause the lamp to extinguish, and restrike time can be excessive.

High-Pressure and Low-Pressure Sodium

High-pressure sodium lamps have an excellent service life, and like the metal halide and mercury vapor lamps, when combined with the proper ballast, can tolerate 40-50 % dips in power. A power interruption of only 1/20th of a second may be enough to cause this lamp type to extinguish and begin its restrike sequence. Restrike is rated as instant hot, meaning that the lamp will not be at its fully rated output until it has returned to its normal operating temperature.

High-pressure sodium luminaires are an excellent choice for lighting systems to be used in conjunction with television surveillance systems, both indoors and outdoors. A possible disadvantage of high-pressure sodium is electromagnetic radiation, which could cause interference with electronic equipment or systems, including alarms.

Low-pressure sodium lamps also have excellent service life and are considered very reliable starters, although they require approximately 8 to 10 minutes to reach full lumen output. This long initial warm-up poses no special problem, however, if the lamps are controlled by a photoelectric switch. If the proper type of switch is used, this lamp will have reached its full rated output prior to a point at which an observer's view would be seriously hampered by diminished natural light. Manufacturers say that 90% of these lamps will reliably restrike after power interruptions of up to 5 minutes, while the remaining 10% will restrike in less than 1 minute.

The only disadvantage of low-pressure sodium lamps appears to be their highly monochromatic yellow light, which offers poor color discrimination. This yellow light, however, has advantages in that it provides better contrast on uneven surfaces than a white light. This contrast and perceived image enhancement works extremely well with a black-and-white closed-circuit television (CCTV) system and records well on film.

Richard J. Gigliotti
and Ronald C. Jason

Source Gigliotti, R., and R. Jason, Security Design for Maximum Protection. (Butterworth-Heinemann, Boston, 1984).

LINE SECURITY

An exterior lines approach to line security can consist of starting from the telephone company cable and working inward to the computer itself. Wherever possible, a communications line serving an electronic data processing (EDP) center should run directly between it and the closest telephone company central office (exchange) or other switching facility providing service to the EDP center. Such a direct route would reduce the number of access locations available to potential wiretappers.

Protective Steps

Multiple Drops. No multiple drops should be permitted on the local communications lines carrying data communications or otherwise serving EDP centers.

Some telephone companies terminate cables at several parallel junction boxes (located usually in basements of office buildings, or in back alleys or garages). Such terminations are left available so the telephone companies can accommodate varying demands for telephone service within adjacent buildings without having to dig up streets.

Multiple drops create a security problem because the terminals of a targeted line can exist in exposed conditions in several junction boxes in the vicinity of the actual target. If the wiretapper has legitimate access to a phone in any of the buildings containing the desired terminals, he or she need only find a junction box and make unobtrusive wired connections bridging terminals to the targeted ones to be in a position to intercept the desired signals.

Multiple-Conductor Cables. Whenever multiple conductors are required to satisfy the operational needs of an EDP center, they should be aggregated insofar as possible into cables having the largest number of conductors. Obviously it is more difficult to select the targeted line if the wiretapper has to sort it out from a large bundle of similarly appearing lines.

Phantom Circuits. Lines within cables should be paired. Phantom circuits should not be permitted. This statement refers to the practice of using a common tip (ground) wire for two or more ring (signal) lines. For example, two pairs can each terminate in separate primary windings of a hybrid transformer, the secondary of which has two ring lines and is centertapped with a common tip wire; or, three telephone circuits could share a common ground that terminates at a star transformer primary, the secondary of which is a delta winding. In this case, the three circuits would be carried by three wires instead of four (a common tip wire) or, in conventional practice, six pairs of wires.

The disadvantage of phantom circuits, from a security point of view, is that unless a precise electrical balance is achieved in the transformers, there will be a certain amount of mutual interference between circuits, which is known as cross-talk. When cross-talk exists, an intruder able to gain authorized access to one of the lines involved could obtain unauthorized information being transmitted over one of the other lines.

Interlocked Alarm Lines. Phantom circuits have one favorable aspect from the standpoint of security. Circuits of this kind are used in alarm circuits that are supervised against unauthorized tampering by interlocking two or more circuits. In such an arrangement, it is impossible to defeat one alarm without simultaneously defeating all other alarms whose communications circuits are interlocked with it.

Cross-Talk. Cross-talk can occur even where there are no phantom circuits because of unfortunate juxtapositions of wires, transformers, or other circuit elements. Its existence or non-existence can be established only by actually monitoring one circuit while all possible combinations of interfering circuits are activated with a known signal. Even this procedure is not foolproof because cross-talk can be weather dependent, arising from the effects of temperature and humidity on the electrical properties of shielding and insulating materials.

Shielding. Communications cables should be shielded to protect them from environmental hazards and from compromising radiation. Shielded, twisted pair wire (twisted to provide additional defense against cross-talk) is in common use for communications lines. However, installation malpractice on the part of technicians and wirepersons can undo many of the advantages.

The fact that an ohmmeter indicates zero resistance between the shield and the ground lug of a coupling means nothing in terms of the effectiveness of the shielding. For shielding to be effective, there must exist contact all around the circumference of the receptacle in such a way that every one of the wires making up the shield is involved in the contact. The ground conductor, usually a ferrule (sleeve) that is part of the coupler, and the shield wires must be in intimate and permanent electrical contact, with no intervening layers of oil, dirt, or metal oxide. This can be achieved by conventional soldering practices if properly executed, by use of a modern mechanical joining process such as wire wrapping, or by use of patented connectors.

Floating Grounds. The ground electrode of the receptacle (jack, plug, or connector) must be connected to some source of zero potential like a ground plane or cold-water pipe; otherwise it will become a floating ground, which can be a very efficient, albeit undesirable, radiator. All comments regarding the grounding of power cables and components apply equally well to the procedures used to connect communications cables and components to ground, including the rules about using a large cross-section conductor

and keeping it as short and as straight as possible.

Ground Loops. Sometimes cable shields have to be grounded at various points along their length to prevent undesirable radiation or the formation of what are called ground loops. A cable connecting two computers (central processing units) might have to be grounded every 25 feet.

Cable Protection. There are various defenses that might inhibit a wiretapper from attacking a telephone pair (also called a loop) somewhere along its length or at least warn of intrusion. The simplest protective measure is to use a trap wire. This is a bare, stranded conductor placed in contact with the shield so that when contact is broken, an alarm is sounded. The trap wire can take the form of a second concentric shield electrically insulated from the first, in which case an alarm could be sounded should any part of the two shields come into contact.

The shield can be energized by a tone or other signal monitored in such a way that any tampering with the shield that diminishes or interrupts the tone will indicate an alarm condition. The line can be encased in a leakproof sheath filled with dry nitrogen and alarmed in such a way that an abrupt decrease in gas pressure causes a warning to be sounded.

White noise can be used to trap a line and to defeat induction taps, but if undesirable results are to be avoided, the noise would have to be isolated from both the line and the environment. This could imply use of triple shielding.

Protection of Line Drops. Places where telephone cable serving an EDP center is dropped from utility pole lines should be within clear view of a fixed guard post capable of providing 24-hour surveillance. Where 24-hour surveillance is not possible, daily physical inspection of line drops should be performed. Surveillance or inspection of line drops may uncover not only wiretap attempts, but also the efforts of persons attempting to compromise alarm lines to police or central stations.

Underground Cables. Wherever possible, communications cables serving an EDP center should enter the building perimeter underground. Of course, manhole-size cable tunnels have to be secured against unauthorized entry, as well as any manholes that are within the ambit of responsibility of the company. Cables are sometimes laid in a trench that is later filled with concrete.

The security coordinator should maintain an up-to-date map of all communications cables within the controlled perimeter. He or she should also keep cable record cards telling the use and destination of each pair of every cable. These documents should be given as high a degree of protection as is the information communicated.

No signs should be posted giving information as to the location of communications cables, especially buried ones. Instead, all maintenance personnel should rely on cable maps and records.

Underground cables within the controlled perimeter should be buried to a depth sufficient to protect them from normal grounds maintenance and in no case less than 18 inches. No excavation or other work likely to disturb communications cables should ever be undertaken without the knowledge and consent of the security coordinator.

Protective Blocks. A protective block appropriately tied to safety ground should be installed on the building side of a communications line at the point where it enters the building to protect against lightning arriving over the line.

Interior Lines

Interior communications lines should consist of shielded, twisted pairs with an additional neutral conductor. The neutral conductor would ordinarily be connected to safety ground and the shield to logical ground.

Junction Boxes. All junction boxes should be contained within locked and guarded telephone closets. These should be kept locked except when opened to authorized maintenance.

Personnel should be instructed to be suspicious of telephone repair persons. They should be told to request the person's identification card, then call the telephone company at its officially listed number and personally check the repair person's identity and the fact that he or she is calling on company business.

Disconnect Switches. Positively acting physical disconnect switches should be provided in data communications lines between the computer and remote (or local) EDP devices, including terminals, printers, data storage devices, and processors.

The key ingredient in a disconnect switch is that no means should exist whereby it can be surreptitiously bypassed.

In highly classified government installations, connections are made by shielded multiconductor jumper cable, which is cut to exact size and not only removed but locked away when a connection is supposed to be broken.

Identification of Pairs. There should be no visible designation of the purpose of or destination of any communications line or terminal pair. It is sufficient to number all junction boxes and all pairs of contacts within these boxes sequentially, relying on cable record cards to identify particular lines.

The practice of tagging direct lines or alarm circuits in red is a common breach of security. They are tagged in the first instance to avoid inadvertent open-circuiting, but the tags also tell the wiretapper which wires to tap.

Use of buzzers attached intermittently to extensions and linemen's headphones in order to identify lines for maintenance is another breach of security. The proper procedure would be to get the security coordinator to identify the lines desired in any authorized maintenance situation by reference to the cable record card.

Telephone Extensions. There should be no communications service extensions or interior drops on data communications lines; these lines should run directly from the building junction box to terminal blocks within the computer room. Telephone extensions in an EDP center should be capable of being supervised by reliable management personnel.

Terminal Blocks. Terminal blocks and disconnect devices within the computer room should be aggregated and enclosed within locked telephone closets. It should be possible to unplug in a positive manner any telephone installed within any sensitive area.

Telephone Instrument Security

Only such telephone instruments and apparatus as have been approved for resistance to compromise should be permitted in a sensitive area.

Three principal points apply:

Ringers. The ringing coil of the common telephone instrument can act as an inductive pickup and transmit intelligence to the line even when the handset is in the on-hook position (hung up). To be safe from this source of compromise, disconnect the ringing coil entirely and replace it by a lamp that will come on when an 85-volt (ringing) signal is received. If an audible signal is desired, an electronic buzzer can be used. It can be actuated by a photocell optically coupled to the lamp.

Compromise Devices. Make sure someone has not bypassed the switch hook of the telephone. This technical intrusion technique is known as telephone compromise. Compromise techniques are extremely subtle. They rely on tiny but sophisticated semiconductor switches, among which are zener diodes, four-layer diodes, and semiconductor controlled rectifiers (SCR). They can easily be concealed within the telephone instrument. Indeed, the plastic encapsulated network within the instrument can be replaced with a fraudulent one containing a compromise device. Some handsets have built-in compromise devices.

Theoretically, it is possible to bug a private automatic branch (telephone) exchange with zener diodes so connected and so biased that an external wiretapper can selectively tap internal phone lines. Compromise devices can be detected in most cases by a slight current drain reflected in a drop in the 48-volt potential normally observed on a telephone line when the handset is on the hook. Compromise devices, except for some SCRs, can usually be destroyed by imposing a 900-volt DC pulse on the line (or better, a positive-going pulse of 900 volts followed by a negative-going one).

It may be inconvenient to check every line To this end, telephone line analyzers may be installed that automatically check all lines and all possible combinations of lines (sneak circuits) for compromise, and transmit a device-destroying pulse when one is encountered.

Intrusion Devices. Finally, make sure someone has not installed an intrusion device within the telephone instrument. These usually take the form of an FM transmitter designed to resemble the carbon microphone of a telephone handset. One defense is to mark telephone microphones (called "transmitters," confusingly enough, by the phone company) in some unique and unobtrusive way and check periodically to see that no one has put in another item.

Infinity Transmitters

Other telephone compromise devices include so-called infinities ("harmonica" bugs). These devices can assume many forms. Their function is to turn the telephone instrument into a clandestine listening device when in the on-hook position but to do so only at such times as the wiretapper signals his or her intent, in this way avoiding defeat of the intrusion device by periodic line analysis.

An infinity usually responds to a tone transmitted down the line by the wiretapper after line selection has been accomplished, but prior to transmission of the ringing signal. The tone activates a foreign microphone and amplifier hidden within the target telephone, and bypasses the ringing mechanism so that no ringing signal is heard by the authorized user of the instrument. Infinities may also incorporate noise-activated switches that interrupt the wiretapping process if the handset is lifted from its cradle, so that the user is not alerted to the possibility of compromise by failure to obtain a dial tone.

Since an infinity may be made up of several electrical components, some of which may be hard to camouflage as normal electrical components of a telephone instrument, they can frequently be identified on sight after disassembling the instrument. However, because electronic components are being made smaller and appearing in a greater variety of shapes all the time, it would not be wise to rely too confidently on visual inspection.

Telephone line analyzers often incorporate a feature that attempts to activate infinities by a monotonically rising audio tone prior to making voltage and conductivity tests on the line. However, line analysis techniques can be defeated by using a coded sequence of tones.

Limiting Telephone Access

A cardinal principle of line security is to not allow telephones into sensitive areas. If their introduction cannot be avoided, they should be physically and completely disconnected any time something is going on in the area around them that you would prefer hostile interests know nothing about.

All telephone bugging (installation of R-F intrusion devices) and compromise require an initial physical access to the target instrument. Such physical access must be accomplished in any secure area by intrusion, subversion, or defection.

Ultimately, a highly technical security problem can be recast in familiar form as one relating to installation of physical barriers and ensuring the integrity of key personnel.

Symptoms of Wiretapping

When there is a suspicion of wiretapping, the corporate security officer should be alerted immediately. The big question is: How do you know when you are being wiretapped? A good wiretap makes no noise and draws little or no power from the line, so weird noises are usually meaningless, and a voltmeter, however sensitive, is of little value as a detection device.

Although wiretapping is a silent process, tapping noises on the line may mean someone is installing a tap; such noises arise from the wires being momentarily shorted, partially shorted, or open-circuited by tools. Advantage can be taken of this state of affairs by installing a tape recorder actuated by a noise-activated switch and notch filter to remove the omnipresent dial tone.

These items should be permanently connected across the line to be protected. Not only do you thereby record all telephone calls, dialing impulses, and ringing signals, but you may also detect the fact that someone has tapped the line.

Absence of the dial tone can signify compromise, although a professional compromise attack will probably not cause you to lose the dial tone. On the other hand, you might be justified in becoming suspicious if a friend tells you "your phone is always busy" and you know for a fact it is not.

Defense against Wiretapping

Balanced capacitance bridges, if installed on a clean line, will register a deflection if any wiretap device is installed, save for one using a non-contacting inductive pickup. The only defense against the latter is to create a high-electrical-noise environment in any location a wiretapper might use as a listening post.

The time-domain reflectometer, an instrument designed to locate faults in electric power distribution lines, has been used to detect telephone wiretaps. The main problem is that the device picks up line discontinuities that are usually not wiretaps at all.

Most telephone companies will check out your line if you complain about wiretapping. Their help will be given subject to three provisions: (1) if they have time, (2) if their records are up to date as to where junctions occur, and (3) if some law enforcement agency does not have a legally authorized tap on your line.

If the telephone company finds an illegal tap, they will remove it and in all probability never tell you, just reporting, "We checked and your line is clear." Which, of course, it will be -- then. The phone company may or may not notify the police. Behavior in this regard tends to be highly variable from place to place.

Quite probably, in most private companies it will be left to the corporate security officer to direct the application, to communications lines, terminals, and equipment, of any physical or electrical defensive measures that may seem appropriate. The only sure defense against wiretapping is encryption. Voice traffic can be digitized and encrypted.

John M. Carroll

Source Carroll, J.M., Computer Security, 2nd Edition. (Butterworth-Heinemann, Boston, 1987).

LITIGATION: A LOSS TO PREVENT

Most security practitioners are well versed in the basic concepts of an effective loss prevention program: preventive measures employed before a loss occurs and reactive evaluations assessing the program after a loss. Unfortunately, most security professionals apply these measures only to the prevention of short-term losses due to theft, embezzlement, destruction, and such violent crimes as rape, assault, and robbery. An inadequate amount of attention is given to the long-range risks of these crimes. One of those risks is a lawsuit.

Knowing Current Trends

Security managers need to take a progressive approach to warding off risks. Such an approach should include regular analysis of case law affecting the security industry. In the past, loss prevention programs may have been limited to traditional approaches because of insurance companies' reluctance to define the reasons a particular case is difficult to defend, the long period of time between incident occurrence and final resolution, and the general lack of understanding among security practitioners of case law. Now security professionals must study developments in security law, the trends in inadequate-security litigation, and the common factors that have led juries to conclude the defendant's level and quality of security was inadequate.

No industry standards currently exist that define the legal acceptability of adequacy of a security program.

In some limited circumstances, however, standards have been imposed by statute, regulation, or contract. For example, certain contractors for the Department of Defense must meet the regulations of a proprietary security department for a contractor with a secret clearance. Many states have imposed statutory obligations on business owners, such as holding landlords responsible for entranceway door locks.

Aside from these limited circumstances, owners of hotels, colleges, apartment complexes, and retail stores may have little idea what is expected of them regarding their security programs. Many property owners are not even aware they have an obligation to provide an environment relatively safe from crime.

Ignorance of these statutes, however, will not hold up in court. Likewise, formulating a security plan after a lawsuit has been filed will not lessen liability. One approach to evaluating the quality of security services or systems is to review existing legal opinions in security cases and apply the various criteria used by the courts.

However, there are rarely enough cases in any one jurisdiction to establish a clear definition of adequate security. The national trend should be evaluated to identify the emerging standards. The law is still new in this arena and as a result is subject to change.

California and Massachusetts, like many other states, used to apply the "prior similar acts" rule, which required the plaintiff to show that a similar crime had occurred previously on the defendant's property. The prior crime was supposed to have put the defendant on notice that an act of this type was foreseeable and therefore avoidable. Plaintiffs who failed to prove prior acts were precluded from recovering any damages from the defendant.

Now courts will consider factors other than prior similar crime to establish liability. Security practitioners must know what these factors are in order to assess the quality of their security programs. Security experts and consultants hired by either plaintiff or defense lawyers will apply these factors to evaluate a case before it goes to trial.

The factors presented most often in court fall into six general categories: prior crime activity, security operations, employment practices, physical security measures, environmental conditions, and management-related issues. This list is not comprehensive, but it gives an overview of the issues considered relevant in assessing security programs.

Prior Crime Activity. Although some states have done away with the requirement that prior crime be shown, it is still strongly persuasive to show an unsafe environment. Prior similar crime, if close in time and type, may have a devastating effect on the defense of a case. Prior dissimilar crime is also effective to show generally unsafe conditions.

One type of crime often leads to another. For example, conditions that allow for property crime may also allow for violent crime. A landowner's knowledge of prior similar crime and subsequent failure to warn of the risk is frequently cited in inadequate-security cases. Complaints about problematic tenants, guests, customers, or visitors have been used as evidence of notice to the landlord of unsafe conditions. Similarly, the failure to evict or otherwise remove such undesirable people can lead to liability.

Security Operations. Staff size is a relative issue because there are no industry standards for what would be the appropriate number of security personnel to employ in a given location or business. The security practitioner must do what the expert or consultant would do -- compare the immediate property with other similar properties, allowing for differences in size, crime rate, location, and demographics. This approach is referred to as the "community standard," a standard that the courts will usually accept as representative of the practices of a particular industry.

Employment Practices. Hiring practices, training, and supervision fall under this category. Hiring or screening problems become evident when a security officer or other employee is hired without adequate screening and commits a crime or tort. In states where it is expressly forbidden for a security contract agency to hire convicted felons, a record check is essential. The level of background check required will vary depending on the potential risk posed by the employee. For example, employees given master keys or access to vulnerable members of the population (such as children or the elderly) should be investigated more extensively.

Training issues are raised when the employee is unable to perform the function of the job because of inadequate or irrelevant training. Supervision problems include the failure to discipline and the retention of personnel who show a tendency toward violence.

Physical Security Measures. Quality and quantity of hardware are both factors in many inadequate-security cases. Questions are raised not only about the sufficiency of certain hardware such as locks, closed-circuit television (CCTV) cameras, keys, lighting, and barriers, but also about whether the equipment was properly maintained and was in working order when the crime occurred.

Environmental Conditions. An external or outdoor factor can be shown to have contributed to the crime if it created an environment conducive to the activity. The nature of the facility (such as an all-women's college), overgrown shrubbery or foliage that gives an assailant a place to hide, and the accessibility of the facility (in an urban setting or next to a wooded area) have all been cited as relevant factors leading to liability in security cases.

Management-Related Issues. Such factors as falsely advertising that an apartment building has 24-hour security or promoting a facility as a family motel have been successfully argued as directly relating to harm suffered by a plaintiff. Additionally, oral statements by the sales staff, information contained in brochures, or the misleading appearance of security (an alarm panel disconnected but not removed) have led to so-called reliance theories of liability that numerous plaintiffs have succeeded in proving.

Liability for inadequate security seems limited only by the creative skills of the plaintiff's counsel and the willingness of juries to accept the factors outlined previously by granting large awards. Security professionals must keep abreast of recent case law and its effect on their particular businesses, voluntarily incorporating these underlying factors into their loss prevention and security programs before a lawsuit forces them to.

Norman D. Bates

LODGING SECURITY: SECURING A BUDGET MOTEL

Most hotels and motels are concerned with security and have measures in place to prevent crimes against patrons. At the same time, however, hotels and motels continue to be targeted by criminal elements.

The Budget Motel

According to the American Hotel & Motel Association, the budget motel typically provides no frills, has one to three stories with 20 to 125 rooms, and makes up 80% of the total domestic lodging community. Security in the lodging environment presents a wide range of challenges if only because the lodging business is in operation every hour of the day, every day of the year. At a budget motel the challenges are especially difficult. Why is this the case? Part of the answer lies in the observation that a budget motel usually has:

•Exterior entries to rooms, some with sliding doors.

- Numerous remote entries and exits.
- Parking right outside each room's door.
- Limited staff with few or no security personnel.
- Little or no physical security.
- Limited capital resources.

Inexpensive safeguards can usually be implemented at a budget motel, but the more significant and costly safeguards tend to be put on the back burner. Unfortunately, it is the absence of the significant safeguards that leads to litigation. ·On the one hand, budget motel management may recognize the need to upgrade security and appreciate the attendant liability risk, but on the other hand, may lack the financial resources to do anything about it. Even with new construction or retrofitting for expansion or other non-security purposes, management may be unable to find enough capital to fund needed security improvements.

With the exception of safe deposit boxes at the front desk, which limit a motel's exposure to property loss, no codes or laws require a motel to provide physical security. Courts across the nation have mandated that motels must merely take "reasonable" precautions to protect their guests from physical harm.

The public has become more educated concerning personal safety. In the last few years, for example, guests have insisted on sprinkler systems and 24-hour security. In an over-built lodging market with heavy competition and fewer people traveling, hotel and motel owners are responding to their customers' concerns about personal safety.

Six Basic Steps

Six very fundamental security steps that involve time but little cost can be implemented at the budget motel. These include:

Step 1. Managing by walking around (MBWA) involves getting into the trenches and seeing what's going on in the business, and getting close to customers and employees. The really small "Mom and Pop" motels practiced MBWA before Tom Peters put a label on the concept. The larger, multi-unit motel chains are often lacking in this valuable practice.

MBWA is a caring attitude that is imparted to employees and guests alike. Many security professionals emphasize having a written policy and program, and although written materials can be helpful, they cannot engender the caring attitude and genuine concern that must be projected for security to succeed.

Step 2. A background investigation that includes contacting prior employers and making criminal records checks should be conducted before employees are hired. This is important because applicants may falsify prior employment information in order to conceal personal defects that make them unsuitable for assignment to high-trust jobs.

The value of background checking is apparent at the budget motel where only one or two employees are present in the evening hours. At stake are the care and custody of the motel and its assets, and the protection of the patrons and their valuables. These are awesome responsibilities that cannot be placed into the hands of people about whom little is known.

Step 3. Employees need to be involved in security. One way to promote involvement is to make employees aware of security risks, how the risks affect the motel, the staff and the patrons, and what the staff can do to offset risks. The American Hotel & Motel Association offers a series of training video workshops on the basics of lodging security. Workshops cover everything from awareness to handling disturbances.

Another consideration is to motivate employees to carry out their security responsibilities, especially with respect to emergency response procedures. Programs that provide rewards, such as a deserved thank you from a supervisor, a certificate of appreciation, recognition by co-workers, a day off or a merit bonus, can go a long way to building a security program.

It is not unusual in the lodging industry for an employer to pay for performance as opposed to paying for time spent on the job. Quality and quantity of work, especially work that is central and essential to the business, is recognized as having a higher value than hours spent at the workplace. Incentive programs can include financial rewards for excellence in security.

Step 4. Having a liaison with local law enforcement is crucial to the small property operator. Without adequate police protection, the budget motel is at extreme risk. The property management can contact the local crime prevention unit to identify the criminal threats confronting the motel and to learn what the police and the management can do to improve security at the property. At a minimum, the local management needs to know the nature of the police services that are available, the manner in which those services are performed, and the officers who deliver the services.

Step 5. The motel manager needs to communicate with neighbors. The idea is to share information about crime in the neighborhood and to look out for each other's interests with respect to spotting and reporting suspicious activity. Neighbors can also share details of their successes and failures in setting up countermeasures to local crime. These are the kinds of activities that defend against allegations that the motel management was negligent by not recognizing crime risks that can impact its patrons and by not having a security program at least equal to that of nearby competitors.

The motel manager should be active in the local business organizations, especially with organizations that serve the lodging industry, such as the local chapter of the American Hotel & Motel Association. The contacts and information obtained through networking can be invaluable.

Step 6. Patrolling of the premises should be done during the hours of darkness and whenever crime presents a threat to property or people. Patrolling can be handled on a proprietary basis by designating in-house employees to perform the patrol (as full-time or add-on duties) or patrolling services can be handled on a contract basis with a security guard company.

Whatever the approach, four considerations are important. First, screen the persons to be selected for patrolling. Ensure they are drug-free, psychologically stable, trustworthy, and possess the physical ability to meet the rigors of constant movement in an outdoor environment. Second, provide the selected persons with the knowledge and skill to do their jobs effectively. Teach them how to look for the indicators of crime and hazardous conditions, and how to respond when the indicators are present; make sure they understand the limits of their lawful authority; and motivate them to convey an interested and caring attitude in their dealings with people. Third, give them the proper tools to carry out their jobs. Distinctive uniforms, inclement weather gear, flashlights, and a means of communication are essential. Fourth, give them plenty of supervision and lots of positive guidance.

This article has presented only a few of the elements of a fully developed motel security program. The key message is that the budget motel management, constrained and driven by cost imperatives, is often unable to provide a full range of security measures. Although the risks may be well understood, management lacks the necessary financial resources to implement what the prudent security professional would consider to be an adequate, reasonable security program.

There are nonetheless certain basic security steps that can be taken with only a modest expenditure of funds. These are: (1) manage by walking around (MBWA); (2) screen job applicants, at least those who will be in positions of trust; (3) make security a responsibility of all employees; (4) work with local law enforcement; (5) communicate with neighboring businesses; and (6) patrol the premises.

Robert L. Kohr, CPP, CSP

Sources

Boyer, J., Get Back to Basics With Security. (Lodging, 1989).

Ellis, R.C. Jr., Security and Loss Prevention Management. (The Educational Institute of the American Hotel & Motel Association, East Lansing, MI, 1986).

Kohr, R.L., Accident Prevention for Hotels, Motels and Restaurants. (Van Nostrand Reinhold, New York, 1991).

LODGING SECURITY: THE ZONE APPROACH SURVEY

Unlike other security specialists, the lodging security manager operates in an environment where the protected group is nearly always changing. With the exception of the employees working on the property, the guest population changes nearly everyday. A wide spectrum of society is represented in the guest population; also represented are the problems the guests bring with them.

As with any facility security program, the security manager will develop a loss prevention plan and program based on the results of a survey. Ideally, although seldom the case, the survey will occur prior to the facility being constructed. The survey of a hotel is similar to that of a survey for any other facility, except possibly that more attention must be paid to the surrounding area.

The foreseeability of crimes is a concept that has great significance at lodging facilities, requiring careful analysis and formulation of effective countermeasures. Lodging operators have been placed on notice by the courts that the owner/operator "may be liable for failure to warn guests and to prevent criminal assault where prior criminal activity in the area should have made the attack on the hotel guest foreseeable to the owner/operator."

In the case of *Peters v. Holiday Inns, Inc.*, 278 N.W. 2d 208 (1979) the court stated:

> (T)he conduct of hotel innkeepers in providing security must conform to the standard of ordinary care. In the context of the hotel-guest relationship, it is foreseeable that an innkeeper's failure to maintain adequate security measures not only permits but may even encourage intruders to rob or assault hotel patrons.

Lodging industry professionals are clearly faced with a duty to act to protect guests. The security survey is an element in meeting the duty. Following is a survey approach suitable to a lodging facility.

The Zone Approach

In this approach, the facility, the land it sits on, and the surrounding neighborhood are compartmented in four zones. Zone 1 is the neighborhood immediately surrounding the property; Zone 2 is the parking and recreational areas surrounding the lodging facility; Zone 3 is the facility itself; and Zone 4 comprises the guest rooms within the facility.

Zone 1. The security manager can begin by introspectively asking: "What's happening in the neighborhood that will have an impact on this particular building?" Obviously, if the hotel staff

is afraid to walk the sidewalk in front of the property after sunset, there is a real problem. While the hotel staff may be aware of crime in the immediate area and may in fact have developed personal strategies for dealing with it, the guests will have no awareness, no warning, and no personal defense mechanisms at hand. A good way for the security manager to begin to appreciate the crime problem is to walk the area during various times of the day and week, and determine first hand the types of activities occurring on the fringes of the property.

A next step for the security manager is to establish working relationships with officers in local, county, and state law enforcement agencies. These may be the supervisors of patrol operations in the neighborhood, vice squad officers, and robbery and burglary detectives. The security manager can learn from them the types and frequencies of crimes, the criminal methods of operation, and the nature of the criminal threats, e.g., whether the criminals act individually, in small teams, or as large gangs. Printouts of crime statistics relating to the neighborhood should be obtained and studied, along with the Federal Bureau of Investigation's (FBI's) Uniform Crime Report. Notes should be made of these liaison activities and held for possible use in defending against litigation that may later arise.

The analysis of information collected through personal observation, interviews of knowledgeable law enforcement professionals, and crime statistics will help the security manager during the remainder of the survey to focus on vulnerabilities that may be exploited by the crime threat. The security manager will follow a logical progression from analysis of threat to analysis of vulnerability to formulation of countermeasures. This is also another way of describing how the security manager will construct an overall protective program. As a small example: in a walk-through of the neighborhood the security manager observes gang activity (threat); joggers make up a good percentage of the clientele (vulnerability); the security manager asks for increased police patrol presence along the jogging route (countermeasure).

Zone 2. This area begins at the property boundary and extends to the wall of the first building. In nearly all cases, this area will include parking areas. The swimming pool, tennis courts, and other outdoor recreational facilities might also be in this area. The Zone 1 analysis will provide clues to the types of security problems that can be anticipated in Zone 2. Other factors requiring consideration are:

•The Perimeter.   The security manager should examine the boundaries of the property to determine needs for psychological deterrents (e.g., signage and lighting) and physical barriers (e.g., fences, walls, and landscaping). It may be possible to inexpensively create boundaries by linking a natural barrier, such as a stream, with a hedge row, or by installing a short fence that extends from a fence or structure on neighboring property.

Lodging facilities are often constructed amid shrubbery and trees. Although esthetically pleasing, these offer concealment to criminals who would prey on unsuspecting guests walking on the grounds or moving to and from their vehicles in the parking areas.

•Parking Areas. Parking schemes for guests vary widely in the lodging industry. There is close-in parking, in which the motel guest's vehicle is parked within a few feet of the guest's room, garage parking, valet parking, on-street parking, parking lots in walking distance, and parking lots with shuttles to the facility. Within the limitations imposed by the type and configuration of parking areas, the security manager must set up safeguards that primarily protect the guests and secondarily protect their vehicles.

•Exterior Lighting. Good lighting is both a deterrent to crime and an aid in detecting and apprehending criminals. Lighting is a basic security tool that can also be pleasing to the eye; for example, when it is artfully integrated with foliage and water.

Security lighting in a parking area is essential. Unfortunately, a parking area is sometimes not lit properly because management wants to avoid projecting an image that the lodging facility is in a high crime area.

In open general parking areas it is recommended that between 0.9 footcandles and 0.6 footcandles be maintained on the pavement. Lighting may go as low as 0.2 footcandles when there is a low level of nighttime activity. In covered parking facilities, the recommended illumination levels increase to 5 footcandles for general parking and pedestrian areas; 10 footcandles for ramps and corners; and 50 footcandles at entrance areas.

•Recreational Areas. The security manager must consider the routes and means of transportation utilized by guests going to and from outlying recreational areas; the times of utilization; the types of guests (e.g., children, young adults, older adults, senior citizens); and the valuables they may be carrying with them. These considerations will aid the security manager in assessing the security risks involved.

The nature of the recreational activity is also a consideration. A swimming pool, for example, may be used at all hours of the day or night when it is fenced or inside a locked building/area where entry is controlled, and where some degree of staff attention is given to the safety and security of guests while using the pool. However, if the pool is near an unfenced/unprotected perimeter, the relative security of the using guests may drop to a level that would require either closing the pool during high-risk hours or increasing the protection. Hiking, walking, jogging, and biking on unattended trails presents similar risks.

•The Exterior Walls of the Lodging Facility. The innermost line of defense in Zone 2 is the exterior of the lodging facility. Passage through the walls can be made by guests and trades people at any number of entrances. The control of access through the entrances is typically by lodging staff whose training and experience permit them to discriminate between authorized persons and unwelcome visitors.

During late evening hours when traffic into the lodging facility is minimal, many or all of the remote entrances can be secured, requiring persons to enter through one or a few entrances that are under the direct observation of staff. Unwelcome visitors who are able to pass through an entrance unchallenged or by subterfuge would be confronted with the safeguards of Zone 3. The term *unwelcome visitor* is substituted for the term *intruder* because Zones 2 and 3 are essentially public areas.

It is not the movement of people through public entrances that is of greatest concern to the security manager -- it is the movement of criminals through exterior doors and windows that lead directly into guest rooms or into areas containing the lodging operator's assets. Questions of interest to the security manager are: Which doors and windows are easily

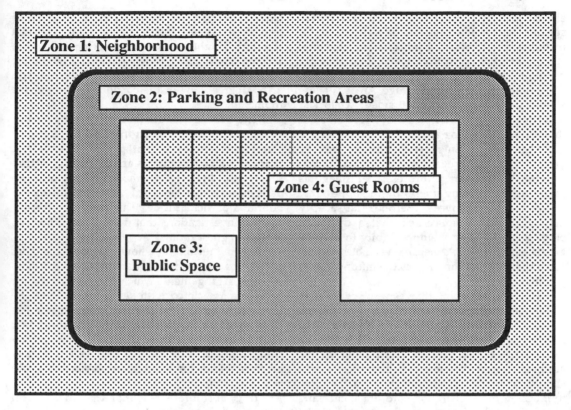

Four Zones in Lodging Security

accessible and what are their vulnerabilities to intruder attack? Which doors and windows need to be locked or grilled? Can windows be arranged to permit opening for air passage but not human passage? What are the fire code implications?

Zone 3. This zone consists of public space that may include restaurants, lounges, shops, rest rooms, and reading areas. Guest room corridors and fire exit stairwells are technically public but from a practical standpoint the security manager will insist that the lodging staff be alert to suspicious persons in these areas. The main thrust of security with respect to Zone 3 is not to keep people out but to exercise subtle controls over human activity inside the zone.

•Security Awareness Training. Security awareness should be second nature for all employees. It means being aware of the methods that criminals use, being able to spot suspicious persons and activities, and knowing what to do when the indicators are present. An

awareness technique that incorporates both courtesy and attentiveness is for staff to greet persons who are on the premises and to offer assistance when it appears they are not sure of their bearings. To the guest, the employee making the greeting is seen as a helpful person; to a criminal looking for the opportunity to commit a crime, the employee is seen as a potential adversary and witness.

•Hold-Up Vulnerability. Robberies at motels, motor lodges, and hotels occur more frequently than property owners care to admit. The foreseeability issue is strongly connected to robberies because of the potential for injury or death to guests and employees. Data gathered in the Zone 1 analysis will indicate the probable nature of the robbery threat. Lawrence Fennelly, in his book, *Handbook of Loss Prevention and Crime Prevention*, offers these precautions: (1) remove any excess cash to a night deposit or safe location, and maintain a very limited night bank; (2) lock the office or lobby after a given hour so that it can be opened only by the release of an electric lock by the night clerk after the person seeking entry has revealed identity; and (3) install a silent alarm connected to a central station or other point from which assistance can be summoned.

•Linen Rooms and Storage Areas. These should be locked when unattended. Unlocked and unattended closets on guest floors result in theft of housekeeping assets.

•Lobbies.   Employees should not be permitted to congregate in the lobby for two reasons. First, an unprofessional image is presented to arriving guests by the appearance of too many employees. Second, the security manager will be concerned that a dishonest employee will have the opportunity to observe guests entering with expensive valuables and act upon this information or pass the information to a confederate.

On the latter point, thieves who specialize in victimizing lodgers will wait near the registration desk looking for a prospective victim (the "mark") as he or she checks in and hoping to overhear the registration clerk mention the assigned room number. Registration clerks should be trained to simply point to the room number on the registration card when checking guests in. For example, while pointing to the room number the clerk would say, "Mr. Smith, you'll be staying in this room."

•Service Doors. Service doors should be locked when not in use and equipped with an intrusion-detection capability.

•Guest Corridors. Lighting should be sufficient to spot suspicious persons or activities. Staff moving through guest corridors should be alert to doors that show evidence of lock tampering or forced entry.

Zone 4. The guest room is the traveler's home away from home; a sanctuary from the rest of the world. The major separating point between the sanctuary and outsiders is the guest room door.

•Doors and Keys. The door should be a solid wood or steel door. In most areas, local building codes and/or fire codes will specify doors with a specific fire rating. Hollow core doors should never be used at the entry point to a guest room.

The door should be equipped with at least one viewing port or peep hole. With the recent enactment of the Americans with Disabilities Act (ADA) serious consideration should be given to providing two peep holes in every door. One at a standard height and one at wheelchair level to accommodate guests in wheelchairs. These view ports or peep holes should provide the guest with a 180-degree view of the corridor outside of the room.

The door lock is another important element. Whenever possible electronic locking systems should be employed that permit a "key/lock change" with every guest's arrival and departure. Electronic locks also make it possible to determine which key card was used to open a door at a particular time. This audit trail feature can aid investigations that involve unauthorized entries to guest rooms.

It is not uncommon, however, to find smaller properties continuing to use the standard lock-in-knob arrangement, which is well known for problems associated with key control. Even the best hardware can be defeated when a key has been stolen or duplicated. The worst thing that can happen is for a master key to be compromised. Professional thieves are always on the lookout for lodging employees who will sell or rent master keys.

It is absolutely essential that mechanical locks be changed immediately whenever a key is missing.   This includes keys that the guest forgets to turn in. The guest room should not be sold to another guest until the locks have been changed.

Each employee must turn in at the end of the work shift any lodging facility keys. It should be policy that only a responsible manager, such as the general manager, chief engineer, or manager of security, will be permitted to take keys off of the property.

If the facility cuts its own mechanical keys, accounting should be made of keys that are cut and of the key blanks that serve as the raw stock. Keys should be identified using some standard form of identification, such as the marking system of the American Hardware Association.

The door should be equipped with a deadbolt with at least a 1-inch throw and self-closing hinges that cause the door to swing into a closed and locked position. The self-closing feature must be reliable because guests will expect the doors to always and perfectly close behind them; if the feature fails, resulting in a loss or injury to the guest, the management can expect a claim for damages.

The sliding glass or patio door often used in resort properties must be capable of resisting forced entry, including the technique of lifting a door panel out of its sliding track. The rule of thumb is to augment the locking capability of a sliding glass door with the use of a secondary device, such as a charley bar.

•Valuables. Consideration must also be given to where a guest will store valuables. Nearly all states have some version of an innkeeper's law requiring the lodging operator to provide safe deposit boxes for guests. Consideration should also be given to providing a guest with an in-room safe.

•Room Checks. The survey should determine why and how often employees enter guest rooms. Entry is usually related to the need to make heating, ventilation, and air conditioning (HVAC), mechanical, and plumbing checks, but includes also the need to determine damage to or theft from rooms. More important, these checks make it possible to discover if a guest inside a room is ill or injured. The standard practice is to conduct a check of each room in every 24-hour period.

Unlike office building security, where the office population is generally stable, the lodging security approach is tailored to address the unique problems of an unstable, ever-changing guest population. In coming to grips with these unique problems, the lodging security professional must take into account the diversity and the changing nature of the clientele. The relatively young lodging guests, those in their 30's and 40's, have different values and expectations than guests who are younger or older; additionally, the United States has an aging population that is increasingly interested in travel.

The security manager must be able to balance the need for security, the guest's desire for privacy, and the organization's need to reduce liability and losses. The lodging security professional must be able to develop sound plans based on applicable case histories, state law, and local ordinances that protect employees and property without violating the rights and expectations of the user group.

Philip C. Sunstrom, CPP

Sources

Federal, R.K., Avoiding Liability in Hotel Security. (Strafford Publications, Inc., Atlanta, 1987).

Fennelly, L.J., Handbook of Loss Prevention and Crime Prevention, 2nd Edition. (Butterworth-Heinemann, Boston, 1989).

Kaufman, J.E., IES Light Handbook. (Illuminating Engineering Society of North America, New York).

Rusting, R.R., Hotel Emphasizes Access Control Outside, Electronic Security Inside. (Hotel/Motel Security and Safety Management, Rusting Publications).

M

MANAGEMENT: HISTORICAL ROOTS

Efforts to organize the work of people have surely existed since people started living in tribes, but few descriptions of managed work were recorded prior to about 200 years ago. Before then, work activities were fairly simple and involved relatively small groups. Typically, the workplace was tiny by contemporary standards and the workforce consisted of a single craftsman and a handful of apprentices. The craftsman was the equivalent of today's line supervisor and directly observed the work in progress. The tasks carried out by the apprentices involved relatively low levels of technology and hence were not complicated to manage.

The Industrial Revolution

In the late 18th century, the Industrial Revolution sweeping across Europe spread quickly to the United States. In his classic book, *The Wealth of Nations*, Adam Smith stole a glance into America's future when he recognized the great increases in work output offered by the use of machines.

America provided fertile ground for cultivating a system of mechanized factories. Funds needed to form manufacturing companies were willingly provided by a monied class in search of profit. The lack of tariff barriers between the states, coupled with an expanding network of roadways and waterways, facilitated large-scale movements of mass-produced goods.

Nature's generous endowment assured a large and dependable supply of raw materials. The advent of the steel plow opened the West to agricultural production, and the factories that produced farm equipment and other work-enhancing machines provided jobs that attracted large numbers of people to urban industrial centers.

The growth of the factory system led to mass employment, which in turn provided incomes that made mass consumption possible. Consumer demand for mass-produced goods enabled mass production to prosper. At the same time, improvements being made in agricultural techniques freed a large part of the work force from food production. With abundant farm land and industrial raw materials, the young American republic developed a balance of agriculture and industry.

The Industrial Revolution was essentially a shift of the production process from small workshops to large factories. Many more people were employed, each working on only one part of the manufactured article and having little contact with those who were making the other parts. Specialization of labor introduced new requirements for managing production. Coordination of separate work efforts was crucial and at the same time more difficult to achieve.

The beginning of the Industrial Revolution was marked by the absence of recorded references to management practices. While managers likely discussed common problems among themselves and thereby improved their skills, little or no exchanges of ideas in writing were circulated and passed on to succeeding managers. In the latter part of the Industrial Revolution, descriptions of management practices began to appear mainly in the professional journals of management societies. It was during this time that the faint outlines of a management movement first appeared. The movement unfolded in three phases.

The Scientific Management Era. Frederick W. Taylor observed that workers were pretty much free to carry out their job assignments at their own paces by their own methods. He used the scientific method of logical inquiry to experiment with work methods in search of better ways to perform jobs.

Although not all of the ideas that came to be known as scientific management originated with Taylor, he brought them into a comprehensible whole, put them into operation, and verified that they worked. Taylor published his findings in *Principles of Scientific Management*. He stressed that his concepts provided a method for labor and management to work together. Taylor's pioneering efforts, however, were widely misunderstood at the time.

Taylor is often referred to as the Father of Scientific Management, but he was not the only expert in this area. Among others, Frank and Lillian Gilbreth developed the principles of motion study, through which jobs were broken into component movements and studied so that wasted motions and fatigue could be reduced. Henry L. Gantt invented the "Gantt Chart" for the scheduling of work and the checking of progress against plans.

Similar management research was taking place in Europe as well. For example, Henri Fayol, chief executive of a large French mining and metallurgical firm, studied management from the top down, with emphasis on overall administration. He published widely on management practices applicable to industrial and governmental organizations.

The Human Relations Era. The pioneers of scientific management, although clearly oriented to efficiency in production, recognized the human element in management. Elton Mayo's study of workers' social needs emphasized the need to take workers' attitudes into account and to recognize them as important contributors to production.

The emphasis by Mayo and others did not downplay the prevailing interest in efficiency. It simply added a new dimension to the field of management, i.e., that management's legitimate interest in getting the work done has to be tempered with an interest in the people who do the work. Technical systems for performing work through social interactions of workers quickly evolved, and the term *sociotechnical systems* came into use to describe the merger.

The Management Science Era. Management science had its beginnings during World War II. Mathematical analyses of data led to decisions that improved the effectiveness of the war effort. In the late 1940s these analytical methods began to be applied to problems of government and industry. Management science often involves the use of models, such as equations and formulas, to describe and provide an understanding of a problem and to identify the optimum solution.

Management science brought a change in the approach to solving work problems. Computers and other scientific tools capable of dealing with large and complex problems are routinely used for business purposes. The modern manager is expected to have strong quantitative skills.

The Age of Technology

In the early craft shop environment, tasks were performed with humans controlling the process and providing the energy to perform the work. In the transition to mass production, people controlled the operation of machines directly but the energy was provided by another source. The next improvement was automatic control in which the machine could sense its manipulations, compare them to preset requirements, and adjust accordingly. Today's automated systems provide instructions to machines, the machines comply, and provide feedback.

Without question one of the greatest triumphs of technology was the electronic computer, and business was profoundly changed as a result. Many of the early applications were to mechanize routine clerical operations, such as payroll and accounting, and as software advanced so did the use of computers in performing more difficult work tasks.

Computer-controlled equipment can make decisions based on signals generated at the points of production. For example, automatic material-handling equipment can move objects to locations depending on the signals they receive; robots can perform operations with the items being produced; and machines equipped with racks of tools and automatic tool changers can carry out commands, all without human intervention.

While technology can be used to improve efficiency and productivity, much can be gained from new management practices. The concept of just-in-time (JIT) production, which originated in Japan, is an example. JIT is founded on the simple notion that costs can be avoided by employing a minimum of inventories to make products. Companies operating in this way coordinate their operations so that one work center produces only what is required by subsequent work centers; production is timed to occur at the moment when the necessary components arrive. Successful implementation of JIT requires reliable sources of supplies and effective preventive maintenance to avoid breakdowns on the line.

Service Sector Growth

As changes have taken place in the management field, the types of operations being managed have changed as well. Operations have spread across wider geographical areas; they have come to use more and increasingly varied technologies; they have become increasingly diversified; and the aggregate mix of operations has changed, with service operations assuming increasing importance.

In this century, great changes have occurred in the American workplace. The number of persons needed to produce food has decreased while the service sector has increased. The increase in service jobs was almost three times as great as the decline in other industries — enough to absorb displaced farm workers and provide many of the additional jobs required by a growing work force.

The direction of growth has been fueled by advances in technology. The shift is clearly in the direction of service operations. Among these is the increasing demand for security-related services.

Much has been said and written about the dramatic growth and the vast future potential of the security services industry. If the past 200 years can serve as an indicator of challenges to management, lively times lie ahead. Managers in the field of security can look forward to even greater changes and greater opportunities for reward.

John J. Fay, CPP

Sources

Dilworth, J.B., Production and Operations Management: Manufacturing and Nonmanufacturing. (Random House Publishers, New York, 1986).

Emmons, H., et al. Quantitative Modeling for Decision Support. (Case Western Reserve University, Cleveland, 1987).

Heyel, C., Encyclopedia of Management, 3rd Edition. (Van Nostrand Reinhold Company, New York, 1982).

Levine, S.N., Dow-Jones Business and Investment Almanac. (Dow-Jones Irwin, Homewood, IL, 1984).

MANAGEMENT: HOW TO HIRE AND MANAGE A CONSULTANT

Many businesses use consultants to increase productivity or generate fresh approaches. Consulting is a growth business, particularly in the security management segment. Security management consultants have long been an important element in security programs of all sizes and types. The *Hallcrest Report II*, for example, shows steady growth in the security consulting business and projects that consulting income will exceed $1 billion by the year 2000.

How Security Consultants Help

The security field is far too complex to expect security directors to be experts in all aspects of the field, so a consultant is retained to provide technical expertise or to evaluate and design a security system. The best consultants render objective advice and opinions, and become a sounding board for the security staff's ideas. A consultant can help combat various types of mental blinders, and help management see problems that would go unnoticed by people within the system.

Often consultants act in a forensic capacity, helping clients during negligence litigation. They may act as a consultant to an attorney or provide expert testimony as an expert witness. A security management consultant may offer independent, third-party insight to help the court separate fact from fiction.

It is the consultant's role to assist in determining the foreseeability of a crime as a vital portion of the defense in security negligence suits. If a shopping center is sued for security negligence, for example, consultants will likely be hired to determine if the crime was reasonably foreseeable. The consultant's testimony will be based on crime history in the area, similar occurrences, and the input of local police to determine the duty and standard of care the shopping center owed to its patrons.

Finally, consultants may be called upon to help companies as they downsize their security staffs. Consultants can design a system to supplement smaller security staffs and maximize security resources. Electronic systems, for example, can be engineered to improve security, while reducing personnel. Its one-time cost can replace ongoing and increasing labor costs.

Defining Needs

A company should first define the problems it seeks to solve before soliciting proposals from consultants. The standard procedure is for the company to submit an RFP (request for proposal) to security consultants. The RFP can take many forms, usually dictated by the complexity of the project. It can be a simple one-page letter or a long and elaborate document, but it is important that it spells out management's security requirements so potential consultants can respond properly. The RFP should define the desired outcome, not necessarily the problem.

On the other hand, not all situations demand a written RFP or the interviewing of numerous consultants. The RFP can be a simple verbal discussion between the client and prospective consultant. The late Howard Shenson, a noted management consultant, wrote in *How to Select and Manage Consultants* that in 83% of the time only one consultant is solicited and interviewed for a project. Therefore, the RFP can simply be a verbal discussion between the client and prospective consultant.

A listing of consultants can be obtained from the International Association of Professional Security Consultants. This nonprofit association counts among its members the leading consultants in a variety of specialized areas. Referrals are made at no charge and are based upon matching management needs with qualified consultants.

Management may also find consultants by networking within its professional group of peers or by referring to advertising in trade publications and directories, such as the *Security Industry Buyers Guide* or the *Consultants and Consulting Organizations Directory*. The latter is published by Gale Research and is available at most public libraries.

A listing of forensic experts can be requested from the Premises Liability Defense Information Center.

The Proposal

Proposals from prospective consultants should allow management to sample the consultant's written communication skills, the consultant's understanding of management's security needs, and how best to solve the security problems. Proposals usually outline the scope of the project, how the consultant will approach and resolve it, and detail the fees and other terms. Consultants usually work by contract, which are usually provided after the proposal is accepted.

Fees

Methods of structuring fees vary, but fall into three basic categories.

For projects with a tightly defined scope, a fixed-fee contract is the norm. After thoroughly analyzing the project, the consultant will determine its cost. If more time is required than estimated, the fee remains the same and the consultant absorbs the difference. Most clients with long-term assignments are comfortable with a fixed contract fee.

The consultant may also estimate the project based on daily or hourly rates. The consultant will estimate the time needed to meet security needs and submit a detailed fee schedule. While most estimates are accurate, the cost of the project could exceed the proposal of an hourly or daily rate.

Per diem fees are often used to cover expenses with the exception of travel costs, which are billed separately. Most consultants bill for expenses they incur during the project for transportation, lodging, and other support services. These charges are usually stated clearly in the contract to avoid misunderstanding.

Some consultants expect a portion of the fee before beginning the work. This deposit is credited to the balance due at the end of the project. If the job extends over the period of a month, progress billings can be made for fees and expenses incurred the previous month.

Finally, some consultants will agree to a retainer to ensure their availability in the future. Retainers are commonly used after a consultant has completed a project and management wants to keep the consultant on to implement the recommendations.

A client's most prevalent fear when hiring a consultant is an excessive fee, studies show. Price shock can be avoided by fully explaining what management expects from the arrangement.

Management should not let the fee be the determining factor in hiring a particular consultant. Management should look instead to the expertise that the consultant brings to the situation and whether that expertise corresponds to a successful resolution of the issue. Lastly, management should gauge how comfortable it feels with the consultant as a working participant.

Qualifying the Consultant

While many people may purport to be security consultants, the actual number of consulting firms and employed consultants is quite small. The moniker of consultant is sometimes assumed by security professionals between jobs or by people selling a product or service. A true consultant will be objective, and will not push a specific product or service.

Asking a consultant for a list of references also may not ensure quality of service. After all, would anyone list a reference not likely to give a glowing recommendation? It's better to review other hallmarks of a professional consultant, such as their credentials and experience, accreditation as a Certified Protection Professional (CPP), and membership in professional associations. The International Association of Professional Security Consultants, for example, has strict standards for membership.

The prospective consultant should provide a curriculum vitae, which will detail experience, education, professional certifications, honors, and affiliations. This should not be confused with a resume, which includes other elements and has a different purpose.

Getting the Most from a Consultant

To ensure that the project is successful, management must send signals to other employees that the project is supported at the highest level. To do that, top management should show interest, for example, by being involved in the planning and execution of the project.

The client should select a responsible manager or supervisor to serve as project coordinator. The coordinator should be familiar with the company's operations and have sufficient authority to clear obstacles that may stand in the way of project activities. The coordinator also will be responsible for providing information and access needed by the consultant to carry out project work. For example, the project coordinator should prepare background information on the company and its personnel, and should be prepared to provide timely responses to requests for information to save the consultant's time and reduce costs.

An initial meeting should be held with all the people involved in the project to review its scope and how the consultant will attain the goals. Management's commitment to the project should be expressed and the consultant should be given the opportunity to resolve with management any unclear issues before beginning the work. The timetable, including major milestones and deadlines, should be agreed and adjusted.

Progress Reports

Depending on the scope of the work, progress reports may be needed during the project. They may be written or oral, depending on management's preferences. Regularly scheduled progress meetings will help resolve questions raised during the project and refine the direction of the work.

Final Report

A final written report from the consultant will distill the consultant's work into a workable and meaningful form, including a plan for action. A complex problem usually engenders a complex report, but even when this is the case the report is likely to contain familiar elements. For example, a final report will often describe the circumstances that spurred management to engage a consultant in the first place, it will define the problem and present the possible solutions or alternatives, and it will outline how work should be carried out to attain a successful conclusion. The bulk of the report should contain the consultant's findings and recommendations. Depending on specific requirements, implementing the plan may be phased. If so, the plan should include a suggested timetable.

If the assignment to the consultant was technical, the final report could take the form of a system design, including drawings and design specifications. Once the design is delivered, the consultant can assist in bidding negotiations, supervising the system's installation, and acceptance testing.

Life after the Consultant

A fear management may have about retaining a consultant is that a consultant can be like a controlled substance -- once management gets hooked, it will be unable to function without a regular fix. In actuality, the consultant's aim is to bring the problem to a permanent resolution. The truly professional consultant is not seeking to be hired by the client as an employee, but to be a one-time partner in helping the client deal with a particular problem or project. Of course, as new challenges surface to confront management, the consultant will hope to be invited to help. Once a relationship has been developed between a client and a consultant, future work becomes even more productive and cost-effective.

Steve C. Kaufer, CPP

Sources

Cannon, J.T., No Miracles for Hire. (American Management Association, New York, 1990).

Shenson, H.L., How to Select and Manage Consultants. (Lexington Books, Lexington, MA, 1990).

MANAGEMENT: A SECURITY STRATEGY FOR THE NINETIES

Three observations are in order. First, today's security manager operates in a rapidly evolving business world. The fast-paced and highly competitive nature of business is forcing companies to continually find new ways to be productive at lower cost. The new ways of doing business bring new security risks.

Second, every important decision made by a security manager depends upon technical knowledge. Important security decisions are never risk-free, and technical knowledge is often the critical factor in arriving at the best possible alternative.

Third, the first and second observations are intertwined. In the dynamic workplace of the 1990s, security risks are rising around us and they are shrouded in complexities that call for technical knowledge. Our best response is to craft a security strategy that matches the needs and tempo of the times.

A Rapidly Evolving Business World

Nearly every business of significant size is organized along lines that permit simultaneous management of two main activities -- the core activities at the heart of the enterprise and the support activities that contribute to the core. The core work, being essential to the business and having value that needs to be protected against loss or compromise, is usually assigned to proven and trusted employees. The support work, while important, usually does not produce any significant or sustainable advantage to the business. The support staff can be varied, running

the gamut from unskilled blue collar to highly skilled white collar employees.

The nature of staffing in large American companies began to change in the early 1990s. Driven by powerful economic imperatives, companies started looking for ways to cut costs and many are finding relief through outsourcing, i.e., transferring support work to external vendors. Labor costs are cut by replacing higher-paid permanent employees with lower-paid temporary and contract employees.

Many managements are concluding that support work is mainly done in-house for reasons of convenience, not of criticality nor even of efficiency.

Central to the outsourcing approach is a belief that a company can realize the full value of its essential core activities at a lower overall cost. The approach also holds to the idea that in freeing itself of the need to provide support services from in-house resources, a company can attain greater flexibility and a sharper focus for managing the core activities.

Although it is too early to judge, outsourcing appears to be more than just a passing fad destined to disappear when economic times improve. The trend is both growing and becoming entrenched, and may well become a natural order of business.

What are the implications for security management? In a broad sense, it means the security manager must understand the risks created by the organizational adjustments that are part of the outsourcing process. The security manager must be attentive, for example, to exposures that arise when the electronic data processing function is outsourced to a vendor whose other clients include competitors. How can the security manager be assured that the vendor will exercise great care in keeping sensitive data out of the hands of competitors?

The exposures are not always easy to find and even more difficult to close. But there is at least a general approach that the security manager can take. It is based on the common sense observation that exposures will in large measure arise in the nature of the support work that is outsourced. The magnitude of potential loss is often a function of the technical knowledge that goes into the work. It stands to reason that a contract scientist who learns the chemical formula for the company's best selling product is in a position to do much more harm than a Kelly girl temp who does the filing. The loss potential increases relative to a job's complexity.

Conversely, the opportunity to prevent the loss or detect its early occurrence decreases relative to the complexity of the job. This is because in an outsourced situation there is likely to be few, if any, individuals remaining in the core workforce who have the technical insights necessary to see or appreciate the effect of an exposure in a complex operation. Complicating matters is the fact that the underlying technical information and performance behaviors change with time and with the nature of the business.

Even after losses show up on the ledger, the company may not find within its in-house resources anyone able to properly diagnose the exposure and prescribe a correct remedy.

The Importance of Technical Knowledge

The security manager, or even the entire security staff, cannot possibly possess technical knowledge so broad and so deep that every risk can be anticipated, understood, and put to rest. We can expect, however, that the security manager will personally acquire a reasonable range of technical skills, provide the same for security staff, and above all else, know where to find technical assistance that is not available in-house.

We can view technical knowledge from many perspectives. One is to see it as a dimension of business, operating in three human competencies: access, quality, and teamwork.

Access. Access is knowing where to go for the right information, service, or product, at the best price. It often means networking internally and externally, and building sound relationships with vendors and peers. Establishing solid relationships with suppliers builds a bridge for acquiring technical assets. Bridge building also occurs in the transfer of "best practices" between security practitioners in different companies or even different industries.

Quality. Quality is the optimal balance between cost and technical excellence to meet security objectives. It includes quality control and quality assurance. Quality control is the responsibility of the supplier; quality assurance derives naturally from confidence in the relationship. In a mature connection between client and vendor, cost and quality will occur together, to the advantage of both parties.

Teamwork. Teamwork is the bringing together of people who each contribute from complementary specialties. It is a competency which also gives to the players the right information, services or product. A team or teams may be the security department or the security department in tandem with various product suppliers and consultants. Team composition will vary according to the mission, with each member contributing a different set of skills and abilities. Teamwork calls for sustained leadership and goal orientation.

In a single sentence, these three competencies operate to obtain *access* to the essential information, services and products that fuel the security function, assuring their *quality* and integrating them through *teamwork*.

The ability to predict, quantify, and control the full menu of risks is the security manager's highest mark of excellence. To predict which is restricted by the limitations of human understanding and current technology is to identify the nature of the threat; to quantify is to measure uncertainty through the application of science and experience; and to control risk is to manage resources logically and flexibly.

The truly competent security manager will appreciate the technical knowledge required to comprehend each risk, know where the knowledge is available, and be positioned to acquire it when it is needed.

A Security Strategy

The strategy proposed here has six elements:
- •Improve on quality and cost.
- •Forge close links to customers.
- •Establish close relationships with suppliers.
- •Make effective use of technology.
- •Operate with minimum layers of management hierarchy.
- •Continuously improve the security staff.

The six elements are mutually reinforcing and, indeed, form a single, integrated strategy.

Improve on Quality and Cost. The measuring stick of security performance is high quality at a reasonable cost. The facets of quality are excellence, reliability, and speedy delivery of services.

The successful security operations are those that strive to be the "best in class" in all the main performance activities. A characteristic of the leading performers is an emphasis on competitive benchmarking, i.e., comparing personal and unit performance with the industry's leaders, and setting goals to measure progress.

Forge Close Links to Customers. Successful security managers make concerted efforts to develop close ties with their customers. This is less like making friends through public relations and more like getting into "the mind" of the customer so as to increase the manager's ability to respond rapidly and appropriately to the users of security services.

Establish Close Relationships with Suppliers. Traditionally, cooperation with suppliers has been achieved through the coercive power of the buyer. What is encouraged here, however, is the creation of partner relationships in which price is not always the single most important factor. Coordination with external vendors is crucial to a security manager in acquiring technical knowledge, i.e., the right information, services or product.

If a key element of strategy is to position the in-house security staff to be a leader in using technical advances in support of the mission, it follows that the security manager will be active in developing partnerships with the suppliers of technology. The idea is to select a small number of capable suppliers and work with them to find the correct balance between cost and quality. A partnership arrangement has little room for second-guessing and beating suppliers down to the last penny.

Make Effective Use of Technology. A security strategy linked to technology will expect the security manager to know the work-enhancing technologies available in the marketplace and to use them wisely. Being wise about technology involves recognizing that newer is not always better -- and even when a technology is in fact better, the final payoff has to exceed the costs of applying it. In short, technology must earn its way into a company's processes.

In looking for a technological solution, don't try to reinvent the wheel and don't refuse a workable technology simply because it does not perfectly match the situation. Try very hard to get the solution right the first time. Retrofitting can be costly. A common mistake is to expect more than the technology can deliver.

A consideration is the working relationship between the security employees and the equipment or routines that make up the technology. This is not so much a matter of ergonomics but of the symbiotic linkage of man and machine. In companies where technology is routinely applied, the security employees are better able to adjust when a new or more complicated technology is acquired for their use.

Operate with Minimum Layers of Management Hierarchy. Organizational structure, i.e., the horizontal distribution of departments and the vertical arrangement of managerial layers, varies considerably from company to company. Today's trend (which is part of the outsourcing phenomenon) is toward greater functional integration and fewer layers of management, both of which promote speedy delivery of services and a strong responsiveness to customer needs. These are virtues to be cherished by any prudent security manager.

Execution of the security strategy in a flatter, leaner organization will in most cases rely upon a small, yet well-rounded staff of the highest quality, working in partnership with suppliers who bring to the arrangement a broad array of technical talent. The talents that come quickly to mind are computer security specialists, electronic countermeasures technicians, forensic auditors, questioned document examiners, architects, access control specialists, et al. Fortunately, the security profession, although very broad and mature in terms of what it does, continues to evolve better ways to protect assets.

Continuously Improve the Security Staff. All of the first five strategy elements require departures from the conventional way of dealing with employees. The changes called for will need a new mindset, a new commitment, and strong leadership. Progress will seldom be comfortable as old ideas are cast off and refashioned.

The improvement of security staff will require large doses of learning. The modes of teaching can include counseling, tutoring, formal classroom instruction, and on-the-job training. The constant in the process will be continuous development of employees -- not just continuous development to get the strategy up and going, but continuous development throughout the employees' working lifetimes.

The desired outcome of staff development will be technical competency, quality output, teamwork, and a flexibility that permits the acceptance of daunting challenges.

John J. Fay, CPP

MANAGEMENT: SELLING SECURITY

Are we security managers or business managers? Many of us who are responsible for the loss prevention function in an organization are not seen by others as both, and worse yet we do not see ourselves in that dual role. We can correct those misperceptions by educating our peers and superiors about the complexities of security and by improving our business skills. This will enable us to more effectively communicate the value of security as an essential business function. It will also help us acquire the resources we need to carry out that function.

When a security manager finds it difficult to get the resources needed to run an effective loss prevention function, the reason is often related to poor communication. Security has often been perceived as a "necessary evil." Top management may see security as a profit drain and line management may see it as an impediment to operations. This thinking is, of course, parochial and inaccurate but is likely to prevail in the absence of effective communication by the security manager.

A helpful step is to communicate information on the current and future effects upon the organization of crime rates and trends. Examples might include the effects of employee drug abuse on productivity and costs, the potential for information loss associated with a work environment dependent upon desktop computers, and the likelihood of willful damage by disgruntled employees during a period of downsizing. The security manager should also communicate historical or actual data that support the need for security, e.g., loss reports, recoveries, and restitution.

Effective communications will include a strong emphasis on profit enhancement. In selling security as a revenue-producing function, the security manager must show a positive balance between costs and benefits, and must often overcome the traditional view that security adds nothing to the bottom line. Showing security in this light is more than just pointing to the occasional instances when major losses were prevented; it relies on regular production of supportable facts and figures that portray the security function as a consistent contributor to the profits. These data reside in many nooks and crannies and may relate to widely differing business activities, such as pre-employment screening, inventory management, accident prevention, information storage, etc. The resourceful security manager will gather the data and present them in credible and meaningful formats.

A critical part of demonstrating security as a profit-enhancer is the budget. Conceptually, a budget will reflect cost experiences (the costs of last year) and anticipated spending (the costs of the current and near-term future years). The security manager will be challenged to present a budget that takes into account the cost realities of the recent past and the estimated costs of activities planned for the near future. The budget is a tool for measuring the cost-effectiveness of work completed or in process, and work planned to be done. Planned work includes profit-enhancing endeavors, which may be standard, institutionalized protective activities or totally new efforts.

Budgeting documents, such as annual and monthly overhead reports, will often array figures that reflect line-item spending over a 3-year span (previous year, current year, and future year). The budget is a mechanism for demonstrating the relationship between the costs of security and the derivative benefits. The astute security manager will translate derivative benefits into dollars and compare those dollars against operating costs. Derivative benefits can take the form of thefts that were deterred, injuries prevented, and claims avoided.

Security and profits go hand in hand. A task of the security manager is to sell that concept to the decision makers. Once understood, the organization can move toward a secure, safe, and productive working environment.

Bonnie S. Michelman, CPP

MANAGEMENT: SERVICE OPERATIONS IN SECURITY

Security services do not produce tangible outputs, although tangible products, such as access control hardware, are often provided or operated as an element of service. Security services are always customer-centered. The customer often has some contact with the service provider, although the customer does not have to be present when the service is actually being delivered. Each type of security service operation has its unique characteristics. When viewed in sufficient detail, a security service operation can be seen as dynamic, that is, changing through time.

Three characteristics of security service operations can be recognized:

•Productivity generally is difficult to measure because the products of service operations are somewhat intangible. Intangible products are difficult to evaluate because they cannot be held, weighed, or measured.

•Quality standards are difficult to establish and to evaluate. No one knows for certain the amount of loss that was avoided because a security officer was present as a psychological deterrent or because the officer acted in a particular way to discourage or prevent a criminal act.

•Persons who provide security services generally have contact with the customers. The marketing and customer relations aspects of the service often overlap the operations function. For example, the relationship between the security services account representative and the client contact is often considered to be a very important component of the total services.

Managers of Security Services

Some companies have executives with titles such as vice president of operations, director of investigations, and account manager. In a good-size security services company, many persons serve in managerial positions, representing disciplines in planning, financing, marketing, and so forth. A company's management team, from the top executive right down to the supervisors of line workers, is at the center of directing and controlling services.

In working through others, managers exercise skills in two dimensions:

•Technical Competence. Since managers make decisions about the tasks that other people are to perform, they need a basic understanding of the processes and technologies that drive the company's internal systems, and they need adequate knowledge of the work they manage. Technical competence is usually obtained through training and experience.

•Behavioral Competence. Since managers work through others, their work necessarily involves a great deal of interpersonal contact. A good manager will have the ability to work with other people. Managers, and those being managed, often work in groups. Groups exist because people find they can achieve more, both in output and in social satisfaction, by working together.

Managers are responsible for seeing that their companies are successful. A successful security services company will meet at least three basic requirements. The services will be:

•Suited to the company's capabilities and the market's demand.

•Delivered with consistent quality at a level that appeals to customers and serves their needs.

•Provided at a cost that allows an adequate profit and a reasonable sales price.

The operations function plays a major role in accomplishing all of these requirements. Managers at the senior level must ensure that company objectives are consistent with operational capabilities and that the appropriate strengths are developed within operations to be consistent with broad, companywide strategy. In many companies the operations function consumes the greatest portion of company resources, thereby strongly impacting cost and price. Since the operations function produces services, it is largely responsible for quality.

Quality and productivity are two factors frequently mentioned as challenges facing security service companies. Achievement of high quality relates very closely to productivity. Providing a service that has to be repeated because of inadequate performance is both a quality and productivity issue. Consistently providing poor quality services leads to certain death in the services industry.

The idea of productivity is broader than just achieving high output per worker hour. It means balancing all factors of operations so that the greatest output is achieved for a given total input of all resources.

Examples of Service Managers' Functions

Planning
Establish the mix of services
Schedule the how and when of services
Plan the capacities of major work groups
Plan the company's locations
Arrange facilities and equipment
Decide shifts and work hours
Establish improvement projects
Organize changes to new processes

Directing
Establish provisions of union contracts
Establish personnel policies
Establish employment contracts
Issue job assignments and instructions
Issue work rules and procedures

Organizing
Centralize or decentralize operations
Organize by function, specialty, or location
Establish work assignments
Assign responsibility
Arrange supplier and subcontractor networks

Controlling
Encourage pride in performing as expected
Compare costs to budgets
Compare actual labor hours to standards
Inspect quality levels
Compare work progress to schedule

Motivating
Challenge through example, objectives and expectations
Encourage through praise, recognition, and other intangible incentives
Motivate through tangible rewards
Motivate through enriched jobs and challenging projects

Coordinating
Coordinate through use of forecasts and schedules
Observe actual performance and recommend needed performance
Report, inform, communicate
Coordinate sales, purchasing, deliveries
Respond to customer inquiries

Developing Employees
Show and encourage better ways
Give "stretch" assignments
Support employees in training programs

Even when security service companies offer the same menu of services, each company will be a uniquely different entity. Many factors account for the differences but the factor that clearly stands out is called management.

A security services company spends a great percentage of income and employee effort carrying out activities that stem from decisions made by managers. As these activities progress and evolve, they determine the current worth and the potential destiny of the company. A company's achievements can be enormous when all of its separate parts work in harmony and pull together to meet carefully established goals.

John J. Fay, CPP

Sources
Dilworth, J.B., Production and Operations Management: Manufacturing and Nonmanufacturing. (Random House Publishers, New York, 1986).

Heyel, C., Encyclopedia of Management, 3rd Edition. (Van Nostrand Reinhold Company, New York, 1982).

MANUFACTURING SECURITY: INSPECTIONS TO REDUCE LOSS

Nearly all security programs at manufacturing facilities include regularly scheduled security inspections. In some programs, the inspections are perfunctory, address a single department or operation, and consist of not more than a review of procedures conducted during a single, short visit that is followed by an equally perfunctory form letter to the responsible line manager. In other programs, the inspections are comprehensive and detailed, involve many days and several visits, including consultations with numerous responsible managers, and are followed by lengthy reports of findings and recommendations. In this article, we will look at the inspection process as an opportunity to do something constructive that lies somewhere between these two extremes.

Records of Openings and Closings

Many manufacturing facilities today are covered after-hours by an alarm system that may be monitored from a central station. Where central stations are used, it is almost always possible to arrange to receive reports from the alarm company of any unusual openings and closings outside of normal hours.   These are often supplemental reports prepared independently of the regular daily opening and closing reports provided by the alarm company.

In the case of installations with proprietary alarms, these systems may come equipped with an automatic printer or recorder that indicates not only the openings and closings of any doors in the installation, but also any tampering with the console or the printer.

For locations that cannot be covered by a central station system or a proprietary system with a built-in recorder, a time-recorder lock can be installed on the main entrance of the facility. The time-recorder lock in turn is tied to sequence locks on other doors. In this way, the security manager can obtain the same permanent record of unusual openings and closings offered by more sophisticated systems.   These records can be invaluable when looking for a particular pattern of surreptitious entries or exits at the facility.

In addition to studying records of openings and closings for holiday, Sunday, and nighttime openings, a security manager should also be alert to the 2- or 3-minute opening that occurs just after closing of the facility at the regularly scheduled time. A dishonest employee may have stashed company property near the exit with the intention of stealing it after other employees have left for the day. The thief will re-enter the building within several minutes of its closing on the pretext of getting a forgotten umbrella or handbag and, while not observed, remove the stashed property. The pretext is usually for the benefit of fellow workers leaving the facility at the same time as the keyholder.

Theft in this manner is far more difficult to detect when employees work in collusion. Ideal opportunities for theft are presented to security officers employed at an alarmed facility during other-than-normal working hours. For example, two security officers, one coming on duty and one going off duty, could conspire to move company property out of the facility when the alarmed door was opened at the time of shift change. The alarm company's report of the opening would not reflect anything unusual. The security countermeasures can include stakeout surveillance of the door at shift time or a concealed video camera activated by movement.

Employee Locker Inspections

Employee lockers are another very productive area that should be inspected in detail. Although it is unusual to find any hard evidence of theft in such locations, the security manager can frequently pick up other clear-cut indications of violations of company rules and regulations. Often, the major violators of certain rules can also be identified later among the dishonest employees of a location.

The one consideration that may play a part in determining the method used for locker inspections is whether or not the employer's actions are limited by an agreement with a collective bargaining unit. An agreement might provide that the employee must be present when his or her locker is inspected, and if not, the fruits of the inspection cannot be used against the interests of the employee. In large plants, where it would be impractical for every employee to be present during a locker inspection, a compromise might be worked out in which a shop steward would act as an employee representative during an inspection.

At any rate, with or without representation by or on behalf of employees, locker inspections should be conducted without prior warning and at irregular intervals. Private padlocks should be prohibited and lockers should be equipped with locks that can be opened by the employer.

Work Stations

In most plant settings, employees have particular areas where they perform their functions and in these areas they tend to place their personal effects. The containers for accumulated personal items may be cabinet and desk drawers, foot lockers, and similar compartments controllable by the employee to some extent. These areas are places where problem employees are likely to conceal alcohol, drugs, drug paraphernalia, weapons, stolen company property, and the evidences of dishonesty, such as false production records, shipping labels, and work orders.

Sensitive Areas

A manufacturing plant is likely to have one or more security-sensitive areas that merit inspection. These can include vaults or rooms where very expensive products or raw materials are stored, such as precious metals, security cages for valuable but less expensive items, and file rooms containing sensitive documents. Of a different nature, but of interest to security, are waste containers. An inspection of these might uncover items in the process of being stolen, stashed alcohol and drugs, and debris indicative of on-the-job alcohol and drug use.

Lavatories

Inspections of lavatories can be revealing as to indicators of theft. Particular attention should be given to toilet water tanks, not only the inside of the tank but also the space between the rear of the tank and the wall; the area underneath wash basins; and any small access doors to plumbing traps, and the like. Shelving, ventilation duct work, dispensers of various types, as well as all types of refuse containers, should be examined closely. In a facility that produces or stores items of wear, such as hosiery and underwear, the inspection should be particularly alert to old items in trash containers. It is common for women to discard worn panty-hose in trash containers in the women's lavatory and simply replace them with a new pair from stock. Usually, along with the old discarded pair, the security manager can also find the packaging material from the stolen product.

The Full Case Area

In distribution centers or warehouse areas, the security manager should pay particular attention to the full case area. If at the time of the inspection the security manager observes that full cases are being processed for filling customers' orders, the security manager should ask that such cases be taken from the full case area to an open stock or order-filling area. The security manager can then inspect the remaining full cases.

Cases in the full case area should be intact and sealed. Dishonest employees will sometimes deliberately break open a full case with a forklift blade or some other object in order to make it easy to steal items from the container. The contents of apparently damaged cases should be checked for missing items.

J. Kirk Barefoot, CPP

MICROWAVE MOTION DETECTORS

While ultrasonic motion detectors generate inaudible acoustic energy patterns and recognize a disturbance in those patterns caused by a moving intruder, microwave motion detectors generate an electromagnetic energy pattern that serves the same function. Also, ultrasonic motion detectors consist of a single control unit with multiple transducers. However, most microwave detectors are self-contained units; that is, the detector antenna, signal processor, and power supply are contained in a single unit. Microwave detectors are, however, available with multiple transceivers connected to a common control unit. Even though each of the multiple transceivers contains its own signal processing circuit, they share the same power supply and alarm relay in the control unit. With multiple transceiver detectors, each transceiver usually generates a smaller energy pattern than the single unit detectors. In application of the multiple transceiver detectors, additional transceivers are required to protect large volumes; however, each detector can be directed to cover a specific area.

Microwave energy has the distinct ability to penetrate glass, wood, and even cinder block walls to some extent, depending on the frequency and antenna direction. Therefore, microwave motion detectors can be used where the volume of the facility to be protected is large, and when it is advantageous to detect intruders through internal partitions and walls. Microwave detectors can also be used in place of ultrasonic motion detectors for volumetric detection when air turbulence in the area requiring protection might cause false alarms with ultrasonic detectors.

The microwave motion detectors described here are for indoor applications only. Indoor microwave detectors should never be used outdoors unless they are designated for outside use by the manufacturer; however, outdoor microwave detectors can certainly be used indoors. The reason indoor detectors should never be used outdoors is that indoor units recognize a Doppler frequency shift produced by a moving target to detect intruders. Moving trees and waving grass can produce Doppler frequency shifts similar to those produced by a moving intruder. This type of motion can cause serious false alarm problems.

Although the resistance to higher-frequency microwave energy passing through wood, sheetrock, and brick is greater than for the lower-frequency energy, the energy can penetrate the walls. The fact that it can penetrate walls has both advantages and disadvantages. An advantage occurs when an intruder is detected by the microwave energy penetrating partitions within the protected volume; but, if it detects someone or something moving outside the protected area, or even outside the building, that is a definite disadvantage. The fact that microwave energy is difficult to contain should be considered in locating and directing the detector-transmitted energy within the area requiring protection.

The shape of the transmitted energy pattern is a function of the antenna configuration. Detectors are available with antennas that generate both omni-directional and directional energy patterns. Omni-directional antennas generate a circular donut-shaped, hemispheric or ellipsoid energy pattern, while directional antennas generate broad teardrop-shaped patterns to protect long corridors.

Robert L. Barnard

Source Barnard, R.L., Intrusion Detection Systems. (Butterworth-Heinemann, Boston, 1982).

MILITARY SECURITY

The military has a wide range of assets that it must protect. Many of the military's assets warrant protection based on their intrinsic value alone. Others, such as weapons, warrant protection for the additional reason that the potential harm to the public resulting from their falling into the wrong hands could be catastrophic. People are another asset about which the military is concerned, although their value is hard to measure quantitatively.

Military security relies heavily on the application of regulations. There are regulations that tell the military security community how to secure nearly everything the military owns. Security, including that required by regulation, also relies on the assessment of the risk associated with the asset's compromise. The risk may include considerations of the value of the asset and the likelihood that aggressors will attempt to compromise. The asset value typically includes an assessment of the degree to which the asset's loss may affect the user's mission and the time required to replace the asset in addition to its cost.

For assets such as classified information and weapons, the consequences of the asset's compromise beyond those to its immediate user are also commonly considered. The likelihood of aggressor activity depends on such considerations as the value of the asset to the aggressor, the availability of the asset elsewhere, the history of or potential for aggressive acts against the asset, and the vulnerabilities of the asset. Higher-risk assets warrant higher degrees of security.

Establishing security beyond that required by regulation depends on threat and vulnerability analysis. Threat analysis may be built upon risk analysis results. A threat statement that is in sufficient detail to serve as a basis for security engineering design includes the likely aggressors; how they are likely to attempt to compromise the asset (their likely tactics); and the weapons, explosives, and tools they are likely to use in carrying out those tactics. Considering these threat parameters and the existing conditions surrounding the asset, including existing security measures, allows the security designer to establish the vulnerabilities of the asset. The goal of the security engineering design, then, is to mitigate the asset's vulnerabilities subject to the operational requirements of its user. An additional consideration is the degree to which the asset will be protected against the threat, or the level of protection. This is commonly based on some measure of the asset's value.

Because the military is an organ of national security, much of the information it handles is classified and a significant amount of all military security efforts are directed at securing it. Similar security is afforded other high-value assets and weapons. Securing these assets depends on both procedural and physical security.

Procedural security measures commonly include limiting access to the information or asset to those who require access to it. In highly sensitive situations, it sometimes is necessary to institute the two-person rule, in which no individual can have access to the information or asset alone. While much of controlling access is done through physical measures, much also depends on procedural measures. These include procedures for classifying information, for accountability of information and assets, and for handling them. There are also many procedures related to protecting information on data processing equipment such as computers or communications lines.

Physical measures in information and high-value asset security focus on the storage of the information or assets when they are not in use. The common philosophies behind information storage are to either prevent theft of the information or to ensure that it is obvious when the information has been compromised. The philosophy behind high-value asset security is commonly limited to preventing theft. Measures to prevent theft usually take the form of vaults, safes, or secure structures in which the information or asset can be stored. Safes are generally procured on the open market based on strict government specifications. Vaults and other secure structures are usually constructed in place of common building materials such as reinforced concrete and steel. They are designed to resist forced entry. Vaults may also be of modular construction that is procured similarly to safes. Where the goal is only to ensure that the compromise of the information is evident, vaults are constructed such that aggressors would have to force their way in, making it obvious that they have done so.

In the storage of information or high-value assets, additional security measures such as intrusion-detection systems and access control are frequently applied. Intrusion detection systems detect aggressors as they attempt to gain access to the information. The resulting alarm allows personnel to respond to the location to attempt to prevent the aggressor from compromising the asset. Access control limits who has access to a vault, safe, or storage structure by requiring them to know a combination or have a key in the case of mechanical locks, or by requiring them to have an entry credential or a combination in the case of electronic entry control equipment. More sophisticated electronic entry control equipment includes devices that validate identity based on biological features such as finger or voice prints, or retinal patterns. Both access control and intrusion detection can be supplemented or performed by guards. In military security, the use of guards is relatively common; however, this practice is being minimized where possible due to declining money and humanpower budgets.

Physical security of computers and communications systems processing classified information may also include special shielding or attenuation measures applied to prevent aggressors from eavesdropping on the electronic emanations from the equipment and means to prevent transmissions from being intercepted. The latter may involve encrypting the data.

Security of other military assets varies widely based on the type of asset and how it is stored. Many military assets are stored in outside storage areas. Security of such assets, such as aircraft or vehicles, commonly relies on perimeter barriers, such as fences, which may or may not be supplemented with intrusion-detection systems or guards. For many of the lower-value or lower-risk assets stored inside of buildings, such as personal equipment or common tools, security is limited to minimizing the opportunities for pilferage through providing locked rooms or containers, and applying deterrent measures such as lighting and intermittent checks by guards. Higher-value assets such as sensitive communications equipment or controlled substances (drugs) stored inside buildings may be provided security approaching that of classified information or other high-value assets and weapons.

Security of personnel, including military and civilian personnel and their dependents, entails prevention of personal crimes and prevention of terrorist acts. Prevention of personal crime is provided by applying crime prevention measures such as lighting and police patrols. Security against terrorist acts is much more complex. Protection of personnel within buildings consists of designing the buildings to resist the effects of terrorist weapons and explosives. Security against terrorism also entails alert law enforcement personnel and good intelligence.

Curt P. Betts, P.E.

MOTIVATION: MASLOW AND THE SECURITY SUPERVISOR

The success of a security supervisor in leading subordinates rests on his ability to motivate them. The supervisor needs interpersonal skills that will take him far beyond being likable and popular. Leadership is not a matter of earning admiration but of inspiring people to work together constructively. The supervisor's principal task is to create a climate for work in which employee efforts are organized and directed toward the goals of the organization. To effectively discharge that task the supervisor must understand the human needs, differences, and emotions of those being supervised.

Motivation is an extremely important factor in supervision. The willingness of employees to apply themselves to productive work activities is linked to how much personal value they find in the work itself. The supervisor's challenge is to discover the personal rewards that people find in their work, then innovate the rewards into their work, and at the same time maintain the expected levels of productivity.

Maslow's Theory

A commonly accepted theory of motivation was advanced by A.H. Maslow[1]. The theory describes people as having needs in five categories: physiological, safety, love, self-esteem, and self-actualization. According to Maslow, human needs operate in an ascending hierarchy that begins with a natural striving to satisfy the physiological needs and ends with self-actualization. In this hierarchy, which can be abstracted as a pyramid, a higher need does not provide motivation until all lower, more basic needs are satisfied. When a need is satisfied, it ceases to be a motivator.

The physiological needs are a human's basic requirements for nourishment, water, air, and rest. A person's focus will be entirely on these needs for as long as they continue to be unmet. Once met, the individual's focus shifts upward to the next level.

The next level is the requirement to be free from harm. The safety and security of the individual dominates. Like the underlying physiological needs, this level is concerned with survival and self-preservation.

At the third level, the individual strives for love and belonging. Affection and human relationships are the focal points.

Self-esteem comes next. These needs relate to what a person thinks of himself. They include achievement, competence, independence, status, and recognition. Self-esteem needs are similar to love needs because both are social in orientation.

The highest order of needs is self-actualization. At this level the individual expresses himself through the exercise of personal capabilities. Satisfaction is derived through self-fulfillment. It is the development of one's own potentiality and the manifestation of creative urge.

The major principles of Maslow's theory can be summed up by observing that:

• A human is a continuously wanting animal. When he is fulfilled in one need, he develops desires in another.

• When a person's needs have been satisfied, they cease to motivate. A person must be confronted with a need before he is moved to initiate, change, or sustain his behavior.

• Identical needs may be satisfied in different ways. A person who needs money will be motivated to acquire it. The method of acquisition, however, could be to earn the money or steal it.

• A given style of behavior may satisfy more than one need. A person who works hard to earn money may want the money to buy food (physiological), pay the mortgage (safety), or gain prestige (self-esteem).

Maslow in the Security Environment

A person's natural striving to establish human relationships and to experience self-esteem are present as much in the workplace as in any other setting. A security employee, whether working at the line level or in management, has social needs that include friendship with co-workers and acceptance within the work group. The extent and intensity of individual efforts will vary, however. An individual who satisfies social needs outside of the workplace may exhibit less striving than someone whose entire social experiences are dependent on co-workers.

Attempts to satisfy the higher needs of self-esteem are often expressed by security employees in the form of seeking recognition as a standout performer or as a valued contributor to the attainment of group goals. Most of us never stop looking for assurance that we are held in high regard by our peers, and even when we obtain that assurance today, we will seek it tomorrow and every day thereafter.

Basic to an understanding of human needs is the recognition that people respond to other people and situations as they are perceived, not as they actually are. If an employee sees work as a path to the attainment of a personal goal, he is likely to be motivated at work. A second employee may not have a goal or a goal that requires much effort and as a result will not see work as a means to his personal ends. A third employee may have a goal so lofty that he will view the job as an impediment.

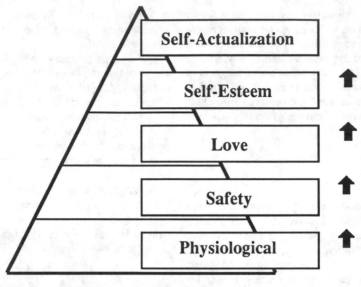

Maslow's Hierarchy of Needs

It is not enough anymore for a supervisor to simply assign work. The supervisor has to establish conditions, within reason, in which employees can fulfill their belonging, self-esteem, and ego needs. The supervisor in some respects can be likened to a buffer that accommodates the demands of the organization and the personal needs of the employees. Using a variety of motivational techniques, the supervisor creates an arrangement that allows employees to meet personal aspirations while at the same time meeting the organization's work requirements.

The supervisor must appreciate that different employees will have different needs and that their needs will affect their motivations. The supervisor has to recognize and assess the differences when they are manifested and to administer supervision accordingly. A critical ability in the supervisor's personal inventory will be a combination of knowledge and skill that addresses the ego needs of subordinates. It is an ability resting on an understanding of motivation and a deft touch in working with people.

John J. Fay, CPP

Source Fay, J.J., Approaches to Criminal Justice Training, 2nd Edition. (University of Georgia Press, Athens, GA, 1988).

Note

1. Maslow's propositions were offered in an article titled "A Theory of Human Motivation," which appeared in Psychological Review 50, pp. 370-396, 1943.

MUSEUM SECURITY

"Museum security" is a general term applied to the protection of a variety of sites that fall loosely under the category of "museum." Museums might include museums of a classical sense -- the type of building containing art or artifacts -- but they might also include "house museums," where the building itself is as much of an artifact as the objects it contains. Museums might also include historic sites such as the Statue of Liberty or Mount Vernon, or facilities with other types of specimens more reminiscent of national parks than museums with walls. There are many types of museums, each posing different security problems.

It has been said that "We are born and we die. In between we wander. Museums are places where the marks of our wanderings are preserved." More specifically, museums are places where we collect and maintain (including protect) art, artifacts, and anything else that society deems important. Museum security, by its nature, is really museum "protection," as the role of the modern museum security practitioner involves aspects of safety, fire prevention and protection, and conservation, as well as classical security concerns. This description, however, concentrates on the "security" aspects of museum protection.

Museums differ from other facilities and institutions in that they do not lock their assets away in vaults. They hang them on the walls. In fact, they invite everyone to approach and sometimes even touch them. Museums are primarily educational institutions and the educational mission often comes into conflict with the protective mission in so far as the need to display objects that might best be protected by being locked in a safe is concerned.

Museums also have a concern for conservation of the displayed object. While it might seem to be a conflict for a museum to display a $100 million work of art on the wall and not place it safely in a vault each night out of concerns that moving it might cause harm, this is the type of conflict that constantly exists in the museum setting. Security practitioners who intend to work in the museum security field must reconcile this conflict if they are to be successful, for there is one reality in providing security for a museum. The reality is that the security practitioner will often have to adapt his or her protective measures to the "rules of the game," and the rules of the game for working in a museum say that museum objects *WILL* be displayed, studied, shipped, and placed in jeopardy as part of the museum's mission. The most frequent reason for failure of museum security managers is the insistence upon protecting the museum by conventional means and an inability to work within the framework of a museum setting.

It is as though the museum's governing board says to the security manager:

Our objects are precious and valuable. But they are only valuable if we can use them for education and enjoyment. If we lock our objects away in a vault and display reproductions, their true value will be lost and they will be wasted. The artist or creator of the object intended them to be seen and enjoyed. So it is worth the risk to place these often irreplaceable objects on display. Now you go out there and don't let anything happen to them!

The task of the museum security manager is to make every effort to work within the framework of the museum where objects will, by their nature, be in jeopardy. A good museum practitioner will provide creative solutions to museum security problems so that the precious objects are protected.

There are the other rules of the game, too. Often, museum security managers face problems unique to museums. Recommendations to place precious paintings behind protective glazing may be met with objections that doing so will change the color balance of light, affect the scholarly study of the object, or result in intolerable glare to the viewer. Recommendations to affix a sensor to the back of a picture will surely result in objections based on conservation principles universal worldwide, as it is common museum practice to not touch even the canvas backing on a picture with anything other than an acid-free white cotton glove. Recommend running wires to each picture for an alarm system and you soon learn that most museums are "changing environments" and the whole row of pictures will move 3 feet to the left, only to move 4 feet to the right a month later as new works are hung. Practitioners who recommend alarming or sprinklering a historic house museum soon learn the realities of "aesthetics" or "historic fabric." More than one major national historic site will not allow any exterior lights at night so as not to disturb the authentic feel of life in the 18th century without electricity. Many lack electricity to power alarms. Most will not allow holes to be drilled for alarm wires — even when the holes are in attics or closets, out of public view. Attics and closets are just as historic to the preservationist as walls and ceilings. Surface running of wires is also out of the question due to the impact on historic fabric, or how the house appears visually. Even in modern museums, the building is often a work of art created by a contemporary architect master. The placement of motion detectors or cameras is often unacceptable.

The security practitioner faces many problems and he or she must overcome them if security is to be provided. While the basic principles of security apply to museums, how they are applied and what tools are used to solve security problems will depend upon the skills and creativity of the practitioner. In one museum you may have to develop an expertise for protecting objects in display cases, while in another you protect two-dimensional works hung on walls. Move to a new job and you may find that your "collection" is stored in specimen jars containing alcohol. Now even your collection has become a fire hazard to your building! In another type of museum like the huge Smithsonian Institution you will protect everything from the Hope Diamond to animal specimens roaming a game preserve. In addition to classical museums, many libraries and archives have museum collections and displays. Even corporations are developing corporate art collections, often without any consideration to specialized security.

It is not unusual for major art museums to display a quarter-billion dollars in value in only one gallery. The largest art theft in U.S. history involved 12 objects valued at $200 million, probably carried out of the building in one load by two men. A recent art exhibit in Europe easily topped a billion dollars in value. The entire contents of the exhibit could have fit inside a mini-van.

There are about 6,500 museums listed in the directory of the leading museum professional association, the American Association of Museums. Of these, only about 500 have a security professional above the guard level in charge of their security and on-site. Many have a non-professional such as a registrar or building manager in charge of security, but most of the major museums do have full-time professional security management.

The American Society for Industrial Security (ASIS) has a Standing Committee on Museums, Libraries and Archives. The American Association of Museums (AAM) has a security committee, as well. The leading conference on museum security is the *National Conference on Museum and Cultural Property Securrity* sponsored by Smithsonian Institution in Washington, DC, and it is held each February. While there are no "standards" on museum security, the leading publication to guide museums in establishing a security program is *The Suggested Guidelines in Museum Security* (published by ASIS), which was adopted by both of the previously mentioned committees in 1989-1990 and are requirements of many museum insurers. The guidelines are intended to be a "minimum common denominator" of security for all museums in North America. Such a de facto standard is necessary because museums regularly borrow and lend valuable objects to one another, and it is desirable to have a measure of security when engaging in such activity.

The major elements of good museum security are: access control, parcel control, and internal security. If you can control who comes and goes and where they go once inside, and if you can control what is carried in and what is carried out, and if you can hire honest employees and keep them honest, your museum will be relatively secure.

Museum access control is often difficult. It involves admitting individuals with different levels of security clearance to different areas of the building. Access is also controlled by time of the day. For example, a conservator (the person in charge of protecting the physical well-being of the collection from such hazards as humidity, temperature, dirt, etc.) may find it necessary to have access to storage 24 hours per day, while the access for the curator (the person actually in charge of the collection) can be restricted to business hours. Problems with access control come when museums are requested to provide access to visiting scholars who wish to study for long periods of time in collection storage. The tendency of the museum is to grant such scholarly requests because sooner or later every museum needs such acccss to the collection of another museum, but a substantial portion of museum thefts have occurred as a result of dishonest scholars or staff (including several dishonest security officers), so such unrestricted access can no longer be permitted. Access control is maintained via conventional methods such as locks, alarms, sign-in procedures, identification (ID) cards, visitor badges, and guards. Museums often have extensive alarm systems using saturation or near saturation motion detection. This is due to the fact that the best way to "break in" to a museum is not to break in at all, but to come in during normal operating hours and stay behind after closing. Museums using extensive motion detection can pick up the movement of a "stay behind" immediately.

Museum parcel control not only involves the removal of collection objects in employee lunch boxes, museums are also equally concerned about the razor blades or spray paint that can come into the museum, since vandalism is a serious problem in most museums. Parcel control is maintained by conventional means such as restrictions on the size and number of parcels that can be carried into the museum, alarms on objects and display cases, and parcel searches upon departure from the building.

Internal security is somewhat conventional, as well. Employees must be pre-screened and steps must be taken to keep them honest -- or identify those who have become dishonest since being hired.

To protect a museum it is important to know how a museum operates. For example, if you do not understand how museum objects are cataloged and tracked on paper, you cannot know how they can be stolen by manipulation of the paper trail. The easiest way for an employee to steal from a museum is to simply manipulate the records. Therefore, safeguards need to be worked into the registration system to avoid this, particularly as museums computerize their collection records.

Since the security manager is often responsible for other aspects of protection, he or she often serves as a "troubleshooter," looking for problems before they occur. Since museums are constantly in a state of change due to the changing nature of exhibits, he or she must know how construction and renovation will impact on security and fire protection. It is not unusual for security managers to review new construction blueprints, for example, to look for water mains running through high-value collection storage or phone or electrical panels, which might require regular service access, located inside high-security storage rooms.

Museum security practitioners need to know about the following specialty areas of security: display cases, burglar and fire alarms, motion detection, key control and retrieval, line security between the museum and the central station, fire protection and suppression (said to be the most devastating threat to museums), historic fabric, museum aesthetics, wireless technology (used increasingly to alarm objects), how art and collection thefts occur, museum conservation, disaster planning, training, and policy development. The limited resources of many museums results in the security manager being a "one-man band." He or she will not have a training officer or a technician except in the larger institutions, so these skills are important.

Museum thefts are primarily crimes of opportunity but there are a growing number of thefts that are well-planned daylight thefts. One recent theft involved a team of criminals using an electric screwdriver to dismantle a case and remove many large objects in broad daylight. While nighttime break-ins are relatively rare, as are daylight robberies, they do occur. The threat from visiting scholars and employees is very real.

Most museum objects of low value, such as historic artifacts, are never recovered and are stolen by "collectors" or souvenir hunters. Lower-value art is most often stolen for re-sale, while masterpieces are stolen for the purpose of extorting the insurer to get the object back. Most museum vandalism involves several categories of damage. They are: damage to historic buildings and artifacts by collectors who want a piece of the "real object," such as a piece of Babe Ruth's uniform or a chip of Plymouth Rock; damage to modern art that is not understood or appreciated by the viewer; damage to art that is irresistibly touchable, such as acrylic or textiles; damage to sexually explicit art (some people can't resist drawing in body parts on nudes); or the signing of pictures by individuals who, for some strange reason, find it interesting to do so. "Political art and artifacts" are always in jeopardy. During the Iranian hostage crisis a traveling exhibit of Persian objects was in danger, and during the Polish hostilities and while a Vatican collection under the control of a Polish Pope traveled in the U.S., special precautions were taken. When a title card on an object in the Alexander the Great exhibition incorrectly referred to Alexander as being Greek, nationalists in his Macedonian homeland threatened the museum showing the art.

Whether you are protecting a museum containing baseball cards or Rembrandts, it is a good idea for the museum security professional to learn about the collection being protected. There is a tendency in the museum field for museum "professionals," as museum staff call themselves, to look closely at the credentials of anyone lacking a PhD in art history, anthropology, history, botany, or whatever degree best serves the institutions. Museums are academic institutions and many entry-level PhD's earn about the same as senior security guards, so senior staff expect a great deal from their "overpaid" security managers. There is a tendency to expect security personnel to move about "gracefully" within this environment if one is to be successful. Having a basic knowledge of the impressionist school of painting would not be a bad idea for a museum security manager in an art museum with an impressionist collection. Since museums are academic institutions, practitioners are required, more so than in other industries, to communicate effectively both verbally and in writing.

Museums often sponsor and stage special events. It is not unusual for museums to offer evening viewing hours, hold formal wine and cheese openings (opening night parties to kick off fund-raising events or new exhibits), or to hold lectures in their auditoriums. Many larger museums are affiliated with or actually house schools and colleges, and some house professional theaters or performing arts centers. Many museum buildings have faculty or staff offices requiring after-hour access. Some even find it necessary to hold lectures or college classes in high-value, high-density collection storage. The mixed use of space provides another dimension to the problems museum security managers face.

The changing nature of museums and the seasonal aspects of exhibit staging make it necessary to employ a large and changing staff of security guards. Many museums operate with a core of full-time professionals and supplement gallery protection with part-time seasonal personnel. This compounds the training, scheduling, and recruitment aspects of museum security, and is a constant drain on security management and support resources.

Probably the most creative aspect of museum security involves the ability of the security manager to adapt technology not intended for museum protection to suit his or her needs. The museum market is small and not directly targeted by manufacturers of security products. Few, for example, make alarms specifically for protecting pictures or motion detectors attractive enough for use in an historic house museum. Successful museum security managers will keep up with the market and with technology, and will be able to adapt equipment to solve their unique problems. While there are strict rules governing what we may and may not do in protecting museums, all of the problems are surmountable. All we have to do is think creatively.

Steven R. Keller, CPP

N

NATIONAL CRIME INFORMATION CENTER (NCIC)

NCIC is a nationwide, computerized information system dedicated to serving criminal justice agencies -- local, state, and federal. The NCIC goal is to help these agencies perform their duties by providing a readily available computerized filing system of accurate and timely criminal justice information. For NCIC purposes, "criminal justice information" is defined as "information collected by criminal justice agencies that is needed for the performance of their legally authorized and required functions."

The NCIC serves criminal justice agencies in the 50 states, District of Columbia, Commonwealth of Puerto Rico, U.S. Virgin Islands, and the Royal Canadian Mounted Police in Canada. The full development of state computerized systems is strongly urged so that NCIC, which complements these systems, can become fully effective. It is through these state systems that NCIC becomes largely available to all criminal justice agencies.

NCIC provides virtually uninterrupted operation, 24 hours a day, 7 days a week. The Federal Bureau of Investigation (FBI) funds all computer operations in FBI Headquarters, including all equipment, programming, and personnel costs.

In addition, the costs of communication lines and modem costs from Washington, DC, to state and federal computer centers are borne by the FBI. Although the NCIC is operated by the FBI, approximately 70% of NCIC usage is by state, local, and other federal agencies.

An NCIC Advisory Policy Board recommends general policy to the FBI director with respect to the philosophy, concept, and operational principles of the NCIC. The board is composed of 30 representatives from criminal justice agencies throughout the United States, thereby providing the users a voice in the overall management of the system.

NCIC's day-to-day management responsibilities are shared with a single state agency in each state, referred to as an NCIC Control Terminal Agency, as well as with Federal Service Coordinators in federal agencies serviced

by the system. These agencies and coordinators train, audit, and generally oversee terminal locations within their jurisdictions.

In addition, they provide feedback to the FBI for improving operations and implementing enhancements. Without this assistance, the FBI could not easily manage NCIC access by the more than 30,000 terminals servicing over 60,000 agencies across the nation.

NCIC records are stored in 12 separate files: Stolen Vehicles, Stolen Articles, Stolen and Recovered Guns, Stolen License Plates, Stolen Securities, Stolen Boats, Wanted Persons, Missing Persons, Unidentified Persons, Foreign Fugitives, and U.S. Secret Service Protection.

The Interstate Identification Index subsystem also provides access to criminal history records maintained in the Identification Division and state identification bureaus.

Federal Bureau of Investigation

Source Public Affairs Pamphlet. (Federal Bureau of Investigation, U.S. Department of Justice, Washington, DC, 1992).

NATIONAL CRIME SURVEY (NCS)

The NCS is a survey of victimization in the United States conducted by the Bureau of Census and supported by the Bureau of Justice Statistics (BJS). The survey is conducted twice per year and consists of interviews of persons in a nationally representative sample of American households. Data collected by the Bureau of Census are analyzed by BJS, which publishes numerous reports describing the nature and level of criminal victimization nationwide.

The NCS project began in 1979 in response to an evaluation by the National Academy of Sciences and a recommendation of the National Criminal Justice Information and Statistics Service, the predecessor of the BJS. The NCS is widely regarded as an objective and critical measure of the impact of crime on American citizens.

Bureau of Justice Statistics

Source Public Affairs Pamphlet. (Bureau of Justice Statistics, U.S. Department of Justice, Washington, DC, 1992).

NATIONAL HIGHWAY TRAFFIC SAFETY ADMINISTRATION

The National Highway Traffic Safety Administration (NHTSA) was established as a separate organizational entity in the Department of Transportation in March 1970. It succeeded the National Highway Safety Bureau, which had previously administered traffic and highway safety functions as a constituent organizational unit of the Federal Highway Administration.

NHTSA's programs are authorized under three major laws: the National Traffic and Motor Vehicle Safety Act; Chapter 4 of Title 23 U.S.C.; and the Motor Vehicle Information and Cost Savings (MVICS) Act. The first law provides for the establishment and enforcement of safety standards for vehicles and associated equipment and the effectuation of supporting research, including the acquisition of required testing facilities and the operation of the National Driver Register (NDR).

Title 23 U.S.C., Chapter 4, provides for coordinated national highway safety grant programs to be carried out with the states, together with supporting highway safety research, development, demonstration, and highway safety education and information programs. An amendment to this law, enacted in October 1982, authorized a program of alcohol safety incentive grants to the states to reduce traffic safety problems resulting from persons driving while under the influence of alcohol.

The administration has assigned high priority to several highway safety programs of special interest to state and local law enforcement agencies, such as police traffic services, drunk driving, motor vehicle occupant restraint usage, emergency medical services, and traffic records.

The third law provides for the establishment of low-speed collision bumper standards, consumer information activities, diagnostic inspection demonstration projects, and odometer regulations. An amendment established the secretary's responsibility for the administration of mandatory automotive fuel economy standards, which was delegated to NHTSA.

National Highway Traffic Safety Administration

Source Public Affairs Pamphlet. (National Highway Traffic Safety Administration, U.S. Department of Transportation, Washington, DC, 1992).

NATIONAL INSTITUTE OF JUSTICE

The National Institute of Justice (NIJ) supports basic and applied research into crime, criminal behavior, and crime prevention. Programs are evaluated for their impact on crime control and on the performance of the criminal justice system. Experimental programs are funded to test the effectiveness of different approaches to law enforcement and criminal justice problems. A wide range of information is available for distribution to interested individuals and organizations through NIJ's National Criminal Justice Reference Service.

Following termination of the Law Enforcement Assistance Administration (LEAA) in 1982, the Justice Assistance Act of 1984 re-authorized and re-structured the Department of Justice's program of assistance to state and local criminal justice agencies.

The Office of Justice Programs (OJP) coordinates the activities of and provides staff support to the Bureau of Justice Statistics, National Institute of Justice, and Office of Juvenile Justice and Delinquency Prevention. The support services include consolidated budget development and financial management, personnel, civil rights compliance, and congressional and public affairs activities. In addition, OJP administers the Public Safety Officers' Benefits program, the Prison Industry Certification program, and the Regional Information Sharing Systems program.

National Institute of Justice

Source Public Affairs Pamphlet. (National Institute of Justice, U.S. Department of Justice, Rockville, MD, 1992).

NATIONAL INSTITUTE ON DRUG ABUSE (NIDA)

NIDA is a federal agency created by Congress under the Drug Abuse Office and Treatment Act of 1972. It began operating in 1974 to provide a coordinated response to the growing enigma of illicit drug use. Prior to NIDA, the federal drug effort was scattered across many agencies, financial support for grassroots treatment programs and drug-related research was plagued with uncertainty, and conflicting policy aims often produced confusion.

With NIDA's inception the various federal drug programs were in large measure consolidated into a single agency.

NIDA is organizationally a part of the U.S. Department of Health and Human Services. It is associated with counterpart agencies in the areas of alcohol abuse and mental health under the Alcohol, Drug Abuse, and Mental Health Administration (ADAMHA), within the Public Health Service. The vast majority of NIDA's funds are funneled to state and community-based programs in the form of grants and contracts.

John J. Fay, CPP

Source Fay, J.J., The Alcohol/Drug Abuse Dictionary and Encyclopedia. (Charles C. Thomas Publishers, Springfield, IL, 1988).

NAVAL INTELLIGENCE

The term "naval intelligence" is used to describe the formal organization that collects, produces, and disseminates intelligence information of naval interest. The naval intelligence organization is headed by the Director of Naval Intelligence (DNI), who is responsible to the Chief of Naval Operations (CNO). The CNO is required by Navy regulations to "collect, evaluate, and disseminate all types of intelligence information required within the naval establishment."

The Office of Naval Intelligence has historically been associated with all aspects of U.S. Navy intelligence. Over the years, this has included the naval attaché system, naval intelligence postgraduate and language schools, amphibious intelligence, air intelligence, fleet intelligence centers, operational intelligence, commerce and travel, photographic intelligence, scientific intelligence, security policy, telecommunications, censorship, counterintelligence, and investigations.

Naval Investigative Service

The Naval Investigative Service (NIS) maintains a worldwide organization to fulfill investigative and counterintelligence responsibilities.

Organizationally, NIS consists of a headquarters located in Suitland, Maryland; various field commands called Naval Investigative Service Offices (NISOs), each of which is under a commanding officer; and subordinate operating units called Resident Agencies. There are about 110 NIS units, including the various headquarters and field commands, both afloat and ashore.

Field-element locations are determined by workload requirements. Daily tasks include the conduct of criminal investigations for and the provisions of counterintelligence support to the Navy Department and the shore commands and operating forces. NIS collects, analyzes, and disseminates information of internal-security significance to Navy and Marine Corps commands.

Office of Naval Intelligence

Source Public Affairs Pamphlet. (Office of Naval Intelligence, Department of the Navy, Washington, 1992).

NAVAL INVESTIGATIVE SERVICE

The Naval Investigative Service (NIS) is a centrally directed, largely civilian, worldwide organization responsible for conducting criminal investigations and counterintelligence operations for the Department of the Navy.

NIS special agents are the successors of the operatives and agents who served as part of the Office of Naval Intelligence (ONI) in World War I. ONI's responsibilities grew in the years that followed World War I and, in 1939, President Franklin D. Roosevelt directed ONI to investigate Navy cases relating to sabotage, espionage, and subversive activities.

During World War II, ONI's mission continued to expand to include personnel security inquiries, war fraud cases, and other intelligence-related activities. Later, the investigations of other felonious crimes was added to the mission of ONI.

After World War II, a small group of civilian special agents was retained and their jurisdiction was extended by the Secretary of Navy. When the United States entered the Korean Conflict in 1950, a major build-up of the civilian special agent corps began.

The name Naval Investigative Service (NIS) was adopted on February 4, 1966, to distinguish the Navy's investigative service from the rest of ONI.

Unlawful acts by or against Department of the Navy personnel (including civilian employees and contractors) that result in property damage, financial loss, or serious personal injury carry the additional threat of impairing the Navy's ability to effectively carry out its mission. Criminal detection and investigation, therefore, are important responsibilities and account for the majority of the work done by the NIS.

In an age of rapidly advancing technology, the protection of classified naval information from unauthorized disclosure is vital to national security, as is the safeguarding of naval material from damage or destruction. The role of the NIS in this regard is a dual one: to assist the Navy and Marine Corps in protecting its assets, and to apprehend those who would allow them to be compromised.

Counterintelligence, therefore, is the business of protecting naval information from espionage, naval personnel against subversion, and Navy installations and equipment from sabotage. The NIS special agent is authorized, for that purpose, to use various measures against organizations hostile to the interests of the United States. (In the United States, NIS counterintelligence activities are coordinated with the Federal Bureau of Investigation; overseas they are coordinated with the Central Intelligence Agency.)

Assassination, kidnapping, and hostage taking are hazards faced by American military personnel at some overseas bases and diplomatic posts, and sometimes by foreign visitors to the United States. NIS special agents are frequently called upon to help prevent such acts by providing Protective Service Details (PSDs).

Overseas, NIS works closely with the security agencies and police forces of the host countries. In the United States, NIS works closely with the counterpart local, state, military, and federal law enforcement and intelligence agencies.

Naval Investigative Service

Source This Is the NIS. (U.S. Naval Investigative Service, The Department of the Navy, Washington, DC, 1992).

NEGLIGENCE

Negligence is the doing of that thing which a reasonably prudent person would not have done, or the failure to do that thing which a reasonably prudent person would have done in like or similar circumstances. It is the failure to exercise that degree of care that reasonably prudent persons would have exercised in similar circumstances.

Tort law has attempted to refine the concept of negligence by subdividing it into narrower categories. Degrees of care and degrees of negligence are closely related but separate approaches in refining negligence. Degrees of care is the amount of care that is reasonable for a given situation. It depends on various factors, including the relationship between the parties and the nature and extent of the risk inherent in that situation. For example, transporting school children requires a higher degree of care than hauling watermelons.

Degrees of negligence embraces the idea that negligence may be classified as slight or gross. This has been a persistent theme in tort law and criminal law. There are statutes in which the term negligence is preceded by some adjective, such as "slight" or "gross." In most cases, the statute applies only to a particular situation or activity.

Slight negligence is the failure to exercise great care. It is not a slight departure from ordinary care. Technically, it is the failure to exercise greater care than the circumstances would ordinarily require. On the other hand, gross negligence is something more than ordinary negligence but only in degree. It is less than recklessness, which is a different kind of conduct showing a conscious disregard for the safety of others. The distinction is important since contributory negligence is not a defense to wanton misconduct but is to gross negligence. A finding of reckless misconduct will usually support an award of punitive damages whereas gross negligence will not.

Contributory negligence is an act or omission amounting to want of ordinary care on the part of a complaining party, which, concurring with the defendant's negligence, is the proximate cause of injury. Contributory negligence generally applies to a condition of employment, either express or implied, with which an employee agrees that the dangers of injury ordinarily or obviously incident to the discharge of required duties will be at the employee's own risk.

Negligent conduct is an element of various tort causes of action. The components of the cause of action for negligence are: (1) a duty owed by the defendant to the plaintiff, (2) a violation of that duty by defendant's failure to conform to the required standard of conduct, (3) sufficient causal connection between the negligent conduct and the resulting harm, and (4) actual loss or damage. The plaintiff's contributory negligence, if any, will reduce or defeat a claim. In many jurisdictions, contributory negligence is a defense to be pleaded and proved by the defendant, but in some jurisdictions the plaintiff must allege and prove his freedom from contributory negligence as a part of his case.

Negligent conduct can be alleged in an employer's hiring practices. The term *negligent hiring* refers to a concept that holds an employer directly liable for an employee's harmful conduct after the employer failed to exercise reasonable care in hiring the employee. Although similar to respondeat superior, this concept can extend to situations that occur outside of the workplace. For example, assume that during working hours a security officer makes a date with a female employee. During the date (off the employer's premises and during non-working hours) the officer rapes the other employee. She learns that the employer was aware that this same officer had assaulted other women whom he had met at work, but had hired him anyway without warning her or other female employees. The employer can be charged with failure to exercise reasonable care in the hiring and retention of a dangerous employee.

The "reasonable person" concept applies objective standards of reasonableness when judging whether conduct is negligent. The law does not make special allowance for the particular weaknesses of a person acting negligently. Conduct that creates an unreasonable risk of harm is no less dangerous because the actor lacked the capacity to conform to an acceptable level of performance. While it may seem unfair to hold some people to standards they cannot always meet, it would be more unjust to require the innocent victims of substandard conduct to bear the consequences.

The standard is usually stated as reasonable care, ordinary care. or due care, and is measured against the hypothetical conduct of a hypothetical person, i.e., the reasonable human of ordinary prudence. Such a person is not the average or typical person, but an idealized image. He is a composite of the community's judgment as to how the typical citizen ought to behave in circumstances where there is a potential or actual risk of harm. The reasonable person is not perfect or infallible. He is allowed mistakes of judgment, of perception, and he may even be momentarily distracted. Above all, he is human and prone to errors, but such errors must have been reasonable or excusable under the circumstances.

The law of negligence distinguishes between liability for the consequences of affirmative acts (misfeasance) and liability for merely doing nothing (nonfeasance).

Almost any inaction can be characterized as misfeasance if the court is so disposed, and often inaction is substantially the equivalent of active misconduct. The failure to repair defective brakes may be seen as active negligence. A fundamental question is whether there is a sufficient relationship between the one who failed to act and the one injured as a result.

A common example is the absence of a duty to go to the aid of someone needing help (when such help is not required by some pre-existing status or relationship). A person skilled in administering cardiopulmonary resuscitation is not required to aid a victim needing such assistance, unless the person happens to also be a paramedic hired for that purpose.

Duties of affirmative action that would not otherwise exist may be voluntarily assumed. It is commonly held that one who freely undertakes to render aid to another assumes a duty to act with reasonable care, and once the duty is assumed it may not be abandoned. This rule is thought by many to have the negative effect of discouraging rescuers.

John J. Fay, CPP

Source Fay, J.J., Butterworths Security Dictionary: Terms and Concepts. (Butterworth-Heinemann, Boston, 1987).

NEGLIGENT HIRING/RETENTION

Employers have incurred liability for negligent hiring and/or retention of employees who engage in criminal acts at and outside the workplace. Liability for a negligent hiring may depend upon the background investigation conducted by the employer; the position for which the employee is hired; and the risk of harm or injury to third parties, including clients, customers, and other employees.

Because a thorough background investigation is necessary to minimize employer liability, competing privacy interests between the employee and employer must be balanced.

Overzealous information collection, or use of information that is not job-related, should not be permitted to disqualify an applicant or terminate an employee. To protect employee privacy interests, a specific job-relatedness should be shown by the employer for a background investigation. This should safeguard the employer's concern of avoiding negligent hiring claims and preserving employment privacy interests. To establish a negligent hiring, the following must be proven:

•The existence of an employment relationship;

•The employee's incompetence;

•The employer's actual or constructive knowledge of this incompetence;

•The employee's act or omission causing the injuries; and

•The employer's negligence in hiring or retaining the employee as the proximate cause of the injuries.

These criteria are important because they show that the employer was put on notice of the responsibility to evaluate the employee's qualifications.

Negligent hiring claims have arisen against employers when a young boy was sexually assaulted and murdered by a former inmate employed as a carpentry instructor [1]; a tenant was raped by a housing inspector [2]; a customer was fatally shot [3]; a customer was assaulted [4]; and a known forger was employed who engaged in illegal business activity [5]. The employer's duty to insulate himself from negligent hiring liability does not end once an applicant is selected. A continuing employer responsibility exists to retain only competent employees while onserving ongoing employment privacy considerations [6].

Kurt H. Decker

Sources

Decker, K., Employee Privacy Law and Procedures. (John Wiley & Sons, Inc., New York, 1987).

Decker, K., Employee Privacy Forms and Procedures. (John Wiley & Sons, Inc., New York, 1988).

Decker, K., A Manager's Guide to Employee Privacy Law, Procedures, and Policies. (John Wiley & Sons, Inc., New York, 1989).

Decker, K., The Rights and Wrongs of Screening. (Security Management, January, 1990).

Notes

1. *Henley v. Prince George's County*, 305 Md. 320, 503 A.2d 1333 (1986).

2. *Cramer v. Housing Opportunities Commission*, 304 Md. 705, 501 A.2d 35 (1985).

3. *Giles v. Shell Oil Corp.*, 487 A.2d 610 (D.C. App. 1985).

4. *Abbot v. Payne*, 457 So.2d 1156 (Fla. Dist. Ct. App. 1984).

5. *Pruitt v. Pavelin*, 141 Ariz. 195, 685 P.2d 1347 (1984).

6. *Welsch Mfg. v. Pinkerton's Inc.*, 474 A.2d 436 (R.I. 1984).

NUCLEAR REGULATORY COMMISSION

The Nuclear Regulatory Commission (NRC) regulates the civilian uses of nuclear materials in the United States to protect the public health and safety, the environment, and the common defense and security. This mission is accomplished through: licensing of nuclear facilities and the possession, use, and disposal of nuclear materials; the development and implementation of requirements governing licensed activities; and inspection and enforcement activities to ensure compliance with these requirements.

The NRC was created as an independent agency by the Energy Reorganization Act, signed into law October 11, 1974, which abolished the Atomic Energy Commission (AEC). The NRC, which took over the regulatory functions of the AEC, formally came into being on January 19, 1975. The Energy Research and Development Administration, also created by the Energy Reorganization Act, took over the other functions of the AEC and is now part of the Department of Energy.

When he signed the legislation, President Gerald Ford said, in part:

The highly technical nature of our nuclear facilities and the special potential hazards which are involved in the use of nuclear fuels fully warrants the creation of an independent and technically competent regulatory agency to assure adequate protection of public health and safety. NRC will be responsible for the licensing and regulation of the nuclear industry under the provisions of the Atomic Energy Act. This means that

NRC will be fully empowered to see to it that reactors using nuclear materials will be properly and safely designed, constructed and operated to guarantee against hazards to the public from leakage or accident. NRC will also exercise strengthened authority to assure that the public is fully safeguarded from hazards arising from the storage, handling and transportation of nuclear materials being used in power reactors, hospitals, research laboratories or for any other purpose.

Basic Functions

The NRC carries out the three basic functions that follow. In addition, the NRC is responsible for licensing the export and import of nuclear facilities, equipment, and materials.

Licensing. The agency reviews and issues licenses for the construction and operation of nuclear power plants and other nuclear facilities, and it licenses the possession and use of nuclear materials for medical, industrial, educational, research, and other purposes. Regulatory authority for nuclear materials licensing has been transferred to 29 states under the NRC's Agreement States Program.

Inspection and Enforcement. The NRC conducts various kinds of inspections and investigations designed to ensure that licensed activities are conducted in compliance with the agency's regulations and other requirements, and enforces compliance as necessary.

Regulatory Research and Standards Development. The NRC is mandated by law to conduct an extensive confirmatory research program in the areas of safety, safeguards, and environmental assessment. In addition, the agency establishes regulations, standards, and guidelines governing the various licensed uses of nuclear facilities and materials.

Nuclear Regulatory Commission

Source Fact Sheet/USNRC. (The Nuclear Regulatory Commission, Washington, DC, 1992).

NUCLEAR SECURITY: COMMERCIAL APPLICATIONS OF NUCLEAR TECHNOLOGY

The development of commercial applications of nuclear technology was initiated by the Atomic Energy Act of 1954 (Public Law 83-703), which declared it would be the policy of the United States that:

a. the development, use, and control of atomic energy shall be directed so as to make the maximum contribution to the general welfare, subject at all times to the paramount objective of making the maximum contribution to the common defense and security; and

b. the development, use, and control of atomic energy shall be directed so as to promote world peace, improve the general welfare, increase the standard of living, and strengthen free competition in private enterprise.

To effectuate these policies, the stated purposes of the Act are to provide for:

a. a program of conducting, assisting, and fostering research and development in order to encourage maximum scientific and industrial progress;

b. a program for the dissemination of scientific and technical information, subject to appropriate safeguards, so as to encourage scientific and industrial progress;

c. a program for Government control of the possession, use, and production of atomic energy and special nuclear material, ...

d. a program to encourage widespread participation in the development and utilization of atomic energy for peaceful purposes to the maximum extent consistent with the common defense and security and with the health and safety of the public;

e. a program of international cooperation to promote the common defense and security and to make available ... the benefits of peaceful applications of atomic energy ...; and

f. a program of administration which will be consistent with the foregoing policies and programs, with international arrangements, and with agreements for cooperation, ...

The Act established the Atomic Energy Commission (AEC) and authorized it to "... establish by rule, regulation, or order such standards and instructions to govern ... (uses of nuclear material) ... as the Commission may deem necessary or desirable to promote the common health or to minimize danger to life or property." The Act also authorized the AEC to "prescribe such regulations or orders as it may deem necessary ... to guard against the loss or diversion of any special nuclear material ... to prevent any use of disposition thereof which the Commission may determine to be inimical to the common defense and security ... to govern any activity ... including ... the design, location, and operation ... in order protect health and to minimize danger to life or property."

The Energy Reorganization Act of 1974 (Public Law 93-438) created the U.S. Nuclear Regulatory Commission (NRC) and what is now the U.S. Department of Energy (DOE) out of the AEC and assigned the commercial regulatory responsibilities to the NRC. Protecting the public health and safety has been the primary basis for AEC and NRC regulatory activities.

To accomplish its regulatory responsibilities, the NRC develops rules and regulations that are set forth in Title 10, "Energy," of the Code of Federal Regulations, publishes implementing guidance in Regulatory Guides and other documents called NUREGs, licenses acceptable activities, and ensures that the activities do not endanger public health and safety through a variety of inspection programs and enforcement actions.

Many of the guidance documents, although written for NRC's licensees, could provide useful information for anyone interested in developing a sound security program. Some of these documents are listed in the Sources section at the end of this article.

International Programs

The Nuclear Non-Proliferation Act of 1978 (Public Law 95-242) was enacted by Congress to provide for more efficient and effective control over the proliferation of nuclear explosive capability and the direct capability to manufacture or otherwise acquire such devices. Such proliferation was considered a grave threat to the security interests of the United States and to the continued international progress toward world peace and development.

Since many "non-nuclear" nations were eagerly seeking sources of energy, the Act encouraged reliable sources of supply for reactors and fuel to nations that adhere to effective non-proliferation policies. The NRC licenses the export of nuclear materials, equipment, and technology intended for use in peaceful nuclear activities with the concurrence of the U.S. Department of State, and in consultation with the U.S. Arms Control and Disarmament Agency and the U.S. Department of Defense (DOD). Such export licenses are granted only where adequate physical security measures will be maintained, and where existing safeguards assure non-proliferation and environmental protection. Section 202 of the Act requires the DOE and the NRC "to provide training in the most advanced safeguards and physical security techniques and technology, consistent with the national security interests of the United States, to nations that have acquired or may be expected to acquire nuclear materials or equipment for peaceful purposes."

The Treaty on Non-Proliferation of Nuclear Weapons gives the International Atomic Energy Agency (IAEA) of the United Nations, which is based in Vienna, Austria, authority to inspect worldwide commercial applications of nuclear materials to ensure that such materials are not diverted and used in military applications.

Many NRC employees, on a leave of absence, work for the IAEA. The IAEA had been relatively unknown to the American public until its efforts to determine whether Iraq was developing nuclear weapons became prominent news after the 1991 Persian Gulf War.

Design Basis Threat

The Department of Defense and DOE, along with the NRC, have each developed a design basis threat to be used in the design of security systems for the protection of nuclear technology and materials under their responsibilities. The adversary attributes in each case are based upon

ACTIVITY/FACILITY	ADVERSARY ACTION OF CONCERN
Nuclear Power Reactors	Radiological Sabotage
Fuel Fabrication Facilities	Theft or Diversion
Non-Power Reactors	Theft, Diversion or Sabotage as deemed appropriate by the NRC
Materials in Transit	Primarily theft or diversion of unirradiated material. Also, radiological sabotage or dispersion of radioactive material

intelligence data and the resource to be protected. In all three instances, the specific size of the adversarial force is classified information. The NRC's unclassified design basis threat is characterized as several persons. Obviously, the loss of a nuclear weapon has the most serious consequences, which is reflected in DOD's design basis threat.

There are two adversary actions of concern to the NRC: radiological sabotage and theft or diversion of a formula quantity of strategic special nuclear materials (i.e., 5 kilograms of material enriched [1] to 20% or more in the U-235 isotope). For radiological sabotage, which is any deliberate act that could directly or indirectly endanger the public health and safety by exposure to radiation, the NRC has established the following:

(i) A determined violent external assault, attack by stealth, or deceptive actions, of several persons with the following attributes, assistance and equipment: (A) Well-trained (including military training and skills) and dedicated individuals, (B) inside assistance which may include a knowledgeable individual who attempts to participate in a passive role (e.g., provide information), an active role (e.g., facilitate entrance and exit, disable alarms and communications, participate in violent attack), or both, (C) suitable weapons, up to and including hand-held automatic weapons, equipped with silencers and having effective long range accuracy, (D) hand-carried equipment, including incapacitating agents and explosives for use as tools of entry or for otherwise destroying reactor, facility,

transporter, or container integrity or features of the safeguards system, and (ii) An internal threat of an insider, including an employee (in any position).

Note that there is both an "external" threat and an "internal" threat. For theft or diversion of a formula quantity of strategic special nuclear material (the type and quantity that could be used to fabricate a nuclear weapon), the NRC modified the previous design basis threat to increase the number of adversaries from several persons to a small group capable of operating as two or more teams. The insider threat is increased from a single insider to a conspiracy.

The NRC staff continually reviews intelligence information concerning the threat and keeps the characterization of the design basis threat current and transmits a threat advisory to the licensees where appropriate.

Types of Activities and Facilities

There are several different types of activities and facilities licensed by the NRC. Each type presents a different threat to public health and safety. Thus, different security program objectives are developed for each type of activity or facility. Because of differences in engineered safety systems that achieve certain other objectives required by the NRC's regulations, there is a plethora of security program designs.

Security Philosophy and Requirements

The general fundamental NRC philosophy is that as the quantity and enrichment of nuclear material is reduced, the concerns for theft, diversion, and sabotage are also reduced. Accordingly, NRC security requirements are tailored to the degree of the adverse consequences associated with a given threat.

For example, nuclear power reactors and activities associated with a formula quantity of nuclear material are required to provide high assurance of success against the applicable design basis threat. For activities and facilities associated with less than a formula quantity, the required measures are reduced in stages. For example, moderately significant nuclear materials require measures that would minimize the possibility for unauthorized removal of the material and facilitate the location and recovery of missing material. In this case, early detection and response is considered important so intrusion alarms and a capability to immediately respond and assess unauthorized penetrations or activities are required. Nuclear materials of lesser significance require measures similar in purpose to those measures required for moderately significant materials, except that detection of loss can be after the fact since thefts at several widely dispersed facilities would be needed to obtain a significant quantity of material to fabricate a weapon. Furthermore, the material is in a form that would require specialized equipment, processing, and knowledge before it would be usable, all factors that would lead to successful recovery.

The fundamental design philosophy used in the nuclear industry, no matter if it is for a critical engineered safety system (e.g., the reactor coolant system, containment facility, instrumentation, emergency core cooling system, or electrical distribution system) or a security system, is both defense in depth and redundancy. For example, before an adversary can reach an objective at a nuclear power reactor or a fixed site where a formula quantity of nuclear material is used or stored, they will encounter at least two barriers and two alarm systems separately monitored in two separate alarm stations.

The NRC's regulations concerning security are set forth as performance requirements. For example, a fuel fabrication activity involving a formula quantity of nuclear material is required to provide a security system with performance capabilities that:

• Prevent unauthorized access of persons, vehicles, and materials;

• Provide for authorized access and ensure detection of and response to unauthorized penetrations of specified areas;

• Permit only authorized activities and conditions, and permit only authorized placement, movement, and removal of nuclear material within or from specified areas;

• Provide a response capability to ensure the above capabilities are achieved, and that adversary forces will be engaged and impeded until off-site assistance forces arrive;

• Include a security system design with sufficient redundancy and diversity to ensure maintenance of the performance capabilities; and

• Include a testing and maintenance program to ensure the effectiveness, reliability, and availability of the physical protection system, such that any defects in activities and devices will be promptly detected and corrected.

To ensure that the general performance objectives and performance capabilities are achieved, the NRC also requires that the physical protection system must, for example [2];

• Detect attempts to gain unauthorized access or introduce unauthorized material across area boundaries by stealth or force by using:

1.   Barriers to channel persons and material to entry control points and to delay any unauthorized penetration attempts by persons or materials sufficient to assist detection and permit a response that will prevent the penetration; and

2.   Access detection subsystems and procedures to detect, assess, and communicate any unauthorized penetration attempts by persons or materials at the time of the attempt so that the response can prevent the unauthorized access or penetration.

• Detect attempts to gain unauthorized access or introduce unauthorized materials by deceit using:

1.   Access authorization controls and procedures to provide current authorization schedules and entry criteria for persons, vehicles, and materials, including under emergency conditions. The access authorization system must be designed to accommodate the potential need for rapid ingress or egress during emergency conditions and situations that could lead to emergency conditions; and

2.   Entry controls and procedures to verify and assess the identity of persons and materials before permitting entry, and to initiate response measures to deny unauthorized entries.

•Detect unauthorized activities or conditions using:

1. Controls and procedures that establish current schedules of authorized activities and conditions in defined areas;

2. Detection and surveillance subsystems and procedures to discover and assess unauthorized activities and conditions and communicate them so that response can stop the activity or correct the conditions. Detection aids must include two continuously manned alarm stations designed to be resistant to acts intended to prevent directing the response to an alarm, at least one of which must be in a bullet-resisting environment;

•Establish a security organization to:

1. Provide trained and qualified personnel to carry out assigned duties and responsibilities; and

2. Provide for routine security operations and response to emergencies and contingencies.

•Establish a plan for responding to safeguards contingency events.

•Provide equipment for the security organization and facility design features to:

1. Provide for rapid assessment of contingencies;

2. Provide for response that is sufficiently rapid and effective to achieve the objective of the response; and

3. Provide protection for the assessment and response personnel so that they can complete their assigned response duties.

•Provide communications networks to:

1. Transmit rapid and accurate security information among on-site forces for routine security operations, assessment of a contingency, and response to a contingency; and

2. Transmit rapid and accurate detection and assessment information to off-site assistance forces.

•Ensure that a single adversary action cannot destroy the capability of the security organization to notify off-site response forces of the need for assistance.

•Provide for:

1. Testing and maintenance of systems and components, including the employment of compensatory measures in the event of failure or degraded performance;

2. Comprehensive program audits every 12 months;

3. Responses by on-site security personnel and local law enforcement authorities, including exercises to ensure adequate capability and the development of contingency plans; and

4. Background investigations, psychological evaluations, drug testing, training, and behavioral observation to ensure that personnel are reliable and trustworthy, and safely and competently perform their duties.

The foregoing is supported with performance requirements relating to the qualifications and training of security personnel. In addition, to cope with a spectrum of potential contingencies, NRC licensees are required to establish and maintain a Safeguards Contingency Plan, which includes the data, criteria, procedures, and mechanisms necessary to effect the actions and specifies the individual or organizational entity responsible for each decision and action.

Loren L. Bush

Sources

Atomic Energy Act of 1954 (Public Law 83-703).

Energy Reorganization Act of 1974 (Public Law 93-438).

Nuclear Non-Proliferation Act of 1978 (Public Law 95-242).

NUREG-0320, Intrusion Alarm System. (Nuclear Regulatory Commission, Washington, DC, February, 1978).

NUREG-0484, Vehicle Access and Control Planning Document. (Nuclear Regulatory Commission, Washington, DC, November, 1979).

NUREG-0485, Vehicle Access and Search Training Manual. (Nuclear Regulatory Commission, Washington, DC, November, 1979).

NUREG/CR-0508, Security Communication Systems for Nuclear Fixed Sites. (Nuclear Regulatory Commission, Washington, DC, April, 1979).

NUREG/CR-0509, Emergency Power Supplies for Physical Security Systems. (Nuclear Regulatory Commission, Washington, DC, October, 1979).

NUREG-0674, Security Personnel Training and Qualification Criteria. (Nuclear Regulatory Commission, Washington, DC, May, 1980).

NUREG-0907, Acceptance Criteria for Determining Armed Response Force Size at Nuclear Power Plants. (Nuclear Regulatory Commission, Washington, DC, February, 1983).

NUREG-0908, Acceptance Criteria for the

518   Nuclear Security: Commercial Applications of Nuclear Technology

Evaluation of Nuclear Power Reactor Security Plans. (Nuclear Regulatory Commission, Washington, DC, August, 1982).

NUREG-1045, Guidance on the Application of Compensatory Measures for Power Reactor Licensees. (Nuclear Regulatory Commission, Washington, DC, January, 1984).

NUREG/CR-1467, CAS-SAS Operational Work Station Design and Procedures. (Nuclear Regulatory Commission, Washington, DC, November, 1980).

NUREG/CR-1468, Design Concepts for Independent Central Alarm Station and Secondary Alarm Station Intrusion Detection Systems. (Nuclear Regulatory Commission, Washington, DC, November, 1980).

NUREG/CR-5721, Video Systems for Alarm Assessment. (Nuclear Regulatory Commission, Washington, DC, September, 1991).

NUREG/CR-5722, Interior Intrusion Detection Systems. (Nuclear Regulatory Commission, Washington, DC, October, 1991).

NUREG/CR-5723, Security System Signal Supervision. (Nuclear Regulatory Commission, Washington, DC, September, 1991).

Part 73, Physical Protection of Plants and Materials, Title 10, Energy. (Code of Federal Regulations, 10 CFR Part 73, U.S. Government Printing Office, Washington, DC, 1992).

Regulatory Guide 5.44, Perimeter Intrusion Alarm Systems, Revision 2. (Nuclear Regulatory Commission, Washington, DC, 1980).

Regulatory Guide 5.66, Access Authorization Program for Nuclear Power Plants. (Nuclear Regulatory Commission, Washington, DC, June 1991).

Notes

1.   Enrichment is a process of artificially increasing the proportion of the fissionable isotope U-235 to the fertile U-238. An efficient design of a nuclear weapon requires material enriched more than 90%. Fuel for nuclear power reactors is enriched to 3-5% and would not cause a nuclear detonation.

2.   Space permits only a limited sampling of the requirements. For more details, see 10 CFR Part 73.

O

OPERABLE OPENING SWITCHES

Operable openings are doors, windows, gates, hatches and other openings that present opportunities for gaining access to restricted areas. Hence, operable opening switches are devices that detect unauthorized passage through the openings. The switches used for this purpose are called balanced magnetic, magnetic, mechanical contact, and tilt switches.

An important consideration in selecting a switch for a door is to evaluate the durability of the door itself. Doors range in durability from very substantial vault doors to easily defeated hollow-core doors. The durability of the door is an important consideration because an intruder who cuts or breaks through to gain access will not cause the operable opening switch to activate for the simple reason that the door remains in the closed position.

Another consideration with respect to doors and windows is that they should be tight against their surrounding frames in order to prevent false alarms induced by wind, rain, and similar innocent forces.

A switch used to protect a door should be installed along the top near the leading edge, if possible. In this position there is greater displacement between the door and door frame than at any other position. Because the displacement is greater at the leading edge, the sensitivity of the switch is not as critical in terms of alarm position, and the switch will not be as sensitive to small displacements if the door is slightly loose.

Balanced Magnetic Switch

A balanced magnetic switch is an assembly containing a balanced magnet usually mounted to a door or window frame. The electrical contact is a three-position reed switch mounted adjacent to an adjustable biasing magnet in the assembly. The reed switch is held in the balanced or center ("no alarm") position by two interacting magnetic fields. The primary field is generated by the balancing magnet and the secondary field by a small biasing magnet. As long as the magnetic

field remains balanced around the reed switch, the contacts remain in contact in the center position. If the balancing magnet is moved or the magnetic field is unbalanced by an external magnet, the switch becomes unbalanced and initiates an alarm.

Contact Switches

The magnetically and mechanically activated contact switches are commonly used to detect the opening of protected doors and windows. Magnetic contact switches are similar to balanced magnetic switches only inasmuch as they are both magnetically activated.

The magnetic contact switch is a two-position reed switch held either in an open or closed position when the door or window is closed. The no-alarm contact position depends on whether the signal monitoring circuit recognizes an open or closed contact to initiate an alarm. In a circuit where the monitor recognizes an open circuit as an alarm condition, the switch would be installed such that when the door is opened the switch opens and initiates an alarm.

In general, the contact switch is mounted on the door frame with the activating magnet mounted on the door.

Mechanically activated contact switches are available with either push-button or lever actuators. Pushbutton switches are normally mounted in the hinge side of the door frames. When a door is opened, the switch contact opens and initiates an alarm.

Since the pushbutton switch is mounted on the hinge side of the door frame, the position where the door is opened far enough to initiate an alarm is critical. If the door can be opened far enough to slide a thin piece of metal over the pushbutton, the switch can be defeated. Lever-type switches are usually installed on a door frame along the top of the door so that when the door is closed it holds the switch closed. When the door is opened, the lever opens, allowing the switch contacts to open.

Robert L. Barnard

Source Barnard, R.L., Intrusion Detection Systems. (Butterworth-Heinemann, Boston, 1982).

OPERATIONS SECURITY

Background

Operations security (OPSEC) is an assessment and analytical process for determining whether an organization's routine activities expose its proprietary information. The process was developed by the U. S. Air Force during the latter half of the Vietnam War. The Air Force found that its B-52 bombing raids against jungle encampments were ineffective. Although targeting intelligence was good and bombs were delivered on the targets, post-bombing assessments revealed very few enemy casualties. A critical examination of the bombing program disclosed two weaknesses: the routine pre-mission coordination data were being intercepted, and enemy spotters at sea and on land were reporting the direction of incoming bombers. The enemy's intelligence units were able to determine the targets and evacuate the areas before arrival of the aircraft.

The OPSEC process is well established in the Department of Defense and its contractor organizations as a safeguard for protecting classified government information. In the business sector, where competitive intelligence is intensifying on a global scale, OPSEC programs are gaining favor by security managers.

How the Process Works

OPSEC concepts are generic and applicable to many different situations. Each situation, however, will require a bit of tailoring to fit the circumstances of the situation and the needs of the organization. Five steps are involved.

Step 1.   Identify those bodies of information (paradigms) that must be protected.   The paradigms might include strategic planning, financing, marketing, production, and so forth. Rank each paradigm by cost. Consider the cost it would take a competitor to develop the bodies of information independently.

Consider also the cost of business opportunity that would be lost by disclosure of the information.

Step 2. Within each paradigm, set up groups as follows:

•Group 1: Information That Is Already Public. In this group would be any information that has been released outside of the company. Examples would include advertisements, public notices, general correspondence, bid offerings, requisitions, and so forth.

•Group 2: Information That Cannot Be Protected. In this group would be information that is worth protecting but cannot be absolutely protected because it must necessarily be communicated outside of the company. Examples would be litigation details communicated to the company's outside legal counsel, financial details released to lenders, scientific details provided to research consultants, marketing ideas turned over to advertisers, and payroll details contained in computer bases available to electronic data processing (EDP) contractors.

•Group 3: Information Critical to the Organization That Must Be Protected. In this group would be a relatively small mass of truly essential information that, if exposed, would hurt the organization. Examples would include trade secrets, proprietary processes, research and development results, marketing plans, and similar types of information that must be carefully safeguarded. An important protective caveat for Group 3 information is to not dilute security effectiveness by placing too many types of information into this group.

Step 3. Within each of the information types placed into Group 3, identify the keystone details. What is a keystone detail? It is a finite piece of protectable information essential to understanding the paradigm. Examples of keystone details would be a manufacturing plant's planned output, a new or modified product, a stock offering, a Chapter 11 filing, bid figures, the geographical areas of interest to oil explorers, and so on.

Step 4. Assess the security controls afforded to each keystone detail and make enhancement recommendations where appropriate. Keystone details can be thought of as taking one or a combination of four forms:

•Knowledge that is information residing in the minds of people. It cannot be locked up or erased.

•Documents are tangible representations of information. They include written materials, photographs, films, video, and audio tapes.

•Data are pieces of information recorded on magnetic or optical media that cannot be read without the aid of a mechanical interpreter.

•Applications include models, prototypes, and samples. Keystone details at this level of evolution may not be protectable.

Each form of keystone detail will exhibit unique migration characteristics and will therefore call for unique security controls. The security manager must know the migration paths and establish barriers to prevent disclosure.

Step 5. Analyze the effect of proposed or existing security controls upon the use of information. This analysis will be in the nature of weighing the cost and the inconvenience of security against the benefits of preventing loss associated with undesired disclosure. Analysis must be done periodically, at least once per year.

G.H. Zimmer, CPP

ORGANIZATION: FORMAL AND INFORMAL ORGANIZATIONS

The Formal Organization

The organizational structure of a department within a company will reflect a logical division of tasks and clear lines of authority and responsibility, both within the department specifically and within the organization generally.

An organizational chart is two-dimensional. On the horizontal plane the chart indicates the division of work, and on the vertical plane it defines levels of authority or rank. Although all charts will reflect these two dimensions, organizational charts will differ in widely varying degrees. This is true because organizational structures are the products of the human intellect reacting to the pressures of efficiency, economy, politics, and other variables.

The reality of organizational structure is the inevitable conflict between rational and irrational issues. It might, for example, be rational, based on considerations of productivity and cost, to place a particular function in Department A. Irrational issues, such as internal politics and opportunities for personal advantage, might dictate placing the function in Department B. Conflicts and compromise are not alien to organizational charts.

A tendency in structuring an organization is to build functions around people rather than determine the functions and then fill in the boxes with qualified individuals. This tendency can be overwhelming to the security manager who is told that he has no choice except to use existing humanpower to carry out work functions, even when the functions have changed in response to crime threats. Because the existing humanpower is unequal to the real tasks, the security manager assigns functions on the basis of ability rather than genuine work needs. When this occurs, it is testimony to the questionable belief that it is easier to tinker with the organization's structure than to change the abilities of people.

The ideal structure is developed by identifying the functions that are necessary to the attainment of organizational goals, arranging the functions into logical work units, and staffing the work units with qualified people.

An organizational chart depicts what is called the formal organization, i.e., an arrangement of people designed and formally approved by management to operate in furtherance of organizational goals. An equally important arrangement of people is called the informal organization.

The Informal Organization

The informal organization also sets goals, has a hierarchy of functions and of people, and communicates among its members. Its goals and functions, however, will often conflict with those of the formal organization, and leadership will rest on qualities other than the assignment of authority from management.

Some organizational theorists will refer to the informal organization as the "real" organization. A more accurate description might be to call it the engine that makes the formal organization work. Although the engine has been designed by management to work in particular ways, it is cantankerous and chooses to chug along in other ways that are at least tolerable and in some instances superior to expectations.

Examples of activities by the informal organization in a security organization include subordinates taking problems around the supervisor to employees they believe are better qualified even though lacking in authority, obtaining supplies and equipment through channels not officially approved, and operating "grapevine" communication networks.

Informal organizations, and there may be many within a single formal organization, exist whether management likes it or not. Some are quite obvious and even demand recognition, albeit unofficial, and others are subtle and may not even be known to or understood by management. Enlightened managements have recognized and even encouraged informal organizations. A security manager would make a serious mistake to ignore them because their opposition to security could defeat even the best practices.

Charles A. Sennewald, CPP

Source Sennewald, C.A., Effective Security Management, 2nd Edition. (Butterworth-Heinemann, Boston, 1985).

ORGANIZATIONAL BUREAUCRACY: A NEW VIEW OF THE SECURITY FUNCTION

Since the early 20th century depiction of the organization as a *bureaucracy* by the German academician, Max Weber, we have seemed to be stuck with the concept of placing every function into little organizational "boxes" or "bureaus." Worse, this concept assumes that all of these functions stand alone. Since Weber's work was "discovered" in the post World War II era in the United States, *bureaucracy* became the conventional wisdom for creating order out of the chaos of that re-building period for the economy. The computer era, which started about this time, seemed to be a perfect environment for the concepts of compartmentalization and bureaucracy -- and they were avidly accepted through the 1950s, 1960s, and 1970s.

Toward the end of that period (aided by the "professionalization" movement in security that was spearheaded by the American Society for Industrial Security), some of the more enlightened sectors of business, industry, and government began to address security as an important issue. Many attempted to move the functions of security (now enhanced with titles such as loss prevention and assets protection) up to the departmental level. This added stature to the "security manager" or "loss prevention manager"

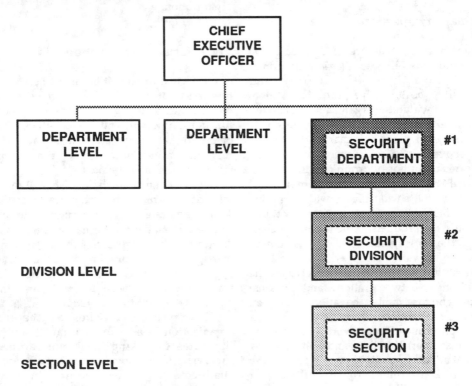

Security as Usually Found on a "Conventional" Organization Chart

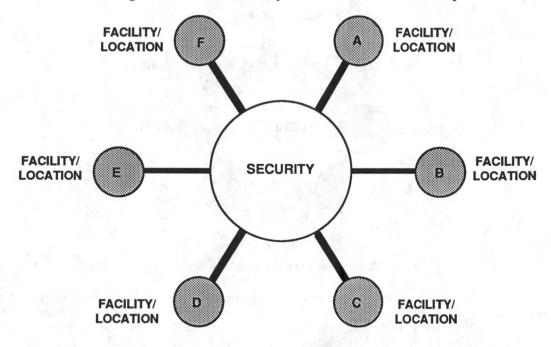

Security as a Facilities/Location Model

in dealing with the rest of the organization. Security became a function that attracted attention at the executive level as increased rates of riots, labor stoppages, executive kidnapping, terrorist activities, and sky-jacking filled the front pages of the papers and the evening television news.

The 1980s saw the beginnings of a movement toward the recognition of the role of security in protecting the "bottom line" of business and governmental activities.   Increased fraud, embezzlement, computer crimes, drugs in the workplace, employee theft, and massive litigation surfaced and were recognized as more harmful than "common crime."

The American Society for Industrial Security had grown to over 26,000 members by the end of the 1980s and the role of security had expanded to touch every other function in any organization. The knowledge required of a security manager and his/her people had, by necessity, also expanded to meet the multi-faceted challenges to be faced in the 1990s.   As the 1980s drew to a close, security operations began to *cost* more and more, while faced by the difficulty of justifying its *value* despite the cost. How do you measure something that *doesn't happen* because a good security/loss prevention program stopped it from happening? In a period of cut-back economics,

security is too often the first victim of the corporate ax -- especially when it is viewed as a neat little "box" that can easily be removed without disturbing the other "boxes" on the organizational chart.

The function of security, especially in tight times, really needs to be moved up to the departmental (policymaking) level and viewed as a "profit center" by protecting the assets, personnel, and profits of *all* the departments. The development of policy and procedures to protect assets and personnel throughout the organization should clearly include the "department director for security/loss prevention" or similar title. Clearly, how the role of security is seen in an organization is often determined by where it is placed on the organization chart. How far the security program is placed from the level of policymaking can determine the amount of impact security can have on the operations (and profits) of the company. The security manager should try to have as much access to the presidential/vice presidential level as possible. In most companies, the security function is typically placed at one of three levels:

•The Department Level. With direct access to the top policy-making levels of the company, this is the most preferred level for security as it

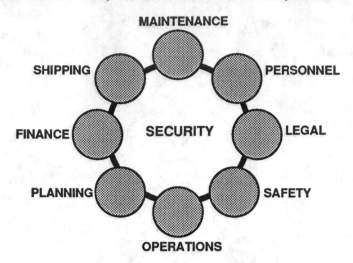

Security as a Departmental Partner

gives the security function a high profile and professional status.

• The Division Level. The security manager reports to a functional director. It is a common arrangement, but its effectiveness is very dependent upon what functional department security reports to.

• Any Level Below Division. This seriously impacts security's ability to make real impact upon policy. It is the least preferred.

How do you sell this concept to management? This article presents new ways to look at an organization and the clear importance of security when seen from those viewpoints. It is very important to view security as a "central" part of an organization, rather than as a "box" buried deeply in some unrelated department.

If management thinks of the security program as another major *profit center*, one that impacts every facility and functional location in the company by prevention of losses and protection of assets, management develops a much different appreciation of the security task. Shown is a view of security as it impacts on a company with six different (generic) facilities/locations and how security is the *only* factor that is constant and connects with each of them.

Security can also be seen as the function that most impacts on *every* department. Whether a company is a large multinational giant or a small local business, the company's various departments have vulnerabilities and risks that can only be properly assessed and addressed by the security function, in concert with those

departments. This concept applies whether the security program is operated by one-person or a massive force of employees and equipment. Once management is able to see that security programs and their personnel can touch every department in the company, security's role can easily be enhanced and enlarged to handle many of the departmental concerns that cannot be addressed by the 9 a.m.-to-5 p.m. staff and employees. This simple concept is why the overlapping areas can be explored as a total team effort. *Maintenance* needs to know where to find potential problems, *Shipping* needs to be on the lookout for fraud and waste, *Personnel* needs to follow up on allegations by employees, *Safety* needs to have all the eyes it can find, etc. All the other departments (in addition to the samples shown) should find *value* in the security task if they are shown how it can be achieved. This is yet another preferred way to describe the security function to management, regardless of the type of company or its size. Security managers ignore this at their peril.

Security is also made up of a large number of activities that impact on every aspect and program in the company. In a large company, these may be accomplished by different sections of the security program; in a small company, they may all be accomplished by the same person. The important point to remember is that these activities impact *all departments* and *all facilities/locations* in each kind and size of company. It is much more sensible to have these activities centralized under a single security program than to spread such activities throughout

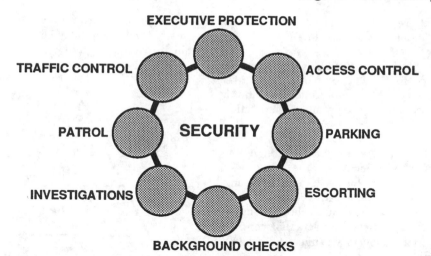

Security as Seen in Regard to Activities

the company with the resulting duplication and inefficiency. This simple concept is yet another way to show the overlapping that occurs when you view security as a *central factor*, rather than a peripheral area in a company's operations and activities. Explored as a total team effort for a company, security becomes a vital part of all facilities, departments, and activities. It is also critical that the policies and procedures for the security program also rely on the corporate and departmental policies, and procedures from which they have been derived.

Now that we have discovered how to view security from at least three new viewpoints, we can free our minds from the inflexible "wiring diagrams" of bureaucratic organizational concepts developed for the early 1900s and adopted wholesale from the 1950s to the 1980s. We can find new ways to demonstrate how loss prevention, personnel security, safety, assets protection, access control, and all the other functions lumped together under "security" are linked with every facility, function, and operation in the organization. Viewed this way, security becomes an integral part of every facility, department, and activity -- instead of a separate "box" fighting for the same shrinking budget.

Clifford E. Simonsen, Ph.D., CPP

Source Simonsen, C.E., Breaking Bureaucratic Bonds. (Security Management, September, 1991). Reprinted in part with permission from Security Management magazine, American Society for Industrial Security, Arlington, VA.

ORGANIZATIONAL PRINCIPLES

The structure of an organization is nothing more nor less than a vehicle for the realization of a purpose. An organization's structure cannot think or act, yet it is absolutely essential to the accomplishment of work because it facilitates the orderly activities of people.

A soundly designed organization will operate in agreement with five widely accepted principles:

•Work should be divided logically.

•Lines of authority and responsibility should be clear and direct.

•Span of control should be within manageable limits.

•Unity of command should prevail.

•Work should be focused on organizational goals.

Each of these principles has meaningful application within a security organization.

Logical Division of Work

The manner of apportioning work influences productivity. Work can be divided along five lines: (1) purpose, (2) process or method, (3) clientele, (4) time, and (5) geography.

Purpose. The most common way to divide work is by purpose. In a security department, for example, work can be apportioned along two general lines: a loss prevention unit to prevent and reduce losses, and an investigation unit to investigate reported losses and make recommendations to prevent recurrence.

Process or Method. Work can be organized according to the method of work. Examples might be a security communications section, a polygraph section, or a pass and identification section.

Clientele. Work can be divided according to the people served or affected by the work. An example here would be the background screening personnel who deal only with prospective and new employees, store detectives who concentrate on shoplifters and dishonest clerks, or contract security account managers who interact daily with client representatives.

Time. A 24-hours-per-day security officer operation is an example of work that is arranged according to time, and within that daily span there may be other work assignments that are influenced by time, for example, an officer who escorts departing employees to their automobiles during certain hours of the early evening shift.

Geography. The security officers at the garage entrance, the main lobby, the loading dock, and the warehouse are geographically dispersed. Each has a well-defined territory to be protected. The security supervisor for these locations also has a territorial responsibility that encompasses all of the separate locations. Job titles like shop foreman, district supervisor, regional manager, and national director denote work that is arranged according to geography.

Clear Lines of Authority and Responsibility

When jobs are plotted out on paper their interrelationships often take on the appearance of a pyramid. At the top of the pyramid is the one or few persons who direct the affairs of the organization, and at the base are the many who carry out directions that flow from the top. The height of the pyramid will be determined by the number of authority levels. A tall pyramid will have several or many levels and a flattened pyramid will have only a few. Authority levels can be seen in positions that go by such names as chairperson, president, vice president, director, deputy director, manager, assistant manager,

supervisor, and so forth. When the organization has many levels, there may be smaller pyramids within the overall pyramid.

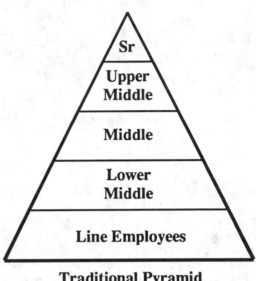

Traditional Pyramid

Flattened Pyramid

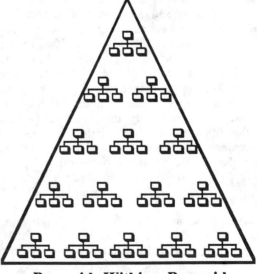

Pyramids Within a Pyramid

Ideally, the authority and the responsibility of each job in the organization will be clearly defined. A variety of documents can serve as the defining tools, e.g., formal delegations of authority, financial memos, spending authorizations, position descriptions, and mission statements. For security officers, authority and responsibility documentation can be general instructions that establish authority rules concerning searching, detaining, and the use of force, and responsibility can be spelled out in special instructions and post orders.

Span of Control

This principle holds that there is a limit to the number of subordinates who can be supervised effectively by one person. The optimum span of control will vary according to the degree of sophistication of the interactions between supervisor and subordinates. At higher levels, the number of supervised subordinates will be fewer than at lower levels where work tends to be less sophisticated. The maximum number of employees who can be effectively supervised at the base of the pyramid is commonly understood to be 12.

Unity of Command

The principle of unity of command says that an employee should be under the direct control of one immediate superior. This idea means also that only one supervisor should be involved in overseeing single tasks or functions, even when more than one subordinate performs the tasks or shares the functions.

Violations of the principle of unity of command occur more by oversight than design. When the principle is violated, it is usually because someone has failed to properly delineate the supervisor's role.

Achievement of Organizational Goals

The final principle has to do with focusing on the rationale or purpose of the organization. The business organization in a macro sense will have a focus on profit-driven goals, and in the micro sense a department within the organization will have a focus on achieving goals that contribute to the larger purpose. For example, an organization in the manufacturing industry might focus on goals to enhance profit while departments within the organization might have complementary goals that deal with cutting costs and increasing sales. The security department's contribution to the bottom line could be reducing loss.

Almost all organizations practice what is called "management by objectives" (MBO). The MBO approach assigns to employees and to groups of employees one or more objectives that are specific, measurable, and directed at achievement of the organization's goals. Performance appraisal, promotion, compensation, bonuses, and the like are strongly influenced by how well the objectives are met.

Charles A. Sennewald, CPP

Source Sennewald, C.A., Effective Security Management, 2nd Edition. (Butterworth-Heinemann, Boston, 1985).

P

PARKING RAMP SECURITY

With the ever increasing security problems occurring in parking ramps, security managers are constantly looking at new ways to improve their physical security systems. Usually there is no single remedy to answer all the problems.

There are pros and cons to all current working systems and new systems that are being considered for increased protection. As an example, many parking ramps and parking lots are increasing the number of security officers both to tour the facility and provide escort service for customers. Although this practice should reduce greatly the perceived dangers that many customers have regarding parking ramps, it is a very costly remedy that would be impossible to accommodate during peak hours. Also, when touring a ramp, it is impossible for a guard to be everywhere at once.

Another suggested remedy is adding closed-circuit television (CCTV) equipment. Although this remedy is less costly than guard service, it cannot provide the same feeling of security that is projected by a live guard. Also, it is virtually impossible for CCTV equipment to cover every nook and cranny of a parking ramp due to columns and low-ceiling height.

A third remedy is to install a sound system in the parking ramp proper to monitor activities that go beyond what would be considered the normal threshold level. Some systems are effective in stairwells, elevator lobbies, and in elevators where noise can be monitored easily. Sound systems are, however, somewhat limited in the ramp proper where noises made by cars and birds can be confusingly similar to the human scream.

An alternative remedy might be a combination of security officers, CCTV, and sound systems. Additional security personnel working on a structured guard tour and connected by radio to a security center would provide deterrence, rapid response, and an enhanced comfort level for customers.

To enhance the performance of the security personnel, strategically located CCTV camera locations should be provided and monitored by personnel at the central site. From this location, a second tour of the facility can be accomplished quicker and provide backup to the live guard tour. This puts security personnel in every location of the ramp every minute of the day.

By adding a sound system, a method is created in which the central monitoring personnel can both monitor remote activities and respond immediately to let people know that help is on the way. If this sound system is augmented with the public address announcements regarding security at a regulated time interval, it would further enhance the security comfort level of customers.

In addition to the previous remedies, certain things such as painting walls, increasing the lighting, and videotaping critical entrance and exit locations can add to the overall security.

On a final note, the owners and operators must be cognizant of the fact that liability and exposure is greater with a security system that is not working vs. having no security system at all. Whatever the decision, a structured check of new and existing systems performance should be done on a routine basis and system maintenance should be performed throughout its life.

Jack Morris

PARKING SECURITY

The control of parking is a major activity for most organizations. This responsibility is sometimes considered to be within the purview of the security function, and it is sometimes assigned elsewhere in the organization. The context of control does not always include protection. Some argue that parking control is not a true function of security and that it is a separate area of support services.

In any case, the protection of people and property within a parking area should be a responsibility of the security department. This protection responsibility includes preventive patrols, escorts, response to calls for services, investigation of security-related incidents, and closed-circuit television (CCTV) monitoring, when utilized as a component of the protection system. Providing protection to persons utilizing parking lots or parking garages accounts for a high percentage of the nation's security systems. According to the Bureau of Justice Statistics, approximately 10% of all reported rapes by strangers take place in parking lots or parking garages. Further, the American Trial Lawyers Association reports that approximately 20% of lawsuits for negligent security involve parking areas.

The parking accommodations of different facilities present unique control and protection problems. The one constant factor is that there is never enough parking space. The shortage of spaces is most acute on weekday afternoons when day-shift employees are still at work and the arriving second shift must find parking spaces. Once the day shift leaves, there is generally an abundance of parking spaces. Because the security department is generally responsible for enforcing parking regulations, it receives the brunt of employee, visitor, and patient dissatisfaction with the real or perceived lack of parking facilities.   Unfortunately, this dissatisfaction with parking has a direct negative effect on the image of the security department.

Types of Parking Areas

Parking areas can generally be categorized as street parking, surface (or grade) lots, freestanding structures, and structures that are physically connected to facilities. The recent trend favors connected structures, and some facilities are being built above existing parking structures. Security considerations and requirements will vary according to the type of parking area.

Although the application of security safeguards may vary from parking area to parking area, the objectives are the same: establish a user-friendly feeling and high perception of safety. The perception of good security and feeling of safety must be backed up by reality. In this respect, frequent patrols, high visibility of security officers, and availability of officers to provide assistance are essential.

Street Parking. Parking on side streets around the facility presents an interesting problem for the security program. This parking is on public property, and in a sense it is outside the realm of the organization's protection responsibility. In a practical sense, however, employees who are assaulted and vehicles that are broken into do affect the organization. Thus, it is not uncommon for security to escort employees or visitors off property. Security escorts should be restricted to a maximum of one block, and this restriction should be strongly upheld by the management. When security officers are more than one block

from the property, they are not providing visibility or surveillance for the facility. The escort service may help one person to the detriment of others.

Street parking can cause community relations problems for the organization in addition to protection problems. Neighboring homeowners generally resent cars parked along streets all day because they restrict homeowner use and bring increased pedestrian traffic and litter.

Surface Parking Lots. Surface parking lots are slowly disappearing from large and urban areas. The cost of land and the fact that many facilities are landlocked and cannot acquire additional property, generally results in the construction of parking structures when parking areas must be expanded or replaced. Security for surface lots generally consists of access control, fencing, lighting, security patrols, and observation posts. CCTV is not widely used for surface lots because of its low cost/benefit ratio.

In extremely large lots, emergency call stations should be installed.   Of specific importance in surface lots is that landscaping be placed and properly maintained to eliminate hiding areas, reduced visibility, and reduced lighting levels. Don't neglect the proper signage to indicate authorized parking, hours of operation, and trespassing signs, if appropriate.

Parking Structures. As land values increase and the available land around facilities decreases, parking structures become a cost-effective alternative to surface lots. Modern structures are designed to be user-friendly and produce a feeling of greater safety. Among the new design features are raised ceilings, increased lighting, bright colors, and legible signs.

Parking structures provide concentrated parking, but at the same time create new security problems.   Many potential problems can be eliminated or minimized through proper security design, which should begin with the first architectural drawing.   Architectural firms without security design experience should advise their clients of this and take steps to obtain expert security advice. The basic security considerations for parking structures include the following:

•The structure should provide the maximum span of vision on the parking levels and should eliminate interior support columns and dark corners.

•Lighting should comply with the standards of the Illuminating Engineering Society. Also, the Parking Consultants Council of the National Parking Association has established guidelines for minimum illumination in parking structures. It is important to have a clear understanding of the vertical height to which the standard is referring: Pavement level, 3 feet, or 6 feet above the pavement.   Many local light and power companies will provide lighting level measurements at little or no charge.   The installation of lighting should take into consideration the failure rate of the system. At any given time approximately 18-22% of the system may be inoperative, according to industry standards. Thus, the lighting standards should be exceeded by approximately 25% so minimum lighting levels are maintained during these failures.

A common method to counteract the effect of burned-out lamps is to use several lamps in one fixture. The interior of the structure should contain some light-colored surfaces (for example, supporting columns and walkway areas). Light-colored paint increases the effectiveness of lighting and conveys a feeling of security for those who use the facility.

•Stairwells and elevators should be enclosed in glass.

•Stairwells should open onto the facility's property, not the street.

•Emergency exit doors can be effectively alarmed as part of the access control system.

•Emergency telephones, or call stations, should be connected directly to the central security station or the facility's telephone operator. Call stations must be conspicuously marked in two different ways. First, they should be marked to be identifiable from great distances. Large signs may be needed within the structure to announce and point to emergency call stations. Second, the station should be prominently marked so callers can accurately describe their location. Some communications equipment shows the caller's location at the answering point; however, it is still desirable to indicate the location in the structure at the telephone.

•Openings on the ground floor large enough to allow people to climb through or to pass objects, such as car batteries, through should be eliminated.   Decorative wire mesh or other barriers can be installed that meet the security objective yet provide light and visibility.

•All entrances/exits should be capable of being closed during low traffic periods, including gates that prohibit pedestrians and vehicles from entering the structure.

•Crash bars should be installed on stairwell emergency exit doors.

•Frequent security patrols should be scheduled. The frequency will depend on the time of day, local crime rate, location, and other security safeguards that have been applied within the structure.

•Cashier booths should be placed outside the structure so cashiers can be afforded a better view of loiterers, stairwells, traffic, and activities in general .

•Entrances and exits should be placed so that they are accessed from within the property, rather than from a side street.

•Covert parking area surveillance posts should be provided. Ideally, there will be one or two posts on each level, allowing security to view any part of the structure.   One-way glass observation posts are generally used. All enclosed areas, such as equipment spaces and storage areas, provide an opportunity for observation posts with little additional cost. By simply including a small window, an added element of security can be achieved.

Cost overruns in construction seem to be a standard. When cost overruns occur, security is generally the target of cost cutting. Even when planned security applications are eliminated, the proper security design can accommodate later retrofitting at a favorable cost.

CCTV Monitoring

Many questions arise concerning the use of CCTV for parking security. The first question is whether a CCTV system is needed. Sometimes it is decided that an area should be monitored before the need has been established. The use of CCTV is somewhat prevalent in parking structures, yet many of these structures have various design elements that do not lend themselves to CCTV.

All CCTV systems require effective monitoring, regardless of the size of the system, and this is extremely difficult to achieve. If effective monitoring is in place, the reaction to monitored incidents is of equal importance. The response of security, police, or fire personnel must be quick and properly directed. CCTV is a protection tool to be used only by properly trained personnel.

Opponents of CCTV point out that it does not give directions, it does not generate people-to-people public relations, and it does not respond to incidents. The live monitoring or recording of an incident does little good without a quick response capability. In fact, CCTV may prove to be a liability rather than an asset. The argument that CCTV may help solve a crime is a poor justification for the system when the primary objective is to prevent the crime.

The cost of a CCTV system does not end with its purchase and installation. Systems require monitoring, maintenance, and replacement expenditures as an ongoing cost. A 20% failure rate of hardware can be expected in the first 24 months of operation. Maintenance may be required 24 hours per day, and weekend and off-hours are quite expensive. From a liability standpoint, equipment must be repaired immediately, or alternative security safeguards must be implemented until the problem is rectified.

Shuttle Service and Valet Parking

Some organizations that have been unable to acquire adjoining land on which to expand their parking facilities have instituted shuttle service. Suitable parking areas are sometimes available nearby but too far for users to walk. Shuttle buses have proved effective.

In the typical shuttle system, security department employees drive a passenger van between the parking lot and the facility during the early morning and late afternoon hours. When an employee needs to leave during the middle of a shift or is held over past the closing time of the lot, security is contacted and a special trip is made for that employee. The larger systems may have a continuous shuttle vehicle operating during the hours the site is operational.

Organizations have tried many incentives to entice employees to use off-site parking areas. Among these are the following:

•Comfortable waiting areas (heated and air-conditioned).

•Complimentary coffee, rolls, and morning papers.

•Coupons for free food in the company cafeteria.

•Weekly prize drawings.

•Car washes while the vehicle is parked for the day.

•Attended parking lots.

The main complaint of shuttle users is the waiting time. Thus, organizations must ensure that they have sufficient resources before embarking on a shuttle program.

The use of valet parking is not new, but it is growing. The shortage of convenient parking is the greatest stimulus to the valet parking system, but proponents also cite the marketing advantage of this program. Most facilities charge for valet parking; others offer the service free.

Organizations that undertake a valet parking program should provide adequate supervision, and they should review their insurance to determine whether they have the proper coverage. The hours of operation should be clearly stated, and the procedure for retrieving cars after hours should be established. Security often becomes involved in the after-hours retrieval of cars.

Types of Parkers

Those who use facility-provided parking can be divided into several distinct categories, including day-shift employees, afternoon-shift employees, night-shift employees, visitors, vendors, and service representatives. All have specific and individual needs that must be considered. The most common approach is to assign each category to a specific parking area.

During the day, the nearest parking is generally assigned to visitors, vendors, and service representatives due to their short-term use of parking space. Senior executives of the organization usually demand and receive special attention when it comes to parking.

Afternoon-Shift Employees. The afternoon-shift employees are the ones who feel the inadequacy of parking space because the day shift is still on duty when they arrive. A common solution is to designate a special "3 to 11" area (named for the hours of the afternoon shift), which is opened approximately an hour before the afternoon shift reports for work. Entry to this area is generally controlled by a security officer unless automatic controls are installed. This area, which is vacant during the morning hours, can also be used to accommodate people attending morning meetings, but must be tightly controlled to ensure that these temporary parkers have cleared the space by the required time.

The fact that afternoon-shift personnel return to their cars late at night presents special security vulnerabilities. For safety reasons, it is desirable that these employees park together. Maximum security officer coverage in the parking lots is advisable during late-night and early-morning shift changes.

Enclosed observation posts offer several advantages. Not only do they provide a shelter for security officers, but also they are another visible safeguard.

Late-Night Shift Employees. Late-night shift employees have many places to park and, left to their own options, may create a fragmented configuration. There should be a designated area for these employees, which is typically as close as possible to the designated night entrance(s). By concentrating these employees and their vehicles into a specific area, a maximum amount of protection for both the employees and vehicles can be provided.

Automated Controls

An automatic, card-activated gate is considered to be cost-effective for parking areas with as few as 20 spaces. Automatic gates with a minicomputer offer many control features, including the ability to set time parameters for card use, to invalidate a card at the output unit, and to provide data on the attempted use of invalidated cards. In addition, some systems render cards invalid once they have been used to enter the parking area and until they are used to exit. This feature, known as anti-pass back, prevents one card from being used by several people. Card-activated gates are predominantly used at the entry and exit points of parking areas; however, there are various applications where the gate is utilized to segregate a specific area internally within the area.

Traffic Flow and Space Allocation

In determining traffic flow and space allocation, the trend toward small cars is both an advantage and a disadvantage. When most cars were the same size, parking spaces could also be uniform.

This limited the number of available spaces, but it made space allocation a rather simple matter. Today, the size of the space needed for small cars and the width of the traffic aisles can be reduced. The problem is to determine how many spaces of each size are required at a given time for a particular parking lot or whether certain areas should be designated for all big cars or all small cars.

Not only are one-way traffic lanes with angled parking expedient, but they are also safer than straight, or 90 degree, parking. The difficulty of parking in a space angled 90 degrees and the excessive size of the traffic lanes required generally make this type of design unsatisfactory. When possible, the entrance and exit to the parking area should be separated.

During periods of low demand, it is recommended that certain parking lots, sections of lots, or parking structure floors be closed off. This improves the safety of people walking to or from their vehicles. Naturally, the closed areas should be those that are the greatest distance from the facility. The more concentrated the parking, the greater the number of people going to and from vehicles, which to some extent deters assaults, vandalism, and break-ins. In addition, by closing lots, the security patrol area is reduced, allowing a more concentrated preventive patrol.

Pay Parking

Recent trends have favored pay parking. When pay parking is the responsibility of the security department, security can be transformed from an overhead cost to an income-producing department. Some organizations completely fund their security operation from parking revenues. The outpatient and visitor parking areas produce the most revenue due to high turnover.

The method of collecting parking fees should be closely examined. For employee parking, a monthly fee can be deducted from the payroll checks at relatively little cost. The visitor lots can be controlled by automatic equipment, which has a high initial cost but can prove economical over a short period of time. The decision to use personnel to collect parking fees should be carefully evaluated because theft appears to be the rule rather than the exception. In addition, providing for accounting controls and backup personnel in case of absences proves much more costly than automatic equipment. When automatic equipment is used, stringent controls should be established regarding the collection of money from the machines, and these controls should be audited periodically.

Parking System Violators

Parking violators present a control problem. Fire lanes must be designated and patrolled to ensure that vehicles do not block the lanes, and lots must be checked to ensure compliance with the parking plan. Most security departments issue parking violation notices to help control illegal parking. Various other methods of increasing severity may be necessary to correct abuses. These methods include issuing city parking tickets, immobilization devices, and towing. The immobilization device, sometimes known as the boot, has proved effective in many parking control programs. It forces the violator to report as directed, and thus the organization can exert good control.

Warning letters and follow-up by department supervisors are common procedures for dealing with employee violators. In one system, the first violation earns the employee a warning notice, and subsequent violations result in successively higher fines, which are collected through automatic payroll deductions. This system works; however, strong administrative support is required.

Computers and Parking Control

The use of computers is becoming commonplace in the administration of parking control systems. Software programs are readily available that permit tracking of parking violations, and efficient issuing and control of parking permits. Most software programs are designed to run on IBM or a compatible personal computer (PC) using DOS. Local Area Network (LAN) versions are also generally available.

Once the data base of information is established, the various programs allow a multitude of search capabilities. In addition to helping manage the day-to-day program, the computer allows the periodic production of activity and planning reports.

Russell Colling, CPP

Sources

Kennedy, D., The Violent Crime Gender Gap. (Security Management, October, 1992).

Monahan, D.R., and T.F. Saemisch, Parking Structure Lighting. (The Parking Professional, December, 1990).

PARK POLICE

The U. S. Park Police, a unit of the National Park Service, Department of the Interior, is a uniformed police agency with full police and investigative powers in all areas administered by the National Park Service. In addition to its headquarters in Washington, DC, the force has a field office in New York City and one in San Francisco. The force also provides Regional Law Enforcement Specialists to the National Park Service Regional Offices for training and advisory purposes.

Several types of patrols are used to ensure visitor and park protection -- these include foot, cruiser, horse-mounted, marine, motorcycle, motor scooter, helicopter, and plainclothes patrols. In addition to routine crime patrol and protection, U.S. Park Police officers must also serve as hosts and information specialists to millions of visitors who visit force-patrolled park areas -- both in the nation's capital and in field office areas. The force also responds at the request of other governmental agencies as situations warrant.

U.S. Park Police

Source Public Affairs Pamphlet. (U.S. Park Police, National Park Service, Department of the Interior, Washington, DC, 1992).

PASSIVE INFRARED MOTION DETECTORS

Infrared motion detectors detect the body heat of thermal energy at the frequencies corresponding to the body temperature of 98 degrees F. They also detect changes in the background thermal energy caused by someone moving through the detector field of view and shadowing the energy emanating from the objects in the background. The field of view of an infrared detector is similar to the acceptance field of view of active motion detectors. With active detectors, energy within the acceptance field of view of the receiver or transceiver is received and sent to the signal processor. The field of view for infrared detectors is the area or areas in front of the detector that are in view of the detector's thermal sensor element.

Detecting changes in the background, radiant energy is usually the more sensitive mode of detection, depending on the radiation characteristics of the objects in the field of view of the detector. All objects with temperatures above absolute zero degrees Kelvin (-273 degrees C) radiate thermal energy; therefore, regardless of the temperature of the protected room, each object in the room emanates energy. The magnitude and frequency of the radiated energy depends on the absolute temperature and surface finish of the objects.

The characteristics of the background energy pattern depend on whether the objects in the detector field of view are dark or shiny, assuming they are all at the same temperature. Dark objects are more efficient radiators than shiny objects; therefore, a background of objects with different surface finishes will create a greater variation in the radiated thermal energy reaching the sensor when someone passes through the sensor's field of view than when the background is one constant surface. In general, the probability of detecting someone moving through a varying background will be higher than detecting the same person moving through a constant background. This is especially true in areas where the temperature is about 98 degrees F.

Thermal sensors are responsive to thermal energy with wavelengths between about 1 and 1,000 microns; however, the most popular detection range for infrared detectors is between 8 and 14 microns. The peak radiation for most objects at room temperature occurs at wavelengths of about 10 microns. In an indoor environment, the radiant energy of the exposed skin is also within the 8- to 14-micron wavelength. Clothing reduces the energy incident on the thermal sensor; however, in most applications the magnitude of the radiant energy is adequate for detection.

Thermistor bolometers and thermopile sensors are used to detect thermal energy in the infrared frequency range. Thermistor bolometers can detect radiant energy with wavelengths from the longest infrared to the shortest ultraviolet. Radiant energy impinging on the sensor raises its temperature, causing a change in resistance in the semiconductor oxide material. Infrared detectors using thermistor bolometers monitor the resistance to detect changes characteristic of someone entering the detector's field of view.

Thermopiles are multijunction thermocouples. Each thermocouple consists of a pair of thermoelectric junctions of dissimilar metals. One junction is shielded from the incident radiation and the second junction is blackened to improve absorption. The difference in the junction temperature between the two dissimilar metals produces an electromagnetic force (emf). Detectors using thermopile sensors monitor this emf to detect radiant energy changes in the detector field of view.

Robert L. Barnard

Source Barnard, R.L., Intrusion Detection Systems. (Butterworth-Heinemann, Boston, 1982).

PERFORMANCE APPRAISAL

Performance appraisal is the ongoing process of setting objectives and assessing individual and collective behavior and achievements during a finite period of time. It is primarily about counseling and feedback on ways to improve performance at an individual and team level, and the quality of work relationships. Performance improvement results from people being clear about priorities and objectives, what skills need to be enhanced, and which types of behavior can help to this end. This comes from open, positive, and constructive discussion between supervisors, individuals, and teams, and agreement on how to focus on doing the job better.

In the appraisal process, a security manager evaluates, coaches, counsels, and develops subordinates on a continuing basis throughout the reporting period, usually 1 year. In the conduct of these activities, the manager's performance is subject to appraisal, as well.

Setting Objectives

Near the close or at the very beginning of the reporting period, the manager and his direct subordinates, individually or as a team, meet for the purpose of setting performance objectives. Objective setting ensures that the manager and the people to be rated are in agreement as to what should be achieved.

The objectives are specific, measurable, relevant, and time-related. Although firm when formulated, they can be amended and supplemented throughout the reporting period. Objectives will vary according to the type of work involved, but will normally relate to business results and expected standards of performance. Objectives can also relate to personal development. For example, the security manager may encourage a subordinate to attain the Certified Protection Professional (CPP) designation. While attainment of an objective along these lines is not directly related to a specific work output, few can dispute the job relatedness of skills and knowledge acquired in pursuit of CPP status.

To the uninitiated, objective setting may appear to be more trouble than it is worth. Objectives can be difficult to formulate and sometimes impossible to agree on. They cause problems when the manager and subordinates cannot come to terms because the objectives are irrelevant, unchallenging, or overly demanding. The manager might reject a subordinate's suggested objectives on the grounds they lack sufficient work value, are not in line with business goals, or are simply too easy. The subordinate may resist the manager's objectives (especially when they are passed down from above like Moses' tablets) because they appear inflexible or carry the risk of failure.

Posing certain questions may be helpful to manager and subordinate alike in formulating an objective:

•Does the objective make good sense? Is it important to the subordinate, the manager, the department, and the company?

•Does it mesh with departmental or organizational goals?

•Does the objective fall within the manager's area of responsibility and authority?

•Does it carry risks operationally? Financially? Politically?

•Will top management support it?

•Will the subordinate (and others who may contribute) have the knowledge, skill, and resources to complete the objective?

•Can achievement of the objective be verified in some measurable way?

For most jobs, six to eight objectives will be sufficient, and it is possible that some or all of them will change or evolve as work progresses. Objectives will sometimes be contingent upon

factors beyond the manager's ability to control, such as higher-level approval of a planned project, availability of funds or equipment, and a dependence upon the work of others outside the manager's supervision.

In determining objectives, it is useful to focus on the action steps required for achievement of expectations. A single objective can incorporate several action steps. If the objective is to "develop and administer a training module for entry level security officers," the action steps could include writing a lesson plan, preparing or acquiring audiovisuals, constructing a test to measure learning, setting a training schedule, arranging for the place of training and needed training equipment, preparing certificates of completion, and making a record of attendance and scores. Time frames or deadline dates can be established for each action step, they can be programmed to occur in a particular sequence, and they can be assigned to several individuals in a team effort.

Objectives can be of two types: base and stretch. A base objective involves tasks that are integral to the job and sometimes routine in nature. Writing a report of investigation is an integral part of a security investigator's job and is fairly routine, at least to the investigator. A productivity gain might be possible by performing this task in a different manner. The manager and his investigator may agree on an objective calling for the investigator to revise the report writing method. A stretch objective goes beyond the norms of job expectations. It typically addresses a major problem, challenge, or opportunity. Achievement of the objective, if it can be done, will bring a substantial reward to the organization. It may seek to raise quality, increase productivity, reduce costs, create new markets, etc.

Once the objectives are set, they need to be put into writing, and any later changes to them should also be written down and acknowledged by the manager and subordinates with signatures or initials.

Reviewing Performance

On a continuing basis and at pre-established intervals, the manager and subordinate meet to review progress. The subordinate is invited to comment on performance with respect to the agreed objectives, highlighting areas of success,

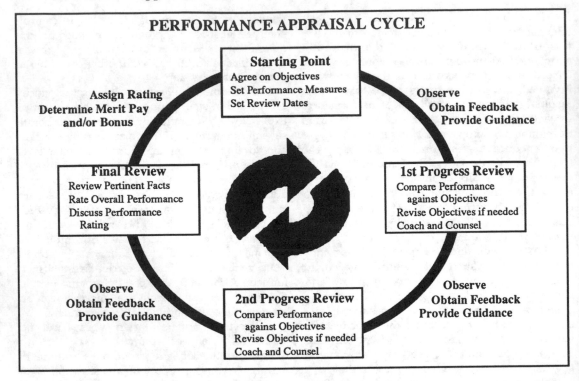

PERFORMANCE APPRAISAL CYCLE

Starting Point
Agree on Objectives
Set Performance Measures
Set Review Dates

Observe
Obtain Feedback
Provide Guidance

Assign Rating
Determine Merit Pay
and/or Bonus

Final Review
Review Pertinent Facts
Rate Overall Performance
Discuss Performance
Rating

1st Progress Review
Compare Performance
against Objectives
Revise Objectives if needed
Coach and Counsel

Observe
Obtain Feedback
Provide Guidance

2nd Progress Review
Compare Performance
against Objectives
Revise Objectives if needed
Coach and Counsel

Observe
Obtain Feedback
Provide Guidance

improvement, and difficulties encountered. The manager coaches and counsels as needed. A review meeting is also a time for revising, canceling, or creating objectives in light of experience.

The meeting is often documented, sometimes with the use of a form. The subordinate may be invited to comment, such as offering suggestions about how performance on particular objectives could be improved. The documentation can serve as a discussion point at the next review meeting. The usual practice is to not make any formal rating of the subordinate until the final review meeting of the reporting period.

The Performance Appraisal Cycle

Evaluation of performance is a process that continues uninterrupted. While significant events relating to performance may occur at points over time and are certainly worthy of consideration, they are not the sole criteria for making an overall judgment.

The process described here operates cyclically, that is, it transitions to a starting point from the ending point of a previous period, passes through one or more phases marked by pre-set

time intervals, and moves to the starting point of the next cycle.

The Starting Point. Manager and subordinate agree on objectives for the upcoming cycle, agree on the measures that will be used to evaluate performance, and agree to meet on or about particular dates for the purpose of reviewing progress. Between progress reviews, the manager observes the subordinate's performance, obtains feedback from the subordinate, and provides appropriate guidance or assistance.

Progress Reviews. On specified dates, usually at the end of the first, second, and third quarters of the reporting period, manager and subordinate meet to compare performance against the objectives. The objectives are revised, if needed, and the subordinate is coached and counseled, if needed. During the final progress review, the subordinate's overall performance is considered, forming a foundation for a written rating.

The Ending Point. The end of one cycle and the start of the next tend to blur. Between the final progress review and the end of the cycle, the manager selects a performance rating; writes the performance report and obtains the subordinate's comments and signature on the report; determines the subordinate's merit pay increase or bonus, if any; and begins to develop with the subordinate a new set of objectives for the upcoming cycle.

Merit Rating

A chief purpose of performance appraisal is to administer salary in a manner that takes into account the separate contributions of individual employees. Through a systematic rating procedure, usually called merit rating, a manager is able to make equitable decisions regarding salary awards based on appraisal records. Despite constant complaints about the imperfections of procedures that link performance to pay, such procedures are usually objective and provide information that often cannot be obtained in any other way.

Merit ratings are designed to replace subjective, general impressions with judgments that are formed from empirically derived evidence. Generally, the evidence is quantitative in nature, capable of analysis, and collected over a period of time, such as 1 year. When soundly developed and systematically administered, merit ratings can stimulate the person being rated, particularly when the rating methodology provides opportunities for manager and subordinate to discuss ways and means for focusing performance on meaningful work outputs. This aspect of appraising is in the nature of making a "reality check."

A merit rating system requires the rater to make objective judgments and present supporting evidence. The rater is confronted with two questions: "What is the standing of the rated person, relative to others, in terms of receiving a financial reward for work contributions?" and "What proof is there to support that standing?"

Unfortunately, the appraisal process is sometimes used only as a tool for making merit, salary, and promotion determinations, as opposed to harnessing the process to the larger issue of improving productivity. In some organizations, supervisors have come to view the appraisal process as a necessary evil to be endured. They admit the process may have some value to the human resources staff but little value to the tasks of supervision or to the enhancement of work output. Appraising becomes nothing more than filling out forms.

Conducted casually, performance appraisal can be destructive. Without a clear focus and a commitment at all levels, the process can poison supervisor-subordinate relationships and seriously detract from optimum productivity. The rater and the rated person can be soured on the process and management's credibility damaged.

Evaluating human performance in the workplace is both essential and difficult. Evaluating is essential because it provides the data for making important decisions -- decisions that affect the profitability of the organization and the aspirations of employees. Evaluating is difficult because it is continuous, complex, and fraught with hazards at every turn. The negative outcomes of an imperfectly administered program can be substantial, but so also are the positive outcomes.

John J. Fay, CPP

Sources

Performance Appraisal and Goal Setting. (Management Paradigms, Plano, TX, 1990).

Guidance Notes on the Performance Appraisal Process. (BP, London, 1991).

PERFORMANCE APPRAISAL: EVALUATING SECURITY PERSONNEL

The style and manner of conducting the annual performance reviews of all employees in a corporate security department are set at the top. A good opportunity for providing the desired example will be in the approach used by the director of corporate security to evaluate his or her immediate subordinates. The procedures used by the director can be emulated by the subordinates and cascaded down through the department.

The director's procedures, which will follow the corporation's formal program, will likely include a standard appraisal form and a checklist of points to be covered, such as the subordinate's performance targets for the rating period. The forms and the processes they dictate tend to require the superior and subordinate to sit face-to-face and address specific criteria. There is no room during the process for talking in generalities.

Performance appraisal forms come in many sizes and shapes. They vary widely among corporations, and even within a single corporation there are likely to be at least two types: one that is used for rating salaried employees (i.e., supervisors and managers) and one for rating hourly employees (i.e., line workers). The form for salaried employees will cover performance behaviors that are expected of supervisors and managers, such as open thinking, influencing and motivating others, sharing achievement, bias for action, knowledge of human behavior, concern for impact, self-confidence, ability to coach and develop subordinates, and skill in developing teamwork. The form for hourly employees will tend to look at other performance traits, such as quality and quantity of work output, punctuality, reliability in meeting deadlines, ability to work without continuous supervision, skill in working harmoniously with others, dependability, and enthusiasm.

A measuring scheme of some type will be applied to determine the rating. Some schemes apply numerical values to the various performance traits, with some traits weighted higher or lower according to their importance. The overall rating label can be a number, such as 3.5 on a scale of 5, or 70 on a scale of 100, or a term such as exemplary, outstanding, or effective.

An employee's rating will also likely be determined by the extent to which the employee met certain performance targets or objectives. For salaried employees, the targets tend to relate to management issues, such as departmental productivity and cost containment; for hourly employees, the indicators might be individual productivity and attendance on the job.

Performance appraisal is made meaningful when the person being rated understands that real-life job accomplishments will be the measures of performance. Accomplishments in the sense used here are the work-related outcomes that are visible and measurable at the end of the rating period. Examples might be the percentage of reduction in cost that the security director achieved in administering the departmental budget, the number of cases solved by the departmental investigator, and the number of safety hazards reported by a security officer.

Performance targets are therefore job-related. Generally, they are set by the supervisor with some bit of negotiation with the subordinate, although it is not unusual for the subordinate to be tasked with developing the targets. In some organizations, the subordinate will be asked to identify one or a few targets that result in self-

development, such as attainment of CPP status or completion of a particular training course. The targets are set at the starting point of the rating period, they serve as focal points in performance review meetings throughout the rating period, and they are the key indices for the performance report at the end of the period.

Performance appraisal is conducted at least annually on a formal basis, that is, by making a record of the performance. It is often conducted semi-annually or quarterly on a less formal basis, that is, by a meeting between the supervisor and subordinate to discuss performance and progress toward achievement of targets. In theory and in fact, the appraisal process is continuous and occurs in the normal give and take of feedback between supervisor and subordinate.

A central purpose of performance appraisal is to apprise the supervisor of a subordinate's contribution to the collective efforts of the organization and to apprise the subordinate of how he or she is perceived as a contributor in terms of job performance. The appraisal is an opportunity for the supervisor to administer praise and constructive criticism, and for the subordinate to obtain direction. It is important that communication be two-way.

One technique that can help set up a give-and-take dialogue is for the subordinate to use the appraisal form in making his or her rating and to turn it in prior to the appraisal meeting. The subordinate's assessment can be revealing; for example, the subordinate might describe contributions that would otherwise have escaped the supervisor's consideration in making an objective evaluation, or the subordinate might ask for certain training or suggest changes with high promise for improvement. If nothing else, the self-appraisal will give insights to the issues that the subordinate feels are important. Allowing them to be put on the table, along with the supervisor's perceptions, can result in a positive and productive meeting Supervisors who use this technique report that initially the self-appraisals and the supervisor appraisals may be in disagreement, but over a period of time they tend to come into fairly close alignment.

An adjunctive purpose of performance appraisal is to evaluate employees against each other or against job standards so that decisions can be made with respect to training, assignments, transfers, promotions, bonuses, and merit increases. Performance appraisal therefore has an important influence on an individual's earning power and movement within the company, both laterally and vertically. The process is called "career pathing" and it involves effort by both the individual and the supervisor; the individual demonstrates competence and promise while the supervisor provides monetary reward and opportunities for development and advancement.

J. Kirk Barefoot, CPP

PERIMETER PROTECTION: ELECTRIC-FIELD SENSORS

Electric-field sensors generate an electrostatic field between either a pair or an array of wire conductors and detect distortions in the field caused by anyone approaching the sensor. The electrostatic field is generated by an alternating current induced on the "field" wire by a crystal-controlled generator. That portion of the electrostatic field coming in contact with or close to the "sense" wires induces electric signals in these wires that are monitored by the signal processor. Under normal operating conditions, the induced signals are constant; however, when someone approaches the sensor, the electrostatic field is distorted, thus altering the induced electrical signal. When the characteristics of the altered signal satisfy the processor alarm criteria, the detector initiates an alarm.

The signal processor is part of the control unit located in or near the electric-field sensor. Signals from the sense wires enter the signal processor and are passed through a band-pass filter. The filter rejects the high-frequency signals that might be caused by wind vibrating the field and sense wires, and the low-frequency signals that might be caused by foreign objects striking the fence wires. The signals must also simultaneously satisfy several signal processing criteria before an alarm will be initiated. The first criterion is that the amplitude of the signal must exceed a certain pre-set level that is a function of the intruder's size and proximity to the fence. This criterion is imposed to discriminate against small animals that might otherwise cause false or nuisance alarms. A second criterion is that the movements of the intruder approaching the sensor must be in the frequency range of the band-pass filter to be accepted by the signal processor. As already mentioned, this criterion is imposed to alleviate alarms from wind and blowing debris. The third

and final criterion is that the signal must be present at the processor for a pre-set period of time. This pre-set time criterion minimizes false alarms caused by electromagnetic fields generated by lightning and also provides additional protection against nuisance alarms caused by objects blowing or birds flying through the sensor wires.

Another feature of the signal processor is that it has a self-adjusting circuit that automatically adjusts the detector sensitivity to compensate for objects moved close to the sensor. This means that cars, buses, or other metal equipment could be located near the electric-field sensor for protection. Anyone who attempts to move the object will initiate an alarm.

Excessive movement between the wire conductors or between the conductors and the fence fabric would induce low-frequency signals on the sense wire that might be interpreted by the signal processor as valid intrusion alarm signals. For the same reason, the chain-link fence fabric should be tight to reduce the relative motion between the fence and sensor. Line supervision for the wire conductors is provided by a terminator installed between the sense and field wire at the end of the electric-field sensor. Two terminators are required for three-wire sensor configurations.

Electric-field sensors can provide perimeter protection for many industrial and commercial installations. An application feature is that the sensors will follow the ground contour and perimeter configuration. If they are mounted to the perimeter fence, the sensors do not occupy a lot of space inside the fence. When the electric-field sensor is mounted on the perimeter fence, it has a high probability of detecting anyone climbing over or cutting through the fence and a fair probability of detecting a low-crawling intruder attempting to crawl under the fence and detector. Therefore, if the intruder can be expected to lift the fence fabric and crawl under, the bottom of the fence fabric should be secured either to the ground or to a bottom rail to prevent it from being easily lifted. This will increase the difficulty to enter under the fence, forcing the intruder to climb over or cut through the fence fabric.

Robert L. Barnard

Source Barnard, R.L., Intrusion Detection Systems. (Butterworth-Heinemann, Boston, 1982).

PERSONAL SECURITY ASSIGNMENTS

The success of a personal security mission depends on many considerations. The key consideration is planning. Planning requires attention to the following details:

- Coordination with other agencies.
- Importance of the dignitary.
- The probable threat against the dignitary.
- Equipment required.
- Means of communication.
- Emergency procedures.
- Contingency or alternate procedures.
- Orientation of security personnel concerning the assignment.
- Relations with new media.

The Security Detail

When the protected person is highly important, it is likely that he or she will have a security detail permanently assigned for protection. A security detail frequently consists of the person in charge, a personal security officer, an advance team, a residence team, and a baggage team.

The Person in Charge. The person in charge of the personal security detail has overall responsibility for accomplishing the objectives of the assignment. He or she coordinates such matters as itinerary, protocol, press policies, and the amount of exposure to the public desired by the principal. The person in charge establishes liaison with supporting intelligence and law enforcement agencies.

The person in charge also coordinates the utilization of resources of humanpower and equipment, and approves the security plan formulated for the assignment.

The Personal Security Officer. This person is somewhat like a bodyguard who provides close-in protection for the principal and normally accompanies the principal away from the office or residence. The personal security officer is the principal's main liaison with the personal security force and with the security personnel provided by the responsible protective agency. The personal security officer communicates with the person in charge and, whenever possible, with the advance team on a daily basis. The personal security officer is usually the person to brief the principal concerning the security arrangements established for the assignment.

The Advance Team. This team is responsible for conducting on-site security inspections before the arrival of the principal and his party to determine and complete personal security arrangements. The advance team is usually tasked to:

- Initiate working relationships with the responsible protective agency and its project officer.
- Initiate liaison with appropriate intelligence and police agencies.
- Examine arrival and departure terminals, and make appropriate security arrangements to ensure security of the principal and his party.
- Conduct a reconnaissance of local travel routes and establish necessary security and traffic control points. Also, make recommendations regarding the speed, composition, and order of a motorcade if appropriate.
- Initiate working relationships with management and security personnel at the place where the principal will reside during the period of the assignment.
- Inspect the buildings and grounds selected as the sites for functions involving the principal, and, on the basis of the inspection, establish appropriate security arrangements.
- Coordinate transportation and arrange for the security of baggage of the principal and his party.
- Inspect the principal's vehicle and conduct a security briefing for all drivers.
- Prepare sketches, maps, and photographs as may be required to fully inform the person in charge and the personal security officer.

The Residence Team. This is a security team that provides protection at the principal's place of stay on a 24-hour-a-day basis. This team maintains a log and various registers, screens telephone calls, checks packages, and exercises control over visitors.

The Baggage Team. This team is responsible for maintaining the security of the baggage of the principal and his official party when in transit. This team may accompany the official party, or it may be drawn from resources under the control of the responsible protective agency. The baggage team does not personally handle the baggage of the official party, but supervises such details. The baggage team conducts baggage counts and answers directly to the personal security officer.

Every detail of security in the performance phase of the assignment must be carefully planned in advance. There is always, however, the possibility of sudden changes of plans. This requires that flexibility be an important element in planning for the personal security assignment. Contingency for alternate plans must be prepared in the event circumstances cause deviation from the original plan. Factors that must be weighed in the development of plans include the importance of the protected person; the amount, duration, and nature of exposure desired by the principal or required by the circumstances; the factors of geography; and modes of transportation.

Persons assigned to personal security duties should recognize that within the democratic framework it is virtually impossible to provide absolute personal protection. Protective security officers must accept the legal and sociological constraints and within those limits reduce the opportunity of kidnap or assassination to the extent possible. A chief operational concept in creating protection is in-depth deployment of the protective force. The potential attacker is forced to penetrate layers of protection before reaching the target. A single-layered security shell, no matter how resistant, will crack when struck with sufficient force, thereby losing the protection it was designed to provide. The shell around the principal should consist of a number of protective layers, each of which becomes increasingly difficult to penetrate as an attacker moves inward toward the target.

Concentric protection, or defense in depth, can be thought of as a pattern of rings radiating out from the protected person. At a minimum, concentric protection consists of an inner and outer ring. The concept is applicable whether the principal is at home, at work, or in travel. In high-risk situations, the number of rings may be increased, made mobile, or supplemented with extra equipment. Under routine circumstances, the concentric pattern remains fairly fixed, but the protective screen exists at all times.

After-Action Report. An after-action report is made as soon as possible after the operation. It is written in narrative style, with emphasis placed on problems encountered and procedures used to resolve them. The after-action report should include detailed recommendations for improvement of performance in future personal security missions. The report provides a history file and is a valuable document for planning future security missions of a similar nature.

John J. Fay, CPP

Source Special Agent Manual. (Georgia Bureau of Investigation, State of Georgia, Atlanta, 1978).

PERSONNEL SELECTION: SELECTING THE SECURITY MANAGER

Making the right choice among candidates for the position of security manager can be a difficult and critical step in providing for the protection of an organization's assets. The selection process should begin with an understanding of what constitutes the profile of a good candidate.

Examining the Main Qualifiers

There are four main areas of consideration when selecting a security manager: organizational fit, skills and knowledge, education, and experience. Although organizational fit is obviously important, it cannot be applied as a disqualifier based on subjective considerations, such as the applicant's race, gender, or sexual preferences. Organizational fit is an appropriate selection factor, for example, when the applicant is expected to perform within a highly structured work environment where extremely inflexible lines of authority and responsibility prevail. Not every applicant will be able to survive under those conditions. Making the right selection has consequences both to the efficiency of the organization and to the needs of the applicant.

Also generally recognized as standard measurements of an applicant are skills, knowledge, and abilities. Education and experience, which are facets of these standards, can be fairly easily determined by verification of the applicant's academic and work credentials. Technical skills and knowledge, which tend to be objective and precision-oriented, can be measured through performance and written examinations, but the so-called "soft" or managerial abilities are somewhat elusive to precise assessment. Very often, the evaluation of these elements is made through the traditional process of applicant interviewing.

**A SAMPLE LIST OF JOB INTERVIEW QUESTIONS
WHEN SELECTING A SECURITY MANAGER**

1. What education, including seminars and training workshops, have you completed that would relate to this position?

2. What experience do you have that would relate to this position? What is your current or former job title? How many persons supervised? What was your reporting relationship in the organization?

3. Do you have any experience in parking programs and parking control? High-rise building security? Executive protection? Computer security? Guard service management?

4. Have any employees under your supervision achieved recognition, promotion or the like? Explain your role in contributing to their achievements.

5. Do you hold any degrees/certifications, or licenses that would relate to this position?

6. What degrees, certifications or licenses do you anticipate acquiring within the next few years?

7. Have you ever been commended officially or given an award for professional work performance or achievements?

8. What budgeting experience do you have? What were the dollar amounts of budgets you managed?

9. What experience do you have in using desk top equipment?

10. What experience do you have as an investigator?

11. What experience have you had in crime prevention programs?

12. What experience have you had working with department level managers?

13. Describe your professional successes and accomplishments.

14. Describe any professional experience in which you did not achieve what you set out to achieve and why.

15. What are your professional goals now? Where do you see yourself five years from now professionally? How do you plan to get there?

16. What reasons can you give as to why you should be the successful candidate for this position?

The Resume and the Application

Information communicated to the organization in the resume and the application form is essentially one-sided and flows in one direction. These evaluation devices are also one-dimensional because they portray the applicant abstractly. Although they often serve as discussion point reminders during interview of the applicant, their real value may lie in using them during the background investigation process to verify the applicant's representations with respect to education, training, certifications, licenses, professional affiliations, publications, prior employment, and work experience.

Interview Preparation

A good interviewer of applicants will bring to the interview session a blend of objective and intuitive judgment. Objectivity will ensure fairness, consistency, and similar positive outcomes that will benefit both the employer and the candidate. Intuitiveness can allow insights and perceptions that go beneath the surface of the image presented by the candidate during the relatively short period of "sizing up" time afforded by the interview. The seasoned interviewer will be sensitive to "red flags" that may signal problems known to the interviewer through past work experiences, and the really skilled interviewer will use behavior-provoking questions to elicit the nonverbal and verbal indicators of internal anxiety that may be associated with deception.

Preparation for the interview can begin with a checklist that identifies factors for facilitating an analysis of the candidate's nonverbal behaviors. Such a checklist might be as follows:

1.   Ensure that the interview room will be private.

2.   Arrange the interview room so that the space between the interviewer and the candidate will not be blocked by a desk, table, or other objects that might interfere with face-to-face communications.

3.   Ensure that the chairs of the interviewer and candidate are of the same height and provide equivalent comfort.

4.   Provide the interviewee with a chair that is not so relaxing as to induce slouching or leaning, such as placing the chair next to a table.

5.   Position the chairs about 3 to 4 feet apart.

By developing a package of pre-assembled notes, the interviewer will prepare questions to be asked, a checklist for recording answers, important points to be covered and emphasized, and materials that were submitted by the candidate, such as the resume and application. In the interviewer's package there may also be a written agenda for providing structure and direction of the interview.

A Structured Interview

The agenda is likely to reflect a step-by-step progression that begins with a greeting, comfortable small talk, an explanation of the organization and the department and their respective missions, and the nature of the position to be filled.

After the preliminaries are out of the way, the interviewer may move to a series of questions that probe the specifics of the candidate's qualifications. The questions will be job related, that is, they will relate to the skills, knowledge, and abilities that the job incumbent must exercise in order to be effective in the job. The accompanying list of questions is a sample.

In addition to taking notice of the candidate's answers with respect to the demands of the job, the interviewer will be evaluating the candidate's personality. If one accepts the notion that the principal objective of the candidate will be to persuade the interviewer that the candidate is the best person for the job, the candidate's ability to persuade will be a dimension worth observing closely. Is persuasive ability a job-related skill for a security manager? You bet it is. Other dimensions of the candidate's personality will bear watching as well, such as poise under fire, quick thinking, and verbal articulation.

Modern security management has evolved into a universally recognized business profession. The profession is constantly undergoing change, with more and more requirements being placed on security managers. The ordinary definition of a generalist security manager now includes many organizational skills, such as budgeting and data processing, that until recently were considered specialties outside of the security realm. The process of selecting a security manager must take into account the changing nature of the job and include an objective and detailed examination of the candidate's skills, knowledge, and abilities as they relate to the employer's expectations.

B. Steve Bias, CPP, CFE, CPO

PHOTOGRAPHY IN INVESTIGATIONS

Photography is an essential tool for the investigator. As a tool it enables the investigator to record the evidence of a crime. Photographs made of a crime can be stored indefinitely and retrieved when needed. There is no other process that can record, retain, and recall criminal evidence as effectively as photography.

Photographs are also a means of communication. They tell something about the objects photographed or the scene of a crime that is helpful in clarifying the issues when testimony is given in court. Because photographs are meant to communicate information honestly, the investigator-photographer has a great responsibility. His photographs must portray a situation as it would be observed by anyone who stood in the same position as the camera and viewed the scene from where the photograph was made.

Photographs by themselves are not substantive evidence. Photographs accepted in court must be attested to by a person who saw the scene and can truthfully state under oath that the photographs accurately represent what the person saw at the scene. In the ordinary, nonlegal field of photography, only the finished photographic print is of interest, but in criminal investigative work, all photographic procedures are subject to review and inspection by the court. Obviously, this rigid requirement makes it imperative that investigative photography conform to high standards of quality and ethics.

Photographic Techniques

The most frequent factor contributing to inferior photographic results is over exposure of the negative. This produces soft, grainy images of low contrast and brightness. Exposure recommendations for any given film are based upon the requirement for a so-called average subject. This is a photographic subject that contains light, medium, and dark tones. If a photographic subject consists of all light tones, the subject would be very low in contrast and high in brightness. If the recommended speed for a given film for use with a so-called average subject were ASA 80, the fact that the photographic subject contained all light tones means that less exposure is required. If, on the other hand, the subject consisted of all dark tones, the subject is low in contrast and is therefore reflecting very little light. In this case the investigator-photographer adjusts his equipment to provide more exposure. For example, less exposure would be called for when the photographic subject is a nude body of a white bleached blonde lying on white sand; or at the other extreme, highly blackened wool at the scene of an arson will require greater exposure than an average subject in order to obtain shadow detail. In short, the investigator must learn to evaluate his photographic subject by contrast and brightness, and to make appropriate adjustments.

Another common difficulty is a dirty lens. Dirt and oxidation may form on the back surface of the lens, as well on the front. Both the outer and inner surfaces of the camera lens should be checked frequently and cleaned when necessary.

Loss of detail in photographic prints is a common problem. This is usually caused by movement of the camera at the time the shutter is released. This problem can be reduced through the use of a rigid tripod and a fast shutter speed.

Sharpness, or image definition, suffers when the diaphragm of a lens is stopped down, i.e., adjusted from its largest opening to its smallest opening. When a lens is stopped down, three things happen:

• The aperture is reduced and less light passes through during a given period of time.

• The depth of field increases.

• The image definition improves to a point (although in a few special cases the definition softens at the smallest apertures).

To obtain good definition the following general rules apply:

• Use a tripod whenever possible.

• For outdoor photography with a hand-held camera, set the aperture as required by film and light conditions, and use a faster shutter speed.

• For flash pictures use an electronic flash.

Photography plays a vital part in establishing points of proof for certain types of crime, particularly crimes involving physical violence. The characteristics and location of relevant objects need to be captured in accurate detail and permanently recorded until presented at trial. If a crime scene is altered through carelessness or haste, it can never be restored to its exact original condition, and as a consequence, vital elements of proof may be lost forever. In addition, the significance of certain aspects of a crime scene may not be apparent, although later they may powerfully affect a guilty or innocent conclusion. The first step in the investigation of any crime is to photograph completely and accurately all aspects of the scene before any of the objects of evidence are removed or otherwise disturbed. Photographs should also be made after victims have been removed. It is much better to take too many photographs rather than not enough.

When taking photographs at a scene, the objective should be to record the maximum of usable information in a series of photographs that will enable the viewer to understand where and how the crime was committed. The term *crime scene* refers not just to the immediate locality in which the offense occurred, but relates also to adjacent areas where important acts took place immediately before or after the commission of the offense. The number and types of photographs will be determined by the total circumstances of the crime.

Photographs of the broad area of the locale of the crime scene should be supplemented by closer shots of portions of the crime scene so that important details are made apparent. Each object within an area should be photographed so that it can be located readily in the overall pictures, thus enabling the viewer to gain a clear picture of its position in relation to other objects at the scene and to the overall scene.

Procedures. At an indoor crime scene location at least four photographs will be required to show the room adequately. Moving in a clockwise direction, each photograph will overlap a portion of the preceding photograph so that 360 degree coverage is made of the area. Obviously, when an area is large or contains many pieces of evidence, the number of photographs will be far in excess of the minimum four. Medium-distant, as well as close-up, photographs should be made of important objects. Two lenses are usually sufficient for crime scene photography. A wide-angle lens is useful for interior photographs and a normal angle lens for outdoor photographs.

Lighting. Indoor lighting is rarely satisfactory for photographic purposes. The investigator must take into account the need for additional illumination. Depending upon the size, shape, and location of a crime scene, the investigator may elect to provide additional illumination through photoflood, photoflash, or electronic flash equipment.

Markings in the Field of View. Because a court may object to the presence of rulers or similar measuring devices in a crime scene photograph, it is recommended that the photographs be taken first without the marker and then with the marker. Measuring devices that are used to show the relative size of and distances between objects should be placed in such a manner that they will not obscure any important part of the evidence.

The final determination of the admissibility of photographs is made in court and often depends upon legal points that have little to do with the investigator-photographer. The investigator's contribution to the admissibility of photographs relates mainly to their accuracy and to the custody of them prior to trial.

All evidence must be protected and accounted for from the time it is found until it is offered in evidence. The law requires that the person presenting physical evidence in court be prepared to prove such evidence could not have been altered or replaced. This means that an investigator must be able to account for negatives and prints at all times. This does not present any great problem when photographs taken by the investigator are developed, printed, and secured within in-house resources. Problems can arise, however, when film is processed or placed into the custody of an outside agency. When this occurs, chain of custody procedures must be followed.

To be admissible, a photograph must be verified by a person who viewed the scene, object, or person represented in the photograph, and is able to state that it is an accurate and truthful representation. In other words, the photograph must be a fair and accurate representation of the scene of the crime. Depending on the desires of the court, this issue can be addressed through testimony given by the investigator who took the photographs or by some other competent witness present at the time the photograph was taken.

An investigator who is required to give testimony regarding photographs he or she took at a scene should be prepared to testify regarding safekeeping of negatives and prints, and to explain the details of the photographic procedures followed.   An understanding of the rules of evidence and an application of common sense is usually sufficient to ensure that photographs taken in connection with a crime will be admissible in court.

John J. Fay, CPP

Source Special Agent Manual. (Georgia Bureau of Investigation, State of Georgia, Atlanta, 1978).

PHYSICAL SECURITY: COUNTERMEASURES DEVELOPMENT

Designing a security system that effectively responds to identified threats and vulnerabilities presents a formidable challenge to the security system designer. A rational adversary who has targeted an asset for gain must consider the potential success of the attack in relation to the risk of being detected and apprehended. The owner of the asset, on the other hand, must seek to mitigate asset exposure with the right selection of countermeasures to ensure that the threat will be unsuccessful. Ultimately, a protective system's success is measured based on the cost-effectiveness of individual measures to counter threats, reduce vulnerabilities, and decrease risk exposure.

System designers must anticipate threats and quantify risks. They must then anticipate the worst possible consequences and ultimately weigh the cost of any countermeasure recommendation against the perceived cost-benefit or reduced potential for loss. Determination of cost-effective protective measures and their integration is the result of a structured decision process that considers the individual and collective contribution of each asset protection strategy according to the complete system's requirements.

The countermeasure selection process can be employed by design engineers and security managers alike to select from a wide range of available physical, electronic, operational, and procedural countermeasures to reduce identified vulnerabilities of assets to an acceptable or manageable level. The end result is a security design concept upon which subsequent phases of design can be based. Even after the final design is completed and the system is installed and operational, countermeasures must be regularly evaluated according to changes in perceived threats, risks, and opportunities for increased effectiveness in the mix of countermeasures.

Role of the Security Designer

The designer can be either the user/owner or a representative such as a security consultant or architect/engineer. The designer should always strive to achieve a synergistic relationship among the various components and subsystems selected. Selection of appropriate security equipment, procedures, humanpower levels, facilities, and information is accomplished on the basis of the most reliable and effective combinations to meet the known and expected capabilities of the threat.

However, the designer is usually constrained by limited budgets, soaring personnel and equipment costs, and the ever-increasing presence of external and internal threats. This demands a comprehensive "systems approach" to countermeasures selection that focuses on the total integration of all possible countermeasure options, minimizes asset vulnerability and risk exposure, optimizes initial and follow-on system cost, and keeps subsequent operational costs under control.

The designer can select protective measures from the following complete range of subsystem options:

•Facilities and architectural solutions designed to deny access to, deter, and delay an adversary.

•Physical security equipment designed to assist in detection of, and assess the severity of intrusion attempts and unauthorized activities.

•Communications and control/display systems that collect, integrate, transmit, and display alarm and other data for operator response, and to control response forces.

•Security personnel to conduct day-to-day security program operations, management, and system support, and respond to non-routine events.

•Security procedures and other information to guide security operations, and provide direction and control.

The culmination of the security designer's art is a fully integrated system that incorporates countermeasures based on: criticality of individual assets; dynamics of threat; vulnerability reduction alternatives; risk exposure mitigation options; and the cost-effective mix of personnel, technologies, and procedures in an optimum system configuration.

The Countermeasures Selection Process

The countermeasures selection process incorporates six sequential steps leading to a complete design concept. Experience has shown that the process must be both structured to ensure designer thoroughness and considered early in the design phase of a project.

In Step 1 of the process, assets that require protection are identified, and their criticality to the organizational mission is determined in Step 2. Next, in Step 3, threats to individual assets are considered in terms of potential threat sources and the attractiveness of these assets to potential aggressors. In Step 4, likely modes of aggressor attack against individual assets are evaluated. Areas in which existing countermeasures do not adequately address the threat are identified as facility vulnerabilities in Step 5. In Step 6, an assessment is made of the financial, regulatory, and operational constraints to candidate countermeasures selection.

Based on the results of the designer's analysis, asset-specific measures are considered for final selection and inclusion in the overall protection program.

The designer selects individual protective measures based on an initial statement of program objectives and functional statements of desired protection levels made by the owner. Finally, individual countermeasures are selected by the designer and integrated into a cohesive protection solution. Preliminary cost estimates for the initial installation and expected total life cycle of the complete system are also established. Costs for those physical security countermeasures necessary to meet operational and vulnerability reduction objectives are always a prime consideration for the designer.

The accompanying chart shows the range of countermeasure elements and related subsystems that are considered by the designer to build a totally integrated program to counter an adversary's objectives. Protective measure options are normally arranged by the designer into mutually supportive subsystems such as access control measures, detection measures, structural and architectural measures, assessment/surveillance measures, command,

control and display requirements, and operational and humanpower considerations

Countermeasures Selection and Integration

The countermeasure options are further defined by the designer in terms of countermeasure application at the asset, facility, or site level. Asset-specific measures are those applied to the asset and its immediate surroundings. These include barriers, detection zones, and a host of other options that give the designer flexibility in choosing which measure or collection of measures is appropriate based on the environment and anticipated attack scenario.

Generally, however, asset-specific measures are applied within the room housing the asset or within close proximity to an asset. The selection of individual measures at the asset begins the methodical design process outward through the facility housing the asset and the site within which the facilities are located. Consequently, facility-specific measures are those applied where assets are housed and site-specific measures are those applied between the facility and a pre-established site perimeter.

Countermeasures selection always begins at the asset. Even in cases where multiple assets are housed within a single facility, a protective design strategy must be formulated for each individual asset. This ensures that asset-unique requirements will be addressed by the designer. However, there are instances in which multiple assets are stored or situated within a single room or compartment of a facility. In this case, the designer must aggregate the vulnerability reduction measures for all of the assets.

Asset-specific protective measures can include a wide range of countermeasure options.

Architectural measures may include interior barriers combined with enhanced structural features that provide the desired level of protection at the asset, facility, or site level. Architectural measures also include the designer's selection from a number of environmental design options that concentrate on the design and use of space. Natural access control and surveillance are examples of environmental design options.

Detection and assessment measures may include a combination of point and area sensors along with duress alarms, closed-circuit television (CCTV) assessment, and area lighting. Interior

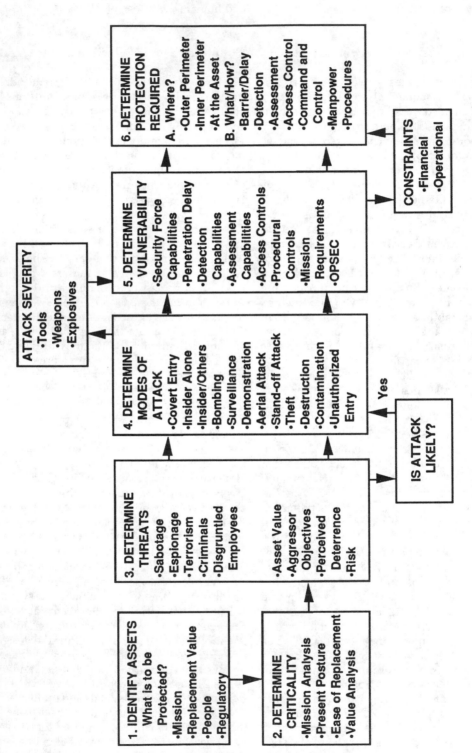

Countermeasures Selection Process

control measures may include personnel access control within the facility and access restriction at or near the asset. Security personnel should be positioned to be available for response to intrusion attempts, while asset-specific procedures may require the periodic check of asset locations by security patrols.

Each potential countermeasure presents an option for the designer in implementing an optimum protective design strategy. Depending upon the criticality of the asset, and likelihood and severity of attack, the designer may choose one measure or a combination of measures for inclusion in the security design. The designer's selection and integration of countermeasure options should be based on organizational mission, security operational requirements, overall system performance characteristics, and cost-effectiveness criteria.

Candidate countermeasures also must be identified in terms of their individual and overall contribution to facility or asset protection from an integrated perspective. For example, the delay capabilities of architectural barriers will modify the designer's selection of sensor and access control subsystem elements.

In addition, the availability and operational capabilities of the security force will, in some form, help dictate the optimum selection, configuration, and placement of various security technologies. Technologies are specifically selected based on their performance, reliability, maintainability, cost, and vulnerability reduction potential.

Considered individually, these elements may offer little in the way of complete protection for critical assets. However, if the system designer has correctly used the information provided in the user's security system concept, the result should be a system that effectively combines individual countermeasures to counter current and future threats at reasonable cost.

Compartmentalization

Facilities with multiple assets that are spatially distributed present the designer with more difficult countermeasures selection options. Not only does the process become more complex, but so does the basis of design. The approach used by most security designers is to compartmentalize protective measures.

The compartmentalization allows the designer to define inner perimeters of a larger controlled space and build security measures inward from the points of access/egress unique to the protection requirements of the asset. The perimeter typically will be defined by physical barriers through which access is monitored electronically or procedurally. Within the facility, several compartments may be contiguous and share common protective measures. A single access control point may be established within the common space to limit costly humanpower allocation or to maximize the efficiency of electronic access control and detection through the creation of a single zone.

The designer's compartmentalization scheme must also consider security force response time to intrusion attempts and the element of delay built into the protection scheme. The inherent penetration delay time of the facility or compartment housing the asset may dictate the need to establish a response capability within the facility or to select additional protective measures to increase structural penetration delay time.

Groups of facilities that share a common boundary or perimeter require that the designer focus not only on the asset and individual facility, but also on the site. Generally, sites with multiple facilities will have common or shared security requirements, and some sites will even have a perimeter fence line and manned guard booth at an entry point to separate the area from the general public.

Countermeasure Cost-Effectiveness

The designer's consideration of countermeasure options will depend to a large extent on the cost-effectiveness of individual countermeasures. Cost-effectiveness criteria that might be used by the designer include operational restrictions, nuisance alarm susceptibility, installation cost, maintenance costs, probability of detection, mean time between failures, contribution to humanpower reduction, degree of vulnerability reduction, and reduced risk, normally expressed in consequence of loss or destruction.

While any one of these criteria may result in selection or rejection of a countermeasure alternative, the range of acceptable countermeasures must be linked together to form a system-level impression of overall cost and

AREA TO BE PROTECTED

ELEMENTS	SUBSYSTEMS	SYSTEM
Natural features, fences walls, portals, restricted areas, clear zones, locks & automated response devices.	BARRIER/ DELAY SUBSYSTEM	
Sensors (exterior, interior, point, space, and duress), Primary & secondary power, electronic aids.	DETECTION SUBSYSTEM	
Towers, booths, CCTV, fixed posts, patrols, audio (remote), security lighting.	ASSESSMENT SUBSYSTEM	
Alarm reporting, data control, displays.	CONTROL AND DISPLAY SUBSYSTEM	**OBJECTIVES** •Overt/Covert Penetration •Mission Attainment •Escape
Radio (base/mobile), data links, telephone, PA/intercom, electronic search aids.	COMMUNI- CATION SUBSYSTEM	INTEGRATED SECURITY SYSTEM ← ADVERSARY
Security mgt, line operations, support services, weapons, vehicles, protective gear.	PERSONNEL & EQUIPMENT SUBSYSTEM	**OBJECTIVES** •Detect •Delay •Deter •Respond/Engage •Prevent Escape
Special purpose portals, ID Badges, automated access, personnel ID and verification.	ACCESS CONTROL SUBSYSTEM	With a High Degree of Reliability and Assurance
Personnel standards, training, plans, procedures, performance assessment, access controls, crisis mgt.	PROCEDURES SUBSYSTEM	

Countermeasure Elements and Subsystems

effectiveness. This is the most difficult task because most organizations do not collect and report security incidents on a regular basis. This lack of data, coupled with the fact that quantifying the contribution that security makes to an organization's goals is difficult if not impossible to accomplish, all make it difficult for the designer to estimate the cost of applying security measures in relation to reduced exposure or risk.

In order to justify security expenditures for countermeasures, it must be shown both on an individual asset and collective system basis that the projected costs of the system are justified in relation to the projected cost of the losses.

Most managers set goals and measure results in financial terms. The security function should not be made an exception to this standard. The designer as either manager or consultant should determine the appropriate protection to afford to critical assets using a structured countermeasures development process. The ultimate integration of the various protective measures selected is the most critical step in the design process and is totally dependent upon a variety of resource and policy issues.

The cost-effectiveness of candidate protective measures and the ultimate system they combine to form must be evaluated in terms of cost of protection vs. potential losses avoided. True system integration can only result from a structured countermeasures selection process that considers the criticality of assets, the capabilities of potential threats, the likely outcome of attack attempts, and the collective contribution of individual asset, facility, and site-protection strategies in quantifiable terms.

Richard P. Grassie, CPP
and William J. Schneider

PHYSICAL SECURITY: LANDSCAPING AS A PERIMETER BARRIER

Security professionals who have studied environmental design agree that an early step in planning for the construction of a building is to examine the site and surrounding grounds. The planner's focus will be on identifying protection opportunities that may be present in the external environment. Because the objective will be to take advantage of available crime-resisting features, the planner's thoughts will be on barrier systems that blend with and capitalize on what nature has already provided. The barrier systems most often considered are walls and fences. A type of perimeter barrier sometimes overlooked is landscaping.

Landscaping can be particularly effective in establishing a property line, both physically and psychologically. The boundaries delineated by landscaping can delay unwanted intrusions and serve also as a subtle signal that uninvited entry is not wanted.

Thorny plants can discourage trespassers when strategically placed. They are available in a variety of sizes to fit different situations. The carissa plant comes in three heights: emerald blanket, which is a dwarf variety; boxwood blanket, which is of intermediate size extending up to 6 feet; and grandiflora, which tops out at 7 to 8 feet. Thorny plants, of course, pose a hazard to children and a challenge to maintenance crews.

Shrub masses and low ground cover in immediate proximity to buildings can be effective in discouraging break-ins through cellar and ground floor windows. The needle-sharp thorns of the pygmy date palm plant, for example, will discourage even the most determined intruder, and the shape and size of the plant is ideal for windows that are left open to facilitate air circulation. Other plants that provide similar protection are the Jerusalem thorn and cinnecord.

Hedges, ferns, and bushes can also deter and delay. They add at least one degree of difficulty in gaining access through a window and several degrees of difficulty in making a quick, unencumbered departure -- especially when the intruder is carrying stolen items.

Earth berms can be useful in some situations, for example, where an intruder moving over the top of a berm would be silhouetted against the horizon or background lights.

Landscaping can be an answer to the problem of wall graffiti. Bare walls can be shielded with climbing ivy, thorny bougainvillea, carissa, and wild lime.

When lighting is used in concert with trees, the direction of illumination should be downward. The number of lights, their placement, and relative power of illumination will be determined by the number of trees, their spacing, and their fullness. The lighting arrangement among trees that shed leaves will be different than that for trees that do not shed.

Lighting patterns will also vary according to purpose. If the purpose is to visually watch the lighted area, the observer's vision should be facilitated with well-distributed lighting at intensity levels that protect against glare and night blindness. If the purpose of lighting is to monitor with closed-circuit television (CCTV) cameras, the pattern will need to conform to lens specifications.

Finally, one important note of caution is appropriate. When improperly designed or installed, landscaping can work to the advantage of the criminal. Shrubbery around windows and doors, favored break-in entry points, can give comfort to burglars; earth berms can create blind spots; and trees can mask intruder movement in lighted areas. These are not reasons to ignore landscaping as a valid design option, but they do merit critical consideration. On balance, the incorporation of landscaping into exterior barrier schemes makes great sense. The security professional should understand this fact and act accordingly.

Randall Atlas, Ph.D., AIA, CPP

PHYSICAL SECURITY: LIGHTING

Two major purposes of lighting are (1) to create a psychological deterrent to intrusion and (2) to enable detection. Good lighting is considered such an effective crime control method that the law in many locales requires buildings to maintain adequate lighting.

One way to analyze lighting deficiencies is to go to the building at night and study the possible methods of entry and areas where inadequate lighting will aid a burglar. Prior to the visit, contact local police as a precaution against mistaken identity; recruit their assistance in spotting weak points in lighting. Look for locations where a burglar could hide and make sure that openings (e.g., doors and windows) are illuminated.

What lighting level will aid an intruder? Most people believe that under conditions of darkness a criminal can safely commit a crime, but this view may be faulty in that one cannot generally work in the dark. Three possible levels of light are: bright light, darkness, and dim light. Bright light, as we know, affords an offender plenty of light to work, but enables easy observation by others and will therefore deter crime. Without light, a burglar will find it difficult to jimmy a door lock, release a latch, or

remove whatever barrier prevents easy access. However, dim light will provide just enough light for the intruder to break and enter while at the same time hinder observation by authorities. Support for this view was shown in a study of crimes during full moon phases -- when dim light was produced. In this study, the records of 972 police shifts, at three police agencies, for a 2-year period, were studied to compare nine different crimes during full moon and non-full moon phases. The crime showing the greatest difference between full moon and non-full moon phases was breaking and entering.

Protective Lighting

There are four basic types of lighting systems:

•Continuous Lighting. This system is in widespread use and applied to light a specific area continuously. A light fixture mounted on a pole is a standard design.

•Entry Lighting. Openings along a perimeter or at doors are sites for entry lighting.

•Movable Lighting. Searchlights are movable and capable of directing a beam of light on a specific area or something moving. They are operated manually and engaged primarily as an auxiliary lighting source.

•Emergency Lighting. This system is primarily for backup in case the continuous lighting system goes out. An on-site power source is vital to this system.

Light Sources

The commonly utilized light sources are:

•Incandescent. These lamps are of the kind found in the home and referred to as light bulbs. Light is produced by the resistance of a filament to an electric current. They provide immediate illumination when turned on, but have a relatively short life. Manufacturers produce a variety of sizes and wattages.

•Gaseous Discharge. Mercury and sodium vapor lamps represent this type. Illumination is produced when electrical current passes through a tube of conducting and luminous gas. These lamps have a longer life and yield more light than incandescent lamps. A chief disadvantage of the gaseous discharge lamps is that they are slow to light when cold and re-light when hot. Mercury vapor lamps result in a blue-white color light. Sodium vapor affords a golden-yellow light; it is often applied where fog is a problem since this light source is capable of penetrating fog. High-pressure sodium lighting reportedly uses 50% less energy to produce the same amount of light as mercury vapor lighting. However, the cost and maintenance may make them prohibitive.

Some citizen groups have opposed sodium lighting for three major reasons: (1) it may affect sleeping habits, (2) it conflicts with aesthetic values, and (3) a general dislike of the glow given off by the sodium vapor lamps.

• Fluorescent. This gaseous discharge light source is installed in buildings. It has good efficiency, is low cost, but each individual light has a short range of coverage.

• Quartz Lamp. These lamps result in a bright white light and an intense glare. They are characterized by high wattage (to 2,000 watts) and the ability to afford light almost as quickly as an incandescent lamp. They are applicable to perimeter lines and areas where detailed work is conducted.

Lighting Equipment

A variety of lighting equipment is on the market. For instance, street lights are stationary and part of a continuous lighting system. Incandescent or gaseous discharge lamps are used in street lights. Fresnel lights have a wide flat beam, which is directed outward to protect a perimeter. Glare is produced in the face of those approaching the perimeter. A floodlight saturates an area with a beam of light while also creating considerable glare. Floodlights are stationary, although the light beams can be aimed at selected positions.

Philip P. Purpura, CPP

Sources   Purpura, P.P., Security and Loss Prevention, 2nd Edition. (Butterworth-Heinemann, Boston, 1991).

PLANNING: A SYSTEMS PERSPECTIVE

What is the systems perspective? A key characteristic of the systems perspective is that there are interactions among the subsystems of a system. When actions take place in one subsystem, other subsystems are affected.

Example: The criminal justice system is composed of three major subsystems -- police, courts, and corrections. If during one day, 100 public drunk arrests are made by the police, then the court and corrections subsystems must react by accommodating the arrestees.

There are many other examples of systems: a loss prevention department, a business, government, an automobile, the human body, and so on. All systems have subsystems that interact and affect the whole. In a loss prevention system, for instance, the subsystem called investigations is dependent for information on the subsystem called patrol. In turn, the patrol subsystem depends on the investigation subsystem for in-depth follow-up investigations.

Similar to other systems, a loss prevention department can be analyzed in terms of inputs, processes, outputs, and feedback. An illustrative example is a loss prevention department's immediate reaction and short-term planning concerning an employee theft. The loss prevention department receives a call from a supervisor who has caught an employee stealing. This is the input. The process in the analysis of the call is planning and from that an action is taken, e.g., loss prevention personnel are dispatched to the scene. The output is activity at the scene, such as questioning and note taking. Feedback can involve communications between the investigating loss prevention officers, the loss prevention manager, and the supervisor who made the original complaint. Feedback helps to determine if the output was proper and if corrections are necessary.

The inputs of goals and objectives relate to upper management's expectations of the loss prevention function. Resources are basically money, material, and personnel. Information, research, reports, and statistics all aid in planning and day-to-day decision making. The output is the loss prevention program activities that evolve from planning. Feedback, an often overlooked activity, is essential for modifying current plans and developing new plans. An integral aspect of feedback is evaluation. Programs and strategies may need modification. Evaluations help to justify programs and strategies, and make it possible for the loss prevention manager to give a credible answer when asked: "How do you know the loss prevention plans and strategies are working?"

Philip P. Purpura, CPP

Source Purpura, P.P., Security and Loss Prevention, 2nd Edition. (Butterworth-Heinemann, Boston, 1991).

POLYGRAPH TESTING

The polygraph technique is most widely used today by the law enforcement community in one of two ways -- as part of the pre-employment screening process for police candidates, and as a forensic technique to help resolve the investigation of criminal offenses.

More than half of the large police departments in the United States use polygraph testing in the pre-employment screening process. Police agencies have found that polygraph testing is a very effective means to identify high-risk candidates. A large number of high-risk candidates for police work continue to be identified by polygraph testing. These include applicants with behavioral histories in felony thefts, burglaries, robberies, the use and sale of illegal drugs, bribery, car thefts, and various sexual offenses.

The value of polygraph testing is further illustrated by the fact that in most of these cases, the applicants had already successfully passed a series of selection hurdles that included mental, physical, and psychological tests, as well as credit and background investigations.

For decades the law enforcement community has used polygraph testing as an investigative aid to:

- Verify the statements of victims;
- Establish the credibility of witnesses; and
- Evaluate the truthfulness of suspects.

The most valuable aspect of the investigative use of polygraph testing is to help exonerate the innocent person suspected by reason of circumstantial evidence. It is particularly valuable in those investigations that rely only on testimonial evidence. At the same time, polygraph testing is very helpful in investigations involving multiple suspects by narrowing the focus of the investigation. Regardless of the circumstance in which polygraph testing is used, the test results are not the sole basis on which decisions are made; rather, polygraph results are used in conjunction with other screening or investigative information.

All federal law enforcement agencies either employ their own polygraph examiners or use the services of examiners employed in other agencies. Staff examiners and quality control programs exist in the Federal Bureau of Investigation (FBI), Secret Service, U.S. Army Criminal Investigation Division (CID), U.S. Marine Corps CID, Air Force Office of Special Investigations (OSI), Naval Investigative Service (NIS), U.S. Customs, U.S. Marshals Service, Defense Criminal Investigation Service, Internal Revenue Service, U.S. Capitol Police, Metropolitan Police of the District of Columbia, and others. Also, all U.S. intelligence agencies use polygraph tests in the pre-employment screening process.

Accuracy

In the past 75 years, over 250 studies have been conducted on the accuracy of the polygraph technique. Since many different conditions and factors were involved in the research, and since the polygraph examination is a very complex process, it has been difficult to draw from the data a precise figure for the accuracy of polygraph testing in all settings. Nevertheless, the preponderance of available information indicates that when a properly trained examiner utilizes an established testing procedure, the accuracy of the decisions made by polygraph examiners is generally in the range of 85-95% for specific issue investigations.

One of the problems in discussing accuracy figures and the margin between the statistics quoted by proponents and opponents of the polygraph technique is the way the figures are calculated. At the risk of oversimplification, critics (who often do not understand polygraph testing) want to classify "inconclusive" test results as errors. In the real-life setting, an inconclusive result simply means that the examiner is unable to render a definite conclusion. In such cases, a second examination is usually conducted at a later date. To illustrate how the inclusion of inconclusive test results can distort accuracy figures, consider the following example: If 10 polygraph examinations are administered and the examiner is correct in 7 decisions, wrong in 1 and has 2 inconclusive test results, we calculate the accuracy rate as 87.5% (8 definitive results, 7 of which were correct). Critics of the polygraph technique would calculate the accuracy rate in this example as 70% (10 examinations with 7 correct decisions). Since those who use polygraph testing do not consider inconclusive test results as negative, and do not hold them against the examinee, to consider them as errors is clearly misleading and certainly skews the figures.

To date there has been only a limited number of research projects on the accuracy of polygraph testing in the pre-employment context, primarily because of the difficulty in establishing ground truth. However, since the same physiological measures are recorded and the same basic psychological principles apply in both the specific issue and pre-employment examinations, there is no reason to believe that there is a substantial decrease in the accuracy rate for the pre-employment circumstance. The few studies that have been conducted on pre-employment testing support this contention. While the polygraph technique is not infallible, the research clearly indicates that when administered by a competent examiner, the polygraph test is the most accurate means available to determine truth and deception.

Errors

While the polygraph technique is highly accurate, it is not infallible and errors do occur. Polygraph errors are generally caused by the examiner's failure to properly prepare the examinee for the examination, or by misreading the physiological data on the polygraph charts. Errors are usually referred to as either false positives or false negatives. A false positive occurs when a truthful examinee is reported as being deceptive; a false negative when a deceptive examinee is reported as truthful. Some research indicates that false negatives occur more frequently than false positives; other research studies show the opposite. In either case, any error is damaging, particularly the false positive. To protect against the occurrence of errors, examiners utilize a variety of procedures to identify the presence of factors that may cause false responses, and to ensure an unbiased review of the polygraph records, the following should be taken into account:

•An assessment of the examinee's emotional state.

•Medical information about the examinee's physical condition.

•Specialized tests to identify the overly responsive examinee and to calm the overly nervous.

•Control questions to evaluate the examinee's response capabilities.

•Factual analysis of the case information.

•A pre-test interview and detailed review of the questions.

•Quality control reviews.

If a polygraph examinee believes that an error has been made, there are several actions that may be taken:

•Request a second examination.

•Retain an independent examiner for a second opinion.

•File a complaint with the state licensing board.

•File a complaint with the U.S. Department of Labor.

Questions and Results

Personal and intrusive questions have no place in a properly conducted polygraph examination. Many state licensing laws, the Employee Polygraph Protection Act, and the official policy of the American Polygraph Association contain language to the effect that the polygraph examiner cannot inquire into any of the following areas during pre-employment or periodic employment examinations:

•Religious beliefs or affiliations.

•Beliefs or opinions regarding racial matters.

•Political beliefs or affiliations.

•Beliefs, affiliations, or lawful activities regarding unions or labor organizations.

•Sexual preferences or activities.

In a law enforcement pre-employment polygraph examination, the questions focus on such job-related inquiries as the theft of money or merchandise from previous employers, falsification of information on the job application, the use of illegal drugs during working hours, and criminal activities. The test questions are limited in the time span they cover, and all are reviewed and discussed with the examinee during a pre-test interview. There are no surprise or trick questions. In a specific-issue polygraph examination, the relevant questions focus on the particular act under investigation.

According to the various state licensing laws and the American Polygraph Association's Standards and Principles of Practice, polygraph results can be released only to authorized persons. Generally, those individuals who can receive test

Four criteria must be met before an employer in the private sector can ask an employee to take a polygraph examination:

1. The request must be relative to an ongoing specific investigation involving an economic loss to the employer.

2. The employee must have had access to the property, money or area central to the investigation. Access can mean physical presence or special knowledge, such as the combination to a safe.

3. The employer must have a reasonable suspicion that the employee was involved in the incident under investigation. Reasonable suspicion goes beyond having access, and incorporates such factors as a witness's statement, suspicious behavior on the part of the employee, or contradictions between the employee's statements and documented records.

4. At least 48 hours prior to the examination the employer must give to the employee a written statement which describes the nature of the loss and the investigation, as well as the basis for the employer's "reasonable suspicion."

In addition, the Employee Polygraph Protection Act (EPPA) requires that the polygraph examiner follow certain procedures in the administration of the examination. Examples of these include a minimum duration of 90 minutes for the examination, and reading a statement to the employee which enunciates certain rights under the Act.

Courtesy of the American Polygraph Association

results are limited to the examinee and anyone specifically designated in writing by the examinee; the person, firm, corporation, or governmental agency that requested the examination; and others as may be required by law.

American Polygraph Association

Source Public Affairs Pamphlet. (American Polygraph Association, Severna Park, MD, 1992).

POSITION EVALUATION

Position evaluation is the determination of an appropriate grade level for a specific position or job. In this context, the evaluation process is focused on the nature of the job, not on the qualities of the job incumbent. Because grade level is the chief determinant of salary or wage and other job benefits, the process of position evaluation is both critical and sensitive.

Certain key pieces of information are necessary to make an accurate determination:
- The nature and function of the job.
- How the job fits into the organization.
- The extent of accountability built into the job, including the dimensions and quantity of accountability.

Grade level determination is an attempt to systematize or make objective what would otherwise be a subjective endeavor. The employer, in trying to sort out and make sense of the comparative values of different work functions in the organization, recognizes that the best he can do is introduce some order into making what are essentially human judgments. Although many evaluation schemes use numbers and other seemingly objective criteria, the process is more art than science.

The Position Description

The basic work of evaluating positions is done by managers who assemble and analyze information about the positions to be rated. This activity often produces a document called a position (or job) description.

Although position description documents come in many sizes and varieties, the form will typically contain particular items.

Identifying Details. These include job title, department, major business unit, location, and so forth.

Nature of the Position. A description is made of the overall purpose and chief objectives of the position and the nature of activities, such as guard force management, investigations, or special

☐ Position Revision/Update
☐ New Position

POSITION DESCRIPTION

Position Title_____ Manager of Security _____

Name of Person_____ John Q. Doe _____

Department_____ Administration _____

Location_____ Houston, Texas _____

Reports to: (Name)_____ William J. Anderson _____ (Title) ___ Chief Executive Officer ___

NATURE OF POSITION

Responsible for planning, leading, organizing, and evaluating security operations at all Company locations. Identifies exposures to crime-related loss, damage, or compromise of assets, and recommends corrective actions. Carries out proactive prevention strategies, and counsels the chief executive officer and other senior managers concerning significant loss exposures and deviations from established controls. Directs investigations of criminal activity directed against the Company and unethical conduct on the part of Company employees. Maintains working relationships with peers in private sector organizations and criminal justice agencies.

This key position is responsible for providing a wide range of assets protection services which include protecting executives, implementing physical and procedural safeguards, overseeing security officer operations, and promoting security awareness among employees at all levels.

Decisions are frequently required in matters that involve complex legal and business issues. The incumbent must necessarily possess a blend of business knowledge, analytical skill, decisiveness and practical field experience.

The major emphasis and challenge is for the incumbent to maintain an effective security program without incurring declines in efficiency and productivity.

ORGANIZATIONAL RELATIONSHIPS

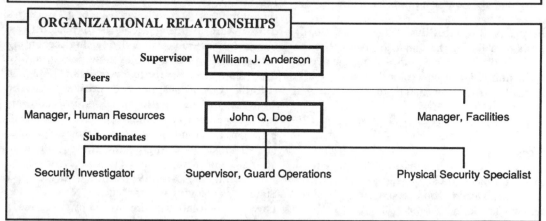

POSITION DATA

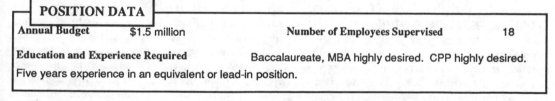

| Annual Budget | $1.5 million | Number of Employees Supervised | 18 |

Education and Experience Required   Baccalaureate, MBA highly desired. CPP highly desired.
Five years experience in an equivalent or lead-in position.

projects. The description, presented in a narrative style, might begin with, "The incumbent is responsible for...," or words to that effect.

Organizational Relationships. In this section will be an identification of the person to whom the position reports, those reporting to the position, and those who hold comparable positions. These are often displayed in the style of an organizational chart The position titles are almost always identified and, in some organizations, the names of the incumbents are included.

In evaluating a position, it may be helpful to identify the equivalent jobs, i.e., the peers of the job holder. The salary grades of the equivalent jobs can be used as a baseline for determining the grade of the position being evaluated.

Position Data. The pertinent data for this section of the form would include the annual budget of the activity performed, the number of employees supervised, the nature and amount of funds that are affected by the incumbent, licensing, education, and experience requirements, and the extent and nature of contacts maintained by the incumbent. For example, it might be pertinent to reflect that the position of security manager requires Certified Protection Professional status, an advanced degree in business administration, and five years of responsible experience in security management or administration.

Principal Accountabilities. This section usually consists of a list of the major job tasks that the incumbent performs in accomplishing the overall purpose and chief objectives of the job. The task statements are often listed in the order of importance or frequency.

John J. Fay, CPP

Sources

Heyel, C., Encyclopedia of Management. (Van Nostrand Reinhold, New York, 1982).

Position Description Preparation Guide. (BP America, Cleveland, OH, 1992).

POSTAL INSPECTION SERVICE

The Postal Inspection Service is this nation's oldest federal law enforcement agency. Its origins can be traced to the American Colonial Postal System and the appointment of Benjamin Franklin as Postmaster of Philadelphia in 1737. Postal inspectors are federal law enforcement agents. They have the power to make arrests, carry firearms, serve warrants and subpoenas, and investigate crimes against the Postal Service. The mission and directives of the Postal Inspection Service have been the same from its early inception and through to present time, i.e., to protect the integrity and public trust of the Postal Service.

The need to protect the privacy and personal rights of the individual is a concept on which the United States of America was founded. In the American colonial period, this concept was a principal goal of freedom-seeking individuals who emigrated to the American Colonies. The idea that an individual's personal papers have a special degree of privacy when entrusted to the mails is called the "Sanctity of the Seal." This idea was the basis for the creation of what is now the Postal Inspection Service.

The Sanctity of the Seal demanded that the Colonial Postal System oversee and regulate the several post offices in the Colonial System. This was done by appointing Benjamin Franklin as Postmaster of Philadelphia with broadened powers to regulate the several post offices and bring the postmasters to account. In 1737, Philadelphia was an important trend-setting city in the colonies. Precedents set by Benjamin Franklin in Philadelphia were carried on throughout all the colonies. Among Franklin's duties were auditing accounts of post offices, improving the transit of mail, devising accounting procedures, and establishing new post offices in expansion areas. Thirty-five years later (1772), the colonial postal system had grown with the colonies. A new position of "surveyor" was established to carry on the responsibility set forth by Franklin. In 1801, the postmaster general issued an order changing the title surveyor to special agent, with expanded investigative duties.

During the early 19th century, the United States was enjoying its formulative "Nation Time." Laws and regulations were created by Congress to meet the needs of the new nation. A separate office of Instructions and Mail Depredation was formed in 1830 to be the investigative and inspection branch of the Post Office Department. Federal laws were enacted by Congress making violations against the "Post Office Department" federal crimes. In 1835, a director was named as head of the investigative and inspection branch with assigned duties clearly mandated. In 1880, at the request of the postmaster general, Congress changed the title from special agent to chief post office inspector. The modern era of the Postal Inspection Service had begun.

Investigative Responsibilities

The Postal Inspection Service is the law enforcement arm of the U.S. Postal Service. The Inspection Service is charged with maintaining the security and integrity of the Postal Service. This responsibility includes protection of U. S. mail, postal facilities, and employees from criminal attack. It also includes protecting the American public from criminal attack whereby the Postal Service is used as a vehicle, including mail fraud schemes, mail bombs, and narcotics trafficking. The Postal Inspection Service also provides an audit function for the Postal Service. The Inspection Service performs financial audits and service evaluations, and works closely with postal management to improve service in all areas.

This mission is no simple task. It is accomplished through criminal and administrative investigations. There are basically six divisions in the investigative responsibilities set forth for the Postal Inspection Service:

Internal Crimes. Investigations focus on employee involvement in criminal actions. The most common of internal investigations are mail thefts and mistreatment of mail by employees. Also included is financial depredation (theft of postal monies/embezzlement) and abuse of workers compensation benefits. Internal investigations also focus on use or sale of narcotics in the workplace.

External Crimes. Investigations center on attacks of the Postal Service from the outside. The most common external crimes investigations are mail thefts, burglary of a postal facility, armed robbery, or assault of a postal employee.

Mail Fraud. These investigations are known as "white collar crime." Mail fraud is the use of the mail usually in a scheme to deceive and defraud people. Insurance fraud and "Get Rich Quick" schemes are common examples of mail fraud. These cases can be criminal or civil in nature and can contain forfeiture of assets.

Prohibited Mailings. These are investigations into the shipment of illegal materials or articles through the mail. Most common prohibitive mailing investigations include pornography, narcotics and other controlled substances, and mail bombs or explosive devices sent through the mail.

Audit. The audit function includes three primary types: financial, operational, and developmental. Financial audits include the review of financial transactions, verification of account balances, and evaluation of systems of accounting and administrative controls. Operational audits provide postal management with an independent review of postal operations to improve efficiency and maintain a higher level of customer satisfaction with the mail service. Developmental audits are conducted to provide independent and objective evaluations of new systems and equipment during the proposal, design, development, and implementation stages.

Prevention/Security. The program of the Inspection Service is a two-tiered program. In one tier it is geared to anticipate, recognize, and assess crime risk by analyzing crime trends and developing countermeasures. In the second tier it implements on-site physical security, such as guards, barriers, alarms, and procedures. Another function is to conduct background investigations of Postal Inspection Service candidates.

Statutory Authority

The criminal investigative program of the Postal Inspection Service is authorized by several federal statutes passed by Congress over the last 200 years. There are well over 100 federal statutes directly related to postal crime. This means federal laws enacted to protect the Postal Service from criminal attack, as well as protecting the American citizen from criminal attack using the U.S. mails. As recently as 1988, Congress further empowered the Postal Inspection Service to investigate postal offenses and civil matters relating to the Postal Service.

The most well-known and widely used federal statute is the Mail Fraud Statute, Title 18, U.S.C., Section 1341, passed by Congress in 1872. Title 21, U.S.C., is also important as Sections 853 and 881 expand both the civil and criminal forfeiture powers of the Inspection Service. Title 39, U.S.C., in its entirety deals directly with the Postal Service and authority thereof.

The Postal Inspection Service is the only federal entity to perform civil, criminal, administrative, audit, security, and inspector general functions within one organization. The Inspection Service works directly with the Department of Justice seeking both civil remedies and federal prosecution of crimes through the U.S. Attorney Offices and the federal courts. It is also not uncommon for prosecution of postal crimes to be sought in the state and local courts, as well.

Organization

The National Headquarters of the Postal Inspection Service is located in L'Enfant Plaza, Washington, DC. The chief postal inspector, the inspector general for the Postal Service, reports directly to the postmaster general of the United States.

The Postal Inspection Service maintains an office in every major city in the United States. There are 30 inspection service divisions nationwide. These include offices in Alaska, Hawaii, and Puerto Rico. In addition, the field offices can draw support from five management support groups and five crime laboratories across the country. This configuration makes it possible to cover the United States and its territories with just over 2,000 postal inspectors.

Although small compared to other agencies, the Postal Inspection Service has always been very proud of its accomplishments and place in American history. Unofficially nicknamed "The Silent Service," the Inspection Service has been involved in many prominent and successful investigations over the years. A few examples are:

• Between 1937 and 1941, postal inspectors were called upon to plan, protect, and transfer 500 railroad cars carrying $15.5 billion in gold from New York to Fort Knox. The transfer was accomplished without incident.

• In 1972, postal inspectors investigated the notorious Clifford Irving Hoax. Mr. Irving defrauded two publishing companies of several hundred thousand dollars, claiming exclusive rights to write billionaire Howard Hughes's biography. Analysis and investigation proved that Irving provided forged documents as the basis of the exclusive rights.

• In 1988, postal inspectors investigated the Wall Street Insider Trading Scandal. This investigation led to the conviction of stock arbitrageur Ivan Boesky.

• In 1989, a task force led by postal inspectors was responsible for the conviction of tele-evangelist Jim and Tammy Faye Bakker on mail fraud charges.

• Also in 1989, inspectors investigated Leona Helmsley, the millionaire hotel magnate, who was convicted on mail fraud charges.

• Another important case was the investigation and conviction of "junk bond king" Michael Milkin et al. in the Drexel, Burnham, Lambert mail fraud case. This case included millions of dollars in forfeiture.

• In 1990, the Postal Inspection Service investigated Chrysler Motors Corporation for mail fraud. Chrysler then paid criminal fines in the amount of $7.6 million to the U.S. Postal Service after the conviction.

Richard Laboda

PRE-EMPLOYMENT SCREENING

Employee crime is preventable and its prevention is profitable. When sales are recorded accurately, high labor costs disappear and inventory shrinkage is curtailed. With true sales reporting, employee turnover can be curbed and customer satisfaction enhanced. All this may be accomplished merely by hiring the right employee -- that is, the honest employee -- and keeping that employee honest.

The task of hiring an honest employee and keeping him or her that way is not a simple one. Criminals and hard workers are not easily distinguishable. It would be nice if honest applicants wore blue suits and con men wore plaid, but they don't. The honest and the dishonest, on the surface, look alike -- but beneath the surface they are as different as night and day.

Although a number of sophisticated devices are available to help employers screen prospective employees -- paper and pencil tests, the polygraph, voice stress analysis, etc. -- this discussion of hiring the right employee will be limited to evaluation methods that are not currently nor likely in the future to become restricted by law.

As a practical matter, no screening policy or procedure should ever be adopted without the endorsement of legal counsel. Although sophisticated screening measures are useful, they should never be used as the sole criterion for making a hiring decision. Common sense goes a long way when it is time to decide whether to hire a person.

The quality of employees hired will directly affect profitability. The cost of loafing and dishonesty is hard to pin down, but the cost of staff turnover might provide a handle for determining the stakes involved in a successful hiring program. It can cost $5,000 to hire a management trainee and $50,000 to hire a corporate officer. These figures include advertising, interviewing, transportation, and training.

A few simple tools are available to help management sift out poor applicants at the pre-employment stage, so an understanding of existing tools is critical. First and foremost, the importance of using a complete and accurate employment application form cannot be overemphasized. A hindsight review of an employment application following a crime against a company will usually provide a list of red flags the personnel or security department should have noticed before a job offer was extended.

Possible red flags include fabrications, exaggerations and conflicting dates of employment, education, and military service. Also, there will be the usual omissions of explanations for how time was spent between critical dates. Most important, the applicant's failure to sign and date the application should be considered a major red flag.

Persons responsible for making hiring decisions should be aware that the first three digits of a social security number, commonly referred to as the social security prefix, identifies the state where the number was issued. (See the accompanying chart of prefixes.)

It is not uncommon to discover a counterfeit application by checking a prefix list. The interviewer should ascertain whether the applicant's school, employment, or military service locations correspond to his or her social security prefix. For instance, if the applicant claims that he or she is a born and bred Kentuckian, the interviewer should be concerned if the applicant's social security prefix indicates the number was issued in New York. There are honest explanations for some red flags, but all require further inquiry.

Another tool that may prove quite helpful at the pre-employment stage is the cursory reference check. Quite commonly, dishonest applicants provide some truth in their references. For instance, they might provide the correct name of a former employer and change the location, or provide the proper city and state of their school but change its name. These deceptions can come to light by simply using the services of long-distance information. The application reviewer should never only use the references and phone numbers provided by the applicant. Personal and work references given by a criminal are likely to produce excellent recommendations that may be totally false. The reviewer should ask to speak to past and present co-workers other than the persons named on the form.

Interviewers are encouraged to watch out for the "storyteller" applicant. This individual will claim to have been a Medal of Honor winner or a finalist in the British Open. The interviewer should corroborate any spectacular claims made by the applicant. Generally, such a claim can be supported or dismissed by a simple call to the reference librarian at a public library.

Crisscross directories can be found in large public libraries and are available by subscription in most major cities. They are a helpful tool for checking the applicant's name, address, and telephone number. As a rule of thumb, an applicant claiming to have been at an address for 2 years or longer should appear in a crisscross directory.

The value of corroborating an applicant's address and telephone number lies in the fact that dishonest applicants do not normally provide accurate information in these areas. An inexpensive way to verify applicant address information is to forward company brochures and benefits description packages to the applicant via certified, receipt-requested mail.

Other red flags include claims of honorable discharge as a reason for leaving the military. Beware of applicants who claim less than full terms for their period of service. Also, the term "self-employed" accurately describes both honest applicants and career criminals. Old telephone directories and county clerk files are a free and relatively easy way to confirm or disprove self-employment. Medical histories that show a pattern of workers' compensation claims or wounds caused by guns or knives should receive extra scrutiny.

Social Security Number Prefixes

000-003	New Hampshire	318-361	Illinois	518-519	Idaho
004-007	Maine	362-386	Michigan	520	Wyoming
008-009	Vermont	387-399	Wisconsin	521-524	Colorado
010-034	Massachusetts	400-407	Kentucky	525-585	New Mexico
035-039	Rhode Island	408-415	Tennessee	526-527	&
040-049	Connecticut	416-424	Alabama	600-601	Arizona
050-134	New York	425-428	&	528-529	Utah
135-158	New Jersey	587-588	Mississippi	530	Nevada
159-211	Pennsylvania	429-432	Arkansas	531-539	Washington
212-220	Maryland	433-439	Louisiana	540-544	Oregon
221-222	Delaware	440-448	Oklahoma	545-573	&
223-236	West Virginia	449-467	Texas	602-626	California
232	&	468-477	Minnesota	574	Alaska
237-246	North Carolina	478-485	Iowa	575-576	Hawaii
247-251	South Carolina	486-500	Missouri	577-579	Washington (DC)
252-260	Georgia	501-502	North Dakota	580-584	Puerto Rico &
261-267	&	503-504	South Dakota	596-599	Virgin Isl, Guam
589-595	Florida	505-508	Nebraska		American Samoa
268-302	Ohio	509-515	Kansas	586	Philippines
303-317	Indiana	516-517	Montana	700-728	RR Retirement

Note: Some numbers are shown more than once because they have been transferred from one state to another, or have been divided for use among certain geographic locations.

Counterfeit applicants are very often practiced, believable liars. The reasons they give for being unable to provide verifiable data about their past histories can be quite convincing. One of the most common reasons put forward is that the former employer went out of business and cannot be contacted. A lack of references is a reason to look further, not to stop.

Management hires should be subjected to a thorough background investigation as soon as they accept an offer of employment. A good source of vital statistics can be a bonding application filled out by the new hire. The honest person will appreciate the relationship between a truthful bonding application and a smooth entry into the job.

On the other hand, the dishonest applicant will correctly understand that untruthful details on the bonding application will very likely be discovered. At this point, there is a chance that the dishonest applicant will decide to not accept the job after all. Even if the dishonest applicant decides to push forward, he or she would most probably not be initially assigned to a position of high trust that could harm the company substantially. By the time the individual would be in such a position, the background investigation would have revealed the untruths.

Many new hires in fact do not go onto the job until after completing a training course. The company's critical assets, such as cash or sensitive information, are not accessible to the new hire during the training period, and while training is being conducted, the background investigation is underway.

In addition to the various pre-employment and post-employment screenings, the employer should ensure that each new hire is informed of policies and procedures that govern personal conduct. This process of orientation would logically include specific identification of the prohibited behaviors, the penalties for violations, and the methods the employer will use to enforce rules. Because the employee's understanding of the rules can be an issue in proving a violation and administering a penalty, the employer should obtain from the new hire a written acknowledgment that the policies and procedures have been understood and accepted.

This is not so much a tactic of administration but of psychology. The new hire who receives clear and explicit instructions about the employer's expectations with respect to protecting assets is more likely to start his or her new job with a personal sense of responsibility to the care and custody of the owner's assets. The psychological message can be both positive and negative. On the positive side, the new hire will know where the employer stands on behavioral issues and will be pleased to work in an environment that upholds the values of honesty and respect. On the negative side, the employee is impressed with the certainty of punishment, fairly and consistently administered. This is not a new concept. Cesare Beccaria, an 18th century criminologist, commented that it is not cruelty or severity that renders punishment an effective deterrent, but its certainty.

Francis James D'addario, CPP

Source Reprinted from the November 1990 issue of Security Management magazine with permission of the American Society for Industrial Security, 1655 North Fort Myer Drive, Suite 1200, Arlington, VA 22209.

PRE-EMPLOYMENT SCREENING: A BASIC PHILOSOPHY

Statistics relating to financial losses because of employee theft, as well as alcohol and illegal drug use by employees, are staggering. For example, the Fireman's Fund Insurance Company reported that 30% of annual business failures are the result of internal theft. A congressional report estimates that companies lose about $70 billion annually in lost productivity and health expenses due to job-related drug abuse. Up to 40% of industrial fatalities and 47% of industrial injuries can be linked to alcohol abuse and alcoholism.

Ironically, even though statistics indicate a greater need for employers to identify dishonest job applicants, legislation restricting areas of pre-employment evaluation and screening procedures is also increasing. For example, several states have passed legislation that prohibits employers from asking questions about an individual's social use of alcohol and the Federal Employee Polygraph Protection Act of 1988 greatly restricts most private employers' use of the polygraph technique for pre-employment screening. Despite these restrictions, with increased frequency courts are holding employers liable for negligent hiring practices if the employer does not adequately

screen job applicants. As one court ruled, "The employer is expected to exercise a reasonable standard of care" in the selection of new employees.

The approaches available to an employer to reduce acts of employee misconduct include establishing measures that: (1) identify employees who violate the law and/or company rules, (2) discourage misconduct through internal controls and supervision, and (3) screen out job applicants who, if hired, are likely to engage in misconduct. While an effective security program involves all three of these approaches, the least costly approach in terms of dollars, time, and liability is an effective screening program at the front end to weed out the "bad apples."

The purpose of pre-employment screening, therefore, is to assess applicants in terms of their propensity to engage in undesirable conduct if hired. The idea of screening is not to automatically reject every applicant having a history of misconduct, but to calculate the probable effect that the hiring of an applicant will have upon the company. These include lost revenue from theft, decreased productivity because of current drug or alcohol use, and liability risks as a result of dishonest or unlawful conduct. Pre-employment screening, then, is intended to predict the applicant's future behavior or performance if hired.

One means of forecasting a job applicant's behavior is through the use of written tests designed to evaluate psychological characteristics that are believed to predict future performance. Because these instruments do not directly assess the applicant's behavior, they are considered inferential tests. One category of these tests evaluates a job applicant's personality traits (Minnesota Multiphase Personality Inventory, MMPI) (California Psychological Inventory, CPI) which may indicate a propensity for certain behaviors. However, the most frequently used written test to predict dishonesty evaluates the job applicant's attitudes. The principle behind such tests is that an individual who has developed strong attitudes toward honesty is less likely to engage in dishonesty than an individual who possesses weaker attitudes toward honesty.

While written personality or attitude tests are relatively inexpensive to administer, psychologists agree that the most valid predictor of future behavior is an individual's past behavioral patterns. For example, a job applicant who has stolen repeatedly from previous employers is more likely to steal in the future than an applicant who has not stolen from previous employers. Pre-employment screening designed to identify past acts of dishonesty or misconduct represents a direct measure of the applicant's behavior.

The difficulty in evaluating a job applicant's past behavior is that dishonest applicants are likely to lie about past acts of dishonesty on a questionnaire or during a typical interview. For this reason, specialized pre-employment procedures are used to identify deception and elicit truthful responses. Examples of these include the polygraph technique, face-to-face behavioral interviews, and interactive computer interviews. Other sources of information that can identify an applicant's past behavioral patterns are background investigations, record checks, and drug testing.

Brian C. Jayne

PRE-EMPLOYMENT SCREENING: PRIVACY ISSUES IN HIRING

The use of personnel selection techniques in employment has traditionally raised concerns over statutory employer liability based on allegations of unfair discrimination as defined by Title VII of the Civil Rights Act of 1964 [1] and state fair employment laws, but given our increasingly litigious society, security and personnel professionals must now be aware of other growing sources of employer liability associated with screening programs. Such liabilities include, but are not limited to, claims of defamation, infliction of emotional distress, negligent employment, and invasion of privacy. Although each of these causes of action is an important consideration in employment screening, today, invasion of privacy is probably at the forefront due to current scrutiny from the judiciary and legislatures.

Basis of Recovery

Invasion of privacy claims can be based on a number of sources -- the U.S. Constitution, state constitutions, state laws, and common law torts. Although the U.S. Constitution and most state constitutions protect parties only against governmental invasions of privacy, the common

law and state laws are generally applicable to the private employer. With many states recognizing a common law right to privacy and with various new privacy-based legislative initiatives, even private sector employers can expect to defend against a growing number of such cases. The current and future growth of such litigation is reflected by a recently reported statistic from the Bureau of National Affairs [2]:

> In workplace privacy cases, the nationwide average jury verdict award from 1985 to 1987 was $316,000. In contrast, from 1979 to 1980, no such cases were heard.

Although invasion of privacy claims can be based on the improper collection, use, maintenance, or disclosure of information, probably the most pertinent and publicized issue currently, is the invasiveness of various hiring criteria (e.g., clinical-based pre-employment tests, drug tests, background checks, credit checks, interviews, etc.). Although invasive inquiries may be warranted, depending on job requirements, personnel and security professionals must be aware that requesting such information can be a lightning rod for privacy-based complaints.

Legislation

A recent example of the growing trend in privacy-based legislation is the Employee Polygraph Protection Act [3]. Although a variety of public policy issues led to the introduction and passage of this legislation, the major impetus was ostensibly privacy issues. For example, in his testimony at the hearing before the Senate Labor and Human Resources Committee, the New York State Attorney General stated[4]:

> Not only are so-called lie detectors shockingly inaccurate, their use constitutes one of the most significant threats to the fundamental right of privacy that we as Americans enjoy...Those who take the test suffer the indignity of being attached to a machine that scrutinizes their bodily functions and are often asked questions about personal aspects of their lives which are none of their employers' business.

More recently, at the state level, the Oregon Interim Senate Committee on Labor conducted a forum in 1990 to address privacy issues in the employment context. Subsequently, during the Oregon legislature's 1991 regular session, the Senate Labor Committee considered a variety of legislation related to the privacy issues that had been addressed at the forum. These issues stemmed from perceived abuses in the use of electronic monitoring (SB 862) [5], credit reports (SB 963) [6], handwriting analysis (SB 834) [7], and psychological testing (SB 792) [8] to screen job applicants and/or to evaluate the performance of current employees. Although none of these bills were enacted by the Oregon legislature, their proposed language and purpose was obviously focused on privacy. For instance, SB 963 sought to ensure that credit reporting agencies deleted information regarding a job applicant's "age, marital status, and dependents" from reports to employers, while SB 792 sought to restrict the use of invasive questions (e.g., family relations, sexual preferences, religious orientation, etc.) on pre-employment psychological tests, where employers can show a business necessity and that the information is essential to effective job performance.

Another privacy-related topic that is most recently receiving a great deal of attention from legislators involves employer inquiries into applicant/employee activities off the premises of the employer during non-working hours. In response to this practice, many states have enacted legislation or have recently introduced legislative initiatives to prohibit such inquiries [9]. Although the impetus for many of these bills is to prevent employers from discriminating against smokers, the language is often broad enough to encompass a whole range of activities that the employer may find undesirable (e.g., moonlighting, engaging in high-risk athletic activities, political activities, etc.).

Judicial Challenges

One of the most heavily litigated areas of employee privacy is the use of drug testing. Applicants and employees object not only to the intrusive process of having their urine or blood tested for chemicals, but also because such testing may reveal information about their activities and lifestyle outside the workplace. Both public and private sector employers who utilize drug tests have been the focus of privacy litigation challenging such practices [10].

Another practice that has received increased attention is the use of clinical personality tests for screening employees. Because many of these tests were originally developed for the purpose of diagnosing psychological disorders in a clinical setting, they often contain highly personal questions that can be offensive to people seeking employment. The most well-known and commonly used of these clinical personality tests is the Minnesota Multiphasic Personality Inventory (MMPI).

Although there has been extensive research on the MMPI and it is well respected in the psychological community, its acceptance by employment applicants has been significantly less than enthusiastic. Questions regarding political beliefs, sexual preferences, and family relations are perceived as unreasonably invasive by many applicants and have resulted in lawsuits and applicant complaints.

In one such case in Rhode Island (*Tucker v. Town of Glocester Police Department*), [11] an applicant to the police department filed a complaint regarding inquiries on the MMPI that dealt with religious beliefs. The Rhode Island Commission for Human Rights arrived at a settlement between the parties when the police department agreed to delete from the MMPI three items relating to religious beliefs.

In another widely publicized California case (*Soroka v. Dayton Hudson Corp.*), [12] Soroka, an applicant for a Store Security Officer (SSO) position with Target Stores was required to take the MMPI and another well-known personality test, the California Psychological Inventory (CPI). Although he was hired for the job, Soroka stated that he was upset by having to complete the tests. In his class action suit against Dayton Hudson, Soroka claimed, among other things, invasion of privacy and discrimination under certain California statutes. In addition, Soroka sought a preliminary injunction to prohibit Target from administering its testing program until the ultimate outcome of the case.

Although Soroka's motion for a preliminary injunction was denied at the trial court level, a California appeals court granted it, stating:

"...Target's inquiry into the religious beliefs and sexual orientation of SSO applicants unjustifiably violates the state constitutional right to privacy..." and that such inquiries are discriminatory under California statutes [13].

Although this decision applies to invasive clinical tests, the court's opinion went no further in restricting the use of testing by California employers. In fact, the court stated that "the preliminary injunction would only limit Target's use of the [MMPI/CPI] in its present form" and "...Target is free to use other, legally proper methods to determine the emotional stability of its SSO applicants" [14]. Thus, the court did not seek to restrict all forms of pre-employment psychological testing -- only those types of clinically oriented tests that contain unjustifiably invasive items. It is important to note that under the California appellate court's decision, even if a pre-employment test is found to be an invasion of privacy, it does not automatically prohibit its use. Rather, if a test is considered by the court to be invasive, an employer may still justify its use by showing a compelling interest for such use. In other words, use of such clinically oriented tests as the MMPI and CPI may be justified for some positions in which emotional stability is critical.

Since legislation and judicial challenges regarding employee privacy are likely to continue to become more commonplace, security and personnel professionals must be circumspect in using pre-employment devices to ensure that only job-related information is considered. Invasive inquiries and procedures should be exclusively limited to use when the employer is able to show a strong business or societal interest. Given the litigious nature of society, coupled with the growing number of privacy-based legislative initiatives, it is also imperative for such professionals to monitor judicial decisions and legislation to ensure maximal compliance and insulation from liability.

David W. Arnold
and Rachel A. Ankeny

Notes

1. Civil Rights Act of 1964, 42 U.S.C. §§2000e-5(g) (1988).

2. Shephard, I. M., and Duston, R. L., Workplace Privacy: Employee Testing, Surveillance, Wrongful Discharge, and Other Areas of Vulnerability (1987).

3. Employee Polygraph Protection Act of 1988, 29 U.S.C. §§2001-2009 (1988).

4. Reviewing the Use and Abuse of Polygraph Testing in the Workplace, 1987: Hearings on H.R. 1212 Before the Senate Comm. on Labor and Human Resources, 100th Congress, 1st Sess. (1987) (statement of Robert Abrams, Attorney General, State of New York).

5. S.B. 862, 66th Or. Leg. Ass., Reg. Sess. (1991).

6. S.B. 963, 66th Or. Leg. Ass., Reg. Sess. (1991).

7. S.B. 834, 66th Or. Leg. Ass., Reg. Sess. (1991).

8. S.B. 792, 66th Or. Leg. Ass., Reg. Sess. (1991).

9. See e.g., IL P.A. 87-0807; L.B. 951, 92nd Neb. Leg., 2d Sess. (1992); H.B. 2274, 52nd Wash. Leg., Reg. Sess. (1992); S.B. 340, 17th Alaska Leg., 2d Sess. (1992); H.B. 1322, 86th Mo. Gen. Ass., 2d Reg. Sess. (1992); H.B. 3272, 16th Hawaii Leg. (1992).

10. See e.g., *National Treasury Employees Union v. Von Raab*, 109 S.Ct. 1384 (1989); *Wilkinson v. Times Mirror Corp.*, 215 Cal.App.3d 1034 (1989).

11. *Tucker v. Town of Glocester Police Department*, RICHR No. 88 ERE 319-19/19 (Jan. 16, 1991).

12. *Soroka v. Dayton Hudson Corp.*, No. A052157 (Cal. Dist. Ct. App. Oct. 25, 1991) (order granting preliminary injunction).

13. Ibid. at 21.

14. See ibid. at 27.

PREGNANCY DISCRIMINATION

The Pregnancy Discrimination Act is an amendment to Title VII of the Civil Rights Act of 1964. Discrimination on the basis of pregnancy, childbirth, or related medical conditions constitutes unlawful sex discrimination under Title VI. Women affected by pregnancy or related conditions must be treated in the same manner as other applicants or employees with similar abilities or limitations.

An employer cannot refuse to hire a woman because of her pregnancy-related condition as long as she is able to perform the major functions of the job. An employer cannot refuse to hire her because of its prejudices against pregnant workers or the prejudices of co-workers, clients, or customers.

An employer may not single out pregnancy-related conditions for special procedures to determine an employee's ability to work. However, an employer may use any procedure used to screen other employees' ability to work. For example, if an employer requires its employees to submit a doctor's statement concerning their inability to work before granting leave or paying sick benefits, the employer may require employees affected by pregnancy-related conditions to submit such statements.

If an employee is temporarily unable to perform her job due to pregnancy, the employer must treat her the same as any other temporarily disabled employee; for example, by providing modified tasks, alternative assignments, disability leave, or leave without pay.

Pregnant employees must be permitted to work as long as they are able to perform their jobs. If an employee has been absent from work as a result of a pregnancy-related condition and recovers, her employer may not require her to remain on leave until the baby's birth. An employer may not have a rule that prohibits an employee from returning to work for a predetermined length of time after childbirth. Employers must hold open a job for a pregnancy-related absence the same length of time jobs are held open for employees on sick or disability leave.

Leave for child care purposes is not covered by the Pregnancy Discrimination Act. However, Title VII requires that leave for child care purposes be granted on the same basis as leave granted to employees for other non-medical reasons, such as non-job-related travel or education. Any health insurance provided by an employer must cover expenses for pregnancy-related conditions on the same basis as costs for other medical conditions. Health insurance for expenses arising from abortion is not required, except where the life of the mother is endangered.

Pregnancy-related expenses should be reimbursed exactly as those incurred for other medical conditions, whether payment is on a fixed basis or a percentage of reasonable and customary charge basis. The amounts payable by the insurance provider can be limited only to the same extent as costs for other conditions. No additional, increased, or larger deductible can be imposed.

If a health insurance plan excludes benefit payments for pre-existing conditions when the insured's coverage becomes effective, benefits can be denied for medical costs arising from an existing pregnancy. Employers must provide the same level of health benefits for spouses of male employees as they do for spouses for female employees.

Pregnancy-related benefits cannot be limited to married employees. In an all-female workforce or job classification, benefits for pregnancy-related conditions must be provided if benefits are provided for other medical conditions. If an employer provides any benefits to workers on leave, the employer must provide the same benefits for those on leave for pregnancy-related conditions. Employees with pregnancy-related disabilities must be treated the same as other temporarily disabled employees for accrual and crediting of seniority, vacation calculation, pay increases, and temporary disability benefits.

U.S. Equal Opportunity Commission

Source Facts about Pregnancy Discrimination. (The U.S. Equal Opportunity Commission, Washington, DC, 1992).

PREMISES LIABILITY FOR NEGLIGENT SECURITY

As a general principle of American common law, there is no duty on the part of any individual or organization to provide protective security services to any other individual or organization unless a special relationship exists between them. In recent years, the courts have established that a special relationship may exist and, therefore, that a duty to provide reasonable security may exist, as between a landlord-tenant, commercial landlord-business invitee, common carrier-passenger, employer-employee, teacher-student, and innkeeper-guest [1]. In other words, those individuals in control of a property or a relationship have a duty to provide reasonable security to those dependent upon them for such protection. While a landlord is not expected to insure the safety of a tenant or invitee, as in strict liability, those security measures that are appropriate to the level of threat must be taken. Where such measures are not taken and this failure is the proximate cause and cause in fact of a plaintiff's injury, the landlord or property operator may be found negligent in tort [2]. The implications for the modern security manager are quite clear. If a customer, guest, or tenant is injured on company property, as in the case of a criminal attack, for example, the company may be liable for compensatory or even punitive damages. In order to try to avoid such liability, the security manager should determine to what extent such a criminal event is reasonably foreseeable and should implement those measures that can reasonably be expected to prevent such a crime. Once again, since it is unlikely that all crimes can ever be prevented, the security manager can only be expected to take reasonable measures. Where reasonable preventive measures have been taken, and a crime still occurs, in theory there should be no liability.

Foreseeability

The operative word in this discussion is "reasonable." There are a number of ways a security manager can determine if a crime is reasonably foreseeable.   In those court jurisdictions that follow the "prior similar acts" rule, evidence of the prior occurrence of a crime on or near the premises which is similar to the crime currently the subject of litigation will often serve to establish foreseeability, or actual notice. Generally, police departments can provide a computer printout detailing all crimes reported at a given address for a 2- or 3-year period prior to the occurrence of the crime generating the lawsuit. Calls for police service (i.e., radio run logs) can also be used in a more limited fashion for this purpose.   The general criminal history of a neighborhood or city can also be established through police department annual reports and Federal Bureau of Investigation (FBI) Uniform Crime Reports.   Of great importance in the assessment of foreseeability are the security incident reports generated for the property in question.   Crime analysis conducted by security department personnel can establish whether any pattern is developing and thus whether crime is foreseeable.

A growing number of jurisdictions are following the "totality of the circumstances" rule, which takes a more comprehensive approach to determining whether or not a given crime, or type of crime, was reasonably foreseeable [3]. Sometimes known as constructive notice, the existence of a number of environmental and social factors can be taken to suggest that a crime was

reasonably foreseeable, even in the absence of prior crimes of a similar nature [4]. For example, a condominium complex within a 1- or 2-mile distance of a low-income public housing project may attract burglars since most crime is committed relatively close to home.   Bus terminals, shopping center parking lots, some bars and fast food restaurants, and video arcades are known as "crime magnets" because of the opportunity for property crimes and crimes of violence.

Hospital parking lots are more likely to be patronized by vulnerable females after business hours due to the nature of the employment pool and the need for 24-hour staffing.   This fact combined with the presence of drugs on campus, potential violence in the emergency room, and the particularly vulnerable nature of patients and emotionally spent visitors can foretell crime. Commercial establishments easily accessible from expressways and not characterized by nearby pedestrian traffic can be uniquely vulnerable to holdup. While the scenarios listed previously do not exhaust the circumstances wherein constructive notice may be found, they do illustrate the wide range of possibilities.   In general, wherever potential victims and motivated perpetrators come together in the absence of natural or organized surveillance, crime may be foreseeable [5].

Adequacy of Security

If a security manager determines that a certain amount or type of crime is reasonably foreseeable, he or she should establish security measures appropriate to the level of threat. To the extent possible, these efforts should deter the criminal, deny him a target, delay him in his efforts, or, at the least, allow his efforts to be detected. Where appropriate, security will also be able to respond and detain. Again, the law is reasonable in that it does not require a maximum security response to a minimum security threat. In order to determine whether property and individual protection rises to the level of crime foreseeability, loss prevention personnel should assess their security hardware, software, and personnel.

Security hardware generally refers to "target hardening" and would include perimeter controls such as barriers and alarms. While fencing alone is rarely an adequate barrier as a stand-alone security measure, the addition of a zoned alarm system relying upon a variety of sensor types greatly improves its usefulness. Lighting levels may also be a part of the physical security system and would hopefully allow security personnel to detect and identify intruders. Some lighting may also serve to incapacitate intruders through glare. The relationship between lighting and crime prevention is not completely straightforward, however, since an increase in lighting levels does not always lead to a decrease in crime. There is a difference between visibility (lighting levels) and observability (whether or not an intruder can be seen due to blocked sight lines or the absence of personnel). While closed-circuit television (CCTV) systems have gained widespread acceptance, the "narcotic effect" of prolonged viewing by security officers and the fact that cameras cannot hear or smell may serve to modify their overall usefulness. Locks, of course, must be appropriate for the protective job to be done but, once again, the law does not expect a landlord to secure a rarely used storage garage to the same extent as he or she would secure Fort Knox.

Security software may be taken to refer to the policies, procedures, rules, and regulations implemented by an organization to protect its assets, which would include, by definition, both invitees and licensees. In a badge identification system, for example, is it corporate policy to have all employees comply by wearing their badges at all times, including the president? Is there a policy in place to require a security survey on an annual or periodic basis? Does a large retail store have a policy of concern for parking lot safety that it implements through a procedure wherein loss prevention personnel routinely maintain surveillance of outside areas? It is generally good security practice to provide pertinent employees with written policies, procedures, rules, and regulations, and to clarify for them the fact that, while procedures allow for a certain degree of discretionary variance, rules and regulations are mandatory. Security awareness training for all employees is a policy that has gained widespread corporate support in recent years.

With regard to security personnel, there are a number of concerns for security management. Are there enough security officers, for example, to provide adequate coverage? If numbers have recently been reduced, such a reduction in force ought to have been due to a reduced threat level rather than to budget reasons alone. While

security patrols cannot be taken to automatically constitute a preventive measure, as was learned in the Kansas City police patrol experiment, such patrols may still provide residual deterrent effect. During litigation, issues concerning negligent hiring of employees will arise. Background checks appropriate to the sensitivity of the position are expected. Negligent training may be argued if an individual has not been properly prepared for the task to be performed. Security managers must avoid negligent assignment of a given individual to a post where job demands exceed his or her skills and must not negligently retain such an employee when it becomes apparent the stress of the assignment exceeds the ability to cope. Negligent retention would also apply to other "danger indications" pertaining to any employee, such as drinking or using drugs while on the job, fighting, bringing weapons to work, etc. [6]. Negligent entrustment would entail, for example, providing a vehicle or weapon to an employee unable to use them properly. Also, security personnel must not be negligently supervised. Finally, security management must not fail to direct security personnel by providing them with unclear policies and procedures or none at all.

The provision of effective security services is an art rather than a science. Although research into what constitutes proper security under a variety of conditions continues, a tremendous amount of discretion is involved in making security decisions.

As a general guideline, security managers must determine the level of foreseeability of a given threat. If they have actual or constructive notice of a criminal threat, for example, then protective measures that can meet and, it is hoped, defeat this threat should be implemented. No landlord is an insurer of a visitor's safety, however, and can only be expected to take reasonable precautions. Where a crime occurs even in the presence of reasonable security measures, no liability should attach.

Daniel B. Kennedy, Ph.D., CPP

Sources

Bottom, N., Security/Loss Control Negligence. (Hanrow Press, Columbia, MD, 1985).

Kennedy, D., Premises Liability: Crime Foreseeability and the Adequacy of Security. Paper presented at 11th Annual Conference of the

International Society of Crime Prevention Practitioners, Detroit, MI, 1988).

Kennedy, D., Facility Site Selection and Analysis Through Environmental Criminology. (Journal of Criminal Justice 18, 1990), pp. 239-252.

Kuhlman, R., Safe Places? (Security Planning and Litigation, The Michie Co., Charlottesville, VA, 1989).

McGoey, C., Security: Adequate or Not? (Aegis Books, Oakland, CA, 1990).

Tarantino, J. and M. Dombroff, Premises Security: Law and Practice. (John Wiley & Sons, New York, 1990).

Notes

1.   Landmark cases which have shaped common law in this area include *Kline v. 1500 Massachusetts Avenue Apartment Corp.*, 439 F. 2d 477 (D.C. Cir. 1970), concerning landlord liability to tenant and *Garzilli v. Howard Johnson's Motor Lodges, Inc.*, 419 F. Supp. 1210 (E.D.N.Y. 1976), concerning innkeeper liability to guest.

2.   In some cases, damages may be awarded a plaintiff under contract law. For example, it may be argued that a renter enters into a form of contract with a landlord through an implied warranty of habitability concerning the premises to be let.

3.   A clear explication of this approach may be found in Gregory Eisland, "Attacks in Parking Lots: Driving Home Liability of Owners," Trial 26 (September, 1990): 108-113. See, also, *Exxon Corp. v. Tidwell*, 816 S.W. 2d 455 (Tex. App.-Dallas, 1991).

4.   For one scholar's elaboration on "absolute" foreseeability vs. "relative" foreseeability, see Lawrence Sherman, "Violent Stranger Crime at a Large Hotel: A Case Study in Risk Assessment Methods" (Security Journal Vol. 1, 1989), pp. 40-46.

5.   Currently, one of the more popular theories of criminal etiology deals with these three elements. See Marcus Felson, "Routine Activities and Crime Prevention in the Developing Metropolis" (Criminology Vol. 25, 1987), pp. 911-931.

6.   Personal communication (1991) from Frank Carrington, Esq., noted expert on crime victims' legal rights. See also Frank Carrington and James Rapp, Victims' Rights: Law and Litigation (Matthew Bender & Co., New York, 1991).

PRIVACY: INTERNATIONAL ISSUES

Within the context of the employment relationship, "privacy" has clearly emerged as a major force in U.S. business and governmental decision making.   Such areas as applicant screening, employee hiring and retention, drug testing, workplace surveillance, use of medical records and histories, access to personnel records and databases, and lifestyle inquiries have all come under the close scrutiny of our courts and legislatures with respect to privacy. Indeed, within the U.S. legal system privacy law has evolved into a distinct discipline [1].

Given the extraordinary impact of privacy to U.S. business personnel practices, it would logically follow that such practices could be reasonably adapted within multinational corporate environments. However, although employment privacy is perceived similarly by most free nations in terms of definition, operationally it reflects quite dissimilar perspectives. Accordingly, U.S. security, legal, and human resource professionals who are affiliated with overseas business organizations must gain a thorough working knowledge and appreciation of privacy issues relevant to employment relationships. Only with such a working knowledge can requisite workplace standards and operational integrity be attained.

Conceptual Similarities

The concept of workplace privacy among major businesses in the United States, Canada, western Europe, and Scandinavia is universally compatible. For example, the basic U.S. premise of a conditional but legally enforceable expectation of privacy for employees is echoed among business entities to the north and overseas [2].   In essence, these countries are in firm agreement that individual and collective employment privacy rights are essential, but must be continually assessed with respect to the legitimate needs of business. In Sweden, for instance, it is recognized that individual privacy rights cannot receive absolute protection. Rather, Swedish law is intended to provide safeguards against, "...unwarranted encroachments of personal integrity..." [3]. Similarly, U.S. case law and statutes, Canada's "Privacy Act," and the Council of Europe regulations provide for reasonable balances between business requirements and employee rights to privacy. Conceptually, at least, the trading nations of the west and Scandinavia agree in principle to the essential tenets of privacy with respect to the employee-employer relationship.

Constructive Differences

The aforementioned countries are in philosophical agreement that individual privacy rights are essentially "...developed as an individual response to the power of the modern state" [4]. Concerning the extension of such rights to the workplace, however, one notices that state protective responses and authority vary considerably among the United States and other western nations. A summary follows [5].

United States. Privacy protections are essentially provided for from three independent sources: (1) case law, (2) legislation (e.g., Polygraph Protection Act of 1988), and (3) state constitutional proscriptions.

Canada. All citizen privacy rights come from one uniform source -- The Privacy Act.

Europe. Individual privacy rights are codified in the European Convention of Human Rights. Also, the Council of Europe, which includes the European Community and the European Free Trade Area, has adopted specific procedures, such as the use of personnel data, that parallel Canada's Privacy Act.

The unique empowerment of the European Convention and the Council of Europe with regard to the individual rights of all citizens is essential knowledge to enlightened and responsive U.S. business management. With the expansion of influence of the European Community in the world market, the Convention and the Council will assuredly gain in power and authority among member nations. As of this writing, for instance, a majority of the European Community (EC) countries have adopted the Convention into their domestic law. Also, another significant example of the commonality shared among the EC nations is that the European Court of Human Rights is perceived as a court of last resort when national judicial processes have been exhausted.

Sweden. Much like the United States, Swedish privacy interests are prescribed largely through legislation. The Data Act, Credit Information Act, and Debt Collection Act, form a central part in the protection of individual privacy rights. The Swedish National Labor Board, County Labor Boards, and ultimately the Labor Exchange represent the enforcement arm of Swedish government for legislative compliance.

Practical Differences

Philosophically and culturally, personnel practices that affect privacy matters are widely divergent between the United States and the rest of western European and Scandinavian countries. For example, the conduct of typical U.S. pre-employment applicant investigations in a European country may be both impractical and illegal. Also, accepted U.S. workplace search procedures may be considered totally invasive and unacceptable by our European, Scandinavian, and Canadian counterparts. Specific differences relative to multinational privacy concerns and practices are summarized as follows [6].

Personnel Data. The Council of Europe and the Privacy Act of Canada recommend that employers obtain most required personal data from employees directly, rather than from outside sources, as is customary in the United States.

Psychological Testing and Attitudinal Questionnaires. Non-U.S. companies seem to place greater emphasis in the use of such employment aids than do U.S. businesses.

Criminal Records. U.S. companies generally perceive more of a need for compiling criminal histories on prospective employees than do the non-U.S. firms.

Search and Surveillance Practices. U.S. companies tend to rely more upon workplace search practices and video surveillance than non-U.S. companies.

Off-Duty Conduct. In general, employer restrictions on certain off-duty or lifestyle choices of employees are more restrictive in the U.S. than overseas (e.g., dating and marital relationships with competitors). However, such restrictions are not looked upon favorably by a majority of all businesses in the west.

Third Party Disclosure of Employment Information. Non-U.S. companies strictly limit such disclosures to either official governmental agencies, judicial bodies, or potential employers. It is interesting to note that European companies are much more likely to share basic employment data with prospective employers than is the case in the United States. Of course, in all companies, disclosure of sensitive personal data, such as health records, is highly restricted. In Sweden, for example, unauthorized disclosure of personal data by a person entrusted with a "personal register" can result in imprisonment of 1 year plus a substantial fine.

The U.S., Canadian, European, and Scandinavian businesses are all surprisingly consistent with respect to their definitions and interpretations of employment privacy. However, employee privacy interests are applied dissimilarly among the countries in such areas as pre-employment applicant screening, workplace searches and surveillance activities, third-party disclosures of personnel data, access to employment records, lifestyle inquiries, and testing procedures.

Possible explanations for such differences in personnel practices between other western nations and the United States include: (1) the heterogeneity of the U.S. workforce, and (2) the significant litigation potentials associated with negligence in hiring and retention of employees in the United States.

In a multinational business environment, the recognition of variations in personnel practices with respect to individual privacy concerns can lead to the effective implementation of quality-driven employment programs.   For U.S. businesses, in particular, the hiring and retention of the most qualified employees in overseas locations will depend upon their essential responsiveness to diverse legal, cultural, and political constraints.

Robert D. Hulshouser, CPP

Sources

Berenbeim, R.E., Employee Privacy, Research Report No. 945. (The Conference Board, New York, 1990).

Decker, K., Employee Privacy Law and Practice. (John Wiley & Sons, New York, 1987).

Flaherty, D.H., Protecting Privacy in Surveillance Societies. (The University of North Carolina Press, Chapel Hill, NC, 1989).

Ivri, K., The Protection of Integrity. (Personal Information and Personal Registers, Skandia, Stockholm, Sweden, 1988).

Notes

1. Decker views "employment privacy law" as an emerging legal discipline in the U.S.

2. See Berenbeim, p. vii, for an explanatory review of privacy considerations in the workplace.

3. This quote was taken directly from an English translation of Ivri's presentation in Swedish (p. 1).

4. Berenbeim's development of a central theme for privacy rights is reflected by this statement (p. 1).

5. This is a brief synopsis of a far more detailed analysis. See Berenbeim, pp. 2-9.

6. See Berenbeim and Ivri for a thorough explanation of privacy concerns in the U.S., Canada, Europe, and Sweden.   Berenbeim provides an excellent comparison of privacy rights and protections in the United States, Canada, and Europe.

PRIVATE SECURITY: HISTORY AND DEVELOPMENT IN THE UNITED STATES

The concepts and security practices that form the basis for modern American security can be traced to early England. Colonists settling in a new and alien land banded together under a system of mutual protection and accountability that stemmed from early Anglo-Saxon times. Prior to American independence, protection of the colonists and their property was the responsibility of town constables and sheriffs, supplemented in many towns, in English tradition, with watchmen who would patrol the streets at night. These watchmen remained familiar figures and constituted the primary security measure until the establishment of full-time police forces in the mid 1800s.

As security problems kept pace with the rapid growth of the country, public pressure mounted for increased and more effective protection. Attempts were made to add daytime complements to support and supplement the night watchmen, but it soon became apparent that the watch system was neither adequate nor efficient. This realization led to the formation of public police departments with full-time, paid personnel. The first public police force in the United States was established in 1844 in New York City, and by 1856 police departments had been set up in Detroit, Cincinnati, Chicago, San Francisco, Los Angeles, Philadelphia, and Dallas, Although these early police departments were generally inefficient and often corrupt, and their personnel poorly trained, they represented a vast improvement over the old watchman system. The Civil Service Act of 1883 was instrumental in rectifying many problems of the early police departments.

The emergence of public police departments, however, did not mean the end of private citizen involvement in the protection of life and property. Public law enforcement agencies were in their most incipient stage and could not keep pace with the mounting problems of crime in their communities. The incidence of crimes against property had become acute. The coupling of these facts forced industrial and business organizations to recognize the need for some form of effective security to protect their assets. Thus, in the 1850s major components of the private security industry were developed in answer to this need.

Allan Pinkerton formed the North West Police Agency in 1855 to provide protection for six midwestern railroads, and the Pinkerton Protection Patrol in 1857 to provide a private watchman service. For more than 50 years, Pinkerton's was the only company in the country engaged in interstate activities, such as the provision of security for many of the railroads. Pinkerton's also provided security for industrial concerns and was even hired as an intelligence-gathering unit for the Union Army during the Civil War. Today, Pinkerton's, with numerous services and activities, is the largest security organization in the world.

In 1858, Edwin Holmes began the first central office burglar alarm operation, which evolved into Holmes Protection, Inc. When the American District Telegraph Company (ADT) was formed in 1874, use of alarms and detection devices spread to provide protective services through the use of messengers and telegraph lines. By 1889, the use of electric protection for industrial and commercial enterprises in New York City was well established.

In 1859, Washington Perry Brink formed his truck and package delivery service in Chicago.

He transported his first payroll in 1891, thereby initiating armored car and courier service. By 1900, Brink had acquired a fleet of 85 wagons. Seventy-five years later his security business was grossing more than $50 million in revenue each year.

During the 1800s, with the westward expansion of the United States, railroad lines moved into sparsely settled territories that had little or no public law enforcement. Trains were subject to attack by Indians and roving bands of outlaws who robbed passengers, stole cargo, dynamited track structures, and disrupted communications. In order to provide adequate protection of goods and passengers from the constant dangers, various states passed railway police acts that enabled private railroads to establish proprietary security forces, with full police powers, for the protection of assets. In many towns and territories, the railway police provided the only protective services until governmental units and law enforcement agencies were established.

At the turn of the century, labor unions began to proliferate and to use strikes as a forceful tool for change. Because many factories were located in areas that had no effective public police forces capable of maintaining order, private security agencies were called in by management to quell the disturbances surrounding strikes and to protect lives and property. During this period, two firms were established that are now major security corporations. In 1909, Baker Industries, Inc., entered the fire control and burglary detection equipment business. That same year, the head of the Federal Bureau of Investigation's (FBI's) predecessor agency (the Bureau of Investigation) formed the William J. Burns International Detective Agency, now a multinational corporation with 117 U.S. offices and more than 30,000 employees.

Industry Formation

Prior to and during World War I, the concern for security intensified in American industry, due not only to urbanization and industrial growth, but also to sabotage and espionage by politically active nationalists.

At the end of World War I, there were other significant developments in private security. A Burglary Protection Council was formed and held its first meeting in 1921, the results of which thrust Underwriters' Laboratories into the business of establishing specifications for, testing of, and certifying burglar alarm systems and devices.

During the 1940s, World War II proved to be a significant catalyst in the growth of the private security industry. Prior to the awarding of national defense contracts, the federal government required that munitions contractors implement stringent and comprehensive security measures to protect classified materials and defense secrets from sabotage and espionage. The FBI assisted in establishing these security programs. As a result of the heightened emphasis on security within the government/military sphere, industry became increasingly aware of the need for plant security, and its value in protection of their assets.

After the war, the use of private security services and products expanded from the area of defense contractors to encompass all segments of the private and public sectors. For example, in 1954, George R. Wackenhut and three other former FBI agents formed the Wackenhut Corporation as a private investigative and contract security firm. In just 20 years this firm established itself as the third-largest contract guard and investigative agency in the country.

Although no accurate data are available, federal government regulation has been a significant factor in the growth of proprietary security over the years. Another major factor has been the increased awareness of companies of the importance of crime reduction and prevention as it relates to company property. In response to this need, both small and large companies have increased proprietary security functions. Thus, it can be concluded that the growth of proprietary security has paralleled that of contractual security.

Technological Impact

Technology has played an important role in the growth of the private security industry. For example, with the application of advanced technology to the security industry, even one of the oldest security devices, the lock, was subject to revolutionary changes: combination locks, combination time locks, delayed action time locks, combination locks with surveillance and electronic controls, and eventually access-control systems that use the technology of television and minicomputers.

The same advances in electronics technology that improved the quality of television and radio have had significant impact upon the security market, broadening it to include additional consumer areas. This new technology has fostered the development of large-scale, totally integrated security systems run by computers that control not only access, but also refrigeration, heating, air-conditioning, and fire detection. Additionally, technological advances have reduced component cost and size, leading to the introduction of security measures now commonly in use, such as low-light-level (LLL), closed-circuit television (CCTV) cameras, and electronic article-surveillance devices.

Other factors, in addition to the rising crime rate, account for this technologically intensive growth in private security services. For example, the Insurance Services Office recommends that insurance companies offer a premium credit or reduction when commercial and industrial property is protected by burglary and detection systems certified by Underwriters' Laboratories. The Federal Bank Protection Act of 1968 mandated increased security measures and equipment for federal banks after they had sustained 23 deaths, 61 injuries, and $15 million in losses from robberies, burglaries, and larcenies in 1967.

Today, as a result of ever-rising crime rates, coupled with the enormous demands placed upon public law enforcement agencies and their lack of adequate resources to deal with these demands, private security has become a multibillion-dollar-a-year industry, and the number of private security personnel surpasses that of public law enforcement in many localities. Moreover, present crime and financial statistics indicate that the industry will continue to experience significant growth in future years.

Philip P. Purpura, CPP

Sources

Davis, A., Bank Security -- It Is the Law. (Industrial Security, October, 1969).

Green, G., and R.C. Farber, Introduction to Security. (Security World Publishing Company, Los Angeles, 1975).

Kakalis, J.S., and S. Wildhorn, Private Police Industry: Its Nature and Extent. (Government Printing Office, Washington, DC, 1972).

Morn, F., Discipline and Disciplinarians: The Problem of Police Control in the Formative Years.

(Paper presented at the Annual Meeting of the American Historical Association, 1975).

Ursic, H.S., and L.E. Pagano, Security Management Systems. (Charles C. Thomas Publishers, Springfield, IL, 1974).

Report of the Task Force on Private Security. (U. S. Government Printing Office, Washington, DC, 1976).

PROBATION

Probation is a criminal sentence that requires the offender to meet conditions under supervision in the community. A probation officer usually monitors the offender for these conditions and enforces rules of conduct. A court imposes probation either directly or in lieu of a partially or fully suspended jail or prison term. Probation is often combined with some time in jail or prison. Violations of the conditions of supervision may result in imposition of a suspended sentence, resentencing, or continuation on probation.

Judges generally have discretionary powers to grant or deny probation as the sentence for an offense. States, however, sometimes legislate statutes that bar or require the use of probation. For example, New York's "predicate felon" law precludes probation for any person with a prior felony conviction. Minnesota's sentencing guidelines direct judges to grant probation for persons convicted of larceny regardless of prior convictions and require the judges who depart from the guidelines to justify the sentence imposed.

Judges alone set the sentence, except in most of the 36 states with a death penalty where death sentences are set by a jury and except for 6 states where sentencing of non-capital cases is by the verdict jury (the jury that convicted).

Judges very often receive a sentencing recommendation. An unknown percentage of the time the prosecutor recommends a sentence. Sometimes the verdict jury recommends a sentence, but the practice is rare: 10 states permit a jury recommendation in death penalty cases and 4 states in non-capital cases. Most often, sentence recommendations come from the probation department in a pre-sentence investigation report (PSI).

A PSI provides a judge with detailed information on the convicted offender's criminal and social background. Based on that background, a PSI also usually recommends a sentence. When imposing sentences, judges do not always follow the recommendations of the probation department's PSI. Judges may reject a probation department recommendation for reasons such as:

•The recommendation conflicts with a plea agreement reached between the prosecution and the defense; or

•The recommended sentence may be viewed as too harsh or too lenient, given the gravity of the offense and the extensiveness of the offender's criminal history.

Felons released on probation to the community are required, as a condition of their freedom, to comply with the orders of the court. Imposed standard conditions frequently include having the probationer meet with the probation officer on a periodic basis, maintain steady employment, remain in school, or avoid certain places or people. Judges may also impose special conditions, often tailored to specific offender characteristics usually revealed in the PSI. Financial conditions can be imposed on felony probationers. Penalty types and amounts vary widely among states, even counties in the same state.

Probationers are often either arrested for a new felony or charged with violating a condition of supervision. Disciplinary hearings, usually held by the original sentencing judge, are the principal means for determining whether a violation of the conditions of supervision has occurred and what penalty to impose. Outcomes of an arrest or a disciplinary hearing range from dismissing the charge and continuing the felon on probation to revoking probation and sending the felon to prison or jail. In addition, absconding from the jurisdiction during the probationary period may result in the issuance of a bench warrant. Absconding, new felony arrests and convictions that result in a sentence to confinement, and revocation of the conditional sentence to probation all represent unsuccessful outcomes.

Imposition of a jail or prison term usually follows more than just failing to perform community service, missing a meeting with the probation officer, or committing some other technical violation of supervisory conditions. Many unsuccessful probationers sent to prison or to jail will have had at least one new felony arrest. Besides the duty of ensuring that probationers fulfill special conditions, probation agencies often have the responsibility to oversee court-ordered payments.

Many probation departments assign an entering probationer to a level of supervision based upon the criminal and social history documented in the PSI. The assigned supervision level generally specifies the required frequency of contact between the probation officer and the offender. A goal of intensive supervision is to reduce the likelihood of continued criminal activity.

Felons comprise about half the adults under supervision of probation agencies. While serving their sentence, the felons are usually monitored by a probation officer who enforces rules of conduct. Two related issues about the growing number of felons under supervision in the community have not been systematically and fully assessed. These are the public safety consequences of having large numbers of persons under conditional supervision and the capability of probation personnel to monitor an expanding number of felons.

Bureau of Justice Statistics

Source Langan, P.A., and M.A. Cunniff, Bureau of Justice Statistics Special Report. (U.S. National Institute of Justice, Department of Justice, Washington, DC, 1992).

PROJECT MANAGEMENT

Literature provides numerous definitions of what a project and project management are. The consensus is that a project is a work effort designed to attain a defined goal on time, within budget, and according to pre-determined quality standards and specifications. Project management is a combination of techniques (planning, organizing, controlling, directing, evaluating progress, communicating, and reporting) used to successfully carry out a project. Security professionals are often required to manage or participate in projects, such as designing and installing an alarm system, making physical security upgrades, and converting a security force.

Definitions

1.   A deliverable is a product that is achieved on a project.

2.   A project plan is a written document that defines what work is to be done, how it is to be accomplished, what funds and personnel are required, when it is to be completed, and what deliverables are to be produced.

3.   A work breakdown structure (WBS) is a tool for dividing the activities or products of a project into the manageable parts necessary to accomplish the project and produce the deliverables; it defines the elements of project work, depicts the relationships between the work elements, and defines the work to be done. The WBS is subdivided to the lowest level needed to define discrete work elements, manage work, facilitate cost control, and report progress. The total project work effort is divided into major groups, subdivided into tasks and subtasks, as required. These subdivisions or elements of work are called WBS elements.

4.   Work authorizations grant authority and responsibility to do work on a project; they specify work to be done, staff assigned to do the work, schedule, budget, milestones, and deliverables.

Project management and its associated techniques are necessary to ensure that cost overruns are minimized or precluded, schedules are clearly identified and met, costs are related to progress, and quality product(s) are delivered. An understanding of project management principles and techniques is necessary for modern security professionals, since they are often confronted with problems that require complicated solutions and to which project management techniques can be applied, whether internal projects or contractual work are involved.

Organization and Staffing

The project manager is the person with the responsibility and authority for planning, organizing, directing, monitoring, and controlling project activities. Typical responsibilities include:

•Selecting the appropriate technical approach.

•Preparing and updating the project plan, including the WBS, schedule, and budget.

•Monitoring and controlling tasks, the budget, and progress.

•Communicating with the project team, contractors, vendors, etc.

•Ensuring that reports are made to line management.

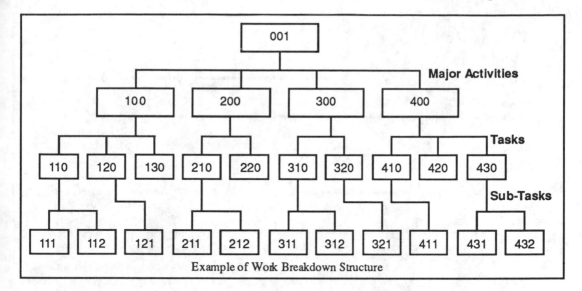

Example of Work Breakdown Structure

•Ensuring that deliverables are made on time and within budget.

Typical authorities are:

•Arranging for use of facilities, staff, and equipment.

•Approving work authorizations and appropriate change orders or variances.

•Requiring status reports from project staff.

•Making purchases and executing contracts.

The organizational structure for a project includes the project manager; task leaders, who are subordinate supervisors to the project manager responsible for accomplishing major WBS elements; project staff; and consultants and contractors.   In many cases, the project management team may not directly report to the line organization, but may draw staff from the line. To make the best use of resources, the project may use horizontal, rather than vertical, work flow.

This should not disrupt the vertical line organization, but rather supplement it, requiring the project manager to coordinate activities horizontally between line organizations, from which the staff resources for a project may be drawn.

Rarely can all staff resources for a project be drawn from the same element in a functional vertical organization, because selecting the most appropriate project members often requires that they come from different levels and units of the formal organizational structure. This is referred to as a matrix organization. For example, a project established to upgrade a computer security system may require a project manager, with functional task leaders and staff drawn from various organizational elements (security, internal audit, management information systems, and a number of operational elements) to ensure that the necessary technical expertise is available and that all functional concerns and operational needs are addressed. Thus, projects are often organized along matrix rather than functional lines, permitting simultaneous operation of the formal functional organization and the project organization.

Another organizational alternative is to have project staff directly report to a project manager who has line responsibility. This alternative, however, does not have the flexibility needed for short-term projects, but is better suited to long-term projects where the technical skills of the project team can be stabilized.

Project Planning

A project plan is a tool to assist the project manager in keeping the project focused and to provide a basis for forecasting the project's completion date and cost.   As the project progresses, the plan may require revision to account for changes in direction or to adjust for variances.

The project planning process involves the following steps: (1) study the work requirements, (2) establish project objectives, (3) define deliverables, (4) define tasks, (5) establish the

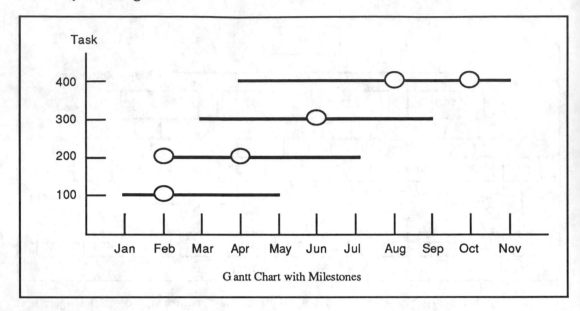

Gantt Chart with Milestones

logical flow of work, (6) establish the project schedule, (7) establish the budget, and (8) allocate resources.

The requirements for the project are usually described in a statement of work. A good statement of work prescribes such requirements as the type of deliverable(s) expected, when the deliverables are due, how work completion will be measured, what the criteria or standards are for deliverable acceptance, and to whom the deliverables are to be sent.

After the requirements are reviewed, project objectives should be defined. Objectives are clear and precise statements that define actions to be taken, the end product, and a target date for completion (for example, "Develop a security force weapons training program by March 31, 1993.") They are precise derivatives of the project requirements. Project requirements and objectives define the project deliverables.

Defining tasks and dividing the project into manageable parts are accomplished through the development of the WBS. A WBS breaks the total project into elements that can be used for issuing work authorizations, budgeting, scheduling, status reporting, and performance tracking.

Scheduling identifies the start and completion dates for all tasks (as well as interim milestones), establishes the logical flow or order in which work will occur, and provides the basis for controlling the project and tracking status. After the WBS is prepared, the schedule can be developed. Understanding of the project objectives is also a major consideration in scheduling. Deliverables should be clearly indicated in the schedule.

Two types of schedules are commonly used. For relatively simple projects, a Gantt chart or bar chart with milestones can be used. This type of chart can show the duration of work efforts and simultaneous activity. For complex projects, network diagrams showing interdependencies between tasks are preferred. This method of scheduling shows the interrelationship between activities and indicates which activities must be completed before others can begin. Another common tool is PERT (Program Evaluation and Review Technique). PERT is a control tool that depicts the network of tasks and activities for a project and when they are to be done. PERT can also show a project's critical path (the sequence of activities with the longest scheduled time). A key element that must be established for PERT is the total elapsed time required to do the work from beginning to end. Project scheduling can be done manually, but a variety of project management software compatible with most computer operating systems is available.

Developing a budget is another planning element that provides the means to manage project costs. Preparing a budget requires assigning costs to each WBS element and tying the budget to the schedule; this is called a time-phased budget. Cost estimates should include internal labor, materials, purchased goods, travel, computer usage, purchased services (architects, engineers, consultants, and contractors), facilities

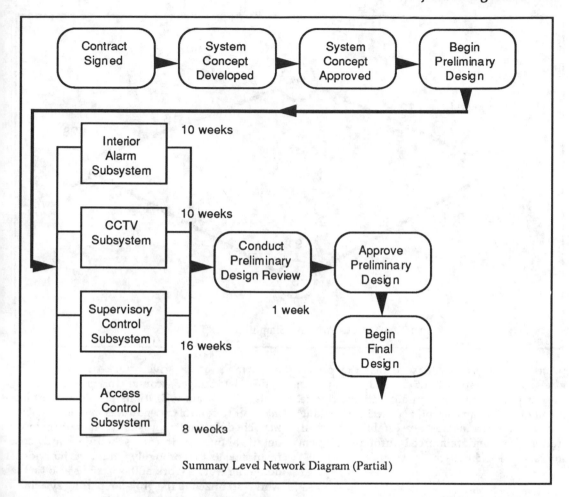

Summary Level Network Diagram (Partial)

or equipment use, printing and drawings, mail, and other direct or indirect costs. A prerequisite is usually a resource plan that allocates labor, materials, and other costs for each WBS element by month, consistent with the schedule requirements. The resource plan should be included in the project plan, in order to ensure that line management is aware of staff and other resources required to support the project. Potential problems between line and project managers can thus be identified and resolved before the plan is approved.

The products of the planning process should be incorporated into a project plan that includes the statement of work and requirements, project objectives, technical approach and specifications to be met, the WBS, project tasks, a schedule with milestones for each WBS element, a budget, a resource plan, the deliverables, and limitations and possible problems. The plan is then typically approved by management, and the implementation process begins. The plan should be reviewed often and revised as changes or variances occur.

Directing and Leading

Directing and leading projects require the same management skills as any other business venture. Project management requires emphasis on team building, communications, problem solving, decision making, and conflict resolution. Successful project managers require technical know-how, but human relations skills are equally important. Typically, members of project teams have diverse technical backgrounds and must be molded into an effective work group or team. The

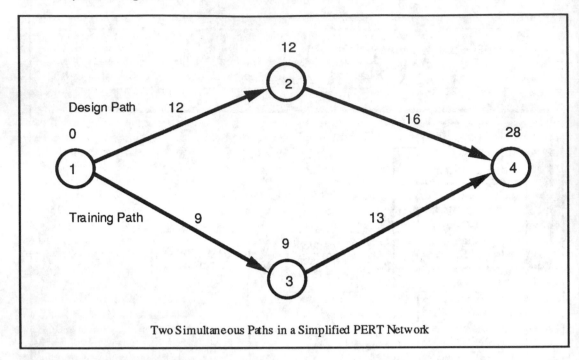

Two Simultaneous Paths in a Simplified PERT Network

project manager must ensure that the project goals; roles, responsibilities, and authorities; project procedures for communications, conflict resolution, change control, and decision making; and team relationships are established, clear, understood, and reinforced through frequent interaction and feedback.

Controlling the Project

Controlling is a process that involves measuring progress against specified objectives, evaluating the cause of and corrective actions necessary to address variances from planned performance, and taking corrective action to deal with either favorable or unfavorable variances. The project manager must control the work effort assigned to each member of the project team, project quality, the schedule, and the budget. A management information or reporting system and regular project reviews are also essential to ensure project control.

Work authorizations are used to grant authority to perform work on a project. When a given task is to be initiated, a work authorization should be prepared by the project manager or task leader. Valid cost accounts should be reflected in work authorizations to ensure that work

performed on a given task is tied to an appropriate budget account. This aids in tracking costs. Work authorizations enable the project manager to control expenditures in sequence with the schedule, and they should contain enough detail about technical, schedule, and cost requirements to thoroughly inform the individual doing the work. Work authorizations also tie the work authorized to the project reporting system.

Quality involves satisfying project specifications or other requirements, ensuring that technical performance or other deliverables meet established and acceptable criteria, and ensuring that the appropriate methodology or material is used. To ensure quality, it is crucial that performance objectives and specifications for project deliverables be indicated in writing. To ensure that quality standards are met, each project should have a quality process that includes independent reviews of both the technical input and the final deliverable, whether it is a written product, hardware, software, functional system, or item of construction.

Schedule control requires frequent monitoring, clear milestones, good communication, and a means to routinely detect problems. Project meetings, reviews, and monitoring the status of progress through personal interaction or the project reporting system are key management tools. The frequency of these activities is determined by the nature of the schedule and the length of time between milestones.

Budget control consists of specifying budgets for all WBS elements, measuring the costs incurred against the budget and identifying variances, measuring progress achieved in relation to costs incurred (referred to as earned value), and taking action where variances exist. To manage costs effectively there must be a system to record all costs, tie them to the WBS and schedule, and report them in such a way that project status can be reviewed readily. Automated systems that report costs are available and should be used.

Periodic reporting and reviews to line management are necessary to ensure project control. Key elements normally addressed are actual progress and expenditures against the schedule and budget, status of deliverables, forecasts to completion, future planned activities, staffing and resource needs, major variances and corrective actions, and problems to be addressed and their resolution. The benefits of reporting and reviews are that they promote communications, eliminate surprises, and enable the project manager to identify variances and to initiate corrective action.

Change Management

Projects and project plans are dynamic. Plans must often be revised, generally because of variance between the actual amount of work done, amount spent, or schedule and the plan. Variances can also result from technical changes directed by management or insufficient availability of funds.

When a variance occurs, the project manager must assess its impact. If it is negative (work behind schedule or cost overrun), the project manager must determine whether the variance is minor, and can thus be corrected within existing project parameters, or whether the variance may adversely impact project requirements. The cause of the variance must also be determined, and the project re-planned accordingly.

After taking these steps, the project manager generally has two options. If the variance can be adjusted without affecting the scope of work, a "work-around plan" is appropriate. A work-

around plan is a modified project plan, including the schedule, costs, and staff resources to accomplish the work, with necessary adjustments in one or a combination of these elements. If devising a work-around plan will not allow the project to meet objectives, increased costs or schedule slippage may become necessary. Appropriate changes are negotiated, and the project is re-planned according to the negotiated schedule and/or budget.

If variances occur because of a change in the project scope or re-direction by the party for whom the work is to be done, the changes in work scope are negotiated and formalized, and the project is re-planned accordingly.

Project Management Files

All projects should have an organized set of files that can easily be used to administer the project. This ensures that pertinent information is available to the project manager, that there is a smooth transition if project managers change, and that actions are documented for historical review, reference for later projects, and backup for legal actions, if required.

Typical contents of a project file are:
- Contractual documents
- Project plan (schedule, budget, resource plan)
- Cost data
- Documentation of meetings and reviews
- Correspondence
- All documentation on deliverables

Project Closure

Formal closure of a project requires a plan to document that all project requirements have been met or that the project has been terminated. If the project is complex, a plan for orderly closeout is crucial. The plan for closure should include at least: actions required, who is responsible for the actions, and a schedule. If the project was completed under a contract, appropriate contractual actions must also be completed.

Dale A. Moul

Sources

Archibald, R.D., Program Management, in Mali, Paul (Editor), Management Handbook:

Operating Guidelines, Techniques and Practices. (John Wiley & Sons, New York, 1981).

Cleland, D., and W. King (Ediors), Project Management Handbook. (Van Nostrand Reinhold Company, New York, 1983).

Cleland, D., and W. King (Editors), Systems Analysis and Project Management. (McGraw-Hill Book Company, New York, 1968).

Dinsmore, P., Human Factors in Project Management. (American Management Association, New York, 1984).

Essentials of Project Management. (Battelle Memorial Institute, Columbus, OH, October, 1990).

Hansen, B.J., Practical PERT. (American Aviation Publications, Washington, DC, 1964).

Hitt, W.D., A Guide for Project Management. (Battelle Memorial Institute, Columbus, OH).

Kerzner, H., Project Management: A Systems Approach to Planning, Scheduling and Controlling, 2nd Edition. (Van Nostrand Reinhold Company, New York, 1984).

Koontz, H., and C. O'Donnell, Management, (McGraw-Hill Book Company, New York, 1976).

Lock, D., Project Management. (Gower Press, Epping, Essex, England, 1977).

Martin, C., Project Management: How to Make It Work. (AMACOM, New York, 1976).

Miller, R.W., How to Plan and Control with PERT. (Harvard Business Review, Vol. 40, No. 2, March-April 1962).

Moder, J.J., C.R. Phillips, and E.W. Davis, Project Management with CPM, PERT, and Precedence Diagramming, 3rd Edition. (Van Nostrand Reinhold Company, New York, 1983).

PROPRIETARY INFORMATION: A PRIMER FOR PROTECTION

In 1780, a drunken pattern-maker working for James Watt, the inventor of the steam engine, bragged at the local pub that circular motion could be obtained from a reciprocating engine. When challenged, the man chalked a rough sketch on the bar top. James Pickard, a button maker, realized the possibilities and obtained a patent ahead of Watt. The case was eventually heard in the courts, and Pickard's claim was upheld, although there was no doubt that Watt was the inventor. This early example supports the security manager's often stated thesis that proprietary information is subject to compromise when protective measures are not in place or not being followed. The loss of proprietary information can have a direct relationship to the bottom line, and when loss is severe it can mean the difference between success or failure of the organization.

Legal scholars tell us that in order to recover damages resulting from the theft of proprietary information, it must be demonstrated that the owner:

• Clearly regarded and identified the information as proprietary in nature;

• Had a clear policy that required employees to treat the stolen information as proprietary; and

• Actively took steps to protect the information.

A first step, then, is to identify the genuinely critical information. Too often, the more sensitive critical information is ignored while costly measures are directed at protecting information that has little value. A rigorous approach is appropriate when determining what types of information are worth safeguarding.

A good way to start is to think what would happen if particular information was to fall into unfriendly hands. A number of possible scenarios can lead the thinking process to an identification of what should be protected, the adversaries, the probable nature of attempts by adversaries to acquire the information, the exposures of the information to the hypothesized attempts, and an estimate in dollars of the value of the information.

This thinking process asks probing questions that relate to criticality and vulnerability. What information, in what form, is critical to the company or to a key operation? How much of that information is vulnerable to exploitation? In what ways is the information vulnerable and to whom? What is the worth of the information, what are the replacement costs and the costs of lost business opportunity? How much is the company willing to spend to protect information?

The answers will not be arrived at easily. They will emerge only after key managers have been interviewed, pertinent business data have been collected and analyzed, and an estimate made of threats and threat capabilities.

Information Classifications

When the truly sensitive information has been differentiated from non-sensitive information, an understanding of it will be helped by defining it in one or a very few categories and assigning to each category a descriptive designator. The designators can be anything, except that companies involved in safeguarding government classified information are not authorized to utilize the government's designators, i.e., TOP SECRET, SECRET, and CONFIDENTIAL, or any combination thereof, e.g., "Company Confidential."

In setting up a classification scheme there will be a temptation to keep it simple, which is certainly sensible, but the aim for simplicity should not go so far as to dictate that every form of sensitive information will be placed in a single classification. If one looks at the sum of all sensitive information residing in a business organization, at least two major groups stand out: that which deals with purely business matters and that which deals with matters relating to employees on a personal level. Thus, a two-level system would be a good choice, especially since it would be relatively easy to differentiate between business information and personal information.

If we look, however, at the business information category we may see that certain types of information (e.g., trade secrets) are clearly more important than others. The information that we perceive to have a lesser sensitivity may still be too sensitive to exclude from protection. Thus, a three-level system may be a better choice than the one- or two-level systems.

Systems that use a single classification level tend to be inflexible, and those that use more than two classification levels tend to be complex and difficult to manage. If there is a need for security protections that cannot be provided within the organization's existing system, the answer may be to use code names, such as Project X or Operation A, to denote the special protections that apply to those very limited groups of information applicable to the project or operation.

Designations and definitions for a three-level scheme might be as follows:

• ABC SENSITIVE. That information which, if revealed in any manner to unauthorized persons, could unquestionably damage the operational, competitive or financial position, or public image of the company or any other party to which the company owes a duty of protection. Examples include production figures, takeover or merger plans, litigation strategies, trade secrets and formulas, and marketing plans.

• ABC RESTRICTED. That information, the unauthorized disclosure of which, would be prejudicial to the interests of the company or which would cause embarrassment to or difficulty for the company. This category of information would include information of commercial value, or which is subject to legal or confidential agreement, or contains controversial or contentious views. Examples include financial statements, bid proposals, succession plans, and reports of investigation.

• ABC PRIVATE. That information which is private to the individual and is only to be opened by the addressee. Examples include personal health reports, salary data, and performance ratings.

Proprietary Information Program

The authority for administering protection to information is derived from policy, that is, a statement of management. A policy will state the business necessity for information protection, the goals and objectives of the policy, the means for achieving the goals and objectives, and will identify the entities and positions affected by the policy. A policy is broad, provides direction, and sets a tone. A policy is carried out by directives, commonly referred to as procedures, that are much more specific and detailed. The activities generated by the policy and the procedures can be called a program; in this case, a proprietary information program. The major elements of the program could include the following:

Access. Decisions will need to be made as to the entitlements or privileges of access. Will access be limited to the need to know or will there be some flexibility in making proprietary information accessible for some other reason? Choices on access may not be controllable if the information falls within the purview of the Defense Industrial Security Program. In this case, that proprietary information to which some recipients do not have a need to know should be placed in an addendum that can be protected in the proprietary information program.

How will access rights be documented and how often will they be reviewed? Will job applicant and employee screening be a decision point in granting access? A consideration will be the reality that the likelihood of compromise increases as the number of persons having access increases. On the other hand, information is valuable to the organization to the extent it is used. A balance must be struck between the protection of information and the use of it.

Accountability. The program may impose accountability on persons and on supervisors of persons. Receipts, log books, a numbering system, and periodic inventories may be instituted for all or just the more sensitive categories. A missing item should automatically trigger an investigation, a report of investigative findings, and recommendations to prevent recurrence.

Classification and Declassification. Who will have classification authority? The choices can be the originator of the information, the head of the department in which the information originated, a manager one level above the originating department, a classification of information coordinator, a classification team representing a number of organizational interests, and so on. For reasons of stability and continuity, the classification authority should be vested in positions as opposed to persons because positions tend to be constant whereas persons are subject to attrition and turnover.

Other issues to be settled are whether or not classification authority can be delegated; and what criteria are to be used in determining if classification is warranted and, if so, determining the appropriate classification level. In this latter regard, strict rules should be in force to prevent non-sensitive information from being classified and sensitive information from being assigned inappropriately high classifications.

Declassification should be automatic when the information is no longer sensitive. The same mechanisms in place to apply classifications would be correct for removing them. Periodic review of classified holdings can help in purging materials that should no longer be subject to special handling and control. A related consideration is downgrading and upgrading of classifications. The management may find it helpful to lower or raise classifications relative to changes in sensitivity.

Communications and Transmissions. The unnecessary distribution of proprietary information outside the circle of those members of staff directly concerned with it wastes time and effort, and leads inevitably to compromise and possible damage to the organization's interests. For this reason, the distribution of proprietary information must be kept as low as possible. This can be helped by circulating one copy among the essential addressees, using the established transmission controls (e.g., receipting, numbering, marking, sealing, double-enveloping, and encrypting) suitable to the classification, rather than by distributing to each addressee a separate copy.

Detailed instructions should be prepared and followed with respect to the distribution of proprietary information via mail channels within the organization, postal and non-postal channels outside of the organization, electronic mail, telex, facsimile, and computer systems that communicate with one another.

Computer Systems. Organizations are increasingly dependent upon computer systems, and the data these systems store, process, and transmit can be of vital importance. The policy and practices for protecting proprietary information will need to reflect the differences in computer systems, which can range from small and simple desktop devices to large and complex mainframe equipment.

Protection is more than just physically safeguarding the hardware, software, and data storage media; it involves backup and recovery, and passwords for accessing files and moving through protected computer gateways and networks.

The manner of protecting computer-related proprietary information can also be influenced by data protection legislation. Obtaining protection under a law designed to protect owner rights might require the owner to register or to meet standards concerning computer access, data retrieval, and storage. This can vary between jurisdictions, therefore a review by the company's legal function would be in order.

Destruction. The general rule is to destroy classified documents by burning, shredding, or pulping when no longer required. Printing ribbons, cassette tapes, microfiche, microfilm, and the like should be destroyed as efficiently as documents. With proper equipment, destruction can be done entirely in-house, it can be contracted to an outside vendor (whose integrity should be verified), or by a combination of both approaches.

Generally speaking, the more sensitive categories are destroyed in-house while less sensitive proprietary information is destroyed by vendors (if volume is an issue).

Education and Awareness. The proprietary information policy must be clear and unambiguous. It must be thoroughly announced when initiated and be continuously reinforced thereafter. The methods for developing awareness can include orientations at time of hire, formal initial training, refresher training, newsletters, posters, and verbal reminders by supervisors at meetings and in discussions with subordinates.

Enforcement. The protection of proprietary information program will be crippled when it does not have a means for enforcing policy and taking action against violators. Those persons given enforcement responsibilities must accept them, must be able to spot violations, must be able to intervene to correct the violations, and must be able to document the violations and refer them to management for the appropriate disciplinary action. Disciplinary actions should correspond to the severity of the violation.

Legal Review. The policy and implementing procedures should be reviewed initially and periodically by legal counsel to ensure that the program protects ownership rights to proprietary information and that liabilities to the organization are not created by the manner of administering the program

Management Support. The program can be only as good as the support it receives from management. Support is evidenced when management treats proprietary information according to the rules followed by other employees, affirms enforcement and disciplinary actions, and speaks in support of information protection. For the program to succeed, enforcement must be effective; and for enforcement to be effective, management must be entirely supportive.

Marking. The practice of marking can include applying to the sensitive material a stamp or legend that identifies the classification, a number or code, or other distinctive mark; placing a classified document into a specially marked folder or covering the front page of the document with a specially marked cover sheet; and numbering the pages of the document. Related to marking is the preparation of classified documents for transmittal by using a return receipt method, inserting inner envelopes within outer envelopes, and sealing envelopes and packages with tamper-resistant and tamper-revealing tape.

A stamp or legend should be applied regardless of format, i.e., documents, drawings, transparencies, film, or tape. It should be carefully constructed as to form and legal content to ensure no misunderstanding about ownership.

Non-Disclosure Agreements. Employees, contractors, and others who will have access to proprietary information in the normal course of their employment should be required at time of hire (and periodically thereafter) to sign an agreement pledging them to not violate the organization's rules regarding proprietary information. The agreement may relate to protection of such information generally and/or it may relate to a particular kind of information, such as work on a research project.

When a signatory to an agreement leaves employment, a debriefing is made to remind the individual of non-disclosure obligations that may continue. It is helpful at the debriefing to obtain a signed acknowledgment of the continuing obligations. Implied in this step is the prospect of legal action for a failure to comply.

Policy and Procedures Review. A review of the policy and its associated procedures should be made at regular intervals to bring them in line with changes that may have occurred since the policy and procedures were first written or last reviewed. Changes can be forced upon the program by external forces, such as the enactment of a law, or by internal forces, such as a major shift in the management's philosophy.

Releases of Information. The disclosure of proprietary information through the press, radio, television, publications, teaching, public speaking, and the like may be permitted by policy providing, of course, that permission is obtained in advance.

Requests for releases of information should be channeled to a knowledgeable person or designated office so that a review can be made of the information to be released. The information is likely to be in the form of financial and operating reports, technical papers, and promotional materials for use at trade shows and seminars.

Reproduction. Unsupervised copying machines present an opportunity for the unauthorized reproduction of proprietary information. Reasonable steps should be taken to guard against improper use of copying equipment. When proprietary information is being copied according to the existing rules, a responsible member of the department charged with protection of the information should oversee the copying operation to ensure that no extra copies have been left on the machine or in trash bins nearby. Other questions come into play: Should subcontractors be hired to reproduce proprietary information? Who can approve reproduction? Should in-house copying be done in one or a few designated areas?

Storage. Generally speaking, proprietary information not in use is stored in containers that correspond to their classification levels as established in the company's proprietary information policy. For example, materials with the highest classification might be stored in a steel safe fitted with a combination lock, materials in the second highest classification stored in a metal filing cabinet fitted with a locking bar, and materials in the lowest classification stored in a locked desk or credenza. The composition and construction of storage containers can be adjusted in relation to whether the facility is protected around the clock by roving security officers or whether the facility is equipped with an intrusion-detection system.

For large volumes of proprietary information, such as might be the case in an organization involved in research, a central library may be appropriate. The library holdings might be recorded on computers, and check out of files by authorized users might be managed by a computer-assisted technique, such as bar coding.

Lonnie R. Buckels, CPP
and Robert B. Iannone, CPP

PROPRIETARY INFORMATION: TECHNICAL SURVEILLANCE COUNTERMEASURES INSPECTIONS

Intense competition and rapidly evolving markets are just a few of the external forces that are changing the ways we do business. Upper managers are pushing decision situations down the corporate ladder to operational managers, the operational managers are spread across large expanses of geography, and the decisions they make are based on great amounts of detail pulled from many centers of expertise. Businesses are working hard to generate meaningful information, to open the information to greater numbers of key players, and to maintain a working dialogue with affected groups in widely separated places.

Business information, including the most sensitive possessed by an organization, is valuable to the extent it is put to work. Although a security manager would like sensitive information to be constantly kept under lock and key, the reality is that information exists to be used. Further, in a fast-track environment many types of information will have a relatively short life span, meaning that it must be put to advantage fairly quickly in order to wring value from it.

The security dilemma is that when information is in the process of being used, with attendant value flowing from such use, it is most vulnerable to compromise. The attendant loss flowing from compromise can be many hundreds of times greater than the utilitarian value attached to the moment of use. Herein lies the problem and the challenge to the security manager.

When is sensitive information at greatest risk? Experience tells us that those who are determined to acquire someone else's secrets will focus on two opportunities: when secrets are brought into the open for discussion, such as at a conference, and when they are transmitted from one place to another, such as messages across an electronic network. In short, sensitive information is at risk when it is being communicated.

The risk is considerably heightened when the business sphere is global. The dollar stakes are higher and political aims are often intertwined. We see, for example, the extraordinary ambitions of Eastern Bloc countries and former Soviet republics to establish business ties with the non-Communist world. The newcomers to Western-style democracy are discovering that capitalism is fueled by technology and until they develop a technological base and become producers and suppliers instead of consumers, they will be junior partners in the economic alliances they wish to forge.

A picture can be drawn that the American business sector, situated as a major repository of technology, is a natural target for those who desperately need technology to become competitive but lack the time and the resources to develop it on their own. An era of industrial espionage on a global scale is being ushered in, and the United States is among the few who have the greatest to lose.

The communications networks that support international commerce are notoriously vulnerable to surreptitious attack, and although efforts have been undertaken by governments to establish some modicum of secure transmissions, the principal protection must come from the network users. Self-protection has even more validity with respect to sensitive information disclosed at conferences and meetings. The owner of the information is the exclusive protector.

This section discusses a form of self-protection called the TSCM inspection, that is, making an organized search for technical surveillance devices. The places of search are typically at corporate offices and off-site meeting places. They include at the corporate offices the chief executive officer's suite, executive conference and dining rooms, the telecommunications center, and the telephone switching room, and off site the search activity might be of the facilities at a resort hotel where a senior management meeting has been scheduled. Findings from the inspection become the basis for taking steps to counter actual or potential surveillance attempts.

A handful of major corporations retain on staff one or a few technicians whose primary duties involve making TSCM inspections. The technicians are usually highly trained, are likely to have had prior experience with a federal law enforcement or intelligence agency, and are supplied with an array of electronic sensing equipment. Most companies, however, choose to obtain the inspection service from a TSCM provider. The guidance here is applicable to either situation, although written for the security manager who engages a provider.

The first contact made by the security manager to the TSCM provider should be via a communications medium separate from the site that is to be inspected. The idea is to not tell a wiretapper that you are about to inspect the phone line that is tapped.

The TSCM provider will want certain details in advance of the inspection. For example:

•The number of phones, identity of manufacturer, and model numbers.

•The number and size of rooms.

•The location of rooms relative to each other.

•The number of floors and buildings involved.

•The type of ceiling, for example, fixed or moveable.

•The types of audiovisual and communications devices, computers, and other special electronic equipment on site.

•The forms of electronic communications and networks in use at the place to be inspected, including local area networks, microwave links, and satellite teleconferencing facilities.

The security manager should expect the TSCM provider to supply all equipment required to carry out a comprehensive inspection. The equipment used should be the products of manufacturers that are recognized by TSCM professionals. Homemade equipment or general purpose receivers and analyzers are almost always lacking in the special capabilities required for TSCM inspections. The following described pieces of equipment are standard:

•Telephone analyzer or time domain reflectometer capable of evaluating telephone systems equipment and cables, including both fiber optic and wire.

•Tuneable countermeasures receiver or countermeasures spectrum analyzer with continuous coverage from 10 kilohertz to 2,000 megahertz and a capability to analyze power lines, demodulate subcarriers, and provide a panoramic visual display of any video signal present, with a capability to extend frequency coverage as may be required by circumstances.

•Non-linear junction detector for detecting hidden tape recorders, non-operating transmitters, and remotely controlled transmitters. This instrument can also aid in detecting devices that use transmission techniques that go beyond the frequency range of countermeasures receivers.

•Countermeasures amplifiers.

TSCM technicians must be thoroughly grounded in countermeasures work, be current in their knowledge of state-of-the-art equipment, and be schooled and experienced in computer-based and digital telephone systems.

Subcarrier and frequency hopping are special techniques that should be applied. All detected signals must be identified as either legitimate or suspect. The source of a legitimate signal might, for example, be an FM broadcast station. A suspect signal would be one that is found to emanate from the area being inspected and cannot be attributed to a legitimate source.

Electronic emissions from computers, communications equipment, and teleconferencing facilities should be evaluated to determine their vulnerability to interception. The TSCM provider must be sufficiently competent to both detect readable emissions and formulate sensible, cost-effective recommendations to prevent exposure of sensitive data to unauthorized parties.

Telephones and telephone lines within the area under inspection should be examined with a telephone analyzer, a time domain reflectometer, and a TSCM audio-amplifier. These instruments check for devices that allow listening of conversations over the telephone and within the office or area nearby, even when the phone is not in use. In addition, each phone should be disassembled and closely checked for illicit devices or wiring. A good technician will easily recognize non-standard objects and wiring that are the tell-tale signs of unauthorized listening.

Telephone satellite terminals and frame rooms, as well as station and distribution cables in the areas of concern should be inspected. Computer-based telephone systems should be evaluated for programming problems.

A thorough physical search should be made, with particular attention to areas adjoining rooms where sensitive communications occur. The walls between the rooms require careful inspection, and exiting wires need to be examined, including in some cases, electrical testing of wires for audio signals. Ceilings, radiators, ducts, electrical outlets and switches, picture frames, furniture, lamp fixtures, and plants all deserve the TSCM technician's attention.

Selected objects, such as desks, tables, chairs, and sofas, can be examined with a non-linear junction detector. This instrument uses a low-power microwave beam to detect energy reflected from electronic components such as diodes, transistors, and integrated circuits. These components are integral to radio transmitters, tape recorders, and other eavesdropping devices. Also, microwave transmitters, remotely activated transmitters, and transmitters that operate on infrared and ultrasonic principles can be spotted with a non-linear junction detector.

At the conclusion of the inspection, the TSCM provider should meet with the security manager to verbally discuss the work performed, the findings, and the recommendations. A fully detailed written report should be submitted within 30 days.

Safeguarding proprietary information is a concern for all companies of substance. TSCM inspections can be a security manager's tool for reducing the organization's exposure to loss or compromise of valuable information.

Richard J. Heffernan, CPP

PROPRIETARY INFORMATION: TRADE SECRETS, COPYRIGHTS, AND MATTERS OF LAW

Any company information considered to be of value (proprietary), and hence worth protecting through legal means, must be both useful and not publicly known. The terms *proprietary information* or *intellectual property* are interchangeable and are often used to describe information which is private and important to a business. The important information on which a business is based may be technical, that is, explaining how to do or make something, or general, including customer lists or lists of prospects.

Knowing what important proprietary information exists is a necessary first step to establishing legal rights. The information identification and classification process (identifying the business information base) is a way to do this. Establishing ownership of technical information developed in the course of business requires employee contracts that clearly state that any ideas coming from the employees' work belong to the company. Such contracts should be used generally for any high-technology business and in special situations (e.g., scientists, engineers, and chiefs) for any business.

Selecting from Legal Protection Alternatives

Legal protection alternatives are useful in some cases for protecting company information, but the business itself must also take reasonable actions to recognize value and make an effort at protection.

Patent

A patent is an exclusive right to use an idea that is both new (hence the patent search necessary before granting) and useful. The owner of a patent does not particularly care if the idea is exposed, since he or she has exclusive rights to it under law for a limited time. In fact, the very act of patenting exposes the idea, because it is published by the U.S. Patent Office. Therefore, in some cases, a company may decide not to use a patent but rather to rely on trade secret practices.

Patents are expensive to obtain, and extensive delays may be encountered in the process. After a patent is granted, enforcing one's rights may be very difficult. Another company's product may look like one already patented, but it may be next to impossible to prove that it has been manufactured in the same way. A court may invalidate a patent if a similar previous invention, also patented, is discovered. The second company might also be cited for infringement.

Trade Secret

Information qualifies as a trade secret and can be defended as such in court if the company has identified the material as valuable and secret, has set up a system for identifying and protecting such material, and has required that its employees actually follow the protection system. The value of a trade secret depends on the profits it produces; a secret that has never produced profits may not be considered to have any value and hence may not be protected by law. There are still risks, however. Others outside the company could independently discover the same information and if they also keep it a secret, it can be shared in secret, and the legal protection still applies.

One advantage a patent has over a trade secret involves the licensing of a process or technology. The licensee probably would feel more secure if the information were patented; the patent provides a clear legal right, while trade secrets are always open to a challenge in court.

Copyright

A copyright protects the arrangement of certain information, not the information itself. Music, for example, consists of an arrangement of a common set of notes. The notes can be used by anyone, but the arrangement of the notes in a copyrighted score makes the particular piece private property.

Copyright can be claimed by the originator of a work simply by indicating the copyright symbol, ©, the year of origination, and the name of the claimant. Copyrighted materials can be registered with the U.S. Copyright Office, thereby allowing suits to be brought in defense.

A copyright has advantages over trade secrets in certain cases. A copyright is an absolute reservation of privilege to a specified person or company, but a trade secret implies that others may know of the information and share it. The issue of business strategy vs. copyright or trade secret protection for information is a complex one, and experienced legal counsel is needed.

Practical Application

Most businesses choose to use trade secret law as the basis for protecting valuable business information. James Pooley, in his excellent reference work *The Executive's Guide to Protecting Proprietary Business Information and Trade Secrets*, suggests that information protection has three goals:

1. To prevent theft.
2. To discourage theft by establishing the value of the trade secrets and the difficulty of stealing them, as well as the fact that any unauthorized user will face prosecution.
3. To maximize the appearance of the program as one designed to meet the first two goals.

The owner of information can accomplish these goals by:

•Establishing an information management program to identify the company's critical information.

•Classifying such information to indicate value.

•Setting up information management practices ensuring protection through regular, required employee actions involving proper marking and handling of valuable information.

In the landmark case *Motorola vs. Fairchild Camera and Instrument Corp.*, which invalidated Motorola's claims for trade secret protection, the judge noted that "there were no signs in the area warning of trade secrets, no warnings given to those taking tours, and no statement requiring nondisclosure agreements required to be signed or acknowledged." He further pointed out that outsiders could see, time, and operate the "secret" machines and even observe a "secret" process through a microscope. Thus, although Motorola had given lip service to trade secret protection, its failure to set up and operate a procedure for protecting the information denied it the protection of law.

If a business wishes to protect its proprietary information, it must take prudent and careful actions in a consistent manner. That means a well-conceived information protection program.

James A. Schweitzer

Source Schweitzer, J.A., Managing Information Security. (Butterworth-Heinemann, Boston, 1990).

PROXIMITY AND POINT SENSORS

Proximity and point sensors are available that detect persons approaching, touching, or attempting to remove valuable items or attempting to penetrate areas containing valuable items.

Proximity Sensors

Capacitance Proximity Detectors. These protect metal items such as safes and file cabinets. They detect changes in the electrical capacitance between the item being protected and an electrical ground plane under the protected item. Capacitance detectors can also be used to protect valuable items such as art objects by mounting the detectors on a metal surface isolated from the ground plane.

A capacitor is an electronic component that consists of two conductor plates separated by a dielectric medium. A change in the electrical charge or dielectric medium results in a change in the capacitance between the two plates. One plate is the metal item being protected and the second plate is an electrical reference ground plane under and around the protected item. The metal object is isolated from the ground plane by insulating blocks. This leaves only air around and between the metal object and ground. Therefore, air is the dielectric medium.

In operation, the metal objects are electrically charged to a potential that creates an electrostatic field between the metal object and reference ground. The strength of the field is certainly non-lethal but is adequate enough to cause a detectable change in the capacitance if anyone approaches or touches the protected object. The electrical conductivity of the intruder's body alters the dielectric characteristics. The dielectric changes result in a change in the capacitance between the protected item and the reference ground. When the net capacitance change satisfies the alarm criterion, an alarm is activated.

The detector sensitivity can be adjusted to detect an intruder approaching a protected item or adjusted to a lesser sensitivity level requiring the intruder to actually touch the item. Although some detectors can be adjusted to detect an intruder at a distance up to 4 or 5 feet from the protected object, this level of sensitivity is not recommended unless it is required for some specific application. The level of sensitivity should be limited to detect the intruder at a distance of about 6 inches or even require him to actually touch the protected item in order to initiate an alarm.

A lower sensitivity will not affect the response time but will help reduce false alarms. If the detector sensitivity is adjusted to detect an intruder 4 feet from the protected item, the electrostatic field close to the item would be very sensitive, perhaps sensitive enough to cause false alarms, even to changes in humidity.

The sensitivity of capacitance detectors is affected by changes in relative humidity and the relocation of other metal objects closer to or farther away from the protected item. Changes in the relative humidity vary the air dielectric characteristics. An increase in the relative humidity causes the air conductivity to increase and reduces the capacitance. Conversely, a decrease in humidity or a drying of the air reduces the conductivity. When a metal object is moved close to a protected object, it is electrically coupled to the protected object by the electrostatic field. The object basically increases the size of the capacitor plate and reduces the capacitance monitored by the detector.

The capacitance detector signal processor is basically a balanced bridge circuit with the protected metal object as part of the bridge. Anyone approaching or touching the protected object changes the capacitance, thus unbalancing the circuit and initiating an alarm. Initially, the circuit must be adjusted either automatically or manually to balance the bridge. If the circuit is manually adjusted, then every time metal objects are moved close to or away from the protected object, the circuit must be rebalanced. Sometimes at the change of seasons the manually adjusted sensors need readjusting to compensate for changes in humidity.

Pressure Mats. These can be used as proximity detectors to detect anyone approaching valuable objects and they can be used as barrier detectors to protect entrances leading to areas requiring protection. Pressure mats are available as individual mats for multiple application purposes and as continuous runners that can be cut to any length. Individual mats are typically used for protecting small areas such as at entrances, under windows, or on steps. Runners are installed under carpets to cover larger areas such as in the area of a safe.

Pressure mats consist of a series of ribbon switches positioned parallel to each other approximately 3 inches apart along the length of the mat. Ribbon switches are constructed from two strips of metal in the form of a ribbon separated by an insulating material. It is constructed so that when an adequate amount of pressure, depending on the application, is exerted any place along the ribbon the metal strips make electrical contact. Individual ribbon switches are available in lengths up to 20 feet, but the switches used in pressure mats or runners are about 2 to 3 feet long. The series of switches forming the mat are electrically wired in parallel, and the assembly is sealed between two plastic sheets or molded in rubber to form a durable, weatherproof mat.

Point Sensors

Pressure Switches. These can be mechanically activated contact switches or single ribbon switches used in pressure mats. An open switch becomes a point sensor when the item requiring protection is placed on the switch, thus closing the contacts. Anyone lifting the item causes the switch to open and initiate an alarm.

Mechanical Vibration Transducers. These are secured to the item being protected rather than to the mounting surface like most mechanical contact switches. When the protected object is moved, the forces required in the act of movement will cause the vibration transducer to initiate a series of open-circuit pulses. These pulses are detected by the supervisor circuit and initiate an alarm. Items

being protected by vibration transducers should be physically secured to their mounting surfaces to ensure that adequate force is required to initiate an alarm as the item is being removed. Signal wires to the transducer should be kept short and well-secured.

Robert L. Barnard

Source Barnard, R.L., Intrusion Detection Systems. (Butterworth-Heinemann, Boston, 1982).

PUBLIC RELATIONS: DEALING WITH THE MEDIA DURING A CRISIS

An organization is much like a living organism in the sense that it reacts to external stimuli, and when the stimuli are unpleasant, as would be the case during a crisis, the organization experiences stress. An external stimulus contributing to an organization's stress in a crisis is the uncompromising search by the news media for information. A significant incident affecting the organization, such as a major accident or crime, will stimulate public interest and consequently set the news media on the trail.

At the outset of a crisis, the organization faces two critical tasks simultaneously: first, deal with the crisis, and second, communicate the facts. Great pressure is on the organization to launch an effective response and at the same time intelligently present the details of what happened and what is being done in response. The target of communications set by the organization is the public broadly, and the vehicles for getting to the target are television, radio, and press agencies.

Business people are learning to be aware of public concerns when commenting on broad issues in which corporate interests are involved. Executives generally look ahead when making public statements. They do so to avoid the impression of not caring for public health or safety when company profit may be at risk. This can be difficult when liability is a possible outcome and legal counsel urges management to be careful in avoiding language that suggests culpability. However, if management is overly circumspect, the business may suffer public relations losses. Losses of this type include damage to public confidence and increased regulatory restrictions imposed by legislators responsive to the public mood. The long-term costs of political and regulatory responses are likely to greatly outweigh the short-term costs of accepting responsibility when it is due.

Interacting with the Media

Certain problems of a security nature can be anticipated in dealings with the media. They include access control at the scene of the incident, disruption of business operations resulting from attempts by the media to acquire information, and unauthorized release of information from sources within the organization. Also, when the security manager is a central persona in responding to contingencies, which is almost always the case, he or she will be sought after by the media.

Being responsive to media requests for information is especially important during emergency response operations. The usual procedure is for media inquiries to be channeled to one office or person, typically called the Public Information Office or PIO. A PIO representative is designated in advance to speak for the organization, to meet with news representatives, and to arrange and be present at media interviews of company employees. The PIO is often sensitive to the needs of the news media, particularly with respect to time. While the media are racing to report the news, the PIO is concerned about releasing details that are both accurate and considerate of the organization's view.

Incidents involving death, serious injury, substantial property loss, damage to the environment, and risk to the public constitute significant news. The PIO serves as a "control valve" for preventing the release of distorted versions and providing some modicum of protection against disclosures that may be harmful to the organization or its individual employees.

Whether business likes it or not, the media will present news in a manner intended to attract attention, and in the process will make news reporting more important than the news itself. The outcome can be distortion of facts.

When an incident of any magnitude arises, the news media will want, indeed demand, the facts. Oftentimes they will be asking for details even before the organization's management is aware of the incident. Through arrangements with governmental response agencies, such as police and fire departments, media employees learn of incidents on a real-time basis. Television,

radio, and press reporters are likely to arrive at the incident scene with the first responders.

When the organization's headquarters is located a considerable distance from the site of the incident, which will frequently be the case, senior management will expect a knowledgeable manager at the scene to act as the organization's spokesperson, at least until arrival of more senior persons. The on-scene spokesperson can initially provide all available details as quickly as possible. Of concern in accidents will be precisely what happened, how, when, and where; the number of persons involved and their names; the nature and extent of deaths and injuries; and the nature and extent of property damage, including non-organizational property and the environment.

A security manager, especially one who also has operational safety responsibilities, may be called upon to perform spokesperson duties. Direct media contact with an operational manager is usually better, at least from the media's point of view, than contact through a PIO representative or other intermediary. Misunderstandings frequently develop whenever a critical incident is being developed by the media, and an absence of personal contact between the media and persons close to the situation contribute to misunderstanding and distrust.

A security manager tabbed for interview must be wary of offhand remarks that could give a wrong impression, and should also avoid leaving out important details. Being quoted out of context can be minimized by speaking in short sentences and repeating constantly the key phrases that convey the organization's point of view. This requires rehearsing, and is particularly important in television interviews where reporters are obliged to select only the briefest, most salient comments from an interview that may have taken an hour or more to tape. If at all possible, a PIO representative should be present to listen objectively and intervene to correct errors on the spot.

Rumor and exaggeration are the organization's nemesis in a time of crisis. Accuracy, although difficult to maintain in the very early stages of an incident, is a priority. Information flowing from the scene has to be carefully weighed as to the extent of casualties and damage. A golden rule is to not release the names of persons killed or injured until the next of kin have been notified, to not speculate as to the causes of the incident, and to not mention dollar amounts concerning damage and loss. Another rule is to avoid saying "no comment." Corporate counsel may like this response because it closes off a line of questioning that could be troublesome, but use of the term suggests to the media and the public that the organization has something to hide.

The organization and the media each have a right to be wary of deception. The organization may feel it has an overriding and legitimate reason to be reserved in its response, and the media know from prior experiences that businesses have engaged in denials and half-truths. Good reporters usually can see through a lie and have it in their power to make the organization look worse for it. Reporters hungry for a headline story may be more attuned to negatives than positives. Some may have an anti-business bias or be ignorant of business needs. Fortunately, most reporters genuinely want to present a responsible view and will work with an organization that deals squarely with them.

If saying the wrong thing can hurt the organization, why not impose a policy of silence? The problem with this approach is that speculation, conjecture, and rumor take the place of facts. Fiction and fantasy rapidly fill the vacuum of official silence. By saying nothing, the organization makes itself vulnerable to unfounded perceptions. In a world strongly influenced by mass communications, perception takes on a reality all its own.

The principal cause of tension between business and the media is their different perspectives. Business operates through policies it believes are proper and is resolute in defending policies in the face of criticism. Executives are resentful when taken to task by reporters who do not understand the policies and the reasons for them. Reporters, on the other hand, feel that their function is to report what they find, even when their findings run counter to long-established business practices and beliefs.

On-Scene Functions

The PIO's contingency plan will customarily call for sending a representative to the scene of a major incident. When the incident is significantly destructive, such as an oil spill or plant explosion, the representative will almost certainly be accompanied by one or more senior managers, possibly including the organization's chief executive officer. Virtually no crisis incident is too small or unimportant to warrant senior management attention.

Some of the media-related functions that require prompt attention at the scene are:
- Verifying key details, such as casualties and damages.
- Meeting and escorting reporters.
- Setting up and making announcements at press conferences.
- Updating and reporting developments as they evolve.
- Clearing the statements and comments of management.

To the extent that circumstances permit, the PIO representative will set up a press center at or close to the scene of the incident. The center could be on the organization's premises, at a hotel nearby, or at any safe and reasonably convenient place having telephone facilities. It is not necessary or even appropriate for the PIO to provide food or refreshments at press center meetings, but it is a given that news personnel will receive honest answers with least possible delay. The answers are delivered courteously and in a manner ensuring that all news personnel receive information the same way at the same time.

Verbal announcements are often supplemented with written materials designed to facilitate accurate reporting. Working from written materials, the PIO spokesperson is able to focus on facts that are fully known. Dangerous conjecture, which will sometimes arise in the face of insistent questioning, can be avoided by commenting only on what has been put into writing.

Also, in the case of releasing the names of persons injured or killed, the chances of word-of-mouth name errors are reduced by providing a written list.

As an incident winds down, the PIO may hold one or more follow-up meetings with the news media. By then, the causes of the incident and the extent of damage may be known and open to discussion. Positive messages would include assurances to the community with respect to safety and the restoration of jobs destabilized by the incident; progress reports on assistance given to families and repairs made to property and the environment; the effectiveness of the organization's preventive and responsive actions;

and credit to local response agencies that assisted in bringing the emergency under control.

The Role of the Security Manager

As touched upon earlier, the security manager has a full plate during a major incident. Depending on the nature of the incident, there can be requirements to provide first-responder medical assistance, establish access control at the incident scene, and protect people and assets exposed to continuing risk. Meeting these requirements involves coordination with many persons inside and out of the organization. Within the organization, and surely this will be a key element in contingency planning, the security manager interfaces with the PIO.

The services performed by a security manager that relate narrowly to the media fall generally under access control. Three services stand out:

•Preventing entrance to an unsafe incident scene by unauthorized personnel. After an incident has been declared safe, the security manager may be involved in escorting media representatives interested in taking pictures, making notes, and in some controlled situations, interviewing employees at the scene.

•Preventing close-in access to PIO representatives and senior managers at meetings with the press. Distraught relatives of victims and issue-oriented persons antagonistic to the organization may use a press meeting to physically attack the organization's spokespersons.

•Preventing access to travel conveyances utilized by senior managers. A person, deranged or motivated by revenge and/or the desire to gain attention to a cause, may attempt to place a bomb aboard or otherwise sabotage the plane or automobile used to transport key members of the organization.

The security manager must understand and be prepared to support the important functions carried out by the organization's public information office during times of crisis. Security support to the PIO cannot be properly executed if it is based on a misunderstanding of the PIO function or if there is insufficient preparation in crisis management. A security manager simply cannot wait until an emergency occurs to determine and fill PIO needs. All of the planning for the handling of public information matters must be done well in advance.

The quality of security support is examined, to the security manager's credit or discredit, at the conclusion of a crisis when the organization summarizes the lessons learned. A manager who puts effort into learning PIO needs and in developing a support capability assures a quality response for the organization and a creditable rating personally.

John J. Fay, CPP

Sources

Finn, D., The Business-Media Relationship: Countering Misconceptions and Distrust. (AMACOM, New York, 1981).

Fire Protection Handbook. (National Fire Protection Association, Quincy, MA, 1986).

Heyel, C., Encyclopedia of Management. (Van Nostrand Reinhold, New York, 1982).

Q

QUESTIONED DOCUMENTS: THE COLLECTION OF KNOWN WRITINGS

A set of absolute rules cannot be applied to the conduct of any investigation, and no two cases involving questioned documents will be exactly alike. The implication? Use the information in this section as a guide and be prepared to season it with liberal amounts of common sense.

An exemplar is a collected writing, obtained from an individual at the request of another, usually an investigator. It is a sample of an individual's handwriting or hand printing, and relates to a case under investigation in which the individual is somehow involved. A standard is a known writing made during the normal course of an individual's activity, usually prior to the incident under investigation. Hand-printed entries on an employment application form and signatures on canceled checks are examples of standards.

Standards are particularly valuable to the document examiner because they allow comparison with characteristics that appear in exemplars. If a disguise is attempted by the writer of exemplars, the examiner may be able to detect the attempt in the examination of standards. Exemplars and standards are often called known writings because authorship is known.

In addition to linking a suspect to the questioned text or signature, exemplars and standards are often used to eliminate the victim from consideration as the author. They are also valuable in determining attempts to simulate or trace the writing of the victim. Exemplars and standards should be collected from the victim in every case, even when the indications of guilt point strongly elsewhere.

Obtaining Known Writings

Exemplars are made from dictation without allowing the writer to view the questioned document. No assistance should be given to the writer as to spelling and punctuation. An error in spelling or punctuation that appears in both the questioned document and an exemplar would be noteworthy. As each exemplar is completed, the investigator removes it from the writer's sight. The objective is to not make it easy for the writer to create a consistent disguise among all the exemplars by copying one after the other.

Each exemplar is placed on a separate piece of paper. The shape and size of the paper corresponds to the shape and size of the questioned document. The writer is directed by the investigator to place the exemplar in the same area or space as it appears on the questioned document. If the questioned writing is on a form, such as a credit application, the investigator would want to obtain a quantity of the same credit application stock. Blank forms would be handed one at a time to the writer. An absolutely incorrect procedure would be for the writer to put all of the exemplars on one piece of paper, one immediately below the other.

Exemplars need to be made of all writings that appear on the questioned document. For example, if a check is the questioned document, the writer should be asked to write not only the maker's signature, but the "Pay to the Order of" entry, the date, and the check amount in words and numbers. A point to keep in mind is that a document may bear writings made by more than one person. Because a person did not write a questioned signature does not mean he or she did not write some other portion of the document. In check cases, it is not unusual for one person to fill out the check and get an accomplice to sign it.

How Much Is Enough?

This question is answered with the observation that the chances for obtaining a definitive opinion increase relative to the number of exemplars provided to the questioned document examiner. Case circumstances will sometimes dictate a need for collecting a large number of exemplars and standards. Consultation with a document examiner is recommended before making the collections. As a general rule, a greater number of known writings is required for analysis when the questioned writing is meager, and vice versa. Also as a general rule, the collected standards should reflect a mix of writings that were made just prior to and shortly after the time frame of the document in question. A signature made 10 years before or after a signature in doubt will not be very meaningful to the examiner.

Typically, a questioned signature will require the investigator to obtain 12 to 15 signature exemplars, plus 12 to 15 known signature standards. A note or letter to be examined will require two to three repetitions, depending on length, and an address on an envelope or package will require about 25 exemplars. If the questioned document is typewritten and lengthy, such as a letter, two to three repetitions of the exact text should suffice, but if the typewritten text is short, such as a signature block, at least 25 exemplars will be needed.

Because some people can write equally or nearly as well with either hand, the investigator should ask the writer at the beginning of an exemplar collecting session to provide one or two samples from each hand. If the investigator is satisfied that the writer is proficient with only one hand, further exemplars by the weak or "unaccustomed writing hand" will not be necessary. If the investigator is not satisfied on this point, exemplars from both hands should be collected. When the questioned writing appears to have been made by the weak hand, the investigator will want to obtain a sufficient number of samples made with that hand.

A questioned writing that is illegible or unreadable is called an abbreviated writing. Generally, an abbreviated writing occurs when the author writes with speed so as to save time. A person with a long name who writes the name many times a day is likely to develop an abbreviated signature. When an abbreviated signature is questioned, the investigator should attempt to acquire standard signatures that would have been made under conditions that called for speedy writing, and also obtain exemplars under similar conditions. An investigator wanting to introduce speed into the exemplar-taking process can dictate rapidly or require so many exemplars that the writer may resort to abbreviation.

Original Documents Are Critical

A properly conducted analysis requires the examiner to work with the original document. Although remarkable advances have been made in the technology of document reproduction, the examiner cannot make definitive judgments based on a copy. Particular characteristics present on the original are simply not transferred to a copy. Indications of pressure of the writing instrument

on the paper and constituents of ink are examples of characteristics that lie outside the examiner's analysis when working from a copy. A good examiner will not render unqualified opinions in such cases, and many examiners will refuse to accept work or give opinions involving reproductions.

It will happen, however, that the original of a questioned document has been lost or destroyed, leaving only a reproduction. The examiner may be asked to make an analysis with the understanding that the finding could be inconclusive, qualified, or limited.

An original is sometimes not readily available for analysis because it is an official record entrusted to a custodian whose authority does not extend to allowing replacement of an original with a certified true copy. The investigator will need to direct his request for the original to a higher level in the custodian's organization or petition a court. An alternative solution, although decidedly less desirable, would be for the examiner to conduct the analysis at the place of custody. Because the examiner utilizes equipment that is not easily transported, this approach is like bringing the hospital to the patient.

In addition to giving the examiner materials to evaluate, the investigator needs to provide certain details, such as the writer's date of birth and date of death, if applicable; whether the writer was left-handed or right-handed; the duration of formal schooling of the writer; the profession of the writer; the country where the writer learned to write; the state of the writer's health on the date the questioned document was executed; the dates of execution for standards; and the date exemplars were obtained.

Selecting a Document Examiner

A security manager or investigator in need of forensic document examination services has to differentiate between examiners who apply scientific-based techniques in the analysis of questioned writings and people who assess personalities based on handwriting. So-called graphologists and graphoanalysts will sometimes claim, often in public advertisements, the ability to judge questioned documents. More art than science, their techniques focus on writing characteristics that purport to reveal the writer's personal traits, such as deceit and dishonesty.

A competent document examiner will hold diplomate status conferred by the American Board of Forensic Document Examiners (ABFDE), which is the only recognized national certifying board in this discipline. Recognition of the ABFDE is derived from the field, principally two professional organizations: the American Academy of Forensic Sciences and the American Society of Questioned Document Examiners. The ABFDE diplomate will:

- Possess a baccalaureate degree.
- Have completed a 2-year, full-time training program at a recognized document laboratory.
- Have completed an additional 2 years of full-time independent document work.
- Practice forensic document examination on a full-time basis.
- Have passed a comprehensive written and/or oral examination.

A professionally concerned examiner will attend seminars, workshop, and training courses to maintain or enhance competency. Some of the better specialized courses are offered by the U.S. Secret Service and the Federal Bureau of Investigation (FBI). Participation in professional associations is an indicator of professional commitment. National associations of interest include the Questioned Document Section of the American Academy of Forensic Sciences, the American Society of Questioned Document Examiners, and the International Association for Identification.

A qualified examiner will own or have access to a professional library of forensic document literature and an assemblage of technical equipment, such as a stereoscopic binocular microscope and hand magnifiers, an electrostatic detection apparatus for detecting and visualizing indentations on paper, a video spectral comparator for detecting differences in inks, test grids for detecting alterations to typewritten documents, and a variety of special cameras and films for documenting the examiner's findings. Finally, a very important qualification is the recognition extended to a forensic document examiner by civil and criminal courts and administrative bodies for the provision of expert witness testimony.

Checking out the credentials of prospective examiners and making a careful selection before authorizing the work may very well be the most critical activity in a case. It could mean the difference between establishing the truth of the

situation in doubt, and if taken to court could mean the difference between winning and losing. At stake may be large sums in litigation costs, awards, and punitive fees. The best advice to the security manager or investigator charged with making an inquiry is to do the homework necessary to choose a competent examiner.

Hans M. Gidion

QUESTIONING TECHNIQUES

Security professionals like to make a distinction between "interview" and "interrogation" and, of course, there is a difference. An interview is the questioning of a person who has or is believed to have facts of official interest. The person questioned usually gives, in his own words, an account of the incident under investigation, or offers information concerning a suspect. The person being interviewed is usually a witness, victim, or complainant. An interrogation, on the other hand, is the questioning of a person suspected of having committed an offense, or of a person who is reluctant to make a full disclosure. The person being interrogated is a suspect, or may be a reluctant witness.

Both definitions have one thing in common; each seeks to obtain information through questioning. The differences arise in the manner of questioning and the type of person being questioned. It is not unusual for an information-gathering session to switch back and forth between interview and interrogation, depending on the degree of cooperation or hostility encountered.

The most consistently available and most valuable sources of information in the majority of inquiries are the people involved. The inquiry obtains information from people for a variety of reasons; initially to establish the facts of a crime, including determination of whether or not a crime actually occurred. During initial phases it is important to verify information given by other persons connected with the case, or tie in facts gleaned from an examination of physical evidence. Information collected from the victim, complainant, or witnesses may lead to identification of offenders and accomplices. Prompt and properly conducted interviews can produce investigative leads, additional physical evidence, and develop background information regarding motives, habits of the criminal and other details that contribute to a fuller understanding of the crime. Interviews can also lead to a discovery of unreported crimes, or connect criminals with unsolved crimes. The function of interviewing has many important uses.

A person charged with conducting an investigation must make himself thoroughly familiar with the elements of proof pertaining to the specific offense under investigation. A working knowledge of criminal law helps the investigator evaluate the relevancy of information he receives, and allows him to detect incriminating comments made during an interview.

In the interrogation of a suspect, for example, a knowledge of what is required to establish criminal intent will assist the investigator to steer his questioning in a direction intended to reveal motive and pre-meditation.

Obstacles

Human factors strongly influence interviews. The skilled interviewer recognizes this critical point. He strives to understand and deal with the motives, fears, and mental makeup of the person from whom he wishes to acquire useful information. The line of questions and interview techniques are selected on the basis of an assessment made by the investigator of the interviewee's psychological makeup.

Perception. An important factor to be assessed is the interviewee's ability to correctly observe what happened in his or her presence. Observation is an ability that can be sharpened through training and practice. A security manager, for example, is conditioned to be a keen observer of persons, places, things, and events. The average person does not possess strong perceptive skills and among different people there are certain to be different skill levels. This point has been illustrated many times in controlled situations where a single event is observed by several persons. As each person recounts his or her observations of the event, we are surprised at how many different versions are offered of the same incident. Why is this so? Psychologists tell us that perception is conditioned by:

• Differing abilities to see, hear, smell, taste, and touch.

• The location of the viewer in relation to the incident at the time of occurrence. Distance and geographical perspective affect vision.

• The amount of time intervening between occurrence and interview.

• The number and nature of events that occur during the interval between occurrence and interview.

What are the implications of these factors? Well, for one thing, the interviewer should attempt to discover if the person being interviewed has physical disabilities that impair the senses. If it is known, for example, that a witness has a vision problem, the investigator should be careful in accepting at full value statements that are based on what the witness saw. It is far better to discover problems in a witness's perception at the outset of an investigation than to have such problems exploited at time of trial by the defendant's lawyer.

It might be helpful during an interview for the investigator to ask the interviewee to place himself or herself on a map or a sketch that depicts the physical layout of the scene at the time of the incident. The position of the interviewee in relation to other persons and objects can help the investigator evaluate how much the person could have seen, heard, or smelled. This technique also discourages fanciful elaboration by the person being interviewed.

Because human memory erodes over time, interviews should be conducted as quickly as practical. Memory not only fades, but becomes colored, either consciously or unconsciously, by what the witness is exposed to after the incident. Remarks made by other witnesses or newspaper accounts may cause an interviewee to fill in the gaps of his own memory with details about which he has no direct knowledge. A witness may even form his own opinion of guilt or innocence and shape his testimony accordingly. This possibility is reduced when the interview is conducted soon, that is, before the witness has time to form personal judgments that distort the truth. Prompt interviewing also affords a suspect less time to formulate an alibi or to "get his story straight" with fellow accomplices.

A person who is subjected to stressful, exciting, or injurious events after observing an incident is likely to forget details. To illustrate, assume a pedestrian observes a speeding motorist strike another pedestrian and drive away from the scene. The witness is caught up in a series of actions in which he renders first aid and transports the seriously injured victim to the hospital. What the witness has experienced in the immediate aftermath may cause him to have a faulty recollection concerning the hit and run vehicle.

Prejudice. It is not unreasonable to expect every interviewee to be prejudiced to some degree. The strength and targets of prejudice vary among people. The investigator should be alert to prejudice and deal with it when it surfaces. One way to keep information from being distorted by prejudice is to require detailed, specific answers during an interview. If allowed to talk in generalities, a prejudiced person will make statements that are partially accurate and partially misleading. By remaining within a narrow line of discussion aimed at a specific issue, the investigator forces the interviewee to respond with information that is free of bias.

Hostility. Suspects are naturally reluctant to talk, and we expect them to be uncooperative and resistive to interviewing. Sometimes we are surprised (and dismayed) when we discover that witnesses and even victims show an unwillingness to talk. Finding the reason for hostility is a first step in overcoming it.

Fear of Self-Involvement. The fear of self-involvement is a common obstacle to information collection. Many citizens are unfamiliar with investigative methods and are afraid to assist. Also, a person may have committed a separate offense at some previous time and is fearful it will come to light. Some persons think that crimes that do not happen to them directly are not their business, or they believe that the misfortunes that befall victims are of the victims' own making. Many people are very private, disliking publicity in general, and some people fear reprisal by the criminal or his associates. The investigator who knows the underlying reason for resistance is better able to work around it.

Inconvenience. No one wants his or her lifestyle disrupted. We are all pretty much animals of habit and we dislike it when the routines of our daily living are upset because we are kept waiting or inconvenienced by an unexpected event. Some people will actually disclaim knowledge of criminal matters because they wish to avoid questioning. We are also aware of witnesses being required to wait several days in courthouse hallways and then not be called to the stand. Even when a witness is compensated for lost time, there is a residue of resentment against a process that penalizes citizens in the name of civic duty.

Resentment. Among some people resentment runs deep and wide. It may manifest itself in a dislike for authority generally. Resentment can appear in the form of blind loyalty to the accused person. We are talking here not of the American tradition that pulls for the underdog, but of the unreasoning attitude that criminals are victims of a repressive society.

Personality Conflicts. Occasionally an interviewee and interviewer will get along beautifully right from the start. More often an interviewing session will begin with mixed feelings and, through the normal give and take of interpersonal communications, a foundation of mutual respect and cooperation will develop. Sometimes, but infrequently, interviewer and interviewee will for one reason or another find it impossible to communicate at all. When this happens the conflict usually has its roots in the attitudes of the interviewee. A successful interviewer will adjust his own personality in relation to the person being questioned; he is skillful at changing his vocabulary and demeanor; he avoids saying and doing things that are abrasive; and he shows respect for the interviewee as a person. In those cases where the investigator is unable to overcome a basic personality conflict, the best course of action is to voluntarily withdraw in favor of another questioner. This should not be regarded as failure, but recognition of a human factor that must be accommodated in the interest of achieving a successful investigative outcome.

Types of Non-Suspect Persons

Now, let's examine the types of persons frequently encountered in interviewing situations who are not subjects of the investigative process. There is usually no requirement to have a witness to a non-suspect interview. When an investigator feels, however, that the person to be interviewed may have some guilt, it is appropriate to have another person present. When a woman is interviewed, either as a suspect or non-suspect, it is good practice to have another person present (preferably a female) or hold the interview in an open room or semi-public area. This affords some protection from a later accusation of sexual impropriety.

In those instances when a non-suspect interview calls for the presence of a witness, only one should be used and the witness should remain neutral, unless planned otherwise. Too many persons present during an interview, or even a single antagonistic person, can cause the interviewee's statement to be later challenged on the grounds it was obtained under duress.

Victims. Because nearly all crimes involve persons as victims, interviews are used to develop the basic facts of the crimes. In some instances the nature of a crime or the victim's condition as a consequence of the crime will reduce the amount of information obtainable. The interview of a victim is likely to occur anyplace: at the hospital, the victim's home, or a location not always of the investigator's choosing.

Although we can normally expect a victim to be cooperative, we cannot expect the information to be highly reliable. A victim may be overly eager to please, or may inflate the severity of the crime as a means to obtain sympathy or a larger insurance payoff. The investigator also has to guard against the possibility that a victim may be a principal to the crime.

When a victim is not cooperative, it may be due to fear of retaliation by the offender. Uncooperativeness can also stem from fear of publicity, or a belief that the amount of personal effort in cooperating exceeds the value of bringing an offender to justice.

Witnesses. A witness is any person, other than a suspect, who has information concerning an incident. Victims, complainants, accusers, laboratory experts, and informants are simply types of witnesses.

Witnesses to an incident are not always easily available to the investigator. It may be necessary to learn a witness's identity and seek that person out for the purpose of obtaining relevant information. A smaller number will not come forward voluntarily and some may actively seek to avoid contact. Human factors account for the reluctance of some people to cooperate.

For a person to be considered a witness it is not necessary for the person to have directly observed a criminal incident. A witness may be a person who can testify as to the actions and whereabouts of a suspect before and after the crime was committed, who knows facts or heard the accused make certain remarks, or who has information concerning the accused's motive. Also included as witnesses are specialists who can give expert and impartial testimony in court regarding analyses of evidence.

A special kind of witness is the informant. Although an informant may not be called to testify in court, investigators can obtain valuable leads from persons who, for pay or other consideration, will furnish information about criminals and their activities.

Complainants. The person who makes the initial report of a crime is called a complainant. A complainant is usually a victim or a person close to a victim. The motivation of a complainant may not always be honorable. A person may report criminal activity for revenge or to divert suspicion from himself.

Interviewing the Non-Suspect Person

Time Is Not a Luxury in Investigations. The rule rather than the exception is that an investigator will have very little time to prepare for interviews of non-suspect persons. Persons who are not immediately contacted after the commission of a crime may become entirely unavailable at a later time, and when the interval is long, details begin to slip from memory. To the extent that an investigator has time, preparation should include the following steps [1].

Obtain the Facts of the Case. The investigator should fix in his mind all that is currently known of the who, what, when, where, how, and why facts. He needs to pay particular attention to specific details, especially those that have not become public knowledge and may therefore be known only to the offender.

Know Something about the Interviewee. Background knowledge of the person to be interviewed will enable the investigator to select a suitable questioning technique. An understanding of the interviewee's connection to the crime helps the investigator evaluate the accuracy and truthfulness of information offered. Knowing something about the interviewee also helps the investigator establish rapport. Examples of background facts include age, place of birth, nationality, address, educational level, habits, companions, prior arrests and convictions, and hobbies.

Determine the Information to Be Sought. The investigator who knows the elements of proof for the crime he is investigating is better prepared to ask questions that bring out the relevant facts. For example, if the law requires that proof be shown of the accused's use of a dangerous weapon the investigator is alerted to the need to obtain a detailed description of the weapon in order to establish that a weapon was used and that it was capable of causing serious injury. In complex cases, the investigator can prepare a set of questions to consult during the interview. The questions should be formulated to reveal critical points but still allow the interviewee to tell his story in his own words.

Care should be taken to neither overestimate or underestimate the interviewee as a potential source of information. Preparation in the context used here is essentially self-preparation, especially of the mind. The investigator readies himself for an encounter with an individual who may be friendly or hostile, communicative or reticent, full of facts or devoid of facts, truthful or lying. The best start that an investigator can make is to have a thorough grasp of case facts, know something about the suspect, and know what information is necessary to bring the case to a successful conclusion.

Selecting the Time and Place. Although it is always useful to talk to a witness as soon as possible after an incident, it is sometimes more valuable to postpone an interview until other facts have been determined. Interviews that are scheduled in a logical sequence will permit the investigator to build upon information obtained previously and to avoid re-interviewing persons in order to fill missing gaps or remove contradictions.

Generally, cooperative witnesses can be interviewed first with uncooperative witnesses put on hold until a fuller understanding of the case has been obtained. Also, it might be desirable to delay an interview until physical evidence has been examined at a laboratory, or records have been checked for the presence of pertinent data.

Except for those witnesses who were necessarily interviewed at the scene, it is appropriate to interview non-suspects at times and places of their convenience. The relaxed, psychologically comfortable atmosphere of the witness's home may help the investigator obtain valuable information in a paced, unrushed interview. There is, of course, no objection to conducting a non-suspect interview at the investigator's office if that is the desire of the witness.

The situation is different with hostile and reluctant witnesses. If resistance is anticipated, it is to the investigator's advantage to conduct the interview in an environment psychologically comfortable to him. When an uncooperative witness objects to being interviewed at the investigator's office, a neutral meeting place might be suggested.

Making the Introduction. The investigator should introduce himself courteously and make sure the interviewee is aware of his correct identity. Remember that an introduction works both ways. The person to be interviewed should be asked to identify himself or herself. This puts the interviewer and interviewee on a name basis, and it establishes identity. The investigator, depending on the circumstances, may ask the interviewee to produce a driver's license or some other piece of identity.

A quick introduction gives an appearance of haste. It may cause the interviewee to think his information is of little importance. A few minutes spent in a proper introduction are not wasted. Of even greater importance is the fact that an introduction provides an ideal opportunity for the investigator to assess the interviewee and select an appropriate interviewing technique. A good introduction also affords the interviewee time to overcome nervousness and relate to the investigator as a person.

The closing moments of the introduction should be used to make a general statement about the case without disclosing any of the specific facts. This not only sets the stage for discussions which follow, but also removes the possibility of a later claim by the witness that he was not informed that the matter was officially under investigation.

Establishing Rapport. What is meant by rapport? In the context used here, rapport is the condition of harmony or agreement between interviewer and interviewee in which interpersonal communications are obtained.

The attitude and actions of the investigator during the initial moments of an interview will determine success or failure. The first few minutes almost certainly determine the tenor of the session [2]. The investigator should be friendly, but professional. The objective is to get the interviewee into a talkative mood, and to guide the conversation toward the interviewee's knowledge of the case. Where possible, the interviewee is encouraged to tell his complete story without interruption.

Interviewing Techniques

After rapport has been established and the interviewee is communicating, the investigator must guide the conversation in productive directions. For those interviewees who require no stimulation to continue talking, the investigator can wait until the story has been told and then review it, and request clarification of confusing points. Matters that were not touched upon by the interviewee can be covered at the end. For some persons, occasional prodding is necessary to keep a conversation moving. A common mistake of the fledgling interviewer is the tendency to interrupt or dominate a conversation to such a degree that the interviewee is not permitted to tell his story. Knowing when to ask a question is every bit as important as knowing what to ask and how to ask. Following are some questioning techniques for non-suspects.

Ask One Question at a Time. Too many questions at one time can be confusing for any person. Questions should be segregated one from each other, and the investigator should not proceed to the next question until he has obtained the fullest answer possible to the previous question. It is important also to pose questions intermittently. A constant series of questions is less desirable than a conversation punctuated by occasional questions inserted to clarify or stimulate.

Use Simple Questions. Long and complex questions lead to confusion and irritation. Legal terms and security jargon are unfamiliar to many people. The person being interviewed may reply that he doesn't know the answer to the question when in fact he simply didn't understand the question in the first place. Some people, when confronted with a misunderstood question, will become embarrassed and respond negatively.

Avoid Implied Answers. There is not much point in asking a question that provides its own answer. Suggesting answers defeats the whole purpose of the interview. An example of a question with an implied answer is "Was the weapon a caliber 0.38 revolver?" A better question might be "What kind of a weapon was it?"

Avoid "Yes" and "No" Questions. The idea in interviewing is to encourage elaboration. Short answers can omit valuable facts. Besides, the interviewee may feel he is being treated unfairly if he is limited to one-word answers. While a "yes" or "no" reply can be considered very specific, such answers are not always absolutely accurate and can be misleading in the absence of details.

Avoid Embarrassment to the Interviewee. Remarks, gestures, or facial expressions that can be interpreted as ridiculing should be avoided. When dealing with the non-suspect interviewee, it is usually not difficult to separate deliberate misrepresentation from unintentional mistakes. If honest errors are made, they should be resolved with tact and courtesy.

Control Digressions. While it is extremely important to get an interviewee to talk, it is equally important to confine talking to the issues at hand. Long, rambling discourses are time consuming and unproductive. The investigator must keep the discussion from drifting into irrelevant matters and excessive detail. The use of precise questions is effective in limiting the range of information being offered. Questions that are highly specific require answers that are not easily shifted to side issues. A technique called shunting can also be useful in controlling digression [3]. A shunting maneuver allows the investigator to bring the interviewee back to the original line of discussion. A shunt might occur by saying, "Let's return to that point where you said the suspect was wearing a baseball cap." The shunt is an inoffensive interruption because it appears to rise out of an interest in what the person has said.

Radiate Confidence. How many times have we been infected by the enthusiasm of others? People who think and act in positive ways influence those around them. The investigator who looks and acts in a confident manner projects an image of success. His overall demeanor and appearance lead others to believe he is in command of the situation and has a habit of success. The comments and questions of the investigator are expressed in positive terms. He avoids negative remarks like, "I don't know if there is much we can do in this case, but I need to talk with you anyway." Statements of that type practically guarantee failure. It would be far better to say, "I intend to get to the bottom of this matter, and I am sure you will be able to help."

Concluding the Non-Suspect Interview

When the investigator terminates the interview of a non-suspect person, it is appropriate to display appreciation for cooperation received. This applies not only to interviewees who have been completely cooperative from the very start, but also to those who initially or occasionally had to be motivated to furnish information. It is not unusual during the closing phase of an interview for the individual to request confidentiality of information provided. Although it is never a good practice for an investigator to release official information, absolute assurances can never be given concerning releases of information.

The closing of an interview is not necessarily the termination of communications between the investigator and the interviewee. On the contrary, an effective closing can result in the acquisition of valuable information. A person who may not have been fully cooperative during the body of the interview may drop his guard after questioning has ceased and the investigator has put away notes and other materials. Pertinent facts that may have been suppressed during the interview might be disclosed as the interview is being ended. Details that escaped the investigator earlier can be brought to the surface even while making a farewell hand-shake.

Preparing to Interrogate Suspects

Interrogation should be preceded by careful planning. Although an interrogation should not follow an inflexible, predetermined script, a general "game plan" can be very helpful. Knowledge of the case enables the investigator to determine what information he needs to obtain and how much the suspect can be expected to possess. The investigator may want to prepare a list of questions and to arrange topics of discussion in a logical sequence so that the interrogation will progress smoothly and important points will not be overlooked.

Statements of witnesses, in addition to information derived from physical evidence, are carefully examined for the purpose of reconstructing the crime mentally and anticipating the suspect's admissions and denials.

The general rule is that witnesses and suspects should be interviewed as soon as possible after the crime has happened. With respect to the witness, the value of a timely interview lies in the freshness of details and the opportunity for the investigator to obtain valuable investigative leads. Regarding the suspect, however, the value of a timely interrogation lies in reducing the changes for fabrication of an alibi, or in keeping accomplices from synchronizing their separate stories. While speed may be helpful, hasty preparation can lead to a weak interrogation. The timing of an interrogation cannot be fixed by some absolute rule that applies in all situations. Rather, an interrogation is conducted whenever it is to the maximum advantage of the investigator. He determines when the maximum advantage is present, based on an assessment of many factors.

The interrogation is scheduled so that other activities do not interfere. Interrogation is normally time consuming and never hurried. A time limit should not be placed on an interrogation. However, the investigator cannot conduct an interrogation under any circumstances that suggest duress. This includes the conditions, as well as length of the interrogation. It is not possible to state at what time an interrogation becomes too long. The investigator should operate from a premise that a court will inquire as to the amount of time a suspect was interrogated and the conditions of the interrogation. The interrogator must be able to prove that he was considerate of the suspect's need for food, water, personal hygiene, and sleep.

An interrogation is conducted at a place where facilities are available for recording the interrogation, where secretarial assistance is available if needed, where witnesses are available to observe the interrogation as a safeguard against possible charges of abuse or coercion, where control of the physical environment is ensured, where interruptions are minimal, where the suspect can be reasonably contained, and where privacy is guaranteed.

An interrogation room is typically plain but comfortably furnished, devoid of pictures or items that can distract attention. It is desirable to have recording devices, a two-way mirror, and similar equipment built into the structure of the interrogation room. The interrogation room must be neither so hot nor so cold as to raise defense counsel contentions that information was extracted through physical discomfort. Furniture should consist of three comfortable chairs and a small table large enough to write on, but not large enough for the suspect to hide behind. Pens, pencils, forms, ashtrays, wastebaskets, and like items should be in place prior to beginning. If the room is equipped with a telephone, it should be disconnected or removed for the purpose of reducing possible interruptions. Most important, any article or item in the room that might serve as a weapon should be removed.

The suspect should be seated at the side of the table. This removes a physical barrier between the investigator and the suspect, and enables the investigator to fully observe the suspect's body language. If there is a window in the interrogation room, chairs should be arranged so that window light falls on the face of the suspect rather than the investigator or witness. Chair arrangement should also preclude the suspect from being able to gaze out a window.

Interrogating Suspects

The skill of an interrogator depends in large measure upon his ability to accurately assess the suspect, and to select a general approach and a combination of interrogation tactics and techniques that eventually succeed. As to the assessment, the development of this ability remains largely a matter of practical experience, even though a lack of experience can be compensated for by pure native ability and keen psychological insight. While the "sizing-up" of a suspect is essentially a subjective process, there are usually a sufficient number of facts known to the investigator, which permits a judgment as to the probable guilt of a suspect prior to interrogation. There are suspects whose guilt is reasonably certain as shown by physical evidence, statements of witnesses, and other available facts. On the other hand, a lack of essential facts and evidence will cause some doubt or uncertainty as to guilt. Most suspects can be placed into one of these two classifications [4].

For each, recommendations can be made in respect to general approaches for starting an interrogation. Once started, the investigator relies upon his knowledge of human behavior to correctly evaluate his suspect. He seeks to discover the "key" for obtaining a full and truthful disclosure. Discovering the key is frequently a matter of trial and error in the application of interrogation tactics and techniques.

The Suspect Whose Guilt is Definite or Reasonably Certain. A direct approach is normally used to interrogate a suspect in this classification. The investigator assumes an air of complete confidence with regard to evidence or witness statements that point to the suspect. He stresses the strength of the evidence and how it implicates the suspect beyond any reasonable doubt. The investigator behaves in a brisk, accusatory manner and displays a complete belief in the suspect's guilt. The investigator acts as if a statement from the suspect is not really important because the quantity and quality of evidence already on hand is more than enough to bring the investigation to a positive conclusion. The investigator suggests that his interest in talking with the suspect is not to learn if he committed the crime, but to learn why. The suspect is made to believe that the interrogation session is an opportunity for him to tell "his side of the story," including any mitigating or extenuating circumstances that brought him to a commission of the offense.

The Suspect Whose Guilt is Doubtful or Uncertain. An indirect approach is generally more successful when interrogating a suspect whose guilt is questionable. In the indirect approach, the questioning is designed to establish a detailed account of the suspect's activities before, during, and after the time the offense occurred. Facts that are definitely known should be used in formulating questions to test the suspect's reactions. If the suspect lies regarding an established fact, this is suggestive of guilt. A crime in which a suspect's involvement is sketchy usually has little or weak evidence. The few certain facts known to the investigator must be cautiously guarded and revealed to the suspect in such a way that he will be forced to either distort or to confirm what is definitely known. If, as the interrogation progresses, the investigator becomes increasingly convinced of the suspect's guilt, he may wish to switch to a more direct approach.

Interrogation Tactics and Techniques

The number and kinds of possible tactics and techniques used during an interrogation are limited only by the interrogator's imagination. There are, of course, limitations to what an interrogator can do or say. These limitations are expressed in constitutional safeguards, case law, appellate decisions, and a variety of other rules or procedures that apply to suspect rights. A good rule of thumb to follow when deciding to employ a particular interrogation tactic or technique is for the investigator to ask himself this question, "Does a possibility exist that the action I take could result in an admission of guilt by an innocent person?" If the answer to that question is "yes," then the tactic or technique should not be employed. To illustrate, assume that an interrogation is about to take place of a suspect whose guilt is uncertain and the crime involves a degrading sexual act. It would be highly improper for the interrogator to imply that a failure of the suspect to make a full confession would necessarily require interviews of the suspect's family and friends. If such a tactic were employed, a possibility exists for the truly innocent person to confess because he feared the loss of love and respect from family and friends. By applying the rule of thumb just mentioned, an investigator can keep himself from answering charges of unethical, if not illegal, conduct.

Following are descriptions of the more common interrogation tactics and techniques. In them the reader will see their applicability to different kinds of suspects in different kinds of situations.

Sympathy. A person who has committed a crime in the heat of passion is normally responsive to a sympathetic and understanding attitude. Crimes that involve the use of threat or violence have emotional overtones. Violent crimes are generally committed by people acting from the heat of passion, anger, or revenge. The interrogator should treat suspects of these crimes as rational people who, under the pressure of circumstance or extreme provocation, committed acts that are out of keeping with their true personalities. The interrogator should present a rationalization of the crime by pointing out that "it could happen to anyone" and minimize the moral seriousness of the act by alluding to the frequency by which such crimes occur. The investigator attempts to gain the confidence of the suspect. He might make reference, for example, to any similarities of good citizenship that appear to exist between himself and the suspect.

Sympathy can be mixed with confidence by pointing out the evidence linking the suspect to the crime. Signs of stress and nervous tension can be pointed out to the suspect as indicators of guilt. The suspect should be repeatedly urged to "get it off his chest." Euphemisms should be used in place of words like *stab* and *steal*.

Repugnant acts and low motives can be treated by the interrogator as "out of character" for the suspect. The idea is to help the suspect "save face" by putting forth an understandable excuse. Even if an excuse is genuine, it does not cancel out the crime. Before the suspect can be brought to a point where he is willing to talk about the crime (at least his version of it), the interrogator needs to remove or soften the unpleasant characteristics of the act.

The sympathetic technique is also particularly useful in dealing with the first offender. A person who has not been subjected to interrogation at some previous time is likely to respond to an understanding attitude. It is natural for a first offender to experience feelings of regret and penitence. A skilled interrogator will play upon these feelings by acting considerate and helpful. In fact, a showing of such feelings toward a first offender is not always false. There have been many cases where investigators, through compassion and understanding, have turned youthful first offenders away from disrespect for laws.

Reasoning. In this technique the suspect is told that guilt is already established, or that it will be established soon, and that there is nothing else to do but make an admission. The investigator points out to the suspect the futility of denying guilt. Every denial is met with logic and facts that refute the suspect's assertions. Laboratory reports, photographs, fingerprint lifts, and similar items can be very useful in convincing a suspect that lying is useless. The thrust of this technique is to appeal to the suspect's common sense as opposed to giving sympathy.

Point Out the Symptoms of Guilt. A suspect who believes that his appearance and verbal expressions are betraying him is placed in a vulnerable situation. His belief that he is showing signs of guilt has the effect of lessening his ability to deceive, and as a result brings him closer to the admission stage [5].

Nonverbal symptoms of guilt can be very revealing. Kinesics, the study of nonverbal communications, teaches us that the body can communicate what we are not saying. Body positions, motions, gestures, and facial expressions are forms of silent language that convey inner thoughts and emotions. Some people find it easy to use words to mask their true feelings, but no one can completely control the body's natural reaction to intense inner feelings. While the brain can learn to lie, the body does not know how.

Documenting the Interrogation

Documenting an interrogation consists of three main phases: note taking, electronic recording and obtaining written statements [6].

Note Taking. Note taking is the most common method for recording information obtained in an interrogation. Note taking is used during interviews as well, but because interrogation notes may be called as evidence at time of trial, they take on special significance.

Note taking for interviews vs. interrogations has another difference. When interviewing a witness, note taking is frequently open and obvious. The investigator can hardly conceal the fact that he is writing in a notebook while obtaining information from a witness. Indeed, some witnesses expect an investigator to take many notes and some will feel slighted if their every word is not written down. Only in a few cases will witnesses be visibly disturbed by note taking, but for obvious reasons suspects will display contrary attitudes. Because suspects are inclined to conceal the truth, it bothers them to observe an interrogator taking notes. The interrogator can overcome this problem to some extent by taking mental notes, or by using a third party. The taking of mental notes allows the suspect to continue without being distracted by efforts to take notes in pace with the flow of information. Mental note taking has its limits, of course. After a period of time the interrogator reaches a mental absorption point where details can be lost. The use of a third party, such as a stenographer, removes this disadvantage. Any discomfort that a suspect might feel regarding visible note taking can be reduced by placing the third party behind the suspect.

Even when written notes are taken by the interrogator, the suspect should be permitted to tell his story at least once before the investigator lifts pencil to paper. Notes are seldom taken in a fully narrative form. They tend to consist of key words denoting salient points, abbreviations, and highly personalized forms of shorthand. Points notated while the suspect talks become points for questioning later in the interrogation; they serve also as a record of the suspect's remarks.

Electronic Recording. Audio and video are the two principal methods for electronic recording of interrogations. The audio method continues to be used, although in recent years, with the advent of compact and relatively inexpensive closed-circuit television (CCTV) equipment, much greater use is being made of video systems.

While audio is practical in terms of cost, installation, economy of space, and concealment, it lacks the extra dimension of visual effect. Video recording leaves little doubt as to the identification of persons present at the interrogation, objects examined or handled during the interrogation, the environment of the interrogation, and the activities of the interrogators.

Video allows a jury to see the suspect nod, shrug, and make other telling movements that convey guilt. Video tape can be used to capture images of the suspect re-constructing the crime through physical actions, such as the way in which he held a gun, stabbed with a knife, or jimmied a window.

Electronic recordings should be carefully kept in their entirety, together with any stenographic transcripts made. A chain of custody should be established and maintained because of their possible use in legal proceedings.

Written Statements. Perhaps the most incriminating type of written statement is the one in which a suspect writes a confession in his or her own handwriting, signs the confessions, and has it witnessed by the interrogator and one other person. A prosecuting attorney will prize this kind of statement because it enhances admissibility at time of trial and makes a stronger impression upon a jury. Statements exclusively prepared by suspects are relatively uncommon because of the difficulty in persuading suspects to write them.

Also, the investigator may not wish a suspect to write his own statement because in so doing certain critical points that relate to elements of proof are likely to be omitted. The investigator knows that to prove the charge against the suspect certain facts will need to be conclusively shown. Getting these facts into a statement prepared by the suspect is extremely difficult. The investigator may prefer instead to prepare a typed statement himself, based on what the suspect said and get the suspect to sign it.

When preparing a typed statement, common sense is called for. The text of the statement should reflect the general vocabulary of the suspect. A confession obtained from a suspect having a sixth grade education deserves skepticism when it includes large words and highly complex sentences. If a suspect speaks with profanity, the typed statement he signs should contain profanity. The actual sentences spoken are used, although they may not necessarily appear in the same order given by the suspect.

It sometimes happens that a suspect will refuse to sign a typed statement, or a statement written for him. Even though an understanding may have existed at the outset of the interrogation that the suspect would sign, he is under no compulsion to do so. If the suspect declines to sign, the investigator should try to obtain a verbal acknowledgment in the presence of witnesses that the information contained in the prepared statement is true and correct. If the suspect refuses to do even this, the investigator has only the oral testimony of himself and the witness that the suspect provided the information contained in the statement. Obviously, this will have less credibility with a jury.

John J. Fay, CPP

Sources

Inbau, F.E., and J.E. Reid, Criminal Interrogation and Confessions. (Williams and Wilkins Company, Baltimore, 1967).

Law Enforcement Investigations. (U.S. Government Printing Office, Washington, DC, 1977).

O'Hara, C.E., Fundamentals of Criminal Investigation. (Charles C. Thomas, Springfield, IL, 1970).

Police Reference Notebook. (International Association of Chiefs of Police, Gaithersburg, MD, 1970).

Special Agent Manual of the Georgia Bureau of Investigation. (Georgia Bureau of Investigation, Atlanta, 1976).

Specter, A., and M. Katz, Police Guide to Search and Seizure, Interrogation and Confession. (Chilton Books, Philadelphia, 1967).

Stuckey, G.B., Evidence for the Law Enforcement Officer. (McGraw-Hill Book Company, New York, 1968).

Swanson, C.R., N.C. Chamelin, and L. Territo, Criminal Investigation. (Goodyear Publishing Company, Santa Monica, CA, 1977).

Tobias, M.W., and R.D. Peterson, Pre-Trial Criminal Procedure. (Charles C. Thomas, Springfield, IL, 1972).

Notes

1. See Law Enforcement Investigations, pp. 101-102.
2. See Fundamentals of Criminal Investigation, p. 91.
3. Ibid., p. 94.
4. See Inbau and Reid, Criminal Interrogation and Confessions, pp. 23 - 24.
5. Ibid., p. 33.
6. See Swanson et al, Criminal Investigation, p. 157.

R

RAPE PREVENTION

The security professional holds a special responsibility for helping employees prevent being assaulted. Rape is a particularly odious form of assault. Fortunately, it is a crime susceptible to prevention, largely through engaging in avoidance tactics and knowing what to do if attacked.

Although the legal definition of rape will vary from state to state, it is generally accepted that rape is first and foremost a crime of force. The rapist uses or threatens to use violence in what is essentially an exercise of power. The primary motive of the rapist is not to attain sexual pleasure, but to feel a sense of superiority by dominating the victim.

Rape has no boundaries. Males have been victims as well as females. Anyone, regardless of age, race, economic status, and physical appearance can be victimized. Victims have included infants, mentally retarded persons, and the elderly.

Rape is also unlimited as to time and place of occurrence. It is not something that happens mainly at night or in ghetto areas. Rapes occur at all times of the day in the poorest and wealthiest sections of cities, suburbs, and rural areas all across America.

Many rapes take place in the victim's home and frequently the rapist is there by invitation. This is so because the rapist is likely to be a friend, relative, or work associate. In some cases, he is an estranged husband or lover, and in about 9 of every 10 reported cases, is of the same race as the victim.

Violence is an element of the act and only about 3 of 10 incidents will involve the use of a weapon. Only very infrequently will a rape end in murder. This is not to suggest that the crime is any less serious, but it does point to the high probability that the victim will survive.

There has never been any truth to the notion that rape is an invited crime, meaning that the victim invited rape because of the way she dressed or behaved. The idea that the rapist was provoked by the victim's sexual advances reflects a dishonored and mistaken view that rape is motivated by sexual desire.

There is also little evidence to support the proposition that women use accusations of rape as a means of obtaining revenge. On the contrary, there is evidence to show that women accusers often suffer further harm by being stigmatized in their communities and abandoned by friends and loved ones.

Another disturbing reality is that a rapist will usually continue to rape until caught and removed from society. The only effective remedy is for the victim to report the crime and assist in the investigation and prosecution. This can be difficult and unpleasant for the victim, but is essential in preventing repeat occurrences of the crime.

Setting Up Personal Defenses

The rapist, like most criminals, will prefer the "easy target," that is to say, a woman who has the appearance of vulnerability. If the rapist can be made to believe that a particular woman would be difficult to overcome, he will look elsewhere for easier prey. A good defense, then, is to display strength -- not in the physical sense, but in character and personality. How is that done? It is done through expressions of self-confidence, capability, and control of events. Strength can be shown by actions and appearance. It is also manifested in what is said and how it is said.

Assertiveness is one of the most powerful indicators of strength. It is a behavior that can enable one to act in his or her own best interest. Assertiveness is largely verbal in nature and is an excellent weapon to use when confronted with a threatening situation. A verbal response that says "no" without any doubt or hesitation could be all that's required to defuse a potentially dangerous encounter.

If a simple refusal is not sufficient, a woman should not be afraid to make a scene. Embarrassment is an acceptable alternative to the risk of the possible consequences of giving in. A woman can use her voice to attract attention, to make people nearby aware of her need for help, and to tell them how they can help, such as by staying close or calling the police.

From childhood people are taught to be courteous and friendly. These are valuable teachings, but they should not have priority in situations that can lead to rape. Traits that are trusting and passive give encouragement to the

Rape Avoidance Tips

On Foot

•Avoid walking, jogging, or running alone, especially at night.

•Walk with your head up, and make eye contact with people you encounter. Be alert for persons who may be watching or following. Try not to carry items with packages that would make it difficult to react or escape.

•When using public transportation, plan the trip so that getting on and off conveyances will be at stations that are well lighted and populated. Sit near the driver or conductor, and don't fall asleep or even give an impression of being unaware of the surroundings.

•While waiting for a bus or train, stand with other females or near an attendant's booth. If accosted, attract attention by talking loudly. Run and scream if needed.

•After getting out of a vehicle, look around. If someone suspicious is nearby, cross the street and change direction. If followed, don't be afraid to run and scream. Head straight for the nearest lighted business or residence. If the area is deserted, break a window or do something to attract attention. If shelter is obtained, call the police.

•Walk near the curb and avoid passing close to shrubbery, dark doorways, vacant lots, closed parks, or parked cars. Shun short-cuts, especially through backyards, closed buildings, parking lots, and alleyways. A rapist's greatest asset is his ability to surprise, to attack when you least expect it.

•Be very cautious about talking to strangers in the street, especially when asked to give directions. Once stopped, you are only one step away from being taken into the rapist's control by force or threat of violence.

•If your route passes close to a group of men, walk around them or cross the street. Know the area you walk in. Learn what stores, restaurants, or gas stations are open late. If alone, be extra aware of activity close by. Listen for footsteps and voices nearby. Walk in a brisk, businesslike, and confident manner. Rapists prefer women who appear to be passive, afraid.

•When arriving home, have the door key ready. Look around to see if anyone is loitering nearby in a position to gain entry when the door is open. If you are being driven home, ask the driver to wait until you are safely inside.

Behind the Wheel

•Your best protection when driving is to be in a mechanically dependable vehicle. Other important preventive measures are to plan the route in advance and have enough gas and money to cover an emergency.

•Park in areas that are well lighted and busy. When walking to your car, have your car keys ready; look under and around the car; and always look in the back seat before entering to make sure someone isn't hiding there. Keep your car in gear and the doors locked when stopped in traffic. If threatened, blow the horn and drive away.

•Whenever practical, drive your car on well lighted and more heavily trafficked roads -- even if the distance is longer -- and drive with doors locked and windows rolled up enough so that no one can reach in.

•If you are being followed, drive to the nearest place where you can obtain help. Good choices would be a police or fire station, a gas station or convenience store, or a well-lighted residence.

•Don't hitch hike if your car breaks down. It's much safer to attract attention to your need for help by tying a flag to the aerial or door handle, placing a sign in the window, putting the hood up, and turning on the flashers. Then get in the car, lock all the doors, roll up the windows, and turn the engine off. If someone stops to offer help, roll your window down far enough to ask that the police, a mechanic, or a relative or friend be called.

In Buildings

•Whenever you enter an elevator, stand near the control panel and alarm button. If you're attacked, hit the alarm button and as many floor buttons as you can.
•Take extreme care in apartment houses and office building elevators. It's safer to remain in the lobby for a few minutes than to ride alone with someone who frightens you. Be careful if the elevator stops at the main floor and a stranger inside doesn't exit. Even if he tells you he pressed the wrong button, tell him to go ahead - that you're waiting for someone.
•Avoid using stairwells and basement laundromats and garages when you're alone. These places are favored hunting grounds for muggers and rapists.

On a Date

•Date peope that you know fairly well or who are recommended by trusted friends. Inquire about a prospective date. If in doubt but still interested, arrange for the date to take place with friends or as part of a group activity. Another alternative would be to date at a public location, such as a restaurant or theater.
•Let your date know in advance what your expectations are concerning intimacy. For the potential rapist, this would be a strong message that you are not an easy person to control or intimidate. This is important because many rapists choose victims who they believe will have the least resistance to an attack. By appearing confident, capable, and in control, you will be setting up a preventive barrier.
•Be prepared to provide your own transportation home. This may mean carrying change for a phone call or cash for a taxi. It means, too, that you should never accept the offer of a ride home from a person you've just met -- no matter how pleasant or attractive he may seem to be.
•Hold your consumption of alcohol to a level consistent with your ability to detect the early warning signals of a possible rape attack and to take preventive steps.
•Trust your instincts. The warning signals are often subtle. The signals may appear as feelings of uneasiness, fear, or a sense of not being in control of the situation. They may even be accompanied by physical reactions, such as sweaty palms and a racing heartbeat. Your mind and body are telling you to be careful.
•If unsure about the way things are heading, avoid getting into a one-on-one situation. Ask to be with other people or tell your date you want to go home. Don't be concerned about seeming foolish or being rude. It is far better to offend than to find youself in jeopardy. If the date ends on a sour note, don't try to make up for it by inviting a person you can't trust to come into your home at the last moment.
•There are no hard and fast rules as to what actions will deflect a rape at the moment it begins, but the tactics that have worked for many women include running away, attracting attention by screaming or making loud noises, being assertive and refusing to be intimidated, acting crazy, and fighting back. Tactics will vary according to the woman and the circumstances.

What to Do If Attacked

Escape

•Your best defense against rape is escape. In terms of personal security, your legs are to run with; your voice is to scream with.
•If you are forced to fight, fight dirty. Bite; kick; gouge eyes with keys, a pen, your thumbs, your nails. And all the time you fight, keep screaming to attract attention.
•Claim to have a venereal disease or act as if you are throwing up.

Use a Weapon?

•Probably your worst defense against rape is a lethal weapon, such as a gun or knife, that might be used against you.
•There are, however, a variety of every day items you can use defensively. Many women today carry plastic lemon containers filled with ammonia. Other women habitually walk with a key ring clenched in their fist, with keys protruding between the fingers.   A hat pin, pencil, corkscrew, or an umbrella used like a cattle prod can be a good protective weapon.

Make Noise

•Gaining in popularity are pocket-size alarms and police whistles. But whatever device you feel comfortable using, make sure it's in your hand ready for use when there's any chance of danger.

Get Medical Attention

•If you are raped, you will want to get medical treatment right away. Make sure that medical personnel know you are a rape victim so that they will take precautions to ensure that the treatment procedures do not destroy or damage evidence that will be critical to a thorough police investigation.
•Even if there is no physical injury associated with the rape, you will need to be medically examined. The first step is to call the police. You may also want to call a relative or friend for moral support.
•While waiting for medical or police help to arrive, do not shower, bathe, or clean yourself or alter the clothing you had on at the time of the attack. Resist the natural impulse to wipe away the reminders of the attack. Your body, the clothing you wore, bedsheets, and anything that the rapist came into physical contact with are important sources of trace evidence, such as semen, blood, hairs, fibers, and fingerprints.
•Medical attention will also be important in respect to tests for AIDS, venereal disease, and pregnancy.

After-Care Assistance

•The rage and helplessness that are part of the trauma accompanying rape will always be difficult to deal with, but they can be countered through professional help.

rapist. Traits that decent people see as valuable social attributes are often seen by the rapist as evidences of weakness, and women who are weak are preferable targets.

Being assertive and being rude are not necessarily the same thing. To be assertive for the wrong reasons can be rude, but not so when the reason is self-protection. It is not rude to assert one's rights, especially when there is an element of risk, and it is not over-reacting to refuse a request or decline to go along with someone else's wishes. The operative word in this context is caution, not rudeness.

Body language, for example, is a powerful indicator of strength. The way a woman walks, stands, and sits can tell a great deal about her attitudes and the way she interacts with her environment. If a woman looks confused, timid, anxious, or lost, she may unwittingly set herself up as a target. Body language can project a strong, self-assured outward appearance.

Eye contact is another indicator. The way a woman meets the eyes of other people can be a silent message that says, "I am in control of the situation and I am not afraid." How a woman dresses and carries herself conveys information about her values and the way she thinks. It is not a matter of dressing to convey success, but to present an overall statement of capability.

A woman has the right to decide who will touch her and when. If someone is too close or touching in an unacceptable way, a woman has the right to move away and the right to tell the person to stop — no matter who the person may be.

When a rapist can't find an opportunity, he may seek to create one. A common tactic is to gain the victim's trust and then draw her into a situation where she is most vulnerable to attack. The ploy to gain trust might be simple, such as offering or requesting help, or it might be more sophisticated, such as staging a phony crisis. Examples include pretending to be a repairperson or pretending to be injured in order to get inside the victim's home; and causing a mechanical malfunction in the victim's automobile and then offering to fix it in exchange for a ride home. Being skeptical is not a signal of weakness or rudeness, but of competence. It tells the potential rapist that his target cannot be easily fooled or maneuvered into a trapped position. In most cases, a firm "no" will be sufficient.

Keeping track of the immediate environment can be important. When a woman moves from one locale to another, she should make a conscious effort to notice the possible dangers that may be present, the routes of escape, and people or things that are available as helping resources. For example, going from a shopping mall to a car in order to drive home involves several distinctly different environments, each one of which requires an assessment of potential danger. When leaving the mall to enter the parking area, a woman's mind should be focused on the changed nature of her surroundings. The same sense of awareness needs to be present as the environment shifts to the interior of the automobile, first inside the parking lot, then on the street, and ultimately in the driveway or garage at home.

A woman's chances of responding successfully in a threatening situation will be much higher when she responds immediately. She will need to resist the natural tendency to believe the threat will go away by ignoring it. In most cases, it won't, and the rapist will be encouraged by the prospect of a non-resisting victim. A successful initial response might be nothing more than showing an awareness of the threat and being prepared to deal with it.

Setting Up Physical Defenses

A discussion of rape prevention is not complete without mention of the things that can be done to set up safeguards of a structural or procedural nature. These are the physical devices and routines that protect a woman when she is alone.

The home as a focal point in rape is underscored by the fact that most rapes occur where the victim lives. It will help to think of the home as a fortress to be defended. Where are the entry points and which points are less protected than others? How can unwanted persons be kept out, or better still, how can they be discouraged from even trying?

Start with the items that give comfort and confidence to an intruder. Consider, for example, places of concealment that might be created by shrubbery that has grown up around windows, especially windows that do not face toward the street or neighbors. Natural hiding places like this can be easily removed with a little trimming and some thoughtful placement of exterior lights. It is important to know the places around the home where an attacker might lie in wait.

Outside lights and one or two interior lights should be left on at night or during the day if return to the home is expected during the hours of darkness. At night, blinds and draperies should be drawn so no one can watch from outside.

An unlocked lock has no value except to the person it is designed to keep out. Exterior doors need to be securely locked -- whether one is at home or not. They should have strong deadbolts, and when moving into an apartment the locks or lock cylinders should be changed. The bedroom door should be locked when retiring for the night. The same guidance applies to window locks. Keys should not be hidden near doors, such as over door frames, under mats, or inside flower pots. All the security devices in the world will not be of any value unless there is a decision to use them consistently and intelligently.

A woman at home alone should never open the door to a caller she does not know. The peephole can be used to check an uninvited caller, and when in doubt about someone who shows up on a supposed business matter credentials can be passed under the door. A stranger should not be allowed to come in to use the telephone just because the person says it's an emergency. The alternative may be to offer to summon help while the person waits outside.

Women living alone should list only their last name and initials in phone directories and mailboxes. A woman living alone should be careful about letting that fact be known.

Cautions need to be taken in elevators. If alone with no people about, a woman should not enter an elevator with a stranger. It's not a case of being rude, just safe.

The police need to be called right away when danger is at hand, such as a prowler moving around the home. Knowing or having the police department phone number handy will help in making a quick report. Having a phone in a lockable interior room will provide an added layer of protection and more time to call for help if someone is trying to break in. Possessing a firearm for protection is discouraged by many police departments. Lethal force is justified only in extreme circumstances, such as defense of one's life. The best course of action may be to flee.

A woman should use the telephone on her terms. She should ask callers to identify themselves and when an unfamiliar voice asks, "Who is this?" the answer might be "What number did you call?" or "Who do you want?" If the caller isn't legitimate, that very likely will end the conversation. If it's the kind of caller that remains silent, the best thing to do is hang up.

It is not a good idea under any circumstances to give information over the phone to strangers. For a woman to tell a stranger she is home alone is an invitation to trouble. Children and babysitters should also be cautioned about what they say over the telephone. If wrong number calls, hang-up calls, late calls from strangers, or other oddities persist, the telephone company's business office can be contacted for assistance. The telephone company can help you deal with such calls.

Women who reside in apartment houses or dormitories should not wander outside at night or go alone to the laundry room or garage.

A woman should use a neighbor's phone to call the police when arriving home and finding a window or door forced open. Entering the home while the criminal is still inside would be very dangerous.

Many local law enforcement agencies conduct no-charge crime prevention surveys of homes. A survey is usually designed to identify the home's vulnerability to unwanted entry and ways to counter the vulnerability.

The "It Can't Happen to Me" Syndrome

A school-aged girl says she's too streetwise to get raped and a housewife says she lives in too nice a neighborhood. These false assumptions contribute to the "it can't happen to me" syndrome that is unfortunately present in far too many sexual assault incidents. While the number of known incidents continues to be high, the police believe that only about 1 in 10 is ever reported by the victim. That is why every woman – regardless of age – should learn and practice all conceivable precautions.

Fear of retaliation by assailants and fear of embarrassment are two very strong reasons that keep victims from filing complaints. Date rape is on the increase, and it is not restricted to teenagers and college students. Fortunately, new approaches and resources are becoming increasingly available to help rape victims cope with both the trauma of the crime and the uneven processes of justice.

When avoidance fails, a victim must be prepared to respond quickly and decisively. Many females are capable of responding successfully to assault, and each woman under attack has the option of choosing a response that is best for her under the circumstances present at the time. Surely the best course of overall action is to remove the rapist's opportunity by thinking and acting preventatively.

John J. Fay, CPP

Source Rape Avoidance: Personal Safety Program. (Security Department, BP Exploration, Inc., Houston, 1990).

RECORDS CHECKS

The use of records in investigating the present and past activities of a subject is an irreplaceable tool for the investigator. Records checks can be utilized in various inquiries from pre-employment backgrounds to insurance claims investigations. The question presents itself: Which records are available for inspection and which are not?

Contrary to common belief, no central source of information exists from which an investigator can determine all that he or she needs to know on a particular subject. A number of sources are required to develop the most basic profile of an individual. As there is no central source of information, likewise, there is not one single law that addresses the legality of accessing all information. Investigators must familiarize themselves with a number of laws at both the state and federal levels to determine what may be legally accessed and under what circumstances.

In certain instances, records may be accessed simply by the asking. On the other end of the spectrum, records may only be obtained on the presentation of a subpoena. In most instances even the more sensitive records can be accessed with a release from the party under investigation. The standard release present at the end of an employment application will often suffice in providing access to employment-related information. However, specific releases may be required for specific records.

General Records Sources

In general terms, records can be classified into three categories:

1. Public records accessible to members of the public, which include: county criminal records, records of lawsuits, judgments, Uniform Commercial Code (UCC) liens, secured transactions, property tax records, deeds, mortgages, divorce records, marriage records, voting records, estate records, estate taxes, bankruptcy, and other records normally found in county and federal courthouses.

2. Those records accessible to a limited audience for legitimate and recognized purposes. These normally involve governmental records such as criminal conviction records (to be distinguished from arrest records that normally are not publicly available), driving records, and vehicle ownership. These records can normally be obtained by completing a form and specifying the purpose of the request. They are typically housed in the state capitol.

3. Those records to which access is strictly limited. They include both governmental and private records, and usually require a specific release or subpoena to obtain. Examples are credit records, income tax records, medical records, school records, and other sensitive records normally maintained in specific offices.

Credit reports are seriously limited and should be avoided unless their access falls within one of the provisions provided for in the Fair Credit Reporting Act. For the most part, these reports can be lawfully accessed when the investigation relates to employment, issuance of credit, or other legitimate business purposes involving the consumer.

Liability for Access of Information

There are several instances where the private practitioner may be liable for accessing information improperly. In most instances liability occurs when records and information are amassed for reasons not considered legitimate, records are secured in an illegal manner, or the reporting of information falls outside permissible parameters.

Whether records are immediately accessible or not, an investigator can be sued for invasion of privacy in instances where the gathering of information on an individual is not for a recognized legitimate reason. While developing an intelligence profile for employment purposes, credit purposes, insurance purposes, or in response to litigation is legally authorized, compilation for other reasons will likely represent an unreasonable intrusion into the subject's privacy and may result in legal action. Similar allegations can be made in instances where records are illegally accessed.

Although information may be legally available from a specific records source, the extent of information that may be reported is often restricted. For example, bankruptcies over 10 years old, criminal convictions over 7 years old, and judgments in court that have no bearing on the scope of the investigation and which would tend to place the subject in a less-than-complimentary light may not be reported.

In instances where records are illegally accessed, used, or reported upon, the private practitioner, his or her employer, and in many instances, the source of such information, may be subject to criminal and/or civil penalties. These sanctions apply regardless of motive behind the illegal access of information or the circumstances surrounding such access.

Although not legally required in all instances, to provide some level of insulation to the investigator, a release should be obtained from the subject of an investigation indicating that he or she has given permission for the investigation. However, the investigator should keep in mind that the subject will normally be guaranteed review of any report filed in connection with the investigation if the report is used in consideration of the subject matter for which it was instituted. Therefore, the investigator must be careful to report precisely the information obtained and any qualifiers that may relate to it. In a case under litigation a release is not usually required; however, the scope of the investigation should be limited to that subject matter reasonably related to the issue under investigation.   Developing information that maintains no bearing on the issue at hand may serve as the basis for a suit alleging an invasion of privacy.

Laws Governing Records Release

A number of laws address records access, reporting, and release. Brief discussions of the more common laws will follow. However, these are not the only laws that address the compilation and assimilation of information.

Those laws that most frequently impact upon records access include: The Fair Credit Reporting Act of 1971, Federal Consumer Credit Protection Act of 1976, Freedom of Information Act of 1966 (amended 1974), Department of Justice Order 601-75, state criminal history records codes, and state motor vehicle records codes.

Further, although certain investigations are lawful, inquiring into matters prohibited by law such as race, date of birth, or other restricted information will inevitably result in violation of the law. Investigators should thoroughly verse themselves in the regulations that apply in their jurisdiction on the types of information lawfully accessible and the permissible scope of information developed. Additional laws that may relate to specific investigations include: The Equal Employment Opportunity Act of 1972, The Americans with Disabilities Act, The Equal Credit Opportunity Act of 1974, The Bankruptcy Act of 1979, the Age Discrimination in Employment Act of 1967, The Privacy Act of 1974, The Civil Rights Act of 1964, The Immigration Reform and Control Act, The Tax Reform Act of 1976, and others, including comparable state laws.

A Common Error

The effectiveness of an investigator is often measured by his or her ability to call forth confidential sources that provide information not otherwise attainable. While such efforts may provide much needed information, the actions of the investigator are, nonetheless, illegal. Further, in spite of the existing laws governing access and release of information, many investigators, aware

of the potential dangers, ignore the laws under the misguided perception that no one will know. In most investigations, if the source of information is not immediately apparent, it is not impossible to determine how the information was accessed. Records are maintained with reporting agencies noting who accessed information on a particular party and when.

In those instances where identifying a source is difficult, investigators very well may be asked under oath to explain the manner in which they came to possess specific intelligence. Unlike their public counterparts who are granted certain rights to maintain confidentiality over their sources, such is not the case with the private practitioner. Therefore, under subpoena at either a deposition, trial, or other legal proceeding, the private practitioner very well may be required to identify the source of information. In the truest sense, there are no confidential sources in the private sector.

Illegally obtained information is risky at best. Ironically, the risk is more often than not unnecessary. Sufficient information can be obtained through legal channels.   If the information required is imperative, a subpoena often serves as a capable vehicle to overcome most obstacles. Therefore, for reasons of ethics and professionalism, illegally accessing information should be routinely prohibited both formally and informally by all private practitioners. Both clients and supervisors should likewise be re-introduced to the realities of unnecessary immediate gratification.

John Dale Hartman

RELIGIOUS DISCRIMINATION

Title VII of the Civil Rights Act of 1964 prohibits employers from discriminating against individuals because of their religion in hiring, firing, and other terms and conditions of employment. The Act also requires employers to reasonably accommodate the religious practices of an employee or prospective employee, unless to do so would create an undue hardship upon the employer.   Flexible scheduling, voluntary substitutions or swaps, job re-assignments, and lateral transfers are examples of accommodating an employee's religious beliefs.

Employers cannot schedule examinations or other selection activities in conflict with a current or prospective employee's religious needs, inquire about an applicant's future availability at certain times, maintain a restrictive dress code, or refuse to allow observance of a Sabbath or religious holiday, unless the employer can prove that not doing so would cause an undue hardship.

An employer can claim undue hardship when accommodating an employee's religious practices if allowing such practices requires more than ordinary administrative costs. Undue hardship also may be shown if changing a bona fide seniority system to accommodate one employee's religious practices denies another employee the job or shift preference guaranteed by the seniority system.

An employee whose religious practices prohibit payment of union dues to a labor organization cannot be required to pay the dues, but may pay an equal sum to a charitable organization.

Mandatory "new age" training programs, designed to improve employee motivation, cooperation, or productivity through meditation, yoga, biofeedback or other practices, may conflict with the non-discriminatory provisions of Title VII.

Employers must accommodate any employee who gives notice that these programs are inconsistent with the employee's religious beliefs, whether or not the employer believes there is a religious basis for the employee's objection.

U.S. Equal Opportunity Commission

Source Facts about Religious Discrimination. (The U.S. Equal Opportunity Commission, Washington, DC, 1992).

REPORT WRITING

An often ignored aspect of investigations is report writing. The private practitioner must understand those liabilities that relate to report writing. In general, private agents are liable for their report when:

1.   The information within the report is false and therefore defames or libels the subject of the investigation.

2.   The information contained within the report places the subject in a false light and therefore invades a person's privacy.

3.   The information, although true, is unrelated to the investigation and therefore

represents a public disclosure of a private fact that would embarrass the subject.

4.   The false or unrelated information was publicized by the investigator to a number of people either in writing or orally. When false information is given oral publicity, the injury is known as slander. Testimony provided in court is usually protected from allegations of libel and slander; however, it is unlikely that unsubstantiated, irrelevant, or immaterial information will be accepted. Usually, opposing counsel will object to the introduction of such evidence.

These liabilities do create a "Catch 22" situation. The investigator's duty is to report the information provided and to not edit or otherwise change it. There are certain actions that may be taken to avoid these liabilities; however, they are not always fail-safe.

1.   Obtain more than one source of information.

2.   Be precise in reporting the information developed and avoid personal assessments. Limit the report to precisely what a witness said.

3.   Be certain that the sources of all information are specifically identified. Note the date, time, and place of any interview or contact, and the identity of any witnesses present at the time.

4.   Assign more than one agent on interviews or contacts of a particularly sensitive or important nature.

5.   Always question the motives behind information provided by witnesses. Where issues of reliability exist, question witnesses on the reasons they are providing testimony. In certain instances, discreet background inquiries into any possible relationship between the witness and the subject of the investigation may be in order.

6.   Where appropriate, use qualifiers such as, "It was alleged..." Any description provided on personal observations should be limited to a factual account of precisely what was seen. Preface these accounts with qualifiers such as "apparently," "approximately," "possibly", etc. Any uncertainty should be specified. Do not attempt to draw factual conclusions from non-factual impressions.

7.   Be critically detailed. Document all activities or information in as much detail as possible. What may seem unimportant at the time may be extremely important in proving the case later. There is no such thing as too much

documentation so long as the documentation is appropriate.

8. Avoid providing opinions. Such subjective assessments invite challenge by adversaries. If an opinion is critical, separately segregate the opinion within the report and ensure it is appropriately identified. Such opinions are generally not permitted in court unless agreed to by stipulation between the attorneys for both sides. An exception involves those instances where the investigator is serving as a court-recognized expert witness.

9. Do not present impressions. Impressions of what may have occurred are of little worth in court. The fact that the investigator has considerable experience in performing the job may be of some comfort to him or her; however, with few exceptions, it is the court that determines guilt, innocence, or negligence.

10. Limit the number of people who see the investigative report and limit discussions of the investigation to those who have a "need to know." This only includes those directly involved. Viewing of materials and discussions of a case outside those few who have direct involvement in the investigation will likely be viewed as an actionable publication of false or private information.

Further, the laws relating to licensed investigators provide civil and criminal penalties for unauthorized release of information.

11. Buttress all reports with a warning on the cover sheet. Designate the information as "Confidential and Privileged" and for "Authorized Viewing Only."

12. Maintain copies of reports that can be used for future reference.

13. Following any testimony given in relation to the report, maintain a continuing log on the challenges made to the report, the successful responses to the challenges, and the changes in format that may be required.

14. Develop standardized and legally approved scripts or formats to be used in reporting particularly sensitive or detailed issues.

15. Ensure that the information relates to the issue at hand and does not involve extraneous information that, while titillating, does not reasonably relate to the issue in question.

16. All reports should be reviewed by supervisory or senior personnel to ensure no questionable items are maintained within the report.

17. Refer all outstanding questions to competent legal counsel.

18. Gauge any information reported to a simple standard, "How will this appear in court?"

19. Remember that all writings made in an investigation are subject to subpoena by adversaries. The same care taken in a report should likewise be made in memoranda, notes, and any other documentation generated.

John Dale Hartman

RESTAURANT SECURITY: LOSS PREVENTION PRINCIPLES

Principles

While the principles of loss prevention are applicable in many working environments, they are particularly appropriate to restaurant operations.

Crime Is Preventable. Crime is never inevitable and always preventable. Support for this proposition is founded on the observation that a criminal usually selects a target based on three expectations: the fruits of the crime will be worthwhile, the criminal act will succeed, and the act will proceed with not much difficulty.

A restaurant management can assess its crime risk by comparing the three expectations against crime-sensitive conditions, such as geographic location, ease of access to and from the premises, police support, characteristics of the clientele and the employees, hours of operation, amount of cash on the premises, and the adequacy of electronic/physical safeguards and procedural controls.

A crime-sensitive condition that deserves close scrutiny is the characteristics of the restaurant's workforce. Dishonest employees commit internal theft and attract dishonest customers, poor supervisors and managers provide opportunities for crime and are seen by criminals as easy targets, inadequately trained employees fail to exercise controls that guard against crime, and drug-abusing employees steal to support their addictions and make mistakes that open the door to crime.

Cash Attracts Thieves. Another sensitive condition is cash. Cash attracts thieves. Robbers who target restaurants want money. The best deterrent to robbery is to reduce the amount of cash available to the minimum amount necessary to conduct business. This means making frequent "bleeds" from the cash drawer and timely transfers of cash to the bank.

It Can Happen to You. Inattention to procedures is an open invitation to robbery. Many managers and employees who have been victims admit having violated one or more anti-robbery procedures. The rationale was that they believed it would not happen to them.

Trust but Verify. Misplaced trust leads to theft. The greatest threat to loss of money and inventory is from employee theft. Employees see and remember everything a manager does wrong or fails to do. Eventually, one or more of them may take advantage of these failures. While most employees are honest and trustworthy, at least a few are not. The dishonest employee is not easily identified and frequently goes to great lengths to appear reliable and trustworthy in order to take advantage of a careless or naive manager. The solution is to protect money, inventory, and other assets, and enforce controls in a fair and consistent manner.

Conventional wisdom says that 10% of the people are totally honest, 30% will steal if given the opportunity, and the remaining 60% may be tempted to steal under the right circumstances. Our experience tells us also that three elements contribute to the commission of a crime: the need or desire of the criminal, availability to the criminal of the skills and tools needed to commit the crime, and the opportunity to act.

The first two are difficult to control. Managers can attempt to control the desire to commit a crime by hiring honest people, but social and economic pressures can cause normally honest individuals to succumb to temptation.

It is also beyond management's control to deny individuals the skills or tools that may be used to commit a crime. The only remaining recourse is to influence the opportunity to commit the crime.

Controls Are Necessary. Physical safeguards, procedures, and accountability are necessary controls in reducing the opportunity to commit crime, especially internal theft. Studies have shown that internal theft rests on three conditions: the employee feels a need (real or imagined) to

steal, the employee sees an opportunity to steal, and the employee rationalizes the stealing.

Loss can be considerable even when only one employee takes advantage of an opportunity to steal. It is virtually impossible for a manager to absolutely ensure that every employee will be so personally honest that theft will not occur. Neither can the manager control employee rationalizations about theft because rationalizing is very human and to be expected. The manager can, however, exercise a great deal of leverage in eliminating the opportunity to steal.

Management Attitudes Affect Security. The concern of supervisors and managers for protecting the employer's assets is expressed in a multitude of actions that include orienting new employees concerning expectations of honest behavior, providing employees with initial and refresher training designed to prevent crime, insisting on strict adherence to loss control procedures, and most of all, in personal behavior that reflects integrity.

Integrity means more than just being honest. It means doing the right thing and this applies to the quality of work as much as it does to the protection of assets. It should be no surprise that there is often a strong correlation between a smoothly operated restaurant and a respect for assets. When food is properly cooked and customers properly served in a clean, well-maintained setting, the odds are fairly high that the manager has a positive attitude toward security and that his or her subordinates emulate that attitude.

Employee Involvement Is Essential. The key to successful crime prevention is employee involvement. Employees need to be empowered to help in protecting assets in much the same way they are empowered to improve customer service. Despite the demanding work schedules typical of restaurant operations, management must set time aside for educating employees in crime prevention and allowing them to contribute their ideas and efforts.

Employees who are members of an opening or closing team need to be made aware of the robbery risks, they need to understand why it is necessary to leave as a group, and to appreciate that their individual safety is ensured when doors are locked and entry access is controlled during non-serving hours.

Theft at Work Affects Everyone. A myth continues that honest employees will come forward and report theft because they do not wish to work in a dishonest environment. The reality is that honest employees will usually just quit without explaining why. When management actively involves employees in efforts to rid the workplace of crime in all its forms, crime decreases and workers gain both the satisfaction of being contributors to the common effort and the ease of mind that comes with working in a safe and secure environment.

Crime Prevention Is Cost-Effective. Research findings suggest that over half of the businesses that fail do so because of employee dishonesty. Loss from theft is paid from net profits and has a great impact on restaurant profitability. In the restaurant business it is fair to say that for each dollar lost through theft the restaurant must generate $4 in new sales to compensate for the loss at the bottom line. As a practical matter, it is not possible in a short period of time to recover from a significant theft loss, such as the disappearance of a day's receipts, because the nature of the business does not provide opportunities for rapid and large increases in sales. Because recovery from the setback is difficult, if not impossible, the logical alternative is to keep the loss from occurring in the first place.

Crime Prevention Improves Employee and Customer Safety and Security. In addition to internal theft are the many loss-producing outcomes associated with robbery, burglary, vandalism, and personal injuries and property damage suffered by employees and customers. The value of a crime prevention program is impressive when its costs are weighed against the costs of loss and the severe impact of such losses on profit. Employees and managers working together can significantly reduce their exposure to crime and make their workplace safer and more secure.

Richard L. Moe

RESTAURANT SECURITY: RISKS AND COUNTERMEASURES

To appreciate the magnitude of the restaurant industry, consider these facts:

•One out of four retail business locations is an eating or drinking establishment.

•Nine million people are employed in the food service industry.

•Nearly 5% of all employees, age 16 and older, are employed by eating and drinking establishments.

•Eating and drinking establishments comprise the largest segment of the retail industry.

•One of three adults eats in a restaurant in a typical day.

•Eating and drinking establishments employ almost 60% of managerial/administrative personnel in the retail industry.

Security in the restaurant industry has two principal objectives: to protect employees and customers from crime, and to protect the employer's assets from loss.

Risks and Countermeasures

The restaurant industry is divided into concept segments, such as full service, fast food, sit down, carry out, etc. Each segment is confronted with a different set of risks. Establishments that are open during late evening hours have a higher degree of exposure to robberies, drug activity, and violence than is the case for establishments that close during early evening hours. Other factors, such as geographical location, clientele, and whether drinking alcohol occurs on the premises, will determine the risks.

As a result, security programs in the restaurant industry vary widely and reflect the unique risks associated with the nature of the business.

The risks commonly characteristic of restaurant operations are robbery, violence directed against customers and employees, employee theft, burglary, and drug and alcohol abuse. The last two -- burglary and drug and alcohol abuse -- are the least significant because they are controllable to some extent and the losses they produce are significantly lower than the first three. Robbery, violence, and internal theft are significant because they impact heavily in two critical dimensions: injury and death, and loss of assets.

Robbery

Robbery is most often committed with the aid of a lethal weapon and is accompanied by stress and fear on the part of the robber and the victim, thereby creating a potential for serious injury or death. Further, because many robbers are under the impairing influence of a drug or alcohol, or are seeking funds to satisfy a craving, they are likely to act violently. A more disturbing fact is that the robber will kill people in order to eliminate them as witnesses. This fact has implications in the restaurant industry for two reasons. First, many robbers will frequent a restaurant one or more times before the robbery in order to work out a plan. The robber may realize during the commission of the crime that a restaurant employee may be able to provide information leading to arrest.

Second, many robbers are former employees of the restaurant and they are known to their former co-workers. The motive for violence is built into the situation and carries over to customers who may be in the establishment at the time of the crime.

The most vulnerable times for robbery are the closing and opening periods. In view of this, the security professional will develop and restaurant staff will follow opening and closing procedures designed to minimize exposure. Procedures usually include two hard and fast rules: at least two employees will be in the restaurant, and cash will be held to the minimum.

Violence

Violence can involve disputes among employees, among customers, and between employees and customers. It can also involve indiscriminate acts by street gangs and drug dealers whose internal disputes are often settled in parking lots. Indicators of gang-related problems at a restaurant are gang graffiti on rest room walls and the wearing of gang colors by employees. A waitress who is a gang member's girl friend can attract to the restaurant gang members who bring with them the kinds of violence peculiar to gang activities.

Gambling, prostitution, and drug selling are crimes that incite violence, and the persons involved often coordinate their activities from public telephones at restaurants. On-the-job drug abuse by employees engenders disruptive, if not violent, behavior, and because drug abusers are drug buyers, the sellers of drugs are attracted to restaurants that employ abusers. Persons who sell drugs are not limited to that criminal activity alone and may see on the premises an opportunity to commit other crimes, such as robbery and theft. The presence of a manager in the dining room/service area has been found to be effective in defusing and controlling potentially violent situations.

Employee Theft

Employee theft is the most frequent criminal event facing a restaurant operator. The reasons are pretty obvious: cash attracts thieves and most restaurant sales are cash transactions, and employees have the greatest opportunity to steal because they have access to the assets and are familiar with the operation.

The focus of successful restaurant operators is toward hospitality, which implies trust, openness, and a positive outlook.

Many operators place too much trust in those individuals responsible for cash and inventory. If this trust is not tempered with the proper controls even the most reliable employee may eventually succumb to the temptation to steal. This trust has been described as "irresponsible trust." Often an owner/operator will complain that their most trusted employee has let them down by resorting to theft. These same individuals must share the blame by not enforcing controls on a consistent basis.

One of the most frequent methods of employee theft of cash is by manipulating sales transactions. Both mechanical and electronic cash registers can be manipulated to disguise a theft. Manipulations include improper voids, discounts, and other reductions to sales. In addition to not recording sales transactions, other methods most commonly used to steal money include misuse of coupons, gift certificates, complimentary passes, and credit cards. To minimize such opportunities, it is vital to establish and maintain, on a consistent basis, inventory and audit procedures.

Richard L. Moe

RETAIL SECURITY: CONDUCTING AUDITS

An audit program is an excellent tool for store management to use in looking at units of the company for the purpose of determining adherence to policy, sound business practices, and approved operating procedures.

Audits are generally conducted by the internal audit department or the security department, or by both departments working in tandem. The internal audit department is usually a part of the corporate or higher-level organization and is therefore free from the influence of the management groups that are subject to audits. The security department may also be a corporate or higher-level unit or a part of a regional or local arrangement. The security department, depending on its position within the organization, will enjoy a lesser or greater degree of freedom in conducting audits. For the purposes of this piece, we will discuss auditing that is conducted by a security department.

The security manager's first task in planning an audit program is to decide overall goals and strategy. For this, some guidance from senior management may be necessary. Questions that may require answering include: "Is the purpose of the program to achieve absolute compliance, compliance in spirit, or something in between?" and "What sanctions will the security manager have at his or her disposal to achieve compliance?" These are essentially questions of responsibility and authority that translate during program execution to practices that may include relieving an employee on the spot when an audit discloses a serious violation, such as theft.

After the policy issues have been sorted out, the security manager will need to select an audit methodology. One of the common methodologies involves three steps: (1) conduct the audit, (2) hold an exit interview, and (3) prepare a written report.

Conducting the Audit

It may be helpful to begin with a discussion of the forms typically used in conducting audits. The formal investigative process of the audit usually features a form that can be filled in, such as with "yes" or "no" check marks and places for comments. The form can vary according to the retail operation being audited. Whatever the nature of the form, when completed it can serve as a script for discussions during the exit interview and for writing a final report.

The checklist audit form is relatively easy to use and to read, but may be lacking in challenge to the auditor. The checklist is usually a collection of standards drawn from established policies and procedures. Since policies direct the "what" of work and procedures direct the "how" of work, items on the checklist correspond to the essential work areas and the manner of the work. The checklist seeks to determine whether particular rules are being followed, whether particular practices are routinely in place, and whether particular jobs are structured in conformance to policy goals and approved operating procedures.

In this auditing approach, the auditor is likely to be seen walking around the facility making "yes" or "no" check marks on a form attached to a clipboard. A "yes" check might indicate compliance and a "no" check indicates non-compliance. The form may have space for comments adjacent to the "no" check marks and a general comments section at the end of the form for more detailed notations or for explanations that go beyond the scope of the form.

The checklist approach is subjective in that it relies on the auditor's judgmental observations. A checklist, however, can be made less subjective by applying weighted numerical values to the various items. Weighting can be based on criticality, frequency, and other criteria. Greater weight, for example, might be given to an item that involved target hardening of cash (a critical asset) as opposed to an item dealing with signage around a register. Increased weight might also be applied to a frequently performed task that has bearing on a current problem. If the problem is losses from bad checks, a highly weighted task would be the verification of the identity of a check-cashing patron.

The form can be used also as a snapshot of how well the facility is being managed. A reader of the form can instantly note the problem areas, although the reasons for the problems and the solutions to them may not be readily apparent.

A variation of the checklist is a fill-in-the-blank form. It is similar to the checklist, but instead of making check marks and brief notes the auditor enters a short written narrative following each item on the form. The design of the form encourages the auditor to expand his or her thinking beyond the black-and-white boundaries of check marks. Gray areas, which may be mildly problematic or may be precursors of serious problems ahead, are more likely to be noticed when the auditor is challenged to apply analytical thinking.

While the forms used to facilitate the audit process will vary, they share three common characteristics: (1) they are tools, valuable to the extent they are skillfully applied; (2) they provide a method or a system of organization for collecting, analyzing, and reporting factual details; and (3) they conform to the functions being audited.

This last characteristic of audit forms gives recognition to the fact that audits are carried out in different ways for different reasons. Following are discussions of audit approaches.

In the formal audit approach, the auditor evaluates all of the operations in one facility at one time. Since many operations are examined, the possibility of a large number of exceptions being noted is probable. An audit report reflecting numerous problems can be misinterpreted by upper management and can make the manager appear incompetent. Depending on the report of the auditor, the result can be a very damaging document that embarrasses the manager of the unit, calls for extreme action in the minds of upper management, and in the end, throws the facility itself into turmoil. This type of reaction can be avoided by concentrating only on the major exceptions and by including in the report the manager's corrective or planned corrective actions.

The problem also can be avoided by developing an audit format that examines only specific areas of responsibility; for example, cash handling, warehouse operation, register operation, paperwork, etc. By dividing the entire operation of a facility into segments, an auditor can perform smaller audits and give detailed suggestions for improvement.

An audit report that gives the manager a smaller set of exceptions to be corrected can help the manager avoid the hopeless feeling that often comes with the requirement to correct a seemingly insurmountable mountain of problems. The smaller audit allows for more frequent visits to the same facility, which may be helpful to managers in tapping into the security expertise of the auditor.

The frequency and intensity of audits will be influenced by the geographical locations of the stores. This has more to do with sound business practices and the cost-effectiveness of the audit program. In cases where only one store exists in a distant or remote location, an extensive audit of all systems would make the trip more cost-effective and necessitate less frequent visits. When several stores are clustered in a single geographical area, the auditor is likely to want to audit them all each time a visit is made to the area. It is usually recommended that the type of audit be varied between stores since the managers will communicate among themselves following the first one or two audits and take steps to mask the discrepancies on which the auditor seems to be focusing.

Another tack would be to vary the auditing schedule. The auditor could choose to examine four or five stores in 2 days several times a year, or audit one or two stores in 5 days once per year. Convenience to the auditor must, of course, be balanced against cost-effectiveness. In this latter regard, the use of abbreviated audits works well when auditing subsystems.

A subsystem in the sense used here is a single major function of a store's total operations. Examples of subsystems include functions related to pre-employment screening, cash handling, warehouse inventories, safety, security officer services, purchasing, etc. Subsystems are often examined in terms of paperwork and control procedures.

A paperwork audit scrutinizes the documents processed or generated within the subsystem. It is concerned with paperwork as the evidence of work performed. If the subsystem being audited was the pre-employment function, the auditor would want to examine employment application forms, forms used by supervisors to verify previous work history of applicants, integrity testing results, and so forth.

A technique associated with paperwork auditing is called sampling. Assume for example that the subsystem being audited involves refund procedures. The auditor selects for examination every fifth refund and finds a total of 10 discrepancies after looking at 20 documents. The projected error rate based on the refund documents that were sampled is 50%. This is a high error rate that calls for correction. A low error rate, however, is not always positive. A single error in a sample size of 100 can be significant when the dollar amount of the single error is significant.

Sampling should be conducted so that the work of several employees is evaluated. A sampling of documents processed by one employee can be misleading if the employee happens to be exceptionally competent or incompetent.

A procedural audit directly examines work in progress. An auditor concerned with subsystems related to safety and security could personally observe if employees followed fail-safe practices and wore protective equipment, and whether the security officers patrolled the parking lot and escorted patrons to their cars.

A "paper hammer" audit is the term applied to the examination of a problem store or of a store under new management. The objective of the audit is to get a quick and dirty reading of major problems that call out for immediate correction. Because the audit typically extends across the board to all aspects of store operations, the report is lengthy and filled with many exceptions.

A follow-up audit is an audit for the purpose of determining if the corrective actions set forth in an earlier audit have been taken and are in fact effective as remedies to the diagnosed problems. Although a follow-up audit takes a backward glance, it sometimes identifies problems not seen earlier or created since. Corrective actions that were poorly conceived or executed sometimes give rise to new problems or new dimensions to old problems and are identifiable in a follow-up audit.

The Exit Interview

At the conclusion of each audit an interview is scheduled with the store manager. During this meeting all of the findings and possible resolutions to the problems are discussed. The exit interview serves at least two purposes. First, it will keep the manager from being caught by surprise when the audit report is published. Second, the interview allows the manager to explain or contest any of the findings. The manager, for example, may produce additional documentation or employee testimony that would change an audit finding. For the auditor, the manager's reactions during the interview may suggest a need to fully document particular exceptions that the manager finds objectionable. An important outcome of the interview should be a feeling of assurance on the part of the manager

that the final report will reflect nothing in addition to what was discussed during the interview.

The exit interview is also the appropriate forum for the auditor to suggest actions to resolve the identified problems, to encourage feedback from the manager concerning his or her interest and intention to take corrective actions, and to participate with the manager in mapping out a game plan for action. A give and take of ideas between the auditor and manager may produce the best possible solutions since the auditor has global knowledge of what has worked and not worked at other stores in similar situations, and the manager has specific knowledge of the unique circumstances at the particular store in question.

In some few cases the auditor may not be able to formulate a corrective action in time to present it during the exit interview. This can result from a corrective action being dependent upon the availability of a particular product or upon the approval of a third party. When this happens, the auditor can hold a second exit interview or communicate his recommendation to the manager at a later time, but before the written report is prepared.

The manager is more likely to commit to action steps that he or she shared in developing. The manager may also see some advantage to begin making changes immediately, if only to be cast in a better light when the auditor's written report arrives on the desk of the manager's superior.

The Written Report

The audit is documented by a fully detailed report. The usual format has three sections: introduction, findings, and recommendations.

The introduction may contain administrative details such as the authority for conducting the audit, the purpose of the audit, the name(s) of the auditor(s), starting and ending dates, the name or number of the store audited, the subsystems or functions audited, the names of key persons who provided information or assistance, and other parameters.

The second section is the main body of the report because it contains the findings. The usual approach is to organize the findings in groups according to function. For example, all of the findings related to cash handling would be in one group and all findings related to warehousing would be in another, and the groups might be listed in some order of importance. Within each group the findings would be presented, again in some logical order, e.g., by criticality, severity, or seriousness. Headings are arranged to lead the reader through the report.

Each finding is presented factually, clearly, and briefly. The principal readers of the report are persons in managerial positions. The author of the report must assume they possess good judgment and intellect, and will not be receptive to editorializing and inappropriate emphases. Including a long list of minor discrepancies may, for example, look like the author is trying to stack charges. The report author should strive to create a product that reflects a quality effort in terms of objectivity, accuracy, cogency, grammar, syntax, spelling, and punctuation.

Where it is possible to do so, the titles of positions or jobs should be used in lieu of employee names. People tend to move into and out of jobs but the jobs themselves remain fairly stable. A report that identifies people could be confusing if the people involved change jobs after the report has been published. Also, from the standpoint of objectivity and fairness, the criticisms inherent in a finding should not appear to focus on individuals. The focus should be on the job, not the holder of the job.

The third section of the report reflects recommendations. It helps the reader when the recommendations are numbered or coded in a manner that will allow the reader to refer back to the corresponding exception(s).

The auditor should describe agreements reached with the manager during the exit interview and any corrective actions that may be underway. This would include problems that were in the process of being corrected when the audit began. Each recommendation can be accompanied by a time schedule. An action step may be of a nature that it can only be taken after other conditions have been met, such as implementation of a separate but related recommendation. These can be described as linked events along a time continuum and as actions that sequentially overlap each other. The auditor may choose to prepare a map or chart that depicts a schedule for bringing various actions together.

Another factor that must be taken into consideration when drafting recommendations is cost. A positive balance between benefit and cost is essential. Recommendations that come with hefty price tags will be seen as unrealistic and may reflect poorly on the auditor as a business person. It may help the auditor get into the right frame of mind by hypothesizing that the costs of the recommendations will be paid out of the auditor's budget instead of the manager's budget. When the auditor and manager confer in good faith and harmony, they are often able to find new and innovative ways of implementing corrective changes at no cost or even with a reduction in cost.

A recommendation that simply says "follow company policy" is not helpful. It may be appropriate for the auditor to recommend that an established procedure be followed, provided the procedure includes specific directions. Procedures referenced in the report can be attached as exhibits. The key point here is that recommendations have to reflect actions that are unambiguous, tangible, and measurable. A follow-up audit to assess compliance will focus on these specifications.

The best audit in the world has no value if it is not read by people who are in a position to do something about it. The minimum distribution of the audit report should be to the store manager and other directly involved supervisors (certainly to those who participated in the exit interview), and to the manager in the chain of command one level higher. When a follow-up audit reveals that little or no action was taken, the auditor may find it necessary to send the original report and the follow-up report to one or more senior managers situated two levels above the store manager.

E. Floyd Phelps, CPP

RETAIL SECURITY: PHYSICAL SAFEGUARDS

Preventing loss rather than reacting to a loss is the basis of physical security. Physical security prevents opportunities for theft and acts as a visual deterrent. In many cases these physical safeguards are inexpensive and can be incorporated into the design of each facility.

Experts agree that retail loss by theft results more from internal sources (employees) than from external (shoplifters) sources. However, this can vary between stores because of the location. A good loss prevention program concentrates equally on external and internal theft potential. Money is the most vulnerable asset and merchandise is second, but measures should be implemented to protect both.

Key control plays a major role in physical security. Each facility should have a distinctive master system on a key that cannot be easily duplicated. The issuance of these master keys should be restricted to management. If employees need frequent access to certain areas and management supervision is not required, an operating key that can also be operated by the store master should be carried by that employee. Often these keys can be issued temporarily and do not leave with the employee at the end of the shift. Managers should not loan their keys to employees, even for a short time. Policy should dictate that store keys cannot be duplicated and that all lost keys are reported. No store identification should be on keys and the locks should be changed each time a key is lost.

Employee parking is an important part of physical security. A designated area should be assigned for employees. This area should be at the far end of the parking lot, away from the store. Employees should not be allowed to park behind the store or next to the receiving door. Employees should be reprimanded for parking near the building. The security benefit is that it is harder for an employee to remove merchandise from the store unnoticed if they must carry the items across the parking lot. A second benefit is that it keeps the parking next to the store free for customers, which are the life blood of retailing.

Employees should be required to enter and leave through a supervised designated door during hours that the store is closed to business. During business hours employees should enter and leave the front door. Warehouse receiving doors and rear doors to the store should be secured when they are not attended. There should be no exceptions.

Most retail outlets have a vault room or cashier's office where funds are reconciled and deposits prepared. Philosophies differ among retail security authorities as to whether the area should be inaccessible to the public or in full view as in grocery stores. However, unless there is a great demand on funds by the public, such as check cashing, the secured unidentified vault room is preferable. This room should be restricted to authorized personnel. Visitors and other employees should be forbidden. Money should

be locked in the safe when the room is unattended. The practice of "day lock" should not be allowed. Day lock is a term used when the door of the safe is temporarily secured by turning the dial a short distance to the left. In this position the door can be opened by turning the knob to the right until it stops. This method is used by lazy managers who do not want to re-dial the combination each time the safe needs to be opened. The door to the room should remain locked at all times, even when the vault cashier or accountant is on duty. A peep hole should be installed to allow the vault cashier to see who is outside and if they are under duress before the door is opened. It is recommended that this room be alarmed and a capacitance proximity detector placed on the safe. This type of device protects metal items and activates if anyone approaches or touches the exterior of the safe.

A number of factors should be weighed before installing an intrusion alarm system in the remainder of the store. These factors include the areas that need protecting, and the cost of the installation and maintenance of the system compared to the items being protected. In most cases an intrusion alarm is an extremely cost-effective way to protect merchandise and cash during closed hours.

The use of guard rails and turnstiles can play an important role in preventing theft. All traffic should be routed through cash stands with personnel on duty. This allows for visual contact of anyone leaving the store, whether or not they purchase anything.

Electronic article surveillance (EAS) systems can act as both a deterrent and apprehension tool. These systems are expensive and are usually placed in selected stores with a high external theft problem. To use the system a special tag that is difficult to remove is placed on the merchandise. If the tagged item moves through a strategically placed sensor, an alarm sounds. These systems use three methods to allow legitimate customers through the system without a problem. They are: (1) tag removal, (2) tag deactivation, and (3) passing the tag (merchandise) around the sensor. The use of this equipment requires consistency and continued training of employees.

The use of closed-circuit television (CCTV) can prevent and document both internal and external theft. This equipment is also expensive and must be used properly to achieve success. Active cameras, as opposed to dummy cameras, should be used and the monitoring station should be in an area where it can be viewed by management at all times, whether or not a recording device is used. In most cases recording equipment should be used. Areas that should be monitored would be cash stands, vault room, exit doors, expensive merchandise, and the warehouse area.

Small, stand-alone alarms are available to protect vulnerable display merchandise. These alarms use contacts that are fastened to the merchandise and wired to a monitoring device. If the contact is removed, an alarm sounds. Usually several display items in the same general area can be connected to one monitor.

A merchandise storage cage can be used to protect popular or "high-ticket" items. The customer views the floor models that can be examined and handled. When the customer purchases the item it is delivered to the cash stand or picked up at a specified delivery area.

Trash removal also presents vulnerability. Salable items can be removed along with the trash. The most effective way to prevent loss is to have a compactor installed with the delivery chute mounted into the wall of the store, allowing trash to be discarded without anyone leaving the store. Whether or not a compactor is used, all boxes should be flattened to ensure that no merchandise

is left in any containers. The use of clear plastic trash bags is also recommended.

Exterior lighting is important. Proper lighting can create a safer atmosphere and reduce liability and vulnerability. Exterior lights should be checked regularly to ensure they are functioning properly.

Emergency doors should remain secured with panic alarm locking devices, which sound an alarm if opened. These locks should be compatible with fire codes and must be checked regularly to ensure that they are operating properly. Employees should be trained to respond if the alarm sounds.

The merchandising philosophy of the company plays an important role in the use of any or all of the measures described. Many merchandisers want all merchandise accessible to the customer with no restrictions. Many companies store merchandise for sale outside of the store unattended, allowing the customer to retrieve what they have purchased using the "honor system." Much of this merchandise remains unattended when the outlet is closed.

A security manager must introduce his ideas and plans, realizing that all of them may not be accepted. The security manager must then ensure that management is aware of the risks involved.

E. Floyd Phelps, CPP

ROBBERY PREVENTION TIPS

•Keep in the cash drawer the smallest amount of cash needed to operate and use a drop safe or similar robbery-resistive container to store excess cash.

•Make bank deposits at least daily, vary the time and route, and use two people to make the deposits or use a courier service.

•Do not allow unneeded cash to build up.

•Place notices in prominent places on the premises which announce the cash protection procedures.

•Arrange for maximum visibility of the cashier's counter from outside the premises.

•Provide initial and refresher training to store personnel concerning excess cash; post warning signs and provide training on what to do when a robbery occurs.

•Maintain liaison with local law enforcement, especially with those officers who patrol in the immediate neighborhood.

•Install alarm equipment and CCTV, or a capability to photograph a robbery in progress, post warning signs that such equipment is installed, and mount cameras so they will serve as psychological deterrents.

RETAIL SECURITY: SYSTEM DESIGN

A large retail department store provides a unique challenge to the security system designer. Because customers, employees, and vendors are allowed relatively free access to areas within a building, the integrity of a security system design is often compromised. An effective security system design must be flexible enough to work within the framework of the retail sales environment, as well as during after-hours equipment maintenance, and to survive changes in security management philosophy. It must function efficiently during special events and the Christmas season sales crunch with its sudden influx of customers and temporary employees. The security design should accommodate system upgrades and be expandable, while not being totally dependent upon minimum security staffing levels to operate the system.

Design for Three Modes of Operation

Most large retail department stores have three primary modes of operation that require different levels of security. It is important to recognize this practical aspect of the retail business and design the security system accordingly. The initial security system concept must be flexible enough to accommodate daily retail sales and related activity while being capable of providing maximum security after hours.

Sales Mode. The first mode of operation is daily sales. During this period, merchandise is on display with relatively free access by customers, employees, and vendors. Most alarms are deactivated, and most common area doors are unlocked. The security emphasis during this period is primarily loss prevention: shoplifting, employee and vendor theft, robbery, and fraud. Customer safety is also a concern.

Non-Sales Mode. The second mode of operation involves activity just before and just after normal business hours when the store is prepared and repaired for the day ahead. With the public excluded, perimeter doors are secured with the exception of the employee entrance and possibly the receiving and loading dock areas. Certain stockroom areas and sensitive areas can be secured, and access controls activated. Employees and vendors still have access to certain interior areas. The security emphasis during this period is on access control and employee and vendor theft.

After-Hours Mode. The third mode of operation involves the after-hours period when the store is vacated. The security emphasis is to ensure that all remaining personnel have exited and then to completely lock down and secure the store. The primary concern is burglary prevention and perimeter intrusion detection. A secondary concern is internal intrusion detection for the customer or employee who may hide inside the vacated store and burglarize it. Because most city fire codes require unrestricted egress from a building, early detection of lock-ins is an important task in retail security design. Fire detection and life safety are also important, but will not be discussed in detail here.

Because of these contrasts in facility usage, retail security design must be multi-functional to accommodate each mode of operation. The most cost-effective security system will integrate intrusion and activity detection, video surveillance, access control, and theft deterrence devices.

Common Design Flaws

The most common reason why retail security systems fail to function effectively is that a hardware package has been installed without an understanding of how the system will be utilized or supported. Another problem develops if a security designer with a limited initial budget focuses on perimeter intrusion detection only, without consideration for use of the same sensors for interior activity detection while the building is occupied. The most costly errors occur when a security designer does not plan for system growth, future integration, and for hardware and software compatibility. Retail security will always be plagued by budget fluctuations; that is why systems should be designed modularly, to be built upon year after year.

A Typical Example

Take for example, a large retail department store located in a four-story building that intends to operate the first three floors for retail sales; the top floor for management offices and credit/cashier functions; and the basement for shipping/receiving, main stockrooms, and support staff operations. The store is part of a new regional mall with three public access points at ground level and interior access from the mall side at three levels.

In this example, the anticipated business hours are 9:00 a.m. to 9:00 p.m., 6 days per week, and 9:00 a.m. to 5:00 p.m. on Sundays. Cleaning crews access the facility at 6:00 a.m. each day. Management and employees may arrive as early as 6:00 am and may remain on the premises as long as 2 hours after closing. Occasional special events such as inventory, stocking, and promotions can extend facility usage into the night. Facility maintenance of escalators, elevators, and heating and air conditioning usually occur after hours as well.

Since the store's security needs vary depending on the time of day, the system components are designed to serve equally well during each period. The heart of the security system is housed in an intelligently designed console; a single security operator can monitor both alarm and video functions, and perform dispatcher duties as well. This proprietary system is designed to capture alarm data and video signals after hours, even though monitored by a central station.

The security console incorporates a computer-based access control system to monitor card reader data and alarm status via a graphic interface of each floor plan. The video surveillance cameras are monitored by a high-speed, multi-format, system controller that has record/playback capability for 16 camera inputs, captured on a single Super-VHS video tape. The system operator is able to view multiple color cameras on a single 25-inch color monitor, either in compressed mode or by calling up individual cameras to full screen size after receiving external alarm input annunciations. A second video system is installed in the security manager's private office to view hidden pinhole surveillance cameras and to back up the main system.

While the store is closed and vacated, traditional intrusion-detection methods are applied. These are designed to suit the particular retail environment. Perimeter alarm protection includes the standard door contacts with interior motion sensors as backup. The store's glass doors and windows will be shaken, have faces pressed

against them, and have police flashlights shone through them, all of which may activate poorly placed internal motion or heat sensors.

A combination of detection devices and physical barriers is designed into the store's interior protection scheme. Interior motion sensors and door contacts are zoned separately, so they can report the location and path traveled by an intruder. A design strategy of lockable back hallway doors and basement recall capability for the elevators forces a "lock-in" intruder to use either the fire stairs or the escalators to move from floor to floor. By forcing the intruder to move through the protected area, the motion sensors electronically track him throughout the store while the color video cameras record the event.

During after-hours maintenance, the system is designed to allow for specific detection device shunting while still monitoring the remaining square footage. While the store is occupied but closed to the public, the same devices are designed to monitor access to sensitive areas. The proprietary alarm and video system is supervised by on-site security personnel during this period.

Janitorial staff and employees are issued mag-stripe cards to control access to their respective work areas and stockrooms. The access control software captures the data from each card reader for later review by security personnel.

The fine jewelry and cashier areas will have an alarm controller sub-system installed with robbery, panic, and safe alarms. These specialty departments use a combination of a mag-stripe card and a digital keypad to access the alarm function. This method provides for dual supervision by the security staff and specialty department personnel.

The multi-camera record/playback capability of the video controller is particularly beneficial as employees approach these sensitive departments. Pre-programmed function keys allow the console operator to monitor live activity in all key areas simultaneously at the push of button, while still recording the remaining camera locations on one video tape. Similarly, when the receiving dock raises the roll-up doors each morning, local alarm annunciation at the console alerts the guard to call up the camera to full screen mode to view this area. Since all 16 cameras are being recorded automatically, one guard can effectively monitor all areas.

During business hours, strict access control is neither reasonable nor desirable in a retail store.

Most perimeter and interior alarm sensors will be deactivated. However, security has daytime monitoring capability for sensitive stockroom areas in the basement and can monitor the loading dock doors when not in operation.

All fire doors and emergency exits are monitored along with holdup and panic alarms for the jewelry department and cashier. The management offices have separate duress alarms installed under each desk, which report to the security console in an emergency.

Video surveillance cameras are heavily relied on during business hours because of expected security staff fluctuations. Each floor has six color camera domes installed and pre-wired for pan-tilt-zoom capabilities. Only three domes per floor contain cameras; the pre-wire allows for movement to any drone location. The basement level, employee entrance, loading dock, and shipping areas all have domes with cameras installed. The fourth floor cashier and management office area also have live cameras and domes.

The sophisticated, multi-camera, video controller system is designed to fit the current aggressive management policy regarding employee theft and shoplifting. However, this design will accommodate other, more passive philosophies in the future as well. The current design technology will allow a single console operator to follow a shoplifter from camera to camera and from floor to floor, while automatically recording the entire event on video tape and dispatching undercover security personnel.

The system design takes advantage of two electrical utility closets located at opposite ends of each floor. Much of the video cable is routed through these rooms down to the security console. Break-out boxes are installed in each electrical room to facilitate maintenance of the video cables and to allow for cost-effective modifications.

The covert video surveillance system is designed to interface partially with the installed dome system. Additional coaxial cable is pulled during the construction phase branching out from each dome location to all appropriate areas for use with pinhole surveillance applications. Other coaxial cable is pulled independent of the dome installations as well.

This design shortcut requires some coaxial cable switching at dome sites, at break-out boxes, or at the security console, but saves hundreds of hours and thousands of dollars when system growth is desired.

The covert video surveillance inputs are routed separately to the security manager's office for privacy. As a cost savings measure, this covert system will utilize manual switching, a smaller monitor, single-camera input recording, and lack camera directional controls. However, the system is pre-wired to accommodate future upgrades.

Vendor Support Can Affect Design Decisions

Local support from access control and video surveillance vendors often affects which design path to follow. Each component of a fully integrated security system must be able to operate independently, should other components fail or need repair. The access control computer and video controller will require rapid local repair service and replacement capability, should they go down. The use of exotic system components is not recommended without solid local vendor support and service capabilities.

Another important design consideration is to plan for manual backup systems for both alarm and video systems. Also, during construction, consider using 3/4- or 1-inch conduit when pulling video coaxial cable, instead of 1/2-inch, to allow for additional cable in the future.

The business of retail sales has not changed much over the years, but thanks to technology, controlling losses is becoming more manageable with a well-designed, integrated security system.

Chris E. Mcgoey, CPP, CSP

Source McGoey, C.E., Effective Security Design Must Be Flexible. (Access Control, August, 1991).

RISK ANALYSIS

Risk is associated with virtually every activity one can think of, but in the present context it is limited to the uncertainty of financial loss, the variations between actual and expected results, or the probability that a loss has occurred or will occur. In the insurance industry, the term *risk* is also used to mean "the thing insured," for example, the XYZ Company is the risk. Risk is also the possible occurrence of an undesirable event.

Risk should not be confused with perils, which are the causes of risk and are things such as fire, flood, and earthquake. Nor should risk be confused with hazard, which is a contributing factor to perils. Almost anything can be a hazard: a loaded gun, a bottle of caustic acid, a bunch of oily rags, or a warehouse used for storing paper products. The end result of risk is loss or a decrease in value.

Risks are generally classified as "speculative" (the difference between loss or gain, for example, the risk in gambling) and "pure risk," a loss or no-loss situation, to which insurance generally applies.

The divisions of risk are limited to three common categories:

- Personal (having to do with people assets).
- Property (having to do with material assets).
- Liability (having to do with legalities that could affect both of the previous categories, such as errors and omissions liability).

What Is Risk Analysis?

Risk analysis is a management tool, the standard that is determined by whatever management decides it wants to accept in terms of actual loss. In order to proceed in a logical manner to perform a risk analysis, it is first necessary to accomplish some basic tasks:

- Identify the assets in need of being protected (money, manufactured product, and industrial processes to name a few).
- Identify the kinds of risks that may affect the assets involved (internal theft, external theft, fire, or earthquake).
- Determine the probability of risk occurrence. Here one must keep in mind that such a determination is not a science but an art -- the art of projecting probabilities.
- Determine the impact or effect, in dollar values if possible, if given loss does occur.

A risk assessment analysis is a rational and orderly approach, and a comprehensive solution to problem identification and probability determination. It is also a method for estimating the anticipated or expected loss from the occurrence of some adverse event. The key word here is *estimating*, because risk analysis will never be an exact science. Nevertheless, the answer to most, if not all, questions regarding one's security exposures can be determined by risk analysis.

Analysis provides management with information on which to base decisions, such as: Is it always best to prevent the occurrence of a situation? Should the policy be to contain the effect a hazardous situation may have? Is it sufficient simply to recognize that an adverse potential exists, and for now do nothing but be aware of the hazard? The eventual goal of risk analysis is to strike an economic balance between the impact of risk on the enterprise and the cost of protective measures.

A properly performed risk analysis has many benefits. It can:

- Show the current security posture (profile) of the organization.
- Highlight areas where greater (or lesser) security is needed.
- Help to assemble some of the facts needed for the development and justification of cost-effective countermeasures (safeguards).
- Serve to increase security awareness by assessing the strengths and weaknesses of security to all organizational levels from management to operations.

Risk analysis is not a task to be accomplished once and for all time. It must be performed periodically in order to stay abreast of changes in mission, facilities, and equipment. Since security measures designed at the inception of a system have generally proved to be more effective than those superimposed later, risk analysis should have a place in the design phase of every system. Unfortunately, this is seldom the case.

The major resource required for a risk analysis is humanpower. For this reason, the first analysis will be the most expensive, as subsequent ones can be based in part on previous work and the time required will decrease to some extent as experience is gained. The time allowed to accomplish the risk analysis should be compatible with its objectives. Large facilities with complex, multi-shift operations and many files of data will require more time than the single-shift, limited production locations. If meaningful results are expected, management must be willing to commit the resources necessary to accomplish this undertaking.

The Role of Management in Risk Analysis

The success of any risk analysis undertaking will be strongly contingent on the role top management takes in the project. Management must support the project and express this support to all levels of the organization. Management must delineate the purpose and scope of risk analysis. It must select a qualified team and formally delegate authority, and management must review the team's findings.

Personnel who are not directly involved in the analysis process must be prepared to provide information and assistance to those who are conducting the analysis and, in addition, to abide by any procedures and limitations of activity that may ensue. Management should leave no doubt that it intends to rely on the final product and base its security decisions on the findings of the risk analysis team. The scope of the project should be defined and the statement of scope should specifically spell out the limitations of the analysis. It is oftentimes equally important to state specifically what the analysis is not designed to accomplish or cover. This will serve to eliminate any misunderstandings at the start rather than at the conclusion of the exercise.

At this point it may be well to define and explain two other terms that are sometimes used interchangeably with risk. They are: *threats*, anything that could adversely affect the enterprise or the assets, and *vulnerability*, weaknesses, flaws, holes, or anything that may conceivably be exploited by a threat. Threats are most easily identified by placing them in one of three classifications or categories: natural hazards, accidents, or intentional acts. Vulnerabilities are most easily identified by collecting information from interviewing persons employed in the facility, by field observation and inspection, by document review, and, in the case of hardware or electronics, by conducting tests designed to highlight vulnerability and expose weaknesses or flaws in the design of the system.

Threat occurrence rates/probabilities are best developed from reports of occurrence or incident reports whenever this historical data exist. Where the data do not exist, it may be necessary to reconstruct them by conducting interviews with knowledgeable persons.

Risk Exposure Assessment

Before any corrective action can be considered, it is necessary to make a thorough assessment of one's identifiable risk exposure. In order to accomplish this, it is essential that three factors be identified and evaluated in quantitative terms.

The first is to determine the types of loss or risk that can affect the assets involved. Here examples would be fire, burglary, robbery, or kidnapping. If one of these were to occur, what effect would the resulting disruption of operations have on the company? If the chief executive officer, on an overseas trip, were to be kidnapped by a terrorist group, who would make the day-to-day operating decisions in his absence? What about the unauthorized disclosure of trade secrets and other proprietary data? After the risk exposure potentials are identified, one must then proceed to evaluate those threats that, should they occur, would produce losses in quantitative terms.

To do this we proceed to the second factor: estimate the probability of occurrence. What are the chances that the identified risks may become actual events? For some risks, estimating probabilities can be relatively easy. This is especially true when we have documented historical data dealing with identifiable problems. For example, how many internal and external theft cases have been investigated over the past year? Other risks are more difficult to predict. Sabotage, industrial espionage, kidnapping, and civil disorder may never occur or may occur only on a one-time basis.

The third factor is quantifying loss potential. This is measuring the impact or severity of the risk, if in fact a loss does occur or the risk becomes an actual event. This exercise does not become final until one develops dollar values for the assets previously identified. This part of the survey is necessary to set the stage for classification evaluation and analysis of the comparisons necessary to the establishment of countermeasure priorities.

Some events or kinds of risk with which business and industry are most commonly concerned are as follows:

•Natural catastrophe (tornado, hurricane, earthquake, volcanic eruption, and flood).

•Industrial disaster (explosion, chemical spill, structural collapse, and fire).

•Civil disturbance (sabotage, labor violence, and bomb threats).

•Criminality (robbery, burglary, pilferage, embezzlement, fraud, industrial espionage, internal theft, and hijacking).

•Conflict of interest (kickbacks, trading on inside information, and unethical practices).

• Miscellaneous risks, threats, or loss factors (bookkeeping errors, unaccounted for inventory losses, traffic accidents, alcohol and drug abuse, absenteeism, gambling, and improper leave or time clocking).

Admittedly, some of the listed events are unlikely to occur. Also, some are less critical to an enterprise than others. Nevertheless, all are possibilities and are thus deserving of consideration.

James F. Broder, CPP

Source Broder, J.F., Risk Analysis and the Security Survey. (Butterworth-Heinemann, Boston, 1984).

RISK ANALYSIS: CRIME DEMOGRAPHIC RESEARCH

A crime demographic survey should be conducted for all at-risk properties that are open to the public. The crime history of a premises is usually a good indicator of which assaultive crimes are likely to occur in the future. Only then can security measures be implemented that address the foreseeable risk of harm.

Crime Record Research

The primary purposes for researching crime records are to establish the frequency and types of crimes that have occurred on the premises, and to establish the frequency and types of crimes that have occurred in the surrounding area. Crime history research will also reveal the characteristics of perpetrators, times of crime, specific locations on site, and criminal methods.

Information sources for a crime demographics analysis for a premises or surrounding area can be as formal as statistics or as informal as a field interview. Crime records, for instance, may be generated by a computer, logged by hand in a ledger, or recalled by witnesses.

Crime record research involves more than gathering prior crime statistics. It involves developing knowledge of the environment surrounding a premises and making judgments regarding which relevant crime types should be collected and for what distance away from a premises. It involves interviews in the field with

premises residents, employees, neighbors, and police beat officers. It is impossible to evaluate crime foreseeability or the effectiveness of on-site security programs without field research.

Crime Research Sources

Crime data is usually obtained from five primary sources: (1) Uniform Crime Reports (UCR) [1]; (2) National Crime Survey (NCS) [2]; (3) local law enforcement; (4) in-house security reports; and (5) field interviews.

Except for UCR and NCS, all other sources of records have a time decay factor to consider. Ideally, local crime records should be obtained annually to update analysis and to observe increases or decreases of crime trends.

Uniform Crime Reports (UCR)

The Uniform Crime Report Program (UCR) has been managed by the Federal Bureau of Investigation (FBI) since 1930 in an effort to collect crime statistics in a consistent manner across the nation. Information compiled by UCR contributors is forwarded to the FBI either directly from the local law enforcement agency or through a state-level UCR program. Approximately 41 states have mandatory reporting requirements in an effort to develop accuracy and consistency in reporting.

Seven criminal offenses were initially chosen to serve as an index for gauging fluctuations in the overall volume and rate of crime. Known jointly as the Crime Index, these offenses include the violent crimes of murder (including non-negligent manslaughter), forcible rape, robbery, aggravated assault, and property crimes of burglary, larceny-theft, and motor vehicle theft. By congressional mandate, arson was added as the eighth index offense in 1979.

UCR crime statistics are collated by region, geographic division, state, and city. The number of incidents reported is divided into the area population and indexed as the crime rate per 100,000 population. Problems with these statistics arise due to the fact that certain population rates must be estimated since the last census. Certain crime rates must also be estimated due to variations in crime classification methods and reporting procedures. Also, cities and towns with populations of less than 25,000 must extrapolate their numbers to come up with a comparative index rating.

Most states use similar criteria to develop a statewide and even a countywide crime index. Although these statistics provide interesting trend comparisons, they offer little benefit in determining crime foreseeability for a neighborhood community or specific site. These statistics do not take into consideration the nature of a particular premises or the effectiveness of its crime prevention programs.

Many criminologists are critical of the UCR data, claiming that it is inaccurate for the reasons cited previously, and because it fails to factor in the amount of unreported crimes. They also argue that the policy of tracking only eight select crimes does not give a true picture of the national crime problem.

National Crime Survey (NCS)

The NCS is a victimization survey created in the mid-1960s, which has been conducted annually since 1973. A sampling of the population is surveyed at random to determine who has been victimized. The surveys are conducted either by telephone, by mail, or by in-person interview.

Victimization surveys have determined that only about half of all felonies are reported to the police. The surveys discover the victims who do not report crimes, and their sex, age, race, and income level. The NCS has often produced different crime trends than the UCR, and often in opposing directions for the same time periods surveyed. Although informative like the UCR, the NCS provides little benefit to help us evaluate crime foreseeability on a particular premises.

Law Enforcement Records

Law enforcement crime records can provide a wealth of information. Quality and quantity of records will vary depending on the jurisdiction, technology, and policies on releasing information. Since the early 1980s, most progressive police departments have computerized their records. This means that in those jurisdictions, computer printouts can be generated that will break down crime records by date, location, crime type, case number, and responding officers. It is sometimes

possible to obtain crime records for a specific address, entire block, beat, census tract, district, or division, depending on one's needs. Certain types of crime can be isolated for the same given locations.

Some agencies maintain records only on microfiche, which must be viewed and recorded by hand. Still others require hand searching of individual incident reports to obtain the records. Whatever the technology, records are usually accessible for at least 1 year, after which they become more difficult to obtain.

Some police agencies will request a fee before releasing records. However, if a business contacts the chief of police or crime prevention unit, many of the formal requirements may be waived. It should be standard practice to obtain relevant crime reports for at least 2 years prior to the implementation of a security program.

Calls for Service

A little known source of police records is what is known as "calls for service." These records are obtained from the police dispatch computer files. Although these records are used for a different purpose, they can produce a useful statistic. Most modern police dispatch computer systems can sort their files electronically by address and retrieve a list of calls to a particular location for the past several years. The disadvantage is the possible inaccuracy of the information. Occasionally, addresses and crime type are given incorrectly to the police dispatcher. Many victims will report a petty theft as a robbery or a domestic dispute as an assault.

In-House Security Reports

The second major source for site-specific crime records is security reports, if any, written by on-site security personnel. Whether proprietary or contract, security guards usually complete daily activity and crime incident reports, as well as other memoranda. These reports are usually more informative than police crime reports because they describe the day-to-day activities of the premises. However, many crime incidents are reported directly to the police and not to the security guards. For example, most people call the police directly to report a purse snatch in a shopping center parking lot rather than report to mall security. Because of this fact, a combination of both police and security reports is necessary.

Larger companies with regional security personnel should develop periodic crime summaries and statistical analysis for management. These documents will not only show criminal activity for a particular premises, but often will rank and compare it to other similar operations within the organization.

Size of Relevant Crime Radius

Obtaining prior crime records for a physical premises is always relevant. For evaluation of the total demographics, it is necessary to research crime records for the surrounding area to determine what level of criminal activity is present in the same environment as the property. It can be determined whether the premises in question is operating with a higher, lower, or similar crime experience as its environment. In some cases of either very high or low crime records on-site, the crime records off-site will become less relevant. For example, any reasonable person should conclude that six armed robberies per year in a convenience store is high, or that an 8-year crime-free history in an apartment complex is very low. Additional records of off-site crime activity will be of little value in evaluating security program effectiveness.

It would not be practical to set a standard search radius in all cases due to the vast number of variables possible. A good rule of thumb is to start with the smallest crime-reporting segment available from the police and move outward as required to obtain a reasonable sampling. Sometimes major physical or psychological barriers -- a freeway, railroad track, or river -- may significantly alter crime rates from one area to another adjacent area. It may be necessary to obtain records from two separate jurisdictions if the premises is situated on the city boundary line.

Of importance is what area around the premises is considered to be its environment. An environment for a business is the area from which it draws the majority of its business. Depending on the nature of the business, that area could be several blocks, several miles, or somewhere in between. An environment for a residential facility is more likely to be only the immediate neighborhood of several blocks. For example, when evaluating the robbery history of a convenience store on a major thoroughfare, it may be more useful to research the robbery history of similar businesses along the same route for 1 mile in each direction rather than a residential community immediately surrounding the site.

Field Interviews

It is impossible to evaluate crime demographics for a premises from behind a desk. One or more visits to the site and surrounding neighborhood are required to gain an understanding of the environment. The environment may be impacted by a school, a shopping center, a sports stadium, or park. This impact may be daily, nightly, or only on a scheduled basis. These special circumstances must be considered in the overall review process.

In addition to the site survey, there should be field interviews conducted of premises residents, employees, neighbors, and local businesses. The purpose of this interview process is to gain feedback on the reputation of the premises and validate the accuracy of police crime records. Although personal interviews are subjective in nature, one can obtain a better picture on how others view their environment. In the event that crime records are unavailable, these field interviews may be the only means of assessing the risk factors.

New operation or shut down of a high school, shopping center, movie theater, or recreation park nearby can have a major impact on crime activity on a premises. This condition may invalidate police crime statistics. Owners or management have been known to significantly alter the nature of a business or level of security and therefore its future crime potential. Sometimes reviewing crime statistics before and after a change in business status will clearly reflect the effect of the change on the criminal activity.

Locating and interviewing police beat officers who patrolled the area should be standard procedure. If crime records are only available for a larger geographic area than desired, these beat officers can be extremely valuable in isolating the high- and low-crime pockets.

Police officers who are familiar with the day-to-day operation of a premises will often be well qualified to comment on crime problems they have encountered. In addition, most police officers have their own opinion on the relative security of a site compared with other similar locations in their reporting area.

The identification of all components of the crime demographics, from statistics to field interviews, is a necessity for every effective security program. This research may prove critical later on in court should a company be sued for not providing adequate security.

Chris E. Mcgoey, CPP, CSP

Source McGoey, C.E., Security: Adequate...or Not?: The Complete Guide to Premises Liability Litigation. (Aegis Books, Oakland, CA).

Notes

1.   See *Crime in the United States, Uniform Crime Reports*, an annual publication of the Federal Bureau of Investigation, Washington, DC.

2.   See the *Criminal Victimization in the United States, National Crime Survey*, a publication of the Bureau of Justice Statistics, U.S. Department of Justice, Washington, DC.

RISK ANALYSIS: DEVELOPMENT OF A SECURITY PROGRAM

Security affects every aspect of an organization, cutting across the spectrum of business disciplines from fundamental administrative tasks to professional staff functions. Be it a business or government agency, security has far reaching implications. Indeed, security has a rippling effect, where an action in one area impacts another, often quite subtly.

However, security frequently is approached on an ad-hoc basis, without consideration for the domino effect of security actions. In many instances security measures are implemented following an isolated event. As a consequence, security systems and procedures are applied in answer to the event, without consideration for broader implications. This approach often results in resources expended in areas that may not be the most important.

Security master planning approaches security differently. A wide array of issues are analyzed before security measures are implemented, ensuring an appropriate distribution of resources, while not creating new exposures in the process. Through master planning a range of

vulnerabilities are identified and categorized on the basis of criticality. These are organized so that security measures are applied in a complementary and supportive manner.

In contrast to the ad-hoc approach, master planning begins with a broad-scope analysis of an organization, developing an understanding of its goals and objectives. Within this context, individual components are assessed resulting in resources directed at the most serious problems.

Security master planning ensures that individual components are understood within the broader context of an organization's primary purpose. It is a holistic approach premised on the notion that organizations are a web of interrelated components that must be understood before imposing security systems and procedures.

Often it is assumed that security vulnerabilities and needs are obvious. However, this rarely is the case. More often than not, the Achilles heel of an organization is hidden and must be flushed out through a master planning study. This approach is analogous to a health care diagnosis. It is based on the belief that a vulnerability may be the result of a seemingly unrelated malady.

The guiding philosophy for master planning is to understand the broad picture, analyze the full breadth of needs, and develop a plan consistent with the results.

At the onset of a project, questions are structured to provide a broad understanding of an organization. For example:

• What is the organization's business, or purpose?

• What type of description best characterizes the organization: a service company, manufacturer, deliverer of government services?

• Who are its competitors?

• What is the organization's long-range plan? Is it 3 years, 5 years, 10 years?

From these questions a baseline understanding of an organization is formed, providing a framework for assessing and categorizing individual components. This macro view establishes parameters for defining priorities and for defining critical elements. This approach facilitates an understanding of interrelationships and of subtle effects that each microcomponent has on the whole.

Consequently, a study begins with establishment of the macropicture. Subsequent steps progress from the big picture view to a narrower, more focused point of attention. This progression, however, unfolds within a context ensuring that a wide range of factors are considered as a plan develops.

The processes noted in this document are a guideline for conducting a master plan study. However, each study should be structured based on the requirements of a specific project.

Project Approach

A security master plan encompasses four major phases: asset definition, threat assessment, vulnerability analysis, and selection of security measures. It is a stepped approach in which each step leads to the next.

The overall objective is to define the organization's requirements and to organize those requirements in a prioritized ranking. Upon conclusion of a master plan, a new project should be initiated for implementation of the plan. At this point, system design projects may be commissioned, security guard force specifications developed, and formal policies and procedures drafted. The master plan provides the foundation for this effort, ultimately leading to implementation.

It is important to note, however, that a master plan is not intended as an implementation exercise, nor a specification task.   More importantly, it defines requirements and establishes parameters for prioritizing.

Asset Definition. The asset definition phase of a study establishes the priorities for a security plan. It is important to note that it would not be feasible to protect every asset against every possible threat. With that as an assumption, a process must be used to determine which assets will be protected. In this phase, assets are listed and classified based on criticality.

Defining assets should not be limited to property, equipment, goods, and other tangible materials. Intangibles, such as company image and employee morale, may be of great importance.

A starting point in asset definition is to interview members of senior management for the purpose of defining the organization's mission, strategy, and goals. The macroview that is unfolded at the upper level will identify the organization's inventory of major assets, certainly the big ticket items that, if lost or damaged, would cause serious problems. These interviews can also set the stage for insightful interviews of key personnel in middle management and at the front line of operations.

Of interest will be the manner in which middle managers and front line supervisors apply resources entrusted to them for carrying out the organization's strategy and goals.   It often happens that the resources being applied to the enhancement of a major asset have a significant value as well. For example, heavy equipment used in an extractive environment, such as in mining for ore or drilling for oil, can cost nearly as much as the raw materials they are acting upon. Although many assets will be obvious, some will not be readily apparent.   In the preceding example, the interviewer might give thought to the geologists who provide the brain power and to the safety program that is so essential to employee morale and the company's public image.

A qualitative classification based on criticality should be applied to the identified assets.   A classification scheme could include three levels:

- •Vital. Loss of a vital asset would prove fatal to the operation.
- •Important. Loss would be disruptive, but not catastrophic.
- •Secondary. Loss would be unpleasant, but relatively insignificant.

Threat Assessment. The next phase in a study is the threat assessment. A multitude of potential threats confront virtually every organization, from criminal acts to natural disasters. Potential threats must be defined in broad terms, including both internal and external threats, natural disasters, and other harmful acts.

Potentially harmful events must be identified and analyzed. The list will vary by organization, but the usual categories are criminal, natural, and accidental.

An analysis of criminal threats begins with compilation of data on losses experienced by the organization.   A review of insurance claims, security records, safety claims, and other internal records can provide a history of reported losses. Crime data on local, national, or international criminal trends can provide a framework for assessing exposure.   This data provides a quantifiable measure of exposure within certain constraints.

Two data sources stand out. The first is the Uniform Crime Reports (UCR), which reflects reported crimes. The second is the National Crime Survey (NCS), which presents statistical estimates based on sampling techniques. Although NCS figures are arguably faulty, they can serve as quantifiable inputs to a qualitative analysis.

When developing a plan for a specific facility, it is important to examine data on crime within a 1-mile radius of the facility. Failing to make a reasonable effort to protect against reasonably foreseeable crimes may leave the organization vulnerable to litigation, should an incident occur that results in injury and damage.

In addition to identifying threats, this phase of a study serves to eliminate potential threats from consideration. Where an organization clearly is not vulnerable to a threat, a determination may be made to eliminate it from consideration, or at least minimize it.

This phase also involves personal interviews with law enforcement agencies to obtain their view of the threats facing a particular organization. Often crime data will not present an accurate view of criminal trends. In some instances data is skewed for an assortment of reasons. The viewpoints of qualified law enforcement officials can help compensate for statistical shortcomings.

To assess risks associated with natural disasters, data can be drawn from internal records, civil disaster agencies, the Federal Emergency Management Agency (FEMA), the Army Corps of Engineers, and other sources.

Accidents should be a substantial point of consideration. Accident data can be obtained from persons working in safety, security, risk management, environmental quality, health, and human resources.

The overall goal is to identify applicable threats and eliminate others. The list of possible threats should narrow as an assessment progresses, and can be categorized as:

- Highly Probable. Expect an event to occur.
- Possible. Circumstances are conducive for an event.
- Unlikely. Possible but unlikely.

Vulnerability Analysis. The next step is to analyze vulnerabilities by correlating assets and threats, and then by defining the process for victimization. This process -- the method by which an asset may be targeted by a particular threat -- is the definition of an asset's vulnerability.

The objective of a vulnerability analysis is to identify potential points for attack. This analysis illuminates the physical, operational, and procedural weaknesses conducive for an assailant to succeed. Through this exercise corrective measures may be identified and implemented to counter the vulnerability and to reduce target attractiveness.

It is important to note, however, that there are many different types of attackers. Correction of one particular vulnerability may not correct all vulnerabilities. Moreover, the implementation of one corrective measure may expose another vulnerability from a different type of attacker. Consequently, a thorough analysis of all threats and vulnerabilities is required to ensure that priorities are clearly established and defined, resources are allocated based on priorities, and security measures are selected appropriately and integrated in a supportive and complementary manner.

The analysis begins with a listing of assets, noting the asset's classification. Each asset is then correlated with those threats that apply to the particular asset. Scenarios are constructed in the analysis suggesting the events that need to occur for an asset to be the victim of a threat. Through these contrived scenarios, the points of vulnerability are exposed.

Security Measures. The vulnerability analysis establishes criteria for the final phase of a master plan, the selection of security measures. Selection is predicated upon the vulnerability analysis and is intended to channel resources to protect the most vital assets against the most probable threats.

An important concept in this phase is a social psychological theory, the theory of social control. According to this theory, people are controlled by formal and informal controls. Formal controls are represented by systems, laws, and rules. These are coercive influences that control behavior. Informal controls are comprised of peer pressure along with social norms and mores. These are the subtle, yet persuasive elements that compel conformity. Informal controls are considered the more effective of the two and the more long lasting. According to the theory, there is an inverse relationship between the two modes of control. As one becomes more prevalent, the other decreases.

Consequently, attention must be focused on preserving informal controls. This means that the application of security measures must be balanced by the impact that security measures (formal controls) will have on informal controls.

The list of possible security measures encompasses a broad range of selections from policy and procedure considerations to physical security systems. The overall goal is to make selections so each operates in concert with the others, while all serve as support for each other.

The range of security measures generally falls within one of the following classifications:

- Policies and Procedures
- Electronic Security Systems
- Physical Barrier Protection Systems
- Security   Personnel   Tasks   and Responsibilities

Policies and Procedures. These provide a foundation for a security plan. Management's direction is stipulated in the form of policies and the process for implementation is defined in procedures. The following highlights specific topics for which policies are needed. It also notes issues for procedure development.

- Accounting systems are essential for detection of internal crimes. Job and process cost techniques in managerial accounting are essential aspects of business management. Standard costs are established for materials, labor, and overhead that are used for budgeting purposes and for measuring the efficiency of operations. Variances from standard costs are a management tool to evaluate the effect of decisions. Variances, however, may also serve as a tool for security in detecting fraud. Policy should state that variances will be reconciled and that security should investigate circumstances that cannot be reconciled. Policy also should indicate that auditing should audit for fraud and other defalcations, not just for compliance with standard accounting practices.
- Computer security is a fundamental protective function of a modern business organization. Computer operations often produce data that is vital to the company. Policies and procedures should be developed to protect computer systems operations. Policy should require establishment of a computer security plan. This plan should follow the same format as the

overall master plan with a definition of assets, threat assessment, vulnerability analysis, and selection of countermeasures.

- A drug and alcohol abuse policy should be developed and indicate the conditions for termination. It should define policy for drug and alcohol screening or testing, and indicate employee assistance that may be available.
- An emergency management policy should state the company position for establishment of emergency plans. These plans should establish a sequence of events to implement in the event of an emergency.
- A policy on information classification should clearly define types of information, classification levels, declassification methods, and penalties for failing to comply. It should establish procedures for classification of trade secrets, company confidential data, and proprietary data.
- A policy on personnel security should state the hiring practices, the prohibited behaviors, the measures that enforce the policy, and disciplinary sanctions. These may include conducting background investigations, monitoring workplace performance to detect aberrant and unacceptable behavior, conducting attitude surveys, debriefing terminated employees, operating security education and awareness programs, and conducting lifestyle and undercover investigations.
- Apply risk assessment techniques for reviewing and revising the security plan.
- Facility access should be granted consistent with a well-understood and carefully followed system that incorporates credentialing, positive personal identification, and access privileges.

Electronic Security Systems. Electronic security measures may be applied to deny, deter, delay, and detect unauthorized intrusions, and to announce hazardous conditions, such as smoke and toxic gas releases. These essential tasks can be assisted by an electronic security system consisting of a central control and reporting capability, intrusion-detection sensors, access control points, closed-circuit television (CCTV), fire detection and suppression devices, communications and annunciation devices, and a tamper-detecting feature.

A generic system should be recommended as opposed to a particular product or model, except in rare circumstances. The main idea should be to define the tasks to be performed by the system, establish performance criteria, and suggest a workable design. The recommendation should be general and unrestrictive. Important features and functions can be described, but not in great detail and not to the extent that the recommendation appears to be "carved in stone."

Physical Barrier Protection Systems. These should be applied in conjunction with electronic security and may include fencing, hardened enclosures and portals, vehicle barriers, bullet-resistant materials, a security command center, special access accommodations for emergency response vehicles and personnel, and heating, ventilating, and air conditioning (HVAC) designs that support protective systems.

Security Personnel Tasks and Responsibilities. Security departments may be structured as a legalistic unit, a service-oriented unit, or a mixture of legalistic and service.

The legalistic unit is characterized by formality. It is detached from people operating the facility and impervious to extenuating circumstances. This type of unit enforces rules rigorously. Its approach is unfriendly and unrelenting. For example, a legalistic unit is appropriate for a nuclear weapons facility, where security is assigned to protect highly sensitive materials and where there is no tolerance for mistakes, nor any room for compromise.

A service-oriented unit is more informal and personable. It is structured to assist people operating the facility and to be accommodating. This approach would be appropriate at a high-tech or research facility.

A mixed unit engenders characteristics of both the legalistic and service-type unit. A facility engaged in nuclear research, for example, might incorporate both approaches.

Whatever the nature of the unit, management needs to be clear as to its operating philosophy, the role of security within the overall organization, and the expectations it has of security personnel.

The process of developing a security plan provides a framework for establishing priorities with the help of a risk analysis. The plan will assess a broad range of issues with a clear intent to bring to light and correct problems before a program is implemented. This is vitally important when security systems are a part of the plan, if only because such systems require an

extensive amount of design. If conflicts and problems are not defined before a design is initiated, the design will meander as changes ensue from the resolution of conflicts. This is costly and time consuming, often resulting in systems that simply never meet the organization's needs.

Planning minimizes the number and degree of changes that occur during design. Most important, however, planning facilitates the formation of a security program that provides a balanced approach and channels resources to the organization's most pressing concerns.

Sal Depasquale, CPP

RISK MANAGEMENT: AN OVERVIEW

Risk management is the process by which a company identifies its potential losses and takes steps to avoid or reduce them. It can be a complex operation, and in a large company may mean the expenditure of millions of dollars annually.

Risk management involves the application of one or any combination of several techniques. In this discussion we are concerned with techniques that manage risk with respect to a company's valuable assets.

A first technique is to eliminate risk altogether by taking some action that will absolutely prevent the asset from being stolen or damaged. Elimination of risk is rarely an acceptable option. An example might be for a jewelry store to place all of its wares in a bank vault and never bring anything out until after a customer has paid for a purchase based on pictures.

A second technique is having someone else take the risk, usually in return for some benefit. This is called transfer of risk, the most common form of which is the taking out of insurance. Another option is to retain the risk, that is, to be willing to accept the cost of loss. When a loss is not covered by insurance, it is referred to as an unreimbursed loss. This type of full loss acceptance is not as common as partial loss acceptance, in which a company accepts losses up to a certain amount (insurance deductibles) or losses over a certain level (policy limits).

The technique of risk control calls for actions such as placing cash deposits immediately into a security container and damage prevention by removing all flammable materials from an area

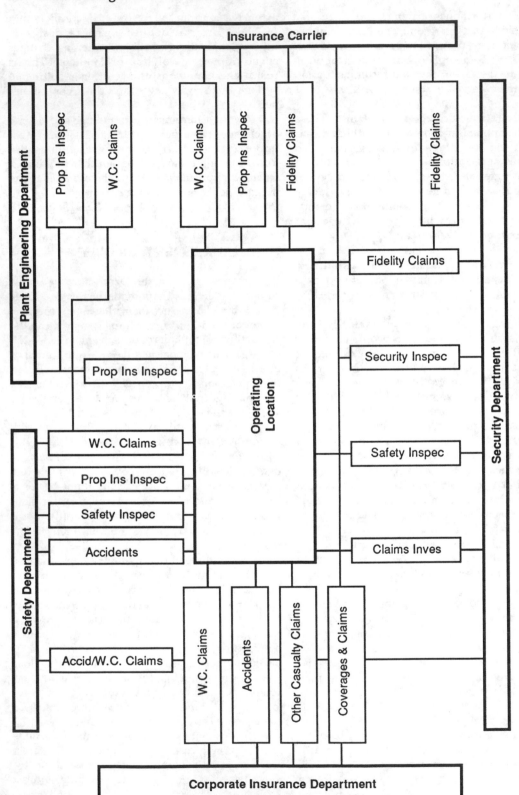

Risk Management Matrix

where valuables are kept. Risk control is a line management responsibility that is almost always carried out with input from a security manager.

It is now generally accepted that risk control is superior to risk transfer. Measures that protect assets can be much more cost-effective than measures that relieve loss through insurance. Premiums are expensive, often much more costly than security safeguards; and regardless of coverage, full compensation is virtually impossible. Avoidance of loss has become the first line of defense in most organizations with insurance as a backup protection against losses that may be impossible to entirely avoid.

A total risk control program would include elements of security, safety, property conservation, environmental protection, and emergency planning. Because concern over potential loss is shared by all responsible business persons, risk management is widely understood and practiced. In large companies a fairly senior manager will be the organization's designated coordinator of risk management functions. This responsibility will often fall on the shoulders of the corporate security director.

Risk Management Interrelationships

As each manager in an organization exercises risk control actions in meeting their responsibilities for the care and custody of assets, interactions among the managers and their subordinates occur both naturally and inevitably. The accompanying matrix depicts risk management relationships typical in a manufacturing organization.

J. Kirk Barefoot, CPP

RISK MANAGEMENT: DETERMINING INSURANCE REQUIREMENTS

Risk management is the process by which an entity identifies its potential losses and selects a treatment of them. Losses can be due to a variety of factors, such as theft, internal crime, or vandalism. Also, losses through fire, safety problems, and product or third-party liability are among the leading concerns of most risk managers.

Risk analysis can be used for many things, but its end result is a definition of the effect risks have on a particular company in terms of the potential for loss. The analysis should tell where, when, and how the risk is likely to be incurred. It should also tell the extent of loss or liability if the risk is incurred and how badly the company would be injured if this loss or liability is, in fact, incurred.

The risk manager must then design a program to cover the company's losses, exposures, and liabilities. When the program is designed, the company is faced with three basic options in dealing with most risks:

- The risk can be avoided, eliminated, or reduced to manageable proportions.
- The risk can be assumed or retained.
- The risk can be transferred to a third party.

The transfer to a third party generally implies transfer of liability to an insurance carrier.

The process of eliminating or reducing risk to manageable proportions is somewhat self-explanatory. This is usually done by programming security, safety procedures, and hardware to do away with the problem or reduce it to an acceptable or manageable level of severity. This is also referred to as risk control or loss control.

In assuming the risk, the company makes itself liable for the loss, if any, to be incurred. If the potential loss is deemed to be within the limits of what is an expected and otherwise acceptable loss, the risk may be recognized for what it is and just left alone. No effort is made to control, eliminate, or minimize the risk. No action is taken to correct the situation and no insurance is purchased to cover the risk. In some cases, a company may develop some form of self-insurance where the exposure or liability is assumed by the company itself. Generally, in most instances of risk assumption or retention the risk is perceived to be small enough that management is willing to assume total responsibility by absorbing any losses that may occur out of operating expenses.

When a company transfers a risk, the risk manager, who usually works in conjunction with an insurance broker, endeavors to find the best insurance program available from those carriers in the marketplace that provide the needed type of insurance coverage. This is no simple task and includes, among other things, determining the best deductible and premium payments available, which in the case of large companies often runs into the hundreds of thousands of dollars annually.

Risk management is constantly faced with the problem of the selection of the best method (or if necessary, some combination of methods) of handling each pure risk. Regardless of the method or combination of methods used, some basic considerations affect most insurance programs. To be insurable, risks must substantially meet the following requirements:

• The risk should be worth the cost and effort to insure.

• The risks are calculable through large numbers of similar risks.

• Losses can be clearly established as to occurrences and amounts.

• Losses must be accidental in nature, unexpected, and unintentional on the part of the insured.

Crime Insurance

Crime insurance is usually obtained to supplement a company's program. Although the presence or absence of insurance has no deterrent effect on crime, it does reimburse the company in whole or in part for losses sustained in a burglary, a robbery, or from internal theft. Crime insurance should, like other coverage, be tailored to meet the specific needs of the client.

As a minimum, most crime insurance programs begin with "3D," or comprehensive dishonesty, disappearance, and destruction, a blanket crime or broad-form storekeepers policy. This coverage will usually reimburse a company for losses due to employee dishonesty or counterfeit currency, as well as loss of money, securities, or merchandise through robbery, burglary, or mysterious disappearance. These policies also generally cover certain types of check forgery and damage to the premises or equipment resulting from a break-in.

Some forms of specialized crime insurance coverage for specific needs include:

• Mercantile Safe Burglary Policy. This covers loss of money, securities, and valuables from a safe or vault, and also pays for damage to the container and any other property damage as a result of the burglary.

• Mercantile Open Stock Policy. Mostly used by retail firms as coverage against burglary or theft of merchandise, furniture, fixtures, and equipment on premises, and will pay for damage to property resulting from burglary.

• Fidelity Bonds. This insurance coverage reimburses the employer for loss due to embezzlement and employee theft of money, securities, and other property. Bonds cover certain positions; employees who handle money, cash receipts, and merchandise are usually bonded.

• Forgery Bonds. This program reimburses merchants and banks for any loss sustained from the forgery of business checks.

Insurance premiums vary for these programs according to the type of business, store location, number of employees, maximum cash values, amount of security equipment installed on premises (alarms), and prior losses. Merchants operating in some high-risk crime areas and needing insurance most are often the least able to afford the premiums. Further, it is difficult to find insurance companies willing to underwrite crime coverage in some high-risk areas. Companies that experience a number of robberies or burglaries usually face escalating premiums, or worse, canceled policies.

For many small businesses and commercial enterprises, insurance and an antiquated burglar alarm may be the only form of protection affordable. For large companies and corporations, the reverse is true.

It is generally believed by knowledgeable corporate management, especially risk management, that insurance should only be used for protection against risk that cannot be avoided or controlled through the effective use of property, casualty, and security techniques. (In the insurance industry, property protection is synonymous with fire, and casualty is synonymous with safety.) This change in philosophy has come into vogue because more and more managers are getting the message that prevention, through risk avoidance, elimination, or control, is the best solution to the preservation of corporate assets. It is also recognized that most insurance programs do not fully compensate a firm for loss regardless of the coverage.

An analysis is normally done at the time the risk manager chooses to explore insuring this risk. Generally, the basic coverage provides reimbursement for loss of monies surrendered as a ransom payment for actual or alleged kidnapping or following receipt of a threat to injure or kidnap an insured person. Some of the various features that are usually incorporated into the policy contract are as follows:

•Business premises extension reimburses for any monies that must be brought in from outside for any kidnap situation if the money is lost while it is on the premises.

•Transit extension reimburses for any monies that are stolen between leaving the premises and reaching the kidnappers.

•Reward extension includes coverage for monies paid to informants whose information leads to the arrest and conviction of the individuals responsible for the kidnapping.

•Personal assets extension reimburses the insured persons for their personal assets that are used as ransom payment if the demand is made on the insured person and not the corporation.

•Negotiations, fees, and expenses reimburse for reasonable fees and expenses incurred to secure the release of a hostage, including interest on a bank loan to pay a ransom payment.

•Property damage coverage extension provides coverage for threats to cause physical damage to property.

•Defense costs, fees, and judgments cover costs resulting from any suit for damages brought by an insured person.

There are some general requirements, mostly concerning secrecy and the fact that the company has kidnap and ransom insurance coverage, of which the security professional should be aware. Here the caution is that specific details of each policy must be studied and adhered to in the event of a kidnap, for otherwise the incident may be non-insurable. Some considerations are:

•The ransom or extortion demand is specifically made against the named insured.

•The extortionate demand is made during the time frame of coverage as set forth in the policy.

•The company has taken every reasonable precaution to ensure that the knowledge of the existence of the coverage is not disclosed to anyone except senior officials of the corporation.

•If a kidnap occurs, the company should:

1.   Determine if the abducted person is insured under the company's policy. (Note: not all policies cover all employees.)

2.   Notify the police and/or Federal Bureau of Investigation (FBI) prior to payment. Comply with police and FBI instructions and recommendations.

3.   Notify the insurance company at the earliest practical time.

4.   Record the serial numbers of bills comprising the ransom payment.

Some underwriters (insurance carriers) require that immediately upon obtaining coverage, written policy and procedural guidelines be established to eliminate the possibility of confusion with regard to the handling of these matters. A prudent course of action is to develop a crisis management program specifically tailored to the requirements of the insured corporation. One of the benefits of contingency planning is to eliminate confusion before the crisis occurs, because once it happens, confusion usually reigns supreme in the absence of a well-thought-out and rehearsed plan.

James F. Broder, CPP

Source Broder, J.F., Risk Analysis and the Security Survey. (Butterworth-Heinemann, Boston, 1984).

RISK MANAGEMENT: QUANTIFYING AND PRIORITIZING LOSS POTENTIAL

The strength of the chain is measured by the weakest link. Very strong security in one area will not compensate for very weak security in another. In order to proceed to correct conclusions and then to recommendations for corrective action, it is necessary to quantify or prioritize the loss potential. For the professional, here lies a most difficult task -- the task of measurement or quantification of exposure.

Given adequate historical or empirical data, loss expectancy can be projected with a satisfactory degree of confidence. On the other hand, where there are insufficient data for reliable forecasting because the data either have not or cannot be collected, one is left with the nagging impression that conclusions will be nothing more than an exercise in educated guessing.

Many risks are classified as things that might happen but that have not yet occurred. Such risks can either be accepted or can be minimized, using prescribed preventive measures. Acceptance assumes that the risk is not sufficiently serious to justify the cost of reduction, or that recovery measures will ensure survival, or that the cessation of operations is an acceptable alternative if the risk should occur in its most serious magnitude. Minimizing the risk presupposes that it is or may be serious enough to justify the cost of eliminating or reducing the possibility of its occurrence, and that recovery measures alone will

Hazard Severity	Probability				
	Not Possible	Probable	50/50	Not Probable	Not Possible
Catastrophic	1	1	1	2	3
Critical	1	1	2	3	3
Marginal	2	2	3	3	3
Negligible	3	3	3	3	3

LEGEND
Probability: The chances of occurrence.
Hazard Severity: The consequences of occurrence.
Catastrophic: Death and/or very high dollar loss.
Critical: Severe injury or illness and high dollar loss.
Marginal: Minor injury or illness and moderate dollar loss.
Neglible: No injury or illness and little or no dollar loss.
1: Unacceptable risk.
2: Acceptable risk with limitations.
3. Permissible risk.

Risk Assessment Matrix

not always be effective in ensuring survival. Also, the remaining alternative -- cessation of operations -- is simply not an acceptable business option.

It is at this juncture that quantifying or prioritizing the loss potential becomes the hallmark of the true professional. Real talent comes into play when one is able to diagnose problems correctly and recommend necessary countermeasures to solve these problems without engaging in overkill. Granted, when we err it must be on the side of prescribing more rather than less security, but not to the level that turns a college campus, hospital, or hotel into a concentration camp.

There are always trade-offs when one considers the implementation of a new or improved security program. Cost is the most obvious. Less obvious and oftentimes overlooked is the inconvenience new security systems cause to personnel.

The probable impact on employee morale, especially if the employees perceive (rightly or wrongly) that the inconvenience caused them is greater than the threat, can often cause more harm than if management did nothing at all.

Assessing Criticality or Severity

Some will refer to this stage of the survey as assessing criticality or assessing the severity of occurrence. Regardless of the name of the process, it is vital that one search for and locate the proper benchmark to approximate adequately dollar values for the loss potentials previously identified. Once this is done, the task of comparing the cure to the disease becomes simplified. One can then design a list of meaningful priorities based on a common denominator -- the dollar.

One technique in use is the three-stage approach involving prevention, control, and recovery. Prevention attempts to stop security incidents before they get started. Control seeks to keep security incidents from impacting assets and/or, if impact occurs, to minimize the loss. Recovery restores the operation after assets have been adversely affected.

Many professionals take the approach that prevention is sufficient, and yet they opt for the installation of various control measures. It is one thing to install fire alarms that act to signal a serious situation, it is another to control and then recover from the effects of a fire. Similarly, it behooves a corporation not only to have adequate security in place to prevent kidnap attempts, but to design a contingency plan to deal with the kidnap event should preventive measures fail and the event become an actuality. In addition, nothing mentioned previously -- prevention, detection, control, or contingency planning – will preclude the necessity of having adequate insurance to help recover from a serious fire or ransom event.

Another technique for assessing security is to prepare a segmented schedule of overhead, installation, and operating costs for the security project. All costs identified must then be directly chargeable to expected benefits. In this process it is crucial to show that the benefits (risk prevention or reduction) will outweigh the cost. This is referred to as a cost/benefit summary and is useful for both existing and proposed security programs and projects.

The Decision Matrix

Another simple technique for prioritizing loss potential is the use of a decision matrix as an aid in making decisions about handling risk. The matrix uses the adjectives *high, medium,* and *low* as factors to measure both frequency and severity of loss.

The quantifying or prioritizing of loss potential should take into account the fact that there are both "intuitive" security control concepts, such as the installation of a burglar alarm at a warehouse, and security control concepts based on detailed cost/benefit analysis. An example of the latter is a multiple-stage electronic card access control system for the research and development laboratory of a computer manufacturer. The procedure for both will take into full consideration the following:
- Available information resources.
- Reliable probability relationships.
- Minimum time, and resource requirements and availability.
- Maximum incentives for management cooperation.
- A realistic evaluation of existing or planned security control effectiveness.

The means of protection designed must always be tailored to the specific risk as viewed in the real day-to-day working environment of the specific corporation being studied. The application of controls simply because they are recommended by a standard or practice without regard to risk in the real-world environment often results in controls that are inappropriate, ineffective, and costly.

The exercise of estimating risks for a specific undertaking is, at best, an imprecise measurement. The definition of risk using highly specific numbers has not always been validated by experience. Several well-known authorities have concluded that order of magnitude expressions such as low, moderate, and high to indicate relative degrees of risk are more than adequate for most risk control surveys.

The use of the terms *low, moderate,* and *high* equate roughly with probability ranges of 1 - 3, 4 - 6, and 7 - 10, respectively. One is cautioned here to remember that even a "low" risk should be taken seriously where the potential damage (or danger) is assessed as being moderate to high.

James F. Broder, CPP

Source Broder, J.F., Risk Analysis and the Security Survey.   (Butterworth-Heinemann, Boston, 1984).

RISK MANAGEMENT IN THE HOSPITAL SETTING

The term *risk management* is relatively new compared with security. However, the workings of a risk management program are not new, and the concept is not complex. That is not to say, though, that the application of the elements of a risk management program is simple.

The hospital security administrator may be more comfortable with terms such as *liability control, total security,* or *loss prevention.* These terms are essentially synonymous with risk management. The latter is defined differently in different hospital organizations and by different individuals.

Risk control begins with the identification and classification of the risks within a hospital. Once the risk has been identified, each risk must be viewed in terms of frequency, severity, and variability. First, this involves specific incidents and includes those risks that require some immediate action due to the high probability that the risk may lead to potential malpractice, worker's compensation, loss, or a general liability claim. Second, it involves areas where no specific incident has occurred, but circumstances indicate that the risk could result in a specific incident or claim. An example might be the foreseeability of a criminal act. Although a specific claim has not been made, the risk must be identified and measured, and appropriate preventive programming must be applied.

Beginnings of Risk Management

The promise by insurance companies, during the medical malpractice insurance crisis of 1974 to 1976, of reduced insurance premiums based on in-house risk identification, evaluation, and reduction or elimination undoubtedly provided the initial motivation for boards of directors and administrators to organize more formally the risk management function.   Subsequent strong support from the American Hospital Association, the Joint Commission on Accreditation of Hospital Organizations (JCAHO), state laws, and certain limited federal regulations catapulted risk management to the forefront of the new hospital management concepts.

A risk management program becomes more critical as an organization moves toward a self-insured program.   With self-insurance the financial issue becomes a matter of cash flow as opposed to simply budgeting an amount to be paid as an insurance company premium.

Components of a Risk Management Program. Although it varies from institution to institution, a written statement of function, authority, and responsibility is absolutely essential to the effective functioning of a risk management program. The security effort is only one of the several components of risk management. Numerous elements can be integrated into a coordinated program.

As one can see from its various elements, the risk management program is largely a staff function. The risk manager must report at least to the assistant administration level to ensure that the program has visibility, stature, and implied authority.

Risk Management and Quality Assurance. Risk management and quality assurance both are directed toward improving patient care and reducing liability. The basic difference between these two areas is in their emphasis. In risk management the focus is on potential liability throughout an institution.   Quality assurance relates to a greater degree to patient care.

In 1980 the American Hospital Association formed the Interdisciplinary Task Force on Quality Assurance and Risk Management. The task force concluded that the risk management and quality assurance functions sometimes overlap, and, "when they do, their purposes and methods are almost indistinguishable."

Centralization of Information. A basic foundation of the risk management program is the maintenance of a central record system. All incidents and accident reports, committee minutes, follow-up investigative reports, support documents, and correspondence are thus readily available.

The incident report is the basic document of the risk management program. It forms the basis for the investigation, review, and evaluation of the incident.   The form must be comprehensive enough to ensure completeness yet simple enough to enable a wide variety of personnel to complete it accurately.

The hospital risk manager should work very closely with the hospital attorney. Incident reports should be part of the attorney's working documents to prevent them from being discovered as evidence in litigation.

Committee/Team Approach. The key to a successful program is top-level administrative support of a risk management committee. The committee usually comprises representatives from the medical staff, administration, quality assurance, legal department, insurance department, and other appropriate areas. In some cases risk management teams are formed to review incidents before discussions begin at the formal meeting.   The team's role sometimes includes settling minor claims and preparing recommendations on incidents for the committee. Security and safety personnel are often involved with either the committee or the team because of their involvement with general liability claims or incidents.

Interrelationship of Security and Risk Management. The philosophy of a sound security program closely relates to a good risk management program; both should attempt to prevent a negative occurrence. This is done by attempting to identify a potential incident and taking corrective steps to prevent it, or at least to minimize its negative impact.

In the infancy of hospital security, guards, as they were known, provided rounds to deter crime and reduce the threat of fire, loss, or injury. This closely relates to the exposures that risk managers deal with: property loss, loss of key people, loss of net income, and liability exposure.

Even though the term *risk management* has only recently been formalized, security and safety personnel have been practicing this philosophy for many years. When both areas work together, a sound loss prevention system is developed.

As described, security and safety personnel tend to develop expertise in many general risk management principles. In Florida, for example, certification as a Certified Healthcare Protection Administrator through the International Healthcare Security and Safety Foundation automatically qualifies an individual to become a Certified Healthcare Risk Manager. Many security and safety professionals have expanded their expertise to become successful risk managers.

In any case, security managers need to adopt the management philosophy used by administrators, risk managers, quality assurance personnel, and JCAHO: (1) identify potential for loss or problems in advance, (2) analyze the problem, (3) examine all alternatives, (4) select the best technique, (5) implement the chosen technique, and (6) monitor and improve the technique.

Russell Colling, CPP

Sources

Monagle, J.F., Risk Management: A Guide for Health Care Professionals. (Aspen Systems Corporation, Rockville, MD, 1985).

Roll, F.G., Safety/Security and Risk Management. (Journal of Healthcare Protection Management, International Association for Hospital Security, Vol. 5, No. 1, Fall, 1988).

ROBBERY: INVESTIGATIVE CONSIDERATIONS

The crime of robbery is a serious offense capable of being carried out by a variety of means. Crime statistics show that robbers are not always men and that robbers come from a wide range of age, racial, social, economic, and occupational groups. The robber's principle motive is usually to obtain money, or property that is easily converted to cash. Robbery is also a crime that is sometimes committed in conjunction with another crime, such as murder or rape, and because robbery is a form of larceny that uses violence as its means, the investigative techniques used in larceny and assault cases have application to robbery cases.

Types of Robberies

Mugging. Mugging is a type of robbery committed by the muffling of the victim's mouth (or by choking) while forcibly taking property from the victim's possession. The amateur or inexperienced mugger will usually act on the earliest opportunity to victimize a lone person. He will act on the spur of the moment, usually with little or no preparation, and is acting in response to some urgent need for money, as for example the drug addict in early withdrawal who needs money to buy his next fix. At the other extreme is the experienced mugger who usually selects his target carefully and formulates a plan that includes a concealed location and an unobstructed escape route. His victims are chosen on the basis of the valuables they are expected to be carrying. The experienced mugger looks for high return at low risk. When a particular mugging method proves successful over a period of time, the experienced mugger will establish a modus operandi or pattern of activity.

A common example of a mugger's operandi is the yoking technique. The largest of a group of two or three muggers subdues the victim from behind by a strangle-hold on the neck. If there are three or more muggers the victim's arms are pinned while the last mugger, usually the smallest, searches the victim's pockets and removes valuables. Other similarities in the mugger's method of operation might include use of the same or similar locations such as parking lots or stairwells; weapons used, if any; the manner of approach; opening statement to the victim or other conversation leading up to the incident; and the use of violence inflicted in certain ways upon the victim. A particularly dangerous type of mugger is the sadist-flagellant robber whose primary motive is sexual gratification through inflicting injury on his victim. The theft aspect of the crime is merely a secondary consideration.

Robberies of Places. Banks, stores, and residences are common robbery targets. As is the case with mugging, this type of robbery can be committed by amateurs or professionals. The amateur robber is capable of traveling to and from the place of robbery in his own car or with a leased car, sometimes leased in his own name, or may travel on foot or even by bicycle. Because the inexperienced robber is certain to be nervous during the commission of the crime, he is apt to use violence unnecessarily. The experienced robber is likely to retain his composure and is comforted by the preparation and planning that has preceded the act. He knows what he is doing, is operating on a schedule, and realizes the risk of causing injury. He will usually use a stolen car, which he later abandons, or he might rent a car in a false name and use stolen plates.

Vehicle Robberies. The target of the crime is frequently a commercial-type vehicle carrying cash or high-value cargo. Vehicle robberies are more likely to be committed by experienced, professional robbers because of the requirements to obtain "inside" information concerning the valuables being transported, the schedule of the vehicle, and its defense capability. A vehicle robber needs also to stop his target, extricate the valuables, and safely get away.

Investigative Techniques

Robberies that are committed on the spur of the moment by amateurs or robberies that are committed by professionals only after long and intricate planning have at least one thing in common: they are both difficult to solve. Many robberies are committed during hours of darkness or under conditions that make it difficult for the robber's features to be seen by the victim. Adding to this is the fact that the attention of the victim is frequently focused on the weapon, thereby making it difficult for the victim to provide a good description of the suspect.

A robbery is usually reported fairly soon after it has happened. The investigator who is called to the scene of the robbery should follow the basic steps of crime scene processing. The crime scene is usually larger than the normal crime scene because it covers that territory where a robber may have lain in wait for his victim, the approach routes of the suspect and victim, the place of the robbery, and the escape route of the suspect. Persons who were present immediately before, during, and after the incident are potential witnesses. The investigator should question witnesses, as well as the victim, to determine the following:

• A description of the robber to include words used, voice peculiarities, gestures, mannerisms, and clothing.

• The direction and type of approach used by the suspect.

• A description of valuables taken.

• The victim's action prior to the robbery.

• The direction traveled by the robber when he left the scene and the method of travel.

After the victim has had time to compose himself and the investigator has had time to make a careful examination of the crime scene, a second interview should be conducted. The victim may remember details after he has settled himself emotionally and the investigator may have to ask specific questions to clarify details or develop leads on the basis of evidence discovered. The second interview can also be used as an opportunity to prepare a composite likeness of the suspect.

If an automobile is involved in the robbery, the investigator should obtain a detailed description of it from as many persons as possible. In addition to making a routine stolen vehicle check, the investigator should contact car rental agencies. When a rental automobile is used in the commission of a robbery, it is possible that a description will be obtained from the clerk who handled the rental transaction. If and when an abandoned vehicle used in a robbery is located, latent fingerprints and items recovered from it will provide valuable leads. Items of clothing found in the car or close to it should be checked for laundry marks or other peculiarities that may provide leads to the identity of the suspect. Footprints at the scene of an abandoned stolen vehicle should not be ignored. Valuable leads can also be developed from discarded items such as newspapers, matchbooks, and cigarette butts that are inside or around the vehicle.

When a robbery has occurred indoors, there should be an intensive search for latent fingerprints. Furniture, counter tops, and anything else that could have been touched by the robber should be processed for latent prints. Notes handed to a teller, discarded deposit slips, or counter checks not only provide opportunities to obtain fingerprints, but can also link the robber to the crime through handwriting analysis.

Some robbers feel a need to restrain their victims using such items as rope or adhesive tape. When rope has been used and to the extent that it is possible to do so, the investigator should obtain the rope with any knots still intact. The type of knot used by the robber may provide a link to him and to other crimes he may have committed. It may also be possible to trace the type of rope to a particular dealer. Adhesive tape has an especially high potential as evidence because it may be possible to obtain fingerprints from either side of it. It may also be possible to match the torn edge of the tape to the end of a roll of tape found in the possession of the suspect.

When interviewing witnesses or victims, the investigator should concentrate on determining the exact words used by the robber. The use of particular words or groups of words is valuable in matching the crime against previous robberies. The speech, gestures, and mannerisms of the robber are sometimes the only leads an investigator may be able to develop.

Any discussion of robbery is not complete without mention of the critical importance that informants can play in the identification and arrest of robbery suspects. While there is no replacement for hard work in developing physical evidence and testimony from people having knowledge of a robbery, there is tremendous value in obtaining the right piece of information from a confidential source who is in a position to know or acquire information beyond the influence of the investigator.

John J. Fay, CPP

Source Special Agent Manual. (Georgia Bureau of Investigation, State of Georgia, Atlanta, 1978).

S

SAFETY AUDITS

To be effective, safety audits should be a part of an established, well-organized safety program. The program provides the vehicle to implement and support the changes indicated by the audit findings.

The audit index (a document that establishes the guidelines for the audit) should be tailored to the needs of the organization and facility. The items to be examined on the index should be established from a number of sources, including Occupational Safety and Health Administration (OSHA), governing fire codes, predictable occurrences, safety guidelines provided by the manufacturer for equipment utilized at the facility, and housekeeping requirements.

Each index should include a section for problems that are not covered by the formal document, but which are observed and recognized as unsafe conditions or potential hazards. Every exception to the established guidelines should be noted in writing for use as a checklist to correct the condition.

The designation of the person or position to perform the audit should be established as a part of the audit program. In many companies the safety audits are performed as a function of the security department. A number of successful programs rely on management in the facility to perform the safety check. If the latter approach is selected, some mechanism must be established to ensure that the required attention and action is placed on the generation of the audit.

The audit must require a physical examination of each of the items, as opposed to completing the document from memory while seated in an office. To avoid neglect of this program, an established follow-up audit should be conducted periodically by a supervisor of the facility or a member of the security department. Where possible, the audits should be conducted on a monthly basis.

Whether the audit is conducted by a member of the security department or of the unit's staff, distribution of the finalized report should include the facility manager, that manager's supervisor, and the security and/or safety manager.

An excellent way to ensure audits are conducted and that action is initiated is to form a safety committee. Each of the findings can be discussed at the meeting of the committee, as well as the solutions to each problem. This not only allows for a more workable solution for the unit, but also builds a commitment to the agreed solutions.

Fire safety can be included as a part of the safety audit or established as a separate audit. However, fire safety is extremely important and must be examined as regularly as other safety considerations. The safety checklist should include the location of each of the fire extinguishers. These units should be checked monthly to ensure that they are in place and in working order. Each extinguisher should be re-certified each year and a tag that documents this check placed on the unit. The audit should include a test of the fire suppression equipment and any alarms regulating this equipment. The survey should include the examination of panic hardware, exit lights, and any other emergency-need equipment, such as emergency lighting.

A safety check should include the examination of any equipment while in use. The use of protective devices and gear by the operators of safety-sensitive equipment should be documented. Equipment in which safety features have been installed should be examined to ensure that these protections are not removed or circumvented. Heavy equipment, such as forklifts, should be examined, not only for safety features, but also for maintenance and operational or structural problems.

A complete list of all persons authorized to use the equipment should be posted next to each piece of equipment. This list should be corroborated by documentation, which indicates that age restrictions are not ignored, proper training has been given, a mandatory period of supervised operation has been completed, and that proper use of the required safety equipment was explained to the operator.

A signed certificate should be on file to ensure that the operator acknowledges the training and agrees to use safety protection equipment. The list should be checked against the certificate on file.

E. Floyd Phelps, CPP

SAFETY PROGRAMMING IN THE HOSPITAL ENVIRONMENT

The equipment, processes, and procedures used to cure illnesses and mend injuries combine to create an environment requiring a high level of safety programming. Despite this recognition of need for hospital safety programs by the public, employees, patients, insurance companies, the Joint Commission on Accreditation of Healthcare Organizations (JCAHO), and a whole host of governmental agencies, hospitals generally remain only partially committed. The general attitude is one of doing only what must be done to comply with the law and JCAHO standards.

OSHA and NIOSH

The purpose of the Occupational Safety and Health Administration (OSHA) Act of 1970 (U.S. Public law 91-596) is to ensure safe and healthful working conditions for employees and to preserve human resources. An initial goal of the Act was to reduce the employee accident rate by 45% in 3 to 5 years, and although the goal was considered realistic, it has never been achieved for a variety of reasons.

The law authorized the National Institute for Occupational Safety and Health. The institute's mission is to develop and establish recommended occupational safety and health standards, conduct research, and develop experimental programs to further new and improved practices and standards for worker safety.

A real step forward for hospital security is found in a 1988 NIOSH publication called *Guidelines for Protecting the Safety and Health of Health Care Workers.* In it NIOSH acknowledges that the assault of employees in and around hospitals is a growing problem and suggests 16 general guidelines for protecting workers from assault. These guidelines should not be construed as standards, but they are certainly a first step in developing awareness and fostering good security practices.

OSHA has launched a far reaching and costly program for preventing the spread of hepatitis B virus (HBV), which is a life-threatening bloodborne pathogen. Approximately 9,000 healthcare workers each year contract HBV. An OSHA standard that went into effect in July 1992 requires all employers to offer, at no cost to the employee, a series of three vaccinations to any employee who may be exposed to blood or other potential infectious materials as part of their job duties. Included in these employee groups are healthcare workers, morticians, law enforcement/correctional officers, launderers, and others.

Foundation of the Safety Program. Accident prevention is the key element of any safety program, and it is an integral part of the total healthcare process. Besides the JCAHO and the enactment of pertinent legislation, what prompts the establishment to make a good safety effort? At least one robust motivator for a workplace safety program is that accidents cost money. Any safety program established solely on the premise that management does not want its employees, patients, or visitors to suffer the pain of accidental injury is doomed to be ineffective or, at best, have very limited success.

Safety is not the organization's primary concern; its basic mission must come first. A safety program is neither more nor less important than supply, personnel, budget, or other administrative functions that are vital to the total operation of the healthcare facility. It should, however, become a part of the facility's every operation in order to contain costs and enhance the quality of every facet of the organization.

Safety activity in its broadest sense revolves around

- Management and personnel involvement
- Accident investigation and reduction of the probability of recurrence
- Facility inspections
- Policy and standards

Obviously each of these activities has many subcategories that are necessary elements of a successful safety effort.

Accident Reporting. The prevention of accidents is, of course, the primary objective of the safety effort, but accidents cannot be reduced unless problems are first identified. Identification of the problems through inspection must be supplemented by good accident and hazard reporting. Reporting accidents is the responsibility of every employee, and the stimulation and motivation of this responsibility are continuing functions of the protection program.

Timeliness of reporting is important. In organizations of any size, reports are often delayed because several people must sign or evaluate the document. At least one copy should be forwarded to the designated administrative office by the end of the shift during which the incident occurred. Even though this copy may not be complete, it serves as a timely notification of the incident.

Patient Accidents.   Reporting   patient accidents is generally the responsibility of the nursing service because it clearly falls into the realm   of   patient   care.   Only   in   rare circumstances would a security officer be called on to conduct an investigation or to file a report. These circumstances include a suicide or an attempted suicide, the disappearance of a patient, a fire, an assault, and when a patient accident occurs in a public area of the facility.

Employee Accidents. The responsibility for reporting employee accidents is usually assigned to the head of the department where the employee works. Thus, responsibility is fixed through the chain of command. Where the accident occurred is not germane to the responsibility of reporting it. The accident report should include the medical care that was rendered. Also, initial reports should not be overly complicated or time consuming; this will result in the delay or failure to report accidents.

Accident reports prepared by departmental heads are often incomplete. Supervisors intent on finishing their departmental responsibilities tend to complete the accident report as quickly as possible and often leave out important causative facts regarding the cause of the accident.   Another major problem is that supervisors often view the report as a fault-finding rather than a fact-finding tool. Supervisors,   either   consciously   or subconsciously, try to protect the employee and the department from being "blamed" for the occurrence.

In some organizations all employee accidents are reported via telephone to the security department. A security officer then responds to the scene of the accident and is responsible for the investigation and the reporting process.   More complete recording generally results from this system. It is much more efficient to train security staff in the proper completion of an accident report than to train the many department supervisors of an organization.   This approach is highly recommended for all organizations that have an organized security department.

Visitor   Accidents.   The reporting and investigation of visitor accidents is frequently neglected, despite the fact that the visitors are the source of many litigation proceedings against healthcare facilities. The basic problem appears to be that the responsibility for reporting visitor incidents is not fixed on a specific individual or department.   Because it is everyone's responsibility, it is sometimes not accomplished.

In one hospital the emergency room completed the incident report and forwarded it to the administration. Nurses simply recorded what the visitor stated were the facts.   A deficiency of this system was revealed when the security department was assigned the responsibility of investigating all visitor incidents. The new system required that employees who witnessed a visitor accident notify security. In addition, the emergency room personnel were required to call security if a visitor reported to the emergency room as the result of an accident on hospital property.

Hazard Reporting. Accident prevention also requires the reporting and correction of hazards. In their own areas, all employees should become the eyes and ears of the safety effort. There are two types of hazards.   Major hazards are generally reported immediately. However, no one bothers to report minor hazards, such as a broken piece of floor tile or a loose piece of molding. As for accident reporting, the system for reporting safety hazards must be simple. For organizations that maintain 24-hour security staff, a simple telephone call is the obvious method for reporting hazards.

Safety Inspections.   Employees cannot realistically report all hazards.   Periodic structured safety inspections are a necessary element of the safety program. The inspections of certain areas may require technical, operational, and procedural expertise.

653 Secular Humanism v. Natural Law

Regardless of the inspection area, the prime goal is to locate unsafe conditions and to observe unsafe acts. Where the latter are noted, the inspector should not correct the employee unless it is a matter of extreme urgency. Corrective behavior is the responsibility of the department supervisor, who must be made aware of the unsafe practice. The unsafe act may be an individual situation, or it may indicate the need for re-training an entire group of employees.

Security professionals do not always agree on the proper frequency of inspection. Inspections may be periodic, continuous, intermittent, or based upon a special need. Regardless of nomenclature, the entire complex must be inspected at least yearly, and certain areas should receive more frequent inspections as required by law or by good safety management. Safety inspections help to promote employee awareness. A safety inspector's presence in various hospital work areas, interacting with employees, forces employees to think about safety, however briefly. The activity of the safety inspector is tangible, not just a concept in the employee's mind.

Americans with Disabilities Act (ADA). This federal Act, signed into law in July 1990, prohibits discrimination by employers and businesses of persons on the basis of physical and/or mental disabilities. There is a phase-in period by size of organization so that by July 1994 the Act will apply to all employers with 15 or more employees. The human resources function of organizations will have the primary responsibility for compliance; however, safety departments will also be heavily involved, especially in the area of making "reasonable accommodation" for disabled persons in the workplace.

Need for Safety Professional. There is hardly an authority in existence who does not believe that a good safety program will not only pay for itself, but also save money and prevent human suffering. Why, then, is it so difficult to obtain funding for a safety professional from a hospital administrator?

One reason may be that the work of the safety person seems abstract. Furthermore, the immediate results of the safety program are not always readily apparent. The positive results of a good safety program may not be evident, at least

in financial terms, for several years. Finally, the intangibility of safety in the mind of the administrator often means that the safety effort is assigned a low priority. Many administrators simply do not fully understand the relationship between safety and quality patient care.

Russell Colling, CPP

Source Guidelines for Protecting the Safety and Health of Healthcare Workers. (U.S. Health and Human Services, September, 1988)

SECULAR HUMANISM v. NATURAL LAW

The American public generally accepted natural law, sometimes called the Judeo-Christian ethic, until recently. Secular humanism is a competing ethic which is quickly gaining adherents in our society. The successful protection of assets requires a knowledge of the ethical systems brought into the workplace, by management and line employees. Few persons operate solely under one system. For example, natural law is often applied at home and secular humanism at work.

Secular Humanism

The ethic is consequence oriented. Moral reference points are floating, not fixed. The individual's moral obligation is limited to taking the best course of action "for him" while taking into account all of the circumstances. The duty to obey the law becomes an empty concept unless it directly adds to the consequences. There is a duty to be honest only if that is the best thing to do under all the circumstances. The best result, for the individual, is always the goal sought. Each moral decision is approached from a subjective and situational perspective. This is a type of cost-benefit approach, cost being pain and benefit being happiness. Morality can only be defined as happiness as seen from one individual's point of view. As one example, greed may be seen as good. Another aspect of secular humanism is the belief that man is considered no more or less important than any other species.

Secular humanism naturally leads to a visible loss of trust in the workplace and overall ethical decline. This is true because, in effect, there are no rules, no absolute moral judgments. The work place is not seen as a community with shared goals and ethics.

Diversity abounds with each individual, or group of similarly minded persons, agitating for special privileges. Unfortunately, each one feels the same way. Laws, rules, and regulations are to be obeyed only if the results will benefit the special group or individual. It becomes difficult to know who to trust since everyone creates his or her own ethical universe.

Natural Law

This ethic is sometimes called the law of nature, instinctive and principal-based. Natural law has been discovered in ancient Hindu, Chinese, and Greek writings. Adherents to this system argue that there is a higher law, and that we are obligated to obey it. Moral awareness and duty are characteristic of natural law.

A familiar example to most Americans is the Golden Rule -- "Do unto others what you would have them do unto you." Thus, even while some may steal, no one wants his own property stolen. The natural law is said to condemn such things as wickedness, evil, and greed. By it we are made ashamed of adultery, theft, murder, and other crimes.

The basis for human law is natural law. Society needs a common moral code that binds us together -- without it society leans toward chaos and self-destruction. Under natural law, we are obligated to do what is right whether or not the consequences are of benefit to us as individuals.

Ends, or consequences, are uncertain and should not be considered in making an ethical decision. Ends cannot be justified by the means utilized – in either public or private transactions. Values are shared and reinforced by society as a whole. Accountability is stressed for personal and business choices. The value of human life is paramount over all other species. Finally, ethical choices revolve around reference points that cannot be moved.

Norman R. Bottom, Jr., Ph.D., CPP

SCREENING EMPLOYEES

Employers have a legitimate need to know certain things about their employees. The employee's ability, honesty, and prior employment history are clearly reasonable job-related inquiries for an employer to scrutinize in its employment screening process. Workplace privacy, however, becomes more difficult when an employer wants to know if the employee smokes marijuana at home, is a homosexual, or socializes with the "wrong" kind of people; i.e., do these inquiries serve legitimate job-related purposes? It is against these employee privacy interests that the employer's "need to know" in screening job-related information must be balanced.

Workplace Privacy

Workplace privacy concerns the nature and extent of an employee's right to be free from unwarranted non-job-related employer intrusions. It arises whether or not an employment relationship is created. Involved are employment information: (1) collection for hiring decisions; (2) storage, retention, and maintenance; (3) internal use in making decisions after hiring; and (4) disclosure to third parties. Accompanying these employment information interests is employee lifestyle regulation at and outside the workplace.

After an application is submitted, employers use various procedures to verify employee information. Verification is the selection method that checks applicant information accuracy. Almost every qualification an applicant offers for employment consideration can be verified. Verification sources include previous employers, schools, colleges, military records, certifying or licensing bodies, public records, and so forth. Public records include those from courts, law enforcement agencies, licensing bureaus, tax assessors, and financial departments.

Certain verification information may be irrelevant and not job-related. To safeguard employee privacy interests and minimize employer litigation exposure, procedures and policies must be developed to counteract these problems.

Credit checks, arrest records, criminal convictions, reference checks, skill testing, employment records, and medical records offer particular employer screening problems.

Credit Checks

Credit information collection, maintenance, use, and disclosure present significant employee privacy concerns by potentially revealing non-job-related data affecting speech, beliefs, and associational interests. Federal and state statutes place certain restrictions on credit information used for employment purposes. Non-job-related credit reports may violate federal and state fair employment practice (FEP) statutes. A requirement that applicants and employees have a good credit record may have to be justified by a legitimate job-related business necessity.

To ensure that employee privacy interests are observed in undertaking a credit check, an employer should [1]:

•Select a reputable credit agency and periodically review the choice;

•Notify the applicant and/or employee that a credit check will be performed and indicate to the individual:

1. The types of information expected to be collected that are not collected on the application, and, as to information regarding character, general reputation, and mode of living, each area of inquiry;

2. The techniques that may be used to collect the information;

3. The sources that are expected to provide the information;

4. The parties to whom and circumstances under which information about the individual may be disclosed without authorization and the information that may be disclosed;

5. The statutory procedure by which the individual may gain access to any resulting record;

6. The procedures the individual may use to correct, amend, or dispute any collected record; and

7. That information in any report prepared by a consumer reporting agency may be retained by that organization and subsequently disclosed by it to others.

•Obtain the applicant's and/or employee's written consent for undertaking a credit check;

•Not share the information received with potential creditors;

•Limit credit checks to job-related information and purposes;

•Consider credit information highly confidential and sensitive; and

•Certify that credit information will only be used for job-related purposes.

Arrest Records

Many employers believe that arrest history is critical, or at least relevant, to employment. Arrest information raises employee privacy concerns because it indicates only that a law enforcement agency believed that probable cause to arrest existed for some offense. It does not reflect guilt, nor that the person actually committed the offense.

Refusing employment or terminating employees because of arrest records is not permitted without evidence that it is job-related to the employer's business. Certain state statutes prohibit arrest record inquiries. Even when a legitimate pre-employment inquiry is made regarding arrest records, an applicant's rejection based solely on an arrest record may violate federal and state FEP statutes. The following should be considered regarding arrest records and their possible employment use:

•Whether the state's statute prohibits arrest record inquiries;

•That a differentiation be made between arrest and conviction;

•That a careful evaluation be made of the frequency and severity of arrests;

•Age at time of the arrest;

•The elapsed time since an arrest;

•The whole individual: that is, his or her aptitude, abilities, interests, and educational level, rather than one aspect of personal history;

•The job's nature and its relation to the employability of those with arrest records; and

•Geographic location of the incidents involved.

Criminal Convictions

Criminal convictions present different employee privacy concerns than do arrests. A conviction is a societal judgment regarding an individual's actions. Unlike arrests, a conviction record is complete. Guilt and accountability have been finalized.

Even though an employer may take legitimate employment actions based on criminal convictions when it correlates to the offense's nature, gravity, and time elapsed since the conviction to job-relatedness, privacy concerns remain over subsequent use and disclosure that impact associational and lifestyle interests. Conviction record use may violate federal and state FEP statutes. Employers must consider a conviction's legitimate job-related circumstances regarding impact and effect before determining that employment would be inconsistent with safe and efficient business operation. These circumstances include:

• The job and its responsibilities;
• The time, nature, and number of convictions;
• Each conviction's facts;
• Each conviction's job-relatedness;
• The length of time between a conviction and the employment decision;
• Employment history before and after the conviction;
• Rehabilitation efforts;
• Whether the particular conviction would prevent job performance in an acceptable businesslike manner;
• Age at the time of the conviction; and
• The conviction's geographic location.

Reference Checks

Reference checks represent another employer effort to compile and verify the most complete and accurate information regarding applicants. Requesting detailed references from former employers is one precaution an employer can take during the hiring process to limit its vulnerability to employment litigation. By failing to request references, the employer may risk negligent hiring liability. Negligent hiring arises out of employee acts committed while in the employer's service but outside the employee's employment scope. While an employer generally is not liable for employee acts outside of the employment's scope, employer liability for negligent hiring has been found where an employee was responsible for others' safety or security.

Some states statutorily regulate employee references. Federal or state FEP statutes, along with claims for invasion of privacy and defamation, may also offer employee protection. In checking references, the following should be considered:

• Obtain the employee's written permission to check references;
• Check references before making the final job offer;
• If a discrepancy exists between facts or recommendations, a more extensive investigation should be undertaken;
• Be skeptical of all subjective evaluations, especially those that do not include verifiable acts or behavior; and
• View silence as an indication for further investigation; an employer may attempt to avoid wrongful termination litigation by negotiating a settlement with an employee that includes no favorable references.

Skill Testing

It has generally been considered that skill testing offers an objective standard by which to predict job performance. Some tests, however, eliminate minorities from certain positions by favoring education levels typical of a white, middle-class background. Performance by the economically disadvantaged on some tests has been poor.

Educational and industrial psychologists have played a major role in developing tests that attempt to predict job performance. These tests remove some of the subjectivity used in employee selection. Employment testing has developed into a highly sophisticated and technical field with its own language, its own standards, and its own complex methodology.

For employee privacy, testing can have a significant impact on information collection, maintenance, use, and disclosure. Depending upon the test, it may reveal privacy interests present in the employee's speech, beliefs, information, association, and lifestyle. These privacy concerns are essentially protected by federal and state FEP statutes.

Under the Civil Rights Act of 1964 (Title VII), the Uniform Guidelines on Employee Selection Procedures have been developed. The guidelines define a selection procedure broadly as any measure, combination of measures, or procedure used as a basis for an employment decision, including hiring, promotion, membership, referral, retention, selection, training, or transfer. Selection procedures include traditional paper and pencil tests, performance tests, training programs, probationary periods; informal or casual interviews; unscored application forms; and physical, educational, and work experience requirements.

Title VII does not prohibit employers from giving or acting on the results of a professionally developed ability test where the test, its administration, and action on it are not designed, intended, or used to discriminate. However, a professionally developed test must be job-related. To safeguard employee privacy interests in testing, the employer should:

• Not over rely on tests;

• Use other screening methods, including interviews, background verifications, and reference checks, along with tests;

• Use test results as added information, not as the sole criteria to disqualify an employee;

• Contact the test's developer to re-check the test if someone receives an extremely poor score but has good recommendations, job performance, and so forth;

• Use tests at the end of the hiring process when applicants have been narrowed to the best choices;

• Maintain test score confidentiality; and

• Ensure that the test is in fact job-related and does not measure extraneous non-job-related factors.

Employment Records

Employer methods for collecting, maintaining, accessing, using, and disclosing employment information vary. Certain employment record aspects are regulated by federal and state statutes. These statutes generally set forth what employment information may be collected, along with providing for employee access and right to review and copy record contents. Some statutes permit employees to place a counterstatement in the record when information is incorrect or challenged.

Overall considerations for preparing employment record privacy procedures and policies should include:

• A uniform system of collecting, maintaining, accessing, using, and disclosing employment information;

• Preserving and protecting employee privacy confidentiality;

• Collecting employment information by reviewing [2]:

1. The number and types of records maintained;

2. Information items;

3. Information uses made within the employer's decision-making and nondecision-making structure;

4. Information disclosure made to those other than the employer; and

5. The extent to which employees are aware and regularly informed of the uses and disclosures that are made of this information.

• Fair information collection procedures and policies concerning applicants, employees, and former employees that [3]:

1. Limit information collection to that which is job-related;

2. Inform what records will be kept;

3. Inform of the uses to be made of this information;

4. Adopt procedures to ensure information accuracy, timeliness, and completeness;

5. Permit review, copying, correction, or information amendment;

6. Limit internal use;

7. Limit external disclosures, including disclosures made without authorization, to specific inquiries or requests to verify information;

8. Provide for a regular policy compliance review;

9. Contain an employment application with a waiver authorizing the employer to disclose employee file contents to those to whom the employee grants access, that is, reference checks by subsequent employers, and to make a credit check where applicable;

10. Indicate on the file when and where these employee reviews took place;

11. Restrict information access to those with a need to know and those who are authorized outside of the employer, such as law enforcement and regulatory officials;

12. Ensure that information retention conforms to applicable law; and

13. Contain a privacy clause.

Medical Records

Medical records may contain employee personal details regarding age, life history, family background, medical history, present and past health or illness, mental and emotional health or illness, treatment, accident reports, laboratory reports, and other scientific data from various sources. They may also contain medical providers' notes, prognoses, and reports of the patients' response to treatment. Should this medical information be disclosed, it could cause embarrassment, humiliation, damage to family relationships, or even employment termination, while infringing privacy rights related to speech, associations, and lifestyles.

A privacy interest in medical records has been partially acknowledged, and the employee privacy interest in preserving medical record confidentiality has been recognized by federal and state privacy statutes. Society's legitimate need for this information may supersede an employee privacy interest even though an employee's medical records, which may contain intimate personal facts, are entitled to privacy protection. Employee privacy rights must be evaluated against the public interest represented by certain government investigations.

Employers should take precautions to protect medical information confidentiality by restricting access to managerial employees who have a legitimate job-related business interest in obtaining the information. Except in emergency situations, employers should avoid seeking medical information directly from an employee's physician without prior employee consent. Employee hospital records should be accorded similar deference.

In developing medical record procedures, the employer should consider the following [4]:
• Medical information disclosure;
• The relationship between the employee and employer regarding any third party requesting the information;
• The employee's privacy interest in not releasing the information;
• The employer's statutory or other duty to disclose the information;
• Identity of the person making the request;
• The request's purpose;
• Restricting disclosure to only necessary information.

When an employee who is the subject of medical information maintained by an employer requests correction or amendment, the employer should:
• Disclose to the employee, or to a person designated by him or her, the identity of the medical information's source;
• Make the requested correction or amendment within a reasonable time period if the person who was the information's source concurs that the information is inaccurate or incomplete; and
• Establish a procedure for an employee who is the subject of employer medical information to present supplemental information for inclusion in the employer's medical information, provided that the supplemental information's source is also included.

Kurt H. Decker

Sources
Decker, K., Employee Privacy Forms and Procedures. (John Wiley & Sons, Inc., New York, 1988).

Decker, K., A Manager's Guide to Employee Privacy Law, Procedures, and Policies. (John Wiley & Sons, Inc., New York, 1989).

Decker, K., Employee Privacy Law and Procedures. (John Wiley & Sons, Inc., New York, 1987).

Decker, K., The Rights and Wrongs of Screening. (Security Management, January, 1990).

Notes
1. See Privacy Protection Study Commission, Personal Privacy In An Information Society, pp. 250-251 (1977).
2. Ibid., p. 235.
3. Ibid., pp. 237-238.
4. Ibid., p. 263.

SEARCH AND SEIZURE

The Fourth Amendment to the Constitution of the United States guarantees the right of the people to be secure in their persons, houses, papers, and effects against unreasonable searches and seizures. The words used in the Constitution are directed at unreasonable searches and seizures conducted by the government. Unfortunately, however, the

Constitution does not go on to define what is meant by the term "unreasonable," nor does the law discuss any provision for punishment of persons who violate the Fourth Amendment. It has been left up to the U.S. government and the various states to create definitions of search and seizure violations, and to provide suitable punishment when violations are proven. At the federal level, Title 18 of the United States Code provides fines and imprisonment for persons found guilty regarding searches. Most states have tended to model their search and seizure laws in conformance with the federal law. Where differences might exist between a particular state and the overall guiding federal law, the difference is more likely to be a matter of semantics rather than spirit or intent of the law.

In addition to possible criminal prosecution for violations of law regarding illegal search and seizure, the offending person is likely to be charged in a civil suit for damages resulting from the violation. A defense is possible, however, if it can be shown that the searching official was acting in good faith, according to an official duty. An official who uses bad judgment and conducts an illegal search has an excuse, but when the search is conducted illegally by intent, or not in connection with official duties, then the official can be charged with a violation.

Basic Concepts

The law on search and seizure requires an understanding of certain basic concepts.

Search. The term "search" denotes the examination of an alleged or suspected offender or his house or other building or property. The examination must be conducted in the normal course of enforcing the law or maintaining order. The examination must have a purpose of looking for some specific item or items. Items looked for will fall into one or more of the following categories: contraband, tools of a crime, fruits of a crime, or incriminating evidence. For an examination to be properly called a "search," the person conducting the examination must have some legal status. Not only must the searcher be duly empowered by law to make searches, but he must also possess a specific authority for conducting a particular search at a particular place at a particular time to look for particular

items. There are several ways for a searching official to demonstrate his authority to search. Most common among these is the search warrant. The term "search" does not include other kinds of "looking" functions. For example, an inspection of a place with a view towards reducing fire hazards is not a search. The close examination of an entry pass by a security officer is not a search.

The plain view doctrine is a rule of law that states it is not a search within the meaning of the Fourth Amendment to observe that which is open to view, provided that the viewing officer has a lawful right to be there. No warrant is required to seize items in plain view. Plain view exists when an officer who had justification for intrusion in the course of official duties inadvertently comes into contact with contraband in open view, and prior to the discovery was unaware of the existence of the contraband before coming upon it unexpectedly. The doctrine relies on the presumption that the officer has a right to be in a place where evidence or contraband is seen in an area open to plain viewing. An example would be an officer who is called to the scene of an assault and observes cocaine on a coffee table. The officer is legally on the premises and can seize the cocaine. However, if the cocaine was viewed by an officer observing through an open window, not in connection with official police business, the plain view doctrine would not apply. In this case, a search warrant would be required to make a search and seizure.

Seizure. The term "seizure" denotes the taking of contraband, fruits of a crime, tools of a crime, or incriminating evidence. The person taking the items must be empowered to make the seizure, and the items seized must be protected until disposed of in some proper fashion. If, for example, the item seized is a stolen ring, the ring will be safeguarded as evidence until the trial is completed. When the judicial action against the offender is ended, the ring will be returned to the owner. For some kinds of seized items, final disposition might be destruction. Narcotics, certain kinds of weapons, and illegal whiskey are examples of items that are usually destroyed after court action has ended.

Search Warrant. The term "search warrant" means a written order issued by competent legal authority that directs a search to be conducted. The warrant specifies who is to conduct the search, who or what place is to be searched, and the items to be looked for during the search. The warrant is made valid for only a certain limited period of time. In some cases a warrant might direct that the search be made at some particular time of night or day, but a warrant is never prepared so that the searcher can wait many days or weeks before deciding to carry out the warrant. A warrant is issued on the basis of a need that exists at the time the warrant is requested. The need cannot be interpreted to spread out over a long period of time. It should also be noted that the word "warrant" itself means an order. Although the person or agency carrying out the warrant was the requester of the warrant in the first place, it is the issuing judge who gives the order for a search to be conducted. A warrant is therefore not simply a permit granted to someone to conduct a search, it is an order to do so. That order is very specific in what must be done. The warrant will name a person or small number of persons who will carry out the warrant. The warrant will name the person, place, or property to be searched. Knowing the details of the area to be searched is sometimes of great importance to the requester of a warrant. For example, it might be very important to know that the building to be searched has a separate shed. Unless the shed is included in the warrant, it cannot be lawfully searched. It might be that the items to be looked for are in the shed. A little advance knowledge on the part of the searcher is important in getting a properly worded warrant. Along the same line, it is important that the warrant include mention of all items that are useful as evidence. If the case involves a search for an automatic rifle, the person requesting the warrant would want to include mention of ammunition, ammunition clips, magazines, or parts pertaining to the type of automatic rifle involved. If the warrant simply names the rifle as the item to be looked for, the searcher cannot technically seize anything except the rifle and misses the chance of getting other pieces of evidence related to the same crime. Advance preparation in the wording of a warrant is therefore important.

A warrant is specific in one other regard. The judge's order will direct that any seized property be taken to some designated place or agency. Seized items are sometimes regarded as property of the court until such time as the items are properly disposed of, with disposition instructions normally issued by the court in writing. The proper safeguarding of seized property requires that the property be inventoried at the time it is seized. The inventory is placed into writing, usually on a receipt type of form that lists all items taken. The copy of the receipt is given, with the search warrant, to the person from whom the items were taken. If no such person is available, the receipt and search warrant are left at the place of seizure. The original copy of the receipt remains with the seized items and is used to account for the property from the time of seizure until the time of final disposition.

Affidavit.   The term "affidavit" describes a written document that is used to support or justify the issuance of a search warrant. An affidavit is nothing more than a written statement made under oath. It sets forth details that provide the issuing judge with enough information for him to conclude that a crime was committed and that a search of a certain place will probably reveal the presence of some evidence pertaining to that crime. The affidavit therefore provides the type of information that is sometimes called "probable cause."

An affidavit might read as follows:

I, John Doe, having been duly sworn, on oath depose and state that at 11:30 p.m., July 1st, 1993, at the premises of ABC Company, 1000 Main Street, Houston, Texas, a person unknown did steal a carton containing a Carrier air-conditioning unit, model X, serial number 123456, valued at $800.00. The affiant further states that Alfred Aware, a security officer at the premises, reported that at 11:30 p.m., July 1st, 1993, he observed a person exit a rear loading door of the building and place a large carton into the rear of a station wagon. Before Mr. Aware could reach the scene, the station wagon fled the area. Mr. Aware did, however, note the license plate number of the station wagon. A check with the license plate bureau revealed the owner of the suspect station wagon to be Billy Badguy, a tenant at 1115 North Street,

Houston, Texas. An interview with Mrs. Betty Busybody, landlady at 1115 North Street, revealed that after midnight on July 1st, 1993, she observed Mr. Badguy carry a large carton into his rented room. She described the carton as having writing that said the carton contained a Carrier air-conditioning unit. In view of the foregoing, the affiant requests that authorization be issued for a search of rooms at 1115 North Street, Houston, Texas, that are rented and controlled by the person identified as Mr. Badguy, and that such authorization include seizure of a Carrier air-conditioning unit, serial number 123456.

Signed, John Doe

Sworn to and subscribed before me this Third Day of July 1993, at Houston, Harris County, State of Texas.

Signed, Lawrence Law, District Attorney

In this fictionalized sample of an affidavit, the most important pieces of information were provided by a security officer. The security officer provided the time, date, place, a description of the property stolen, and certain other details that led to an identification of the suspect.

In other words, the security officer observed and made notes as to the who, what, when, where, and how of an offense. It is this kind of basic information that will add up to a total picture so as to provide probable cause for a judge to issue a search warrant. The basic information in the affidavit demonstrates firstly that a crime happened. The affidavit then leads to a reasonable conclusion that some evidence of that particular crime will probably be found at a certain place. When these requirements are satisfied, a judge will likely grant the request for a search warrant.

A few other terms need to be explained regarding searches. We have already mentioned the terms "contraband," "fruits of the crime," "tools of the crime," and "incriminating evidence." Items to be looked for and seized in connection with a search will fall into one or more of these four categories.

Contraband. Contraband is any item that, by itself, is a crime to have. Bootleg whiskey is contraband because possession of it is against the law. The same holds true for certain types of firearms, explosives, illegal narcotics, marijuana, pornographic materials, and counterfeit money. Search warrants are issued to cover the seizure of contraband when it is known in advance that contraband is present at a certain place. If such contraband is seized without getting the search warrant, the seizure is illegal; however, contraband that is discovered accidentally can be seized without a warrant. In regard to contraband, it can always be seized. How it was seized will determine whether the contraband can be used as evidence against the person responsible for it.

Fruits of the Crime. This is a term referring to that advantage which is derived by the criminal who commits a crime. A stolen television set and swindled money are all examples of fruits of crime.

Tools of the Crime. This term refers to the devices used in the commission of the illegal act. Tools in this sense obviously include burglary devices such as a jimmy, lock pick, bolt cutter, and so forth. Tools also include a worthless check, a false document, or even a fraudulent advertisement.

Incriminating Evidence. The term "incriminating evidence" covers a wide range of items. In this category are items that tend to show involvement of a suspect or an accomplice in a criminal activity. The item could be a shirt bearing blood stains acquired during the crime, it could be a diary containing references to a crime, it could be a photograph showing some relationship to a crime, or it could even be a tape recording of accomplices discussing a crime.

Reasonableness. An understanding of the foregoing terms will be of assistance in understanding further concepts associated with search and seizure. One other term, which is common to everyday language, should be looked at in respect to the matter of legal searches. The term "reasonable" is sometimes used to describe the nature of a search conducted with authority of a search warrant. Since probable cause has to be present for a search warrant to be issued, it can be said that the search was reasonable. The term reasonable then becomes almost identical with words like "constitutional," "lawful," or "legal." The term "unreasonable" is therefore just the opposite of "reasonable" in meaning. "Unreasonable" has often been used to describe searches that were conducted without benefit of a search warrant. An example of an "unreasonable search" would be an examination of a place for the purpose of finding any kind of evidence that might possibly be used against a person. This type of search is unreasonable because it is not specific in terms of what item or items are expected to be found. Such a search is exploratory and is in the nature of a fishing expedition.

Search without a Warrant. This does not mean that only searches conducted with warrants can be properly called reasonable. A search with a warrant is certain to be reasonable, but other searches can be considered reasonable, if they are conducted under certain conditions. Let us look at those situations in which it is possible to conduct reasonable searches without the use of a search warrant.

Search Incidental to Arrest. Perhaps the most common type of search is the search made in connection with an arrest. A check of a person's possessions at the time he is taken into custody is mainly intended to discover the presence of weapons that can be used against the arresting person. The arresting person has a right to protect himself from attack by a weapon concealed on the body of the arrested person. A search at the time of arrest is mainly directed toward this consideration. A second consideration for the arresting person is to see if the offender has any evidence on his person that is connected with a crime. It is important that the evidence be taken before the suspect has an opportunity to destroy or discard it. A frisk or wall search will normally reveal the presence of weapons or destructible evidence. The frisk and wall search are called precautionary searches because they are designed to take precautions against attack and against the chance of losing valuable evidence. Property in the possession of the arrested person can be searched. This would include packages, brief cases, and the like. The place under immediate control of the arrested person can be searched for evidence connected to the crime. Thus, when a person is arrested in his private office, the unlocked areas of the office can be legally searched. If the arrest is made in a building lobby, the lobby cannot be searched because it is not under immediate control of the suspect at the time of arrest. Vehicles driven by an arrested person can be searched, but only those areas of the vehicle that are controlled by the suspect. The trunk of a vehicle is not considered to be under control of the suspect at the time of arrest. If it is felt that a search of the trunk will probably yield evidence connected to a crime, a search warrant can be requested. If the arrested person is a woman, the search can include only the purse, coat, parcels, baggage, or other articles not worn by her.

The Emergency Search. Another type of lawful search and seizure is the looking for and taking of criminal goods before those goods can be disposed of. This form of search is in the nature of an emergency action that is taken to prevent the removal, destruction, or further hiding of property illegally held by a suspect. To illustrate, assume a company employee discovers that three rolls of 25-cent pieces are missing from a box containing the company's petty cash fund. The employee calls the security office and explains that he knows the missing rolls of quarters were in the box minutes prior to the time the cleaning man had access to the cash box, and the cleaning man is getting ready to leave the company premises. Under circumstances like this, a search of the cleaning man would be justified. A search is justified because facts show that a crime was committed, that the stolen property is probably in the possession of the suspect, that the suspect is leaving and there is no time to obtain a search warrant, and that to recover the stolen property it is necessary to take emergency action before the suspect can leave with the stolen money.

Search with Consent. Another kind of search not requiring a warrant is search by consent. The consent must be freely and intelligently given. Consent cannot be obtained through the use of threats or trickery. The person giving permission to search his person or property must do so in a completely willing manner. For the consent to be intelligently given, the person must be able to recognize the consequences of permitting a search. A person who is too young, too old, too drunk, retarded, ill, or insane cannot intelligently give consent to a search. Also, mere submission or giving in to a request for consent is not the same as giving a free consent. In order to demonstrate that consent to search was freely and intelligently given, the security officer should obtain the consent in writing. The writing itself, the words used, and the physical act of writing help to demonstrate that the consent was properly obtained.

Any consent obtained must be obtained from the person who has a right to give the consent. A hotel manager cannot give consent to search a paying guest's hotel room. A person sharing an apartment cannot give consent to a search of another person's property within the apartment. This is an important point to remember when asking for consent to conduct a search.

Purposes of a Search

It can be said that a search and seizure action has two overall purposes. One is to discover and obtain evidence that will bring the criminal to justice. The other is to recover property that belongs to another person. A search and seizure that achieves both these purposes is what we strive for.

Sometimes, because of improper methods in a search, the goal of justice is not realized. Evidence is inadmissible in a court of law if it was obtained as the result of an unlawful search or seizure. The law also goes on to provide that other evidence obtained later, quite lawfully, cannot be used if it was connected in any way with a preceding unlawful search. For instance, assume that an unlawful search resulted in the discovery of a notebook containing information that led to the identification of other accomplices and hiding places of stolen property. Any evidence discovered from lawful searches made of the accomplices and the hiding places cannot be made in court. For this reason it is important to keep in mind the major points of law dealing with search and seizure.

John J. Fay, CPP

SEARCH AND SEIZURE: FOURTH AMENDMENT PROTECTIONS

The Fourth Amendment to the United States Constitution specifically provides:

> The right of the people to be secure in their persons, houses, papers, and effects against unreasonable searches and seizures, shall not be violated, and no warrants shall issue, but upon probable cause, supported by oath or affirmation, and particularly describing the place to be searched, and the persons or things to be seized.

In general, the Fourth Amendment addresses the manner in which searches and seizures of evidence may be made and the manner in which arrests of individuals may be conducted by government officials. With certain exceptions, neither arrests nor searches or seizures may be made without a warrant.

Private Searches and Seizures

With the exception of Montana and California, private security agents are generally not held to Fourth Amendment standards. From an investigative standpoint, they are limited in the benefits the Fourth Amendment provides. In particular, private agents cannot independently obtain and execute a search warrant in connection with an investigation. However, a private agent can swear out an affidavit for a search warrant. A district magistrate can then act on the affidavit and issue a warrant. The execution of the warrant must, though, be made by a public agent. Therefore, private investigations are coordinated with public authorities when actions such as searches pursuant to a warrant are required.

In those instances when an actor consents to a search and related seizure, no warrant is required and the private actor can proceed without the assistance of public authorities. Under these circumstances, the actor should be asked to execute a written consent to search and seize. As in the case of any other consent, the consent must fall within the guidelines provided previously.

Private Arrest Contemporaneous with Investigations

As with search warrants, a private agent cannot obtain and execute an arrest warrant. Again, though, the private agent can swear out a complaint against a particular actor. If approved, the district magistrate can either issue a summons, which can be sent through the mails, or issue an arrest warrant. A police officer or the constable for the magistrate can then proceed on the warrant and arrest the subject.

In general, arrests without warrants are common in those instances where a serious offense is committed in the presence of another and in instances where there is probable cause to believe such an offense has occurred or is about to occur. A distinction is made between public and private practitioners when the act is not actually witnessed. With few exceptions, private security officers cannot proceed in effecting an arrest on probable cause regardless of the extent of their beliefs.

While an eventual arrest may or may not occur in a private investigation, the private agent should be aware of the general parameters of security arrest powers. In general, private security powers of arrest are either addressed in specific state statutes or in court opinions. In many instances there is a state statute specifically addressing the parameters under which a private security officer may make an arrest. In other instances the statutes relating to arrests may be limited to retail theft (shoplifting) with other guidelines provided by the courts for other crimes. In still other instances the entire body of law relating to arrest exists in court opinion.

In instances where arrest authority is specified by statute, a private practitioner should be familiar with the parameters of those statutes. In those instances where the courts have established the existing law relating to private agent arrest, this section will provide some general guidelines. These guidelines, however, do not apply in all jurisdictions. For practical purposes, the reader is encouraged to study the court opinions of the jurisdiction in question.

Generally, under common law, any private citizen can effect an arrest without a warrant for felony offenses committed in his or her presence. In certain jurisdictions this has likewise been expanded to misdemeanor offenses that specifically involve breaches of the peace committed in the citizen's presence. Certain other jurisdictions have expanded the felony arrest law to include those instances where the citizen possesses probable cause to believe a forcible felony has been committed.

In most jurisdictions, unless a private agent has received specific, official commissioning as a "private police officer" or "special police officer," he or she is considered a citizen and is mandated by those laws relating to citizen's arrest without a warrant. One exception relates to security officers employed in the retail arena. In these instances, a security officer is often provided statutory authority to "apprehend and detain" an actor for an offense of retail theft occurring on or about his or her employer's property. This statutory authority will often exist contemporaneous with "citizen arrest" common law generated by the courts for other crimes. Furthermore, in certain instances the retail theft laws are written to provide a security officer with authority to apprehend and detain on probable cause for retail theft.

One more clarification must be made on private sector powers of arrest. Considerable confusion has occurred on whether a private agent can make an "investigatory stop." An investigatory stop or "Terry Stop" involves the stopping and questioning of parties who are reasonably expected to have committed a crime or are in the process of committing a crime. During these stops the subject may be questioned on his or her identity and the nature of his or her activities. If, during the questioning, the officer has reason to believe that the subject possesses a weapon, a limited search of the subject's outer clothing may be made for weapons. Under what has been referred to as the "hard/soft rule," any hard object that reasonably may be believed to be a weapon may be removed by the officer and inspected.

This type of stop is not considered an arrest, but a legal mechanism under which an officer can make a reasonable inquiry on the activities of a person he or she has reason to believe may be involved in criminal activity. The officer does not have to have probable cause to believe criminal activity is afoot, only the lesser standard of a reasonable suspicion. Any limited search resulting from such a stop is permitted for the safety of the officer alone and is not considered a search in the constitutional sense.

In general, private agents are not given authority to make this type of stop. For the most part, private agents can only detain a subject for the commission of a crime committed in their presence. In some instances this has been expanded to include arrests pursuant to probable cause. There have been no provisions in the law enacted that allow the private practitioner to interfere with the freedom of another citizen because of a belief something may be occurring.

The significance of this last point is that regardless of the degree of probable cause that may be present that a subject committed a particular crime, the private security officer cannot independently move in apprehending the subject unless the officer has been granted specific authority to do so.

John Dale Hartman

SECRET SERVICE

At the close of the Civil War, between one-third and one-half of all U.S. paper currency in circulation was counterfeit. On July 5, 1865, the Secret Service was created as a bureau under the Department of the Treasury to combat this threat to the nation's economy. Within less than a decade, counterfeiting was sharply reduced.

During its early years, the Secret Service investigated many cases unrelated to counterfeiting. These cases included the Teapot Dome oil scandals, the Ku Klux Klan, government land frauds, and counterespionage activity during the Spanish-American War and World War I. As other federal law enforcement agencies were created, the investigative jurisdiction of the Secret Service became limited to treasury-related crimes.

The Protective Mission

In 1901, President William McKinley was assassinated in Buffalo, New York. He was the third President killed in 36 years, and the public demanded protection for U.S. presidents. As a result, Congress directed the Secret Service to protect the new president, Theodore Roosevelt. In 1906, Congress finally enacted legislation making presidential protection a permanent Secret Service responsibility.

Protective responsibilities expanded greatly after that time, and the Secret Service completed a number of temporary protective duties. These assignments included providing security for the Declaration of Independence, the U.S. Constitution, the Gutenberg Bible, and other valuable documents during World War II; providing protection for a number of foreign leaders who visited the United States during World War II; and providing protection for Leonardo da Vinci's "Mona Lisa" while on exhibit in the United States.

Secret Service protective responsibilities have increased dramatically since the days of President Roosevelt. Today the service protects:

•The president, vice president, the president-elect, vice president-elect, and their immediate families.

•Former presidents and their spouses;

•Children of former presidents until age 16;

•Visiting heads of foreign states or governments and their spouses, and other distinguished foreign visitors to the United States;

•Major presidential and vice presidential candidates and their spouses;

•Other individuals at the direction of the President.

The Investigative Mission

The Secret Service continues to suppress the counterfeiting of currency and securities of the United States and of foreign governments. The service is also responsible for investigating the fraud and forgery of U.S. checks, bonds, and other obligations.

In 1984, Congress passed legislation expanding Secret Service investigative jurisdiction further to include fraud related to false identification documents and devices; fraud and related activities involving credit and debit cards; investigative authority relating to computer fraud; and, at the direction of the Secretary of the Treasury, authorization to investigate fraud associated with the electronic funds transfer system of the U.S. Treasury. In 1990, Congress further expanded the jurisdiction of the Secret Service regarding criminal violations against federally insured financial institutions, to include savings and loan investigations.

The Secret Service Uniformed Division

The first formal attempt to provide security at the White House occurred during the Civil War. The "Bucktail Brigade" (members of the 150th Regiment of the Pennsylvania Volunteers) and four officers from the Metropolitan Washington Police Force were assigned to protect White House property.   On September 14, 1922, President Warren G. Harding created the White House Police under the supervision of the White House military aide's office.

President Hoover decided that White House police officers and Secret Service agents at the White House could better coordinate their efforts if they were under centralized control.   In 1930, Congress placed the White House Police under the supervision of the U.S. Secret Service.

White House Police responsibilities expanded sharply in 1970 to include security for foreign diplomatic missions in the Washington DC area.   At the same time, the force was renamed the Executive Protective Service.   In 1977, the name was changed again to the U.S. Secret Service Uniformed Division.

Today, Uniformed Division officers provide security at the White House, the vice president's residence, buildings in which presidential offices are located, the U.S. Treasury Building and the Treasury Annex, foreign diplomatic missions in the Washington, DC, metropolitan area, and foreign diplomatic establishments in other parts of the United States as the president may direct.

Uniformed Division officers carry out their protective responsibilities through a network of foot patrols, vehicular patrols, and fixed posts. They provide additional assistance to the overall Secret Service protective mission through special support programs such as the canine, magnetometer, and countersniper units.

U.S. Secret Service

Source The Secret Service Story. (U.S. Secret Service, Department of the Treasury, Washington, DC, 1992).

SECURITY CONSULTING

The term "security consultant" means different things to different people. In a broad sense, the term can apply to anyone offering security products, services, advice, or expertise.   In a narrow sense, it refers to a branch of the security profession in which individuals and firms with specialized knowledge and skills provide independent, non-product-affiliated consultation to clients on a fee plus expense basis or similar arrangement.

The International Association of Professional Security Consultants (IAPSC) is the leading professional association specifically for this group of security practitioners, representing both the member consultant and the consumer. The IAPSC imposes a strict code of ethics upon members, and its view of the security consultant role carries a great deal of weight in defining the profession.   The IAPSC says that security consultants are independent, non-product-affiliated individuals or firms that offer security management, technical, or forensic consultation. This definition also includes professional security educators and trainers.

The IAPSC says that security consultants have nothing to sell but their expertise and advice, although it permits members to publish and produce consulting products such as books, manuals, training programs, and other information sources that are extensions of the consulting practice.   Generally, these consulting products offer advice and expertise.   Members may not represent or sell security products or other services such as guard or humanpower services, nor may they engage in certain types of private investigations.   The goal is to reduce the possibility of a conflict of interest so that the advice of a security consultant is totally independent and free of conflict or the appearance of conflict of any type.

Security consultants fall into specialized areas and it is rare for one consultant to offer services in all areas.   Even a single specialty will require many years of education, training, and practical experience before the practitioner reaches a level of marketable competency. Some consulting firms will offer a variety of specialized services, using a combination of in-house staff and outside associates.   Associates are often part-timers who work on an as-needed, project-by-project basis.   Some consulting firms will affiliate with other firms in order to expand the range of services.   Of course, a senior security practitioner of the caliber and with the experience one would expect of a security consultant probably came up through the ranks in several industries and gained a range of skills. Therefore, few consultants offer only one specialized service, but consumers should beware of the jack of all trades consultant who is an expert in everything. He is either a true Renaissance man or someone who can't make a living in his specialty and finds it necessary to move into other fields to make ends meet. One sign of a true expert in the consulting field is that he or she is successful as a specialist rather than as a generalist.

Security management consultants offer "pro-active" advice such as preventive surveys, humanpower and cost reduction audits, and evaluations designed to improve the overall management and efficiency of the security operation. Most often they conduct security surveys that look at the management aspects of security for a client.

Technical security consultants offer a range of technical services from value surveys designed to ascertain if there are cost savings in redefining the alarm system service or maintenance agreement with the vendor to highly technical electronic system designs. Many technical security consultants work on projects under contract with architects and engineers. In this capacity they advise the architect on physical security design, lighting, alarms, closed-circuit television (CCTV), access controls, and related matters. They are closely involved with security codes and standards such as the standards of Underwriters Laboratories as they relate to alarm and electronic systems. They often advise on foreseeability issues as well. They often produce bid documents such as system design or performance specifications, blueprints, device and hardware schedules, bid forms, requests for proposals, detail drawings, etc. They provide project management during the installation of the electronic system or a construction project. Technical security consulting is highly specialized and involves considerable risk to the consultant due to the possibility of error and omission lawsuits.

Forensic security consultants are often referred to as "expert witnesses" but it is not necessary to testify in court to provide forensic consultation. Forensic consultants in the security specialty advise clients before, during, and after litigation. They advise on how to properly secure a premises to avoid litigation and they advise the court during litigation on various aspects of the case in question. This is done through research reports submitted to the attorneys or the court, through depositions, testimony, or other means. Forensic consultation requires constant research on the part of the consultant to keep up with the current state of the art in security and current case law. This aspect of security is highly specialized and requires great attention to detail on the part of the expert advising the court or clients. While any security "expert" can testify in court, those who make testifying a profession had better be good at it because there will always be opposing experts.

Security educators and trainers are individuals who teach security and loss prevention subjects at a college level or who provide training services on a consulting basis to clients. Some provide evaluations of corporate loss prevention or of law enforcement training programs and advise on improvements. Some offer training seminars and programs.

While the previous categories of security consultant cover most of the consulting activity, there are other specialized services offered as well. They might include executive recruitment of security managers for a client, or consultation to insurers and law enforcement on matters that they do not encounter frequently enough to gain their own expertise, such as recovery of stolen art or stamp collection theft investigation. Generally, consultants who engage in "high-level," specialized investigation do so as advisors, turning their cases over to law enforcement or to private investigators before arrests are made. The hourly rate for consultants is typically twice that of private investigators, precluding them from involvement in investigative activities of a routine nature.

Most security consultants are "niche consultants," that is, they specialize in one or more of the many security-sensitive industries, or they have unique qualifications in a fairly narrow security discipline. For every work activity having a security implication, there will be one or more persons who possess or claim to possess special knowledge and skill. Complementing these are technical experts who provide electronic countermeasures that protect against covert listening devices, experts who design access control systems, and so on. Add to these the many experts in forensic matters, such as questioned document examinations, tool marks, fingerprints, and biological fluids. Don't forget also the area consultants who understand security as it is practiced in certain geographic regions such as the Caribbean, South America, or the Middle East, where language, politics, and culture are important concerns.

Security consultants are usually independent contractors who own their own businesses, but many work for larger firms as staff consultants. It has been estimated by the IAPSC that fewer than 1,000 full-time non-product-affiliated security consulting firms operate in the United States and Canada, but there are hundreds more individuals who engage in security consulting on a part-time basis.

Security consulting is a rewarding profession for the practitioner who has become recognized in his or her specialty or in the security profession as a whole. While compensation for the more successful security consultants is about equal to the top compensation packages of security managers in the same specialty of security, many choose security consulting because they prefer the independence of working for themselves. Each year 10 - 15% of individuals who hang out their shingles give up consulting. This is due in part to lack of preparation and capitalization. Because it usually takes at least 1 full year to build even a modest consulting practice, the fledgling consultant needs to have a well-researched business plan and be prepared financially to carry out the plan during the start-up period.

The ranks of consultants will swell when employers cut back and will shrivel when employers are in a hiring mode. During a down trend, many of the displaced security professionals will turn to consulting, and most of these will be among the first to leave consulting during an up trend. Those that leave consulting often do so because they find the work and travel schedule to be intolerably demanding. Successful security consultants, not unlike their counterparts in the corporate environment, put in long, hard hours to reap the rewards.

Security consultants generally charge an hourly or daily fee about equal to that charged by general management consultants to industry, with technical and forensic security consultants commanding slightly more. They pay their own benefits and taxes, and devote a considerable amount of time to non-billable functions. For example, a security consultant who works steadily at a rate of 40 hours per week may find at the end of the year that the billable time will total about 1,100 hours, with non-billable time in the range of 1,000 hours. The billable hours were spent working directly for clients while the non-billable time was spent marketing one's services and performing a variety of administrative functions.

Consumers can often find qualified consultants by contacting the IAPSC or other professional associations that screen their members prior to admitting them to membership. They often provide referrals or directories to consumers.

The use of security consultants has been growing steadily in the United States and Canada in recent years, but the trend has been for consumers to use the services of the more recognized experts. Security practitioners who are widely published, for example, find it less difficult to break into the profession. A client tends to want to contract with an individual who is immediately recognizable as an expert. High visibility is often equated with excellence, at least in the mind of the client.

The client also wants a consultant who knows security and knows the nature of the client's line of business. It is not sufficient, for example, to know how to detect embezzlement without at the same time knowing the arena of the suspected embezzlement. Success in detection will depend on a solid understanding of the client's industry and the client's unique business operations. In the area of electronic equipment, security consultants are increasingly expected to be on the leading edge of the technology and to be proficient in related scientific areas such as computer-assisted design techniques.

To the client, a security consultant can be an attractive alternative to carrying a professional on the regular payroll. The major incentive is the money that can be saved by not having to pay fringe benefits, such as medical insurance and paid holidays. A minor incentive is having to pay for security services only when needed. While thoughtful employers will not favor this type of band-aid approach, many small and mid-size employers have no other choice.

Steven R. Keller, CPP

SECURITY DESIGN: PRELIMINARY CONSIDERATIONS

Security is a topic on the minds and budgets of a growing number of owners, as is evidenced by the rapidly expanding supply of security technology and the increased attention being paid to the cost-effective integration of facility monitoring systems. The demand for more secure facilities, coupled with computerized technology and its growing integration capabilities, is making access control and intrusion detection a science of its own. Unfortunately, the design of a system incorporating these security functions far too often emphasizes the technological aspects of access control and intrusion detection rather than the basic design considerations associated with the system's intended use.

Security needs and requirements must be determined early in the project programming and definition process. Burglary, industrial espionage, shoplifting, riots, vandalism, assault, rape, murder, and employee theft are crimes that imperil lives and drive up the cost of doing business.

As crime increases, owners and their architect/engineers alike are being called upon to address security problems by incorporating security into the design and construction in all building types.

Designing a facility without security in mind can lead to expensive lawsuits, injuries, and retrofitting of protection measures after the facility is complete. As a result, the designer needs to factor basic security system design and integration considerations into the design. These include, at a minimum, the purpose and objectives of the security system, the physical and operational environment, and the anticipated complexity and responsiveness of the system to be employed. The security designer must consider these factors early in the design process, regardless of whether he or she is focusing on a new or planned upgrade effort.

Determining System Objectives

Security concerns need to be defined by the owner, with subsequent assistance in formulating system objectives and design details provided by a security architect/engineer. With the proliferation of security devices, along with rapid advances in system technology, security planning requires specialists with a working knowledge not only of the devices themselves, but also of the various integration possibilities for joining discrete systems for increased facility monitoring effectiveness. Electronic intrusion detection, perimeter protection, surveillance, and access control techniques are contributing elements in a total security system and design approach. Each technique has distinct technological and operational characteristics, and environmental reactions, along with differing requirements for installation and maintenance.

In order to determine what security strategy is most cost-effective and appropriate, the following questions should be answered by members of the project team:

1. For What Is the System to Be Used? For example, is the system designed to prevent escape or intrusion? For high or low security? Profile security? Interior or exterior detection or both? What are the methods of responding to alarms? Length of delay from time of criminal entry? To justify the use of an electronic access control system, the owner will need to know what assets and areas are to be protected along with what the potential loss or damages will cost. Each security situation is unique; there are no package solutions.

2. What Are the Operational Aspects of a Security System, and What Are Their Priorities? The type of alarm system needs to be defined, as well as the allowable false alarm rate tolerance. The proposed transmission system from sensors to alarms needs to be considered; for example, radio waves, hard wired, dedicated circuits, or multiplexed fiber-optic systems. What is the backup system in power and hardware? How are the alarms to be assessed for effectiveness, e.g., with closed-circuit television (CCTV), lights, horns, bells, or printed records? Should the system have tamper alarms, self-tests, or lightning protection? Each security system requires careful forethought on subsequent implementation and operation.

3. What Are the Environmental Impacts That Affect the Security System? Examples of such conditions are weather, water surfaces, wildlife, vegetation, corrosive condition of acid rain, or salt. Information is needed on topographic conditions of the site and

humanmade impacts such as physical structures, traffic patterns, and industry controls.

Answers to these questions will allow the owner and designer to focus on the best strategy for asset protection within budget and operational constraints. Arriving at the best security strategy for the intended environment requires that they also factor in some preliminary considerations into the design strategy.

Preliminary Considerations

The security design process is a key element in the overall project development plan. Most designers perform their design and integration tasks according to specific phases. Generally, these phases of the design process include, in order of accomplishment:
- Survey and Report
- Conceptual Design
- Preliminary and Final Design
- Bid and Construction
- Turnover and Operation

It is imperative that the requirements for security systems be incorporated at the earliest possible phase of planning. Requirements for security systems normally result from the initial Survey and Report phase, are formally identified as functional requirements and are reflected in an initial security design solution in the Conceptual Design phase. These requirements are the principal responsibility of the owner/user to develop, and they form the basis for quality control and review of the more detailed phases of engineering and system implementation planning. Establishing and baselining system requirements early-on in the design process can allow the design team to avoid the costly oversight and disruptive consideration of security requirements at later phases of major design and construction.

Each site or facility to receive a security system will offer the designer unique differences in local circumstances and conditions. As a result, the requirements for individual facility protective measures must be evaluated on a case-by-case basis. Specific factors that need to be evaluated when designing integrated systems include:
- The mission criticality of the facility and its assets.

- The threats anticipated for each of the assets, including current threat assessments and owner concerns.
- The vulnerability and consequence of loss for each asset to be protected given the anticipated threats.
- Local security response force capabilities.
- Design constraints such as monetary, operational, and environmental limitations.

The previous list of preliminary considerations leads the designer to a determination of functional requirements for each facility to be protected. Once the functional baseline of the system has been established, other considerations become the basis of selecting appropriate security measures. These include the physical and operational environment, the need for protection-in-depth, and the complexity and sensitivity of the subsystems to be employed. The system designer must consider these factors in the analysis of proposed security measures, including upgrade efforts.

Security System Selection

Each type of security system is intended to perform a specific function within a total system design. Basic factors to be considered in selecting security measures include, but are not limited to, the physical environment, operational environment, and the need for protection-in-depth of critical assets. The end results of the failure of the designer to consider these factors are a non-responsive system, an ineffective system, and an unacceptable level of false and nuisance alarm occurrences. A discussion for each of these basic design considerations will follow.

The meanings of the terms *false* and *nuisance* alarm are important to our discussion. Without a proper understanding of these terms, the designer is likely to overlook important sources of system degradation.

A false alarm is an alarm indication that results from the malfunction anywhere in the system hardware or software between the outermost sensor and the control and display central annunciator. A nuisance alarm is an alarm condition that is caused by sensor system response to outside stimuli such as environmental conditions, vehicle traffic, electrical power line disturbances, electromagnetic interference, and vibration-causing machinery, to name a few.

Both sources of system degradation, false alarms and nuisance alarms, demand that the designer carefully consider the physical environment and operational environment, as well as the most effective protection-in-depth schemes.

Physical Environment. The state-of-the-art of electronic security systems presents a series of options for the designer that will result in the selection of best, acceptable, or unacceptable technology and other countermeasure options. In particular, sensor and CCTV elements are designed to perform within specific environmental parameters and failure to adhere to accepted application requirements for each technology will lead to degraded performance, excessive nuisance alarms, or both. In addition to the real system performance costs associated with a degraded detection and assessment capability, hidden costs of such misapplication are in the real dollar cost of repair/retrofit and in the loss of owner confidence in the system.

The security system designer needs to carefully analyze the physical environment to determine and document the host of physical environment variables that may adversely affect the performance of electronic components. In the exterior physical security environment these include the factors of wind, temperature extremes, fog, foliage, salt, rain/standing water, condition of fence fabric, location of underground utilities, and other environmental influences that would cause sensor and other technologies to not respond within specified performance limits. The selection and placement of interior sensors must consider the heating, ventilating, and air conditioning (HVAC) location; heat sources; transient light; vibration; moving machinery; dust; and moisture/humidity. The assignment and positioning of CCTV must consider the aspects of sun glare, even and sufficient distribution of artificial light, temperature, wind, and the monitoring location.

Thus, the most critical consideration for the security designer is that the initial requirements analysis phase of system design should identify all potential sources of environmentally generated stimuli which could adversely impact overall system performance. The subsequent preliminary design phase will then be able to accommodate these design constraints through the selection of the appropriate technology, combining technology with other measures and/or modification of the environment.

Another aspect of the physical environment to be considered by the designer is the notion of security control through environmental design. This concept involves a review of the physical environment to be protected and the use of facility and site design concepts to reduce the inclination of the physical environment to support criminal behavior. Environmental design strategies include the use of natural access control through placement of walkways, natural surveillance through the elimination of unsafe areas, and the use of improved lighting. Included within the environmental design approach are concepts of individual territoriality, effective use of space, and manipulation of the natural environment to deter potential threats.

Operational Environment. Operational issues place two types of constraints on the architect and engineer as designers: physical and owner-required. An example of the former is a facility perimeter that must adapt to site constraints, property availability, or usage. Owner-required issues include the need to compartmentalize certain operations, limitations on location and design of access control portals, and placement of handicapped access. Distinct owner groups must maintain their own separate operations that include their own safety, efficiency, and a variety of other mission performance criteria within which the security system must adapt.

Each of these unique requirements may result in selection or rejection of specific security system solutions. Rejection of a technology is usually due to an inability to operate effectively within the operational environment or as a result of a potential for impeding routine organizational operations. Specific examples of these instances include rejection of CCTV assessment in the manufacturing environment and rejection of access control portals at a key entrance gate.

Protection-In-Depth. Depending upon the criticality of the asset in terms of mission or replacement value, the security designer attempts to establish a series of integrated protective measures around the asset(s) to be protected. The strategy of forming layers of protection is known as designing for protection-in-depth. The purpose of the protective layers is to make it progressively more difficult for an intruder to reach critical targets and to escape undetected. These protection-in-depth schemes also build time delays into the intruder's path to the asset, calculated to allow for arrival of the response force and neutralization of the threat before reaching the asset.

Technology selection and placement is critical to forming effective protection-in-depth schemes and must be made in such a pattern as to maximize the potential that the intruder will pass through the desired detection pattern. A well-conceived security system should detect penetration attempts as far away from the asset to be protected as is practical, and at several points along the path of the intruder to the asset.

The area where the system detects an intrusion is defined as a zone or line of detection. A comprehensive system protecting highly critical assets may require multiple lines or zones of detection. The security designer determines the number of zones to be implemented and their configuration according to the perceived degree of protection required to ensure a rapid response. Also considered are the possible intrusion schemes that might be launched against the defense and the neutralizing capacity of the security forces.

Security System Performance

The security system designer must constantly strive to make the probability of detecting and assessing the nature of an intrusion 100% and the potential for nuisance and false alarms 0%. Both objectives in their extremes are ideals and most likely unattainable given our relevant inability to absolutely control the environment, technology limitations, and unexpected threat capabilities.

Probability of detection of individual sensors and detection configurations is the ratio of the total number of successful test intrusion detections to the total number of attempted test intrusions. Probability of detection can be expressed in terms of individual sensors or as an indication of the complete security system, considering all of its individual components together.

Most commercially available interior systems individually claim a probability of detection (PD) of 0.95 (being capable of detecting greater than 9 out of 10 intrusions), while other sensors designed to operate in harsh or outside environments generally are rated to have a PD of 0.90 for each sensor. This latter rating is usually based upon tests of actual intrusions by relatively knowledgeable intruders into the sensor field in a controlled environment. A higher overall system rate can be obtained by combining sensors in a protection-in-depth scheme. Combining sensors in a protection scheme can increase the likelihood of intruder detection and correspondingly the probability of detection.

In any event, PD ultimately needs to be evaluated as a system *performance goal* rather than as a measure of *individual sensor performance*. The probability of successfully detecting an intrusion will depend upon the inherent performance of the component, the method and appropriateness of technology deployment, the type and number of sensors deployed, the environment in which the technology operates, the individual sensor PD, and the competence and knowledge of the intruder.

False and Nuisance Alarms.   Security systems should be designed and installed to generate the absolute minimum number of nuisance and false alarms per unit of time. As mentioned previously, false alarms are differentiated from nuisance alarms in that the former are caused by non-intrusion internal phenomena inherent to the system, such as a malfunction, while the latter are valid alarms generated by physical stimuli or environmental phenomena.

Careful equipment selection, system design, and effective installation can substantially minimize nuisance (and false alarms) to an acceptable level. Because nuisance alarms are so dependent upon controlling the environment or reducing the sensitivity of the sensing equipment and cannot be completely controlled in the typical installation, the technique of assessing alarm annunciations through CCTV or direct visual observation covering the sensor field is normally used. When properly configured, CCTV permits automatic assessment of a sensor zone in a state of alarm.

The design requirement to maximize system probability of detection and protection-in-depth within constraints does not mean that the designer should saturate a building or site with sensors, cameras, or other technological devices. The designer must perform the critical integration function of determining an acceptable level and mix of electronic, physical, and procedural measures that will work together to maximize intruder delay, detection, assessment, and speed of response. While this mix will be unique for each site or facility, cost trade-off analyses conducted during the initial design phase will force the selection of certain countermeasures against a perceived threat.

Although nuisance alarm sources must be considered in an overall negative light, they nevertheless do provide an actual test of the system to respond to various phenomena. Ideally, all sources of false alarms should be eliminated from the system by the designer and installer, although it is often operationally difficult to differentiate between false and nuisance alarms. The security system designer needs to establish acceptable levels of nuisance alarm criteria and false alarm rates, and take particular note of these requirements in the design specifications, subsequent installation, and test of system components.

Integration Considerations

A decade ago, the security manager's portfolio of protective technology options was limited to relatively simple sensors, basic yet expensive CCTV, archaic photo identification systems, and unidimensional access control systems. Access control systems in particular relied more on humanpower than technology. In cases where technology was integrated with personnel and procedures for access control, managers were faced with reliance on complex processing systems that had limited applications and required major capital expenditures. Today, the security industry offers a wide assortment of capable protective technologies and integrated systems at affordable prices.

Integrated protective systems can include: guard personnel, responsive procedures for contingencies, detection sensors, automated access control elements, CCTV, fiber-optic communication and transmission lines, and multiplexed control and display equipment to tie all the various elements together into one central monitoring location. Ultimately, integrated security systems are designed to detect and communicate intrusions and other alarm conditions to a central control location for response.

Thus, the adequacy of the security force response depends largely upon the ability of the security command and control function to assess reliably the nature of the alarm, and to communicate the circumstances and conditions in the alarm zone to the available response force. The use of CCTV, which is tied into the sensor annunciation system, permits the security system operator to immediately view the alarming sector, to validate the alarm, and to communicate relevant information to the response force. The designer must consider the most cost-effective means to accomplish this system objective.

The advantages of employing integrated systems are obvious. Integrated security systems can be used to reduce the cost of providing essential security services. Integrated systems permit more economical and efficient use of humanpower usually assigned to building patrols and fixed guard posts. Integrated intrusion detection and access control systems have become electronic extensions of the security organization by permitting remote monitoring of critical locations at a lower initial equipment cost vs. continuing humanpower expenditures.

In addition, integrated security technology can be used in place of other physical security measures that cannot be employed because of safety regulations, operational requirements, appearance, layout, cost, or other reasons. Security technology can augment guard personnel to provide additional protective measures at critical entry points or within a building's high security or sensitive areas. Technology can also provide increased protection-in-depth where the use of multiple protective measures for increased system reliability is considered essential by the owner.

Upgrades. The system designer should ensure that future expansion or upgrades, such as adding new alarm points and electronic access controls, and expanding CCTV coverage, are included in initial system designs and that future upgrades do not force the retrofit of costly control and display equipment. Most state-of-the-art alarm and video control systems are modularly expandable and permit future growth. The integrated system should have an expansion capability sufficient to accommodate modular additions throughout the life cycle of the installed system. A 7- to 10-year life cycle is generally accepted as a baseline for off-the-shelf commercial systems. The designer should consider maximum enhancements projected over this period based upon the continual re-assessment of threats and resultant effectiveness of installed countermeasures.

Simplicity and Maintainability. The security system designer also must keep the system as simple as possible, and carefully consider the interaction of people and hardware. How will an alarmed area be assessed? What throughput rates must be accommodated for controlled entrances? Who is available to monitor a simple alarm system for a small protected area? In particular, at the alarm control and monitoring location, it is important to know the operational limitations imposed on the system design in terms of operator sophistication and the inventory of functions to be performed while monitoring the alarm and display.

System and component maintainability is also a critical concern for non-redundant items, as is the probability that an item can perform its intended function for a specified interval under stated conditions.

As a common system descriptor, mean-time-between-failure (MTBF) is a basic measure of reliability for repairable hardware items. MTBF is the mean number of life units during which all parts of the hardware item perform within specified limits, during a particular time interval under defined conditions. Mean-time-to-repair (MTTR) is a basic measure of maintainability, defined as the sum of corrective maintenance times at any specific level of repair, divided by the total number of failures within an item repaired at that level. The designer must keep these two concepts in mind when preparing the initial and final security designs with specific technologies selected on the basis of these and other criteria.

Alarm Zone Configurations. Unless carefully specified in design and construction documents,

system installers may often connect sensors in series to simplify the installation task and to reduce installation costs. This may result in the annunciation of each device in the series as one alarm at the control and display annunciator, without giving the console operator the benefit of knowing which device in the area is causing the alarm. This type of sensor integration is called daisy-chaining. The opposite is called point-for-point integration, where each sensor is wired separately to a common control unit and, upon alarm, the sensor is readily identifiable as the source of the alarm by the control operator.

Where direct point-for-point annunciation is a design goal, care should be taken in designing and specifying the control network so that the control console will display an individual sensor zone, CCTV sector, or specific point, as well as facilitate troubleshooting and maintenance. For example, all sensors in a single room may be combined on a single zone because it may not seem important for the system operator to know which window or door was penetrated. From the response management point of view, it may be important that each sensor be annunciated individually so that the point of intrusion can be determined and the response force directed accordingly.

Different types of sensors may be annunciated separately by sensor zone so that the security system operator can differentiate between sensor types and location. For example, door contact switches would annunciate attempted entry from one approach, the microwave or infrared sensors would annunciate when the intruder enters the room, and the capacitance sensor would annunciate when the intruder attempted to penetrate a given asset (e.g., a safe). This has the added advantage of providing operator assessment of intruder progress across or through the sensored area.

Additionally, at some level within the system, the identification of individual sensor alarms must be possible to enable maintenance personnel to expeditiously identify sensors for maintenance or repair. Wiring sensors individually to the control unit substantially eases troubleshooting, and reduces maintenance cost, as a trade-off against initial increased wiring costs.

Codes and Regulations. Finally, the designer must ensure that the security system hardware complies with the applicable codes, standards, and regulations that are in effect for a specific site at the time the design is prepared. This includes safety and legal protective measures such as posted notices. Additionally, security system components located in areas where fire or explosion hazards may exist due to flammable gases or vapors, flammable liquids, combustible dust, or ignitable fibers must be made intrinsically safe. Intrinsically safe components are those that are incapable of releasing sufficient energy to ignite a specific atmospheric mixture under normal operating conditions. Methods of accomplishing intrinsic safety include either limiting the level of voltage and current, or housing components within sealed conduit or enclosures that would prevent the release of hazardous energy.

System integration of protective measures is the primary objective of the security system design process. The designer must effectively combine all physical protective measures with security personnel and procedures. The designer's selection of which security measures are more effective depends upon several factors, e.g., the availability and capability of the security force to respond within a specific time, the value of the asset, the criticality of the mission, the capabilities of the adversary, budgetary constraints, and a host of other factors. These are all basic considerations factored into the design effort from the beginning.

System integration is totally within the hands of the security manager as he or she ponders the choices appropriate to individual asset protection schemes. Principal design considerations include the physical and operational environment, and the need for the designer to base his or her protection scheme on the need for protection-in-depth. Whether the security system designer is working with the design of a relatively small system with detection and control display devices or a large system with multiple elements, all the subsystems must be integrated into a total systems approach.

Richard P. Grassie, CPP
and Randall I. Atlas, Ph.D., AIA, CPP

SECURITY DESIGN AND INTEGRATION: A PHASED PROCESS

Introduction

Critical assets can offer extremely attractive targets for a variety of threats. Threats can range from unsophisticated activist groups to highly sophisticated, well-armed and trained professional career criminals or narco-terrorists. While the nature of the threat is key to security design and integration efforts, in many cases the consequences of loss for a small or medium firm due to even a medium-level threat can be catastrophic when a key business asset has been compromised.

Security managers are becoming increasingly convinced that the best defense against dynamic threats and potential catastrophic loss is a fully integrated security program that carefully and effectively blends architectural, technological, and operational elements into a flexible, responsive system. The design and integration process described below is one approach that can be employed by security managers to effectively counter threats and substantially reduce risk or consequence of loss. The process is generic and requires that the manager overlay his or her own security problem in order to arrive at an effective design solution.

Some security organizations place undue emphasis upon the selection and application of security personnel or equipment alone without equal consideration of the full range of options and countermeasures that comprise a totally integrated security system. Security managers must avoid the tendency to emphasize a single solution or approach and they must strive to achieve a virtually seamless mix of security countermeasures designed specifically to address anticipated threats and risks. More important, soaring humanpower and equipment costs coupled with the risk posed by the ominous insider threat demand the effective application of state-of-the-art security countermeasures at key locations to reduce asset vulnerability and keep operational costs under control.

The Security Design and Integration process applies equally to the security manager as system user and the architect/engineer as system designer. This approach will ensure the

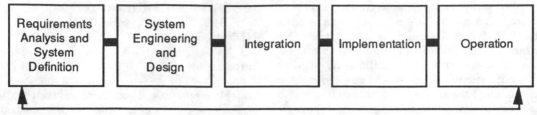

The Design and Integration Process

proper selection and combination of humanpower, procedures, information, facilities, and equipment into a fully responsive and operationally effective system at a reasonable cost.

System Objectives

Simply stated, a security system is an integrated combination of barriers, technologies, personnel, and procedures designed to safeguard personnel, property, and operations. System objectives generally address deterrence, denial, detection, delay, assessment, and response options based upon a precise definition of threat and user requirements.

It is essential that the security manager recognize that complete systems incorporate a wide range of measures to achieve stated objectives. In the case of a fully integrated security system, protection objectives are achieved through the selection and integration of protective measures from the following range of subsystem options:

• Facilities, architectural barriers, and space definition to deter and delay the movements of an adversary.

• Physical security equipment designed to detect, assess, and, in some cases, respond to intrusion attempts and unauthorized activities.

• Communications and control and display networks to collect, integrate, transmit, and display alarm and other data for operator response and to control activities of the response force.

• Security personnel to conduct day-to-day security program operations, management and system support, and response to non-routine events.

• Security procedures to guide security operations and provide overall security program direction and control.

The Design and Integration Process

The essence of design is to invent an order or arrangement of components and details of a system in accordance with a plan. In all cases, whether for security or any other function, a system is designed for a purpose. In the case of security design, the plan is to select and incorporate the various physical elements, personnel, and procedures into a unified system that reduces and controls vulnerability based upon an identified threat.

Engineering design usually involves six project stages, namely: study and report, preliminary design, final design, bidding or negotiation, construction, and operational. While these engineering stages are familiar to the architect and engineer, for the security manager, some adjustments are necessary in order to arrive at a process that includes not only the functions of engineering design, but also the integration of tangible and intangible elements resulting in a responsive protection system design.

The essence of integration is to make a whole by bringing together individual parts. For the security manager, system integration is the art of fusing security equipment, facilities, personnel, and procedures together seamlessly in a manner that produces pro-active asset protection.

The end result is a fully integrated security system that responds effectively to dynamic threats and risks during crisis conditions and, at the same time, functions imperceptibly during normal conditions. Whereas design results in the various security elements responding to a threat or risk, integration fuses them into a workable, day-to-day strategy for effective asset protection.

Security system design and integration begins with a thorough requirements analysis and concept definition. Facility and site protection plans are always based on the identification of critical assets requiring protection and the identification of appropriate countermeasures for each asset. Barriers, electronic hardware, personnel, and procedures are selected to interplay at key locations within the design scheme to form an integrated subsystem protection scheme.

The system concept is formed through the collection of integrated approaches at each asset, facility, and group of facilities sharing a common boundary. Given the diverse missions found in organizations, the integration of protective measures and resources does not involve a static set of environments. Because threat is normally dynamic at each asset or facility requiring protection, the fully integrated system concept must allow for various scenarios, system redundancy based on criticality, and collective management of available resources in order to achieve the best possible protective design solution. The security manager is always the final authority on system options based on requirements stated early in the process and resource constraints.

Based on the approved concept, the System Engineering and Design phase brings the system through the various phases of design steps from preliminary to final design. The end result is a complete system solution. The integration function that follows the design phase is merely a design review phase where the final design and integration solution is formally reviewed by the security manager based upon previously stated requirements.

This Integration phase is absolutely critical for the security manager to be ensured that the integrated design solution addresses all stated requirements. More importantly, design solution validation is essential before hardware is acquired and construction is begun. Once validated, the system is ready for the final phases of Implementation and ultimate Operation by the end user. Feedback on the effectiveness of the system, which is based upon the dynamics of threat and changing missions, is continuously fed into the front-end requirements phase.

Requirements Analysis and System Definition

Experience has shown that the System Design and Integration process must be front-loaded in order to arrive at a valid security concept. This means the process cannot be expected to yield sufficient results unless it is based upon a thorough analysis of threats and risks, and the relative exposure of individual assets to these conditions. Thus, the Requirements Analysis phase is critical to develop an optimum system configuration and to determine the relative cost-effectiveness of various physical security options.

Initially, assets that need protection are identified, and their criticality to the facility or organizational mission are determined. Next, the attractiveness of these assets to potential threats and their likely modes of attack are evaluated. Finally, areas in which existing security measures do not adequately address the threat are identified as vulnerabilities.

Based on the results of the on-site requirements analysis, asset-specific countermeasures are applied at various locations on and around the asset to be protected. Selection of individual countermeasures is made by the designer based upon an initial statement of system objectives and functional requirements, such as detecting unauthorized entry and controlling access. The designer and security manager must consider the full range of potential countermeasures, to include architectural barriers, intrusion detection, access control, and assessment subsystems, as well as procedural and personnel intensive countermeasure combinations appropriate to each asset.

Finally, the security concept or design solution is reached through the selection of the best combination of individual, complementary countermeasures for specific assets. The accumulation of the various countermeasure selections for each asset are considered collectively in terms of total protection afforded and potential for unnecessary redundancy.

The overall concept for protection of all grouped assets is then factored into a cohesive design solution and preliminary life cycle cost estimates are prepared.

The security manager is the final arbiter of which conceptual design solution is offered for more detailed consideration and design in the next phase.

Design solution documentation that forms the basis for subsequent engineering and detailed design includes basic schematic representations or drawings, basic level of

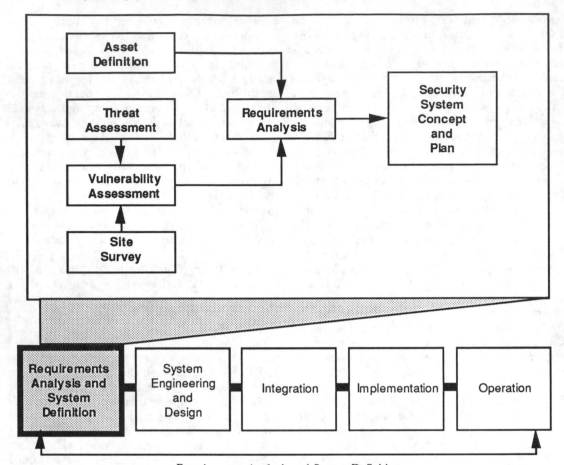

Requirements Analysis and System Definition

information specifications, and a preliminary "order of magnitude" cost estimate of subsystem and overall system costs in equipment, materials, and labor.

The conceptual design drawings will usually include an overall site plan, a building footprint, building elevations, and a system block diagram that depicts the major components and their connectivities in forming a total protection system.

System Engineering and Design

The System Engineering and Design phase uses the system's conceptual design as a basis and results in a detailed engineering design solution. The security manager is responsible for providing the designer with an established system goal, a full set of functional requirements

upon which the design can be based, and a complete system concept that clearly defines how the total system and its elements will function to counter identified threats and reduce vulnerabilities. These are all expected outputs of the initial conceptual design phase incorporated in a security plan.

The engineering design consists of both a preliminary and final design. The preliminary design defines the total project through construction and operation and includes preliminary design drawings, outline specifications, a design analysis, and a total project cost estimate. The final design results in complete design documentation to include detailed drawings, specifications, cost estimate, bid requirements, contract forms, and contract conditions. The engineering design also addresses and resolves all of the integration issues associated with the resultant total system

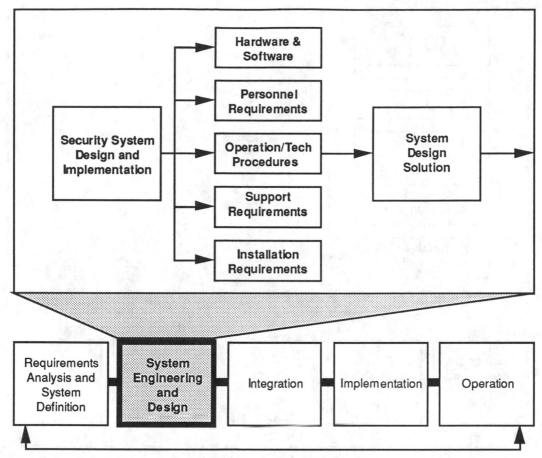

System Engineering and Design

and its key elements. Apart from the identification of equipment and subsystem interface, the engineering design also addresses a concept of operations that describes in clear terms the interplay of personnel and procedures with equipment.

The system designer leads a team effort that concentrates on the development of asset-, facility-, organizational-, and site-specific protective measures to deter, delay, deny, detect, assess, and respond to a variety of threats. Typical protective measures detailed in the engineering design phase include architectural barriers, interior and exterior detection technology, closed circuit television (CCTV) assessment/surveillance equipment and associated support lighting, data transmission and communication, alarm and signal field collectors, and annunciator equipment for control and display. The security manager must

consider appropriate response procedures along with security force weapons and equipment sufficient to counter the design basis threat.

These protective measures must be identified in terms of their individual characteristics and overall contribution to facility/asset protection from an integrated perspective. For example, the delay capabilities of selected architectural barriers may modify the designer's choice of associated sensor and access control subsystem elements. The determining criteria applied in this case would be to measure the delay/denial capability of the barrier in conjunction with an appropriate sensor keyed to the threat scenario and to sufficient response force reaction time. In essence, the availability and operational capabilities of the security response force will dictate the optimum selection, configuration, and placement of various protective measures.

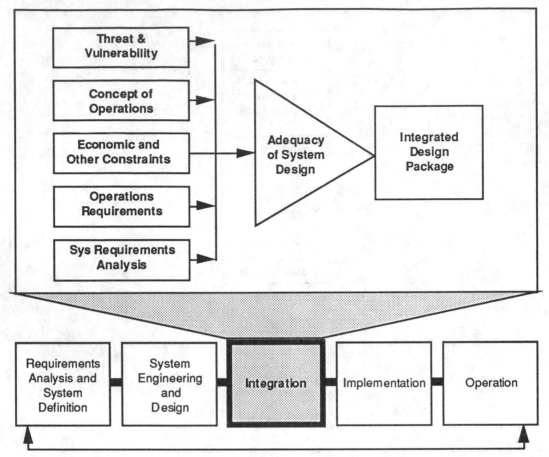

Integration

In another example, the designer may focus on the combination of specific technologies such as microwave and infrared sensors to ensure maximum probability of detection using complementary technologies. Each of the various protection options available to the security designer represent a complete inventory of choices that may be selected and combined with other protection options to form a completely integrated physical security system.

Considered individually, countermeasures likely offer little in the way of complete protection for critical assets. Collectively, a carefully chosen combination of measures keyed specifically to facility and site-unique requirements comprise a wholly effective, integrated approach to asset protection. Selection of the best measures is based on the designer's determination of individual and collective performance, reliability, maintain-

ability, cost, and vulnerability reduction potential.

The designer's principal function is to select the various components, elements and subsystems and integrate them into a complete system design. In all cases, selecting and balancing combinations of asset protection measures according to perceived threat and desired results is the key to design integration.

System Integration

System design and integration has been presented as a complete process accomplished by the security manager and security architect/engineer. Although the integration function is exercised by both in every phase of the process, it is also a major phase between design and implementation. Upon completion of the system engineering design, both the security manager and design engineer need to carefully review the designed system and ask the critical integration question: How do all of the selected protection measures and components required for their operation fit together for total system effectiveness?

Integration is singled out as a major phase to emphasize the importance of reviewing and balancing the engineering design according to validated requirements and constraints before proceeding to the costly later phases of construction and operation. In effect, the Integration phase is really a formal, detailed final design review elevated to a major phase in the process.

While not normally recognized as a major design phase, System Integration is an essential step between final design and implementation where the security manager validates the system design in accordance with previously established requirements. It is at this point that the security manager considers the adequacy of the complete final system design solution in terms of previously determined threats and vulnerabilities, the security manager's concept of security operations, economic and other constraints, organizational operations, and overall system requirements. In effect, system integration is really the final design review elevated to a major phase.

The Integration phase confirms the primary objective of the earlier design process to incorporate the various subsystem elements (architectural barriers, sensors, data transmission media, controllers, CCTV, etc.), with personnel and procedures resulting in an integrated approach to asset protection. During Integration, each subsystem, along with its associated component(s), needs to be evaluated by the security manager and the designer according to its individual contribution to vulnerability reduction and contribution to the total system protection effort. Each measure offers trade-offs in terms of costs and benefits. Subsystem integration reflected in the final design represents the culmination of choices appropriate to individual asset protection decisions.

The end result of the Engineering Design phase is a completely integrated security system consisting of various subsystems and their associated elements, which collectively counter an adversary with a high degree of reliability and assurance.

System Implementation

Implementing the security system involves preparing facilities, acquiring hardware, installation, testing and evaluation, training, and establishing a comprehensive logistics and maintenance support system.

In terms of eventual system performance, proper completion of the steps in this phase, namely system installation, will to a large extent determine successful operation and responsiveness of the final system.

It is at this crucial phase that the security system designer can lose control of the desired results. Project controls need to be exercised with respect to the design specifications to ensure quality control. The security manager has overall responsibility for quality assurance, test, and acceptance issues. On-site quality control of system installation is essential to successful system performance. The designer plays a key role in this phase by carefully considering key installation activities when on-site inspection can confirm that design requirements are being met.

The designer must be completely familiar with the devices being installed and ensure that all items, right down to cable connectors, meet the design specifications and are appropriate for the conditions and environment in which they will be used.

Quality assurance representatives are responsible for monitoring compliance with technical design requirements and they must be given the authority to stop the project upon determining that the system will not meet the requirements and objectives established at the beginning of the process.

Field system checkout and performance tests need to be monitored closely. The system test results, prepared at the end of each test phase, should be documented fully by the testing agency and verified by user security representatives. Likewise, shop drawings and other engineering submittals required by the specifications and statement of work need to be reviewed for acceptability.

Formal acceptance of the installed system should be made only after the user has

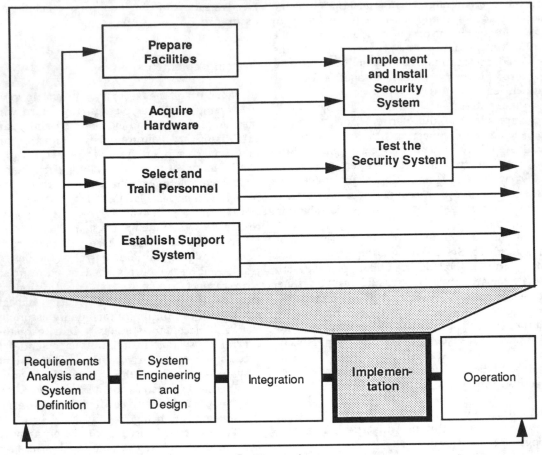

Implementation

confirmed that all quality control provisions have been satisfied.

System-level training for operators, maintainers, and supervisors should also be scheduled at the conclusion of this phase.

System Operation

The System Operation phase involves the actual operation of the accepted system by the user organization. Key aspects of this phase include preparing and submitting as-built drawings, and the final receipt of technical manuals for system operation and maintenance. A principal element of this phase is the assumption by the user of responsibility for system support.

One pricing option involves the forming and training of a dedicated maintenance team to perform the routine preventative and troubleshooting procedures on a regular basis. Another option is to contract out all maintenance to a qualified firm.

Regardless of the option chosen, all maintenance personnel need to understand system operation and be able to test, troubleshoot, and replace modular components and repair certain components. In some cases, multiplex control and display manufacturers offer diagnostic software to troubleshoot system, subsystem, and component failures.

All operational systems should be evaluated on a regular basis—at least yearly—based on a continuing threat and vulnerability analysis, and changes in organizational missions. System hardware should also be tested regularly to verify that system performance has not been degraded. Some experts recommend repeating original system-level acceptance tests semi-annually. Lastly, sustained training of all system

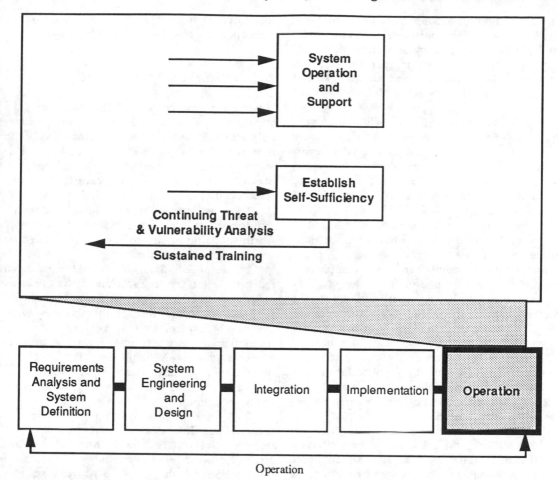

Operation

personnel, including operators, maintenance, and supervisory personnel, is mandatory.

Effective security system integration not only includes security hardware selection and application, but also must take into consideration existing procedures, architectural measures, and security resources. This requires a thorough understanding of the System Design and Integration process, as well as the roles and responsibilities of each member of the project team.

Adherence to the phased steps of the process is critical to effective system design and operation. After selecting assets deemed critical for protection, the security manager must systematically determine potential threats and their characteristics, the attractiveness of critical assets to threats, potential attack modes, and potential attack severity. Finally, with the aid of a project team that understands that the most

effective, flexible, and economical security system is one that has an appropriate blend of personnel, procedures, and technology, an integrated security system can be designed.

Richard P. Grassie, CPP

SECURITY SURVEY: AN OVERVIEW

One approach to determining whether or not there is a need for a security survey is first to examine what services an experienced security expert can provide and then to seek information on security (crime)-related losses at the particular place of business. The security expert can either be in place, that is to say a member of the staff of the enterprise, an outside consultant, or both.

Security-related problems that can be evaluated by a security survey include theft, fraud, forgery, arson, burglary, robbery, malicious damage, personnel screening and investigation, theft of trade secrets, industrial espionage, executive protection, kidnap, extortion, bomb threats and bombings, and emergency and disaster planning, to name but a few.

If the company or facility being considered has a security plan, the survey can establish if the plan is up-to-date and functional in every respect. Experience has shown that many security plans were established as the need dictated, without regard to centralization and coordination.

Upon review, many such plans resemble a crazy quilt affair. More often than not these plans need to be brought together in such a manner that the component parts complement instead of contradict one another.

If the facility has no security plan, then the survey can establish the need for one and develop some or all of the following security services, most of which are commonly found in an industrial setting. By conducting a comprehensive survey of the entire facility—its operations and procedures—one can identify critical factors affecting the security of the premises or operation.

The next step is to analyze the vulnerabilities and recommend cost-effective protection. This will assist the client in developing policies and procedures to do the following:

• Protect against internal and external theft.
• Develop access control procedures.
• Establish lock and key control procedures.
• Design, supervise, and review installation of anti-intrusion detection systems.
• Establish an executive protection program.
• Provide control over the movement and identification of employees, customers, and visitors on company property.
• Review the selection, training, and deployment of security personnel.
• Assist in the establishment of emergency and disaster plans and guidelines.
• Identify the internal resources available and needed for the establishment of an effective security program.
• Develop and present security seminars for management.

The previous list is by no means all inclusive. It does set forth some of the frequently encountered programs and systems reviewed or developed as a result of a security survey.

Selling Security to Management

It is not uncommon to find that management's attention is gained only after a serious problem points to the lack of adequate protection. The first reaction is often one of overkill. The response pendulum swings from complacency to paranoia when the facts indicate that proper response should be somewhere in between.

There are some things a security director can do to convince management that security is worth spending money to obtain. Methods that have proven successful are:

1.   Establish dialogue with the decision makers. First try to ascertain feelings about security. What do they really want a security program to accomplish, if in fact they want anything? Do not be surprised to learn that some management personnel regard security as a necessary evil. Marshal the facts. Research the history of security losses experienced by the company and use this information to develop trend projections.

2.   When presenting data to support the security position, deal in principles and not personalities. Use the technique of non-attribution for all unpublished sources of information. With published sources, such as interoffice memos, excerpt the pertinent data if possible. Avoid power struggles. Maintain a position of objective neutrality.

3.   Be professional about security. Explore every avenue to acquire the needed information, such as developing contacts with other security professionals who share similar problems. Don't re-invent the wheel.

4.   In making a proposal, hit the highlights and make it as brief as possible. Save the details for later. In any proposal that will cost money, develop the cost figures as accurately as possible. If the figures are estimates, label them as such and err on the high side.

5.   It is a wise person who knows his or her limitations. If outside help is needed, do not be reluctant to say so. Such areas as electronics, computers, and sophisticated anti-intrusion alarm systems are usually beyond the capabilities of the security generalist. Do some studying. Know where to go to get help.

SURVEY CHECKLIST

1.   Security Policy

Y/N   [ ] _____   1.1.   Is there a written security policy emphasizing the importance of protecting people, property, and processes against risk of injury, loss or damage from criminal, hostile, or malicious acts?

1.2.   Does the security policy address:

Y/N [ ] _____	1. Theft or destruction of property?
Y/N [ ] _____	2. Burglary?
Y/N [ ] _____	3. Theft of process or trade secrets?
Y/N [ ] _____	4. Assault?
Y/N [ ] _____	5. Bomb threats?
Y/N [ ] _____	6. Arson?
Y/N [ ] _____	7. Civil disturbances?
Y/N [ ] _____	8. Drug and alcohol violations?
Y/N [ ] _____	9. Ethics and conflict of interest violations?
Y/N [ ] _____	10. Fraud?
Y/N [ ] _____	11. Sex offenses?
Y/N [ ] _____	12. Contraband violations?
Y/N [ ] _____	13. Other?

_____

_____

1.3.   Is the security policy:

Y/N [ ] _____	1. Communicated in writing to all employees?
Y/N [ ] _____	2. Referred to during new employee orientation?
Y/N [ ] _____	3. Referred to in group meetings?
Y/N [ ] _____	4. Contained in some manual?
Y/N [ ] _____	5. Referred to in management training programs?

1.4.   Does senior management support the security policy?

Y/N [ ] _____	1. By periodic written communications?
Y/N [ ] _____	2. By regular security tours?
Y/N [ ] _____	3. By participating in security program audits?

2.   Security Standards and Procedures

Y/N   [ ] _____   2.1.   Are there written standards for management performance in the security program?

Y/N   [ ] _____   2.2.   Are security program standards communicated to all levels of management?

Y/N [ ] _____   2.3.   Are security instructions and procedures defined in a program manual?

3.   Program Objectives

Y/N [ ] _____   3.1.   Are annual security program objectives set for the organization?

% [ ] _____   3.2.   What percentage of managers have developed written security program objectives?

% [ ] _____   3.3.   To what degree are security program objectives being achieved?

4.   Security Organization/Administration

Y/N [ ] _____   4.1.   Has a person been designated in writing to coordinate the security program?

Y/N [ ] _____   4.2.   Does this person have direct access to senior management on security program matters?

Y/N [ ] _____   4.3.   Are security responsibilities written into appropriate managers' job descriptions?

Y/N [ ] _____   4.4.   Is performance to security standards included in managers' performance reviews?

Y/N [ ] _____   4.5.   Is there some form of regular contact with law enforcement or other outside agencies to plan for assistance on security incidents?

Y/N [ ] _____   4.6.   Are people who are selected for regular and augmenting security duties screened for suitability and reliability?

5.   Management Training

% [ ] _____   5.1.   What percentage of managers received an orientation to the security program?

Y/N [ ] _____   5.2.   Is this orientation completed within one month of appointment to a management position?

% [ ] _____   5.3.   What percentage of managers have had a formal training course on fundamentals of security?

Y/N [ ] _____   5.4.   Are written materials used in this formal security management training course?

Y/N [ ] _____   5.5.   Is there a program which requires managers to attend formal security update training at least every three years?

% [ ] _____   5.6.   What percentage of managers required to have this update training have had it?

6.   Employee Training

% [ ] _____   6.1.   What percentage of employees receive an orientation to security program standards?

Y/N [ ] _____   6.2.   Are written materials included in the orientation?

Y/N [ ] _____   6.3.   Are signs and notices posted in appropriate places to reinforce knowledge of security standards?

% [ ] _____   6.4.   What percentage of employees, who are assigned specific security duties, receive formal training in how to perform their duties?

Y/N [ ] _____   6.5.   Are training manuals used to aid and reinforce security training?

Y/N [ ] _____   6.6.   Are records kept to verify security training and identify employees needing such training?

7.   Security Needs Established

Y/N [ ] _____   7.1.   Has a survey been made to determine the need for security measures, systems, and devices?

                       7.2.   Has this survey determined the need for:

Y/N [ ] _____   1. Intrusion alarms?
Y/N [ ] _____   2. CCTV?
Y/N [ ] _____   3. Fencing of perimeter, barring doors and windows?
Y/N [ ] _____   4. Computer protection systems?
Y/N [ ] _____   5. Lighting?
Y/N [ ] _____   6. Security officers?
Y/N [ ] _____   7. Vaults or protected storage?
Y/N [ ] _____   8. Signs?
Y/N [ ] _____   9. Controlled access?
Y/N [ ] _____   10. Workplace searches and inspections?
Y/N [ ] _____   11. Other?

                       _____

% [ ] _____   7.3.   What percentage of the needs, as determined by the survey, have been met?

7.4.   When were the security needs last reviewed and updated?

1 year ago   3 years ago
2 years ago   Not done

8.   Access Control

Y/N   [ ] _____   8.1.   Are methods taken to control entry and movement of people and vehicles as a security measure?

8.2.   Do these measures seek to control:

Y/N   [ ] _____   1. Employees?
Y/N   [ ] _____   2. Service technicians and consultants?
Y/N   [ ] _____   3. Contractors and sub-contractors?
Y/N   [ ] _____   4. Visitors?
Y/N   [ ] _____   5. Sales personnel?
Y/N   [ ] _____   6. Intruders?
Y/N   [ ] _____   7. Other? _____

Y/N   [ ] _____   8.3.   Are the allotment and duplication of keys controlled?

9.   Intangibles Control

Y/N   [ ] _____   9.1.   Are all people who have access to sensitive information required to sign a pledge to protect that information from improper release?

Y/N   [ ] _____   9.2.   Are there procedures to protect developments through copyrights, patents, trademarks, logos, and other organization identification?

Y/N   [ ] _____   9.3.   Are technical papers, speeches, and other presentations reviewed for protection of sensitive information before release?

Y/N   [ ] _____   9.4.   Are news releases, interviews, and other communications to the public reviewed for protection of sensitive information before release?

Y/N   [ ] _____   9.5.   Are access codes used to protect computer system files against improper entry to information?

10. Security Loss Reports

10.1.   How often are inventories, accountings, and records checks made to identify security losses?

Every month   Every 3 months   Every 6 months Once per year   Every other year   Not done

Y/N   [   ] _____   10.2.   Are security losses investigated with the findings and actions reported on a standard incident report form?

10.3.   Does the security program require a complete investigation of incidents involving the following:

Y/N   [   ] _____   1. Cash shortages?
Y/N   [   ] _____   2. Irregularities in financial accounts?
Y/N   [   ] _____   3. Equipment and materials shortages?
Y/N   [   ] _____   4. Expendable supplies and inventory shrinkages?
Y/N   [   ] _____   5. Production losses from disturbances?
Y/N   [   ] _____   6. Computer theft?
Y/N   [   ] _____   7. Other security losses?

11. Security Inspections

11.1.   How often are inspections of facilities and operations made to verify compliance with security standards?

Every month   Every 3 months   Every 6 months   Once per year   Every other year   Not done

Y/N   [   ] _____   11.2.   Are checklists used to guide security inspections?

Y/N   [   ] _____   11.3.   Are the results of security inspections communicated in writing to senior management?

Y/N   [   ] _____   11.4.   Is a copy of the inspection report given the affected supervisor for follow-up actions?

Y/N   [   ] _____   11.5.   Is there a written follow-up procedure to ensure that appropriate remedial actions have been taken?

12. Security Plan for Emergencies

Y/N   [   ] _____   12.1.   Are security requirements included in all emergency plans for both natural and technological incidents and disasters?

12.2.   Do these emergency plans include:

Y/N   [   ] _____   1. Kidnapping or taking of employees as hostages?
Y/N   [   ] _____   2. Bomb threats?
Y/N   [   ] _____   3. Civil or labor disturbances?
Y/N   [   ] _____   4. Control of looting and vandalism?
Y/N   [   ] _____   5. Alternate protection when alarms and control systems are damaged or deactivated?
Y/N   [   ] _____   6. Coordination with local security agencies or other outside sources of assistance?
Y/N   [   ] _____   7. Spectator control?
Y/N   [   ] _____   8. Executive protection?

Y/N   [   ] _____   12.3.   How often are drills held to train employees in emergency
                                 actions and test their performance?

Every month   Every 3 months   Every 6 months   Once per year   Every other year   Not done

13.   Records and Reports

Y/N   [   ] _____   13.1.   Is there a central file of security incident investigation
                                 reports?

Y/N   [   ] _____   13.2.   Are investigation reports kept in an active file for at least
                                 two years?

Y/N   [   ] _____   13.3.   Is there a central file of security inspection reports?

                                 13.4.   How often are security loss analyses prepared and distributed
                                 to managers?

Every month   Every 3 months   Every 6 months   Once per year   Every other year   Not done

14.   Reference Library

                                 14.1.   Evaluate the adequacy of the library of security reference
                                 texts.

Y/N   [   ] _____   14.2.   Does the organization receive security periodicals to update
                                 program knowledge?

Y/N   [   ] _____   14.3.   Are security articles or other written materials distributed to
                                 managers at least quarterly to update their security management
                                 knowledge?

15.   Enforcement

Y/N   [   ] _____   15.1.   Are there written guidelines on enforcement of security
                                 standards to aid supervisors in equitable enforcement?

16.   Security Management Audits Conducted

                                 16.1.   How often is an evaluation made of key security program
                                 indicators to determine effectiveness of the programs?

Every month   Every 3 months   Every 6 months   Once per year   Every other year   Not done

Y/N   [   ] _____   16.2.   Are the results of these program audits communicated to
                                 senior management?

Source: Top Shelf, Inc., Bellaire, Texas

6. Suggest that management hire an outside consultant. Competent security professionals have nothing to fear by obtaining a "second opinion." Often, the "expert from afar" has greater persuasion over management than members of their own staff. More often than not the consultant will re-inforce the security position by reaching the same conclusions and suggesting the same or similar recommendations.

7. Use the right timing to present viewpoints. Recognize that management's priorities are first and foremost the generating of profit. In order to capture management's attention, one should wait for the right time and circumstances to present a proposal. It is difficult to predict when this may occur. Therefore, develop the facts and have them ready at a moment's notice for presentation.

8. Develop a program of public relations. Security represents inconvenience even under the best of circumstances. Once management is thinking favorably about a proposal, the next step is to sell it to everyone in the organization. Most employees enjoy working in a safe and secure environment. Use this attitude to advantage in convincing employees that the program was designed as much for their safety and security as for the protection of the assets of the corporation.

Do homework in a thorough manner and be patient. Few are those who have been able to sell 100% of the security program to management the first time out of the starting blocks.

James F. Broder, CPP

Source Broder, J.F., Risk Analysis and the Security Survey. (Butterworth–Heinemann, Boston, 1984).

SENSORS: AIRCRAFT, BOAT, AND VEHICLE APPLICATIONS

Parked Aircraft Protection

Permanently installed aircraft protection sensors fall into two distinct categories. In the first are sensors that are permanently installed in the exterior skin of the aircraft, which on activation establish a detection pattern around the aircraft. Most commonly, the devices utilized for this application are variations of omni-directional, range gated, pulsed monostatic microwave devices. Depending on the size of the aircraft, between 1 and 4 sensors, typically located in the front and rear portions of the fuselage, and possibly at the wing tips, might be required. The detection pattern extends out, and forms a continuous circle of detection approximately 10–15 feet wide surrounding the aircraft. Movement inside the circle of detection, such as would be associated with the movement of wing tips and rotor blades in the wind, are not detected, and movement of airport ramp vehicles outside the zone of detection are likewise ignored.

In the second category, the sensors are installed on the interior of the aircraft and are very similar to traditional interior intrusion-detection system (IDS) protection. A typical installation might include sensors at the following perimeter access points:

- Main cabin doors
- Radome
- Wheel wells
- Baggage compartment doors
- Emergency window exits
- Ground power access ports
- Refueling access ports
- Engine access panels
- Onboard auxiliary power unit access
- Avionics bays

In addition to perimeter protection, most internal aircraft systems utilize motion detection sensors, typically either passive infrared or photoelectric, on the interior cabin and cockpit areas of the aircraft. Motion-detection protection is often installed in the exterior wheel wells, and occasionally in the baggage compartment. Interior motion-detection sensors may be permanently installed or affixed to appropriate locations, as necessary, using Velcro tape which remains in place.

An onboard controller is generally located in the cockpit of the aircraft, and may be powered by one or more solar panels deployed on top of the aircraft dashboard. Communications between the sensors and the onboard controller is accomplished through a wired data bus, or radio frequency (RF) links.

Communications from the onboard controller to the central station, airport security office, or pilot's belt annunciator are usually through an RF link; however, cellular telephone communications devices are becoming more popular.

Boat Protection

The basic concepts and devices associated with the protection of boats, using permanently installed interior sensors, are identical to those associated with aircraft protection, and equally as effective. Communications techniques between the sensors and onboard controller, and the onboard controller and annunciator, are also identical.

A typical installation might include perimeter-detection sensors at the following locations:
- Main cabin access doors
- Refueling access points
- State rooms and owner's cabin doors
- Bridge and flying bridge access doors
- Electronics and navigation equipment bay access hatches
- Safes
- Engine room access doors or hatches

In addition to perimeter protection, most internal boat protection systems utilize motion-detection sensors, typically either passive infrared or photoelectric, to protect the interior of cabins, staterooms, and engine rooms. Additionally, interior protection is often installed on the bridge, flying bridge, and in the radio room, if any.

As with aircraft protection systems, interior motion-detection sensors may be permanently installed, or affixed to appropriate locations, as necessary, using Velcro tape, which remains in place.

Boat protection systems are often used to monitor equipment status, as well as intrusion detection. Status monitoring can include such things as hydraulic pressures, bilges and bilge pumps, anchor status, and engine pressures and temperatures.

Unlike aircraft protection systems, boat protection systems do not ordinarily use exterior hull-mounted sensors.

Vehicle Protection

Vehicle protection systems have been available for many years. They typically consist of mechanical switches installed on personnel doors, engine hood, trunk, trailer cargo doors, and other similar access points. In addition to the perimeter sensors, a series of specialized sensors for use in vehicle protection systems have been developed.

- Current drain sensors are wired into the vehicle's electrical system, and sense the current drain associated with the lighting of the vehicle's interior lights when a door is opened.
- Ultrasonic motion-detection sensors are available specifically configured for installation in a vehicle's interior.
- Vibration sensors are installed in the vehicle's engine compartment, and will alarm if an intruder attempts to violently enter a vehicle or tow it away.

Vehicle protection systems draw their power from the battery system, and this can be a problem if not properly dealt with. One of the primary methods of attacking vehicle protection systems is through the use of a long, sharp object that is extended through the vehicle's front grill and into the battery. Puncturing the battery causes the electrolyte to leak out, rendering the battery powerless in a few seconds. The intruder may then attack the vehicle in any desired fashion. To counter this vulnerability, metal protective plates should be installed around the vulnerable sides of the battery.

Traditionally, vehicle protection systems have annunciated alarms audibly, through a siren or other noise-making device. Some recent systems use an RF link to annunciate on a belt pager worn by the driver, and some utilize a cellular telephone system. When cellular communications are utilized, the system is useless if the monitoring central station is not aware of the location of the vehicle. In addition to the traditional annunciation options, circuitry can be added to these systems to disable the vehicle's ignition system, fuel system, or both on activation of an alarm.

Martin L. Vitch, CPP

SENSORS: BARRIER PENETRATION DETECTORS

Barrier penetration detectors detect cutting and breaking types of forced entry through walls, ceilings, windows, doors, vaults, etc. They detect penetrations either by sensing the physical phenomena caused by the physical attack on the barrier or by detecting the actual penetration. Vibration detectors and heat sensors detect physical disturbance phenomena; foil tape, breakwire, and gridwire screen detect actual barrier penetrations. Audio detectors, especially those detectors designed to detect actual penetrations, can certainly be used as barrier penetration detectors.

Two types of vibration detectors are available to detect the phenomena generated by physical attacks on barriers. One type detects low-frequency structural vibrations; the second type detects high-frequency breaking glass vibrations. Structural vibration detectors, used for detecting physical attacks on walls and ceilings, detect the low-frequency energy generated by penetration attacks. Glass breakage detectors, used for protecting glass windows or showcase glass, detect the high-frequency energy generated as the glass is broken. Heat sensors detect the heat generated by a torch cutting through metal walls or doors.

Foil tape, breakwires, and gridwire screens detect the actual penetration through walls, ceilings, windows, and the like. These devices depend on the forced entry to break the foil tape or wire. Foil tape and gridwire screens are primarily used to protect windows; however, they can also be used on the inside of walls to detect penetrations.

Structural Vibration Detectors

Structural vibration detectors detect the low-frequency energy or vibrations generated by a forced attack on the physical barrier where they are installed. Although vibration detectors can be used to detect penetrations through barriers constructed from any rigid construction material, caution should be exercised before using them to protect walls of lesser structural integrity, such as sheet rock or thin metal. These types of barriers are more prone to vibrate from external forces that might cause false alarms. In general, if the valuables are worthy of barrier penetration detection, they should be stored behind masonry walls.

The low-frequency energy generated in a forced attack on a barrier is sensed by transducers that are secured directly to the barrier being protected. Two basic types of transducers are used to detect forced entries. One type is the piezoelectric transducers; the other is the mechanical contact switch. Piezoelectric transducers sense the mechanical energy and convert it into electrical signals that are proportional in magnitude to the mechanical vibrations.

Electrical signals from the piezoelectric transducers are amplified and sent to the signal processor over shielded or coaxial cables. Shielded cables are required to shield the piezoelectric low-voltage signals from outside electrical interference. Otherwise, electrical interference could totally mask valid signals and probably cause the detector to false alarm. With shielded cables, only valid signals are received and analyzed by the signal processor. To reduce false alarms from single accidental impact on the protected barrier, most vibration detectors use an adjustable pulse-counting accumulator in conjunction with a manual sensitivity adjustment. The count circuit can be set to count a specific number of pulses having a specified magnitude before it will initiate an alarm. Then, when the number of pulses with amplitudes equal to or exceeding the preset threshold is accumulated, an alarm is initiated.

The second type of transducer, the mechanical contact switch, uses a seismic mass that makes the electrical connection between the switch contacts, or it uses a seismic mass to open a switch contact. A seismic mass is simply a small weight that responds to an externally applied external force that causes the weight to accelerate. For instance, if a small object is placed on a table and the table top struck sharply, the object will bounce. The height of the bounce depends on how hard the table top is hit. This is basically how the mechanical switch functions. When the force of the impact on the protected barrier is adequate to bounce the seismic mass, the contact is opened, generating a momentary open circuit.

In the mechanical switch that uses a seismic mass to make electrical contact, the mass is free to vibrate along a vertical axis, returning to rest on the contact under its own weight. Every time the mass is accelerated or bounced from the contacts it causes a momentary open circuit.

In the unrestricted seismic mass switch, the size of the mass and the spacing between the electrical contacts are designed so that the detector can differentiate between small impact from normal activity and the large impacts from a forced entry. When the mass forms part of the movable switch contact arm, the force impacts accelerate the mass, which opens the contacts.

The difference between the mechanical switches that use a spring-loaded seismic mass and those that use an unrestricted mass is that the spring-loaded mechanical switches rely on the force of the spring to close the contacts, and the unrestricted switch relies on the weight of the seismic mass to make the contact. Since the spring-loaded switches rely on a spring to make the contacts, they can be mounted in any orientation on the wall or ceiling. They usually have an adjustment screw for varying the force on the contact to satisfy the particular application requirement. The switch with the unrestricted seismic mass must always be mounted in a vertical position so that the seismic mass will return to rest on the electrical contacts.

Glass Breakage

Glass breakage detectors are similar to the structural vibration detectors. The difference is that the piezoelectric and mechanical transducers are designed to respond to the higher frequency energies generated in breaking glass and not the low-frequency structural vibrations. In fact, one of the cautions about selecting glass breakage detectors is their response to low-frequency vibrations. If they are sensitive to low frequencies, they will be prone to false alarms caused by someone knocking on the protected glass.

Another difference is that the signal processor should initiate an alarm on the first signal from the piezoelectric transducer or series of pulses from the mechanical transducers. Glass breakage detectors should not be connected into a pulse-count circuit as with structural vibration detectors. They should respond to the first impact on the window because most often only one impact is required to break out the window.

Heat Sensors

Heat sensors respond to the physical phenomena of an intrusion by detecting the heat generated by a cutting torch or burn bar while cutting through a metal barrier such as a safe or vault door. The sensor consists of a thermostat that opens an electrical contact when the temperature of the mounting surface reaches a preset temperature. The detection temperature for heat detectors used to protect metal barriers is between 135 degrees F and 165 degrees F.

A thermostatic heat sensor uses a mechanically restricted bimetallic strip that distorts with increasing temperature until the present temperature is reached. At this time, the bimetallic strip has distorted to its limit and snaps open. When it opens, the electrical contacts open and an alarm is activated.

Foil Tape

Foil tape is a metallized conductive tape used to protect window glass and other barriers against forcible penetration. In the case of windows, the tape should be secured around the perimeter of glass windows within 2 to 4 inches of the window frames. When the glass is broken, the glass severs the supervised foil tape, thus initiating an alarm.

Often foil tape is installed on a glass window in a closed loop pattern. A closed loop is formed when the installer starts applying the tape in one corner of the glass and continues around the periphery of the glass until he returns to the starting point, connecting the tape to the terminal strip where he started. This type of installation can be surreptitiously compromised during normal open hours by electrically shorting or bridging between either the ends of the foil tape or the terminal connections with a piece of conductive material. The intruder can then return after closing and knock out the window to gain entry without being detected.

To eliminate this type of compromise, the tape should be installed so that it can be electrically supervised at the alarm signal transmitter with either double circuit protection or end-of-line impedance terminations. Double circuit protection supervises one section of the foil with one electrical polarity provided by an electrical DC source, which could be a battery connected across the ends of the foil tape. If the foil tape is cut, there is an open circuit and if the circuit is electrically shorted, there is a loss of signal.

Either attempted compromise initiates an alarm. An end-of-line impedance termination, either a resistor or a resistor/capacitor network, is monitored by a balanced bridge network by the alarm signal transmitter.

If the foil is cut or shorted, the bridge becomes imbalanced, initiating an alarm. Regardless of the type of circuit supervision, an alarm should be initiated if the foil tape is cut, broken, or electrically shorted. Normally the foil circuit should be supervised 24 hours a day, whether the area is open or closed. Continually supervising the circuit will increase the possibility of detecting attempts to compromise the protection.

Breakwire Grids

A breakwire grid is a closely spaced grid pattern formed by a continuous electrical wire forming a closed electrical circuit. The breakwire can be installed directly on the barrier requiring protection or it can be installed in a grill or screen that is, in turn, installed on the barrier or over an opening requiring protection. Breakwire grids should be continually supervised and when a forcible entry penetrates the protected surface and breaks the wire, the electrical continuity is interrupted and an alarm is initiated.

Robert L. Barnard

Source Barnard, R.L., Intrusion Detection Systems. (Butterworth-Heinemann, Boston, 1982).

SENSORS: BURIED LINE SENSORS

Buried line sensors protect an area along the ground just above the sensor transducer cable or sensors by detecting anyone crossing the protected zone. Someone who crosses the sensitive area induces both seismic energy and exerts pressure in the ground. Buried sensors are available that detect strain and seismic energy. Another type of buried line sensor is available that detects the presence of ferrous metals being carried or worn by the person crossing the transducer cable, as well as detecting local induced pressure.

Piezoelectric transducers are used primarily to detect short-range pressure disturbances in the ground, and geophones are primarily used to detect longer-range seismic waves. These are basically the same devices used for the fence disturbance sensor transducers, and in some cases they are the same device.

Geophone Transducers

Buried geophones detect the low-frequency seismic energy induced in the ground by someone crossing the protected area above the sensors, and convert this energy into electrical signals. The electrical signals correspond to the frequency of the induced seismic energy, and they are proportional in amplitude to the magnitude of the energy. These induced signals are sent to the signal processor, where they are filtered before entering the signal processor. The band-pass of the filter corresponds to the seismic energies with frequencies or signatures typical of someone crossing the geophone sensors. When the characteristics of the induced signals satisfy the processor alarm criteria, an alarm is initiated.

A geophone consists of a movable spring-balanced coil of fine wire suspended around a permanent magnet. The coil of fine wire is cylindrical to slide over the magnetic rod fixed to the geophone housing. When the geophone is acted upon by the seismic energy, the permanent magnet vibrates with the geophone housing at the frequency of the induced energy. The vibrating magnet moves in line with the coil of fine wire, which tends to stay near rest. It stays near rest because the fine spring holding the wire coil in suspension around the magnet offers very little resistance to the moving geophone housing. As the magnet vibrates in the coil, the magnetic lines of force associated with the permanent magnet induce an electromotive force (emf) in the coil This emf, or electrical signal, is the signal that is monitored by the signal processor.

Geophones are very sensitive to detecting even low-level seismic energies generated by moving objects anchored in the ground such as trees, fences, light poles, or telephone poles. When these objects are subjected to wind loads, the overturning forces are absorbed by the ground. As the winds vary, the objects move, inducing seismic energy in the ground. To help reduce the need for the signal processor to differentiate between these energies and valid intrusion signals, the geophones should be installed a reasonable distance from this type of object. A reasonable distance is difficult to define because of all the varying parameters in any given installation. However, the following minimum distances can be used as guides:

about 30 feet from tree-drip line, 10 feet from fences, and a distance about equal to the height of the light pole or telephone pole away from the pole.

Piezoelectric Transducers

Piezoelectric transducers detect the stresses or pressure induced in the ground by anyone crossing the protected area above the sensor line. The transducer consists of a quartz crystal that is secured to the transducer case such that when an external pressure is applied to the transducer the crystal generates a voltage. In operation, when someone steps on the ground above the transducer, the pressure from the person's weight stresses the piezoelectric crystal. The stressed crystal generates an electrical signal that is proportional to the applied pressure. When the characteristics of the signal satisfy the processor alarm criteria, an alarm is initiated.

Strain/Magnetic Line Sensors

The combined strain and magnetic line sensors detect both the pressure or strain induced in the ground by someone crossing the sensor line and the presence of ferrous material carried or worn by the person crossing. The sensor consists of a passive transducer cable and an alarm electronics module. The passive transducer cable uses a magnetic material wound with a pair of sense coil windings. This assembly is wrapped with a stainless steel jacket and covered with an outer plastic jacket. The two sense windings are wound on the magnetic core and connected together in a manner to cancel far-field seismic and magnetic disturbances.

In operation, the residual flux density of the ferromagnetic core material and the flux density of the earth's magnetic field remain constant during normal circumstances. The weight of anyone crossing the sensitive area above the transducer cable stresses the ferromagnetic core material. The induced stress alters the magnetic flux that generates a voltage in the sense winding overlay around the coil. A voltage is also induced in the sense winding when someone crosses the transducer cable carrying or wearing ferrous material. In this case, the ferrous materials

distort the earth's magnetic field. The changing magnetic field alters the coil magnetic flux density, generating a voltage in the sense winding. Signals resulting from either the mechanical stresses or from the presence of ferrous materials, or these combined signals, are processed and analyzed by the signal processor in the alarm electronics module. Before the signal is analyzed and when their characteristics satisfy the established alarm criteria, an alarm is initiated. The purpose of the dual-channel signal processing is to reduce false alarms from wind and electrical interference.

Robert L. Barnard

Source Barnard, R.L., Intrusion Detection Systems. (Butterworth–Heinemann, Boston, 1982).

SENSORS: PORTABLE AND RAPID DEPLOYMENT APPLICATIONS

Applications

The sensor applications that immediately follow are intended to be illustrative of the common potential applications, rather than being all inclusive. In each case, the basic concept is that sensors will be deployed around the area requiring protection, and removed or relocated when they are no longer necessary.

Replacement of Inoperative Sensors. When an exterior perimeter sensor becomes inoperative, it may take some time to repair. Traditionally, this has meant, depending on the criticality of the system, dedicating a guard to the inoperative section of the perimeter, increasing patrol frequency in the area, or simply accepting the vulnerability and hoping that it is not obvious to a potential intruder. In this application, data is transmitted either directly, or through repeaters to the site-monitoring facility.

Supplemented Protection in Times of Increased Threat. Unfortunately, increases in threat levels are not predictable with sufficient advance warning to permit the design and application of additional permanent protection. Portable rapid deployment sensors can be quickly set up and activated to provide additional protection as needed. As with the replacement sensors, these devices typically transmit to the site-monitoring facility.

Special Events and Temporary Requirements. Trade shows, conventions, exhibits, and similar events often result in large quantities of high-dollar-value equipment being displayed in areas where there is little or no permanent protection. Portable and rapid deployment sensors can be placed within or around exhibits to provide a level of protection commensurate with their value. For the most part, sensors deployed in this manner will transmit to the exhibition security office.

Utility Sites. Utility sites, particularly construction locations, often involve substantial high-dollar-value equipment that must be left on site for an extended period of time. Since these sites are typically remote, alarms are typically transmitted to an on-site receiver where they are forwarded to the monitoring facility through either telephone lines or cellular communications.

Cargo Containers. Shipping containers, particularly those containing high-dollar-value cargo, are frequently left unattended in vulnerable areas for considerable lengths of time. At cargo storage facilities, this condition can be prolonged over days or even weeks while the cargo is assembled and routed. Alarms are typically transmitted to a site security office.

Construction Sites. Frequently construction sites, both residential and commercial, are the victims of vandalism and theft of construction materials. Materials stored on a construction site can be of high-dollar-value, and virtually untraceable; thus, there is a need for temporary intrusion-detection system (IDS) protection. Alarms from the deployed sensors are typically transmitted to an on-site receiver, and converted to either telephone or cellular communications as appropriate.

Trucks in Transit. Trucks en route present several problems. Theft from the vehicle and theft of the vehicle are both major concerns. While some vehicles carry two drivers, allowing one to be awake at all times, most trucks are single-driver vehicles that must stop for meals, rest and sleep, bad weather, and vehicle service.

Even if the stops are made at truck terminals, truck stops, and other similar locations, the vehicle must often be left unattended for substantial periods of time. Protection for these vehicles is typically carried in the vehicle cab and deployed as necessary around the vehicle. In addition to protection deployed around the vehicle, this situation may call for devices such as cargo net/tarp, breakwire, or other similar sensors applied directly to the cargo. This type of system typically uses the radio frequency (RF) link to transmit from the sensors to the vehicle, and then a cellular telephone system to transmit from the vehicle to a monitoring station.

Railroad Classification Yards and Sidings. Trains are continuously routed onto sidings and may remain there unattended for a few hours to a few days while trains are re-configured for further transportation. Devices are typically carried in the caboose and deployed around cars carrying sensitive cargo. Alarms may be sent to the railroad yard office, or through a cellular communications system to a central station.

Aircraft and Aircraft Parking Areas. Without exception, aircraft represent a high-dollar-value item, which in itself is deserving of protection. When the aircraft is loaded with cargo, it becomes an even greater target. Attacks against aircraft may include theft, pilferage, attempts to sabotage the aircraft, and attempts to secrete contraband aboard. Protection devices are typically carried in the aircraft cargo hold and deployed on landing. Alarms are transmitted to either the airport security office, or to a belt pager device worn by one or more crew members.

Port Facilities, Boats, Wharves, and Docks. A variety of protection requirements present themselves in the seaport environment. Cargo, either in-transit, or being re-configured for shipping (containerization, conversion from rail to boat, etc.), is highly vulnerable to pilfering. Items are often left outdoors and unattended overnight, on wharves and in storage areas. Additionally, it may be necessary to deploy sensors along a dock or wharf to detect individuals attempting to either enter or leave a ship. Alarms are monitored either at the port security office, onboard a ship, or through a cellular network.

698   Sensors: Portable and Rapid Deployment Applications

Automobiles. Automobile protection is typically associated with executive protection situations; however, it may also be appropriate for courier vehicles or vehicles delivering small high-dollar-value items. Devices are typically carried in the trunk of the vehicle and deployed when the vehicle is parked. Monitoring is typically accomplished by the driver through a belt-mounted pager-type device.

Sensors

There are a wide variety of portable and rapid deployment sensors available today, and the number seems to be increasing daily. Technologies range from old, traditional IDS sensors, which have been re-configured into an appropriate package for exterior rapid deployment use, while others are devices specifically developed for this application.

Microwave. Portable and rapid deployment microwave sensors are simply traditional fixed-installation devices, packaged with a portable battery power supply, charger, and tripod-mounting assembly.

This sensor is available with either an internal or external communications capability. Microwave systems are available in both bi-static and monostatic configurations, and in both high- and low-band operating frequencies.

Range Gated, Sharp Cut-Off, Pulsed Radar. This sensor is designed to accommodate some of the unique requirements associated with aircraft and helicopter protection. Typically, two devices are positioned under the aircraft so that their detection patterns extend out and form a continuous circle of detection approximately 10–15 feet wide surrounding the aircraft. Movement inside the circle of detection, such as would be associated with the movement of wing tips and rotor blades in the wind, are not detected and movement of airport ramp vehicles outside the zone of detection are likewise ignored. An internal communications system reporting to either a belt pager or the airport security office is provided with this sensor.

Air Couple RF Field Sensor. Consisting of a series of cable support posts, a signal processor, and 100 meters of sensor cables, this device is available only in a portable, rapid deployment version. A 100-meter zone of the sensor is human portable and can be erected in approximately 30 minutes. It has both internal and external communications capabilities.

Support posts are driven into the ground along the 100 meter length of the zone. Two cables are extended from the signal processor and affixed to the support poles, with one near the ground and the other about waist high. When activated, an RF field is established extending from the ground, to approximately 3–4 feet high. Disturbance of the field initiates an alarm.

Photoelectric or Laser "Fences." This is an adaptation of the standard configuration exterior photoelectric technology, with the addition of a battery power supply, and a tripod mount. The system is available with both infrared (IR) and laser light sources, and with either internal or external communications.

Passive Infrared. The passive infrared technology is essentially identical to that currently in use for both interior and exterior traditional applications. In fact, one of the devices is assembled by simply adding a tripod-mounting system, and battery power supply to an existing sensor.

Detection configurations available include virtually all traditional patterns, 90-degree to 360-degree volumetric coverage, long range, and curtain coverage.

Some of the more creative packaging concepts include self-contained traffic cones and "towers" containing the sensor, power supply, transmitter, and battery charger onboard. Other configurations are generally based on either tripod mounting, or application to surfaces, typically vehicle interiors, with double-sided tape.

Magnetically Deployed Vibration Sensor. This is a standard, seismic mass-based vibration sensor, battery, and RF transmitter in a housing with a magnetic backing. The assembly is typically magnetically attached to either the interior or exterior of a metal cargo container or any metal enclosure. If an intruder attempts entry into the container or enclosure, an alarm is transmitted. An internal communications system is supplied with the sensor. This device might report to a cellular telephone reporting system, or through an RF link to a site security center.

Magnetic Contact Sensor. This sensor is a standard magnetic or balanced magnetic switch, as appropriate, fixed into position with either two-sided tape or Velcro. The sensor is typically installed on truck cargo doors, or container access doors, and operates in a manner identical to that of any other magnetic switch. Detection is limited to the opening of protected doors. An internal RF communications system is supplied. This sensor may report to a site security center, a cellular communications device, or a data logger.

Breakwire Loop Sensor. The breakwire loop consists of a transmitter, and a section of thin wire. The wire is extended through an object such as a sealing point, lock hasp, or other similar item. Breaking the wire transmits an alarm. This sensor is often used on vehicles and cargo containers in place of or in addition to frangible seals. Data communications are supplied through an internal transmitter assembly, and the sensor reports to a site security center, a cellular communications device, or a data logger.

Fiber-Optic Cargo Net Sensor. This is a fiber-optic continuity type sensor, consisting of a net of jacketed fiber-optic cables, bonded together at the crossover points. Any break in the fiber-optic loop continuity will initiate an alarm. This configuration allows the sensor to be used as a "cargo net" type covering for virtually any type of material, cargo, or vehicle.

This device is supplied in a "sensor only" configuration. The end user must add the power supply, external communications system, and any necessary tie downs to hold the fiber-optic net in place.

Sensor Tarps with Vibration Pack. Rather than the fiber-optic cargo net configuration, this device utilizes a heavy canvas tarp that is deployed over the top of the material to be protected. Two configurations are available. One is imprinted with large announcements warning that it is a sensor system, while the other is unmarked. Incorporated into the tarp is a vibration detector, which senses movement, and an internal communications system. Alarms

may be transmitted to a vehicle-mounted cellular telephone system, or to a site security center.

Seismic. The seismic sensor consists of a series of geophones attached at 10-foot intervals to an interconnecting cable. Each geophone has a spike protruding from its bottom; the spike is inserted into the ground to hold the sensor in place. Other than the surface installation, this device is identical to the standard geophone sensor. It is supplied in a "sensor only" configuration. The end user must add the power supply, external communications system, and battery.

Martin L. Vitch, CPP

SENSORS: PORTABLE VS. PERMANENT

For many years the concept of intrusion detection, both interior and exterior, was one of permanently installed, fixed location systems. Because the equipment was permanently installed, any changes that became necessary were difficult and costly to make. Unfortunately, due to the difficulty and expense, needed changes were often not made. This left many systems, which were originally effectively designed and installed, with large "holes" in the protection they now offered.

The introduction of wireless technology alleviated the problem to some limited extent, but for the most part this technology was confined to interior residential applications. Point identification monitor and control systems allowed some system re-configuration with little re-wiring, as long as the new sensor location was near one of the data busses; however, the problem did not really come close to a solution until the recent introduction of a variety of portable and rapid deployment sensor systems for exterior applications.

Portable and rapid deployment sensor systems offer a number of distinct advantages over permanent fixed installations. As a group, the sensors are:

- •Mobile. They can be relocated as necessary, often in a matter of minutes.
- •Reusable. Rather than being simply abandoned, sensors no longer needed in a particular area can be stockpiled.

•Cost-Effective. Resources do not have to be expended to install or support extensive data communications wiring systems.

•Require No Design Lead Time. Intrusion-detection system (IDS) designs, particularly those requiring new or re-configured data communications wiring, can require substantial lead time. Portable rapid deployment sensor systems virtually eliminate the design lead time problem.

•Require Minimal Installation Time. Installation of most permanent systems is a lengthy process. Most portable and rapid deployment sensors install in less than 1 hour per zone; many in less than 10 minutes.

•Modular. Sensors can be added or subtracted to existing zones, or new zones can be created in a short period of time, with relatively little cost.

Unfortunately, there is a down side to portable and rapid deployment sensor systems. Because there is virtually no site preparation associated with the installation of these devices, the experienced nuisance alarm rate will be somewhat higher than with a permanent installation.

Since most portable and rapid deployment devices are battery powered, the question of battery recharge or replacement can become a major factor. Battery life varies from system to system, and is effected by several factors, including:

•The basic power requirements of the sensor and transmitter.

•Sizing of the battery pack, and the availability of space within the sensor for additional batteries.

•The operating environment, particularly the air temperature.

•Frequency of supervisory transmissions.

•Frequency of nuisance alarms.

Based on the factors above, and the characteristics of the system in use, battery life may range between 24 hours and 10 days, with the majority of systems falling into the 24–72 hour range.

If large numbers of sensors are utilized, careful planning is necessary to ensure adequate sensor rotation and re-charge, or battery replacement and re-charge as appropriate. Failure to do so can lead to a massive system failure as multiple batteries go dead at the same time.

Self-Protection

Self-protection capability is an important consideration. Some sensors are self-protecting, that is the sensor is completely surrounded by a detection field. The 360-degree passive infrared sensor is typical of a self-protecting device. Other sensors require that they be deployed in pairs, or other multiples so that each sensor can be located within the protection field of another. Unfortunately, some sensors have no self-protection capability, and are substantially vulnerable to compromise.

Alarm Communications and Annunciation

Obviously, communications between the individual sensors, and a monitoring location is a key factor. Most communication between these devices is accomplished over radio requency (RF) transmission links. Some are self-supervising, sending a supervisory transmission to the monitor at periodic intervals, some as often as every 10 seconds. Others are totally unsupervised, transmitting only alarm, or low-battery indications.

The RF communications link for these systems may report back directly to a security force monitoring station, to a pager-type device carried by one or more guards, or to a local receiver, which is then hard wired into a traditional IDS data transmission system.

Communications and annunciation equipment associated with portable and rapid deployment sensor systems fall into five categories.

1. Internal communications systems incorporate the RF transmitter, antenna, and other necessary components directly into the sensor package. The sensor is procured with the transmitter installed and ready for activation. Systems of this type typically utilize their own proprietary annunciation system.

2. External communications systems, consisting of RF transmitters, receivers, and necessary accessories, are procured independently of the sensors, and are typically installed by the end user. Many manufacturers construct their sensors leaving internal space available for installation of the transmitter package, and provide batteries to power the external communications equipment.

3.   Cellular telephone systems are utilized in a somewhat different manner than the RF devices. Assuming the presence of an adequate cellular network, cellular telephone systems are typically utilized to communicate directly with either a proprietary monitoring facility, or a commercial central station located many miles from the protected site. Cellular systems can be adapted to use with any portable or rapid deployment technology; however, they are often associated with vehicle protection systems, cargo protection systems, executive protection devices installed in hotel rooms, and other systems that may move a considerable distance each day. Where RF systems are generally tied to fixed-position RF antennas, limiting the placement of the sensors, cellular systems are restricted only by the presence of the cellular networks, which are increasing in coverage daily. The key to successful operation of a cellular telephone-based system is assuring that the monitoring facility is notified each time the system relocates. This is true even in the case of a vehicle-mounted system when frequent stops are routine. Notification must identify the location of the system and identify the appropriate response force, such as the local or state police, and telephone number.

4.   Audible/visible annunciation options are available with several different systems. Audible annunciation may consist of bells, sirens, horns, or in at least one case, the repeated playing of a loud taped message similar to "STOP!! You are entering an unauthorized area." Visible annunciation components include flashing lights, strobes, and rotating beacon lights.   As with most portable and rapid deployment systems, battery capability is critical. While the typical battery system may support the sensor and transmitter for extended periods of time, audible and visible annunciation systems may deplete the battery within a matter of minutes.

5.   Data loggers are used in situations where it is necessary to be able to ensure the integrity of a cargo, rather than immediately annunciate an alarm.   This application is particularly important in military systems, which involve complex weaponry or communications equipment.   While intrusion detection is important, it is equally or more important to be able to verify that the equipment has not been tampered with or compromised.   When the cargo arrives, the data logger is read to determine if the cargo has been compromised.

Automated Response and Activated Barrier Systems

Often, particularly in cargo in transit applications, a response to an alarm is not possible, and the use of a data logger is unsatisfactory. In these situations the use of automated response and activated barrier systems should be considered. Probably the most commonly encountered version of this type of response is the dye bomb often included in money taken in a bank robbery. The bomb explodes, dying the money and the perpetrator, making identification of the individual easy and the money useless.

Cargo in transit, enclosed in a shipping container, can often be protected in this manner through a product called sticky foam. On activation, a foam generator fills the container with a dense, extremely sticky foam substance, which makes it virtually impossible for an intruder to enter the container or remove anything from it. Several other technologies are available to accomplish the same end result. This should be considered a last resort since the cleanup after activation of one of these devices can be expensive and time consuming.

Martin L. Vitch, CPP

SENSORS: SPECIAL SITUATIONS

Occasionally, situations are encountered that do not lend themselves to traditional intrusion-detection sensors or application techniques. To provide protection in these instances, a series of special application sensors have been developed. Some of the special application sensors are simply traditional exterior sensors with slightly modified packaging, signal processing, or both. Others are unique devices specifically developed for a single application.

Underwater Detection

The ability to detect intruders underwater can be an essential part of a site security system. Applications for this type of detection include:

•Sites with substantial waterfront exposure as part of their perimeter.

•Nuclear power plant cooling water inlets/outlets.

•Harbors and commercial seaports.

•Marinas.

•Streams and canals passing through security areas.

There are several technologies associated with underwater detection. For the most part, devices available today are combined devices that serve as both an intrusion-detection sensor and a barrier. Several devices that operate independently of any barrier component are being developed and may reach the market shortly. Currently available technologies include:

Underwater Breakwire Fiber-Optic Sensor. This is a fiber-optic continuity-type sensor consisting of a fiber-optic cable, embedded in a rigid, reinforced support system of waterproof, rubberized material. The fiber-optic cable is arranged in a mesh configuration approximately 4–6 inches on center, and can be custom manufactured in any desired size. For very large areas, such as harbor and marina entrances, anchorages, canals, and similar sites, several large sensor panels can be interconnected and extended almost indefinitely. Any break in the fiber-optic continuity will result in an alarm. Note that this device serves as both a physical barrier and a sensor. In smaller sections this device is an effective culvert sensor.

Underwater Microbending Fiber-Optic Sensor. This sensor is composed of a series of fiber-optic cables, contained within a watertight hollow metal framework. When an intruder attempts to penetrate the sensor, movement of the hollow metal tube causes movement of the internal fiber-optic cable. The fiber-optic cable movement alters the characteristics of the transmitted light signals, and that alteration is detected as an alarm. This sensor is custom manufactured by the supplier in the dimensions required for each application.

Underwater Capacitance Detector. A metal conductor is encased in a rugged, waterproof, heavy insulating jacket, and fabricated into a grid approximately 8 inches on center. The resulting panels, pre-fabricated in any desired

size, are installed as needed and serve as both a barrier and a sensor. A capacitance-detection module establishes and monitors the capacitance of the cable with reference to ground. If the cable is cut, the insulation is broken and the cable is grounded through the water causing an alarm.

Strain-Sensitive Cable in Waterproof Conduit. This sensor utilizes the traditional exterior strain-sensitive cable sensor, installed in a waterproof conduit assembly, which is custom fabricated into the configuration required for each application. This device also serves as both a barrier and a sensor. Unlike the previous devices, which are factory assembled as underwater sensors, this device is manufactured on-site from the standard strain-sensitive cable sensor and readily available materials. In application, due to the potential difficulty in assembling the waterproof conduit assembly, this configuration is generally reserved for smaller areas.

Culverts

Culverts and similar terrain features that cross the perimeter of a site can present a difficult problem in intrusion-detection systems (IDS) design. Often they represent a direct path into the site, and are ignored in many systems. A good culvert sensor should be reliable, and incorporate some method of cleaning out debris, which tends to accumulate behind the sensor structure. In many instances this is accomplished by hinging one side of the sensor structure, allowing it to swing out for easy clean-out. After clean-out, the sensor structure is affixed in place with appropriate locking devices.

All of the technologies associated with underwater detection systems may be used for culvert protection. The following additional technologies and techniques are also useful.

Re-Bar with Strain-Sensitive Cable. This arrangement is generally used in situations where areas under the perimeter fence are subject to washout, erosion, or other natural phenomena that creates sufficient space between a fence and the ground to allow an individual to crawl under the fence undetected. To counter this vulnerability, steel reinforcing rods are driven into the ground approximately 4 inches apart along the length of the washout. Additional reinforcing rods are welded to the vertical rods horizontally at 4-inch intervals up to the bottom of the fence, and the entire assembly is welded to the bottom of the fence.

The end result is an extension of the "fence" below the actual bottom of the fence fabric into the ground. The strain-sensitive cable is then deployed along the welded reinforcing rod array to provide IDS protection. The primary drawback to this arrangement is an almost certain nuisance alarm problem when the culvert is actively carrying runoff.

This arrangement can also be used to protect traditional pipe and culvert assemblies when removal for the purpose of cleaning debris out of the culvert is not a concern.

Mechanical Vibration Sensors. In this application, a metal frame of steel reinforcing rods or other similar material is installed inside the culvert. An exterior mechanical vibration sensor is affixed to the metal framework. Any attempt to penetrate through the culvert will alarm the mechanical vibration sensor.

As with the strain-sensitive cable application, this arrangement will create an almost certain nuisance alarm problem when the culvert is actively carrying runoff.

Vehicle Locator Systems

With automobile prices and auto theft increasing almost daily, the recovery of stolen vehicles is becoming a major goal. While not a true intrusion-detection sensor, a system has been developed to enable law enforcement officials to quickly locate a stolen vehicle, sometimes with the responsible party still inside. This system is currently available on a limited basis in some areas of the country.

A radio transponder device is installed in the protected vehicle. The transponder remains in a passive state until the vehicle is stolen. When the victim notifies law enforcement officials of the theft, the transponder is activated by a radio signal, and begins transmitting. The transponder's signal is used to pinpoint the location of the vehicle, sometimes to within a few feet.

Protection of Pipes

Industrial sites often have large diameter pipes transiting across sensitive area perimeters. The pipes carry process materials, steam, and other substances necessary for operation of the facility, and in many cases, are clustered together forming what amounts to a bridge across the perimeter.

The diameter of the pipes often make it impossible for a guard to clearly see the top of the assembly, allowing a potential intruder to use the pipe bridge to gain undetected penetration of the perimeter. Since the pipes are often higher than the site perimeter lighting, an intruder may escape notice by site security forces on routine patrol.

Relocation of the pipes underground may be impractical due to cost, disruption to process, and interference with the operation of some perimeter sensors and buried cables.

Two technologies are typically used to formulate this type of protection.

•The exterior capacitance sensor has proven effective when arrayed along the length of the pipe. A collar is fabricated and installed on either end of the pipe assembly, and the capacitance detection cables are extended between the collars. Any attempt to use the pipes as a bridge forces the intruder into contact with the capacitance sensor, thereby causing an alarm.

•The taut-wire technology may be arrayed and utilized in a manner identical to that of the capacitance sensor.

Vibration sensors are unsuitable for this application due to the effects of wind-induced motion, motion of material through the pipes, and the effects of rain on the pipes' horizontal surface area.

Protection of Power Lines

Power and communications lines passing over a site perimeter have always presented a problem. A potential intruder can use the wiring as a bridging aid, allowing undetected penetration of the perimeter. Since the power and communications lines are typically higher than the site perimeter lighting, an intruder will generally not be seen by site security forces on routine patrol.

Relocating the utility wiring underground can be expensive, disruptive to existing buried cables, and may interfere with the operation of some perimeter sensors.

Adjustable strain gages, essentially digital scales, can be inserted into the cable messenger line, if any, or the guy wire supporting one of the supporting telephone poles. The strain gages are adjusted to alarm when a predetermined weight or strain is detected on the cable. An intruder attempting to cross the perimeter, using the protected cables as an aid, will be detected by the strain gage and an alarm will be transmitted.

Protection of Conduit

Sensitive data is frequently transmitted from place to place through cables enclosed in metal conduit for protection. Often the conduit travels through uncontrolled areas of a facility, allowing potential access to the conduit for tampering. An intruder can separate the conduit at the joints, or simply saw through the metal pipe gaining access to the data transmission cables. Using one-way screws, sealing joints with epoxy, and using expensive rigid galvanized conduit may eliminate the disassembly vulnerability; however, the cutting attack vulnerability remains.

A simple method of protection in this situation is the use of the exterior electret transducer, strain-sensitive cable sensor. The sensor is wrapped around the conduit, with approximately one complete revolution every 18–24 inches, extending for the length of the conduit run. Any attempt to penetrate the conduit, by either disassembly or sawing, will be detected by the sensor.

Communications Tower Protection

Communications, lighting, and closed-circuit television (CCTV) towers are often vulnerable to climbing by unauthorized individuals, and are rarely afforded IDS protection.

Recently, two different devices have been used successfully to protect towers. A small, short-range, monostatic microwave sensor can be installed approximately 10 feet above the base of the tower with the detection pattern pointing up, or a capacitance sensor can be arrayed around the tower approximately 10 feet above the ground. In both instances, persons walking on the ground below the sensor are not detected but any attempt to climb the tower causes an alarm.

Long-Range Audio Detection

Long-range audio detection devices are effective detection devices for use at remote sites. Essentially these devices are highly directional microphones, capable of detecting normal conversation at distances of up to 1 mile, and whispered conversations at distances up to 150 feet.

Typically, these devices are mounted on CCTV pan and tilt units so that they can be used to scan the exterior perimeter for noises associated with intruders.

Environmental Sensing

Modern IDS is capable of monitoring a wide variety of conditions not necessarily associated with the detection of intrusions. A truly integrated IDS may include monitoring for the purpose of facility or energy management, process controlling, and equipment maintenance requirement monitoring. Virtually any condition that can be sensed can be monitored by an IDS. Some of the capabilities include:

- Water presence or level
- Gas detection
- Low or high temperature
- Equipment status—on or off
- Equipment utilization hours
- Activation of heating, cooling, and other environmental systems
- Activation of interior lighting
- Water flow in pipes
- Fire detection
- Fire suppression

The capability of the modern IDS to accept integration of a wide variety of capabilities increases its commercial utility and can, in many instances, be the factor that convinces corporate management to invest in the system.

Martin L. Vitch, CPP

SENTENCING OF CORPORATIONS: FEDERAL GUIDELINES

In 1984 the Sentencing Reform Act established the U.S. Sentencing Commission. The Commission's mandate was to create guidelines designed to eliminate disparity in sentences being meted out by federal courts. The idea was to replace a very loose sentencing approach with an approach that would be consistent and impose punishments equal to the crimes committed.

In creating the Commission, Congress was making it clear that indeterminate sentencing had grown excessively lenient and that a tougher stance on crime was needed. Congress instructed the Commission to "insure that the Guidelines reflect the fact that, in many cases, current sentences do not accurately reflect the seriousness of the offense." The Commission's response to Congressional concern was its stated objective to "avoid unwarranted sentencing disparities among defendants with similar records who have been found guilty of similar criminal conduct while maintaining sufficient flexibility to permit individualized sentences when warranted by mitigating or aggravating factors not taken into account in the establishment of general sentencing practices."

Accordingly, the Commission established Guidelines for determining sentences, including whether to impose a sentence of probation, fine, or imprisonment, and if so, how long and/or how much; whether the defendant should be placed on supervised release after imprisonment; and whether multiple sentences should run concurrently or consecutively. Most observers agree that the Guidelines have generated more and longer prison terms and heavier fines.

In 1988, the mandate of the Commission was expanded to include development of Guidelines for the sentencing of corporations. The stated purposes were to (1) substantially increase most of the fines imposed on companies convicted of crime, (2) introduce a concept of "corporate probation," and (3) call for self-reporting of crimes discovered by corporate management. The interesting and important part is that a corporate defendant's culpability can be mitigated by having a program in place to detect violations and by self-reporting of offenses prior to investigation. In effect, a corporate defendant has a measure of control over the leniency or severity of its sentence by its own action taken before and after its violation of the law. The Guidelines provide strong incentive for compliance and self-policing. Indeed, the U.S. Sentencing Commission has said that the purposes of the Guidelines are to "provide just punishment, adequate deterrence, and incentives for organizations to maintain internal mechanisms for preventing, detecting and reporting criminal conduct."

On November 1, 1991, the Guidelines became law. If the same tough stance that has been applied in individual sentencing is carried over to business organizations, corporate management should be concerned. A sense of foreboding can be found in the new corporate Guidelines in the statement that the "goals and purposes of sentencing for organizations are identical to those for individuals."

At present, the impact of the law on corporate behavior is uncertain, but many commentators anticipate that because sentences will be defined and judicial discretion reduced, punishment for corporate crime will be more predictable. It is certain, however, that the intent of the government is to seek increased penalties against companies for anti-trust and other violations. The Department of Justice is on record about its intent to vigorously pursue corporate offenders.

The Guidelines

Prevention and Detection. The Guidelines call for a credible effort to detect and deter crime. The elements of a compliance program are spelled out. Anything less will expose a corporation and its officers to substantial punishment.

Remedies. A convicted organization must notify the victims of the crime and take appropriate action to compensate them or remedy the harm. Full restitution either as part of the sentence or as a condition of probation is provided, trust funds for victims may be ordered, and community service is an option.

Fines. Fines are assessed using a complicated formula that considers the seriousness of the offense and the culpability of the offending organization. The first step is to determine a

COMPLIANCE POLICY
CONCERNING CORPORATE CONDUCT
(Sample)

The Company and each of its subsidiaries will establish and maintain an effective compliance program that conforms to the standards established in the Sentencing Guidelines promulgated by the U.S. Sentencing Commission. The program will be designed, implemented, and enforced with the purpose of being effective in preventing and detecting criminal conduct.

The Company will exercise due diligence in attempting to prevent and to detect criminal conduct by its employees and agents. To those ends the Company will establish and maintain the policies and practices set forth as follows:

1. The Company will determine the likelihood that there is a substantial risk that certain types of criminal offenses may occur.

2. The Company will establish and maintain compliance standards and procedures to be followed by its employees and agents which are reasonably capable of reducing the prospect of criminal conduct.

3. Specific high-level individuals within the Company shall be assigned overall responsibility to oversee compliance with such standards and procedures. Division and subsidiary presidents and vice presidents in charge of corporate staff functions are hereby assigned such responsibility for their respective divisions, subsidiaries, and departments.

4. The Company will not delegate substantial discretionary authority to any individual it knows, or through the exercise of due diligence should have known, had a propensity to engage in illegal activities.

5. The Company will take reasonable steps to communicate effectively its standards and procedures to all employees and other agents.

6. The Company will take reasonable steps to achieve compliance with its standards. Such reasonable steps include the establishment of monitoring and auditing systems that are reasonably designed to detect unlawful conduct by employees and agents, and establishing, monitoring, and publicizing a reporting system whereby employees and other agents can report abuse by others within the organization without fear of retribution.

7. The Company will consistently enforce its standards through appropriate disciplinary mechanisms, including, as appropriate, discipline of individuals responsible for the failure to detect an offense.

8. If a criminal offense is detected, the organization must take all reasonable steps to respond appropriately to the offense and to prevent similar offenses.

9. Each division and subsidiary will establish one or more committees to assist the president of the division or subsidiary in the implementation and enforcement of this program.

10. These compliance statements are intended to establish a procedural framework; they are not intended to set forth in full the substantive compliance programs and practices of the Company and its subsidiaries. Additional standards for compliance are established and maintained by virtue of the practices, procedures, and policies of the Company and the form of organization that manages the Company, and those additional practices, procedures, policies, and organization are an integral part of the compliance program.

base fine that is the greater of the dollar value of the gain to the offender/loss to the victim, or an amount determined by a table of fines set out in the Guidelines.

The second step is to determine a "culpability score" based on aggravating and mitigating factors. Aggravating factors might be foreknowledge by management, concealment of the offense, and a history of prior offenses; mitigating factors might be the existence of a compliance program, prompt reporting of the offense, and cooperation in the investigation. The culpability score is cross-referenced to minimum and maximum multipliers.

In the third step, the multiplier is applied to the fine. A low culpability score can lead to a fine smaller than the base fine while a high culpability score may lead to a fine many times larger.

To illustrate, assume that the victim's damages were $100,000 and that the court used this amount as the base fine. The judge noted that the culpability score is 10 points based on aggravating factors. In looking at the Guidelines table, the minimum multiplier is 2 and the maximum is 4. The judge can set the fine no lower than $200,000 and no higher than $400,000.

Probation. In addition to requiring payment of damages and a fine, the judge can place a company on probation for up to 5 years. Probation is mandatory if at the time of sentencing the company does not have in place an acceptable compliance program. When this happens, the court will impose a program that it will periodically monitor.

Developing a Compliance Program

The first objective of a compliance program is to keep from violating criminal laws; the second objective is to achieve the lowest possible culpability score if the first objective is not met.

A compliance program to meet these objectives will include:
• Written policy, directives, and procedures to guide employees.
• The assignment to specific senior management of responsibilities for the proper execution of the compliance program.
• Steps to prevent giving discretionary authority to individuals whom the company knew or should have known had a propensity to engage in illegal acts.
• An education component for informing employees of their personal responsibilities under the program.
• A monitoring and auditing system to detect deviations from compliance, including a mechanism for employees to report suspected criminal conduct without fear of retribution.
• Consistent enforcement of compliance standards with appropriate disciplinary sanctions.
• Steps to prevent recurrence of offenses, including needed changes to the program.

The Federal Sentencing Guidelines add a new dimension to corporate accountability by emphasizing compliance programs, self-policing, and reporting of offenses. The sentencing judge is bound to a highly defined, essentially mathematical scheme when determining sentences. The result in many cases will be heavy fines and invasive probation.

John J. Fay, CPP

Sources

Amendments to the Sentencing Guidelines for United States Courts. (Federal Register, Vol. 57, No. 91, 1992).

Fett, L., New Corporation Sentencing Guidelines: Perils and Possibilities of Compliance Programs and Self-Policing. (American Corporate Counsel Association, Washington, 1991).

Machlowitz, D.S., Designing and Implementing Corporate Compliance Policies. (General Instrument Corporation, Lyndhurst, NJ).

Murphy, J.E., Corporate Compliance Programs: Counsel's Role. (American Corporate Counsel Association Docket, Washington, DC, Fall, 1989).

Nord, N.A., Sentencing Guidelines Up the Ante for Corporate Compliance Programs. (American Corporate Counsel Association Docket, Washington, DC, Fall, 1991).

Olson, J.F., and D.C. Mahaffey, Criminal Exposure in the Corporate Environment. (American Corporate Counsel Association, Washington, DC, 1992).

Sentencing Guidelines and Policy Statements for Federal Courts. (Federal Register, Vol. 57, No. 1, 1992).

SONIC MOTION DETECTORS

Sonic motion detectors are similar to ultrasonic motion detectors inasmuch as they both use air as their signal transmission medium. The primary difference between the two is that sonic detectors fill the volume requiring protection with energy in the audible frequency range (typically 800 hertz) instead of with ultrasonic energy (above 20 kilohertz). Since the audible energy is lower in frequency than inaudible ultrasonic energy, the audible energy has longer wavelengths and, consequently, is less sensitive to air currents that might distort ultrasonic energy patterns.

It is also less sensitive than ultrasonic motion detectors to small moving objects in the zone of detection such as insects, cats, or rodents. This sensitivity difference results from the fact that the wavelength of sonic energy is much longer than ultrasonic energy. Therefore, the distortions generated by the small animals are not as significant as they are with the ultrasonic detector.

Sonic detectors consist basically of a control unit that contains the power supply and signal processor, and the central unit can operate from one to eight transceivers. The transmitter section of these units fills the area requiring protection with acoustical energy, while the receiver section collects the reflected acoustical signals for the signal processor. The transmitted acoustical energy is reflected by the walls and other objects within the protected area, thus generating standing wave patterns of acoustical energy. Any disturbance in these energy patterns that satisfies the detector alarm criteria initiates an alarm, as is the case with the ultrasonic and microwave motion detectors.

Sonic motion detectors monitor the received acoustic energy for both a change in the amplitude of the received energy and a Doppler frequency shift in the standing wave pattern. These changes can be detected by comparing the frequency spectrum of the reflected signal with that of the transmitted signal. When both the standing wave amplitude change and the frequency shift satisfy the detector alarm criteria, an alarm is initiated.

Robert L. Barnard

Source Barnard, R.L., Intrusion Detection Systems. (Butterworth–Heinemann, Boston, 1982).

T

TERMINATION INTERVIEWS: DEALING WITH EMPLOYEE REACTIONS

For two reasons the security manager needs to be knowledgeable about the do's and don'ts of conducting termination interviews: first, there will be the need from time to time for the security manager to personally inform a subordinate that his or her services are no longer required, and second, the security manager may be asked to be present when trouble is expected at a termination interview of someone else's subordinate.

Types of Reactions

It is very unlikely that any manager, security or otherwise, has the breadth of understanding and skill sufficient to anticipate and completely deal with the full range of potential reactions that are possible in a termination interview. Nonetheless, it is important for the interviewer to be aware of some of the responses that can be expected. These include: stunned reaction, severe trauma, sorrow, and belligerence.

Stunned Reaction. In this case, the termination notice is received as almost good news, the employee seems to be fully composed and in control, the session is proceeding well, and the interviewer is gaining assurance that there will be no problems. The fact may be that the employee is stunned by the news and unable to respond in a manner that reflects true inner feelings. People who react this way may lack the capacity to vent and if they hold back the stress, which will build over time, they can potentially explode hours, days, or weeks later. To the security manager, this is a concern because of the possibility that the explosion will be directed at the company, its management, or workers.

It can also happen that the employee will be so taken aback by the termination notice that he or she will not mentally process the implications and, in effect, act is if the interview is nothing more than a routine meeting. The employee simply chooses to not hear the bad news.

Severe Trauma. Employees who react to termination with uncontrolled weeping, absolute silence, or what appears to be shock have probably entered the stunned reaction phase and are incapable of moving out of it. It can be very unnerving when the employee clearly appears to need help and the interviewer, who would like to give help, lacks the capacity to do so.

It occasionally happens that the interviewer, motivated by a desire to help, will hint at or promise to assist the employee in some way that is not permitted by the terms of the discharge. This is clearly not a good move for the employee because the offered help cannot be delivered, and for the interviewer it may result in a charge of a breach of promise, not to mention senior management dissatisfaction.

When the employee cannot be returned to a normal state, the interviewer should bring a treatment professional into the picture. A company, especially when multiple terminations are involved, would be wise to have skilled counselors available nearby when interviews are being held.

Sorrow. Many employees will respond initially with expressions of disappointment and hurt. A lesser number will express anger, betrayal, and resentment. These are all natural reactions that can be healthy because they are venting mechanisms. The interviewer can expect the employee to move from these normal expressions of sorrow to practical questions about what happens next, such as benefits and pay.

Belligerence. An interviewer will be apprehensive about encountering an employee who over-reacts when informed of termination. Although it is true that violence is possible, experience indicates that the odds are low that it will occur. Experience also indicates that when the interviewer approaches the situation with perceptible apprehension and is primed to respond with stiff resistance, the odds change greatly in favor of a confrontation.

The critical factor, then, when confronted with a potentially belligerent employee is to maintain self-control and not escalate the belligerence. On the other hand, the interviewer should not be defensive to the point of agreeing with the employee. Calmative gestures, such as

---

TERMINATION PROCEDURES
(Sample)

1. Each employee selected for termination will be informed privately and individually by the employee's departmental manager.
2. The manager will prepare a checklist of items that are to be collected during or immediately following the interview.
3. The Human Resources Office will provide to the manager a script to be learned in advance of and followed during the interview.
4. The manager will go to the employee's work station and escort the employee to the manager's office or other private area for the purpose of conducting the interview.
5. During the interview, the manager will reach agreement with the employee concerning removal of the employee's personal property from the premises. Two options are suggested: removal during the same workday of the notice with removal assisted and supervised by a responsible person designated by the manager, or removal during non-working hours while under escort by a security officer.
5. At the conclusion of the termination interview, the manager will escort the employee to the Human Resources Office and introduce the employee to the Outplacement Counselor.
6. The Outplacement Counselor will explain company benefits available to the employee and will schedule the employee for further counseling at the off-site Placement Center.
7. If the employee, during interviewing or counseling, exhibits problematic behavior or becomes ill, the Security Office will be asked to provide assistance.

---

a smile, a shrug, an open posture, and soft silence, may be useful in helping the belligerent person restore his or her composure.

Disparaging comments against the interviewer and the company are in the realm of normal behavior and to be expected but certainly there are limits to the abuse that the interviewer should tolerate. Threats of harm and intimidating physical contact are outside the limits of acceptable conduct. Should unacceptable conduct occur, the interviewer has three options: (1) warn the employee that the behavior must cease immediately, (2) call for assistance, and (3) conclude the interview.

Managing the Interview

Preparing for the termination interview increases the probability of producing the desired results, reduces the stress placed on the interviewer, and helps keep the process on a professional level. Getting ready means reviewing the reasons for terminating the employee, anticipating the range of reactions that may be exhibited by the employee, and determining a strategy and a set of tactics for controlling the reactions. Getting ready also means scheduling the interview at a suitable place and time, ensuring that the employee will appear (even to the extent of personally escorting the employee to the interview), knowing what should be collected from the employee (keys, credit cards, money owed, desktop assets, etc.), arranging for security assistance that may be needed to counter a belligerent reaction or human resources counseling assistance to deal with an emotional reaction, and setting up a procedure for the employee to leave the work site with personal property in hand. The interview process can also be enhanced by resolving to be empathic and a good listener.

Specific actions to take in preparing for and conducting the interview are:

• Develop a plan for conducting the interview. Write a script of things that must be stated. Rehearse the statements.

• Anticipate problems that are likely to occur. Anticipation is made with respect to each individual, as well as to the whole process of interviewing. If help is anticipated, such as having a security officer on standby, arrangements should be made ahead of time.

• State the purpose early in the interview. Avoid small talk; get to the point in a business-like (but not necessarily cold) fashion.

•Maintain direct eye contact in a manner that projects openness and honesty.

•Be sure the employee understands that he or she has been terminated; that certain rights and benefits apply; that certain follow-up steps will be taken by the company; and that the employee will be expected to do certain things, such as repay loans, turn in assigned keys and equipment, and take away personal items.

•Allow the employee to vent emotions, but in the process stay committed to the interview plan and the script.

•Keep the meeting as brief as possible and close the meeting on a positive note.

Things not to do include:

•Don't read from the script. Memorize the key points and the order in which they are to be presented. If needed to stay on track, glance at the script from time to time.

•Don't use words, terms, or phrases that are open to interpretation. Being precise in language will help eliminate later claims based on misunderstanding.

•Don't promise or give any hint of help that can't be delivered. For example, don't promise to provide the employee with a written letter of recommendation when the company's policy allows only a confirmation of prior employment.

•Don't use words that imply or remotely suggest discrimination. For example, don't suggest that the terminated employee's duties will be given to a younger person or that the employee's political attitudes are out of harmony with those of the management.

•Don't suggest that the terminating employee has an opportunity to change the decision to discharge or to negotiate a change in the terms of the discharge.

•Don't say more than is necessary. After the necessary information has been conveyed, any further talking should be done by the employee.

•Don't use platitudes, homilies, or engage in philosophical discussions, such as how the economy is at fault.

•Don't make comments which indicate that the discharge decision was based on anything other than job-related factors. A discussion of the employee's personal traits and habits, insofar as they do not directly impact performance, has no place in the interview.

•Don't give the impression that the discharge is a retaliation for something that the employee may have done wrong.

Termination Interview Checklist

1. Collect the following items:
    •Company identification card, key card, and credit cards.
    •Mechanical keys to entrances, offices, desks, etc.
     •Beeper, pager, and portable telephone.
     •Desk top assets used at home.
     •Files, documents, books, and manuals.
     •Unused travel tickets.
     •Outstanding loans and cash advances.
2. Obtain a written acknowledgment of the employee's understanding of continued confidentiality obligations.
3. Ensure that the following items used by the employee remain at the work site:
    •Desk top assets.
    •Artwork and plants.
    •Work products.
    •Classified materials.
4. Cancel the employee's worksite and computer access privileges.
5. Debrief the employee concerning classified information.
6. Obtain a final expense report.

Retaliation in this sense is different than punishment consisting of discharge as the appropriate disciplinary action.

•Don't be defensive or admit in any way that the termination is unjustified or improperly administered.

John J. Fay, CPP

TERRORISM: COMMUNICATING WITH KIDNAPPERS

Communications problems vary according to the type of kidnapping. From the standpoint of negotiations and kidnappings, there are two types: political and ransom. In the case of a political kidnapping, the kidnappers' specific demands—usually the release of imprisoned comrades—are part of a larger set of political goals. Political kidnappers also want publicity, to inspire fear, demonstrate government impotence, and win adherents. Achievement of these other objectives may be of equal or greater importance than the specific demands.

Strictly ransom kidnappings may be carried out either by terrorists or ordinary criminals. Victims are selected on the basis of their value, measured only in economic terms, and their vulnerability. Ransom kidnappers may also seek other goals, but the paramount objective in ransom kidnappings is the ransom. Political kidnappers usually select government officials as their victims; ransom kidnappers prefer businessmen or members of wealthy families, though not all kidnappings uphold this distinction. German terrorists in 1977 kidnapped Hanns-Martin Schleyer, a prominent and influential German industrialist, for primarily political purposes. In 1981, Italian terrorists released Ciro Cirillo, a Christian Democrat politician in Naples, in return for a ransom of approximately $1.5 million.

With regard to communications, the principal difference between the two types of kidnappings is that in political kidnappings communications take place directly or indirectly between the kidnappers and public authorities. In most ransom kidnappings, communications take place between the kidnappers and a private party, sometimes with a deliberate effort by both to conceal communications from the authorities.

Political Kidnappings

Political kidnappings of diplomats or other government officials are employed by terrorists as a means of gaining international attention and exerting leverage over the local government, on whom they usually levy their demands. A political kidnapping is an act of propaganda; inherent within it is a desire to communicate. Holding a hostage guarantees that the kidnappers will be heard. On the other side, the government not only is concerned with obtaining the safe release of a hostage or hostages; it also wants to communicate its position in the contest with the terrorists. When the hostage is an official of another government, that government also must communicate its concerns about the safety of one or more of its citizens, its policy with regard to political kidnappings, and its attitude toward the local government.

For the news media, a political kidnapping is a good story, a genuine drama; human life hangs in the balance. There are disagreements, confrontations, ultimatums, brinkmanship, and rumors. The noise level is high.

Political kidnappings create many communications problems. Resolution of these

kidnappings requires communication between at least two parties: the terrorist kidnappers and the government. Governments themselves are, of course, complex organizations comprised of separate entities that sometimes act independently of one another, each having its own means of communicating. This diversity magnifies the problem. When opinions are divided on how to handle the kidnapping, the government may be saying several things at once.

When terrorists seize diplomats, two governments are automatically involved, the local government and the government of the hostage. The captive's government in such a situation may comprise two principal entities: a task force assembled in the capital of the captive's country to manage the crisis and the embassy on the scene. If the kidnapping occurs outside a country's capital, a regional government and a local consul are added to the network.

Kidnappers in some cases have contacted the hostage's family as a means of increasing pressure; or the family, dissatisfied with the handling of the incident by officials, may try to initiate direct contact with the kidnappers. In a few cases, hostages have been made to participate in meetings with the press or have been permitted to write letters or make appeals, and thus they too become part of the communications. In some cases intermediaries are used. Often they have something to say themselves, and they become yet another component in the complex communications net.

The Hard- and Soft-Line Debate. The problem is not simply that a lot of people must somehow communicate with a lot of other people. There are many prohibitions. The local government often does not want to talk to the kidnappers, or at least does not want to be seen doing so. Communications themselves are viewed by many as a concession that gives terrorists equal status with the government. The local government may not want the embassy or the hostage's family to communicate directly with the kidnappers either, or at least not without government supervision; and the local government often will try to prevent the terrorists from communicating with the public. It may go so far as to prohibit publications by the news media of terrorist communiqués. In other words, the local government usually wants to cut off the terrorists, bury the crisis, remain in charge, and conduct its business in private.

The prohibition against direct communications with the kidnappers also applies to the captive's government. Since the mid-1970s, a growing number of countries have adopted a no-concessions policy in dealing with political kidnappings. Sometimes such a policy precludes direct communications between the government and the kidnappers. Moreover, most governments regard the host or local government as being responsible for the safety of diplomats assigned to it. Direct communications incur the risk that the terrorists will shift their demands to the captive's government and lift the responsibility from the shoulders of the local government.

The kidnappers may try to get around the local government's and the embassy's unwillingness to communicate by dealing directly with the hostage's family. The kidnappers, the hostage, and the hostage's family often have a community of interests. All would like to see the kidnappers' demands met so the hostage can be released. Kidnappers may try to manipulate the family in order to exert private and public pressure on the government to make concessions. For that same reason, government officials generally try to keep the family from becoming directly involved. The family's single-minded dedication to the safe release of the hostage makes it unconcerned with abstract policies about terrorism. The family may be willing to offer concessions, exert pressure on the government for concessions, or publicly criticize officials for "abandoning" the hostage.

Generally, terrorists kidnap diplomats or other government officials for political reasons. When they want cash, they abduct businesspersons, who are more lucrative targets. However, in a few of the episodes involving government officials, the kidnappers have made demands directly on the hostage's family, usually for a cash ransom. This happened in the case of Terrence Leonhardy, the American consul general in Guadalajara, Mexico. In that incident, the kidnappers instructed the family not to inform local authorities.

A Multiple-Message Problem. The different parties involved in a political kidnapping aim their communications at different audiences. The terrorists probably have the most ambitious program in this regard. Their specific audiences include their perceived constituents, the local population in general, the American public, a world audience, other potential targets whom they might attack in the future, and other terrorists. A different message is aimed at each audience. They must inspire their perceived constituents. They must show the local population that the local government is ineffective, incompetent, and impotent. To the public in the captor's country they must explain their cause and thereby undermine its support for the local government. The message to the world is the desire for publicity and recognition. They want to instill terror among local and foreign officials. They must demonstrate their superiority over rival terrorist groups.

The local government must communicate with the terrorists, the local population, and, to a lesser degree, the world. Again, there are different messages for each, and sometimes the messages are contradictory. The local government publicly tries to persuade the terrorists that it will make no concessions, that they can gain nothing from the kidnapping and must release their hostage. Privately, the government may at the same time indicate its willingness to reach some sort of compromise to save the life of the hostage. The local government tries to convince the local population—its principal audience—that the government remains in charge, that it will not capitulate to terrorists, that it is competent.

The captive's government talks to the terrorists, to the local government, and to its own public. It tries to persuade the terrorists that kidnapping will not pay and that they must release the hostage. At the same time, it may or may not try to persuade the local government to open a dialogue with the terrorists and come to some kind of agreement that will bring about the safe release of the hostage. The captive's government must also address the public at home. This is probably the primary audience before whom the government must appear strong, unyielding to terrorism, and managerially competent.

One serious problem is that most of the messages are public. In a sense, everyone reads everyone else's mail. Since each actor's objectives differ with regard to different audiences, the total traffic may be confusing and conflicting. The terrorists must figure out if the local government is throwing down the gauntlet or signaling its readiness to bargain. The local government may sometimes be confused as to whether the captive's government places greater emphasis on preserving a policy of no concessions or on securing the safe release of the hostage. In one case involving an American diplomat kidnapped abroad, U.S. policy was communicated publicly and privately in double-edged language, which stated that the U.S. government's policy was not to accede to demands of terrorists holding hostages, but the responsibility for the protection of American diplomats abroad lay with the host government. In this case, the host government demanded to know what exactly that sentence meant. Did the United States want the man back or not? In fact, the officials in Washington, DC, who drafted the phrase saw it as a means of preserving a previously established no-concessions policy while opening a window for the local government to cut a deal.

There is no easy solution to this problem. It simply must be kept in mind that in addressing one audience, a government may be causing difficulties in its communications with another audience. This argues for coordination of communications, and it suggests that the fine language of diplomacy may not always be applicable to the more practical problem of dealing with terrorist kidnappers in a crisis situation.

Uses and Misuses of the News Media. In most political kidnappings, the kidnappers and the government communicate with each other through the news media. Terrorists have also communicated through aboveground spokespersons, they have left messages for government officials to find, and sometimes they have established direct telephone contact. (Telephone contact is generally characteristic of negotiations for cash ransom.) In all private means of communication, the terrorists have the initiative. Governments devote a great deal of effort to figuring out how to contact the terrorists directly without addressing them publicly through the news media. Who can get in touch with them? Known sympathizers? A certain journalist? The leaders of other governments? Imprisoned comrades?   Even if a means is

found, the government can seldom be confident that its messages are accurately conveyed to the kidnappers.

In a few of the political kidnappings, an intermediary was used.   While such intermediaries are sometimes necessary, they can be dangerous from the government point of view, and must be chosen and handled with care. The intermediary is rarely a neutral communicator.   To be acceptable to the kidnappers, he may have to be someone who sympathizes with their cause to some degree. He may exploit his role to publicly blast the government.   Even the politically neutral intermediary may begin to see himself, not as a passive conveyer, but as an active arbitrator in a dispute. He may become increasingly dedicated to arranging a compromise, and may become impatient and begin to publicly criticize the government for not making concessions. Entrusting communications to an intermediary almost invariably translates into eventual concessions; and if the government is not prepared to negotiate, there is no need for an intermediary.

Communicating through the news media has both advantages and disadvantages. One disadvantage is the usual unwillingness of the local government or the captive's government to be seen in public communicating with terrorist kidnappers. Another is the desire to send a variety of messages—tough on terrorists, humane with regard to the hostage and his family, unyielding on the matter of concessions but willing to talk about a settlement—that are intended for different audiences but that will be read by everyone. A third disadvantage is the high volume of background noise. A political kidnapping commands the attention of the national and international press. Newspersons seldom wait for official briefings. They dig for news, ask for interviews, call their informants, and reach for rumors. They also have two governments to work on. Each government's message must compete with a barrage of public statements by high-level officials, off-the-record comments, tips, and rumors as interpreted by the press. The message to the terrorists, if there is one, may get lost. There is one unseen advantage to using the media rather than direct negotiations for communication. There is no capability for instant reply. In critical moments, one does not want to assume a position without thinking out the consequences and communicating with the other party involved. Each side has time to consider its moves and coordinate its position.

Terrorists naturally want all the attention they can get. They may even make media coverage or publication of their communiqués a part of their demands. Sometimes the local government may try to suppress messages sent by the terrorists by prohibiting their publication. In one case, however—the 1976 hijacking of a TWA airliners by Croatian extremists—a Federal Bureau of Investigation (FBI) official communicated the hijacker's demand that several newspapers print their manifesto on the front page and asked that newspapers go along with the demand. The U.S. secretary of state was incensed when he heard about the request, as he considered it a violation of the U.S. no-concessions policy. Although the press went along with the request in this case, the news media are generally reluctant to relinquish command of their space to terrorists or governments.

On several occasions, public statements by high-ranking officials have complicated negotiations and narrowed options. Two American examples come to mind. In 1973, Palestinian terrorists, members of Black September, took over the Saudi Arabian embassy in Khartoum. In return for the release of their hostages—who included one Belgium and two American diplomats, the ambassador and the deputy chief of mission—the terrorists demanded, among other things, the release of the imprisoned assassin of Senator Robert Kennedy. For the first 2 days, the terrorists took no action. Sudanese officials informed them that a high-ranking American official, the under secretary of state, was on his way to Khartoum. Meanwhile, in the course of a routine press conference at the White House, reporters asked President Nixon if the United States was going to release Kennedy's killer. The president replied that the United States would never give in to terrorist blackmail. This comment was broadcast to the Middle East and re-broadcast to Khartoum. The terrorists reportedly heard it on their radio. Shortly after that, they murdered the one Belgian and two American hostages.

It would be irresponsible to blame their deaths on the president's statement. Less than 3 months before the Khartoum incident, a team of

Black September terrorists holding the Israeli embassy in Bangkok had agreed to a compromise and were strongly criticized within the group. Black September was anxious to demonstrate its resolve at Khartoum. The United States could never have agreed to the release of a convicted assassin, so there was little room to negotiate. On the other hand, the terrorists had appeared willing to wait for the arrival of the American under secretary. The president's statement may have inadvertently undercut a stalling tactic.

In another case, the former U.S. attorney general inadvertently revealed in a Washington press conference that an American diplomat had been kidnapped in Mexico. The kidnapping of the American vice consul in Hermosillo occurred 5 days before the attorney general's conference, but authorities had kept it secret while attempting in vain to deliver the ransom demanded by the kidnappers. Once the secret was out, the news media in both Mexico and the United States made inquiries. The authorities, who were still hopeful of delivering the ransom and saving the hostage, had to make careful replies; they did not want to frighten off the kidnappers. As it turned out, the attorney general's revelation was irrelevant. The kidnapper, a lone criminal who was later apprehended, had already murdered his hostage and fled. Had this not been the case, however, the attorney general's remarks might have caused serious complications.

In neither case were the high-ranking officials to blame for the diplomat's deaths. In one case terrorists, and in the other an ordinary criminal, pulled the trigger. They alone are culpable, but the examples are instructive of the difficulties that can be caused by off-the-cuff remarks during a political kidnapping.

Hoax calls and claims will often equal or exceed genuine communications from the kidnappers. We have seen this in other cases. In some cases, groups unconnected with the kidnapping may make demands; publicity seekers, nuts, or pranksters may get into the act; or the kidnappers themselves may send false messages—"The hostage has been condemned and executed, his body may be found...." These are designed to keep public attention focused on the kidnapping and government tensions high. To assure itself that the claimants actually have the hostage and that he is still alive, the government may demand proof. Governments also have exploited the existence of rival claimants to confuse the kidnappers and entice them to provide additional information. Where further dialogue—particularly over the telephone—is likely, the kidnappers or the government may establish a code to ensure that the right calls will get through without delay.

Kidnappings as Governmental Crises. Not all problems derive from the difficulty of communications between governments and terrorists. The kidnapping of a foreign official creates a major crisis for any government. In such a crisis, the local government closes in on itself. Decisions are made by the chief of state and a few close advisors. The minister of foreign affairs, the ambassador's normal point of contact, may not be part of the inner decision-making group. This is particularly true in Third World countries where the key figures are likely to include the president, the ministers of defense and interior, and chiefs of the armed forces. The foreign minister is often a respected figure but not part of the inner circle. On tough issues like terrorism, political survival takes precedence over foreign relations. How does an ambassador get to the people who count? Other contacts, the defense attaché, the military mission, an intelligence counterpart, or a personal acquaintance may become crucial sources of information and communications.   In some cases, these are not enough and it is necessary for the ambassador to talk directly to the chief of state. In the past, this has been accomplished by sending a letter from the head of state to the captive's country to be hand-delivered to the local chief of state.

In one episode, U.S. embassy officials feared that the local president's inattention to the problem after his government agreed to the terrorists' demands but before the deal was consummated might provide an opportunity for elements within the government who opposed the concessions to sabotage the settlement. In this case, they persuaded the chief of state to come back from his weekend retreat to guarantee that the deal would go through.

Communications between the capital of the captive's country and its embassy have sometimes been a problem. The kidnapping of a diplomat inevitably generates a certain amount of debate regarding policy. "No concessions"

ceases to be an abstract issue. A life is at stake and that changes things. Diplomats are skilled at resolving differences with vague or double-edged language, but compromise language used to bridge differences in the capital may not be understood by embassy officials who were not privy to the original debate and therefore may not see the intent of the words.

Political Kidnappings: Lessons Learned

There are no general rules for solving these communications problems, just as there are no formulas for dealing with political kidnappings. Each case is unique. At the same time, there do seem to be some general principles that government officials might try to adhere to:

1.   The less said in public the better. The volume of communications is enormous. Anything said is likely to be lost in the noise, or worse, misinterpreted with tragic consequences.

2.   Off-the-cuff remarks by high-ranking officials should be avoided altogether. They are likely to get attention they do not deserve. They may inadvertently complicate affairs, foreclose options, and further elevate an event that is likely to have a tragic outcome.

3.   The government must speak with a single voice; all communications should be coordinated. The off-the-record interview may have greater effect than the official briefing.

4.   The various audiences should be identified. Those communicating should think about the message to be sent and the effect it is likely to have on the other parties. It must be remembered that everything will be heard by everyone.

5.   The government's public responses should be kept as low-key as possible. The U.S. government is at the margin; its ability to determine the outcome of a political kidnapping in a positive way is limited. The kidnappers may decide to murder an American official, and we cannot stop them. In such a circumstance, there is no reason to elevate the confrontation.

6.   Messages should be blunt and simple. This admonition is likely to curdle the hearts of diplomats, but a kidnapping is a time of crisis. The volume of noise is high. Subtle messages are seldom received.

7.   Policy   ought   not   to   equate communications   with   negotiations   and

concessions. Communicating and negotiating are different things.

8. Beware of intermediaries. They are seldom neutral or passive. They will drive the government toward concessions and denounce it for not making them.

9. Committee language does not work. It will not be understood by those not present at the debate.

Ransom Kidnappings

Corporations face many of the same problems faced by governments communicating with terrorists, as well as some unique problems. Like governments, corporations have to address several different audiences simultaneously. To the kidnappers, the corporation must communicate that it wants to get its person back and know what it will take to do so.

This is not always easily accomplished since the corporation cannot contact the kidnappers directly. It must wait for their call or attempt to communicate its willingness to negotiate terms through means of public statements. These public statements must not undermine the company's efforts to bargain with the kidnappers.

To the family of the hostage, the company must communicate that it is making every reasonable effort to obtain his safe release. This can become extremely difficult during ransom negotiations. In the eyes of family members, if the company's primary objective is the safe release of the hostage, then the company ought not to imperil the hostage by attempting to reduce the amount of ransom it is willing to pay; it ought to promptly pay whatever the kidnappers demand. If it is not willing to do so, then its paramount interest is not the safe release of the hostage.

This conflict raises the question: To what degree should companies inform families of the course of the negotiations? In some cases, company negotiators have chosen not to keep the family informed of progress of the negotiations. This, however, is a perilous course. For one thing, it generates bad feelings that can lead to family members criticizing the company in interviews with the press and making direct appeals to the kidnappers. By keeping the family in the dark, the company also assumes a

greater responsibility for the outcome of the event. Ultimately, bitter feelings and the company's assumption of sole responsibility for all decisions can lead to lawsuits. Whatever the legal merits of any legal action, it does a corporation little good to be seen being sued by wives or widows of hostages. Without making family members direct participants in the negotiations, which all experts advise against, the corporation should try as much as possible to keep the family apprised of their progress. This may involve selecting one member of the family, not necessarily the wife, as a point of contact.

To the public, the corporation must communicate that it is not a callous institution that values its profits above human life. On the other hand, some corporations have stated in public that they will not pay ransom for kidnapped employees. Such statements may be intended to deter would-be kidnappers or reduce ransom demands, or are instead meant to assure a local government that the company is complying with laws against the payment of ransom (while perhaps secretly negotiating).

In cases where kidnappers make demands beyond cash ransom, such as concessions to the work force, the corporation must also communicate to workers and workers' representatives. To workers, it must communicate that the kidnappers' demands are unreasonable, and that although they might benefit workers in the short run, the long-run effect will weaken the company and could eventually cost jobs.

Kidnappers' demands for concessions to workers create special problems for both corporate management and labor union leadership. If the corporation goes along with the kidnappers' demands, its own ability to control the company is reduced; it undermines the authority of the union. If the corporation rejects the demands, the workers see themselves losing something they might otherwise have gained.

Similarly, if union leaders endorse the kidnappers' demands, their own leadership will be outflanked, and the kidnappers may be seen by workers as the new vanguard in resolving future labor disputes. If the union opposes the demands, it may be seen as acting contrary to the workers' interests.

Rejection of the demands is probably in the interests of both company and union. However, concessions may be necessary to save a life. At a minimum then, corporate management and union labor leadership ought not to appear divided on the issue. Ideally, the two will act in tandem, denouncing terrorism, resisting certain kinds of demands, agreeing as to what concessions might be possible in extraordinary circumstances. That requires coordination, which in turn requires communication. However, communication during negotiations becomes difficult when corporate management suspects that the kidnappers may have confederates within union leadership who might communicate corporate positions and strategies to the kidnappers—which sometimes has been the case—or when corporate management suspects that union leadership is exploiting the kidnapping for its own purposes. Beyond being aware of this problem there are no general rules to deal with it.

To corporate executives and other professional employees, the corporation must communicate a message of reassurance: that the company is paying close attention and devoting sufficient resources to their physical security, adding that their security also depends greatly on measures they take as individuals, and that the company will do everything reasonable to secure the release of any employee who is kidnapped.

To government authorities, if they know about the kidnapping, the corporation may want to communicate several messages. One may be its concern over the general problem of security and the necessity that the authorities pay close attention to it. A second message may be to dissuade the government from imposing any limitation or taking any precipitate action that will imperil the life of the hostage. A third message may be that the corporation is complying with the law.

Whether to inform authorities of negotiation, if they do not already know about them, is a major decision for the corporation. Where governments prohibit negotiations with kidnappers or the payment of ransom, corporations and families have sometimes tried to keep contacts with kidnappers secret or move the negotiations to another country. This persistence entails many risks for corporations and negotiators, who in some cases have been jailed. Most ransom insurance policies require that local authorities be informed. Corporations must usually wait for kidnappers to contact them. In the absence of communications, corporate officials have at times in desperation made public statements or inserted ads in newspapers indicating a willingness to discuss terms or proposing specific offers. Corporate officials have also on occasion tried to reach kidnappers indirectly through known figures in the criminal underworld or political underground, but usually contacts in this area are the preserve of government.

Terrorist Tactics of Communication. Terrorists use communications as a tool in the negotiations. Their most common tactic is to delay their initial contact or suspend communications during the negotiations to increase pressure on the corporation and family. Silence for days, weeks, or even months has a devastating effect on the family and colleagues of a hostage, softening them for the negotiations. When kidnappers confront hard negotiators on behalf of a corporation or family, they will frequently insist on talking to the family directly. This tactic often follows a long period of silence, making it difficult for the negotiator to maintain control. Another tactic kidnappers use is to involve the hostage in the negotiations directly, permitting him to write letters or tape messages, pleading for the company or family to yield to the kidnappers demands.

Brian M. Jenkins

Source Jenkins, B.M., Terrorism and Personal Protection. (Butterworth-Heinemann, Boston, 1985).

TERRORISM: RE-ENTRY OF THE HOSTAGE

It's not over when it's over. Much of the former hostage's anxieties and bitterness relate not to the period of captivity, but to experiences after release.

To begin with, the former hostage feels that he has gone through an experience that no one, save perhaps another former hostage, can understand. Being kidnapped is a harrowing, frightening experience. It is only natural that most hostages have had some problems coping with it. Some may have discovered that they did not perform as bravely as they expected they would. Rightly or wrongly, the hostage often feels he has done something for which he should feel guilty. In retrospect, he may feel that he was too frightened or too docile, or that he collaborated with his captors to a greater degree than was necessary to survive.

The former hostage may have found himself identifying with his captors during captivity and still may do so. We know now that many hostages develop positive attitudes toward their captors. Upon release, they part company amiably, wish each other well. Some former kidnap victims recall their "hosts" almost fondly, noting that "they were exceptionally polite— especially for terrorists." Some speak of them with admiration: "They were dedicated men." "Their sincerity should be respected." Some hostages develop something close to affection for their captors. A few fall in love.

Some former hostages justify the actions of their captors, refuse to testify against them, defend their logic—and it bothers them. One former hostage admitted that he found himself identifying with the terrorists even after they cold-bloodedly murdered another hostage; this deeply disturbed him.

Another former hostage, whose finger was mutilated by his kidnappers to increase pressure on authorities to meet their demands, later explained, "Sure, they cut off the end of my finger, but from their point of view it wasn't atrocious. For them it was logical; the ransom hadn't been paid" [1].

Grateful for having been spared? Fearful of retribution? Uncommonly compassionate? Latently sympathetic toward the political aims of the captors? None of these phrases fully explains why hostages and captors may become temporary comrades. Some elements of brainwashing are inherent in the situation: fear, fatigue, disorientation in space and time, sensory deprivation. The hostage may be isolated, blindfolded, or locked in a dark room, unable to hear more than muffled voices.

Political extremists may lecture hostages on their political goals, but they seldom make any serious attempt to indoctrinate, convert, or recruit them. More often, the hostages are informed that they are simply pawns, bargaining chips, against whom the captors bear no personal malice, but who, unfortunately, may have to be killed if the kidnappers' demands are not met.

These are hardly ideal conditions under which to forge even temporary friendships. How does one explain it? Some of the reasons are simple and obvious. Others reveal how the human mind deals with extreme threats.

The hostage instantly tries to establish his own identity, some human bond with his captors. He knows he must move out of the category of human item to be bartered and become a human being—an individual he hopes it will be harder to kill. He may ask his captors about their lives, how they became terrorists, what they want to achieve, or he may tell them about himself. "I talked as hard as I could," wrote one former hostage, "explaining that we didn't share political philosophies but I ought to hear their side of the story."

While the hostage probably does not share the political goals and certainly does not approve of the tactics of his captors—least of all their choice of victim—it is difficult to talk with anyone for hours or days without seeing at least something of their point of view. The hostage also quickly recognizes that his interests and those of his captors coincide. Both would like to see the demands met. The hostage's life depends on it.

These obvious reasons alone do not account for the change of heart. Another process is taking place that the hostage may not be aware of. Its essential ingredient is the inescapable threat of death, with the outcome a mere matter of whim from the hostage's point of view. The captors may kill him whether their demands are met or not. It is entirely up to the captor, omnipotent, a virtual god, with absolute power over life and death, before whom the hostage is helpless, frightened, humiliated, virtually an infant. Under these circumstances, the hostage unconsciously begins to assimilate—and even imitate—the attitudes of his captors.

Psychologists have come to label this set of reactions the Stockholm syndrome. Generally, they advise potential hostages not to resist these natural feelings, for they work both ways. The kidnappers also begin to develop a certain friendship with their hostage. In a close vote on whether a hostage will be executed or a split-second decision whether to pull the trigger during an assault by police that relationship could save the hostage's life.

The fact that seizing hostages has become so common, that the reactions of hostages have become the subject of scholarly research, newspaper articles, and television talk shows, does not prevent the former hostage from criticizing his own performance while in captivity or make him immune to criticism by others.

One observer, highly critical of the performance of hostages after their release, wrote in a popular magazine,

"It is ... fair to expect that after their danger is safely past, hostages might avail themselves of the single form of resistance still remaining, which is to refuse to accede in retrospect to the aims of those who have victimized them....What is at issue here is not their (the hostages') gratitude but its peculiar nature, a sympathy for their captor and his cause which approaches ideologized collaboration." [2] Such comments are unfortunately typical of the judgmental attitude many assume toward the former hostage, and that he comes to expect. Before the term Stockholm syndrome became popular, another term was used: the Turncoat syndrome.

Critical of his own performance in captivity, the hostage expects such criticism from others. He did heroically escape. He may ask himself if he has, in fact, been brainwashed. He typically believes that others do not think well of him.

In nearly all of our discussions with former hostages, the question was asked, "How did I do?" This question reflects the victim's doubts about his performance as a hostage measured against some yardstick of self-esteem, motion-picture heroes, or standards of behavior inferred from the attitudes and comments of others. Most of us, having been spared the experience of captivity, of helplessly facing death, can live with our illusions of how we would perform, but the hostage feels embarrassed both during and after the episode. He has caused his company, his government, his family, and his friends considerable trouble and perhaps considerable expense. The way his colleagues, friends, and relatives treat him after his release may add to his sense of embarrassment.

Some former hostages feel permanently stigmatized by their experience. It is a reaction also noted in young men who suffer heart attacks. The victim may write himself off, as he

believes others will, as "damaged merchandise" whose career is through. Whether a kidnapping in fact has adverse effects on a person's career is hard to tell, but it is certainly seen that way by former hostages. Diplomats who have been kidnapped complain that being kidnapped has the same effect on one's career in the foreign service as being declared *persona non grata* in a diplomatic post. Diplomats are sometimes declared *persona non grata* for reasons of personal conduct, but in many cases they are "PNG'd" for carrying out the instructions of their own government, for example, by delivering a speech that some local official finds objectionable. They assert that, whatever the reason, having been declared PNG carries a stigma that follows a person through his career—and so does having been kidnapped.

The universe of diplomats who have been kidnapped is too small to permit confirmation of this perception. Many kidnap victims were senior diplomats who retired soon after the episode. Some re-evaluated their life and careers during captivity and elected to leave the foreign service. Of those who remained, some had their careers disrupted by a sudden unanticipated change of posts due to the kidnapping; they had to take whatever job was available. Others found that departmental concerns about their physical or emotional health led to assignments designed to give them a break, which, in terms of career progress, translated into being put on the shelf for a while. Still other former hostages understandably refused to serve again in the region where they had been kidnapped, or in another area of the world where kidnappings were a problem, where they and their families would again face all of the stringent security requirements, all of the anxieties. The resulting mid-career change of regions was disruptive to their careers. This was particularly true of diplomats serving in Latin America, who normally receive repeated assignments in the region.

Corporate executives who have been kidnapped have faced similar, as well as some different, problems. If not in top management positions, their corporate careers also were disrupted by the need for sudden transfer, the possibility of being shelved for a period, or their unwillingness to serve again in a high-risk area. In addition, the fact that the corporation had been compelled to pay a large ransom for their safe return obligated them to the company, at least in their eyes, in a way that was not conducive to career advancement. They could not easily leave to accept a better offer elsewhere after the corporation had paid a million-dollar ransom. They could not easily demand a better position or a raise in pay. The degree to which these perceptions are translated into reality and how former hostages have in fact fared in the corporate world since their release is not known.

This is part of a more generalized feeling among hostages of discomfort at being indebted to their company or family, especially if a ransom is paid. Colleagues and relatives may unwittingly add to this feeling of indebtedness, saying without saying, "We paid a lot for you."

Most hostages feel a strong need to tell the whole story. Sometimes they are discouraged from doing so by well-meaning friends or relatives who are concerned that describing the whole episode will be painful or embarrassing for the former hostage, and perhaps for them too. In some cases, former hostages have withheld the whole story even from their closest intimates, not only because it might be painful, but also because they anticipated judgment. It is interesting to note that in our interviews, former hostages frequently said that this was the first time they had told the whole story, and to a total stranger! Asked how they felt about it, most of them said that it was a relief.

The well-meaning intent of relatives and colleagues to protect the former hostage from re-living the episode may in fact reflect their own embarrassment and may accentuate the feelings of embarrassment he is already experiencing. In some cases, former hostages appear to have been treated much the same as rape victims. Both of them are told not to talk about it; the entire episode is to be swept away, kept in the closet. Both kinds of victims also tend to feel that they are on trial.

In a cruel way, they are on trial. Most victims of terrorist kidnappings were selected because they represented governments and were therefore good bargaining pieces, because they represented political or economic systems or specific policies opposed by the terrorists, or because they worked for large corporations or belonged to wealthy families that could be compelled to pay large ransoms. Their personal behavior had very little to do with their kidnapping, except for the fact that they were

available to the kidnappers, or at least, they were more available than other potential victims. Yet, many of us harbor medieval notions that bad things happen only to people who somehow deserve them. Rape victims confront this attitude: if a woman did not wear attractive clothes, walk down dark streets at night, or otherwise "induce" her attacker, she would not have suffered this terrible experience.

So it is with the former hostage. If he had followed every recommendation in the security briefing, he would not have been kidnapped. The former hostage is always vulnerable on that score. Not one former hostage can claim to have followed every bit of security advice, but neither can people who have not been kidnapped.

The judgment of others, however, goes deeper than the implied lapse of security. At its core, it represents a reaction to fear, which is what terrorism is all about. We find it difficult to accept the idea that virtually any one of us could be selected, stalked, yanked off the street, and threatened with death by terrorists. "That cannot happen to me. If it happens to someone else who is just like me, there must be a reason, something I don't know about, something he did that made him a victim and not me. I am different." Our own fear persuades us to blame the victim for his misfortune.

Although it may be therapeutic for the former hostage to relate the whole story, the most inappropriate and damaging moment for him to do so is before the microphones and cameras of the news media immediately on his release. At that moment he is exhausted, a bundle of mixed emotions—grateful to be alive, still frightened, angry, confused, impatient. Moments before, he probably thought he was going to be killed as kidnappers blindfolded him and thrust him into a car, or as police rushed through the doors of his cell. He may still be emotionally attached to his former captors. He is not likely to know all of the details that led to his release. Lacking facts, his judgment impaired, he may blurt out statements that he will later regret. It is a disservice to the former hostage to expose him to this situation. Fortunately, this is a lesson that has been learned, and most hostages are insulated from the press for a least a few days after their release.

With time, the former hostage begins to build up certain defenses against the criticism he expects to receive. He may begin to reconstruct his memory of the episode; certain parts are left out; self-deprecating humor may be injected into the account to mark the painful parts; the humor has an edge; the listener is challenged. Sometimes the whole episode is reduced to minor importance. Some former hostages recount their kidnappings as if they had been tea parties, although their colleagues recall that at the time of their release they were too emotionally shaken to even speak.

Psychological problems experienced by former hostages vary considerably. They include insomnia, nightmares, tremors, impotence, loss of appetite, restlessness, difficulties in concentration, loss of motivation, fear of the dark, fear of crowds, fear of being left alone, a sense of detachment, and feelings of alienation. A few former hostages have suffered breakdowns. One former hostage's hands trembled severely whenever he recalled the incident. Others would not sleep at night or slept with guns at their side. The wife of one former hostage noted that her husband "gulped his food" after his return. Some became more emotionally detached, whereas others sought physical contact—embracing and kissing friends. Some former hostages recall that they suffered no noticeable difficulties on their return, but only later began to experience the same symptoms other former hostages spoke about. Most of the symptoms fade with time. Sleep problems may last a year or more. Fear may persist for years.

Indeed, many former hostages appear to retain a great fear of their former captors and all other terrorists. Even years later, thousands of miles away, some mentioned that they had to be careful of what they said. They attribute vast, worldwide power to underground groups. Incidents that recall their captivity—a stranger approaching them on the street, a newspaper account of another kidnapping, being momentarily unable to find a light switch in a darkened room—could set off strong sensations of fear, including vivid memories of the sights, sounds, and smells of captivity.

Some former hostages experience more profound and permanent changes. Many said that they were not the same person on return. The experience is cataclysmic. It may change the hostage's personality, his outlook on life, or his lifestyle. Many hostages review their lives during captivity. Career goals that previously drove the corporate executive may become less important. Others have mentioned that they are less certain about their ability to predict and plan for the future [3]. One former hostage tended to be more impulsive in his decisions. Still another was considered by his colleagues to have become more unpredictable.

Puzzling to colleagues and superiors, these changes can also cause problems within the corporation. A case in point is that of Baron Edouard-Jean Empain, chairman of one of the largest companies in Europe. Kidnapped and held for 63 days, 20 pounds lighter, barely able to walk due to a muscular condition related to his captivity, Baron Empain temporarily stepped down from the chairmanship on his release. He dramatically altered his previously conservative lifestyle and became a playboy. Describing his new outlook on life, he said, "The thing I regretted during my captivity was not having taken sufficient advantage of life, not having seen enough places, known enough girls [4]." After 7 months, the Baron settled down somewhat and announced that he wanted to resume his position as chairman, but his fling with flamboyance offended and concerned the deeply conservative family and board members, who worried that he might no longer be suitable for the job. Ultimately, the baron did regain control of the corporation.

Many former hostages blame subsequent physical ailments on their captivity or believe that captivity exacerbated previous health problems. Former hostages have suffered heart attacks or strokes; others have developed phlebitis or other problems associated with the circulatory and nervous systems. It is not certain whether these are in fact related to physical treatment and stress suffered during captivity, or whether they may be related to the stress brought on by the post-release problems of re-adjustment, family tensions, and concerns about careers. Medical science has only recently come to trace numerous physical problems to emotional stress.

In addition to having health problems, former hostages have complained about being accident-prone. Studies have in fact shown that former prisoners of war (POWs) experience a higher-than-normal incidence of accidents, along with a higher incidence of alcoholism and suicide, compared with similar populations who have not been captives. Accidents, alcoholism, and suicide, of course, are related. Again, it is not clear whether these problems are the direct result of the experience of captivity or the result of the post-release experience. If they are the result of captivity, then prompt treatment can mitigate the problems. If they are caused by post-release experiences, then preventive measures are possible through education and counseling.

The former hostage remains a prisoner of our perceptions, his ordeal protracted by callous ignorance or unwarranted concern. If possible problems of re-adjustment are not recognized and handled competently and sympathetically, the former hostage suffers unnecessarily. On the other hand, to describe all the possible re-adjustment problems of the former hostage is to paint a portrait of a hypersensitive, guilt-ridden, psychological cripple who may at any moment suffer a coronary or drive his car over a cliff. Noting that "people are careful around us," some former hostages complain that friends and colleagues treat them "as if we were nuts or that we would go nuts [5]." Former hostages express similar resentment toward eager psychiatrists who insist that they must have serious problems and must require treatment.

The portrait presented here is an artificial one, because it is built of the complaints and concerns of many hostages. It resembles in its totality no single former hostage. Although most former hostages have experienced some of the problems described here, most have found that re-entry difficulties were mild and disappeared in a few months, swept away by the joy of being alive.

The former hostage gets a great deal of attention. He is lionized by the press, pampered by his family, watched closely for symptoms of re-adjustment problems. Family members are often overlooked, but they suffer problems, too. During the period of a loved one's captivity, they go through tremendous stress, maintaining their composure, sometimes kept in the dark by government and corporate officials, sometimes compelled to decide exactly how much money their father, or husband, or wife is worth—the final offer to be made by negotiators. They are prepared for the worst by friends and relatives, inwardly rejecting the possibility that the hostage may be killed.

Family members have experienced nervous breakdowns and miscarriages, have become dependent on alcohol or drugs. The release of a hostage permits an emotional release in the family, but the result is not always happy. Relatives have mentioned that their concern for the well-being of the homecoming hostage forced them to suppress their own pent-up feelings of anger and fear. The wife of one former hostage admitted that she treated her husband terribly on his return and months later felt very guilty about it. In interviews, family members also often ask, "How did I do?" These reactions suggest that government and corporate efforts to ease the re-entry problems of the former hostage should also take into account the re-adjustment problems of his family.

Not all the effects of having been held hostage are negative. Some former hostages have channeled their recollection and feelings into constructive efforts, writing books, lecturing those who face the threat of kidnapping, and helping the families of kidnap victims. Some hostages have undergone profound religious experiences in captivity and a subsequent deepening of religious faith. Captivity may imperil some relationships, exacerbating conflicts among couples trying to return to a pre-kidnapping normality that no longer exists because the experience has changed at least one and probably both partners; in other cases, separation and the threat of death and loss have deepened relationships. Friends and family note that many former hostages display an enviable zest for life, that they have become more patient, more tolerant, and more generous toward their fellow human beings.

Brian M. Jenkins

Source Jenkins, B.M., Terrorism and Personal Protection. (Butterworth–Heinemann, Boston, 1985).

Notes
1.   See, for example, "The Kidnapped Baron," Newsweek, October 16, 1978, p. 24.
2   Dorothy Rabinowitz, "The Hostage Mentality," Commentary, June 1977, pp. 70–72.
3.   This point was noted by Robert G. Hillman in "The Psychology of Being Held Hostage," American Journal of Psychiatry, 138:9, September 1981, pp. 1193–97. See also Frank M. Ochberg, "The Victim of Terrorism: Psychiatric Considerations," Terrorism, Vol. 1, No. 2, 1978, pp. 147–168.

4. Don Holt, "Kidnapped Baron Regains Corporate Power," Fortune, November 6, 1978, pp. 6, 49.

5. Victoria Marina, "Siege Leaves Mark on 2 Hostages," Los Angeles Times, May 20, 1979.

TERRORISM: THE PAYMENT OF RANSOM

Terrorist groups finance themselves primarily through armed robberies, extortion, and kidnappings for ransom. It is difficult to say with any precision how much ransom terrorists have collected in recent years. Family members and corporate officials are naturally reluctant to discuss the amounts paid for the safe return of relatives or company executives, and many ransom kidnappings are not reported at all. It has been estimated that during the 1970s corporations paid between $150 and $250 million dollars in ransom to terrorists [1]. Since then, kidnappings have increased and ransoms in excess of $1 million are not uncommon. The total amount of ransom paid probably lies in the region of several hundred million U.S. dollars and could be much more.

How did it come about that corporations started routinely paying ransom to terrorists? To answer that question, one must go back to the first terrorist kidnappings of corporate executives in Latin America at the beginning of the 1970s. The Tupamaros in Uruguay carried out a number of abductions in the late 1960s, but these were primarily for propaganda purposes. The terrorists sought to embarrass the government by kidnapping members of the country's business elite and personal friends of the president of Uruguay, then obtaining information from their hostages about corruption involving business and government officials that the terrorists could use to discredit the political and economic system. It is in Argentina that one finds the precedent for the contemporary practice of kidnapping corporate executives to finance terrorist organizations.

The precedent-setting case was the abduction in May 1971 of Stanley Sylvester, the honorary British consul in Rosario, Argentina, and the manager of the Swift Company's meat-packing plant. The kidnappers made no demands on the Argentine or British governments, both of whom by 1971 had adopted no-concessions policies. Instead, they demanded that the Swift Company re-hire 300 workers who had been dismissed by the company, reduce work quotas for Swift employees, terminate indiscriminate firing of workers, provide medical attention and reduce cold working conditions in the packing plant, distribute $50,000 worth of food to specified working-class neighborhoods, and publish the kidnappers' communiqués in all the public media. The company promptly agreed and Sylvester was released 1 week after his abduction.

The kidnapping of Sylvester marked the first time in the world that a terrorist organization had forced an international corporation to change working conditions in its plant and distribute goods to the poor. The kidnapping of the executive of a foreign corporation also marked a departure for the terrorist organization, which had until then limited its operations to assaults on police and military installations, and gained its funds from bank robberies—the traditional Bolshevik method of financing revolution.

At the outset, the Sylvester kidnapping apparently caused considerable debate within the terrorists' ranks. The kidnapping was planned and executed by the Rosario group without approval of the terrorist group's national command. The Rosario group hoped to win sympathy among the workers, provoke the government into repressive measures on behalf of the foreign business community, and force the national leadership of the terrorist organization to adopt a new tactical-strategic line of attack. The demand to pay for the distribution of food was something additionally calculated to appeal to the workers. It was not yet seen as a means of financing terrorist operations. Although the kidnapping of Stanley Sylvester fell within the terrorists' broad aims of improving the lot of the workers and eliminating foreign enterprises from Argentina, the group's national leadership considered the kidnapping a departure from orthodox revolutionary tactics and also feared that such an act of terrorism would lead to increased police repression that would imperil the group itself [2].

Thus, the kidnapping and ransoming of Stanley Sylvester represents an innovation, not one carefully designed or even imagined by its perpetrators at the time as a method of financing terrorist operations, but rather something they fell into, and not without internal debate. Had the operation failed, the national leadership's objections would have been justified, and ransom kidnappings might have for a time remained in the domain of ordinary crime. As it turned out, however, the demands were met.

Viewing the outcome of the Sylvester case as a success, Argentine terrorists struck again in March 1972, this time kidnapping Oberdan Sallustro, president of Fiat of Argentina. They demanded that the Argentine government release 50 prisoners, and that Fiat reinstate 250 workers who had been fired in a labor dispute and provide $1 million in the form of school supplies and shoes to children in poor areas of the country. Fiat accepted the ransom demands but the Argentine government refused to release any prisoners and warned that Fiat executives would be prosecuted for "illicit associations" unless they broke off contact with the kidnappers. Police launched an all-out search and discovered where Sallustro was being held. Sallustro was killed when police assaulted the hideout.

The government's strong response in the Sallustro case did not arrest growing terrorism in Argentina or prevent further kidnappings. The kidnappers switched from extracting corporate funds for philanthropic enterprises on behalf of the workers and the poor to demanding direct cash payments. In June 1972, terrorists kidnapped the president of the Buenos Aires branch of the Italian Banco di Napoli. They demanded and received $200,000 in ransom. In September, another terrorist group kidnapped the Dutch head of Philips Argentina and demanded $500,000 ransom. In November, an Italian industrialist was kidnapped in Buenos Aires. He was released after $500,000 was paid.

The ransom demands began to escalate. In December 1972, terrorists in Argentina kidnapped the managing director of a British firm and held him for $1 million ransom. In April 1973, terrorists kidnapped an American executive of the Kodak Corporation and held him for $1.5 million. In June 1973 they kidnapped a British executive and demanded $7.5 million in ransom. In October 1973, the kidnappers of a Swissair executive demanded $10 million in ransom. In March 1974, the kidnappers of an Esso plant manager reportedly received $14.2 million in ransom; and in September 1974, the kidnappers of the Born

brothers, directors of the Bunge and Born Company, one of the world's largest trading conglomerates, demanded an incredible $60 million ransom. The pattern of corporations paying ransom for kidnapped executives was set.

In the early 1970s, however, this kind of terrorism was a new phenomenon. Political kidnappings were still comparatively rare occurrences, targeted almost entirely against government officials and diplomats. The corporations faced with ransom demands in these first cases probably had no notion that they were establishing precedents that would later become customary practice for the corporate community worldwide, ones that would ultimately give rise to a new service industry of kidnap and ransom insurance and hostage recovery consultants.

If corporations had little notion of establishing precedents for the future, they did have precedents set in the past on which to base their decisions, and the precedents pointed toward paying ransom. Most kidnappings up to that time had been carried out by common criminals who demanded ransom from the family of a victim. Families almost always paid, and the authorities often cooperated in the hope that in taking delivery of the money, the kidnappers would expose themselves to arrest. In countries with effective law enforcement establishments, kidnappers usually were caught. Even in the rare cases in which a family was unable or unwilling to meet the kidnappers' ransom demands, the authorities usually arranged a bogus payment to bring the kidnappers to the surface.

The growing number of airline hijackings that had occurred by the early 1970s provided another kind of precedent. Here again, the practice was to yield to the demand of hijackers. Faced with threats to passengers and crew members and expensive aircraft, airline companies agreed to the demands of hijackers whether they wanted to simply change the destination of the plane or asked for money and parachutes. There was no notion that passengers or employees would be imperiled by refusals to comply with the demands of hijackers.

It should also be recalled—particularly by governments who now wish that corporations would follow their lead and adopt no-ransom policies—that in the early 1970s when the corporations first confronted terrorists demanding ransom, many governments themselves routinely yielded to the demands of terrorists holding hostages. Between 1969 and 1971, the government of Brazil released prisoners on four occasions to save the lives of foreign diplomats kidnapped by terrorists in that country. In July 1970, the Greek government released seven prisoners in exchange for the safe release of passengers held aboard a hijacked Olympic Airways plane. In September 1970, Switzerland, Germany, and the United Kingdom released prisoners to obtain the safe release of airline passengers held hostage by Palestinian hijackers in Jordan. In 1972, West Germany released the terrorists responsible for the Munich incident in return for the release of hostages aboard a hijacked Lufthansa airliner, and in 1975, the German government released German terrorists to obtain the freedom of a kidnapped German official. Between 1970 and 1973, the governments of Guatemala, Haiti, the Dominican Republic, and Mexico all yielded to the demands of terrorists holding government officials or foreign diplomats.

The United States, currently an advocate of a no-concessions policy, also had a different view at the time of the first kidnappings. Because of the presumed influence that the United States exercised over local governments, urban guerrillas abducted American diplomats. While not in sympathy with the kidnappers, the United States realized that in many cases, the local governments were in fact authoritarian regimes whose opponents were subject to arbitrary arrest: the political prisoners whose release was demanded in exchange for the release of an American diplomat might be just that—political prisoners.   On March 24, 1970, a U.S. Department of State spokesperson announced as a matter of policy—the first such policy pronouncement on the topic—that the United States favored the release of political prisoners if it were the only way to free kidnapped American diplomats. This policy did not begin to change until 1971, and a firm no-ransom policy did not really emerge until 1973. Even then it was debated within the government.

Argentina was the first country to pronounce a no-concessions policy in March 1970, although it occasionally departed from this policy in subsequent incidents. Guatemala and Uruguay followed later that year. No-concessions policies,

however, were not widely adopted until the middle of the 1970s, and many countries continued to yield to terrorists holding hostages. As late as 1977, the government of Japan paid $5 million dollars to Japanese Red Army terrorists who had hijacked a Japan Airlines plane. In 1978, the government of Nicaragua paid $500,000 to Sandinistas holding hostages in the national assembly building. In 1981, the government of Italy found a way of negotiating a $1.5 million ransom paid to the terrorist kidnappers of an Italian politician in Naples, despite a no-concessions policy that had been declared and adhered to during the Moro kidnapping.

With so many governments publicly yielding to terrorist demands, in many cases releasing convicted felons, it was not likely that corporations were going to adopt a contrary position and refuse to pay ransom for sequestered executives. Once the precedent was established in the corporate community, it became increasingly difficult in subsequent cases to take a position out of line with widespread corporate practice.

The nature of the terrorists' demands in the first kidnappings of corporate executives also made it hard to refuse. The terrorists demanded not cash for themselves, but financial backing of various philanthropic efforts, such as the deliveries of food to the poor demanded by the kidnappers of Stanley Sylvester. Large foreign corporations could not easily refuse to provide such charity even under duress. (At the same time, corporate philanthropy itself provided no immunity against terrorist kidnappings.) Later, terrorist kidnappers switched from philanthropy to cash payments paid directly to the terrorists.

If, in the early 1970s, the corporations had foreseen a long struggle with terrorism in which the companies were to be the unwilling financiers and principal targets of terrorists, they might have thought differently, but no one saw this coming. For one thing, companies did not take a collective view when faced with kidnappings; although as the problem persisted, particularly in Argentina, the corporations did begin to share information and take a more united stand in demanding government action. In each kidnapping, the corporation was very much on its own and saw its problem as an isolated event. There was a presumption that once it got through its kidnapping, paid its ransom, obtained the release of its executive, it would not again be attacked. In Argentina this perception was mostly correct. Companies were seldom targeted again in subsequent kidnappings, at least, not by the same group. In Italy, it was a different story. There, the Red Brigades repeatedly attacked the same corporations.

Arguments for the Payment of Ransoms

Few corporations have adopted no-ransom policies, but the debate over the decision to pay or not to pay ransom repeatedly surfaces. There are many obvious arguments in favor of paying ransom, the principal one being humanitarian. Paying ransom is often the only way to save the life of the hostage, and for the corporation, the life of a valuable employee. A willingness to pay ransom also aids employee morale and recruiting.

While some employees might derive comfort from a publicly declared no-ransom policy, figuring that it will make them less of a target to would-be kidnappers, it is more likely that a no-ransom policy would make it more difficult for a company to recruit personnel for areas where kidnapping is a problem. Clearly, the death of an employee resulting from a decision not to pay ransom would have an adverse impact on employee morale. It could also have a disastrous impact on the corporate image, particularly when the corporation is foreign and the hostage a local employee. Refusal to pay ransom, moreover, could result in lawsuits—even though it has never been established in a court of law that a company is obliged to pay ransoms.

A further argument for the payment of ransoms is that delivery of the money may assist the authorities, if they have been notified, in apprehending the kidnappers. This expectation holds in the United States and a few other countries, but not in many Third World countries where the adversaries are sophisticated terrorist organizations.

Paying ransoms is not costly. Although multimillion-dollar ransoms are not uncommon, ransom insurance policies reduce a company's expenditure to the deductible, usually something around several hundred thousand dollars. In the United States, at least, the amount is tax deductible.

Paying ransoms is by now a widely accepted corporate practice and for most corporations, it is a one-time affair. A company whose executive is kidnapped is not likely to have to go through the same experience twice in the same country. In some cases, corporations have sought and received assurance from terrorist kidnappers that if they pay the ransom, their employees will not be kidnapped again. No enforcement of such a bargain is possible, of course, and it does not work in countries where several independent groups are active. In cases where a company is subject to repeated kidnappings and other terrorist actions directed against its employees that are financed by the ransoms it pays, the arguments against the payment of ransoms are stronger.

Arguments against the Payment of Ransoms

There are several arguments against the payment of ransoms. Of most merit is the argument that ransom payments merely finance further terrorist activity, which certainly is not in the country's or the corporate community's long-term interest. Put it this way: a million-dollar ransom can support 10 to 20 full-time terrorists for a year, or it can buy an arsenal of weapons. Suppose a terrorist organization with an established record of assassinations and bombings demanded that a corporation deliver 500 machine guns and enough dynamite to make several hundred bombs. The humanitarian argument in favor of saving the life of a single hostage would be outweighed by the obvious violence these weapons would bring. In such a case the corporation probably would refuse.

The willingness of corporations to pay large ransoms has made them a lucrative target. Then, would not a policy of not paying ransom provide a deterrent to terrorist kidnappings? It might, if all the companies agreed and stuck to a no-ransom policy, but the evidence is mixed. A declared no-concessions policy did not reduce terrorist hijackings and other hostage seizures aimed at extracting concessions from the government of Israel, although the record shows that Palestinian terrorists successively reduced their original demands in an unsuccessful attempt to entice Israel into making a compromise. No-concessions policies did not reduce terrorist kidnappings in Uruguay, Argentina, or Italy. Terrorist kidnappings declined when the terrorist groups were destroyed.

A careful examination of government policies on ransom and terrorist kidnapping trends finds little convincing evidence to support the assumption that no-concessions policies are a deterrent. On the other hand, as we have seen already, a no-concessions policy announced by the Argentine government in 1970 may have shifted terrorist sights to the corporate community; and no doubt the willingness of corporations to pay sizable ransoms provided an incentive to further kidnappings of corporate executives. To whom would the risk be displaced if all the corporations in the world were to magically agree to pay no more ransom? Probably individual families would be faced with the ransom demands, as they already have been in many cases. That trend may save corporations money but would not necessarily solve recruiting and morale problems. Nor can it be automatically considered a positive achievement in a broader definition of the public good, except that families generally have less financial resources than large corporations and are less able to pay large ransoms. Shifting the ransom burden to families would theoretically reduce the volume of funds going to the terrorists.

Two further arguments against the payment of ransom are that the government and corporate stockholders may object. Stockholders have on occasion objected to ransom payments but the single case to reach the courts failed. Governments may express their objection to ransom payments by administrative means—ruling ransom payments not to be deductible, imposing restrictions on currency exchange—or in legislation by outlawing "illicit associations" with terrorists or the payment of ransom itself. Such laws, however, can have unintended adverse effects.

For governments, the arguments for and against yielding to the demands of kidnappers are different. Here the issue is not simply the payment of cash, but a matter of governance: terrorists seldom seek access to the national treasury. Instead, they demand political concessions, most often, the release of imprisoned terrorists. This constitutes subversion of the judicial system, and if conceded to, represents an abdication of the government's responsibility to protect all citizens who may be endangered by releasing imprisoned terrorists or making other concessions that strengthen the terrorists' group. Finally, a government can demand more of its officials than can a corporation. A person may be asked to risk his life for his country, but seldom can he be asked to die for his company [3].

Should Paying Ransom Be Outlawed?

Governments have adopted various approaches toward kidnapping. Some governments, while following no-concessions policies in dealing with any demands that kidnappers may levy on the government, have not tried to interfere with the payment of ransom by private parties. Other countries have outlawed the payment of ransom by making it illegal under any circumstances to give money to terrorist organizations or by making it a crime to act as an intermediary between a hostage and terrorists in a kidnapping.

Such laws are not evenly enforced. Some governments have used laws against ransom simply to keep ransom payments out of the newspapers, which could encourage more kidnappings, but have not tried vigorously to prevent negotiations or prosecute those who pay ransom. In still other cases, laws outlawing the payment of ransom have been used by government authorities to ensure that government authorities are brought into the case. Companies whose executives are kidnapped are informed that they may negotiate a ransom but are warned to keep government authorities posted on the negotiations or risk prosecution. Another approach may be to use the law to discourage certain kinds of corporate concessions that are unacceptable to the government. For example, a government may not object to a quietly arranged cash payment but will object to a corporation agreeing to pay for the publication of terrorist manifestos in newspapers around the world. The government will warn the corporation that its executives will face prosecution if they make such a concession. In other countries, the target of a no-ransom law may be aimed at the transfer of funds abroad. To avoid taxes and currency regulations, some families have faked kidnappings and conducted phony negotiations that end in large sums of money being transferred out of the country to family accounts abroad.

Laws against ransom make the target of a ransom a participant in the crime. In addition to the negative aspects of criminalizing victims of crime, a law against ransom, if enforced, can become an obstacle to effective law enforcement. Faced with prosecution, many companies probably—and certainly families—will attempt to negotiate with kidnappers secretly. Argentina went through this experience in the early 1970s when it warned that companies paying ransom could be prosecuted. Cooperation with Argentine police ceased as companies secretly negotiated ransom payments. Argentina subsequently dropped the idea of outlawing ransom payments. Cooperation with the authorities increased somewhat, but the apprehension and conviction record was dismal and the kidnappings continued until the terrorist groups were destroyed.

In the United States, where ransom kidnappings have been carried out by ordinary criminals rather than political terrorists, ransom payments are almost always arranged, with Federal Bureau of Investigation (FBI) officials present, and the kidnappers are almost invariably apprehended as a result. Owing to the apprehension and conviction record, kidnapping remains a comparatively rare crime in the United States. It is noteworthy that while some corporations favor laws against ransom as a means of relieving them of making life and death decisions, most corporations oppose such laws.

How Much Ransom?

As ransom demands escalated in the 1970s, and before the purchase of ransom insurance policies had become more common and less costly, corporate heads asked: How much ransom should a corporation pay? A ransom of several hundred thousand dollars would not impose a great burden on most corporations, but what if terrorists asked for $50 million or $100 million? It is difficult enough to set a price on human life, although economists, insurance companies, and the courts do so all the time. It is

also impossible to say how much ransom is appropriate as a final offer or will suffice in any particular case. Kidnappers demanding $5 million have settled for several hundred thousand. In other cases, terrorists demanding $10 million have refused offers of $5 million.

In a sense, the question is the wrong one. There is no "correct" price for a hostage any more than there is a "correct" price for a Rembrandt. The final amount depends on many things. The rank of the individual is a factor in the company's decision. A million-dollar ransom may not seem unreasonable for an executive who receives an annual salary of a half million—an expression of the value the company places on him.

While not to be used as a formula for calculating ransom, a rough idea of how much an individual is worth to a corporation can be worked out if we set the present value of his future services to the company as the discounted sum of his future earnings. Suppose, for example, a 45-year-old executive draws a current salary of $100,000 a year. If we figure in a 10% discount (a standard often used) to reflect the corporations' expected internal rate of return from the employee's 20 remaining years before retirement, his present value would be $850,000 [4]. Most corporations do consider at least their senior employees as investments. This approach may not work for easily replaced lower-level employees. However, for reasons relating to its public image, there might be tremendous public pressure on a corporation to pay ransoms for low-ranking employees.

It is difficult historically to find much relationship between the rank of an individual kidnapped and the amount of ransom ultimately paid. Such values are set, of course, when a company purchases a ransom insurance policy. (It is the author's own impression that ransom insurance policies have had a leveling effect on ransom payments by providing teams of skilled negotiators who are able to significantly reduce the initial ransom demands of the kidnappers, and by providing broad policies that cover all employees instead of just a handful of men at the top.)

Another important factor appears to be the "going market rate." In countries where kidnapping is a frequent occurrence, professional negotiators may have a fair idea of how much the kidnappers are likely to accept.

This, however, is frequently distorted. Terrorist kidnappers may be especially desperate for a quick settlement to pay for a shipment of guns; or while holding several hostages from several firms, they might be willing to satisfy their short-term cash needs with a quick settlement of one case. The terrorists could also decide to kill one of their hostages in order to encourage others to settle quickly on their terms.

Terrorists, if they are at all sophisticated, are going to have a pretty good idea of a corporation's financial situation prior to the kidnapping of one of its executives. We know now from arrests and interrogations that in many cases terrorists had confederates within corporations who had provided the kidnappers with details of its operations. A corporation must take special precautions to ensure that kidnappers are not receiving information from its response or negotiating team even during a kidnapping. Terrorist kidnappers are also going to know how much they or other groups active in the country have ultimately settled for. Unless the corporation has received information from government sources or other companies, or has contracted consultants who are familiar with previous cases in the country, it will operate at an informational disadvantage.

Concessions Other Than Cash

Paying money is the easiest thing a company can do. Concessions other than cash can cause major problems for corporations. In a number of cases, kidnappers have tried to develop constituencies among workers by demanding that companies re-hire workers who have been dismissed or make other concessions to the labor force. Such concessions are sometimes more difficult to resist because they may be popular. Terrorists have been skillful in exploiting labor disputes or situations where workers are exposed to dangerous conditions and accidents have occurred. For the corporation, however, such concessions involve both economic and management issues. Re-hiring workers, increasing wages, or other economic concessions directly affect profits— more so than a single ransom payment, complicate relations with labor unions where they exist, and undermine management itself. The question becomes not one of concessions, but one of who is going to run the corporation: corporate management or a group of terrorists.

Demands that corporations pay for the publication of terrorist manifestos have caused serious problems between corporations and governments. Understandably, governments are opposed to the worldwide publication of manifestos that are calculated to embarrass the government. In the Niehous case, the Venezuelan government threatened to nationalize the local assets of Owens-Illinois for agreeing to publish terrorist manifestos.

In all probability, while governments continue to resist terrorist demands, corporations will continue to pay ransom. With continuing kidnappings, the growth of ransom insurance, and the appearance of hostage recovery consultants, kidnapping has become an institutionalized form of extortion.

Brian M. Jenkins

Source Jenkins, B.M., Terrorism and Personal Protection. (Butterworth–Heinemann, Boston, 1985).

Notes
1.   The low estimate was made by E. Patrick McGuire, "International Terrorism and Business Security," The Conference Board Information Bulletin, No. 65, New York, 1979, p. 6. The higher estimates come from Terrorism and International Business (Business International Corporation, New York, 1979), p. 2.
2.   Details of the Stanley Sylvester case are based upon a detailed case study of the episode by Edward Gonzalez of the Rand Corporation, Santa Monica, CA.
3.   For further discussions of the arguments for and against ransom, see Brian M. Jenkins, "Should Corporations Be Prevented from Paying Ransom?" Series No. P-5291 (The Rand Corporation, Santa Monica, CA, 1974); or an excellent article by Paul Wilkinson, "Kidnap and Ransom—To Pay or Not to Pay?" International Security Review, March/April 1983, pp. 32–36.
4.   The author is indebted to Arthur J. Alexander for this point.

TESTIFYING IN COURT

The person who has investigated a case is often the most important witness in the trial of that case. He may be the only person with a comprehensive understanding of a crime sufficient to give a complete, coordinated view of what happened. He is, therefore, the main communications system through which evidence of a crime is transmitted to the finder of fact at trial.

The importance of a good presentation by the investigator on the witness stand cannot be overemphasized. Hours and hours of the most competent investigation and preparation may be wasted if the results are improperly presented in court. The trier of fact (usually the jury) comes into court having no prior knowledge of what happened or who is guilty or innocent. The picture the jury gets depends largely on the ability of the investigator to testify truthfully and accurately, and to do so in a manner that impresses everyone present that he is intelligent, honest, competent, and fair. The defense attorney will do everything legally permitted to twist the evidence in his client's favor. If the investigator is confused, hazy, or unsure of important facts, the jury will be similarly confused and hazy. However, if he presents a clear-cut report containing all elements of proof in a calm, unprejudiced manner, the jury will see the case in the same light.

Furthermore, a verdict of guilty accomplishes little if an investigator has testified so poorly that he affords the accused good grounds for a new trial or for a reversal on appeal. Neither does a guilty verdict accomplish the good it should unless the trial has been conducted in such a manner that everyone in the courtroom has been impressed with the dignity and justice of the proceedings. Public confidence in our system of justice is essential to its proper function.

Preparation before Trial

Effective testimony in court depends to a large extent on preparation. Preparation begins with the first notification that a possible crime has been committed. All facts, observations, and actions having to do with the case should be carefully recorded in notes, reports, and photographs, keeping in mind that the information may eventually be introduced in court. Proper investigative procedures cannot be stressed strongly enough, because there are often long delays between the investigation of a case and the trial, and unless information is recorded, much of it is sure to be forgotten in the interim.

Knowledge of the Case. As the time of trial draws near, the investigator should make a complete review of the case and refresh his memory of the facts by carefully reading through all notes and reports. He should also examine physical evidence that has been collected, in the event that it has to be identified or referred to in court. Then he should put his thoughts together so he can visualize the whole case in the sequence in which it happened. Testimony presented to a jury as a chain of events in the order that they occurred is both interesting and convincing.

An investigator may be allowed to refresh his memory on the witness stand by referring to his notes or reports. However, if he does, the defense counsel has a right to examine these notes and question him about them. Therefore, the investigator should discuss with the prosecuting attorney the advisability of taking notes to the witness stand.

Also, the prosecuting attorney may want to confer with the investigator about the facts of the case at a pre-trial session. At this session, the prosecuting attorney may try to re-awaken the investigator's senses to recall parts of the investigation that he deems essential to the case and to go over the investigator's testimony. This is entirely proper and, at this time, the investigator should make sure that the prosecuting attorney knows all the facts of the case, whether favorable or unfavorable to the defendant. The prosecuting attorney may not, however, tell the investigator what to say or influence the investigator to deviate from the truth in any way.

Knowledge of the Rules of Evidence. Besides knowledge of the case being tried, the investigator testifying in court should have a basic knowledge of the rules of evidence. This knowledge will help him to better understand the proceedings and enable him to testify more intelligently, removing the opportunities for delay and confusion that can occur in the mind of the investigator when placed under pressure in the courtroom.

Appearance and Attitude. When an investigator appears in court, he must observe the highest standards of conduct. The minute he walks to the witness stand, he becomes the focal point of interest and observation by the public.

The key thing for an investigator to impress in his mind when testifying in court is that he is engaged in a very solemn and serious matter. He should look and act accordingly. While waiting to testify, the investigator should not linger outside the door of the courtroom smoking, gossiping, joking, laughing, or engaging in other similar conduct. This distracts attention from the proceedings and shows little regard for the serious nature of the occasion. Rather, the investigator should be seated quietly in the courtroom while awaiting his turn to take the stand, unless he is directed to wait in the witness room.

An investigator's appearance while testifying should be neat and well-groomed. He should wear a clean suit, tie, and shined shoes. Neither should he wear dark glasses, smoke, chew gum, or generally fidget around while on the witness stand. A favorable impression is created if the investigator sits erect but at ease in the witness chair and appears confident, alert, and interested in the proceedings.

Testimony during Trial

Our system of securing information from a witness at a trial is by the question and answer method. The questioning by attorneys on direct examination serves merely to guide the witness in his testimony and to indicate the information that is required. After direct examination, the witness may be subject to cross-examination by the opposing counsel. The questions on cross-examination will have the opposite purpose of those asked on direct examination. Cross-examination questions may be devious, deceptive, or innocent in appearance, masking the opposing counsel's real objective, which is to discredit or minimize, to as great an extent as possible, the effect of the witness's testimony. The investigator is usually a witness for the state. Direct examination is by the prosecuting attorney, with cross-examination by counsel for the defense.

There are no definite rules for testifying effectively in court because each case has its own peculiarities. However, there are general guidelines for answering questions that should be followed in most cases and some specific suggestions designed to aid the witness on cross-examination.

Answering Questions on the Witness Stand

When taking the oath, the investigator should be serious and stand upright, facing the officer administering the oath. He should say "I do" clearly and positively and then be seated to await further questioning.

The investigator should listen carefully to the questions asked and make sure he understands each question before answering. If he does not understand, he should say so, and ask to have the question repeated. He should then pause after the question long enough to form an intelligent answer and to allow the attorneys and judge time to make objections.

Answers to questions should be given in a confident, straightforward, and sincere manner. The investigator should speak clearly, loudly, and slowly enough so that all in the courtroom can hear, and he should avoid mumbling or covering his mouth with his hand while talking. He should look at the attorney asking the questions but direct his answers toward the jury. Simple conversational English should be used, and all slang and unnecessary technical terms avoided. Most importantly, the investigator should be respectful and courteous at all times despite his feelings toward the people involved in the case. He should address the judge as "Your Honor," the attorney as "Sir," and the defendant as "the Defendant."

The essential rule to be observed above and beyond all others is to always tell the truth, even if it is favorable to the defendant. Facts should not be distorted or exaggerated to try and aid a conviction, nor should details be added to cover up personal mistakes. Once it has been shown that an investigator has not truthfully testified as to one portion of his investigation, no matter how small and inconsequential, the jury may reject the truthfulness of all other testimony which he may offer. On the other hand, an investigator's testimony will appear strong if it is a truthful recital of what he did and observed, even though it reveals human error on his part and favors the defendant in some parts.

Answers to questions should go no further than what the questions ask for. The investigator should not volunteer any information not asked for. If a question requests a "yes" or "no" answer and the investigator feels it cannot properly be answered in this manner, he should ask to have the question explained or re-worded, or request the right to explain his answer. He may state that he cannot answer the question by "yes" or "no." This should alert the prosecuting attorney to come to his assistance.

Answers to questions should be given as specifically as possible. However, figures for time, distance, size, etc., should be approximated only, unless they were exactly measured by the investigator.

When an investigator is referring to a map or plan in his testimony, he should identify the point on the map as clearly as possible so it becomes part of the trial record. For example, he should say "the northwest corner of the room" rather than just point to the spot and say "here" or "there." If the investigator does not understand the map or plan that is to be used at trial, he should tell the prosecuting attorney before trial and go over it with the person who prepared it.

If a wrong or ambiguous answer is given, it should be clarified immediately. It is far better for an investigator to correct his own mistakes than to have them pointed out to the jury by the defense attorney or a subsequent witness.

If a judge interrupts or an attorney objects to an investigator's testimony, the investigator should stop talking instantly. However, he should not anticipate an objection when a difficult question is asked but should only pause long enough to form an intelligent answer.

Under no circumstances should an investigator memorize his testimony. It will only sound rehearsed and false, and will not inspire the confidence of the jury. Instead, the investigator should have a thorough knowledge of the facts of the case and organize them in his mind so he can recite them as a narrative. If a particular fact or circumstance becomes hazy or is forgotten, the investigator may be allowed to refresh his memory from his notes as long as this does not become a habit. It is worth noting that if

an investigator does refer to notes, they may be examined by the opposing counsel. If for any reason, the judge criticizes an investigator's conduct in court, the investigator should not allow it to disturb his composure. The best policy is to ask the court's pardon for the error committed and proceed as though nothing had occurred.

Cross-Examination

In a criminal trial, it is the duty of counsel for the defendant, as an officer of the court and as an attorney, to use every legal means to secure the acquittal of the client or the best possible verdict under the circumstances. Since the investigator is often a chief witness for the state, the defense attorney, in order to win, must normally discredit or nullify the investigator's testimony, or at least minimize its importance in the eyes of the jury. To do this, he may use every device legally available to him. He may attempt to show that the investigator did not have the proper opportunity to observe the facts, or that he was inattentive or mistaken in his observations. He may try to make it seem like the investigator is lying or leaving out facts which are favorable to the defendant. In trials of crimes that happened some time ago, the defense counsel may try to show that the investigator's recollection of the entire event is bad and that he knows nothing without his notes. He may even try to show that the investigator has a grudge against the defendant. One of the ways of doing this is to goad the investigator into losing his temper to give the appearance of being personally antagonistic to the defendant. Under the proper circumstances, all these approaches are legal and available for the use of defense counsel.

The best defense against the techniques and devices of the defense attorney is thorough preparation. If the investigator has carefully observed the facts at the time of their occurrence, made complete and sufficient notes, reviewed his notes and reports carefully to fix the events in his memory, and testified truthfully, he need have no fear of cross-examination. Nevertheless, there are a few important suggestions regarding cross-examination that help prevent the investigator from falling into the traps laid by a clever defense attorney. Some of these suggestions have been mentioned previously and others apply exclusively to cross-examination.

•The investigator should not become angry or argumentative with the defense attorney. This is exactly what the defense attorney wants. Rather, the investigator should stick to calmly answering all questions unless an objection is sustained by the judge.

•The investigator should make very clear by his attitudes and statements that he has no personal feelings against the accused. If an accused has been nasty, insulting, or even has assaulted the investigator, the defense attorney may make much of such occurrences to persuade the jury that the investigator has a personal grudge in the matter and is "out to get" the accused. Jurors, being only human, are quick to resent any evidence of overbearing conduct or personal animosity on the part of the witness. The investigator, in this situation, should make clear that such things are common occurrences in his line of work and that they have no bearing on the matter as far as the facts are concerned.

•The investigator should not be afraid to admit mistakes made either in his investigation or his prior testimony. No one is perfect and an investigator admitting his errors himself will give defense counsel less fuel for attacking his credibility.

•If a defense attorney's question is not clear, the investigator should tell the court and ask to have it re-stated. An answer to an ambiguous question may very likely be a setup for a contradiction later on.

•The investigator should never be afraid to admit that he had discussed his testimony before trial with the prosecuting attorney, his superiors, or other investigators. This is entirely proper and accepted procedure. However, defense counsel, in the way he asks the question, may try to make it seem improper, and thereby trick the witness into a lie.

•If defense counsel seeks to cut off an investigator in the middle of his testimony, the investigator may turn to the judge and request an opportunity to explain his answer. This request will usually be granted.

Conduct after Trial

When an investigator leaves the witness stand, he should do so quickly and quietly, and either return to his seat or leave the courtroom if no longer needed. He should not linger to talk to the prosecutor. If he should have additional information or ideas to tell the prosecutor, they should be written down and passed to the prosecutor with a minimum amount of display. When an investigator leaves the courtroom he should not loiter to talk or gossip with others and, most important, he should not talk to jurors if it is a jury trial.

Convincing and effective testimony by the investigator is essential to successful operation of the criminal justice system and depends on proper preparation, approach, and experience. The suggestions outlined previously are designed to familiarize the investigator with court procedure and improve his testimony as a witness. The preparation and individual effort required in this endeavor is a minimum expectation.

John J. Fay, CPP

Source Special Agent Manual. (Georgia Bureau of Investigation, State Government of Georgia, Atlanta, 1979).

TORTS

A crime is a public wrong and a tort is a private wrong. A public wrong is remedied in a criminal proceeding and a private wrong is remedied in a civil proceeding. A single act in some instances will constitute both a crime and a tort. For example, if a person commits an assault and battery upon another, he commits a crime (a public wrong) and a tort (a private wrong). The law will seek to remedy both wrongs, but it will do so in different ways.

The state will move on its own authority to do justice by bringing a criminal action against the offender. The victim is also entitled to bring action against the offender in a civil suit. Tort law gives the victim a cause of action for damages in order that he may obtain sufficient satisfaction. The victim, however, pursues a civil remedy at his own discretion and in his own name. Whether the victim wins his lawsuit or not, the judgment will not prevent prosecution of the offender by the state.

The civil injuries involved in tort cases usually arise from acts of negligence. The fact that by his own negligence the victim contributed to the harm done may afford the offender a defense in a civil action of tort, but it does not constitute a defense to the offender in a criminal prosecution.

The single characteristic that differentiates criminal law from civil law is punishment. Generally, in a civil suit the basic questions are:

•How much, if at all, has the defendant injured the plaintiff, and

•What remedies, if any, are appropriate to compensate the plaintiff for his loss?

In a criminal case, the questions are:

•To what extent has the defendant injured society, and

•What sentence is appropriate to punish the defendant?

Tort Law Purposes

Tort law has three main purposes:

•To compensate persons who sustain a loss as a result of another's conduct.

•To place the cost of that compensation on those responsible for the loss.

•To prevent future harms and losses.

Compensation is predicated on the idea that losses, both tangible and intangible, can be measured in money.

If a loss-producing event is a matter of pure chance, the fairest way to relieve the victim of the burden is insurance or governmental compensation. Where a particular person can be identified as responsible for the creation of the risk, it becomes more just to impose the loss on the responsible person (tortfeasor) than to allow it to remain on the victim or the community at large.

The third major purpose of tort law is to prevent future torts by regulating human behavior. In concept, the tortfeasor held liable for damages will be more careful in the future, and the general threat of tort liability serves as an incentive to all persons to regulate their conduct appropriately. In this way, tort law supplements criminal law.

Damages: Compensatory and Punitive

When one person's tortious act injures another's person or property, the remedy for the injured party is to collect damages. The common law rules of damages for physical harm contain three fundamental ideas:

•Justice requires that the plaintiff be restored to his pre-injury condition, so far as it is possible to do so with money. He should be reimbursed not only for economic losses, but also for loss of physical and mental well-being.

•Most economic losses are translatable into dollars.

•When the plaintiff sues for an injury, he must recover all of his damages arising from that injury, past and future, in a lump sum and in a single lawsuit.

If the defendant's wrongful conduct is sufficiently serious, the law permits the trier of fact to impose a civil fine as punishment to deter him and others from similar conduct in the future. Punitive damages (also called exemplary or vindictive damages) are not really damages at all since the plaintiff has been made whole by the compensatory damages awarded in the same action. Punitive damages are justified as:

•An incentive for bringing the defendant to justice.

•Punishment for offenses that often escape or are beyond the reach of criminal law.

•Compensation for damages not normally compensable, such as hurt feelings, attorneys' fees, and expenses of litigation.

•The only effective means to force conscienceless defendants to cease practices known to be dangerous and which they would otherwise continue in the absence of an effective deterrent.

The Intentional Tort of Intrusion

Interference with the right to be "let alone" can be grouped into four categories: intrusion, appropriation of one's name or likeness, giving unreasonable publicity to private facts, and placing a person in a false light in the public eye. The latter three of these are founded upon improper publicity, usually in the public press or electronic media. They are beyond the scope of this concept and will not be discussed.

Intrusion is an intentional tort closely related to infliction of emotional distress. Both torts protect a person's interest in his mental tranquillity or peace of mind. A person has a basic right to choose when and to what extent he will permit others to know his personal affairs.

Essentially, intrusion is an intentional, improper, unreasonable, and offensive interference with the solitude, seclusion, or private life of another. It embraces a broad spectrum of activities. It may consist of an unauthorized entry, an illegal search or seizure, or an unauthorized eavesdropping, with or without electronic aids.

The tort is complete when the intrusion occurs. No publication or publicity of the information obtained is required. It is, of course, essential that the intrusion be into that which is, and is entitled to remain, private. Additionally, the harm must be substantial. The intrusion must be seriously objectionable, not simply bothersome or inconvenient.

John J. Fay, CPP

Source Fay, J.J., Butterworths Security Dictionary. (Butterworth–Heinemann, Boston, 1987).

TRADE SECRETS

How do trade secrets differ from other kinds of corporate confidential information? What unique requirements do the courts expect of a company to uphold ownership of a trade secret and the exclusive right to its use?

A trade secret is generally understood to be information that provides its owner a competitive advantage, is not generally known, and that the owner takes reasonable measures to keep secret. One of the most accepted definitions originated in a court case in Ohio and was restated by the United States Supreme Court in *Kewanee Oil Co. v. Bicron Corporation*:

> "...a trade secret may consist of any formula, pattern, device or compilation of information which is used in one's business, and which gives one an opportunity to obtain an advantage over competitors who do not know or use it. It may be a formula for a chemical compound, a process of manufacturing, treating or preserving materials, a pattern for a machine or other device, or a list of customers."

In this case, the court also summarized the key attributes of a trade secret:

•The subject of a trade secret must be a secret that is not of public knowledge or of general knowledge in the trade or business.

•The necessary element of secrecy is not lost, however, if the holder reveals the trade secret to another in confidence and under implied obligation not to disclose or use it.

•The holder of a trade secret is protected against unauthorized disclosure or use by those either under agreement or contract not to disclose the secret or who gain the secret by improper means.

•Improper means include theft, wiretapping, aerial reconnaissance, physical force, trespass, and criminal bribery. In general they are means which fall below the generally accepted standards of commercial morality and reasonable conduct.

•The courts may permit a person to use the holder's trade secret if the person discovered or developed the same secret independent of the holder or through reverse engineering, or if the holder does not take adequate measures to protect the secret.

•If a trade secret is discovered or developed by a person hired by a company to do such research and development, the trade secret generally belongs to the company, not the developer. Likewise, if the employee is not specifically assigned such work, but uses the employer's premises or materials or work time to develop the secret, the employer generally would have a claim to the secret.

Most states have criminal statutes against theft of trade secrets. Civil remedies include orders to stop using or disclosing the secret, and the payment of damages to the holder. Often, trade secret disputes are settled out of court by an agreement that the offending party will pay royalties to the complaining party for the right to use the secret in a limited way.

In writing policies and procedures, many experts refer to three basic requirements for calling a piece of information a trade secret: (1) it must be secret—that is, not generally known, (2) it must have some commercial value, and (3) it must be protected by the person or company claiming to own the secret.

The protective measures the owner of the secret needs to take include:

•Restricting visitors and those without a "need to know" from having access to areas where they could learn the secret.

•Labeling documents that contain the secret "Confidential" or "Company Proprietary," or with a similar designation.

•Having those to whom the secret is disclosed sign agreements to protect the secret and not disclose it to others without authorization.

•Properly disposing of unneeded documents containing the secret by shredding or depositing in locked bins.

When going to court, one of the most difficult problems for the owner of a trade secret is to protect the idea from disclosure during the trial process. The plaintiff most likely will not have to reveal the secret in the complaint or petition, and if disclosure is necessary for "the ascertainment of the truth," the courts will often allow evidence to be given in the privacy of the judge's chambers.

Determining the Value of a Trade Secret

In a landmark court case on the value of trade secrets, the court said it would entertain "any reasonable value" that could be articulated and supported with reasonable arguments. In other words, there is no one method of setting a value that is reasonable to all circumstances. The information security practitioner needs to understand several different approaches to value, and apply the one that best fits the situation. Let's look at some of these approaches:

•If the owner purchased the secret from the patent holder, the purchase price can establish its value. Similarly, when a company licenses technology from another, the royalty or licensing fee can determine the value.

•If the secret is vital to the product, as in the recipe to a unique soft drink, the value of the secret can equal the value of the entire market.

•If the secret contributes to the total product in a measurable way, the value of the secret can be the percent of contribution it makes to the whole product. For example, if a secret manufacturing process cuts manufacturing costs by a third, the value of the secret process is equal to the dollars represented by that one-third reduction in manufacturing costs.

Value can be measured by either gain or loss. In the case of a trade secret theft, the court will entertain either the dollars lost to the victim company or the dollars gained from the secret by the company who misappropriated it.

The cost to develop a secret process can be used to calculate its value and should include the materials and equipment used in the development, the human-hours spent, a portion of the developer's overhead (indirect costs, real estate, phone bills, utilities, etc.), money paid for related technology, patents, or licenses, and deferred costs (the costs to other projects caused by delay from allocating resources to the secret's development).

In the case of a misappropriation, costs of defending the secret (investigation and legal costs), loss of market share or reputation, and the financial implications of having the secret disclosed to the public through the litigation can be added to the other values mentioned. Exclusively possessing the secret often makes it much more valuable than it would be if it was widely known.

Practically speaking, the security professional and corporate executive should make certain that employees are informed of their obligations to protect the company's confidential information and are aware of the various ways that trade secrets can be compromised. The company should have a policy on the protection of confidential information and procedures detailing how documents should be protected, labeled, stored, and disposed of. Guidelines governing oral disclosure of confidential business information should be included in the procedures, and sound physical security measures should be taken to protect the sensitive areas of the company. Non-disclosure agreements should be part of the employee's employment agreement, and vendors and contractors should also sign non-disclosure agreements. Since leaks of confidential information are often unintentional, employee education campaigns go a long way to protect a company's valuable trade secret information.

Trade secret law is complex and the advice of a competent attorney with a specialty in intellectual property should be sought in these matters.

Don Greenwood

TRAINING: LIABILITY FOR NEGLIGENT TRAINING

Contract security officers, their employers, and the clients they serve continue to be named in lawsuits alleging a wide variety of civil violations. Two factors appear to be at work. First is the increasingly litigious nature of society, and second is an expanding social conscience that favors the little guy. The pattern that emerges from civil actions reveals a pronounced targeting of persons in authority positions, such as security officers and the people who hire and manage them.

Because misconduct litigation is a prominent and highly profitable specialty in the practice of law, there are many who seek careers in it. Seminars on the subject are offered around the country, and how-to manuals are available to guide the novices. Expert witnesses, many of them current and former security professionals, are paid to testify for plaintiffs.

The usual path of pursuit in civil litigation is the negligence theory. In this approach the argument is not that the injurious conduct was malicious in nature, but that the injury and damages resulted from a failure to perform a duty with due care. Liability is the result of negligence or failure to give proper attention or care to one's duty. For the liability to be recognized, it must be the cause of a deprivation of rights secured by the Constitution.

Within the negligence theory, there is a particular vulnerability to accusations of improper training. The courts have consistently ruled in favor of plaintiffs who can show injury caused by negligence resulting from the absence of training or the administration of faulty training. The citizenry and the law impose an affirmative duty upon employers to provide their employees with requisite knowledge and skills. When jobs contain the potential for abuse and injury, as is the case with many jobs in security, the affirmative duty to provide training is expected to be met without qualification.

More often than not, the injured party will file suit against the offending officer, as well as the officer's superiors. The plaintiff's charge will frequently allege that the officer acted intentionally to cause injury and that the superiors should also be held accountable for being negligent in failing to take preventive action.

When a suit is pursued along these lines, the officer and superiors are very apt to come into sharp and bitter disagreement. The officer will argue that his or her actions conformed with policy, procedures, and the training provided by superiors. The superiors will argue that their subordinate's actions were inconsistent with the standards established for the officer. The conflict is certain to weaken their separate defenses and cast a shadow of doubt in the minds of jurors.

The damages that may be assessed in a negligence case are of three types: direct, punitive, and nominal. Direct damages may include such things as medical expenses, lost wages, and the costs of replacing or repairing property. Punitive damages are usually assessed when an element of fraud, malice, or oppression is present. The third type is called nominal damages. If assessed, the amount is usually set at $1, hence the term nominal.

In the concept of proximate cause, a single wrongful act may be caused by two or more persons acting at different points in time. For example, a security officer might make an unlawful arrest. The officer says his action was based on knowledge imparted to him through training given by the officer's employer. The concept of proximate cause supports the plaintiff's charge against the officer and any other persons who contributed to the unlawful arrest. In this example, the contributing persons could be the instructor, the officer's supervisor, and so on right up to senior management.

Lawsuits that allege insufficient instruction serve as reminders that the days of training on a catch-as-catch-can basis are over. Today the techniques of quality control have as much meaning in the classroom as in any work environment where excellence is the minimum standard. Further, the general public holds high expectations concerning training. The media have helped shape public perceptions, and when training expectations fall short, the community is angered and the injured parties seek justice through the courts.

Any response strategy to counter the potential for civil litigation should be aimed at eliminating in the training domain any conditions that might contribute to charges of improper instruction. Even the finest training operation must anticipate that negligent training lawsuits will be charged. The best answer to charges will be a positive defense based on accurate and detailed documentation.

Five tactics should be included within the strategy:

- Validate training
- Administer training to specifications
- Evaluate the trainees
- Keep accurate records
- Impose instructor standards

Validate Training

Validation means to ensure through an objective process that the training provided corresponds to duties associated with the job. The key objectives of validation are to verify that: (1) doctrinal content and skills development are correct, (2) instructional methods are appropriate and effective, and (3) training is relevant to the workplace and answers the day-to-day needs of job incumbents.

One of the more objective and commonly used techniques of validation is task analysis. Information drawn from task analysis gives to the curriculum designer a wealth of facts obtained from incumbents and others close to the job. The data reveal with high accuracy and specificity the nature and conditions of the trainees' future work environment.

A curriculum constructed from task analysis data will establish the baseline tasks of the job and will highlight tasks that, if not performed or performed incorrectly, could lead to litigation. Further, the task analysis approach uncovers the knowledge and skills that support each task. For example, if a task requires a security officer to use his revolver in defense of human life, the officer must be taught how to handle and fire the revolver (skills), and he must know the deadly force law and be able to differentiate between threatening and non-threatening situations (knowledge). The curriculum will require each officer-trainee to perform the skill part of the task, demonstrating a competency to pre-determined standards. The knowledge part of the task might be tested by written examination, again in accordance with high standards.

By far, the most important specifications are the tasks. They serve as the focal points and basic framework of instruction. Other course specifications, such as practical exercises and tests, are derived from and influenced by tasks.

When a curriculum has been validated (i.e., determined objectively to be job relevant) and when instructional activities have been executed according to plan, the opportunities for negligence are largely, if not entirely, removed and a strong defense is constructed against accusations of improper training.

Administer Training to Specifications

A minimum of logic must prevail for a training course to be made resistant to charges of negligence. Logic tells us that the success of a training operation cannot exceed the combined capacity of its component parts. The instructors, the logistics, and the students might all be top notch, but the training will be less than successful if the program is poorly conceived or carried out haphazardly.

The curriculum can be the training supervisor's most valuable tool for planning, organizing, and controlling. If the tool is ignored or used without skill, the training will suffer. Sadly, some training supervisors regard a curriculum as something to be merely tolerated, deserving not much more than lip service, and certainly not something to be followed. After all, they might argue, the curriculum was put together by people who have no real appreciation of the problems that confront trainers.

Serious implications are present in a situation where control is lacking over what is being taught and learned. When a training supervisor ignores a curriculum, so will the instructors. It does not take much imagination to speculate on the variety of civil liability risks that are created when instructors and their supervisors are allowed to teach according to their own dictates. The appropriate remedy is to make clear that curriculum specifications are not negotiable and that if the curriculum requires a change, for whatever reason, it will be done through an established process.

Training in progress can be monitored in several ways to ensure that the curriculum is being followed. Trainees can be asked if they personally participated in certain programmed activities; classrooms and training areas can be visited to verify that trainees are engaged in activities that support the training objectives; and tests, scores, critique sheets, and other written materials that reflect the details of training can be examined.

It is far better to discover imperfections during training than to wait until the imperfections produce undesirable consequences on the job. Mistakes noted as they happen are easier to correct and are free of the potential for complaints and redress in the courts.

Evaluate the Trainees

Students are evaluated in two dimensions, general and specific. Generally, they are appraised in terms of personal appearance, demeanor, attitude, motivation, and similar characteristics. In the specific dimension, students are evaluated in objective terms, that is, by the administration of tests. Two types of tests are appropriate in security officer training programs: written examinations to measure knowledge attainment, and performance examinations to measure skill development.

Since every task (or training objective) is either knowledge-oriented or skill-oriented, determining the appropriate type of test is not a problem. If the task is to "name the limitations on the use of deadly force," the test is by written examination, and if the task is to "operate a handy-talky radio," the test is by performance or doing.

A written examination may contain one or more classes of questions such as essay, write-in, matching, true/false, and multiple choice. The questions can range from subjective to objective, and operate from the principles of discrimination, recall, and recognition. Subjective questions have a lesser value in entry-level training programs because most knowledge-oriented tasks are either performed correctly or incorrectly, with no tolerance for "in-between" responses. Subjective questions are also difficult to grade and depend on the interpretations and judgments of the grader. By contrast, objective questions do not have these limitations and lend readily to task-centered training.

In testing important knowledge, more than one question needs to be asked, not just to convey importance to the student, but to obtain assurance that the student really possesses the knowledge and did not guess the answer.

The issue of whether or not a question is easy or hard is not a consideration. Certainly, a question should not give away its own answer. The purpose is to determine fairly if the student has attained the required knowledge. Testing is not a contest of wits between the test writer and the student.

Everything that is taught should be tested. Testing some tasks and not others is not an acceptable practice. Neither is testing extraneous and nice-to-know information or information not included in the curriculum. Testing all and only what has been taught is an effective, direct approach.

The testing concept is the same for the skill-oriented task, but with conditions and standards spelled out. For example, if the task being tested is to operate a handy-talky, the test might require the student to turn the radio on, adjust for squelch, and send a message using the 10 series code. Grading would focus on the time required to perform the task and the number of errors made in turning the radio on, adjusting it, and speaking the message using the correct code numbers.

Testing a skill-oriented task is especially demanding of an instructor's time, energy, and resourcefulness. The instructor has to find a testing location and furnish it with the required equipment, recruit assistants, organize the students and get them to the testing location, and conduct the tests.

Instances of instructors allowing some students to pass without being tested or without achieving the minimum competency levels are most likely to occur in the performance examinations. The preventive steps are to make sufficient time available for testing, precede testing with lots of practice, provide plenty of help to the primary instructor, and give slower learners special attention prior to and during the testing.

Establishing a spread among learners or comparing learners against each other is not necessary. The idea is to find out if the student has reached an acceptable level of competence. This is what we would call a pass/fail situation. It is both pointless and misleading for a grade to be assigned to a task. Why even try to compute a task grade or even a composite grade when the only measurement that really counts is whether or not the student has satisfactorily performed the task?

Keep Training Records

Because documentation can serve as a strong defense to a charge of negligent training, keeping records of every aspect of a student's progress from start to finish makes very good sense. At the front end are documents which reflect the qualifications that a student brings to the course. Licenses, entrance examination scores, aptitude and psychological test scores, high school and college transcripts, and certificates of prior training are examples. These items are indicators of the student's entering abilities and predictors of course performance.

If a course applicant does not meet prerequisites but is nonetheless allowed to enter, a record should be made of who granted the waiver and why. This should serve as a red flag, not to stigmatize the student but to alert the staff to a need for special teaching attention. Whatever extra efforts are expended by the staff and the student to overcome the deficiency should be made a matter of record.

Documents associated with course administration run the gamut from the opening day schedule to the graduation agenda. Within this large collection of written materials are two broad classes: documents that relate to training activities generally, and documents that relate to students individually. One way to organize what can surely be a very large mass of paperwork is to place the general documents in a single, large file and the student documents in separate dossiers.

The general file is for documents from one single course offering, not all offerings of the same course. The general file can be broken down into subcategories such as correspondence and memoranda, course announcement and schedule, curriculum or program of instruction, lesson plans, student handouts, class roster, attendance sheets, etc. Related to the file, but maintained apart from it for security reasons, are the written examinations.

Lesson plans and handouts are excellent documents for refuting negligent training claims. They reflect what the instructors taught and what the students were expected to learn. For example, a lesson plan on self-defense tactics would require an instructor to emphasize the risk of injury to a person being restrained by a choke hold. The student handout would reinforce that important teaching point. The lesson plan and handout would directly rebut a claim of improper training of the choke hold. One note of advice: put preparation/revision dates on lesson plans and handouts.

The attendance sheets can also be important. If the officer in the example just given falsely represents that he was not in class on the day the lesson was taught and the handout distributed, thereby imputing negligence to the training agency, the attendance sheets provide an opportunity for refutation.

A student's dossier contains items that reflect entry into the course, participation in it, and departure from it. There might be evidence of registration, issuance of supplies, disciplining, counseling, academic problems, absences, makeup and remedial training/re-testing, special honors earned, and test results.

From the standpoint of potential civil liability, test results are extremely significant because they substantiate that important, job-related tasks were learned by the trainee. It also helps when the test results are recorded in a format that describes the tasks tested, the names of the evaluator and approving official, whether re-teaching and re-testing were needed, and the initials or signature of the trainee in acknowledgment of the record's entries.

Impose Instructor Standards

Without good instruction, it will not matter if students are bright and eager, facilities first-rate, and the administration efficient. All of these elements are important, but the controlling element will certainly be the competency of instructors.

Instructor qualifications are typically fixed by legislation in states where security officer training is mandated. A certification process will accompany enforcement in almost every case. Instructor certification may specify minimums that relate to education and training accomplishments, field experience in the subject area to be taught, and successful completion of an approved instructor training course.

An instructor's competency can be judged in two areas: knowledge of subject, and ability to teach. If either area is deficient, it is reasonable to expect that the instructor's performance will be correspondingly deficient.

Each of us at one time or another has been the victim of the knowledgeable instructor who, despite good intentions and best effort, was just not able to get his message across. By contrast, the instructor who is weak in the subject area but strong as a teacher is apt to be less noticeable. Through superior communications, a small amount of information can be stretched a long way.

The exceptional instructor will be solidly proficient in both subject matter knowledge and teaching abilities. The average instructor will have a combination of strengths and weaknesses in each area, and the below-average instructor will be significantly weak in at least one area. If required to select a below-average instructor, a training director would not want the instructor's weakness to be in topic knowledge. This is a problem that cannot be corrected easily or quickly. An instructor who lacks a solid command of his or her subject needs to return to the field and gain more knowledge through job experience and self-development.

The instructor who knows the topic to be taught but cannot teach very well can be improved with much less difficulty and in a reasonable period of time. A certain amount of improvement will inevitably result from the teaching experience itself, and from the process of instructors interacting and learning from one another. Surely the most dramatic improvement can result from attendance at an instructor training course.

A training course for instructors is typically 1 or 2 weeks long and covers topics such as learning theory, instructional strategies and methods, learning aids, lesson plan writing, and development of practical exercises. The 1-week course has only enough time to explain basic teaching concepts; the 2-week course will additionally allow the trainee to make one or more graded presentations using lesson plan materials, learning aids, and handouts developed while in the course.

Where instructor training is required as a condition of certification, the certifying agency will most likely conduct or make available a range of approved courses. In addition to a course that prepares an instructor to teach generally, specialized instructor training courses in firearms may be provided.

The absence of legislated requirements should not be seen as a rationale for not upgrading instructors, and under no circumstances should it be seen as a legal defense to complaints of incompetent instruction. Even where minimum standards prevail, a very persuasive argument can be made that such standards are, after all, only minimums. There is no law against establishing instructor standards where none exist or in setting standards above what are minimally expected. Having no instructor standards or choosing to operate with minimums is an assurance of mediocrity.

Security managers need to reduce risks associated with inadequate and poorly operated training programs. A question to be asked is not whether a security manager can afford quality training, but whether he can afford not to have it.

John J. Fay, CPP

Source Fay, J.J., Approaches to Criminal Justice Training, 2nd Edition. (University of Georgia Press, Athens, GA, 1988).

U

ULTRASONIC MOTION DETECTORS

A basic ultrasonic motion detector consists of a transmitter, receiver, and control unit. The control unit contains the signal processor, power supply, and standby battery. In operation, the detector transmitter generates an acoustical energy pattern that fills the zone of detection. Energy reflecting from the walls, ceiling, and floor, and objects within the energy pattern and entering the receiver's field of acceptance, is processed and analyzed by the signal processor. As long as the reflected energy is at the same frequency as the transmitted energy, there is no alarm; but anyone moving in the energy pattern produces a Doppler frequency shift that changes the reflected signal. When the signal characteristics satisfy the processor alarm criteria, the detector initiates an alarm.

Most ultrasonic detectors operate at a specific frequency in the frequency range between 19 and 40 kilohertz. Acoustical energy generated at frequencies above 19 kilohertz is considered inaudible to the average human ear and is defined as ultrasonic energy. A feature of ultrasonic energy is that it will not penetrate physical barriers such as walls; therefore, it can be easily contained in closed rooms. Since acoustical energy will not penetrate physical barriers, the walls of the protected room either absorb or reflect the energy. Since most walls absorb very little ultrasonic energy unless they are covered with a very soft material, such as heavy drapes, most of the energy is reflected. This reflected energy helps fill the zone of detection, making it more difficult for an intruder to escape notice.

There are two basic ultrasonic motion-detector configurations. The first configuration consists of a number of transceivers connected to one common control unit. A transceiver is a single unit that has a transmitter and receiver in one housing. In case of an ultrasonic transceiver, it has a separate transducer that transmits and receives ultrasonic energy. The second detector configuration consists of a number of separate transmitters and receivers also connected to one common control unit. The number of individual transceivers or separate transmitters and

receivers in a specific installation depends primarily on the size and configuration of the area requiring protection. The limiting factor on the number of transceivers or receivers and transmitters connected to a single control unit is the maximum allowable number of units designated by the manufacturer.

Piezoelectric and magnetostrictive transducers are used in ultrasonic motion detectors to convert electrical energy into acoustical energy and vice-versa. In the piezoelectric transducer, the crystal is mounted in the center of a circular diaphragm mounted in the front of the transducer housing. When an alternating current is applied to the crystal, it physically expands and contracts at the frequency of the alternating current. This expansion and contraction causes the mounting diaphragm to vibrate, which in turn causes the air in front of the diaphragm to vibrate. This vibrating air is the acoustical energy. Conversely, reflected acoustical energy exerts an external force on the receive transducer, causing the crystal mounting diaphragm to vibrate. These vibrations stress the crystal, which generates an output signal for the signal processor. The signal is proportional to the strength of the reflected energy.

Piezoelectric transducer crystals are optimized to operate over a rather narrow-frequency band. Although they operate very well at these frequencies, their ability to transmit and especially to receive energy at frequencies much above or below their design frequency is marginal. Although the piezoelectric transducer frequency response is considered narrow, the transducers are quite capable of receiving an ample signal to detect a moving intruder. A moving intruder produces a Doppler frequency shift containing frequency components that range between 20 to 800 kilohertz on either side of the primary operating frequency. The amplitude and range of the frequency shift depend on the moving intruder's size, speed, and direction. The "speed" is not just the velocity of the intruder's body; it also includes the velocities of swinging arms and legs.

Magnetostrictive transducers perform the same functions as the piezoelectric transducers; but, instead of a vibrating crystal, the magnetostrictive transducer uses a laminated nickel rod wound with a wire coil. When the coil around the nickel rod is excited by an alternating current, the resulting magnetic field expands and contracts the rod at twice the frequency of the impressed field—twice the frequency because it expands and contracts the rod on both halves of the alternating electromagnetic field.

A permanent magnet is used to bias the coil and cancel out the flux generated on one half-cycle of the impressed electromagnetic field. Removing one half-cycle of the impressed field, or halving the frequency, reduces the transducer frequency to the original alternating current frequency.

In the piezoelectric transducer, the crystal mounting diaphragm excites the air medium, but in the magnetostrictive transducer the nickel rod is connected to the base of a hemispherical-shaped aluminum shell or to some other shaped diaphragm that excites the air medium. When the nickel rod expands and contracts, it vibrates the hemispherical shell or diaphragm that generates the acoustical energy pattern.

The receive transducer is identical in configuration to the transmitting transducer. Reflected acoustical energy impinging on the hemispherical shell or diaphragm stresses the nickel rod in compression and expansion at the frequency of the reflected energy. The compression and expansion of the nickel rod generates a signal for the processor that is proportional to the strength of the reflected energy.

Most ultrasonic motion detectors are designed to operate at lower ultrasonic frequencies because low-frequency acoustical energy is less affected by air currents. The lower operating frequencies, approximately 19.6 kilohertz for the magnetostrictive type transducers and 25 kilohertz for the piezoelectric transducers, are also compatible with the construction characteristics of the individual transducers.

Although the detector operating frequencies have been described as low frequencies, the acoustical energy at these frequencies is still out of the audible frequency range for most human ears.

However, the frequencies are high enough so that the detector operation is not affected by common audible noises occurring in the protected areas. Resorting to higher operating frequencies above 25 kilohertz to further isolate the detector from common noises would result in a loss of coverage due to the resistance air imposes on the propagation of ultrasonic energy.

Robert L. Barnard

Source Barnard, R.L., *Intrusion Detection Systems.* (Butterworth–Heinemann, Boston, 1982).

UNDERCOVER OPERATIONS

An enlightened executive group will correctly conclude that hard-core thievery is part of today's business environment. Accordingly, it will realize that identification of the offenders and their separation from the payroll are essential to the viability of the organization.

One of the oldest investigative approaches, second only to interrogation, is the use of undercover agents. Undercover investigation can be defined as a deep-as-possible penetration of the adversary's operation for the purpose of gathering information valuable in defeating the adversary. Many investigations today would be impossible to conclude satisfactorily without undercover operations.

Selecting and Managing the Operative

Among the several elements necessary for a successful undercover investigation is selection of the right type of individual for the correct job. Not only should the security manager give consideration to the particular skills necessary in the undercover role, but even more important, the security manager should be sure that the agent selected is able to blend successfully with the work force.

Basic Qualifications. Ethnic or racial background can be an important consideration in the selection of an undercover agent, but more important the selected individual should have the ability to make friends easily, possess a keen understanding of human nature, be perceptive and intelligent, have an above-average memory, and be good at inductive reasoning.

A good undercover operative will also be skilled or at least trainable as an effective witness when providing testimonial evidence at trial and other judicial or administrative proceedings. A

	"Off-the-Street" Operative	Criminal Justice Graduate
1. Likely to blend in?	Yes	No
2. Likely to be good at roping?	Yes	No
3. Likely to know legal issues?	No	Yes
4. Likely to make a good witness?	No	Yes
5. Likely to be a good report writer?	No	Yes

personal trait that underlies effectiveness as a witness is credibility. The agent must come across to the trier of fact as honest and loyal. Given the nature of undercover work, on the surface the agent may appear to be devious, thus requiring the agent as a testifying witness to project a demeanor of rectitude.

Screening and Controlling. In view of the qualifications stressed previously, it is not surprising that a sizable and unacceptable percentage of undercover agents continue to prove themselves to be other than basically honest people. Case critiques often reveal that in the course of investigations, agents have engaged in impermissible thievery, have kept drugs for personal use or re-sale, have falsified reports, and incriminated otherwise innocent employees.

At a minimum, each applicant should be administered one or more screening tests designed to evaluate honesty, personality, and aptitude for the work. The Reid Report and the Minnesota Multiphasic Personality Inventory (MMPI) can be useful in this regard. When permitted by the Polygraph Protection Act, the applicant should be administered a polygraph test. Polygraph is very effective in detecting a history of prior conduct that would render the applicant unsuitable for undercover work.

The applicant should also be thoroughly interviewed, even to the point of interrogation. A skillfully conducted interview can be very revealing both with respect to the applicant's background and his or her ability to react under pressure. Intense interviewing of the undercover agent is also recommended on a periodic basis during the course of the investigation as a means of discovering and discouraging undesirable conduct. The questions should focus on:

• Accurately identifying and accounting for any company property taken by the operative as part of the attempt to infiltrate the criminal operation under investigation.

• Accurately accounting for any funds or other assets entrusted to the operative for use in advancing the investigation.

• Ensuring that case progress reports submitted by the operative are accurate and truthful.

• Ensuring that the operative has not concealed or failed to disclose significant facts about the investigation.

• Ensuring that the operative has not compromised the investigation by discussing his or her role with others, or by engaging in activities that would reveal that role.

In-House vs. Agency Investigations

The employer requiring an undercover investigation has the option of using operatives selected from in-house resources or operatives provided by an outside contract agency. There may be a tendency on the part of management to use an existing employee (most probably someone from another company location) or hire someone.

The rationale may be founded on the advantages of control that can be exercised over the operative; loyalty from the operative; a lower salary cost for an in-house employee compared to a contract employee, especially if the investigation drags on; and the possibility of placing the employee into a non-undercover assignment at the completion of the investigation. Very often, the in-house person will be selected on the basis of prior education in criminal justice or experience as a police officer.

On the other hand, management may be persuaded by its own logic or the representations of the security director to use an operative provided by an outside contract company that specializes in undercover work. The contract operative may or may not have a background in police education or work, but will most likely have been trained in undercover operations and will have some experience as an operative. Some other points are as follows:

Cover Stories.   Cover stories are an extremely important part of any undercover operation. The more complex the case and the greater the sophistication of the criminal suspects, the more attention must be given to the preparation of the cover story. An agent can only be as effective as his cover story is acceptable, i.e., the story must fit the role being played by the agent and the agent's personal style must correspond to both the story and the role. Three rules to observe are: (1) keep the story simple, (2) make it believable, and (3) keep it as close to the truth as possible.

Coaching and Supervising. The individual's experience in undercover work will determine the amount of preparation and direction needed to be given by the handler. Some experienced agents are able to take a case and work it with little or no supervision. The novice agent will require extensive supervision and help.

When the agent lacks experience and is the employee of a contract agency, the security manager handling the investigation may decide to participate personally in coaching and supervising. Very often this has less to do with a lack of confidence in the competency of the agent or the agent's employer and more to do with raising the comfort level of the security manager. It may also relate to the security manager's desire to be personally knowledgeable of case progress in order to be ready to brief senior management on short notice.

There is no set of rules for making contact with an agent. The initiative for making the contact is most often by the agent and occurs in a pre-arranged manner within a flexible schedule. The pre-arrangements will conform to the nature of the case. In one case the agent may call his or her handler several times a week on particular nights and meet with the handler once per month at a location agreed upon by them; in another case, which may be more important and complex, telephone calls will be daily and meetings at a frequency of at least once a week.

The contact between agent and handler can also be through mail, facsimile transmissions, voice messages placed into an electronic mail box, and reports sent to a computer through a telephone modem.

A word of caution is in order regarding the selection of a meeting site.   Months of productive investigative activity can be undone by the chance encounter of the agent and handler with people who know the agent in the context of the undercover role. The temptation to meet in a public place, such as restaurant, bar, or park, should be resisted in favor of a closed setting, such as a motel room.

Roping. Roping is an art applied by the undercover agent in gaining the trust and confidence of a suspect. The objective is to elicit from the suspect admissions of past or current criminal acts or to be positioned physically to observe the suspect's criminal acts. In order to achieve the objective, the agent must be seen by the criminal as a fellow criminal. The applicable adage is "It takes a thief to catch a thief." Roping, of course, carries a high probability that the suspect's later legal defense will allege entrapment. Roping frequently requires push and pull on the part of the handler. To get the investigation moving and focused upon the suspect, the handler may find it necessary to prod the agent into particular actions, and at other times the handler may see it necessary to restrain the agent from activities that could be construed as entrapment.

Finding a Balance. In the initial stage of the undercover operation, the operative will endeavor to maintain a balanced relationship between employees who are essentially honest and those who are not. The operative at first cannot alienate either group because from the group of honest employees the operative seeks information about the criminal activities of the dishonest group and their players, and from the dishonest group the operative seeks acceptance and status in order to be positioned as an eyewitness to crime and to obtain physical evidence of it. The operative eventually aspires to be invited to become part of the criminal enterprise. When the invitation is made, the operative will conspicuously swing away from the orbit of the honest group in order to be accepted by the dishonest group.

Making Buys. When the criminal enterprise involves theft and re-sale of stolen goods or

Undercover Operations
A Short Glossary Of Terms

Burn. To be exposed or come under suspicion as an undercover agent. In many cases, the agent will be able to throw off suspicion by:
- Laughing it off at the first accusation.
- Becoming angry and making counter-accusations at the accuser at the second accusation.
- Being physically confrontational at the third accusation.

Cover. The protective guise of the undercover agent that facilitates infiltration and conceals the true nature of the agent's affiliations. A cover story will be simple, believable and correspond as closely as possible to the agent's real life situation.

Deductive Reasoning. That mental process of deducing from a number of facts that are uncovered, the perpetrator or suspect. This is a common way of investigation used by police detectives and security agents who are not working undercover. It is the reverse of inductive reasoning.

Entrapment. In a security investigation not involving law enforcement, the act of an undercover agent to induce a person to commit a crime or violate a workplace rule which was not contemplated by the person, for the purpose of instituting criminal prosecution or adverse administrative action. The mere act of furnishing the opportunity where the person is predisposed to commit the crime or rule violation is not entrapment. In law, entrapment can only be committed by persons working as agents of the government.

Handler. The person in direct communication with the undercover agent who provides instructions and guidance; meets with the agent; receives reports and evidence; and generally serves as the agent's counselor and confidant. The handler may or may not be the person in charge of the undercover operation.

Inductive Reasoning. This is the mental process by which an agent may go about building his case. It is the opposite of deductive reasoning and is sometimes described as a sixth sense. Some agents have it instinctively, while others develop it over a period of time. Some police and security people never do develop this trait. Inductive reasoning enables an operative to focus his activities on likely suspects and then look to develop the facts to clinch his case.

Informant. A person who knowingly or unknowingly provides information of interest to a matter under investigation. An informant is often motivated by financial reward, assistance of some type or fear. Loyalty, good citizenship and altruism are occasional motivators. The term informant does not describe an undercover agent who is a trained and dedicated professional.

Introduction. The acceptance of the undercover agent into the society of the criminal group under investigation, usually through the recommendation of a member of the group. The introduction results from a successful roping.

Operative. A term synonymous with agent; the person doing the undercover work. Also called op.

Roping. The art of identifying and gaining the confidence of a member of the criminal group under investigation. Roping leads to introduction (obtaining acceptance by the group) and the collection of information and evidence.

Staging. Activity that supports a cover story. It typically consists of placing the undercover agent into a neighborhood in close proximity to the criminal group or activities and allowing sufficient time for the undercover agent to obtain familiarity with surroundings and people, settle into the role and carefully set up the roping.

Source: J. Kirk Barefoot, CPP, Security Consultant, Savannah, Georgia.

trafficking in drugs, the agent may need coaching in how to make a buy. The agent needs also to know what not to buy. It would be illogical and out of character in a larceny operation for the agent to buy stolen company property that is within the agent's ability to steal, but there may be an advantage in a drug operation for the agent to purchase drugs being sold in the workplace.

Outside Agents.   Some cases require investigative assistance outside of the workplace, such as agents to follow suspects from the workplace to locations where stolen property may be stored, fenced, or sold, or to act as buyers of stolen property. The supervisor of the case will make the decision to introduce outside agents, will determine the manner and methods of communicating with them, and will approve or disapprove contact between the outside agent(s) and the undercover agent. In this last regard, for example, the undercover agent might be instructed to "finger" a suspect leaving the work premises by giving a signal to an outside agent who has the task of following the suspect.

Maintaining Perspective

The undercover supervisor has to maintain an overall perspective on the entire case. The typical undercover case will end up with an identification of a large number and wide variety of dishonest employees. The process of identification will proceed slowly at first, then accelerate, and then perhaps slow down, suggesting that all of the suspects have been identified. What may be happening is that the undercover operative has lost an enthusiasm for ferreting out new suspects or is bogged down in relationships with already-identified suspects and has little time or opportunity to expand the case. If this possibility is overlooked by the case supervisor, he or she may be tempted to close down the investigation on the incorrect proposition that all of the guilty employees have been identified. This is essentially a judgment call influenced by the supervisor's interpretation of case facts. A balanced perspective is to not let guilty employees slip through the net by premature shutdown and at the same time not let the company continue unnecessarily to be damaged by the criminal enterprise.

By keeping the "big picture" in mind, the supervisor sees to it that the case is developed to its logical conclusion so that maximum identification is made of dishonest employees and that sufficient evidence has been collected to sustain a successful prosecution.

Premature Exposure. It sometimes happens that the undercover agent will "push the panic button" and cause the supervisor to terminate the investigation or recommend this action to senior management.   Rather than take precipitate action, the supervisor should take a hands-off approach and allow things to settle, provided, of course, that the agent's safety will not be jeopardized by a failure to intervene.

Limited Progress Reports. Knowledge and details of an undercover investigation should be provided to those few managers whose functions require them to be informed. The imperative of the need-to-know rule is driven not by reasoning that some managers cannot be trusted, but by the common-sense observation that managers who are aware of an undercover investigation may have to engage in play-acting in order to maintain confidentiality. Managers may make inadvisable comments or be unable to conceal their feelings about suspect employees. Even with coaching and with good intentions to not compromise the investigation, the personal value system of a manager may not permit the manager to be silent or to act as if nothing is going on. It may not be possible for a manager to refrain from doing something corrective and in the process tip off the suspects. If progress reports are to be made, they should be verbal and general in nature.

J. Kirk Barefoot, CPP

UPWARD FEEDBACK

Upward feedback is a process or mechanism for communication between managers and their subordinates that can be mutually beneficial. Upward feedback has four objectives: (1) to improve communication between the manager and his or her team, (2) improve teamwork, (3) identify management practices where change will result in managing people more effectively, and (4) create an action plan to which all members of the team commit.   Upward

The Upward Feedback Process

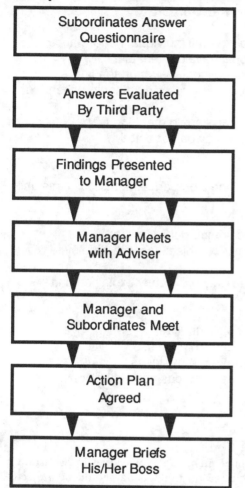

- Subordinates Answer Questionnaire
- Answers Evaluated By Third Party
- Findings Presented to Manager
- Manager Meets with Adviser
- Manager and Subordinates Meet
- Action Plan Agreed
- Manager Briefs His/Her Boss

feedback is marked by open thinking, personal impact, empowerment, and networking.

Performance feedback can be a key tool in helping a manager improve personal performance by giving the manager a better understanding of his or her abilities to lead others.

Research into the reactions of managers receiving feedback reveal a sequence of reactions called **SARAH.** It begins with Shock, followed by Anger and Rejection, moves to Acceptance, and concludes with a request for Help. A natural instinct is to react to what first appears to be personal criticism. When a manager is able to get past the initial surprise, annoyance, and rationalization, he or she is ready to accept the feedback as valid and then to accept help.

The Upward Feedback Process

The process usually begins by distributing a questionnaire to the persons who report to the manager. The questionnaire is anonymous and contains questions relating to management practices that are widely held to be supportive of effective teamwork. (The person filling out the questionnaire will be asked to rate each practice in certain dimensions; for example, the relative importance that the respondent places upon the practice and the degree to which the manager uses the practice.)

The completed questionnaires are sent to a third party, such as an outside consultant or a specialist within the organization's human resources department. The questionnaires are scored, with significant variances noted. An example of a significant variance might be that the respondent considered conflict resolution within the team to be highly important but rated the manager very low in effectively resolving conflict. A report is generated in the scoring process and it may present findings in the form of numerical data, such as bar charts, and short narratives describing outstanding strengths and weaknesses.

The report provides a snapshot of team members' perceptions. The report is provided to the manager. A one-to-one meeting between the manager and an upward feedback adviser assists the manager in moving through the SARAH process. In this meeting, the manager sizes up the information, raises issues and questions with the adviser, identifies areas that need to be clarified, and develops an agenda and a plan to meet with the team to review the findings of the report.

The next step is to hold a team meeting chaired by the manager, with the adviser present to facilitate the process. The adviser's role also includes easing the comfort level of the manager and the team, and serving as an objective third party. The role of the manager is to actively solicit observations and examples pertinent to the feedback report, listen carefully and probe for understanding, and look for improvement opportunities. The desired outcomes are that the manager will gain from the team members a clearer, truer understanding of the feedback and determine a foundation for action.

Immediately following the team meeting, the manager and the adviser confer privately.

TEAM BUILDING PRACTICES
THROUGH UPWARD FEEDBACK

•Meeting frequently with employees to review their overall individual performance.
•Working with people to determine realistic personal development plans.
•Accurately representing the views, opinions, and feelings of staff up the line.
•Anticipating future business opportunities and requirements, and planning ahead to meet them.
•Maintaining the right balance of skills within the work team to meet the team's objectives.
•Making problems and their cases clear so that they may be corrected.
•Being effective at initiating and sustaining change.
•Effectively resolving conflicts.
•Understanding and clarifying the best interests of the Company and the business unit.
•Involving others in decisions where necessary.
•Maintaining high standards for the team's work.
•Relating the total reward system to the excellence of job performance.
•Agreeing on challenging and achievable performance objectives with employees.
•Sharing power in the interest of common goals.
•When tasks or projects are assigned, making sure they are clearly explained and understood.
•Managing time effectively.
•Providing equal development and advancement opportunitites to all employees.
•Creating a sense of enthusiasm about the work team's direction.
•Encouraging employees to be innovative to improve the business.
•Being innovative and creative in responding to changing business conditions.
•Being supportive and helpful with employees.
•Making tough decisions.
•Striving to set team goals, as well as individual goals.

They review and obtain clarity on what was said. The adviser provides objective commentary and assists the manager in "reading between the lines." The manager is led to explore areas where change is appropriate and to make a personal commitment for improvement steps. In this regard, the manager develops a draft of a realistic action plan that incorporates personal and team objectives.

Finally, the manager sets up a meeting with his or her boss to identify ways to fully support achievement of the objectives in the action plan. Included on the agenda should be a discussion of the training, education, or other resources that may be needed to carry out the plan. The manager should circulate the agreed action plan to team members. This helps confirm that the feedback has been heard at a level higher than the manager and that commitments have been made to act on the key areas.

John J. Fay, CPP

V

VIDEO SIGNALS: TRANSMISSION OPTIONS

As important as choosing the proper equipment when designing a closed-circuit television (CCTV) installation is the method by which signals will be sent from the camera to the monitoring point. Advances in technology have provided options to what was one choice: coaxial cable.

Coaxial Cable

The ubiquitous coax cable continues to be the most widely used means of sending a signal from camera to monitor. The standard RG59U cable can carry a video signal to a maximum distance of 1,000 feet. To span greater distances, an RG11U cable with a thicker center conductor can be specified, increasing the range to 2,400 feet. Adding video line amplifiers increases distance, typically to 3,400 feet for RG59U cable and to 8,600 feet for RG11U. The actual length of the cable affects capacitance and can lead to loss of high-frequency response and a degraded picture. Metallic cables such as coax cannot be used in hazardous environments, such as some manufacturing plants and oil refineries. The signals might spark an explosion. Environments sensitive to electromagnetic interference (EMI) should also avoid the use of metal coax cables. Without proper protection, coax cable can subject equipment to which it is connected to lightning and other high-voltage surges.

Microwave

For applications with line-of-sight between the camera and monitoring point, microwave can provide cost-effective signal transmission for up to 15 miles. This type of transmission is especially useful when the locations are separated by property not under the control of the system owner, avoiding right-of-way easements.

Microwave transmission in its basic form sends signals one way, from the camera to the

monitor. More complex bi-directional transmitters are required to control switching, pan-tilt operation, and provide two-way audio. Both black-and-white and color signals may be transmitted.

Weather conditions such as heavy rain, snow, and fog can reduce the operating range of microwave by a third, degrading the picture or completely losing it. System manufacturers can provide charts to help determine the frequency and duration of outages in any particular area.

Microwave is one of the few CCTV transmission technologies requiring licensing by the Federal Communications Commission (FCC). While the procedure is not complicated, companies are available to assist in licensing the transmitters.

Slow-Scan Telephone

Utilizing standard dial network telephone lines, phone line video transmits still-frame video images, with a new "snapshot" every 3 to 70 seconds. The speed of the frames is dictated by the amount of change that has taken place from the previous frame.

Using a combination of transmitter and receiver, the image is stored in a digital memory prior to transmission. The image is then converted line-by-line into low-band audio tones. The process is reversed at the receiver and turned into an image that can be displayed on a standard monitor.

Recently developed systems use standard personal computers (PCs) with special interface boards for video connections. The PC operates the system and provides video image storage. One hour of video storage uses approximately 10 megabytes of disk space.

Because regular telephone lines are used, the distance between two points is only limited by the availability of phone lines. This technology is also ideal for temporary or covert installations, wherever phone lines are available.

Radio Frequency

The use of FM frequencies is a new option for video signaling, with an effective range of up to 5 miles for either black-and-white or color images. Longer ranges are attainable with repeaters.

The broadcast nature of the signal does not require line-of-sight. The FM frequency increases the range and allows signals to penetrate buildings and foliage without distortion. Reverse transmission allows equipment control via the radio signal. No licensing is required to operate the system; however, current FCC regulations prohibit transmission of audio over the frequency.

Fiber Optics

Like coax cable, fiber optics form a physical link between the camera and monitor. While the perceived difficulty in installation and cost keeps some away, fiber optics' increased transmission range, signal clarity, and resistance to EMI make it the fastest growing segment in transmission methods.

A transmitter device that attaches to both the camera and the monitor converts a standard video signal into an optical signal. Two emitter types, the light-emitting diode (LED) and the injection laser diode (ILD), are the optical sources used in transmission.

The LED is less expensive and used typically for shorter distances of less than 4 miles, transmitting over a multi-mode fiber. The ILD is normally suggested for distances over 6 miles using single-mode fiber cable.

The light signal is modulated over the fiber-optics cable using either the AM or FM baseband. AM signaling equipment is normally less costly, but requires adjustment after installation. Fiber attenuation does not affect the FM band, and allows for other signals, such as voice or CCTV equipment control, to be multiplexed onto the cable.

Fiber is increasingly being used in integrated systems, allowing a single cable for transmission of CCTV, card access, and alarm point monitoring signals. The nature of fiber optics eliminates ground loops, a problem that can plague some coax installations. Because it is non-metallic, it can be used in hazardous environments.

Infrared

Infrared is point-to-point technology that has a transmission distance of up to 4 miles. The system transmitter generates an infrared beam to a collector lens system at the receiver which focuses the energy into a photodetector. The signal is then decoded into a usable message.

A range of sub-carriers is available to permit the transmission of bi-directional audio and camera signaling. Infrared links can also transmit computer communications with built-in RS-232.

Twisted-Pair Cable

While it might not always be possible or economical to run a coax or fiber cable from one building to another or across the street, a pair of wires might be available. A spare, unused in-house phone line or other spare wire may be already in place, allowing installation with little cost related to the cabling.

Connecting a transmitter to an incoming video device via a 75-ohm cable converts the video image into a composite signal, which is sent to the amplified receiver over the spare wires and ultimately to the monitor or other device.

Laser

Another form of short-distance line-of-sight technology, laser provides signaling for distances of approximately 1 mile. The relatively short distance is necessary because power must be reduced for safety.

At the transmitter, the input signal from the camera is modulated into a laser beam and sent to a receiver where the light is focused onto a photoconductor. For bi-directional communications, two simplex systems are coupled together and operated at the same wavelength.

Steven C. Kaufer, CPP

VIOLENCE IN THE WORKPLACE

Across America, violence in the workplace is increasing. Virtually unheard of until the 1970s, workplace violence has since tripled. According to the Bureau of Labor Statistics, murder is the ranking cause of death at work. During the 1970s and 1980s, while national homicide rates were declining along with the population of murder-prone 18- to 21-year-olds, the numbers for workplace murder were increasing at an alarming rate. Violence has become a standard form of expression in the American culture. As much as 30% of the population has replaced other forms of communication with violence as a means of sending messages. Individuals are using violence as a shortcut to getting what they want. Today, violence as a means of expression is finding its way increasingly into the workplace.

A Variety of Sources

Violence may come from an employee, former employee, an estranged spouse, a jilted suitor, or someone outside the company with a grudge. Researchers have identified the most common characteristics of a person prone to using violence in the workplace:

- **Male.** While women make up a large part of the American workforce, almost all incidents are carried out by men. Psychologists believe that the violence-prone male is most often a loner with no family or friends to form a support system. The job for this individual is often his only connection to others. Losing it brings about a traumatic psychological loss.
- **Age 30 to 40.** Most incidents involve a white male in his 30s or 40s. A person in his 20s often rationalizes the loss of a job as an opportunity to seek a better position. The individual in his 40s, who has a migratory job history because of his violence-prone behavior, views the loss of job as another act against him by those in power. The frustration and feelings of failure can trigger a violent reaction.
- **Migratory Job History.** The employee's methods of dealing with supervisors and co-workers and disregard of company policies contribute to frequent job changes.
- **Chronically Disgruntled.** The nature of the loner, coupled with the frustrations and disappointments in his life, often lead to a constant state of anger.
- **Perceptions of Unfairness and Injustice.** This individual externalizes blame; his troubles are always someone else's fault. People who commit suicide often blame themselves for everything that goes wrong. Those who blame others for all their troubles often seek revenge against those people. The

violence-prone person rarely accepts responsibility for things that go wrong.
- **Influence of Violence.** During the course of post-incident investigations it is often discovered that the violent individual watched violent television and movies, and read soldier-of-fortune type magazines. These programs and publications helped them validate their own violent attitudes.
- **Drug and Alcohol Use.** Existing aggressive moods and behavior can be magnified by drug usage. Alcohol has a disinhibiting effect leading to the release of pent-up anger. The illegal use of stimulant drugs, such as phencyclidine (PCP) and the amphetamines, is a contributor to violent conduct. Abuse of controlled substances can also be linked to the transitory job history of some violence-prone employees.

Types of Violence

Two basic types of violence have found their way into the workplace. Instrumental violence is used to force another person to do or stop doing something. Expressive violence results from fear, confusion, rage, or other feelings. Workplace violence is often a mixture of both types.

Violence Is Not Spontaneous. A violent reaction to a given situation is possible from any individual, but it takes less to provoke a person who is predisposed to violence. An unstable person contemplating violence often gives warning signs of the impending act. Troubled by the fear that he intends to hurt someone, he may give signals as a call for help. If the calls for help are undetected or ignored, the individual may regress to a lower level of action in dealing with the situation.

Violence is generally not spontaneous, particularly among employees. Supervisors and co-workers have an opportunity to spot warning signs and early aberrant behavior. The key is to educate supervisors and employees to recognize the signs and follow the organization's established procedures for intervention.

One of the most important steps an employer can take is to establish a central clearing point to gather and analyze potentially dangerous behavior. This information should be kept apart from the employee personnel files. Warning signs reported by knowledgeable supervisors and co-workers can be helpful in diagnosing the situation, assessing the risk, and taking appropriate preventive steps.   For example, an employee might have a violent reaction or over-reaction to a new company policy, threaten a co-worker, or close a savings account at the credit union. These are warning signs. Other signs include:

• Repeated violations of company policies and rules.

• An "everyone is against me" attitude.

• Threats, verbal or physical, against supervisors or fellow employees.

• Comments about past incidents of violence.

• A plan to "solve everything."

An early warning program may be the organization's only chance to prevent seriously violent incidents. Developing and maintaining the program should be carried out in a positive fashion, that is, it should be projected as a concerned and caring activity, not unlike that of an accident prevention program. Care must be taken to ensure that the program is not perceived as an expression by management that the workplace is full of unstable employees or that management has no confidence in the ability of the employees to work in harmony.

Violence Can Begin at Home. The National Institute of Mental Health reports that 20–50% of American couples have suffered regularly from violence in their relationships. These statistics emphasize that domestic violence is a real threat, and one that is present in all socioeconomic classes.

Employers should recognize that domestic violence generates a potential for violent acts at work. Even when a violent act is committed outside of the workplace, the employer carries the trauma of it to the job and productivity is negatively impacted.

The Costs of Violence

Both dollar and psychological costs are associated with a violent act in the workplace. The effects of violence can continue long past the event. Employee victims have reactions similar to other victims of violence. He or she can suffer from anxiety, depression, become withdrawn, increase the use of alcohol or drugs, and experience a wide range of emotions.

Employees, and not necessarily those who were directly victimized by an act of workplace violence, may experience the post-traumatic stress syndrome. In the aftermath of a serious incident, a large percentage of the employee population may be focused almost entirely on the incident. The quality and quantity of work drops off as people are absorbed in the details of what happened. Many of them are working out their psychological stresses. At the same time, management may be expecting workers to be able to deal with the consequences of violence because, after all, they are adults and should be able to cope with stress. This short-sighted attitude will prolong recovery.

Litigation in the aftermath of violence is a very real threat to the viability of an organization. Civil suits against employers for violence in the workplace is increasing, and very large compensatory and punitive awards are common. Negligence on the part of the employer can be alleged in the hiring procedure, in the training program, in duty assignments, in workplace rules, in the manner that rules were enforced or not enforced, and in the manner of supervision.

Under the theory of negligent hiring and retention, an employer can be liable for the violent act of an employee when the employer possessed or had access to information indicating that the employee had a potential for violence and the employer failed to take reasonable steps to prevent it. The message here is that an employer owes a standard of care to employees who might be injured by an employee whose past or current conduct suggests a penchant for violence. The care can be exercised by not hiring or by discharging violence-prone people, by assigning violence-prone employees to duties in which they cannot hurt others, or by informing the other employees they are at risk when working with the violence-prone employee. The last two options are really not workable, leaving the employer with the no-hire/discharge option.

Dealing with the Violent Employee

Discharging a potentially violent employee is not possible (and not recommended) in the absence of actual violence or other conduct that provides the just cause for discharge. The employer, however, can refer the "troubled employee" to a diagnostic or treatment professional. Treatment in most cases is counseling. Unfortunately, employees who most need assistance seldom choose to use it. The very problems that trouble them make them resistant to accepting assistance. This is particularly true when the assistance is offered by the employer, who in the mind of the employee may be seen as an adversary and the source of the employee's problems.

When the assistance has been refused or has not been effective, the employer may be in a position to terminate the employee on grounds and in a manner that will not invite a wrongful termination suit. If discharge is the course of action, the security manager should recommend the following steps:

• Fire the worker at the beginning or the end of the shift, and do not allow the worker to return to the work area.

• Make the firing a statement of fact, not a discussion or debate with the employee.

• Have all needed paperwork at hand, so the worker does not have to go to another part of the building.

• Have a security officer standing by, briefed on the situation and prepared to act if needed.

• Do not allow the employee to return to the work area unescorted. A weapon could be secreted there.

• Retrieve all identification, company charge cards, key cards, and keys, and invalidate the employee's computer access privileges.

• Clearly state that the person will be arrested for trespassing should he or she return uninvited.

• Make the person aware of any company-provided benefits, including counseling, that may be available after termination.

If handled sensitively, the exit interview can help defuse intentions to retaliate.

Screening Out the Violent Applicant

A person prone to violence will most likely have a history of violent acts that are described in legally accessible records. The records of greatest interest can be found in civil and criminal court repositories. The employer is free to examine or engage an agent to examine those records. Such an examination is quite legal and is central to the process we call pre-employment screening.

Pre-employment screening includes also a verification of data provided by the applicant in a job application. Prior employment history is an important area for verification. Although it is true that former employers are generally reluctant to do more than verify prior employment, what they choose to not say or decline to answer can be revealing.

If the dates of employment, as listed on the job application, do not match the records of the former employee, the applicant may be attempting to conceal work with another employer that was characterized by violence or a period of time spent in jail or prison. Gaps in employment history reflected on the job application also indicate these possibilities. Remembering that violence-prone workers often have a migratory job history, applicants who have many jobs of short duration deserve closer scrutiny.

Written pre-employment testing may also give insight to an applicant's character. Responses to such testing can pinpoint drug or alcohol abuse, prior thefts, anti-social behavior, and a host of other problems that could spell trouble. Properly administered and evaluated, these tests can paint an accurate picture of an applicant's fitness for employment. Moreover, exercising due diligence while hiring is vital to protect against a negligent hiring claim should the applicant later engage in violent behavior.

Steve C. Kaufer, CPP

VOLUMETRIC MOTION DETECTION

Active Detectors

Active volumetric motion detectors generate their own energy pattern and analyze the disturbance in that pattern for that portion of the energy reflected back to the receiver from a moving intruder. The disturbance in the energy pattern is referred to as a frequency shift or, in particular, a Doppler frequency shift. A Doppler frequency shift can best be explained by the classic example found in most elementary physics books. A person standing near a railroad track observing an approaching train and hearing the blowing whistle will first hear an increase in the pitch of the whistle and then hear a distinct lowering in the pitch as the train passes. Pitch increase is a result of the compression of the whistle sound waves as the train approaches and the decrease in the pitch is a result of the expansion of the sound wave as the train moves away from the observer. The change in the whistle pitch illustrates a wave principle that was discovered by the Austrian physicist Christian Doppler and it is applicable to all wave motion.

The most popular active volumetric detectors using the Doppler principle are the ultrasonic and microwave motion detectors. As already mentioned, ultrasonic motion detectors generate an inaudible acoustic energy pattern and process the Doppler frequency shift caused by an intruder moving in the detection zone. Microwave motion detectors basically operate by the same principle, except that they generate an energy pattern of electromagnetic energy. Because they do transmit electromagnetic energy, the detector operating frequencies and power output are regulated by the Federal Communications Commission (FCC). The FCC has allocated five operating frequencies for microwave motion detectors. The lowest frequency is 915 megahertz and the highest is 22,125 megahertz; however, most microwave detectors operate at a 10,525-megahertz frequency.

Another, but less popular, active volumetric motion detector is the sonic detector. Unlike ultrasonic detectors, sonic detectors generate an audible instead of an inaudible acoustic energy pattern and detect phase changes in the energy pattern, as well as Doppler frequency shifts caused by someone moving in the detection zone. Audibility of the sonic energy is probably the reason for the limited application of sonic motion detectors; however, there are applications where the sound is not a problem and in fact it could be a deterrent against an intruder who might otherwise consider entering the protected area.

Passive Detectors

Passive motion detectors detect energy generated by the intruder. In other words, passive detectors do not generate their own energy patterns. They detect the presence or change in energy as a result of the intruder's presence, or they detect energy generated during the intrusion. Two types of passive volumetric motion detectors are the infrared motion detector and the audio detector.

Infrared motion detectors detect a change in the thermal energy pattern resulting from a moving intruder and initiate an alarm when the change in the energy satisfies the detector alarm criteria. Audio detectors are not motion detectors per se. They depend on the intruder to generate noises, either breaking in or moving within the protected area. When the noise level reaches the detector alarm threshold, an alarm is activated.

Robert L. Barnard

Source Barnard, R.L., Intrusion Detection Systems. (Butterworth–Heinemann, Boston, 1982).

VULNERABILITY AND THREAT IDENTIFICATION

The primary purpose of vulnerability identification is to make the task of risk analysis more manageable by establishing a base from which to proceed. When the risks associated with the various systems and subsystems within a given enterprise are known, then the allocation of countermeasures can be more carefully planned. The need for such planning rests on the premise that security resources, as with all other resources, are limited and therefore must be allocated wisely.

Risk control begins locally, with identification and then classification of risk. To accomplish this task it is necessary to examine or survey all of the activities and relationships of the enterprise in question and develop answers to these basic considerations:

• Assets. What does the company own, operate, lease, control, have custody of or responsibility for, buy, sell, service, design, produce, manufacture, test, analyze, or maintain?

• Exposure. What is the company exposed to that could cause or contribute to damage, theft, or loss of property or other company assets, or that could cause or contribute to personal injury of company employees or others?

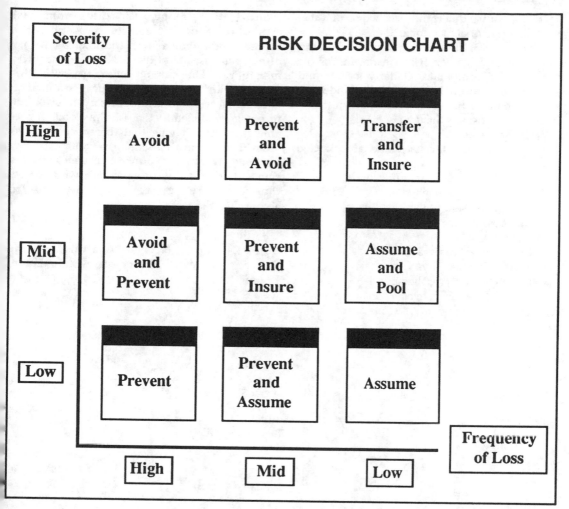

RISK DECISION CHART

Severity of Loss	High	Mid	Low

(The chart shows, for each Severity/Frequency combination:)

High severity:
- Avoid
- Prevent and Avoid
- Transfer and Insure

Mid severity:
- Avoid and Prevent
- Prevent and Insure
- Assume and Pool

Low severity:
- Prevent
- Prevent and Assume
- Assume

Frequency of Loss

High   Mid   Low

• Losses. What empirical knowledge is available to identify the frequency, magnitude, and range of past losses experienced by this and similarly located companies performing a like service or manufacturing the same or a similar product?

Security professionals use many techniques to develop data for risk identification. They may review company policies, procedures, and organizational activities to ascertain what risks have been identified and how they are perceived as management responsibilities. They may review insurance and risk-related files, including claims and loss records. Interviews with the heads of departments that have experienced loss exposures develop information on the organization and functioning of loss control procedures, if in fact any exist. Conducting inspections and interviewing management and other personnel in enough locations and activities develops a complete picture of the company's risk exposures as a basis for later evaluating loss control procedures and their effectiveness.

The tools necessary to accomplish the previously mentioned are the ability to conduct comprehensive interviews; the ability to conduct inspections and to make field observations of operations, procedures, humanpower, and electronics applied in security systems; and the ability to identify, obtain, and analyze pertinent records.

Another technique is to develop asset data. To do this one completely identifies all company assets, tangible and intangible, in terms of quantity and quality. Then one identifies the location of all company assets, as well as obvious exposures that may exist at these locations.

Next, one must determine the value of these assets in terms of actual dollars.

The identification of company assets, coupled with a history of loss exposure for the company and companies similarly located and engaged, will normally be sufficient to identify most of the major risks involved.

Risks will usually include:

- Crime losses.
- Natural, human-caused and acts of God disasters.
- Liability of officers and directors.
- Environmental damage.
- Comprehensive general liability.
- Business interruption and lost business opportunity.
- Errors and omissions liability.
- Professional liability.
- Product and service liability.

As can be seen from even a cursory review of the previously identified risks, the scope of risk identification alone, separate from risk evaluation and risk control, presupposes a degree of education and practical knowledge not often possessed by the individual security manager.   The person charged with this responsibility must have the education, training, and practical experience necessary to seek out, recognize, and identify the risks involved. It goes almost without saying that the process of risk identification, evaluation, and control in any dynamic organization, public or private, requires constant attention by professionals who possess the necessary knowledge and tools to accomplish the task.

James F. Broder, CPP

Source Broder, J.F., Risk Analysis and the Security Survey.   (Butterworth–Heinemann, Boston, 1984).

W

WAREHOUSING SAFEGUARDS IN THE RETAIL SECTOR

Many retail operations have their own distribution centers that make purchasing and delivery of merchandise timely and more cost-effective. In addition, many companies have warehouse operations in each of their outlets to receive, price, and store merchandise. This piece will concentrate on the warehouse operation of the stand-alone retail outlet and the warehouse operation that regulates the flow of merchandise in and out of the outlet.

Retail operations purchase three basic categories of merchandise. Although these types include a variety of items, they will fall into the buying categories of basic stock, special purchases, and sale merchandise. Each of these types of merchandise require different handling. The first is regular stock purchased to maintain the specified stock level necessary for day-to-day operation. This merchandise must move through the warehouse operation quickly to ensure maximum exposure to customer traffic. The second type is merchandise purchased in large quantities, not because of immediate need, but to take advantage of a special purchase price to increase profit margin or to buy seasonal merchandise such as patio or Christmas items. These items must be stored for extended periods of time and used as needed. The third type is merchandise purchased for an advertised sale. These items are also usually purchased in large quantities to ensure sufficient stock to satisfy customer demand and are usually negotiated at a one-time special purchase price. These items must be stored until the advertisement is published.

Losses in a warehouse operation result from four causes: (1) paperwork errors in receiving; (2) damage to merchandise making it unsalable; (3) pricing errors, which place the merchandise on the sales floor below the established retail price; and (4) theft, both internal and external.

Because of high turnover, low salary, and minimal experience level of most warehouse employees, it is important that an on-site supervisor or warehouse manager be present to train and monitor the work. This ensures the quality and precision of the processing of merchandise to prevent loss.

In most retail outlets, the manager of the store is less familiar with warehouse operations than any other facet of store operations. The manager, if not knowledgeable in this area, relies heavily on information, whether correct or incorrect, supplied him by the warehouse manager and other warehouse personnel. Many problems would be less likely to occur or re-occur if this were not the case. The proficiency of the manager to research questionable transactions and understand why they occurred can allow for the development of procedures that prevent further occurrence of the problem.

To prevent loss it is important that merchandise be received in an organized manner. The process begins when the merchandise is received off the delivery truck. The carton count of each shipment must be verified. The freight bill should be noted with the date, time, person receiving the merchandise, the carton count, and any notations of cartons short or with visible damage (holes, dents, crushed, etc.) on both the carrier's copy and the store copy. If visible damage or missing cartons are involved, the delivery driver should initial the store copy of the freight bill.

Truck drivers should not have free access to the warehouse. If there is a reason for them to enter the interior of the store, they should be escorted. This avoids the temptation to take merchandise out of the rear of the store while warehouse employees are busy unloading the shipment. Drivers, depending on the regulations of the delivery company, should be involved to some extent in the unloading process. They are at least required to move the merchandise to the rear door of the truck for removal by store personnel.

When the transaction is complete, the merchandise should be moved inside the warehouse to the receiving area to be "checked-in." Shipments must not be left outside unattended. Each shipment should be logged as it is received. The log should reflect the date, time, vendor, carton count, the purchase order number, and the freight carrier. This can be done on a notebook or a receiving log designed for this purpose, which can be purchased from an office supply store.

The purchase order should then be "pulled," each carton opened, and the contents verified and recorded in the receiving column of the purchase order. Exceptions such as wrong or damaged merchandise should be noted during this process. If any concealed damage is observed, the transfer company should be notified immediately and arrangements made to settle the claim which usually involves an inspection of the merchandise. These claims are strengthened by notations of visible damage to cartons noted at the time of delivery on the freight bill.

Often paperwork errors occur because of laziness. It is easier to list the quantities shown as shipped on the packing list accompanying the shipment than it is to count each item. Merely inserting the quantity ordered as the quantity received also avoids locating and counting each item, especially on large shipments of many items. The packing slip should be removed and secured by the warehouse manager until the shipment is completely received. Then the figures should be compared for accuracy. Any discrepancies should be checked prior to the merchandise leaving the warehouse.

Controls must be established for merchandise leaving the store. All merchandise removed from the store should be accompanied by the proper documenting paperwork. Companies that operate multiple outlets in one geographical location encourage the transfer of merchandise between stores to reduce inventory and maximize sales. Employees and members of management often make these deliveries in their own vehicles. Where possible, these deliveries should be made during business hours, and the removal and paperwork documenting the transfer done by warehouse personnel or someone other than the designated delivery person. This will ensure that the correct items and amount of merchandise is removed, and that no additional merchandise is taken at the same time. Managers must also comply with the warehouse procedures. If a manager is making a delivery after store hours, the merchandise and paperwork should be placed in the manager's vehicle by a warehouse employee, prior to store closing. This will prevent accusations or confusion later if a question arises.

Merchandise shipped from the store using a postal service such as United Parcel Service (UPS) and the U.S. Postal Service should be documented and reviewed by the warehouse manager or store manager to ensure that the shipments represent valid transactions (i.e., return of merchandise to a vendor or a special order to a customer). This method of shipment can be used by employees to ship merchandise that has not been purchased to themselves, relatives, or friends with no detection. Such shipments must be referenced to paperwork, which ensures the legitimacy of the shipment.

Damage to merchandise is another big cause of loss. This can occur when merchandise is received because warehouse personnel are not properly trained and supervised on the use of equipment such as the fork lift or pallet jack. Entire shipments can be damaged by improper handling of large equipment used to move the merchandise. The merchandise should be moved as little as possible. The more times an item is moved from place to place, the more the chances of damage. Damage is often caused by warehouse personnel using a box cutter to open cartons. Training in the use of a box knife and care by the user can avoid costly loss.

A procedure should be established to handle damaged merchandise. Employees should not be allowed to purchase damaged merchandise at a reduced price. To do so would create an incentive to damage items that they wished to purchase. The price for a damaged item should be set by the store manager. Care should be taken to destroy or mark (i.e., spray paint) damaged merchandise if it is discarded instead of sold. This would prevent someone from retrieving the item from the trash container and returning it for a refund.

Many vendors have a liberal return policy for damaged or defective merchandise. Return of the merchandise allows the store to re-coup funds for these items. Warehouse employees should be aware of items that can be returned for credit. Items can sometimes be repaired instead of destroyed. Management must be involved in the destruction of damaged merchandise.

Pricing errors occur when a receiving clerk is in a hurry or does not pay attention to what he or she is doing. The warehouse manager should double-check pricing. Another way to ensure correct pricing is by having one clerk make all price labels, locate the merchandise, and fasten the labels. However, this is usually not a possibility with the skeletal staffing of warehouse operations.

Pricing guns and machines should be secured when not in use and should not be readily available to non-warehouse employees. Price changes or pricing by other employees should be done with the approval/knowledge of store management. Employees must be instructed to not leave pricing guns unattended. A procedure should be established to "check out" and "check in" pricing guns that are used in areas other than the warehouse. This will prevent loss or misuse of the gun.

Theft of merchandise from both internal and external sources is a problem in warehouses that have little or no established controls. In addition to taking merchandise, a truck driver can take advantage of an inattentive receiving clerk and place merchandise back on the truck after it has been received or by offering to help count the cartons and intentionally falsifying the number of cartons "off-loaded." Employees should be made aware of this tactic.

Vendors can also be a problem. Company representatives who order and stock merchandise as a part of their contract with the retail outlet should not be allowed to roam the warehouse unsupervised. They should be required to enter and leave through the front door of the store, and not enter and leave through the warehouse. They should not be allowed to "check in" their own merchandise. This would allow them to declare merchandise that was not received as delivered. Representatives often remove damaged or defective merchandise from the store as a part of their agreement. This should be processed and documented by warehouse personnel just the same as any other shipment leaving the store. An effective way is to have the vendor, after completing his other duties in the store, drive his vehicle around to the delivery door, and pick up the merchandise and sign for it.

The receiving door/area should not be an entry or exit from outside the store to anyone, including warehouse and other store personnel. Ideally it should only be used for receiving. Employees should not be allowed to park their vehicles in or around the receiving area. Operating hours of the warehouse should be posted and the area secured after these hours. Receiving doors and rear doors should not be used after hours except in the case of an emergency with the supervision of management. This prevents not only unobserved theft, but also vulnerability to robbery and hijacking via an unsecured and unattended rear entrance.

Some stores require employees to enter and exit through the warehouse area prior to store opening and after the store closes. If such a procedure exists, the employees should be supervised. This procedure also increases the vulnerability to armed robbery.

Trash removal also usually involves the warehouse area. Stores should have a compactor so that trash removal is accomplished from the interior of the store. This avoids merchandise being carried out with the trash and retrieved later. All boxes should be broken down (flattened) before being thrown out. This keeps items from being concealed in boxes designated as trash. Even in the case of a store using a compactor, breaking down boxes prevents salable merchandise from being accidentally discarded in a box thought to contain only packing material. Many retail stores have started selling flattened boxes as scrap paper, adding extra money to the "bottom line."

E. Floyd Phelps, CPP

WEINGARTEN RULE

As police officers must observe the Miranda decision when interrogating suspects, the private security official must be familiar with and know when to follow the Weingarten rule in questioning employees.

In two separate but similar cases, *NLRB v J. Weingarten, Inc.* [1] and *ILGWU v. Quality Manufacturing Company et al.* [2], the U.S. Supreme Court ruled that employees who belong to unions are entitled to union representation during questioning by an employer or the employer's agent. The high court ruled that such interrogation that can result in disciplinary action entitles the employee to representation if he or she requests same. Failure to honor such a request "interferes with, restrains and coerces the individual right of the employee to engage in concerted activities for mutual aid or protection."

Without question, the decision complicates the work of many security officials whose companies are organized by a union. The court did not state that representation must be offered in all cases—only if it is desired. Furthermore, the court did state that the employer or his agent may elect to terminate the interview if such a request for union representation is made. This option can be pointed out to the employee, as well as the fact that the employee would not gain any of the benefits that might result from such an interview. In other words, the employer may proceed on a course of action with whatever facts are already at hand, and the employee may take his chances with the consequences.

If the interview or questioning proceeds with a shop steward or business agent present, the court affirms the union's role as that of a representative who is present to assist the employee and who may attempt to clarify the facts or suggest other employees who may have knowledge of them. The employer, however, is free to insist that he is only interested, at that time, in hearing the employee's own account of the matter under investigation [3].

As in any far-reaching court decision, there are always additional rulings and decisions growing out of the original. Four of the more notable decisions that have further clarified the Weingarten rule are:

- *Lennox Industries Inc. v. NLRB* CA 5 NOR 79-3890, 79-3894, 2-17-81.
- *Southwestern Bell v. NLRB* #80-2072 (BNA 10-17-82 #32).
- *Montgomery Ward v. NLRB* No. 81-1248 (BNA 12-17-81 #242).
- *Pacific Telephone v. NLRB* CCA9 July 15, 1983/82-7466.

With thorough knowledge of the previous material and the various appellate court decisions that followed, the security official is prepared to choose from four options when union representation is requested. These are:

1.   Grant the request and summon the shop steward to the proceedings.

2.   Deny the request and terminate the interrogation.

3.   Point out to the employee that the company is prepared to take disciplinary action based on the facts at hand, *sans* union representation. (Note: if the employee withdraws his or her request, this should be confirmed in writing and witnessed.)

4.   Recommend the company take disciplinary action, based on the evidence at hand, and do not attempt an interrogation.

J. Kirk Barefoot, CPP

Notes

1.   *NLRB v. J. Weingarten, Inc.* 485 F. 2d 1135 (1973).

2.   *ILGWU v. Quality Manufacturing Co.* 95 S. Ct. 972 (1975)

3.   Ibid.

WHITE COLLAR CRIME

The term "white collar crime" is a general description that relates broadly to a wide variety of specific crimes. It may take the form of consumer fraud, illegal competition, deceptive practices, check and credit card fraud, tax evasion, bankruptcy fraud, bribes, kickbacks, pay-offs, computer-related crime, pilferage, insurance fraud, fencing stolen property, securities fraud, and similar offenses.

The white collar criminal can be a bank executive who embezzles or a shipping clerk who pilfers. The essential characteristic of white collar crime, however, has more to do with the nature of the offense rather than the status of the offender. White collar crime is a non-violent crime; it involves deceit, corruption, or breach of trust. The offense frequently involves lying, cheating, or stealing through misrepresentation. It can be committed against private individuals, business corporations, non-profit organizations, and government units.

A problem in addressing white collar crime is the absence of valid measures for determining if criminal activity is present and to what extent. A difficulty in detecting its presence is the fact that a victim is not aware that he is being victimized, and when discovery is made, it may be too late to take effective action against the offender. In a sense, white collar crime is an invisible crime.

The invisibility of the crime is complicated by two other factors: an unwillingness of the public to vigorously prosecute white collar criminals and the failure of investigators to keep pace with increasingly complex schemes.

The Nature of White Collar Crime

In most crimes there is a "crime scene," but with white collar crime the offense is not readily apparent and is usually in progress. The investigator needs to detect the crime and work backwards to identify the principals. Following are general characteristics of white collar offenses:

- Detection is frequently accidental.
- Offenses are frequently reported anonymously.
- There is usually no complainant.
- The scheme has been in existence over a long period of time.
- The crime tends to cover a large geographical area, often spanning several prosecutorial jurisdictions.
- The scheme tends to involve several specific violations of law.
- The principals are usually well known, respected, intelligent and, in some cases, influential.
- The scheme is sometimes difficult to decipher.
- Evidence tends to get "lost or destroyed" when the principal learns that an investigation is in progress.

Types of White Collar Crime

Following are brief discussions of the more common types of white collar crime.

Advanced Fee Schemes. These are designed to obtain fees in advance for services the promoter has no intention of providing. They usually occur when the offender claims to have means of obtaining buyers for one's business, property, securities, or other assets, or to have access to sources of loan financing. These usually occur when property is hard to obtain.

Pyramid Schemes. These are investment frauds by which an individual is offered a distributorship or franchise to market a particular product. The contract also authorizes the investor to sell additional franchises. Promoters represent that the marketing of the product will result in profits, but that the selling of franchises will result in quicker return on investment. Therefore, investors expend greater energies on selling franchises than on sale of products. Finally, a point is reached where the supply of investors is exhausted, leading to the collapse of the pyramid. Often, too, the product itself is overpriced, and no real effort is made by promoters to sell the product.

Chain Referral Schemes. These involve sales of grossly overpriced products through false representation that the cost will be recovered by commissions the promoter will pay on sales to the purchaser's friends, if only the purchaser will permit them to be contacted with the same proposition.

Ponzi Schemes. These are basically investment frauds. Operators solicit investors in a business venture, promising extremely high financial returns or dividends in a very short time. The operator never invests the money in anything, but does pay "dividends" to the investor by giving him back some of his original investment. This is done as an inducement to investors to put up additional funds, or to solicit others to do so. During the early stages, the investor may even be able to liquidate his investment if he wishes, plus interest. This makes the operation more credible to others. When the operator has accumulated sufficient funds for his purposes, he flees the area.

Business Opportunity Schemes. These are a number of schemes and deceptions concocted to attract victims into participating in an allegedly lucrative business venture. They may appear in almost any type financial dealing, e.g., vending machines, product dispensing, distributorships in limited areas, multi-level sales organizations, etc. The schemes may differ in form, but may have basic identifiable similarities, such as:

- Financial investment by the victim in advance.
- The victim's investment is "covered" by company inventory, buy-back agreements, or escrow accounts.
- The promoter convinces the victim that the company will work closely with him to ensure success. This usually includes management and marketing aids, training, and saturation advertising.

The best way to identify potentially fraudulent business opportunity schemes is to attempt to identify the misrepresentation. Some of the common indicators of misrepresentation are:

- Claiming affiliation or association with a larger or well-known company.
- Presenting a misleading credit rating, such as a false Dunn & Bradstreet report.

•Citing false business and personal references (e.g., Better Business Bureau, Chamber of Commerce, and well-known individuals).

•Inflating marketing experience and national sales.

•Misreporting the size of the firm.

•Promoting a unique product or service that has a high public demand and need.

•Projecting unrealistic sales and profits.

•Presenting doctored marketing surveys.

•Claiming easy selling, working during spare time and/or at home, such as filling orders for retail stores and selling via direct mail.

•Offering exclusive territory with leads and potential customers furnished.

•Offering a re-purchase or buy-back option.

•Providing free training, free servicing, and repair of the product to be marketed.

•Representing that the manufacturer or sponsor will provide saturated advertising.

•Advising that the offer to "get on board" will soon expire.

•Changing the contract or deleting clauses before signing.

Planned Bankruptcy Scheme. This is a merchandising swindle based on the abuse of credit that has been established, either legitimately or fraudulently. The scheme usually consists of:

•Overpurchasing of inventory on credit; then:

•Selling or other disposing of the merchandise obtained;

•Concealing the proceeds;

•Not paying the creditors; and

•Filing a bankruptcy petition, either voluntarily or involuntarily.

The new company is organized, a bank account opened, and operating space is leased. The company begins making purchases from a number of suppliers and making payment promptly to establish credit. The operators then use this credit to find other suppliers and order more merchandise, while slowing payments to the original suppliers.

The orders for goods from all suppliers are increased while the goods are sold to fences below cost. The operators now either abscond or gut the business and file bankruptcy. This can also be accomplished in one step by buying a business with a good credit rating. Organized

crime has been particularly active in this type of scheme.

Merchandising Schemes. Many times these schemes are visible, blatant, and occur in the retail marketplace. All are frauds based on a twisting of the truth for increased profits. Some include:

•Bait and Switch. A product or service is promoted with no intent to sell it as advertised. The customer is lured to the seller by an extraordinarily good buy and upon arrival the salesperson tries to induce the customer to buy a higher-priced product or service. Hence the name, "bait and switch."

•Phony Sales. The unscrupulous businessperson relies on the customer's desire for a bargain. These may take the form of fire, liquidation, or going out of business sales. The advertising must be shown to be fraudulent.

•Deceptive Sales Contest. Through a variety of means, the deceptive businessperson promotes a contest in which the victim is led to believe that the chance of winning is much greater than it really is.

•Short Weighing. This practice involves substantially more than simply cheating a customer in the weighing of produce in a grocery store. Producers at the packaging stages of production can fill containers of their product 9/10 the capacity and charge retailers for the entire amount. Investigative efforts directed at a package-by-package basis seems a waste, but considering mass marketing practices, this can be extremely lucrative for the dishonest firm.

Service and Repair Schemes. Since in the affluent society many of our appliances, automobiles, or other mechanical devices need repair from time to time, this can be a very lucrative scheme. Repair schemes, regardless of the product involved, give dishonest repairpersons the chance to "lowball" the customer. Lowballing occurs when a customer takes a product in for repair, and is quoted a ridiculously low bid for the repairs. The operator has no intention of fixing the product at this price, but the lowball price will induce the customer to authorize the repairs.

Once the repairperson has the product in his possession, he tends to discover other malfunctions or worn parts, and the repair price is adjusted upward.

The most difficult element to prove is that from the beginning the repairperson intended the original estimate only as an enticement to obtain the repair job under false pretenses.

Land Schemes. Increasing in frequency, land schemes are marked by high-pressure sales tactics in which many misrepresentations are made, such as the location of the land, value, utilities available, title validity, prospect for future profitable sale, the installation of roads, or other improvements. The land is often sold sight unseen with the use of deceptive photographs, appraisal reports, and false promotions as to free bonuses, refunds, and closing costs. Targets are usually retirees, middle-income families seeking vacation resort property, and investors lured by promises of lucrative returns.

Home Improvement, Debt Consolidation, and Mortgage Loans. In recent years, all of these have been combined into one overall scheme. Homeowners already heavily burdened with debt have been the victims. The homeowner is offered a loan sufficient to pay off all other debts, as well as finance a home improvement, and is promised that the one monthly payment is less, or at least no larger, than the combined payment now being made. The large amount of the loan offered may stem from the criminal's intention to quickly sell the note at a discount to a finance company. To do so profitably he knows the amount borrowed must sufficiently exceed the cost of the home improvement work so as to offset the discount. The finance company, a third party, assumes legal possession of the promissory note, collects the monthly payments as a holder in due course, and disowns all responsibility for any misrepresentations that may have been made in its creation. In this type of scheme, promoters rely on the bewildering terms of the signed documents and numerous put-off tactics to forestall serious consequences when the home improvement falls in arrears, is poorly done, or is not done at all.

Home Solicitation Schemes. In this type of scheme, the operator represents that an individual may receive a product at no cost because the operators wish to showcase the product in the neighborhood. He will often say that the person was selected because of his reputation in the community. The victim is then asked to sign a contract that supposedly reflects the terms of the oral agreement. It is, in fact, a long-term sales contract that requires the consumer to make additional purchases for as long as 10 years.

Personal Improvement Schemes. Promoters prey on the victim's need to improve himself. These may come in the form of joining a health spa, attending a trade school, computer dating service, losing weight, learning to dance, becoming more attractive, etc.

Medical Frauds. In this illegal activity will be found a number of schemes that involve defrauding of government-sponsored medical programs.
 • Double Billing. Others billed include the patient, Medicare, Blue Cross, Medicaid of another county or state, or state insurance (Workers' Compensation).
 • Over-Billing and Billing for Services Not Performed.
 • Billing for Services Provided by Another. This is done by gaining access to another provider's records and billing for the other's as yet unbilled services. This frequently occurs where many doctors work at the same location and records are centrally maintained.
 • Ping-Ponging. The victim is given unnecessary treatment at the same time needed services are performed.

Welfare Frauds. These involve the acquisition of public assistance funds by those not entitled to such funds, for example:
 • Receiving payments while employed.
 • Receiving payments with an undisclosed source of support that would otherwise disqualify the person from receiving funds.
 • Receiving funds for individuals no longer residing in the household.

Food Stamp Frauds. The individual may improperly receive food stamps in much the same way that welfare frauds are committed. The following are examples:
 • Misrepresenting current income or property.
 • Receiving support from an undisclosed source.
 • Trafficking in the sale of stamps for cash.

Official Corruption. Many times the investigation of other white-collar type crimes, such as bid-rigging or frauds against government programs, have corrupt public officials at the core. Often the only way to identify these frauds is when they are brought to the attention of the investigator by informants. To succeed, these investigations must be discreetly conducted.

Bid-Rigging. Generally, large public contracts are awarded by means of competitive bidding. Sometimes providers of the bids will agree on which one will submit the lowest bid, and although it is the lowest bid received, it is usually inflated because of the rigging. Oftentimes, this is very difficult to prove because the rigging is the result of a tacit understanding rather than a provable conspiracy. Sometimes the bidders may have divided the public market among themselves, or the competitors may rotate the lowest bids. Either way, the competitive bidding process is no more than a sham.

Commercial Bribery. This includes payments, kickbacks, and rebates. Through the offer of a bribe, a responsible corporate official may be persuaded to purchase inferior supplies from one firm, or to overlook deficiencies or irregularities by a contractor and thus certify payment for unsatisfactory work. The cost of the corruption is ultimately passed on to the consumer.

Insurance Fraud. This type of fraud basically occurs in four ways:

•Fraud Committed by Insurance Agents. Agents who become involved in this type of fraud usually practice a form of the Ponzi scheme. They are normally independent, travel large territories, and sell a variety of types of insurance. They purport to represent legitimate insurance companies, and often use forms and promotional materials of the major companies. Since all premium payments, policy changes, and claims are processed through the agent, the agent simply fails to forward the payment to the company. Barring a rash of claims at once, the agent can operate successfully over a number of years by simply paying the claims out of the premiums. State insurance agent licensing laws makes this type of fraud fairly easy to detect, but this has not seemed to decrease the incidence of this fraud.

•Fraud Committed by Claim Adjusters. An adjuster's investigation is the basis for insurance settlements. The most common fraud is when the adjuster conspires with claimants or repairpersons. Exclusive dealing arrangements and falsely inflated bills are the hallmark of this type. They also often substitute claimants.

•Fraud Committed by Individual Policy Holders. False customer claims are the largest source of insurance fraud. Sometimes this involves the "staging" of accidents.

•Fraud Committed by Organized Rings of Phony Claimants. Although many times an individual will commit frauds involving "staged" accidents, an increasing number of false claims are the result of organized rings of economic criminals who work together. The annual loss suffered by legitimate insurance companies is enormous in terms of fraudulent accident and health claims—losses that impact increasingly on the rising cost of insurance to the general public.

Computer-Related Frauds. Most computer crime is not detected and most of what is detected is not reported. This type of fraud is very difficult for the investigator because of lack of expertise and because the computer can be programmed to wipe out the evidence of a crime. Many schemes involve fraudulent conversion of confidential information stored within the memory banks. For this type of criminal, data is money and power.

Credit Card Frauds. Several distinct crimes are included in this classification.

•Falsely acquired credit cards by misrepresentation, including identity, age, employment, etc.

•Use of the card to defraud merchants or other providers.

•Professional credit card rings who deal in counterfeit, lost, stolen, or misdelivered credit cards.

These losses are in the millions annually. As always, the economic consequences are borne by the honest consumer in terms of increased prices.

Charity Frauds. The most common form of this type of fraud involves solicitation of money for an ostensibly worthwhile cause by an individual who has no intention of turning the money over to the organization if, in fact, one does exist. Also, professional fund raisers solicit donations for legitimate charities but fail to disclose that because they are professional they take for themselves a large percentage of the funds.

Check Kiting. This is the practice of drawing checks on accounts whose balances consist substantially of uncollected funds (checks that have not cleared). Using two different banks, the kiter can cover checks drawn on one bank by checks drawn on the other. The key to the scheme is the time required for the bank to actually collect deposited funds (checks).

John J. Fay, CPP

WIRELESS VIDEO TRANSMISSION

Most closed-circuit television (CCTV) security systems transmit video, audio, and control signals via coaxial cable, two-wire, or fiber-optic transmission means. These techniques are cost effective, reliable, and provide an excellent solution for transmission. However, there are applications and circumstances when wireless transmission of CCTV and other signals are necessary or advantageous compared with the "hard-wired" systems. The hardware costs for these wireless radio frequency (RF), microwave, and lightwave systems are considerably higher than any of the copper wire or fiber-optic systems, and should only be used when absolutely necessary, as when their use avoids expensive cable installations (e.g., across roadways) or for temporary applications.

There are several methods by which the CCTV signal from the camera can be transmitted to the receiver through the atmosphere without having to use any hard-wire or fiber connection between the two. The most familiar technique is the transmission of commercial television signals received by the home consumer television set with the RF signal being broadcast through the atmosphere from some distant transmitter tower on the very high frequency (VHF) and ultra-high frequency (UHF) channels.

Commercial broadcasting is, of course, rigidly controlled by the Federal Communications Commission (FCC) whose regulations dictate precise usage. Microwave transmission is also controlled by the FCC. Rules

are set forth with licensing required for certain frequencies and power levels which limit usage to specific customers (government versus private) and applications. The government exercises strict control over wireless RF and microwave video atmospheric transmission. Some low-power RF transmitters suitable for short links (less than a mile) are available for use without an FCC license, and some microwave links are approved after a frequency check is made.

Following are descriptions of wireless TV transmission using RF over VHF or UHF channels, microwave (ground-to-ground station satellite), and lightwave transmission using infrared (IR) beams. It should be noted that the results obtainable with hard-wired copper wire or fiber-optic video transmission are usually predictable, with the exception of an unknown interference that might occur due to the copper wire cables running near electromagnetic radiating equipment. The results obtained with wireless transmission are generally not as predictable. This is because of the variable nature of the atmospheric path through which RF, microwave, or a light beam must travel, as well as the specific transmitting and propagating characteristics of the particular wavelength or frequency of transmission.

Each of the three different wireless transmitting regimes have different transmission properties because of the wide diversity of transmission frequencies (RF versus microwave versus lightwave).

Radio Frequency

RF is a wireless video transmission means used primarily by government agencies, but finding increasing use in commercial security applications as a result of the removal of government restrictions. Video transmitters and receivers transmit a monochrome or color video signal over distances of several hundred feet to several miles using small, portable, battery-powered equipment operating anywhere in the frequency range of 150 to 980 megahertz (MHz), covering the full VHF and UHF frequency spectra.

The RF link constitutes the lowest carrier frequency in wireless video transmission. RF energy can penetrate most nonmetallic and

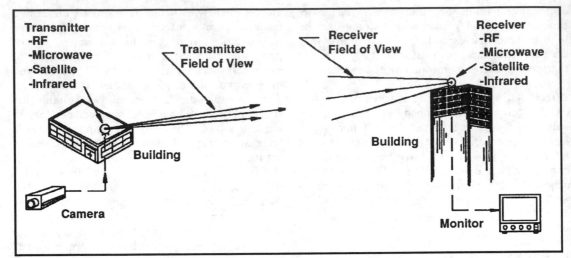

Wireless Transmission Techniques

visually opaque materials, go around corners, and does not require a line-of-sight path (receiver in sight of the transmitter) when transmitting from one location to another. RF frequencies range from 150 to 450 MHz in the VHF spectrum and 450 to 1000 MHz in the UHF spectrum.

The RF frequencies are, however, susceptible to attenuation and reflection by metallic objects and ground terrain or large buildings and structures. These intervening signal attenuations sometimes produce unpredictable and unsatisfactory results.

Microwave

Microwave frequency video transmission systems require line-of-sight between the transmitter and receiver, and are more sensitive to obstructions in the line-of-sight path than RF. Any metallic, moist, or wet objects cause severe attenuation and/or reflection, often rendering a system useless. Metallic objects can sometimes be used to advantage. By reflecting the microwave energy off a metallic pole or flat surface (in a mirror-like fashion), the beam can be deflected and redirected around a corner. This reflection of the microwave beam reduces the energy reaching the receiver and reduces the effective range of the system. Most microwave frequencies penetrate through dry, nonmetallic structures such as wood or dry-wall,

thereby making non-line-of-sight transmission possible.

Microwave systems applicable to television transmission operate with allocated frequencies in bands from 1 gigaherz (GHz) (i.e., 1000 MHz) to 40 GHz.

Since microwave frequencies approach those of light, they are transmitted and received by parabolic-shaped reflector antennas or metallic horns. These reflectors must be contoured accurately so that the transmitter beam pattern directs the energy toward the receiver antenna, and the receiver antenna collects the energy coming from the transmitter.

Signal fading can occur due to changes in the atmospheric conditions between the transmitter and receiver, a problem which must be taken into account in the design. This fading can result at any frequency, but, in general, is more severe at higher microwave frequencies (20 to 40 GHz).

Terrestrial (ground-based) microwave transmission equipment can transmit video, audio, and control signals over distances from several hundred feet to 25 miles in line-of-sight conditions. The system operates at a carrier frequency of 2450 to 2483 MHz with a power output of 1 watt, requires an FCC license for operation, and can only be used for government applications. The system transmits monochrome or color video with excellent quality, has a subcarrier channel for audio communications, and is powered from 117 volts

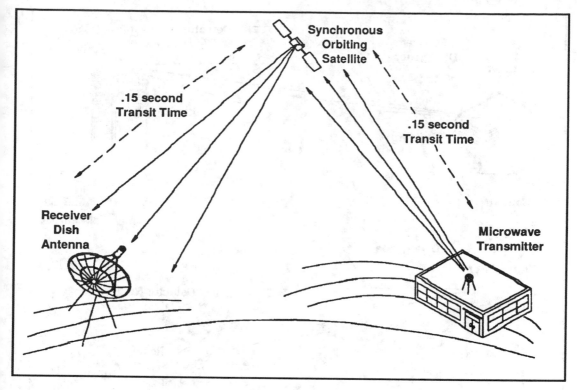

Satellite Television Transmission System

alternating current (AC) or 12 volts direct current (DC).

In outdoor applications it can transmit with good quality over a range of 1 mile. A high-gain directional antenna is available to extend the operating range to several miles. A benefit in operating at a microwave frequency is that it prevents casual interception by most of the population, thereby making the transmission semi-covert.

A system for government and industrial users to transmit at longer ranges (up to 3 miles) uses the 21.8 to 23.2 GHz frequency spectrum. In addition to transmitting the video channel, the system is capable of providing up to three voice or data (control) channels. The data channels may be used to control pan/tilt, zoom, focus, and iris at the camera location. FCC licensing is required, and approval is given after an authorized interference survey is made to verify that no interference will result in other equipment operating in the area.

A frequency in widespread use in government and industrial applications operates at 10.525 GHz with an output power of 15 milliwatts. An FM-modulated color or monochrome video signal is transmitted over a distance of 3500 feet. The system also operates as a video intrusion detection system. When the transmitter and receiver are located to intercept movement by a person, vehicle, or other object passing through the beam, the beam interception causes the microwave detection system to register an alarm. Prior to the alarm occurring, a video camera located at the distant end transmits a picture of the intruder. After the intrusion is cleared, the video camera continues transmitting the video picture.

Video signals can be transmitted over microwave links using satellites. They are in extensive use for earth-to-satellite-to-earth communications. The orbiting synchronous satellite relays the microwave signal to and from the earth dish antennas.

Large dish-shaped antennas are used at motels, commercial and government buildings, etc., to transmit and receive video and other signals over great distances. The feed horn directs the microwave signal into a low noise amplifier (LNA) which amplifies the weak signal

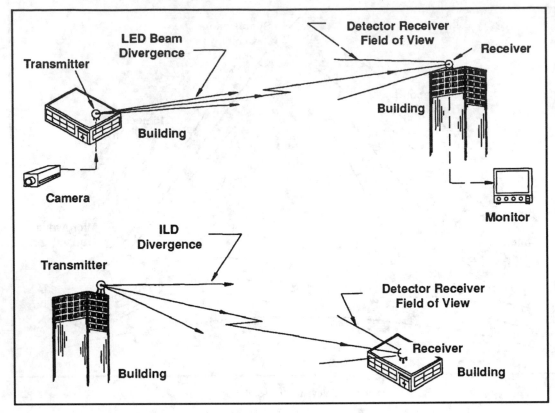

IR Atmospheric Video Transmission System

and eventually transmits it by cable to the monitoring location. They can be compared to fiber-optic cables that transmit light along their path. The LNA is the first active electronic component in the receiving system that acts on the video signal and is analogous to an audio preamplifier. The microwave signal from the LNA is transmitted via coaxial cable and converted to a VHF or UHF RF frequency and displayed on a television receiver, or converted further to be displayed on a CCTV monitor.

Infrared Atmospheric

The light beam generated in the IR atmospheric video transmitter is converted from the electrical video signal by either a light-emitting diode (LED) or infrared laser diode (ILD). The receiver uses a silicon diode IR detector and amplifier to convert the light signal back to an electrical signal and drive the coaxial cable and CCTV monitor. Either the LED or ILD is used,

depending on the transmitter-to-receiver distance and how secure the link must be. Short-range transmissions of up to several hundred feet are accomplished using the LED. The ILD is used for longer ranges up to several miles under clear atmospheric conditions. The advantages of using the LED are its lower cost, wider beam, and easy alignment procedure. The LED produces a 10 to 20 degree beam width, making it relatively simple to align the transmitter and receiver.

The beam width of a typical ILD transmitter is 0.1 or 0.2 degrees, making it more difficult to align and requiring that the mounting structure be very stable to maintain alignment. Additionally, the building structure must not sway, creep, vibrate, or produce appreciable twist due to uneven thermal heating (sun loading). LED and ILD systems can transmit the IR beam through most forms of transparent window glazing; however, some have a high tin content that causes severe signal attenuation with attendant poor video quality. The suitability of the window can only be determined by testing, which should be performed prior to system installation.

ILD atmospheric transmission provides a secure video, audio, and control link which is hard to tap because the tapping device -- a laser receiver -- must be positioned into the laser beam, which is hard to accomplish without being detected.

Lightwave Transmission Path Considerations

LED and ILD atmospheric transmission systems suffer video signal transmission losses caused by atmosphere path absorption.   At certain wavelengths the molecular absorption in the air is so great that it totally blocks communications. Lightwave transmission wavelengths are chosen at atmospheric windows where the attenuation is small enough to be tolerated.

Light signals are absorbed by dust and aerosol particles present in the atmosphere. These may reach very high concentrations near a body of water. Improved performance in these locations is achieved by locating the link as high above the ground as possible.

Fog is a third factor causing severe absorption of the IR signal. In areas where fog occurs, the local weather conditions must be analyzed and taken into account when specifying an atmospheric link, since the presence of fog will greatly influence link down time.

Turbulence in the atmosphere causes a refractive index variation in the signal path (similar to the heat waves seen when there is solar heating in air -- the *mirage effect)* and its subsequent wind-aided turbulent mixing. The net effect of this turbulence is to move or bend the IR beam in an unpredictable direction so that the transmitted radiation does not reach the remote receiver.   To compensate for this turbulence, the transmitter beam is made wide enough so that it is highly unlikely that the beam will miss the receiver. This wider beam, however, means that the beam intensity is less; therefore, the received signal on average will be less than that received from the transmission of a narrower beam.

Several techniques are available to transmit video, audio, and control signals through the atmosphere by wireless means.   These techniques should only be used after it has been determined that the conventional techniques of coaxial, two-wire, and fiber optics are impractical.

Herman A. Kruegle

WOUNDS: TRAUMA CAUSED BY SHOOTING AND CUTTING

In gunshot cases, a bullet entrance wound is usually a neat, round hole made by a bullet entering the body. The shape of an exit wound will vary according to where it exits (whether through a fleshy or bony structure), the shape of the bullet as it exits (whether pristine or flattened), and the motion of the bullet (whether spinning or tumbling).   Exit wound shapes include marks that are stellate (star-like), slit-like, everted (inside-out), and irregular.

A bullet exit wound is typically a ragged or torn hole made by a bullet leaving the body and is usually much larger than the size of the bullet.

An abrasion collar is a narrow ring around the entry of a bullet hole in the skin. The skin, being resistant and elastic, will be stretched by the impacting bullet. A narrow ring around the bullet hole is formed by the abrasive action of the bullet. The ring may also contain residues from the surface of the bullet.

A contact or tattooed gunshot wound is a close-range wound characterized by gunpowder tattooing in and around the bullet hole. The tattooing consists of charring at the entry point, and powder grains and combustion products embedded in the skin. The wound results when the muzzle of the gun has been firmly applied to the skin at the instant of firing.   When the muzzle is against a bony structure, such as the head, the blast causes a lacerated, charred wound that shows flame burns of the skin and hair from the rapidly expanding explosive gases. Smudges from carbon deposits appear within the subcutaneous tissue, muscle, and bone. A distinct abraded and contused imprint, with the laceration in the shape of a star, will very likely appear on the skin.   When the muzzle is in contact with soft flesh, such as the abdomen, the star-shaped laceration and flame burns are not present because the exploding gases of the muzzle blast are dispersed without resistance into the abdominal cavity.

A near-contact gunshot wound results when the muzzle, at time of discharge, is approximately 2 inches or less from the victim but not in contact with the skin. The wound is rounded with inverted abraded edges, surrounded by a zone of scorching, soot deposits, and compact tattooing from powder grains embedded in the skin.

A close-range gunshot wound is a wound caused when the muzzle, at time of discharge, is 2–24 inches from the victim. As the distance between a gun and the skin is increased, the flame burns diminish and powder grains embedded in the skin (tattooing) are spread in a widening circle around the bullet entry hole. Eventually, the tattooing effect disappears. When a bullet fired at close range first passes through clothing or some other substance, the tattooing effect may not be visible at all, thereby giving the appearance of a distant shot.

A distant wound is a wound caused by a bullet that traveled in excess of at least 2 feet from muzzle to victim. A distant wound is apparent by the absence of flame, smoke, and tattooing marks characteristic of a shot made in contact or in close contact with the victim. When a bullet penetrates the body perpendicular to the skin, it produces a round wound with abraded margins, called a collar abrasion. When a bullet penetrates the skin at an angle, the direction from which it enters the skin is indicated by a triangular abrasion and undermining of the skin. A bullet that grazes but does not penetrate the skin will produce a rectangular abrasion of the skin, called a bullet rub.

A beveled wound or a tangential gunshot wound results when the skin is penetrated at an angle. One margin of the wound is beveled and the other margin overhangs it. A residue track may be visible.

Marks from shotgun wounds have similar characteristics and are potentially classifiable as to the distance separating the victim and the shotgun muzzle at time of discharge. Four classifications are generally recognized: (1) the direct contact wound, which shows an imprint of the muzzle on the skin or which indicates contact by massive destruction of bone and tissue; (2) the up-close or loose-contact wound, which shows a small diameter entry pattern having abraded edges surrounded by a zone of considerable scorching, soot, and powder residue; (3) the close-range or near-range wound, which has a larger diameter entry pattern consistent with a discharge at 4–6 feet and shows abraded, scalloped margins, wad-impact abrasion, and wide dispersal of powder residue, soot, and smoke stains; and (4) the distance wound, which has a very large-diameter entry pattern consistent with a discharge at greater than 6 feet and shows scattered, small, round pellet holes with abraded margins.

In cutting and stabbing cases, a cleavage line wound is a gaping wound produced by cutting or stabbing perpendicularly to a cleavage line. The wound will appear to have been caused by a large blade or a deep cutting action. The gaping aspect, however, results from a distortion of the muscle fibers that provide a normal tension to the skin. Defense wounds are often found on the victim's hands and arms. The wounds evidence the manner in which the victim maneuvered to fend off the attacker. Wounds made by cutting instruments are called incised wounds.

A wrinkle wound results from a cutting or stabbing action that produces multiple cuts or punctures along the line of the blade, with interspersed areas of uninvolved skin. Wrinkle wounds are usually associated with obese or elderly victims.

John J. Fay, CPP

Source Fay, J.J., Butterworths Security Dictionary. (Butterworth–Heinemann, Boston, 1987).

Z

ZERO-BASE BUDGETING

In any operation of size and complexity, budgeting will be an essential element of management planning and control. Three purposes of budgeting stand out:

- Estimate the costs and expected revenues of planned activities.
- Provide a warning mechanism when variances occur in actual costs and revenues.
- Exercise uniformity in the matter of fiscal control.

The master budget is the comprehensive or overall budget. It is the forecast of all transactions within a given period, set up in a manner that will deliver timely reports of financial results to responsible managers. The comprehensive budget enables the preparation of financial statements, such as the profit and loss statement and balance sheet. Within the comprehensive budget can be found a variety of smaller budgets that address the activities of departments and functions within the business. A budget director may be assigned to coordinate preparation of the individual budgets, and the process of preparation may follow a particular approach or technique.

A security manager's budget may include a major purchase. A preparatory step in considering a large expenditure is to determine the cost-benefit ratio. The ratio is attained by dividing costs by benefits. For example, if the installation of an access control system is estimated to cost $500,000 with an anticipated service life of 10 years, and annual guard costs will be reduced $100,000 per year as a result, the cost-benefit ratio is 0.5:1, meaning that the costs are half of the benefits or the benefits are twice as great as the costs. The ratio in this example was arrived at by multiplying the annual guard cost savings by the number of years of useful service that can be expected from the access control system. This figure ($1,000,000) represents the benefit, and is divided into the cost of the system ($500,000). When the ratio is less than 1, it is favorable; and it is unfavorable when it is higher than 1.

The budgeting process can be extensive, perhaps requiring a budget committee, typically consisting of the chief executive officer, the chief financial officer, and the budget director. The committee would develop spending policy and manage overall costs.

The Zero-Base Approach

A technique growing in popularity is zero-base budgeting. The technique serves several important purposes of management. It facilitates planning, decision making, the allocation of resources, and, in particular, cost containment.

The zero-base approach utilizes a planning and budgeting process that requires each manager to:

- Establish objectives for his or her function and gain agreement on them.
- Define alternatives for achieving the objectives.
- Select the most practical alternative of achieving the objectives.
- Break the alternative up into incremental levels of effort.
- Assess the costs and benefits of each incremental level.
- Describe the consequences of disapproval.

The budget submission is described in decision packages, each reflecting one of the incremental levels. All packages are ranked in order of priority, and those above a pre-defined level of affordability are approved and funded while all others are deferred or eliminated.

In this approach, a manager's budget for the upcoming period starts with zero dollars. Funds are placed into the manager's budget only to the extent that planned expenditures have been justified in detail. By starting from a zero-base point, the manager is forced to engage in fresh, innovative thinking that cuts costs and drives productivity.

A manager looks at planned activities in terms of purpose, cost, and value added. The benefits to be derived are weighed against the benefits that will be lost if the planned activity is carried out at a lesser level or not done at all. An inherent requirement is to explore different alternatives for achieving the same results. For example, the security manager may analyze the pros and cons of using an in-house security officer service or contracting with an outside agency.

The essence of the approach is in its search for alternative ways. The manager is asked to imagine that his or her operation does not exist and to start from scratch in constructing the operation from a zero base. Questions that a manager might critically examine include: Is it best to continue as before or find different ways to conduct business? Is there a value in consolidating, reorganizing, merging, automating, or contracting? What can be cut, or can the operation be eliminated entirely?

Zero-base budgeting forces managers to look at different levels of effect for performing an activity. The levels may range from zero activity to maximum or optimum activity. At each spending level, the manager would show the costs and the corresponding effect.

A security manager, for example, might be required to analyze a guard operation arranged to function at the 50%, 75%, and 100% levels of spending. The security manager would describe the probable outcomes of operating at different cost levels. The approach brings the manager to examine other alternatives for getting the job done, and at the same time gives to management the alternative of reducing or eliminating an activity.

Putting zero-base budgeting to work is not without difficulties. Because it involves a decentralization of the planning process, many more people become players, many of them for the first time. This dictates a need to educate and train, both in terms of teaching the process and in giving to the players the skills of participative management. To some, the approach is threatening—the name itself suggests risk. A great deal of salesmanship is often needed.

The centrality of objectives to the process requires that the organization have a well-defined set of goals and strategies. It often happens that an organization will not have made the effort to establish a coherent game plan, or is unable or unwilling to share the game plan with all the players.

Because the process involves an aggressive search for alternative ways, it presupposes that managers will be innovative, creative, and unafraid of risk. Also, because zero-base budgeting generates new ideas, managers spend more time examining, discussing, and deciding. The process goes beyond simply allocating costs; managers are pushed to the consideration of issues at the heart of the business.

On the plus side, the zero-base approach brings planning, budgeting, and decision making into one self-contained process. The process leans less toward "bean counting" and more toward functional analysis and decision making that is closer to the operating level.

Zero-base budgeting has the capability to pinpoint unnecessary work and duplication of effort. It produces objectives consistent with overall organizational goals, and allows management to pick and choose among the objectives with due consideration of resource constraints.

John J. Fay, CPP

Sources

Austin, A.L., and L.M. Cheek, Zero-base Budgeting. (AMACOM, New York, 1979).

Heyel, C., Encyclopedia of Management. (Van Nostrand Reinhold, New York, 1982).

A

K

L

M

median divider 7
medical fraud 765
medical record 658
medical review officer (MRO) 256
merchandising fraud 764
mercury arc lamp 130
mercury vapor lamp 471
merit rating 537
metabolism of marijuana 250
metabolite 256
metal detector 7
metal halide lamp 471
metal-oxide semiconductor 118
MICR 53
microprocessor-controlled device 10
microwave 433, 751
microwave detectors 449, 698
microwave motion detector 498
Military Police Corps 47
military record 68
military security 499
mini-lens 124
Minnesota Multiphasic Personality Inventory 565
Miranda rights 463, 467
miscellaneous charges orders 56
misfeasance 511
mistake of fact 226
MMPI 565
modulated beam 72
monostatic microwave sensor 704
monthly analysis 108
mortgage loan fraud 765
MOS 118
motion to quash 464
motivation 500
motive 195
Motor Vehicle Information and Cost Savings
(MVICS) Act 508
mouth-to-mouth resuscitation 14
movable evidence 291
MRO 256
MTBF 674
MTTR 674
mugging 647
multiple drops 472
multiple level access 3
multiple reader 3
multiple-conductor cables 472
multiplexer 4
museum security 502

N

National Crime Information Center 311, 421, 507
National Crime Survey 507, 632, 637
National Criminal Justice Reference Service 508
National Highway Traffic Safety Administration
(NHTSA) 508
National Institute for Occupational Safety and
Health 651
National Institute of Justice 508
National Park Service 533
National Security Council 403
National Traffic and Motor Vehicle Safety Act 508
national automobile altered numbers file 311
national driver register 508
national fraudulent check file 311
national motor vehicle certificate of title file 311
national security information 152
national stolen art file, 311
national stolen coin file 311
national vehicle identification number standard
file 311
natural law 653
Naval Intelligence 509
Naval Investigative Service 509
NCIC 311, 421, 507
NCS 507, 632, 637
NDR 508
near-contact gunshot wound 771
necessity defense 226
needle stick 16
negligence 464, 567
negligence theory 738
negligent conduct and hiring 510
never-alone principle 165
NHTSA 508
niche consultant 667
NIDA 508
NIDA guidelines 248
ninhydrin 242NIS 509
no-ransom policies 727
nominal damages 738
non-directive counseling 189
non-drug crimes 243
nonfeasance 511
nonlinear junction detector 275, 587
nonverbal and verbal behavior 428
NRC 512
NTSC 118
Nuclear Non-Proliferation Act of 1978 514
Nuclear Regulatory Commission 512

Q

R

V

W

X

Y

Z